Welsh Husting
1885-2004

Welsh Hustings 1885-2004

Compiled by
Ivor Thomas Rees

CYHOEDDWYR
DINEFWR
PUBLISHERS

Published in 2005 by
Cyhoeddwyr Dinefwr Publishers
Rawlings Road, Llandybie
Carmarthenshire, SA18 3YD

A CIP catalogue record for this book is
available from the British Library.

ISBN 1-904323-09-X

Printed and bound in Wales by
Dinefwr Press Ltd.
Rawlings Road, Llandybie
Carmarthenshire, SA18 3YD

I DELYTH
gyda llawer o gariad a diolch

Foreword

By Professor Emeritus, Sir Glanmor Williams, KBE FBA

I have known the Revd Ivor Thomas Rees for over fifty years, ever since he was a lively and articulate undergraduate at what was then the University College of Swansea. Since that time he has exercised a long, active and fruitful Christian ministry and now, in retirement, he is still doing so, to great effect. He has always revealed himself to be a minister with a profound and sincere concern for political service and social welfare, especially as they affect his native Wales. Although he has spent much of his career outside his own country, since his retirement to Swansea, he has pursued more diligently than ever his researches into the lives and interests of those who have been active in Welsh parliamentary and assembly politics. The outcome has been the compilation of this meticulous work of research, for which I am delighted to write a foreword. Its readers will find that they can turn to it as a reliable and valuable reference book for biographical information about all candidates (successful and unsuccessful) for Welsh parliamentary and assembly seats in the nineteenth and twentieth centuries. They will also discover how pleasurably they can browse through it and pick up many surprising and fascinating titbits about political life. One of the most charming *obiter dicta* emanated from S. O. Davies, M.P. for Merthyr Tydfil from 1934 to 1972. When he was offered the freedom of the borough in 1970, he refused it, declaring that his election as an Independent Labour candidate was "sufficient honour from our people." I recommend this book wholeheartedly to all those who have the slightest interest in the life and politics of modern Wales.

Preface

1945 saw the end of World War II and the Labour Party's landslide victory in the General Election. It had one major disappointment for a Rhondda schoolboy. I was unfortunate enough to live in one of the two constituencies in mainland Britain where the sitting member was returned unopposed! Liverpool Exchange was one and Rhondda West was the other. The only election experience I enjoyed was on the school bus from Treherbert to Porth one morning when I saw Harry Pollitt, the Communist Leader, step out of a large open tourer to kiss a baby just as Kitchener Davies passed by in his tiny car surmounted by an enormous loudspeaker.

So began my interest in the people who contest elections. A couple of years later when browsing on the reference shelves of Treherbert's small public library I came across *Whittaker's Almanac* and discovered the 1945 election results within. It took a couple of Saturday visits to copy out the Welsh results. Some time later I transferred my affections to the Central Library at Pentre where I discovered *Who's Who in Wales 1937* from which I proceeded to copy the 1935 election results – I was hooked!

Then, sometime after my ordination in 1956, I thought of doing an M.A. degree on *Religion and Politics in the Rhondda*. I did not discuss the idea with anyone but began collecting biographical data on candidates. That pursuit took over and by the 1970s I had a card index of parliamentary candidates in the United Kingdom from 1918 (now in the National Library's Political Archive) and in Wales from 1885. Pressures of work had grown and I lost interest in the research until we retired to a small house in Swansea which had no space for the card index. The enthusiasm with which the Political Archive accepted it re-awakened my interest and for the past seven years or so I have sought information on candidates for Welsh constituencies in parliamentary, European and assembly elections. This book is the result.

Let me say that I am not an academic historian. As far as I know, it is the only work dealing with all candidates. There is ample information available on MPs with lots of books on outstanding figures. I am particularly concerned to record and honour those people, largely forgotten, who have protected and enlivened our democratic processes by fighting elections, often for lost causes. I have sought to set down all the information available (apart from criminal records for the most part) to me. I hope it will of some value to political historians as well as providing interest and pleasure for general readers interested in people or politics or both.

Finally, I must record a debt of gratitude to many people: those friends and relatives whom I have pestered for many years to supply me with election addresses and newspaper cuttings; the staff of reference libraries up and down Wales for a great deal of patient help and interest and especially at Swansea's Reference Library and the National Library of Wales, and John

Graham Jones of the Political Archive for his encouragement in my researches. Three people who have shown interest in this work and eased my way into thinking of its publication, namely, Professor Prys Morgan, Professor Sir Glanmor Williams, my teacher long ago, and Professor David Farmer who has given me a push when it seemed necessary. Then there are several hundred candidates, successful and unsuccessful, who took the trouble to return my questionnaires. My greatest debt is to my wife, Delyth, for her patience and help, especially in a great piece of proofreading. Then I must express my deepest thanks to Mr. Emyr Nicholas, Mr. Eddie John and all at Dinefwr Press.

So I offer this volume to anyone who is interested in the political and sociological history of modern Wales.

Ivor Thomas Rees

AB ELIS Rhys Gwyn: Plaid Cymru, Blaenau Gwent 2003. **Mr. Rhys ab Elis:** Born London, 8 May 1946, s of a precision machine toolmaker & a civil servant. Presbyterian Church of Wales. Educated London Secondary Modern School. Civil Servant 1962-92, retired. Joined Plaid Cymru 1968. Member: Cymdeithas yr Iaith. Contested Swansea BC 1970, Newport BC 1999. Interests: Equality for Welsh speakers; Welsh civil rights; Public Transport, Crime Prevention. Hobbies: Celtic Culture, Travel by Public Transport, Inland Waterways, Early Music. Languages: Welsh, English, Irish, German, French. Of Newport.

AB OWAIN Evan Melvyn: BA. (Wales). Liberal Democrat, Caernarfon 2001. **Mr. Mel ab Owain:** Born Caernarfon, 5 November 1958. Educated Ysgol Aberconwy, Conwy; St. David's University College, Lampeter. Court Administrator, Caernarfon Magistrates Court. CAB Manager, Rhyl. Liberal Democrats Seat Officer, Wales & West Midlands. Agent, Conwy 1992, South Sussex & Crawley Euro 1994, Islwyn 1995, Beckenham 1997, West Bromwich West B/E 2000. Balchder Bro Project Officer (Countryside Council for Wales & Wales Council for Voluntary Action. West Clwyd Regional Representative, British Trust for Ornithology. Liberal Democrat Prospective Parliamentary Candidate, Conwy 2004. Interests: Environment, Eastern Europe. Hobbies: Ornithology, travel, painting. Languages: Welsh, English. Of Abergele.

ABBOTT Henry: Conservative: Ogmore, 1929. **Mr. Henry Abbott:** Born Swansea 1882, s of Alfred Abbott, bootmaker. Partner in a Swansea family boot making business. An active socialist until 1914. Joined Conservative Party 1924.

ABRAHAM William (*Mabon*): PC1912, JP (Glam). 1887 Hon. LLD (Wales) 1918. Labour MP: Rhondda 1885-1918, Rhondda West 1918-20. **Rt. Hon. William Abraham:** Born Cwmafan, 14 June 1842, s of Thomas Abraham, miner & copper smelter & Mary Abraham. Calvinistic Methodist Elder, Lay Preacher & Precentor, Teetotaller. Married 1860, Sarah Williams. (Died 1900) 7c (+ 5 died). Educated Cwmafan National School. Door boy in mines at 10, Worked later in tinworks. Worked in Chile, returned to Wales 1870, Caercynydd Pit, Waunarlwydd. Secretary, Waunarlwydd Lodge, Associated Society of Mine-

William Abraham (Mabon).

workers 1871. District Treasurer, West Glamorgan & Carmarthenshire District 1872. Member NEC 1872, Full-time Agent, Loughor District, Dec 1872 after being dismissed from work for union activities. Agent, Cambrian Miners' Assn. Rhondda 1877. Miners President on Sliding Scale Association 1875-1903. First President: South Wales & Mon Colliery Workmen's Federation 1888-98; South Wales Miners' Federation 1898-1912. Treasurer: International Miners' Congress 1902; MFGB. Member, Rhondda School Board 1885. Vice-Chair: Miners' Provident Society. Company Director: Edinburgh & Glasgow Insurance Co. Ltd. 1889-1910. Royal Commission Member: Mining Royalties 1889, Labour 1891. Member, Gorsedd of Bards 1889 (known by his bardic name of *Mabon*). Languages: Welsh, English. Of Pentre (1881). Estate £33,315. Died 14 May 1922. Further Reading: E. W. *Evans: Mabon*, 1951.

ABSE Leopold: Labour: Cardiff North 1955, MP: Pontypool, B/E 1958-1983, Torfaen 1983-87. **Mr. Leo Abse:** Born Cardiff, 22 April 1917, s of Rudolph & Kate Abse & brother of poet Dannie Abse. Jewish Humanist. Married 1935, Marjorie Davies (Died 1996), 2c (2) 2000, Ania Czeputkowska. Educated Howard Gardens High

School, Cardiff, London School of Economics. RAF 1939-45. Journalist in Italy 1945. Solicitor. Company Chair: 1964-65, Resigned over policy of importing Japanese cars. Joined Labour 1934. Recruiter for Republican Cause in Spanish Civil War. Cardiff CC 1954-59. Chair: Welsh Parliamentary Party 1976-87, Welsh Parliamentary Labour Group. Member, Advisory Council, British Humanist Society. Leading opponent of devolution 1979, Campaigner against Capital Punishment 1969, sponsor/co-sponsor: Private Members' Acts on divorce, homosexuality, family planning, legitimacy, widows' damages, industrial injuries, congenital disabilities, children. Member: Council, Institute for Study & Treatment of Delinquency 1964. Chair: Winnicott Clinic of Psychotherapy 1988-91. President, National Council for the Divorced & Separated 1974-92, Vice-President, British Assn. for Counselling 1985-90. Chair: Parliamentary Friends of Welsh National Opera 1985-87. Vice-Chair, Centre for Crime & Justice Studies. Court Member: National Museum of Wales 1981-87, University of Wales 1981-87. Regents Lecturer, University of California 1984. *Books: Leo Abse, Best Dressed Man Award, Clothing Federation 1962. Of London & Livorno, Italy.* Leo Abse: *Private Member 1973, Margaret, daughter of Beatrice 1990, Tony Blair – the Man Behind the Smile 2002, Wotton My Enemy – Can I live with Germany in the European Union, Fellatio, Masochism, Politics and Love, 2000.*

ACWORTH Bernard: DSO RN. (Ret) FRAS. Liberal: Pontypridd 1931, Independent National: Putney B/E 1942. **Captain Bernard Acworth:** Born 1885, s of Revd Herbert Summers Acworth & Rose, d of Colonel Money-Dougal, Ratho. Anglican. Married Phyllis Doreen Bushfield, 4c. Educated HMS *Britannia*, Royal Naval College, Greenwich. Royal Navy 24 years (submarines). Freelance Journalist. Naval Correspondent, *Morning Star, Observer* & *Yorkshire Post*. Fellow, Royal Ornithological Society & American Ornithological Union. Founder/President, Evolution Protest League (campaigned in retirement against Darwinism, aviation, and the oil-firing of warships, and large battleships, (Professor, David Egerton, lecture. Science and the . . . 2002). Died 16 February 1963. *Books: Bernard Acworth, The Navies of Today and Tomorrow – a study of the naval crisis from within 1931.* Further Reading: *C. S. Lewis' Letters to Acworth on Evolution 1944-60.*

ADAMS Catherine: Plaid Cymru, South Wales/West Euro 1994. **Ms. Catherine Adams:** Born 1972, d of a mining engineer & a special needs teacher. Educated University of Wales, Aberystwyth (International Politics); President Student Representative Council. Joined Plaid Cymru 1988, Chair: Plaid Cymru Youth Movement 1989.

ADAMS David Rowland: Conservative: Neath, 1992. **Mr. Rowland Adams:** Born Bryncoch, 21 March 1963. Married Amanda Adams, 1s. Educated Mynachlog Nedd Primary School, France Hill Comprehensive School, Camberley. Computer Projects Manager EASAMI (GEC). Surrey Heath BC 1987-. Languages: Welsh, English.

ADAMS Patrick Henry Walter: Green Party: Montgomery 1992, North Wales Euro 1989**. Mr. Patrick Adams:** Born 1 April 1949. Educated an Oxford school, Wolverhampton Polytechnic. Ex-Local government officer. Ex-Natural Environment Research Council, Oxford. Biologist & Smallholder (1984). Oxford CC (Labour) 1979-84. Of Meifod.

ADAMS Paul: BSc (Wales). Socialist Labour Party, South/East List 2003. **Mr. Paul Adams:** Born Pontypool, 3 March 1977, s of Michael Adams, factory inspector, & Gloria Adams, housewife. Methodist. Educated Pontllanffraith Comprehensive School; University of Wales, Cardiff (Politics/Economics). Civil Servant, Inland Revenue. Member, Labour Party 1995-99. Joined Socialist Labour Party 1999. Peace Campaigner. Interests: Anti-Imperialism, Anti-Globalisation. Hobbies: Films, Reading, Walking, History, Travelling. Languages: English, a little French & Spanish.

AERON-THOMAS John L: Liberal National: Gower 1945. **Mr. John Aeron-Thomas:** Born Swansea, 1921, s of Gwilym E. Aeron-Thomas & gs of John Aeron Thomas MP for Gower (qv). Educated Cambridge University. Lieutenant TA 1939, Army, 1939-43, Captain, wounded at El Alamein & invalided out. Law student at time of election. Barrister, Inner Temple 1947. Timber Importer, Company Director: Insurance Company 1952, Harlech TV. Managing Director, Emlyn Brick Company, Deputy Chair: *South Wales Argus*. Regional Director, Lloyds Bank. Chair: CBI Welsh Area 1971. Member, Council for Wales 1971. Director, Swansea Festival. Scout Commissioner, Mumbles, Glamorgan. Died 29 January 1984.

AINGER Nicholas Richard: Labour MP: Pembroke, Carmarthen West & Pembrokeshire South 1997-. **Mr. Nick Ainger:** Born Sheffield, 24 October 1949, s of Richard Ainger & Marjorie Ainger. Married 1976 Sally Robinson, 1d. Educated Northup Grammar School, Staveley; College of the Distributive Trades. Rigger, Marine & Support Services, Ltd, Pembroke Dock 1977-92. TGWU Shop Steward 1978-82, Branch Secretary 1978-92. Joined Labour Party 1979. Chair: & Secretary, Pembroke CLP. Dyfed CC 1981-93. Member: Co-operative Party, Amnesty International, Greenpeace, RSPB, Dyfed Wild

Life Trust. PPS Secretary of State for Wales 1997-2001. Welsh Whip, June 2001. Hobbies: Reading, The Arts, Walking, Swimming. Lived in South Wales from 1976.

AINLEY Stephen Michael: BScEng 1992. Green Party & Plaid Cymru: Newport East 1992, Green Party, Wales Euro 1999. **Mr. Steve Ainley:** Born Yorkshire 1951. Carpenter, Environment Studies Student, Pontypool & Usk College of Further Education. Of Pontnewydd.

AKEN Marion – see ST. CLAIR Lindi.

ALDRIDGE Raymond William: Severnside Libertarian Party, Cardiff South-East 1979. **Mr. Raymond Aldridge:** Born Grangetown, Cardiff, 1952. Educated Cardiff High School, Llandaff Technical College. Ship's Officer. Contested Cardiff CC 1973. Manifesto: Legalisation of Prostitution & Cannabis.

Miquad Al-Nuami.

AL-NUAMI Miquad: BSc PhD FIEE CEng. Labour, Assembly South/East 1999. **Professor Miquad Al-Nuami:** Born Mosul, Iraq, 20 May 1945, s of Omar Al-Nuami & Zaineb Al-Nuami, came to Britain, 1962. Married 1968, Lindsay Thomas, college lecturer, Newport CBC. 2s. Educated Universities of Birmingham & Loughborough. Professor of Radio Communications, University of Glamorgan. Specialist in IT, international networking & research development. Newport BC 1988-96, Newport CBC 1996- (Stow Hill ward). Member: All Wales Ethnic Minority Assn (AWEMA). Interests: Economic Development, Community Development, Equality. Hobbies: Classical Music, Opera, Gardening, Reading. Languages: Arabic, English. Of Newport.

ALI Parvaiz Arshad: BSc 1979 MSc 1980 (Birmingham) PhD 1983 (Wales). Labour, South/West List 2003. **Dr. Parvaiz Ali:** Born Glasgow, 4 March 1958, s of Rahmat Ali, businessman, & Hamida Begum, housewife. Islam. Married 1983, Nasreem Kauser, 1s 2d. Educated University of Birmingham, University of Wales. Consultant Clinical Scientist. Head of Nuclear Medicine Services, Singleton Hospital, Swansea. Chair, Welsh Osteoporosis Advisory Group. Vice-Chair, Swansea West CLP. Member: Board, Health Protection Agency 2003-07; South Wales Police Authority 1995-99. Hobbies: Walking, Badminton. Languages: English, Urdu. Of Sketty, Swansea.

ALLEN Charles Francis Egerton-: JP (Pembs) BA. (Oxon) 1870. Liberal MP: Pembroke & Haverfordwest, 1892-95. **Mr. Charles Egerton-Allen:** Born 14 October, 1847, s of Charles Allen, JP, Bengal Civil Service, & Mary, d of James Allen, nephew of H. G. Allen (qv). Anglican. Married Elizabeth Georgina, d of William Wilcox of Whitburn, Sunderland. Educated Eton; St. John's College, Cambridge. Barrister, Inner Temple 1871. Government Advocate, Rangoon. Lecturer in English Law, Presidency College, Bengal 1876. Recorder of Rangoon 1883-84. Tenby BC. Of Tenby. Estate £9,354. Died 31 December 1927.

ALLEN Henry George: QC 1880 JP (Pembs & Carms) BA 1837 MA 1840 (Oxon). Liberal MP: Pembroke 1880-85, Pembroke & Haverfordwest 1885-86. **Mr. Henry Allen:** Born 29 July 1816, s of John Hensleigh Allen MP (1818-26) of Heywood, Tenby. Educated Rugby School; Christ Church, Oxford. Barrister, Lincolns Inn 1841, Bencher 1881, Recorder of Andover 1857-72, Chair: Pembrokeshire Quarter Sessions 1879-95. Pembrokeshire CC. Ald. 1895, 1st Vice-Chair: 1888-92, Chair: 1894-95. Of Pakeston, Pembs. Estate: £61,207. Died 25 November 1908.

ALLISON George Edmund: MA (Oxon). Conservative: Pembroke 1935. **Mr. George Allison:** Born 1912. Educated Oxford University. Bank Clerk 1925-28, 1931-.

ALLISON John: CBE 1975 JP. (Swansea). 1966 DL (W. Glam) 1975 Labour, Barry 1970. **Mr. John Allison:** Born 4 October 1919, s of Thomas William Allison, Quarry Owner (Mayor of Swansea 1941). Married Elvira Gwendoline Lewis. Educated Glanmor Secondary School, Swansea Technical College. Professional Musician, Quarry Consultant. Chair: quarrying company until 1968, Musical Instrument Retailing Company 1957-. Joined Labour Party 1946. Member: National Executive, Musicians Union, Welsh Development Corporation, Welsh Air

Advisory Cttee, Vice-Chair: Welsh Rivers Authority. Swansea CC 1957-74, Alderman, Leader of the Council, Deputy-Mayor 1966-67, 1972-73. West Glamorgan CC 1977-. Of Morriston, Swansea.

ALTIKRITI Sura: BSc MSc (Wales). Vote 2 Stop the War Party, South/Central: **Ms. Sura Altikriti:** Born Wolverhampton, d of Osana Tunfeq Altikriti, medical consultant, & Wakar Hamdan Tokan, housewife, (family left Iraq after Sadam Hussain took power). Islam. Married 1995, Faris I. Atnaemi, university lecturer. Lecturer in Computing, Merthyr College. Member: Management Cttee, Cardiff Women's Workshop; All Wales Saheli (help & guidance for ethnic groups in Wales); Assn of Islam Professionals; Human Relief Aid. Youth Club Supervisor. Interests: Human Rights. Hobbies: travel, Social Activities. Languages: English, Arabic. Of Cardiff.

AMYES Rodney M: BA (Liverpool) Conservative, East Flint 1970. **Mr. Rodney Amyes:** Born May 1934. Educated Liverpool Collegiate School; Liverpool University, Chair: Liverpool University Conservative Assn. Company Director, Liverpool printing works. Lancashire Fusiliers & RAEC, Liverpool CC 1961-.

ANDERSON Donald: PC Dec 2000 BA. (Wales) 1960. Commander's Grand Cross, Order of Merit (Germany). Labour MP: Monmouth 1966-70, Swansea East Oct. 1974-. Announced his intention to retire at the next general election 2003. **Rt. Hon. Donald Anderson:** Born Swansea, 17 June 1939, s of David Robert Anderson, fitter & Eva Mathias. Baptist origins, Methodist local preacher, worships too with URC. Married 1963, Dr. Dorothy, d of Revd Frank Trotman, Methodist missionary in Bolivia, 3c. Educated Swansea GS, University of Wales, Swansea (1st), Hon. Fellow. Foreign Office 1960-64, Lecturer in Politics, University of Wales, Swansea 1964-66, Joined Labour Party 1957, Director, Campaign for European Political Community, Barrister 1969. Kensington & Chelsea BC 1973-74. PPS 1969-70. Chair: Welsh Labour Group 1977-78, Select Cttee on Welsh Affairs. Opposition Spokesman, Foreign & Commonwealth Affairs 1983-92, Defence 1992-94, Legal Affairs 1994-95. Member, Speaker's Panel of Chairmen 1995. Chair: Parliamentary Christian Fellowship 1990, National Prayer Breakfast 1989, Campaign for the Homeless. Vice-Chair: All Parties Methodist Group, Joint Vice-Chair: Council of Christians & Jews Group. Senior Vice-President, Assn. of West European Parliamentarians for Africa (Southern) 1984-, Member, North Atlantic Assembly 1992. Chair: Foreign Affairs Cttee 1997. Leader, UK Delegation to North Atlantic Assembly. Joint Chair: Parliamentary Ecclesiastical Group. Chair:

Donald Anderson.

Commonwealth Parliamentary Assn, All Party South Africa Group 1997-. Joint Vice-Chair: Council of Christians & Jews Group. Vice-Chair, Methodist Group. Secretary, Christian Fellowship Group. Joint secretary: Europe Group. Consultant, Royal Society of Chemistry. Vice-Chair, Executive, Inter-parliamentary Union 1985-88. Senior Vice-President, Assn. of West European Parliamentarians against Apartheid 1992-. President: Gower Society 1976-78; Boys' Brigade of Wales; Swansea Male Voice Choir. Hon. Freeman, City of Swansea 1999. Hobbies: Church Work, Walking. Of London & Swansea.

ANDREW Stewart J: Conservative: Wrexham, 1997. **Mr. Stewart Andrew:** Born 25 November 1971. Educated David Hughes Comprehensive School, Menai Bridge. Personal Assistant, Ynys Môn Conservative Assn. Dept. of Social Security official 1992-94. Area Organiser, British Heart Foundation 1994-. Founder Chair: Môn Young Conservatives1989, Chair: Welsh Young Conservatives1991-93, North Wales Euro Council 1993. Beaumaris TC. Wrexham Maelor BC 1995-. Freeman, City of Chester. PPC Vale of Clwyd, Sacked after talks with Labour Party 1998, Joined Labour Party, 8 November 1998, returned to Conservative Party, May 2001. Languages: Welsh, English. Of Wrexham.

ANDREWS Leighton Russell: BA (Wales) MA (Sussex). Labour AM, Rhondda 2003-; Liberal/ Alliance Gillingham 1987. **Mr. Leighton Andrews:** Born Cardiff 8 November 1957, s of Thomas Leonard Andrews, finance officer, & Ada Margaret (Peggy) Squires, teacher. Married 1996, Ann Beynon, BT National Manager, Wales, 1s 1d. Educated Poole Grammar School; University of Wales, Bangor; Sussex University. Head of Public Affairs BBC. Parliamentary Officer, Age Concern. Lecturer, School of Journalism, Media & Culture, Cardiff. Consultant Adviser to businesses and organizations on their social, green and ethical responsibilities. Former lobbyist & charity director. Vice-Chair, Liberal Party National Executive; member Liberal Party Council; Vice-Chair, Standing Cttee. Vice-President, National Union of Students. Director, 1987 International Year of Shelter for the Homeless. Co-founder, Yes for Wales Campaign 1997 Referendum. Interests: Economic Development, Social Policy, Housing, Culture, Media. Of Llwynypia.

ANGLEZARKE Barbara A: BA Wales). Plaid Cymru: Cardiff South & Penarth 1992. **Ms. Barbara Anglezarke:** Born Lancashire, 4 June 1959. Educated University of Wales (Archaeology). Cardiff. Officer, Housing Department Special Needs Unit. Sustainable Funding Officer, Brecon Beacons National Park. Cydcoed Project Officer, S. E. Wales. Member, The Princes Trust Cymru. Came to Wales 1978.

ANKERS William David Mervyn: JP. (Anglesey). Liberal: Anglesey 1974, Oct. **Mr. Mervyn Ankers:** Born Holyhead 1924. Educated Holyhead Grammar School; Sloane School, Chelsea. Tobacconist until 1974. Business Consultant 1974. Holyhead UDC 1957-64.

ANSTEY Duncan Josef: BA (Hallam). Liberal Democrat, Merthyr Tydfil & Rhymney 1997, South East List 1999. **Mr. Duncan Anstey:** Born Monmouth, 29 December 1966, s of Arthur Anstey, printer. Roman Catholic. Married Valerie Ann Anstey, teacher. Educated Monmouth Comprehensive School, Crosskeys Tertiary College, Sheffield Hallam University. Marketing Development Manager, Director, Regeneration Trust, PHAB Wales. Strategy Co-ordinator, Torfaen CBC Social Inclusion Unit. Gwent CC 1997. Monmouthshire CC 1996- (Group Leader), Deputy-Leader, Independents/Liberal Democrats Group. Member, Friends of the Earth. Sub-aqua diver, Gardening, local Charity Trusts. Of Dingestow, nr. Monmouth.

ANSTEY Roger Hilary: BSc (Bristol. Liberal: Swansea East Oct 1974, Langstone 1970. **Mr. Roger Anstey:** Born Birmingham 1934. Married 2c. Educated Reading School, Bristol University.

Works Shift Manager, BP Baglan Bay. Investment Executive. Swansea CC1973-. Member: Gower Society, Conservation Society.

AP GWENT Gruffydd Rolant: LlB (Wales). Plaid Cymru: Swansea East 1970, Oct.1974, 1979. **Mr. Guto ap Gwent:** Born Swansea, 9 May 1942, s of Mervyn Gwent Hughes Jones, medical practitioner, & Gwladwen Ann Jones, housewife. Welsh Independent Church Secretary. Married 1983, Margaret Evans, dentist, 1s. Educated Lon Las Welsh School, Llandovery College, University of Wales, Aberystwyth. President, College Law Society. Solicitor 1970. Member: Gower Society, Royal Institution of South Wales, Cymdeithas yr Iaith Gymraeg, Celtic Congress, AUT. Joined Plaid Cymru 1964, Vice-Chair, Swansea West. Contested Swansea BC 3 times. Interests: Human Rights, World Peace. Hobbies: Gardening, Walking, Countryside, Art. Languages: Welsh, English, French. Of Kittle, Gower.

AP GWILYM Thomas Eurfyl: BSc. PhD 1969 (London). Plaid Cymru: Merthyr Tydfil 1979. **Dr. Eurfyl ap Gwilym:** Born Penparciau, Aberystwyth, November 1944. Married Siwan, 4c. Educated Ardwyn School, Aberystwyth, University College, London (Bio-physics). Industrial Economist. Management Trainee, Unilever 1969. Senior Manager, John Williams. Group of Companies, Executive Director, Corporate Strategy & Acquisitions, Terence Chapman, London, Non-Executive Director: Principality Building Society June 2000; SOFT Group plc. Joined Plaid Cymru, 1966, Director of Research, 1973, Chair 1976-78. Member: Audit Cttee. National Museums & Galleries of Wales 2002. Languages: Welsh, English.

AP RHYS Thomas: BA (Wales) 1923. Labour, Caernarfon Boroughs 1929. **Mr. Thomas ap Rhys**: Born Bangor, gs of Michael D Jones. Welsh Independent. Educated Friars School, Bangor, University of Wales, Bangor (Engineering student). Joined Army 1914, blinded on active service. Married Evelyn, his nurse at St. Dunstans, 3c. Trained in typing, Braille & massage. Returned to Bangor (1st Economics & Philosophy). Languages: Welsh, English. Of Bangor.

AP ROBERT Gwilym Robert Jones: BA. (Wales) MA. (Oxon) PhD. (Hartford). Plaid Cymru: Ebbw Vale Oct. 1974, 1979. **Revd Dr. Gwilym ap Robert:** Born May 1926, s of Revd Robert John Jones, & brother of Hywel (q.v.). Married Educated Cardiff High School, University of Wales, Cardiff, Mansfield College, Oxford, Hartford Theological Seminary, Connecticut. Welsh Independent Minister, Ordained 1954, Addoldy, Glynneath 1954-59, Aberystwyth 1959-64, Porth 1966-74, Bethel, Caerphilly 1994-, Lecturer, University College, Cardiff 1964-. Member:

Welsh Cttee of 100, Chair: Welsh Cttee for Aid to Bangladesh, Member, AUT. Languages: Welsh, English.

AP ROBERT Hywel Wyn Jones: MA (Oxon). Plaid Cymru: Cardigan 1970. **Mr. Hywel ap Robert:** Born Pontyberem 19 November 1923, s of Revd Robert John Jones, Welsh Independent Minister & brother of Gwilym (qv). Welsh Independent. Married Elizabeth Davies, 2c. Educated Cardiff High School, Corpus Christi College, Oxford. Army 1941-46. Barrister, Middle Temple 1950, Prosecuting Counsel, Post Office, Crown Recorder 1971, Cardiff & South Glam Stipendiary Magistrate 1972-75, Circuit Judge 1989-94, Judge, Cardiff Crown Court 1993-94. President, Penarth Society. Hon. Member, Gorsedd, 1973. Languages: Welsh, English. Died August 2001.

ARBUTHNOT James Norwich: PC 1998, BA 1974 MA (Cantab). Conservative: Cynon Valley 1983, B/E 1984, MP. Wanstead & Woodford 1987-97, Hampshire NE 1997-. **Rt. Hon. James Arbuthnot:** Born 4 August 1952, s of Sir James Arbuthnot Bart MP (Dover) & Mary Jane, d of Alexander Duff. Married 1984, Emma. Louise, d of Michael & Daphne Broadbent, 1s 3d. Educated Wellesley School, Broadstairs, Eton (Captain of School, Secretary, Eton Political Society 1968), Trinity College, Cambridge (Law), London College of Law. Barrister (non practising), Inner Temple 1975, Lincoln's Inn 1977. Member of Lloyds. Kensington & Chelsea BC 1978-87, Deputy Mayor 1983-84. Deputy Chair: Chelsea Conservative Assn1980-82, President, Cynon Valley Conservative Assn. PPS 1988-92. Asst. Whip 1992-94. Under-Secretary, Social Security 1994-95. Minister, Defence Procurement 1995-97. Chief Whip 1997-2001. Shadow Secretary for Trade 2003-. Headed William Hague's Campaign to become Leader. Hobbies Playing Guitar, Cycling.

ARCHBOLD Edward: Labour: Cardiff Central 1935, Portsmouth 1929, Balham & Tooting 1924, 1923. **Mr. Ernest Archbold:** Southend Hairdresser. Former Labour Colleges Lecturer in Lancashire. Southend BC.

ARMSTRONG George Elliot: 2nd Bart 1892 CMG 1917 MA. (Cantab). Conservative: Pembroke & Haverfordwest Jan 1910, Southampton Dec 1910. **Commander, Sir George Armstrong:** Born 1866, s of Sir George Carylon Hughes Armstrong, 1st Bart, Proprietor of The Globe & Alicia, d of Revd J. C. Furlong. Married1890, Edith Annie. d of Adolphus Foss, 3c. Educated HMS. Britannia. Royal Navy 1878-92, 1914-18. Journalist, The Globe 1892 & Proprietor. Died 30 March 1940.

Klaus Armstrong-Braun.

ARMSTRONG-BRAUN Klaus: BSc MSc. Green Party, North List 1999, North Wales Euro 1999, Euro Wales 2001, Alyn & Deeside 2001. **Mr. Klaus Armstrong-Braun:** Born Krakow, Poland, 1940. Went to an orphanage at Essen, Germany, 1941, evacuated to an orphanage at Dublin 1944, foster homes 1944-54, Dr. Barnados's, Chester 1954. Single. Educated Chester FE College; Liverpool Polytechnic Manchester; Metropolitan University; University College, Chester. Apprentice & Hydraulic Engineer, Hydraulic Engineering Co. Chester 1960-64, Goods Clerk, LMS. Chester 1964-66, Work Study Inspector, Chester Steam & Tractor Depots 1966-75, Divisional Cripple Wagon Controller, Stoke & North Wales Division, British Rail 1975-80, Workshop Supervisor, Wagon Shops, British Rail, Chester 1980-85. Joined Chester Green Party 1989. Broughton & Bretton ComC 1991-95. Flintshire CC (Saltney-Stonebridge) 1995. Interests: Social, Environmental & Economic Justice (Poverty, Transport, Incinerators, Social Housing, Local Employment & Economies). Hobbies: Ultra Distance Running (100 miles), Mountain Trails, 24-Hour Track Races, Church & Mixed Voice Choirs, Composing Music & Poetry, Playing & Coaching Badminton. Of Broughton.

ARNOLD Anthony Dowdeswell: MBE. Conservative: Merthyr Tydfil 1955, Newport 1959, 1970. **Mr. Anthony Arnold:** Born Cardiff, 1929. Married (1) 1957, Beatta Brookes (qv) divorced, (2) Shirley Arnold. Educated Repton. Royal Artillery 1947-50. Average Adjuster, partner in family firm. Joined Young Conservatives 1950. Chair: Wales & Mon Young Conservatives1952-54, 1957-58, National Vice-Chair: 1957-58, President, Wales Area Young Conservatives, Chair: Wales & Mon. Area Conservative Political Centre, Cardiff SE Conservative Assn, City of Cardiff Conservative Assn, Agent, Carmarthen East & Dinefwr 1997, 1999.

ARROWSMITH Margaret Patricia: BA (Cantab). Independent Socialist: Cardiff South-East 1979, Stop South East Asia War: Fulham 1979, Radical Alliance: Fulham 1966. **Miss Pat Arrowsmith:** Born 2 March 1930, d of George Ernest Arrowsmith & Margaret Vera Kingham. Married & Separated 11 August 1979, Donald Gardener, Lesbian relationship 1962-76. Educated Farringtons, Stover School, Cheltenham Ladies College, Newnham College, Cambridge (History), Ohio University, Liverpool University (Cert.Soc.Sc). Many jobs including Community Organiser, Chicago 1952-53, Cinema Usher 1953-54, social care worker, Liverpool Family Service Unit 1954, Child Care Officer 1955, Nursing Assistant, Deva Psychiatric Hospital 1956-57, Peace News Reporter 1965, Gardener, London Borough of Camden 1966-68, Researcher, Society of Friends Race Relations Cttee 1969-71, NCCL Case Worker 1971, also on farms, cafes, factories etc, Organiser: CND, Direct Action against Nuclear War, Committee of 100 Campaign for Nuclear Disarmament 1958-68, Asst. Editor, Amnesty International 1971-94, retired. Novelist, Poet & Writer. Gaoled eleven times as political prisoner 1958-85 (twice adopted as Amnesty International Prisoner of Conscience), Active supporter of United Troops Out Movement, Anti-Nazi League, Gay Liberation, Women's Lib, Leader, NUJ Branch, War Resisters International, CND, TGWU. 'Pro-Welsh Home Rule & the Welsh Language' (1979 election). Of London. *Books: Pat Arrowsmith (autobiography): I should have been a Hornby train 1995.*

ARWYN Eirian Heledd: Plaid Cymru, South/West List 2003. **Ms. Eirian Arwyn:** Presbyterian Church of Wales. Plaid Cymru activist in Cardiff North. Languages: Welsh, English. Of Cardiff.

ASH Angela: Labour, South/East List. **Ms. Angela Ash:** Born 20 July 1952, of farming family. Qualified in social work. Runs own training & research business. Interests: Sustainable Economic Development, Health & Social care. Of Usk.

ASHFORTH John: BA MA. Natural Law Party, South/East List 1999, Euro Wales, June 1999, Preston, 1997. **Mr. John Ashforth:** Born Chesterfield, 9 October 1953, s of Clifford Ashforth, engineer. Unmarried. Lived in Lancashire 17 years. Senior Lecturer, Central Lancashire University, Preston. TM Teacher. 1980 & Writer. Ex-BBC photographer. Interests: Ecology. Hobbies: Swimming, Cycling, Travel, Yoga, Cinema. Of Skelmersdale.

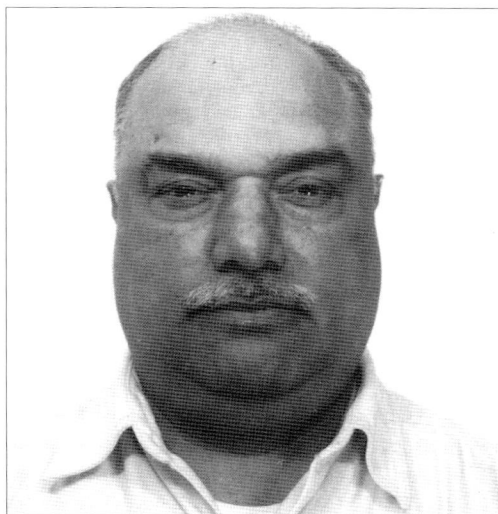

Mohammed Ashgar.

ASGHAR Mohammed: BA (Peshawar). Plaid Cymru, Newport East 2003. **Mr. Mohammed Asghar:** Born Peshawar, Pakistan 30 September 1945, s of Mohammad Aslam Khan, civil servant, & Begum Katoon, housewife. Islam (Sunni). Married 1982, Firdaus Ashgar, 1d. Educated Peshawar University (political science), Nash College, Newport. Chartered Accountant; Principal of a firm of accountants 1983. Chair, Newport East Plaid Cymru. Interests: Economy. Hobbies: Listening to World News, Flying, Cricket, Athletics, Badminton. Languages: English, Urdu, Punjabi. Of Newport.

ATKIN Leon: People's Party: Swansea East B/E 1963. **Revd Leon Atkin:** Born Spalding, 26 July 1902. Married Ethel May, 2s. Mechanical Engineer. Worked in mines. Began leading worship at 13. Trained for Methodist Ministry at Handsworth College, Birmingham. Methodist Probationer Minister at St. Johns, Risca 1930 & Barged Central Hall 1931. Took in 28 young unemployed at the Central Hall and refused to send them home, also rejected a Methodist plan to send him to Cornwall. Pastor, St. Paul's Congregational Church, Swansea 1933-39, Joined army as a gunner 1939, Army Chaplain 1940-45, won legal Battles against deacons over right to return to the church 1945. Removed from Congregational Year Book 1952. Congregational Union sought unsuccessfully to open negotiations for his recognition as a minister. Swansea BC 1936-64. Elected as Labour member but resigned from Labour Party 1947 when asked to give up his seat and transfer to another ward; formed People's Party. Retired from ministry due to ill-health 1970. Prosecuted for non-payment of rates on the vestry, which he turned into a flat for himself and family and for showing films on Sunday evenings. Turned church crypt into a *'recognized haven for the homeless and others with social problems'*. Died 27 January 1976.

ATKINSON Gareth Martin: Liberal/Alliance: Blaenau Gwent 1983. **Mr. Gareth Atkinson:** Born 1962. Educated Mid-Gwent College of Further Education, Pontypool. Apprentice, Dunlop Semtex. Unemployed.

AUBEL Felix Franc Elfed: BA MTh PhD (Wales) 1995. SDP: Cynon Valley 1983, B/E 1984. Joined Conservatives 1984. Conservative: Caernarfon 1987, Ceredigion 1997, Preseli 1999, Brecon & Radnor 2001. **Revd Dr. Felix Aubel:** Born 21 September 1960, s of a Yugoslav refugee grocer father & Welsh mother. Partner, Mary Davies, complimentary health practitioner & Assembly candidate 1999. Educated Ysgol Gymraeg Rhydfelin; University Of Wales, Lampeter & Cardiff. History Teacher, Chislehurst & Sidcup Grammar School 1989-92. Lecturer in History, University College, Lampeter, Welsh Independent Minister, Ordained 1993: Aberaeron Group of Churches, 1993-. Disagreed with SDP over devolution & defence and joined Conservatives 1984. Chair: Cynon Valley Young Conservatives 1985-87. Active in Keep Britain Out Campaign 1975. Chair: Cynon Valley Young Conservatives 1985-87. Hobbies: Antiques, Numismatics, Cinema., Theatre, Visiting places of historic interest. Wrote chapter on the Conservative Party in Wales in The Conservatives and British Society 1880-1990. Re-adopted as parliamentary candidate for Brecon & Radnor 2003; withdrew as parliamentary candidate for Brecon and Radnor 2004. Languages: Welsh, English. Of Aberaeron.

AULT John Anthony: Liberal Democrat, Merthyr Tydfil & Rhymney 2003; Wyre 1992; European Election 1994. **Mr. John Ault:** Born 5 August 1970. Educated Grange School, Hertford; Edge Hill College of Higher Education. Hotel & Catering Trade. Member: Young Liberal Democrats National Executive 1989-91. Appleton ComC 1991-. Liberal Democrat National Campaigns & Media Officer for North-West England. Agent, Eddisbury, Wigan, Preston & Ogmore by-elections. Welsh Liberal Democrats Campaign Manager. Hobbies: Driving around Wales in his Mini or Triumph Herald, Cricket, Football. Of Cardiff.

AUSTIN Dennis J: Liberal: Rhondda, Feb. & Oct. 1974. **Mr. Dennis Austin:** Born Nottingham, 1937. Married 5c. Educated Mansfield Grammar School. Royal Navy submariner, 12 years. Colliery worker. Owner & Landlord, Britannia Hotel, Porth. President: Porth & District British Legion. Secretary, Rhondda Federation of Ratepayers' & Residents Assns. Contested local elections.

AYLIFFE Janet: Natural Law Party, Mid & West List 1999; Lancashire Central Euro 1994. **Ms. Janet Ayliffe:** Of Skelmersdale.

AYLWIN Jonathan Paul: BScEcon (Wales). Liberal Democrat, South/Central List 1999. **Mr. Jonathan Aylwin:** Born Taunton, 2 October 1977, s of Norman George Aylwin, builder's labourer, & Maureen Hilary Hawkins, teacher. Educated University of Wales, Cardiff (Politics). Cardiff CC (Cathays) 1999-. AM's constituency manager. Joined Liberal Democrats 1996. Chair: Cardiff Students Liberal Democrats, Liberal Democrats Youth & Students, Wales. Member Liberal Democrat Youth & Students Executive. Interests: Transport, Housing. Languages: English, French. Of Cardiff.

BADGER Pauline Edwina: Liberal Democrat, Ynys Môn 1992. **Ms. Pauline Badger:** Born 12 June 1947. Educated Wallasey High School; Liverpool College of Occupational Therapy. Occupational Therapist.

BAGRAM Charles Ernest: Conservative: Bedwellty 1922. **Captain Charles Bagram**: Born 1881. Barrister, Inner Temple 1903. Presidency Magistrate, Calcutta: Resigned to serve in Great War. Royal Flying Corps & RAF. France. Courts Martial Officer, London.

BAILEY Christopher Homfray: Independent Liberal: Cardiff South-East 1974, Feb, Liberal: 1974, Oct. withdrew in favour of Conservative 1979 & left the Liberals to find a last minute replacement. **Mr. Christopher Bailey:** Born Wales, 1931. Married 1956, Sarah Ann McMaster, d of a Chelsea businessman, 1s 1d. Educated Oundle School. Apprentice in ship repairing; Royal Navy stoker, then commissioned (national service). Managing director, family owned C. H. Bailey, 1958. Millionaire & Company Chair, Bristol Channel Repairers. Hobbies: Rugby, Swimming, Water Polo. Died Cape Town, South Africa, 23 August 2002.

BAILEY George N. A: OBE 1995 MA (Edin) MBA (Henley) PhD. Conservative: Aberavon 1983. **Dr. George Bailey:** Born Northumberland 14 December 1944. Married Janet, 2c. Educated Allhallows School, Edinburgh, Edinburgh University, Exeter University, Kings College, London. Research Director. International Strategic Management. External Examiner, Staffordshire Business School, ESERP Spain. Greater London CC 1967-. Surrey Heath BC (Executive Member for Environment).

BAIN William James Alexander: BEM. Conservative: Aberdare 1955. **Mr. William Bain:** Born Newport, Isle of Wight 1905. Educated Banchory Academy, Scotland, RAF Cranwell. RAF Apprentice 1921-23. RAF 1923-31, Unemployed 1931-32, then worked as a navvy, forestry worker and taxi driver. Foreman-in-Charge, British Overseas Aircraft Corporation Engine Testing Site, Nantgarw. Chair, Barry Divisional Conservative Trade Unionist Council. Whitchurch PC 1949-67, Cardiff CC 1967-. Of Rhiwbina, Cardiff.

BAKER Andrew Charles Stuart: Conservative: Swansea West 1997. Mr. **Andrew Baker:** Born 6 November 1965. Educated Monkton House Grammar School, Cardiff, South Glamorgan Institute of Higher Education. Business Development Consultant. Chair, Cardiff Central Young Conservatives 1989. Vice-President, Wales Area Young Conservatives 1993-94. Vice-Chair: Cardiff Central Conservative Political Cttee until April 1998. Contested Cardiff CC 1991, S. Glam CC 1993.

BALL John Graham: BScEcon. PhD (Wales) 1996. Plaid Cymru: Swansea East Feb. & Oct. 1974, 1999, 2001, B/E September 2001. **Dr. John Ball:** Born Gorseinon, 14 December 1947, s of Mervyn Robert Ball, public service vehicle driver/car park manager. Married (1) 1971 (Elizabeth) Morwen Davies, divorced 1s 1d (2) 2001 Deborah Williams, teacher. Educated Cwmbwrla School, Dynevor Grammar School, University of Wales, Cardiff & Swansea. GPO Engineer 1965-71, Manager, Addis Hardware, Swansea 1971-74, Manager Avvco 1974-76, Store Buyer, Calor Gas 1980-83, Advisor, Welsh Development Agency 1984-90, Business Manager, Welsh Development Agency 1990-94, Senior Lecturer, Swansea Business School 1994-. Chair: Swansea Associate Section, Institute of Post Office Electrical Engineers, West Glamorgan Executive, Plaid Cymru. Member: ACTSS, Plaid Cymru Transport Research Group. Swansea CC 1976-79. Interests: Education, Economic Development. Hobbies: Railways, Travel, History. Of Brynhyfryd, Swansea.

BALL Martin: PhD (Wales) 1985. Liberal: Swansea West 1979. **Professor Martin Ball:** Born February 1951. Educated Exeter School, University of Wales, Bangor, University of Essex. Lecturer, Linguistics & Speech Therapy, Mid Glamorgan Institute of Higher Education; University of Wales Institute, Cardiff. Professor of Phonetics & Linguistics, University of Ulster. Course Director until December 1998. Professor in Communicative Disorders, University of Louisiana, Lafayette. President, International Clinical phonetics & Linguistics Assn 2000-. Editor, *Clinical Linguistics & Phonetics* 1986-. Associate Editor, Journal *of Multilingual Communication Disorders* 2002-. Co-Editor, book series, *Methods in Speech & Language Disorders* 1998-. Administrative Editor, *Journal of Celtic Linguistics*

1990-94. Editorial Board Member, *Journal of Celtic Language Learning* 1994-; *Advances in Speech Pathology* 1997-; *Welsh Journal of Education* 2001-; *International Journal of Language & Communication Disorders* 2002. Co-Editor, *Belfast Working Papers in Linguistics, 13.* Languages: Learned Welsh, English. *Books: The Use of Welsh – a Contribution to Sociolinguistics 1988, Welsh Phonology 1988, Mutations in Welsh 1984, Vowel Disorders (with Fiona Gibbon) 2002.*

BANKES John Eldon: PC 1915 GCB 1927 Kt 1910 KC 1901 MA (Oxon). Conservative: Flint District 1906. **Rt. Hon. Sir John Bankes:** Born Llaneurgain 1854, s of John Scott Bankes, Plas Sychtyn. Anglican. Married1882, Edith Ethelstone (died 1931) 4c. Educated Eton, University College, Oxford. Barrister, Inner Temple 1878. Chancellor, Diocese of St. Asaph 1908-10. Chair, Flintshire Quarter Sessions 37 years, Judge, Queens Bench 1910-15, Lord Justice of Appeal 1915-27. Chair, Flintshire CC 1932. Member, Governing Body of the Church in Wales. Died 31 December 1946.

BARD Stephen Richard: GDBM PCGE MA(Ed). Liberal Democrat, Blaenau Gwent 2003. **Mr. Steve Bard:** Born, Worcester 21 May 1961, s of William Richard Bard & Marie Yvonne Bard. Church in Wales. Educated Nantyglo Comprehensive School; Salford College; Bath College of HE. Teacher. Church Treasurer. Conductor, Abertillery Male Voice Choir. Treasurer: Blaenau Gwent Liberal Democrats. Football referee, Hobbies: Skittles. Blaenau Gwent BC. 13.3.2003. Languages: English, a little German Of Six Bells, Abertillery.

BARHAM Alan Cyril: Referendum Party: Conwy 1997, UK Independence Party, Euro, 1999, Conwy, 2001. **Mr. Alan Barham:** Born Upminster, 26 January 1938, s of Cyril William Barham, process engraver/hotelier, & Sheila Ross Mona Barham, court dressmaker. Disbeliever. Married 1965, Christine Brereton Cliff, legal secretary, 1s 1d. Writer & Broadcaster. BBC Radio Journalist 1968-2000. With Murder Incorporated (arranges who-dunnit weekends) 2000-. Trefriw & Llarhychyn ComC (Chairman, 10 years). Interests: Left of Right & Telling the EU to get lost. Of Llanbedr-y-Cennin, Conwy.

BARKER George: JP. (Mon). Labour MP: Abertillery B/E 1920-29. **Mr. George Barker**: Born Hanley, Staffs 13 March 1858, s of William Barker, handyman (died 1860) & Elizabeth Barker. Married 1884, Margaret, d of Edward & Sarah Sadler 2s 2d. Educated Norwood National School. Started work at 8, pulling milk cart. Colliery door boy at 10. Soldier (Buffs) 1876-83, (Zulu War 1879, Straits Settlements 2 years).

Miner in Wales 1883. Colliery Overman in China 1902; Western Valleys Miners' Agent 1908-2. Executive Member: SWMF 1898, 1908- & MFGB. Member: ILP & Co-operative Movement, Member, Bedwellty Board of Guardians. Estate £1524. Died 21 October 1936.

BARLOW John Emmott: 1st BArt1907 JP. Liberal: Denbigh District 1886, Knutsford 1885; MP Frome 1892-95, 1896-1918. **Sir John Barlow:** Born Adswood Grove, nr Stockport 1857, s of Thomas Barlow JP & Mary Ann, d of George Emmott CE. Married 1895, Hon. Anna Denman (Liberal candidate) d of 2nd Baron Denman. Educated Tottenham School. Civil Engineer. Barrister 1884. Company Chair & Landowner. Cheshire CC Alderman. Of Hazel Grove & Colwyn Bay. Estate £120,069. Died 17 September 1932.

BARR Christopher John: Conservative: Merthyr Tydfil B/E 1972, Bradford 1970, Colne Valley 1959. **Mr. Christopher Barr:** Born May 1933. Married Dain Barr, 3d. Educated Argentina, Cleckheaton Grammar School, Pocklington School, York. Royal Artillery, 1951-53. Computer Bureau Salesman, Managing Director, family commercial business. Spenborough TC 1966, Alderman.

BARRACLOUGH Jean: BSc DipEd (Wales). Liberal Democrat, Bridgend 2001. **Mrs. Jean Barraclough:** Born Rhondda 29 August 1930. Divorced, 1s 2d. Educated University of Wales, Aberystwyth (Chemistry/Geology) and Cardiff (Education). Science Teacher, 27 years, Bookshop owner. President: Porthcawl Chamber of Trade. Cttee Member: Porthcawl Horticultural Society. Member: Porthcawl U3A. School. Governor. Of Porthcawl.

BARRATT Michael Frank: Conservative, Ogmore 1987. **Mr. Michael Barratt:** Born 1935, Married. Educated Havelock Grammar School, Grimsby, Liverpool Polytechnic. Solicitor at Dorking 1953. Brighton BC. Chair: Brighton CPC 1985.

BARRETT Lorraine Jayne: Labour AM Cardiff South & Penarth, 1999. **Mrs. Lorraine Barrett:** Born Ynyshir 18 March, 1950. Married 1972, Paul Franklyn, s of David & Hazell Barrett, Atheist. Married Paul Barrett, rock & roll manager, 1s 1d. Educated Rhondda County Grammar School for Girls. Nurse, Llandough Hospital, 1955-70. Secretary, 1970-74, Personal & Political Assistant to Rt. Hon. Alun Michael MP. 1987-89/. Penarth 1991-99, Vale of Glamorgan BC.1995. Member: TGWU, Labour Party National Policy Forum, Welsh Labour Party Executive Cttee. Founder/Director, Penarth Youth Project (Youth Information Shop/Café). Vale of Glamorgan BC 1995-99

School governor. Assembly 1999. Deputy Chief Whip 1999, resigned 10/2/2000. Chair: Labour/Co-operative Group in Assembly. Interests: Education, Lifelong Learning, Culture, Sport, Welsh Language, Equality of Opportunity, Broadcasting Standards, Voluntary Sector Partnership. Hobbies: Reading Horror & Thriller Books, Walking, Cinema. Of Penarth (1969).

BARRETT Wycliffe Alan: Labour: North List 2003. **Mr. Wycliffe Barrett:** Born Bolton, Lancs. 23 February 1954, s of Wycliffe Constantine Barrett, electrical engineer, & Pauline Edna Barrett, clerical assistant. Married 1984, Fran Mason, Independent Chair, Child Protection Conference, 2d. Educated Smithills Secondary School, Bolton; Cardiff College of Further Education, Cyncoed (CQSW & DipSocial Work, Cert Training, etc). Staff Development & Training Officer, Cardiff CC. Ex-social worker. President, National Race Cttee 1992-2000. Chair: Regional Race Cttee 1992-2000; CENTREX Police Review Panel on Community Relations. Member: GMB South Western Regional Council. Branch Secretary, GNB. Interests: Socialist ideology, Democracy, Right to Vote. Hobbies: Reading, Cooking, Flying, Exercise & Body Building, Travel. Languages: English, Greek. Of Cardiff.

BARRITT William Moorhouse: Liberal: Barry 1979. **Mr. William Barritt:** Born Bridgnorth, Shropshire, 18 February 1932, s of Joseph Luther Barrett, headmaster. Church of England. Married 1955, Patricia Barritt, teacher, 2s 2d. Educated Bridgnorth Grammar School. Chartered Accountant. Chair: Barry Liberal Assn, Vale of Glamorgan Liberal Assn. Treasurer: Liberal Party of Wales, Lloyd George Society. Hobbies: Sports (Cricket, Soccer), Building Walls, Steam Railways.

BARTLETT, David Charles: BA (Wales). United Socialists, Assembly, South Central List 1999, Welsh Socialist Alliance, Cardiff South & Penarth 2001; Socialist Alternative, Cardiff South & Penarth 2003. **Mr. Dave Bartlett:** Born Milford Haven 1953. Educated University of Wales, Cardiff (History & Politics). Works in magistrates' court & adult literacy teacher. Member, Welsh Socialist Alliance. Labour Party member, Cardiff South & Penarth for 15 years, left in disgust at New Labour's move to the Right and abandoning working people in favour of big business. Secretary, CRISIS (Campaign to Save Cardiff Royal Infirmary). Member, Socialist Party & Welsh Socialist Alliance. Interests: National Health Service, Renationalisation, Restoration of Student Grants. Hobbies Sport, Reading, A Pint. Of Cardiff.

BARTLEY Stephen James: BA (Glam). Green Party, Cardiff Central 2001. **Mr. Stephen Bartley:** Born Haverfordwest, 26 September 1976, s of Edward Bartley, civil servant, & Jane Bartley. Buddhist. Educated Queens Park High School, Chester, University of Glamorgan. Local Civil Servant. Joined Green Party 1999. Editor, *Green Wales*. Interests: Sustainable Development, Agriculture, Environment, Human Rights. Hobbies: Buddhist Practice, Reading, Writing, British Sign Language, *The Archers*, Kung Fu. Languages: English, German.

BARTON Robert: Liberal Democrat: Swansea East 1992. **Mr. Robert Barton: Educated** London Business School. Principal Lecturer in Marketing. Woking BC.

BASKERVILLE Derek James: Plaid Cymru: Ebbw Vale 1970. **Mr. Derek Baskerville:** Born Ebbw Vale 1942, s of a wire rope splicer. Married Eironydd, teacher. Educated Ebbw Vale Grammar School, UWIST. Senior Statistician, British Steel Corporation, Llanwern. Joined Plaid Cymru 1961, founded Caldecott Branch. Of Caldecott.

BATCUP Madoc Robert: Plaid Cymru: Newport East 2001. **Mr. Madoc Batcup:** Born Swansea, 28 April 1954. Married 2c. Educated Wrekin College, Shropshire, Selwyn College, Cambridge, Council of Legal Action, Institut d'etudes Europeens, Brussels, Council of Legal Education. Barrister. With Swiss Bank Corporation 1983-93, Executive Director, London Oxford Capital Markets plc 1993-. Interests: European Union, Euro, Genetic Engineering, Welsh Economy. Hobbies: Photography, Diving, Travel (Japan & Asia). Languages: English, Japanese, French. Of Twickenham.

BATEMAN Luke Henry: Labour: Monmouth 1924, 1929, Bristol East, 1918, 1922. **Mr. Luke Bateman:** s of William Bateman. Railwayman. President, Bristol Brotherhood Movement. Of Bristol.

BATES, Michael John: CertEd 1970 BA (Open) 1970. Liberal Democrat, AM Montgomery 1997-. **Mr. Mick Bates:** Born Loughborough, 24 September 1947, s of George Bates & Lily Bates. Married Buddug Thomas, 1s 1d. Educated Loughborough College School; Worcester College of Education; Open University (Education & Science]). Science Teacher at Barrow-in-Soar, Shrewsbury & Market Drayton 1970-77. Farmer, 1977-. Chair, Primestock Producers (Farmers' Co-op). Branch Chair, NFU, Llanfair Caereinon. Chair, Powys NFU 1991. Powys CC. (Llanfair Caereinion) 1994-99. Chair, Llanfair Caereinion. Public Forum. Vice-Chair: Powys Eisteddfod Finance Cttee 1989. School Governor. Founder Member & Chair, National Assembly

Sustainable Energy Group (NASEGO. Lib Dem Assembly Spokesperson on Agriculture & Rural Affairs, Environment, Planning & Transport & European Affairs. Chair, Legislation Cttee. Hobbies: Sports, especially Rugby, Charity fundraising, Painting, Walking, Folk Music, Bob Dylan.

BATTERSBY Roy J: Workers' Revolutionary Party: Merthyr Tydfil & Rhymney Feb. 1974, Dundee East, 1979. **Mr. Roy Battersby:** Born 1937. Married 1997 Judy Loe, actress (partner from c.1977) 4s 1d. Educated grammar school, University College, London, London School of Economics. Television & Film Director. Member WRP 1968-80. Member: ACTT, WRP Central Cttee. *Filmography: Brotherly Love, In Defence 2000, Catherine Cookson's Moth, A Touch of Frost (TV Series) 19922. The Black Candle 1991, King of the Ghetto 1986, Mr. Love 1985, Winter flight 1984, The Home Front 1983, The Body 1970.*

BATTLE, Maria: Labour, Ceredigion Assembly 1999, Ceredigion B/E Feb. 2000. **Ms. Maria Battle:** Born Merseyside 1957. Anglican (choir, youth club leader & Sunday school teacher) 2c. Educated Convent of Mercy, Liverpool, Milan, Sheffield University. Articled to South Glam. CC. Solicitor & independent consultant, Manager, NCH Cymru Action for Children. Ex-principal local government officer on planning, education, highways & social services. Carmarthenshire CC. Member, National Council for Family Proceedings, Special Needs. Director, Age Concern Ceredigion. Policy Officer, Welsh Office, Children's Society. Asst Commissioner (Legal & Admin) to the Children's Commissioner for Wales 2001-.

BEANY Captain (Barry Kirk): Real Bean/New Millennium Bean Party: Neath B/E 1991, Aberavon 1992, 1997, South Wales West Euro 1994, 1999, Ogmore B/E 2002, Cardiff Central & South/Central List 2003. **Captain Beany:** Born Neath, 23 September 1954, s of Barry Kirk, steelworker, & Wynne Howard Kirk. Church of England. Educated Sandfields Comprehensive School. Computer Programmer, BP Chemicals, Port Talbot, unemployed. Voluntary Charity Fundraiser. Contested BC elections as The World's Greatest Lover Candidate, Sold Rosettes at Neath by-election to help buy child's electric wheel chair, started dressing as Captain Beany in the 1980s after sitting in a Bath of Baked beans for a day to raise money for charity, Regularly paints head red, wears a red cape and tights, represents Beans, home planet of Baked beans. Founder/Leader, New Millennium Bean Party 26 June 200. Placed £50 bet on self to win, 2001, winnings for SCOPE (cerebral palsy charity), would donate deposit if saved. Hobbies: Social-

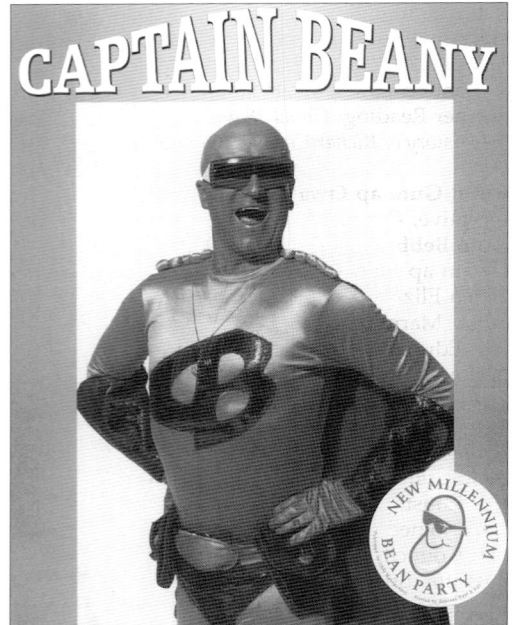

Barry Kirk ('Captain Beany').

ising, Music. Keeping Fit, Charity Fundraising. 4th place in Kellogg's *Best of British Eccentrics* Contest 2002. Of Sandfields, Port Talbot.

BEASLEY Trefor: Plaid Cymru: Aberdare 1955. **Mr. Trefor Beasley:** Born Llangennech 1918, s of William Beasley. Married Eileen Beasley, 2c. Educated Llangennech elementary school. Began work at 14, miner at 17, sacked for trade union activity, Lodge delegate at 20, Secretary, Llangennech Lodge NUM. Llanelli RDC 1955-. Chairman, Carmarthenshire Cttee, Plaid Cymru. Constantly refused to pay rates because Demand Notes were printed only in English 1955-1960, when the council agreed to his request. Twice summoned before magistrates & bailiffs sent in. Languages: Welsh, English.

BEAUMONT-THOMAS Lionel: MC. 1917 JP. (Hereford). 1922. Conservative: Llanelli 1923, Pontypool 1924. MP Kings Norton1929-35. **Colonel Lionel Beaumont-Thomas:** Born 1 August 1893, s of Richard Beaumont-Thomas, Alvington Court, Gloucestershire. & Nora, d of James Anderson, Lowestoft. Anglican. Married (1) Pauline Grace, d of Sidney Marriott (secretly at Registry Office because of his mother's disapproval) 4c. Divorced 1934, (2) 1934, Iseult Marjery Bland. Educated Rugby School. Company Director 26 years, Deputy Chair, Richard Thomas Ltd1931-. Freeman of the City of London. Member, Haberdashers Company. Herefordshire CC 1925-. Joined Army Reserve, 1912, Lieutenant, RA 1914, Captain 1915, Major 1917,

Retired from TA 1923, Ministry of Economic Warfare 1939, General Staff 1940, Colonel 1942, Member, Middle East Mission 1942. Of Madeley, & London. Died, Lost at Sea, December 1942. Further Reading: *David Wainwright, Men of Steel, the History of Richard Thomas and his family 1986.*

BEBB Guto ap Owain: BA (Wales) ALBA. Conservative, Ogmore B/E 2002, Conwy 2003. **Mr. Guto Bebb:** Born Wrexham, 9 October 1968, s of Owain ap Emrys Bebb, chartered accountant, & Helen Elizabeth Bebb, teacher. Calvinistic Methodist. Married 1993 Esyllt Penri, translator, 1s 1d. Educated Ysgol Syr Hugh Owen, Caernarfon, University of Wales, Aberystwyth (History). Freelance Business Consultant' Partner, Egin Partnership, Partner, Hole in the Wall Bookshop, Caernarfon. Wine Editor, Barn. Joined Plaid Cymru 1987; Chair: Plaid Cymru, Caernarfon Constituency 1996-2001, Caernarfon Agent 2001. Joined Conservatives. October 2001. Member: Council, Europe Yes, Euro No, Chair: Business for Stirling, Gwynedd CAB Board. Conservative Prospective Parliamentary Candidate, Conwy 2004. Interests: Economic Development, Welfare State, Europe. Hobbies: Reading, Music, Fine Wine. Languages: Welsh, English, French (very little). Of Bontnewydd.

BEBB William Ambrose: BA 1918 MA 1920 (Wales). Plaid Cymru: Caernarfonshire 1945. **Mr. Ambrose Bebb:** Born Goginan, 4 August 1894, s of Edward Hughes Bebb, farmer, & Anne Jones. Presbyterian Church of Wales Elder & Sunday School Teacher. Married 1931, Eluned Pierce Roberts, 7c. Educated Tregaron County School, University of Wales, Aberystwyth, Sorbonne & Rennes. 1920-25. Lecturer in Celtic, Sorbonne. Lecturer in History, Bangor Normal College, Lecturer & Head of Scripture Knowledge Department. WEA & Extra Mural Lecturer, historian, Writer. One of the founders of Plaid Cymru. Bangor CC. 1939-46, Candidate 1937. Languages: Welsh, English, French. Died 27 April 1955. *Books: W Ambrose Bebb: Y Baradwys Bell Llydaw, Pererindodau 1941, Dydd-Lyfr Pythefnos neu y Ddawns Angau 1939, Dydd-Lyfr 1941, Dydd-Lyfr 1942, Ein Hen Hen Hanes, Machlud y Mynachlogydd, Llywodraeth y Cestyll, Cyfnod y Tuduriaid, Machlud yr Oesoedd Canol, Canrif o Hanes Y Tŵr Gwyn, Yr Ysgol Sul, yr Argyfwng.*

BELL Ronald McMillan: Kt 1980 QC 1966 MA (Oxon) 1942 BA. 936. Conservative: Caerphilly B/E 1939, MP Newport B/E May-July 1945, Buckinghamshire South 1950-74, Beaconsfield 1974-. **Sir Ronald Bell:** Born Cardiff 14 April 1914, s of John Bell. Church of Scotland. Married 1954, Elizabeth Audrey Goswell, 2s 1d. Educated Cardiff High School & Magdalene College, Oxford. Secretary & Treasurer, Oxford Union

1936, President, Oxford University Conservative Assn 1935. Barrister, Grays Inn 1938. RNVR 1939-45, Lieut-Commander. Paddington BC 1947-49. Advisory Director, Michael Clark & Associates (PR) 1960-61. Conservative spokesman on Defence 1965-66. Died 27 February 1982. *Books: R. M. Bell, Crown Proceedings 1948.*

BELL Stephen William: Socialist Labour, South Central List 1999, Wales Euro 1999, Welsh Socialist Alliance, Torfaen 2001. **Mr. Steve Bell:** Born Panteg (father, shop steward at Ebbw Vale steelworks). Married c. Teacher at Cardiff. Member NUT. Member, Labour Party 1986-92, supporter of Militant. Chair: Hounslow Anti-Poll Tax Federation, delegate to London Anti Poll Tax Federation 1984-95. Worked in Department of Employment, Branch Chair/Secretary CPSA, Regional CPSA Organiser. Active in getting Union branches and NUM lodges to 'twin' during miners' strike 1984-85 and Pit closures 1992. Chair: Hounslow Anti Poll Tax Federation. Founder Member/Chair, Reclaim our Trade Union Rights Campaign in South Wales. Member: Gwent Campaign to Defend Asylum Seekers. Member, Labour Party 1986-92. Secretary, Torfaen Socialist Labour Party,. Member NUT. Founder Member/Chair: Gwent Branch, Welsh Socialist Alliance. Hobbies: Music, Local History, Sport (member Llanwern Rugby XV). Of Cwmbran.

BELL William Mather: Conservative: Pontypool 1970. **Mr. William Bell:** Born May 1930. Married 6 c. Educated Bedford School. Garage Owner & Motor Trader. Managing Director, Motoring Services Ltd. Youth Secretary, East Midlands RFU. Bristol CC 1961-. Bedfordshire CC.

BELLAMY David Arthur James: Vote 2 Stop the War, Mid & West List 2003. **Mr. David Bellamy:** Born Pembroke, 15 June 1943, s of Arthur Bellamy, carpenter, & Edith Hurn. Married Jennifer Keal, artist, 1d. Artist & Writer. With wife runs courses on painting in UK & abroad. Produced 5 videos on painting. Of Erwood.

BELLIS John Herbert: LlB (Liverpool). Liberal: Conway 1959. **Mr. John Bellis:** Born Penmaenmawr 11 April 1930, s of Dr. Thomas & Jane Bellis . Married 1961, Sheila Helen McNeil Ford, 3c. Educated Friars School, Bangor; Liverpool University. Admitted solicitor, 1953. Army 1953-55, Lieutenant, Welch Regt. Solicitor at Penmaenmawr 1958-84. Chair, Industrial Tribunals, Manchester Region 1984-92, Nottingham Region 1992-. Languages: Welsh, English.

BELZAK Stephen: BA (Wales) 1980. Liberal Democrat: Pontypridd 1992. **Mr. Steve Belzak:** Born London, 15 May 1958, s of Stefan Belzak &

Beatrice Mary Belzak, factory workers. Protestant. Married 1982, Verity Keep, clerical officer, 1d. Educated Pontypridd Grammar School; University of Wales, Cardiff (Politics & Economics). Legal Executive 1986-94. Lecturer, University of Wales Cardiff Business School & School of Lifelong Learning; Lecturer, Humanities School 1997- & MA student. Guest Lecturer, Coleg Glanhafren. Chair, Rhondda-Cynon-Taf Liberal Democrats -1997, Taf-Ely BC 1983-96. Rhondda/Cynon/Taf BC (Cilfynydd) 1999-. Pontypridd TC 1991-. Member, Institute of Legal Executives 1993. Hobbies: Reading, Writing, Current Affairs. Of Cilfynydd.

BENNETT, Caroline Jeanette: BA. (Reading). Liberal Democrat, Assembly, Islwyn 1999. **Ms. Caroline Bennett:** Born Luton, 6 November 1972, d of Michael Bennett, care worker, & Patricia Edith Christine Bennett, senior care assistant. Baptised Methodist, Married Catholic. Married 31/8/2001 Andrew Hucker, retail supervisor. Educated Brookfield Primary School, Cwmbran, Brynmawr Comprehensive School; Reading University (Linguistics with Language Pathology). Speech & Language Therapist, NHS Trust. Secretary, Caerphilly Liberal Democrats. Contested ComC & CC elections. Volunteer, Homestar, single parents' charity, extensive fundraiser for charities. Interests: Health, Education, Youth Work, Animal Rights. Hobbies: Arts, Literature, Dancing, Theatre, Cinema. Of Ystrad Mynach.

BENNETT Ernest Nathaniel: Kt 1930 JP. MA (Oxon). Labour MP: Cardiff Central 1929-31, National Labour 1931-45, Candidate: Westbury 1918, Banbury 1922, St. Pancras South West 1923, 1924, Joined Labour Party 1916. Liberal MP: Woodstock 1906-10. **Captain, Sir Ernest Bennett:** Born Gorleston, Suffolk, 1873, s of Revd George Bennett, Rector of Bede, Suffolk, & Anna Bennett. Anglican. Married Marguerite Kleinwort, 3c (incl. Sir Frederick Bennett, Conservative MP). Educated Durham School, Hertford College, Oxford (triple 1st). Fellow of Hertford College 1891, Lecturer, Wadham, Lincoln & Hertford Colleges. War Correspondent: Crete 1897, Sudan 1898. Volunteer Ambulance Corps, South Africa 1898-1900, Oxfordshire Volunteers, South Africa 1902, Ottoman Army 1911-12. British Red Cross Commissioner 1914-15, Army, 1915-18. PPS 1909, Asst. Postmaster-General 1932-35, Temporary Chair of Committees. Member: Archbishops' Commission on Church & State; Indian Franchise Cttee 1922; British Delegation, League of Nations 1934; Council, Psychical Research Society; Governing Body of the Church in Wales. Member of the Right Club, set up by Captain A. M. Ramsay MP to create an united front of those anxious to bolster Chamberlain's appeasement policy. The only National Labour candidate for a Welsh seat. Of Aberangell & London. Died 2 February 1947. *Books: E. N. Bennett, Apparitions and Haunted Houses 1939.*

BENNETT Nicholas: BSc 1991 MBA Liberal Democrat, Ynys Môn 2001. **Mr. Nicholas Bennett:** Born St. Asaph 29 April 1969, s of Nicholas Bennett, licensee, & Catherine Ellen Bennett, solicitor's clerical officer. Church of Wales. Married 1994, Nia Gwenllian Bennett, personnel officer (of Llanfairpwll) 1s 2d. Educated Ysgol Goronwy Owen, Benllech; Ysgol Gyfun Llangefni; University of Wales, Aberystwyth (Political Science). Research Assistant, Richard Livsey MP., Economic Officer, Ynys Môn, Regional Policy Adviser, Wales European Centre, Brussels 1995-99, Director, Newidiem (economic development consultancy), Founded DARPAR, his own economic development consultancy. Economic Development Officer, North West Wales, Special Adviser to Liberal Democrat Assembly Cabinet Members. Contested Ceredigion DC 1991. Interests: Europe, Regional, Policy, Social Justice, Welsh Language. Hobbies: Reading, Running, Family Life, Rock Music. Languages: Welsh, English, Intermediate French. Of Cardiff.

BENNETT Nicholas Jerome: MA (Sussex)1974. Conservative MP: Pembroke 1987-92, Candidate: Hackney Central 1979, Reading West 1997. **Mr. Nicholas Bennett:** Born 7 May1947, (ggs of Socialist, Tom Mann, & gs of an editor of *Daily Worker*). Educated Sedgehill School, London; Southwark & Wallworth Colleges of Further Education; North London Polytechnic; Sussex University. Teacher & lecturer 1976-85. Education Officer, Borough of Havering. PPS 1980, Under-Secretary for Wales 1990-92. Managing Partner, Sussex Associates, public affairs & education consultants 199. Joint Vice-Chair, Conservative MPs' Backbench Party Organisation Cttee 1989-90, Joint Secretary Conservative Transport Cttee 1987-88. Lewisham BC 1974-78. Co-opted Member, ILEA 1978-81.

BENNETT William: JP. MPS. Labour: Cardiff East 1935, Guildford 1918, 1922, 1923, Hitchin B/E June 1933, Harborough B/E November 1933, Hitchin 1931, MP: Hitchin 1929-31, Joined National Liberal Party 1937. **Mr. William Bennett:** Born Oakhill, Somerset 7 April, 1873, s of Samuel Bennett. Married 1899, Ethel Mary Murrin, 1d. Educated Bath Grammar School, Metropolitan College of Pharmacy. Pharmaceutical Chemist 1896. London CC Alderman 1934-37. Of Battersea. Died 4 November 1937.

BENNETT-COLLINS Heather – see COLLINS Heather Bennett.

BENNEY Clifford Terence: Plaid Cymru: Cynon Valley 1992; Wales Euro 2004. **Mr. Terry Benny:** Born Abercynon 13 April 1947. Married, c. Educated Bryngolwg Secondary Modern School. Legal Executive, solicitors' office. Founder Member, Merthyr/Cynon Action for the Homeless, Cynon Valley Hospital Broadcast Service, Rugby Club Choir, Chair, Mountain Ash YMCA. Joined Plaid Cymru 1972. Secretary, Mountain Ash RFC Supporters Club. Cynon Valley DC 1987-. Rhondda-Cynon-Taf BC. Schools governor. Interests: Housing, Licensing, Social Services, Hobbies: Rugby, Singing. Of Mountain Ash.

BENSON Robin Noel: Vote 2 Stop the War Party, Mid & West List 2003. **Mr. Robin Benson:** Born 1963. Married 3c. Housing Adviser, national housing charity, working with homeless and badly housed people. Runs a community-based circus. Long-standing peace campaigner. Active community development volunteer. Of Llawhaden, Pembs.

BERESFORD Michael Simon: Natural Law Party: Gower 1992. **Mr. Michael Beresford:** Wales Director, Transcendental Meditation, Wales. Member, NLP Executive Council. Emigrated to Canada.

BERMAN Rodney Simon: BSc PhD (Glasgow). Liberal Democrat: Rhondda 1997, South/Central List 1999, 2003, Cardiff South & Penarth 2001, 2003. **Dr. Rodney Berman:** Born Glasgow, 20 April 1969, s of Stanley Harris Berman, teacher, & Maxine Berman, part-time secretary. Jewish by birth, atheist by belief. Educated Woodfarm High School, Thornlie Bank, Glasgow; Glasgow University (Pharmacology); Research Fellow, Welsh National School of Medicine. Senior Researcher, Liberal Democrat Group, National Assembly. Contested Cardiff CC elections 1995. Cardiff CCC (Plasnewydd) 1999. Leader, Liberal Democrat Group, 2000, Leader of the Opposition. Member, Cardiff Harbour Authority. Chair/Secretary, Cardiff Central Liberal Democrats. Chair, South Wales Central Liberal Democrats. Interests: Making government at all levels more responsive, consultative & accountable to electorate, Education, Environment. Hobbies: Computers, Photography, Travel, Cinema, Cookery. Languages: English, very basic French. Of Cardiff.

BERRY David: Referendum Party: Preseli 1997. **Mr. David Berry:** Born 1934. Married Susan, 3c. 26 years in Management, self-employed in tourism. Of Preseli (1971).

BERRY Peter Sain ley Berry – see SAIN LEY BERRY P. G.

BEST Keith Lander: TD MA (Oxon). Conservative MP: Anglesey 1979-87, Ynys Môn 1983-87. **Mr. Keith Best:** Born 10 June 1949, s of Peter & Margaret Louise Best. Married1990, Elizabeth Margaret Gibson, 2d. Educated Brighton College, Keble College, Oxford. Barrister, Inner Temple 1971, Lecturer in Law 1973. Member of Lloyds. TA 1970-76: Major. Brighton BC 1976-80. PPS 1981-84. Resigned as MP just before the 1987 election after being found guilty of fraudulently obtaining British Telecom shares. Director, Prisoners Abroad 1989-93, Chief Executive. Languages: Learned Welsh, English. Of London. *Books etc: K. L. Best, Write Your Own Will 1978; The Right way to Prove a Will 1981.*

BESTIC Penni: Plaid Cymru: Cardiff West 1992. **Ms. Penni Bestic:** Born 4 May 1953. Educated Johannesburg, West Sussex College of Design. Graphic Designer. Theatre Designer, Aberystwyth 1975-79. Member of Argraff, a design & photocopying co-operative. Information Officer, Disability Wales. Plaid Cymru spokesperson on employment. Of Cardiff from 1979.

BESWICK Paul Michael Olajade: BSc. Green Party List 2003. **Mr. Paul Beswick:** Born Bury, Lancs. 13 October 1966, s of Professor M. O. A. Durojaiye, psychologist, & Susan Myra Beswick, Lecturer in English. Zen Buddhist (lapsed Roman Catholic). Educated University (Management Sciences). Community Worker. Secretary, Friends of the Earth (Wales) 2000-02. Roads Protester 1995-97. Interests: Environmental Policy; Ecological Sustainability. Hobbies: Kung Fu, Tai Chi, Meditation. Languages: English, Beginner's Spanish. Of Penarth.

BETTELL-HIGGINS David E: Liberal: Merthyr Tydfil Feb. & Oct. 1974. **Mr. David Bettell-Higgins:** Born July 1949. Married 4c. Educated Blackwood Secondary Modern School; Pontypool FE College. Owns a DIY business. Of Cefn Coed.

BEVAN Allan James: Workers Revolutionary Party Candidate for Aberavon 1974, Oct. **Mr. Jim Bevan:** Born Halifax, 1943, s of a rugby league player. Married 2c. Fitter, Port Talbot. Of Cwmafan.

BEVAN Aneurin: PC 1945, JP 1928. Labour MP: Ebbw Vale 1929-. **Rt. Hon. Aneurin Bevan:** Born Tredegar 15 November 1897, s of David Bevan, miner, and Phoebe, d of John Protheroe, blacksmith. Married Jennie Lee, MP. Educated Sirhowy Central School. Miner 1911. Chair, Tŷ Trist Miners' Lodge Cttee 1916; Delegate to SWMF 1917. An eye problem kept him out of the

Aneurin Bevan.

army but he became known as an opponent of the Great War. Student, Central Labour College 1919-21. Unemployed 1921-24. Miners' Disputes Agent 1926-29. Tredegar UDC 1922-29. Monmouthshire CC 1928-31, Chair, Ebbw Vale CLP 1923-29. Expelled from Labour Party for supporting Popular Front 1938. Opposed the National Government throughout the war and was particularly critical of Winston Churchill & Ernest Bevin. Member, Labour Party NEC 1944-, Labour Party Treasurer 1956-. Editor, *Tribune* 1942-45. Minister of Health 1945-50: created the National Health Service, Minister of Labour 1951, resigned office, April 1951 in opposition to the scale & speed of re-armament expenditure & Whip withdrawn. Deputy Leader, October 1959. Died 6 July 1960. *Books: Aneurin Bevan, Why Not Trust the Tories 1944, Democratic Values 1950, In Place of Fear 1952.* Further Reading: *Vincent Broom, Aneurin Bevan (1953); John Campbell, Nye Bevan & The Mirage of British Socialism 1987, Huw T. Edwards, Aneurin 1, Rhif 1 1961, Michael Foot: Aneurin Bevan; Mark M. Krug, Aneurin Bevan, Cautious Rebel (1961); Jennie Lee, This Great Journey (1963), My Life with Nye (1980); David Llewellyn: Nye, the beloved Patrician; Kenneth O. Morgan: Labour People: Leaders & Lieutenants (1987; Dai Smith: Aneurin Bevan & the world of South Wales 1993; D. Ben Rees: Cymry Adnabyddus 1952-1972, 1978.*

BEVAN David H: Independent Caerphilly 1974, Feb. **Mr. David Bevan:** Born 1939. Married 2c.

Educated Caerphilly Grammar School. Technician, Mineral Exploitation Department, University of Wales, Cardiff. Treasurer: Caerphilly Shelter Group.

BEVAN Digby John: Plaid Cymru: Newport West 1987. **Mr. Digby Bevan:** Born 1952. Married. 1s. Civil Engineer, with a Cardiff housing assn. Chief Executive, Cymdeithas Tai Cantref cyf, Newcastle Emlyn. Chair, Council of Welsh Federation of Housing Assns 2002. Worked with irrigation projects in West Indies, Australia, Sri Lanka & Malaysia.

BEVAN Michael James: Conservative: Islwyn 1983. **Mr. Michael Bevan:** Born Pontywain 6 August, 1944. Married, 1 stepson. Educated Cross Keys Primary School, Pontywain Secondary Modern School. Sales & Marketing Administrator: Westland Helicopters, Lansing Henley Forklift Trucks, Pontllanffraith 1978-. Member: Welsh Conservative Executive. Milbourne PC. Interests: Foreign Affairs, Housing.

BEVAN Philip James: Plaid Cymru, South/East List 1999. **Mr. Philip Bevan:** Caerphilly CBC (Morgan Jones Ward). Cabinet Member for Education & Leisure 1999; Chair: Corporate Safety Cttee, Industrial Liaison Working Party; Members Services Working Party. School Governor. Member, Court: University of Wales, Cardiff; University of Wales, Aberystwyth; Coleg Harlech. Chair: Educational Support Initiative (ESIS). Member: National Playing Fields Assn; University of Wales Audit Cttee. Of Caerphilly.

BIDDULPH Joseph Anthony: Pro-Life Alliance, Pontypridd 2001, South/East List 2003, Christian Democratic Party, Wales Euro 2004. **Mr. Joe Biddulph:** Born Handsworth, Birmingham, 19 January 1951, s of Frederick George Biddulph (clerical officer) & Maud Harriet Biddulph, Roman Catholic. Married 1973, Margaret Rose Hudson (support worker), 4s 1d. Writer & Publisher in specialist areas including African languages & Heraldry. Editor, *Pro-Life Magazine.* Unemployed for several years. Lived at Pontypridd since 1975. Chair: Cwm Tâf Credit Union. Member: Pontypridd Bite for the Night homeless shelter, Ulster Scots Language Society. Chair, Plaid Cymru, branch & constituency 1980-81. Contested BC for Plaid Cymru and as Independent. Interests: An unremitting search for social justice particularly in regard to the jobless and in the workplace. Hobbies: Book Collecting, Dendrology, Church Architecture, Nonconformist History, Singing, Jazz, Dialect & Scots Language, Walking, Travelling by Public Transport, Photography. Languages: Reading knowledge of Welsh.

English, reading knowledge of seven other languages, smattering of dozens.

BIGGINS Thomas Henry: Conservative, Clwyd South 2001. **Mr. Tom Biggins:** Born Whitchurch, Shropshire, 4 September 1960. Educated Shrewsbury School, Oxford. Company Secretary, S. Biggins Ltd (family's wholesale cheese business (founded by great-grandfather) 1982-. Chair, North Shropshire Conservative Assn 1996-99. Shropshire CC 1997 (re-elected on General Election Day). School Governor. Member: Pengwern Boat Club. Interests: Rural Economy, Law & Order, Local Government. Hobbies: Historical Matters. Of Whitchurch, Shropshire.

BIRCH Evelyn Nigel Chetwode, Baron Rhyl of Holywell 1970: PC 1954. OBE 1945. Conservative MP: Flint 1945-50, West Flint 1950-70. **Rt. Hon. Nigel Birch:** Born 18 November, 1906, s of General Sir Noel Birch. Anglican lay reader. Married 1950, Hon. Esme Glyn, d. of 4th Baron Wolverton. Educated Eton. Stockbroker. Had saved £45,000 by 1939 and retired to study politics. TA, KRRC & General Staff 1939-45, Lieut-Colonel. Under-Secretary, Air 1951-52, Parl-Secretary, Defence 1952-54, Minister of Works 1954-55, Secretary for Air 1955-57, Economic Secretary to the Treasury 1957-58, Resigned over policy 1958. Director, London and Manchester Assurance Co. Farmer of £60,000 Hampshire farm, previously farmed in Flintshire. Died 8 March 1981. *Books: E. N. C. Birch, The Conservative Party 1948.*

BISHOP Mark Andrew: MA (Cantab). Conservative: Cynon Valley 1987, Cambridge 1992, **Mr. Mark Bishop:** Born 12 July, 1958. Anglican lay reader. Married Christine. Educated Leys School, Cambridge; Downing College, Cambridge, Cambridge, Inns of Court Law School. Chair, Cambridge University Conservative Assn. President, Cambridge Union 1980. London Barrister 1981. Standing Counsel, Department of Trade & Industry. Treasurer, Battersea Conservative Assn. 1983-85. President, Coningsby Club.

BLACK David Michael: Christian Labour & Centre Alliance: Pontypridd B/E 1989, Vale of Glamorgan B/E 1989, Mid-Staffordshire B/E March 1990, Bootle B/E Nov. 1990, UK Independence Party: Reading 2001. **Mr. David Black:** Insurance Clerk, of Reading. Founder of the Christian Alliance: Stood as a family Man on a policy of anti-Communism, anti-abortion & anti European Community and favouring self-government for Wales in an independent Great Britain.

BLACK Peter Malcolm: BA. MA. Liberal Democrat, Swansea East, 1999, 2003. A.M. South/West List 1997. **Mr. Peter Black:** Born Clatterback, Wirral, 30 January 1960, s of John Malcolm black & Joan Arlene Black. Roman Catholic (not practising because of theological differences). Married (1) Divorced 1984 Patricia Mary Hopkin, divorced 1995 (2) August 2000, Angela Lynette Jones, Executive Officer, Swansea Housing Assn. Educated Wirral Boys Grammar School, University of Wales, Swansea (English & History). Research Assistant, West Glam. Social Services Dept. 1982-83, Civil Servant, Land Registry for Wales, 1983-99. Swansea CC 1984- (Group Leader, 1984-99, Leader of the Opposition). Chair, Liberal Democrats Wales, Secretary, Liberal Democrats Wales Finance & Administration Cttee. Spokesperson on Local Government, Environment & Housing 1999. Deputy Minister, Local Government, October 2000-03. Chair: Education & Lifelong Learning Cttee 2003. Interests: Housing, local government. Hobbies: Science Fiction, Poetry, Film, Theatre, Cats, Poetry. Of Manselton, Swansea.

BLACKBURN Graham Robert: BA.(Cantab). Liberal Democrat: Torfaen 1983, 1987. Mr. **Graham Blackburn:** Born 25 May 1939. Married a teacher, 4c. Educated Newport High School, St. Catherine's College, Cambridge. Engineer. General Manager & Director, British Steel Corporation Workshops. Of Crickhowell.

BLACKMAN Anne: Independent, Caerphilly 2003. **Ms. Anne Blackman:** Born Abercynon, 19 December 1946, d of Michael Scannell, Mines Contractor. Roman Catholic. Married 1973 Thomas Michael Blackman, industrial chemist. Ex-bank official. Nelson ComC 1991-. Caerphilly CBC 1995-. Member: Gwent Assn for the Blind, Wales Council for the Blind. Interests: Environment, Community. Hobbies: Cooking, Gardening, Music. Of Nelson.

BLACKWOOD Jonathan: MA (St. Andrews) MA PhD (London). Plaid Cymru Wales Euro, 2004. **Dr. Jonathan Blackwood:** Born Glasgow, 4 July 1973, s of David Blackwood, land surveyor, & Phyllis Paterson Blackwood, secretary. Married 2001, Kathryn Hilsden, conservation officer, Torfaen BC. Educated Kelvinside Academy, Glasgow; St. Andrew's University (1st Art History); Courtauld Institute of Art, London University. Curator of Collections, Kettle's Yard, Cambridge University; Lecturer in Media & Culture, University of Glamorgan 2001. Chair, Cathays Branch, Plaid Cymru. Interests: Environment, Equal Opportunities, Europe, Constitutional Affairs, Education, Culture, Sport, Welsh Language. Hobbies: Soccer (Newport County), Cricket (Glamorgan), All forms of music, Reading, Visual Arts from 1700, Social & Political History, Contemporary Politics. *Books: Jonathan*

Blackwood, Winifred Nicholson (English painter) 2001; Joint Author, Wales: many Talents, many Cultures.

BLAKEBOROUGH-POWNALL Roger: BA (Cantab). Liberal: Gower 1979. **Mr. Roger Blakeborough-Pownall:** Born September 1944. Educated Rhyl Grammar School; Queens College, Cambridge. Solicitor.

BLAUSTEN Richard: Conservative: Merthyr Tydfil & Rhymney Valley 1983. **Mr. Richard Blausten:** Born 18 December 1948. Married, 1 d. Educated Clifton College, Bristol, Sheffield University. Editor *Insurance Mail & Media International*. Editor & Publisher, Mitre House Publishing (*Charities Management Magazine, IFA Review, General Insurance*). Chair, English Speaking Union Debating Society 1979-81. Barnet BC 1974-82, Chair, Education Committee.

BLEWETT Charles A: JP CE MIME. Labour: Cardiff North-West, Feb. & Oct. 1974. **Mr. Charles Blewett:** Born 1922. Married 3 c. Miner 1936, Army 1939-45, Captain, Chartered Engineer, Colliery Manager, NCB Industrial Relations Officer. Penallta Colliery Lodge Secretary, NUM 1964. President, local OAPs Association.

BLOMFIELD-SMITH Rosamund: Conservative, South Wales East Euro 1994. **Mrs. Rosamund Blomfield-Smith:** Married Clive Blomfield Smith, 2 stepsons. Company Director 2001; Chief Executive, Housing Finance Corporation 2001-2002; Investment Banker 1982-2002. Member: National Rivers Board; Council & Audit Cttee, Water Aid. Wandsworth BC 1990- (Vice-Chair: Policy & Finance Cttee). Hobbies: Gardening, Playing Piano, Tennis. Speaks 5 European languages & reads 11. Of Ross on Wye.

BODY Richard Bernard Francis Stewart: Kt. Conservative: Abertillery B/E Dec 1950, Rotherham 1950, Leek 1951, MP Billericay 1955-59, Holland with Boston 1966-97, Boston with Skegness 1997-2001. **Sir Richard Body:** Born 18 May 1927, s of Lieut-Colonel Richard F. Body. Married 1959, Marion, d. of Major H. Graham OBE. Educated Reading School. RAF 1945-48. Barrister (Middle Temple) 1949. Farmer, Stockbroker & Underwriting Member of Lloyds (6 syndicates). Vice-President, Small Farmers' Assn. Joint Master Windsor Forest Bloodhounds. Chair: Open Seas Forum 1971-, Society for Individual Freedom 1987-, Consumer Watch 1988. Joint Chair, Get Britain Out Campaign 1975. President, Cobden Club 1981. Vice-President, Selsdon Group. Member, Association of Scientific Workers. Resigned Conservative whip 1994-94, in protest at increase in UK contributions to EU Budget. Chair, Select Cttee on Agriculture 1983-87. Of Stanford Dingley, nr. Reading. *Books: Richard Body, The Breakdown of Europe, 1998.*

BOND Henry Coulson: JP (Carms) 1896. Conservative: Carmarthen Boroughs B/E 1912. **Mr. Henry Bond:** Born 27 July 1864, s of Frank Walter Bond JP DL. Wargrave Court, Berks. Anglican. Married 1891 Frances Edith, d of Major Francis Beaumaris Buckeley, Linden Hill, Berks. Educated Rugby. Steel Manufacturer: With father founded South Wales Tinplate Co. (13 mills) & Cwmbwrla, amalgamated with Richard Thomas & Co 1898, Merged with Cwmfelin Steel & Tinplate Co 1918, Chair, Richard Thomas & Co Ltd. 1920-31, Director: Grosvenor Steel & Tinplate Co, Whitford Steel & Carbonisation Co Ltd, Raglan Colliery Co.Ltd, New Sharleston Raven Tinplate Co Ltd, Swansea Naval Colliery Ltd, South Wales Tinplate Corporation. President, National Federation of Iron & Steel Manufacturers 1926-27. High Sheriff of Carmarthenshire 1920-21. Of Wargrave Court, Berks. Estate £54,769. Died June 1937.

BONE Peter William: ACA1977 Conservative: Islwyn 1992, Mid & West Wales Euro 1994, Pudsey 1997, Wellingborough 2001; Re-adopted as candidate for Wellingborough 2003. **Mr. Peter Bone:** Born Billericay 19 October 1952, s of William & Marjorie Bone. Anglican. Married 1981, Jeanette Beatrice Sweeney, 1s 1d. Educated Westcliff on Sea Grammar School. Chartered Accountant. Financial Director, Columbia Precision Products Ltd. Essex, 1977-83. Chief Executive, High Tech Electronics plc. Managing Director, Palm Travel (West) Ltd & of property companies 1990-. Press Secretary, Paul Channon MP 1982-84. Southend BC 1977-86. Member, All Wales Conservative Policy Group. Chair, Islwyn Conservative Assn. Hobbies: Playing Cricket & Golf, Running in London Marathons.

BONNER-EVANS Elenor Elisabeth: Plaid Cymru: Swansea East 1992, Assembly List, Mid & West Wales 1999. **Miss Elenor Bonner-Evans:** Born 10 July 1970. Student Union Officer, President, Powys, Dyfed, West Glamorgan Area, National Union of Students. Member, Council, University of Wales. Youngest candidate in Wales 1992. Languages: Welsh, English. Of Llanwrin, Machynlleth.

BOOTH Richard William George: MBE 31.12.2003 MA (Oxon) Hon. Dr. Regeneration (US University). Socialist Labour, Mid & West List. Revival Party Candidate for Brecon & Radnor, 1983. **Mr. Richard Booth:** Born 12 September 1938. Married 1987, Hope Escourt Stuart Barrie. Educated Rugby, Oxford University. Worked at City of London accountants for 3 weeks. Bookseller since 1961. Opened second-hand book-shop at Hay on Wye 1962. Chair, Richard Booth (Booksellers) Ltd. the world's largest second hand bookshop. Founding Father, centres of bookselling at Hay 1961, Redu 1984, Veckerell 1988, Montolieu 1989. Bredvoor 1992, Fjaerling 1996, Dalmellington 2992. Chair, Welsh Book-sellers Assn. Hobbies: Creating a monarchy in Hay. Of Hay on Wye. *Books: Richard Booth: Countrylife Book of Collecting 1976, Independence for Hay 1997, My Kingdom of Books, 1999.*

BOULT Myr Anna: Conservative, Cardiff West 1999, Aberavon 2003. **Mrs. Myr Boult:** Born London, 1951. Educated Mountain Ash Gram-mar School, University of Wales, Cardiff, (Law) Aberystwyth & Lampeter (Research into British Government Policy Decisions in Palestine). Married 2c. RAF Air Traffic Controller 1968. WRAF Representative, Lord Nuffield Trust. Commercial Officer, Welsh Industrial Estates Corporation early 1970s. Supervisor, Mid Glam-organ FE Department. Chief Executive Officer, New York based corporation. Company Director & Political Research Analyst. Community Worker. FE Supervisor. Founder Member: South & West Wales Business Women's Club. Royal Welsh Agricultural Society Judge. Deputy Chair, Carmarthen East & Dinefwr Conservative Assn. Member: New York Forum Club. Interests: Health, Law & Constitution, Middle East politics. Hob-bies: Opera, Music, Watching Rugby. Of Ffair-fach, Llandeilo.

BOURNE, Nicholas Henry: LlB LLM (Wales) LLM (Cantab). Conservative, Brecon & Radnor, 1999, 2003. A.M. Mid & West List 1997. Contested Worcester, 1997, Chesterfield B/E 1984. **Professor Nick Bourne:** Born Newark 1 January 1952, s of John Morgan Bourne, technical author, & Joan Edith Mary Bourne, housewife. Church of England. Educated King Edward VII School, Chelmsford; University of Wales (1st); Trinity College, Cambridge. Visiting Scholar, Harvard Law School. Barrister (Grays Inn) 1976. Supervisor in Law College, Cam-bridge, 1974-82. Principal, Chart University Tutor 1979-81. Company Secretary, Chart Director of Studies, Holborn Law Tutors Ltd. 1988-91. Senior Lecturer in Law, South Bank University, 1991-92. Dean of Law, Swansea, Law School. 1992-96. Assistant Principal, Swansea Institute, 1996-98. Visiting Lecturer, Hong Kong University, 1996-. Lecturer & Author. Member: NE Thames, Regional Health Authority, 1990-92, West Glamorgan Health Authority, 1994-97. President, Cambridge University Conservative Lawyers. Treasurer, Cambridge University Conservative Assn. Chair, St. Marylebone Young Conser-vatives. Hon. Lawyer, Bow Group. Chair, Gower Conservative Assn. Vice-Chair, Conservative

Nicholas Bourne.

Party in Wales. Chair, Conservative Political Centre, Wales. Conservative Chief Spokesperson in Wales. Contested Welsh Conservative leader-ship 1998, Member, National Assembly Advisory Group 1997. Executive Member Just Say NO Campaign 1997, Conservative Spokesperson for Wales 1998. Member, West Glam Regional Health Authority, Iechyd Morgannwg Health, Doctors & Dentists Pay Review Body, British Heart Foundation, Society of Authors, Institute of Directors, United Oxford & Cambridge Club. Member, Assembly: Mid & West Regional Cttee, South West Regional Cttee, European Affairs Cttee. Hobbies: Tennis, Squash, Badminton, Cricket, Walking, National Trust, NSPCC. Of Aberystwyth.

BOWEN David John: KC 1938 MSc (Wales). Liberal: Aberdare 1924, National: Neath 1945. **Mr. David Bowen:** Born Pentre 13 February 1885, s of John & Eliza Bowen. Married 1912, Mabel Staniland Cobb. Educated elementary school, entered mines at 14, Student at Univer-sity of Wales, Cardiff. Lecturer in Geology, Mining and Mining Surveying, Camborne School of Mines, Asst Professor of Mining, University of Leeds 1909-10, Head, Dept. of Mining, Leeds 1911-13. Consulting Mining/Civil Engineer 1911-14. Royal Engineers 1914-19, Major. Barrister, Lincolns Inn 1920, Bencher. Languages: Welsh, English. Of Richmond on Thames. Died 27 November 1950.

BOWEN Delme – see BOWEN, Ifor Delme.

BOWEN Evan Roderic: QC LlB. Hon. LLD 1972 (Wales) MA (Cantab). Liberal MP Cardigan 1945-66. **Mr. Roderic Bowen:** Born Cardigan 6 August 1913, s of Evan Bowen JP & Margaret Ellen Twiss. Presbyterian. Educated Cardigan County School, University of Wales, Aberystwyth, St. John's College, Cambridge, Brussels. Barrister, Middle Temple 1937, Master. Army, 1940-46, Captain, Judge Advocate General's staff. Recorder: Carmarthen 1950-53, Merthyr Tydfil, 1953-60, Swansea 1960-64, Cardiff 1964-67. Chair, Montgomery Quarter Sessions 1959-71. Chair, Welsh Parliamentary Party 1955. Deputy Chair of Ways and Means 1965-66. President, Liberal Party. National Insurance/DSS Commissioner for Wales 1967-86. Member: Lord Chancellor's Committee on Leasehold Reform. Chair: Cttee on Bilingual Traffic Signs 1972. Hon. Fellow Trinity College, Carmarthen. President, University College of Wales, Lampeter 1979-82. Languages: Welsh, English, Of Llandaff. Died July 2001.

BOWEN Geraint: BA 1938 MA (Wales) 1942 MA (Liverpool) 1952 PhD (Wales) 1978 DipEd 1943. Plaid Cymru: Wrexham 1950. **Dr. Geraint Bowen:** Born Llanelli, 10 September 1917, s of Revd T. Orchwy Bowen, Independent Minister & Ada Bowen. Married Zonia Margarita North, 2s 2d. Educated Llanelli, Llangywun & New Quay Primary Schools; Aberaeron Grammar School, University of Wales, Bangor. Teacher: Tonyrefail 1945-47; Ruabon 1947-61. HMI Schools 1961-75. Editor, *Y Faner* 1977-8, Poet, Winner National Eisteddfod Chair, Mountain Ash 1946. Member, Gorsedd of Bards. Archdruid of Wales 1979-81. Member; Council of Welsh Academy. Languages: Welsh, English. Of Corris *Books: Geraint Bowen, Mynegai i Gerdd Dafod John Morris Jones 1947, Gwasanaeth y Gwŷr Newydd 1970, Atlas Meirionydd 1973, Bwyd Llwy o Badell Awen 1977, Cerddi 1984, Golwg ar Orsedd y Beirdd 1992, O Groth y Ddaear 1993, Bro a Bywyd W. J. Gruffydd 1994, Y Drych Kristnogawl 1996, Hanes Gorsedd y Beirdd (gyda Zonia Bowen) 1992; Editor: Y Traddodiad Rhyddiaith 1970, Y Traddodiad Rhyddiaith yn yr Oesau Canol 1974, Y Traddodiad Rhyddiaith yn yr Ugeinfed Ganrif 1976, Ysgrifennu Creadigol 1972, Y Gwareiddiad Celtaidd 1976.*

BOWEN Ifor Delme: BSc PhD DSc FRMS. Plaid Cymru: Pontypridd, 1992, 1997, 1999, 2003, South West List 1997, Cardiff West 2001. **Professor Delme Bowen:** Born Dafen, Llanelli, 20 March 1944, s of Benjamin Ifor Bowen, coalminer, & Sarah Eirwen Bowen, farmer. Married 1968 Dr. Sandra Maureen Bowen, 3s 1d (divorced). Educated Amman Valley Grammar School, University of Wales, Cardiff. Research Demonstrator, 1969-76, Senior Lecturer, 1976-80, Reader, 1980-86, Professor of Cell Biology, University of Wales, Cardiff, 1986-94. Taf-Ely BC.1987-94,

Cardiff CCC.1999-. Llantrisant-Pontyclun ComC. 1991-92, Pentyrch/Creigiau ComC. (Chair). Chair: Cardiff NW Conservation Group. Member: Court, University of Wales, National Museum of Wales. Member: Plaid Cymru National Council, AUT. Languages: Welsh, English. Interests: Science, Education, Agriculture. Hobbies: Canvassing, Travel, Celtic History. Languages: Welsh, English, French. Of Cardiff.

BOWEN James Elscombe: MBE 1961. Conservative: Ebbw Vale 1951, 1955. **Mr. Jim Bowen:** Born Cowbridge January 1917. Educated Cowbridge Grammar School. Bank Clerk. Area Secretary, National Union of Bank Employees. Royal Navy 1939-45. Member, Monmouthshire County Rugby XV.

BOWEN John William: Kt. 1953 CBE 1939 JP (London). Labour: Newport 1918, 1922, 1923, 1924, Crewe 1931, 1935, MP Crewe 1929-31. **Sir William Bowen:** Born Blackpill, Swansea 8 May 1876, s of John Bowen, railwayman. Anglican. Married 1903, Eva Sanger (died 1953) of Waunarlwydd, 3s. 1d. Educated Gowerton. Started work as a postal messenger. President, Swansea Branch, Postmen's Federation, 14 years. General Secretary, Union of Post Office Workers. President, Post Office Employees Approved Society. Fellow of the Faculty of Insurance. Chair: North East Metropolitan Hospital Board, Ruskin College, Workers Travel Association. London CC Alderman 1951, Chairman 1949-52. Died 1965.

BOWEN Miriam Patricia: Socialist Labour, Mid & West List 1999; Euro Wales 1999. **Ms. Miriam Bowen:** Born 1975, d of Peter Bowen (qv) & Patricia Bowen (qv) & s of Martha Page-Harris (qv). Of Pembrokeshire (1981).

BOWEN Patricia Ann: Socialist Labour, Preseli 2001. **Mrs. Trisha Bowen:** Married Peter Bowen (qv) 2d (Miriam Bowen & Martha Page-Harris [qv]). Smallholding for 20 years. Small art & craft business. Environmental campaigner & part-time swimming teacher. Languages: English. Of Pembrokeshire (1981).

BOWEN Peter: Socialist Labour, South/East List 1999. **Mr. Peter Bowen:** Married Patricia Bowen (qv) 2d (Miriam Bowen & Martha Page-Harris (qv). Of Pembrokeshire (1981).

BOWEN-DAVIES Catherine: JP (Glam). Conservative: Caerphilly 1931, PPC Bedwellty 1939. **Mrs. Catherine Bowen-Davies:** Born d of Walter Davies, compositor, & Margaret Catherine, d of Henry Williams. mason, Aberaman. Married (1) Thomas Quinton, divorced), (2) Elystan Bowen-Davies (died 1947, estate £63,944), 2s (1 killed 1940, 1 fell from office block). Educated University of Wales, Cardiff, Paris. President: Rhondda East Women's Unionist Assn, Vice-President: South Wales Guild of Empire, Caerphilly Conservative Assn, Member: Primrose League Grand Council 1924, Red Cross Central Cttee. Succeeded husband as Chair, Davies, Middleton & Davies 1947. International Bridge Player. Member: Cambrian Archeological Assn. Hobbies: Bridge, Flying. Prosecuted, 4 November 1947 with others for embezzlement & theft, two others sentenced to 12 months imprisonment 19 December 1947.

BOWIE Nigel David: Conservative, Mid & West List, 1999. **Mr. Nigel Bowie:** Of Solfach.

BOX, Miss Clarissa: Conservative, South/Central List 1999. **Miss Clarissa Box:** Of Cardiff.

BOX Donald Stewart: Conservative: Newport 1955, B/E 1956, MP: Cardiff North, 1959-66. **Mr. Donald Box:** Born Llandaff 22 November 1917, s of Stanley Carter Box & Elizabeth Bassett. Anglican. Married Margaret Rose (Peggy) Davies, 1d. Educated Llandaff Cathedral School, St. John's School, Pinner, Harrow County School. RAF ranks 1939, commissioned 1941, Flight-Lieutenant 1945. Clerk, Cardiff Docks 1934. Stockbroker 1945, Member, International Stock Exchange, Director: N. M. Rothschild (Wales) Ltd. Partner: Margaret Box Relocations. Chair, Cardiff South-East Conservative Assn. President, Cardiff Southeast Young Conservatives, Jt Vice-Chair, Conservative Parl Finance Cttee. Died 12 July 1993.

BOYD Gillian Mary: JP 1993. BSc. Green Party, North List 2003. **Mrs. Gilly Boyd:** Born Rubery, Worcs. 16 June 1933, d of Cyril Edward Hugh Minns, Chartered Electrical Engineer, & Emmeline Mary Minns, company secretary. Christian Mystic. Married 1956 Dr. James William Boyd, Veterinary Surgeon, 4s. Educated Preparatory School; Endowed Grammar School; Bristol University Veterinary School (Inter BVSc; Liverpool University (Psychology; Dip.Coms. DipTHP). Lecturer in Psychology & Counseling; Relate & BPS counsellor. Labour Party Branch Chair & Secretary. Secretary, Ecology Party, Green Party. Guide Captain 8 years. Chair: Merseyside Humanist Assn; Executive Member, British Humanist Assn. Branch Chair GRTA 10 years. Founder member: NAWCH, WHERE, CASE. Secretary, Phoenix Action Group against waste powered kiln. Interests: Green Issues, Healthy Foods, Recycling, Abuse of Power, Empowering Women, Conflict Resolution. Hobbies: Organic Gardening, Philosophy, Hill Walking, Native American Culture, Singing, Poetry. Languages: English, French, German. Of Penmynydd, Flintshire.

BRACE Mark: Conservative: Ebbw Vale 1929. **Mr. Mark Brace:** Born Risca, 1862, nephew of Rt. Hon. William Brace (qv). Educated Bolt Street Elementary School, Newport. Started work at 14 at W. A. Baker engineering works. GWR. Apprentice, Swindon. Worked for Admiralty on submarines in Great War. Organiser, National Council of Industry 15.5.1931. Formerly a Liberal, a well-known Newport Anti-Socialist speaker. Member: South Wales & Mon Public Economy Assn. Declined Abertillery nomination 1922.

BRACE William: PC 1916. Labour MP: South Glamorgan 1906-18, Abertillery 1918-20. **Rt. Hon. William Brace:** Born Risca 23 September 1865, s of Thomas Brace. Baptist Sunday School Teacher & Lay Preacher. Married 1890, Nellie, d of William Humphreys, 1s 1d. Educated Risca Board School. Miner, 1877. Miners' Agent 1890. President: SWMF, West Mon Liberal Assn, Mon Free Church Federal Council. Vice-President, Welsh National Liberal Federation. Member, Royal Commission on Coal Supplies. Under-Secretary, Home Office 1915-18. Chief Labour Adviser, Department of Mines 1920-27. Died 12 October 1947.

BRADLEY Richard Blaine: Alternative Liberal Democrat, Conwy 1997. **Mr. Richard Bradley:** Born 1965. Conwy Liberal Democrats' Campaign Manager & Chair, Llandudno Branch. Territorial Army Officer.

BRADLEY-BIRT Francis Bradley: JP FRGS LCS BA (Oxon.). 1897. Conservative: Merthyr 1929. **Lieut-Colonel Francis Bradley-Birt:** Born 25 June 1874, s of John Bradley-Birt of Birtsmoreton Court, Worcs. Anglican. Married 1920, Lady Norah Spencer-Churchill, d. of 8th Duke of Marlborough. Barrister, Inner Temple 1897. Indian Civil Service 1898. District Magistrate & Member, Legislative Assembly of India 1921-23. Landowner & Writer. Lord of the Manors of Birtsmoreton & Berrow. Patron, Parish of Birtsmoreton. Died 11 June 1963.

BRADNEY David: BSc (Sheffield). Green Party, Ceredigion & Mid & West List 1999; Wales Euro 2004. **Mr. Dave Bradney:** Born Walsall, 30 December 1945, s of Arthur Bradney, shoe repairer, & Bessie Doreen Bradney. Agnostic. Partner Diana Jane Weeks, 1d. Educated Dr. Morgan's Grammar School, Bridgwater; Sheffield University (Biochemistry); University of Wales, Cardiff (Dip. Journalism). Journalist, sub-editor weekly newspaper. Joined Green Party 1987, Wales Representative 1995, party newspaper editor, 1988-92. Editor, England & Wales Green Party newspaper 1988-92. Co-Chair, Green Party Regional Council, Press Officer & Treasurer, Wales Green Party. Moved to Wales from London, 1991. Green Party, Wales Euro 2004. Of Rhydlewis, Llandysul.

BRADNEY Joseph Arthur: Kt 1924 CB 1911 TD 1912 JP DL (Mon) JP (Rads) CStJ FSA MA (Cantab). Conservative: Radnorshire 1892. **Colonel Sir Joseph Bradney:** Born Greet, Salop1859, s of Revd Joseph Bradney, Rector of Greet & Sarah Decima d of Revd David Jones, Rector of Hope Bagot, 1 of 3c. Anglican. Married (1) 1883 Rosa (died 1927), d. of Edward Jenkins JP DL (2) 1927 Florence, d. of Francis Egerton Prothero of Malpas Court, 3s 3d. Educated Harrow, Trinity College, Cambridge. Landowner. Captain, Militia 1882-92, Lieut-Colonel 1892, Hon. Colonel, 1899, Army 1915-18, Chair, Monmouthshire TA Assn. Monmouthshire CC 1894-28, Alderman 1924-28, Chair 1921-22. Of Llanfihangel-ystern, Llewern, Mon. Estate £43,642. Died 21 July 1943.

BRAID David Oswald (also known as David Franklin-Braid): Independent (Battle of Britain Christian Alliance Party), Ogmore B/E Feb.2002, Independent, Preston 2001, Anti-Corruption Pro Family Christian Alliance, North west England Euro 1999, Wigan B/E Sept. 1999, Multi-Racial Anti-Corruption, Liverpool, Riverside 1997. **Revd David Braid:** Born 1937. RAF 20 years. Ordained 1982. Minister, African Church, Liverpool. Voted Best lifesaver in Riverside 1981. Founder, Battle of Britain Christian Alliance Party 2000. Of Ormskirk, Lancashire.

BRANSBY-WILLIAMS Morgan Edward: Liberal: Llandaff & Barry 1945. **Lieut-Colonel Morgan Bransby-Williams:** Born 1916, s of George Bransby-Williams MICE & Dorothy Maud, d of Edward Thorp of Cheadle Hulme. Married 1944, Susan, d of Brigadier Francis Lymm, 3d. Educated Clifton College, Bristol & RMC Sandhurst. Royal Artillery 1936-, Seconded to Belgrade Embassy 1949-50. Russian Interpreter. Contested Surrey CC 1964, 1967, 1970. Member, Surrey Education Cttee.

BRAND Henry Robert, 2nd Viscount Hampden: Liberal Unionist Cardiff District 1886, Liberal MP Hertfordshire Dec. 1868-Feb. 1874, Stroud July-Dec1874 (unseated on petition Dec. 1874), 1880-86. **Hon. Henry Brand:** Born Devonport 1841, s of Rt. Hon. Henry B. W. Brand, 1st Viscount Hampden (Speaker of the Commons) & Eliza, d of General Robert Ellice, succeeded 1892. Anglican. Married (1) 1864, Victoria, d of H. E. M. Van-der-Weyer (died 1865) (2) 1868, Susan, d of Lord George Cavendish. Educated Rugby. Lieutenant Coldstream Guards 1855-63, Captain 1863-65. Surveyor General of the Ordnance 1883. Of Temple Dinsley, Herts. Died 22 November 1911.

BREESE Charles Edward: JP (Caerns). Coalition Liberal MP: Caernarfonshire 1918-22. **Captain Charles Breese:** Born 26 March 1867, s of

Edward Breese, Clerk of Peace for Merioneth. Anglican. Married 1894 Janet Beatrice, d of Rev. Paul Stedman, Norfolk, 1 d. Educated Shrewsbury School. RWF Volunteers 1887-98, RWF 1914-17. Solicitor with interests in quarrying industry. Hon. Treasurer, Welsh National Liberal Federation 1903-, Chair, Executive, Cambrian Archaeological Assn. Provincial Grand Secretary, Freemasons Lodge of North Wales 1903-10, Grand Treasurer 1918, Caernarfonshire CC. Received the Coalition Coupon from Lloyd George Nov. 1918, 4 days after Caernarfonshire Liberals had adopted Ellis Davies & adopted as Coalition candidate at a subsequent meeting. Languages: Welsh, English. Of Porthmadog. Estate £15,149. Died 15 August 1932.

BRENNAN, Kevin Denis: BA (Oxon) 1982. PGCE (Wales) 1985. MSc (Glam). 1992. Labour MP Cardiff West 2001. **Mr. Kevin Brennan:** Born Cwmbran, 16 October 1959. Married Amy Brennan, 1d. Educated St. Albans RC School, Pontypool; Pembroke College, Oxford (PPE); University of Wales, Cardiff; Glamorgan University. President, Oxford Union. With Cwmbran Community Press 1982-84. Teacher (Head of Economics, Radyr Comprehensive School 1985-94). Political Adviser to Rhodri Morgan AM 1995-2000. Cardiff CC 1991-2001, Chair, Economic Scrutiny Cttee 1999-2000, Vice-Chair, Finance Cttee 1999-2002, Economic Development 1996-99, Chair, Finance 1996-99. Member: Fabian Society, Socialist Health Assn, Labour Campaign for Electoral Reform. Chair, Cardiff says YES campaign 1997. Hobbies: Sports, Music. Languages: Learning Welsh, English. Of Canton, Cardiff.

BRIENZA Gerardo: BSc. 1980. Pro-Life Alliance, Neath 2001, South West List 2003. **Mr. Gerry Brienza:** Born Windsor, 1958, son of Guiseppe Brienza & Genoeffa Iasa. Independent Reformed Church, Converted 1979. Married 1985. Ruth Helen, 3s 1d. Educated Maidenhead Grammar School; Portsmouth Polytechnic (Civil Engineering). Design Engineer, Winchester, Freelance Sit Engineer, Bridgend, worked for several civil engineering contractors 1986-95. Site Agent/ Supervisor, Swansea CCC 1995. Member. LIFE Group 1984-85, CARE in 1990s. Chair, Pro-Life Alliance, Wales. Of Gorseinon 1990-95, Cadoxton-juxta-Neath (1995).

BRIERLEY Paul: Conservative, Delyn 2001, North West England Euro 1999. **Mr. Paul Brierley:** Born Bolton 5 August 1959. Married Diana (Accountant) 1 stepson. Educated Liverpool Polytechnic. Qualified quantity surveyor & project Manager/Principal of Family Business. Sub-post Master at Salford. Chartered Quantity Surveyor. Contested local elections. Karate Black

Belt, under 21 international team. Interests: Social Security, the Constitution. Hobbies: Sport, Hill walking, Dog training, Raising money for Hospice & Children's Hospital. Of Bolton.

BRIGHT John Albert: JP (Lancs). Liberal: Montgomery District 1900, MP: Birmingham 1885-95 Joined Liberal Unionists 14/4/1889 but returned to Liberals. MP Oldham 1906-1910. **Mr. John A. Bright:** Born Rochdale 1848, s of Rt. Hon. John Bright, MP & Margaret Elizabeth, d of William Leatham of Wakefield. Unitarian (?) Married 1883, Edith Eckersley, d of William Tuer Shawcross, Foxholes, Rochdale. Educated Grove House School, Tottenham, University College, London. Company Director: John Bright & Bros Ltd. cotton spinners, Rochdale, London & North Western Railway Co Ltd. Of Rochdale. Estate £212,539. Died 11 November 1924.

BRIGHTON Paul John: BA (Exeter). Liberal: West Flint Feb & Oct 1974, North Wales List, 1999, Alyn & Deeside 2003. **Mr. Paul Brighton:** Born Maidstone, Kent, 2July 1942, s of Samuel John Brighton, civil servant (died 1998), & Moldred Elizabeth Grimwood. Married 1971 Sarah Grizel Waterhouse, 1s 1d. Educated Eastbourne College 1962-65. Lindisfarne College, Ruabon; University of Sussex (History) and Brighton (CertEd). VSO for 2 years. History Teacher, Holywell Grammar School, Head of Sixth form, Hawarden Grammar School, retired 2002). Joined Liberal Party 1960. Member: NAS, Assn. of Liberal Trades Unionists, Liberal International, Grwp Pennant (local history). Secretary, Delyn Liberal Democrats. Delyn BC 1987-91; Whitford ComC. 1991-. Interests: International Affairs. Hobbies: Reading, History. Languages: English. Lived in Wales since 1972. Of Carmel, Holywell.

BRIMMACOMBE Terence Frank: Plaid Cymru: Monmouth Oct. 1974. **Mr. Terry Brimmacombe:** Born Haverfordwest 1942. Married Susan Brimmacombe, of Hampshire, 2c. Educated Haverfordwest Grammar School. Regular Army (NCO) 1961-70. Construction Executive and partner in retail trade. Associate, Institute of Administrative Management. Poet & lyricist. Member, International Songwriters' Assn. Of Abergavenny.

BRISBY Tania Alexandra Teofana Beatrice: MA (Oxon). Conservative, Bridgend 2001. **Ms. Tania Brisby:** Born London, 11 September 1963, d of Michael Douglas (civil engineer, died 1965)) & Liliana Daneva Brisby, BBC Word Service & Editor, *World Today* [died 1998] & gd and ggd of Prime Ministers of Bulgaria. Church of England. Married Julian Georgiev Popov (writer & educational consultant, 1st Vice-Chancellor of the New Bulgarian University, established 1990) 2s. Educated St. Paul's Girls' School, London, Christ Church, Oxford (scholarship 1979, Modern Languages). Company Director (finance & corporate communications). Worked in North America, Europe & Japan. European Union Aid Programme adviser to non-Communist government of Bulgaria 1991-94. Joined Conservative Party 1995, Chair, Camberwell & Peckham Conservative Assn 1998-2000. Member: Royal Institute of International Affairs. Interests: International Affairs, Education, Economy. Hobbies: Riding, Sailing, Skiing, Opera, Piano. Languages: English, German, Italian, Bulgarian. Of London.

BRITTON Robert Alexander: Liberal Democrat: Alyn & Deeside 1992. **Mr. Robert Britton:** Born Cardiff 4 July 1945. Married 2s.Educated Monckton House School, Cardiff, Inns of Court School of Law. Barrister 1973. With Home Office. Hobbies: all sports. Of Gerrards Cross.

BROAD Andrew: Independent Wales Party, South/East List 2003. **Mr. Andrew Broad:** Born Abertillery, miner's son. Miner, Six Bells Colliery. Welsh Guards (Falklands) 1980. Postman. Chair: Blaenau Gwent IWP. Contested Blaenau Gwent BC B/E 13/3/2003, where he was the party's first ever candidate).

BROCKWAY Archibald Fenner, Baron Brockway 1964, Hon. LLD (Lancaster). ILP: Cardiff East B/E 1942, East Leyton 1931, Upton B/E 1934, Norwich 1935, Lancaster B/E 1941; Labour: Lancaster 1922, Westminster Abbey B/E March 1924, Eton & Slough 1964, Labour MP: East Leyton 1929-31, Eton & Slough 1950-64. **Mr. Fenner Brockway:** Born Calcutta, 1 November 1888, s of Revd W. G. Brockway, London Missionary Society. Married (1) 1914, Lilla, d of Revd W. Harvey Smith, 4 d. divorced, (2) Edith Violet King 1s. Educated Eltham College. Journalist: offices of monthly *Quiver* on leaving school. Joined staff of *The Examiner* 1907, Sub-Editor, *Christian Commonwealth* 1909, *Labour Leader* 1911, Editor, *Labour Leader* 1912-17. Liberal sub-agent, Tunbridge Wells 1906. Joined SDF and then ILP. Secretary, No-Conscription Fellowship 1917. One month's imprisonment under DORA August 1916, and three months, six months and two years hard labour under Military Service Act. Joint Secretary, British Cttee Indian National Congress & Editor of *India* 1919, Joint Sec. Prison System Enquiry Cttee.1920. Organising Secretary, ILP 1922, General Secretary, ILP 1928, 1933-39. Editor, *New Leader* 1926-29, 1931-41. Chair, No More War Movement & War Resisters' International 1923-28. Executive Member, Labour and Socialist International 1926-31. Political Secretary ILP 1939-46, Rejoined Labour Party 1946. Member, International Cttee for Socialist Movement for United Europe 1947-56, Chair, Movement for Colonial Freedom, British Asian & Overseas Socialist Fellowship 1959-. Died 28 April 1988. *Books: Fenner Brockway, Inside the Left, Outside the Right, Towards Tomorrow, Not Out. (Autobiography).*

BRODRICK Annie Gwendolyn: JP (Denbs) 1920. Conservative: Denbigh 1922, 1924. **Hon. Mrs. Gwen Brodrick:** Born, d of Hugh Robert Hughes JP of Kinmel Park, Lord Lieutenant of Denbighshire & Lady Florentia, d of Earl of Ravenswold. Anglican. Married (1) 1892 Major-General Edward Lloyd Wynne CB Coed Coch (died 1893) 1s killed 1916 (2) 1896 Hon. Laurence A Brodrick (died 1915) s of Viscount Middleton, 1d. Hon. Member, Gorsedd, withdrew as PPC 1929 after leg amputation. Estate £129,115. Died 8 September 1929.

BROOKE Eric William: BSc (Herts). Liberal Democrat, Pontypridd 2001. **Mr. Eric Brooke:** Born 23 March 1971. Unmarried. Educated St. Peter's High School, Exeter, Exeter College, University of Hertfordshire, Hatfield (Computer Science). President, Hertfordshire Students Union, National Executive, NUS. Campaigns Development Adviser NSPCC. General Election Manager, Liberal Democrats. Wales, Political Adviser, Lembit Opik MP. Member: Friends of the Earth, Amnesty International, British Youth Council. Interests: Education, Environment, Human Rights, Youth. Hobbies: Hiking, Drama, Reading, Socialising, Computers, Music. Of Cardiff.

BROOKE Peter Leonard, Baron Brooke of Sutton Mandeville 2001: PC 1987 CH 1992 MA (Oxon) MBA (Harvard) Hon. DLitt (Westminster) 1999. Conservative: Bedwellty Oct. 1974, MP City of London & Westminster South B/E 1977-97, Cities of London & Westminster 1997-2001. **Rt. Hon. Peter Brooke:** Born March 1934, s of Rt. Hon. Henry, Baron Brooke of Cumnor & Baroness Brooke of Ystradfellte. Anglican. Married 1964, Joan, d of F. G. Smith of Brazil, 2s. Educated Marlborough, Balliol College, Oxford, Harvard Business School, Vice-President, National Union of Students 1955-56, President, Oxford Union 1957, Harkness Fellow 1957-59. Joined *Financial Times* 1960, Managing Director, Spencer, Stuart & Associates 1961-68, Chair 1968-69, President: Spencer, Stuart & Associates (New York) 1969-71, Spencer, Stuart International 1971. Member of Lloyds. Camden BC 1968-69. Asst. Whip 1979-81, Lord Commissioner 1981-83, Under Secretary, Education & Science 1983-85, Minister of State Treasury 1985-87, Paymaster General & Chair, Conservative Party 1987-89, Secretary of State for Northern Ireland 1989-92, resigned to contest Speakership 1992, Secretary of State for the Heritage 1992-94. Chair, Building

Societies Ombudsman Council, President, British Antique Dealers' Assn. Pro Chancellor & Chairman of the Council, University of London.

Beata Brookes.

BROOKES Beata: CBE 1996. Conservative, MEP North Wales 1979-89; contested Widnes 1955, Warrington 1963, Manchester Exchange 1964. **Miss Beata Brookes:** Born 21 January 1931. Married Anthony Arnold (qv) divorced. Educated University of Wales, Bangor. Social Worker, Company Secretary (tourism & catering), Farmer. Member: NFU. National Vice-Chair: Young Conservatives. Chair: Wales Young Conservatives. Treasurer: West Flint Conservative Assn. Interests: Education, Agriculture.

BROOKES Jennifer Jane: UK Independence Party, Wrexham 2001. **Mrs. Jane Brookes:** Born Market Drayton, 3 September 1946, daughter of Charles Parry, accountant, & Marjorie Parry. Christian. Married 1974, Denis Brookes, air traffic controller, 1d. Educated Tunstall Hall College. Housewife. Hobbies UKIP Walking, Gardening. Languages: English, German.

BROOKS John Edward, Baron Brooks of Tremorfa 1979: DL (S. Glam) 1994. Labour: Barry Feb & Oct 1974. **Mr. Jack Brooks:** Born 12 April 1927, s of Edward George Brooks & Rachel White. Married (1) 1948 divorced 1956, 3c (2) 1958, Margaret Pringle 2s. Educated Coleg Harlech, University of Wales, Cardiff. Steelworker. Secretary/Agent Cardiff SE Labour Party. Member, TGWU. Chair: Cardiff City

Labour Party, Labour Party, Wales 1978-79. Cardiff CC 1971-, South Glamorgan CC1973-, Labour Group Leader 1973-77, 1986-, Chair 1981-82. Opposition Defence Spokesman in Lords 1980-81. Steward, British Boxing Board of Control 1986-, Vice-Chair, Chair 2002-. Chair: Welsh Sporting Hall of Fame. Board Member, Cardiff Bay Development Corporation. Hon. Freeman, City of Cardiff 2000. Hon. Fellow, University of Wales, Cardiff. Of Cardiff.

BROWN David John: UK Independence Party, South/Central List 2003. **Mr. David Brown:** Retired local government officer. Of Canton, Cardiff.

BROWN Richard Graham: Liberal Democrat, Mid & West List. **Mr. Richard Brown:** Born 1958. Educated University of Wales, Aberystwyth. Legal Assistant. Montgomeryshire DC. (Chair, Environmental Health), Powys CC. (Vice-Chair, Environmental Health, House & Trading Standards, Chair, Ethics). Member: Montgomeryshire Health Council, Prince of Wales Committee. Governor, University of Wales, Aberystwyth & Bangor. President, Haughton Village Hall Cttee. Governor, two primary schools. Interests: Amateur Dramatics, Community Work. Of Llandrinio, Powys.

BROWN William Glanville: TD MA (Oxon). Liberal: Cardiff Central 1935, St. Albans 1964. **Mr. Glanville Brown:** Born Cardiff 19 July 1907, s of Cecil G. Brown, Cardiff Town Clerk Cardiff & Edith Tyndale Brown. Married (1) 1935 Theresa Margaret Mary Harrison 1 s, divorced 1946 (2) 1948, Margaret Isobel Dilks (died 1988). Educated Llandaff Cathedral School; Magdalen College School; Magdalen College, Oxford. Barrister, Inner Temple 1932. Army 1939-45. Junior UK Prosecuting Counsel, Tokyo 1946-48. Member: National Arbitration Tribunal 1949-51, Industrial Disputes Tribunal 1959, Deputy Chair various Wages Council 1950-64. Lecturer in Germany for UK Embassy 1965-73, Joint Legal Editor, translation of Treaty of Rome & other European Community documents for Foreign Office 1962-63, Member: Mental Health Tribunal, NE Metropolitan Regional Health Board 1960-79. Fellow, Institute of Linguists. Of Northwood Hills, Middlesex.

BRUSSATIS Ralph Rayner: DTM& H DFFP MECPI III State Examination FRG. Natural Law Party, South Wales East Euro 1994. **Dr. Ralph Brussatis:** Born Munster, Germany 6 May 1957, s of Friedrich Wilhelm Udo Hugo Otto Paul Brussatis & Anneliese Brussatis. Protestant. Unmarried. Educated Germany; Lancing College, Sussex; University for Human Medicine, Hanover. Medical Practitioner (State Examination in Medicine 1989). Member: Amnesty International, Earthwatch, Life Foundation, Oxfam. Came to UK 1991. At Royal Gwent Hospital at time of election. Languages: English, French, German. Of Liverpool.

BRYANT Christopher John: BA (English) 1983 (Theology 1986) MA (Oxon). Labour, Wycombe 1997; MP Rhondda 2001. **Mr. Chris Bryant:** Born Cardiff, 1 January 1962 s of Rees Bryant, IT Manager, & Anne Grace Goodwin, Make-up artist. gs of a Welsh rugby international. Anglican. Partner, Alex Craig. Educated Cheltenham College, Mansfield College, Oxford (English), Ripon College Cuddesdon, Wimbledon. Anglican priest: Curate, High Wycombe 1986-89. Youth Chaplain, Diocese of Peterborough 1986-91. Resigned orders 1991. Agent, Holborn & St. Pancras 1992-93. Freelance Author 1996-. Joined Labour Party 1986. Head of European Affairs, BBC 1998-2000. Member, Oxford University Conservative Assn. Chair, Christian Socialist Movement 1993-98; Labour Movement for Europe 2002. Associate, National Youth Theatre of Great Britain. Member: Fabian Society, Co-operative Party, MSF. Hackney BC 1993-98. Member: Ferndale RFC. Member, Select Cttee on Culture, Media and Sport. Hobbies: Swimming, Gym, Theatre. Languages: English, Spanish, French. Of Stanleytown & London. *Books: Chris Bryant, Glenda Jackson (authorised biography), Stafford Cripps, the first modern chancellor 1997, Common Purpose (History of Christian Socialist Movement).*

BRYANT Conrad Lawson: CPFA. Plaid Cymru, Pembroke, 1992, Preseli 1999. **Mr. Conrad Bryant:** Born Gilfach Goch, 11 March 1947. Married Janet, 1s. Educated Tonyrefail County Grammar School. Chief Accountant, Pembrokeshire CC. Borough Treasurer & Housing Manager, Haverfordwest B until 1974. Chief Accountant, Port Authority. Member, Plaid Cymru National Executive, 10 years, Treasurer, 4 years, Vice-President, 2 years. Chair, Pembroke Plaid Cymru. Treasurer, National Library of Wales. Board member, Torch Theatre Co. Treasurer/Team Manager/Hon. Auditor, Cleddau Athletic Club. Hobbies Athletics, Rugby. Of Neyland (1971).

BRYANT Oliver: Liberal: South Mon 1886. **Mr. Oliver Bryant:** a member of the Bryant family, of Bryant & May, Manufacturers of *'England's Glory'* Matches. Barrister. Of London.

BRYNACH Siôn: BA MLitt (Oxon). Plaid Cymru, Assembly, Vale of Clwyd & North List 1999. **Mr. Siôn Brynach:** Born Bangor, 4 April 1968, s of Saunders Davies (Bishop of Bangor 2000) & Cynthia Davies. Church in Wales. Married 1993, Catharine Laura Brynach, 1s.

Educated Ysgol Gyfun Ystalyfera, University of Wales, Bangor, Jesus College, Oxford. British Gas PRO. Archbishop of Wales' Media Manager 2000. Interests: Economic Development Energy, Environment. Hobbies: Dog-owner April 1968, Languages: Welsh, English, some German. Of Cardiff.

BUCKLAND Robert James: BA (Durham). Conservative: South Wales West Euro 1994, Islwyn B/E 1995, Preseli 1997, Mid & West Wales List, 1999, Wales Euro 1999. **Mr. Robert Buckland:** Born Llanelli 22 September 1968, s of William Thomas Roger Buckland, solicitor & Barbara Jayne Glenys Buckland, housewife. Anglican. Married 1997, Siân Caroline Pugh Reed, bank manager, 1s 1d. Educated Old Road Primary School, Llanelli' St. Michael's School, Bryn, Llanelli; Hatfield College, Durham. Barrister 1991. Chair, Llanelli Young Conservatives 1985-87. Chair: Welsh Conservative Candidates Assn; Llanelli Conservative Assn; Swansea West Conservative Assn; Mid & West Wales Conservative Euro Council 1993. Agent, Llanelli 1987. Coordinator Llanelli & Gower Young Conservatives anti-drug misuse campaign. Welsh Conservative Health Spokesman 1997-99. Dyfed CC 1993-97. Contested Swansea CCC 1999. Interests: Criminal Justice, Europe, Education, Constitutional Affairs. Hobbies: Wine, History, Music. Of Swansea.

BUCKLEY Richard W: Conservative: Neath 1983. **Mr. Richard Buckley:** Born 7 September 1947. Married Sharon Buckley, 4c. Educated Harrow County School, Watford College of Technology, Manchester Polytechnic. Design Consultant, Managing Director. Brent BC 1974-76. Of London.

BUCKLEY William Joseph: JP (Carms). Liberal Unionist: West Carmarthenshire 1895. **Mr. William Buckley:** Born Llanelli 1852, s of James Buckley JP & Elizabeth Buckley, Penyfai. Anglican. Married 1895, Muriel (died 1928) d of Lieut-Colonel John Howell, Trefynydd, Penyrheol & Mary d of Thomas Phillips, Llangadog. Landowner, Farmer & Businessman, Chairman, Buckley's Breweries. Founder-Chair, Carmarthenshire Stud Co. High Sheriff, Carmarthenshire 1897. MFH, Penllergaer Hunt. Bought Maesgwynne Hunt 1892; MFH of both until 1898. President: National Eisteddfod 1895, Llanelli Agricultural Society 1892, Carmarthenshire Agricultural Society. Chair, Carmarthenshire Agricultural Society, Carmarthenshire Chamber of Agriculture. A founding Vice-President, Pontarddulais RFC 1881. Languages: Welsh, English. Of Llanelli.

BUFTON John Andreas: Referendum Party: Montgomery 1997, UK Independence, Ceredig-

ion B/E 2000. **Mr. John Bufton:** Born Rhayader 1963. Married Amanda 1d. Educated Rhayader High School. Employed at Royal British Legion factory, Llanwrthwl. Sales & Marketing Manager, Pengerrig Garden Hotel & owner of a fruit and vegetable shop. Rhayader TC 1987-, Mayor, 1995-96, Powys CC (Ind) 1995-99. Of Rhayader, then Liverpool.

BULMER-THOMAS Ivor: CBE MA (Oxon) 1937 FSA. Hon.DSc (Warwick) 1979. Stella Della Solidarieta Italia 1948. Conservative: Newport 1950, Joined Conservative Party 1948, Labour: Spen Valley1935, MP Keighley 1942-50. **Mr. Ivor Bulmer-Thomas:** Born Cwmbran 30 November 1905, s of A. E. Thomas, added Bulmer 1952. Anglican. Married (1) Dilys, d. of Dr. W. Llewelyn Jones, Merthyr Tydfil (died 1938) 1 s (2) 1940, Joan Margaret, d. of E. F. Bulmer of Hereford, 3c. Educated Jones' West Monmouth School, Pontypool, St. John's College, Oxford, Magdalen College, Oxford, Scholar of St. John's, Double 1st Cross Country and Athletics Blue, Welsh International Cross-Country runner, 1926. Gladstone Research Scholar, St. Deiniol's Library. Editorial Staff *The Times*, 1930-37, Chief Leader Writer *News Chronicle* 1937-39. Army, 1939-45, Captain, Royal Norfolk Regt. 1941. Acting Deputy Editor, *Daily Telegraph* 1953-54. Parl-Secretary, Civil Aviation 1945-46, Under-Secretary, Colonies 1946-47. Member, House of Laity, Church Assembly 1950. Chair, Executive, Historic Churches Preservation Trust. Hon. Director, Friends of Friendless Churches. Secretary, Ancient Monuments Society. Died 7 October 1993.

BURKE Charles Patrick Towers: Conservative: Rhondda West 1955, Gravesend 1951. **Colonel Charles Burke:** Born Australia 1905. Roman Catholic. Married. Educated Sidney, Adelaide & Melbourne, and St. Joseph's Institution, Singapore. Barrister, Grays Inn 1927, Practised in Malaya 1927-41. Officer, Singapore Volunteer Corps 1928-42, Royal Hampshire Regt 1942-6, Deputy Chief Legal Officer, Westphalia. Hon. ADC to Governor of Malaya 1938-42. Holborn BC 1949-53. Of London.

BURNHAM Derek William Lawrence: MA (Oxon). Liberal Democrat, Ynys Môn 1997, Clwyd South & North List 1999, Alyn & Deeside 2001. **Mr. Derek Burnham:** Born Liverpool, 23 December 1949, s of Geoffrey Cowlishaw Burnham, company director, & Marion Lilian Lawrence, bookseller. Unitarian. Married 1975 Eleanor Burnham (qv) 1s 1d. Educated William Hulme's School, Manchester, University College, Oxford (Geography). Soccer blue. International Business Consultant. Chief Executive, Innovation Company operating in European Objective

One. Worked with German & Italian linked companies. Regional Director, Welsh Development Agency. Managing Director, Wrexham Dunlop. Personnel Manager, Pilkingtons, St. Asaph. Competent linguist. Regional Manager, Liberal Democrats. Member: CBI Welsh Council, European Regional Development Cttees, Institute of Welsh Affairs. Interests: Politics in General, Lifelong Liberal. Hobbies: Music, Literature, Arts, Walking, Sport. Languages: English, French, some Italian. Of Rossett, Wrexham.

BURNHAM Eleanor: JP BA (Manchester Met) MACINA. Liberal Democrat, Alyn & Deeside 1997, Delyn & North List. 1999, Clwyd West 2003. AM North Wales, 20/3/2001. **Mrs. Eleanor Burnham:** Born Wrexham, 17 April 1951, d of Meirion Roberts, farmer, & Emily Eileen White, ex-nurse/matron; brought up on a farm at Cynwyd, Corwen. Methodist. Married 1975, Derek (qv). 1s 1d. Educated Tywyn School, Radbrook College, Shrewsbury, Manchester Metropolitan University. Business Consultant, advising on charity fundraising & arts festival. Soprano singer (Llangollen winner). Interests: Politics in General, lifelong Liberal. Languages: Welsh, English, some French & Italian. Resigned as ppc for Chester on appointment to Assembly. Of Rossett, Wrexham.

BURNIE Robert John Dickson: JP(Swansea). Liberal MP Swansea Town 1892-95. **Mr. Dickson Burnie:** Born Dawlish 1842, s of John Dickson Burnie, builder (member of a Dumfries-shire family) & Elizabeth Stamp. Married 1866, Georgianna, d of Nicholas Elliott, 4s 1d. Educated John Nicholls Academy, Dawlish. Clerk, South Devon & Cornwall Railway Co 7 years, Asst Secretary, Bristol & South Wales Wagon Co 1864, Co Secretary: Cheltenham & Swansea Wagon Co(Cheltenham) 1866, Co Secretary, Swansea Wagon Co 1869 (Managing Director,1877). Director: Taylor & Co. Swansea BC 1877 (Chair, Finance Cttee, Alderman, Mayor 1883-84. Laid foundation of library and art gallery opened by Mr. Gladstone). Chair, Swansea Harbour Trust (Chair, Finance Cttee). Treasurer, South Wales Liberal Federation. Vice-President, Royal Institution of South Wales. President: Swansea Chamber of Commerce, Swansea Devonian Society. Provincial Grand Master, Independent Order of Oddfellows. Freemason. Captain 3rd Glamorgan Volunteers. Led the campaign to abolish tolls on the bridge connecting Swansea & St. Thomas and for the founding of the library and art gallery. Treasurer, Anti Tithe League in Wales. Lived a very private life for ten years. Of Swansea. Estate £13,416. Died 6 March 1908.

BURNS Alistair: BA (Open). Liberal: Blaenau Gwent 1992. **Mr. Alistair Burns:** Born 5 January

1962. Unmarried (1992). Educated Dollar Academy, Open University. Principal Laboratory Technician. Member, Institute of Professionals, Managers & Specialists.

BURNS David Frederick: Civil Rights/Welsh Political Prisoner Candidate for Gower B/E 1982. **Mr. David Burns:** Born 1959. Roman Catholic. Trainee Computer Programmer. Member, Workers' Army for a Welsh Republic. In custody from May 1982 on two charges of acting with intent to cause an explosion at the Army Recruitment Office, Pontypridd, Cleared on one count and acquitted on the other, Cardiff Crown Court, December 1983. Of Cardiff.

BURNS Simon Hugh McGuigan: MA (Oxon). Conservative: Alyn & Deeside 1983; MP Chelmsford 1987-97, Chelmsford West 19?. **Mr. Simon Burns:** Born 6 September 1952, s of Major Brian Stanley Burns MC & Shelagh Mary Nash. Married 1982, Emma Mary, d of David & Susan Clifford (divorced), 2c. Educated Christ the King School, Accra; Stamford School; Worcester College, Oxford. Secretary, Oxford University Conservative Assn 1972-75. Founded Rutland Young Conservatives 1970. Journalist. Personal & Research Assistant to Mrs. Sally Oppenheim MP 1975-80. Policy Executive, Institute of Directors 1983-87, Company Director *What to Buy?* 1982-83. PPS 1989, Asst Govt Whip1994-95, Whip 1995-96, Under-Secretary, Health 1996-97. Hobbies: Swimming.

BURNS Terence John: Socialist Labour: Cardiff Central 1997. **Mr. Terry Burns:** Born Markham Village 1946, miner's son. Apprentice Fitter at 15. WEA Tutor. Joined AEU & Labour Party 1961. Left Labour Party 1987. Member, MSF. Of Whitchurch.

BURREE Nicholas Charles: BA.(Wales). Liberal Democrat, Llanelli 1997, Mid & West List 1999. **Mr. Nick Burree:** Born Surrey, 14 February 1956, s of Thomas Henry Burree, steel fitter, & Margaret Nathalie Morgan, district nurse. Unmarried. Educated Park Street Primary School, Llanelli; Llanelli Boys Grammar School; St. Davids University College, Lampeter (2a History); University of Wales, Aberystwyth. Teacher of History & Politics, St. Michael's School, Llanelli 1982. Llanelli BC (Elli Ward) 1991-95. Contested Carmarthenshire CC (Glanymor) 1999. Chair, Welsh Liberal Democrats 1998-2001; Treasurer 2000-02. Chair: Candidates Cttee 1997-2001; Policy Cttee 1995-98, Press & Media Officer 1999-2000, Member: Executive 1995-2002, Policy Cttee 1994-98, Candidates Cttee 1997-2001, Campaigns Cttee 1994-95, 1999-2000, Conference Cttee 1993-97, Finance & B Administration Cttee 2000-2002. Party Spokesperson on Education

1996-97. Chair: Llanelli Liberal Democrats 1988-91, 1995-97, 2000-02, Carmarthen East, Dinefwr & Llanelli Liberal Democrats 2001-. Chair/Secretary/Treasurer, Llanelli Liberal Assn at various times 1979-88. President, Lampeter Student Liberal Assn 1976-77, Treasurer 1975-76. Member, Federal (UK) Conference Cttee 1998-99. Member: ATL, amnesty International, Howard League for Penal Reform, Charter 88. Interests: Pro Europe, Welsh Assembly Constitutional Affairs, Education, Civil Liberties. Hobbies: Reading (Detective/Sci-Fi & Political Biographies), Cinema, Popular Music. Languages: English. Of Llanelli.

BUSBY [CATO] Christopher Charles: BSc (London). PhD (Kent). Green, Mid & West Wales Euro 1994, North List 1999; Mid & West List (as Cato) 2003. **Dr. Chris Busby:** Born Paignton, Devon, 1 September 1945, son of Colonel Walter Robert Busby & Enid Lorna Whiigham-Teasdale, teacher of music. Pagan. Married 1967, Lorraine Hebron, teacher, 2s 5d. Lives with partner, Molly Scott Cato (qv), 1d. Educated St. Mary's School, Nairobi, Brockenhurst High School, Erith Grammar School, London University (1st Class Special in Chemistry), Kent University (Raman spectro electrochemistry), Environmental Scientist, developed interest in health effects of ionizing radiation since 1987; Radiation & Health Expert, employed by Irish government to research Sellafield & Health. Scientific Secretary, European Cttee on Radiation Brussels. Member: International Society for Environment Epidemiology; UK Ministry of Defence Oversight Cttee of Depleted Uranium. Joined Green Party 1990, Member Regional Council National Speaker (Shadow Cabinet) in Science & Technology. Green Party, Wales Euro (Reserve) 2004. Interests: Science Advice; Direct Action. Hobbies: Sailing, Music. Languages: English, French, German. Of Aberystwyth.

BUSH Eluned Mair: BSc (Exeter), DipVocGuid (Reading), MA (Wales). Plaid Cymru, Cardiff North 1987, 1992. Cardiff West & South/Central List 1999, Cardiff West & South/Central list 2003. **Mrs. Eluned Bush:** Born Ferndale 10 March 1944. Married Keith Bush (qv). Educated, Ferndale Grammar School, University of Exeter (Economics & Statistics), University of Reading, University of Wakes (Special Study of Welsh Education in Gwent). Careers Adviser, University of Wales, Newport. Senior Careers Adviser, Gwent County Council. Joined Plaid Cymru 1967. Member: Plaid Cymru National Council, NALGO Contested Rhondda BC & Cardiff CC. Of Llandaff, Cardiff.

BUSH Keith: BSc LlB (London). Plaid Cymru: Cardiff South East Feb & Oct. 1974, Bridgend

1983. **Mr. Keith Bush:** Born Briton Ferry May 1948, s of Hopkin George Bush & Gladys May Greener. Married 2c. Educated Tregaron County School & Imperial College, London. Planning Engineer, East Steel Works, Cardiff. Member, AUEW. Barrister 20 years. Crown Court Recorder. Member, National Assembly Counsel General's Staff (Transport, Planning & Environment). Legal Adviser, Richards Commission. Contested Neath local elections 1971, 1973, Cardiff CCC 1999. Left Plaid during 1984 Conference, Chair: traditionalist Hydro Group, Re-joined June 1987. Languages: Welsh, English. Of Cardiff.

BUSHBY Edmund Fleming: Kt. 1926. Conservative: Wrexham 1923, 1929, Withdrew in favour of Liberal 1931. **Sir Edmund Bushby:** Born Liverpool 14 November 1879, s of John Cannell & Emily Bushby. Anglican. Married 1907 Elaine, d of John Heap Hutchinson. Educated Sedbergh School. Spent 11 years in USA. Founded company of Bushby Brothers Cotton Merchants 1910, Director, Royal Insurance Co Ltd., Chair, Wrexham & East Denbighshire Water Co. Retired 1923. Army 1914-18: Lieutenant, King's (Liverpool) Regt. High Sheriff of Denbighshire 1931. Bought Bronwylfa Estate, Wrexham 1919. Died 11 July 1943.

BUSHELL John Gunther: ARCM FTCL ABSM PhD. Liberal Democrat: Islwyn B/E 1985, South Wales Euro, 1994, Gower 2001, **Dr. John Gunther Bushell:** Born Penang, 1959. Married Patricia Bushell, 2s. Educated Lee Mason C of E School, Birmingham College of Music. Music Teacher, Derbyshire 1980-89, West Glamorgan 1989-93. Director/Conductor, European Youth Brass Ensemble & String Consort, Director/Conductor, National Youth Brass Ensemble of GB & NI. Secretary, Swansea Branch, AMA. Swansea CC (Ind) B/E March 1994-97, Swansea CCC 1997-. Swansea leader, "NO" Campaign in Referendum 1997. Joined Conservative Party March 1998. Agent to Richard Lewis, Referendum Party 1999. Announced resignation from Conservative Party to fight the extension of Swansea Airport, 4 October 2003. Hobbies: Music, Travel, Sport. Of Dunvant, Swansea.

BUTLER Christopher John: BA 1973 MA PhD (Cantab). Conservative: Brecon & Radnor B/E 1985, MP Warrington South 1987-92, Contested Wales Euro 1999. **Dr. Christopher Butler:** Born 12 August 1950, s of Dr. John Wyn Butler & Eileen Patricia O'Neill. Church of England. Jacqueline Clair, d of R. O. F. Harper of Lymm, 1s. Educated Cardiff High School, Emmanuel College, Cambridge (Anthropology). Market Research Consultant, 1975-77. Conservative Research Dept 1977-80, Prime Minister's Staff 1980-83, Special Adviser, Secretary of State for Wales 1983-85.

Market Research Consultant 1985-86. Political Adviser, Richard Luce, Minister for the Arts 1986-87. Secretary Leasehold Reform Group 1989-92, Secretary, All Party Drugs Misuse Cttee 1989-92. Freelance Journalist. Parliamentary Consultant in public policy, Charities Trust plc, public policy unit, 1992. Company Director, Butler Kelly Ltd. political consultants. Interests: Wales, Small Businesses, Anti Single Currency. Author, Cardiff Mysteries. Hobbies: Deltiology. Languages: Welsh (just about), English, French. Of Kent.

BUTLER Gareth: BSc PGCE (Wales). Plaid Cymru: Newport East 1987. **Mr. Gareth Butler:** Born Newport 18 November 1956. Educated Dyffryn High School, Newport, University of Wales, Aberystwyth, (President SRC 1980). Education Adviser. Plaid Cymru Director of Language Policy 1993. Aberystwyth TC. Ceredigion DC 1987-/ Ceredigion CC (17 years in all). Contested Ceredigion CC (Aberystwyth East) 1999. Interests: Parliament for Wales. Languages: Welsh. English. Of Aberystwyth.

BUTLER Keith D: SDP/Alliance: Cynon Valley 1987. **Mr. Keith Butler:** Born 26 December 1953. Married Commercial Manager, Hereford United Football Club, ex-Worcestershire County Cricket Club. Vice-Chair, SDP Area Council, Member, Council for Social Democracy, Founding Member: Assn of SDP Councillors. Broadhall PC. Malvern Hills DC.

BUTLER Rosemary Mair Jane: Labour, AM. Newport West 1997. **Mrs. Rosemary Butler:** Born Bargoed, 21 January 1943. Married 1966, Derek, s of Thomas Charles Butler, lecturer in Art & Design, 2d. Educated St. Julian's High School, Newport. Chiropodist. Joined Labour Party 1971. Newport BC. 1973-99, Mayor, Chair, Leisure Services Cttee. 14 years, Member: Museums. & Galleries Commission, Council for Museums. In Wales Executive, Sports Council for Wales, -1999, Broadcasting Council for Wales, -1999. Governor, University of Wales, Newport. Director of Tourism, South & West Wales. Secretary for Education under 16s, 1999-Oct. 2000. Nominated by cabinet for Deputy Presiding Officer but defeated by John Marek. Interests:

Europe, Local Government, Arts, Sports, Culture. Languages: Learning Welsh, English. Of Newport.

BUTLIN Michael G: Liberal Democrat: Caerphilly 1987. **Mr. Michael Butlin:** Born 23 January 1942. Married 2s. Educated Kingston College. With computer manufacturing company. Member: British Computer Society, Lloyd George Society. President: Dyfed NUT 1987-88. Member, regional party executive.

BUTTON Victor John: Green Party: Alyn & Deeside 1992. **Mr. Victor Button:** Born Chester, 19 July 1943, s of Albert James Button, Post Office worker, & Helen Margaret Peake. Humanitarian. Married 1984 Jacqueline Mary Button, shop Manager, 2s 2d. Educated Chester College, Chester College of Further Education. Electrical Engineer: senior partner in family electrical repair/retail business at Chester. Joined: Labour Party 1984, Green Party 1986. Branch Secretary, Green Party. Sealand ComC, Clwyd CC. Area Tree Warden. School governor. Secretary: Creating Wealth (promoting self-sufficient/reliant, Vegan, organic communities). Interests: Green & Socialist Politics. Hobbies Music. Languages: English.

BYASS Sidney Hutcheson: 1st Bart 1926 JP DL (Glam) MA (Oxon). Conservative: Aberavon, 1922, 1923. **Sir Sidney Byass:** Born Reigate 1862, s of R. Nicholl Byass & Mary Hutchinson. Anglican. Married Eveline Stratton 3c. Educated Radley College, Oxford University. Came to Wales 1885. Steel & Tinplate Manufacturer; Director, docks & railway companies. Chair: Port Talbot Pilotage Board, Port Talbot Education Cttee, Llandaff Diocesan Board of Finance. President: Port Talbot & Aberavon Hospital Board, Aberavon Conservative Assn, Port Talbot Cricket Club, Aberavon RFC. Member, Governing Body of the Church in Wales. Margam UDC (Chair). Charter Mayor of Port Talbot 1920, 1st Freeman of Port Talbot. Vice-Chair, Glamorgan Quarter Sessions. Of Llandough Castle, Cowbridge from 1914. Estate £101,570. Died 18 February 1929.

CAIACH Siân Mair: MB BS. (London) 1981 FRCS (Glasgow) 1987 MRCS (Eng) LRCP (London) 1981. Plaid Cymru: Cardiff Central 1987; Gower 2001, 2003. **Dr. Siân Caiach:** Born Gelligaer, 8 October 1957. Partner, Kevin, 4c. Educated Gowerton Grammar School; Hall Bank School, Barnsley; Charing Cross Hospital Medical School. Orthopaedic Consultant 1981. Consultant Orthopaedic Surgeon, Prince of Wales Hospital, Llanelli. Suspended 2002. after 'blowing whistle' on private practice. Forensic Medical Examiner. Member: MPU, ASTMS. Joined Plaid Cymru 1976. Llanelli RDC. Interests: Health, Women, Agriculture. Hobbies: Free Range Chickens. Lives on 45-acre smallholding (sheep, goats, chickens). Of Llanelli.

CAIRNS Alun Hugh: Conservative: Gower 1997, Bridgend, 1999; AM South/West List 1999-. **Mr. Alun Cairns:** Born Clydach 30 July 1970. Baptist. Married Emma Turner, solicitor. Educated Ysgol Gyfun Ystalyfera. Regional Business Development Counsellor, Lloyds, Bank, Cardiff. Joined Conservatives 1987; Deputy-Chair, Wales Area Young Conservatives 1995. Conservative Assembly Spokesperson: Economics & Welsh Language 1997; Economic Development & Europe. Chair, South West Wales Regional Cttee 2001. Conservative Prospective Parliamentary Candidate, Vale of Glamorgan 2004. Hobbies: Running, Squash; Raising Money for Motor Neurone Disease. Languages: Welsh, English. Of Ewenny.

CALLAGHAN Leonard James, Baron Callaghan of Cardiff 1987: PC 1964 KG 1987 Grand Cross First Class, Order of Merit, Germany; Hon. LLD: Wales 1976; Sardar Patel University, India 1978; Birmingham 1981; Sussex 1988. Labour MP Cardiff South 1945-50; Cardiff SE 1950-83; Cardiff South & Penarth 1983-87. **Rt. Hon. James Callaghan:** Born Portsmouth 27 March 1912, s of Chief Petty Officer Leonard Callaghan. Ex-Baptist Sunday School Teacher. Married 1938, Audrey Elizabeth Moulton 3c. Educated Portsmouth Northern Grammar School. Joined staff of Inland Revenue 1929. Asst. Secretary, Inland Revenue Staff Assn 1936-47. Royal Navy 1939; Lieutenant RNVR 1941-45. Parl-Secretary, Ministry of Transport 1945-50. Chair, Cttee on Road Safety 1948-50. Parl & Fin Secretary, Admiralty 1950-51. Delegate, Council of Europe 1948-50, 1954. Consultant to the Police Federa-

James Callaghan.

tion of England and Wales & Scottish Police Federation 1956-64. President, United Kingdom Pilots' Assn 1963. Visiting Fellow, Nuffield College, Oxford 1956-57. Member, Labour Party NEC 1957-67; Treasurer, Labour Party 1967-76, Chair 1973-74. Opposition Spokesman on Financial Affairs 1961-64; Chancellor of the Exchequer 1964-67; Home Secretary 1967-70; Opposition Spokesman: Home Affairs 1970-71, Employment 1971-72. Director, National Bank of Wales 1972-74. Foreign Secretary 1974-76; Prime Minister 1976-79; Leader of the Opposition 1979-80; Father of the House of Commons 1983. President, University of Wales, Swansea. Hon. Fellow: University of Wales: Cardiff 1978, Swansea 1992; University of Portsmouth 1981. Hon. Freeman: Cardiff 1975, Sheffield 1979; Portsmouth 1991, Swansea 1993. *The Spectator's Elder Statesman of the Year* Award 1997. Languages: English. Further Reading: *Kenneth O. Morgan, James Callaghan, 1997.*

CALLAN Justin Patrick: UK Independence Party, Cardiff South & Penarth 2001. **Mr. Justin Callan:** Born Cardiff 28 March 1938, s of William Callan, weaver, & Florence Ethel Callan. Married 1963, Mary June Webster, 3d. Army 1972-1998; Gas Fitter/Plumber. Member: Referendum Party; Democracy Movement. Interests: Democracy, Truth, Justice & Fair Trading System. Hobbies: Work, Photography, Walking, Wild Life. Of Cardiff.

CAMERON Alistair Ronald: BA (Bristol). Liberal Democrat: Newport East 1997, 1999, 2001; Euro Wales 1999; South-West England Euro 2004; prospective parliamentary candidate, Tewkesbury. **Mr. Alistair Cameron:** Born 8 April 1960. Unmarried. Educated Greenhill School, Tenby; Bristol University (History); Bristol Poly (Dip. Personnel). Personnel Officer, British Energy, Gloucester. Cheltenham BC (Deputy Leader; Chair, Housing & Personnel Cttees). School Governor. Liberal Democrat Prospective Parliamentary Candidate, Tewkesbury 2003. Interests: Housing, Social services, Environment. Hobbies: Travel, Horse Riding, Football, Scuba Diving. Of Cheltenham.

CAMERON John: JP (Mon). Conservative: West Mon, Dec 1910. **Mr. John Cameron:** Born 25 December 1873. Married 1s 2d. Chair: Ebbw Vale Football Club. Chair, West Mon Conservative Ass. President, Ebbw Vale Conservative Assns. Ebbw Vale UDC. Chair, Governors, Ebbw Vale County School. Member: Bedwellty Board of Guardians, Ebbw Vale CO Tribunal, Ebbw Vale War Pensions Cttee. Of Victoria, Ebbw Vale. *An ardent sportsman.* Died 28 October 1918.

CAMPBELL Charles: KCMG 1905 CB DSO. Conservative: North Mon, Jan. 1910. **Vice-Admiral, Sir Charles Campbell:** Born St. Andrews 26 March 1847, s of John Campbell. Anglican. Married (1) Esther Constance Fairlie (2) Florence Geraldine Ross. Educated Staplehurst; Royal Naval Academy, Gosport; HMS *Britannia.* Officer, Royal Navy, Retired 1906. ADC Queen Victoria & Edward VII 1899-1902. Of Kensington. Estate £4,500. Died 8 February 1911.

CAMPBELL C. Ian: BSc(Psych) CertEd (Bristol). Labour: Clwyd North-West 1983. **Mr. Ian Campbell:** Born Pembroke, 1936. Married Thalia, 3s 1d. Educated Bristol University. Teacher. Unemployed. Served RNR & RNVR. Board of Trade Yachtmaster. RNLI crewmember. Secretary, Aberystwyth Child Poverty Action Group. Of Borth, Ceredigion.

CAMPBELL Hugh Frederick Vaughan, 4th Earl Cawdor: Viscount Emlyn 1827, Baron Cawdor 1796. JP (Carms Pembs) DL (Carms & Nairn) BA 1893 MA (Oxon). Conservative: Pembrokeshire B/E 1898; PPC Guildford (resigned on health grounds). **Captain, Hon. Hugh Campbell:** Born Golden Grove, Carms. 21 June 1870, s of 3rd Earl Cawdor (qv Viscount Emlyn) & Edith Georgiana, d of Christopher & Lady Caroline Tourniour. Succeeded to Viscounty 1898; Earldom 1911. Married 1898, Jean Emily Mary, d of Revd Lord John Charles Thynne. Landowner (101,657 acres in five estates, annual rent, 1910, £44,662).

Captain, Carmarthenshire Yeomanry. Landowner. Of Cawdor Castle, Nairn, Golden Grove, Carms, & Richmond. Estate £100,631. Died 7 January 1914.

CAMPBELL John Ross: MM 1917. Communist: Ogmore 1929; B/E 1931, 1931; Greenock 1945, 1950; Woodford 1951. **Mr. J. R. Campbell:** Born Paisley 1894, s of John Campbell. Married 1920, Sarah Marie O'Donnell, 2d. Educated Paisley Elementary School. Army 1914-18, lost toes on one foot. Joined British Socialist Party 1912; founder member, Communist Party 1920. Editor: *Glasgow Worker* 1921-22, Workers Weekly 1924-26; Industrial Editor, *Daily Worker* Editor -1939, 1949-. The publication of the *Don't Shoot* appeal to troops by the *Daily Worker* and the withdrawal of the mutiny charge (Arrested May 24 & Oct. 25 1924 & subsequently released in the *Campbell case*) was an important element in the fall of the 1924 Labour government; served six months for seditious conspiracy 1925-26. Member: Communist Party Executive 1923-, Communist Party International Executive 1925-35. Leading figure in Party 1922-29; lost influence in 1929 *coup d'etat*; a worker-intellectual; His support of British entry into the war in 1939 led to his removal from the *Daily Worker* and his being sent to district work in Scotland; restored to editorship 1949. Of Cricklewood, London.

CAMPBELL Robert John: Conservative: Swansea District Jan 1910. **Mr. Robert Campbell:** Born Kilmarnock 5 November 1866. Engineer, worked at bench from age of 10. Member, Amalgamated Society of Engineers. Woolwich BC. 1906-. Of Plumstead, Kent.

CAMPBELL Suzanne Margaret: FPC. Liberal Democrat: Vale of Glamorgan 1997. **Mrs. Suzanne Campbell:** Born Pembroke, 27 March 1945, d of Edgar Owen Jones, carpenter/cabinet maker, & Margaret Loraine Mears. Church in Wales. Married John Barry Campbell, veterinary surgeon, 5d. Educated Pembroke Grammar School; Haverfordwest FE College. Nurse 8 years; Independent Financial Adviser 1987; Semi-Professional Vocalist. Chair: South Wales Federation of Independent Financial Advisers; Wenvoe & District Community Action Group; Member: Equity, Amnesty International, Greenpeace, RSPCA, League against Cruel Sports. Contested local elections 1992-2000. Interests: Social Justice; Improving Animal Welfare. Languages: English, a little French. Of Wenvoe.

CAMPBELL William Darling Mill: UK Independence Party, Vale of Clwyd 2001. **Mr. William Campbell:** Born Edinburgh, 7 November 1959, s of George Campbell, farmer, & Isabella Elizabeth Campbell, housewife. Methodist. Married 1987, Hazel Laureen Stark, veterinary nurse, 3s. Educated Casteltown Primary School; Thurso High School; Edinburgh University. Veterinary Surgeon. Interests: Anything to re-instate UK Home Rule! Hobbies: Attend Church, Charity Work, RSPCA, Send-a-Cow. Languages: English, French.

CANNING Jeffrey: AIB. Plaid Cymru, Assembly, Bridgend 1999. **Mr Jeff Canning:** Born Cardiff, 9 June 1959, son of Stanley canning, warehouse manager, & Carol Barnett. Agnostic. Married 1979, Wendy Canning, health service worker, 2d. Joined Bank 1973. Lending Manager, Barclays Bank. Member, Banking, Insurance & Finance Union. Auditor, TUC Wales, 1997- Member, Advisory Board, New Deal Employment Scheme, Bridgend. Joined Plaid Cymru 1974. National Treasurer, Plaid Cymru. Creigiau & Pentyrch ComC. Interests: Socialism/Nationalism. Hobbies: Scuba diving, Sailing. Languages: Welsh, English. Of Creigiau.

CAPLAN Leonard: QC 1954 LlB (Liverpool) 1920. Conservative: Pontypool 1935; North Hammersmith 1945; Kensington North 1950, 1951. **Mr. Leonard Caplan:** Born Merthyr Tydfil 28 June 1909; s of Henry Caplan of Liverpool. Jewish. Married (1) 1929 Tania Finkelstein 2d (div. 1974) (2) 1977 Mrs. Herkovits, New York (div. 1989). Educated Grocers Company School; Liverpool University. Barrister, Grays Inn 1935; Middle Temple 1949; Master of the Bench, Grays Inn1964, Treasurer 1979. Army 1939-45, Major. Chair, College Hall, London.

CARBUTT Edward Hamer: 1st Bart 1892 MIMechE. Liberal MP: Monmouth District 1880-86. **Sir Edward Carbutt:** Born 22 July 1838, s of Francis Carbutt JP, Chapel Allerton, Leeds. Unitarian. Married 1874, Mary, d of John Rhodes of Leeds. Manufacturing Engineer. Partner, Thwaites & Carbutt, Bradford. Leeds BC 1877, Mayor 1878. Chair, West Riding Liberal Assn. Of Llanwern House, Newport & London. Estate £103,192. Died 8 October 1905.

CARLILE Alexander Charles, Baron Carlile 1999: QC 1984 LlB (London) 1969. Liberal (Democrat): East Flint Feb. 1974,1979; MP Montgomery 1983-97. **Mr. Alex Carlile:** Born Rossett, 12 February 1949, s of Irwin Falik, MD. & Sabina Lozenska (fought in Warsaw uprising), Polish Jews. Married 1968 Frances, d of Michael & Elizabeth Soley, 3d. Educated Heathfield College, Risworth; Epsom College; Kings College, London; Inns of Court Law School. Barrister, Grays Inn 1970. Recorder 1986; Deputy High Court Judge 1998-. Hon. Recorder of Hereford 1996. Liberal Democrat Spokesman: Legal Affairs 1989; Trade & Industry, 1990; Foreign &

European Affairs 1988-89. Jt-Sec. All Party Lawyers Group. Treasurer, All parties United Nations Group. Vice-Chair, All Parties War Crimes Group; Civil Liberties Group. Lay Member, General Medical Council 1989. Member: Public Records Advisory Cttee; Council, Howard League 1989. Adviser (unpaid) Overseas Doctors Assn. Chair, Welsh Liberal Party 1980-82, Leader 1992-97. Chair; NACRO Cttee on Children & Crime. Non-executive director, medium sized manufacturing co. Chair: Carlile Review, child protection in NHS (Assembly of Wales). Vice-Chair: Great Britain/East Europe Centre. Co-Chair: Return of Britain to UNESCO. Fellow: Industry and Parliament Trust. Appointed by Home Secretary as Independent Reviewer of Terrorism Legislation 2001. Hobbies: Music, Theatre, Fine Arts. Languages: Moderate Welsh speaker, English. Retired to give more time to his family. Of Berriew, Welshpool.

CARMICHAEL Evelyn George Massey: OBE JP (Staffs) 1923 MA FSA. Conservative: North Monmouthshire Jan. 1910 **Mr. Evelyn Carmichael:** Born1871, s of Lieut-Colonel G. L. Carmichael. Anglican. Married 1908 Dorothea Helen, d of Sir James Colquohoun of Luss; 3d. Educated Harrow; Oriel College, Oxford. Barrister. Chair: Court of Referees; Munitions Tribunal for Coventry, Worcs & Herefordshire; Wrekin Conservative Assn. Of Newport, Salop.

CARPENTER Peter: BA (Cantab). Unitax Independent: Monmouth B/E 1991. **Mr. Peter Carpenter:** Born Cambridge 1938. Educated Cambridge University (Natural Sciences). Teacher 12 years (6 at Monmouth School). Set up Caer Llan Conference & Field Studies Centre, Lydart, Monmouth, 1969. Designed & built Caer Llan Berm House, Lydart (earth sheltered Berm house & one of the ten most energy saving buildings in Europe 1980-87). Secretary, British Earth Sheltering Society. Unitax aims to have only one tax.

CARR Gwenllian Angharad: BA (Wales). Plaid Cymru: Cardiff West 1997. **Ms Angharad Carr:** Born Bangor 3 June 1971, d of Tony, Welsh History Lecturer & Glenda, translator. Married Jan. 1997, George Herd. Educated University of Wales, Bangor. Organiser, North Wales Assn of Students 1994-95; President, Wales NUS 1995-96; Welsh Language Convenor, University of Wales Bangor; NUS; North Wales Convenor 1993-94. Journalist. Policy Officer, Council for Racial Equality; Policy & Marketing Officer, Welsh Language Board. Languages: Welsh, English.

CARRINGTON Anthony Richard: The Monmouthshire Candidate, Monmouth 1999. **Mr. Anthony Carrington:** Born 1958. Married

Alyson Carrington, 1s 1d. Blaenau Gwent BC Highways Dept. Inspector. Blaenau Gwent BC 1987, (Vice-Chair, Personnel). Monmouthshire CC (Llanelly Hill) 1995-99 (defeated), Chair, Personnel, 1997-99, Vice-Chair, 1997-98, Chair of the Council, 1998-99. Llanelly Community Clr 1987-, twice Chair. Resigned from Labour Party in protest at the Party's Selection Procedure Project 99. Contested CC By-election (Independent), July 2002. Of Gilwern.

CARTER Dennis B: BA MEd Labour: Clwyd South-West 1983. **Mr. Dennis Carter:** Born 1943. Married 2c. Educated Preston Secondary Modern School; Birkenhead Technical School; Chester College of Education; London University; Exeter University. Bank Clerk, Forestry Commission Worker; with Bowater Paper Co. Teacher. Head-teacher, Taliesin Junior School, Shotton. Member: Socialist Education Assn, CND, NUT. Hobbies: Ornithology.

CARTER Michael James: ARICS. AIArb. Conservative: Gower 1970. **Mr. Michael Carter:** Born Cornwall 1936. Married Wendy McAdam (actress) 2c. Educated South Africa; King's College, Taunton. Chartered Surveyor. In building trade 1954-66. Lecturer in Surveying. Member: Falmouth Rugby XV, Round Table, Scouts, Monday Club, NUT. Kingston-upon-Thames BC until 1973. Achieved biggest pro-Tory swing in Wales in the election: Pro death penalty; anti foreign aid; Resigned 1973 from borough council and as PPC for Eton & Slough because of his right wing disagreement with Heath government policies.

CATO Sarah Margaret (Moli) Scott – see Scott-Cato, Sarah.

CATON Martin Philip: Labour MP Gower 1997. **Mr. Martin Caton:** Born Bishop Stortford 15 June 1951, s of William John & Pauline Caton, shopkeepers. Married Bethan, d of Hermas & Menai Evans, 2d. Educated Newport Grammar School, Essex; Norfolk College of Agriculture; Aberystwyth College of Further Education. Scientific Research Officer, Welsh Plant Breeding Station. Political Assistant to David Morris MEP. Swansea CC 1988-97; Joined Labour Party 1975. Member: CND Cymru; SERA. Environmental group. Interests: Devolution, Environment, Local Government Finance. Member, Select Cttee: Welsh Affairs. Interests: Planning, Education, Europe. Hobbies: Reading, Walking, Theatre, Thinking about gardening.

CAVENAGH Stephen John: Conservative: Carmarthen 1992. **Mr. Stephen Cavenagh:** Born 1964. Educated Malvern College. Farmer (family dairy 7 sheep farm). Branch Chair, NFU & Young Farmers' Club. Chair: NFU Branch. Carmarthen East & Dinefwr Conservative Assn (2001). Of Llandovery.

CAVES Barbara: Natural Law Party: Cardiff South & Penarth 1997; Assembly South/Central List 1999. **Mrs. Barbara Caves:** Born Birmingham, 21 March 1941, d of Alan Walter Osborne, soldier, & Helen Osborne. Married 1963, Michael William Coynes, director of own company,1d. Educated Secondary Modern School. Local Govt Officer, Birmingham; personal assistant to managing director of a Birmingham Advertising Agency. Teacher of Transcendental Meditation 1983; Staff of TM Academy Wales 1994-; formerly at Kent TM Academy & TM Academy/Conference Centre, Derbyshire; Teacher of Vedic Science; Teacher of Personal Development. Interests: Peace, Prosperity for All Mankind. Hobbies: Colour/Harmony in many forms. Languages: English; some Sanskrit. Of Roath, Cardiff.

CAVILL Terrance: British National Party (BNP), Newport West 2001; Euro South West England 1999. **Mr. Terry Cavill:** Born 1955. Single. Farmer. BNP Regional Organiser for South Wales; Branch Organiser, Cardiff & The Valleys. Of Itton, Mon.

CAYZER Charles William: 2nd Bart 1905 MA (Oxon). Conservative: Monmouth District Jan. 1910. **Sir Charles Cayzer:** Born Bombay 19 July 1869, s of 1st Bart. Married Annie Mabel Harriet, d of Thomas Jennings White QC. 6c. Educated Rugby; Christ Church, Oxford. Shipowner: Partner, Cayzer, Irvine & Co. Chair, Clan Line Steamers 1890-1911. Of 22, Lewes Crescent, Brighton. Estate £115,662. Died 20 July 1917.

CEMLYN-JONES Elias Wynne: Kt 1941 JP. Liberal: Brecon & Radnor 1929; South Croydon 1923. **Sir Wynne Cemlyn-Jones:** Born Amlwch 16 May 1888, s of John Cemlyn Jones, solicitor, & Gaynor Hannah, d of John Elias Jones, Penmaenmawr. Anglican. Married 1914 Muriel Gwendolin d. of Owen Owen, stores owner; 4c. Educated Mostyn School; Parkgate; Shrewsbury School; London and abroad. Barrister. Private Secretary, Rt. Hon. Sir E. J. Ellis-Griffith MP 1912-14. Army 1914-18, Captain RWF. Anglesey CC 1919, Alderman 1928. Chair CC Selection Cttee; Anglesey War Agricultural Exec. Cttee. Member: Central Advisory Water Cttee. Small Holdings Advisory Cttee; Council of Welsh National School of Medicine; Central Whiteley Council for the Health Service. Vice-President: Council Councils Assn; National Museum of Wales, National Library of Wales, Court of the University of Wales, University College of North Wales. Languages: Welsh, English. Died June 1966.

CHADWICK Andrew: Liberal Democrat: Clwyd South 1997. **Mr. Graham Chadwick:** Born 23 October 1953. Educated Aireborough Grammar School, Leeds. Development Professional since 1982. Voluntary Sector Consultant. Save the Children Fund Co-ordinator, Ethiopia, 1992-95. Oxfam Co-ordinator, Bosnia.

CHALKE Richard David: CBE 1951 JP (Glam) 1929 BA 1898 MA 1901 LlB 1901 LLD Dublin 1903. Liberal: Rhondda East 1929; Swansea East 1931. **Dr. R. D. Chalke:** Born Neath Abbey 1869, s of Henry, police sergeant, & Jane Chalke 1 of 6c. Anglican. Educated Treorchy Board School; Higher Grade School; Cheltenham Training College; Trinity College, Dublin. Married 1924, Elizabeth Catherine JP CC d of Revd Philip Jones, Pontypridd, 1s 1d. Teacher 1890. Headmaster: (1st) Ferndale Higher Grade School 1892-98; Porth Higher Grade School & Teacher Training Centre 1898-1926. Captain, 6th Volunteer Battalion, Welch Regt. 1st Chair, South Wales League of Young Liberals. Chair: East Glamorgan Liberal Assn; Welsh League for Taxation of Land Values; Hon. Sec. Welsh Democratic League; Member: Central Welsh Board; Court of the University of Wales, University College of Swansea, University College of South Wales & Mon., Welsh National School of Medicine; President, Welsh RFU, Welsh Secondary Schools Rugby Union; Porthcawl UDC 25 years. Of Porth, then Porthcawl. Died 13 September 1962.

CHAMBERS Jill Frances: BA CertEd. Conservative, Neath & South/West List, 1999. Born 1949. **Mrs. Jill Chambers:** Married 6c. Educated University (History). MP's office manager. Managing director, property company & farm business. Joint owner with Tony Marlow (ex-MP) of Pembrokeshire farm where GM trials were planned 2001. Officer. School Governor. Voluntary administrator, hospice charity. Deputy-Chair: Neath Chair: Neath Conservative Assn (2001). Of Castle Cenlas, Mathry, Haverfordwest.

CHAPMAN Christine: BA (Wales) MSc (Econ) 1992, PGCE 1995. Labour AM Cynon Valley 1999. **Mrs. Christine Chapman:** Born Porth, Rhondda, 7 April 1956, d of John Price & Edith Jean Price. Married 1981, Dr. Michael Chapman, s of Don & Mai Chapman, 1s 1d. Educated Rhondda Grammar School for Girls, Porth; University of Wales, Aberystwyth (History & Classical Studies); South bank Polytechnic (Dip. Careers Guidance); University of Wales, Cardiff. Supervisor, Mid-Glam Community Services Agency 1979-80, Mid-Glam Careers Service 1980-83; Seconded to Mid-Glam Business Partnership 1996-99. Director, Mid-Glamorgan Careers Ltd 1996-99. Contested Taf-Ely BC 1991,

Rhondda/Cynon/Taf BC 1995-99. Ynysbwl ComC. 1995-99. Chair, school governors. Interests: Women's issues; Health; Education. Hobbies: Gym, Running, Swimming, Playing piano, Women's history. Deputy Secretary, Education & Economic Development. Chair: Assembly Objective One Monitoring Cttee. Of Ynysybwl.

CHAPMAN Martin: Welsh Socialist Alliance, Aberavon 2001. Brought up near Stoke on Trent, family from Neath/Briton Ferry/London. Lives with Partner Nimisha Trivedi (qv), 1s. Chair: Welsh Socialist Alliance; Campaign Organiser, Swansea 2003. Of Brynmill, Swansea.

CHAPMAN-WALKER Peter John Fairchild: OBE. Conservative: Abertillery 1929, East Bristol 1931, Holborn & St. Pancras South 1950. **Mr. Peter Chapman-Walker:** Born 1907. Married Educated Marlborough; The Sorbonne. London Solicitor 1930 & farmer (200 acres) at Ware. Hertfordshire Regt & Services Reconnaissance Department 1939-45, Lieut-Colonel. London CC (Westminster). Died March 1958.

CHRISTON Bernard Miles: Liberal: Cardiff South-East Feb. 1974, Blackpool South 1970. **Mr. Bernard Christon:** Born Carlton, nr. Goole, Yorks. April 1937 (grandparents from Abergavenny). Married Educated Selby Technical College; Bradford Technical College. State Registered Nurse. Laboratory Technician. Medical Representative of a pharmaceutical company. District Sales Manager for Wales & South-West. Member: Institute of Medical Laboratory Technicians; Royal Society of Health; North-Western Liberal Federation Executive; Preston Council for Community Relations. Joined Liberal Party 1963. Contested Fulwood UDC 14 times. Of Bridgend.

CHURCHMAN Stephen William: Liberal Democrat, Caernarfon 2003, Barking 1992. **Mr. Steve Churchman:** Born Dagenham, Essex, 4 August 1962, s of Frederick Alfred Churchman, builders' merchant, & Violet Louisa Churchman, office worker. Married 1981, Wendy Marion Churchman, shopkeeper, 1s 1d. Educated Mayesbrook Comprehensive School, Dagenham; Technical College. Draftsman. Technical Auditor, British Rail & Balfour Beatty. Shopkeeper. Barking & Dagenham BC 1986-90, 1994-99 (Deputy Group Leader). Contested Gwynedd CC B/E 2003. Liberal Democrat Press Officer, Barking 1984-86; Barking Agent 1987, 1992, 1997. Liberal Democrat Campaign Co-ordinator, Conwy & Caernarfon. Member: TSSA, Reptile & Amphibian Society Cttee. Interests: Housing, Planning. Hobbies: Herpetology; Gardening. Of Gandolbenmaen.

CIRCUS Philip J: MA MPhil DCA FISP. Conservative: Llanelli 1987. **Mr. Philip Circus:** Born 8 May 1951. Married Gaenor. Educated Westcliff High School; Ealing College of Higher Education; Southampton University. Barrister. Director of Legal Affairs, Institute of Practitioners in Advertising. Principal, Lawmark (Market Law Advisory Service). Chair: CBI Customer Affairs Cttee; Advertising Law Group. Member; Government working parties on prices, credit & environmental labeling; National Consumer Council; Mail Protection Scheme Board; ITC Advertising Advisory Cttee; Cttee of Advertising Practice 1977 (Vice-Chair, Sales Promotion & Direct Response Panel). Advertising Law Consultant, Newspaper Society. Head of Legal Affairs, Institute of Sales Promotion. Programme Adviser on marketing law, Hawkesmere plc. Member, Editorial Advisory Board, Business Law Review. Richmond on Thames BC 1982-86. Reigate & Banstead BC 1999-; Deputy-Leader 2002-03. Mayor of Reigate & Banstead 2003-04.

CLAGUE Gwyn Alexander: Democratic Alliance of Wales, Assembly, North List 1999. **Mr Gwyn Clague:** Married Pauline Valerie Clague, 1d. Fire Officer. Loss Prevention Manager. In UK North Africa and Middle East. Denbighshire CC (Prestatyn South) 1999-. Founder, Democratic Alliance of Wales. Of Prestatyn (1971).

CLARK Godfrey Lewis Bosville: JP DL (Glam) MA FRAS. Conservative: East Glamorgan 1885. **Colonel Godfrey Clark:** Born 30 November 1855, s of George Thomas Clark JP DL & Ann, d of Henry Lewis JP of Greenmeadow. Anglican. Married 1883, Alicia Georgiana, Caroline, d of Henry L. Strong, 3s. Landowner. Company Chair: Rhymney Railway Co. Ltd; Vale of Glamorgan Railway Co. Ltd; Cardiff Gas Coke & Light Co. Ltd. Captain, Shropshire Light Infantry (Militia), Hon. Major; Hon. Colonel, Glamorgan Volunteers. Chair: Pontypridd Board of Guardians 20 years; Llantrisant & Llantwit Fardre RDC; Glamorgan Joint Standing Cttee. Of Talygarn, Pontyclun. Estate £320,539. Died 11 February 1918.

CLARK Hugh Westcott: BA. PGCE. (Wales). Liberal: Abertillery Feb. & Oct. 1974. **Mr. Hugh Clark:** Born Newport, 2 March1935, s of Raymond Thomas Clark, electrician, & Ethel Winefred Palmer. Church of Wales. Married 1959. Valerie May Clark, teacher, 1s. Educated Corporation Road Primary School, Newport; Hathersleigh Secondary Modern School; Gwent College; Independent Gwent College of HE; University of Wales, Cardiff (History). Clerical Worker, British Steel Corporation, Llanwern (in 1974); FE College Lecturer. Member, BISAKTA. Chair: Welsh League of Young Liberals; Newport Liberal Democrats –May 2002. Contested Newport BC 1999; Newport BC 1964-67; Dec. 1999. Interests: Education, Finance. *Books: Hugh Clark: The Maindee Book, The Maindee Companion, New Stories* 1981. Of Newport.

CLARKE Eric John James: Keep Britain United Party: Carmarthen 1979. **Mr. John Clarke:** Born Newport 1926. Married 6c. Quality Control Inspector, Standard Telephones Ltd. Newport. Chair, Gwent Ratepayers' Assn. Secretary: Skateboarding Assn. of Wales & UK Skateboarding Federation. Contested Newport BC twice. Responded to E. Brisbane Jones' (qv) advert for a candidate for this election. Of Newport, Gwent.

CLARKE David: United Socialists, North List, 1999. **Mr. David Clarke:** Community activist. Of Old Colwyn.

CLARKE James Henry: BSc. Liberal Democrat, Ynys Môn & North List 1999 **Mr. James Clarke:** Born County Meath, Ireland, 1950. Married 1971 Susan, 1s 1d. Mature Student (Engineering). Laboratory Technician. Ex-Fire Service. Business Manager Joined Liberals 1974. Member Welsh Executive Cttee. Secretary, Welsh Liberal Democrat Council. Ynys Môn CC 1987-91. Interests: International affairs, Job creation, Economic development & re-generation. Hobbies: Travel. Of LlanfairPG.

CLARKE Jeffrey John: BSc(Soc). Liberal Democrat: Preseli 1997; Alyn & Deeside 1999. **Mr. Jeffrey Clarke:** Born Cardiff 19 March 1962. Married 2c. Educated Keele University. Criminal Defence Barrister. Legal Assistant, South Pembs DC. Welsh Liberal Democrat Spokesman on Justice & Home Affairs. Languages: English. Of Chester

CLARKE Owen – see CLARKE Robert Owen Lear.

CLARKE Peter: Conservative: Newport West 1997; Fife Central Oct 1974. **Mr. Peter Clarke:** Born April 1947. Married Lilian Strickland, writer, 2s. Educated St. Columba's School, Kilmalcolm; Loughborough Grammar School; Bradford University; Balliol College, Oxford. Political Assistant to Enoch Powell, Keith Joseph & Nicholas Ridley. Journalist, *Private Eye*, The Economist; former BBC economics correspondent. National Secretary, National Referendum "NO" Campaign against joining EEC. Co. Chairman, Business Seminars International. Chair, Selsdon Group. Political Assistant to Enoch Powell, Sir Keith Joseph & Nicholas Ridley. Formed PULSE (Campaign to promote competitive tendering for public services).

CLARKE Rina Judith: Labour, Montgomery 2003. **Ms. Rina Clarke:** Born Carmarthen, 1947. Married Timothy Clarke, 4c. Educated Carmarthen Girls' Grammar School; University of Wales, Swansea. Teacher in London. Deputy Head, Cornwall primary school. With Tim, started Zest Foods in a garage in Cornwall; came to Newtown with Zest Foods 1988, sold out 1998. Taught Welsh in local schools. Part time Powys CC Home Tutor. Volunteer manager, Robert Owen Credit Union. Non Executive Director, Dyfed/Powys Health Authority. Languages: Welsh, English. Of Kerry, Powys.

CLARKE Robert Owen Lear: Green Party, South/East List 1999, 2003. **Mr. Owen Clarke:** Educated Quaker school. Engineer & Company Director, retired. Rope Tester, National Caving Assn. Member: Green Party Disputes Resolution Cttee. Active in Peace Movement Hobbies: Caving, Choral Singing, Enjoying life. Of Abersychan.

CLARRY Reginald George: Kt 1936 JP FCIS. Conservative MP Newport B/E 1922-29, 1931-. **Sir Reginald Clarry:** Born Derby 24 July 1882, s of George Clarry FCIS, General Manager Cardiff Gas Co. Anglican. Married 1906, Laura Marian, d of Edmund Sapey 3d. Educated Marling School, Stroud; Technical College. Articled Pupil in Gas Engineering. Resident Engineer, Shoreditch Gas Works. Engineer-Manager-Secretary, Swansea Gas Co. Managing Director, Dyffryn Steel & Tin Plate Works, Morriston. Hon. Adviser, Ministry of Munitions 1915-18. Consulting Engineer & Company Director. Chair, British Road Tar Federation. Freemason. Died 17 January 1945. His election at the 1922 by-election led to the collapse of the Lloyd George Coalition Government.

CLATWORTHY Joshua Thomas: OBE JP (Cardiff). Labour: Cardiff South 1918. **Mr. Joshua Clatworthy:** Born 1867, s of Joshua Clatworthy, iron foreman. Married Caroline (Died 1936) 2c. Grocer's boy. Coal Trimmer. President, Cardiff & Barry Coal Trimmers' Union 1911-31. Member: Cardiff Board of Guardians Governor, Cardiff Royal Infirmary. Cardiff CC. Died 25 July 1948.

CLAY Michael John: DL (S. Glam) 1997 FCA ACA. Conservative: Pontypridd 1979. **Mr. Michael Clay:** Born Cowbridge, 23 July 1929, s of John Charles Clay, cricketer & shipowner, & Gwenllian Mary, d of Colonel H. R. Homfray, Penllyn Castle, Cowbridge. Married (1) 1956 Anne Mary Amelia Gillespie (2) Catherine Vivian Lindsay Picton-Turberville CC. 1s 1d. Church of England. Educated Winchester. Lieutenant, Welch Regiment. Chartered Accountant 1957. Company Secretary, later Managing Director, Wm. Lewis (Agricultural house) Ltd. Cardiff. Practised as Chartered Accountant 1964-94. 1st Chair, Cowbridge RNLI Branch. Chair, Cowbridge Conservative Branch Assn 1972-75. Vice-Chair, Pontypridd Conservative Assn. Election Agent, Pontypridd, Feb. & Oct. 1974. Founder Member, Cardiff & District Society of Chartered Accountants (Chair 1980-82. President: South Wales & Mon District Society of Chartered Accountants 1983-84. Member: Welsh Cttee. Transport Users' Consultative Cttee. Rector's Churchwarden & Treasurer, Llangunnor PCC. Member, Llandaff Diocesan Board of Finance 1984, Vice-Chair 1985-92, Chair 1992-. Chair: Cowbridge Amateur Operatic Society. High Sheriff of South Glamorgan 1991-92. Member: Priory for Wales Finance Cttee, Order of St. John of Jerusalem 1992; Treasurer 1993-. Hobbies: Gardening, Forestry, Training gun-dogs.

CLEGG Steven Mark: Green Party, South/West List 2003. **Mr. Steve Clegg:** Born Kirkham, Lancs. 21 June 1967, s of Brian Clegg, joiner/cabinet maker, & Janet Lacey Clegg, nurse/buyer/shop worker. Pagan. Married 2003, Sarah Jane Clegg, rehabilitation assistant, 1s 1d. Educated Carr Hill High School, Kirkham; Blackpool & Fylde College; University of Bradford; University of Wales, Swansea. Spiritual Healer/Advice Case Worker Centre for Complimentary Medicines. Green Party local press officer & spokesman on Housing, Regeneration, Social/Inclusion. Member: CND, Animal World, World Development Movement, Amnesty International. Interests: Regeneration, Sustainability, Equality, Globalisation. Hobbies: Internal Martial Arts (Zaisi, Wing Chung), Art, Reading, Walking, Cooking, Gardening, Music Festivals. Of Swansea.

CLIFF Janet Mary: BSc. MRES. Green Party, Llanelli 2001; South/West List 2003. **Mrs. Jan Cliff:** Born Ferndale, Rhondda, 17 August 1960, d of Benjamin Gareth Jones, engineer, & Marjorie Morgan, civil servant. Pagan. Married Joseph Timothy Stuart Cliff, archeologist (Agent 2001) 1s 2d. Educated Formby High School; London University. Part-time tutor, University of Wales, Swansea & renewable energy consultant/company director. Vice-Chair, Hendy Village Forum. Volunteer. Swansea community farm. Joined Green Party, London 1981; Secretary, Swansea & Llanelli Green Party; Treasurer, Carmarthenshire Green Party. Interests: Radical Solutions/environmentalism, anti-globalisation. Hobbies: Organic horticulture, Music, Walking, Family. Languages: English; Welsh Learner; French. Of Hendy, Pontarddulais.

CLOVER C. George: Conservative: Aberdare 1945. **Captain George Clover:** Born 1910; spent a great deal of his time in Wales; Captain, Royal Scots Grays; Came forward as a National Candidate, supporting Mr. Churchill . . . *I earnestly appeal to you on a point of national unity to stand four square behind Mr. Churchill, a man who has triumphantly brought this country through the darkest days of its history (election address).*

CLOWES Carl Iwan: BSc (London) 1980, MB BCh (Manchester) 1957, MFCM RCP (UK) 1981, MSc (Social Medicine). DTM. FFPHM. Certificate in Health Economics. Plaid Cymru: Montgomery 1979, 1983, 1987. **Dr. Carl Clowes:** Born Manchester, 11 December 1943, s of Gilbert Clowes, carpenter, & Mary Gwyneth Thomas. Church in Wales. Married 1966, Dorothi Clowes, 2s 2d. Educated Bury Grammar School; Manchester University; London School of Hygiene & Tropical Medicine. Medical Practitioner: Llanelhaearn 1970-82; Health Administrator, Gwynedd Health Authority 1983-88, resigned; Director of Planning, Powys Health Authority 1988-. International Health Care Consultant. Founder-Chair: Antur Aelhaearn 1974-69. Nant Gwrtheyrn Trust 1978-82. Chair: Nant Gwrtheyrn Co; Wales-Lesotho Link. Hon. Consul, Lesotho in Wales. Plaid Cymru Spokesman on Health 1985-90. Interests: Gardening, Art, Music. Languages: Welsh, English.

CLWYD Ann Clwyd Lewis: PC 2004; BA (Wales). Labour: Denbigh 1970; Gloucester Oct. 1974; MP Cynon Valley, B/E 1984-; MEP West & Mid Wales 1979-84. **Rt. Hon. Ann Clwyd:** Born Denbigh 21 March 1937, d. of Gwilym Henry Lewis & Elizabeth Jane Jones. Presbyterian Church of Wales. Married Owen Roberts. Educated Holywell Grammar School; Queen's School, Chester; University of Wales, Bangor. Journalist & Broadcaster: Welsh Correspondent, *The Guardian.* Member: Cardiff & District Hospital Management House Cttee; Executive, Cardiff & District Assn. for Mental Health; Welsh Hospital Board; Royal Commission on NHS 1976-79. Supported Jennie Eirian Davies, Plaid Cymru in Carmarthen By-Election 1957. Joined Labour Party 1965. Contested Deputy Leadership 1992. Dismissed from Front Bench for unauthorised visit to Kurdistan 1995. Parl-Adviser, Society of Telecom Executives. Vice-Chair, PLP Defence Cttee 1985-87; Chair, PLP Health & Social Security Cttee 1985-87, 1991. Member, Select Cttee on Euro Legislation 1987-88. Treasurer, Europe Group 1988. Opposition Spokesman: Education 1987-88; Women's' Rights 1987-88; Overseas Aid 1989. Contested Deputy Leadership of Labour Party 1992. Member, Labour Party NEC 1983-84. Chair: All Party Human Rights Group 1997-; Insight; Vietnam Group; Vice-Chair: Portuguese Group 1997-. Vice-Chair PLP. Prime Minister's Special Envoy to Iraq 2003. Member, NUJ, TGWU, UNA. Interests: Arts, Foreign Affairs, Overseas Development, Women's issues. Hobbies: Walking, Boating. Languages: Welsh, English.

COCKBURN John Alexander: KCMG 1900 KStJ MD (London). Independent Tariff Reform: West Mon B/E 1904, with official backing of Tariff Reform & Unionist Assns. **Hon. Sir John Cockburn:** Born Borsbie, New Brunswick 2 August 1850. Married Sarah Holden, d of Forbes Scott Brown, 1s 1d. Educated Cholmeley School, Highgate; King's College, London (Fellow). Settled in South Australia 1875. Medical Practitioner. Captain, Royal Volunteer Rifles. Mayor of Jamestown, 3 years. Member, South Australia Assembly 1884-1901. Minister of Education 1885-87. Premier 1889-90. Chief Secretary 1892. Minister for Education & Agriculture 1893-98. Agent General for South Australia 1898-1901. Chair, Australian Chamber of Commerce in London. Vice-Chair, London School of Economics. President: Men's International Alliance for Women's Suffrage; International Philological Society 1917-19; Bacon Society; John Payne Society. Hobbies: Archeology, Agriculture, Photography. Of Harrietson, Kent. Estate £20,442. Died 26 September 1929.

COCKWELL Leighton Philip: CertEd (Birmingham). Plaid Cymru: Aberavon 1997. **Mr. Philip Cockwell:** Born Neath, 1st March 1933, s of Harold Llywelyn Cockwell, insurance & estate agent, & Ivy Mary Phillips. Welsh Independent. Married 1960 Gillian Roderick (Died) 2s 1d. Educated Ynysmaerdy Primary School, Briton Ferry; Neath Boys Grammar School; Worcester Teacher Training College. Teacher; Deputy Head, Primary School; Retired. Neath BC 1991-96. Blaenhonddan ComC. 1988- (Chair 1995-96). Neath/Port Talbot CBC. Chair/Secretary, Plaid Cymru Neath Constituency Cttee; Agent 2001. Founder, Neath Archery Club. Hobbies: Photography, Local history, Folklore. Languages: English, a little Welsh. Of Bryncoch, Neath.

COGHILL Roger William: MA (Cantab) 1965. CBiol 1995 MA (Wales) 1997 PhD. Green Party: Pembroke 1992; South Wales East Euro 1994; Torfaen 1997; South/East List. **Dr. Roger Coghill:** Born London 8 September 1957. Married (1) 1966 4c; divorced 1989 (2) 1998, Tamara Galonja, Yugoslav microbiologist, 1s. Educated City of London School; Emmanuel College, Cambridge (2a Classics; Natural Science 1962) University of Wales, Cardiff (Environmental Management). Director of Research & Proprietor, Coghill Research Laboratories, Pontypool. Scientific Officer, Pembrokeshire Against Radar Campaign. Joined Islington Green Party 1986; Gwent Green Party 1988. Treasurer, Torfaen Green Party. *Books: The*

Dark Side of the Brain, 1989; Electropollution, 1990; Electroheating, 1992; All Fall Down, 1994.

COHEN Samuel Israel: MA LlB. Liberal: Newport 1929. **Mr. Samuel Cohen:** Born 1904. Jewish. Cardiff Solicitor. Contested London CC (Mile End) 1928. Author of articles on music & politics.

COLBERT James John: Labour: Delyn 1983. **Mr. James Colbert:** Born 30 January 1936. Material Blender. Member, TGWU. Wrexham-Maelor BC 1979-.

COLE Charles James: JP (Mon). Liberal: Cardiff South 1929. **Mr. Charles Cole:** Baptist. Company Director: Sand & Gravel Co. Chair, Chepstow UDC. Chair: Monmouth Liberal Assn.

COLEMAN Donald Richard: CBE 1979 JP. Labour MP: Neath 1964-. **Mr. Donald Coleman:** Born Barry 19 September 1925, s of Albert Archer Coleman, miner. Anglican. Married (1) Phyllis Eileen Williams (Died 1963) 1c (2) 1966 Margaret Elizabeth Morgan. Educated Cadoxton Boys School, Barry; Cardiff Technical College. Metallurgist: Steel Co. of Wales Research Dept 1954-56; University of Wales, Swansea 1950-54. Joined Labour Party 1948. Member: Co-operative Party 1955, Assn Scientific Workers 1948; BISAKTA 1955, Welsh National Opera Co Chorus, Swansea Amateur Opera Co. Contested Swansea BC 1960. PPS 1964-70. Opposition Whip 1970-74; Council of Europe 1968-73; Lord Commissioner 1974-78; Vice Chamberlain of the Household 1978-79; Opposition Spokesman Welsh Affairs 1981-83. Member, Select Cttee: Overseas Aid, Parl Adviser, Institute of Medical Sciences. Of Bryncoch, Neath. Died 14 January 1991.

COLIN Joan Rosemarie: JP (Carms). SDP/Alliance, Carmarthen 1983. **Mrs. Joan Colin:** Born Glyn Abbey, Pontyates, 22 June 1928. Married (husband runs environmental studies center) 3s. Teacher; Head of Remedial Centre at Brighton. Founder Member, Disablement Income Group. Co-ordinator, Wales (300) Group. Member: National Assn for Remedial Education; Assn for the Welfare of Children in Hospital. Member, Labour Party; joined Council for Social Democracy 1981; member SDP Steering Cttee for Wales; Short listed at Gower by-election 1983.

COLLICK Sarah Jane: Green Party, North List 1999. **Ms. Sarah Collick:** Plays violin in Red Tony Town, 3 piece Rhuddlan band. Of Carneddi, Bethesda.

COLLINS Clive: Referendum Party, Caernarfon 1997.

COLLINS Heather Bennett: Referendum Party, Clwyd West 1997. **Mrs. Heather Bennett-Collins:** Married 6c. Came to Wales 1975. Social Worker. Valuer of antiques & freelance writer. Vice-Chair, Clwyd North-West Conservative Assn. Chair, Clwyd NW Conservative Women's Assn.

COLLINS John V: BA (Wales) 1964. Labour: Cardiff North Feb. & Oct. 1974. **Mr. John Collins:** Born Preston, Lancs. March 1945. Educated Preston Grammar School; University of Wales, Cardiff. Teacher, Newport Comprehensive School. Joined Labour Party 1966. Member NUT. Contested Cardiff CC elections.

COLTMAN-ROGERS Charles Coltman: JP (Radnor Salop & Hereford) DL (Radnor) BA 1876 MA 1879 (Oxon) FLS. Liberal: Radnorshire 1885; MP Radnor Boroughs 1884-85. **Mr. Charles Coltman-Rogers:** Born 12 May 1854, s of Revd John Rogers of Stanage Park. Anglican. Married 1888 Muriel Augusta Gillian CBE d of Major Frederick Barclay Chapman, 4c. Educated Eton; Brasenose College, Oxford. Landowner. Chair, Radnorshire Territorial Army Assn. Council Member: Royal Agricultural Show; Welsh Pony & Cob Society; Welsh National Agricultural Show; Shropshire & West Midland Agricultural Society. High Sheriff of Radnorshire 1882, Vice-Lieutenant 1921, Lord Lieutenant of Radnorshire 1922. Radnorshire CC 1888, Alderman 1889, Vice-Chairman 1896, Chair, Education Cttee. Of Stanage Park, Herefordshire. Died 19 May 1933.

CONNELL Robert Lowden: KBE 1918 JP. Liberal, Pontypool 1922. **Sir Robert Connell:** Born Mersby, Cumberland, 6 December 1867; s of Thomas Connell & Catherine Lowden. Congregationalist. Married 1899, Sarah, d of John Webster, 3d. Educated Ghyllbank, Cumberland. Shipowner: Chair, Lowden Connell & Co. Chair, Army Contracts Cttee. 1917. Deputy Controller: Army Salvage 1918, Surplus Government Property Disposal Board 1919-21. Member, Mersey Docks & Harbour Board. Languages: English. Of Glencapel, Blundellsands. Estate £94,671. Died 27 December 1936.

COOKE Scott Adam: United Kingdom Independence Party, Vale of Clwyd 1997, Independent 2001. **Mr. Scott Cooke:** Born Cardiff. 24 February 1972, s of Leslie James Cooke & Marilyn Jane Brookes. Zen Buddhist. Married 2001. Kerry-Anne FitzPatrick, 1d. Educated Rhyl Grammar School; North East Wales Institute (1 year; left to found pure technology internet services). Web Developer. Interests: Northern Ireland; Europe; One World Government. Hobbies: Dancing; Current Affairs. *Stood for Parliament for UKIP but now support moves for United States of Europe and eventually one world government. (September 2001).*

COOKSEY John Max: Independent, Alyn & Deeside 1992, 2001; North Wales Euro 1994. **Mr. Max Cooksey:** Born Ewloe 3 March 1938, s of Len Cooksey, Steelworker, & Jessie (Cross). Anglican. Unmarried. Educated Ewloe Primary School; Shotton Secondary Modern School; Kesterton College; Birkenhead College. (HNC Electrical Engineering). With Electricity Board 37 years until made redundant; A Level Art student at Deeside College. Shopkeeper & Photographer, retired. Used his redundancy money to fight the elections. Interests: *I hate party politicians.* Hobbies: Photography, Painting, Woodturning. Of Ewloe. Concerned about the Environment. *He is unashamedly an opponent of devolution and is standing as an Independent to show his distaste for the traditional political parties. (North Wales Chronicle 16/4/1999).*

COOMBS Richard Stanley: BA (Wales) 1988 MPhil (Kent) 1994 Plaid Cymru, Alyn & Deeside 2001, 2003; North List 2003. **Mr. Richard Coombs:** Born Heswall, Cheshire, 18 April 1965, s of Roger Victor Coombs, Mersey river pilot, & Ann Elizabeth Berkson, North Wales Tourism. Deist, I believe in God but not religion. Educated University of Wales, Lampeter; University of Kent at Canterbury (MPhil in Cartoons & Caricatures); Scholar at European Film College, Denmark 1995; PhD Research at University College, Dublin 1997-99. Worked in broadcasting prior to eye surgery. Lidl Store Assistant; Charity Worker. Disability Rights Campaigner with National Eczema Society and National Asthma Campaign. Contested Denbighshire CC (Prestatyn SW) 1999. Interests: Low Pay, Disability Issues, European Issues. Director, Equal Opportunity on Plaid Cymru Executive. Registered Disabled. Hobbies: Playing Church Organ, Cribbage, Real Ale; Falkland Islands & Sub-Antarctic. Languages: Learning Welsh, English, Danish. Dual Nationality: UK/Irish. Of Prestatyn.

COOPER Anthony Craig: Labour, Carmarthen East & Dinefwr 2003. **Mr. Anthony Cooper:** Born Saron, Ammanford 1974. Educated University of Wales, Cardiff & Aberystwyth. Communications Officer, Welsh Assn MS. Ex-Welsh Office Agriculture Dept. Languages: Welsh, English. Of Ammanford.

COOPER Willoughby Gervase: Conservative & National Liberal, Wrexham 1950, 1951. **Mr. Willoughby Cooper:** Born Burton-on-Trent 1911. Educated Ashby de la Zouche Grammar School. Engineer & Haulage Contractor. Started his business when 17 with one lorry. Sold up 1945 rather than accept nationalisation. Chair, Midland Area, Road Haulage Assn. Farmer 1945, of Anglesey.

COPE William, 1st & last Baron Cope of St. Mellons: 1945 1st Bart 1928 TD KC 1934 JP DL (Glam) MA (Cantab). Conservative MP. Llandaff & Barry 1918-29. **Major, Sir William Cope:** Born Roath, Cardiff, 18 August 1870; s of Matthew Cope JP of St. Mellons, & Margaret Harrison. Anglican. Married 1900. Helen, d of Major Alexander Dhuldham JP DL Co. Londonderry. Educated Repton & Clare College, Cambridge. Cambridge Rugby Blue 1891; Welsh Rugby XV 1896. Major, Glamorgan Yeomanry. Barrister, Inner Temple 1895. Company Director: Albion Colliery Co. Ltd. Welsh Navigation Colliery Co. Ltd. South Wales Electrical Power Distribution Co. Ltd. Member: Governing Body of the Church in Wales. Vice-Chair, Glamorgan Quarter Sessions, 1933. Civil Commissioner for London & Home Counties, General Strike 1926. High Sheriff of Glamorgan 1932. Lord Commissioner of the Treasury 1923, 1924-29. Of Porthcawl. Died July 1945.

CORDES Thomas: JP DL (Mon) JP (Berks). Conservative, Monmouth District 1880, 1885; MP: 1874-80. **Mr. Thomas Cordes:** Born Hatcham Grove, Surrey 1826, s of James Jamieson Cordes JP of Brynglas, Newport & Mary, d of J. I. Lucas, Hatcham Grove. Anglican. Married Margaret Agnes, d of Admiral of the Fleet, Sir Alexander Milne Bt. Landowner. High Sheriff of Monmouthshire 1871. Lord of the Manor of Sunninghill, Berks. Languages: English. Of Brynglas, Newport; Selwood Park, Sunninghill, Berks. & London. Estate £269,099. Died 14 August 1901.

CORNELIUS Steven: BA 1997 MA (Wales). Plaid Cymru: Brecon & Radnor 1997, Assembly, South/West List 1999. **Mr. Steven Cornelius:** Born Morriston, 14 December 1975, s of a kitchen designer & a physiotherapist. Educated Maesydderwen School, Ystradgynlais; University of Wales, Swansea (1st in Welsh, 1997). Translator, City 7 County of Swansea 1998-99; Public Affairs Executive, Strategy Wales 1999-. Chair: Federation of Plaid Cymru Students. Plaid Cymru Youth Movement. Member: Plaid Cymru Executive. Interests: Education, Combating Poverty, Social Justice; International Development, Foreign Affairs. Hobbies: Reading, Cooking, Travelling, Socialising. Languages: Welsh. English, Spanish; French.

CORNISH Jane Maw – see MAW-CORNISH Jane.

CORNWALLIS-WEST William Cornwallis: JP (Denbs). Liberal MP. West Denbighshire 1885-86, Liberal Unionist 1886-92; Liberal: Lymington 1874; West Cheshire 1880. **Lieut-Colonel William Cornwallis-West:** Born Ruthin Castle, 20 March 1835, s of Frederick Richard West MP Denbigh

District 1826-30, 1847-57; East Grinstead 1830-32, & Theresa, d of Captain John Whitby; & gs of Hon. Frederick West MP Denbigh District 1802-06; Assumed name Cornwallis-West 1895. Anglican. Married 1872, Mary, d of Revd Frederick Fitzpatrick, Co. Leitrem & Lady Olivia. Educated Eton. Barrister, Lincolns Inn 1862. Landowner. Major, Denbighshire Rifle Volunteers 1875; Hon. Colonel 1890. Lord Lieutenant of Denbighshire. Of Ruthin Castle, Flints. & Newlands Manor, Lymington. Estate £10,625. Died 4 July 1917.

CORP Melanie Jane: BA. PGCGE. Plaid Cymru, Vale of Glamorgan, 1997. **Ms Melanie Corp:** Born Cardiff 1 February 1972, d of Eric Raymond Corp, travel agent, & Patricia Jane Morris, senior radiographer. Baptist. Married 1997 Jonathan Edward Parker, teacher. Educated Ysgol Gyfun Glantaf; University of Wales, Lampeter (Welsh). [Post Graduate Certificate in Management]. Employment Worker, Equal Opportunities Commission. Teacher, Head of Department. Barry TC 1995-99. Plaid Cymru Spokesperson on Employment & Training. Interests: Equal Opportunities, Offenders, Homelessness. Hobbies: Drama, Scouts, Singing. Languages: Welsh; English; GCSE French & German. Of Barry; then Narberth.

CORY Clifford John: 1st Bart 1907 JP DL (Glam) 1889 JP (Mon); Commander, Order of Leopold II (Belgium). Liberal, South Mon.1895; Tonbridge 1900; MP: St. Ives 1906-10; 1923-24. **Sir Clifford Cory:** Born Cardiff 1859, 2nd s of John Cory JP DL of Dyffryn House. United Free Methodist. Married 1893, Jane Ann, d of Albert Lethbridge. Educated Privately & on Continent. Captain, Welch Regiment. Company Chair: Cory Bros & Co. coal proprietors & exporters; Barry Railway Co; Vale of Glamorgan Railway Co; Anglo-French & Belgian Corporation. President, South Wales & Mon Coalowners' Assn 1906. Chair: South Wales & Mon Coal Trade Conciliation Board 1906. High Sheriff of Monmouthshire 1905. Glamorgan CC 1892-1910. Governor, University of Wales, Cardiff. Chair, South Wales & Mon School of Mines. Chair: Cardiff Liberal Assn. 1906-11. Of Llantarnam Abbey & London. Died 3 February 1941.

CORY James Herbert: 1st Bart 1919 JP 1906 DL (Glam). Conservative MP. Cardiff District B/E 1915-18; Cardiff South 1918-23. **Sir Herbert Cory:** Born Padstow, Cornwall, 7 February, 1857, s of John Cory, Shipowner, & Mary Couch. Anglican. Married (1) 1879, Elizabeth Hoskin Wills (Died 1898) 4s 1d (2) 1908, Elizabeth Walker CBE. 2d. Educated Tregoney, Cornwall. Shipowner: Director, of shipping, trading, coal, ore, hotels & other companies. High Sheriff of Glamorgan 1913-14. Vice-Chairman, Welsh Parliamentary Party 1920. Chair, Cardiff Conserva-

tive Assn. Of Coryton, Whitchurch. Estate £587,442. Died 7 February 1933.

COTTON Alan Frank Vincent: Plaid Cymru, Monmouth 1997. **Mr. Alan Cotton:** Born Lewisham 6 December 1960. Educated Hundred of Ho Secondary Modern School, Kent. National Power Worker-1995. Student, University of Glamorgan 1995-. Contested Rhondda/Cynon Taf BC 1999. Pontypridd TC (Glyn Coch).

COULTHARD Alan George Weal: Liberal, Pembroke 1964; Resigned as PPC Jan. 1966 for business reasons. Mr. Alan Coulthard: Born Bournemouth 20 January 1924, s of George Robert Coulthard & Cicely Eva Minns. Roman Catholic. Married 1948 Jacqueline Anna, d. of Dr. T. H. James of Fishguard, 4c. Educated Watford Grammar School. RAF pilot 1941-46, Flight Lieutenant. 1st Officer, BOAC 1946-48; recalled to RAF 1948-58 (pilot & staff officer). Barrister, Inner Temple 1959. Asst. Recorder 1970; Recorder, Crown Court, Wales & Chester Circuit 1972-81; Hon. Recorder, Llanelli 1975-81; Circuit Judge 1981-. Chair, Medical Appeals Tribunal for Wales 1976-81. President, Swansea Festival Patrons Assn. 1974-80. Chair, Swansea West Liberal Assn. Secretary, Assn of Liberal Lawyers. Of London. Died 25 June 1988.

COUPER Alastair Dougal: MA (Aberdeen) PhD (ANU Canberra) DSc (Exeter). Vote 2 Stop the War Party, South/Central List 2003. **Professor Alastair Couper:** Born Aberdeen, 4 June 1931, s of Daniel Alexander Couper, builder, & Devina Couper, shop worker. Married 1958 Norma Couper, civil servant, 2s 2d. Educated Nautical School, Aberdeen; University of Aberdeen; Australian National University. Professor FNI FRICS Professor of Maritime Studies & International Transport, University of Wales, Cardiff 1970-; Professor Emeritus. Visiting Professor, Greenwich Maritime Institute. Seafarers International Research Centre, Cardiff. World Expert in Maritime Field. Member: Executive Cttee, Law of the Sea Institute (USA); Pacem in Maribus (Peace at Sea). Member, Labour Party until 2003. *Assembly candidature was a one-off anti-war effort.* Interests: UN, Human Rights, Peace Movement. Hobbies: Writing, Theatre, Hill Walking. *Books: Voyages of Abuse.*

COVE William George: Labour MP Aberavon 1929-59; Wellingborough 1923-29. **Mr. Willie Cove:** Born Treherbert 21 May 1888. A Wesleyan Lay Preacher, he became a Marxist when a student at Exeter. Married. Educated Porth Pupil Teachers Centre & Exeter University. Miner at 14; Teacher. President: NUT 1922; 1st Discharged Soldiers & Sailors Assn. Chair, Welsh Parliamentary Labour Group; PPS 1924. Freeman of

Port Talbot 1957. Estate £9,818. Died 15 March 1963.

COVENTRY George William Reginald Victor: 10th Earl of Coventry 1697, Viscount Deerhurst. JP DL. Conservative, Carmarthen 1922. **Hon. George Coventry:** Born 10 September 1901, s of Viscount Deerhurst (Died 1924); succeeded grandfather 1930. Anglican. Married 1921 Hon. Nesta Donna Philipps, d. of Baron Kylsant (qv), 2d. Landowner; Company Director: London & Thames Haven Oil Wharfs Ltd & King's Line Ltd. MFM. Cambridgeshire 1926-31; Master of Croome Hounds 1932; Hawkestone Otter Hounds 1931. President, Welsh Boxing Assn. Lieutenant, Worcestershire Yeomanry. Languages: English. Of Amroth Castle, Pembs & Groome Court, Worcs. Killed in action, May 1940.

COVENTRY John Bonynge: JP (Worcs) 1930 MA (Oxon). Conservative, Carmarthen 1929. **Hon. John Coventry:** Born 9 January 1903, s of Viscount Deerhurst, brother of George (qv). Anglican. Married 1942, Sybil Duse, d. of Alan Tattam of Sydney NSW. Educated Eton & Magdalen College, Oxford. Stockbroker 1923-27. At Conservative Central Office 1928. Major, Grenadier Guards. Worcestershire CC. Worcester City Alderman 1930, Mayor 1929. Interests: Agriculture. Died 1969.

COWAN Jayne Louise: BSc (Wales). Conservative, South/Central List 2003. **Ms. Jayne Cowan:** Born Cardiff 1973. Educated Howells School, Llandaff; University of Wales, Cardiff. Former Teacher. Press Officer, Conservative Group, Cardiff CC. Of Cardiff.

COWDELL Alan B: Old Labour, Merthyr Tydfil & Rhymney 1997. **Mr. Alan Cowdell:** Born Blackwood, 23 May 1942, s of William Brynley Cowdell, miner, & Hilda May Davies. Agnostic. Married 1983, Brenda Davies, 1s. Educated New Tredegar High School 1955-58; Crosskeys Technical College 1958-63; Coleg Harlech 1968-69. Miner, 8 years. Royal Navy; Worked in factories & hotels. Disabled/unemployed. Contested Merthyr Tydfil BC (Dowlais) as Plaid Cymru candidate 1999. Interests: Constitutional Reform. Hobbies: Ornithology, Numismatics. *Policy 1997: Anything over 25 in a class should be illegal. Totally against privatisation of the health service . . . UNEMPLOYMENT: The word should be scrubbed from the dictionary. I don't think we need the money for DEFENCE; pro capital punishment; castration of rapists & paedophiles . . . I would lock away any MP guilty of sleaze and throw away the key. I think the royal family has run its course. WOMEN should paid a wage for staying at home and looking after the children; A federal Europe will never work; I don't agree with the Common Market. I believe in devolv-* *ing power to the regions but it's got to be done properly. I believe in proportional representation. WM.16/4/97200.*

COWELL-STEPNEY Emile Algernon Arthur Keppel: 2nd Bart (1871) JP DL (Carms). Liberal, Carmarthen District 1874; MP 1876-78; 1886-92; Joined Liberal Unionists 1891. **Sir Arthur Cowell-Stepney:** Born Baden 26 December 1834, s of Sir John Cowell-Stepney, 1st Bart MP. Carmarthen District 1868-74, & Euphemia, d of General John Murray, Co. Donegal. Married 1875, Hon. Margaret de Tapley, d of Baron de Tapley, 1d (judicial separation, 1903). Educated Eton. Clerk at Foreign Office 20 years. Landowner (10,000 acres). Epistimologist. High Sheriff of Carmarthenshire 1884. Emigrated; took U.S. citizenship 1906; became an extensive land proprietor and large-scale agriculturalist. Of Llanelli & Sunninghill, Berks. (& Enderby, British Columbia). Estate £77,048. Died Yuma, Arizona, 2 July 1909 *(body found at Yuma Railway Station when on an eptimological expedition; thought to have died of heat and heart trouble).*

COWEN Jonathan: MA PGCE (Oxon). Conservative, Pontypridd 1997. **Mr. Jonathan Cowen:** Born 25 June 1964. Married Mandy Rachael, 1s 1d. Educated Kilburn Grammar-Senior High School; Worcester College, Oxford (PPE); Oxford Institute of Education; City University (Diploma in Law). Barrister 1986. Joined Conservative Party 1994. Member, Society of Conservative Lawyers. Hertsmere BC 1996-. Vice-Chair, Hertsmere CPC. London Tourist Board Registered Guide. Languages: English, French, German.

COX Alun Geraint: BA (Wales). Plaid Cymru, Merthyr Tydfil & Rhymney 1992, 1997, 1999, 2003. **Mr. Alun Cox:** Born Newport 22 May 1964. Married. Educated Ysgol Gyfun Rhydfelin; University of Wales, Aberystwyth (Politics). President, Welsh NUS 1989-91. Computer Consultant, Economic Development Agency. Contested Ceredigion CC (Llanbadarn Fawr) 1999. Member: Aberystwyth ABC Choir. Interests: Economic Development, The Valleys, Education. Hobbies: Sport, Travel, Reading. Of Porth.

COX Charles James: BA (Bristol). Conservative, Bedwellty 1959, 1964. **Mr. Charles Cox:** Born London, December 1932. Educated Latymers School; Bristol University (Philosophy & Psychology). Teacher of Science & Maths at Twmpath Secondary Modern School 1955-59. Psychologist at Richard Thomas & Baldwin Ltd. Operational Research Dept 1959-; Management Consultant & Lecturer. Chair, Pontypool YCs. Ratepayers' Candidate, Pontypool UDC. (Ratepayers Assn. Wainfelin) 1958. Graduate Member, British Psychological Society. Of Pontypool (1952).

COX Gavin Cameron: Liberal Democrat, Rhondda 2001. BA. (Manchester) 1998. **Mr. Gavin Cox:** Born Blackpool 7 February 1970, s of David Roy Cox, local government officer, & Jennifer May Greenhough, primary school teacher. Christian. Educated Welshpool High School; University of Manchester (Politics & History). Assistant, Assembly Liberal Democrat Group. Communications Officer, RNIB. Interests: Education, Environment, youth affairs, social policy. Hobbies: Travel, Photography, Music, Cooking, Liverpool AFC. Of Cardiff.

Idris Cox.

COX Idris: Communist, Rhondda East 1951. **Mr. Idris Cox:** Born Nantyffyllon 15 July 1899, father a miner & mother a tinplate worker. Marxist; proud of being brought up at Ebeneser Welsh Congregational Church, Garth, Maesteg. Married Dora Robert of Bradford, 2s 1d. Educated Llangynwyd National School; Garth Elementary School; won grammar school scholarship but family circumstances prevented his taking it. Shoe shop assistant at 13, followed by iron moulding foundry, & colliery lamp room. Assistant to coal hewer 1913, until accident returned to lamp room for a while. Miner 14 years. Central Labour College 1923-25. SWMF lodge delegate; Lodge Chair, SWMF 1920. Checkweighman 1925. Vice-Chair, Maesteg Labour Party 1927. Joined the Communist Party at Labour College 1924. NCLC tutor. Communist Party Mid-Glamorgan Area Organiser (unpaid) 1925-27. South Wales Organiser (full time) Feb. 1927; District Secretary 1927. Secretary, Parliamentary Cttee (Politburo) 1929; South Wales

Organiser 1929; Agent Rhondda East 1933 & Merthyr 1934 B/Es. Assistant to R. Palme Dutt, Editor, *Daily Worker.* South Wales Organiser, Communist Party 1929. Secretary, Welsh Council of the Communist Party 1953-70. Member, Parliament for Wales Campaign Contested Glamorgan CC 1934. Languages: Welsh; English. Died 1989. *Books: Idris Cox, Story of a Welsh Rebel (autobiography MSS at archive of University of Wales Swansea).*

COX John Idris: BSc MScEcon. PhD. (London), ARCS. DIS. FIChemE Green Party/Plaid Cymru, Torfaen 1992; Vote 2 Stop the War: South/Central List 2003. **Dr. John Cox:** Born Cardiff. 16 May 1935, s of Idris Cox (qv) and Dora Cox, secretary/women's organiser. Married 1961, Judith Olwen Cox, lecturer, 2d. Educated Cathays High School, Cardiff; Imperial College, London; London School of Economics. Consultant Chemical Engineer. College Lecturer. Former Member, Communist Party. Executive Member, Democratic Left. Vice-President, CND. Torfaen BC 1991-95. Contested Torfaen BC 1987. A founder, Vote 2 Stop the War Party 2003. Interests: Peace and Socialism in a Green World. Of Talywaun, Pontypool.

COX Phyllis Mary R: Plaid Cymru, Newport Feb 1974; Torfaen 1983. **Mrs. Phyllis Cox:** Born Henllys, Mon, July 1935. Moved to Newport 1950. Married Barrie; 2c. Educated Open University. Housewife & Open University Student. Accounts clerk with a local car firm. Member, Plaid Cymru Executive & Spokesperson on Consumer Affairs. Contested Torfaen BC 1999. Of Cwmbran.

CRABB George Howard: Vote 2 Stop the War Party, South/Central List 2003. **Mr. George Crabb:** Born London, 31 December 1942, s of Percival Robert Nathaniel Crabb, civil servant, & Harriet Crabb, teacher. Humanist. Married: 1952, Jeanne Rhoswen Crabb, 1s. Educated: Wandsworth Grammar School; Borough Road Teacher Training College, London; University of Wales, Swansea. RAF (air gunner). Coal miner in South Wales 1945-49. Teacher in Special Education. Retired Headteacher of a Residential Special School for Physically Handicapped Children. Member: Democratic Left; British Humanist Assn; CND Cymru. Vice-Chair, Cowbridge Labour Party, expelled for standing in election Interests: Left Politics. Anti-fascist & peace campaigner. Hobbies: Welsh Language & Literature, Nature Study. Languages: Welsh, English. Of Cowbridge.

CRABB Stephen: BSc (Bristol) 1995. Conservative, Preseli 2001. **Mr. Stephen Crabb:** Born Inverness, 20 January 1973. Married Beatrice, town-planning consultant. Educated Tasker Millward VC School, Haverfordwest; Bristol University (1st Politics). Researcher, Andrew Rowe MP 1995-96. Parliamentary Affairs Officer, National Council for Voluntary Youth Services 1996-98. Campaigns Executive, London Chamber of Commerce 1998-2000, Campaigns Manager 2000-. President, Haverfordwest Interact. Chair, North Southwark & Bermondsey Conservative Assn. Co-founder, Renewing One Nation think tank. Chair, school governors 1998-2000. Election Monitor, Bosnia & Herzegovina, Organisation for Security & Co-operation in Europe, September 1998. Member, Conservative Christian Fellowship. Interests: Education. Hobbies: Running, Swimming, Gym, Member, Blackheath RFC XV. Of London.

CRAWFORD William: UK Independence Party, Alyn & Deeside 2001, 2003. **Mr. William Crawford:** Born Belfast 1944. Army, 24 years, REME, warrant Officer 1. Manufacturer of mobile catering caravans. Caterer, Chairman, Phoenix Catering Ltd. Joined UKIP 1996. Member, UKIP Wales Cttee. Deputy Chair, UKIP Chester. Corporate Member: Institute of Road Transport Engineers. Member, Society of Operations Engineers.

CRAWSHAY Geoffrey Cartland Hugh: JP DL. (Mon) 1934 BA Hon. LLD (Wales) 1953. Liberal, Pontypool 1929; Pontypridd B/E 1931. **Captain Geoffrey Crawshay:** Born Pandy, Mon. 20 June 1892, s of Codrington Fraser Crawshay, of Abergavenny & Emily Howard Cartland. Anglican. Educated Wellington College; University of Wales, Cardiff. Captain, Welsh Guards 1914-24 (founded regimental choir & rugby XV) badly wounded; ADC Governor of India; 1st Chair & Hon. Secretary, Welsh Council for Social Service; District Commissioner for South Wales (Special Areas Act) 1934-39; Regional Commissioner for Wales, Ministry of Aircraft Production 1940-44. Chair, Welsh Board of Health 1945-52; Welsh Land Settlement Society Ltd. Government Director, Treforest Trading Estate. Member, Governing Body of the Church in Wales. High Sheriff of Monmouthshire 1939. Monmouthshire CC. A founder, Contemporary Art Society for Wales. Hon. Member & Sword Bearer, Gorsedd of Bards; Founder, Crawshay Rugby XV; President, London Welsh RFC 1924. Of Llanfair Court, Abergavenny. Died 8 November 1954.

CRAWSHAY William Robert: Kt 1972 ADC 1966 DSO 1945 JP DL (Glam) 1966 HML (Mon) 1970 VL (Gwent) 1974. TD ERD Hon. LLD (Wales) 1975 KStJ 1969 Chevalier Legion d'Hon.neur 1956 Croix de Guerre 1944. Liberal, Newport 1945; Joined Conservative Party 1947. **Colonel Sir William Crawshay:** Born Caversham Park, Oxon 27 May 1920, s of J. W. L.

Crawshay & Hon. Mrs. Clare Egerton (nephew of Geoffrey Crawshay qv). Anglican. Married 1950, Elizabeth Mary Boyd, d. of Lieut-Colonel Guy Franklin Reynolds of Abergavenny. Educated Eton. Commissioned, RWF 1939; Kings African Rifles 1940; Served in Yugoslavia with Marshal Tito; Worked with French Underground, known as Captain Crown; organised force of 16,000; Given Hon. Rank in French Foreign Legion. Colonel, Paratroops (TA) 1947-64. Hon. Colonel 3rd Royal Regiment of Wales 1976-82. Personnel Manager, Stewart & Lloyds 1945-50; Trainee/ Manager, Unilever, 1950-55; Stockbroker, Cardiff 1955. President: British Legion, Wales Area; Monmouthshire Beekeepers Assn; Council for Social Service for Wales & Mon 1947. Chair, Wales Cttee, Arts Council 1968; Territorial & Auxiliary Forces Assn 1966; Monmouthshire Rural Community Council; King George V Jubilee Fund. Member: Council for Wales, 1968; Council, University College, Cardiff, National Museum; Council for Industrial Design; St. John's Council for Monmouthshire; Arts Council of Great Britain 1962-74. ADC to the Queen 1966-71. Succeeded to Llanfair Court on the death of Geoffrey Crawshay. Died 25 January 1997.

CRICHTON-STUART Colum Edmund: JP BA (Oxon). Conservative, Cardiff East 1918; MP: Northwich 1922-45. **Lord Colum Crichton-Stuart:** Born 3 April 1886, s of 3rd Marquess of Bute. Roman Catholic. Married 1940, Elizabeth, Marchioness of Lansdowne, widow of 6th Marquess & d. of Sir Edward Hope. Educated Oxford University. Diplomatic Service 1910: Attaché 1910; Cairo, 1911; 2nd Secretary 1913; Foreign Office 1914-20. Landowner. Lord Lieutenant of the Isle of Bute 1953-57. Of Ardencraig, Isle of Bute & London. Died 18 August 1957.

CRICHTON-STUART Ninian Edward: BA (Oxon). Conservative, Cardiff District Jan 1910; MP Dec 1910-. **Lieut-Colonel, Lord Ninian Crichton-Stuart:** Born 15 May 1883, s of 3rd Marquess of Bute. Married 1906, Hon. Ismay Preston, d of Viscount Gormaston, 1d. Educated Harrow; Christ Church, Oxford; Lieutenant, Scots Guards; Lieut-Colonel, RWF. Keeper, Falkland Palace. Languages: English. Of House of Falkland; Falkland, Fife. Killed in action in France 1915.

CRIDDLE James Brian: BSc (Wales) BA (Open). Plaid Cymru, Blaenau Gwent 1997. **Mr. James Criddle:** Born 16 October 1947, miner's son. Married Rhian (died) d of H. Heulyn Roberts (qv) 3c. Educated UWIST (Applied Science). Teacher (Maths) St. Illtyd's College, Cardiff. Joined Plaid Cymru 1974. Member, Plaid Cymru Executive. Islwyn BC 1976-96, Chair, Finance

Cttee 1977-78. Director, Plaid Cymru Credit Union. Member Rugby XVs: Universities Athletic Union; British Universities; Ebbw Vale, Pont-llanffraith. Languages: Learned Welsh, English.

CROFTON Mary: Socialist Labour Party, South/East: List 1999. **Mrs. Mary Crofton:** Born Limerick, 1918; adopted. Married 5c (1 Died at 12 & 1 in his 30s). Lived in squatters' camp after the war. Came to Newport in late 1960s. Nurse, St. Woollos' Hospital, Newport until 65 and then at nursing home until 80. NUPE shop steward. Active with "Troops Out" Movement. Helped organised Greenham Common Peace March. Secretary, Newport Miners' Support Group 1984-85. Member: CND. Left Labour Party to join Socialist Labour. Interests: Irish freedom, Women's Issues, Racism, Injustice & Disempowerment. Died 4 May 2001.

CRONK John Edward: Referendum Party, Wrexham 1997. **Mr. John Cronk:** Born South London 1935. Married 2s. RAF. Air Traffic Control. Clerk, Philips Electronic Group. Of Prestatyn.

CROSS Kenneth Adrian: Conservative, Mid & West List 1999. **Mr. Kenneth Cross:** Born Merthyr Tydfil, 19 July 1943, son of George Fredrick Cross, engineer, & Phillias Cross. Church of England. Married 1976, Patricia Ann Cross, guesthouse owner (died). 1s. Educated Royal Masonic School for Boys, Bushey. Business Consultant. Chair: St. David's Conservative Branch. No local active or member of any party (2001). Non-Executive Director, Dyfed-Powys Health Authority. Director: West Wales Regional Tourism Partnership. Hobbies: Walking, Music, Reading, Wine. Of Haverfordwest.

CROSS William Glyn: MA DipEd (Oxon). Independent Wales Party, South/Central list 2003. **Mr. Glyn Cross:** Born Shardlow, Derbyshire 16 August 1944, s of William Stanley Cross, financial controller, & Irene Cross, secretary. Practical Christian. Educated Birkenhead School; Oxford University. Chemistry teacher, Cathays High School, Cardiff 1968-70, Aberdare Boys Grammar School 1970-88; private tutor 1988-97. Plaid Cymru activist 1993-99. Contested Cardiff CC 1995. Activist, Parliament for Wales Campaign 1993-97. Cttee Member, Railway Development Society. Member, Friends of the Earth. Interests: Sustainability, Crisis avoidance. Hobbies: Gardening, Music, Architecture, Things Welsh, Rugby. Languages: Welsh, English, French. Of Thornhill, Cardiff.

CRUM-EWING Humphry John Frederick: MA (Oxon). Conservative Swansea East 1959. **Mr. Humphry Crum-Ewing:** Born Sevenoaks, May 1934, s of H. W. E. Crum-Ewing; several members of his father's family were Scottish Liberal MPs. Educated Marlborough College & Christ Church, Oxford. President, Oxford University Conservative Assn 1956. Vice-Chair, Federation of University Conservative & Unionist Assns 1957-58. Royal Navy 1953-55. Company Secretary. Research Fellow, Centre for Defence & International Studies, Lancaster University. Associate Fellow, Royal United Services Institute. Special Adviser, House of Commons Select Cttees. Member: National Cttee; World Assembly of Youth; CAWU. Of London.

CUMING Richard Andrew: Conservative, Merthyr Tydfil & Rhymney 2001. **Mr. Richard Cuming:** Born Torbay 24 March 1962. Married. Ex-Newsagent; Partner in tourist attraction & specialist shopping development. Adviser on tourism. Ex-assistant to Rupert Allason & Sir Frederick Bennett, MPs for Torbay. Hon. Member: Torbay British Legion & Burma Star Assn. Torbay BC 1987-; Leader, Conservative Group 2000. Primary School Governor. Member: Devon & Cornwall Police Authority. Member: Orders & Medals Research Society. Hobbies: Watching sports, Soccer, Rugby, Cricket; Theatre, Travel, Antiques. Of Torbay.

CUNLIFFE Robert Alfred: 5th Bart 1759 JP DL. Liberal Flint District B/E 1874; Denbigh District 1885; MP: Flint District 1872-74, Denbigh District 1880-85; Joined Loyal & Patriotic Union 1886; Liberal Unionist: Flintshire 1892. **Lieut-Colonel, Sir Robert Cunliffe:** Born 17 January 1839, s of Robert Ellis Cunliffe, East India Company's Civil Service & Charlotte, d of Iltyd Howell; Succeeded grandfather 1859. Married (1) 1898, Eleanor, d of Major Egerton Leigh; (2) Cecile Victoria, d of Hon. E. Sackville-West. Educated Eton. Landowner. Lieutenant, Scots Guards 1857; Captain 1862, Retired; Lieut-Colonel, Denbighshire & Merioneth Militia 1872. High Sheriff of Denbighshire 1868; Denbighshire CC 1888-. Of Acton Park, Wrexham. Estate £63,088. Died 18 June 1905.

CUNLIFFE Foster Hugh Egerton: 6th Bart 1759 MA (Oxon). Liberal Unionist, East Denbighshire B/E April 1909. **Major, Sir Foster Cunliffe:** Born 17 August 1876, s of the 5th baronet (qv) & Eleanor, d of Major Egerton Leigh; Succeeded father 1905. Married Cecile Victoria Cunliffe. Educated Eton; New College, Oxford. Fellow of All Souls. Landowner. Army 1914-. Of Acton Park, Wrexham. Estate £135,883. Killed in action in France, 10 July 1916.

CURRAN Edward: JP. Liberal, Cardiff South 1918, Aberavon 1931. **Mr. Ned Curran:** Born Cardiff, 1881, of Irish descent. Roman Catholic. Married 2s 4d. Civil Engineer. Founder/Chair/

Managing Director, Curran Bros. Ltd (foundry & engineering); Cardiff Foundry & Engineering Co; South of Ireland Asphalt Co; Industrial Traders Ltd; Currans Metals & Munitions Co (during Great War). Invented Curran Recuperative Furnace for Treatment of Metals. President, Cardiff South Liberal Assn. Cardiff CC 1915-, 1931-34. Noted for his advocacy of brighter Sundays – open parks etc. Member, Irish League. Estate £135,783. Of Porthcawl. Died 13 February 1937.

CURRIE George Boyle Hanna: MBE 1946 MA LlB. (Dublin). Conservative, East Flint 1950, 1951; Ulster Unionist MP: North Down 1955-70. **Mr. George Currie:** Born Port Ballintrae, Co. Antrim, 19 December, 1905, s of Very Revd William John Currie, DD Presbyterian Minister. Married 1933, Stephanie Maud Evelyn, d. of J. H. Costello of Dublin. Educated Campbell College, Belfast; Trinity College, Dublin. Barrister, Middle Temple 1932; Barrister, Northern Ireland Inns of Court 1947. Squadron Leader, RAF Legal Branch 1939-45. Wirral UDC 1935-50; Chair 1938-39. Died 21 July 1978.

CURRY Stephen David: Independent Wales Party, 2003. **Mr. Stephen Curry:** Born 23 March 1957. Married Christine Curry, 2s 2d. Computer Engineer. South Wales West Regional Co-ordinator, Independent Wales Party. Interests: Fighting for a Welsh Parliament. Languages: Welsh, English.

CURRY Kelvyn: Green Party, Brecon & Radnor & Mid & West List 1999. **Mr Kelvin Curry:** Employed by Powys CC. Seconded to University of Warwick on the development of teaching materials. Director, NatWest Financial Literacy Centre, University of Warwick. Nantmel ComC. 1991-, Radnorshire DC 1993-96 (Vice-Chair, Planning Cttee 1995-6, Chair 1996. School Governor. Trustee, Bryn Titli Wind Farm Trust. Chair: Mediation Mid-Wales. Of Nantmel.

CUTHBERT Jeffrey Hambley: BSc (Wales) MICPP. Labour AM. Caerphilly 2003-. **Mr. Jeff Cuthbert:** Born Glasgow, 4 June 1948, s of William Stevenson Cuthbert, printer, & Jennie Carruthers Cuthbert, music teacher. Religion/ None. Married (2) 1985 Gaynor Catherine Cuthbert, lecturer, 1s 4d. Educated Whitchurch County Secondary School, Cardiff; Glamorgan College of Technology; University of Wales. Cardiff (mining engineering). NCB Mining Surveyor, Markham & Oakdale Collieries. Senior Consultant, WJEC Asset to Industry Unit & Part-time (Evenings) Principal, Aberbargoed Adult Education Centre. Ex-Member, Militant Tendency. Joined Labour Party 1967. Chair, Caerphilly CLP. Member, Amicus Regional Council 20 years; Diabetes UK Campaigners Network; MSF. School governor 15 years. Interests: Trade Union & Labour Movement Activities, Education & Industrial Training. Hobbies: Labour History, Reading, Walking, Travel. Languages Learning Welsh, English. Of Penpedairheol, Caerphilly.

CUTTS Sheila May: Liberal [Democrat], Aberavon, Oct 1974, 1979, 1983. **Mrs. Sheila Cutts:** Born Rumney, Cardiff 1929. Married 2c. Educated Maynard School, Exeter; Exeter University; City of Bath Training College. Teacher. Writer. Flower Farmer. Former Conservative. Of Bere Alston, Devon. *Books: Sheila Cutts, Tales of the Tamar, 1975.*

– D –

DAFIS Cynog Glyndwr: BA MEd 1973 (Wales). Plaid Cymru: Ceredigion & North Pembs 1987, MP: Ceredigion & North Pembs 1992-97, Ceredigion 1997-2000 (resigned to concentrate on Assembly, AM Mid & West List 1999-2003. **Mr. Cynog Dafis:** Born Swansea 1st April 1938, s of the Revd George Davies, Presbyterian Minister, & Annie Davies. Undodwr/Methodist Calfinaidd (Unitarian/Calvinistic Methodist). Married Llinos Iorwerth, d of Iorwerth & Eluned Jones, 2s 1d. Educated Aberaeron Grammar School, Neath Grammar School, University of Wales, Aberystwyth. Teacher (English & Welsh) Pontardawe FE College 1960-62, Head of English, Newcastle Emlyn Secondary Modern School 1962-80, Teacher (English), Aberaeron Comprehensive School 1980-84, Head of English, Dyffryn Teifi Comprehensive School, Llandysul 1984-91, Research Officer, Dept. of Adult Continuing Education, University of Wales, Swansea 1991-92. Chair: Tai Cartref Housing Assn. Member, Select Cttee on Welsh Affairs 1995-97, Education, 1997. Secretary, All Party UK Eurosolar Parl Group. Vice-Chair: Warm Homes Group, Jt. Vice-Chair: All Party Environment Group. Plaid Cymru Spokesman: Education, Environment, Energy, National Heritage & Housing. Contested Plaid presidency, September 2003. Hobbies: Jogging, Reading. Languages: Welsh, English, French.

DAFYDD-LEWIS Avril Ann: BD DipPS (Wales). Caerphilly Constituency Independents 2003. **Revd Avril Dafydd-Lewis:** Born Caerphilly, 6 July 1956, d of Leonard Lewis, Asst. Engineer, Penallta Colliery, & Annie Jane Selwood, nurse (died 1993). Baptist. Married, 1 s, divorced 1978. Educated South Wales Baptist College, Cardiff. Laboratory Technician, St. Cennydd Comprehensive School, Caerphilly until 1987; Student 1987-91; Baptist Minister, ordained 1991. Pastorates, Upper Rhondda,1991-99; Cwmcarn part time 15 months. Secretary: Teen Challenge, Rhondda (support for those influenced by drugs or alcohol). Interests: Health Service, Jobs, Anti-Social Behaviour, Leisure Provision, Education. Hobbies: Gardening, Watercolour painting, Walking, Love of animals. Of Nelson.

DAGGAR George: JP. Labour MP Abertillery 1929-. **Mr. George Daggar:** Born Cwmbran 6 November 1879, s of Jesse Daggar (Dagger), miner, & Elizabeth Russell. Agnostic. Married 1915, Rachel of J. Smith of Bradford. Educated Abertillery British School. Miner at 12. Vice-Chair: Six Bells Lodge SWMF, Central Labour College 1911, Lecturer in economics & industrial affairs, Miners' Agent 1921-29. Abertillery UDC 1919-29. Member, Select Cttee on Mining Subsidence, Chair: Welsh Parliamentary Party 1949-50, Vice-Chair: Parliamentary Labour Party 1949-50. Of Six Bells. Estate £2,712. Died 14 October 1950.

DAILEY Prudence Mary Prior: MA (Oxon) 1988. Conservative, Pontypridd 2001. **Miss Prudence Dailey:** Born Mtarfa, Malta, 10 November 1965, d of Stanley Thomas Dailey & Margaret Prior Robinson, teachers. Anglican. Educated Simon Langton Girls Grammar School, The Kings School, Canterbury, Merton College, Oxford (PPE). General Management NHS 1988-94, Business School Systems Analyst, CSC Computer Sciences Ltd 1994-98, Business Systems Analyst, Toys R Us 1998-. Chair: Oxford East Conservative Assn 1996-2000. Member, Executive, Prayer Book Society 1992-. Member: General Synod of the Church of England 2000-. Interests: Family & community, Constitution. Hobbies: Church activities, Choral singing, Dress making, Crafts. Oxford CC 1992-96. School governor. Of Oxford.

DALTON Edward Hugh John Neale, Baron Dalton, 1960: PC 1940 MA (Cantab) DSc (London) 1921 Hon. DSc (Sydney, Durham 1958) Hon. Manchester). Labour: Cardiff East 1923, Cambridge B/E March 1922, Maidstone 1922, Holland with Boston B/E July 1924, Bishop Auckland 1931, MP: Peckham 1924-29, Bishop Auckland 1929-31, 1935-59. **Rt. Hon. Dr. Hugh Dalton:** Born Neath Abbey, 1887, s of Canon John Neale Dalton KCVO CMG (Chaplain to Queen Victoria) & Catherine Alicia, d of Charles Evan-Thomas P DL, Neath. Married 1914, Ruth (MP Bishop Auckland, Feb-May 1929) d of Thomas Hamilton Fox, 1d (died 1922). Educated Eton, Kings School College, Cambridge, Hutcheson Research Scholar, London School of Economics 1911-13. Barrister, Middle Temple 1914, Army 1914-19, Lieutenant RGA, Attached to Ministry of Labour for special investigations 1919. Lecturer, London School of Economics 1919-20, Sir Ernest Cass Reader in Commerce, London University 1920-25, Reader in Economics 1925-36. Member, Statutory Commission of Cambridge

University 1923. Chair: Labour Party NEC. 1936-37. President, Ramblers' Assn 1948-50. Master, Drapers' Company 1958-59. Under-Sec Foreign Office 1929-31, Minister for Economic Warfare 1940-42, President Board of Trade 1942-45, Chancellor of the Exchequer 1945-47, resigned over a budget leak, Chancellor, Duchy of Lancaster 1948-50, Minister of Town & Country Planning 1950-51, Minister of Local Government & Planning 1951. Hon. Fellow, London School of Economics. Hon. Bencher, Middle Temple 1946. Master, Drapers Company 1958-59. Of London & Wilts. Died 13 February 1962. *Books: Hugh Dalton: Principles of Public Finance 1923, Towards the Peace of Nations 1928, Practical Socialism for Britain 1935, Call Back Yesterday 1953, The Faithful Years 1957, A High Tide and After 1962.* Further Reading: *Ben Pimlott, Hugh Dalton 1985.*

John Edward Daniel.

DANIEL John Edward: MA (Oxon). Plaid Cymru, Caernarfonshire 1931, Caernarfon Boroughs 1935, B/E May 1945, 1945. **Professor J. E. Daniel:** Born Bangor 26 June 1902, s of Revd Morgan Daniel & Anna, d of John Jones, Cwm-aman. Welsh Independent. Married Catherine (converted to Roman Catholicism) d of Revd Rowland Hughes, 5c. Educated Friars School, Bangor, Jesus College, Oxford 1919- (triple First), Fellow, Coleg Bala-Bangor 1925, Professor of Theology 1926-46, Student at Marburg University (Bultmann) 1931, HMI 1946-Joined Plaid Cymru 1928. Editor, *Y Ddraig Goch* 1939-41. Vice-President, Plaid Cymru 1931-35, President 1939-

43. Languages Welsh, English. Died 11 February 1962 (killed in car accident). *Books: J. E. Daniel: Welsh Nationalism: What it stands for 1937, Dysg-eidiaeth yr Apostol Paul 1933.* Further Reading: *D. Densil Morgan: Torri Seiliau Sicr, 1993, Cedyrn Canrif 2001. D Ben Rees: Cymry Adnabyddus 1952-1972; Pennar Davies: Athrawon ac Annibynwyr (1971).*

DANIELS Joanne Samantha: Plaid Cymru, South/East List 2003. Of Caldicot.

DAUNCEY Alexander James: Liberal Democrat. Preseli 2001. **Mr. Alec Dauncy:** Born 1969. Educated University of Wales, Bangor. Lived in West Wales since 1986. Aberystwyth TC. Mayor, 2001-02. Languages: Learned Welsh. English. Of Aberystwyth.

DAVEY Charles M: MA (Cantab). Plaid Cymru: Bedwellty 1970. Mr. Charles Davey: Born March 1922. Quaker. Married Megan Thomas of Maes-ycymmer, 4c. Educated Ampleforth College, King's College, Cambridge (double First). "Bevin Boy", Penallta & Tower Collieries 1940-46. RAF. Education Officer, 5 years. Senior Lecturer, Kesteven College of Further Education -1967, English Teacher, Maesycymmer Comprehensive School 1967-. Of Blackwood.

DAVEY Lester: Green Party: Cardiff South & Penarth 1992. **Mr. Lester Davey:** Born Cardiff 1960. Educated Llanrumney High School. Local Postmaster.

DAVID Elfyn William: LlB (Wales). Liberal: Llandaff & Barry 1923, 1924. **Mr. Elfyn David:** Born Tondu 1894, schoolmaster's son. Married 1929, Dorothy Williams. Educated Bridgend County School, Christ College, Brecon, University of Wales, Aberystwyth. Solicitor 1916. Clerk, South-East Glamorgan Area Assn Cttee 1932. Chair: Cardiff & Barry Liberal Council.

DAVID Frances Ann: BA (Oxon). SDP/Liberal Democrat Candidate for Newport East 1983, 1987, Monmouth B/E 1991, 1992. **Mrs. Frances David:** Born Llanvair Discoed 4 February 1923, d of Geoffrey Ford Rainforth, shipowner. Roman Catholic. Married 1968 Bede Guy Markham David, farmer, 2s 4d, divorced. Educated Caerleon Primary School, Monmouth School for Girls, Sherborne School for Girls, St. Hugh's College, Oxford. Teacher, Deputy Head, Ross on Wye Comprehensive School. Member, Secondary Heads Assn. Briefly a member of Labour Party. Vice-President, Welsh SDP 1990. Vice-President, Welsh Liberal Democrats. Contested Monmouthshire CC 1999. Interests: Education, Third World. Hobbies: Gardening. Languages: English, French.

DAVID Gerald Hill: OBE CEng 1987 FREng FIEE. Liberal: Caernarfon Feb. 1974. **Mr. Gerald David:** Born Swansea August 1934. Married. Educated Newcastle Emlyn Grammar School, Swansea Grammar School, Newport Technical College, University College of Wales, Cardiff. Formerly Telephone Engineer, Standard Cables & Telephones Ltd, electrical officer, Cunard's Queen Mary & Queen Elizabeth, Telephonic Consultant & Managing Director of own firm. Chair, Aerial Facilities Ltd. Of Chesham.

DAVID James John: Communist: Neath 1959, 1964, 1966. **Mr. Jim David:** Born Seven Sisters, March 1920. Married 2c. Educated elementary schools. Miner 1934, Chair: Seven Sisters Lodge NUM, 1949-63, Vice-Chair, Dillwyn Lodge 1963-. Member: South Wales Executive NUM 1963-65, 1966-, Seven Sisters Welfare Cttee, Dulais Valley Band Cttee, Dulais Valley Housing Cttee. Joined Communist Party 1946, Secretary, South Wales District CPGB 1959-60, Chair 1960. Member National Executive. Languages: Welsh, English. Died 23 August 1966, drowning accident USSR.

DAVID Peter: Referendum Party: Aberavon 1997. **Mr. Peter David:** Born 1955. Married 2c. With British Steel Corporation 20 years, Works Officer, Port Talbot. Special Policeman. Trainer, junior AFC XI.

DAVID Trefor: British Empire Party: Ogmore 1950. **Mr. Trefor David:** Born 1895. Married. Educated elementary schools. Miner, 1910, Blacksmith, Army 1914-19. Former member, Plaid Cymru. Penybont RDC. Bridgend UDC April 1933-, Chair: Glamorgan CC 1934-37. Former amateur boxing champion. Charged with Criminal Libel after criticisms of council leaders & officers but acquitted at Swansea Assizes 23 July 1936. Bankrupted. The only candidate ever of the British Empire Party founded by P. J. Ridout, a pre-war fascist. Of Bridgend.

DAVID Wayne A: BA (Wales) 1979 PGCE. Labour: Rhondda 1999, MEP South Wales 1989-94, South Wales Central 1994-99, MP Caerphilly 2000-. **Mr. Wayne David:** Born, Bridgend, 1 July 1957, s of David Haydn David, teacher, & Edna Amelia Jones. Married 1991 Catherine Thomas (his former political aide). Educated Cynfig Comprehensive School, University of Wales, Cardiff (History) & Swansea. Teacher, Brynteg Comprehensive School, 1983-85. WEA Tutor/Organiser, Mid-Glamorgan 1985-89. Policy Adviser in youth Policy, Wales Youth Agency 1999-2001. Vice-President, European Parliament. Labour, Labour Group 1994-99. Cefn Cribwr ComC. (Chairman 1986-87). Hon. Fellow, University of Wales, Cardiff. Vice-President: Council for Wales of Voluntary Youth services. Member:

Fabian Society, AEEU, MSF. Hobbies: Music, Playing oboe.

DAVIDSON Jane: BA. PCGE (Wales). Labour AM Pontypridd, 1999. **Ms. Jane Davidson:** Born Birmingham 19 March 1957, d of Dr. Lindsay Alexander Gordon Davidson & Dr. Joyce Mary Davidson Married 1993, Guy Toger George, s of Alvan & Maisie Stoate, 2 stepsons, 1d. Educated Arundel School, Harare, Park School, Glasgow, Malvern Girls' College, Birmingham University (English), University of Wales, Aberystwyth, Teacher (English & PE, Ysgol Uwchradd Aberteifi & Coedylan School, Pontypridd 1981-84, Development Officer YHA 1984-87, Youth & Community Worker, Dinas Powys 1987-90, Researcher to Rhodri Morgan MP 1991-96, Welsh Co-coordinator, National Local Government Forum Against Poverty 1994-96, Head of Social Affairs, Welsh Local Government Assn. 1996-99. Cardiff CC 1987-96. Arts Council for Wales 12 years. Supported Rhodri Morgan's leadership campaign. Interests: Health, social exclusion, community safety. Chair, Governors, Gwaelodygarth School. Deputy Presiding Officer, Assembly 1999-2000, Minister for Education & Lifelong Learning Oct. 2000. Hobbies: Walking, Swimming, Theatre. Languages: Learned Welsh, English. Of Gwaelodygarth.

DAVIES Alfred: Liberal MP Carmarthen District 1900-06. **Mr. Alfred Davies:** Born 1862, s of Revd John Davies, Congregational Minister, & Mary Kidman Foster of Cambridgeshire. Married 1877, Lydia Edith, d of William Death, 2s. Educated Mill Hill School. Founder-Chair: Davies, Turner & Co., London, President, Davies & Turner, New York, International Carriers. London CC 1889-92. Used patronage to become candidate, rejected by local party 1906 after much bribery of voters. Of Hampstead. Estate £30,697. Died 27 September 1907.

DAVIES Andrew – see DAVIES David Andrew.

DAVIES Alun – see DAVIES: T. A. R.

DAVIES Alun Talfan: Kt 1976 QC 1961 Hon. LLD (Wales) 1973 LlB (Wales) MA LlB (Cantab). Independent: University of Wales B/E 1944, Liberal: Carmarthen 1959, 1964, Denbigh 1966. **Sir Alun Talfan Davies:** Born Gorseinon 22 July 1913, s of Revd W. Talfan Davies. Presbyterian Church of Wales. Married 1942 Eiluned, d of Humphrey R Williams, Stanmore, 1s 3d. Educated Gowerton Grammar School; University of Wales, Aberystwyth; Gonville & Caius College, Cambridge. Barrister, Grays Inn 1939, Bencher, 1969, Recorder: Merthyr Tydfil 1963-65, Swansea 1968-69, Cardiff 1969-71, Crown Court 1972-85, Hon. Recorder of Cardiff 1972-86, Deputy-Chair:

Cardiganshire Quarter Sessions 1963-71, Judge, Courts of Appeal, Jersey & Guernsey 1969-84. Member: Commission on the Constitution 1969-73, Criminal Injuries Compensation Board 1977-85. Founder, Llyfrau'r Dryw, publishers 1940, *Barn* 1962. Chair: Liberal Party of Wales. Member: Court of the University of Wales, University of Wales, Aberystwyth & Swansea. Fellow, University of Wales, Aberystwyth 1984. President, National Eisteddfod Court 1977-80, Court Welsh National Opera 1978-80, Welsh National Centre for International Affairs 1985. Director: Cardiff World Trade Centre Ltd. 1985-97. Chair: Bank of Wales 1991-96 (Deputy Chair: 1973-91) Harrison Cowley (Cardiff PR co). Deputy Chair: HTV & Chair: Welsh Board 1978-83, Vice-Chair: HTV Group Ltd 1978-83, Chair: Aberfan Fund Trustees 1969-88. Languages: Welsh, English. Of Penarth. Died 11 November 2000.

DAVIES Andrew Robert Tudor: Conservative, Cardiff West 2001. **Mr. Andrew Davies:** Born Cowbridge, 8 April 1968. Married Julie, midwife, 2s 1d. Educated Balfour House, St. Athan, Wycliffe College, Somerset. Farmer (1100 acre beef & dairy) in partnership with father & brothers. Vice-Chair: NFU Cymru/Wales. Hobbies: Sport, Reading, Meeting people. Joined Conservative Party 1998. Of St. Hilary.

DAVIES Angharad: BA (Queens) MA (Limerick). Labour: Montgomery 1997. **Mrs. Angharad Davies:** Born Walsall, 18 October1971. Married 2c. Educated Lampeter Comprehensive School, Queens University, Belfast, Limerick University. Political Assistant to Eluned Morgan MEP. Public Affairs Adviser, Royal College of Nursing in Wales. Member: Amnesty, Fawcett Society, TGWU. Organised Ron Davies' campaign for leadership of Labour in Wales. Shortlisted, Caerphilly 1999, 2003, Cynon Valley 1999. Languages: Welsh, English.

DAVIES Arthur: Labour: Montgomery 1924, Liberal PPC Rhondda East-1918. **Mr. Arthur Davies:** Born Llangefni 1877, s of Richard Davies, schoolmaster, & Ellen Davies. Barrister, Inner & Middle Temples. Indian army 1914-19. Bank Manager in South Africa, Lawyer at Rangoon. Languages: Welsh, English.

DAVIES Arthur Gwynne: Conservative: Abertillery 1955, Ebbw Vale 1959. **Mr. Arthur Davies:** Born Ebbw Vale, February 1918. Married 1c. Educated Pantywaun Grammar School, Ebbw Vale Grammar School, Cardiff School of Law. Local government clerk 1934-39. SWB (TA) 1939, Army 1939-45, Lieutenant 1940, Major 1945, 3rd Mon Regt. Barrister, Grays Inn 1947. Chair: Military Hardship & Re-instatement Cttee, Ministry of Pensions local appeals tribunal & industrial injuries tribunal. Joined Conservatives 1934. President: Ebbw Vale Conservative Assn, Monmouthshire Council of Conservative Clubs, Vice-Chair: Wales & Mon. Conservative Clubs Council. President, Monmouthshire Federation of Conservative Clubs. Life Member, Temple Union Society. Died December 1968.

DAVIES Arthur P. S. – see SAUNDERS-DAVIES A. P.

DAVIES Bryan, Baron Davies of Oldham 1997: BA 1961 BSc Econ 1968 PGCE 1962 Hon. LLD (Middx) 1996. Labour: Newport West 1983, Norfolk Central 1966, MP Enfield North, Feb. 1974-79, Oldham Central & Royton 1992-97. **Mr. Bryan Davies:** Born Mon. 9 November 1939, s of George William Davies, painter & decorator & Beryl Parsons. Humanist. Married 1963, Monica Rosemary Mildred Shearing, 2s 1d. Educated Redditch High School, University College, London, Institute of Education, London, London School of Economics. Teacher, Latymer School 1962-65, Lecturer, Middlesex Polytechnic Enfield 1965-74. Secretary, Parliamentary Labour Party 1979-92. Asst Govt Whip 1979, Opposition Spokesman: Higher Education 1993-97, Select Cttee Member: Public Expenditure 1975-79, Overseas Development 1975-79, National Heritage 1992-93. Member, Medical Research Council 1977-79. Lord in Waiting (Whip) & Government spokesman 2000-03. Deputy Chief Whip & Captain of the Yeomen of the Guard 2003. President, Royal Society for the Prevention of Accidents 1999-2000. Committed supporter of Oxfam. Hobbies: Sport, Literature. Of Broxbourne, Herts.

DAVIES Catherine Bowen – see BOWEN-DAVIES C.

DAVIES Christopher Gareth: Liberal Democrat: Gower 1992, Aberavon 2001. **Mr. Christopher Davies:** Born Three Crosses, 28 September 1961. Married Gail, 1s. Educated Gowerton Grammar School, West Glamorgan Institute of Higher Education, Portsmouth Polytechnic. Sales Manager, Allied Dunbar. Portsmouth CC 1986-90. Deputy Welsh Campaign Manager, 1997 election, Director, Assembly Campaign 1999. Chair: Welsh Liberal Democrats.

DAVIES Christopher Trefor: BA Dip.Prac.Theol (Wales), Independent Wales Party, South/Central List 2003. **Revd Christopher Trefor Davies:** Born Bridgend 22 March 1968, s of Trevor Davies, crane operator, & Blodwen Emma Davies, housewife. Educated Llangynwyd Primary School; Maesteg Comprehensive School; University of Wales, Cardiff (Religious Studies); Northern Baptist College, Manchester (Post Ordination MA course). Welsh Baptist Minister. Member,

Plaid Cymru (contested Bridgend BC 1999). Interests: Youth Work. Community regeneration, Health, Disability rights, Crime. Of Sheffield.

DAVIES Clifford Gregory: BA (Wales). Plaid Cymru: Gower 1970, Cardigan 1974, Feb. **Mr. Clifford Davies:** Born Clydach 1940, s of Revd T. W. Davies, Vicar of Clydach. Married Christine (of Bradford), 2s. Educated Brecon Grammar School, Ystalyfera Grammar School, University of Wales, Swansea. Teacher: Head of History, Preseli Comprehensive School 1966 (previously taught at London & Cardiff). Headteacher, Bro Dyfi Comprehensive School, Machynlleth, Education Adviser, Powys CC. Member, Literary Cttee, Haverfordwest National Eisteddfod 1972. Active supporter of UNA work in schools. Plaid Cymru spokesman on Education, Director of Policy 1973. Member, Cardigan Cricket XI. Treasurer, Cilgerran Football Club. Languages: Welsh, English.

DAVIES Cyrus Golyddan: JP (Mon). Liberal: Ebbw Vale 1923. **Mr. Cyrus Davies:** Born Ebbw Vale, 1872, s of Jonathan A. Davies & Jane Davies. Jeweler & Director, Ebbw Vale AFC. Commissioner for Income Tax. Ebbw Vale UDC 23 years, Chairman, 1932-33. Monmouthshire CC 20 years. Trustee, Ebbw Vale Welfare Club. Estate £11,504. Died 14 December 1942.

DAVIES David: JP (Mon Cards) DL (Cards). Liberal: Cardiganshire 1865, MP Cardigan District 1874-85, Cardiganshire 1885-86, Liberal Unionist: Cardiganshire 1886. **Mr. David Davies:** Born Llandinam 18 December 1818, s of David & Elizabeth Davies. Calvinistic Methodist. Married 1851, Margaret, d of Edward Jones, Llanfair, 1s. Educated Llanidloes Day School. Farm Worker at 11, Sawyer, Industrialist (employed 3,000): Coal, railway & dock owner: Director, Brecon & Merthyr, Pembroke & Tenby, Manchester & Milford & Cambrian Railway Companies, Vice-Chair: Barry Dock & Railway Co. Chair: Llandinam School Board, Montgomeryshire CC1889-. Treasurer, University College of Wales, Aberystwyth 1875-87. Languages: Welsh, English. Of Llandinam. Estate £404,424. Died 20 July 1890, after long illness. Further Reading: *Ivor Davies: Top Sawyer (1938), Goronwy Jones: David Davies (1913.*

DAVIES David: 1st Baron Davies of Llandinam 1932: JP (Mont) MA (Cantab). Liberal MP Montgomeryshire, 1906-1929. **Colonel David Davies:** Born Llandinam, 1 May 1880, s of Edward Davies & gs of David Davies MP (qv). Calvinistic Methodist. Married (1) 1910, Anna Penman (Died 1918) 3c (2) Henrietta Margaret Fergusson, 4c. Educated Merchiston Castle School, Edinburgh, Trinity College, Cambridge (2nd History).

Landowner, Coal Owner & Chair: Ocean Coal Co, Wilsons Ltd, United National Collieries Ltd, Burnyeat, Brown & Co, Cambrian & General Securities, Director: railway & banking companies. President: Mining Education Board of South Wales, King Edward VII Welsh National Memorial Assn, Welsh Housing & Development Assn, Welsh League of Nations Union, Football Assn of Wales. Founder Chair: New Commonwealth Society. Colonel, 14th Battalion, RWF 1916-19. Estate £440,040. Died 16 June 1944. *Books: David Davies, The Problem of the Twentieth Century 1930, Letters to John Bull 1932, Suicide or Sanity 1932, Force 1934, Nearing the Abyss 1936, Foundations of Victory 1941, Facing the Future 1942.*

DAVIES David: JP (Swansea) FIJ. Order of Leopold (Belgium) 1920. Conservative, Swansea West 1918. **Mr. David Davies:** Born Llanelli, 20 November 1862, s of Benjamin Davies & Margaret Williams. Anglican. Married 1889, Alice Matthews. Educated Pentip National School, Llanelli. Journalist, *Llanelli Guardian*. Editorial Staff, *Western Mail* 1887-94; Deputy Editor 1889. Editor & Managing Director, *South Wales Daily Post*. Swansea BC 1900-04, 1906-18; Alderman 1916-18, Mayor 1916-17; Chairman, Arts & Crafts Cttee. Chair: Swansea & Merthyr Tydfil Joint Asylum Cttee; Swansea War Savings Cttee; Belgian Refugees Cttee. Member: Swansea Board of Guardians; Swansea Harbour Trust; West Glamorgan Army Corps Cttee; Bohemian Club. Chair: Swansea West Conservative Assn. President, South Wales Branch, Institute of Journalists. Founder: *South Wales Daily Post* Prisoners of War Fund. Freemason. Retired from public life 1923. Died 30 October 1932.

DAVIES David: BA (Wales) 1922. Plaid Cymru: Rhondda East 1950. **Mr. David Davies:** Born Tylorstown 1897. Welsh Independent Deacon, Church Secretary & Lay Preacher. Married Eira. Educated Ferndale Grammar School, University of Wales, Cardiff (1st Welsh). Teacher {Welsh & RE) Tonypandy Grammar School. Chair: East Glamorgan Assn of Welsh Independents 1963-64. Member, Tylorstown Undeb Cymru Fydd. Languages: Welsh, English. Of Tylorstown. Died 21 July 1980.

DAVIES David Andrew: BScEcon. PGCE. (Wales). Labour AM Swansea West 1999. **Mr. Andrew Davies:** Born Hereford, 5 May 1952. Married 1978, Deborah Frost, Marriage Dissolved. Educated Hereford Cathedral School, University of Wales, Swansea, (Diploma in Counselling). Regional Officer, Wales Labour Party 1984-91, Head of Employee Development Assistance Program, Ford Motor Co. (South Wales) 1991-96. Lecturer, Swansea College 1994-97, Special Projects Officer, Wales Labour Party

1997-98, Associate Director, Welsh *Context*, Cardiff based public affairs company 1998-99. School governor. Chair, Swansea West Labour Party. Member, Wales Labour Party Executive. Election Agent to Alan Williams MP & David Morris MEP. Assembly Business Manager 1999-2002, Minister for Economic Development 2002. Hon. Fellow, University of Wales Swansea 2004. Of Sandfields, Swansea.

DAVIES David Charles Thomas: Conservative: Bridgend 1997, AM Monmouth 1999- **Mr. David Davies:** Born London 27 July 1970, s of Peter Davies (qv). Married, 2003, Aliz Harnisfoger of Hungary. Educated Basseleg Comprehensive School, Newport. Clerk, British Steel Corporation 1988-89, Worked his way around the world (including rickshaw driver) 1989-91, Former Youth Hostel Manager & Clerk, British Steel Corporation, General Manager, Burrows Heath, Ltd. forwarders & tea importers 1990. Joined Conservative Party at 13. Treasurer, Welsh Young Conservatives 1995-97, Chair: Newport West Conservative Assn.1993-96, Re-formed Newport West CPC 1997-98. Managed Rod Richards Leader Election Campaign 1998, Chief of Staff 1998. Member: Institute of Logistics, Assoc Member, Institute of Transport Administration. Newport Campaign Manager, Just say NO Referendum campaign. Deputy Leader Assembly Conservatives & Chief Whip 1999. Prospective parliamentary candidate for Monmouth, September 2003. Conservative Prospective Parliamentary Candidate, Monmouth 2004. Interests: Health, Education, Transport, Ensuring a cost-effective Assembly. Hobbies: Surfing, Keep Fit. Languages: Learned Welsh, English. Of Monmouth.

DAVIES David Griffith: JP (Glam) 1925. CertEd (Wales). Liberal: Neath 1931. **Mr. D. G. Davies:** Born Neath Abbey, 1874, s of Evan Davies, iron pattern maker, & Sarah Davies (1 of 6 c. 1881). Ex-Presbyterian Elder, Anglican. Married Margaret, 1s 1d. Educated Dynevor Grammar School, Swansea, University of Wales, Cardiff. Teacher, Aberdare Higher Grade School 1896-1917. Took over uncle's business: D. T. Sims & Co. Builders & Limestone Merchants, Ammanford 1917-19, Neath 1919-46. Ammanford UDC -1919, Neath BC 1919-, Mayor 1925-26, Neath RDC, Neath Board of Guardians, Glamorgan CC 1919-44. Vice-President, Neath Free Church Council, 1928. Languages: Welsh, English. Died 9 March 1957.

DAVIES David Hywel: JP (Pembs) 1952 FCA. Liberal: Monmouth 1964, Carmarthen 1966, B/E 1966. **Mr. Hywel Davies:** Born July 1919. Married. Educated Whitland Grammar School. Chartered Accountant. President, Pembrokeshire Liberal Assn. 1962, Chair: Liberal Party of Wales,

1953. Narberth UDC 1948-, Chair. Pembroke-shire CC 1951-54, 1961-. Member, Court, University of Wales, Swansea.

DAVIES David John: CBE 1966. Labour: Cardigan 1964. **Mr. D. J. Davies:** Born Tregroes, Llandysul, February 1906, s of David Davies (Died 1919). Welsh Independent Deacon. Married 1945, Elizabeth Margaret, d of John James, Maesgwyn, 7c. Educated Llandysul Grammar School. Farmer (500 acres). President, Cardiganshire CLP. 1953-. Vice-President: Cardiganshire, Welsh Agricultural Organisation Society, County Parish Councils Assn. Founder Member, Farmers' Union of Wales. Chairman, Aberaeron RDC. Languages: Welsh, English. Of Tregroes, Llandysul.

DAVIES David John Denzil: PC MA (Oxon). Labour MP: Llanelli 1970-. **Rt. Hon. Denzil Davies:** Born Cynwyl Elfed 9 October 1938, s of Gareth Davies, colliery blacksmith. Married (1) 1963 Mary Ann Finlay of Illinois, 1s 1d, divorced, 1988 (2) 1989 Ann Carlton. Educated Queen Elizabeth Grammar School, Carmarthen, Pembroke College, Oxford (1st, Law). Lecturer in Law, University of Chicago, Leeds University. Barrister. Joined Labour Party 1956. Member, Society of Labour Lawyers. Chair, Welsh Parliamentary Labour Party. Minister of State, Treasury 1975-79. Opposition Spokesman: Foreign & Commonwealth Affairs 1978-81, Defence & Disarmament 1981-83, Welsh Affairs 1983, Defence 1983-88, resigned. Contested Labour leadership 1994. Announced retirement at next election 2003. Hobbies: Gardening, Walking, Rugby, Cricket, Reading. Languages: Welsh, English. Of London.

DAVIES David Keith: SDP: Neath 1983, Vale of Glamorgan B/E 1989, 1992, Aberavon & South West List 1999. **Mr. Keith Davies:** Born 1946. Married Susan 3d. Plant fitter, BP Chemicals, Baglan Bay. AUEW Shop Steward, Chair: Llandarcy Joint Shop Stewards Cttee. Market Researcher. Neath BC 1979-95, Neath-Port Talbot BC 1990 (Leader of Opposition). School Governor. Hobbies: Bowls, Golf, Rugby, Gardening. Of Skewen.

DAVIES David Lewis: JP. (Glam). Labour: Pontypridd 1918, MP B/E May 1931-. **Mr. D. Lewis Davies:** Born 15 December 1892, s of John Owen Davies & Mary Lewis. Baptist deacon. Married 1900, Nora Nurse, 1s. Educated Wood Road Elementary School, Treforest, and evening classes. Miner 1904, Miners Agent. Chairman, Pontypridd UDC. Languages: Welsh, English. Of Treforest. Died 25 November 1937.

DAVIES David Michael Barry: Liberal Democrat: Ceredigion 1997. **Mr. Dai Davies:** Born 9 March 1943. Married (1) widowed 1992, (2) 1995.

Educated Cardigan Grammar School. Chartered Accountant 1979. Cardigan TC 1990-, Mayor 1994-95. Ceredigion DC 1993-97. Ceredigion CC 1996-, Group Leader 1995-. Member, Charter 88. Languages: Welsh, English. Of Cardigan & Llechryd.

DAVIES David Rees: BA MA PhD. Liberal Democrat, Neath, Assembly 1999, 2001. Born Banwen, 1954, son of Handel Davies. Educated University of Wales, Bangor. Traveled extensively, taught in Africa, South America & Middle East. Teacher. Joined Liberal Democrats 1997. Onllwyn ComC 1997. Contested Neath/Port Talbot BC 1999. Interests: Education, Return to Prosperity. Hobbies: Astronomy, Sailing, Scuba diving, Reading, Travel. Of Dyffryn Cellwen, Neath.

DAVIES David Richard Seabourne: JP (Liverpool & Caernarfonshire). Hon. LLD (Liverpool) LlB (Wales) 1927. MA (Oxon). Liberal MP: Caernarfon Boroughs, May-July, 1945. **Professor Seabourne Davies:** Born Pwllheli 26 June 1904, s of David S Davies, sea captain, & Claudia Davies. Presbyterian elder. Educated Pwllheli Grammar School, University of Wales, Aberystwyth (1st), St. John's College, Cambridge (1st). Barrister. Lecturer in Law, London University 1929-45. Nationality Division, Home Office 1941-45, Secretary, Naturalisation Revocation Cttee 1944-5. Professor of Common Law, Liverpool University 1946-71, Dean of the Faculty of Law 1946-56, Warden, Derby Hall 1947-, Public Orator 1950-55, Pro-Vice-Chancellor 1956-60. Member, Standing Cttee on Criminal Law Revision 1959-72. Chair, Liverpool Licensing Planning Cttee 1960-63. President: National Eisteddfod Council 1958, 1973, 1977; Society of Public Teachers of Law 1960-61. Vice-President, London Welsh RFC. High Sheriff of Caernarfonshire 1967-68. Languages: Welsh, English. Of Pwllheli. Died 21 October 1984.

DAVIES David Saunders: Kt 1918 JP (Denbs 1906, Manchester 1895). Coalition Liberal MP Denbigh 1918-22. **Sir David S. Davies:** Born Caeio, Carms, 11 May 1852, s of John Owen Davies. Calvinistic Methodist Elder. Married 1886, Jane Emily, d of Thomas Gee, 1d. Educated Llandovery College. Apprenticed to a Llandovery draper. Governing Director, Pugh, Davies & Co. Ltd, Manchester. Part-Owner & Editor, *Baner ac Amserau Cymru* & *North Wales Times*. High Sheriff of Denbighshire 1915. Chair: Denbighshire County Appeals & Pension Cttee; West Denbighshire CO Appeal Tribunal. Member, CWB Executive. Languages: Welsh, English. Of Denbigh. Died 28 February 1934.

DAVIES Ednyfed Hudson – see DAVIES Gwilym E. H.

Clement Davies.

DAVIES Edward Clement: PC 1947 KC 1926 JP (Mont) Hon. LLD (Wales) BA LlB (Cantab). Liberal MP Montgomery 1929-, (Liberal National 1931-42). **Rt. Hon. Clement Davies:** Born Llanfyllin 1884, s of Alderman Moses Davies, auctioneer, & Elizabeth Margaret Jones. Calvinistic Methodist. Married 1913, Jano Elizabeth, d of Morgan Davies, MD. FRCS London, 3s 1d. Educated Llanfyllin Grammar School, University of Wales, Aberystwyth, Trinity Hall, Cambridge, (1st), Law Studentship, Trinity Hall 1907-11 (Hon. Fellow 1950). Lecturer in Law, University of Wales, Aberystwyth 1908-09. Barrister, Lincoln's Inn 1909, Bencher 1953. Adviser within Office of Procurator General on enemy activities in neural countries and on the high seas 1914. Adviser on Trading with the enemy, Board of Trade, 1918. Secretary to: Master of Probate, Divorce & Admiralty Division 1918-19, Master of the Rolls 1919-23. Junior Counsel to the Treasury 1919-25. Director & Legal Adviser, Unilever Ltd & Lever Bros Ltd 1925. Founder, London Montgomeryshire Society 1929, President, Powys Eisteddfod 1923-29,1943, National Eisteddfod 1938, 1939. Parliamentary Charity Commissioner 1936-37. Chair: Montgomeryshire Quarter Sessions 1935-, Chair: Commons Administration Cttee, Greater London Planning Cttee. Select Cttees Member: Delegated Legislation, Members' Expenses, Political Hon. Scrutiny Cttee. Chair: Parliamentary Liberal Party 1931, Liberal Party 1945, President, Welsh Liberal Federation 1945-48, Leader, Liberal Party 1945-56, President: Approved Societies of Wales, World Assn. of Parliamentarians for World Government. Declined Churchill's offer of a government job 1956. Nominated for 1955 Nobel Peace Prize. Languages: Welsh, English. Of Meifod & London. Died 23 March 1962. *Books etc: Clement*

Davies, Agricultural Law 1910, Finance (1909-10 Act 1910, Agricultural Holdings Act 1912, Law of Auctions and Auctioneers 1913. Further Reading: *Alun Wyburn-Powell, Clement Davies: A Liberal Life, Sept. 2002, David M. Roberts, MA Thesis (Wales) 1975, Clement Davies and the Liberal Party 1929-56; John Graham Jones, Dictionary of Liberal Biography 1998, pages 92-94.*

E. Glyn Davies.

DAVIES Edward Glyn: BSc (Wales). Conservative: Montgomery 1997, AM North Wales List 1999. **Mr. Glyn Davies:** Born Castell Caereinion, 16 February 1944. Married 1944, Bobbie, 4c. Educated Llanfair Caereinion High School. Farmer (Principal, T. E. Davies & Son, Livestock Farmers) & Joint Owner with wife of Granary Restaurants. Montgomeryshire DC 1979-89 (Chairman 1985-89). ComC. Powys CC. Member, Welsh Tourist Board 1989-94. Chair: Development Corporation for Rural Wales 1989-94. Chair: Housing Assn. Welsh Conservative Spokesman on Agriculture & Rural Economy 1999. Hobbies: Sport, including Squash & Rugby, Gardening. Languages: Learned Welsh, English. Of Berriew, Welshpool (1971).

DAVIES Ellis William: JP (Caerns). Liberal: Caernarfonshire 1918; MP Eifion B/E 1906-18, Denbigh, 1923-29, Joined the Labour Party 1934. Resigned over foreign policy & joined Liberal National Party, Feb. 1939. **Mr. Ellis Davies:** Born Bethesda 12 April 1872, s of David Davies, Quarry Clerk & Catherine Elizabeth Williams. Calvinistic Methodist. Married 1901, Minnie, d of Richard Hughes, Porthmadog, 3c. Educated Carnedd School, Liverpool College. Prepared for Calvinistic Methodist Ministry; Clerk in insurance office, Solicitor 1899, Caernarfon & London. Company Director, Selfridge & Co. Ltd, National

Press of Wales & Welsh Insurance Corporation Ltd. Caernarfonshire CC Alderman (Chair: Public Assistance Cttee), Chairman of Council 1939. Member: House of Commons Cttees: Landed Estates 1910, Juries 1911, Mr. Lloyd George's Land Enquiry Cttee, Speaker's Electoral Conference 1916-17, Second Chamber Conference 1917, House of Commons Panel of Chairmen. 1st President, (Asquithian) Welsh Liberal Federation Jan. 1921-. Adopted by Caernarfonshire Liberal Assn. November 1918 but opposed by Coalition Liberal candidate chosen by Lloyd George with whom he had quarrelled. Languages: Welsh, English. Of Caernarfon. Died 29 April 1949.

DAVIES Evan: JP (Mon) 1916. Labour MP Ebbw Vale B/E 1920-29, failed to secure re-adoption in 1929 and was replaced by Aneurin Bevan. **Mr. Evan Davies:** Born Beaufort 1875, s of Evan Davies & Rachel Davies, laundress. Methodist. Educated Beaufort Hill British School. Miner 1887, Chair: & Sub-Agent, Ebbw Vale District SWMF. 1904, Miners' Agent, Ebbw Vale 1913, Member, Miners' Delegation, France, Belgium, Germany 1913. General Secretary, Monmouthshire Assn. of Friendly Societies, National Health Act 1913-16. Ebbw Vale UDC Chair: 1914-16. Keen Temperance worker, greatly involved in war recruiting. Not Readopted by Ebbw Vale Labour Party 1929. Died 1960. Further Reading: *Llafur, Vol. 3, No. 3. 1981: John Graham Jones, Evan Davies & Ebbw Vale, Biographical Material Stenton & Lees: Who's Who of British Members of Parliament Vol. III 1919-45 (Brighton 1979) p.302, Edwin Yates: Labour Personalities in the House of Commons (Watford 1923), S. V. Bracher: The Herald Book of Labour Members (London 1923), Joyce M. Bellamy & John Saville: A Dictionary of Labour Biography), The Labour Who's Who 1924 (London).*

DAVIES Evan: Independent Labour: University of Wales B/E 1943. **Sergeant Evan Davies:** Educated University of Wales, Aberystwyth. Army, based at War Office. Called for Secretary of State for Wales. Of Hengoed.

DAVIES Evan Robert: JP (Caerns). National Liberal: Wrexham 1922. **Mr. Evan R. Davies:** Born nr Pwllheli 12 January 1871, s of Revd D. E. Davies. Calvinistic Methodist Elder. Married 1896, J. C. Jones, 4c. Educated Pwllheli Grammar School, University of Wales, Aberystwyth. Solicitor, Senior Partner, Evans, Davies & Co. Town Clerk of Pwllheli 1896-1920. first Secretary: Caernarfonshire Education Cttee, Director of Education 1903, Secretary: North Wales Training College Cttee, Founder-Secretary, Federation of British Health & Holiday Resorts. District Commissioner, Board of Agriculture 1916-19. Member, Prime Minister's Secretariat 1919-22, Member:

North Wales Munitions Board, Lancashire & Western Fisheries Board, North Wales Advertising Board, Caernarfonshire Labour Advisory Cttee, Caernarfonshire Agricultural Advisory Cttee, Welsh Agricultural Council. Company Chair: Snowdon Railway Co Ltd, Ffestiniog Railway Co Ltd, Central Advertising Service, Ltd & other public companies. Secretary, British Travel Ltd, Pwllheli BC 4 times Mayor. Caernarfonshire CC 1892, Alderman 1894. Languages: Welsh, English. Of Pwllheli & London. Estate £24,267. Died at chapel, 2 December 1934.

DAVIES Ewan Gibson: LlB (London). Liberal: Cardiff South 1924, Llandaff & Barry 1929. **Mr. Ewan Davies:** Born 23 June 1887, s of D. E. Davies, solicitor. Married Educated Cardiff High School, Llandovery College, Cardiff Municipal College, University College, London, Kings College, London (1st, Clements Inn & Daniel Reardon Prizes). Army 1914-18, Captain RWF. Solicitor & Director of colliery & other companies. Secretary, Aberavon Liberal & Labour Assn., Agent 1918, 1922, Member: Wales Rugby XV 1912, Cardiff XV. Vice-President & Vice-Captain, Cardiff Golf Club. President, Cardiff Law Society, Chair: 1951. Vice-Chair: Cardiff Business Club. Member, Court, University of Wales, Cardiff. Short-listed as National candidate, Brecon & Radnor B/E 1939.

DAVIES Frederick William: JP (Glam). (National) Liberal: Gower 1922, 1929. **Mr. Fred W. Davies:** Born Dinas Powys 1875. Married 1900, Susan (1874-1953), d of Christopher Rowlands, Newport, Mon. 3d. Senior Partner: Davies & McCann, builder's merchants & ironmongers, Swansea South Dock. Joint Treasurer, Welsh Liberal Federation 1920. Dinas Powys PC. Glamorgan CC 1922-, 1937-, Alderman. Governor, Gowerton County School. Of Bishopston, Gower. Died 1947.

DAVIES Gary: Socialist Labour Party, South/West List 2003. **Mr. Gary Davies:** Born Wales. Educated Wales. Member, Labour Party *until he realized that they had turned their backs on the principles and values the party was founded on.* Interests: ensuring the dignity and respect of all members of the community; the sick, the aged, the disabled, those who work and the unemployed, and a society free from all forms of discrimination. Hobbies: Football, Rugby, Countryside walks. Of Sarn, Bridgend.

DAVIES George Maitland Lloyd: Christian Pacifist MP University of Wales 1923-24. **Revd George M. Ll. Davies:** Born Liverpool 30 April 1880, s of John & Gwen, d of Revd John Jones, Talysarn. Presbyterian. Married 1916, Lesley, d of Michael Holroyd Smith, 1d. Educated Liverpool. Bank clerk, Bank of Liverpool, Bank Man-

George Maitland Lloyd Davies.

ager 1908-13. Secretary, Welsh Housing Trust 1913-15. Lieutenant TA. Read Fellowship of Reconciliation 1915 Declaration and became a Christian Pacifist. Gave up career to become Joint-Secretary of the Fellowship of Reconciliation. Worked with delinquents 1916 & became a shepherd in Lleyn whilst actively involved in Christian Pacifist activities. Sentenced to two years hard labour for peace propaganda 1917-19, struck off church roll. Refused permission to speak at Presbyterian Church of Wales General Assembly 1920. After the Great War he was a *Missioner for Reconciliation* at home and abroad. Afforded Labour Whip in Commons. Minister, Presbyterian Church of Wales, Ordained 1926, Tywyn English & Maethlon 1926. Worked with Unemployed in Rhondda. Retired to Dolwyddelan 1946. Languages: Welsh, English. Died 16 December 1949 (found hanged at North Wales Mental Hospital). *Books: G. M. Ll. Davies: Ynwrthod â Rhyfel, Essays towards Peace, Around the Malthouse (biography of Joseph Rowntree Gilbert), Atgofion Talysarn, Pererindod Heddwch/Pilgrimage of Peace 1950 (autobiography).* Further Reading: *D. Ben Rees (edit), Herio'r Byd, Oriel o Heddychwyr; E. H. Griffith, Heddychwyr Mawr Cymru; Byron Howells, Troi'r Cledd yn Gaib.*

DAVIES Geraint Rhys: BPharm (London) MRPharmS. Plaid Cymru: Rhondda 1983, 1987, 1992, AM Rhondda, 1997-2003. **Mr. Geraint Davies:** Born Treherbert, 1 December 1948, s of John Haydn Davies (headteacher & Conductor, Treorchy Male Vale Choir) & Sarah Olwen Williams. Baptist deacon. Married Meriel Margaret, d of Horace & Merrill Williams, 3s 1d. Educated Ysgol Gymraeg Ynyswen, Pentre

Grammar School, London University. Pharmaceutical Chemist: with Boots 1970-75; self-employed 1975. Rhondda BC 1987-, Rhondda-Cynon-Taf BC. Chair: Plaid Cymru, Rhondda Branch, Plaid Cymru National Council, Treherbert & District Leasehold Assn Languages: Welsh, English. Plaid Cymru Spokesman on The Valleys. Member Assembly Cttees: Health & Social Services, Environment, Planning, Transport. Interests: Regeneration Policies. Hobbies: Tennis, Music, Reading, Playing Piano. Of Treherbert, Rhondda.

DAVIES Gerald G. C: Conservative: Newport 1979. **Mr. Gerald Davies:** Born1941. Educated Rougemount School, Newport, Wycliffe College, Gloucester. Company Chair: private menswear retailing co. Newport BC -1979, Chair: Housing Cttee, Magor & St. Mellons RDC 1967-70.

DAVIES Gerson Wynn: BA (Wales) 1967. Labour: Conway 1979. **Mr. Gerson Davies:** Born January 1945, s of Baptist minister/ex-miner. Baptist lay preacher. Married 1970, Myra, teacher, 2s. Educated Holyhead Comprehensive School, University College of Wales, Aberystwyth, Jesus College, Oxford (President, Junior Common Room, Member, Dafydd ap Gwilym Society). Barrister, Inner Temple. Adult Education Officer. Open University Tutor, Pembrokeshire LEA. Member: NAS/UWT, Labour Committee on Pneumoconiosis. Director of Education & Community Services for Pembrokeshire. Languages: Welsh, English.

DAVIES Glyn: BA (Liverpool). Communist (Party of Britain): East Flint 1979, Alyn & Deeside, 1999, 2001, North Wales List 2003. **Mr. Glyn Davies:** Born Gwersyllt, Wrexham, 16 March 1939, s of Edgar Davies, miner, mother a hospital cleaner. Atheist. Married 3c. Educated Coleg Harlech 2 years, Liverpool University. Building Worker, Local Government Officer. UCATT branch secretary, Member, Deeside Trades Council, North Wales Regional Cttee, Wales TUC. Contested Flintshire CC 1999. Joined Communist Party 1972, Secretary, Welsh Cttee. Communist Party. Chair: Shotton Working Men's Club. NE Wales Organiser, Trade Unionists against Single Currency. Interests: Marxism, Nationalism, Trade Unionism, Anti-Fascism, Welfare State, Pensions. Hobbies: Reading. Of Shotton.

DAVIES Glyn (Conservative) – see DAVIES Edward Glyn.

DAVIES Gwilym Ednyfed Hudson: BA (Wales) MA (Oxon). Labour MP Conway 1966-70, Caerphilly 1979-83. Joined SDP 1981, SDP Basingstoke 1983. **Mr. Ednyfed Hudson Davies:** Born Llanelli 12 December 1929, s of Revd E.

Curig Davies, Welsh Independent Minister (General Secretary, Union of Welsh Independents) & Enid Hughes. Married Amanda, d of Peter & Elsa Barker-Mill, 2d. Educated Friars School, Bangor, Dynevor Grammar School, Swansea, University of Wales, Swansea (1st Philosophy, 2a, Welsh), Balliol College, Oxford (2a PPE). President: University of Wales: Branch, Student Christian Movement Branch 1948-49, Student Representative Council 1951-52. Lecturer, Extra-Mural Studies, University of Wales, Aberystwyth 1957-61. Lecturer in Political Thought, Welsh College of Advanced Technology 1961-66. BBC broadcaster on current affairs & motoring 1962-66. BBC programme presenter 1970-76. Barrister, Grays Inn 1975. Chair: Wales Tourist Board 1976. Chair: Lincolnshire FM plc. 1991-. Deputy Chair: Ocean Sound Radio 1989- (Director 1986). Director: Southern Radio 1988-, New Forest Nineteenth Century Trust, New Forest Insudtrail Assn Ltd. Member: TGWU, AUT, Member, Select Cttee: Energy 1980-83. Secretary, All Party Tourism Cttee 1979-83. Languages: Welsh, English.

DAVIES Gwilym Prys – see PRYS-DAVIES G.

DAVIES Gwilym Elfed, Baron Davies of Pendyrus 1974: Labour MP: Rhondda East 1959-Feb1974. **Mr. Elfed Davies:** Born Tylorstown, 19 October, 1913, s of David Davies, coal miner. Married 1940, Gwyneth, d of Daniel Rees, 3c. Educated Tylorstown Elementary School. Miner, Tylorstown Colliery 1928-59. Joined SWMF 1929, Lodge Chair, 1934-40, Treasurer 1940-54. Chair: Aberdare & Rhondda District, NUM 1958-59. Joined Labour Party 1929. Executive Member, Rhondda East CLP & Rhondda Borough Labour Party. Joined CWS 1940. Member, St. Johns Ambulance Brigade 1926-46. Glamorgan CC 1954-59. Secretary, Miners' Parliamentary Group 1964. Chair: Welsh Parliamentary Party 1968-69. PPS 1964-68. President: Tylorstown RFC, Pendyrus Male Voice Choir. Of Tylorstown, Rhondda. Died 28 April 1992.

DAVIES Gwynant Huw: Liberal Democrat, Mid & West List, 1999. **Mr. Gwynant Davies:** Asst. Vice-Chair: Montgomeryshire Liberal Democrats. Chair: Machynlleth Liberal Democrats. Of Cwm Llinau, Machynlleth.

DAVIES Henry: OBE 1920. Liberal: Newport 1929. **Captain Henry Davies:** Born Treforest 1860, s of a railway worker. Congregationalist. Married Elizabeth, 3s 2d. Educated University of Wales, Cardiff. Teacher, Head-teacher 1881-92, Lecturer in Mining 1892-1904, Organiser, Treforest Mining Institute 1904-05, Director of Mining Education 1905-26. Army 1915-19: RWF. & Labour Corps, Hon. Major. Cardiff CC 1919,

1926, Member, Merthyr Tydfil School Board & Board of Guardians. Of Cardiff. Estate £1,565. Died 26 October 1930.

DAVIES Henry James Lloyd – see LLOYD DAVIES H. J.

DAVIES Henri Lloyd – see LLOYD DAVIES H.

DAVIES Henry Victor: AIMI. AIEI. Plaid Cymru: Rhondda West 1964, 1966, B/E 1967, 1970. **Mr. Vic Davies**: Born Ystrad-Rhondda, March 1917. Methodist lay preacher. Married Irene (of Yorkshire) 3c. Educated Bodringallt Primary School, Tonypandy Grammar School, Rhondda Technical College, Glamorgan College of Technology. Motor engineering apprentice. Motor Engineer. RAF 1939-45 (three years in Canada). AEU Shop Steward & Branch Official. Engineering Inspector of Factories. Lecturer in Engineering, Pontypridd College of Further Education. Member, CND, UNA Welsh Council. President, Rhondda Cttee. Plaid Cymru, Contested Rhondda BC elections. Spent 3 years in Canada & USA. Languages: Welsh, English. Of Treorchy, Rhondda.

DAVIES Ifor: JP (Glam). MIM. Labour MP: Gower, 1949-. **Mr. Ifor Davies:** Born 9 June 1910, s of Jeffrey Davies. Welsh Independent lay preacher & church secretary. Married 1950, Doreen, d of William Griffiths. Educated Gowerton Grammar School, Swansea Technical College, Ruskin College, Oxford. Accountant, I. Rowland Jones, Ltd. 1931-39, Personnel Officer: ICI 1942-47, Aluminium Wire & Cable Co 1948-59. Official, Statistics Dept. Ministry of Labour 1947-49. Joined Labour Party 1928, Secretary, Gower CLP.1948 Agent. Chair: Welsh Regional Council of Labour, President, West Wales Federation, Labour League of Youth 1935. Member: CAWU, Co-operative Party, Fabian Society, WEA Welsh Executive. Swansea BC, Glamorgan CC. Opposition Whip 1961-64, Lord Commissioner 1964-66, Under-Secretary, Wales 1966-69. Languages: Welsh, English. Of Three Crosses. Died 6 May 1982.

DAVIES Ithel: BA (Wales) 1924. Labour: University of Wales 1935, Joined Plaid Cymru, 1940, Welsh Republican Movement: Ogmore 1950. **Mr. Ithel Davies:** Born Llangynnog 1894, s of Benjamin & Ann Davies. Married 1925, Gwyneth, d of Revd R. E. Davies, Menai Bridge. Educated Clynnog Grammar School, University of Wales, Bangor. Imprisoned as CO 1915-19, beaten for four days, suffered broken nose. Solicitor, Barrister Inner Temple, 1937. Labour candidate, Swansea BC. Joined Plaid Cymru and left in 1949 to be a founder member of the Welsh Republican Movement. Of Waunfawr 1976-.

Languages: Welsh, English. Died 9 September 1989. Further Reading: *Harri Webb, No Half-Way House, Selected Political Journalism.*

DAVIES James Kitchener: BA (Wales) 1925. Plaid Cymru: Rhondda East 1945, Rhondda West 1950, 1951. **Mr. Kitchener Davies:** Born Blaencaron 16 June 1902, s of Thomas Davies, Garw Valley miner and Blaencaron smallholder, & Martha Davies (Died 1909). Given name *Kitchener* at grammar school to differentiate him from another boy. Presbyterian Church of Wales lay preacher. Married Mair I Rees, Ffosyffin, Tregaron (teacher) 3d (qv Manon Rhys). Educated Tregaron County Grammar School, University of Wales, Aberystwyth (1st Welsh). Pupil-teacher, Blaengwynfi 1921-22. Teacher (Welsh) Pentre Secondary Grammar School from 1926. Dramatist, poet and broadcaster. Hon. Member, Gorsedd 1945. Member: Cambrian Combine United Front, Plaid Cymru Executive, Welsh Drama Council, Arts Council Drama Cttee (Wales). Languages: Welsh, English. Of Porth, Rhondda. Died 25 August 1952. *Books Kitchener Davies: Cwm Glo, Susannah, Meini Gwagedd (dramas), Y Tri Dyn Dieithr, Dies Irae, Miss Blodeuwedd, Swn y Gwynt sy'n Chwythu. Further Reading: Mair I. Davies (ed) Gwaith Kitchener Davies, Gwasg Gomer 1980; Ioan Williams, Kitchener Davies 1985; D. Ben Rees, Cymry Adnabyddus; Manon Rhys & M. Wynn Thomas (edit) James Kitchener Davies, Detholiad o'i Waith 2002; M. Wynn Thomas, Keeping the Rhondda for Wales, Cymmrodorion Transactions 1999; M. Wynn Thomas, James Kitchener Davies 2002.*

DAVIES Janet Marion: BA (Wales) BA (Open). Plaid Cymru: Pontypridd 1983, Brecon & Radnor B/E 1985, AM South/West List 1999- **Mrs. Janet Davies:** Born Cardiff, 28 May 1939, d of David Rees & Jean Wardlaw Rees. Married 1965 Basil Peter Ridley Davies (Died Dec. 2000) 1s 1d. Educated Howells School, Llandaff, Trinity College, Carmarthen (mature student, Rural Environmental Studies) Open University. Plaid Cymru: Director of Elections, Senior Vice Chair. Llanharry ComC 1977-, Chair: 1980-81. Taf-Ely BC Council Leader. Member: CND Cymru. Chair: Assembly Public Accounts Cttee 1999, Audit Cttee 2000. Shadow Environment, Transport & Planning Minister March 2002. Hobbies: Gardening, Sailing. Of Llanharry.

DAVIES Jennie Eirian: BA MA (Wales). Plaid Cymru, Carmarthen 1955 B/E 1956. **Mrs. Jennie Eirian Davies:** Born Pencader February 1925, d of Howells, farmer. Presbyterian Church of Wales. Married Revd Eirian Davies (died 1998). Educated Carmarthen Girls' Grammar School; University of Wales, Aberystwyth (1st Welsh). Teacher. Lecturer, Cartrefle Training College, Wrexham. Editor, *Y Faner*. Chair, Plaid Cymru

Women's' Cttee. President, Merched y Wawr. Languages: Welsh, English. Died May 1982. *Further Reading: Cyfrol Coffa Jennie Eirian Davies, 1983.*

DAVIES Joan: Liberal/Alliance, South Wales Euro 1984. **Mrs. Joan Davies:** Of Surrey.

DAVIES Jocelyn Ann: Plaid Cymru: Islwyn B/E 1995, AM South/East List. **Mrs. Jocelyn Davies:** Born Usk, 18 June 1959, d of Thomas Edward (Ted) Davies & [Caroline Lilian] Marjorie Smith. Married Mike Davies, 3c. Educated Newbridge Grammar School, Crosskeys College, Law student at Manchester College, Oxford at time of election. Local Government Officer, Islwyn & Newport 1977-80; student 1995. Schools Inspector. Campaigner, British Dyslexia Assn. Member, Plaid Cymru Executive. Islwyn BC 1987-91. School Governor. Shadow Minister, Planning, Environment & Transport 2000-02, Business manager & Chief Whip March 2002. Interests: Constitutional Affairs, Special Needs Education, Ethnic Minority Issues, Equal Opportunities. Hobbies: Gym, Workout, Watching People. Of Newbridge, Gwent.

DAVIES John Berkeley: BA PGCE (Wales). Independent Green/Save World Climate, Ceredigion B/E 2000, Independent Environmentalist, Kensington & Chelsea B/E 1999. **Mr. John Berkeley Davies:** Born Oxted, Surrey, 6 August 1944, s of William Morgan Davies, pharmaceutical chemist, & Elsie Jean Davies, dispenser & housewife. Church of England. Educated St. Martin's Primary School, Hereford; Hereford High School; University of Wales, Cardiff (History & English). London Teacher (retired). Friends of the Earth Volunteer. Campaigner of stop global warming. Interests: Committed Socialist, Global Warming, GM Foods, Economics of Railways. Green Party disassociated itself from his campaign. Languages: English, a little French. Of London. *I believe the world could face ecological catastrophe and humanity will be wiped out by global warming if we do not drastically reduce greenhouse gas emissions. (Questionnaire 2003).*

DAVIES John Bowen: KC 1926 MA LlB (Cantab) JP (Cards 1915 Glam Mon/Brecs 1936). Conservative: Caernarfon Boroughs 1929. **Mr. J. Bowen Davies:** Born Llandysul 1st February 1876, s of Henry Harries Davies, surgeon & Elizabeth Rose, d of John Jones of Maesycrugiau (cousin of Sir Courtenay Mansel). Anglican. Married 1918, Alice, d of Alderman D. L. Jones DL of Derlwyn, 1s. Educated Epsom College, Downing College, Cambridge. Barrister, Middle Temple 1898, Bencher 1930, Autumn Reader 1942. Stipendary Magistrate, Merthyr Tydfil 1930, Recorder of Merthyr Tydfil 1933-36, Vice-Chair: Glamorgan

Quarter Sessions 1936-, Army 1914-18, Captain. Lay Rector of St. Peter's, Carmarthen, Member: St. David's Diocesan Conference, Carmarthenshire Agricultural Cttee, Glamorgan Joint Standing Cttee. Of Derlwyn, nr. Carmarthen. Died 12 October 1943.

DAVIES John Cledwyn: JP (Denbs) MA (National) Liberal: Denbigh 1935, MP: 1922-23. **Mr. J Cledwyn Davies:** Born 1869, labourer's son, orphaned at 14. Nonconformist. Married Louisa, 2d. Teacher. Headmaster, Holywell Grammar School, Director of Education for Denbighshire 1922, 1923-39. Called to the Bar by the Middle Temple. Denbighshire CC Alderman. Member Welsh Joint Education Cttee. Languages: Welsh, English. Died 31 December 1952.

DAVIES John Eifion Brynmor: Conservative: Caernarfon 1951. **Mr. Brynmor Davies:** Born Colwyn Bay, July 1907. Educated Abergele Grammar School; Colwyn Bay Grammar School; Nottingham University. Farmer. Member: Caernarfonshire County Agricultural Executive Cttee, NFU Council, Served on Ministry of Agriculture cttees & Ministry of National Insurance tribunals. Languages: Welsh, English. Of Colwyn Bay.

DAVIES John Hamlyn: BSc 1972 PhD (London). Plaid Cymru: Brecon & Radnor 1987. **Dr. John Davies:** Born Cardiff 3 May 1944. Married Sue, 2c. Educated Allenbank Secondary School, Cardiff; LLandaff Technical College; London University. Geologist. Unemployed at time of election. Tutor, visiting American groups & Tourist Information Officer at Welsh Bookshop, Llanwrtyd.

DAVIES John Hubert: MA (Oxon). Conservative: Caerphilly 1955, Brecon & Radnor 1959. **Mr. John Davies:** Born Merthyr Tydfil, 1914, s of a company director. Educated Merthyr Tydfil Grammar School, Wadham College, Oxford, Treasurer, Oxford Union. President, Chatham Club. Barrister, Middle Temple 1935. RAMC 1939-45. Member: Bow Group, NFU.

DAVIES John Leigh: Communist: Rhondda West 1931. **Mr. Jack Davies:** Born Rhondda, 1882, one of 11 children. Married 1907 Martha (Died 1997). Started work 1893. Miner 1898-. Chair: Llwynypia Lodge, SWMF, Cambrian Combine Workmen's Cttee, Executive SWMF 1935. Unemployed at time of election. Miners' Agent 1935. Founder member, Rhondda Communist Party 1921. Rhondda UDC -1947. Languages: Welsh, English. Of Llwynypia, Rhondda.

DAVIES John Morgan: BSc 1939 MSc (Wales). Liberal, Carmarthen B/E 1957. Short-listed, Cardigan 1945. **Mr. Morgan Davies:** Born Pont-siân 1917, s of Alderman Griffith Davies. Welsh Independent. Married. Educated St. David's College School, Lampeter; University of Wales, Aberystwyth (1st Agro-Economics). Lecturer, King's College, Durham 1939-44. Principal, Cumberland and Westmorland College of Agriculture 1947-55. Chief Livestock Officer, Fatstock Marketing Corporation 1955. Resigned to contest the by-election. Director, Welsh Agricultural Organisation Society 1958-59. Director, Davies Agricultural Services Ltd. Carmarthen Conservative Assn decided not to oppose Davies. Pro Suez Operation, Anti Welsh Home Rule.

DAVIES John Richard Thomas: Liberal Democrat, Ceredigion 2003. **Mr. John Davies:** Born Aberystwyth 5 June 1960, s of Richard Islwyn Davies & Megan Hefina Davies, farmers. Methodist. Married 1988 Siân Vaughan Evans Davies, 3s 2d. Educated Ysgol Gymraeg Aberystwyth; Ysgol Gyfun Penweddig; Gelli Aur Agricultural College (National Certificate in Agriculture & Farm Management). NFU Policy Adviser 1998-2001. Centre Manager, Food Centre Wales 2001-. Vice-Chair: Welsh Objective 1 Agriculture-Food Forum. Member: Welsh Organisation Food Strategic Group; Welsh Red Meat Strategic Group. Ceredigion CC. Interests: Rural Affairs, Economic Development. Hobbies: Watching Rugby, Current Affairs. Languages: Welsh, English. Of Rhydfelin, Aberystwyth.

DAVIES John Robert: Labour: Ceredigion & North Pembs 1987, 1992. **Mr. John Davies:** Born 23 June 1937. Married Ceri 3c. Educated Gwendraeth Grammar School, St. Luke's College, Exeter. Teacher (Geography) at Lampeter Secondary School. Walsall TC 1970-74. Member: NUT, Cymdeithas Tai Cymru, CND, Executive, Campaign for a Welsh Assembly. Languages: Welsh, English.

DAVIES John Sellick: MBE JP. New Party: Merthyr 1931, Liberal: Evesham 1929. **Major Sellick Davies:** Born Darwen, Lancs. Baptist lay pastor. Educated Taunton School, Brighton Grove College, Manchester University. Accountant. Lecturer, Cardiff Technical College. Executive Member, Welsh National Liberal Federation. Received largest share of vote for a New Party candidate anywhere in UK. Of Cardiff.

DAVIES John Tudor: MA (Oxon). Labour: Montgomery B/E 1962. **Mr. Tudor Davies:** Born Bangor 1916, s of a Presbyterian minister. Married Anwen, sister of novelist Cledwyn Hughes. Educated Oxford University. Teacher 9 years, Further Education Officer for Merioneth, Columnist, *Cambrian News*. Chair: Merioneth CLP. Languages: Welsh, English. Died 7 January 1989.

DAVIES Karl – see DAVIES Robert K.

DAVIES Keith – see DAVIES David Keith.

Davies: Kenneth Wynne: Communist, North List 1999. **Mr. Kenneth Davies:** Born Flint 7 October 1934, s of Thomas Edward Davies, driver, & Annie Blanch Kirby, telephonist. Atheist. Married 1965, Beryl Davies, 2d. Educated Secondary School. Scaffolder. Hobbies: Music, Reading. Of Flint.

DAVIES Lloyd H. – see HAVARD DAVIES Lloyd.

DAVIES Mary: BA (Open) 1992. Conservative, Cardiff South & Penarth & South/Central List 1999. **Mrs. Mary Davies:** Born Swansea 1950. Educated St. Winifrede's Convent, Trinity College, Carmarthen, Open University (Fine Arts). Supply Teacher for children with special needs and remedial support (ex-primary and secondary). Joined Swansea YCs 1968. Vice-Chair, Llanelli Conservative Assn. 1997, Chair 1998. Chair, Co-ordinating Cttee for West Wales Local Govt. 1998. Vice-President, National Society of Conservative and Unionist Agents, Wales Branch. Member: Conservative National Education Society, Conservative Christian Animal Welfare Group, Prince Philip Hospital League of Friends, Raven Trust for the Homeless, Newport. Treasurer, Childline, Llanelli. Hobbies: Church activities, Oil painting, Art history, Tennis, Swimming. Of Llanelli.

DAVIES Mary Elizabeth: Conservative: Aberavon & South West List 1999. **Mrs. Mary Davies:** Born Grangetown, Cardiff 25 May 1949, d of William George Watchorn, shop proprietor, & Gertrude Ivy Mabel Jarvis. Church in Wales. Married, widowed. Educated Grangetown Secondary Modern School, Cardiff; Cleves Secretarial College, Cardiff. Cardiff stockbroker, 20 years. Farmer, upland Carmarthenshire, with late husband. Complementary Medical Practitioner & Antiques Dealer. Ex-Supervisor of assistant receptionists at Lyddon Co. Stockbrokers, Cardiff, PA to company director. Vice-Chair: Crymych Conservatives Branch, Member, Executive, Preseli Conservative Assn. Chair: Welsh Conservative Women for Ian Duncan Smith 2001. Interests: Health, Social Care, Environment, Europe. Hobbies: Music, Walking, Cinema, Theatre, Visiting places of historical interest. Languages: Welsh learner, English. Of Newcastle Emlyn.

DAVIES Owen Glyndwr: MBE TD. National Conservative: Ogmore 1945. **Major Glyn Davies:** Born Bridgend, s of Idris Davies, builder and contractor. Married Sheila, d of W. D. Thomas, postmaster, Brynmenyn. Educated Cowbridge Grammar School. Solicitor, Town Clerk of Cowbridge, 53rd Welsh Division 1939-45. Bridgend UDC at 22, Chairman 1939.

DAVIES Paul Malcolm: Labour, Montgomery 2001. **Mr. Paul Davies:** Born Llanelli 1969, s of miner/coal merchant. Assistant District Nurse, Social Worker for the Homeless at Swansea. School Governor. Chair: Carmarthenshire County Labour Party. Member: Red Cross, GMB. Languages: Welsh, English. Of Llanelli.

DAVIES Paul Windsor: Conservative, Ceredigion, B/E 2000, 200, Preseli 2003. **Mr. Paul Davies:** Born Carmarthen 2 January 1969, s of Timothy Iorwerth Davies & Mary Elizabeth Jones, farmers. Anglican. Married 2003, Margaret Julie Wheeler, management accounts officer. Educated Tregroes Primary School; Llandysul Grammar School; Newcastle Emlyn Comprehensive School. Joined Lloyds Bank 1987. Business Banking Manager, Lloyds TSB Cardigan. Chair, Ceredigion Young Conservatives 1997. Treasurer, Ceredigion Conservative Assn 1997, Deputy Chair 1999. Agent 1997, 1999. Deputy Chair: Mid & West Wales Area Conservative Council 2001-. Treasurer: St. Ffraed's Church, Tregroes, Pontsian Memorial Playground Cttee. Member: Prengwyn & District Sheepdog Trials Cttee. Trustee: Pontsian Memorial Hall. Election Agent 1997, 1999. Llandysul TC (Pontsian) 2000-03. Interests: Business, Rural Economy. Hobbies: Playing rugby & snooker, Reading, Historical attractions. Languages: Welsh, English. Of Llandysul.

DAVIES Raymond T: Labour: Cardiff Central 1983. **Mr. Ray Davies: Born** Cardiff, 9 January 1930, s of George Llewelyn Davies, miner, & Winifred Maud Davies, housewife. 5s 1d. Educated Elementary School; Ruskin College, Oxford. Miner, Steelworker. TU branch secretary. Labour Party ward secretary. Mid-Glam CC. Caerphilly CBC. Not re-adopted by ward Labour Party, Nov. 2003. Sought nomination against Neil Kinnock at Islwyn. Member: Caerphilly Male Choir. Campaigner for Palestinian rights (human shield), against arms trade etc. Interests: International Affairs, Anti Racism, Peace. Hobbies: Choirs. Languages: Welsh, English. Of Bedwas.

DAVIES Rhodri Vaughan: LlB (Wales). Plaid Cymru: Conwy 1987, 1992, 1997. **Mr. Rhodri Davies:** Born Llanfairfechan, 25 November 1947. Married 2c. Educated Friars School, Bangor, University of Wales, Aberystwyth, Guildford College of Law. Solicitor 1971-2003 (Practised at Bangor, then Beaconsfield). Lecturer in Local Government Law, Bristol Polytechnic 1971-76. Ynys Môn BC 1976-, BC. School Governor. Member: National Union of Local Government Secretaries. Languages: Welsh, English.

DAVIES Richard: JP (Caerns. Anglesey 1863) DL 1876. (Anglesey). Liberal: Caernarfon District 1852, MP: Anglesey 1868-86. **Mr. Richard Davies:** Born Llangefni 1818, s of Rhisiart Dafydd, shopkeeper & Anne Jones. Calvinistic Methodist Elder. Married 1885, Anne, d of Revd Henry Rees of Liverpool, 5c. Educated Llangefni National School. Shipowner, shipbuilder & Timber Merchant. 1st Nonconformist JP. High Sheriff of Anglesey 1858, Lord Lieutenant of Anglesey 1884-, Retired from Parliament because of his opposition to Irish Home Rule, declined nomination as a Liberal Unionist but supported Morgan Lloyd 1892, Nicknamed '*Lleugwr (Starver)*' because of his treatment of his sailors. Estate of 3000 acres in Anglesey. Estate £294,446. Languages: Welsh, English. Died Treborth, 27 October 1896. Further Reading: *The Political Career of Richard Davies, Anglesey Antiquarian, Social & Field Club 1979*.

DAVIES Richard Bees: BA (Cantab) MSc (Birmingham) PhD (Bristol). Plaid Cymru: Cardiff South-East 1970, Pembroke Feb. & Oct. 1974. **Mr. Richard Davies:** Born September 1946, s of Dr. D. J. Davies, MOH Pembrokeshire. Early days at Port Talbot & Llanelli. Married 3c. Educated Milford Haven Grammar School; Sidney Sussex College, Cambridge (Mechanical Science); Birmingham University (Transportation & Traffic Planning). Assistant Lecturer (studying effects of new roads), Bristol University 1972, Lecturer in Town Planning, University of Wales Institute of Science & Technology, Cardiff 1972. Professor of Statistics 1990-2003, Pro-Vice-Chancellor, Lancaster University 1998-2003. Vice-Chancellor, University of Wales, Swansea, 2003-. Plaid Cymru spokesman on communications. Languages: Learned Welsh, English. Of Swansea (2003).

DAVIES Robert Karl: BA 1984 MA 1989 PhD. (Wales). Plaid Cymru: Clwyd NW 1987. **Dr. Karl Davies:** Born St. Asaph 26 July 1963, s of R. Keith Davies & Dilys Catherine Hughes. Educated Ysgol St. Elford, Abergele, Ysgol Glan Clwyd, St. Asaph, University of Wales, Aberystwyth (History & Welsh History), President, Welsh Students Union. Director of Research, Plaid Cymru 1985-89, BBC Wales Radio Producer 1989-90, Parliamentary Editor 1990-93. Editor, *Tafod y Ddraig* 1983-86. Chair: Welsh Language Society 1984-85. Chief Executive, Plaid Cymru 1993-2002. Wales Director, National Assn of Head Teachers 2002-. Member, Gorsedd of Bards 2003. Hobbies: Music, Travel, Good food. Languages: Welsh, English, Italian. Of Cardiff.

DAVIES Ronald: PC 1997. Labour MP Caerphilly 1983-2001, AM Caerphilly 1999-2003; Forward Wales Party, Wales Euro 2004. **Rt. Hon.**

Ron Davies.

Ron Davies: Born Machen 6 August 1946, s of Francis Ronald Davies, fitter & Beryl Richards. Married (1) 1971 Anne (nurse) d of Alan & Jean Williams (divorced 1979) (2) 1981, Christine Elizabeth Rees (local government officer & Mid Glam CC) 1d (divorced 2000), (3) 2002 Lynne Hughes 1c. Educated Basseleg Grammar School, Portsmouth Polytechnic, University of Wales, Cardiff. Teacher (Geology) 1968-70; WEA Tutor-Organiser 1970-74; Further Education Adviser, Mid-Glam. LEA 1974-83. Bedwas & Machen UDC [Chair 1970], Rhymney Valley DC 1969-84, Deputy Leader. Labour Whip 1985-87, Labour Spokesman: Food, Agriculture & Rural Affairs 1987-93, Shadow Welsh Secretary 1993-97, Elected to Shadow Cabinet 1992, Stood for Chief Whip 1988, Secretary of State for Wales 1997-98. Elected Welsh Labour Leader Sept.1998. Resigned: as Secretary of State 27/10/1998, as Welsh Labour Leader 29/10/1998. Announced resignation from Labour Party 25 January 2004. Hon. Member Gorsedd 1998. Director, Valleys Racial Equality Council 2003. Forward Wales, Wales Euro 2004. Of Machen.

DAVIES Ronald Albert: Liberal Democrat, Wrexham 2001. **Mr. Ron Davies:** Born Wrexham 10 October 1937. Married Hilda. 3c. Educated Grove Park Grammar School, Wrexham, Wrexham Technical College, Liverpool College of Building. Denbighshire Pupil Architect. Birkenhead Architectural Assistant. Assistant Architect, Cheshire CC. Maintenance Development Officer. Property Information Manager. Wrexham Maelor BC 1987-95. Wrexham CBC 1995-, Mayor 1999-2000. Of Wrexham.

DAVIES Ronald George: National Front: Pontypridd 1979. **Mr. Ronald Davies:** Born 1928. Married 7c. Army. Self-employed Decorator. West Wales Organiser, National Front. Of Peniel, Carmarthen.

DAVIES Ruth Gwendoline: LlB (East Anglia). Pro-Life Alliance, Montgomery 2001; Mid & West List 2003. **Miss Ruth Davies:** Born London, 5 November 1969, d of Jonathan Hugh Davies & Mary Veronica Davies. Roman Catholic. Educated: Dragon School, Oxford, St. Mary's School, Ascot, University of East Anglia, Bar School, London. Barrister 1992. Worked in France and Germany but Montgomeryshire has always been 'home'. Produced Gregynog Passion Play from 1996. Joined Pro-Life Alliance 1997, works at Central Office. Hobbies: Singing. Languages: English, French. Of London.

DAVIES: Stephen Owen: JP (Merthyr) BA (Wales) 1913. Labour MP: Merthyr B/E 1934-Independent Labour 1970-. **Mr. S. O. Davies:** Born Abercwmboi 8 November 1886, s of Thomas Davies, farm labourer & miner & columnist (excommunicated from Soar, Mountain Ash 1904, Died 1909), & Esther Owen, shop assistant. Marxist. Married (1) 1919 Madge (Died 1932) 3d, (2) 1934, Sephora Davies, Gwauncaegurwen teacher, 2s. Educated Elementary Schools, Miner 1898, evening classes (mining engineering). Gwynfryn Academy, Ammanford, University of Wales, Cardiff 1908, as Memorial College, Brecon, student much influenced by theology of R. J. Campbell, College set up sub-cttee to enquire into his theology and ended its sponsorship in 1910. ILP candidate, Cardiff Board of Guardians, when student. Miner at Tumble 1913. Adopted as ILP candidate for Llanelli during war. Checkweighman 1913, Miners' Agent 1918-34, Chief Organiser & Legal Adviser, SWMF, Vice-President, SWMF 1924-34, Executive, MFGB 1924-34, Merthyr Tydfil BC 1931, Alderman, Mayor 1945-46. Governor, National Museum, National Library, University of Wales. Member, Parliament for Wales Campaign. Labour Whip withdrawn 1961. Stood as Independent Labour when refused re-adoption by Merthyr Labour Party on the grounds of age. Offered the freedom of the borough 1970 but refused it saying that his re-election was sufficient Honour from the people. Languages: Welsh, English. Died 25 February 1972. *Further Reading: Robert Griffiths, S. O. Davies: A Socialist Faith. 1983; D. Ben Rees, Cymry Adnabyddus 1952-1972.*

DAVIES: Thomas: JP (Swansea). Liberal Unionist: East Carmarthenshire 1892. **Captain, Revd Thomas Davies:** Born St. Davids 1825. Calvinistic Methodist. Married (1) (2) Jane, 6c. Ship's Captain until 1860. Shipping Broker. Coal Merchant (1881). Ordained as Calvinistic Methodist Minister 1870. Fiery Temperance Orator. Swansea BC 1872-, Alderman, Chair: Works & Sanitary Cttees, Mayor 1881. Member Swansea Harbour Trust. Nautical Assessor, Board of Trade. Member, British Sailors Society. Chairman, Swansea Bench, 1881-82. Of Llansamlet, Swansea, when candidate. Saw no future for steam ships. Languages: Welsh, English. Died Mumbles, 16 January 1905. *Further Reading:* Ivor Thomas Rees, 'Captain Thomas Davies JP', *Minerva (Royal Institution of South Wales), Vol. XII, 2004, 75-80*; Ivor Thomas Rees, 'A Note on Captain Thomas Davies JP (1825-1905), *The Journal of Welsh Religious History, New Series, Volume 4: 2004, 102-108.*

DAVIES T. Alun R: Plaid Cymru, Blaenau Gwent 1992, Cynon Valley 1997. **Mr. Alun Davies:** Born 12 February 1964. Educated Tredegar Comprehensive School, University of Wales, Aberystwyth. Conservationist, with wildlife charity. Public Affairs Manager, Oxfam. Member: Court of the University of Wales.

DAVIES Thomas M: BA (Wales). Celtic Alliance, Assembly, Cardiff West 1999. **Mr. Tom Davies:** Born Pontypridd, 10 April 1941, s of Jack Davies, bricklayer, & Phyllis Ford. Church of England. Married 1966, Elizabeth Meirfon Davies, 3s. Educated University of Wales, Cardiff (Philosophy; state scholar, President of Debates). Worked as steward on Campbell's paddle steamers, merchant seaman, sailing to Australia & Africa. 1st graduate to be sent to Indonesia as VSO. New York East Side Social Worker. Journalist, *Western Mail, Sunday Times (Atticus) & Observer (Pendennis,* 2 years). Full time writer since 1978. Languages: English. Campaigned for a Welsh national publishing house, a fully funded fllm-studio & a national theatre. Of Penarth. *Books –* 15 *including* Novels: *One Winter of the Holy Spirit, Black Sunlight, I Conker, Fire in the Bay. Other Books: Merlyn the Magician, Pacific Coast Highway, Stained Glass Hours, Landscapes of Glory, The Celtic Heart, Road to the Stars, The Visions of Caradoc.*

DAVIES Tudor – see DAVIES John T.

DAVIES Vic – see DAVIES Henry Victor.

DAVIES William: Kt 1893 JP DL (Pembs). Liberal: Pembrokeshire 1876, MP 1880-92. **Sir William Davies:** Born August 1821, s of Thomas Davies, Haverfordwest. Baptist, became Congregationalist. Married (1) 1859, Martha Rees, d of Thomas Morgan of Haverfordwest, 7s 1d (2) Mary Elizabeth Morgan 1d. Solicitor at Haverfordwest 1848. Immense interests in Transatlantic Steam Coal Co. Ltd. Haverfordwest BC. 30 years, Alderman, 1858-83, Mayor, 2 years. Vice-President, Pembroke & Haverfordwest Infirmary. Conserva-

tive Agent, Haverfordwest, Fishguard & Narberth Boroughs, 1851. Of Scoveston & London. Died 23 November 1895.

DAVIES William Edmund Vincent John: BSc PhD (Wales). Independent, Carmarthen West & South Pembs. 1999. **Dr. Edmund Davies:** Born 1960. Married 1980 Brenda Howells, 2d. Educated St. Clears National School, Whitland Grammar School, University of Wales, Swansea (Maths). Senior Resident Affiliate CEGB. Senior Scientific Affiliate British Industrial & Scientific Research Assn 1966-7. Lecturer, Afan tertiary College 1971, retired. Farmer. Carmarthenshire CC/DC 1972-99. Dyfed CC 1974 retired. Chair, 1993. Mayor of St. Clears, 1975-776, 1984-86. Hobbies: Helping people in the community, Bridge, Rugby, Cricket, Soccer, Stock markets. Of St. Clears. *A disillusioned Tory (Carmarthen Journal 16/4/1999).*

DAVIES William Lewis: JP. (Pembs). Independent: Pembroke 1955 (with the backing of Conservative & Liberal Assns). **Mr. Lewis Davies:** Born North Pembrokeshire. Married 1927. Farmer & Managing Director, of a firm of steel specialists at Pembroke Dock which he founded 1947 after establishing factories in Canada & USA. Pembrokeshire CC 1945-, Chair: 1953. President, South Wales British Friesians Breeders Club. Pro Secretary of State for Wales. Languages: Welsh, English. Of Scoveston & London.

DAVIES William Rees Morgan: Kt 1913 KC Hon.g Kong 1908 JP (Haverfordwest & Pembroke) DL (Pembs) BA 1865. Liberal MP: Pembrokeshire 1892-98. **Sir William Rees Davies:** Born Haverfordwest 11 May 1863, s of Sir William Davies, MP (q.v.) & Martha Rees, d of Thomas Morgan of Haverfordwest. Educated Eton, Trinity Hall, Cambridge. Married (1) 1898, Florence Beatrice, (Died 1910) d of John Birkett of Kendal, (2) 1913, Ellen Kathleen, d of W. Blennerhasset Atthill, of Faversham, 1s (William Rees-Davies MP). Barrister, Inner Temple 1887. Asst Secretary (unpaid) to Sir William Harcourt MP1893. Attorney General, Bahamas 1898-1902, King's Advocate, Cyprus 1902-07, Attorney General, Hong Kong 1907-12, Chief Justice of Hong Kong 1912-24. Of Scoveston & London. Died 14 April 1939.

DAVIES William Thomas Pennar: BA Hon. DD 1987 (Wales) BLitt (Oxon) 1936 PhD (Yale) 1943. Plaid Cymru: Llanelli 1964, 1966. **Revd Dr. Pennar Davies:** Born Mountain Ash, 12 November, 1911, s of Joseph Davies, miner, & Edith Annie Moss. Added *Pennar* Congregationalist/ Welsh Independent. Married 1943, Rosemarie Wolff, German refugee, 5c, (q.v. son Meirion Pennar). Educated Mountain Ash Grammar

School 1922-29, University of Wales, Cardiff 1929-33 (1st Latin 1932, 1st English 1933), Balliol College, Oxford 1933-36, Commonwealth Fund Fellow, Yale University 1936-38, University of Wales Fellowship 1938-40, Mansfield College, Oxford 1940-43. Congregational Minister, Ordained, 1940: Minster Road Church, Cardiff 1940-46, Vice-Principal & Professor of Church History, Coleg Bala-Bangor 1946-50, Professor of Church History, Congregational Memorial College, Brecon & Swansea 1950-, Principal 1952-81. Warden, Guild of Graduates, University of Wales 1959-62, Dean of Theology 1967-70. Editor, *Welsh Nation*. National Eisteddfod Adjudicator, Crown Poem & Prose Medal. Chair: Executive, Swansea Council of Christians and Jews, President, Free Church Council of Wales, President, Union of Welsh Independents 1973-74. Pacifist, historian, author, writer, novelist, poet. Languages: Learned Welsh, English. Of Swansea. Died 29 December 1996. *Books: Pennar Davies: The Welsh Pattern 1945, Cinio'r Cythraul 1946, Naw Wfft 1957, Cudd fy Meiau 1957, Anadl o'r Uchelder 1958, Y Brenin Alltud 1974, Gwas y Gwaredwr 1991. Further Reading: Dewi Eurig Davies (ed) Cyfrol Deyrnged Pennar Davies 1981, Meic Stephens, Artists in Wales, Densil Morgan, Pennar Davies 2003.*

DAVIES Yvonne Marie: Plaid Cymru, South/ West List 1999. **Miss Yvonne Davies:** Student. Contested Swansea CC (Castle) 1999. Of Swansea.

DAVIES-EVANS Delme William Campbell: DSO 1919 TD JP DL (Carms). National Conservative: Carmarthen 1931. **Lieut-Colonel Delme Davies-Evans:** Born Highmead, Carmarthen, 25 April 1873, s of Herbert Davies-Evans, Lord Lieutenant of Carmarthenshire & Mary, d. of David Jones JP DL, Pantglas (MP Carmarthenshire 1852-68). Anglican. Married 1903, Gwladys Kathleen, d of Thomas Morris, Coomb, 4c. Educated Harrow. In the Colonies 1899-1903, Lloyds Bank 1903-30, Superintendent Manager, Carmarthenshire. Officer, Pembrokeshire Yeomanry, Lincolnshire & Worcestershire Regts 1914-18. Master of Penylan Hounds 1920-32. President, Carmarthenshire NFU 1921-22, Carmarthenshire County Commissioner, Boy Scouts 1921. Carmarthenshire CC 14 years. Of Penylan, Carms. Died 30 November 1950.

DAVIS Edward Garth Cheney: Referendum Party: Newport East 1997. **Mr. Garth Davis:** Born Newport, 1969. Married Samantha. General Manager, local printing group.

DAVIS Frederick Lewis: JP (Glam) BA LLB (Cantab). Liberal: Rhondda 1885. **Mr. Fred Davis:** Born Canton, Cardiff, 21 January 1863, s of Lewis Davis, Coal Owner (Died 1892). Wesleyan. Married 1886, H. B. d of Robert Smith, Brentham Park, Stirling, 1s. Educated Amersham Hall, Reading, Trinity College, Cambridge. Barrister (Inner Temple) 1886. Apprenticed in coal industry 3 years. Coalowner: Chair: & Managing Director: Ferndale Collieries Ltd.1888. Director: Barry Railway Co. Vale of Glamorgan Railway Co. Markham Steam Coal Co. Oakdale Naval Collieries Ltd. Low Temperature Carbonisation Ltd. North Exploration Ltd. Tredegar Iron & Coal Co. Chair: South Wales & Mon. Coalowners' Assn. at £2,000 per annum 1904. Owners' Representative on Coalfield Conciliation Board. Glamorgan CC 1888, 1889-95. High Sheriff of Glamorgan 1890. Adopted as Liberal candidate after his father withdrew because of pressure of business, defeated by William Abraham who stood as the successful Miners' Candidate, though their political aims and methods were similar. Estate £127,586. Died London, 17 May 1920.

DAWE Ronald: Plaid Cymru: Pembroke 1979. **Mr. Ron Dawe:** Born Ogmore Vale November 1936. Married 2c. Educated Nantymoel Secondary School. Miner 13 years. NUM. Lodge Cttee at 17. Heating & Ventilating Engineer. Joined Plaid Cymru 1953. Ogmore & Garw UDC. Of Haverfordwest, 1976.

DAWSON Robert Hulton: Conservative: Montgomery B/E 1962. **Mr. Robert Dawson:** Born Criggion, Mont. 1924, s of Captain W. H. H. Dawson, Married 3s. RAF Officer 1943-51, RAF staff. Farmer (2 extensive farms) of Criggion.

DAY Arthur Michael: BSc FCIPD MCMI. Liberal Democrat, Swansea West 2001, 2003. BScEcon DipPersMan FECert FCIPD MIMgtt. **Mr. Mike Day:** Born Pontypool 25 July 1953. Evangelical. Married 1977 Chris, 1s 1d. Educated Hereford Cathedral School, Gowerton Grammar School, UWIST. Swansea CC 1999, contested CC 1994, 1995. Personnel Manager, South Glam CC 1974-88, Swansea Institute of Higher Education 1988-2002 (Dean of Business School, Head of Marketing, Asst Dean of Business). Commercial Manager, Digital Technium, University of Wales, Swansea 2003-. Deacon, House Group Leader, Sunday School Teacher, Boys' Brigade Leader, Church Secretary, Project Manager. Chair, Trustees, St. Madoc Christian Youth Camp, Member, Council of Reference, Gweini. Chair, Sketty Primary School Governors, Governor, Olchfa Comprehensive School. Member, Liberal Democrat Welsh Executive. Of Sketty, Swansea.

DAY Simon James: Kt 1997 MA (Cantab). Conservative: Carmarthen 1966, B/E July 1966,

North Cornwall, 1970. **Sir Simon Day:** Born January 1935, s of Liberal candidate, Alderman John A. Day (estate of £340,000 in 1966) & Kathleen Hebditch, & brother of Liberal candidate, Bridget Trethewey). Married Hilary Maureen Greenslade Gomm, 2s. Educated Bedales School, South Devon Technical College, Emmanuel College, Cambridge (History). Royal Navy 1954-56. Farmer, Property Owner & Company Director: Non-Executive Director, South West Water 1989, Regional Director, Portman Building Society 1989-91, Director: Plymouth Sound Radio 1966-80, Plymouth Development Corporation 1993-, Chair: West of England Newspapers Group 1981-86, Lloyds Underwriter 1974, Devon CC 1964-, Whip 1981-89, Deputy Leader 1989, Leader 1991-93, Chair: Governor, Exeter University. Of Ivybridge, Devon.

DE COURCY John Frederick Manuel: FRGS. Conservative: Caerphilly 1945. **Major John de Courcy:** Born Ireland, 1901, s of W. Stephen de Courcy of Co. Galway (s of 8th Duc de Grantmesnil) & Minnie, (d of Frederick & Sophia Schafer-Andries, Scholl Kyburgh) directors of Hollinwood Mission, Oldham 1900-10. Married 1941, Norah, d of Dr. R. P. Beatty of Swindon. 1s 1d. Educated Christ's Hospital, Horsham. Welch Regt. 1939-45, Lieutenant 1940, Major 1941. Journalist & Company Director. Of Co. Meath & East Grinstead. Died 14 April 1950.

DE SILVA Nilmini Priyanga: Liberal Democrat, Vale of Glamorgan 2003; Wales Euro 2004. **Ms Nil de Silva:** Born Swindon 21 October 1973, d of Shantilal de Silva & Indranee Perera. Church of England. Partner, Julian Francis, 2s. Educated Churchfields School; New College, Swindon; University of Wales, Swansea (Ancient History & Civilisation & Welsh Language). Liaison Student, Advertising sales. Research Assistant, Roger Williams MP. Interests: Civil Liberties, Education, Economic Development, Rural Economy. Liberal Democrat, Wales Euro 2004. Hobbies: History, Literature, Swimming. Languages: Learned Welsh, English. Of London.

DE WILDE Alan Robin: QC 1993. Conservative: Merthyr Tydfil 1979. **Mr. Robin de Wilde:** Born 12 July, 1945, s of Captain Roderick Cedric de Wilde & Dorothea Elizabeth Mary Fenningworth. Married 1977, Patricia Theresa Beaucroft, 3s. Educated Dean Close School, Cheltenham, RAF College, Cranwell, Inns of Court Law School. RAF Officer, Barrister, Inner Temple 1971, Bencher 1996. Member: Bar Council 1985-90, 1998-99, 2002-. Fellow, Royal Society of Medicine. Member: Medico-Legal Society. Associate, American Bar Assn. Member: Assn of Trial Lawyers of America; British Neuroscience Assn. Chair: Professional Negligence Bar Assn 1995-97,

Hon. Vice-President 1998. Advocacy teacher trainer, Inner Temple. Chair, Ogden Cttee 2002. General Editor, *Facts and Figures*. Vice-Chair: Chelsea CPC.

DEACON Russell Martin: BA. PGCE. CEED. PhD. Liberal Democrat, South/East List 1999. **Dr. Russell Deacon:** Born Newbury, Berkshire, 11 February 1966, s of Gary Raymond Deacon, police superintendent, & Margaret Jean Smith, medical secretary. United Reformed Church. Married 1990 Tracey Elizabeth Deacon, population health specialist, 1d. Educated: Denefield School, Reading College, Aylesbury College, University of Glamorgan, University of Wales, Cardiff. Senior Lecturer in Government, UWIST. Treasurer, Caerphilly Liberal Democrats. Research Officer, Campaign for a Welsh Parliament. Liberal Democrat Representative: 'Yes for Wales Campaign Cttee. Van ComC (Group Leader). Interests: Supporting candidates from disadvantaged backgrounds. Hobbies: Gardening. Languages: Welsh, English, Limited French. Of Caerphilly. *Books: Devolved Great Britain, Sheffield Hallam Press, Governance of Wales 1964-69, Welsh Academic Press 2002.*

DEARE Susan Lesley: Socialist Labour, South/East List 1999; South/Central List 2003. **Ms Susan Deare:** Brought up in Newport area. BT employee 20 years. Member, POEU Retired carer of elderly relative. Member: CND; WILPF. Joined SLP 1997. Of Ponthir, Newport.

DEERE David Berkerolles Turberville: Conservative: Aberdare 1979. **Mr. David Deere:** Born 1945, s of Richard Payne Turberville Deere, estate agent, & Linda Enid Deere. Church in Wales. Educated St. John's School, Newton, Porthcawl. Estate Agent: partner in family Porthcawl firm of T. Elwood Deere & Son, auctioneers, surveyors, valuers, estate agents. Chair: Porthcawl YCs 1964, Bridgend Conservative Assn (2001). Deputy-Chair (Political) South Wales West Area, Conservative Party. President, Porthcawl Chamber of Trade 1975-76. Member: Mid-Glamorgan Health Authority. Vice-Chair, Iechyd Morgannwg Health Authority. Vice-Chair, Bridgend Local Health Board. Porthcawl UDC. Ogwr BC 1973-. Hobbies: Reading. Of Newton, Porthcawl.

DENNETT Christopher C: Communist: Merthyr Tydfil 1979. **Mr. Chris Dennett:** Born 1945, lived in Merthyr since 1962. Married 2c. Engineer. Member, AUEW.

DEVEREUX Robert Charles: 17th Viscount Hereford (1550): Premier Viscount of England, Bart. 1611. JP (Hereford) JP DL (Brecs) KStJ BA

(Oxon). 1888. Conservative: Breconshire 1906, Jan. 1910. **Hon. Robert Devereux:** Born Tredegar Park 11 August 1865, s of 16th Viscount & the Hon. Mary Anna Morgan, d of 1st Baron Tredegar, succeeded father 1924. Anglican. Married 1892, Ethel Mildred d of John Shaw of Welburn Hall (Died 1945). Educated Eton, New College, Oxford. Landowner. Captain, SWB Volunteers 1889-95. Breconshire CC 1907-. Died 16 April 1952.

DEVINE David William: ACA. Conservative, Neath. **Mr. David Devine:** Born Glasgow, 22 March 1965, s of William Devine, taxi driver & Helen Braithwaite Lockie, civil servant. Church of Scotland. Married 2000, Belinda Jane Moore (NHS medical secretary). Educated Abronhill High School, Cumberbnauld, Napier University, Edinburgh. Chartered Accountant 1989. Financial Accounting Manager, Janssen-Cilag Ltd (pharmaceutical subsidiary of Johnson 7 Johnson) 1996-. Previously worked for English, Welsh 7 Scottish Railways Joined Conservative Party 1982. Young Conservatives Chair: Edinburgh South, Slough, Berkshire, Beaconsfield. Chair: Slough Conservative Assn. Deputy Chair: Aylesbury Conservative Assn. Member: Federation of Small Businesses. Interests: Small Businesses, Environment, Health, Transport. Hobbies: Mountaineering, Hill Walking, Current Affairs. Languages: English, French (moderate).

DEXTER Edward Ralph: CBE 1.1.2001. MA (Cantab). Conservative: Cardiff South East 1964. **Mr. Ted Dexter:** Born Milan 15 May 1935. Anglican. Married 1959, Susan Georgina Longfield, 2c. Educated Radley College, Jesus College, Cambridge. Captain Cambridge University Cricket XI & Golf Team. Army 1956-57, 11th Hussars. Professional Cricketer 1958-68: Captain, Sussex XI 1960-80, England XI, Captain 1962-65. Retired from Cricket 1965. Freelance Journalist 1965-88, Sports Promotion Consultant 1978, Managing Director, Ted Dexter & Associates 1978-. Chair: England Cricket Cttee. TCCB, 1989-93. President MCC Oct. 2001. Hobbies: Golf (*a top class golfer*). Of Ealing. *Books: E. R. Dexter: Ted Dexter Declares. 1966 etc.*

DIAMOND Dennis Oscar: MA (Cantab). Liberal: East Flint 1966, 1970. **Mr. Dennis Diamond:** Born Withington, Manchester, August 1931. Married 5c. Educated Rydal School, Colwyn Bay, Clare College, Cambridge. Solicitor 1957, at Chester. Executive Member, Chester & District Marriage Guidance Council. Member, Rosslyn Park Rugby XV 6 years. Died September 1989.

DIBBLE Elizabeth Catherine: Conservative: Swansea East 1997. **Miss Catherine Dibble:** Born 26 September 1971. Educated Howells School, Llandaff, Leeds University. Recruitment Researcher. Formerly Research Assistant, Bernard Jenkin MP & Tim Kirkhope MP. Chair: Leeds N.E. Conservative Assn.

DILLON Terence A: Labour, North Wales Euro 1979, South Fylde 1974. **Mr. Terry Dillon:** Born April 1942. Married 2c. Educated Ruskin College, Oxford, Trinity College, Cambridge. TGWU research Dept. 3 years. Extra-Mural Staff Tutor, University of Wales, Bangor. Member: Society of Industrial Tutors, Society for Study of Welsh Labour History, Wrexham Trades Council, TGWU. Secretary, Wrexham CLP.

DILLWYN Lewis Llewelyn: JP 1838 DL (Glam). Liberal MP Swansea 1855-85, Swansea Town 1885-92. **Mr. Lewis Dillwyn:** Born Swansea 19 May 1814, s of Lewis Weston Dillwyn, Sketty Hall, Swansea, MP for Glamorgan 1832-37 & Mary, d of John Llewellyn, Penllergaer. Anglican. Married 1838 Elizabeth (Died 1866), d of Sir Henry de la Beech, Banker, Ironmaster & Jamaican slave plantation owner. Educated Bath. Industrialist: Chair: Dillwyn & Richards (Landore Spelter Works), merged to form Landore Siemens Steel Co, Chair: Glamorganshire Banking Co. Director: South Wales Railway Co. then Great Western Railway Co, West London Extension Railway Co, Mexican South Railway Co, American & General Mortgage Corporation, Hallcraft Furnace Ltd. Trustee: Mercantile Investment & General Trust Ltd, United States & South American Investment Fund. Raised 3rd Glamorganshire Rifle Volunteers (Colonel-Commandant). Swansea, botanist & antiquarian. Mayor of Swansea, 1848. Member, Swansea Harbour Board. President: Swansea Ladies Teacher Training College, Swansea Eye Hospital, Royal Institution of South Wales, 1861-62, 1881-2-3-4 (Hon. Curator for Geology 1839-60), Swansea Liberal Assn. Proposed Disestablishment bill almost annually from 1883. Of Swansea, & London. Estate £7,819. Died Royal Hotel, Swansea, 19 June 1892, after collapsing at an election meeting.

DILLWYN-LLEWELYN John Talbot: 1st Bart 1890 JP DL (Glam). MA (Oxon). Conservative: Swansea Town 1892, 1900; South Glamorgan 1885; Cardiff District B/E 1886; West Glamorgan B/E 1888. MP Swansea Town 1895-1900. **Sir John Dillwyn-Llewelyn:** Born 26 May 1836, son of John Dillwyn-Llewelyn JP DL FRS & Emma Thomasina, d of Thomas Mansel Talbot, of Margam Park, 1s (1 s died). Anglican. Educated: Eton; Christ Church, Oxford. Landowner & Director, Great Western Railway. Mayor of Swansea 1890-91. Glamorgan CC Alderman. High Sheriff of Glamorgan 1878. Chairman, Glamorgan Quarter Sessions. Founder & 2nd President, Swansea RFC. President:, Welsh Rugby Union; Royal

John Talbot Dillwyn-Llewelyn.

Institution of South Wales 1884-86, 1896-97 (Hon. Curator, Botany & Entomology 1892-96). Member, Royal Commission on Land in Wales 1896. Member, Governing Body of the Church in Wales. Of Penllergaer, Ynysgerwen & London. Estate £92,546. Died 24 July 1927.

DILLWYN-VENABLES-LLEWELYN Charles Leyshon: 2nd Bart 1890 CB JP (Brecs Rads Glam) DL (Brecs) MA (Oxon). Conservative: Radnorshire 1900, 1906, Dec 1910, MP. Jan-Dec. 1910. **Colonel, Sir Charles Dillwyn-Venables-Llewelyn:** Born Ynisgerwen, Neath 29 June 1870, s of Sir John Dillwyn-Llewelyn qv) & Caroline Julia, d of Sir Michael Hicks-Beach. Succeeded father 1927. Anglican. Married 1893, Katherine Minna, d of Revd Richard Lister-Venables, Vicar of Clyro (heiress of the Venables of Llandinam estate) & assumed the additional name of Venables, 1s. Educated Eton, Christ Church, Oxford. Landowner. Lieut-Colonel, Glamorgan Yeomanry 1908-18, Colonel 1918. Lord Lieutenant of Radnorshire 1929-49. Of Newbridge on Wye. Died 24 June 1951.

DIXON Andrew John: Plaid Cymru: Barry 1979, Vale of Glamorgan 1983, B/E 1989. **Mr. John Dixon:** Born Barry, August 1951 (father a clerk from Newcastle upon Tyne). Married Frances, 2c. Educated Dinas Powys Elementary School; Penarth Grammar School; University of Surrey. Computer Programmer, Wales Gas. Member, NALGO South Wales District Council. Treasurer, Penarth Branch, Shelter. Joined Plaid Cymru 1977; Spokesman on International Affairs, Treasurer 1980. Dinas Powys ComC. Vale of Glamorgan DC.

DIXON John Leslie: BSc (Wales) Liberal Democrat, Cardiff North 2001, Euro Candidate South Wales Central 1995, Wales 1999. **Mr. John Dixon:** Born Brentford, Middlesex, 24 April 1965, s of Leslie Thomas Dixon, lecturer, & Dorothy Jane Theresa Knell, teacher. Engaged to Sara. Educated Hounslow Primary School, Isleworth Grammar School, University of Wales, Cardiff (Microbiology & Genetics). Creative Services Manager. Graphics Designer. Cardiff CC 1999. Press Officer, Welsh Liberal Democrats 1998-99. Liberal Democrat Prospective Parliamentary Candidate, Cardiff North 2004. Hobbies: Rugby (Member Cardiff RFC). Of Cardiff.

DODD Raymond Charles: BSc. Liberal Democrat: Delyn 1987, 1992. **Mr. Raymond Dodd:** Born Birkenhead, 26 September 1945, s of Joseph Dodd, shipyard elecrician, & Cecilia Elizabeth Cook, housewife. Married 1968, Irene Dodd, 2d, divorced. Educated Birkenhead Institute Grammar School; Northern College of Youth Leadership; Liverpool University (part-time). Manager, Daniel Owen Community Centre. Deputy Chief Officer, community development charity. Treasurer & Chair, Delyn Liberal Democrats. Delyn BC 1976-96 (Liberal DemocratGroup Leader 1977-79). Mold TC 1987-. Flintshire CC 1997-. Member, British MENSA. Hobbies: Organising Secretary, British Novelty Salt & Pepper Pots Collectors Club; Restoration Theatre, Public Speaking.

DONALD Nona: Independent, Ynys Môn 2001. **Ms. Nona Donald:** *Not keen to say how old she is (Liverpool Daily Post 24.5.2001).* Married. Spent 32 years in business School. Owner: Soldiers Point Hotel, Holyhead, Plas Coch Caravan & Leisure Park & Yr Ynys Caravan Park, owns 300 acres. *Favours Tories but has voted Liberal and Plaid Cymru.* Of Holyhead (1969).

DONALDSON Angus: MBE 2003. Liberal: Ebbw Vale 1970, Merthyr Tydfil B/E 1972, Feb. & Oct. 1974. **Mr. Angus Donaldson:** Born Bedwas June 1927. Married Barbara, 3c. Educated Basseleg Grammar School. Fitter, Bedwas Colliery, Artificer, Fleet Air Arm. Boxer. Hotelier, Castle Hotel, Tredegar. President, Tredegar Chamber of Trade, Member: Tredegar Round Table, Tredegar Rotary Club, Licensed Victuallers Assn. Tredegar UDC 1967-, Monmouthshire CC 1967-. Caerphilly CBC (Ind). Founder, Caerphilly Independents Assn. Of Bedwas.

DONNELLY Anthony L: Conservative, Gower 1992. **Mr. Anthony Donnelly:** Born 1 September 1950. Married. Poppy Donnelly, 2s. Educated St. Martins Secondary School, Chelmsford; Chelmsford College. Director, small business. Brentwood DC 1967-80. Essex CC 1981-89.

DONNELLY Desmond Louis: Labour MP Pembroke 1955-70, Resigned Labour Whip over *Withdrawal from East of Suez* Jan. 1968, Expelled from Labour Party 27/3/1968, Formed United Democratic Party 1969, Candidate: Pembroke 1970; Labour: County Down B/E 1946, Common Wealth: Evesham 1945, then joined Labour, Joined Conservative Party 1971 but failed in attempts to be a candidate. **Mr. Desmond Donnelly:** Born India, 16 October, 1920, s of Louis J. Donnelly, Assam tea planter, & Aimee Tucker, 1s 2d. Married 1947, Rosemary (Pembs CC 1967), d of Dr. John Taggart, Belfast. 3c. Educated Bembridge School, Isle of Wight. RAF 1939-45, Flight Lieutenant. Journalist & Author. Director, Town & Country Planning Assn. & Editor, *'Town & Country Planning'* 1948-50. Company Director, Pemdock Properties Ltd. 1964-, Consultant, David Brown Corporation Ltd.1954, Philips Industries Ltd. 1965. Governor, University of Wales, Swansea, National Museum, National Library. Of Trefasser & London. Died 4 April 1974 (suicide in hotel bedroom). *Books etc: Desmond Donnelly, The March Wind 1959, Trade with Communist Countries (with Alec Nove) 1960, David Brown's: The Story of a Family Business 1960, No Gains without Pains 1960, Years Ahead 1964, Struggle for the World 1965, The Nearing Storm 1968, Gadarene '68 1968, There is Another Britain 1970.*

DONNELLY Peter Duncan: MB ChB (Edin) MBA (Havard) 1989 MPH (Wales) 1991 MFPHM 1991 DA. (UK). 1988. Conservative: Pontypridd 1992. **Dr. Peter Donnelly:** Born Bangor, 27 November 1963, s of Dr. James Donnelly & Gwyneth Gittins. Married 1988, Joan Dymmock. Educated Perth Academy; Edinburgh University; Havard Postgraduate School of Business Administration; University of Wales, Cardiff. Senior Lecturer in Public Health Medicine, University of Wales, Cardiff -1996. Asst. Director, Breast Test Wales. Locum Consultant in Health Medicine, South Glam Health Authority 1989. Hon. Senior Lecturer, University of Wales College of Medicine & University of Wales, Swansea. Director of Health, PHM Group, Iechyd Morgannwg 1996-. Vice-President, Faculty of Public Medicine of Royal Colleges of Physicians of UK. Cardiff CC 1991-4. School Governor. Hobbies: Hill walking, Skiing, Gardening. Of Cardiff.

DONOVAN John: Computer Democrat: Gower B/E 1982, Neath 1983. **Mr. John Donovan:** Born 1952. Groundsman, Polytechnic of Wales. Plaid Cymru candidate in local elections. *One of two people to respond to an invitation to represent the Computer Democrat Party, name drawn out of hat for by-election. Policy cybernetic semantics, Remove the old divisions which have split society, with no capitalists, no communists, no left, no right, no governors, no governed, all to retire at 50.*

DOUGLAS Heather: Conservative, Cardiff West 2003. **Mrs. Heather Douglas:** Born Cardiff. Church in Wales. 2d. Educated Victoria Junior School, Penarth; Penarth Secondary School; Cleves Secretarial College, Cardiff. Legal Secretary 1988. Cardiff CCC (Plasnewydd) 1999-. Left Conservatives 1997 and Joined Liberal Democrats but returned 2002. Interests: Anything that can help people. Hobbies: Watercolour Painting; Guitar. Of Cardiff (1986).

DOVER Denmore Ronald: BSc (Manchester) 1959. CEng 1975. MICE 1964. Conservative: Caerphilly Oct. 1974, MP Chorley 1979-97, MEP North West England 1999-. **Mr. Den Dover:** Born Warrington 4 April 1938, s of Albert Dover, works manager, & Emma Kirk. Methodist. Married (1) 1959, Marina Wright (divorced 1986) 3c, (2) 1989 Kathleen Edna Fisher. Educated Manchester Grammar School, Manchester University (1st Civil Engineering). Civil Engineer: With John Laing & Son Ltd 1959-69, Chief Executive, National Building Agency 1969-72, Projects Director, Capital & Counties Property Co 1972-75, Contracts Manager, Wimpey Laing Iran 1975-77, Director, GLC Housing Construction 1977-79, Parliamentary Consultant, George Wimpey plc, Director, Cosalt plc. 1988, President, CTU national engineering group. Barnet BC 1968-77. Member, Select Cttees: Transport 1979-87, Environment 1994-97, Severn Bridge Bill 1991. Joint Vice-Chair: Conservative MPs Trade & Industry Cttee. 1994-97. Vice-Chair: EU-Malta Joint Parliamentary Cttee. Member: EU Cttee on Budgets, Cttee on Employment & Social Affairs. Of Boreham Wood, Herts. & Chorley.

DOWN Graham Lindsay: MMIPA. ATT. MSPI. Conservative: Llanelli 1992. **Mr. Graham Down:** Born Bridgend, 28 June 1956, s of Gordon H. Down & Jean Trew. Married Julie Alyson Evans, 2c. Educated Bridgend Grammar School, Brynteg Comprehensive School, Bridgend, Swansea College of Technology, Polytechnic of Wales. Chartered Accountant 1971-90, Principal Partner 1987-90. Insolvency Consultant. Member, Mid-Glamorgan Health Authority 1986-90. Hobbies: Reading, swimming, family life. Of Mathern, nr. Chepstow.

DOXSEY Sidney William: Conservative: Merthyr Tydfil 1964, Cardiff West 1966. **Mr. Sidney Doxsey:** Born Cardiff July 1929. Roman Catholic. Married 3c. Educated St. Illtyd's College, Cardiff. Industrial Bank Representative, Hospital Pensions Officer 9 years. Treasurer, Wales & Mon YCs, Member, YCs National Advisory Cttee. Member, Cardiff Hospital Management Cttee. Cardiff CC 1955-, Conservative Chief Whip 1958. Of Cardiff.

DRAKE Ashley: BA (Wales). Plaid Cymru: Delyn 1992, 1997. **Mr. Ashley Drake:** Born Tonypandy, 14 May 1965. Educated Banbury; Gwent College of Higher Education, University of Wales, Lampeter (Welsh Studies). Publisher's sales representative, Sales Director 1994-97, Joint-Managing Director, Drake Publishing. Asst Regional Director, CBI Wales 1997-2000. Director, University of Wales Press 2003. Joined Plaid Cymru 1984. NUS Wales Area Organiser 1987-89. Plaid Cymru Youth & Students' Organiser 1989-93. Vice-Chair: Plaid Cymru Communications Cttee 1992-94, Member: Greenpeace, Chelsea Football Club, TC. Member: West Glam. Education Cttee, Plaid Cymru Executive, Governor, University of Wales, Aberystwyth. Interests: Education, Environment. Hobbies: Squash, 5-a-side football. Languages: Welsh, English.

DRAKE Robert Geoffrey: BA DipEd (Wales) SDP: Cardiff West 1987, Labour: Walsall South 1966. **Mr. Geoffrey Drake:** Born Tonypandy 6 April 1937, s of Robert Ronald Drake & Alice Simcox, owners of a decorating supplies shop. Married 1959, Marion Elaine, 1s 2d. Educated Tonypandy Grammar School, University of Wales, Swansea. Educational Publisher: Chair: & Managing Director, Drake Group of Companies 1971. Founder Member SDP. Chair: Cardiff West SDP; SDP Council for Wales. Member, CSD CBI & CBI Smaller Firms Council, Exec. British Educational Equipment Assn, Vice-President, Centre for International Affairs. Of Cardiff.

DRAKEFORD Mark: BA BPhil PGCE CQSW PhD. Labour, Cardiff Central 1999. **Dr. Mark Drakeford:** Born Carmarthen, 19 September 1954, s of John Joseph Drakeford, teacher, & Joan Williams, telephonist. Married 1977, Clare Elizabeth Drakeford, teacher. Educated Queen Elizabeth Grammar School, Carmarthen, University of Kent, Canterbury, University of Wales. Lecturer in Social Policy & Applied Social Studies, University of Wales, Cardiff. Former Probation Officer & Project Leader at Ely, Cardiff. Member: Social Policy Action Assn, Child Poverty Action Group, Glamorgan Charity Cricket Club. South Glam. CC 1985-93. Cabinet Advisor for Health & Social Service & First Minister's Official Spokesperson May 2000. Interests: Poverty, Social Policy. Hobbies: Music, Theatre, Cricket. Languages: Welsh, English. Of Cardiff. *Books: Mark Drakeford, (with Jill Campling), Social Movements and their Supporters: The Green Shirts in England 1997, (with Ian Butler) Social Policy, Social Welfare and Scandal 2003.*

DRISCOLL James Patrick: BSc 1949 PhD (Wales) 1952 FREconS FRSA. Conservative: Rhondda West 1950. **Dr. James Driscoll:** Born Cardiff 24 April 1925, s of Henry James Driscoll & Honorah Driscoll. Roman Catholic. Married 1955, Jean Lawrence Williams, 1s 1d. Educated St. Illtyd's College, Cardiff, University of Wales, Cardiff (1st Economics). Royal Navy, Royal Marines & Indian Army 1943-46. Chair: Welsh Young Conservatives 1949-50. Deputy President National Union of Students 1949-51. Chair: University of Wales Asst. Lecturer in Industrial Relations, University of Wales, Cardiff 1950-53. Economist, British Steel Corporation 1953-67. General Manager, Economics & International Affairs Section, British Steel Corporation 1967-71: Managing Director, Corporate Strategy Policy 1971-76; Board Adviser 1976-80; Director 1980-90. Chairman, Webb Estates Ltd 2001-. Senior Partner, Woodcote Consulting Services 1990-94. Member: Grand Council, Federation of British Industries 1957-65; CBI Council 1970-93. Observer. NEDC 1977-91. Fellow, University of Wales, Cardiff 1986. Member, Court, University of Wales, Cardiff 1970-88, 1990-. Vice-Chair, Croydon Municipal Mencap Ltd 1997. Of Purley.

DU CROS Arthur Roy Philip: Conservative: Caernarfon District 1935. **Mr. Roy du Cros:** Born 15 March 1913, s of Sir Arthur Philip du Cros Bart MP & proprietor of the Dunlop Tyre Co. Married 1935 Myra McLarney, d of Gerald Mooney of Kilkenny. Educated Harrow, Oxford University. Law student when a candidate. Barrister 1936. Army 1939-45, Major, RASC.

DUGDALE John: PC 1949 MA. (Oxon). Labour: Cardiff Central 1935, South Leicester 1931, York B/E May 1937, MP: West Bromwich B/E 1941-. **Rt. Hon. John Dugdale:** Born 16 March 1905, s of Colonel Arthur Dugdale, CMG DSO. Married 1938, Irene Constance Haverson, granddaughter of Rt. Hon. George Lansbury MP. 2s. Educated Wellington College; Christ Church, Oxford. Attaché, British Legation, Peking 1927-28. Journalist. London CC.1934-41. Private Secretary, Rt. Hon. Clement Attlee MP 1931-39. Army 1939-45. PPS to Prime Minister Attlee, 1945, Parl & Financial Secretary, Admiralty 1945-50, Minister of State, Colonies 1950-51. Estate £114,943. Died 12 March 1963.

DUGUAY Gabriel Bernard: BEd. Natural Law Party, South Wales East Euro 1994, Gillingham 1997. **Mr. Gabriel Duguay:** Born Quebec. Married Gillian Duguay, 2d, divorced. Educated Montreal University (Business) & Wales. Runner. A founder, Canadian Road Runners Club 1975. Involved in preparing a plan for qualified road measurers and certifiers in Canada for road races (scheme accepted 1999). PE Teacher. Took up Transcendental Meditation 1991. Moved to Wales. Of Gelli, Rhondda, then Kent.

DUMPER Timothy Roland: BSc (Wales) 1970. Liberal Democrat, Assembly, Llanelli 1999, East Devon 2001. **Mr. Tim Dumper:** Born 13 December 1947, s of William George Dumper (died 1992) railway clerk, & Nancy Kathleen Wheatland (died 1994). Free Church of England as teenager, not regular churchgoer. Married 1969 Glynis Lloyd. Family history researcher & district councillor, 2s. Educated Exmouth Grammar School 1959-63, Carisbrooke Grammar School, Isle of Wight 1964-66, University of Wales, Bangor (Psychology), MIPD. Dip. Training Management. Training Officer, Swaziland Railways 1976-78, Training & Education Officer, Southampton Docks 1978-79, Training Officer, Yemen Airways 1979-80, Lecturer, Civil Service Training, Kiribati Government 1980-84, Personnel Officer, Somerset CC 1986-87, Training Officer, North Devon DC 1987-88, self-employed Personnel & Training Consultant 1998-. Joined Liberal Democrats in 1980s. Chair, University of Wales, Bangor, Liberals 1968-69. Interests: Transport, Environment, Devolution, Empowering & involving people, World affairs. Hobbies Quizzes, Music, Drama, Chess, Bridge, Watching sport Languages: a little Welsh, English, school French, some spoken German, Siswati, Kiribati. Re-adopted for East Devon 2003.

DUNCAN Richard Nicholas: United Socialist, Assembly, Neath 1999. **Mr. Richard Duncan:** Lecturer in Languages & Communications, Neath College. Member, Socialist Workers Party. Branch Chair: NATFHE. Campaigner against Racism & Insufficient Health Provision.

DUNN W. F. N. – see NEWTON-DUNN W. F.

DUNWOODY-KNEAFSEY Moyra Tamsin: Labour, Preseli 2003. **Mrs. Tamsin Dunwoody-Kneefsey:** Born Totnes, Devon, 3 September 1958, d of Dr. John Elliott Orr Dunwoody MP, general practitioner, & d of Gwyneth Patricia Phillips Dunwoody MP (d of Morgan Phillips, General Secretary, labour Party). Church in Wales. Married 1993 Mark Robert Kneafsey, company director, 2s 3d. Educated Dartington Primary School, Devon; Burdett Coutts Primary School, Westminster; Grey Coat Hospital, Westminster; University of Kent (English & American Literature); University of the South Bank, London Post Graduate Diploma, NHS Management). Member, Objective One Management Board. Adviser, Small businesses. Member: Women in Enterprise, Mothers' Union. Shortlisted at Merthyr Tydfil 2001. Interests: Socialism. Hobbies: Smallholder, Embroidery, Reading, Current Affairs. Languages: I will speak Welsh, English, French. Of Ambleston, Haverfordwest.

DUVAL Gillian Sorel: Pro Life Party, Mid & West List 2003; Chesham & Amersham 2001; Beaconsfield 1997; South-East England Euro 2004. **Mrs. Gillian Duval:** Born London, 8 November 1944, d of Edward Oliver Blandford, general manager, & Mrs. Blandford, manager & farmer. Roman Catholic. Married 1966, Peter James Duval, IT consultant, 1s 3d. Educated Oystermouth Primary School; Old Palace School, Mayfield, Sussex. Counsellor Trainer. Chair: South England Area, Pro-Life Party. Interests: Right to Life of old, unborn & handicapped; concerned about media censorship on the reality of abortion. Hobbies: Gardening, Internet, Grandchildren. Languages: English, a little French. Of High Wycombe.

– E –

EAGLESTONE Martin Robert: BSc. (Birmingham). Labour, Caernarfon 2001, 2003. **Mr. Martin Eaglestone:** Born West Bromwich, 13 November 1959. Methodist. Married Susan Catherine Eaglestone, physiotherapist, 2s 3d. Educated Waunfawr Primary School; Ysgol Syr Hugh Owen, Caernarfon; Birmingham Polytechnic Town Planning). Technical Assistant, Welsh Office Agricultural Dept. 1982-83; Planning Assistant, Snowdonia National Park 1983-86; Planning Officer, Gwynedd CC 1986-96. Head of Planning Policy, Ynys Môn CC 1996-. Registered Foster Carer. Secretary, Caernarfon CLP. ComC. School Governor. Member, Unison. Menai Bridge ComC. Interests: International Affairs. Hobbies: Current Affairs; Football. Languages: Welsh, English. Of Menai Bridge.

EASTON Clive Gwennap: UK Independence Party, Mid & West List 2003, Wales Euro 2004, Hereford 2001, West Midlands Euro 1999; Referendum Party, Hereford 1997. Born Guildford 21 July 1947. Anglican. Married 1980 Yvonne Ingrid, 1s. Educated King James First School, Isle of Wight, London School of Flying. Freelance Charter Pilot/Instructor 1968-69, Pilot, Skyways Coach Air 1969-70, BOAC/British Airways 1970-98; retired as Senior Captain. Member: Conservative Party until 1995, Referendum Party 1997, UK Independence Party 1998. Chairman, Llanwrthwl ComC. Chair: Herefordshire Keep the £ Campaign. Member: Democracy Movement, Council for Democracy. Hobbies: Rotary, Sailing, Flying, Farming, Home. Of Llanwrthwl.

EBORALL Rachel: BA (Wales) 2001. United Socialists, South/Central List 1999. **Miss Rachel Eborall:** Student, University of Wales, Cardiff at time of election (2a English Literature, Communications & History). Member, Socialist Workers Party, SWSS, Stop the Fees Campaign. Launched *Students against the War* 1999.

EDMONDES Dorothy Caroline: OBE 1920 JP (Glam) 1922, retired 1950. Conservative: Ogmore 1922. **Mrs. Dorothy Edmondes:** Born Usk 1871, d. of John Cole Nicholl, landowner of Merthyr Mawr House & Mary de la Beche (died 1922). Anglican. Married 1898, Major Charles Gresford Irving Edmondes of Old Hall, Cowbridge (died 1911), 2s. Educated at home & Switzerland. Masseuse: Head Masseuse & Administrator, County Treasurer, Soldiers, Sailors & Airforce

Assn., St. Hilary; Bridgend Orthopaedic Clinic, which she established & installed 1917-22. Commandant VAD. Joined Glamorgan Red Cross 1914; President, Life Member; Life Vice-President 1959. Of Erw Fain, Glamorgan. Estate £3,793. Died 1963.

EDMUNDS James Ewart: JP (Cardiff). Labour: Cardiff Central 1918, 1922, 1923; MP: Cardiff East 1929-31. **Mr. James Edmunds:** Born Gilwern 5 August 1892, son of Edmund Edmunds, schoolmaster, & Annie Louise, teacher, d of J. Lucas; spent childhood in Dorset. Married 1920 Keturah, d of Edmund Morgan, Taffs Well 2d. Educated Howard Gardens School, Cardiff; University of Wales, Cardiff Teacher, 1903-20; Newport District Secretary TGWU 1920-. Secretary, Cardiff Trades Council 1911-22, President 2001.1924-28. Chairman, Welsh Divisional Council ILP 1915, 1923. Member, Cardiff Board of Guardians 1903-20. Of Rhiwbina, Cardiff. Died 1962.

EDMUNDS William Rees: JP. Coalition Liberal: Caerphilly 1918, B/E 1921. **Mr. Willie Rees Edmunds:** Born Llanelli 29 August 1874, son of William Edmunds, Five Roads & Mary Edmunds. Baptist Deacon. Married 1912. Sarah (died 1941), d of Thomas Edmunds, Mountain Ash (President, Baptist Union of Wales) 3d. At Cardiff 1897-1900. Solicitor, at Merthyr Tydfil 1900-30. Chairman, Merthyr Tydfil War Savings Cttee. Vice-President, East Glam Liberal Assn. President: Merthyr Liberal Assn 1909-26; Federated Chambers of Trade, Glamorgan & Mon. Chairman, East Glamorgan Welsh Baptist Assn. Member, Welsh National Liberal Council. Acting Returning Officer, Merthyr Tydfil Dec. 1910. Hon Solicitor, Baptist Union of Wales, President 1933. Merthyr Tydfil BC. Lived at Quakers Yard until he retired to Llanelli, 1930. Languages: Welsh, English. Died September 1944.

EDWARDS Alfred Harold: OBE MA (Oxon). Conservative: Flintshire 1906. **Lieut-Colonel Harold Edwards:** Born Llandovery 16 August 1878, son of Revd Alfred G. Edwards (Archbishop of Wales) & Caroline Edwards (1 of 4, 1881) 1of 4c. Anglican. Married 1913, Eleanor, d of E. H. Hayes of St. Asaph, 5s. Educated Eton; Magdalen College, Oxford. Army: South African War 1899-1900; France 1914-18. Estate Agent & Barrister. Probate Registrar, Chester & Bangor (retired 1948). Chancellor, Diocese of St. Asaph. Of St. Asaph. Died 15 May 1964.

EDWARDS Allen Clement: Liberal: Denbigh District 1900; MP Denbigh District 1906-Jan. 1910; East Glam: Dec. 1910-18; National Democratic Party MP East Ham South 1918-22; Progressive Labour, Tottenham 1895. **Mr. Clement Edwards:** Born Knighton 7 June 1869, son of George Benjamin Edward auctioneer, master tailor & draper) & Sarah Ellen Tudge, Villa, Garth Road, 1 of 4c. Anglican, he became a Congregationalist. Married (1) Fanny Emerson (died 1920) (2) 1922 Alice Mary Parker, NDP Secretary, 1s. Educated Knighton National School. Farm labourer at 13; casual work; clerk in solicitor's office. Junior clerk, *British & Colonial Printer & Stationer & Paper Trade Review* 1886. Asst. Secretary, Union of Dock, Wharf, Riverside & General Labourers 1890. General Secretary, Federation of Trade & Labour Unions 1891. Journalist: Labour Editor, *The Sun* 1893-94; Labour Editor, *The Echo* 1894; Special Commissioner, *The Daily News*, 1894-1901. Member: Fabian Society. Editor *The Sun*. Barrister, Middle Temple 1899. Junior Counsel to the Post Office 1913. Contested London School Board 1894. Islington BC 1898. Took part in an anti-socialist crusade in the mining valleys in years before 1914. Vice-President, 1918, Chairman, National Democratic Party 1918-20. Resigned from Liberal Party & supported Labour 1931. Of London. Died 23 June 1938.

EDWARDS Aneurin J. C. – see GLYN-EDWARDS A. J.

EDWARDS Brian Morgan-: BSc Econ (London). Plaid Cymru: Cardiff North 1970, Flint West 1979. **Mr. Brian Morgan-Edwards:** Born Swansea, July 1934. Brought up at Exeter. Married Rona Thomas (died Jan. 2003). Educated Hele's School, Exeter & London School of Economics. Army 1954-56, Sergeant, RAEC. Computer salesman -1968. Independent Financial Consultant: Financial Consultant to a number of London computer leasing companies Oct. 1968. Company Director: Cwmni Recordiau *Sain* 1969. Member, Conservative Party -1967; Joined Plaid Cymru 1967. Secretary, London Branch 1967-68, Gabalfa Branch 1969. Deputy Treasurer, Plaid Cymru. Contested Cardiff CC 1969, 1970. Of Penrhos, Pwllheli. Died suddenly at home, 24 November 2002.

EDWARDS Charles: PC 1940 Kt 1935 CBE 1931 JP (Mon). Labour MP Bedwellty, 1918-50. **Rt. Hon Sir Charles Edwards:** Born Llangunllo, Radnorshire, 19 February 1867; son of John (agricultural labourer) & Catherine Edwards. Congregationalist. Married Margaret Ann, d of William Davies of Abercarn, 1s 1d. Educated

Llangunllo National School. Miner at Sirhowy at 14. Checkweigher; Miners' Agent -1918; Executive SWMF, 1905-18. Risca UDC. Monmouthshire CC. Member, Abertillery Water Board. Labour Whip 1924-31; Chief Whip 1931-42; Lord Commissioner 1929-31; Joint Parl-Secretary, Treasury 1940-42. Of Risca. Died 15 June 1954.

EDWARDS David Elgan Hugh: DL (Cheshire) 1989. LlB (Wales) 1966. Conservative: Merioneth 1970; Stockport North Feb. 1974. **Mr. Elgan Edwards:** Born Rhyl 6 December 1943, son of Howell & Dilys Edwards. Married Carol Anne Smalls, barrister, 2s 2d. Educated Rhyl Grammar School; University of Wales, Aberystwyth. President: Debates, 1964; Law Society 1966, Student Representative Council 1966-67. Barrister, Grays Inn 1967; Recorder, Wales & Chester Circuit 1983-89; Circuit Judge 1989. Chester CC 1974; Chester DC 1973-. Sheriff, City of Chester 1977-78. Hon. Recorder, Chester 1997. Hobbies: Swimming.

EDWARDS David Graham: Conservative, Ogmore 1992, Vale of Clwyd 1997, Assembly, West Carmarthenshire & South Pembs 1999. **Mr. David Edwards:** Born Shrewsbury, 12 November 1965, son of John Arthur Edwards & Edith Ann Ferneyhough. Educated Newtown High School, Harper Adams Agricultural College. Managing Director, Agrafax, (PR & publishing (Eco) 1990, Director, RSP Badges Ltd. Newtown TC. Montgomeryshire DC. (Conservative Group Leader, Chair, Planning Cttee). Powys CC (resigned November 2003). Vice-President, Ogmore Conservative Assn. Chair: Welsh Agricultural & Development Forum. Member: Conservative Welsh Policy Team, Conservative Local Govt. Advisory Cttee, Institute of Public Relations, Guild of Agricultural Journalist, Young Farmers Club. Hobbies: Music, Rugby, Reading. Of Aberbechan, Newtown.

EDWARDS Dyfed Wyn: BMus (Wales) 1980. Plaid Cymru, Clwyd South 2001, 2003 & North List 2003. **Mr. Dyfed Edwards:** Born Rhosllanerchrugog 13 December 1958, Christian. Married Ruth Myfanwy Edwards (artist/graphic artist) 2d. Educated: Rhos, Ysgol Gyfun Rhiwabon, University of Wales, Cardiff. Music Teacher, Connah's Quay 1981-86, Ysgol y Gader, Dolgellau 1986-88; Freelance Musician 1988-92; Owner/Managing Director, *Curiad*, music publishing company 1992-. School governor. Director, Antur Nantlle (enterprise agency). Secretary: Nantlle Branch; Chair: Plaid Cymru, Conwy & Denbighshire; Agent, Clwyd South West 1983; Clwyd West 1997. Interests: International Affairs, Economy, Social Inclusion; Environment. Hobbies: Football, Music. Languages: Welsh; English; Basic French. Of Penygroes, Caernarfon.

EDWARDS Elgan – see EDWARDS David Elgan Hugh.

EDWARDS Frances: Labour: Flint 1931; Darwen 1935. **Miss Frances Edwards:** Born Manchester, 1907, d of a Welsh father & Irish mother. Anglican. Married 1933 Canon Edward Kirkby, Vicar of St. John's, Pendlebury. Teacher at Salford. Labour Party Women's Regional Organiser for the North West. Swinton & Pendlebury BC (Chairman, Maternity & Child Welfare Cttee). Died March 1970.

EDWARDS Francis: 1st Bart 1907 JP (Rads) DL 1892 BA 1875 MA (Oxon). Liberal MP Radnorshire 1900-Jan. 1910; Dec. 1910-1918. **Sir Frank Edwards:** Born Llangollen 28 April 1852, son of Edward Edwards, of The Hand Hotel, & cousin of Archbishop A. G. Edwards. Anglican. Married 1880, Catherine (died 1915) d of David Davies, Aberdare, 1d. Educated Shrewsbury School; Jesus College, Oxford. Solicitor 1879. High Sheriff of Radnorshire 1898. Estate £93,846. Died 10 May 1927.

EDWARDS Goronwy Owen: Independent, Assembly, Conwy, 1999, Conservative, Caernarfon 2003. **Mr Goronwy Edwards:** Born 29 October 1950, son of John David Edwards, farmer, & Jane Ann Edwards. Methodist. Married Eryl Lloyd Hughes, bank clerk, 2s. Left school at 15 due to family bereavement. Telecommunications Consultant Engineer & Farmer. Aberconwy BC 1996-98, Conwy CBC (Caerhuan Ward) 1995- (Chair: Finance & Property Cttee 1996-98). Henryd ComC. 1979. Governor, University of Wales, Bangor. School governor. Chair: Conwy Valley NFU. President: Rowen Young Farmers Club. Of Henryd, Conwy.

EDWARDS Gwilym Meredith: Hon MA (Wales) 1997. Plaid Cymru: Denbigh 1966. **Mr. Meredith Edwards:** Born Rhosllanerchrugog 10 June 1917, son of John Edwards, miner. Presbyterian Church of Wales. Married Daisy, 2s 1d. Educated Rhos Junior School; Ruabon Grammar School. Actor: theatre, television & film. Formerly: Teacher; Chemist at Courthalds. Joined 1st Welsh National Theatre Company at Llangollen 1938; CO 1939: Fireman at Liverpool, Chester & London; & member, Non Combatant Corps. Pilgrim Players, Liverpool, 1945; Ealing Films: *A Run for Your Money, The Blue Lamp, The Cruel Sea, Dunkirk,* etc. BBC Repertory Co. Board Member, Royal College of Music & Drama. Life President, Equity. Patron, Goals for Special Need. Died 8 February 1999. *Books: Meredith Edwards, Ar Lwyfan Awr 1977.*

EDWARDS Hywel Teifi: BA MA Wales). Plaid Cymru: Llanelli 1983, Carmarthen 1987. **Pro-fessor Hywel Teifi Edwards:** Born Llanddewi Aberarth 15 October 1934, s of John Daniel Edwards, carpenter, & Olwen Myfanwy Edwards, housewife. Calvinistic Methodist. Married 1960, Aerona Protheroe, teacher, 1s 1d. Educated Aberarth Primary School; Aberaeron Grammar School; University of Wales, Aberystwyth (Welsh). Teacher. Tutor in Adult Education, University College of Wales, Swansea 1965; Research Professor of Welsh 1989-95. Critic & Literary Historian. Author, writer, broadcaster. Dyfed CC 1977-. Llangennech ComC. Refused to pay for television licence 1997, protesting with 11 others that there was too much English on S4C. Interests: Promoting Plaid Cymru & an independent Wales in the EU, Hobbies: Books, Films, Soccer, and Almost any ball game. Languages: Welsh, English. Of Llangennech. *Books: Eisteddfod 1176-1976 (1976), Gŵyl Gwalia: Yr Eisteddfod ac Oes Fictoria 18858-1868 (1980), Codi'r Hen wlad yn ei Hôl (1989), Eisteddfod (Writers of Wales 1989), Eisteddfod Ffair y Byd, Chicago 1893 (1990), Arwr Glew Enwau'r Glo (1994).* Editor, *Cyfres y Cymoedd* series.

EDWARDS Jeffrey: MBE 31.12.2003 JP. Independent, Merthyr Tydfil & Rhymney. **Mr. Jeff Edwards:** Born Aberfan 1959. Unmarried. Educated Pantglas School, Aberfan (survivor the Aberfan tip disaster 1966). Joined NCB as trainee accountant. Unmarried. Educated London University; University of Wales (Finance & Business Administration). Accountant, worked in private and public sectors; Asst. Secretary, British Coal Corporation. Management Consultant & Company Director. Founder Chairman, Aberfan & Merthyr Vale Youth & Community Project. Mid-Glam CC (Merthyr Vale) 1990s, Leader, Independent Group. Merthyr Tydfil BC 1999 (Merthyr Vale Ward); Deputy Leader of the Opposition, October 1999, Leader, November 1999. Chair: Order of St. John Council, County of Merthyr Tydfil; Hoover Sports AFC; Youth Panel, Merthyr Tydfil Magistrates Court. Member: South Wales Police Authority; Mid-Glamorgan Fire Service; Mid-Glamorgan Probation Service; Board of Visitors, Cardiff Prison; Merthyr Tydfil Courts; Sports Council Eastern Panel; South Wales Miners Convalescent Homes Board. President: Ynysowen Boys & Girls Club FC. School Governor. Hobbies: Travel; Reading; Walking; Politics; Current Affairs; the Stock Market. Of Aberfan, Merthyr Tydfil.

EDWARDS John: DSO BA (Lond). Coalition Liberal MP Aberavon 1918-22; Ind. Liberal: University of Wales 1923. **Lieut-Colonel Jack Edwards:** Born Llanbadarn Fawr 28 February 1882, son of Revd James Edwards & Rachel Jones. Welsh Independent. Married 1932, Gweno Elin, d of Dr. Joseph Davies Bryan, Alexandria,

Egypt, 2s 1d. Educated British School; Neath Grammar School; University of Wales, Aberystwyth. Teacher; Member NUT. Army: Private. RWF 1914; Lieut-Colonel. Barrister, Grays Inn 1921. Welsh Dramatist & Writer in Welsh & English. Member: Aberdare, London Welsh & Middlesex Rugby XVs. High Sheriff of Cardiganshire 1942. Governor, University of Wales, Aberystwyth. Languages: Welsh, English. Of Neath, & Kingston Hill, Surrey. Died 23 May 1960.

EDWARDS John Ellis: Natural Law Party, Mid & West List 1999. **Mr John Edwards:** Of Skelmersdale.

EDWARDS John Hugh: JP (Surrey) BA (London). Liberal MP Mid-Glamorgan, Dec. 1910-18; Neath 1918-22; Accrington 1924-29 (stood in 1934 as Liberal & Constitutionalist, with Conservative support). **Mr. John Hugh Edwards:** Born Aberystwyth 1871 son of Alderman John Edwards, flannel merchant, & Mary Evans. Congregationalist. Married 1934, Doris, d of Sir Samuel Faire, Leicester, Educated Aberystwyth County School; University of Wales, Aberystwyth. Ordained 1899: Congregationalist Minister, Newtown 1899-1905, Dulwich Grove 1905-06; Hanover Church, Peckham 1906-13; Resigned from Ministry 1913. Shared with A. Clement Edwards, & Rev. W. F. Phillips in an anti-socialist campaign in the mining valleys 1910. Abstained on first vote on Conscription Bill, Jan. 1916, but gave support later; Speaker's Conference on Government of Wales & Scotland 1920. Journalist, author & writer. Editor, *Young Wales* 1895-1904. Cardiganshire CC. Purley UDC Chairman 1921; Hazlemere UDC (Chairman 2 years). Governor, University of Wales Colleges, Aberystwyth & Cardiff. Member: Speaker's Conference on Devolution 1919. Church Secretary & Treasurer, Tower Road Congregational Church, Hindhead. Chair: Welsh National Liberal Federation Disestablishment Cttee. President: Guildford & District Free Church Council 1943-44; Hazlemere Rotary Club, Hazlemere Chamber of Commerce; Surrey Federation of Ratepayers; Confederation of Ratepayers' Assns of England & Wales. 19 languages: Welsh, English. Of Purley 1920 & Hindhead c.1930. Languages: Welsh, English. Estate £23,000, of which he left the residue to the Exchequer. Will contested successfully by Mrs Rose Mary Edwards & Mrs. Gladys May Larrsen, Gilfach Goch, sister-in-law and niece, 1945-49. Died at Virginia Water Mental Hospital, 15 June, 1945. *Books: J. Hugh Edwards: From Village Green to Downing Street (biography of David Lloyd George); A History of Wales. Further Reading:* Ivor Thomas Rees, 'The Immaculate John Hugh', *National Library of Wales Journal, Vol. XXXIII, No. 1, Summer 2003.*

EDWARDS John Trefor – see TREFOR-EDWARDS John.

EDWARDS Jonathan G. M: LlB (Southampton). Plaid Cymru: Gower 1987. **Mr. Jonathan Edwards:** Born Fishguard 7 February 1952. Married Vicki, 1c. Educated Cheltenham College; Southampton University. Spent five years with a London shipping company. Barrister, Lincolns Inn, at Swansea. Member: Welsh International Rowing Team; Cymdeithas Tai Dyffryn Teifi; Tŷ Tawe Cttee. Swansea; Guild for the Promotion of Welsh Music. Languages: Welsh, English. Of Porthyrhyd.

EDWARDS Leslie Douglas (*Also known as 'Gibson, Martin Fender'*): Monster Raving Loony Party, Ogmore By-Election 14 Feb. 2002. **Mr. Leslie Edwards:** Born 1945. Teacher: Head of English, Porthcawl Comprehensive School, retired. Official Monster Raving Loony Party Shadow Minister for Jamming; Official Monster Raving Loony Party Welsh Ambassador. Of Bridgend.

EDWARDS Meredith – see EDWARDS Gwilym Meredith.

EDWARDS Ness (Onesimus): PC 1947 JP (Glam). Labour MP Caerphilly B/E 1939-. **Rt. Hon Ness Edwards:** Born Abertillery 5 April 1897. Married Elvina Victoria, 5c (inc. Llinos Golding MP). Educated elementary schools & London Labour College 1919-21. Miner at 13. Chair, SWMF Lodge at 18; Full-time Secretary, Penallta Lodge 1927; Miners' Agent, East Glamorgan 1932; MFGB Executive 1935. Imprisoned as CO. Gelligaer UDC. Visited Czechoslovakia 1939 and organised the escape of 200 Sudeten miners to UK. Delegate, International Labour Conference, Paris 1945. Parl. Secretary, Labour 1945-50; Postmaster General 1950-51. Chairman, Trades Union Group of MPs 1964-68. Of Caerphilly. *Book: Ness Edwards: A History of the SMWF; A History of the South Wales Miners.* Died 3 May 1968.

EDWARDS Owen Meirion: BA (Wales). Labour: Ynys Môn 1997. **Mr. Owen Edwards:** Born 9 August 1970, s of William H. Edwards MP (qv). Married Louise, 1s. Educated Yale Sixth Form College; University of Wales, Cardiff; Inns of Court School of Law. Barrister. ComC. Languages: Welsh, English.

EDWARDS Owen Morgan: Kt 1916 BA (Lond) 1883 BA (Oxon) 1887 Hon DLitt (Wales) 1918. Liberal: MP Merioneth B/E 1899-1900. **Sir Owen M. Edwards:** Born Llanuwchllyn 25 December 1858, son of Owen & Beti Edwards. Calvinistic Methodist. Married Ellen Davies (died 1919) 2s 1d. Educated Bala Theological College;

University of Wales, Aberystwyth 1880-83; Glasgow University (1883-4); Balliol College, Oxford (1st History); Fellow of Lincoln College & Tutor in History 1889-1907. 1st Chief Inspector of Schools for Wales 1907-. Litterateur. Languages: Welsh, English. Joint-Editor: *Cymru Fydd* 1890; Founded *Cymru* 1891; *Cymru'r Plant* 1892, *Wales*, 1894, *Y Llenor* 1895. Died 15 May 1920. Further Reading: *W. J. Gruffydd, Cofiant O. M. Edwards, Cyf. 1.*

EDWARDS Richard John: BA MA PhD. MICSA. Labour AM, Preseli, 1999-2003, retired on health grounds. **Dr. Richard Edwards:** Born Llanelli, 25 August 1956, s of Kenneth Edwards, policeman. Atheist. Unmarried. Educated Queen Elizabeth Grammar School, Carmarthen, University of Wales, Swansea, Birmingham University. Local Government Officer, Hounslow, 1979-81. Lecturer & Researcher, Institute of Local Government Studies 1981-85. Freelance Political Researcher 1985-87. Research Assistant to Alan Wynne Williams, MP 1987-99. Agent, Carmarthen, 1987, 1992. Secretary: Carmarthen Constituency Labour Party. Chair, Dyfed County Labour Party, 1988-91, Carmarthen West & South Pembs CLP 1997-98. Freelance Political Researcher Lecturer 1995-97. Member, Wales Labour Party Executive, 1990-95 (Chair 1995-96). Mayor of Carmarthen 1997-98. Member: Chartered Institute of Secretaries, Age Concern, CAB. Chair: Stroke Club, Access Group, Arthritis Care branch. School governor. Chair: Assembly Environment, Planning & Transport Cttee. Interests: Welfare rights, Disability issues, Rural poverty, Equal opportunities, Access & Disability issues, Nuclear disarmament, GM crops. A leading opponent of the Iraq War and critic of Tony Blair's part in it. Hobbies: Walking, Sport, Cinema, Classical music, Opera. Languages: Welsh, English. Of Haverfordwest.

EDWARDS Robert John: ILP: Newport B/E May 1945, Chorley 1935, Stretford B/E 1935; Joined the Labour Party 1950; Labour & Co-operative MP Bilston 1955-Feb. 1974, Wolverhampton SE Feb. 1974-87. **Mr. Bob Edwards:** Born 6 January 1906, son of a steel erector; Married Edith, d of Eli Sandham, MP. Educated elementary schools & technical college. Chemical Worker. Lancashire Area Organiser, Chemical Workers' Union 1939-47; General Secretary, Chemical Workers' Union 1947-71; National Officer TGWU 1971-76. Editor, *The Chemical Worker*. Served with Republican Army in Spanish Civil War 1936-38. Chairman, Delegations to USSR 1926, 1934. Liverpool CC 1943-48. National Chairman, ILP 1943-48. Founder-President, Socialist Movement for United States of Europe. Vice-President, British Section. European League for Economic Co-operation; Economic Research

Council. Vice-Chairman, Federal Union; PLP Defence Group 1966. Chairman, West Midlands Labour MPs Group 1966; Co-operative MPs Group, 1964; Industrial Common Ownership Group. Member, Estimates Cttee. 1964. Died 4 October 1990.

Nicholas Edwards.

EDWARDS Roger Nicholas, Baron Crickhowell 1987: PC 1979 BA 1957 MA (Cantab) 1968. Hon. (Glam). 2001. Conservative MP Pembroke 1970-87. **Rt. Hon. Nicholas Edwards:** Born 25 February 1934, son of Ralph Edwards CBE. Anglican. Married Ankarat Margaret, d of W. J. Healing, 1s 2d. Educated Westminster School; Trinity College, Cambridge (History) 1954-57. Lieutenant, RWF 1952-54. Director of several underwriting & holdings companies. Writer & Reviewer for Art Journals. Vice-Chairman, Barons Court Conservative Assn. Member, Select Cttee. on Members' Interests 1976-79. Secretary, Welsh Group of Conservative MPs 1972-74; Opposition spokesman on Welsh Affairs 1975-79; Secretary of State for Wales 1979-87. Chairman: National Rivers Authority 1989-96. Company Director: HTV Group 1987-2002 (Chairman 1997-2002); Associated British Port Holdings 1988-99. Deputy Chairman, Anglesey Mining Co. Non-executive Chairman, ITNET 1995. Committee Member, Automobile Assn 1989-96. President, University of Wales, Cardiff 1988-98. Of Abergavenny & London. *Books: Nicholas Edwards, Westminster, Wales and Water (Autobiography) 1998.*

EDWARDS Sandra: Conservative: Swansea East 1979; Joined Liberal Party, 26 January 1982. **Mrs. Sandra Edwards:** Born USA 1941 of Greek parentage. Married 3c. Educated Bennington High School & Mount Holyoake College, Massachusetts. Company Director: National Housing

Corporation Finance Co. Ealing BC 1978-. Westminster CC 1974-78. National Chair: Pre-School Play Groups Assn 1974-78. Founder/Chair, Fair Play for Children Campaign 1973-78. Director, The Volunteer Centre. Of London.

EDWARDS Siân Angharad: Plaid Cymru: Cardiff South & Penarth 1983; 1987. **Ms. Siân Edwards:** Born Barry, 30 August 1948. Educated Ysgol Gymraeg St. Ffransis, Barry; Carmarthen Grammar School; University of Wales, Aberystwyth. Freelance Translator & Scriptwriter. Founder-Member, Welsh Campaign for Civil & Political Liberties. Active in Peace Movement. Member: Plaid Cymru Executive. Chair, Plaid Cymru 1992-93. Languages: English; Welsh. Of Cardiff (1968).

EDWARDS Trefor: BA (Wales). Plaid Cymru: Montgomery 1966. **Mr. Trefor Edwards:** Born Llanuwchllyn 1928. Presbyterian Church of Wales. Married Mair, d of Revd Gomer Roberts, 1s. Educated Bala Grammar School & University of Wales, Aberystwyth. Teacher (Welsh), Llanfair Caereinion -1968; Bala 1968-. Pennillion singer & actor. A founder, Côr Godre'r Aran. Gwynedd CC. Languages Welsh; English. Of Llanuwchllyn. Died 15 November 2003.

EDWARDS William: MBE OBE JP (Anglesey) 1929 FRGS. Labour: Anglesey 1929. **Mr. William Edwards:** Born Llanfedwen 22 August 1863, son of William Edwards & Elizabeth Jones. Baptist. Married 1895, Fanny Ann, d of John Williams. Educated Duchess of Kent School, Llanfair PG; University of Wales, Bangor. (Diploma of the Royal Agricultural Society). Organiser & Lecturer in Agriculture, North Cheshire, 1894-1907; Lecturer in Agriculture & County Organiser (Anglesey), University of Wales, Aberystwyth, 1907. Farmer. Anglesey CC 1910; Alderman 1924; Chairman; Chairman, Education Cttee 1945- (Vice-Chairman 1941). Joint Founder, trade union, with Cyril O. Jones, Undeb Gweision Môn 1909. Chairman: Anglesey Joint Standing Cttee 1937-38; Anglesey War Agricultural Executive Cttee. Member, Court of Governors, University of Wales, University College, Bangor; Welsh Agricultural Council; Royal Commission on Agriculture 1919. Chairman, Anglesey Liberal Assn 1918. Languages: Welsh; English. Of Llanddaniel. Died 1950.

EDWARDS William Edmund Huw: BA (Manchester) 1976 MA (York) 1978 MPhil (York) 1984. Labour MP Monmouth: B/E 1991-92; 1997-. **Mr. Huw Edwards:** Born 12 April 1953, son of Revd Dr. Ifor M. Edwards & Esme Edwards. Welsh Independent. Educated Earlsfield High School, Mitcham; Manchester Polytechnic (Social Science); York University. Research Associate, Low Pay

Unit 1985; Senior Lecturer in Social Policy, Brighton Poly 1985-89; Manchester Poly 1985-88; South Bank Poly 1984-85; Sheffield University 1983-84; Lanchester/Coventry Poly 1980-81; Open University Tutor 1988-89, 1993-96. Member: NATFHE; Gwalia Male Voice Choir; Fabian Society; Parliament for Wales Campaign; Labour Campaign for Electoral Reform 1991. Executive, Shelter Cymru; President, Chepstow Mencap 1992. Select Cttee. Member: Minimum Wage Bill 1997; Welsh Affairs 1991-92. Hobbies: Sports (member, Parliamentary cricket, rugby & soccer teams) Manchester United fan; member, Gwalia Male Voice Choir.

EDWARDS William Henry: LlB (Liverpool) Labour: West Flint 1964; Merioneth Feb. & Oct. 1974; MP Merioneth 1966-74; Withdrew as Anglesey PPC 1983 because of his concern at the leftward trend in the Labour Party. **Mr. Will Edwards:** Born Amlwch 6 January 1938, son of Owen Henry Edwards, smallholder. Married 1961, Dr. Ann Eleri Rogers, 4c (Owen Edwards qv). Educated Sir Thomas Jones Comprehensive School, Amlwch; Liverpool University; London College of Law. Solicitor 1952. Visiting Lecturer in Mercantile Law, Liverpool College of Commerce; WEA Lecturer. Joined Labour Party 1953; Secretary, Amlwch Branch, Labour Party 1954-56; Chairman, Anglesey Young Socialists. PPS 1968-70; Additional Opposition Spokesman: Welsh Affairs 1970; Member, Select Cttee on Agriculture 1967-70; Historic Building Council of Wales 1971-76. Chair: Welsh Labour MPs Group. Member: Parliament for Wales Campaign; Labour Campaign for Electoral Reform; Shelter Cymru Executive 1989-91. Research Associate, Low Pay Unit 1985-97. Editor, *Solicitors' Diary*. Languages: Welsh, English.

EGAN Gerard Patrick: Looney Green: Gower 1992. **Mr. Gerry Egan:** Publican, William Hancock Inn, Mumbles.

EILIAN John - see JONES: J. T.

ELIAS Thomas: BA (Oxon). Liberal: Neath 1923. **Captain Tom Elias:** Born 1887, son of Thomas & Sarah Elias, Abernant, Glyn Neath. Married 1913, Elsie Cameron (Candidate, Southwark SE 1924), d. of Rt. Hon. T. J. MacNamara MP. 2d. Educated Glyn Neath Elementary School; Neath Grammar School; Llandovery College; Keble College, Oxford. Army 1915-17, Captain RWF. Journalist, *Daily Chronicle*; Asst. Editor, *Board of Trade Journal*; Financial Editor, *Daily Express* & *Sunday Express*. Languages: Welsh, English. Of Abernant & Kew.

ELIS Islwyn Ffowc: BA 1946 BD 1949 Hon. DLitt (Wales) 1993. Plaid Cymru: Montgomery

B/E 1962, 1964. **Revd Dr. Islwyn Ffowc Elis:** Born Wrexham 17 November 1924, son of Edward Ifor Ellis, farmer, & Catherine Kenrick. Presbyterian Church of Wales. Married Eirlys Rees Owen, 1d. Educated Llangollen Grammar School; University of Wales, Bangor; Aberystwyth & Bala Theological Colleges. CO 1942. Won Inter-Collegiate Eisteddfod Crown 1944. Minister, Presbyterian Church of Wales, Ordained, 1950. Pastorate: Llanfair Caereinion, Meifod, 1950-56. Lecturer, Trinity College, Carmarthen 1956-63. Translator-Editor, Welsh Books Council project 1963 (fluent in French, Italian and German). Author, novelist & broadcaster 1963-67. Freelance 11967-73. Lecturer, University of Wales, Lampeter 1975-2000. Won National Eisteddfod Prose Medal 1951; Arts Council for Wales Award for Welsh Literature 1962. Joined Plaid Cymru 1944. Editor, *Y Ddraig Goch* 1951. Member, Plaid Cymru Executive. Press & Publications Officer, Carmarthen By-Election 1966. Member: University of Wales Council. Of Lampeter. *Books: Cyn Oeri'r Gwaed 1952, Cysgod y Cryman 1953, Ffenestri Tua'r Gwyll 1955, Yn ôl i Leifior 1956, Wythnos yng Nghymru Fydd 1957, Blas y Cynfyd 1958, Tabyrddau'r Babongo 1961, Y Blaned Dirion 1968, Y Gromlech yn yr Haidd 1970 Eira Mawr 1971, Harris 1973, Marwydos 1974; Editor, Edward Tegla Davies, Llenor a Phroffwyd 1956, Storïau'r Deffro 1959, Twenty-Five Welsh Short Stories (with Gwyn Jones) 1971.* Further Reading: *T. Robin Chapman, Islwyn Ffowc Elis 2000, Rhywfaint of Anfarwoldeb, Bywgraffiad Islwyn Ffowc Elis 2003.*

ELIS Marged Ann: BA (Wales) 1972. Plaid Cymru, Delyn 1999. **Ms. Meg Elis:** Born Aberystwyth 26 October 1950, d of Thomas Iorwerth Elis, author & broadcaster, & Mari Gwendoline Headley, librarian. Church in Wales. Married 1976, Roger Dafydd. 1s 2d. Educated Ysgol Gymraeg, Aberystwyth, Ardwyn Grammar School, Aberystwyth; University of Wales, Bangor. Secretary, Cymdeithas yr Iaith Gymraeg 1972. Translator. Radio Producer, BBC Bangor, mid 80s. Journalist/Editor, *Y Faner*. Head of Translation Unit, Gwynedd CC. Academic Translator & Head of Translation Unit, Ganolfan Bedwyr, University of Wales, Bangor Freelance writer and broadcaster. Member: Institute of Translating & Interpreting, Cymdeithas yr Iaith, Friends of the National Library, Friends of Plas Glyn y Weddw Art Gallery, The Welsh Academy, Greenpeace, Amnesty International, Church in Wales Standing Liturgical Commission, Welsh Consumer Council 1998, Arts Council for Wales, Gorsedd of Bards. Winner of National Eisteddfod Prose Medal 1985. Active peace campaigner. Interests: Culture, Women's Rights, Third World Issues, Peace. Hobbies: Politics, History, Creative Writing, Travel. Languages: Welsh, English, some

French. Of Waunfawr, Caernarfon. *Books: I'r Gad 1975, Carchar 1978, Eglwysi Cymru (with Mary Ellis) 1985, Cyn Ddaw'r Gaeaf 1985.*

ELIS-THOMAS Dafydd Elis, Baron Elis-Thomas 1987: PC 12 August 2004, BA (Wales) 1967 Hon. LLD (Wales). Plaid Cymru: Conway 1970; MP Merioneth 1974-83; Meirionydd/Nant Conwy 1983-87; AM Meirionydd/Nant Conwy, 1999. **Rt. Hon. Lord Dafydd Elis-Thomas:** Born Carmarthen 18 October 1946, son of Rev. William Elis Thomas & Eirlys James. Changed surname to Elis-Thomas by deed poll 1992. Presbyterian, became Anglican. Married (1) 1970 Ellen M. Williams, 3s; divorced (2) 1993 Mair Parry Jones. Educated Ysgol Dyffryn Conwy; University of Wales, Bangor (1st Welsh). Member, Bangor SRC Executive. PhD Research student 1968-71. Tutor, Welsh Studies, Coleg Harlech 1971-74; broadcaster & writer. Joined CND, then Labour Party, then Plaid Cymru. Chair, Plaid Cymru Youth Cttee. Director of Policy. Spokesman on Social, Educational & Cultural Policy 1975; Agricultural & Rural Development 1974. President, Plaid Cymru 1984-91. Member, Select Cttee: Education, Science & Arts. Consultant, S4C and Welsh Development Authority. Member: Welsh Arts Council; Chairman, Welsh Language Board 1993-99. Assembly Presiding Officer, 1999-. Languages: Welsh, English. Of Dolgellau & Cardiff.

ELLIOT George: 1st Bart. 1874 JP (Glam & Mon) DL (Mon & Durham) Conservative MP: Monmouth District 1886-92; North Durham 1868-74 (election declared void) 1874-80; B/E 1881-85; Candidate: South East Durham 1885. **Sir George Elliot:** Born Penshaw, Gateshead, 18 March 1815, son of Ralph Elliot JP deputy manager Whitefield Colliery. Married 1836, Margaret (died 1880), d of George Green of Houghton le Spring. Pitboy at 8; apprentice at 19; Overman 1835; Partner in Colliery 1840. Chief Engineer & Consultant, Lord Londonderry's Durham collieries 1851-60. Proprietor, Kuper & Co. mining cable manufacturers 1840. Partner, Glass & Elliot; Telegraph Construction & Maintenance Co (laid first Trans Atlantic cable 1864); Thomas Powell & Co. 1864. Established Powell Dyffryn Steam Coal Co (16 mines); Crawshay Bailey Iron Works; Dyffryn Steel Co; Alexandra Dock Co. Chairman, George Elliot & Co. rope manufacturers; Pontypridd, Caerphilly & Newport Railway Co. President, Institute of Mining Engineering. Freemason (Grand Master, South East Wales 1877). Of Newport; Aberdare, Durham & London. Estate £575,785. Died 29 December 1893.

ELLIOTT D. H. Owen: SDP/Alliance: Gower 1987. **Mr. Owen Elliott:** Born 1950. Married.

Educated Gowerton Grammar School. Probation Service Assistant at Gowerton. Farmer on family farm 20 years. Membership Secretary, Gower SDP. Llangennith ComC. Of Fairwood, Gower.

ELLIS Nesta Wyn – see WYN ELLIS N. M.

ELLIS Robert Thomas: BSc (Wales) 1944 BSc. (Nottingham) 1952. Labour: West Flint 1966; MP Wrexham 1970-83; Founder Member SDP 1983; SDP/Alliance: Clwyd South West 1983, 1987; North Wales Euro 1984; Liberal-Democrat: Pontypridd B/E 1989. **Mr. Tom Ellis:** Born Rhosllanerchrugog 15 March 1924, son of Robert (miner) and Edith Ann Ellis (W). Presbyterian. Married 1949, Nona Harcourt Williams 4c. Educated Ruabon Grammar School; University of Wales, Bangor; Nottingham University (Mining). Chemist, ICI Penrhyndeudraeth 1944-46; Hons Student 1946-47; Miner, Gresford Colliery 1957-50; NCB. Scholarship, Nottingham University 1950-52; Deputy-Manager, Bersham 1952-57; Asst. Manager, Llai Main 1957-60; Manager, Bersham 1960-70. Member: Assn. of Colliery Managers; Assn. of British Colliery Management; Fellow, Institute of Mining. PPS 1974. Member, European Parliament 1975-79. President: Wrexham Fabian Society; SDP Council for Wales. Vice-Chair, Electoral Reform Society; Member: Russell Cttee on Adult Education. Of Ruabon. *Books: Tom Ellis, Dan Loriau Maelor (autobiography), 2002.*

ELLIS Roger Philip: Natural Law Party, Mid & West list 1999. **Mr Roger Ellis:** Of Skelmersdale.

ELLIS Thomas Edward: BA (London) 1879, BA (Oxon) 1894 MA 1897. Liberal MP Merioneth 1886. **Mr. Tom Ellis:** Born Cefnddwysarn, near

Thomas Edward Ellis.

Bala 16 February 1859, son of Thomas & Elizabeth Ellis. Calvinistic Methodist. Married Annie, d of R. J. Davies, Llangeitho, 1s. Educated Llandderfel British School; Bala County School; Bala Theological College; University of Wales, Aberystwyth; New College, Oxford; 2nd History); parents intended him for the Ministry. Tutor, John Cory family 1886-87; Secretary to Sir John Brunner BT 1867-86. Charity Commissioner (unpaid); Lord Commissioner & Deputy Chief Whip 1892-94; Patronage Secretary & Chief Whip 1894-. Member, Merioneth Education Cttee. 1889-; Central Welsh Board; Court of the University of Wales; Founder-President, UCW Aberystwyth Old Students Assn; Warden, Welsh Guild of Graduates. Received National Testimonial of £1,000, 1889. Languages: Welsh, English. Of Cefnddwyrsarn. Died Cannes, 5 April 1899. *Books: T. E. Ellis: Addresses & Speeches, 1892.* Further Reading: *Wyn Griffith: Thomas Edward Ellis, 1959. Neville Masterman: The Forerunner.*

ELLIS William Armon: CBE 1969 LlB (Wales) 1936. Liberal: West Flint 1950. **Mr. Armon Ellis:** Born Licswyn, 1 March 1913, son of Edward & Margaret Ann Ellis. Baptist. Educated Holywell Grammar School; University of Wales, Aberystwyth (1st Law). Solicitor at Rhyl. Army 1939-45, Major; Deputy Asst. Director GHQ, India Command. President East Flint Liberal Assn 1953. Chairman, Executive, Flint National Eisteddfod 1969; Hon Solicitor, National Eisteddfod; President, Flint Eisteddfod. Hon Member, Gorsedd 1970. Vice-President, Rent Tribunals, Wales. Flintshire CC Alderman. Member: Hon Society of Cymmrodorion. Languages: Welsh, English. Of Licswyn. Died 6 July 1994.

ELLIS-GRIFFITH Ellis Jones: 1st Bart 1919 PC 1914 KC 1910 BA (London) 1888 MA (Cantab). Liberal MP Anglesey 1895-1918 (PPC 1918-21); Carmarthen 1923-24; Candidate: University of Wales 1922, West Toxteth 1892. **Rt. Hon Sir Ellis Ellis-Griffith:** Born Birmingham, 24 May 1869, son of Thomas Morris Griffith (died 1886), builder & Jane, d of William & Eleanor Jones one of 8 children. Calvinistic Methodist. Married 1892, Mary, d of Revd Robert Owen, Mold, 2s 1d. Educated Brynsiencyn; Holt School, nr Wrexham; University of Wales, Aberystwyth; Downing College, Cambridge (Pensioner-Minor Scholar); Captain UCW Cricket XI; President, Cambridge Union1886; Fellow of Downing College. Barrister, Middle Temple) 1887. Recorder of Birkenhead 1907-12. Chairman, Welsh Parliamentary Party 1912; Under-Secretary, Home Office 1912-15, resigned. County Court Judge 1924. Estate £10,884. Languages: Welsh, English. Died at Metropole Hotel, Swansea, 30 November 1926. Further Reading: *T. I. Ellis: Ellis Jones Griffith, 1969.*

ELLIS-JONES William Benjamin Ellis: MB ChB Liverpool) 1942. MRCS LRCP (England) 1942. Liberal: Denbigh 1964. **Dr. William Ellis-Jones:** Born Rhuallt, near Rhyl, September 1918. Educated St. Asaph Grammar School; Liverpool University. Medical Practitioner at Southport. Founder member, Stockport Muscular Dystrophy Group. Chairman, Stockport Round Table.

ELLIS-NANNEY Hugh John: 1st Bart 1897 JP (Caerns). Conservative: Arfon B/E 1880, 1885; Caernarfon District 1890, 1895. **Sir Hugh Ellis-Nanney:** Born 16 February 1845, son of Major Owen Jones Ellis-Nanney MP Caernarfon District March-May 1933, & Mary, d of Hugh Jones, Hengwrtucha. Anglican. Married 1878, Hon. Elizabeth Octavia, d of Baron Clonbrook. Landowner & Agent to Lord Penrhyn. Caernarfonshire CC 1889-President, Caernarfon Boroughs Conservative Assn. 1918. High Sheriff: Merioneth 1877, Caernarfonshire 1890. Of Gwynfryn Castle, Llanystymdwy & Cefnddeuddwr, Merioneth. Estate £61,511. Died 7 June 1920.

ELPHICK Felicity Ann Ledgewater: Conservative, Wrexham 1999, 2001; Wales Euro 2004; ppc Vale of Clwyd 2004. **Mrs Felicity Elphick:** Born Preston, Lancs. 17 December 1947, d of Arthur Edward Jones, paint manufacturer, & Muriel Ledgerwood, political activist. Church of England. Married. 1977, Colin Henry Elphick, company director (retired) & officer for charity 3s. Educated Heathfield, Ascot, Henley Lodge, Bath, Universities of Madrid & Saarbruken, Alliance Francais, Paris, Mrs. Hosters' Secretarial College, London, Courtfield Catering College, Blackpool. Worked with Punch magazine (PA to Alan Coran) & Bertorelli gold manufacturers, Padua. Director, Grange Barton Hotel, Financial Secretary, Brook Home Farm Properties Ltd, Proprietor, Partner Easy Entertaining. Owner, Anglesey holiday cottages. Final Year, A level Politics, 1999. Student at Manchester University (Politics) 2001. Joined Conservative Party 1963. Chair, Fylde YCs, Ynys Môn Conservative Assn, Wrexham Conservative Assn (2001, North Wales Women's Cttee. Parent Carer, Conwy Connect. Interests: Special Needs – Carers & Dyslexics, Feminism, Third World Politics, Political Science & Philosophy. Hobbies: Painting, Reading, Gardening, Bridge, Socialising. Languages: English, Learning Welsh, French, Spanish, Italian, Portuguese, German. Of Llandudno.

EMLYN Viscount: Frederick Archibald Vaughan Campbell, 3rd Earl Cawdor, Viscount Emlyn (1827); Baron Cawdor (1796) PC 1905 JP DL (Carms) & Cairns) MA (Oxon). Conservative: West Carmarthenshire 1885; South Manchester B/E July 1892; Cricklade B/E 1898; MP Carmarthenshire 1874-85; South Manchester 1892-95. **Rt.**

Hon Viscount Emlyn: Born London 13 February 1847, son of 2nd Earl Cawdor of Golden Grove (MP Pembrokeshire 1841-60) & Sarah Mary, d of General, Hon Henry Compton-Cavendish; succeeded 1898. Anglican. Married 1868, Edith Georgiana, d of Christopher & Lady Caroline Tournour of Stoke Rochford. Educated Eton; Christ Church, Oxford. Landowner; Chairman, Great Western Railway 1895-1905. Lieutenant, Carmarthenshire Militia RA 1865; Hon Colonel. ADC to the King. Chairman, Carmarthenshire Quarter Sessions 1888. Carmarthenshire CC 1888-. President, Royal Agricultural Society 1901. Member: Aberdare Commission into Intermediate & Higher Education in Wales. Ecclesiastical Commissioner 1880; Hon Commissioner in Lunacy 1886-93; First Lord of the Admiralty 1905. Lord Lieutenant of Carmarthenshire 1896-.Of Golden Grove, Carms & London. Estate £633,328. Died 8 February 1911.

EMLYN-JONES John Alun: JP (Glam). Liberal: Barry 1950; North Dorset B/E 1957, 1959. **Mr. Alun Emlyn-Jones:** Born Cardiff February 1923, son of J. E. Emlyn-Jones (qv.). Presbyterian Church of Wales. Married. Educated Summer Fields School; Charterhouse School; University of Wales, Cardiff. RAF Bomber Command 1941-45. Sales Manager, manufacturing company on Treforest trading estate. Company Director. Chairman, Cardiff Young Liberals; Member: Liberal Party Council & Executive.

EMLYN-JONES John Emlyn: JP (Cardiff). Liberal: Cardiff East 1929, 1931, 1945; Flint 1945; North Dorset 1918, 1924; MP North Dorset 1922-24. **Mr. J. E. Emlyn-Jones:** Born Cardiff 23 January 1889, son of Revd Evan Jones, Presbyterian minister, & Sarah Elizabeth Davies. Presbyterian. Married 1915, Rhoda Penberthy, d of Captain Richard Care of Cardiff, 1s (qv) 1d. Educated Cardiff High School and France, Spain & Italy. Clerk in shipping office 1906; Shipowner 1911: Joint Managing Director, Emlyn-Jones, Griffin & Co.; Director of many companies. Chairman: Cardiff Anglo-Soviet Society; South Wales Branch, Ibero-American Institute; Cardiff Incorporated Chamber of Commerce; Cardiff & Bristol Incorporated Shipowners' Assn. President, Cardiff & Barry Liberal Council; Pontypridd Liberal Assn; North Dorset Liberal Assn. Freemason. Of Cardiff. Died Nice, 3 March 1952 (killed in air crash).

EMMETT Angela Ann: Conservative: Newport East 1992. **Mrs Angela Emmett:** Born 24 August 1952. Married Educated Gurnley House Convent Grammar School; Thames Valley Management Centre. Executive: BAT Industries, BOC International, Beecham Pharmaceuticals. Chairman: West European Union of Women; Aston

CPC. Vice-Chair, Greater London CPC. Of London.

ESSEX Susan Linda: BA (Leicester). MRPTI. Labour AM Cardiff North 1999. **Mrs Sue Essex:** Born Cromford, Derbyshire, 29 August 1945. Married 1967 Richard Essex, 1s 1d. Educated Leicester University (Geography). Technical Secretary, South Wales Standing Conference 1971-73, Researcher, Equal Opportunity Commission 1985-87; Planner, Mid-Glam CC; Lecturer, City & Regional Planning, University of Wales, Cardiff. 1991-99, Planner, London Borough of Waltham Forest 1995-99. Cardiff CC 1983-96 (Leader), Cardiff CCC 1995-99. Member: Countryside Council for Wales, Royal Town Planning Institute. Interests: Transport, Environment, Planning. Supported Rhodri Morgan's leadership campaign. Secretary for the Environment 2000. Minister for the Environment Oct. 2000; Deputy First Minister & Minister of Finance & Local government 2003. Hobbies: Football, Walking. Of Rhiwbina.

ETHERIDGE Kevin: Liberal Democrat, Islwyn 2001. **Mr. Kevin Etheridge:** Born Tredegar 21 October 1958, son of William John Ken Etheridge & Jean Etheridge. Methodist. Married 2980 Teresa Jane Etheridge, 1s 3d. Educated Ynysddu Secondary Modern School; Crosskeys College. Design. Chair, Islwyn Liberal Democrats; Agent 1983, 1992. Interests: Environment, Education. Hobbies: Family; Dealing with council problems. Resigned from Liberal Democrats, 1.1.2003, when asked to fund his own 2003 campaign at Islwyn. Of Pontllanffraith.

EVANS Alan: Labour: Pembroke 1979; Joined SDP Feb.1982; SDP/Alliance: Vale of Glamorgan 1983. **Mr. Alan Evans:** Born Llanelli 10 February 1939, steelworker's son. Educated Llanelli Grammar School; London School of Economics. Member: school rugby XV; Carmarthenshire youth soccer XI. Teacher. Personal Assistant, General Secretary NUT (Sir Ronald Gould). Chair: NUT Education Cttee. Camden BC 1974-78. Member: NUT; NUGMW.

EVANS Alfred Thomas: BA (Wales). Labour MP Caerphilly B/E 1968-79; Candidate: Stroud 1959, Leominster, 1955. **Mr. Fred Evans:** Born Aberfan 24 February 1914, son of Alfred Evans, miner, & Sarah Jane, mid-wife. Married 1939, Mary O'Morah, 2d. Educated Bargoed Grammar School; University of Wales, Cardiff. Teacher (English) Lewis School, Pengam 1937-49; Head: Bedlinog School 1949-66; Lewis School, Pengam 1966-68. Gelligaer UDC. President, Caerphilly CLP; election agent 1964, 1966. Select Cttee. Member: Estimates; Statutory Instruments. Treasurer: British-DDR Parliamentary Group; Secretary: Anglo-Libyan Parliamentary Group. Of Hengoed. Died 13 April 1987.

EVANS Arthur – see EVANS Henry A.

EVANS David Charles: Independent, Swansea West, Assembly 1999; UK Independence Party, Swansea West 2003. **Mr. David Evans:** Born Swansea, 28 February 1935, son of George Evans, contractor, & Naryanna Evans, dressmaker. Church of England. Married 1963 Daphne Annette Evans, 1s 1d. Educated Dynevor Grammar School, Swansea. Apprentice, Swansea Docks. RAF. Owner, Swansea Building Supplies, retired. Mumbles ComC. -2002 (Chair). Swansea CC 1999. Hobbies: DIY, Gardening, ex-county golfer. Of Mayals, Swansea.

EVANS David Doiran: BSc. MEd. Liberal Democrat, Ceredigion 1999, East Carmarthenshire & Dinefwr 2001. **Mr. Doiran Evans:** Born Cardigan, 16 February 1939, son of Thomas Evans, headteacher, & Margaret Elizabeth Phillips, teacher. Church in Wales. Married 1972 Patricia Ann Head, 1s 1d. Educated Cardigan Grammar School, Trinity College, Carmarthen, Birkbeck College, London, University of Wales, Bangor. PE teacher at Lampeter 1968-89. Headteacher, Education Officer. Retired. Ceredigion CC 1995-99 (defeated). Member, Welsh Liberal Democrat Executive 1996-, Welsh Liberal Democrat Candidates Cttee. 1996-98. Secretary: Ceredigion Liberal Democrats. Interests: Devolution, Of Drefach, Llanybydder.

EVANS David John: Conservative, Pontypridd 1924; Neath 1929. **Mr. David Evans:** Miner. SWMF lodge chairman. Secretary, Wales & Mon Unionist Labour Cttee. Of 48 Miskin Road, Trealaw.

EVANS David John: BSc. Liberal/Alliance, Delyn 1987, North Shropshire 1983, Oswestry 1979, Feb. & Oct. 1974 Wallasey 1970. **Mr. David Evans:** Born Devon 28 February 1947. Married Jean, 3c. Educated Teignmouth Grammar School; Liverpool University; Chester HE College. Teacher; Senior Lecturer in Biology, Chester HE College. Regional Service Manager, Spastics Society. Chairman, Garston Liberal Assn. Chester CC. Member, NATFHE.

EVANS David John: Conservative: Neath 1997. **Mr. David Evans:** Born 7 August 1947. Educated Highams Park Senior High School, Chingford; University of Wales, Swansea. Marketing Executive, Business Seminars International. Joined Chingford YCs. Chair, Welsh Conservative Students. Chief of Staff Conservative Students. Campaign Manager, Conservative Central Office 1992.

EVANS David Lloyd: Independent, Ceredigion, 1999. **Mr. Dai Lloyd Evans:** Born Llanddeiniol, 1

August 1941. Married Margaret, 3s 1d. Educated Llanddeiniol Primary School; Swyddffynon Primary School; Tregaron Secondary School. Farmer. Tregaron RDC 1961, Chair 1968-69. Ceredigion DC 1973-83, 1987-96, Chair, 1994. Ceredigion CC. 1995- (Leader, Independent Group, Leader of the Council, Chair, Education Cttee, Representative on National Assembly working party on Future of Farming Oct. 2000). Leader, Independent Group, Welsh Local Government Assn. Director, Wales European Centre. Chair, West Wales Partnership. Hobbies: Sheep dog training, Harness racing. Languages: Welsh, English. Of Tregaron.

EVANS David Maldwyn: MA (Oxon). Conservative: Montgomery 1987, Newport East 1997. **Mr. David Evans:** Born 13 August 1957. Married 1s. Educated Kingsland Grange School, Shrewsbury; Wrekin College; Mansfield College, Oxford; Inns of Court Law School. Barrister, in Oil & Gas industry. Treasurer, Wycombe Conservative Assn. Chair: Swansea West Conservative Assn. Languages: Welsh, English.

EVANS David Meurig: Conservative: Barry 1950. **Mr. Meurig Evans:** Born Aberaeron 1906, son of Howell T. Evans, Welsh historian. Married 1933, Joyce Diedericke Sander of St. Albans, 4c. Educated Cardiff High School; Aberaeron County School; Cardiff Technical College. Journalist on *Western Mail* & *The Economist* 1925-31. Barrister, Grays Inn 1931. Royal Navy 1939-45, Lieut-Commander. Chairman, Medical Appeal Tribunal for Wales 1952-57: County Court Judge 1957-79. Died 7 March 1983.

EVANS David Owen: Kt 1945 JP (Cards). Liberal MP Cardigan B/E 1932-. **Sir D. Owen Evans:** Born Llanborth, Penbryn 1876; son of William Evans, farmer 168 acres, & Elizabeth Jane Owens. Calvinistic Methodist. Freemason. Married 1899, Kate, d. of David Morgan, Aberffrwd. Educated Llandovery College; Royal College of Science, London; Kings College, London. Civil Servant, 1898-1908. Barrister, Grays Inn 1909-16. Joined Mond Nickel Company 1916; later became Chief Administrative Director, Vice-President and Chairman. Chairman, General Munitions Council, Wales & Mon. Member: Hon Society of Cymmrodorion; Council of University of Wales, Aberystwyth & Swansea; National Library & National Museum of Wales. Approached by Swansea West Liberal Assn 1931. Languages: Welsh, English. Of Llangranog; Maidenhead & London. Died 11 June 1945.

EVANS David Roderick: Kt 2001. QC 1989 LlB LLM (London). Plaid Cymru: Swansea East 1970. **Sir Roderick Evans:** Born Morriston 22 October 1946, son of Thomas James Evans & Dorothy Carpenter. Married 1971 Kathryn Rebecca Lewis, 3s 1d. Educated Bishop Gore Grammar School, Swansea; University College, London. Visiting Lecturer in Commercial Law, University of Wales 1968-69. Barrister, Grays Inn 1970. Chair: Morriston Citizens Action Group; Morriston Branch, Plaid Cymru; Plaid Cymru Research Group; Plaid Cymru spokesman on Fuel & Power. Contested Swansea CC 1970. Crown Court Recorder 1987. Resident Judge, Merthyr 1994-98. Recorder of Swansea 1998-99. Recorder of Cardiff 1999-200. High Court Judge 12 April 2001, with special responsibility for Welsh Language matters, Wales & Chester Circuit. Hobbies: Welsh Ceramics, Reading, Walking. Languages: Welsh, English. Of Sketty, Swansea.

EVANS Delyth – see EVANS Margaret Delyth.

EVANS Dengar Robinson: MPS. Labour: Barry 1959, Chippenham 1951. **Mr. Dengar Evans:** Born Blaengarw, November 1909. Married Margaret, 1s 1d. Educated Garw Grammar School; Welsh National School of Pharmacy. Pharmaceutical Chemist. Member: USDAW; Socialist Medical Assn. Cardiff CC -1965. Died 10 January 2002.

EVANS Dewi Richard: MB ChB (Wales) 1971 MRCP (UK)1975 DObstRCOG 1973 FRCP FRCPCH. Plaid Cymru Neath, B/E 1991, 1992; Swansea East 2003. **Dr. Dewi Evans:** Born Llanllwni, 29 July 1949, son of Daniel Evans & Lizzie Mary Davies, farmers. Welsh Independent. Married 1975, Delyth Margaret Evans, administrative officer, 1s 1d. Educated Peniel Primary School; Queen Elizabeth Grammar School, Carmarthen; University of Wales, Cardiff; Welsh National School of Medicine. Consultant Paediatrician, Singleton Hospital. West Glam CC 1989-93. Neath/Port Talbot BC 1999-. Member, Plaid Cymru Executive. Plaid Cymru Spokesman on Local Government; Election Agent, South Wales West Euro Seat, 1994. Chair: Neath Constituency Plaid Cymru. Interests: Health, Education, Environment, Economy. Hobbies: Politics, Travel. Languages: English, Welsh. Of Alltwen, Pontardawe.

EVANS Doiran – see EVANS David Doiran.

EVANS Elinor B. – see BONNER-EVANS E.

EVANS Emlyn H. G. – GARNER-EVANS E. H.

EVANS Ernest: KC 1937 JP BA (Cantab) LlB (Wales). (Coalition) Liberal MP Cardigan B/E 1921-23; University of Wales 1924-42. **Captain Ernest Evans:** Born Aberystwyth 1885; son of Evan Evans, clerk to Cardiganshire County

Council & Moderator of General Assembly, Presbyterian Church of Wales, & Annie Davies. Presbyterian Church of Wales. Married 1925; Constance Anne, d. of Thomas Lloyd, Hadley Wood, 3s. Educated Llandovery College; University of Wales, Aberystwyth; Trinity Hall, Cambridge. President of the Cambridge Union 1909. Barrister, 1910. Legal Adviser in National Insurance Office, Cardiff. Army 1914-18 Captain RASC. Private Secretary to David Lloyd George, Prime Minister 1918-21. Member: Council of University of Wales, Aberystwyth; National Library. President, Hon Society of Cymmrodorion. Chairman, Cardiganshire & Anglesey Quarter Sessions. Judge of the County Court 1942-57. Of New Quay, then Deganwy. Died 15 January 1965.

EVANS Ernest John: Liberal: Llanelli Feb. 1974. **Mr. John Evans:** Born Llwchwr June 1951. Married 1s. Educated Pontardawe Grammar School. Owner of two retail carpet shops; formerly the youngest ever consultant to Britain's largest pensions office. Of Llanelli.

EVANS Frank: Plaid Cymru: East Flint Oct 1974. **Mr. Frank Evans:** Born Shotton 1938, son of Tom "Taff" Evans BEM. Married Janet, London, 4c. Educated Hawarden Grammar School. ATC. RAF 1956-58. Electrical Engineer at Vauxhall Motors Ltd. Financial Secretary, Chester Area DATA. Vice-Chairman, Plaid Cymru West Flint Cttee; Member, Plaid Cymru Executive. Mold TC. Of Mold.

EVANS Gareth Wyn: JP (Carms) MA PhD (Cantab). Plaid Cymru: Cardigan 1959, 1964. **Dr. Gareth Evans:** Born Talybont, Cards. September 1921, son of Fred Evans, schoolmaster. Presbyterian Church of Wales. Married. Educated Ardwyn Grammar School, Aberystwyth; Peterhouse College, Cambridge. Lecturer in Mathematics, University of Wales, Swansea. Member, Advisory Council for Education in Wales.

EVANS Gwyndaf: BSc. Natural Law Party, Caernarfon 1992. **Mr. Gwyndaf Evans:** Born Bryngwran, Ynys Môn, 4 July 1948, son of William Hugh Evans, farmer, & Jane Ellen Richards, teacher. Methodist. Married 1989, Eibhlin Ide Cody, housewife, 1s. Educated Holyhead Secondary School & University (Electrical Engineering Science). Computer Software Consultant & part-time Farmer. Taught Transcendental Meditation in Wales for several years. Hobbies: Hill Walking, Transcendental Meditation. Languages: Welsh, English. Of, Skelmersdale.

EVANS Gwynfor Richard: LlB (Wales)1934 MA (Oxon) Hon (Wales) 1973. Plaid Cymru: Merioneth 1945, 1950, 1955, 1959; Aberdare B/E

1954, 1964, 1970, Feb. & Oct. 1974, 1979, 1983; MP Carmarthen, B/E July 1966-70, Oct. 1974-79. **Mr. Gwynfor Evans:** Born Barry September 1912, s. of Dan Evans, house furnisher & Catherine Mary Richard. Welsh Independent. Married 1941, Rhiannon Prys, d. of Dan Thomas (qv) 7 c. Educated Barry Grammar School; University of Wales, Aberystwyth; St. John's College, Oxford. Secretary, Cymdeithas Dafydd ap Gwilym; Founder Oxford branch, Plaid Cymru. Solicitor 1939; Market Gardener. Secretary, Heddychwyr Cymru 1939-45 & Editor, 33 pamphlets. Plaid Cymru Executive 1937; Vice-President 1943-45, President, 1945-. Chairman, Union of Welsh Independents 1954-55, Treasurer 1964-. Member: Court of the University of Wales; Council of University College, Aberystwyth; Executive, Welsh Guild of Graduates; Executive, Undeb Cymru Fydd; Broadcasting Council for Wales. Hon Member, Gorsedd of Bards 1965. Carmarthenshire CC 1949-74; Alderman 1955. Society of Cymmrodorion Medal 1984; 1st recipient of the World Wide Wales Award, August 2000. Voted 'Wales' Greatest Living Statesman' in *Western Mail* Poll (8.01.2004). Languages: Welsh, English. Of Llangadog (1939) then Llanybydder. *Books: Gwynfor Evans: Argyfwng Amaethyddiaeth Cymru; Plaid Cymru & Wales 1950; Rhagom i Ryddid 1964, Celtic Nationalism (with others) 1968, Wales Can*

Plaid Cymru leaders.
Left to right: Dafydd Wigley MP & AM;
Gwynfor Evans MP,
and Dafydd Elis Thomas MP & AM.
(Photograph courtesy D. Cyril Jones).

Win 1975, Aros Mae 1971, Land of my Fathers 1974, A National Future for Wales 1975, Diwedd Prydeindod 1981, Bywyd Cymru 1982, Seiri Cenedl 1986, Welsh Nation Builders 19887, Pe Bai Cymru'n Rhydd 1989, Fighting for Wales 1991, Heddychiaeth Gristnogol yng Nghymru 1992.

EVANS Gwynfryn Morris: Labour: Montgomery 1964, 1966. **Mr. Gwyn Evans:** Born Rhosllanerchrugog, February 1931 (W). Educated Ruabon Grammar School; Bangor Normal College; colleges at Portsmouth & Southampton. Teacher. Secretary, Rhosllanerchrugog Branch, Labour Party; Member, Executive, Wrexham Divisional Labour Party; Welsh Member, Labour League of Youth National Cttee 1952-55. Member NUT.

EVANS Helen: BSc PGCE (Wales). Natural Law Party, South/Central List 1999, Euro election, Wales 1999. **Ms. Helen Evans:** Born Aberdare, 20 January 1947, d of Gwilym Glanville Evans, deputy head teacher (died 2001) and Nancy Owens, teacher. Christian. Married, divorced. Educated University of Wales, Cardiff (Biochemistry; Diploma of British Dyslexia Society to teach children with specific learning difficulties). Teacher: London 2 years; Canmore High School, Alberta; Ysgol Gyfun Rhydfelin. TM Teacher. Deputy National Leader, Natural Law Party (NLP no longer politically active, but is political branch of the Transcendental Meditation Movement). Interests: To bring about world peace. Hobbies: teaching about how we can achieve world peace. Languages: Welsh, English. Of Sibford Ferris, Banbury.

EVANS Henry Arthur: Kt 1944. Conservative: Cardiff South 1929, 1945; East Leicester 1923; MP Cardiff South 1924-29, 1931-45; Joined Conservative Party 1923; National Liberal MP: East Leicester 1922-23. **Colonel, Sir Arthur Evans:** Born London 24 September 1898, son of Captain Arthur S. Evans & Ina Mary Bolton. Married (1) 1920, Mary Stewart, d. of John Claflin, Morristown, New Jersey, divorced 1929; 1s (killed North Africa 1942). Educated privately and abroad. Joined Westminster Dragoons 1913; Army 1913-18, Captain, Welsh Guards Reserve List 1920; Army 1939-4, invalided out; Hon. Colonel TA (Retired). Private Secretary, Earl Jellicoe 1931. Company Director & Chairman, Member of the Stock Exchange. Chairman, British Totalisator Manufacturers Conference. Freeman, City of London. Governor, University of Wales, National Library & National Museum 20 years. Member: Hon Society of Cymmrodorion; Royal United Services Institution; Pilgrims; Court & Livery of the Glaziers Company. Vice-President, Wales & Mon. Conservative Assn. Chairman, Welsh Parliamentary Party 1938-39, 1942-43; Welsh Conservative Group 1936-45;

British Group, Inter-Parliamentary Union 1939-45; Parliamentary Select Cttee: Private Bills. Treasurer 1922 Cttee 1922, 1942-44; Vice-Chairman, Anglo-Brazilian Society 1943. Died Paris 25 September 1958.

EVANS Howard William: BEd (Business Education) 1993; HND (Agricultural Marketing & Business) 1989. Liberal Democrat, Islwyn 1995 B/E; Gower 1997, Assembly 1997. **Mr. Howard Evans:** Born Oldswinford, Worcs. 6 August 1966, son of Stanley Jenkyn Evans, teacher, & Jean Gittoes, nurse. Church of England. Married Alannah Ruthen, retail manager. Educated Ounsdale High School; Wufrum College, Wolverhampton, Adams Agricultural College, West of England University. Agricultural Marketing for 7 years; Teacher at Llanelli; ICT Manager, Penyrheol Comprehensive School, Gowerton. Mawr Com.C. 1999 (Vice-Chairman). Clerk, Reynoldston Community council 1996-. Member: NUT, Electoral Reform Society, European Movement. School Governor. Joined Liberal Democrats 1991. Interests: Education, Agriculture/ Rural affairs. Hobbies: Hockey Club, Rugby, Cricket, Gardening, Philately. Of Craigcefnparc.

EVANS Hugh Goronwy: Plaid Cymru: Neath Feb. & Oct. 1974. **Mr. Hugh Evans:** Born 1944. Married Lee Evans, dietician, 1d. Educated Aberaeron Secondary School; Tottenham Technical College, London. Health Inspector, Borough of Neath. Chairman, Neath Branch, NALGO & Member, South Wales District Council. Member, Neath Trades Council. Contested Neath RDC & Glamorgan CC 1972. West Glam CC 1973-. Chair, Neath Branch Plaid Cymru, Agent 1970. Languages: Welsh, English. Of Bryncoch.

EVANS Ieuan W. – see WATKINS-EVANS I.

EVANS Ieuan Wilson: SDP/Alliance: Ynys Môn 1987. **Mr. Ieuan Evans:** Born 11 July 1956. Married. Educated Ysgol Glan Clwyd, St. Asaph; University of Wales, Bangor. Gwynedd County Council staff member. Vice-Chair, SDP Wales Council; Member CSD; Alliance Policy Co-ordinating Cttee Wales. Alliance Wales Spokesman on Local Government. Arfon BC 1985-87. Languages: English, Welsh.

EVANS Ioan Lyonel: JP (Birmingham). Labour/ Co-op MP Aberdare 1974-83, Cynon Valley 1983-; Yardley 1964-70. **Mr. Ioan Evans:** Born Llanelli July 1927, s of Evan Evans, clerk of works & Maria Griffiths. Married 2c. Educated Llanelli Grammar School; University of Wales, Swansea. Midland Bank clerk 1943-45. Army 1945-48. WEA & NCLC Lecturer 1948-50. Secretary: Birkenhead Co-operative Party 1950-53; Birmingham Co-operative Party 1953-64; Labour Agent Small Heath 1955, 1959. Member, West Bromwich Education Cttee. Director, Birmingham Printers Ltd (co-operative). Chairman, Labour League of Youth 1948-50; Member, West Midlands Regional Council of Labour; Exec Cttee, British Assn for World Government. Asst. Whip 1966-68; Comptroller of the Household 1968-70. Director, International Defence &Aid Group 1970-74. Chair: West Midland Group of Labour MPs; Parliamentary Labour Trade Group 1974, 1977; PLP Foreign Affairs Group, 1981-. Member: Council of Europe; Select Cttee. on Welsh Affairs 1981-82. Opposition Spokesman on European & Community Affairs 1982-. Secretary, Welsh Labour MPs Group 1974, 1977-. Languages: Welsh, English, Esperanto. Died 10 February 1984.

EVANS Janet Bronwyn: Green Party, South West Wales Euro 1994, South/West List 1999. **Ms. Jan Evans:** Born 1945. Singer & Song Writer. Ex-language teacher. Member, Christian CND. In wheelchair following childhood polio. Active peace & disabled rights protester. Contested Swansea CC. Languages: Learned Welsh, English. Of Swansea.

EVANS Jason Philip: BA (Plymouth) 1996; MSc (Stirling) 1997. Conservative, Torfaen 2001. **Mr. Jason Evans:** Born Abergavenny, 27 November 1973, son of New Tredegar coal miner. Educated Bedwellty Comprehensive School; Plymouth University (Design); Stirling University (Politics, Management & Communication) & Germany. Political Adviser: Ludgate Public Affairs 1998-2000; Halifax plc. 2001-; & part-time postgraduate lecturer at University College, London 2000-. Chair: Stirling University Conservative Assn 1996-97. Interests: Employment, Law & Order, Economics, Europe. Hobbies: Reading, Mountain Climbing, Running, 'Loud' Music. Of London & New Tredegar.

EVANS Jillian: BA (Wales) 1980 MPhil (CNAA) 1996. Plaid Cymru: Torfaen 1987; South Wales Euro 1989, South Wales East 1994, MEP Wales 1999. **Ms. Jill Evans:** Born Ystrad Rhondda, 16 May 1959, d of Horace Burge & Valma Lois Yeates, teacher. Married 1992 Syd Morgan. Educated Tonypandy Grammar School; University of Wales, Aberystwyth (Welsh); Polytechnic of Wales. Research Assistant, Polytechnic of Wales 1980-85; self-employed Administrator 1985-89; Administrative Public Affairs Officer 1989-93, Project Officer 1994-98, National Federation of Women's Institutes; Welsh Organiser, Child Infertility Support Network 1998-99. Chair, Plaid Cymru National Council 1994-96; Plaid Cymru Alternate Member, Committee of the Regions 1994-98; Representative, European

Jill Evans.

Free Alliance. Plaid Spokesperson on Peace & International Affairs 1986-94. Chair: CND Cymru. Rhondda BC. Rhondda-Cynon-Taf BC 1992-99. Contested Plaid Cymru Presidency 2000. Vice-President, Plaid Cymru, November 2003. Vice-Chair: EU. Cttee on Women's Rights & Equal Opportunities; Member: EU Cttee on Employment & Social Affairs; EU Temporary Cttee on Human Genetics & New Technologies in Modern Medicine; Delegation to the EU-Lithuania Joint Parliamentary Cttee. Interests: Environment, Equal Opportunity. Hobbies: Reading, Gardening, DIY. Of Llwynypia, Rhondda.

EVANS John: OBE 1945 JP (Glam). Labour: Montgomery 1929; MP Ogmore,B/E 1946-50. **Mr. John Evans:** Born Cwmparc 10 September 1875. Married 1909 Elizabeth Parton, 1s 3d. Educated Park Board School, Cwmparc; Ruskin College, Oxford 1907-09. Miner 1887-1907; Miners' Agent. Llynfi Valley 1908-. Maesteg UDC 1916-37. Glamorgan CC 1913-46, 1952- (Chairman: Education Cttee; Standing Joint Cttee; Emergency [Civil Defence Cttee 1939-45], Leader of the Labour Group; Alderman 1925-46; Chairman 1939-41). Cardiff RDC. Member, Royal Commissions: National Health Insurance 1924-25; Justices of the Peace 1948. Of Nantyffyllon & later of Whitchurch. Languages: Welsh, English. Died 18 April 1961. Further Reading: *D. Ben Rees: Cymry Adnabyddus 1952-1972.*

EVANS John: Labour & Co-operative: Carmarthen 1955; Cardiff North 1951, Worcester 1945, 1950. **Mr. Jack Evans:** Born Penygroes, Carms. 1895. Married Ray Bevan. Educated Penygroes Elementary School; Trinity College, Carmarthen. Miner 1909-1914. Army 1914-19. Miner 1919-26. Student 1926-28. Teacher 1928-61. President, Llanelli CLP. Languages: Welsh, English. Of Penygroes. Died December 1962.

EVANS John (Lib-Dem) – see EVANS Ernest John.

EVANS John Benjamin: Conservative: Carmarthen 1959; PPC Brecon & Radnor 1952-54; resigned in protest against Government's agricultural policy. **Mr. J. B. Evans:** Born September 1906, son of saddler (W). Married Educated Llanybydder Grammar School. Political Agent. Joined RAMC as ambulance driver 1939; Captain RASC. Captured at Tobruk 1942, Prisoner of War in Italy 1942-45. Returned home to be Conservative election agent at Cardiff East. Clerk, Newcastle Emlyn RDC 1944-48. Secretary, Carmarthenshire County Branch NFU 1948-56; Secretary, Farmers' Union of Wales 1957-58.

EVANS John Gilbert: BA (Wales). Labour: West Flint 1970. **Mr. John Evans:** Born Ystalyfera 18 December 1935 miner's son. Welsh Independent. Married Marian, d of Revd E. Islwyn Evans, 1s. Educated Ystalyfera Grammar School; University of Wales, Aberystwyth (1st Welsh). Teacher. Lecturer in Education, Caerleon College of Education. Joined Labour Party 1959; Asst. Secretary, Maesteg Labour Party 1964-68. Maesteg UDC 1968-. Member, NUT, Fabian Society.

EVANS John Victor: LlB (Wales) BA 1922 MA (Oxon). Liberal: Pontypridd 1929; Merthyr B/E 1934; Cardigan Short-List 1945. **Mr. Victor Evans:** Born Cwmdare 7 October 1895, son of Henry Howard Evans, Llwynypia, General Manager, Cambrian Collieries. Baptist. Married 1927, Katherine Mary, d of Henry Dawson, Streatham 1 s. (died 1938). Educated Cwmdare elementary school; Christ College, Brecon; University of Wales, Aberystwyth & Christ Church, Oxford (Modern History). President of the Oxford Union 1922; Cymdeithas Dafydd ap Gwilym. Army 1914-18. Barrister Inner Temple 1924. Lecturer in Law, University of Wales, Aberystwyth 1930-35. Warden, Cynon Folk College, Aberdare 1936-39 (following son's death). Civil Servant, Ministry of Economic Warfare 1939-45; Ministry of Supply 1945-. Languages: Welsh, English. Died 15 May 1957.

EVANS Jonathan Peter: Conservative: Brecon & Radnor 1987, 1997; Ebbw Vale Feb. & Oct. 1974; Wolverhampton North East 1979; MP Brecon & Radnor 1992-97; MEP Wales 1999-. **Mr. Jonathan Evans:** Born Tredegar, 2 June 1950, son of David John Evans, estate agent & Tredegar UDC & Harriet Mary Drury. Roman Catholic. Married 1978, Margaret Thomas, 2c. Educated Lewis School, Pengam; Howardian High School, Cardiff; College of Law, Guildford; Lancaster Gate, London. Solicitor of the Supreme Court/Managing Partner, Leo Abse & Cohen; Director,

Jonathan Evans.

insurance companies 1997-99. Independent Consultant to US, Canadian & UK Insurers on London Markets Issues. Member: Welsh Spastics Society; UN Welsh Youth Cttee for Human Rights; Cardiff Civic Society. Chair, Cardiff Young Conservatives. Member: Executive, National Union of Conservative Assns 1991-. Chair: Welsh Conservative Candidates 1985-91; Welsh Conservative Policy Group 1987-91; Executive, Society of Conservative Lawyers. Vice-President: Tory Reform Group. Vice-Chairman, NSPCC in Wales & NSPCC Parliamentary Consultant. Director & Trustee, Welsh national sports centre for the disabled. Deputy Chairman, Tai Cymru 1988-94. Parl-Secretary: Corporate Affairs Ministry 1994-95; Lord Chancellor's Department 1995-96; Under-Secretary, Wales 1996-97. Leader, Euro Conservative Group 12 December 2001 October 2004. Interests: Economic Affairs, Trade Policy, Children, Disability. Hobbies: Watching sport with family, Music, History. Languages: English, French. *Books: Jonathan Evans, Future of Welsh Conservatism, 2002.*

EVANS Keith John: BA (Wales) 1977. SDP/Alliance: Llanelli 1992; Bury South 1993; Liberal Democrat: Carmarthen West & South Pembs 1997. **Mr. Keith Evans:** Born Trimsaran 1 April 1956; Educated Coleshill Comprehensive School, Warwickshire; Wolverhampton Poly; University of Wales, Swansea. Economist: British Steel Corporation, then National Retailers. Freelance Writer & Researcher. Greater Manchester CC 1981-86; Llanelli BC 1991-; Carmarthenshire CC 1991-99; Group Leader; Chairman, Highways & Transportation Cttee. Deputy-Chairman, Llanelli Liberal Democrats. Member: Charter 88; founder member, British-American Assn (member, UK Atlantic Cttee). Member: Royal Institution of South Wales 1988-91. Joined Conservatives, May 2001. Of Burry Port.

EVANS Kenneth: Socialist Labour, Merthyr Tydfil & Rhymney 2001; South Central List 2003. **Mr. Ken Evans:** Born Merthyr Tydfil 16 April 1940, s of Edward John Evans, miner, & Florence Evans, housewife. Church of England. Married, divorced, 2d. Educated secondary modern school. Semi-skilled factory worker. Active trade unionist for 40 years; AEEU shop steward. Member, Labour Party 1984-98, (Secretary, Gurnos Ward Labour Party 12 years) when he joined Socialist Labour Party. Active with Unemployed Action Group. Campaigner against closure of local post-offices. Hobbies: Skittles, Darts, Walking, Political memoirs. Retired to Barry 1996.

EVANS Malcolm Williams: Plaid Cymru, Wrexham 2001, Vale of Clwyd 2003. **Mr. Malcolm Evans:** Born Blaenau Ffestiniog, 29 August 1956, son of Idris Evans, Royal Marines-Slate Quarryman-Chef, & Glenys Davies, hotelier. Church in Wales/Annibynwyr (Welsh Independent). Married 1989, Heather Hind Evans, nurse. Educated Craig y Don Primary School, Blaenau Ffestiniog; John Bright, Grammar School, Llandudno; Bangor School of Nursing. Registered General Nurse, Ysbyty Glan Clwyd; manager, medical practice. Ex-footballer: Bangor City, Rhyl, Caernarfon Town; Wrexham trialist. Mochdre ComC. 1997. Chair: Colwyn Branch, Plaid Cymru; Secretary, West Clwyd Constituency; Member: National Council, Conference Steering Cttee; Vice-Chair: National Assembly Regional Cttee. Chief Steward, National Conference. Member: Conwy Assn of Local Councils Executive; Police & Community Consultative Group. Interests: Health Service; Youth Crime; Miners' Compensation; Pensions; Housing; Agriculture; Student Grants. Hobbies: Fly-fishing; Gardening; Hill walking; Sport, especially football. Mochdre ComC. 1998-. Secretary, West Clwyd Plaid Cymru. Languages: Welsh, English. Of Mochdre, Colwyn Bay.

EVANS Margaret Delyth: BA (Wales). Labour, Mid & West List 1999. Assembly Member, Mid & West Wales List, 1.5.200, on resignation of Alun Michael, retired 2003. **Ms. Delyth Evans:** Born Cardiff, 17 March 1958, d of David Gwynne Evans, civil servant, & Jean Margaret Evans. Brought up at Caerbryn, Carmarthenshire. Partner, Edward Richards, Downing Street Senior Policy Adviser, 1s 1d. Educated Ysgol Gyfun Rhydfelin, University of Wales, Aberystwyth (French), Centre for Journalism Studies, Cardiff. (Post Graduate Diploma in Journalism). Journalist: HTV *Wales at Six* & *Y Byd a'r Bedwar*, BBC. *World at One* 1985-82. Policy Adviser & Speech Writer to Rt. Hon. John Smith MP. 1992-94. Management Consultant, Adrian Elis Consultants 1994. Joined Labour Party 1984. Member: Contemporary Arts Society, Institute of

Welsh Affairs, Special Adviser to First Secretary Alun Michael, 1999. Deputy Minister, Rural Affairs 2000. Interests: Economic Development, Rural Affairs. Hobbies: Keeping Fit, the Arts, Outdoor Activities. Languages: Welsh, English, French.

EVANS Matthew Robert Hatton: Conservative, Newport East 2003. **Mr. Matthew Evans:** Born 1963. Married Tina (regional director, international construction consultancy group) 2d. Educated Crosskeys Tertiary College, Thames Valley University (Hotel & Catering Management). Management in London & Midlands. Founded Matt Snax Caterers 1990, sold out as going concern. School governor. Newport CC 1999. Vice-Captain, Stow Park Lawn Tennis Club. Supporter, Newport RFC, Member: Glamorgan County Cricket Club, Bannatynes Health Club, Newport Golf Club, Welsh Springer Spaniels Club. Friend, Newport Ship. Of Newport.

EVANS Neville Lawrence: BA (Oxon) 1936. Independent Labour: University of Wales B/E 1943. **Mr. Neville Evans:** Born Sheffield, 1914 (father from Carmarthenshire). Educated Sheffield Grammar School; Jesus College, Oxford (Meyricke Exhibitioner in Natural Sciences; 2nd Chemistry). Industrial Chemist, working in a government small arms factory in London. Stood for *socialism, social security and decent education for the children of Wales.*

EVANS Nigel Martin: BA (Wales) 1979. Conservative: Swansea West 1987; Pontypridd B/E 1989; Ribble Valley B/E 1991; MP Ribble Valley 1992-. **Mr. Nigel Evans:** Born 10 November 1957, son of Albert Evans & Betty Brown, newsagents & grocers. Church of England. Educated Dynevor Comprehensive School, Swansea; University of Wales, Swansea (Politics). Newsagent & Grocer 1979-90 (took over family business on father's death). Joined Conservative Party 1974. President, Swansea West Conservatives. Chair, Welsh Candidates Policy Group 1990. PPS 1994-97. Jt. Vice-Chair, Parl. Friends of Music Group. Treasurer, Manufacturing Industry Group. Unpaid Director, Networking for Industry & Small Business Bureau. West Glam CC 1985-91. PPS 1985-91. Conservative Spokesman for Constitutional Affairs (Wales & Scotland) 1997-99; Constitutional Affairs (Wales) 1999-10.11.2003 (Refused re-appointment when the post was removed from the Shadow Cabinet). Vice-Chairman, Conservative Party 1999. Hobbies: Running, Travel, Telecoms, Arts. Of Swansea & Longridge, Preston.

EVANS Richard: LlB (Wales). Conservative: Pontypridd 1983. **Mr. Richard Evans:** Born

Whitchurch, 22 February 1948, stepson of Michael Roberts MP. Married 3c. Educated Whitchurch Grammar School; University of Wales, Aberystwyth. Solicitor. South Glam CC Conservative Whip; Chairman, 1979.

EVANS Richard George: BSc PGDE MPhil PhD (London). Conservative: Neath B/E 1991, Hendon 2001. **Dr. Richard Evans:** Born Finchley, of Welsh parents (uncle was a Resolfen Labour councillor). Married 1991, Lesley, financial consultant, 1s 1d. Educated Harrow (Captain of Football; member, school boxing team, rugby XV); Bedford College, London; London University Institute of Education. Teacher (Maths) 1981-; Deputy Head, Copland Community School 1997-. Director, Sixth Form, College at St. Marylebone Church School. Brent BC. Westminster CC 1986- (Chair, Town Planning & New Technology Cttees). Marathon runner (London marathon 1985, 1987 in aid of Trigger/Horse Riding for the disabled). Friend of RAF Museum, Hendon; MCC; Mill Hill Preservation Society. Season Ticket Holder, Chelsea FC. Interests: Education, Europe. Hobbies: Cricket, Historical Manuscripts & Books, 20th Century British Art, Music, Jazz, Visiting Historical Houses. Languages: English, French. Of Mill Hill, London.

EVANS Richard Thomas: MA (Wales). Liberal: Carmarthen 1935, Llanelli 1923, 1924, 1929; MP Carmarthen 1931-35. **Captain R. T. Evans:** Born Cefn Coed, Brecs 1890. Welsh Independent. Married 1918, Edith, d of Morgan Rhys Williams Educated University of Wales, Bangor & Cardiff (1st Economics). Army 1914-18, Captain SWB & Staff. Deputy Director, Ministry of Labour Industrial Training Department, South Wales. Lecturer in Economics, University of Wales, Cardiff. Cardiff CC Deputy Lord Mayor. Languages: Welsh, English. Of Llandaff. Died 20 July 1945.

EVANS Robert Craig: Christian Democratic Party, Wales Euro 2004. **Mr. Craig Evans:** Charity worker. Of Brynmill, Swansea.

EVANS Roger Kenneth: MA (Cantab). Conservative: Monmouth 1997; B/E 1991; Ynys Môn 1987; Warley West 1979, Oct. 1974; MP Monmouth 1992-97. Mr. Roger Evans: Born 18 March 1947. Anglican. Married 1973, June Rodgers 2s. Educated Clytha Park School, Newport, City of Norwich School; Bristol Grammar School; Trinity Hall, Cambridge. President: Cambridge Union 1970; Cambridge Georgian Group. Chairman, Cambridge University Conservative Assn 1969. Barrister. Crown Court Recorder. Chancellor of the Diocese of Gloucester. Member: Ecclesiastical Law Society; Society of Conservative Lawyers Executive, Country Land-

lords Assn, Gwent Wild Life Trust, NFU, National Trust, CADW. Chair: Friends of Friendless Churches 1998 (Trustee 1983); Prayer Book Society 2001- (Vice-President 1995-2001). Freeman, City of London 1976. Member, Ecclesiastical Law Society 1998. Research Director, Society of Conservative Lawyers 1997-. Under-Secretary, Social Security 1994-97. Hobbies: Architectural & Gardening History, Building, Gardening. Of Trelleck.

EVANS Samuel Thomas: Kt 1908 PC 1910 GCB 1910 QC 1901 BA (Lond). Liberal MP Mid-Glamorgan 1890-1910. **Rt. Hon. Sir Samuel Evans:** Born Skewen May 1859, son of John Evans, Swansea Road (grocer) & Margaret. Welsh Independent. Married (1) 1887, Rachel, d of William Thomas, Skewen (2) 1905, Blanche, d of Charles Royle, Cincinnati. Educated Swansea Collegiate School; University of Wales, Aberystwyth (his parents wished him to enter the ministry but he took up Law). Solicitor 1883; Barrister 1891; the last appointed QC in reign of Queen Victoria. Recorder of Swansea 1908. Neath BC. Solicitor General 1908-10; President of the Probate, Divorce & Admiralty Division, High Court, 1910-; Authority on International Law; Freeman of Neath & Swansea. Languages: Welsh, English. Of London, & Hove. Estate £49,736. Died 13 September 1918.

EVANS William Prys Owen: Independent National: Caernarfonshire 1931. **Mr. William Evans:** Born 1905, son of Colonel Owen Lloyd J. Evans (died 1928) JP DL Broom Hall, Chwilog (one of North Wales' largest landowners) & Lydia, d of John Savin, Pwllheli. Bachelor. Anglican. Educated RN Colleges, Osborne & Dartmouth. Lieutenant, Royal Navy retired. Farmer & landowner. Supported by Caernarfonshire Conservative Assn. Evans provided £500 for election expenses & the rest from Caernarfonshire Conservative Assn. Of Broom Hall, Chwilog. Estate £220,607. Died 6 April 1937. (Killed on his own landing ground when his plane crashed on take-off).

EVANS-JONES Henry: MBE 1972 LlB (Wales) 1931. Liberal: Merioneth 1955. **Mr. Henry Evans-Jones:** Born Ffestiniog. Methodist Circuit Steward. Married. Educated Ffestiniog Grammar School; University of Wales, Aberystwyth. Solicitor. Clerk to Ffestiniog UDC 1947-54. Coroner for Merioneth 1949. Clerk to Magistrates, Ardudwy Uwch Artro & Edeyrnion Districts. Clerk, Governors, Ysgol Sir Ffestiniog. President, Merioneth Liberal Assn. Chair, North Wales Advisory Disablement Cttee. Languages: Welsh, English.

EVEREST Roger Norman Joseph: BA (Wales). Conservative: Caerphilly 1974; One Nation

Conservative: Brecon & Radnor B/E 1985; Europe Conservative: Winchester B/E Nov. 1997; Independent Pro-Europe Conservative, Eddisbury B/E 1999; Independent, Cheltenham 2001. **Mr. Roger Everest:** Born 1939. Anglican. Married Carmel, 2s 2d. Educated Llandaff Cathedral School, Kingswood School, Bath; University of Wales, Cardiff (Charles Morgan Prize in Welsh History, Welsh UNA Scholarship to Geneva). Barrister, Grays Inn 1968. Member, Bow Group; Chairman, Barry Conservative Assn. 1982-83. Removed from approved list of candidates Feb. 1985. Joined Charter for Jobs, April 1985. Supported Pro-Europe Conservative Party in 1999 Euro Elections. Of Sully.

EWART-JAMES Thomas Owen: Conservative: Ogmore 1959. **Mr. Tom Ewart-James:** Born Southend on Sea 1917, s of Revd D. Ewart James (gs. of Revd Dr. John Thomas, Liverpool). Congregationalist/URC lay preacher & elder. Married 4c. Educated Thorpe Hall Preparatory School; Bishop Stortford's College. Worked in Swansea as a youth at steel rolling mills. Civil Engineer, George Wimpey & Co. Managing Director: his own firm of building & civil engineering contractors. Served in Trinidad Volunteers, 1937-38, Horse Guards OCTU 1939, invalided out. Inns of Court Regt (TA) 1940-45. President, Southend Master Builders Assn. Member, National Council of Federation of Building Trade Employers; Government's Joint Co-ordinating Cttee for the Building Industry. Chair: Voluntary Old People's Residential Home; Southend East Conservative Assn. President South East Essex Cambrian Society. Southend BC 1955-. Of Southend-on-Sea.

FAHM Sikuri Tunji: LlB LLM (London) FCIS FRSA FREconS. Labour, South/Central list 2003. **Mr. Tunji Fahm:** Born Lagos, Nigeria, 10 May 1953. Muslim (Shi-ite). Came to Wales as student in 1950s. Married, widowed, 3s 1d. Educated University of Wales, Cardiff; London School of Economics; University College, London; Institute of Advanced Legal Studies, London. Barrister (non practising), Lincolns Inn. Legal Officer, Islwyn BC 1974-95. Principal, Fahm & Co. Solicitors & High Court Advocates. Joint Convenor, Joint Cttee for Ethnic Minorities in Wales. Interests: Welsh Affairs, Equality Issues, Black People & the Criminal Justice system. Hobbies: Golf, Walking, Watching Formula One Racing. Of Blackwood.

FAREY-JONES Frederick William: FRSA KtComm. Civil Merit (Spain) 1958. Conservative: Pembroke 1951, Goole 1950, MP Watford 1955-64. **Mr. Frederick Farey-Jones:** Born Neyland 21 May 1904, s of Evan Francis Jones & Gladys Gertrude Jones. Married Lilian Ada Farey & added her surname, 1s 1d. Educated Queen Elizabeth Grammar School, Carmarthen, Paris, Liege, Vienna. (Diploma in Psychology). Insurance Broker, Company Chairman: Farey-Jones (Insurance) Ltd, Reconstruction Enterprises Assn. Ltd. Airline Operator, Aircraft Manufacturer, Aviation Consultant. Founder: Conference of Air Traffic Operators. Revived Air Transport Assn. Member: Council, Air League of the British Empire. Of Chipstead & London. Languages: Welsh, English, French, German. Died 18 February 1974.

FAIRLEY Richard James Stanley: Liberal: East Flint Oct. 1974. **Mr. Richard Fairley:** Born September 1938. Married 2c. Educated Stowe School, College of Estate Management, Teaching & Law. Barrister, Middle Temple 1968.

FARMER Graham: Plaid Cymru: Aberavon 1970. **Mr. Graham Farmer:** Born Ferndale November 1929. Married 3c. Educated Rhondda Technical College. Electrician. ETU Shop Steward. Plaid Cymru Organiser, Pontypridd. Chairman, Swansea West Plaid Cymru. Languages: Learned Welsh, English. Of Brynmill, Swansea.

FARMER Pryce Michael: QC. BA. (London) 1966. Plaid Cymru: Conway Feb. & Oct. 1974. **Mr. Michael Farmer:** Born Penygroes, Arfon 20 May 1944, s of Sarah Jane Farmer. Married 1975, Olwen Mary, d of Revd Griffith John Roberts, 1s 1d. Educated Dyffryn Nantlle Grammar School, Kings College, London (English). Teacher of History & English, St. David's College, Llandudno 1968-72. Barrister, Grays Inn 1972. Recorder 1995, Judge 2001/. Chair: Special Review Cttee. Anglesey CC, 1998, Circuit Judge 2001. Cttee. Member, Cymdeithas Tai Gwynedd, Member, Rugby XV. Hobbies: Listening to classical music, Reading, Gardening, Watching rugby. Languages: Welsh, English. Of Glynllifon.

FARR Lynne Marie: Green Party, South/Central list 2003. **Ms. Lynne Farr:** Of Llantrisant.

FARREN George: JP (Caerns) FStatS MICE. Liberal Unionist: Eifion 1886. **Mr. George Farren:** Born 1836, s of George Farren, barrister. Married 1876, Rebecca, d of Henry Capel Cundy of London. Educated Kings College, London. Quarry Owner. Of Caernarfon.

FAULKNER Richard Oliver, Baron Faulkner of Worcester: MA (Oxon) Hon. LLD (Luton). Labour: Monmouth Oct. 1974, Huddersfield West 1979, Devizes 1970, Feb. 1974. **Mr. Richard Faulkner:** Born Manchester 22 March 1966, s of Harold Ewart Faulkner & Mabel Faulkner. Married 1968 Susan Heyes, 2d. Educated Merchant Taylors School, Northwood, Worcester College, Oxford (PPE). Joined Labour Party 1961. Journalist & Research Assistant, Labour Party 1967-69, Public Relations Officer: Construction Industry Training Board 1969-70, Editor, *Steel News* 1971, Account Director, P. J. Lyons (PR) Ltd 1971-73, Director, PPR International 1973-74, Co-founder, parliamentary journal, *The House Magazine,* Communications Adviser, Leader of the Opposition & Labour Party (unpaid) 1987 & 1992 elections, Bishops at Lambeth, 1990, Government Relations Adviser, Fyffes Group 1973-, railway trades unions 1975-76, A. C. Parsons & Co 1976-77, Pool Promoters Assn. 1977, British Rail Board 1977, British Hardware Federation 1985, TSB Group 1987, International Parliamentary Union 1988-90, Southampton CC 1989-91. CAMRA 1989, Barclays de la Zoete Wedd 1990-92, Standard Life Assurance 1990, South Glam CC 1991-94, Cardiff Bay Development Corp 1993. Foundation Trustee: Football Trust 1979-82, Secretary 1983-86, Deputy-Chairman 1986-90. Member: Sports Council 1986-

88, anti-hooliganism cttee 1987-90, Court, University of Luton. Non Executive Director, Brighton & Hove FC. Ex-Director: Wimbledon & Crystal Palace Football Clubs, Cardiff Millennium Stadium 1997. Strategy Adviser, Littlewoods Group 1999-, Incepta Group plc 1999-. Chair: Women's Football Assn 1988-91. Vice-Chair: Transport 2000 Ltd 1986. First Deputy Chairman, Football Trust. Jt. Managing Director, Westminster Communications Group Ltd 1989. Merton BC 1971-78. President, Royal Society for the Protection of Birds. Of Wimbledon.

FEELEY Robina Lynn: Liberal Democrat, Meirionydd/Nant Conwy 1997, Clwyd West & North List 1999, Clwyd West 2001, Vale of Clwyd 2003. **Mrs. Bobbie Feeley:** Born Andover, 14 September 1946. Church of England. Lived in Ruthin since 1975. Married Deryck George Feeley, 2d. Educated Andover Girls Grammar School, Eastleigh Secretarial Business College. Retailer of Nearly New Clothes Agency & company secretary to her husband's Goodman Construction Co. Denbighshire DC 1985-96, Denbighshire CC 1996-99 (defeated), Deputy Group Leader. Group. Vice-Chair, Personnel & Licensing Cttees. Chair, Ruthin Steering Group. Director, North Wales Tourism. Member, Glyndwr CAB Management Cttee. Chair: North Wales Liberal Democrats. Liberal Democrat, Wales Euro 2004. Hobbies: Walking, Cooking, Reading, Films, Opera, Swimming, Tennis, Attending race meetings. Languages: Learning Welsh, English. Of Llanfair Dyffryn Clwyd.

FELD Valerie Anne: MScEcon. Labour AM, Swansea East 1999-. **Mrs. Val Feld:** Born Bangor, 29 October 1947, d of James Breem-Turner, dentist, & Evelyn Breen Turner. Married 1969 John Feld, divorced, 179, 2d. Partner, Mike Read. Educated Hillgrove School, Bangor, The Abbey, Malvern Wells, University of Wales, Cardiff. Researcher/Secretary, BBC ITN Tellex Monitors, 1969-72. Voluntary & Community Activities 1972-77, Housing/Welfare Rights Worker, Chorley, 1977-79, Founder/Director, Shelter Cymru 1981-89, Director, Equal Opportunities Commission, Wales 1989-99. Clr. 1975-77. Director. Women's Jazz Archive. Member, Amnesty International, Greenpeace, Cyrenians Cymru. Treasurer, YES Campaign. School Governor. Interests: Economic Development, Housing, Education, Equality Issues. Chair, Economic Development Cttee. (Resigned because of ill health, May 2001). Hobbies: Gentle Walking, Choral Music, Turkish Baths. Languages: Learned Welsh, English. Of Swansea (1979). Died 18 July 2001.

FELLOWS J. Alan: Labour: Bridgend 1983**. Mr. Alan Fellows:** Born Aberavon, steelworker's son 1936. Married Jeanette of Port Talbot 1s 1d.

Educated Dyffryn Grammar School, Port Talbot. Sales Accounts Manager, British Steel Corporation group office, Port Talbot.

FERGUSON Anthony David: BA (Reading). Liberal Democrat: Caerphilly 1997. **Mr. Tony Ferguson:** Born 12 September 1961. Married Debra, 3s. Educated Marlborough, Essex University (Politics). Senior Systems. Analyst, British Telecom. Newbury BC 1992- Deputy Leader.

FERNANDES-VIDAL Antonio: Pro Europe Conservative, Wales Euro 1999. **Dr. Antonio Fernandes-Vidal:** Of London.

FIENBURGH Wilfred: MBE. Labour: Pembroke 1945, MP Islington North 1951-. **Mr. Wilfred Fienburgh:** Born Ilford, November 1919, s of Harry Fienburgh (mother, Bradford CC, g/f a friend of Keir Hardie & early Labour candidate). Married 1940, Joan Valerie d of Captain Thomas McDonnell & Eva McDonnell, Belfast. Educated Bellevue High School, Bradford. Manual Worker. Unemployed 1934-39. Army 1939-45: Rifleman 1939, Commissioned 1940, Major General Staff. Asst-Secretary, Civil Service Clerical Assn 1946-47, Labour Party Research Dept 1947-51. Member: TUC Economic Cttee 1950-51. Vice-Chairman, Political Staff, Westminster Branch, CAWU 1947. PR Consultant, Granada Group 1950. Languages: English. Of Hemel Hempstead, Herts. Died 5 February 1958, after car accident.

FINCH Harold Josiah: Kt 1976. Labour MP Bedwellty1950-70. **Sir Harold Finch:** Born Barry 2 May 1898, s of Josiah Coleman Finch, railway inspector, & Emmie Keedwell. Married 1922, Gladys Hinder, 1s 1d. Educated elementary school. Clerk, Barry Railway Co 1912-19. Secretary, Tredegar District SWMF 1919-34, Compensation Secretary SWMF/South Wales Area NUM 1935-50. Member: NUM National Executive 1951-60. Secretary, Parliamentary Miners' Group 1964-66. Chairman, Welsh Parliamentary Party. Mynyddislwyn UDC 1922-33, Chairman 1932-33. Under-Secretary for Wales 1964-66. President, Islwyn Memorial Society. Of Pontllanffraith & London. Died 1979. *Books H. J. Finch: Guide to Workmen's Compensation Acts 1944, Industrial Injuries Act Explained 1948, Memoirs of a Bedwellty M.P.*

FINCH-SAUNDERS Janet Elizabeth: Conservative, North List, 1999, Wrexham & North List 2003. **Ms. Janet Finch-Saunders: Born** Accrington, Lancs. 28 April 1958, d of Jack Finch, electrical engineer & Conwy BC & Joan Finch, secretary (both parents, Mayor of Llandudno), moved to Llandudno 1969. Church of England/Wales. Married 1986, Gareth Donald Treleaven Saunders, manufacturing optician 1s 1d. Educated Huncoat Primary School; St. Christopher's Secondary School, Accrington; Ysgol John Bright, Llandudno; Llandrillo College (business management). Proprietor of shop & investment services. Deputy Chair: Conwy Conservative Assn 2002. Conservative Agent 2001. Member: Conwy Community Health Council. 2002. Llandudno TC 1995- (Chairman, Community Services 1998). Contested Conwy CC 1998. Hobbies: Boating, Reading, Horseriding. Languages: English. Of Llandudno.

FINLAY Graeme Bell: 1st Bart 1964 ERD LlB (London). Conservative: Ebbw Vale 1950, MP Epping 1951-64. **Sir Graeme Finlay:** Born Chepstow 29 October 1916, s of James Bell Pettigrew Finlay & Margaret Helena, d of John Euston Davies JP (great grand nephew of Henry Richard MP). Married 1953, June Evangeline, d of Colonel Francis Drake, Harlow, 1d. Educated Marlborough School, London University. Army 1939-45: SWB, Major, Gurkha Rifles. Barrister, Grays Inn 1950. President: Hardwicke Society 1950-51. Secretary, Conservative MPs Home Affairs Cttee 1952-57, Vice-Chairman, Housing & Local Govt. Cttee 1956-57. PPS 1952-57. Asst. Whip 1957-59, Lord Commissioner of Treasury 1959-60, Vice-Chamberlain of the Household 1960-64. Deputy County Court Judge 1967-70, Sous Magistrate & Judge of Petty Debts, Channel Islands 1972-. Of Cheltenham. Died 1989.

FISCHER Mark W: BA. Communist (CPGB): Rhondda 1992, **Mr. Mark Fischer:** Born Swansea 1962. 1d. Journalist & Writer. National Organiser, Communist Party of Great Britain.

FISHER Francis Michael: Conservative: Pembroke 1966. **Mr. Michael Fisher:** Born Staffs October 1940. Married 1965. Educated Brewood Grammar School, Staffs, Birmingham College of Advanced Technology. Civil Engineer: Chief Engineer, Sir Alfred McAlpine & Co. Chairman, Lichfield & Tamworth Young Conservatives, Vice-Chairman: Hereford Conservative Assn. Contested Rugeley UDC 1963.

FITZWILIAMS. Edward Crawford Lloyd: CMG 1971 JP DL (Cards & Carms) FRGS FRSI. Order: St. Maurice & St. Lazarus (Italy) White Eagle of Serbia 1916. Conservative: Cardigan 1929, B/E 1932, Withdrew 1931 in favour of Ernest Evans, Liberal. **Lieut-Colonel Edward FitzWilliams:** Born Strathleven, Dunbarton 11 March 1872, s of Charles Home Lloyd FitzWilliams. of Cilgwyn & Margaret Alice Crawford. Anglican. Married 1899, Maud, d of Hawtrey Collins Platt of Brixton, 2s 3d. Educated Wellington College. 3rd Welch Regt 1899, Captain, 1901, South African War 1899-1901, Great War 1914-18. Landowner. Member, Governing Body of the Church in Wales. Wales Area Representative, British Legion. Free-

mason: Grand Deacon of England. Of Cilgwyn, Newcastle Emlyn. Died 10 July 1936.

FLANNERY James Fortescue-: 1st Bart 1904, Kt 1899, JP (Kent, Surrey, Essex, London) HML (London) MInstCE. Conservative, Cardiff District 1906 MP Shipley 1895-1906; MP Maldon 1918-22. **Sir James Fortescue-Flannery:** Born Liverpool, 16 December 1851, s of Captain John Flannery, Seacombe. Anglican. Married 1882 (Edith Mary Emma (d.1936) d of Osborne Jenkin, 1s 1d. Educated Liverpool School of Science. Pupil at Britannia Engine Works, Birkenhead. Inspecting Engineer under Sir E. J. Reed (qv). President: Society of Consulting Marine Engineers; Liverpool Shipbuilders' Guild; Junior Engineers' Institution. Associate of Lloyds & Member, Technical Cttee, Lloyds' Register. Member: British Cttee, Brussels International Exhibition 1897, Milan International Exhibition 1906. Lord of the Manor of Wethersfield & Patron of the living. Recreations: Cycling, riding, shooting, rowing. Of Wethersfield Manor, Essex. Died 1943.

FLOUTIER Sophie Chantal Jacqueline: MA (Concordia). Independent Wales Party, **Miss Sophie Floutier:** Born Montpelier, France, 1970, d of Professor Denis Floutier, & Chantal Boucheine, English teacher. Huguenot. Educated France & Concordia University, Montreal. Art teacher. Interests: Republicanism, Celtic resurgence. Hobbies: Arts, crafts. Lived in Wales since 2000. *I am a citizen of the French Republic who has lived and worked in Wales for the past three years. Possibly the first French citizen to run in a National Assembly election?*

FLYNN Keith Thomas: OBE 1985. Conservative: Cardiff West 1964. **Mr. Keith Flynn:** Born Cardiff, August 1928, s of railwayman (died 1935). Baptist. Married Margaret. Educated Canton High School, Cardiff. Bank Clerk. Royal Navy 1946-49. Chair, Wales & Mon Young Conservatives 1958. Secretary, Cardiff Branch, British Leprosy Relief Assn. Cardiff CC 1966.

FLYNN Paul Philip: Labour: Denbigh Oct. 1974, MP Newport West, 1987-. **Mr. Paul Flynn:** Born Cardiff 9 February 1935, s of James Flynn, postman, & Winifred Kathleen Flynn, housewife. Inactive Roman Catholic. Married (1) 1962, Ann Harvey, divorced (2) 1985, Samantha Morgan, d of Douglas & Elsie Cumpstone, 1s 1d. Educated St. Illtyds College, Cardiff, University of Wales, Cardiff. Industrial Chemist, British Steel Corporation 1962-83. Research Officer, Llew Smith MEP 1984-87, Political Researcher & Broadcaster. Joined Labour Party 1953, Newport BC (Deputy Leader, Chairman Public Works & Transport Cttees) 1972-.74, Gwent CC 1974-82. Secretary: Newport Branch, Child Poverty Action

Group. Co-Author, Report: *Television in Wales.* Chairman, Broadcasting Council for Wales, South Wales Dock Board. Member: Council of University of Wales, Cardiff, Secretary: All-Party Dolphins Group. Member: Labour Party Welsh Executive, NUPE. CND, Welsh Anti-Nuclear Alliance, Opposition Spokesman, Social Security 1988-90, Wales 1987. Select Cttee Member: Transport 1982-87, Joint Vice-Chairman, all party extra daylight group. Interests: Social Security, Drugs, Welsh Affairs, Environment. Hobbies: Photography, Swimming. Languages: Learned Welsh, English, some French. *Books: Paul Flynn: Television in Wales 1974, Common Knowledge – How to be a Backbencher 1997, Baglu 'Mlaen, Gwasg Gwynedd 1998, Dragons Led by Poodles 1999.*

FLYNN Thomas Patrick Godwin: Pro Life Alliance, South/East list 2003. **Mr. Thomas Flynn:** Born Oxford, 3 May 1977. Roman Catholic. Educated Ampleforth College, York; Merton College, Oxford (Classics). Joined Pro-Life Alliance at university. Membership Secretary, Pro Life Party. Interests: Liberty for the Subject, Human Rights. Hobbies: Beer, Cinema. Of London.

FOLLAND Leah Norah: CBE 1939 JP. National Liberal: Gower 1923. **Mrs. Lily Folland:** Born Penclawdd, d of Rev. John Thomas, Baptist minister, sister-in-law of David Henry Williams (qv). Baptist. Teacher at Gorseinon. Married Henry Folland, Swansea Industrialist, M/D. Grosvenor Steel & Co. Director, Richard Thomas & Co 1923 (died, Egypt 1926, Estate £484,474). Council Member & Life Governor, University of Wales, Swansea. President: South Wales Women's Liberal Federation, Swansea Girls Sunshine Club & Home. Member, Appeal Tribunal, Unemployment Assistance Board. Of Blackpill, Swansea.

FOOT Michael Mackintosh: PC 1974 MA (Oxon). Labour: Monmouth 1935, Devonport 1955, 1959, MP. Ebbw Vale B/E 1960-83, Blaenau Gwent 1983-92, Devonport 1945-55. **Rt. Hon. Michael Foot:** Born 23 July 1913, s of Rt. Hon. Dingle Foot MP & Eva, d of Angus Mackintosh MD. Humanist. Married 1949 Jill Craigie (died Dec1999). Educated Forres School, Leighton Park School, Reading, Wadham College, Oxford (Exhibitioner). President, Oxford Union 1933. Journalist, Writer, Author. Asst-Editor, *Tribune* 1937-38, Acting Editor, *Evening Standard,* 1942, Columnist, *Daily Herald* 1944-64, Editor, *Tribune* 1948-52, 1955-60, Managing Director, *Tribune* Publications 1960-, Member: CND, Labour Party NEC 1947-50. Opposition Spokesman: Fuel & Power 1970-74, Secretary of State for Employment 1974-76, Lord President of the Council & Leader of the Commons 1976-79, Deputy Leader of the Opposition 1979-80, Leader of the Opposi-

Michael Foot.

tion 1980-83. *Books: Michael Foot, Guilty Men (with Frank Owen & Peter Howard) 1940, Armistice 1918-39 1940, Trial of Mussolini 1943, Brendan & Beverley 1944, Still at Large 1950, Full Speed Ahead 1950, Guilty Men (with Mervyn Jones) 1957, The Pen and the Sword 1957; Parliament in Danger 1959, Aneurin Bevan (2 vols) 1962 & 1973; Harold Wilson: A Pictorial Biography 1964, Debts of Honour 1980, Another Heart and Other Pulses 1984, Loyalists and Loners 1980, H. G. Wells 1995. Further Reading: Simon Hoggart & David Leigh, Michael Foot, A Portrait 1981; Mervyn Jones, Michael Foot 1994.*

FORD Martyn: BA (Wales). Liberal/Alliance: Swansea West 1987; Conservative, South/West List 1999. **Mr. Martyn Ford:** Born Cardiff, 27 May 1954, son of Trevor Ford, professional footballer, & Anne Louise Ford, housewife. Church of England. Educated Clifton College, Bristol; University of Wales, Aberystwyth. Barrister 1978. Former Prosecutor, Dyfed Powys Police Authority. West Glam CC 1985-96. Chairman, Swansea West Liberals 1984. Joined Conservative Party. Contested Swansea CCC as Conservative. Interests: Anti-Abortion. Languages: Welsh, English. Hobbies: History. Of Sketty, Swansea.

FOREMAN John: New Labour: Cardiff South & Penarth 1997, Independent Labour, Cardiff South & Penarth 1999. **Mr. John Foreman:** Labour Party Member 18 months, expelled when he contested the 1997 election. Of Penarth.

FORESTIER-WALKER Charles Leolin: 1st Bart 1929 KBE 1925 JP 1906 DL (Mon) 1930 KStJ. Conservative: South Mon Jan. & Dec. 1910, MP Monmouth 1918-. **Sir Leolin-Forestier-Walker:** Born Castleton, Mon 6 May 1866 s of Sir George Forestier-Walker, 2nd Bart & Hon. Fanny Morgan, d of 1st Baron Tredegar. Anglican (Chairman PCC). Married 1894 Alice, d. of Colonel Blandy Jenkins, 2d. Educated RMA Gosport. Ceylon tea, coffee and cinchona planter 1884-89. Returned to Gwent mining operations 1908. Landowner. Company Director: Alexandra Dock & Railway Co, Thomas Spittle Ltd, Brecon & Merthyr Tydfil Railway Co, etc. Chairman, Cordes Bros. Led own cricket XI at Machen. St. Mellons RDC 1907-, Chairman from 1909. Monmouthshire CC 1907-25, 1928-31, Chairman 1923-24. Forestry Commissioner 1919-29. Member: Speaker's Conference on Devolution 1919, Commissioner, Board of Control 1921-30. Welsh Church Commissioner (unpaid) 1921. Supported Welsh home rule. Of Rhiwderin. Estate £13,186. Died 13 May 1933.

FORSDIKE George Frederick: OBE JP. Liberal: Cardiff Central 1918, Ludlow 1910. **Mr. George Forsdike:** Born Llanelli 23 October 1872, s of Captain John Forsdike. Baptist. Married 1901 Edith, d of Robert Thomas, Pontypridd solicitor. Educated Dr. Morgan's School, Bridgewater, University of Wales, Cardiff. Solicitor until 1919. Member, Stock Exchange 1919-. Chairman: Cardiff Military Tribunal, With French Red Cross, Verdun 1917. Member, Executive, St. John's Priory for Wales, Executive, National Liberal Federation. Chairman: Cardiff Liberal Assn. Cardiff CC Lord Mayor 1919-20. Freemason. Estate £85,781. Died 17 February 1936.

FORMSTONE Neil Alexander: Conservative, Alyn & Deeside and North Wales List 1999. **Mr. Neil Formstone:** Born Wrexham 1959. Educated North Wales. Self-employed businessman (two seaside businesses & pizza delivery service, of which he is head chef). Joined Young Conservatives 1975. Colwyn Bay BC 1987-96, Conwy BC (Rhiw Ward) 1996-99 (defeated). Lay member, Clwyd Family Practitioners' Cttee. Non-executive Director, Clwyd Family Health Service 1990-94. Panel Member, Gas Consumers' Council for Wales 1996-. School governor. Founder chair, Bay of Colwyn Promenade Day Cttee. Llandudno TC. Contested Conwy BC (Craigydon Ward) 1999. Interests: Better & more cost-effective public services. Hobbies: Walking, Reading, Jet skiing. Of Llandudno.

FOSTER Gareth Glynne: BA (Open). Plaid Cymru: Aberavon Feb. 1974. **Revd Canon Gareth Foster:** Born Bangor 1944. Anglican. Married Linda (1st Plaid Cymru Mayor of Merthyr Tydfil). Educated Hornchurch Grammar School, King's College, London, Chichester Theological College. Church in Wales Minister, Ordained: Deacon 1969, Priest 1970, Canon 2000. Curate: Fairwater 1969-71, Merthyr Tydfil 1971-72 (specialising in community welfare). Rector of Merthyr Tydfil with Cyfarthfa 1972-76. Team Vicar 1976-87. Diocesan Social Responsibilities Officer & Priest in Charge, Abercanaid, 1987. Executive Officer, Board of Social Responsibility 1995-. Chairman, Provincial Sector for Social Policy 1992-96, Member, CCBI Cttee for Inter-Faith Relations 1993, Merthyr Tydfil BC 1973-76, Chairman, Housing Services Cttee 1976-79, Chairman, Plaid Cymru Councillors, Mayor 1980-81. Chaplain to Mayor of Merthyr Tydfil, 2001. Of Merthyr Tydfil.

FOSTER Greg: Communist, North List 1999. **Mr. Greg Foster:** Of Mold.

FOSTER Simon Gruffydd: Independent Wales Party, South/West List 2003. **Mr. Simon Foster:** Born Cardiff 23 December 1961, s of the Revd R. J. Foster, Baptist Minister, & Dr. Griffiths, general practitioner. Religion, Eclectic. Community Economic Development Consultant. Bridgend BC 1999. Nominating Officer/Campaign Co-ordinator, Independent Wales Party. Interests: Monetary Reform. Hobbies: Woodwork, Renovation. Languages: Welsh, English. *I am also a Canadian citizen having spent over half my life there – but am happy to be back fighting for my homeland.*

FOSTER Timothy John: BSc (Eng). 1983. Green Party, Mid & West List 1999, 2003. **Mr. Timothy Foster:** Born Exeter, 19 January 1962, son of Peter Malcolm Foster, Computer Systems. Analyst, & Pauline Train. Quaker/non-aligned. Educated The Judd School, Tonbridge, University (Naval Architecture). MRCA Industrial Design 1986, Certificate in Counselling Skills & Theory 1993, ITEC Diploma A & P/Massage 2001, TEC Diploma Reflexology 2001. Art Student & part time child support worker 1999, Bodyworker-Complementary Therapist. Joined Green Party 1986, Membership Secretary, Wales 1989-91. Contested Aberystwyth TC & Ceredigion CC. Llanbadarn Fawr ComC. Interests: Transport, Energy, Economics, Trade, Third World, Housing, Town Planning, Nutrition/Food. Hobbies: Cycling, World Music, Radio. Languages: Welsh, English. Of Aberystwyth.

FOUWETHER David Thomas: Conservative, Assembly, South/East List 1999. **Mr. David Fouweather:** Born Newport, 17 September 1964, s of Walter Thomas Denis Fouweather, forklift truck driver, & Albimia Selina Harriett Saunders. Church in Wales. Married 1996, Paula Jane Smith, 1 s. Educated Bettws High School, Newport. Prison Officer. Secretary, Newport CPF 1997. Deputy chair: Newport West Conservative Assn 1997, South Wales Area Conservatives 2001. Contested Newport CBC (Malpas) 1999. Interests: Law & Order, Home Affairs. Hobbies: Music, Theatre. Of Newport.

FOWLER Peter Edward Hamilton: Conservative: Caernarfon 1992. **Mr. Peter Fowler:** Born 10 May 1949. Married Educated Loughborough College School, Hertford Grammar School. Chartered Accountant. Member Liberal Party 1974-81: Vice-Chair & Press Officer, Anglesey Liberal Assn. Joined Conservative 1981. Vice-Chair: Conwy Conservative Assn. 1989-91. Member: Press Council 1983-88.

FOX Albert M: Conservative, Ynys Môn 2001, Clwyd South 2003. **Mr. Albie Fox:** Born San Angelo, Texas 17 August 1950, s of Albert Mortimer Fox & Maud Jones (American father & Welsh mother). Returned to Wales 1956. Married 1975 Margaret. 1s 1d. Educated Llandovery College. Royal Navy, AB 1969, helicopter pilot (Queen's Commendation for Valuable Services in the Air). Transferred to RAF 1981, helicopter instructor, RAF Valley 4 years, retired 1992 as Flight Lieutenant. Set up computerised embroidery business 1992. A founder, Sportsman's Assn of Great Britain & Northern Ireland 1997 (to defend shooting sports & pistol shooting), first director. On list for East Carmarthen & Dinefwr. Agent to A Dignan, Country Field Sports & Shooting Candidate for Shrewsbury & Atcham 1997. Joined Conservative Party 1997, Press Officer, Shrewsbury & Atcham Conservative Assn. Shropshire CC 1999- (Chairman, Social Care & Health Cttee 2000). Conservative, Wales Euro 2004. Interests: Armed Forces, Social Health & Care. Ran in London Marathon 2000, 2003. Member, Welsh pistol shooting team, Commonwealth Games 1986. Hobbies: Reading, Keeping Fit, Pistol Shooting, Coaching Shooting Sports, Light Reading. Languages: Welsh, English, Colloquial French. Of Shrewsbury.

FOX-DAVIES Arthur Charles: Conservative: Merthyr Tydfil Jan 1910, Merthyr 1923, 1924. **Mr. Arthur Fox-Davies:** Born Bristol 1871, s of T. E. Fox-Davies & Maria, d of John Fox, Coalbrookdale, Salop. Anglican. Married 1901, Mary E. B. (Maggie) d. of Captain S. A. Crookes, 1s 1d. Educated Ackworth. Barrister, Lincolns Inn 1912. Served in Anti-Aircraft Corps & Naval Law Branch. Weekly Columnist, *South Wales Echo*. Editor, *Burke's Landed Gentry* & *Dod's Peerage*. Gold Staff Officer, Coronation 1910. Holborn BC. Of Coalbrookdale, Salop & London. Died London, 19 May 1928. *Books: Armorial Families*, *The Complete Guide of Heraldry, Heraldic Badges, Book of Public Armour, also wrote Thrillers.*

FRANCE-HEYHURST Jeannie: BA (Wales). Conservative: Montgomery 1992. **Mrs. Jeannie France-Heyhurst:** Born 20 January 1950, d of William Smith & Mair Smith. Married (1) 1979 Anthony Jamieson, divorced (2) 1983 James France-Heyhurst, divorced, 1s 3d. Educated Tywyn Grammar School, University of Wales, Aberystwyth, Inns of Court School of Law. Solicitor. Barrister 1987 & Public Relations Consultant. Founder, Women in Enterprise. Member: MENSA, Executive 300. Of Bunbury Heath, near Tarporley.

FRANCIS Brian Morgan: DipEd. Natural Law Party: Cardiff Central 1992, South/Central 1999. **Mr. Morgan Francis:** Born Pantyffordd, Seven Sisters 1st July 1939, s of Dai Francis, NUM leader. Educated Trinity College, Carmarthen. Teacher, Bethnal Green. Self-Employed Carpenter. Transcendental Meditation Teacher 1969. NLP National Leader, Wales & Spokesman on Welsh Affairs. Languages, Welsh, English. Of Roath, Cardiff.

FRANCIS David Hywel: BA 1968 PhD (Wales). Labour MP Aberavon 2001, South/West List 1999. **Professor Hywel Francis:** Born Onllwyn, 6 June 1946, s of Dai Francis, NUM leader (brother of Brian qv). Married Mair (Assembly candidate 1999) Married Mair Georgina Price 1s 1d (1s died at 17). Educated Llangatwg Secondary School 1958-59, Whitchurch Secondary School 1960, Whitchurch Grammar School 1960-65, University of Wales, Swansea (History). Assistant, TUC London 1971-72, Senior Research Assistant, University of Wales, Swansea 1972-74, Tutor/Lecturer DACE 2974-86, Director DACE 1987-89. Professor of Continuing Education University of Wales, Swansea 1992-99, Professorial Fellow, National Centre for Public Policy 2000-01. Special Adviser, Secretary of State for Wales 1999-2000. National Convenor, YES Campaign 1997. Member: Socialist Educational Assn, National Advisory Cttee on Lifelong Learning 1997, Welsh Office University for Industry Specialists Group. Vice-President, Llafur (Welsh Labour History Society). Founder, Community University of the Valleys, South Wales Miners' Library 1973, Bevan Foundation. Chair: Dulais Partnership & Valleys Initiative for Adult Education. Author. Member: Aberavon RFC, Cwmafan RFC. Chair: Briton Ferry Brunel Regeneration Project. Patron: Friends of St Agnes, Port Talbot. Interests: Community Regeneration, Steel, International Development, Rights of Disabled People & their Carers. Hobbies: Films, Walking, Travel, Rugby. Languages: Welsh, English, some French. Of Creunant.

FRANCIS Elizabeth Ann: Conservative, Merionydd/Nant Conwy 2001, 2003; AM Mid &

West List 2003-. **Miss Lisa Francis:** Born London 29 November 1960 (family from Y Foel, Montgomeryshire), raised at Dinas Mawddwy. Single. Educated Dinas Mawddwy Primary School; Ardwyn School, Aberystwyth; West London Institute of Higher Education. Bilingual Secretary. Hotelier, Aberystwyth family hotel 1984-2002. Proprietor, Property Management Service. Aberystwyth TC. (Chairman, General Purposes Cttee). Chair: Aberystwyth Tourism Action Group. President, Aberystwyth Rotaract Club. Director, Mid-Wales Tourism company 2002. Joined Conservative Party 1996. Deputy-Chair, Membership, Mid & West Wales Conservative Council. Interests: Agriculture, Rural Economy, Tourism, Culture. Hobbies: Modern languages, Travel, Swimming, Sailing. Languages: Welsh, English, French, conversational Spanish. Of Aberystwyth.

FRANCIS Idris Richard: UK Independence Party, Wales Euro, 1999. **Mr. Idris Francis:** Born Swansea. Design Engineer. Member: Assn of British Motorists, Business for Stirling. Of West Meon, Petersfield.

FRANCIS Mair Georgina: DipAd. ATC. MScEcon. Labour, South/West List 1999. **Mrs. Mair Francis:** Born Barry, 29 January 1948, d of Iorwerth Badger Price, supplies officer, & Hilda Hay Price, nurse. Married 1968 Hywel Francis (qv) 1s 1d (1s died at 17). Educated Barry Grammar School, Cardiff Art College, University of Wales, Swansea. Teacher. Researcher. Founder/Manager, Dove Workshops, Dulais Valley 1987. Founder, Dulais Opportunity for Voluntary Enterprise Workshop during Miners' Strike. Co-ordinator: European Community Education Projects 1990-98. Parliamentary Researcher for husband 2001-. Interests: Women's Issues, Peace, Community Development. Hobbies: Films, Music, Gardening, Travel. Languages: English. Welsh, some German. Of Creunant.

FRANCIS-WILLIAMS Benjamin Francis: QC 1885 JP (Mon) MA (Cantab). Conservative: West Monmouthshire 1885, Merthyr Tydfil 1892. **Mr. Benjamin Francis-Williams:** Born February 1845 s of Revd Enoch Williams, Baptist Minister, Merthyr Tydfil. Anglican. Married (1) Willametta (died 1886), d of Revd J. Hughes, Vicar of Ebbw Vale (2) Nora, widow of Major Donald Waterfield. Educated Swansea Grammar School; Shrewsbury School; St. John's College, Cambridge. Barrister, Middle Temple 1867, Bencher 1891. Recorder: Carmarthen 1879-90, Cardiff 1890-. Of Kensington. Estate £23,721. Of London. Died 29 July 1914.

FRANKS Christopher Paul: Plaid Cymru, Vale of Glamorgan 1999, 2001, 2003. **Mr. Chris Franks:** Born Cardiff, 2 August 1951, s of Geoffrey John Franks, engineer, & Maureen Phillips, secretary. Welsh Independent. Married 1979 Christine, lecturer. 2s 1d. Educated Llandaff College (HNC Building). Engineer, Cardiff City Highways & Transport Department. Vale of Glamorgan BC (Group Leader, Chair: Lifelong Learning Scrutiny Cttee). Chair: Plaid Cymru Councillors Assn. School Governor. Interests: Education. Hobbies: Medieval Churches. Of Dinas Powys.

FREEMAN Peter William Bernhard: Labour: Newport 1935, MP Brecon & Radnor 1929-31, Newport 1945-. **Mr. Peter Freeman:** Born London 19 October 1888, s of George James Freeman & Edith Marion Freeman. Theosophist. Married Ella, d of Sir James Torrance 3c. Educated Haberdashers' School, London. Managing Director: J. R. Freeman & Son, cigar manufacturers, Megeot Rolling Mills Ltd 1908-29. Hoxton Poor Law Guardian 1910-12, Penarth UDC 1923-26, Glamorgan CC 1927-31, Cardiff CC 1928-30. Organising Secretary. Wales, Theosophist League 1922-38. Organising Secretary: Animal Welfare Society for Wales. President: Vegetarian Society of Great Britain 1937-42, Society of Industrial & Commercial Accountants. Member: RSPCA Council, Fabian Society. Welsh Open Tennis Champion 1919-21. Campaigned for an international charter to end the cruelty, exploitation and neglect of helpless animals. Pacifist. Millionaire. Of Penarth. Died 19 May 1958. *Books etc: Peter Freeman, The Druids and Theosophy, Brotherhood, Our Young Brothers: The Animals, Our Duty to India, World Peace and Vegetarianism, The Government of the World.*

FREYBERG Bernard Cyril, 1st Baron Freyberg of Wellington NZ & Munstead: 1945: VC 1916 GCMG 1946 KCB 1942 KBE 1942 CB 1936 DSO 1915 & two others Hon. DCL Oxon 1945 Hon. LLD St. Andrews 1922 New Zealand 1944. Liberal: Cardiff South 1922. **Lieut-General, Sir Bernard Freyberg:** Born London 1889. Family emigrated to New Zealand. Married 1922 Hon. Mrs. Barbara McLaren, widow of Hon. Francis McLaren MP & d of Sir Herbert Jekyll. Educated Wellington College, New Zealand. Army: Colonel/ Acting Brigadier 1917-18, Major 1927, Colonel 1931. War Office between wars. GOC New Zealand Forces 1939-45, Lieut-General. Governor General of New Zealand, 1946-52. Deputy Constable & Lieut-Governor, Windsor Castle, 1953. Although adopted by Cardiff South Liberal Assn *he stood as an Independent candidate supporting neither Asquith nor Lloyd George.* Died 4 July 1963.

FRY Graham Thomas Reginald: Tourism & Farmers' Candidate, West Carmarthenshire & South Pembs. 1999. **Mr. Graham Fry:** Born 1948, s of Frederick Charles Fry (died 2000) & Connie Fry (died 1997). Baptist. Married Annette, 3s 1d.

Tenby Hotelier & businessman. Owner, Royal Gatehouse & Royal Lion Hotels & Royal Playhouse Cinema (closed September 2000). Interests: Tourism. Hobbies sport. Of Penhoyle Manor, Penally. *I am a true local who has gleaned a living from Pembrokeshire for the past thirty years. I think it's important for someone to give this election a run.*

FULLER-MAITLAND William Fuller: JP (Brecs) 1875 Essex DL (Essex) MA (Oxon). Liberal MP Breconshire 1875-95. **Mr. William Fuller-Maitland:** Born Stanstead Hall 8 May 1844, s of William Fuller-Maitland JP DL. Garth House, Builth & Stanstead Hall, Essex, & Lydia, d of Lieut-Colonel Prescott. Anglican. Married 1881, Hon. Evelyn Colton Gardner, d of Baron Gardner.

Educated: Harrow, Christ Church, Oxford. Landowner. Patron of 3 livings. "Gentleman" Cricketer. Languages: English. Estate £102,650. Of Garth House, Builth, Stanstead Hall, Essex, London & Brighton. Died 15 November 1932.

FURNELL Patrick Arthur Thomas: MA (Oxon). Liberal: Cardiff South-East 1950, East Grinstead 1959, Lincoln B/E 1964. **Mr. Patrick Furnell:** Born Godalming, June 1927. Married Educated Godalming Grammar School, Trinity College, Oxford (Kitchener Scholar). President, Oxford University Liberal Club 1947. RAF 1948-51, Flying-Officer, Education RAF St. Athans 1950. Lecturer/Tutor, Economics & British Constitution. Of London.

– G –

GARDENER Stephen Michael: Referendum Party: Rhondda 1997. **Mr. Stephen Gardener:** Born, South Wales 1958. Educated, Cardiff (Diploma in Engineering). Engineer. Worked at Ministry of Defence & Plessey Marine (Shop Steward). Owner: auction house & Internet publishing company. Conservative Candidate, Cardiff CC (Llanishen) 1999. Of Old St. Mellons.

GARDINER Graham Webster – see WEBSTER-GARDINER G.

GARDNER Antony Frederick: Conservative: Ogmore 1970. **Mr. Antony Gardner:** Born, July 1925. Church of England. Married, Stella, 2s. Educated, Ashburton School, Croydon. Army: Kings Royal Rifles 1954-56; Special Air Training Service (TA); Training Officer, Army Cadet Force. Joined Wiggins Teape Group 1953; South Wales & West of England Representative 1962-, plus West Midlands 1968. PC & RDC. Chairman, School Managers. Joined Young Conservatives 1958; Chair: Beckenham Young Conservatives; Bristol Federation Young Conservatives 1963-65. Contested London CC 1962. Member, St. Mary Redcliffe PCC. Of Bristol.

GARDNER Harry: Conservative: Llanelli 1951, 1959. **Mr. Harry Gardner:** Born Sussex, October 1900. Married, 3c. Educated, Sir Henry Fermor's School, Crowborough; King Charles School, Tunbridge Wells. Merchant Navy 1915-26, 1939-45; Wood turner; dock labourer in Australia; farm labourer; Maker of fishing rods. Of Tunbridge Wells.

GARDNER Iltyd William Henry: FSA. Conservative: West Monmouthshire 1900. **Mr. Iltyd Gardner:** Born, s of Revd Saul Wright Gardner. Anglican. Married, Minnie Thornton (died 1934). Solicitor. Registrar & High Bailiff of County Court. Abergavenny BC 1908-11; Monmouthshire CC. Member, Governing Body of the Church in Wales. Student of ancient architecture. Conservative election agent West Mon 1892. Hon. Member, North Monmouthshire Hunt. Of Govilon. Invalid 4 years. Estate £19,659. Died 10 February 1935.

GAREL-JONES William Armand Thomas Tristan, Baron Garel-Jones 1997: PC 1992. Conservative: Caernarfon Feb. 1974, Watford Oct. 1974; MP Watford 1979-97. **Rt. Hon. Tristan Garel-Jones:** Born, Gorseinon 28 February 1941, s of Bernard Garel-Jones & Meriel Williams. Married, Catalina Garrigues of Spain, 4s 1d. Educated, Llangennech Primary School; Kings School, Canterbury. Owner of a Madrid language school 1966-70. London Merchant Banker 1970-74; Conservative Central Office 1974-79. Personal Asst: Party Chairman 1978-79. Financial Consultant 1979. PPS 1981, Asst. Whip 1982-83, Lord Commissioner of the Treasury 1983-86; Vice-Chamberlain of the Household 1988-89; Treasurer of the Household & Deputy Chief Whip 1989-90; Minister of State, Foreign Office 1990-93. Teetotaller. Languages: Welsh, English, Spanish.

GARNER-EVANS Emlyn Hugh: LlB (Wales) MA. (Cantab). Liberal: Denbigh 1945, Chester 1935; Liberal National MP Denbigh 1950-59. Dropped by Denbigh National Liberals when Conservatives withdrew support. **Mr. Emlyn Garner-Evans:** Born, Llangollen 3 September 1911, s of Henry & Margaret Garner-Evans. Presbyterian Church of Wales. Educated, Llangollen Grammar School; University of Wales, Aberystwyth; Gonville & Caius College, Cambridge. President: Cambridge Union 1936, Union of University Liberal Societies. Founder Member: World Youth Congress Movement & British Youth Peace Assembly. Editor *New Commonwealth*, 1935-50. RAF 1939-45 Wing-Commander. PPS. Secretary, Parl Cttee on Atomic Energy. Languages: Welsh, English. Interests: International Affairs, Youth problems. Of Llangollen. Died 11 October 1963. *Books: D. Ben Rees: Cymry Adnabyddus 1952-1972.*

GARRARD Llunos Ann: Labour, Llanelli 1999. **Mrs. Ann Garrard:** Born 14 January 1950, d of Hiram Gwyn Jones, headteacher & former miner. Married 1s. Journalist, *Agenda*. Regional Secretary, Wales Law Society. Secretary, Llanelli CLP. Adviser, First Secretary Alun Michael 1999. Short-listed, Rhondda ppc 2000. Interests: Economy, Social Policy, Health. Languages: Welsh, English.

GARROW SMITH Dewi Hywel – see SMITH Dewi Hywel Garrow.

GASKELL Frank Hill: Conservative: for East Glamorgan Jan. & Dec. 1910; PPC South Glam 1913. **Lieut-Colonel Frank Gaskell:** Born, Cardiff 1879, s of Colonel Joseph Gaskell, (Chairman of Hancocks Breweries), & Emily Gaskell, of Llantwit Major. Anglican. Married, Violet Ann Catherine, d of H. P. Charles, Registrar, Neath County Court. 2s 1d. Educated, Dean Vaughan School, Llandaff; Malvern; University of Wales Cardiff. Barrister. Cardiff CC. Army: Boer War, OC 16th Battalion, Welch Regiment. Languages: English. Of Cardiff. Killed in action in France 17 May 1916.

GASS Katrina: BSc. Labour: Monmouth 1987. **Mrs. Katrina Gass:** Born Halifax, 9 November 1946 d of Kenneth Ackroyd, executive director. Married, 1971 Jeremy Gass, university lecturer, 1d. Educated grammar school & university (Social Science, Diploma in Community Work). Programme Officer, Oxfam. Member, TGWU; North Gwent Community Health Council; Beacons National Park Authority; Arts Council for Wales. Gwent CC 1985-95; Monmouthshire CC. 1995-99. Interests: Environment; Developing World. Hobbies: Walking; Photography. Languages: English, French. Of Abergavenny.

GASSON Jacqueline Anne: BSc(Psych). Liberal Democrat: Islwyn 1987, Cardiff West 1992, 1997, 2001, 2003; South/Central List 1999. **Mrs. Jacqui Gasson:** Born, Surrey, 15 March 1938. Married. Educated, Tolworth Grammar School; University of Wales Institute of Science & Technology, Cardiff. Tax Officer; Personal Assistant; Unemployed; Child Protection Officer; Advice Bureau Worker. Cardiff CC 1988- (Whip); South Glam CC 1989-97 (Group Leader); Cardiff CCC 1996- (Whip). Chair: Cardiff Victim Support; Credit Union; Special Schools Governors. Vice-Chair, CAB; Cardiff West Lib-Dems. Member: South Wales Police Authority 1989-93, 1999-; Cardiff Community Health Council 1987-. Interests: Health, Housing, Social services, Crime/policing. Hobbies: Music, Television, Reading (forensic science). Languages: English. Of Caerau, Cardiff.

GENNILARD Andre Charles Leopol: Free World of MS: Brecon & Radnor B/E 1985. **Mr. Andre Gennilard:** Born 1949. President, World of Multiple Sclerosis. Of Tunbridge Wells.

GEORGE David Frederick Roberts: BSc (Reading). Conservative: Cardigan 1970, Gower Feb. & Oct. 1974. **Mr. David George:** Born, Haverfordwest May 1937, s of Dr. W. F. T. George. Married 1969, Lynette Jane Savage (Miss Young Conservatives Wales 1969) 1s 1d. Educated, Mill Hill School; Grammar School; Reading University. Farmer (500 acres); Chairman, Livestock Marketing Co; Director, grain marketing company. Chair: Seedgrowers Assn; Welsh Growers Assn. Management Cttee; Cardiganshire Young Conservatives. Chairman, Conservative Political

Centre in Wales). Publicity Officer, Cardiganshire Conservative Assn. Of Llangoedmor.

GEORGE David Lloyd – see LLOYD GEORGE David.

GEORGE Griffith Owen: TD JP 1952 DL (Glam) 1970 MA (Oxon). Conservative: Llanelli 1945. **Major Owen George:** Born, Hirwaun 5 December 1902, s of John Owen George & Emiah George. Anglican. Married, 1937 Anne Elinor, d of Charles Edwards of Llandaff, 1s. Educated, Westminster School; Christ Church, Oxford. Army 1939-45, Lieutenant RA, Major, staff 1943. Barrister, Grays Inn 1927. Chairman, Glamorgan Quarter Sessions 1966-; Deputy Chairman 1956-66. Deputy Commissioner for Wales, National Insurance Act 1950-67. Crown Court Recorder 1972-74. Chair, Glamorgan Probation Cttee.

GEORGE Gwilym – see LLOYD GEORGE G.

GEORGE Megan – see LLOYD GEORGE M.

GERMAN Michael James: OBE 1998, BA (Open) DET CertEd. Liberal Democrat: Cardiff North Oct. 1974, Cardiff Central 1979, Caerphilly 1999, Torfaen 2003. AM. South/East List 1999. **Mr. Mike German:** Born 8 May 1945, son of Arthur Ronald German & Margaret Molly German. Roman Catholic. Married 1970 2d (divorced 1996). Educated St. Illtyd's College, Cardiff; St. Mary's College, London; Open University (Educational Studies); University of the West of England, PGEM. Primary School teacher 1966-67, Secondary School teacher: Mostyn High School 1967-70, Head of Music, Lady Mary High School, Cardiff 1970-86, Corpus Christi High School 1986-91. Director, European

Mike German.

Unit, Welsh Joint Education Cttee 1991-99. Member: NAS/UWT. Treasurer, Octavia Trust. Director, L'Avenir Ltd. Cardiff CC 1983-94, Cardiff CCC 1993- (Joint Group Leader). Chair of Governors, Gladstone Junior & Infants School, Cardiff. Welsh Liberal Democrat selection Organiser, 1992, 1997. Liberal Democrat Chief Spokesperson in Wales. Leader, Welsh Liberal Democrats Nov. 1998. Chair, National Assembly Legislation Cttee 1999-2000. Deputy First Minister & Minister for Economic Development Oct. 2000-2001; Deputy Prime Minister & Minister for Rural Development & Wales Abroad, June 2002-2003. Hobbies: Travel, Music, Reading. Languages: Learned Welsh, English, French. Of Blackwood.

GETHING Humphrey Vaughan ap David: LlB (Wales). Labour: Assembly, Mid & West List 1999. **Mr. Vaughan Gething:** Born Lusaka, Zambia, 15 March 1974, s of David John Gething, veterinary surgeon, & Beritha Gething, poultry farmer. Educated, Broadwindsor Primary School; Beaminster Comprehensive School; University of Wales, Aberystwyth & Cardiff (Diploma in Legal Studies). Trainee Solicitor 2001. President: Aberystwyth Guild of Students 1996-97; President NUS Wales 1997-98, Aberystwyth Guild of Students 1996-97. Chair, Wales Labour Students 1996-97. Branch Secretary, Aberystwyth Labour Party 1999. Chair: Cardiff & District Branch GMB 2000; GMB Race Cttee Wales & South west 2002. Co-ordinator, Right to Vote Project Board. Policy & Media Assistant, Welsh Labour HQ during 1997 election. Researcher to Loraine Barrett AM 1999. Interests: Education, Minority Representation, Social Justice. Hobbies: sport, especially cricket. Languages English; intermediate French (not fluent). Of Cardiff.

GIBBINS Frederick William: JP (Glam). Liberal MP: Mid-Glamorgan B/E March 1910-Dec. 1910. **Mr. Frederick Gibbins:** Born, Neath 1st April 1861, s of Frederick & Caroline Gibbins (Grandfather was President, Society of Friends) of Dyffryn Clydach. Quaker. Married, 1898, Jennet, d of Jenkin Rees, Penderyn, 2s. Educated, Friends School, Scarborough. Entered tinplate industry 1880; Asst. Manager, Ynyspenllwch works 1884; Tinplate Manufacturer: built Eagle Works, Neath 1890 (sold 1920); Chairman & Managing Director, Eagle Tinplate Co; Chairman, Melyn Tinplate Co; Director, London & Scottish Insurance Corporation & Welsh Insurance Corporation. A Founder, Welsh Plate & Sheet Manufacturers Assn, Chairman 1910-22. Vice-President, Welsh National Memorial Fund (against TB). High Sheriff of Glamorgan 1908. Glamorgan CC (Neath South). A temperance worker, he opened a temperance bar at his Melincryddan works. Adopted by local Liberals to oppose Vernon Hartshorn against the advice of the Master of Elibank,

Liberal Chief Whip who wished to honour the Lib-Lab accord. Estate £44,409. Died 30 July 1937.

GIBBON Colin: National Front: Cardiff West 1979; Walton Feb. 1974. **Mr. Colin Gibbon**: Born, Pontypridd, May 1936. Married, 1d. Educated, Pontypridd Grammar School. Policeman; Royal Navy; Pontypridd Garage Owner 1957. Of Pontypridd.

GIBBONS Brian Joseph: MB ChB BAO 1974 DRCOG 1979 Cert FBA 1979 MRCGP 1980 FRCGP 1995. Labour AM Aberavon 1999. **Dr. Brian Gibbons:** Born Dublin, 25 August 1950, son of a Fianna Foil TD. Educated Keadue National School. Summerhill. College, Sligo, University of Galway. Junior Hospital Doctor, Galway, Roscommon & Sheffield 1974-76, Calderdale General Practitioner Vocational Training Scheme 1977-80, General Practitioner, Blaengwynfi 198-99. Member: Socialist Medical Assn. Vice-President, Gwynfi United FC. Trustee, Gwynfi Boys and Girls Club. School Governor. Deputy Minister, Health Oct. 2000; Deputy Minister, Transport, May 2003. Interests: Health, Education, Community development. Hobbies: Sport, Music, Travel, Bevan Foundation. Of Blaengwynfi (1960).

GIBBS Jennie Thomas: BA (Wales). Liberal: Ogmore 1966, Feb. & Oct. 1974; 1979. **Mrs. Jennie Gibbs:** Born, October 1920. Married, John Gibbs. Educated, Maesteg Grammar School; University of Wales, Aberystwyth. Teacher; Company Director & Hygiene Consultant. Asst. Secretary, Liberal Party of Wales 1962-65; Conference Secretary 1965-66; Opposed establishment of Welsh Liberal Party, 1966. Maesteg UDC 1963-; Glamorgan CC 1967-73; Mid-Glam CC 1973-. Of Maesteg.

GIBSON-WATT James David, Baron Gibson Watt, of the Wye 1974: PC 1974, MC 1943, Bar 1945, DL 1968, MA (Cantab). Conservative: Brecon & Radnor 1950, 1951; MP Hereford B/E 1956-Oct. 1974. **Major, Rt. Hon. David Gibson-Watt:** Born, 11 September 1918, s of Major James Millar Gibson-Watt JP DL & Marjorie Adela; descendant of James Watt. Married, 1942 Diana (died 2000), d of Sir Charles Hambro 3s 2d. Educated, Eton; Trinity College, Cambridge; RMC Sandhurst. Major, Welsh Guards. Landowner, Forester, Farmer, Director, brewing company & Llanwrtyd British Legion Tweed Factory. Radnorshire CC 1946-68. Chair: Livestock Export Council of Great Britain. Member: National Cttee, Forestry Commission for Wales; Council of Welsh Settlement; BBC General Advisory Council; Select Cttee on broadcasting Commons Proceedings 1964. PPS 1962; Asst

Whip 1957-59; Opposition Spokesman: Broadcasting 1965-6; Welsh Affairs 1964-70; Minister of State, Wales 1970-74. Forestry Commissioner 1976-86; Chairman, Timber Growers United Kingdom 1987-90, Hon. President 1993. Chairman, Wales NO Assembly Campaign 1997. Hobbies: Football, Shooting. Of Doldowlod Hall, Llandrindod & London. Died February 2002.

GIMBLETT Michael Willis: LlB (Wales). Liberal: Llanelli Oct. 1974. **Mr. Michael Gimblett:** Born, Llanelli 1936. S of David John Gimblett & Myra (died 2001). Anglican. Married, Margaret, 4c. Educated, Llanelli Grammar School; Llandovery College; University of Wales, Aberystwyth. Solicitor 1963. Member: Assn of Liberal Lawyers. Llanelli BC (Liberal Group Leader). Of Llanelli.

GITTINS Dafydd Noel: Plaid Cymru: Brecon & Radnor Feb. 1974. **Mr. Dafydd Gittins:** Born, Brecon, December 1939, s of Ron Gittins, Camden Arms). Married 1974, Gill Skinner. Educated, Brecon High School; Knightsbridge Computer College; Lufthansa Training Base With Lufthansa (Trade Union Officer). Recording artist & composer, London 1967. Publican, Camden Arms, Brecon. Given £30,000 grant to open brewery. Founded Welsh Distillers 1976, sold to MDT International 1996 & became non-executive director. Involved in: *Chequers* Nightclub, Penally 1996-, Sept. 1997 mining operation at Aberdare; consultancy work & European Commission project on co-operatives. Director, CBI Training & Enterprise Council. Chair: Mid Wales CBI. Jailed for 12 months, 1999, for allowing the sale of drugs at Chequers, Penally, after two years of court appearances, and served four months. Conviction quashed on appeal, February 2000. Languages: Learned Welsh, English, German. *Books: Dafydd Gittins, Dafydd and Goliath (autobiography) 2000.*

GLASCODINE Charles Henry: Conservative: West Glamorgan 1895. **Mr. Charles Glascodine:** Born, Llanelli 25 June 1842, s of Richard Glascodine, Secretary, Llanelli Railway & Dock Co. Anglican. Married, 1869, Elizabeth Helen (died Dec. 1927), d of William Higgs of Stainford, 1d. Solicitor 1868; Barrister, Grays Inn 1885. Asst Clerk of Assize, South Wales Circuit 1901. Deputy Clerk of Arraigns until 1926. Hon. Librarian, Royal Institution of South Wales, President 1900-01. Swansea BC 1878-81. Member, Hon. Society of Cymmrodorion. Languages: English, Welsh learner. Estate £7,013. Died 6 April 1928.

GLYN-EDWARDS Aneurin John: BA (Wales) 1907 LlB (London). Liberal: Cardiff Central 1924; West Bromwich 1922, 1923; Stourbridge B/E 1927; Burnley 1929. **Mr. Aneurin Glyn-Edwards:**

Born, Dolgellau, s of John & Katherine Edwards. Welsh Independent. Educated Dolgellau Grammar School; University of Wales, Aberystwyth (Classics); University of London. Solicitor. Languages: Welsh, English. Of London.

GOLDING Cyril: MSc (Wales) AMIEE. Plaid Cymru: Wrexham 1970. **Mr. Cyril Golding:** Born, Caerau, Maesteg April 1935. Married, Enid, 2s. Educated, Maesteg Grammar School; University of Wales, Swansea (1st electrical engineering). Metropolitan Vickers Electrical Co 1955-59. Lecturer in Electric. Member, Court of University College, Bangor. Asst.Treasurer, Mold Choral Society. Mold UDC 1967-. Of Mold.

GOLDSWORTHY Alison: Liberal Democrat, Wales Euro 2004. **Miss Alison Goldsworthy:** Educated Haberdashers' Aske School for Girls, Monmouth; Bath University. National Chair, Liberal Democrat Youth & Students 2002-03. Liberal Democrat Delegate to European Youth Convention on the Future of Europe. Of Llangybi, Monmouth.

GORDON Robert I. N: Conservative: Torfaen 1987, Watford 1997. **Mr. Robert Gordon:** Born, 29 March 1952. Married, 2d. Educated, Watford Grammar School; Sussex University; Guildford College of Law; London College of Law. Solicitor 1975 at Enfield. Watford BC 1982-90; Group Leader 1984-86. Hertfordshire CC 1989-. Deputy Chairman, Watford Conservative Assn 1984-86. Of Watford.

GORDON-WILLIAMS May L: Conservative: Pontypridd 1929. **Miss May Gordon-Williams:** Born, Cardiff 1906, d of Gordon Williams, solicitor. Anglican. Married, vicar. Barrister (Grays Inn 1928) at Liverpool.

GOSS Julian Beresford: United Socialists, Cardiff Central 1999, Welsh Socialist Alliance, Cardiff Central 2001. **Mr. Julian Goss:** Born 1 October 1946, son of Ernest William Goss, estate agent, & Margaret Goss. Atheist. Married 1968, Teresa Ruth Goss, CAB advisor. 1s 2d. Educated Monmouth School. Bus driver, Cardiff Bus 1978. TGWU Shop Steward. Secretary: Cardiff Welsh Socialist Alliance. Member: Cardiff 3 Campaign, Anti-Nazi League. Active in Miners' Support Group 1984-85, Campaign to prevent imposition of Section 28, and Anti Poll Tax Campaign. Secretary, Welsh Socialist Alliance. Languages: English, French, Spanish. Hobbies: History, Pre-History, Cooking. Of Roath, Cardiff (1976).

GOTTHARD Cerian R. – see SCREEN Cerian.

GOUGH Michael Bernard: BA (Oxon) 1976 MA 1987. Independent, Torfaen 1999. **Mr. Mike**

Gough: Born Newport 30 November 1943, son of Walter Bernard Gough & Iris Winifred Josephine Gough, social club stewards. Married 1967 Gillian Mary Thomas, social worker, 1s 2d. Educated Pontnewydd Primary School, West Mon Grammar School, Pontypool 1966-60, Coleg Harlech 1972-74, Balliol College, Oxford 1974-76 (PPE). Apprentice Patternmaker, GKN Iron Foundries 1960, redundant 1971, Health & Safety Executive factory inspector 1976, Central Health & Safety Adviser, Gwent CC 1978, retired 1996. Former part-time WEA & Gwent HE College lecturer. Works part-time at a residential home for the elderly at Abergavenny. Joined Labour Party 1969, Chair, Coleg Harlech Labour Students. Labour Party Branch Secretary President, Torfaen CLP. Expelled from Labour Party 1999 for opposing an official Labour candidate. Foundry Workers shop steward. Vice-President, Gwent NALGO. Secretary, Court Farm Community Assn. Chair: Afon Llwyd Housing Society. Treasurer, Cwmbran RFC. Cwmbran UDC 1970-74, Torfaen BC 1983-91 (Chair, Finance Cttee 1987-91). Hobbies: Member, Lleisiau Gwent Choir, 1981; Amateur Comedian & Entertainer; Sports (especially rugby, played for GKN XV, Newport Youth XV, Cwmbran RFC, Balliol College XV), Travel, Cycling. Of Cwmbran.

GOUGH Robert William: Plaid Cymru: Torfaen 1997, Assembly, Caerphilly 1999. **Mr. Robert Gough:** Born Llanbradach 12 August 1947, son of David William Gough, Co-op Provision Manager, & Marion Rae Gough. English Baptist. Married 1968, Shirley Patricia Gough, receptionist, 2d. Educated Coed-y-Brain Primary School, Twyn Secondary Modern School, Caerphilly. Bodyshop manager, Fords Main Dealer. Member, Institute of Motor Industry. ComC. 1983 (thrice Chair), Rhymney Valley DC. Caerphilly CBC (Cabinet Member for Economic Development, Tourism and Objective One 1999). Schools Governor & Chair, Governor, Ystrad Mynach College. Chair: Community Legal Services Funders' Forum, Objective 1 Partnership, Objective One Steering Group. Member: Institute of the Motor Industry, Islwyn Borough Transport Board of Directors. Interests: Economic Regeneration. Hobbies: Watching football & other sports, Walking, Gardening. Supporter of Animal Welfare charities, opposed to animal testing & fox hunting. Languages: English. Of Llanbradach.

GOULD James Childs: Conservative MP. Cardiff Central 1918-26. **Mr. J. C. Gould:** Born, Penarth, 1882, s of Richard Gould, stonemason. Married, 1905, Mary Blanche Flagg JP of New Brunswick 2d. Educated, Radnor Road Elementary School, Cardiff; Penarth Higher Grade School. Shipping Office Clerk in South Africa & USA. Manager, New York insurance office -1912.

Founded own business 1912: Governing Director: Gould Steamships & Industrials Ltd; J. C. Gould, Angier & Co; Chair: Richardson, Duck & Co; Blair & Co. (Stockton on Tees); Director: Western Alliance Re-Insurance Co. Member of Lloyds. Chair, Cardiff Maritime Board 1919. Cardiff CC 1917-. Governor: King Edward VII Hospital; Executive, Prince of Wales Hospital. Of St. Mellons. Died 2 July 1944.

GOULD R. Travis: Workers' Revolutionary Party: Merthyr Tydfil 1979; Merthyr Tydfil & Rhymney 1983. **Mr. Travis Gould:** Born, Merthyr Tydfil 1950. Married, 1d. Machine Operator, Moss Gears. Unemployed. Joined: AUEW 1976, WRP 1977. Of Cefn Coed.

GOURLAY Francis Page: Conservative: Caernarfon Boroughs 1931; Spennymoor 1929. **Captain Page Gourlay:** London Stockbroker. Army 1914-18. Travelled Europe, India, Egypt. Chair, Bethnal Green Junior Imperial League. Of London.

GOWER Herbert Raymond: Kt 1974. Conservative: Ogmore 1950; MP. Barry 1951-83; Vale of Glamorgan 1983-. **Sir Raymond Gower:** Born, Briton Ferry 15 August 1916, s of Lawford Gower, Glam CC Architect. Baptist. Unmarried,. Educated, Neath Grammar School, Cardiff High School; University of Wales, Cardiff; Cardiff School of Law. Army Cadet Officer, Observer Corps & Civil Defence 1939, after failing military medical. Solicitor 1944; own practice 1948. *Western Mail* columnist 1951-64; Chairman, Penray Press & *Barry Herald* 1955-64. Director: Airport Hotels Ltd; British Soil Ltd; Broughton & Co (Bristol) Ltd 1961-. Joint Founder & Director, Welsh Dragon Unit Trust 1962-67 & other companies. PPS 1952-60. Court Member: National Museum of Wales 1953; National Library of Wales 1957; University College, Cardiff, 1951; University College, Aberystwyth 1953. Vice-President: Wales & Mon. Conservative Assn; Cardiff Business Club 1953; National Chamber of Trade 1956; South Wales Ramblers 1968. Hon. Secretary: Friends of Wales Society. Member: Welsh Executive & Council, United Nations Assn. Chair: Welsh Conservative MPs Group. President: Conservative Teachers in Wales; London Glamorgan Society 1967-69. Treasurer, Welsh Parliamentary Group 1966. Member: Select Cttee on Expenditures 1970; Speaker's Conference on Electoral Reform 1967-69. Fellow, Institute of Directors 1958. Freeman of the Borough of Vale of Glamorgan 1978. Of Cardiff. Died 23 February 1989.

GRACE David: BSc (London) PGCE. (Wales). Labour, Ceredigion. **Mr. David Grace:** Born, Cwmgwili 1948. Married, Linda, 2s 2d. Educated, Kings College, London, University of Wales,

Aberystwyth. Physics Teacher: Taught in London 17 years; Head of Science, Ysgol Gyfun Preseli. Secretary, Ceredigion Labour Party, 1989-97; Chair 1997-2000, Agent B/E 2000. Chartered Physicist. Member: Institute of Physics; *Menter Aberteifi*, Theatr Mwldan Management Board. Cardigan TC. 1995 Mayor. Interests: Health, Education, Rural Affairs. Hobbies: Fishing, Wall building. Languages: English, Welsh. Of Cardigan.

GRACIA Peter Manuel: LlB (UWE Bristol). UK Independence Party. **Mr. Peter Gracia:** Born 1963. Married 2c. Educated University of the West Country, Bristol (1st & PGDipLaw). Construction Industry Consultant 2000. College Lecturer 7 years. Labour Party Branch Chair. Left to join UKIP. Hobbies: Mountain Walking, Motor Cycling. Of Merthyr Tydfil.

GRAHAM Alan Crosland: BA (Oxon) FSA Order (3rd Class) St. Anne of Russia. Conservative: Denbigh 1929, Darwen 1931, MP: Wirral 1935-45. **Captain Alan Crosland:** Born, August 1896, s of Sir Crosland Graham, of Clwyd Hall & Mary Bond Graham. Married, (1) 1939 Marion, d of M. C. de Plessis of Cape Town, (divorced 1948) 2d (2) 1953 Maria Antionette Louise Pavluc 1s1d. Educated, Rugby; Trinity College, Oxford (History). Army 1915-19: Captain. Private Secretary, Lord Hailsham, Leader of the Lords 1932-35. Chair: Anglo-Polish Parliamentary Cttee. Member: Royal Asian Society, Royal Institution for International Affairs, Viscount Mersey's Cttee for the Preservation of Antiquities in Cyprus. Languages: English. Of Plas Llanychen, nr Ruthin & London. Died 30 May 1964.

GRAHAM William: JP. Conservative, Newport West 1999, 2003; AM. South/East List 1999. **Mr. William Graham:** Born Newport 18 November 1949. URC Elder & Trustee. Married Elizabeth Hannah, d of Joshua Griffiths, 1s 2d. Educated Blackfriars School, College of Estate Management. Quantity Surveyor (Principal, family firm). President & charter member, Caerleon Rotary Club. Deputy Chair, Rougemont School Governors, Newport. Fundraiser, Royal Gwent Hospital Children's Ward, Macmillan National Cancer Trust. Newport BC (Group Leader 1992-94), 1988-94, 1999-. Member URC Wales Trust, Health Help International, Newport Harbour Commission. Gwent CC 1986-90. Deputy Chair, Newport West Conservative Assn. Deputy Business Secretary & Cttee Chair, Welsh Conservative Party 1999. Group Spokesman for Social Justice 2003-. Hobbies: Breeder of pedigree Suffolk sheep, Orchid hybridization, Architectural history. Of Lower Machen.

GRAHAM-PALMER Robert William Henry: BA (Cantab). Conservative: Wrexham 1979, 1987.

Mr. Robert Graham-Palmer: Born, 15 February 1941. Married, 4c. Educated, Radley College, Abingdon; Emmanuel College, Cambridge. Ran family farm at Wrexham (250 Rhosnesi Friesian Herd) 1969. Hotelier; Director: Wrexham & East Denbighshire Water Co; Chairman, Wrexham Training Board Ltd. Wrexham-Maelor BC 1973-83. Chair: Clwyd Country Landowners' Assn; Welsh Cttee, Country Landowners Assn. Of Wrexham.

GRAIL Michael John: Independent Wales Party, Mid & West List 2003. **Mr. Michael Grail:** National Secretary, Independent Wales Party. Of Six Bells, Abertillery.

GRAY Jean Elizabeth: SRN SCM. Liberal Democrat, Torfaen 1997, Assembly 1999. **Mrs. Jean Gray:** Born, Newport, 10 November 1941. Educated, Stow Hill Secondary Modern School, Newport. Clerk/typist in water heating factory; student nurse; GP's nurse/receptionist; school nurse/clerk; Community Midwife 1980-93, retired. Torfaen Group Representative, Royal College of Midwives 1984-92. Joined Liberal 1979. Chair, Secretary & Membership Secretary Torfaen Liberal Democrat Assn. Torfaen BC 1987-94; Cwmbran ComC. 1987-95. Contested Monmouthshire CC 1999. Retired from politics 2000. Interests: Health; Education; Environment; Local government. Hobbies: Family, Travel, Reading, Art. Languages: English. Of Cwmbran.

GRAY-MORRIS: Robert Hugh: JP. MSc. FSMC. FBCO. Referendum Party: Ynys Môn 1997. **Mr. Hugh Gray-Morris:** Born, Welshpool, 12 January 1938, s of William Gray Morris, pharmacist, & Eira Mary Evans. Church of England. Married, 1976 Sonia Marilyn Gray Morris, 1d. Educated, Holyhead Grammar School; Ellesmere College; City University. Ophthalmic Optician, Holyhead since 1985. Joined UK Independence Party. Interests: Campaigning against the Single Currency. Hobbies: Gardening; Reading; Old Cars; Hill Walking. Of Llanddeusant.

GREAVES David Tudor: MLIA (Dip) CeMAP. Referendum Party: Bridgend 1997. **Mr. Tudor Greaves:** Born, Alperton,. Middlesex, 3 March 1933, s of David Charles Greaves, retailer, & Gwendoline Mary Ungoed, dressmaker. Church of England. Married, Gillian Diana Evans. 1d. Independent Financial Adviser. Chairman, Chamber of Trade. Joined Conservatives after 1997 election. Secretary/Treasurer/Chair: Porthcawl Conservative Assn. Interests: Passionate supporter of the pound. Hobbies: DIY, Photography, Water Colours. Languages: English. Of Porthcawl.

GREAVES James C: Liberal, South Wales Euro 1979. **Mr. James Greaves:** Born 1930. Married 1d.

Educated St. Ignatius College, London, University of London. Senior Lecturer, Business Administration, Polytechnic of Wales. Chair: Barry Liberal Assn. Vale of Glamorgan BC.

GREEN Cheryl Ann: BA. Dip. Politics & Government (Open). Liberal Democrat, South/West List, 1999, Bridgend 2003. **Mrs. Cheryl Green:** Born Neath, 22 October 1952, d of Richard Ronald Rees, civil servant, & Elvis Eileen Rees, accounts clerk. Church of England. Married 1971, Thomas William Green, programmer/analyst, 2s. Educated Cynffig Comprehensive School, Open University. Company Secretary (own business). Bridgend BC. (Bryntirion, Laleston, Merthyr Mawr Ward). Leader of the Opposition (Chair: Cross Cutting Issues Scrutiny Cttee). Chair, Bridgend Liberal Democrat Assn. Interests: Policy Development. Hobbies: Walking, Latin American & Salsa Dancing. Languages: Welsh, English, German. Of Laleston.

GREEN Michael Joseph: Communist, North List 2003. **Mr. Mike Green:** Born Sheffield 13 December 1966, s of Joe Green, miner-fitter, & Dorothy Joan Green, housewife. Non-believer. Partner, Sonja Mooney, 1s. Educated, Comprehensive School; College student, 2003-. Ex-miner at Point of Ayr Colliery. Unemployed after motor cycle accident. Denbighshire CC. Member NUM. Campaigner against Imperialism & for Cuba Solidarity. Interests: Marxism, Noam Chomsky. Hobbies: US History, Reading, Cycling, Football, Chess, Pool, Philosophy. Of Rhyl.

GREEN-PRICE Richard: 1st Bart 1874 JP DL (Rads) JP (Hereford). Liberal Radnorshire 1885, 1886; MP Radnor District 1863-69; Radnorshire 1880-85. **Sir Richard Green Price:** Born, 18 October 1803, s of George Green, Canon Bridge, & Elizabeth, d of Colonel Price of Norton Manor (MP Radnor District 1797-1847). Assumed the name of Price when he inherited the estate of his uncle, Colonel Richard Price. Married, (1) Elizabeth, d of Dansey Richard Dansey (2) Laura, d of Richard Henry King MP, 5s 1d. Educated Worcester. Landowner (8800 acres). High Sheriff of Radnorshire 1876. Of Norton Manor, Radnorshire & London. Estate £11,258. Died 11 August 1887.

GREEN-WANSTALL Kenneth: Conservative: Pontypridd 1966. **Mr. Kenneth Green-Wanstall:** Born, Yorkshire June 1918. Married, 1s. Educated, Grimsby Municipal College; Reigate College; Eastbourne College. Factory Inspector; Special policeman; Author, Journalist & Broadcaster. Of Brixham. Died 1974/75.

GREENAWAY Margaret May Miranda: BA BScEcon (London). Conservative: Merthyr Tydfil 1959; Wolverhampton NE 1964. **Mrs. Miranda Greenaway:** Born, November 1916, d of R. G. Heergard Warner. Anglican. Married, (1) John Raymond Brumfit (died) (2) 1942 Dr. Frank Greenaway, Keeper/Research Fellow, The Science Museum, London 5c. Educated Blackheath Grammar School; Kings College, London; London School of Economics. Organising Secretary, Mothers' Union 1956-58; Marriage Guidance Legal Counsellor (Epsom); part-time lecturer in Law, Politics & Economics. Member: Bow Group; South West Metropolitan Regional Hospital Board; Medical, Hospital & Dental Whiteley Council. Surrey CC. Of Ewell, Epsom.

GREENSLADE Peter: Socialist Labour Party, South/West List 2003. **Mr. Peter Greenslade:** Active trade unionist. Of Blaengarw.

GREER Neil: Independent, Merthyr Tydfil & Rhymney 2003. **Mr. Jock Greer:** Born Edinburgh 15 May 1947, baker, & Sarah Ann Greer, housewife. Married Christine 1s. Educated Schools in Scotland; FETC in Wales. Army 23 years. Master Chef. Self-employed gas salesman & Voluntary Action Merthyr Tydfil Caretaker; Taxi driver at weekends. Member: British Legion. Contested Merthyr Tydfil BC September 2002. Hobbies: Chess, Swimming, Golf, Family recreation. Languages: English. Of Penydarren, Merthyr Tydfil (1983).

GREGORY Janice: Labour AM. Ogmore 1999. **Mrs. Janice Gregory:** Born Llwynypia, Rhondda 10 January 1955, d of Sir Ray Powell MP (qv). Methodist. Married 1977, Michael Gregory, consultant, furniture industry, 2d. Educated Pentre Grammar School & Bridgend Grammar School. Constituency Secretary to her father 1991-99. Secretary, CLP Women's Council & Branch Chair. Chair: Women's Section, Welsh Labour Party. Member: Co-operative Party, Fabian Society, USDAW, TGWU. Labour Whip 1999, resigned Feb. 2000 believing that there had been a ploy to oust Alun Michael. Chair: Social Justice & Regeneration Cttee. Interests: Tackling Poverty, Community Regeneration, Health, Children. Hobbies: Family Time, Gardening. Of Pencoed.

GREGORY Jeffrey: Independent, Rhondda 2003. **Mr. Jeff Gregory:** Born Clydach Vale. Ex-Miner. Keen sportsman. Ex-player, Ystrad RFC XV, Tylorstown RFC XV. Welsh short green bowls champion. Inaugurated Rhondda's 1st Rock & Pop Festival. Founder, Rhondda People's Party. Member, RANT (Rhondda against Nantgwyddon Tip). Interests: Needs of young & elderly, education, transport, employment, opposed to legalisation of cannabis.

GREGORY Pauline Carol: British National Party, South/East List 2003, Wales Euro 2004. **Mrs.**

Pauline Gregory: d. of Leonard Owen. Christian. Married. Widowed. Property Manager, retired. Joined BNP after hearing that *Labour was introducing teaching of Japanese in Wales with no opposition from other parties (uncle was a POW).* Interests: "Working to stop this government giving my country away and treating British people as second class citizens." Of Cardiff.

GRENFELL David Rhys: PC 1951 CBE 1935 JP (Swansea) 1922 Hon. LLD. (Wales) 1958 Chevalier de la Legion d'Honneur (France) 1953. Labour MP Gower 1922-59. **Rt. Hon. Dai Grenfell:** Born, Penyrheol, Gorseinon 27 June 1881, s of William Grenfell, Miner & Ann Grenfell. Welsh Independent. Married,1905 Beatrice Morgan 1d. Educated, Penyrheol Elementary School. Miner 1893; attended night school 1900-03. Nova Scotia 1903-05; Manager's Certificate, Nova Scotia 1904; Returned to UK 1905. Pit sinking at Mountain Colliery 1905; Loughor Colliery; Under-Manager Certificate 1906; 1st Class Manager's Certificate 1907; taught at evening classes 1907-11; Miners' Agent 1916; Advisory Agent 1922-35. PPS 1924, 1929-31. Member, Miners' Welfare Scholarship Cttee 1930-35. Member: Forestry Commission 1929-42; Royal Commission of Safety in Mines 1936; Welsh Land Settlement Commission 1935-36; Select Cttee: on Betting 1923; Police Organization 1932; Parliamentary Admin Cttee. 1929-45. Secretary of State for Mines 1940-42. Chair: Welsh Parliamentary Party; Franco-British Parliamentary Group; Welsh Tourist Board 1948-51. Father of the House of Commons 1953-59. Hon. Member, Gorsedd. 1st President, Gower Society. Hon. Member, French National Chamber of Deputies 1953. Rechabite. Languages: Welsh, English, French, German. Of Sketty, Swansea. Died November 1968. *Books: D. R. Grenfell: Industrial Planning 1935, Coal 1947.* Further Reading: *D. Ben Rees: Cymry Adnabyddus 1952-1972.*

GRICE Colin Dudley: National Front: Carmarthen 1979; British National Party: Carmarthen 1983. **Mr. Colin Grice:** Royal Artillery Signaller, 2 years. Qualified draughtsman & surveyor. Worked in sales, farming, driving instruction & publishing. Of Llandysul.

GRIFFIN Helen Mary: BSc. Respect Unity Coalition. Wales Euro 2004. **Ms. Helen Griffin:** Born Pyle, 18 July 1958, d of Gerald Patrick Griffin, steelworker/manager, & Mary Madden, housewife/secretary/student. Educated Bishop Vaughan RC Comprehensive School, Swansea; Swansea College (Psychology/Sociology). Registered Mental Nurse. Writer & Actress. Chair, Swansea Anti-War Demonstrations 2003. Hobbies: Reading, photography, theatre, singing. Languages: Welsh learner; English. Of Swansea.

GRIFFITH Ellis J. – see ELLIS-GRIFFITH E. J.

GRIFFITH John Huw Price: Conservative: Gower 1964; Rugby 1970. **Mr. Huw Griffith:** Born Swansea, July 1930. Married, 4c. Educated, Bromsgrove School. Royal Artillery Lieutenant 1949. Chartered Accountant. Slough BC 1962; Alderman; Group Leader 1964-69. Of Slough.

GRIFFITH Morgan: JP (Mon) 1923. Liberal: Monmouth 1923. **Mr. Morgan Griffith:** Born Llantrissent, Gwent, 1864, s of Griffith Griffith, Gelliwen. Presbyterian Church of Wales Elder. Married, 1888, Rebecca, d of Ioan David, Llansantffraed, Gwent. Educated Bridgwater & Cardiff. Farmer. Chairman, Abergavenny Branch NFU. Royal Artillery. Monmouthshire CC until 25.8.1932. Of Llantrissent, Gwent.

GRIFFITH-BOSCAWEN Arthur Sackville Trevor: PC 1920 Kt 1911 JP MA (Oxon). Conservative Candidate: East Denbighshire B/E August 1906; MP Tonbridge 1892-1906, Dudley 1910-22, Taunton 1922-. **Rt. Hon. Sir Arthur Griffith-Boscawen:** Born, Trevelyan Hall, Rossett, Wrexham 1865, s of Captain Boscawen Trevor Griffith-Boscawen & Helen Sophia Duff. Anglican. Married, (1) 1892, Edith Sarah (died 1919) d of Samuel Williams. of Boons Park, Edenbridge, Kent; (2) 1921, Phyllis Maud, d of William Dereham Educated, Rugby; Queens College, Oxford. President, Oxford Union 1888. Lieut-Colonel, Royal West Kent Regt 1914-16; 19th Hampshire Regt; France 1916-17. London CC 1910-13. PPS 1895-1900; Parl-Sec: Pensions 1916-19, Board of Agriculture & Fisheries 1919-21; Minister, Agriculture & Fisheries 1921-22; Minister of Health 1922-23. Hon. Treasurer, Church Army; Member, Church Assembly. Chairman, Church of England Pension Fund; Welsh Church Commissioners 1923-45. Chair: Commission on Transport 1928-31. Of Pangbourne. Died 1 June 1946. *Books: A. S. T. Griffith-Boscawen: Fourteen Years in Parliament. 1907: Memories, 1925.*

GRIFFITHS Alan Paul: MA (Oxon). Labour: Pembroke 1983. **Mr. Alan Griffiths:** Born, 21 September 1953, teacher's son. Educated, St. Davids Comprehensive School; Jesus College, Oxford (double first in Law). Fellow & Tutor in Law, Exeter College. Barrister, Grays Inn 1981. Called to Bermuda Bar. Oxford CC 1980- (Chairman, Finance Cttee). Member AUT. Secretary, Oxford University Welsh Society. President Oxford Students' Union. Member: Lawyers against the Bomb. Languages: Welsh, English.

GRIFFITHS Albert John: LlB (Wales). Labour AM. Newport East 1999. **Mr. John Griffiths:** Born Newport, 19 December 1956, s of Albert

John Griffiths, British Rail head shunter, & Hannah Griffiths, factory worker/domestic help. Atheist. Married 1978, Alison Kim, d of Donald Henry Hopkins & Lilian Ann Hopkins, 2s. Educated Duffryn Comprehensive School, Newport, Newport FE College; University of Wales, Newport, Bristol Polytechnic, University of Wales Continuing Education Dept. Diploma in Social Science. Lecturer in FE & HE 1988-89, Production Executive 1990, Solicitor 1990-. Member: WEA, Co-operative Party. School governor. Gwent CC 1995-95. Newport CBC 1995-99. Member: Labour Party National Forum. Deputy Minister of Economic Development, 30.4.2001; Deputy Minister for Health 2003. Interests: Social Inclusion, Economy, Education, Environment, International Affairs. Hobbies; Running: raised £3500 for charity in London Marathon, Cricket, Football, Rugby, Circuit training, Reading. Languages: Learning welsh, English, GCSE French. Of Newport.

GRIFFITHS David Brandon: FCA. Liberal Democrat, Clwyd South 2001; Paddington North 1966; Euro, Hertfordshire 1993, Thames Valley 1989. **Mr. David Griffiths:** Born, Conwy, November 1940. Married, Divorced 2c. Educated City of London School. Chartered Accountant (Principal, Griffiths, Hicks); Non-Executive Director, Insplay Ltd; ex-finance director, Ladbrokes Racing. Election Agent 1979, 1987, 1992, 1997. Chairman, Paddington North Liberal Assn. Former Welsh International Sprinter. Trustee & Treasurer, National Benevolent Fund for the Aged. Hobbies: Watching sport, Coins, Tokens. Languages: Welsh, English. Of Bovingdon, Herts.

GRIFFITHS Edward: BSc (Wales). Labour: Denbigh 1966; MP: Brightside B/E June 1968-Oct. 1974; failed to secure re-adoption, Independent Labour: Brightside Oct. 1974. **Mr. Edward Griffiths:** Born, Treuddyn nr Mold, 7 March 1929, s of Robert Griffiths JP. Congregationalist lay preacher. Married, 1954, Ella Constance, d of William G. Griffiths 1s d. Educated, Mold Grammar School; University of Wales, Bangor. Industrial Chemist, John Summers Steelworks, Shotton 1954 – Part-time Director, British Steel Corporation April 1968-74 (resigned to fight by-election). Flintshire CC 1964-67. Member: BISAKTA; Commons House Services Cttee. Vice-Chairman, PLP Power & Steel Group 1974 – Voted Conservative 1979 election.

GRIFFITHS Gwendoline: Communist, South/Central List 1999, 2003. **Mrs. Gwen Griffiths:** Teacher, retired. Museum Volunteer Worker. Plaid Cymru Taf-Ely BC. Left to join Communists *because Communists fight for social justice and self-government across the world,. (1999 Manifesto).* Of Pontypridd.

GRIFFITHS Gwyn – see GRIFFITHS Owain G.

GRIFFITHS Hubert Geoffrey: Conservative: Bedwellty 1929. **Mr. Hubert Griffiths:** Born, Saundersfoot, s of John Griffiths. Member, Hon. Society of Cymmrodorion.

James Griffiths.

GRIFFITHS James: PC 1945, CH 1966 JP (Brecs). Hon. (Wales) 1946. Labour MP Llanelli B/E 1936-70. **Rt. Hon. James Griffiths:** Born, Betws, Ammanford September 1890, s of William Griffiths, colliery blacksmith. Welsh Independent. Married, 1918, Winifred, d of William Rutley, Overton, Hants, 2s 1d. Educated, Betws elementary school; Central Labour College. Miner 1903-20. Branch Secretary SWMF 1907; Miners' Agent, Anthracite Miners' Assn 1925-36; President SWMF 1934-36; Executive Member, MFGB 1934-36. Joined ILP 1905, Branch Secretary 1907. Secretary, Ammanford Trades Council 1916-19; Llanelli Labour Agent 1922-25. Member, Labour Party NEC 1939-59; Chairman 1948-49; Secretary, Welsh Parliamentary Party 1942. Minister of National Insurance 1945-50; Secretary of State for the Colonies 1950-51; Deputy Leader of the Opposition 1956-59; Secretary of State for Wales 1964-66. Member, BBC Advisory Council 1952; Temperance Advocate. Languages: English. Died 7 August 1975. *Books: James Griffiths: Coal 1941, Glo 1945, Pages from Memory, 1969.* Further Reading: *J. Beverley Smith etc: James Griffiths & His Times (Wales Labour Party) 1977.*

GRIFFITHS John – see GRIFFITHS Albert John.

GRIFFITHS John Gwynedd: BA (Wales) MA (Liverpool) DPhil (Oxon) Dlitt Hon. DD (Wales).

Plaid Cymru: Gower 1959, 1964. **Professor J. Gwyn Griffiths:** Born, Pentre, Rhondda, 7 December 1911, s of Revd Robert Griffiths, Baptist Minister, & Jemima Davies, housewife. Baptist Lay Preacher & Deacon. Married 1939, Dr. Kathe Julia Gertrud Bosse, German Archaeologist (died 1998) 2s. Educated, Rhondda County School; University of Wales, Cardiff (1st Greek, Latin; 2nd Hebrew); Liverpool University; Fellow of the University of Wales at Queens College, Oxford Archaeological Assistant, Egyptian Research Society; Teacher: Rhondda County School-1943; Wirral Grammar School; Lecturer in Classics & Professor, University of Wales, Swansea. President UCAC. Plaid Cymru Branch Secretary: Pentre, Bala, Oxford & Swansea West Constituency. Editor, *Y Ddraig Goch & Welsh Nation.* Contested Swansea BC (Llansamlet). Languages: Welsh, English, German, Arabic. Of Sketty, Swansea. Died 15 June 2004.

GRIFFITHS Lesley – see GRIFFITHS Susan Lesley.

GRIFFITHS Llyr Hughes – see HUGHES GRIFFITHS Llyr.

GRIFFITHS Owain Gwyn: LlB (Wales). Liberal (Democrat): Caernarfon 1983; Clwyd North-West 1987. **Mr. Gwyn Griffiths:** Born, 30 July 1956. Educated, Merioneth & University of Wales, Aberystwyth. Solicitor 1980 at Holywell Secretary, Welsh Liberal Party; Vice-Chairman; Member, Welsh Liberal Executive 1976-; Last Chairman, Welsh Liberal Party; Member, Alliance Cttee for Wales. Governor, University of Wales. Member: Standing Conference, Welsh Centre for International Affairs; National Trust; CPRW; Political Archive Cttee National Library of Wales. Joined Assembly Legal Staff. August 1999. Languages: English, Welsh.

GRIFFITHS Rhodri: BA PGCE. Green Party, South/West List 2003. **Mr. Rhodri Griffiths:** Born London, 22 September 1953, s of Gwynne Edward Griffiths, teacher, & Kate Daniel, nurse. Buddhist. Married 2001, Ana Rosa Boyain Y Goita Griffiths, research assistant, 2d. Educated Penlan Comprehensive School, Swansea; Liverpool Polytechnic; University of Wales, Cardiff. Teacher. Green Party Swansea spokesman on Transport. Interests: Transport, Environmental issues, Promoting peace and co-operation. Hobbies: Conservation, Gardening, Painting, Reading, Cycling, Cinema, Travel. Languages: Welsh, English, Spanish. Of Three Crosses, Gower.

GRIFFITHS Richard Ffoulkes: Liberal: Merthyr Tydfil B/E 26 Oct. 1888. **Mr. Ffoulkes Griffiths:** Born, Llangollen 1850, teacher's son. Married (1) 1874, d of Joseph Aston (died 1879) (2) d of

Professor Goadby, 1s 1d. Educated Llangollen Baptist College. Founder-Secretary, Llangollen School Board whilst a student. Baptist Minister, Ordained 1872: Tarporley, Cheshire 1872-77; Stoney Street, Nottingham 1877-81. Agent, Liberation Society. Temperance Speaker. Chancery Barrister 1879. Became a barrister after the comments of a judge in a libel case, where he defended himself. Prominent in *Cymru Fydd.* Belatedly nominated to oppose W. Pritchard Morgan after much uncertainty among the Liberal caucus. Languages: Welsh, English. Died 9 April 1901. *Further Reading:* Ivor Thomas Rees, 'From Grace to Politics via Law', *Merthyr Historian, Vol. 18, 2005, 99-107.*

GRIFFITHS Robert David: Communist Party of Britain: Pontypridd 1997; South Wales Central Euro 1994;, Pontypridd & South/Central List 1999; Newport East 2001, 2003. **Mr. Robert Griffiths:** Married, 3c; Educated, University of Wales, Newport (Labour & Euro Studies). President: Welsh Area, AUEW/TASS. General Secretary, Communist Party of Britain January 1998, when Mike Hicks was ousted. Tutor in Economic & Trade Union Studies, University of Wales, Newport. Author & Broadcaster. Languages: Welsh, English. Of Splott, Cardiff. *Books: Robert Griffiths: S. O. Davies.*

GRIFFITHS Susan Lesley: Labour, Wrexham 2003. **Mrs. Lesley Griffiths:** Born Paisley, Scotland, 8 January 1960. Educated Ysgol Rhiwabon; North East Wales Institute, Wrexham. Church in Wales. Married Gareth Wyn Griffiths. (Wrexham BC) 2d. Political Assistant, Dr. John Marek MP AM (whom she defeated in the party election) and to Ian Lucas MP. Member. *Yes for Wales* Campaign. Interests: Health, Economic Development, Road Safety. Hobbies: Walking, Reading, Music, Watching Wrexham AFC. Of Wrexham.

GRIFFITHS Thomas: JP (Glam). Labour MP Pontypool 1918-29. **Mr. Tom Griffiths:** Born, Neath 1867, s of Thomas & Mary Griffiths. Calvinistic Methodist Elder & Sunday School Teacher. Married, 1891, Mary Elizabeth, d of Dr. Morgan. Educated, Melyn Voluntary School, Neath; Ruskin College, Oxford. Half-time Tinplate worker at 14 at 4d a day. Organiser, Steel Smelters' Union 1899-1916; Divisional Officer, Iron & Steel Trades Confederation 1916-18. Neath BC. Member: Munitions Tribunal; War Dilution Cttee. Labour Whip, 1919-25; Treasurer of the Household 1924. Hobbies: Connoisseur of Nantgarw & Swansea China, Football, Cricket, Bowls. Languages: Welsh, English. Of Neath. Died 8 February 1955. *Books: Thomas Griffiths, The Tinplate and Steel Industries in Russia.*

GRIFFITHS William: JP (Mon). Liberal: Ebbw Vale 1929. **Mr. William Griffiths:** Born, s of the

Revd William Griffiths, Beaufort. Welsh Independent Deacon. Married, Polly 1d. Teacher: Abertysswg & Neath; Head, Abertysswg; Member NUT. Executive; 1st teacher to be appointed to Monmouthshire Education Cttee. Languages: Welsh, English. Estate £947. Of Rhymney Died 11 April 1935.

GRIFFITHS Winston James: BA 1965 DipEd. (Wales) FRSA 1991. Labour MP Bridgend 1987-; MEP South Wales 1979-87. **Mr. Win Griffiths:** Born, Grahamstown, South Africa 11 February 1943, s of Evan George Griffiths & Rachel Ellen. Methodist lay preacher 1966. Married, 1966 Elizabeth Ceri, d of John & Edith Gravell 1s 1d. Educated, Brecon Grammar School; University of Wales, Cardiff. Teacher: Tanzania 1966-68, George Dixon's Grammar School, Birmingham 1969-70, Barry Boys' Grammar School 1970-76, Cowbridge Comprehensive School 1976-79. Vice-President, European Assembly 1984-87. Member: Council for Preservation of Rural Wales; World Development Movement; Christian Socialist Movement; Amnesty International; Voluntary Service Overseas; Socialist Education Assn 1986; Fabian Society; Labour Housing Group; Socialist Health Assn. Vice-President, Wales Aid to Poland. President: Boys Brigade in Wales; Kenfig Hill Male Voice Choir, Porthcawl Choral Society. Vale of Glamorgan BC 1973-76; Dinas Powys ComC 1974-79. Vice-President & ex-Chairman, Parliamentary Global Action for Disarmament, Development & World Reform 1984-87. Opposition Spokesman on environmental protection 1990-92, Education 1992-94, Wales 1994-97; Under-Secretary, Wales 1997-98. Select Cttee Member, Education, Arts & Science. House of Commons Representative, Convention for Charter of European Union Fundamental Rights 1999-2000. Announced he would not contest the next election 2003. Interests: Animal Welfare; Children, Disability, education, European Union, Human Rights, Green Issues, Overseas Development, the Economy. Hobbies: House Plants, ex-Marathon Runner, Of Cefn Cribwr.

GRIFFITHS-JONES Morgan Thomas Laugharne: BSc (Exeter). Natural Law Party, Mid & West Wales Euro 1994. **Mr. Thomas Griffiths-Jones:** Born Buckinghamshire 1949. Educated Exeter University (Engineering Science). Land Agent & Chartered Surveyor; Own Practice 1989. Moved to Cullompton, Devon, as farmer and land agent. South West representative, UK Rural Business Campaign. Took up Transcendental Meditation 1974.

GRIGG Percy James: PC 1942 KCB 1932 KCSI 1936 MA (Cantab) Hon. LL.D (Bristol) 1946. National MP Cardiff East B/E 1942-45. **Rt. Hon. Sir James Grigg:** Born, Exmouth 16 December 1890, s of Alfred James Grigg, journeyman car-penter. Anglican. Married, 1919 Gertrude Charlotte, d of Rev. G. F. Hough. Educated, Bournemouth School; St. John's College, Cambridge (Maths); Wrangler; Hon. Fellow 1943. Civil Servant, Treasury 1913; Royal Garrison Artillery 1915-18; Principal Private Secretary, Chancellors of the Exchequer 1921-30; Chair: Board of Customs & Excise 1930; Board of Inland Revenue 1930-34; Finance Member, Government of India 1934-39; Permanent Under-Secretary, War Office 1939-42. Secretary of State for War 1943-45. British Executive Director, International Bank for Reconstruction & Development 1946-47; Company Director: Imperial Tobacco Company 1947; Prudential Assurance Co. 1948; National Provincial Bank 1949 (Deputy Chairman 1957); Distillers Company 1950; Chairman, Bass, Mitchells & Butler 1961. Hon. Bencher, Middle Temple 1954. Of Tilford, Surrey. Died 5 May 1964. *Books: James Grigg, Prejudice and Judgement.*

GRIGG Richard Rhys: BA. (Staffs). Plaid Cymru, Cardiff Central 2001, Cardiff South & Penarth 2003. **Mr. Richard Grigg:** Born, Cardiff 4 October 1967, s of David James Grigg, self-employed businessman, & Margaret Marrianne Grigg, makeup artist. Agnostic. Married 1998 (Luned) Gwenllian Grigg, journalist. Educated, Ysgol Bryntaf, Glantaf; Staffordshire University (Business Studies); Lancashire University (Dip. Journalism); Open University (Dip. Politics). Producer & Researcher, BBC Wales 1991-99. Mature Student (Law), University of Glamorgan. Managing Director, Launderette, Grangetown 1998-. Lawyer. Chair: Plasnewydd & Adamstown Branch, Plaid Cymru; Vice-Chair: Cardiff Central; Press Officer, Cardiff Region. Interests: Economic policy, Education, Housing, Business, Planning. Hobbies: Cardiff City FC. Languages: Welsh, English. Of Penylan, Cardiff.

GRIST Ian: BA (Oxon) FRSA. Conservative: Aberavon 1970; MP Cardiff North 1974-83, Cardiff Central 1983-92. **Mr. Ian Grist:** Born, Southampton, 5 December 1938, s of Basil William Grist MBE, land agent/garage owner, & Leila Helen Grist. Married, 1962, Wendy Anne White, 2s. Educated, Repton; Jesus College, Oxford (Open Scholarship, History). Teacher until 1960; Plebiscite Officer, South Cameroons 1960-61; Sales Manager, United Africa Co 1961-63; Conservative Party Research & Information Officer, Wales 1963-74. Joined Eastleigh Young Conservatives 1956. PPS 1979-81; Under-Secretary, Wales 1987-90; Chairman, Welsh Conservative MPs Group 1990-. Select Cttees Member: Members' Interests 1984-87, Welsh Affairs 1981-83, 1986-87. Member: Court of the University of Wales 1983-, UWIST 1983-. Member, Conservative Anti-Hunt Council. Chair: Conservative MPs West African Affairs Cttee 1978-87, 1991-92; Welsh Conservative MPs 1990. Vice-Chairman,

Association of Conservative Clubs, Wales 1978-82. Chairman, South Glamorgan Health Authority 1992-85. Of. Cardiff. Died 2 January 2002.

GROSVENOR Richard De Aquila, 1st Baron Stalbridge 1886: PC 1872 JP (Dorset Flint) BA 1858, MA 1859 (Cantab) FRGS AICE. Liberal MP Flintshire 1861-86. **Rt. Hon. Lord Richard Grosvenor:** Born, Dorset, 28 January 1837, son of 4th Marquess of Westminster & Lady Elizabeth Gower, d of Duke of Sutherland, (brother of 1st Duke of Westminster). Anglican. Married, (1) 1870, Hon. Eleanor Frances Beatrice Vesey (died 1876), d of Viscount de Vesci; 1d; (2) Eleanor, d of Hamilton Stubber of Moyne; 5c. Educated, Westminster School; Trinity College, Cambridge. Lieutenant, Royal Navy 1858. Vice-Chamberlain of the Household 1872-74; Patronage Secretary & Chief Whip 1880-85. Director, Alliance Life & Fire Assurance Co. Ltd; London & North Western Railway 1870-1911, Chairman 1891-1911. Dorset CC 1888-; Hon. Colonel, Royal Dorsetshire Yeomanry. Estate £5,083. Died 18 May 1912.

GROVE Florence Craufurd: Conservative: Mid-Glamorgan 1892. **Mr. Crauford Grove:** son of Rt. Hon. Sir William R. Grove (died 1896), Justice of the Common Pleas (of a Swansea family) & Anne Bevan. Barrister. President, The Alpine Club. Author, *Frosty Caucasus* & several plays. Of Melincryddan, Neath, & London.

GRUFFYDD William John: MA (Oxon) Hon. Dlitt (Wales) 1947 Hon. DesL (Rennes) 1946. Liberal MP University of Wales B/E 1943-50. Born, Bethel, Caerns. 14 February 1881, son of John & Elizabeth Griffiths, Gorffwysfa. Married 1909, Gwenda, d of Revd John Evans. Educated Bethel Elementary School, Caernarfon County School (1894), Jesus College, Oxford 1899 (English Literature). Teacher, Beaumaris Grammar School 1904-06; Lecturer, University of Wales, Cardiff 1906-15. Royal Navy 1915-18. Lieutenant RNVR 1916. Professor of Celtic, University of Wales, Cardiff 1918-46. National Eisteddfod Crown Bard, London 1909. Editor, *Y Llenor* 1922-45. Cymmrodorion Gold Medal 1946. Member, Plaid Cymru, 1926; resigned over attitude to the War 1939. Chair: Council of the Welsh Drama League. Member: Government Departmental Cttee on Welsh; Government Cttee on Public Schools. President, National Eisteddfod Council 1945-53. Awarded Cymmrodorion Medal 1946. Died Caernarfon 29 September 1954. *Books: W. J. Gruffydd: The Years of the Locust; Hen Atgofion, 1936; Llenyddiaeth Cymru 1540-1660, Llenyddiaeth Cymry 1450-1600, Math vab Mathonwy, Dafydd ap Gwilym, Beddau'r Proffwydi (drama), Dyrchafiad Arall i Gymro (drama), Cofiant O. M. Edwards, Poems – Telynegion 1900, Caneuon a Cherddi 1906, Ynys yr Hyd a Chaneuon Eraill 1923, Caniadau (1932), plays – Beddau'r Proffwydi 1913, Dyrchafiad*

arall i Gymro 1914, Dros y Dŵr 1928. Further Reading: *Geraint Bowen: W. J. Gruffydd, 1992.; T. Robin Chapman: W. J. Gruffydd, 1944, D. Ben Rees: Cymry Adnabyddus 1952-1972*.

GUEST Christian Henry Charles: Liberal MP Pembroke & Haverfordwest Dec. 1910-18, East Dorset Jan.-Dec. 1910, North Bristol 1922-23, Drake B/E June 1937-45. Candidate: Wandsworth Central 1918. Joined Conservative Party 1937. **Colonel, Hon. Henry Guest:** Born, 15 February 1874, son of 1st Baron Wimborne & Lady Cornelia Spencer-Churchill, d of Duke of Marlborough. Anglican. Married, 1911, Hon. Frances Lyttleton (died 1918), d of 1st Viscount Cobham 1s. Educated, Eton. Army 1892-1918: Lieutenant, Lancashire Fusiliers 1892; Royal Dragoons 1894; South Africa 1899-1902; India 1902-07; Staff College 1907; Riding School; France 1914-15, 1918. PPS 1911-15. Of St. Leonards Grange, Beaulieu. Died 3 October 1957.

GUEST Ivor Churchill, 1st Viscount Wimborne 1918: 2nd Baron Wimborne 1880, 1st Baron Ashby St. Ledgers 1910; 3rd Bart 1838. PC 1910 MA. (Cantab). Liberal MP Cardiff District 1906-1910. Candidate, Plymouth B/E 1898. Joined Liberal Party 1904; Conservative MP Plymouth 1900-06. **Rt. Hon. Ivor Guest:** Born, 1873, son of 1st Baron & Lady Cornelia Spencer-Churchill, d of Duke of Marlborough; succeeded father 1914; Married, 1902 The Hon. Alice Grosvenor, d of Baron Ebury. Educated, Eton; Trinity College, Cambridge. Captain, Dorsetshire Imperial Yeomanry, served in Boer War. Landowner: (73,000 acres) & Director Barclays Bank. President, Liberal National Council 1936-. Of 22, Arlington Street, London SW1 & Ashby St. Ledgers, Rugby. Died 1938. *Western Mail, 1906 Shoni Bob Ochr . . . (when the ex-Tory MP arrived in Cardiff. . . . .*

GUEST Ivor Grosvenor, 2nd Viscount Wimborne 1918: 3rd Baron Wimborne (1880) 2nd Baron Ashby St. Ledger 1910, 4th Baronet of Dowlais. OBE 1953 JP DL (London) MA (Cantab). National MP Brecon & Radnor, 1935-39. Major Hon. Ivor Guest: Born, 21 February 1903, son of 1st Viscount (qv) & Hon. Alice Grosvenor, d of Baron Ebury; succeeded 1939. Married, Lady Mary Fox-Strangways, d of Earl of Ilchester, 3s 1d. Educated, Eton, Trinity College, Cambridge. Army 1939-45 Major, Northants Yeomanry, Landowner & Company Director. Chairman, Stowe School Governors. PPS. Under-Sec Air 1943-45;Liberal Chief Whip, House of Lords 1944-48, Deputy-Speaker, House of Lords 1948-. Of London & Ashby St. Ledger, Rugby. Died 7 January 1967.

GUEST George Mathew: UK Independence, Vale of Clwyd 2001. **Mr. Mathew Guest:** Born, St. Asaph, 1 March 1968, son of Arthur & Olwen

Guest, farmers (W). Educated, Brynhyfryd School, Ruthin. (Diploma in Business & Finance). Works in manufacturing. Chairman, UKIP, North Wales. Interests: Getting UK out of the EU.

GUEST Oscar Montague: MC MA (Cantab). Conservative: Brecon & Radnor 1945; PPC Hornchurch-1949; MP North Camberwell 1935-45; Coalition Liberal MP Loughborough 1918-22. **Major Hon. Oscar Guest:** Born, 1888, son of 1st Baron Wimborne & Lady Cornelia Spencer-Church, d of Duke of Marlborough (1st cousin of Winston Churchill). Married, Kathleen Susan, d of Graham Paterson, 2s 2d (qv. Revel). Educated, Harrow; Trinity College, Cambridge. Landowner & Company Director. Opened factories in Merthyr & Dowlais during World War II. Lothian & Border Horse, 1914-16, Royal Flying Corps 1916-18. PPS 1921-22. Gave up his Camberwell seat in 1945 because his business interests had moved to South Wales. Of Gabalva House, Whitney on Wye. Died 5 May 1958.

GUEST Sarah Revel: Conservative: Swansea East 1955. **Miss Sarah Guest:** Born, 1931, d of Hon. Oscar Guest (qv) & Kathleen Susan, d of Graham Paterson. Educated, Edgebury Park School, Goudhurst; London School of Economics. Private Secretary. Round-World Trip 1952, during which she worked at UN Assembly. Far East tour 1954. Film & Television Producer. Chair, Hay-on-Wye Festival of Literature. Lived in Radnorshire from 1940. *Author: Revel Guest, Lady Charlotte – A Biography of the Nineteenth Century (with Angela John) 1989.*

GUNN John E: Kt 1898 JP (Glam & Cardiff). Liberal Unionist: Cardiff District 1892. **Sir John Gunn:** Born, 28 October 1837, son of Donald Gunn of Achalybster, Caithness. Presbyterian elder, a founder, Windsor Road PCE Church, Cardiff. Married, (1) 1871, Sarah Jane (died 1874) d of Thomas Hill of Cardiff (2) 1877, Harriette, (died 1914) d of James Boyle of Co. Antrim, agent to the Marquis of Bute. Educated, private schools in Westerdale, Harpsdale and Watton. Draper's Assistant on leaving school. Probably came to Cardiff in the 1850s/1860s when Marquis of Bute was extending the docks and his agents went to Scotland to recruit people. Shipowner (bought P. A. Campbell's) & Merchant. Director, J. M. Gunn & Sons; Park Hall Co; Cardiff Railway Co. 25 years; North British Mercantile Insurance Co; Mount Stuart Dry Dock Co; John Bland & Co timber importers; Cardiff Collieries; Western Super Mare Grand Pier Co. Chairman, Bristol & West of England Bank. President, Cardiff Chamber of Commerce 1886-87; Cardiff Chamber of Shipping 1899-1900. Of St. Mellons. Estate £130,878. Died 20 January 1918.

GWYN David Aled Jones: BA MA BD (Wales). Plaid Cymru: Neath 1979. **Revd Aled Gwyn:** Born, Newcastle Emlyn 20 August 1940, son of Gwyn Jones, farmer, & Jenkins. Married, Williams, 2c. Educated, Newcastle Emlyn Grammar School; University of Wales, Aberystwyth; Congregational Memorial College, Swansea. Welsh Independent Minister, Ordained 1966; Henllan, Capel Mair & Cwm Miles 1966-76; Zoar-Maesyrhaf, Neath 1976-82. BBC Radio Cymru Correspondent 1982-; Carmarthen RDC 1969-72; Dyfed CC 1972-76; West Glam CC 1977-81. Joined Plaid Cymru 1955; Chair, Carmarthen Constituency Plaid Cymru 1972-74; Member: Plaid Cymru National Council. Of Whitchurch, Cardiff.

GWYNNE Ivor Hael: JP (Swansea) 1913. Labour: Pembroke 1918. **Mr. Ivor Gwynne:** Born, Briton Ferry 10 October 1867. Married, Ann, 2s1d. Educated elementary school. Errand boy at 11. Tinplate worker. President: Neath Branch, South Wales, Mon & Gloucs Tinplate Workers Union 1871; Tin & Sheet Millmen's Society 1898, General Secretary 1904-; Chairman, Employees Section, Plate & Steel Joint Industrial Council; Tinplate Advisory Officer, Iron & Steel Trades Confederation. Swansea BC 1907, Alderman 1918-; Chairman, Education Cttee 1910-25. Chairman, Swansea Technical College 1915-, Vice-Chairman 1908-10. President, Federation of Education Cttees 2 years. Member: Central Welsh Board; Council, University of Wales, Cardiff; Advisory Cttee for Magistrates; Welsh Labour Corps Executive; Labour Adviser for South Wales, National Service Acts. Of Swansea. Died 29 November 1934.

GWYTHER Christine Margery: Labour AM Preseli 1999-. **Miss Christine Gwyther:** Born Pembroke, 9 August 1959, d of Ivor George Gwyther, marine engineer, & Marjorie Gwyther, office worker. Atheist. Partner, Stephen James May, marine biologist (died January 2003). Educated Albion Square Primary School, Pembroke Dock; Pembroke Grammar School; University of Wales, Cardiff (unfinished degree). Worked in London. Local Government Officer, Pembs CC. Economic development division, supporting small & growing businesses), formerly with Milford Haven Waterway Enterprise Zone 1986, South Pembs. DC 1987-96, Pembrokeshire CC 1996-99, Seconded 2 days a week to UNISON. Joined Labour Party, 1991, Agent, 1997. Vegetarian. Member: Pembrokeshire Business Club, RSPB. Interests: Social Welfare, Health, Employment. Secretary for Agriculture and Rural Affairs, 1999-2000. Chair, Economic Development & Transport Cttee. Interests: Economy, Environment. Hobbies: Cooking, Walking. Of Pembroke Dock.

– H –

HADDRILL Lionel Francis: Conservative: Merthyr Tydfil 1950. **Mr. Lionel Haddrill:** Born Liverpool 1891. Married Mrs. Browning, 2 step-c. Educated elementary schools. Work at 13. Solicitor's office, Post Office & electrical engineering. Army 1914-18 (Royal Engineers sapper). Seaman. Worked in Canada. Liverpool policeman. Electrical engineer & contractor from 1921. Chair, National Federation of the Electrical Assn. Of Rumney, Cardiff.

HADEN-GUEST Leslie Haden, 1st Baron Haden-Guest of Saling 1950: MC MRCP LRCS. Labour: Brecon & Radnor 1935, Central Southwark 1918, North Southwark 1922, South Bucks 1931, MP North Southwark 1924-27, resigned in opposition to party policy on China and stood as Independent Candidate in B/E 1927. Conservative: North Southwark 1931. Re-joined Labour. Labour MP North Islington B/E 1937-50. **Dr. L. Haden-Guest:** Born Oldham 10 March 1877, s of Dr. Alexander Haden Guest. Theosophist. Married (1) 1898 Edith Low (died 1908) 2c; (2) 1910 Muriel Carmel Goldsmid (died 1943) 2c. Educated William Hume Grammar School, Oldham; Owens College, Manchester; London Hospital; Medical Practitioner. Major, RAMC 1914-18, 1939-45. Author & journalist. London CC 1919-22. PPS 1924. Lord in Waiting (Whip) Feb.-Oct. 1951. Opposition Whip 1951. Of London. Died 20 August 1960.

HAIN Peter Gerald: PC July 2001 BScEcon (London) MPhil. (Sussex). Labour MP Neath B/E 1991-; Candidate: Putney 1983, 1987. **Rt. Hon. Peter Hain:** Born Nairobi, Kenya 16 February 1950, s of Walter & Adeline Hain. Married (1) 1975, Patricia, d of Jack Western (separated 2000) 2s (2) 2003 Elizabeth. Haywood, ex-Director, CBI Wales. Educated Pretoria Boys High School; Emmanuel School, Wandsworth; Queen Mary College, London (1st); Sussex University. National Chair, Young Liberals 1971-73. Joined Labour 1977. Civil Rights and Anti-Apartheid Campaigner. Author. Unpaid Director, *Tribune*. Head of Research, Union of Communication Workers 1987-91. Asst Research Officer, 1976-87. Press Officer, Anti-Nazi League, 1977-80. Chair, *Stop the 70 (South Africa) Tour* 1969-70. Secretary: Tribune Group, MPs 1991-93. PLP 1992-94. Labour Whip 1995-96. Opposition Spokesman on Employment, 1996-9. Under-Secretary, Wales 1997-99. Minister of State, Foreign & Commonwealth Office 1999-2001. Minister of State, Trade & Industry (Energy) Jan. 2001. Minister of State for Europe, Foreign & Commonwealth Office, June 2001. Secretary of State for Wales, Nov. 2002 & Leader, House of Commons 2003. Member: Friends of the Earth; Resolfen RFC. Of Resolfen. Hobbies: Sport, Motor racing, Walking, Rock & folk music. *Books: Peter Hain: A Welsh Third Way 1995, Sing the Beloved Country 1996, Ayes to the Left, A Future for Socialism 1995, The Peking Connection 1995, A Putney Plot 1987, Proportional Misrepresentation, The Case against PR in Britain 1986, Political Strikes: The State and Trades Unionism In Britain 1986, Political Trials in Britain 1984, Neighbourhood Participation 1980, Mistaken Identity, The Wrong Face of the Law 1976, Radical Regeneration: Protest, Direct Action and Community Politics 1875, Don't Play with Apartheid : The Background to the Stop the Seventy Tour Campaign 1971.*

HAINES Lila Eilis Maire: Plaid Cymru, Cardiff South & Penarth 2001. **Mrs. Lila Haines:** Born Arklow, Co. Wicklow, 13 June 1948. Married Meic Haines, 2d. Educated University of Wales, Swansea. Business journalist. Taught in Ireland and Cuba. Presenter, Radio Cuba. Freelance Business Journalist. Working mainly for the *Economist*. Head of Plaid Cymru Assembly Research Team 2000. Interests: Economic Development, Community Regeneration, Good practice promoting public investment. Hobbies: Travel, Good books. Languages: Welsh, English, Irish, Spanish. Of Cardiff (1974).

HALFORD Alison Monica: Labour AM. Delyn 1999-2003. **Miss Alison Halford:** Born Norwich 8 May 1940, d of William Charles Halford & Yvonne Bastien. Educated Notre Dame Convent Grammar School, Norwich; Open University (foundation course). Police Officer 1961-92. Metropolitan Police 21 years. Asst. Chief Constable of Greater Manchester 1983. Retired on medical grounds after winning a long-running sex discrimination battle. Won a phone tapping case against the Home Secretary & UK Government in European Court if Human rights. Police Long Service & Good Conduct Medal 1993. Joined Labour Party 1994. Flintshire CC 1995 (Vice-Chair, Personnel Cttee). Hawarden ComC. Member, North Wales Police Authority. Suspended from Labour Group for voting against the Wales Millennium Centre, 5 February 2002.

Hobbies: Golf, Swimming, Gardening, Painting, Cooking, Learning Bridge, Music. Languages: Learned Welsh, English. *Books: Alison Halford, No Way Up the Greasy Pole (autobiography) 1993.*

HALL George Henry, 1st Viscount Hall, of Cynon Valley 1946: PC 1942 JP DL (Glam) 1953 Hon. LLD Wales), Birmingham. Labour MP Aberdare 1922-46. **Rt. Hon. George Hall:** Born Penrhiwceiber, December 1881 s of George & Ann Hall. Anglican. Temperance worker; Married (1) 1910, Margaret Jones (died 1941) 1s (2) 1964 Alice M. Walker. Educated Penrhiwceiber Elementary School. Pitboy at 12. Checkweighman, Penrhikyber Colliery 1911. Mountain Ash UDC 1908-24 (Chair 1916). Chair, Merthyr Tydfil Labour Party 1910, 1918. Member, Governing Body of the Church in Wales. Governor, University of Wales, Cardiff, Civil Lord of the Admiralty 1929. Under-Secretary, Colonies 1940-43. Under-Secretary, Foreign Affairs 1943-45. First Lord of the Admiralty 1945-51. Deputy Leader, Labour peers 1947-52. Consultant: International Combustion (Holdings) Ltd mid 1950s. Director, South Wales Switchgear Ltd 1951. Chair: West of England Enterprises. Temperance worker. Chair, Welsh Youth Cttee 1939. Of Chesham & Penrhiwceiber. Languages: English; limited conversational Welsh. Estate £30,659. Died 8 November 1965.

HALL Walter D'Arcy: MC & Bar Croix de Guerre. Conservative MP Brecon & Radnor 1924-29; 1931-35. **Lieut-Colonel D'Arcy Hall:** Born Australia 10 August 1891, s of Thomas Skarratt Hall, of Weeting Hall, Brandon, Norfolk; Anglican; Married (1) 1920 Anne Madeleine, d of Colonel Charles Brook of Kinmount, Annan, dissolved (2) 1957 Ruth Penelope Owen. Educated Eton; RMC Sandhurst. Landowner. PPS. Of Ewelme Park, Henley on Thames. Died 22 January 1980.

HALLINAN Adrian Lincoln Stuart: Kt 1977 DL (Glam) 1969 Chevalier des Palmes Academiques, France 1965. Conservative Aberdare B/E 1946, Cardiff West 1951, 1955. **Sir Lincoln Hallinan:** Born Cardiff 13 November 1922, s of Sir Charles Stuart Hallinan (qv) & Theresa Holman. Roman Catholic. Married Mary Parry Evans, 4c. Educated Downside. Army 1940-45, Lieutenant 1942. Captain, Rifle Corps TA 1951-52. Barrister, Lincoln's Inn 1950. Recorder, Wales & Chester Circuit 1972-. Cardiff CC 1949-74, Alderman 1961 (Chair, Education Cttee 1962-69; Arts Cttee), Lord Mayor 1969-70. Chair: Governors, Cardiff College of Art; Cardiff College of Music & Drama. Founder-Chair: Cardiff Civic Society; Cardiff 2000 Trust; Cardiff-Nantes Fellowship, 7 years. Member, Court: University of Wales, National Museum, National Theatre of Wales, UWIST. Of Cardiff. Died November 1997.

HALLINAN Charles Stuart: Kt 1962 CBE 1954. Conservative: Cardiff Central 1945; Cardiff West 1950. **Sir Charles Hallinan:** Born Neath 21 October 1890. Roman Catholic. Married Theresa Doris Holman, 4c. Educated Monckton House School, Cardiff; Ratcliffe College, Leicester; Clongowess College, Dublin. Solicitor. Lieut-Colonel, Home Guard 1940-45. Chair: Cardiff West Conservative Assn, Wales & Mon Conservatives. Of Cardiff. Died 24 February 1981.

HAMER Ernest: BSc (Wales). Green Party, South/East List 2003. **Mr. Ernest Hamer:** Born Wrexham 31 July 1927, s of Alfred Cecil Hamer, mine official, & Isabel Hamer, housewife. Church of England. Married 1953 Christine Shirley Hamer, market researcher, 1s 1d. Educated grammar school; University of Wales, Cardiff (Mining). Mine Manager Certificate. 12 years in mines. Steel Works Engineer, retired. Treasurer, Gwent Green Party. Interests: Green Policies. Hobbies: Gardening, Music.

HAMILTON Mostyn Neil: MSc Econ LlB. Conservative: Abertillery Feb. 1974; Bradford North, 1979; MP Tatton 1983-97. **Mr. Neil Hamilton:** Born Fleur de Lis 9 March 1949, s of Ronald Hamilton, colliery manager, & Norma Jones. Married Christine, d of Dr. Holman, MP's secretary. Educated Amman Valley Grammar School; University of Wales, Aberystwyth; Corpus Christi College, Oxford. Barrister. Lecturer in Economics, St. John's College, Portsmouth. Economic Adviser, NCB 1970-71. Director: travel company; Plateau Mining Co 1990. Director, European & Parliamentary Affairs, Institute of Directors. Member: Welsh Conservative Council. Vice-President: League for Introduction of Canine Controls 1984; Small Farmers' Assn 1985-; Cheshire Agricultural Society 1986. *The Spectator's Wit of the Year* 1990. Joint Secretary, Conservative MPs Finance Cttee 1987-90. Vice-Chair, Small Business Bureau 1985-90. Jt. Vice-Chair: Conservative MPs Trade & Industry Cttee 1984-86, 1987-90. Member: Treasury & Civil Service Select Cttee 1987-90. PPS 1986-87. Ass Whip, 1990-92. Under-Secretary, Trade & Industry 1992-94; resigned 25.10.94. Member: Strategy Advisory Group NTL Communications. Declared bankrupt 22 May 2001. He and his wife have undertaken all sorts of entertainment engagements in order to help clear their debts.

HAMMOND Nigel Keith: Conservative: Aberavon Oct. 1974, Swindon 1979. **Mr. Nigel Hammond:** Born February 1938. Educated Abingdon School; London School of Economics; Bristol University. Economics teacher at Abingdon School. Freelance writer & WEA lecturer. Officer TA & RAFVR. Member: Conservative National Advisory Cttee. on Education 1965-70; Wiltshire

Conservative Trade Unionists' Teachers' Cttee; AMA; Bow Group; Oxfordshire Rural Community Council. Written more than 200 articles for periodicals on economics, history & politics. Languages: English. Of Oxfordshire.

HANBURY-TRACY Frederick Stephen Archibald: BA 1870 MA (Oxon). Liberal MP Montgomery District B/E 1877-85, 1886-92. **Hon. Frederick Hanbury-Tracy:** Born 15 September 1848, s of 2nd Baron Sudeley & Emma Elizabeth Alice, d of General H. D. Pennant, Penrhyn Castle. Anglican. Married 1870, Helena Caroline, d of Sir T. E. Winnington, Bart. Stamford Court, Worcs. 5c; Captain, Worcestershire Yeomanry 1872; Major 1890. Landowner. Of Gregynog Hall, Montgomeryshire & Toddington, Gloucs. Succeeded brother Charles (1863-77) as MP. Not re-selected 1894. Of Penybryn Hall, Mont & London. Died 9 August 1906.

HANCOCK Bleddyn William: Plaid Cymru, Pontypridd, Assembly 1999, 2001. Ogmore B/E 14/2/2002. **Mr. Bleddyn Hancock:** Born Merthyr Vale 10 February 1953. Married 15/2/2002. Educated Quakers Yard Grammar School; Afan Taf High School; Polytechnic of Wales, Treforest. General Secretary NACODS. Trustee, Pension Fund. Campaigned for ten years to secure compensation for miners suffering from industrial diseases. Interests: Self Government, Pensions, Welfare Reform. Hobbies: Reading, Travel, War gaming. Of Talygarn, Pontyclun.

HANCOCK Brian John: BSc Plaid Cymru AM Islwyn 1999-2003. **Mr. Brian Hancock:** Born Cardiff 8 August 1950, s of John & Joan Hancock. Married 1972, Elizabeth, d of Wasyl & Gwenllian Kalynca, 1s 1d. Educated Lady Mary High School, Cardiff, Llandaff Technical College, Polytechnic of Wales, Treforest (Chemical Engineering). Diploma in Occupational Safety & Health, Diploma in Loss Prevention in Process Industries. Project/Chemical Engineer, Monsanto Ltd. 1974-76, Shift Production Supervisor & Chemical Engineer, ReChem International Ltd 1976-81. Asst. Plant Manager 1981-85. Specialist Chemical Inspector of Factories, Health & Safety Executive 1985-88. Health, Safety & Environment Superintendent BP Chemicals 1988-92. Self-employed Health, Safety & Environment Consultant 1992 (Brian Harris Associates). Chair, Newport Harriers Athletic Club. Governor, Ysgol Gyfun Gwynllyw & Ysgol Gymraeg Casnewydd. Member, Newport Education Cttee, Member CHEME. Assembly Deputy Whip & Spokesperson on Small Businesses. Interests: Environment, Education, Equal Opportunities. Hobbies: Running. Of Newport.

HANCOCK Frank R: Labour: Monmouth B/E 1939; Salisbury, 1929, B/E 1931; Lewes 1931,

1935; Independent Pacifist: Woolwich East 1950 (backed by United Socialist Movement). **Mr. Frank Hancock:** Born 1884. Quaker. Went from school to solicitor's office. Clerk in City of London. Retired in order to concentrate on peace and socialist propaganda.

HANDO David: BA (London) DipEd MEd (Wales). Liberal: Monmouth 1970, Feb. & Oct. 1974. **Mr. David Hando:** Born Newport, 7 April 1938, s of William Roy Hando, shop assistant, & Gladys Hughes, shop assistant. Methodist Sunday School Teacher. Married Mary Theresa Pugh, school secretary, 3s. Educated Durham Road Junior School; St. Julian's High School, Newport; London School of Economics; University of Wales, Cardiff. Teacher, 3 years in Uganda. Deputy Head, Radyr High School. Chair: Gaer Community Centre, Newport. Youth & Scout Leader. Member: NUT; Shelter; UNA. Vice-Chair, Monmouthshire Anti-Apartheid Movement. Election Agent 1979. Chair: Newport AFC 1989-99; Newport Liberal Democrats May 2002. Interests: Commonwealth, Education, Health. Of Hartridge, Newport.

HANNINGTON Walter: Communist: Merthyr B/E 1934; Wallsend 1929; Bermondsey 1931. **Mr. Wal Hannington:** Born London. Engineer's toolmaker. Formed National Unemployed Workers' Cttee. Later National Unemployed Movement 1921; London Organiser 1920-21. Organised a number of hunger marches. Sentenced to imprisonment 1925. Founder Member, Communist Party; Member, Central Cttee. Member, Minority Movement 1928. Expelled from Party 1938 for opposing policy on National Unemployed Movement. Asst Secretary, AEU. Author of pamphlets. Of London.

HANSON David George: BA 1978 CertEd 1980 (Hull). Labour: Delyn 1987, Eddisbury 1983, Cheshire West Euro 1984; MP Delyn 1992. **Mr. David Hanson:** Born Liverpool 5 July 1957, s of Brian Hanson, deliveryman, then fork lift driver & Glenda Doreen Jones, clerk. Church in Wales. Married 1986 Margaret Rose (candidate for Eddisbury 1997, B/E 1999, TUC officer), d of Ronald Mitchell, 1s 2d. Educated Verdin Comprehensive School, Winsford; Hull University (Vice-President SRC 1978-79). Trainee CWS 1980-81. Manager Plymouth Co-operative 1981-82. Various Posts, Spastics Society 1982-89. Director, Re-Solv (Society for Prevention of Solvent Abuse) 1989-92. Joined Labour Party 1976. Vale Royal BC 1983-92 (Group Leader 1990-92). Northwich TC 1987-91. Member, Select Cttees: Welsh Affairs 1992-96, Public Service 1996-97. Secretary: PLP National Heritage Cttee. 1994-; All-party Prevention of solvent abuse parliamentary group. Hobbies Football, Cinema, Reading, Family Life.

HARAN Sean: BA MSc Econ DipSW. Pro-Life Party, South/West List 2003. **Mr. Sean Haran:** Born,Griffithstown, Pontypool 30 August 1966, s of Patrick Haran, labourer, & Vanessa Haran, shop worker. Roman Catholic. Educated St. Albans RC Comprehensive School, Pontypool; Lancashire Polytechnic; University of Wales, Swansea (Social Work). Social Worker. Of Clydach, Swansea.

HARBEN Henry: Kt 1897 JP DL. Conservative: Cardiff District 1885, Norwich 1880. **Sir Henry Harben:** Born Bloomsbury, 24 August 1823, s of Henry Harben. Anglican. Married (1) Ann, d of James Such (2) Mary, d of Thomas Bullman Cole of Notting Hill. Educated privately. Secretary, Prudential Assurance Co (then President). High Sheriff 1898. Vice-President, Sussex County Cricket Club. Of Warnham Lodge, Sussex, & Brighton. Died 2 December 1912.

HARCOURT William George Granville Venables Vernon: Kt 1873 PC FRS MA (Cantab). Liberal MP West Mon 1885-; Derby, 1875-89; Oxford 1868-75. Independent Liberal candidate, Kirkaldy Burghs 1859. **Rt. Hon. Sir William Harcourt:** Born York 14 October 1827, s of William Vernon Harcourt Vernon Harcourt & Matilde, d of Colonel William Gough (& brother of Edward Harcourt, Conservative MP). A land-owning & clerical family, traced ancestry back to Plantagenet kings. Educated Private Tutor & Trinity College, Cambridge 1847-51 (1st Classics; Maths tripos). Married (1) 1859 Maria Theresa Lister (Died 1863) (2) 1867, Elizabeth, d of John Lothrop Motley, US Ambassador. Barrister, Lincolns Inn 1857. Whewell Professor of International Law 1868-87. Joined Liberal Party in 1840s. Declined post of Judge Advocate General. Solicitor General 1873. Home Secretary 1880-85. Chancellor of the Exchequer 1886-92. Expected to become Liberal Leader after Gladstone but Queen Victoria asked Lord Rosebery to form a government 1894. Liberal Leader in the Commons 1894-98, resigned. Trustee, British Museum. Freeman of Glasgow 1881. Defeated in by-election on appointment as Home Secretary but Samuel Plimsoll stood down in his favour at Derby. When defeated at Derby, Cornelius Warmington stood down in his favour at North Mon. Of London, Nuneham Park, Oxford, & Malwood, Hants. Estate £190,264. Died 1st October 1904. Further Reading: *A. G. Gardiner: Life of Sir William Harcourt, 1913 (2 vols). G. I. T. Machen, Politics and the Churches in Great Britain 1869-1921, Clarendon Press 1987; Ian Machin in "Dictionary of Liberal Biography", 1998, pages 164-167.*

HARDIE James Keir: Labour MP Merthyr Tydfil 1900-; West Ham South 1892-95. Contested Mid

J. Keir Hardie.

Lanarkshire B/E 1888 1895. **Mr. Keir Hardie:** Born Legbrannock, Lanarkshire 15 August 1856, s of a ship's carpenter, & Mary Keir, domestic servant. Congregationalist. Married 1880, Lillie, d of Duncan Wilson, miner, 2s 1d. Messenger Boy 1863. Worked in shipyard & as baker's errand boy. Miner 1866-78. Stationer 1878. Hamilton miners' Correspondence Secretary 1879. Organiser, Ayrshire Miners 1880. 1st Secretary, Scottish Miners' Federation 1886. Founder member ILP. Editor, *Cunnock News* 1882-86. Founder Editor, *The Miner* 182-84, *Labour Leader* 1889-. Secretary, Scottish Labour Party 1888. 1st Chair, PLP 1906-07. Chair, ILP 1893-1900, 1913. Chair, British Section, Socialist International. Estate £426. Health broke down after outbreak of Great War 1914. Died 2 September 1915. *Books: Keir Hardie, From Serfdom to Socialism 1907, India: Impressions and Suggestions 1909, many pamphlets.* Further Reading: *William J. Stewart, J. Keir Hardie, A Biography 1921; David Lowe: From Pit to Parliament, 1923; Emrys Hughes: Keir Hardie, 1956; Kenneth O. Morgan: Keir Hardie, Radical & Socialist, 1975. J. H. Howard, "Winding Lanes", pages 54-55-56; C. Benn, Keir Hardie, 1997; Ian Mclean, Keir Hardie, 1975; F. Reid, Keir Hardie, 1978. Kenneth O. Morgan, Peace Movements in Wales 1899-1945, The Welsh History Review, Vol. 10, June 1981; Anthony Mor-O'Brien, Keir Hardie, C. B. Stanton and the First World War, Llafur 1985, Vol. 4, No. 5, pp 31-42.*

HARDING Andrew Edward: Natural Law Party: Cardiff West 1992. **Mr. Andrew Harding:** Lost contact with NLP.

HARDING John Barrington Geen: OBE 1990 BA (Wales). DipEd. Conservative, Llanelli 1999.

Mr. Barrie Harding: Born Swansea 24 December 1940, s of James Luther Harding, retail trader/outfitter, & Phyllis Eileen Geen. Educated Dynevor Grammar School, Swansea, University of Wales, Cardiff, (German) & Swansea. Teacher, 1965-81, Information Officer, Wales, in preparation for Euro Elections, Teacher, 1989-96, Supply Teacher from 1996, Lecturer, Gorseinon FE College. Joined Conservatives 1974. Agent 1992, 1997, Deputy Chair: Mid & West Wales Area Cttee. Interests: Education, Defence, Preservation of Union of UK within Europe. Hobbies: Photography, Medieval History, Eating out. Languages: English, German, French, Latin, Reads Basic Dutch & Spanish. Of Blue Anchor, Gower.

HARDING William Rowe: MA (Oxon Hon. LLD (Wales) 1971 DL (Glam) 1970. Liberal National: Swansea East 1944, National Liberal & Conservative: Gower 1950, 1951. **Mr. Rowe Harding:** Born Birchgrove, Swansea 10 September 1901, s of Albert & Elizabeth Harding. Anglican. Married 1933, Elizabeth Adelaine (died 1998) d of J. Owen George of Hirwaun (sister of G. O. George qv) 4c. Educated Gowerton Grammar School; Cambridge University. Rugby Captain: University XV; Swansea XV & Wales XV 1924-28; Welsh Amateur Sprint Champion 1922, 1926; Lecturer in Law, University of Wales, Cardiff & Swansea; Solicitor 1924; Barrister, Inner Temple 1928. Chair of Quarter Sessions: Haverfordwest 1948-49; Radnorshire, Breconshire; Deputy Chair: Haverfordwest 1945-48; Pembrokeshire, Carmarthenshire, Glamorgan. Deputy Chair, Glamorgan Local Tribunal for Conscientious Objectors. Chancellor, Diocese of St. Davids 1949-83; Judge, Provincial Court, Church in Wales 1965; Member: Governing Body of the Church in Wales; Council, St. David's College, Lampeter; University of Wales, Swansea, 1956- (Court 1957-). Chair, Glamorgan New Party 1931. Chair: Glamorgan County Cricket Club 1959-76, President 1977; Vice-President, Welsh Rugby Football Union 1953-56; President, Crawshay RFC XV. Captain, Home Guard 1940-45. Judge of the County Court 1953-71. Chair, Swansea Porcelain Ltd 1976. Of Ilston, Gower. Died 10 February 1991.

HARDMAN Frederick: Kt 1982 MBE 1972. Conservative: East Flint 1959, 1964, 1966; Wolverhampton SE 1955. **Sir Frederick Hardman:** Born September 1914, s of Frederick Hardman (killed 1915) & Annie Walsh. Married 1941 Emma Lawson, 1s. Educated Muttenz College, Switzerland. Joined family cotton business. Journalist. RAF 1939-46. Conservative Party Agent 1947-52. Senior Executive, Lecturer & PR Consultant, Rentokil 1952-74. Industrial Relations Consultant 1974-. Director: Telford Development

Corporation 1980. Ironbridge Museum Trust, 1989. Chair, Tawn Printers Ltd. 1983. Vice-Chair, Severn Navigation Restoration Trust, Ltd. Staffordshire CC 1955-58; Madeley. 1988. Member, Court, University College of North Staffs (Keele). President: West Midlands Conservative Trade Unionists, 1980; Vice-President, National Union of Conservative & Unionist Assns 1982, Chair, 1980-81; Chair, Conservative Trade Unionists Assn. Of Ironbridge. Died 6 March 1991.

HARFORD John Charles: 1st Bart 1934 JP (Cards & Gloucs) DL (Cards). Conservative: Cardiganshire 1895, 1900. **Major, Sir John Harford:** Born Stoke Bishop nr Bristol 28 July 1860, Anglican; s of John Battersby Harford JP & Mary Charlotte, d of Baron Bunsen, Prussian Envoy Extraordinary in London. Anglican. Married Blanche (died 1904) d of Rt. Hon. Henry Cecil Raikes, 2s 1d (1s killed in war). Educated Harrow. Landowner, Cardiganshire (5782 acres) & Gloucershire. Chair, Aberayron Light Railway Co. Major, Pembrokeshire Yeomanry. Cardiganshire CC. Chair, Cardiganshire Quarter Sessions 14 years. Trustee, Diocese of St. Davids. Member: Board of Guardians, Court of University of Wales, Aberystwyth; St. David's College, Lampeter. Hobbies: Hunting, Shooting, Fishing. Of Falcondale, Lampeter. Estate £118,876. Died on golf course, 16 July 1934.

HARGREAVES Gerald de la Pryme: Kt 1944 Croix de Guerre (Belgium) BA (Oxon). Conservative: Monmouth District Dec. 1910, Osgoldcross Yorks Jan. 1910; PPC Bedford 1910-18. **Sir Gerald Hargreaves:** Born Birkdale, s of Thomas & Constance Hargreaves. Married (1) 1924 Mary Elphinstone (2) 1955 Mrs. Winifred Elsie Johnson. Educated Eton; Magdalene College, Oxford. Barrister 1905. Bedfordshire Yeomanry 1914-18; Home Guard, 1942-45. County Court Judge, 1922-53. Chair, London CO Tribunal 1939-45. Of London. Died 29 April 1972.

HARMAN Julie Veronica: Green Party: Swansea East 1987. **Mrs. Julie Harman:** Born 1955. Married 2c. Community Trust Development Office. Formerly owned a whole-food shop at Neath. Co-Chair, West Glamorgan Green Party. Of Aberdulais.

HARPER Margaret Mary: BA (Brookes). Conservative, Swansea West 2001. **Mrs Margaret Harper:** Born Bethnal Green, 4 March 1972. Roman Catholic. Married 1999 Mark Harper (accountant & Candidate for Forest of Dean 2001). Educated Our Lady's Convent High School, Hackney; South Islington 6th Form Centre; Brookes University, Oxford (Politics & Retail Management). 1st & only Conservative to be President of Brookes SRC. Client Service, Catalina

Marketing 1997-98; Marketing Executive, Nationwide Building Society 1998-2001; Wyevale Garden Centres plc 2001-. Forest of Dean DC. Interests: Health, Law & Order, Pensions, Economy, Rural Affairs. Hobbies: Music, Reading, Travel, Cinema, Pet Rabbits. Of Newham Bottom, Forest of Dean.

HARPER Peter: BSc (Wales). Conservative: Aberavon 1997. **Mr. Peter Harper:** Born 8 August 1965. Educated Oxted Comprehensive School; University of Wales, Swansea. Self-employed Computer Consultant. Surrey Heath BC. School Governor. Of Surrey.

HARRIES David Brian: BSc (Wales) 1952 BA (Lancaster). Plaid Cymru: Abertillery 1970, 1979. **Mr. Dai Harries:** Born Newbridge January 1932. Married Mary, 4c. Educated Newbridge Grammar School; University of Wales, Swansea; Lancaster University. Army 1952-55, Lieutenant. Lecturer in Chemical Engineering, Polytechnic of Wales. Member, Rugby XVs: Newbridge, University of Wales, Swansea; BAOR; Monmouthshire. Coach: Tredegar XV; Welsh RFU. Secretary, Risca Welsh School Parents Assn. Member: UNA. Contested Abercarn UDC 1967, 1970. Of Newbridge.

HARRIES Norman Bevan: AIOB AIQS. Labour: West Flint Feb. & Oct. 1974. **Mr. Norman Harries:** Born Caerphilly 1928. Nonconformist. Married Brenda, 2d. Educated Caerphilly Grammar School; Cardiff Technical College. Building industry from school; Quantity Surveyor; Lecturer in Construction Management, Salford University. Pastor of a Holywell Church. Secretary, West Flint Labour Party; Agent 1970. Of Holywell.

HARRIES Peter Warren: Labour: Montgomery Feb. & Oct. 1974. **Mr. Peter Harries:** Born Tredegar October 1940. Married 2s. Educated Ebbw Vale Grammar School; Coleg Harlech; University of Wales, Cardiff; Bradford University Management Centre. Left school to work in steelworks. Lecturer in Economics, Montgomeryshire College of Further Education, Newtown. Member: ATTI, Fabian Society. Vice-Chair, Montgomery CLP. Of Newtown.

HARRIS Bryn Clifford Derek: Communist Party of England (Marxist Leninist): Cardiff South-East Oct. 1974. **Mr. Bryn Harris:** Born 1948. Technical Services Dept. East Moors Steelworks, Cardiff. Member, BISAKTA. First candidate to contest a Welsh seat for his party. Of Cardiff.

HARRIS Edward: OBE JP (Swansea). National Liberal: Swansea East 1922. **Mr. Edward Harris:** Born Morriston 1873, s of Thomas & Ann Harris. Married 1s 2d. Solicitor. Clerk: Swansea RDC

1905-. Clerk, LLwchwr UDC. Company Chair: R. E. Jones Ltd; Ben Evans & Co. (department stores). President: Swansea & Neath Incorporated Law Society; Swansea East Liberal Assn until 1922. Member: Consultative Health Council 1919. Chair: West Glamorgan Advisory Assistance Board. Swansea BC 1918- (Alderman; Mayor 1933-34). Freemason: Grand Master & Provincial Grand Master. Captain, Morriston Golf Club. Languages: Welsh, English. Of Mumbles. Died 4 August 1945.

HARRIS Frederick Rutherfoord: LRCS. Conservative MP Monmouth District 1901; Unseated on petition over electoral malpractices. MP Dulwich, Dec. 1903-May 1906; resigned in order to travel. **Dr. Rutherfoord Harris:** Born 1st May 1856, s of G. A. Harris, Judge of the Supreme Court, Madras, & Emma, d of R. Rutherford & Gs of Lord Harris. Went to South Africa 1882. Married Florence, d of Joseph Ling of Kimberley, Rhodesia. Educated Leatherhead Grammar School; Baden University; Edinburgh University. Medical Officer, Kimberley Diamond Mines 1882. Confidential Secretary, Cecil Rhodes. 1st Secretary, British South Africa Co. Progressive Party MP Kimberley 1894-96; Conservative 1898, in Cape Parliament. Returned to UK 1896. Eminent imperialist; friend of Rhodes & Jameson; elected in a campaign of spectacular corruption. Of Llangibby Castle, Mon (1896) & London. Estate £7,194. Died Grand Hotel, Eastbourne, 1 September 1920.

HARRIS Hugh Rhodri: BA (Kent) FCA. Conservative: Caerphilly 1997. **Mr. Rhodri Harris:** Born Cardiff 7 January 1950, s of Morgan Harris, sub postmaster, & Rosamund Harris, housewife. Agnostic. Married 1972 Elizabeth Glynn Hitchens, 2s 2d. Educated Bridgend Boys' Grammar/ Technical School; Kent University. Chartered Accountant: Arthur Anderson & Co. Bankers. Self-Employed 1989-. Chair: South Wales Young Conservatives 1965; Kent University Conservative Assn. Member, Executive, Federation of Conservative Students. Vice-Chair, Greenwich & Woolwich Conservative Assn. Voluntary Information Services Officer, Conservative Central Office 1995. School governor. Member, MCC. Greenwich BC 1992-94, 1998- (Deputy Leader of the Opposition). Contested Greenwich & Lewisham, Greater London Assembly 2000. Interests: Local Government, Education, Finance. Hobbies: Watching Cricket, Listening to Music, Country Walking. Of Blackheath.

HARRIS Jennifer Esther Clare: Pro-Europe Conservative, Wales Euro 1999. Of Hereford.

HARRIS John Noel: BSc MSc (Wales) FIM. Plaid Cymru: Gower Feb. 1974. **Mr. Jac Harris:** Born

Clydach, 1924. Welsh Independent deacon, treasurer & trustee. Married 3c. Educated Pontardawe Grammar School; University of Wales, Swansea. Royal Navy 1942-46, Lieutenant RNVR. Lecturer in Metallurgy. Director, two private companies employing 24 people. Joined Plaid Cymru 1945; Welsh Republican Movement 1950. Plaid Cymru Agent, Gower 1964-74; Treasurer: Cronfa Glyndŵr. Secretary: Welsh Schools Cttee. Died 24 March 2004. Languages: Welsh, English. Of Clydach.

HARRIS John Richard: BSc MSc DipIEE CEng MIEE. People's Representative Party, Swansea West 1999. **Mr. Jack Harris:** Born Hafod, Swansea. Married (1) 2s divorced (2). Educated Mayhill Primary School; Dynevor Grammar School; Swansea College of Technology, Welsh College of Advanced Technology, University of Wales, Swansea (1st Electrical Engineering). Electrical Engineering Apprentice at Felindre Tinplate Works, Electrical & Electronics Engineer. Electronics/Computing Researcher. Computer Software Analyst. Consultant specialising in Nuclear Power Station Simulation. Co-Founder, People's Representative Party, 1999. Of Uplands, Swansea.

HARRIS Kenneth Albert: BA (London). Liberal Democrat, Mid & West List 2003. **Mr. Ken Harris:** Born Baglan, Port Talbot, 10 June 1945, s of Sydney Edgar Harris, rigger/carpenter, & Catherine Jane Harris, housewife. Church in Wales. Married 1967 Ruby Vaughan, bank official, 1s 1d. Educated Dyffryn Grammar School, Port Talbot; London University; Open University; Polytechnic of Wales; University of Wales, Aberystwyth; University of Worcestershire. (Diploma in Careers Guidance; Advanced Diploma in Educational Management). Police Officer 1963-70. Industrial Security Officer BP Chemicals 1970-80. Local Authority Careers Officer, 1981-87). Primary School Teacher 1988-2000; Health Charity Work 2000-2002. Part-time Client Adviser to Disabled intent on running own business. Llanfair Caereinion TC 1984-85. Knighton TC 1999. Powys CC 1999. Joined Liberal Party 1982. Inaugural Chair: Knighton Liberal Democrats 1984. Member: Welsh Liberal Democrat Executive. Hobbies: Watching Sport; Played Rugby, Soccer & Cricket for local teams. & South Wales Police). Languages: some Welsh, English. Of Knighton.

HARRIS Margaret Lydia: People's Representative Party, South/West List 1999. **Mrs. Margaret Harris:** Married Peter Harris (qv). Of Llansamlet, Swansea.

HARRIS Marilyn: BA. Liberal Democrat: Aberavon 1987, 1992; Assembly South/West List

1999. **Mrs. Marilyn Harris:** Born Neath, 14 May 1948, d of David Griffith Melville Jones, excise officer, & Sarah Elizabeth Llewellyn, shop assistant. Married 1968, 2d. Divorced. Educated Dyffryn Grammar School, Port Talbot; University of Wales, Swansea. Analyst Programmer, BP Baglan; Systems Analyst, West Glamorgan CC. Retired. Member: ASTMS. Port Talbot BC 1991-95. Founder Member, Aberavon Liberal Democrat Assn. Contested: Port Talbot BC 5 times. Port Talbot BC. Contested Neath/Port Talbot BC (Cwmafan & Bryn) 1999. Hobbies: Gardening. Of Port Talbot.

HARRIS Martha Jane Page – see Page-Harris M. J.

HARRIS Michael J: BSc (Nottingham) MICE. Conservative: Neath Oct. 1974. **Mr. Michael Harris:** Born Cwmbran 1947. Educated Croesyceiliog Grammar School; Nottingham University. Civil Engineer: London Borough of Ealing Engineer's Dept. President: Nottingham University Conservative Assn 1986-89; Treasurer: London Area Young Conservatives. Of London.

HARRIS Peter Gilbert: People's Representative Party, South/West List 1999. **Mr. Peter Harris:** Married Margaret Harris (qv). Of Llansamlet, Swansea.

HARRIS Robert George: BA (Wales). Labour: Ceredigion 1997. **Mr. Hag Harris:** Born Coventry 8 July 1955, s of Ted Harris, aero-engineer. Married Jan, 3s. Educated King Henry VIII Grammar School, Coventry; University of Wales, Aberystwyth. Vice-President SRC. Local Government Planner, Ceredigion CC 1 year. Labourer, Maesyfelin sawmill. Window Cleaner. Lampeter Music Store Manager. Football Referee. Joined Labour Party 1975. Dyfed CC 1981-85. Ceredigion DC 1991-95. Ceredigion CC 1995-. Lampeter TC Mayor. Languages: Learned Welsh, English. Of Lampeter.

HARRISON Austin: Independent: Caernarfon District 1918. **Mr. Austin Harrison:** Born 27 March 1873, s of Frederick Harrison. Married Mary Medona Greenway, USA. 3c. Educated Harrow; foreign universities. Editor, The *English Review* 1910. Opposed conscription. *Stood to demand the establishment of the League of Nations.* Languages: English, German. Died 13 July 1928. *Publications: The Pan-German Doctrine, England and Germany, The Kaiser's War.* Of London.

HART Edwina: MBE 1998. Labour AM. Gower 1999. **Mrs. Edwina Hart:** Born Gowerton, 26 April 1957, d of Eric G. Thomas & Hannah J. Thomas. Married 1976, Robert B. Hart, 1d. Bank Clerk. President, Banking, Insurance and Finance Union 1992-94. Chair, Wales TUC General Council 1997-98. Non-Executive Director: *Chwarae Teg* (expanding role of women in work force), Wales Millenium Centre. Member: Employment Appeal Tribunal 1992-99; South West Wales Economic Forum; TUC General Council; Broadcasting Council for Wales 1995-99; Council, University of Wales, Swansea 1998-99; Advisory Committee, Equal Opportunities Commission 1989-99; Wales Millennium Centre 1997-99; TGWU; ISTC. Assembly Secretary for Finance 1999-, Minister for Finance, Local Government & Communities Oct. 2000-, Minister of Social Justice 2003-. Hon. Fellow, Trinity College, Carmarthen, 2001. Hobbies: Reading, Music, Cooking. Of Gowerton.

HART Jeremy Graham: Green Party, North List 2003. **Mr. Jeremy Hart:** Born, Bromley, Kent, 21 February 1947, s of Leonard Wilfred Hart, buyer, & Violet May Hart. Christian. Unmarried. Educated Secondary School. Unemployed. Special Constable. Interests: Green matters. Hobbies: Computers, Tropical Fish, Growing Plants. Of Llandudno.

HART Julian Tudor: MB (Cantab) 1952 DCH (England) 1959 Hon. DSc (Glasgow) 1999. Communist: Aberavon 1964, 1966, 1970. **Dr. Tudor Hart:** Born London March 1927, doctor's son. Married Mary; 3c. Educated Dartington Hall, Ontario; Queens College, Cambridge; St. George's Hospital (1947-52). Medical Practitioner 1957, retired 1987. Pneumoconiosis Research Unit, 1957-61. Hon. Professor WISCH, University of Glamorgan. Joined Communist Party 1945; Member: Communist Party Welsh Council; CND Welsh Council. Chair: Socialist Health Assn. Glyncorrwg UDC 1959-69; retired from council in order to concentrate on research into heart disease in South Wales. Contested Glamorgan CC 1962. The 1st GP to be awarded a Glasgow honorary doctorate. Of Glyncorrwg.

HARTSHORN Vernon: PC 1924 OBE 1918 JP (Glam). Labour: Mid-Glamorgan B/E March 1910; Dec. 1910 MP Ogmore 1918-. **Rt. Hon. Vernon Hartshorn:** Born Pontywaun, Cross Keys, 16 March 1872, s of Theophilus Hartshorn, miner, & Ellen Gregory. Primitive Methodist in early life (lay preacher 7 years). Married 1899 Mary Matilda Winsor, 2s 1d. Educated elementary school. Clerk in colliery office at Cardiff Docks. Miner. Checkweighman. Miners' Agent, Maesteg 1905. Vice-President SWMF. Resigned 1920, *because of Bolshevism in the coalfield*. President 1922-24. Executive, MFGB. LP activist. Chair: Welsh Labour MPs Group. Active in recruiting for army 1914-18. Chair, South Wales Conscientious Objectors' Tribunal 1915-18. Risca UDC. Maesteg UDC. Glamorgan CC. Member,

Bridgend Board of Guardians. Paymaster General 1924. Lord Privy Seal (with responsibility for unemployment) 1930-. Of Maesteg. Estate £2,278. Died 13 March 1930. Further Reading: *Hywel Francis & David Smith, The Fed.*

HARVEY Robert Lambart: BA 1974 MA 1978 (Oxon). Conservative: Merioneth, 1979, Caernarfon Oct. 1974; MP Clwyd South West 1983-87. **Mr. Robert Harvey:** Born 21 August 1953, s of Hon. John Harvey & Elena Harvey; brought up at Meifod. Married 1981, Jane Roper. Educated Eton; Christ Church. Oxford (PPE). Chair, Oxford Branch, Bow Group. Secretary, Oxford University Conservative Assn. Journalist, author & broadcaster. Staff Correspondent *The Economist* 1974-81. Asst. Editor 1981-83. Columnist & Leader writer, *Daily Telegraph* 1987-91. Member: Bow Group; NUT; Royal Institute of International Affairs. Select Cttees Member: Foreign Affairs 1984-87, Welsh Affairs 1983-84. Vice-Chair, CARE (Conservative Action to Revive Employment). Hobbies: The Arts, Films, Music, Swimming.

HASLAM Lewis: JP (Lancs) Officer, Order of the Crown of Belgium. Liberal MP. Monmouth District 1906-18; Newport 1918-; Contested Westhoughton 1892, Stamford 1895. **Mr. Lewis Haslam:** Born Bolton 25 April 1856, s of John Haslam, Gilnow House. Married 1893, Helen d of Henry Dixie of Watlington. Educated University College School & University College, London. Cotton Manufacturer. Director: John Haslam & Co; Schweppes Co. Ltd. Chair, Parliamentary Commercial Cttee. Joint Hon. Treasurer, International Parliamentary Cttees. Of Polborough & London. Estate £521,454. Died 12 September 1922.

HASTINGS Wilfred: Green Party, North List 2003. **Mr. Wilfred Hastings:** Born Connahs Quay 30 November 1949, s of Stanley Hastings, works convenor, & Katharina Margarete Hastings, factory worker. World Wide Church of God. Unmarried. Seed Merchants' employee. Secretary/Treasurer, Flintshire Green Party. Member: Green Party Disputes Resolution Cttee. Contested Flintshire CC Supports: Soil Assn, Asthma campaign, RNLI, Red Cross, Society for the Protection of Nature In Israel. Interests: Wales Green Party. Hobbies: Interdenominational Activities, Pen Pals, Public Speaking. Of Connahs Quay.

HASTON James Ritchie: Revolutionary Communist Party: Neath B/E May 1945. **Mr. Jock Haston:** Born Edinburgh. Founder General Secretary (1944) and only parliamentary candidate of the Revolutionary Communist Party, a merger of the Workers' International League & the

Revolutionary Socialist League. In prison at beginning of election campaign (sentenced, with Roy Tearse, Heaton Lee and Ann Keen, to one year's imprisonment June 1944 but sentence was quashed Sept. 1944). Party disbanded 1949. Haston renounced Trotskyism and resigned from Fourth International, June 1950. Further Reading: *John McHugh & B. J. Ripley, The Neath By-Election 1945: Trotskyists in West Wales, Llafur, Spring 1981, Vol. 3, No. 2.*

HASWELL David Brian Langham: BA. PGCE. Plaid Cymru: Vale of Glamorgan, 1992, Cardiff South & Penarth 1997. **Mr. David Haswell:** Born Penarth 6 January 1962. Married Debbie 2d. Educated Stanwell School, Penarth; University of Wales, Swansea & Cardiff. Teacher. Deputy School Co-ordinator, Headlands Special Needs School, Penarth. Chair, Vale of Glamorgan Plaid Cymru; Member: NUT; Sully & Lavernock ComC (Vice-Chair). Of Barry.

HAVARD David Stuart: CertEd. (Birmingham) MA. (Warwick). Labour MP Merthyr Tydfil & Rhymney 2001. **Mr. Dai Havard:** Born Quakers Yard, 7 August 1950. Married. Educated Treharris Secondary Modern School; Quakers Yard Grammar School; Afon Taf Comprehensive School; St. Peter's College, Warwick; Birmingham University. Researcher 1975-76. TUC Tutor in Further Education 1976-82. Maintenance Engineer 1971-75. TUC Tutor in FE 1976-82. Trade Union Official: SPCS Union 1982-86; STE Union 1986-97. Wales Area Secretary, MSF 1998-2001. Candidate Co-ordinator, Birmingham marginal 1992, 1997; Merthyr Tydfil & Rhymney. Member: Co-operative Party. Hobbies: Hill Walking, Horse Riding, Bird Watching. Of Quakers Yard.

HAVARD-DAVIES Lloyd: Conservative: Carmarthen 1970, Brecon & Radnor Feb. & Oct. 1974. **Mr. Lloyd Havard-Davies:** Born Crugybar, November 1919. Married 2c. Educated Llandovery Senior School; Pibwrlwyd Farm Institute; Avoncroft Agricultural College, Worcs. In film industry. RAF 1939-45. Writer & broadcaster. Farmer (150 acres). Chair, Llansawel PC. Member, Carmarthenshire County Executive, NFU; Guild of Agricultural Journalists. Writes & broadcasts in Welsh & English on agricultural & political topics. Interests: Agriculture. Languages: Welsh, English. Of Llansawel.

HAWKINS Mark C: Conservative: Torfaen 1992. **Mr. Mark Hawkins:** Born 27 July 1961. Educated West Monmouthshire Grammar School; University of Wales, Cardiff. Management Consultant. Chair, Torfaen Young Conservatives 1979-82. Of Newport.

HAYES Andrew: MA (Edinburgh) 1997. Conservative: Llanelli 1997, Winchester 2001. **Mr. Andrew Hayes:** Born Gloucestershire 13 August 1963, Welsh Parents. Married Victoria (solicitor) 2s 2d. Educated Hampton School, London; Edinburgh University (History). Corporate Finance Executive, Hill Samuel Bank 1987-90. Director, Hudson Sandler, investment & financial public relations Consultancy 1990-. Founder 1995 Murchisons Pantheon Ltd. (talking book publisher). Chair: Edinburgh University Conservative Assn. Vice-Chair, Vauxhall Conservative Assn; Campaign for British Referendum 1992. Member: Conservative Way Forward. Contested Lambeth BC 1990. Of London.

HAYES Simon: Conservative, Llanelli 2001. **Mr. Simon Hayes:** Born Hampstead, 9 November 1958. Married Miranda 2s 1d. Educated: Clayesmore School, Dorset; turned down place at Durham University and took a year out, working at a Hamburg dockyard. Stockjobber 2 years. Merchant banker with Barings 2 years. Sotheby's auctioneer. Opened freshly ground coffee stall at Lymington market 1982, and then founded Hayes Tea & Coffee. New Forest DC 1987- (Leader 1999 & Policy & Strategy Cabinet Member). Hampshire CC 1997- (Vice-Chair, Social Services Cttee 2000-). Chair: New Forest CLP 1990-92. Member: Hampshire & Isle of Wight Police Authority 1997-. Interests: Crime & Disorder; Local Government; Health & Social care provision. Prospective candidate for Mid Dorset & North Poole 2003. Interests: Crime & Disorder, Education, Local Government, Social Care Provision. Of Lymington.

HAYES-JONES John Rathbone: Independent Welsh Nationalist: Wrexham 1945. **Mr. Rathbone Hayes-Jones:** Born Wrexham 1896. Educated Victoria Council School; Switzerland; Rome (art); Aix en Provence University (law); French School of Law, Cairo. Egyptian Civil Service. Councillor for Mansourah. Magistrate of a mixed tribunal. Flew in from Cairo just in time to be nominated. Director of companies. Of Ruthin. Died 1960.

HAYWARD Edwin Richard: ACT FRGS. Conservative, Carmarthenshire East & Dinefwr 1997; Cynon Valley, 1999, Euro Wales 1999. **Mr. Edwin Hayward:** Born Windsor, 25 October 1956, s of Colonel Edwin William Hayward, military surgeon, & Ms. Pine-Coffin, wartime WRAF. Roman Catholic. Married 1998 Susan Marie Moss, general practitioner, 1s 1d. Educated Wellington College; University of Exeter (Law). Chartered Accountant. 1979-89. Financial Controller, then Associate Sales Director, Financial Ltd. (producing training films. for the City). Director, Cable & Finance Ltd (investment company in media industry) 1985-89. Self-employed

Taxation & Business Consultant. Founded removal and storage business 1983-95 (sold to allow more time for politics). Chair: Exeter University Conservative Assn 1977-78, North Battersea Conservative Assn 1982-83. Treasurer, then Chair, Battersea Conservative Assn 1983-87. Treasurer: Brecon & Radnor Conservative Assn 1993-96 (Asst. Treasurer 1991-93); Welsh Trustee, Radnorshire Wild Life Trust 1992-. Interests: Taxation, Countryside. Hobbies: Sport & exercise (energetic hill walker & cyclist, keen racegoer & subscriber to Glyn Celyn Beagles), DIY enthusiast, Travel, Gardening. Lived in Wales since 1987. Of Llanbister, Llandrindod Wells .

HAYWARD John Joseph: MRCP LRCP (Wales) DObst MRCOG. National: Abertillery 1945; Conservative: Cardiff South East 1950. **Dr. J. J. Hayward:** Born Swansea, 1916. Married 1942, Diana Davies, teacher of Llandysul, 2c. Educated Bishop Gore Grammar School, Swansea; Cardiff High School; Welsh National School of Medicine. Medical Practitioner at Whitchurch 1946-. Royal Navy 1942-45, Surgeon-Commander RNVR. Chair: University of Wales, Cardiff Conservative Assn. 1936-39; Wales & Mon Conservative Political Education Cttee 1946-49; Wales & Mon Conservative Candidates Assn 1946-49. Of Cardiff.

HAYWARD Robert Antony: CBE 1991 BSc. Conservative: Carmarthen Oct. 1974; MP Kingswood 1983-92. **Mr. Robert Hayward:** Born 11 March 1949, s of Ralph & Mary Hayward. Educated Abingdon School; Maidenhead Grammar School; University of Rhodesia (Economics). Personnel Manager, Esso Petroleum 1971-75; Coca Cola Bottlers 1975-78; GEC Large Machines 1978-82. Director, British Soft Drinks Assn 1993-. Rugby Referee. Political Chair, Maidenhead Young Conservatives 1967. Chair: Bedford Young Conservatives 1973. National Vice-Chair, Young Conservatives 1976-77. Coventry CC 1976-78. PPS 1985-89. Member, Select Cttees: Cardiff Bay Barrage Bill, 1991-92; Energy 1983-85.

HEALE Frederick William: National Liberal: Rhondda East, 1922. **Mr. Frederick Heale:** Born Cardigan 1849. Married. Educated Cardigan Grammar School. Married Emma, 5s 4d. Went to work in London at 15. At Coolgardie Goldfield, Australia for 2 years. Private secretary to Earl of Donaghue & Colonel Vivian Lloyd. Chair & Managing Director, firm of London Chartered Accountants. Founder, Polytechnic Institute. Master, 3 Masonic lodges. Declined invitation to be Conservative candidate for Rhondda East 1928. Of Tottenham.

HEARNE Derrick Kenneth: BA (London) 1954. Plaid Cymru: Swansea West Feb. 1974. **Mr.**

Derrick Hearne: Born St. Thomas, Swansea, June 1932. Married 2c. Educated Ystalyfera Grammar School; Kings College, London (Fellow, British Computer Society). Army 1954-56. Computer Organiser, United Nations Health Service 1969- (Adviser, setting up Bulgarian State Computer Bureau); World Health Organisation Consultant, Computer Technology; Director, W.H.O. European Office, Copenhagen 1973-. Joined Plaid Cymru 1962. Author of *The Rise of the Welsh Republic* 1973 which led to his expulsion from Plaid Cymru 1975.

HEDLEY Ernest Hall: CE JP (Glam) 1893 CE. Independent Labour & Radical: Swansea District 1895. **Mr. Hall Hedley:** Born Tynemouth 1855, s of Joseph Hedley. Married (1) 1881 Mary Ann Lewis, Alltycham (2) Marjorie (died 1987). Engineer & Colliery Proprietor. Sought Gower Liberal nomination 1900. Of Pontardawe.

HELME Ernest: DSO & Bar MA (Oxon). Conservative: Swansea District 1906. **Lieut-Colonel Ernest Helme:** Born Walthamstow 1874, s of Richard Mashiter (changed name from Helme) London banker, of Gower & London. & Louisa. Anglican. Educated Winchester; Christ Church, Oxford. Country Gentleman. Lieutenant, Glamorgan Yeomanry. Army, France 1914-18, 15th Carmarthenshire Battalion, Welch Regt. Raised & conducted Glamorgan Yeomanry Male Voice Choir. Landowner. Member, Welsh Industries Assn. Chair, Gower Conservative Assn 1923. Member, Welsh Industries Assn. Of Gower & London.

HEMMERDE Edward George: QC BA 1892, BCL 1896 MA (Oxon). Liberal MP: East Denbighshire B/E 1906-1910, North-West Norfolk B/E 1912-1918; Candidate: Winchester 1900, Shrewsbury 1906, Portsmouth 1910. Joined Labour Party 1920. Labour MP Crewe 1922-24. **Mr. Edward Hemmerde:** Born Peckham, London, 13 November 1871, s of James Godfrey Lorche Hemmerde, manager, Imperial Ottoman Bank, & Frances Pope. Married 1906. Lucy Elinor, d of C. C. Colley; divorced 1922; 1s (killed in accident in Africa 1926) 1d. Educated Winchester (Cricket & Football XIs); University College, Oxford (1st Classical Moderations 1892, 3rd Lit. Hum. 1894, 2nd Jurisprudence 1895). Diamond Sculls, Henley 1900. Barrister, Inner Temple, 1899. Recorder of Liverpool 1909-. Member: English League for the Taxation of Land Values; Liberal Land Enquiry 1912-13. Wrote several plays. Estate £402. Died 24 August 1948. *Books: E. G. Hemmerde, A Maid of Honour, A Butterfly on the Wheel (both with Francis Neilson MP), The Crucible, Proud Maisie, The Dead Hand, A Cardinal's Romance (with Cicely Fraser).*

HENDERSON Arthur Jr: Baron Rowley of Rowley Regis 1966 PC 1947 KC 1939 DL (London) 1948 MA LlB (Cantab). Labour: Cardiff South 1923-24; 1929-31; Kingswingford 1935-50; Rowley Regis & Tipton 1950-66; Candidate: South Portsmouth, 1922. **Rt. Hon. Arthur Henderson:** Born 27 August 1893, s of Rt. Hon. Arthur Henderson MP. Wesleyan Methodist. Married 1958, Mrs. Mary Elizabeth Glickstein. Educated Central School, Darlington; Queens College, Taunton; Trinity Hall, Cambridge. Army 1915-19, 1939-45, Major. President, Cambridge University Labour Club 1920-21. Secretary, Universities Labour Federation 1921-24. Barrister 1921. Joint Under-Sec. War 1942-43; Financial Secretary, War Office 1943-45. Under Secretary, India 1945-47. Minister of State, Commonwealth Relations 1947; Secretary for Air 1947-51. Vice-President: Council of Europe Assembly 1961-62; Parliamentary Group for World Government. Deputy-Chair, UK Branch, Commonwealth Parliamentary Assn. President: Parliamentary United Nations Group. Member: Royal Economic Society; Hardwick Society. Of London. Died 28 August 1968. *Books: A. Henderson, Trade Unions and the Law (with Sir Henry Slesser), Industrial Law, Treatise on Housing Law.*

HERBERT Auberon Mark Henry Yvo Molyneaux: MA (Oxon). National Liberal: Aberavon 1950; Conservative & National Liberal: Sunderland North 1951. **Mr. Auberon Herbert:** Born 1922, s of Colonel Aubrey Herbert, MP & gs f 4th Earl of Carnarvon. Roman Catholic. Landowner & Journalist. Five times rejected for military service on health grounds but served with Polish Armoured Corps 1942-45; Polish Re-Settlement Staff 1945-47. Member, European Movement International Secretariat. Foreign Correspondent, *The Tablet* 1974. A founder & Chair, Anglo-Byelorussian Society. Of London. Died 1974.

HERBERT Ivor John Caradog: 1st & last Baron Treowen 1917: 1st Bart 1907 CB 1890 CMG 1895 JP (Mon) Hon. LLD (Wales) 1933 Order of the Red Eagle (Germany) Commander of the Order of the Cross of Italy; Officer of the Legion d'Honneur (France). Liberal MP South Monmouthshire 1906-17. **Major-General, Sir Ivor Herbert:** Born Raglan 1851, s of John Herbert JP DL & Hon. Augusta Hall, d of 1st Baron Llanover. Roman Catholic. Married 1871, Albertina (Died 1929) d of Baron Londesborough. Educated St. Mary's College, Oscott. Lieutenant, Grenadier Guards 1970; Captain 1874; Brevet Colonel 1908, retired. Military Attaché at St. Petersburg 1886-90. Commander, Canadian local forces 1890-95, with local rank of Major-General; Raised Welsh Army Corps & Director of National Service for Wales 1914-18; Hon. Major-General. Landowner (20,000 acres). Newport BC. Mon-mouthshire CC. Chair: Liberal War Cttee. Chair: School of Slavonic & East European Studies, London University 1933. President: University College, Cardiff; Hon. Society of Cymmrodorion. Lord Lieutenant of Monmouthshire 1913-. Of Llanarth Court, Raglan. Died 18 October 1933.

HERBERT John Arthur: GCIE 1939 JP 1921 DL (Mon). Conservative MP Monmouth B/E 1934-39. **Colonel, Sir John Herbert:** Born 1895, s of Sir Arthur Herbert, GCVO. of Coldbrook, Abergavenny, & Helen Louisa Gammet of Rhode Island (nephew of Lord Treowen qv & ggs of Benjamin Hall MP). Married 1924, Lady Mary Theresa Fox-Strangways, d of 6th Earl of Ilchester, 1s. Educated Wellington College; Havard University. Lieutenant, Royal Horse Guards 1916; Major 1930. ADC to Viceroy of India 1926-28. Retired 1934. MFH Monmouthshire Hunt, 1921-25. Asst Whip (unpaid). Governor of Bengal 1939-. Of Llanover & London. Died 11 December 1943.

HERMAN Peter: Natural Law Party, South/East List 1999. **Mr. Peter Herman:** Married Susan Parry (qv). Airline pilot. Gave a Hon.g hotel on candidature papers. Of Skelmersdale.

HERRIOT Christopher: BA. Socialist Labour, Ogmore B/E 14 Feb. 2002-2003 & South/West List; Motherwell & Wishaw 1997; Paisley South B/E Nov. 1997; Airdrie & Shotts 2001; Hartlepool B/E 2004. **Mr. Chris Herriot:** Born 1959. Married Sue 3c. Educated university (Certificate in Community Education). Miner. Sacked during strikes of 1984-85. Area Manager, Community Education, Caerphilly CBC. Asst. Branch Secretary, Unison. Founder President, SLP Scotland Of Newport.

Chris Herriot.

HESELTINE Michael Ray Dibdin: Baron Heseltine 2001: CH 1997 PC 1972 MA (Oxon) Hon. LLD (Liverpool) 1990. National Liberal & Conservative: Gower 1959; Conservative: Coventry North 1964; MP Tavistock 1966-Feb. 1974; Henley Feb1974-2001. **Rt. Hon. Michael Heseltine:** Born Swansea, 21 March 1933, s of Colonel Rupert Heseltine & Eileen Pridmore. Anglican. Married Anne Williams, 3c. Educated Shrewsbury School; Pembroke College, Oxford (2nd PPE); Hon. Fellow 1986. President, Oxford Union 1954. With Graduates Appointments Registrar, Industrial & Professional Careers Research Organisation. Publisher of Magazines & Property Developer; Chair, The Haymarket Press 1966-70; Director 1970-79. Member, Blue Ribbon Club. Fellow, Institute of Directors. Member, Council of the Zoological Society of London 1987-90. Parl-Secretary: Transport June-Oct. 1970. Joint Parl-Secretary: Environment 1970-72. Minister for Aerospace 1972-74. Chief Opposition Spokesman, Industry 1974-76; Environment 1976-79. Secretary of State for Environment 1979-83. Secretary for Defence 1983-86, Resigned over future of Westland Helicopters Co.1986. Contested Party Leadership 1990. Secretary for Environment 1990-92. Secretary for Trade & Industry (President of the Board of Trade) 1992-95. First Secretary of State & Deputy Prime Minister 1995-97. Hon. FRIBA 1990. Fellow: Leeds Polytechnic 1988; University of Wales, Swansea, 2001. Non-drinker. Of Thenford Hall, nr. Banbury & London. *Books: Michael Heseltine, Life in the Jungle 2000.* Further Reading: *Michael Crick, Michael Heseltine, a Biography, 1997; Julian Critchley, Heseltine 1987.*

HEWINS William Albert Samuel: MA (Oxon). Conservative: Swansea West 1922, 1923, 1924; Shipley B/E 1910, SE Lancashire Dec. 1910, B/E 1911; MP City of Hereford B/E 1912-18. Resigned as PPC for Barnstable to contest Swansea. **Professor William Hewins:** Born, Wolverhampton, 11 May 1865, s of Samuel Hewins, iron master. Roman Catholic. Married 1922, Margaret, d of James Slater, 3c. Educated Wolverhampton Grammar School; Pembroke College, Oxford (Mathematics). Tooke Professor of Economic Science & Statistics, Kings College, London 1897-1903; Director, London School of Economics 1895-1903. Member, London University Senate 1900-03. Secretary, Tariff Commission 1903-17. President, Lingaard Society. Under-Secretary, Colonies 1917-18. Of London. Died 17 November 1931. *Books: W. A. S. Hewins, Trade in Balance 1924; Empire Restored 1927, Apologia of an Imperialist 1929.*

HEWITT Aylwin Owen: Conservative: Pontypool 1951, 1955. **Mr. Aylwin Hewitt:** Born Beddgelert 1923. Married 2c. Educated Porth-

madog Grammar School. RAF 1941-46, Flight Lieutenant. Solicitor 1948. Beddgelert PC 1948-49, Vice-Chairman 1949, Resigned on removal to Ledbury. Branch Secretary, Beddgelert Conservatives until 1949, Ledbury Conservatives, January 1951. Languages: Welsh, English. Of Ledbury.

HEWITT Christopher Stanley: BSc. CertEd. Labour, Montgomeryshire 1999. **Mr. Chris Hewitt:** Born 22 March 1952. Educated University of Wales, Aberystwyth (1st Pure Maths). Maths. Teacher. At DERA, Aberporth 1980-98 (Principal Scientific Officer 1992). Voluntary redundancy 1998. Patron, Fishguard Music Festival. Member: Charter 88. Hobbies: Theatre, Classical Music. Of Cardigan.

HEWSON Malcolm George: Liberal Democrat, Torfaen 1992. **Mr. Malcolm Hewson:** Born 31 December 1958. Unmarried. Educated Leeds University (Statistics/Economics). Computing Systems Analyst, BT. Member: Society of Telecom Executives; Cwmbran Cricket Club. Hobbies: Cricket, Hill walking. Of Cwmbran.

HICKERY Darren Charles: Socialist Labour, South/East List, 1999; Gower 2001. **Mr. Darren Hickery:** Born 1965. Married 1s. Electrician. Examiner. Shop steward. Secretary, Wales Region, Socialist Labour Party. Local Correspondent, *Llwchwr Star*. ComC. School Governor. Contested Carmarthenshire CC (Hendy) 1999. Of Hendy, Pontarddulais.

HICKS Robert Adrian: Kt 1996 BSc (London) FRGS. Conservative: Aberavon 1966; Cardiff North short list 1967; MP Bodmin 1970-74; Cornwall South East 1974-97. **Sir Robert Hicks:** Born Horrabridge, Devon 18 January 1938, s of William Henry Hicks, electrician & Marjorie Hicks. Married Marion Elizabeth Anne Gwyther 1d. Educated Queen Elizabeth's Grammar School, Crediton; University College, London; Exeter University. Teacher, St. Austell Grammar School 1961-64. Lecturer: Economics & Regional Geography, Weston-Super-Mare Technical College 1964-70. Treasurer, London University Conservative Assn. National Vice-Chair Young Conservatives 1964-66. Secretary: Conservative MPs Agricultural Cttee 1970-73. Chair, West Country Conservative MPs 1976-79; Cttee on European Affairs 1979-80; UK Group, Parl Assn for Euro-Arab Co-operation 1982. Select Cttees Member: European Legislation 1979. Parl Adviser: British Hotels, Restaurants & Caterers Assn 1974; Milk Marketing Board, 1985. President, Plymouth Albion RFC 1991. Hobbies: Keen Cricketer. Of Torpoint.

HILL J. Gerald: Liberal: Aberdare Oct. 1974. **Mr. Gerry Hill:** Born Mountain Ash December 1935.

Married 2c. Educated York Street Secondary School, Mountain Ash. Chair & Managing Director, Gerry Hill Holdings Ltd & owner of one of Wales' largest garage chains. Labour Party member until 1973; resigned when Labour chose an English PPC. Member Plaid Cymru 1973-74. Joined Liberal Party May 1974. Aberdare UDC. Killed in helicopter crash 1976.

HILL Richard John: Conservative, Ogmore 2001, 2003. **Mr. Richard Hill:** Born Church Village, 17 January 1962, s of Bryan Royston Hill, steelworker, & Jean Griffiths, civil servant. Church of England. Married Carol Patricia Hill, nursery nurse, 1s 1d. Educated Dyffryn High School, Newport; South Gwent FE College. Royal Marines 9 years. Director, independent financial advisers. Contested Newport CC 3 times. Interests: Taxation, Pensions, Long-term care issues. Hobbies: Rugby, Work. Of Newport.

HILLS Susan: BSc (Nottingham) LlB (John Moore). Plaid Cymru: Alyn & Deeside 1997. **Mrs. Siw Hills:** Born Barry, 9 October 1951. Married Barry 2s. Educated Nottingham University (Psychology); John Moore University, Liverpool (Law). With Industrial Research Council. Area Manager, Wrexham Maelor Housing Dept. Member: Chartered Institute of Housing; Mudiad Ysgolion Meithrin; CADW; National Trust; UNISON. Treasurer, constituency Plaid Cymru. Of Rhydtalog, Wrexham.

HINDS John: JP DL (Carms). Liberal MP: West Carmarthenshire 1910-18; Carmarthen 1918-22. **Mr. John Hinds:** Born Carmarthen, 26 July 1862, s of William Hinds, farmer, & Mary Jones. Baptist deacon. Married 1893 Lizzie, d of R. Powell 1d (1 son killed in Great War). Educated Alcwyn Evans Academy. Farm boy. Apprenticed to Carmarthen draper, 5 years. Own shop at Blackheath 1887. Chair, D. Hinds & Co. (Drapers). Chair, Welsh Parliamentary Party 1920-21. President: Baptist Union of Wales 1920; Drapers Chamber of Trade of the United Kingdom; London Welsh Literary Union. Freemason, Senior Grand Deacon, Grand Lodge of England. Lord Lieutenant of Carmarthenshire. Mayor of Carmarthen 1925-26. Freeman, Carmarthen & City of London. Treasurer, Hon. Society of Cymmrodorion. Of Carmarthen & London. Estate £104,692. Died 23 July 1928.

HINTON Robert N. E: Conservative: Aberdare 1950; Hammersmith South 1951. **Mr. Robert Hinton:** Born March 1901, s of J. Hinton & Miss Kelly of Cardiff. Educated Highgate School. Worked in India & Burma (shipping), South Africa & Malaya. Managing Director, combustion stove manufacturers. Army 1939-46, Southern Command staff officer. Vice-President,

Watford Branch, British Legion. Member: Eastern Gas Consultative Council. Watford BC 1946-. Of Watford.

HITCHON Robert Ernest: Communist: Llanelli 1964, 1966, 1970, Feb. & Oct. 1974, 1983. **Mr. Bob Hitchon:** Born July 1933. Married Delphine, 2c. Educated Llanelli Grammar School; Llanelli Technical College. Apprentice, Nevill's foundry & engineering works 1948. Fitter & Turner. Toolroom machinist, Morris Motors, Llanelli. AEF shop steward & District Vice-Chair. Joined Communist Party 1957. Member: West Wales Area Cttee. & Welsh District Cttee. Communist Party; Contested every local election at Llanelli 1958-70. Of Llanelli.

HOARE Simon James: Conservative: Cardiff West 1997. **Mr. Simon Hoare:** Born Cardiff 28 January 1969. Roman Catholic. Unmarried. Educated Bishop Hannon RC Comprehensive School, Cardiff; Grayfriars College, Oxford. Public Affairs Consultant. At Conservative Central Office 1990-91. PA to Leader, Kingston upon Thames BC 1992-93. With Docolon Holdings Ltd Cardiff 1991-92; Charles Barker Public Affairs 1993-95; Environmental Services Assn 1995; Political Planning Services 1996-. Vice/Chair, Wales Young Conservatives. Chair, Oxford Bow Group. Political Officer, Bow Group. Of Cardiff.

HOBBINS Peter: BA CertEd (Wales) Conservative, Rhondda, 1999, 2001. **Mr. Peter Hobbins:** Born Paderborn, Germany, 20 January 1971, s of Raymond Dennis Hobbins & Eileen Patricia O'Loughlin, Salvation Army Officers. Church in Wales/Church of England. Married 1999, Anne Gaelle Hobbins, teacher, 1s. Educated Bedwellty Comprehensive School; University of Wales, Lampeter (religion, ethics & western society); Trinity College, Carmarthen. Teacher. Worked with inner city children, Boston, Mass 1990 & 1992. Money raiser and youth & community worker for Salvation Army 1991. Teacher (RE, then history, government & politics). TA Officer Recruit (Royal Logistics Corps). Joined Conservative Party 1990. Chair: Lampeter University Conservative Assn; Wales Area Conservative Students. Worked at Ian Duncan Smith's Campaign HQ 2001 (Vice-President IDS Campaign). Lampeter TC. 1995-96. Interests: Devolution, Education, Anglo-American Politics. Hobbies: Cross country & Marathon running, Cricket. Of Tenby (1999), then Orpington.

HOBBS Anthony Robert: Natural Law Party: Cardiff Central 1997; Folkestone & Hythe 1992. **Mr. Anthony Hobbs:** Born 1939. Educated Cambridge University (Diploma in Public Relations). Journalist, *Western Daily Press* 11 years. PR Manager 20 years (a London building company,

Trust House Forte, Pilkington Glass etc); Teacher of Transcendental Meditation 1993-.

HOBSON Phylip Andrew David: Liberal Democrat, Newport West & South/East List 2003; Manchester Central 2001. Green Party, Kensington & Chelsea B/E 1988. **Mr. Phylip Hobson:** Born Newport, 21 September 1968. Roman Catholic. Unmarried. Educated St. Joseph's School, Newport; Institutio Cervantes, Manchester. Worked in publishing & telecom industries. Business Administrative Manager. Chepstow TC. Secretary, Monmouth Liberal Democrat Assn. Member: Welsh Liberal Democrat National Executive. Interests: Environment, Economics, Wales in Europe, Transport. Hobbies: Travel, Gardening, Mountain Biking, Cooking, Writing, Political History. Languages: Learning Welsh, English, French, Castilian Spanish. Of Chepstow.

HODGE John: PC 1916. Labour: West Glamorgan 1900; Preston 1903; MP Gorton 1903-23. **Rt. Hon. John Hodge:** Born Linkeyburn, Muirkirk, Ayrshire 29 October 1855, s of William Hodge, iron works puddler, & Marian Henderson, 1 of 8c. Father, active trade unionist, victimized and family had to move to Glasgow. Wesleyan Methodist. Married 1885, Mary Forsyth (died 1931) 4d. Educated Motherwell Works School; Hutchesonstown Grammar School, Glasgow. Solicitor's Clerk 1868-72. Tinplate Worker, Parkhead Ironworks 1872-79. Grocer for a while. Ironworker, Coatbridge & Motherwell. 1st Secretary, British Steel Smelters, Mill, Iron, Tinplate & Kindred Trades Assn 1886 (joined 1886), President 1931. 1st President, Association of Iron & Steel Trades Confederation. President: Glasgow Trades Council; Trade Union Congress 1892. Made several unsuccessful attempts to be a Liberal candidate before 1900. President: Labour Representation Cttee (twice). Glasgow CC. Manchester CC 1898-1901 (Liberal). Broke with Liberal Party 1900. Vice-Chair PLP 1914, Chair 1915. Minister of Labour 1916-17. Minister of Pensions 1917-19. Temperance Speaker. Policy Labour first, politics second. Estate £2837. Of Blackheath. Died 10 August 1937. *Books: John Hodge: From Workman's Cottage to Windsor Castle, 1931. Further Readings: Kenneth O. Morgan, Wales in British Politics, 1963; Kenneth O. Morgan, The Khaki Election in Gower, Gower xiii, 1961.*

HODGE Philip Herman: Referendum Party, Merionydd/Nant Conwy 1997. **Mr. Philip Hodge:** Born 1956. Apprentice Car Mechanic in family garage. Came to Wales 1976 when family took over a Corris hotel. Owner of a Machynlleth Computer Business. Conservative Branch Chair.

HODGKINSON Christopher Frederick Lloyd: Pro-Conservative, Wales Euro 1999. **Mr. Chris-**topher Hodgkinson: Born Hereford, 23 March 1977, s of William L. Hodgkinson. Educated Hereford Cathedral School. Retail Store Manager. Interests: Business, Economy. Hobbies: Current Affairs, Business, Politics. Of Hereford.

HOFFMAN David Ludwig: BSc. (Sussex). Ecology Party: Pembroke 1983. **Mr. David Hoffman:** Born 1951. Educated Sussex University (Biological Science). Moved to area to work in conservation. Undertook research on history of Pembrokeshire for library service & natural history for county museum. Consultant Medical Herbalist at Cardigan. Lectured widely on ecology, alternative medicine and New Age. Of St. Dogmaels (1973). *Books: David Hoffman, The Holistic Herbalist.*

HOLLAND Christopher Kevin: Plaid Cymru, Newport East 1997, 1999. **Mr. Chris Holland:** Born Newport 25 July 1956. Married 3c. Educated Brunel College, Bristol. Local Government Officer. Secretary, Newport Plaid Cymru. Contested Newport BC 1996. Of Newport.

HOLLER Deborah J: Referendum Party: Torfaen 1997. **Mrs. Deborah Holler:** Born 1965. Married 3c. Hairdresser. Of Newport.

HOOD Alfred: Conservative: East Denbighshire Dec. 1910. **Mr. Alfred Hood:** Born 1862, s of William Hood of New Brunswick. Married 1902, Winifred, d of Sir William Tait, Bart of Liverpool. Educated Privately. Member, Liverpool Stock Exchange. Treasurer, Liverpool Tariff Reform Assn. High Sheriff of Denbighshire 1911-12. Of Liverpool & Rossett.

HOOSON Hugh Emlyn, Baron Hooson of Montgomery: 1979 QC. 1960 JP (Flint & Merioneth) LlB Hon. LLD 2003 (Wales). Liberal: Conway 1950, 1951; MP Montgomery B/E 1962-79. **Mr. Emlyn Hooson:** Born Denbigh 26 March, 1925, s of Hugh Hooson, farmer, & Elsie Hooson. Presbyterian Church of Wales. Married Shirley Margaret Wynne, d of Sir George Hamer HML, Llanidloes, 2c. Educated Denbigh Elementary School; Denbigh Grammar School; Ford Agricultural Institute, Chelmsford; University of Wales, Aberystwyth. Royal Navy Fleet Air Arm 1946-49. Barrister, Grays Inn 1949, Bencher 1968; Vice-Treasurer 1985; Treasurer 1986; Leader, Wales & Chester Circuit 1971-74. Director, Gwasg Gee. Deputy-Chair, Quarter Sessions: Flintshire 1960-71; Merioneth 1960-67; Chair 1967-71; Recorder of Merthyr Tydfil 1971; Swansea 1971; Crown Court 1972-93. Farmer. Chair, Severn Crossing plc until 2003. President: Liberal Party of Wales 1956-57; Welsh Liberal Party 1983-86; Leader, Welsh Liberal Party 1967-79. President: Llangollen International Eisteddfod

1987-93; Denbigh National Eisteddfod; Newtown National Eisteddfod; Llanidloes AFC; Montgomeryshire Amateur Football League; Vice-Chair: North Atlantic Assn. Political Cttee. 1975-79. Governor: Grassland & Environmental Research. Hon. Member, Gorsedd of Bards 1965. President, University of Wales, Aberystwyth, 1971. Hon. Professorial Fellow, University of Wales, Aberystwyth. Chair: Laura Ashley Foundation 1986-97. Hobbies: Welsh country life, Reading, Music, Cricket, Rugby. Languages: Welsh, English. Of Llanidloes. Further Reading: *John Graham Jones in "Dictionary of Liberal Biography", pages 186-188.*

HOOSON Tom Ellis: MA (Oxon). Conservative: Caernarfon1959; MP Brecon & Radnor 1979-. **Mr. Tom Hooson:** Born 16 March 1933, farmer's son (cousin of Emlyn Hooson qv & grandnephew of Tom Ellis MP & I. D. Hooson, poet. Educated Rhyl Grammar School; University College, Oxford. Barrister, Grays Inn. Journalist, *The Times.* Director General, Periodical Publishers' Assn. Executive, Prentis & Varley Ltd 1958-61, Benton & Bowles (New York 1961-70. Europe 1971-76). Director of Communications, Conservative Party 1976-78. Director, publishing company. Founder, *Welsh Farm News.* Chair: Bow Group & *Crossbow.* Vice-President, Federation of University Conservative & Unionist Assns 1960-61. Member, Hon. Society of Cymmrodorion. Languages: Welsh, English. Died 8 May 1985. *Books etc: Tom Hooson (with Geoffrey Howe), Work for Wales.*

HOPE John Campbell: Conservative: Neath 1950; Swansea East 1951. **Mr. Jack Hope:** Born Swansea, April 1908. Married 2d. Educated Swansea Grammar School. Office Boy to Company Secretary, Prince of Wales Dry Dock Co. Swansea. Vice-Chair, Swansea East Conservative Assn. Secretary, Mumbles Conservative Club. Of Swansea.

HOPKIN Daniel: MC 1916 BA 1913 MA LlB 1914 (Cantab). Labour: Carmarthen B/E 1928, 1931; MP 1929-31, 1935-45. **Major Daniel Hopkin:** Born Llantwit Major 11 July 1886, s of Daniel Hopkin, farm labourer, & Ann Price, school cleaner. Married, London, 1919, Edmee Viterbo (died 1965) of Cairo (wealthy Italian family), 1s 1d. Educated Llantwit Major Elementary School; Trinity College, Carmarthen; St. Catherine's College, Cambridge (exhibitioner 1910). Pupil Teacher 1900. Teacher, Blaengarw Council School 1906-08. Private Tutor 1912-14. Army, East Yorks Regt, Gallipoli & France 1914-16; Major, Royal Fusiliers 1916-18 (POW 1918). At Cairo with brother-in-law's engineering company 1919-21. Moved to San Remo, to open school, 1921, but instead returned to Grays Inn.

Barrister (Grays Inn 1924). Major, Pioneer Corps 1939-40. Metropolitan Magistrate 1940-. Chair: Magistrates Assn of Great Britain. Joined a Christian Socialist organisation 1912; Fabian Society 1913. Collapsed in court and died 30 August 1951.

HOPKIN-MORGAN Peter Trevor: QC 1972 MA (Oxon). Liberal: Cardiff Central 1945. **Mr. Peter Hopkin-Morgan:** Born 5 February 1919, s of Cyril Richard Morgan (Managing Director, Morgan, Harris & Co) & Muriel Arcita Hole of Llamas. Anglican. Married 1942 Josephine Mauncy, d of Ben Travers CBE, theatre producer/actor, 4c. Educated Mill Hill School; Magdalen College, Oxford. Army 1939-45, Lieutenant, RWF. Barrister, Middle Temple 1949. Lecturer in Law, University of Wales, Cardiff & Swansea 1950-56. Circuit Judge 1972-87. Deputy Judge 1987. Liaison Judge, Magistrates & JPs 1973-87. Judge, Provincial Court of the Church in Wales. Liveryman, Fishmongers Company. Of Chippenham. Died 30 December 1996.

HOPKINS Arthur: Liberal: Swansea East 1929. **Mr. Arthur Hopkins:** Born 1880. Married 1933 Gwenllian, d of Lake Howell Phillips, Senghenydd. Provision Merchant & Collector of Taxes. President: Caerphilly & District Grocers' Assn. 1931; Nelson Chamber of Trade. Hon. Commissioner, Senghenydd Red Cross. Caerphilly UDC 1919- (Chair, Finance Cttee), Chairman1930-31. Died 10 July 1947.

HOPKINS Kenneth Samuel: BA MA (Oxon) PGCE (Wales). Labour, South/Central List 1999. **Mr. Ken Hopkins:** Born 1927, s of Revd Morgan Samuel Hopkins, Congregational minister. Congregationalist/United Reformed Church. Married 1949 Margaret Lewis, teacher/deputy head, 1d. Educated Rhondda Boys' Grammar School. Porth; St. Catherine's, Oxford. Teacher. Headteacher. Director of Education. Chair, NIACE Cymru. Fellow & Vice-President, University of Wales, Cardiff. Secretary, Rhondda Labour Party. Chair: Wales Labour Party; Wales Labour Party Policy Commission on the Assembly; Welsh Assembly Preparation Group. Member: National Assembly Advisory Group, Labour Party National Policy Forum. Part-time Policy Adviser to Janice Gregory AM. Interests: Local Government, Devolution, Electoral Systems, Europe. Languages: English, a little Welsh, French. Of Porth, Rhondda.

HORNER Arthur Lewis: Communist: Rhondda East 1929, 1931, B/E 1933. **Mr. Arthur Horner:** Born Merthyr Tydfil 5 April 1894, s of James Horner, railwayman (his father walked from Northumberland to Merthyr Tydfil in search of work) & Emily Lewis, Cop-operative store keeper. Brought up Churches of Christ (Church

Arthur Horner.

Secretary). Married 1916, Ethel Mary Merrick, 3d. Educated Elementary School. Worked part-time at barber's shop at 8; then as grocer's delivery boy. Railway telephonist at 11. Known as the 'boy preacher'. At 17 awarded scholarship to Birmingham Baptist College but left after 6 months – college disapproved of his political activities. Joined Rhondda Socialist League. Miner at Standard Collieries, Ynyshir 1906. His anti-war feelings caused his religious beliefs to wane. Joined Sinn Fein in 1916, Dublin Rising; Arrested at Holyhead on the way home; Court Martial led to two years imprisonment at Carmarthen Gaol for incorrigible behaviour; went on Hunger Strike; released 1921. Checkweighman (elected when in prison). Sentenced to One month's Gaol in 1921 for *Inciting to Riot*. Miners' Agent 1933-46. Executive Member, Miners Federation of Great Britain 1933-36. President, SWMF 1933-45. Production Manager, National Coal Board, 1945-46; General Secretary, National Union of Mineworkers, 1946-59. Founder Member, Communist Party of Great Britain 1920; Member, Central Committee 1923-29, excluded 1929; Opposed Party Line over 1939 War & Hungarian *Uprising* 1956. Freeman of Merthyr Tydfil 1959. Died 4 September 1968. *Books: Arthur Horner: The Bureaucracy in the Miners' Federation 1928, Incorrigible Rebel (autobiography) 1960, (with Allen Hutt) Communism and Coal 1928, (with Will Paynter, Outlook for Mining 1958.* Further Reading: *Nina Fishman, Solving the Enigma of Arthur Horner, 2004.*

HOWARD Henry Lloyd Richard: CB.1900 MA. (Oxon). Conservative: Flint District 1895, 1900, Jan. & Dec. 1910. **Colonel Henry Howard:** Born Sunningdale, Berks 19 July 1853, s of Revd R. H. Howard. Anglican. Married Violet Mary Barnard (died 1913) d of Captain H. B. Hankey, 2c. Educated Eton; Christ Church, Oxford. Commissioned 16th Lancers. Flintshire CC. Of Wigfawr. Died 22 December 1922.

HOWARD James Henry: BA (Wales) MA (Liverpool) DD (Princeton) 1936. Labour: Merioneth 1931. **Revd Dr. J. H. Howard:** Born Swansea, 3 November 1877, s of Joshua George Howard, naval officer (descendant of John Howard, prison reformer) & Catherine Bowen, housemaid (parents eloped & father disowned by family); Orphaned at 2 & placed in Cockett Cottage Homes; fostered by Thomas & Mary Davies, Bonymaen. Spoke no Welsh until 15. Educated St. Peter's National School, Cockett, Swansea; Gwynfryn Academy, Brynaman; Newcastle Emlyn Academy; University of Wales, Cardiff; Trefecca Theological College. Miner 1888-98. Minister, Presbyterian Church of Wales. Ordained 1905. Pastorates Terrace Road, Swansea 1905; Tabernacl, Cwmafan 1905-09; Willmer Road, Birkenhead 1905-15; Colwyn Bay 1915-27; Catherine Road, Liverpool 1927-41 (& Warden, Liverpool University Settlement 1927-41); Colwyn Bay 1941-4. Moderator, Vale of Conwy Presbytery. Member: Birkenhead Board of Guardians. Chair, Denbigh CLP. Pacifist. Died 7 July 1947. *Books: J. H. Howard: Crefydd a Chymdeithas 1914, Y Bywyd Llawn o'r Ysbryd, Life beyond the Veil 1917, Which Jesus?, Perarogl Crist, Cofiant a Phregethau William Jones 1934, Jesus the Agitator 1935, Winding Lanes (autobiography) 1938.* Further Reading: Ivor Thomas Rees, 'Aristocrat, Pauper and Preacher', *Welsh Journal of Religious History, New Series, Vol. 4, 2004, 65-79.*

HOWARTH Alan Thomas: CBE 1982 BA 1965 MA (Cantab). Labour MP. Newport East 1997-; Crossed the floor & joined Labour, October 1995. Conservative MP Stratford on Avon 1983-97. **Mr. Alan Howarth:** Born London11 June 1944, s of Thomas E. B. Howarth MC TD. (headmaster of St. Paul's School) & Margaret Howarth. Married 1967, Gillian Martha, d of Arthur Chance, Dublin, 2s 2d; divorced 1996. Educated Rugby School; Kings College, Cambridge. Vice-Chair: Conservative Party 1980-81. Director, Conservative Research Dept. 1979-81. Senior Research Assistant to Field Marshal. Public Affairs Adviser to Baring Brothers & Co. 1982-. Member of Lloyds. Governor: Royal Shakespeare Theatre 1984-; Warwick University 1987-; Birmingham University 1992-. Board Member, Institute of Historical Research 1992. Member, Select Cttee: Social Security, 1996-. Chair, Charities & Voluntary Sector Parliamentary Panel; All-Party Disablement Group. Vice-Chair, Southern Africa/Britain All Party Group. PPS 1985-87. Asst Whip 1987-88. Lord Commissioner of the Treasury 1988-89. Under-Secretary, Education & Science

(Labour) 1998-2001. Member: GMB. Hobbies: Hill walking, Reading, The Arts. A poet.

HOWE Martin Russell Thomson: QC 1996 BA. 1977 MA (Cantab) 1979. Conservative: Neath 1987. **Mr. Martin Howe:** Born London 26 June 1955, s of Colin Thomson Howe, surgeon, & Dr. Angela Brock, haematologist, d of Baron Brock (nephew, of Geoffrey Howe qv). Church of England. Married 1989 Lynda Barnett, 3c. Educated Winchester; Trinity College, Cambridge (Engineering & Law). Barrister, Middle Temple, 1978. Joint-Editor, *Halsbury's Law on Trade Marks, 1984, 985.* Editor: *Russell-Clarke on Industrial Designs (6th Ed 1996).* Member: Society of Conservative Lawyers (Vice-Chair, Executive). Hammersmith & Fulham BC 1982-86 (Chair, Planning Cttee). Interests: European & British Constitutional Affairs. *Publications: Europe & the Constitution after Masstricht (1992), Protecting the Foundations of Nationhood (2001).* Of London.

HOWE Richard Edward Geoffrey, Baron Howe of Aberavon 1992: PC 1972 Kt 1970 QC 1965 JP (Glam) 1966 MA (Cantab) Hon. LLD (Liverpool) 1990; Grand Cross of the Order of Merit of the Federal Republic of Germany 1992. Conservative: Aberavon 1955, 1959; MP Bebington 1964-66, Reigate 1970-74, East Surrey 1974-92. **Rt. Hon. Sir Geoffrey Howe:** Born 20 December 1920, s of Edward Howe, Port Talbot solicitor, & Elizabeth Florence Thompson. Anglican. Married 1953 Elspeth Rosamund Morton Shand, 3c. Educated Winchester; Trinity Hall, Cambridge. (Chair, Cambridge University Conservative Assn 1951; Vice-President, Cambridge University Law Society). Lieutenant, Royal Signals 1945-48. Barrister, Middle Temple 1951, Bencher 1969. Member: General Council of the Bar 1957-61; Executive of *Justice* 1963; Deputy Chair, Glamorgan Quarter Sessions, 1966-70. Chair: Bow Group 1955-56. Managing Director, *Crossbow* 1957-6- (Editor 1960-62). Opposition Spokesman: Labour & Social Services 1965-66. Solicitor General 1970-72. Minister for Trade & Consumer Affairs 1972-74. Opposition Spokesman: Treasury & Economic Affairs 1975-79. Chancellor of the Exchequer 1979-83. Foreign Secretary 1983-90. President: Conservative Political Centre National Advisory Cttee. 1977-79; National Union of Conservative & Unionist Assns1983-84. Company Director: EMI Ltd 1976-79; Sun Alliance & London Insurance Group 1974-79; AGC Research Group 1974-79; BICC plc 1991-; Glaxo Holdings 1991-. Chair, Framlingham Russian Investment Fund 1994. President: Great Britain-China Centre 1992; Consumers' Assn. 1993-. Vice-President: British-American Parliamentary Group. Chair, Ely Hospital, Cardiff, Enquiry 1969. Visitor, SOAS, London University 1991-. Visiting Fellow: John F. Kennedy School of Government, Havard University 1990-; Centre for European Studies 1992-. Member: Advisory Council, Presidium of Supreme Soviet of Ukraine 1991-; Council of Management, Private Patients Plan, 1969-70; Steering Cttee. Project Liberty; Patron, Enterprise Europe 1990-. Special Adviser: European & International Affairs, Law Firm of Jones, Day, Reavis & Pogue. Member: International Councils of J. P. Morgan & Co; Stanford University Institute for International Studies; Bertselsmann Foundation, Bonn. Hon. Fellow: RIBA 1990; Leeds Polytechnic 1988; Freeman, Port Talbot 1992. *Books: Geoffrey Howe, Conflict of Loyalty, 1995.* Further Reading: *J. Hillman & P. Clarke, Geoffrey Howe, a Quiet Revolutionary, 1988.*

HOWELL John Dawkin Arnold: BSc (Bristol). Plaid Cymru: Caerphilly 1959, 1964. **Mr. John Howell:** Born Pakistan, October 1928 (lived with aunt at Nelson 1932-). Married 3c. Educated Llanfabon Primary School; Clifton College, Bristol; Bristol University (Engineering). Engineer (at Hoover Ltd. Merthyr Tydfil). Science Teacher. Contested Cardiff CC 1973.

HOWELL William Tudor: BA BCL (Oxon). Conservative MP Denbigh District 1895-1900. **Mr. Tudor Howell:** Born Pwllheli 15 October 1862, s of Revd David Howell (later Dean of St. Davids) & Ann, d of David Powell. Anglican. Married 1888, Julie divorced (?) 1900. Educated Wrexham Grammar School; Shrewsbury School; New College, Oxford. Barrister, Inner Temple 1887. Of London. Went to Canada & 'disappeared from the scene'. Estate £3,396. Died Canada, 3 October 1911.

HOWELLS Anne L: Plaid Cymru: Aberavon 1987. **Miss Anne Howells:** Born Aberavon, 1956. Educated St. David's College, Lampeter. Plaid Cymru Organiser, Denbigh. University of Wales Press Editor. Languages: Welsh, English.

HOWELLS Geraint Wyn, Baron Geraint of Ponterwyd 1992: Liberal (Democrat) Brecon & Radnor 1970; MP Cardigan 1974-83; Ceredigion & N. Pembs.1983-92. **Mr. Geraint Howells:** Born Ponterwyd, 15 April 1925, s of David John Howells & Mary Blodwen Howells, farmers. Presbyterian Church of Wales Elder. Married 1957, Mary Olwen Hughes, d of M. A. Griffiths, 2d. Educated Ardwyn School, Aberystwyth. Fellow, Royal Agricultural Society. Farmer & champion sheep shearer. Managing Director, Wilkinson & Stairs, Meat Wholesalers, Manchester. Chair, Wool Producers of Wales Ltd. 1977-81. Secretary, Ponterwyd Eisteddfod 1944-c.2000. President: International Sheep Dog Society 1983; Royal Welsh Agricultural Show. Vice-Chair, British Wool Marketing Board 1971-

83. Cardiganshire CC 1952-74. Chair: Liberal Party of Wales, (President 1974-78, Leader 1979-83). Chair, Liberal Party By-Election Unit 1987-88. President, Liberal Democrats Wales. Member: Speaker's Panel of Chairmen 1987-92, Select Cttee. for Wales 1979-87. Lord in Waiting to the Queen. Deputy Speaker, House of Lords 1994. Hon. Member, Gorsedd. Hobbies: Walking, sport. Languages: Welsh, English. Of Ponterwyd. Further Reading: *John Graham Jones in "Dictionary of Liberal Biography", 1998, pages 186-188.*

HOWELLS Gerald: Plaid Cymru: Merthyr Tydfil & Rhymney 1983. **Mr. Gerald Howells:** Born Pontlottyn 1942, miner's son. Married Janice, 1c. Educated Lewis School, Pengam. RAF 5 years. Quantity Controller. AUEW Convenor. Plaid Cymru National Field Organiser.Mid-Glam CC. Rhymney Valley DC. Of Pontlottyn.

HOWELLS Kim Scott: BA 1974 PhD 1979. Hon. Dr. (East Anglia). Labour MP Pontypridd B/E 1989-. **Dr. Kim Howells:** Born Merthyr Tydfil 27 November 1946, s of Glanville James Howells & Joan Glenys Howells. *Raised a Wesleyan but probably now as Agnostic as anyone else at Westminster* (quoted in *Western Mail*). Married 1983 Eirlys, d of William & Glenda Davies, 2s 1d. Educated Mountain Ash Grammar School; Hornsey College of Art; Cambridge College of Advanced Technology; Warwick University. Steelworker, East Moors Steelworks, Cardiff, 1969-70. Miner 1970-71. Lecturer/Tutor, Cambridgeshire College of Arts & Technology 1975-79. Research Officer, Coalfield History Research Project, University of Wales, Swansea 1979-82; South Wales Area, National Union of Mineworkers 1982-89. Freelance Radio & Television Broadcaster 1986-89. Member, Communist Party. Joined Labour Party 1983. Select Committees Member: Welsh Affairs 1989-90, Environment 1990-91, House of Commons Sittings, 1991-92. Opposition Spokesman: Development & Co-operation 1993-94; Foreign & Commonwealth Affairs 1994; Home Affairs, 1994-95; Trade & Industry 1995-97. Under-Secretary, Education & Employment 1997-98. Minister for Consumer Affairs, 1998-99. Under-Secretary, Trade & Industry 1999-2001. Minister for Tourism, Film & Broadcasting, June 2001. Member: Pontypridd RFC; British Mountaineering Council. Hobbies: Mounteering, Films, Literature, Art, Jazz. Of Pontypridd.

HOWELLS Nigel: BSc (Wales). MICAEW. Liberal Democrat, South/Central List 1999. **Mr. Nigel Howells:** Born Haverfordwest, 11 August 1966, s of Brynley Aneurin Howells, builder, & Rhian Thomas. Unmarried. Educated Letterston Primary School; Fishguard Secondary School; University of Wales, Cardiff (Pure & Applied Maths & Astronomy). Chartered Accountant.

Treasurer: Cardiff Central Liberal Democrat; Welsh Liberal Democrats. Cardiff CCC 1999. Interests: Environment, Education. Hobbies: Keep Fit, Rugby (Member Cardiff RFC). Languages: Welsh, English. Of Adamstown, Cardiff.

HOWELLS Phillip Bernard: BA 1980 MBA 1993 DipMan MICM MIMGT MIDM. Conservative, Islwyn 2001. Born Much Wenlock 20 April 1947, son Reginald Bernard Howells, herdsman, & Edith Mary Scott. Church of England. Married (1) divorced (2) 1992 Margaret Howells (died 1997) 2 adopted sons. Educated Shrewsbury Technical High School; Wolverhampton University (Business Studies); Warwick University. Electronics Engineer 1963-66. Army Officer, Royal Regiment of Fusiliers 1966-72. Manager, Ford Electronics Ltd 1972-74. Self-employed 1974-76. Founder-Director, Allen-Martin Electronics Ltd 1976-81. Own Marketing Company 1981. Managing Director, Worcester market research & consultancy company. Management Consultant, Romtec Ltd 1989-96. Managing Director, Routes to Market Interactive Ltd 1996-. Member: national & local cycling cttees. Interests: Small Businesses; Countryside, Farming; Environment; Technology. Hobbies: Sport (keen runner and cyclist), Reading, Music; Voluntary fund raising for charity. Of Budleigh Salterton, Devon.

HOWLETT William: MBE 1959 JP (Glam). Labour: Cardiff North 1950. **Mr. William Howlett:** Born Port Talbot 1899. Married Alice. Steel worker. NUGMW Organiser until 1952. South Wales Organiser Transport & General Workers Union 1952-. Joined Labour Party 1917. Of Cardiff.

HUBBARD Marc Antony: Plaid Cymru, Monmouth & South/East List 1999, 2001. **Mr. Marc Hubbard:** Born Caerleon, 21 April 1958. Married, separated, 2c. Educated Basseleg School; Newcastle University; University of Wales, Swansea. Social Care Consultant. Chair/Secretary, London Branch, Plaid Cymru. Press Officer, Monmouth Branch. Interests: Social Welfare, Public Transport, Sustainable Development, Environment, Freedom of Information. Hobbies: Walking, Cinema, Theatre, Watching Rugby. Of Chesham, Bucks. then Caerphilly .

HUBBARD-MILES Peter Charles: CBE 1987. Conservative: Aberavon Feb. 1974; MP Bridgend 1983-87. **Mr. Peter Hubbard-Miles:** Born Mynydd-Islwyn 9 May 1927, s of Charles Hubbard Miles & Agnes Lewis (father died before he was born). Married (1) 1945 Pamela Wilkinson 5c; divorced 1969; (2) 1975. Educated Lewis School, Pengam. RAF 1945-48. Self-employed businessman since 1948 (Owns hairdresser & tourist gift shops) 1948. Glamorgan CC 1967-74. Mid-Glam CC 1974-83 (Group Leader 1974-83). Ogwr BC 1974-83 (Group Leader; Mayor 1979-80). Porthcawl UDC 1970-74. PPS 1976-83. President: Aberavon Conservative Assn. Chair: Wales Conservative Local Govt. Advisory Council 1979-83. Governor, Bridgend Technical College 1977-81. Of Porthcawl.

HUGHES Albert: JP (Caerns). Conservative: Anglesey 1929, 1931. **Mr. Albert Hughes:** Born Llanrwst. Anglican: Stonemason. Member, Church Defence League 1904-14. Llanrwst UDC 1908-, Chairman. Languages: Welsh, English. Of Llanrwst.

HUGHES Alfred William: FRCS. Conservative: Arfon 1895. **Professor Alfred Hughes:** Born Corris 1 July 1861, s of Captain Robert Pryce Hughes, Quarry Manager, & Jane Hughes (brother of Arthur qv). Anglican. Professor of Anatomy, Kings College, London. With his brother, Arthur he formed and maintained a military hospital in South Africa during the Boer War. Languages: Welsh, English. Died, London, 13 November 1900, of enteric fever, which he contracted in South Africa.

HUGHES Anthony: Natural Law Party: Cardiff Central 1997.

HUGHES Arthur Edward: MA (Cantab). Conservative: Arfon 1906, Jan 1910. **Mr. Arthur Hughes:** Born Corris 1868, s of Captain Robert Pryce Hughes, Slate Quarries Manager, Aberllefeni & Jane Hughes; brother of Alfred (qv). Anglican. Married Mary Vivian Educated Friars School, Bangor; Sydney Sussex College, Cambridge. Barrister, Grays Inn. With his brother Alfred he formed and maintained a hospital during the Boer War. Of New Barnet. Estate £786. Died London, 9 February 1918, after accident.

HUGHES Cledwyn: Baron Cledwyn of Penrhos 1979: CH 1979 PC 1966 Hon. LLD Wales 1970, Sheffield 1992 LIB (Wales) 1937. Labour: Anglesey 1945, 1950; MP 1951-79. **Rt. Hon. Cledwyn Hughes:** Born Holyhead 16 September 1911, s of Revd Henry David Hughes & Emily Hughes. Presbyterian Church of Wales elder & lay preacher. Married 1949 Jean Beatrice Hughes 2c. Educated Holyhead Grammar School; University of Wales, Aberystwyth (Chair, Liberal Society). RAF 1940-46, Flying Officer. Solicitor 1946. Clerk, Holyhead UDC 1946-52. Member of Court: University of Wales; National Library; National Museum. Member: Parliament for Wales Campaign Cttee 1951. Chair: Welsh Parliamentary Party 1953-54; Welsh Labour Group 1955-56. Opposition Spokesman: Housing & Local Government 1954-64. Minister of State, Commonwealth

Relations 1964-66. Secretary of State for Wales 1966-68. Minister of Agriculture, Fisheries & Food 1968-70. Opposition Spokesman: Agriculture 1970-72. Chair: Parliamentary Labour Party 1975-79; TUC/Labour Party Liaison Cttee 1974-79. Member: Cttee of Privileges 1974. Deputy Leader of the Opposition in the House of Lords 1981-82, Leader 1982-92. President of Council, University of Wales, Bangor, 1976-84. Pro-Chancellor, University of Wales 1985-94. President: Assn of Welsh Counties 1990-; Housing & Town Planning Council 1980-92; Age Concern, Wales 1980-85; Society of Welsh People Overseas 1979-81. Hon. Freeman: Beaumaris 1972, Anglesey 1976. Company Director: Shell UK Ltd 1980-84; Anglesey Aluminium Ltd 1980-; Holyhead Towing Co 1980-. Regional Adviser (Wales) Midland Bank Ltd 1979. Chair: Welsh Theatre Co 1981-85. Languages: Welsh, English. Of Trearddur, Anglesey. Died 22 February 2001. *Papers at National Library of Wales.*

HUGHES Colin Lucas: Rhuddlan Debt Protest Campaign, North List 1999. **Mr. Colin Lucas:** Retired civil servant. Chair, Denbighshire School Governors Assn. Contested Denbighshire CC 1999. Of Denbigh.

HUGHES Craig Parry: LIB (Wales) 1938. Conservative: Merioneth 1945. **Mr. Parry Hughes:** Born Merioneth 1918, s of Owen Parry Hughes, clerk, Felinwen. Married Nancy Wayne Brydon, of New York. Educated Dolgellau Grammar School; University of Wales, Aberystwyth. Solicitor. Royal Navy, Able Seaman 1940-43. Asst. Solicitor to Blackpool Corporation until 1945. Resigned to fight the election. Asst Solicitor, West Riding County Council 1947-. Languages: Welsh, English.

HUGHES Dafydd John Lewys – see HUWS D. J. L.

HUGHES Daniel: JP. (Mon). Labour: Monmouth 1931, B/E 1934. **Revd Daniel Hughes:** Born Minera, Denbighshire 1st April1875, s of Robert Hughes, bookseller, & Ann Hughes. Married 1d. Educated Manchester Baptist College. Miner & Steelworker. Baptist Minister, Ordained 1898: Darwen 1898-1902; Grosvenor Park, Chester 1904-06; Churches of Christ, Upper Parliament Street, Liverpool 1906-08 (sent to prison for ten days as a *Passive Resister* 27/2/1907); Calfaria, Llanelli 1908-09; Pontypool 1909-13 (dismissed 1912; broke open church doors and nicknamed *The Sledgehammer Pastor*; Dispute at High Court 1913). Removed from Roll of Ministers of Baptist Union of Great Britain and Ireland 1913. RAMC, Sergeant 1915-19, Machen, 1921-72 (opposed by deacons 1936, who fitted new church locks which Hughes opened with a skeleton key); Detroit

136

Welsh Presbyterian Church 1939-53 (edited *Mawl a Chân* North American Welsh Churches' Bi-Lingual hymn book). Monmouthshire CC 1913-16, 1928-45; Bedwas & Machen UDC (Chairman 1935-36). Languages: Welsh, English, Esperanto. Died 9 May 1972. *Further Reading:* Ivor Thomas Rees, 'Sledgehammer: Daniel Hughes, the Sledge-hammer Pastor, 1875-1972', *Journal of the National Library of Wales, Vol. XXXII, Winter 2001, 147-176.*

HUGHES David Emrys: Natural Law Party, Conwy 1997, North List 1999, Wales Euro 1999. **Mr. David Hughes:** Born Bangor 27 October 1954, s of Cyril Hughes, teacher, & Marjorie Hughes, librarian. Educated John Bright Grammar School, Llandudno. Trained in Science of Creative Intelligence 1974. Teacher of Transcendental Meditation 1975-. Writer. Leader of Natural Law Party, Wales. Anti Genetically Modified Foods Campaigner 1996-. Hobbies: Hill walking (mostly in Snowdonia), Swimming. Of Skelmersdale.

HUGHES Eric – see HUGHES Griffith Eric.

HUGHES Frank Roger Wynne: UK Independence, Cardiff Central 2001, Cardiff West & South/Central List 2003. **Mr. Frank Hughes:** Born, Roath, Cardiff 19 June 1940, s of Charles Richard Hughes (Area Manager, Penmaenmawr & Welsh Granite Co) & Tegwen Mefis (teacher). Protestant. Unmarried. Educated Marlborough Road School, Cardiff; King's College, Taunton; Llandaff Technical College. Local Government Officer 12 years. London Electricity Board (Admin) 9 years. Worked in hotel business (Chester). Insurance Agent (Cardiff). Pensions Administrator (London) 1996. Retired. Joined Referendum Party 1996. Helped founded Democracy Movement Branch, Chair. Joined UK Independence Party 1998. Cttee Member, Wales Branch UKIP. Treasurer UKIP Wales. Chair: South Wales Central Branch, Democracy Movement. Member: Glamorgan Cricket Club; Supporter Cardiff City FC. Hobbies: Reading; Watching Cricket, Rugby & other Sports. Of Llanishen, Cardiff.

HUGHES Glyn – see HUGHES John G.

HUGHES Glyn – see MÔN HUGHES R. G.

HUGHES Glyn Tegai: BA 1949 MA PhD (Cantab). Liberal: Denbigh 1950, 1955, 1959. **Dr. Glyn Tegai Hughes:** Born Chester, January 1923, s of Revd John Hughes & Keturah Evans. Methodist Lay preacher. Married Margaret Cribb of Australia, 2s. Educated Newtown, Tywyn & Liverpool Grammar Schools; Corpus Christi College, Cambridge 1940-42, 1946-51. Army 1942-46, Major RWF. Asst. Adjutant General SEAC. President: Cambridge University Liberal Assn. Chair: Cymdeithas y Mabinogion,

Union of University Liberal Societies. Lecturer in English, Basle University 1951-53. Lecturer in Comparative Literary Studies, Manchester University 1953-63. Warden, Gregynog Hall 1964-89. Member: Liberal Party Council & Executive; Arts Council for Wales (Chair: Literary Panel 1967-76. National Governor for Wales, BBC. Chair: Liberal Party of Wales; North Wales Society for the Arts; Broadcasting Council for Wales 1971-76; Welsh Broadcasting Trust 1988, Undeb Cymru Fydd 1979. Member: Council of Social Service for Wales; Court of National Library & National Museum. Director: Channel 4 Television Co. 1980-87; Welsh 4th Channel Authority 1981-87. Vice-President: North Wales Arts Assn 1974-94. Hon. Fellow, University of Wales, Aberystwyth 2001. Languages: Welsh, English. *Books: Glyn Tegai Hughes, Williams Pantycelyn 1983, Daniel Owen a Natur y Nofel, Bibliography of Comparative Literature in Britain and Ireland* (compiler) 1982, *Romantic German Literature 1979.*

HUGHES Griffith Eric: Labour: Ceredigion & North Pembs 1983. **Mr. Eric Hughes:** Born Aberporth 24 September 1925. Married Shan, school cook, 2d. Educated Cardigan Grammar School. Postman. Member, UPOW. Aberystwyth TC. Ceredigion DC. Dyfed CC 1974-. Member: Wales Council for the Disabled; Development Board for Rural Wales. Resigned from Labour Party 1998. Contested Cardiganshire CC 1999. Languages: Welsh, English. Of Aberystwyth.

HUGHES Gwilym: Plaid Cymru: Conway 1964; East Flint 1966, 1970. **Mr. Gwilym Hughes:** Born Amlwch March 1934. Married Educated Sir Thomas Jones School, Amlwch; Bangor Normal College, 1955-57. Apprentice carpenter 1950-53. RAF 1953-55. Art Teacher, Hull CofE School; Fishguard Secondary School; Ysgol Glan Clwyd. Rhyl UDC 1968-. Contested local elections 1961-67. Founder/Chair: Foryd Drama Group. Secretary, then Chair, Plaid Cymru East Flint; Member, Plaid Cymru National Executive. Languages: Welsh; English. Of Rhyl.

HUGHES Hugh: JP (Denbs). Labour: Wrexham 1918; Resigned as PPC 1920 in order to devote himself to union affairs. **Mr. Hugh Hughes:** Born Easington Lane near Hetton-le-Hole, Co. Durham, 4 November 1878, s of Alderman Edward Hughes JP, General Secretary, North Wales Miners' Assn (died 1925) & Elizabeth (née Hughes). Married Liverpool 1905, Eliza Jane, d of William & Mary Ann Jones, 2s 4d. Educated South Hetton Church School until 1887; Llanasa Church School; declined a place at Newmarket Grammar School. Miner, Point of Ayr, then Trelogan lead mine. Farm blacksmith. Worked at Point of Ayr Colliery; Liverpool Docks Board, then Wrexham coalfield. Checkweighman, Coed Talon Colliery. Financial Secretary, North Wales Miners' Assn 1915-25; Succeeded father as General Secretary & Agent 1925. Executive Member, Miners Federation of Great Britain. President, North Wales Trades & Labour Council 1918. Denbighshire CC 1921-, Alderman 1925. Of Wrexham. Estate £787. Died Wrexham 25 December 1932. Further Reading: *Keith Gildart, Men of Coal, Llafur, Vol. 8, No. 1, 2000.*

HUGHES Huw Moelwyn – see MOELWYN HUGHES H.

HUGHES John Glyn: LIB (Wales) 1946. Labour: Denbigh 1950, City of Chester 1951. **Mr. Glyn Hughes:** Born January 1923, s of a police sergeant). Educated Brompton Avenue Elementary School, Colwyn Bay; Denbigh Grammar School; University of Wales, Aberystwyth. Government of Rhodesia Legal Dept 1946-48. WEA tutor. Barrister. Languages: Welsh, English.

HUGHES John Roberts: Labour: Denbigh 1935, **Mr. John Hughes:** Born 1901. Educated Port Dinorwic & Caernarfon Central Schools; Coleg Harlech. Railway Clerk. Member, Railway Clerks Assn. Llanfairisgaer PC. Languages: Welsh, English. Of Port Dinorwic.

HUGHES John Williams: Liberal: Flint 1945, Anglesey 1955. **Mr. John Williams Hughes:** Born Marianglas 1906. Educated Llangefni Grammar School. Local Government Officer, Anglesey Education Dept 1931-36. Hon. Secretary, Appeal for Ambulances for Spain. With Welsh Ambulance Brigade in Spanish Civil War 1936-38. Army 1939-45; Major, Army School of Education. Journalist, writer, lecturer & broadcaster. Secretary, Hon. Society of Cymmrodorion 1953. Member, English Speaking Union. Languages: Welsh, English. Died 6 March 1977.

HUGHES Juliana Marie-Jane: JP (Carms). BA. DipEd. (Wales). Liberal (Democrat): Carmarthen 1992, Mid-Wales Euro 1984; Carmarthenshire East & Dinefwr 1997, 1999; Wales Euro 1999. **Mrs. Juliana Hughes:** Born Llangennech 30 November 1944, d of Gwynfryn Aaron Williams, mineworker, & Margaret Mia Williams. Church in Wales. Married 1969, John Maelgwyn Hughes, solicitor, divorced, 2s 1d. Educated Llanelli Grammar School; University of Wales, Aberystwyth. Teacher 15 years (Amman Valley & Whitland). House Manager. BBC & ITV Presenter. Hon. Member, Gorsedd. Member, St. Davids Diocesan Board of Social Responsibility. Joined Liberal Party 1982. Chair: Carmarthen Liberal Assn. Member: Welsh Liberal Democrat Party Executive & Policy Cttee; Liberal Democrat Federal Policy Cttee 9 years. Translator of Party documents. Media Spokesman 6 years. Council Member, Macmillan (cancer) Trust. Strongly opposed Assembly Coalition at Liberal Democrat Day Conference Oct. 2000. Interests: Education, Tourism, Legal Matters. Hobbies: Gardening. Languages: Welsh; English; French. Of Rhydargaeau.

HUGHES Loti R. – see REES-HUGHES L.

HUGHES Mark James: Conservative: Merthyr Tydfil & Rhymney 1992. **Mr. Mark Hughes:** Born 23 September 1961, s of Kenneth James Hughes & Diana Russell Bennett. Married 1986, Hazel Jane Pleasaunce. Educated Sheredes School, Herts; Kingsway Princeton College, London. Communications Manager, GKN Stern Osmat 1980-88. Computer Operations Controller, East Herts DC 1985-89. Company Director, Lighting Skills Ltd. Football referee. Joined Conservatives 1979. Chair: Broxbourne Young Conservatives 1983-84. Vice-Chair: North Hertfordshire Conservative Assn 1987-88. Branch Treasurer, National Association of Local Government Officers 1986-88. Royston BC 1987 (Mayor 1990-91). North Herts DC. Member CAB. Of Royston, Herts.

HUGHES Owen Hughes: Conservative: Anglesey 1955. **Mr. Owen Hughes:** Born Llanddulas 1912. Anglican. Married 4c. Educated Llanddulas Church School; Abergele Grammar School; Chester Training College. Teacher. Head, Church Primary School. Royal Navy 1941-43. Home Guard 1943-45. President, West Flint Conservative Assn 1954-55. Languages: Welsh, English.

HUGHES Ralph G: Independent, Ogmore, 1999. **Mr Ralph Hughes:** Born Ogmore Vale, 6 November 1949, s of David John Hughes, electrician, & Winifred Mercia Hughes, Married 1975, Mary Hughes, youth leader, 2d. Educated Nantymoel Secondary Modern School; Bridgend College (Btec national certificate). Driving Instructor. Bridgend BC 1995- (Leader of Independent Group, Leader of Opposition; Chair, Social Services & Housing Scrutiny Cttee). Interests: Democracy with a capital 'D'. Hobbies: Family/grandchildren. Of Nantymoel.

HUGHES Robert: JP (Glam 1896 Mon & Hereford). Conservative, Rhondda 1900; Independent Coalition, Cardiff Central 1918, **Mr. Robert Hughes:** Born Llanegryn, Merioneth 20 February 1857, s of John Hughes & Harriet Owen. Anglican. Married 1896 Annie Williams of Lisvane. Educated Llanegryn National School. Clerk at Eagle Breweries. Manager & Director, Brewing Co. Cardiff BC 1892 & CC. (Alderman 1904, last Mayor & 1st Lord Mayor). Chair: Cardiff Conservative Working Men's Club;

Cardiff Central Conservative Assn. Resigned to contest 1918 election when Gould was adopted as candidate to protest at the choosing of three shipowners by the Coalition. Freemason. Member, Royal Commission on Welsh Monuments; Governor, King Edward VII Hospital, Cardiff. Languages: Welsh, English. Of Cardiff. Died 15 April 1945.

HUGHES Robert: BA QTS. Plaid Cymru, Merthyr Tydfil & Rhymney 2001. **Mr. Robert Hughes:** Born Reading, 27 April 1972, s of Albert Hughes, roofer. Married Hesther 1s 1d. Educated Reading Grammar School; Little Heath Comprehensive School; Open University; University of Wales Institute, Cardiff (Psychology). Student teacher (Welsh) & Barman, Bontnewydd Hotel, Treharris. Contested Merthyr Tydfil CBC B/E 2000. Secretary, Merthyr Tydfil Constituency, Plaid Cymru 1999-2000. Organised Dic Penderyn Festival 2000. Campaigner with *Justice for Miners* Group. Member: Treharris Regeneration Assn. Ex-player, Treharris AFX XI; Member: Trelewis AFC XI; Wales Historical Forum. Interests: Miners' Compensation; Social Deprivation; Social Injustice. Hobbies: Cardiff City FC supporter; Playing & watching football & rugby; Environment action groups. Languages: Learned Welsh, English, French. Of Quakers Yard (1997).

HUGHES R. Meirion: Labour: West Flint 1979. **Mr. Meirion Hughes:** Born Anglesey, February 1948 s of Presbyterian Minister. Married Gay, warden, sheltered housing, 1 d. Educated Alun School, Mold; Bangor Normal College; Liverpool Polytechnic. Ex-Teacher. Social Worker 1972-. Member: NALGO, Vale of Clwyd Trades Council. Hobbies: Rugby, Cricket. Languages: Welsh, English. Of Rhyl.

HUGHES Ronw Moelwyn: KC LlB (Wales) BA LlB (Cantab). Liberal: Rhondda West 1929, Southport 1931; Joined Labour Party 1933; Labour: Cardigan 1935; MP Carmarthen B/E 1940-45, Islington North 1950-51. **Mr. Moelwyn Hughes:** Born Cardigan October 1897, s of Revd Dr. J. G. Moelwyn Hughes, Presbyterian Minister & Moderator, General Assembly, Presbyterian Church of Wales. Married Hon. Mary Louise, d of 3rd Baron Fairfield, 3c. Educated Cardigan Grammar School; University of Wales, Aberystwyth; Cambridge University (1st, Law; Chancellor's Gold Medal in English Law). Barrister, Inner Temple. Army 1916; RFC & RAF 1917-19. Lecturer in Law. Recorder of Bolton 1946-53. Chair: Catering Wages Commission; Cotton Manufacturing Commission; Greater London Water Enquiry 1947. Special Assistant, Controller for Wales, Local Government Boundary Commission. Commissioner for Bolton Football Disaster Enquiry 1946. Birkenhead BC. Ealing BC. Member: Fabian Society; Haldane Society; Society of Teachers of Public Law. Languages: Welsh, English. Of London. Estate £1,437. Died 1 November 1956. *Books etc: R. M. Hughes, 7th Edition, Lord Birkenhead's International Law (edit) 1928, Agency, Bills of Exchange, Money & Money-lending in Halsbury's Laws of England (2nd edit 1931-35), Road and Rail Traffic Act (with Dingle Foot) 1933.*

HUGHES R. G. M. – see MÔN HUGHES R. G.

HUGHES Royston John, Baron Islwyn of Casnewydd 1997: DL (Gwent) 1992. Labour MP: Newport 1966-83; Newport East 1983-97. **Mr. Roy Hughes:** Born Pontllanffraith 9 June 1925, s of John Hughes, collier, & Alice Tucker. Married 1957, Florence Marion Appleford of Coventry 3d. Educated Pontllanffraith Secondary School. Clerical Administrative Officer 1957-59. TGWU Officer, Coventry 1959-66. Secretary, Coventry City Labour Party 1962-66. Coventry CC 1962-66. Chair: Welsh Parliamentary Party 1969-70, Welsh Grand Cttee 1982-84, 1990-97. Member: Council of Europe & WEU 1991, Speaker's Panel of Chairmen 1990. PPS 1974. Opposition Spokesman 1984-88. Joint-Vice Chair: Rugby Union Group 1993-97; All Party Road Group 1983-97; All Party Motors Group 1986-97. Vice-President: Crawshays RFC XV; Glamorgan CCC. Life Member, Newport RFC. President, Newport Athletic Club 1997-. Hobbies; Gardening, Watching Rugby, Cricket & Football. Of Abergavenny. Died 19 December 2003.

HUGHES Thomas Mervyn: QC 1994 LlB (Liverpool). Labour: Caernarfon 1979. **Mr. Merfyn Hughes:** Born Rhuddlan 8 April 1949, s of John Medwyn Hughes, bank manager & Mayor of Anglesey 1877-78, & Blodwen Jane Roberts. Married 1977, Patricia Joan, d of John Talbot FRCS, 3c. Educated Ysgol Abermad, Aberystwyth; Rydal School, Colwyn Bay; Liverpool University. Barrister, Inner Temple 1968. Asst Recorder 1987-91. Recorder 1991. Circuit Judge 12 May 2001. President, Mental Health Tribunal 1999. Member: Wales & Chester Circuit Management Board. Chair: Chester Bar Assn. Member: Law Society Legal Aid Cttee; Amnesty International; TGWU. Hobbies: Current Affairs; Politics; Theatre; Arts; Playing Rugby. Languages: Welsh, English. Of Beaumaris.

HUGHES William: Conservative, Swansea East 1999. **Mr Bill Hughes:** Born Ffair Rhos, Ceredigion 1932. Teacher 15 years. Company Director 40 years. Retired nightclub owner. West Glam CC 1977-89. Swansea CCC 1983-93. Contested CCC (Morriston Ward) 1999. Chair: Gower Conservative Assn 1991-94; Mumbles Conservative Club 6 years; Swansea East Conservative Assn;

Castle Ward Branch. President, South Wales Euro Conservative Assn. Vice-President, Young Conservative Future. Member: Welsh Industrial Council, European Committee of the Regions, Swansea City Forum for Redevelopment of City Centre, Cefn Coed & Llwynderw Hospital Management Cttee, Tŷ Olwen Hospice Action Cttee, Oystermouth NSPCC Cttee. Chair, Oystermouth School Governors. Chair of Finance, Gowerton Urdd National Eisteddfod 1983. Hon. Life Member, Swansea Sportsman's Club. Area Chair, South West Wales Conservative Party, Oct. 1999, resigned July 2001 in order to campaign for the setting up of a separate Welsh party organisation. Languages: Welsh, English. Of Ynystawe, Swansea.

HUGHES-EVANS Idris: Liberal: Denbigh 1960. **Mr. Idris Hughes-Evans:** Born Meifod, Mont, April 1941, farmer's son; moved to Llangollen 1944. Married 1962. 3c. Educated Lindisfarne College, Ruabon. Sales Executive. Welsh Liberal Spokesman on Tourism. Languages: Welsh, English. Of Llangollen.

HUGHES GRIFFITHS Llyr: Plaid Cymru, Carmarthen West & Pembrokeshire South 2001. **Mr. Llyr Hughes Griffiths:** Born Aberystwyth, 25 September 1970. Educated Ysgol Gyfun Bro Myrddin; University of Wales, Aberystwyth. President, NUS Wales. Election Co-ordinator, Assembly & Euro Elections. Political Researcher, Plaid Cymru MEPs. Senior Development Officer, Welsh Youth Agency. Carmarthen TC, Sheriff, Mayor 2000-01. Schools Governor. Chair, Carmarthen & District Forum. Member: CATCH (Campaign for Action on Tenby Hospital); Taft Myrddin Area Forum; Dairy Crest West Wales Action Group. President: Dr. M's Youth Project in Carmarthen; Wales Young Framers' Club National Board of Management. UK Representative, European Bureau for Lesser-Used Languages for Youth. Interests: Voluntary sector, Youth affairs, Europe, Rural affairs. Hobbies: Sport, Music. Languages: Welsh, English. Of Carmarthen.

HUGHES-PARRY John Dafydd: LlB (Bristol). Liberal, West Flint 1979, Delyn 1983. **Mr. John Hughes-Parry:** Born Bristol 1935. Married Valmai, 2s 2d. Educated Clifton College, Bristol; Bristol University. Solicitor (at Holywell 1962). Secretary, Halkyn Countryside Cttee. Joined Liberal Party 1974. Liberal Agent, West Flint. Member: Mold Male Voice Choir; Mold CAB Management Cttee. Hobbies: Rugby, Classical Music & Jazz. Languages: English, French, German. Of Halkyn.

HULSTON Donald Edwin: JP 1979. UK Independence Party, Cardiff North 2001, 2003. **Mr Don Hulston:** Born Acocks Green, Birmingham 2 January 1932, s of Leonard Wilfred Hulston,

sales manager, and Marion Burton, shop cashier. United Reformed Church. Married 1957, Audrey Elizabeth Richmond 1s 1d. Educated Solihull School. Managing Director, small Cardiff wholesale drapery. Active Conservative, 40 years. Member UKIP Welsh Cttee. Chair, UKIP Cardiff & District Branch. Hobbies: Bowls. Of Rhiwbina, Cardiff.

HUME-WILLIAMS William Ellis: 1st Bart 1922 PC 1929 KBE 1918 KStJ QC 1899 MA LlB (Cantab). Conservative: North Mon 1895, Frome 1900, North Kensington 1906; MP Bassetlaw 1910-29. **Rt. Hon. Sir William Hume-Williams:** Born 1863, s of J. W. Hume-Williams, Barrister. Married 1886 Lucy Arbetts, d of James Malet Charter JP DL Somerset. Educated Trinity Hall, Cambridge. Barrister, Middle Temple 1881, Bencher 1906, Treasurer 1929. Recorder: Bury St. Edmunds 1901-05, Norwich 1905. Judge, Midland Circuit. With Munro Ambulance Corps. Flanders 1914-15. Red Cross Commissioner in Russia 1916-17. Of London. Died 4 February 1947.

HUMPHREYS Christine Mary: Liberal Democrat, Conwy 1999, AM North List 1999-2001. **Mrs. Christine Humphreys:** Born 26 May 1947. Married 2s. Educated Llanrwst Grammar School; Kirkby Fields College of Education. Teacher (English) & Vocational Co-ordinator, Ysgol Dŷ Creuddyn, Penrhyn Bay. Colwyn Bay BC (Vice-Chair, Personnel & Planning Cttees). Senior Liberal Democrat Spokesperson, Wales, on Tourism, Transport & Environment. Contested Welsh Liberal Democrat Leadership, November 1988. Deputy Leader, Liberal Democrats, Wales, 1998-2001. Resigned Assembly seat on health grounds, 20.03.2001. Hobbies: Travel, Bird watching, Walking the dog. Languages: Welsh, English. Of Llanrwst.

HUMPHREYS Robert Owen: Liberal Democrat, Bridgend 1999. **Mr. Bob Humphreys:** Born Montgomeryshire 1958, farmer's son. Married Catrin Evans, S4C Journalist, 1d. Educated Ruskin College, Oxford; University of Wales, Cardiff (Economics). Factory Worker. Lecturer in Continuing Education, University of Wales, Swansea. Member: Welsh Liberal Democrat Executive Cttee 1998-, Siarter Cymru-Charter 88 1990-93, Group of the Welsh European Programme Executive. Co-Convenor, *Swansea Says YES*. President: Welsh Liberal Democrats, January 2002. Interests: Community Development, Higher Education, Life Long Earning, Culture, Arts, Electoral Reform. Hobbies: Mountain Climbing (climbed 144 of 185 mountains in Wales), Football, Cinema, Running, Literature, Arts. Of Swansea.

HUMPHREYS William: Conservative: Eifion 1892. **Mr. William Humphreys:** Born 1853. Described when adopted as candidate as s of Thomas Humphreys, Cefn Isa, Llangybi, Caernarfonshire. but told the Registrar of Bankruptcy that he had changed his name from William Humphrey Williams and was the s of Thomas Williams. Calvinistic Methodist but Anti-Disestablishment. Educated Tatton Hall Grammar School. Tenant Farmer, Horse & Cattle Dealer 1876. Took over Aberkin, March 1886 & formed Cattle Partnership. Declared bankrupt in the sum of £6,392. Went to Australia under name of Robinson. Warrant issued for forgery (forging father's signature to a promissory note for £100) and an offence under the Bankruptcy Act (Taking money out of the country). Arrested at Adelaide and brought back under police escort. Appeared before magistrates, 23 July 1895, and sent to Assizes. Appeared before Public Registrar and declared that he had handed over everything but his clothes. Public Registrar's examination closed, 20 November 1895. Languages: Welsh, English. Of Aberkin, near Criccieth. Further Reading: *Yr Herald Gymraeg & Caernarvonshire & Denbighshire Herald).*

HUMPHREYS-EVANS William Ian: Referendum Party: Carmarthenshire East & Dinefwr 1997. **Mr. Ian Humphreys-Evans:** Born 1944, member of a Llandeilo farming family. Married 3c. London Solicitor. Languages: Welsh, English.

HUMPHREYS-OWEN Arthur Charles: JP DL (Mont) BA 1860 MA (Cantab). Liberal MP: Montgomeryshire B/E 1894-1900. **Mr. Arthur Humphreys-Owen:** Born Garthmyl 9 November 1836, s of Erskine Humphreys (added Owen by royal licence to inherit William Owen's Glansevin estate on the death of Mrs. Owen). Anglican. Married 1874 Maria, d of James Russell QC. Educated Harrow; Trinity College, Cambridge. Barrister, Lincolns Inn 1863. Lecturer in Civil Law, Cambridge 1869-70, 1877-83, Law Tripos 1878-81. Landowner (7,736 acres) & Company Chair, Cambrian Railways 1900. Montgomeryshire CC 1889- (1st Chair 1889-90). Governor, University of Wales: Bangor & Aberystwyth. Deputy Chancellor, University of Wales 1895. Chair, Central Welsh Board of Education 1896-1905. Of Glansevin, Berriew. Estate £3,904. Died 9 December 1905.

HUMPHREYS-OWEN Arthur Erskine: JP (Mont) BA (Cantab). Liberal: Montgomery District Dec. 1910. **Mr. Erskine Humphreys-Owen:** Born Berriew, 16 June 1876, s of Arthur Charles Humphreys-Owen MP (qv) & Maria, d of James Russell QC. Anglican. Married 1907 Isabella, d of Sir Edward Sassoon, Bart. Educated Harrow; Trinity College, Cambridge; Germany. Barrister, Lincolns Inn. Landowner. Hon. Attaché, Washington DC 1898-1903; Stockholm, 1903. Lieutenant, SWB (TA) 1907-08; RWF (TA) 1908-10, RWF 1914-18, wounded 1918. Of Glansevin, Berriew. Further Reading: *Kenneth O. Morgan, Peace Movements in Wales 1899-1945, The Welsh History Review, Vol. 10, June 1981, page 401.*

HUNTER JARVIE Thomas: Conservative: Cardiff South & Penarth 1992. **Mr. Thomas Hunter Jarvie:** Born Glasgow 23 March 1944, s of Thomas Jarvie & Doreen Swaithes. Anglican. Married 1971 Christine Minoprio, 2c. Educated Ifield Grammar School, Crawley; Birmingham University. Solicitor. Board Member, Cardiff Bay Development Corporation 1991-. Deputy Chair, Vale of Glamorgan Conservative Assn. President, Bridgend Law Society 1986. Vale of Glamorgan BC 1982-96, 1999- (Mayor 1988-89). Member, Llandaff Diocesan Conference. PCC Treasurer. Of Llanblethian.

HURFORD Jeffrey James: BSc Econ. Welsh Socialist Alliance, Ogmore B/E 14 Feb. 2002. **Mr. Jeff Hurford:** Born London, 18 March 1940, son of James Hurford, stoker, & Evelyn Crick, 1s 2d. Educated secondary modern school; technical college, college of education, university. Teacher, retired. Local organizer: Stop the War Coalition; Valleys Race Equality Council; Anti Poll Tax Movement. Leading activist against racism. Member: Socialist Workers' Party. Chair: PTA. School governor. Interests: Socialism. Hobbies: Gardening, Reading.

HUTCHINGS Ronald William: Referendum Party: Merthyr Tydfil & Rhymney 1997. **Mr. Ronald Hutchings:** Born Taunton 1928. Married (wife died 1996) 3c. Senior Manager in construction industry. Set up his own technical college. Of Cardiff.

HUTCHINSON Geoffrey Clegg, Baron Ilford 1972: Kt 1952 KC 1939 MC 1916 MA (Cantab). National: Gower 1935. Conservative MP Ilford B/E 1937-45, Ilford North 1950-54. **Colonel, Sir Geoffrey Hutchinson:** Born 14 October 1893, s of Henry Omerod Hutchinson VD JP. Anglican. Married Jane Kemp. Educated Cheltenham College; Clare College, Cambridge. Hon. Colonel TA 1948-54. Chair: East Surrey Water Co 1952-54. Company Director, Colne Valley Water Co1948-54. President: British Waterworks Assn 1947; Water Companies Assn. 1951-54; Non County Boroughs Assn. 1937-44. Vice-President: Association of Municipal Corporations 1944-54. Hon. Member, NALGO. Hampstead BC 1949-52 (Alderman 1944-49). Chair: Home Counties Conservative Provincial Council 1946. Hon. Freeman: Ilford 1954, Hampstead, 1956. Member, Church of England Assembly. Chair, National Assistance Board 1964-65. Died 20 August 1974.

HUTT Jane Elizabeth: BA (Kent) 1970 MSc (Bristol). Labour AM Vale of Glamorgan 1999-. **Ms. Jane Hutt:** Born Epsom 15 December 1949, d of Professor Michael S. R. Hutt & Elizabeth Mai Hutt. Married 1984 Michael Hilary Trickey 2d. Educated Highlands School, Eldoret, Kenya; Rosemead School, Littlehampton; Kent University; London School of Economics (Certificate of Qualification in Social Work); Bristol University. Community Worker: Blackfriars Settlement 1970-71, Impact, Cowbridge 1972-74, Polypill, Newport 1974-77. Co-ordinator, Welsh Women's Aid 1978-88, Tenant Participation Advisory Service 1988-92. Director, Chwarae Teg 1992-. South Glam CC (Vice-Chair, Social Services Cttee). Member: Wales New Deal Task Force, Cardiff Community Health Care Trust, New Opportunities Fund (UK) Board. Vice-Chair, Wales Council for Voluntary Service. Special Adviser, MPs Welsh Affairs Select Cttee. Secretary for Health & Social Services 1999; Minister, Health & Social Service Oct, 2000. Hobbies: Music, Walking. Languages: Learned Welsh, English. Of Cardiff.

HUWS Dafydd John Lewys: MB BCh (Wales) 1960 DPM (England) 1963. Plaid Cymru: Cardigan 1979; Cardiff West 1983. **Dr. Dafydd Huws:** Born Aberystwyth, 1937, raised at Llandre. Welsh Independent. Spent early years in Kenya. Married Rhian 1d. Educated Ysgol Rhydpennau, Aberystwyth; Ardwyn School, Aberystwyth; Welsh National School of Medicine. Medical research Council 5 years. Consultant Psychiatrist, Whitchurch Hospital 1970. Vice-President, Cardiff West Plaid Cymru. Chair: Division of Psychiatry, South Glamorgan Area Health Authority; Gwynfe Hostel, Llanishen. Member: Wales Medical Campaign against Nuclear Weapons, UNA. Plaid Cymru Spokesman on Health. Cardiff CC (1st PC member). Languages: Welsh, English. Of Cardiff.

HUWS Haydn: LlB (London). Plaid Cymru: Delyn 1983. **Mr. Haydn Huws:** Born 1953. Married Sara. Educated London University. Caernarfon Solicitor. Gwynedd CC. Chair, Gwynedd Anti-Nuclear Alliance. Languages: Welsh, English.

HUXLEY Norman Llewelyn: Plaid Cymru, Mid & West List 1999. Gwynedd CC (Tywyn). **Mr. Llew Huxley:** Gwynedd CC. Chair 2002. Languages: Welsh, English. Withdrew candidature after Nominations Day. Of Tywyn, Meirionydd.

HYDE Caroline Maureen: Conservative, Merthyr Tydfil & Rhymney and South/East List 1999. **Mrs Caroline Hyde:** Born Swansea, 29 April 1944, d of William Albert Edgar, steel erector, & Edna Pauline Palmer-Davies. Roman Catholic. Married 1968, Henry Anthony Hyde managing director, 1s 1d. Educated Swansea Technical School. WRENS Petty Officer. Local Government Officer. Company Director, retired. Chair: Welsh Conservatives Women's Cttee; Welsh Conservative Party 2002; Mid & West Wales Conservatives Women's Cttee; South Wales West Conservative Women's Cttee; Aberavon Conservative Assn. Group Leader, party parliamentary selection board. Hon. Secretary, Gower Conservative Assn. Member: Conservative Women's Central Cttee; Institute for Welsh Affairs; Swansea Ex-Wrens Assn. Non-Executive Director, Glanymor NHS Trust; Deputy Complaints Convenor. Co-ordinator, Shopping Hours Reform Cttee. Chair, Gower Red Cross. Member: West Glam FHSA/DHA; Institute for Welsh Affairs, Swansea Ex-Wrens Assn. Fund Raiser: Alzheimer's Disease, Marie Curie Fund. Interests: Health, Sports/Leisure, Arts. Hobbies: Entertaining Grandchildren. Of Killay, Swansea, then Murton (2002).

HYDE Clarendon Goulding: Kt 1910 FSS AKC. Liberal: Cardiff District Dec. 1910, Southampton 1900; MP Wednesbury Jan.-Dec. 1910. **Sir Clarendon Hyde:** Born 1858, s of Henry Hyde FSS. Anglican. Married 1886 Laura. d of Canon George Palmer. Educated Royal Institution School, Liverpool; King's College, London. Company Chair, Brazilian North Railways & Director of several companies. Estate £236,164. Of Farringdon, Berks. Died 24 June 1934.

HYDE William: Plaid Cymru: Pontypool 1979. **Mr. Bill Hyde:** Born 1947. Brought up at Manchester & Connahs Quay. Educated Ruskin College, Oxford. Collier 1962. Rigger at Bedwas Colliery. AUEW Shop Steward 3 years. Of Abertridwr. Contested Caerphilly BC 1999.

IDRIS Thomas Howell Williams: JP (London & Merioneth). Liberal, Denbigh 1892, Chester 1900; MP Flint District 1906-Jan. 1910. **Mr. Howell Idris:** Born 15 August 1842, s of Benjamin Williams, farmer, & Catherine Williams. Assumed name of Idris by deed poll Feb. 1893. Married Fina, d of John Trevenna, Pembroke Dock, 6c. Educated Tavernspite National School & Privately. Apprenticed to a chemist 1854. Pharmaceutical Chemist. Chair: Idris & Co. Mineral Water Manufacturers 1889-1907. Director: First Garden City Ltd. President: London Chemists Assn; British Pharmaceutical Conference 1903, 1904. Member: London Water Board; Themes Conservancy Board. Chair, St. Pancras Liberal Assn. London CC 1889-1907 (Chair, Rivers, Water & Main Drainage Cttee). St. Pancras BC Mayor 1903. High Sheriff of Merioneth 1912. Freeman, City of London. Languages: Welsh, English. Of Cader Idris & London. Died 10 February 1925.

IFAN Dafydd Guto: Independent Wales Party, North List 2003. **Mr. Dafydd Guto Ifan:** Born Sharoe Green, Preston, 21 February 1942, s of J. J. R. D. Evans, welder/fitter/blacksmith, & Menna Jones Evans, explosives factory worker. Christian. Married Linda Ifan. Unemployed. Branch & Caernarfon Constituency Secretary, Independent Wales Party & North Wales Co-ordinator. Interests: Helping the weak, Gaining Welsh Independence. Languages: Welsh, Spanish, Scottish Gaelic. Of Llanrug.

INGHAM, Robert Vincent: Labour Clwyd North West 1992; Knutsford B/E & 1979. **Mr. Robert Ingham:** Born 8 November 1931. Married 2s. Educated Llangollen Grammar School; University of Wales, Bangor. Army, Parachute Regt. Physicist, formerly at Royal Armaments Research Establishment, Kent, & Nuclear Power Station, Harwell; Worked on Channel Tunnel Ventilation. Chair, Institution of Professional Managers & Specialists. Member, 1st Battalion, Parachute Regt. Assn. Macclesfield BC 1986.

INGLEFIELD Susan – see INKIN Susan.

INKIN Geoffrey: Kt 1993 CBE 1974 MBE 1971 DL (Gwent) 1983-89. FRSA. Hon. MRICS 1994. Hon. Dr. University of Glamorgan 1996. Conservative. Ebbw Vale 1979. **Sir Geoffrey Inkin:** Born 2 October 1934, s of Noel D. Inkin & Evelyn Margaret Inkin 1961. Married (1) 1961 Susan Elizabeth Sheldon 3s (divorced 1998) (2) 1998 Mrs. Elizabeth Inglefield (qv). Educated Dean Close School; RMC Sandhurst; Officer Training College, Camberley; Royal Agricultural College, Cirencester. Officer RWF 1954-74 (Malaysia 1955-57; Cyprus 1958-59). OC 1st Battalion RWF 1972-74. Gwent farmer. Gwent CC 1977-83. Member, Gwent Police Authority 1979-83. Chair, Cwmbran Development Corporation 1983-87; Cardiff Bay Development Corporation 1987-2000; Land Authority for Wales 1986-. Member: Welsh National Opera 1987-91; Council: UWIST 1987-88; University of Wales, Cardiff, Council, 1988-. Of St. Brides Major.

INKIN Susan Lilias: MA (TC Dublin). Conservative, Pontypridd and South/Central List, 1999, Vale of Glamorgan 2001. **Susan, Lady Inkin:** Born Edinburgh, 20 May 1944, d of Henry Turcan, malster. Anglican. Married (1) Christopher Samuel Inglefield (2) 1998 Sir Geoffrey David Inkin 2 stepsons. Educated Edinburgh; Moreton Hall, Shropshire; Chatham Hall, Virginia; Trinity College, Dublin (English & Anglo-Saxon). Garden Design Adviser & Interior Design Consultant. Chair, South Wales Region, Riding for the Disabled Assn. 1986-94. Chief of Staff, National Assembly Conservative Group 1999. Chair, Governors, Monmouth School for Girls. Interests Agriculture, Environment, Constitutional matters. Hobbies: All Field Sports, Gardening, Golf, Travel, Music, Opera. Languages: English, French. Of St. Brides Major.

IRRANCA-DAVIES Ifor Huw: MSc. (Wales). Labour, Brecon & Radnor 2001, MP Ogmore B/E 14 February 2002-. **Mr Huw Irranca-Davies:** Born Gowerton, 22 January 1963 (Nephew of Ifor Davies MP qv). Roman Catholic. Married Joanna Irranca (radiographer) & added her family name to his, 3s. Educated Gowerton Comprehensive School; Crewe & Alsager College; Swansea Institute. Manager; Local Government Officer. Director, Ystalyfera Development Trust (Vice-President). Course Director, Business Faculty, Swansea Institute of Higher Education. Joined Labour Party 1981. Chair Neath CLP. Vice-President; Chair, Secretary Ystalyfera Ward Party. Vice-President, Ystalyfera Development Trust. Member: GMB; Co-operative Party; Sustrans. Contested Neath/Port Talbot CBC 1999. Lost selection for Swansea East Assembly

B/E 2001 by one vote. Languages: Learned Welsh, English. Of Ystalyfera.

ISHERWOOD Mark Allan: BA (Newcastle) 1981 ACIB. Conservative, Alyn & Deeside 2001, 2003. AM North Wales List 2003-. **Mr. Mark Isherwood:** Born Bramhall, Cheshire, 21 January 1959. Married Hilary, 2s 4d. Educated Stockport Grammar School; University of Newcastle upon Tyne (Politics). Trainee Manager, Cheshire Building Society 1981-91. Commercial Business Development Manager, NWS Bank plc 1989-90. Area Manager, Cheshire Building Society 1990-. Member, Federation of Conservative Students 1977-81. Chair, Round Table. Treasurer, Alyn & Deeside Conservative Assn. Contested Flintshire CC 1999. Treuddyn Community Clr. 1999. Housing Assn Voluntary Board Member, 8 years. Chair, school governors. Chair, Round Table. Conservative spokesman on Finance 2003-. Interests: Small businesses, Public services, Jobs. Hobbies: Family, Dog, House & Garden, Static Caravan, Sailing. Of Mold.

IWAN Dafydd Iwan Jones: BArch (Wales) 1968. Plaid Cymru Anglesey Feb. & Oct. 1974; Conwy 1983. **Mr. Dafydd Iwan:** Born Brynaman August 1943, s of Revd Gerallt Jones & Elizabeth Jane Jones, teacher of music & languages (gs of Revd Fred Jones, a founder of Plaid Cymru). Welsh Independent lay preacher. Married 1968 (1) Marion Eames, 2s, divorced (2) Bethan 2s. Educated Ammanford; Llanuwchllyn; Bala Grammar School; University of Wales, Aberystwyth (1 year); University of Wales. Cardiff. Architect. Folk & pop singer. 1st record 1966. Composed some 200 songs; released 17 albums, including 7 CDs, 3 live videos, several songbooks. Managing Director, *Sain* Recording Co (founder 1969). Joined Cymdeithas yr Iaith 1963 (Chair 1968-71; Vice-Chair 1971-72; Editor *Tafod y Ddraig*. Chair: Plaid Cymru Youth Section 1982-83. Involved in road signs campaign: one-month prison, 1969; postponed sentence 1969; prison 1970-71, 1980. Chair: Gwynn music publishing co. Board Member, Arianrhod. Trustee, Portmeirion Foundation. Member: Amnesty International; Conscience (for the right not to pay taxes for weapons of mass destruction). Founder member: Nant Gwrtheyrn Language Centre; Antur Waunfawr foundation for people with learning difficulties. Chair: Bontnewydd Community Centre. Awarded Order of Gwynfor Evans for his lifelong services to Wales by the Gwynfor Evans Welsh American Assn 2001. Hon. Fellow, University of Wales, Bangor & Aberystwyth. Vice-President, Plaid Cymru 10/4/2002). Hobbies: Rugby, Art, Music. Of Caeathro. *Books: Dafydd Iwan, Cân dros Gymru (autobiography) 2002.*

– J –

JACKSON Charles James: Kt 1919 JP FSA. Conservative: East Glamorgan 1895. **Sir Charles Jackson:** Born Monmouth 1849, s of James Edwin Jackson, architect of Monmouth & Cardiff. Married Agnes Jackson. Barrister, Middle Temple 1888. Newspaper Proprietor. Chair, *News of the World.* Author: books on porcelain & pottery. Freeman, City of London 1922. Of Cardiff. Died 23 April 1923.

JACKSON Emma: BA (Cantab). Green Party: Pontypridd 1992. **Ms. Emma Jackson:** Born 1969. 1d. Educated Brecon & Monmouth Schools; Cambridge University. Research Assistant, Glamorgan Polytechnic.

JACKSON Henry M. – see MATHER-JACKSON H.

JACKSON Huw Vaughan: BA (North London) Oxon MEd (Wales). Plaid Cymru: Newport West 1997. **Mr. Huw Jackson**: Born Caerphilly 8 April 1953. Married Ann, 1d. Educated Caerphilly Grammar Technical School; North London Polytechnic; University of Wales, Cardiff. Civil Servant, Home Office, Cardiff 1976-79; Teacher. Deputy Head South East London school. Joined Plaid Cymru 1967. Chair, Plaid Cymru, England Region 1996-. Vice-Chair, London Branch 1995- & Secretary 1994-.

JACKSON William Frederick, 1st & last Baron Jackson of Glewstone 1945: Labour MP Brecon & Radnor, B/E 1939-45. **Mr. W. F. Jackson:** Born 1893, s of George Jackson JP, fruit merchant of Smithfield (George Jackson & Co Ltd) & Minnie Jacks of Birmingham. Married 1923 M. Hope Gilmour JP. Educated King Edward High School, Birmingham. 14th Warwickshire Regt 1914-18; Sergeant, invalided out. Managing Director, Glewstone Farms & Fruit Plantations 1918-. Herefordshire CC 1931-46. Member, Liberal Party. Joined Labour 1931. Of Glewstone, Herefordshire. Invalid from 1946. Died 2 May 1954.

JACOB Andre Robert: Mid & West Wales Pensioners' Party, Mid & West List 2003. **Mr. Andre Jacob:** Born Paris 5 February 1957, s of Frederick Brynmor Jacob, motor executive, restaurateur and swimming pool manager, & Mauricette Emilienne DeLattrre, restauratrix. Married, 2s divorced 1995. Occupational Therapist & Mental Health nurse. Treasurer/Chair/Secretary: COHER,

Unison. Member: Cymdeithas Owain Llawgoch; Bois y Castell Choir. ComC. Interests: Plaid Cymru. Hobbies: History, Eisteddfodau. Languages: Welsh, English, German, Italian, reads Russian. Of Salem, Llandeilo.

JAKEWAY Kevin: BA. Green Party, Rhondda 1997, South/Central List, 1999. **Mr. Kevin Jakeway:** Born Trebanog, Rhondda, 9 October 1962, s of a colliery winder & a factory worker. Educated Porth Grammar Technical School; Gwent College of HE; Cardiff Business School; Cardiff Institute of HE (3D Design, PG Dip. Business, PG Dip. Interior Architecture). Designer-craftsman. Development Manager, Clydach Vale Community Centre & founder/co-ordinator, Rhondda Community Exchange (local exchange trading system) from 1996. Director, Valleys Furniture Re-cycling. Company Secretary, CUP arts (community music project). Network Co-ordinator, UK Office VAN (Voluntary Arts Network) January 2002. Freelance Consultant to the Voluntary & Community Sectors. Resigned from Labour Party (because of its disregard for environmental issues and its drift to the Right). Joined the Green Party 1996. General Secretary, Wales Green Party 1996-97. Member: Steering Group, to set up Rhondda Credit Union, Clydach Vale Parent Support Group. Vice-Chair, Treherbert Forum. Contested Rhondda-Cynon-Taf (Clydach Vale) 1999. Interests: A socialist and committed to the ideas of Local Community Ownership and the devolution of power to the lowest possible level, Culture & in particular the myth that is 'Welsh Culture', Employment, Structure of Society. Hobbies: Art, Design, Music, Walking. Of Rhondda.

JAMES Carwyn Rees: BA (Wales). Plaid Cymru, Llanelli 1970. **Mr. Carwyn James:** Born Cefneithen November 1929, s of Michael James, miner, & Anne James. Welsh Independent Deacon/Church Secretary. Educated Gwendraeth Grammar School; University of Wales, Aberystwyth. Royal Navy 1947-49. Teacher (Welsh): Carmarthen 1954-56; Llandovery College 1956-58. Lecturer in Welsh & Drama, Trinity College, Carmarthen 1969-74. Rugby Player: Welsh Secondary Schools XV (Captain 1948); Llanelli, 1969; Barbarians & Wales XV. Rugby coach: West Wales Selection 1967, Llanelli, British Lions 1969, Wales and Italy 1977-79. Offered trial for Cardiff City XI. Member: Court,

University of Wales; University of Wales, Aberystwyth; Welsh Cttee. Duke of Edinburgh Awards Scheme, Urdd Gobaith Cymru, UCAC. Co-Editor: *Campau, Barn* (Educational Section). Hon. Member, Gorsedd 1977. Languages: Welsh, English. Declined MBE 1971. Died 10 January 1983, (heart attack at Nabolsky Hotel, Amsterdam. Further Reading: *Alun Richards, Carwyn.*

JAMES Charles Herbert: JP. Liberal MP: Merthyr Tydfil 1980-88. **Mr. Charles James:** Born Merthyr Tydfil, 1817, s of William James, brewer, & Margaret James. Brought up Wesleyan, became Unitarian. President, Unitarian Assembly. Married 1842 Sarah, d of Thomas Thomas, Bristol. Educated Taliesin Williams School, Merthyr Tydfil; Gouldstone School, Bristol. Solicitor, 1838. Chair, local Nonconformist Cttee. which invited Henry Richard to be candidate 1868. Of Merthyr Tydfil. Died 3 October 1890.

JAMES Craig: Brannigan's Monster Raving Loony Party, Cardiff Central 1997. **Mr. Craig James:** Of Penarth.

JAMES Deborah: Green Party, South/West list 2003. **Miss Deborah James:** Born Swansea, 14 December 1967, d of Reginald John James, engineering manager, & Beverley James, data processing clerk. Church of England. Educated Pentrepoeth Junior School, Swansea; Morriston Comprehensive School, Swansea. Contested Swansea CC 1.5.2003. Interests; Local Issues. Hobbies: Swimming, Keep fit. Of Ynystawe, Swansea.

JAMES Glyndwr Powell: Plaid Cymru, Rhondda West, 1955, 1959; Rhondda, Feb. & Oct. 1974, 1979. **Mr. Glyn James:** Born Llangrannog 26 March 1925, s of David James, Carpenter, & Mary Hannah Powell; one of 8 children. Presbyterian Church of Wales lay preacher. Married Hawys, d of Revd John Williams, Ferndale 2c. Educated Cardigan Grammar School; Glamorgan Technical College (HND Mech). Apprentice, Bridge End Foundry, Cardigan 1937-42; Mining Engineer 1942-83, Part-time Organiser South East Wales, Plaid Cymru 1960-64. Part-time BBC actor. Rhondda BC 1960-. Mayor of Rhondda. Hon. Alderman 1991. Glamorgan CC 1961-64, 1967-69. Joined Plaid Cymru 1944. Languages: Welsh, English. Of Ferndale.

JAMES Irene Mary: Labour, AM Islwyn 2003. **Ms. Irene James**: Born Cwmcarn, 7 September 1952, miner's daughter. Educated West London University. Special Needs Teacher, Risca Primary School. Agent to Don Touhig MP 2001. Interests: Jobs, Health, Education. Of Cwmcarn.

JAMES Jimmy – see JAMES Timothy David Richard.

JAMES Mair: SDP/Alliance, Ogmore 1987. **Mrs. Mair James:** Born Caerau 5 February 1934. Married 3s. Educated Maesteg Grammar School. Charity's Social & Fundraising Officer. Chair, Vale of Glamorgan SDP. 1986. Languages: Welsh, English. Contested Vale of Glamorgan BC 1987.

JAMES Michael – see JAMES Richard Michael.

JAMES Peter Terrence: Conservative, Pontypool 1966; Southampton, Itchen Feb. & Oct. 1974. **Mr. Peter James:** Born April 1941. Anglican. Educated St. John's Preparatory School. School, Chepstow; Hereford Cathedral School. Solicitor & Director of several companies. Joined Chepstow Young Conservatives 1960. Branch Chair, National Society for Mentally Handicapped Children; NSPCC.

JAMES Richard Michael: Liberal, Cardiff West Feb. & Oct. 1974, Devonport 1979, Bournemouth West 1983. **Mr. Michael James**: Born 8 March 1934. Married 1c. Educated Canton High School, Cardiff; Llandaff Technical College; University of Wales, Cardiff (part-time study). Legal Assistant. Estate Agent (Director, Phoenix, James & Co. Paignton). Chair, Cardiff West Liberal Assn. 1971. Contested Cardiff CC 1968, 1969, 1970. Moved to Paignton from Cardiff.

JAMES Siân Catherine: Labour, Monmouth 2003. **Mrs. Siân James:** Born 24 June 1959, d of Melbourne & Martha Griffiths. Married 1976, Martin Ray James, hill farmer, 1s 1d. Educated Cefn Saeson Comprehensive School, Neath; University of Wales, Swansea (mature student). Trainer, West Glam Video Workshops, Field Officer, Young Farmers' Clubs. South Wales Organiser, *Save the Children Fund*. Communications Manager, Parc Prison, Bridgend until 2003. Shortlisted for Blaenau Gwent parliamentary candidature, Dec. 2003; prospective parliamentary candidate, Swansea East 2004. Of Neath.

JAMES Stephen Randall: BA (Bristol). Conservative, Gower 2003. **Mr. Stephen James:** Born Morriston 1979. Educated Glanymor School; Burry Port; Gorseinon; Bristol (completing MA). Joined Conservatives 1994. Chair: Llanelli Young Conservatives 1995-98. Vice-Chair, Llanelli Conservative Assn 2002-. Burry Port TC. 2002. Hobbies: Golf, Football, Rugby, History, Christian Theology. Of Burry Port.

JAMES Terence: United Socialists, South/Central List 1999. Mr. Terry James: Housing worker at Cardiff. Unison shop steward. Lifelong Socialist. Member, Socialist Workers' Party; Anti-Nazi League. Of Llanedeyrn, Cardiff.

JAMES Timothy David Richard: BSocSc. (Birmingham) 1980. Conservative: Vale of Clwyd 2001; Bolsover 1992; South-East Staffordshire B/E 1996. **Major Jimmy James:** Born Oxford 22 January 1952 (family from Llansamlet). Married Jane 3d. Educated Marlborough; RMC Sandhurst; Birmingham University (International Studies). Australian Army 1971-73. British Army 1973-90. Career Consultant. Deputy Director, Management Consultancies Assn 1990-94. Charity Fundraising Consultant: Craigmyle & Co 1995-97; Jimmy James Fund Raising Consultancy 1997-. Northamptonshire CC 1993-97. Deputy Chair: Wellingborough Conservative Assn. 1998-99. Member: Royal United Services Institute for Defence Studies; International Institute for Strategic Subjects; Institute for European Defence and Strategic Studies. Interests: Agriculture; Education; Defence; Promoting Inward Investment into North Wales.

JANES Ian: BScEcon PCGE. Labour, Brecon & Radnor 1999. **Mr. Ian Janes:** Born Tredegar, 24 May 1959, s of Ronald Thomas Janes, steelworker, & Priscilla June Janes. Christian. Educated Tredegar Comprehensive School; University of Wales, Cardiff. Lecturer in Accountancy, Coleg Gwent. DC 8 years. Tredegar TC 1990-99 (Mayor 1994-95, youngest ever). Chair, Blaenau Gwent YES Campaign. Treasurer, Blaenau Gwent CLP 1996-2000, Chair, 2002-03. Director, development trust. Member: Institute of Welsh Affairs. School governor. Interests: Economic Development, Constitutional Reform. Hobbies: Member: Glamorgan County Cricket Club, Ebbw Vale RFC. *World Wide 1st Prize Winner, ACCA Paper 7, Taxation, December 2000.* Of Tredegar.

JANNER Barnett, Baron Janner (1970): Kt 1960, Hon. LLD (Leeds) 1957; BA (Wales) FRSA. Liberal, Cardiff Central 1929; Whitechapel & St. George's B/E 1930, 1935; MP Whitechapel & St. George's B/E 1931-35. Joined Labour Party 1936. Labour MP Leicester North West 1950-70. **Sir Barnett Janner:** Born Barry 1892, s of Joseph Janner. Jewish. Married 1927, Elsie, d of Joseph Cohen, (s, Grenville Janner, MP). Educated Barry Grammar School; University of Wales, Cardiff (President SRC). Solicitor 1919. Labour Party Adviser on Rents. Member: Executive, Jewish Claims on Austria. Chair: Lords & Commons Solicitors Group. Vice-President: Assn. of Municipal Corporations; Leasehold Reform Assn of Great Britain (ex-Chair); Conference of Jewish Claims against Germany Inc. President: Board of Deputies of British Jews 1955-64; Assn of Jewish Friendly Societies; Zionist Federation of Great Britain and Ireland. Chair: Anglo-Israeli Parliamentary Group; Anglo-Benelux Parliamentary Group. Contested Cardiff CC as Ex-Servicemen's Candidate 1920. Of London. Died 6 May 1982.

JARMAN Andrea Kathleen: BSc MSc PGCE RAScert TEFL. Natural Law Party, South/West list 1999. **Miss Andrea Jarman:** Born Neath 20 August 1942, d of Thomas Francis Jarman, medical practitioner, & Lindesth, laboratory technician. Educated University of Wales, Aberystwyth. Teacher (Maths) & later ESOL in adult education. Teacher of Transcendental Meditation under auspices of Maharishi Mdhesh Yogi. Hobbies: Walking, Circle dancing, Music, Travelling. Languages: Learning Welsh; English, French, Italian, German, Norwegian, Swahili. Of Cardiff.

JARMAN Pauline: Plaid Cymru, Cynon Valley 1983; AM South/Central List 1999. **Mrs. Pauline Jarman:** Born Mountain Ash 15 December 1945. Married 1965, Colin, s of Douglas & Gwyneth Jarman, 2s. Educated Mountain Ash Grammar School. Export Officer, AB Metals, Abercynon 1961-63. Import/Export Officer, Fram Filters, Treforest 1963-65. Import Officer, AB Metals, Abercynon 1965-66. Chief Cashier, GUS Caerphilly 1966-69. Pharmacy Assistant 1973-78. Self-employed Shopkeeper 1978-. Cynon Valley DC 1976-96 (Mayor 1987-88). Mid-Glam CC 1981-96. Rhondda-Cynon-Taf BC 1996- (Plaid Cymru Group Leader; Leader of the Council 1999). Chair, school governors. Member: Cefnpennar & District Welfare Assn. Trustee Rhondda-Cynon-Taf Multiple Sclerosis in Wales. Of Mountain Ash.

JARVIE Thomas H. – see HUNTER JARVIE T.

JEFFREYS Rhys Vincent Wynn: BSc (London) MSc (Wales). Local Independent Labour, Neath B/E 1991. **Mr. Rhys Jeffreys:** Born Creunant 1938. Welsh Independent Deacon. Married Marilyn Jeffreys, school secretary, Ysgol Gymraeg Castell Nedd, 2s. Educated Neath Grammar School; Apprenticeship, British Thompson Houston, Rugby; Night School; City & Guilds College, London (Engineering), NCB Scholarship to Royal of School of Mines of Imperial College, London (1st Mining engineering; Governors' Prize in Mining Engineering). Member, University Air Squadron, Cadet Pilot RAFVR. Safety Officer, Glyncastle Colliery, Resolfen. Mine Manager 1963. Lecturer, Swansea. Engineer: Cefn Coed, Seven Sisters, Banwen, Dillwyn, Blaennant & Glyncastle Collieries until 1963. Private mines from 1963: Brynaman, Bryn, Maesteg, Tairgwaith, Glyn Neath, Resolfen. Owner, small coal mine. Chair: South Wales Small Mines Assn 1979; Federation of Small Mines of Great Britain. Languages: Welsh, English. *Neath needs a Welshman and a local man.*

JENKING Joyce Lilian: UK Independence Party, Cardiff West 2001. **Ms Joyce Jenking:** Born Cardiff 17 June 1934, d of David Richard

Morgans, bus driver, & Doris Kathleen Morgans. Anglican. Married 1953, William Ernest Clark, owner/butcher, 3s 1d. Educated Canton High School for Girls, Cardiff. Book Keeper, retired. With husband, spent 2 years in Cyprus as holiday representatives & ran a bar in Spain for 2 years. Treasurer, UKIP Welsh Cttee 1998. Interests: Freeing Britain from Corrupt Dictatorship, which is the Common Market. Hobbies: Reading, Walking, Travel. Languages: English, a little Spanish. Of Cardiff.

JENKINS Arthur: JP (Mon) 1936. Labour MP Pontypool 1935-. **Mr. Arthur Jenkins:** Born Varteg, Mon, 13 February 1896, s of John Jenkins, miner, & Eliza Perry. Married 1911 Hattie, d of William Harris (Blaenavon Steelworks Manager) 1 son (Rt. Hon. Roy Jenkins). Educated Varteg Council School; Ruskin College, Oxford 1908-09; Central Labour College 1909-10; private school in France 1910-11. Miner 1908-16. Deputy Miners' Agent, Eastern Valleys 1918-21. Miners' Agent 1921-35. Vice-President, SWMF 1934-36. Secretary, Pontypool Trades & Labour Council 1911-18. President, Pontypool CLP 1918-32. Sentenced to imprisonment for riotous assembly during 1926 General Strike. Abersychan UDC. Monmouthshire CC 1918-35, Alderman 1927, Chair 1932-33. Member: County Councils Assn, Royal Commission on Licensing 1929-31; Minister of Pensions Special Grants Cttee, Labour Party NEC 1925-29, 1931-33, 1935-37. Member: Labour Party Commission of Enquiry into Distressed Areas 1936-37. PPS Clement Attlee, Deputy Prime Minister 1940-45. Parl. Secretary, Planning July-August 1945. Parl. Secretary, Education, August 1945-. Of Pontypool. Estate £1631. Died 25 April 1946.

JENKINS Elgar Spencer: Kt 1996 OBE 1988 BA (Oxon) FRSA. Conservative, Ebbw Vale 1970. **Sir Elgar Jenkins**: Born Rhondda, June 1935. Anglican. Educated Monmouth School; St. Edmund Hall; Oxford; St. Luke's College, Exeter. President, Oxford University Conservative Assn 1995. RAF officer 1956-59. Teacher (History & Social Studies), Bath & Bristol comprehensive schools 1962-73. Deputy Head, Cardinal Newman School, St. Gregory's Catholic Comprehensive School, Bath 1973-78. Chair: Bath & District Health Authority 1989-93; Local Government Management Board 1990-96. Member, National Advisory Cttee on Libraries 1995-. Bath CC 1966-72, 1973-96 (Mayor, Leader of the Council, Cttees Chair). Bath & NE Somerset DC. Member: Member: Assn of District Councils 1985-96 (Leader of Conservative Group 1991-96). Deputy Chair 1991-93, Vice-Chair 1993-96. Vice-President, Conservative Political Council. Member, Court 1968-96 & Council, 1968-69, University of Bath & Chair of Trustees. Member: Bath Archeo-

logical Trust 1994-. Hobbies: History, Reading. Of Bath.

JENKINS Ieuan Lewis: BA (Wales). Plaid Cymru, Merioneth 1966. **Mr. Ieuan Jenkins:** Born Abertillery. Married Ann 3s 1d. Educated Lewis School, Pengam; University of Wales, Cardiff. Post Graduate Course in Agriculture. Organiser, Welsh Agricultural Organisations Society until 1949. Youth Employment Officer for Merioneth 1949. Member, Plaid Cymru Executive.

JENKINS James: Liberal, Merthyr 1929. **Mr. James Jenkins:** Born Treherbert 1877, s of John Jenkins, Methodist. Miner. Mining Engineer: Waunfelin Colliery, Pontypool, Mynydd Maen, Pontypool 1925. LEA Lecturer in Mining. Vice-President, Wesley Brotherhood. President, Monmouth Liberal Assn. Member, Monmouthshire Education Cttee. Of Pontypool.

JENKINS John Verdi: National Liberal, Merioneth 1955. **Mr. Verdi Jenkins:** Born Login 1904, s of William Jenkins (Gwilym o'r Glyn). Married Gwyneth, 1d. Educated Whitland Elementary & Grammar Schools; Jones West Mon. School, Pontypool. Temporary Postman. Sub-Postmaster, Hayes, Middlesex until 1932. Asst General Secretary, National Federation of Sub-Postmasters, 1932-34. Barrister, Grays Inn, 1934. East Carmarthenshire Coroner. Carmarthen BC. 1945-48. Carmarthenshire CC 1946-. Member, Carmarthen Health Authority. School governor. Hobbies: Gardening, Sea Fishing. Languages: Welsh, English.

JENKINS Mike Geraint: United Socialists, Merthyr Tydfil & Rhymney 1999. **Mr. Mike Jenkins:** Born Aberystwyth 16 January 1953, s of David Geraint Jenkins, various jobs, and Sheila Mary Budge, teacher. Atheist. Married 1976, Marie Francis Jenkins, teacher, 1s 2d. English Teacher, Pen-y-dre school on Gurnos estate & Writer. Worked in Germany & Northern Ireland. Author. Member, Cymru Coch. Secretary: Merthyr Branch, Welsh Socialist Alliance. Chair, Anti-Opencast Group. A founder, Red Poets Society. Awarded Arts Council of Wales Book o f the Year Award 1998. Member, CND, Anti-Apartheid Movement, Anti Poll Tax Unions. Involved in miners' strike. Interests: Welsh Socialist Republican. Hobbies: Football, Theatre, Music of all kinds, Cinema. Languages: Welsh but not fluently, English, some German. Of Merthyr Tydfil. *Books: Mike Jenkins: Wanting to Belonging (short stories), Red Landscapes (poems) 2000; Tangled in thorns, Fires and the Comet, Coulda bin summin!*

JENKINS Samuel Roberts: BA (London). Liberal, Caerphilly 1923, Gravesend 1906. **Revd**

S. R. Jenkins: Born Newtown 1868, s of Revd David Miles Jenkins & the daughter of Griffith & Maria Griffith (& niece of Samuel Roberts [SR]). Married Jennie Ellison 1s (died in Italian POW camp). Educated Coleg Bala-Bangor; University of Wales, Bangor 1894-98. Congregational Minister, Ordained 1894. Pastorates: Glanrafon, Bangor 1894-98; Market Square Merthyr Tydfil 1898-1902; Princes Street, Gravesend 1902-09; Seaforth, Liverpool 1913-19; Trafalgar Road, Birkdale 1924-Barrister, Middle Temple 1910-13. Secretary, Liverpool District, Lancashire Congregational Union 1917-, Chair 1928-29. Editor, *Merseyside Congregational Magazine* 12 years. Died 18 October 1944.

JENKINS Timothy: UK Independence Party, Swansea East, 2001, Assembly B/E 2001, Wales Euro 2004. **Mr. Tim Jenkins:** Born Haverfordwest 9 May 1962, s of Brian Jenkins, company director, & Eluned Jenkins. Unmarried. Educated Butron Voluntary Church School; Haverfordwest Boys Grammar School; North Wirral College; College of Maritime Studies, Warsash. (HNC & OND Marine Engineering, Chief engineer's Combined Certificate). Merchant Navy Engineer Officer. Interests: Europe, Defence, Shipping. UK Independence Party, Wales Euro 2004. Hobbies: Swansea City FC, Fishing, Boating, Walking. Languages: English, Basic Cantonese. Of Swansea.

JENKINS William: Kt 1931 JP (Glam) KStJ. Labour MP Neath, 1922-. **Sir William Jenkins:** Born Cymer Afan 1871 s of Miles Jenkins, collier, & Annie Jenkins. Welsh Independent Deacon. Married 1895, Hannah Evans 3c. Educated Glyncorrwg National School. Attendant to navvies building Rhondda & Swansea Bay at 11. Coal miner, Blaengwynfi Colliery, at 13. Checkweighman, Cymer Drift 1899. Secretary/Agent, Western District 1906; Miners' Agent, Afan Valley. Member, SWMF Executive. Glyncorrwg School Board 1900. Glyncorrwg UDC 1904-; Chair 1908-16, 1927-28. Glamorgan CC 1906- (Chair, Education Cttee 1918-), Alderman 1920-; Chairman 1919-21. Member: School Board 1900-; Glamorgan Conscientious Objectors Tribunal, 1916-18. Branch President, Discharged Soldiers & Sailors Assn. Member: Council, University of Wales; Central Welsh Board; Glamorgan War Pensions Cttee. Chair: Federation of Education Authorities for Wales 1926-27 Glamorgan Joint Standing Cttee; Bridgend School for the Blind. Vice-President, County Councils Assn. of England & Wales. Member, Speaker's Panel of Chairmen. Languages: Welsh, English. Of Cymmer Afan. Died 8 December 1944.

JENKINS William Albert: Kt 1938 JP (Swansea) 1928 KStJ FCIS Knight, Order of Danneborg (Den) 1933; Gold Cross, Order of George I (Greece) 1938; Chevalier de la Legion d'honneur (France) 1947. National Liberal MP: Brecon & Radnor 1922-24; Liberal National, Llanelli B/E 1936. **Sir William A. Jenkins:** Born Swansea 9 July 1878 s of Daniel (examiner, railway vehicles) & Elizabeth Williams of St. Thomas. Congregationalist. Married Beatrice (died 1967) d of Frederick Tyler. Educated Danygraig Elementary School; Swansea Higher Grade School. Office Boy at Swansea Docks at 13. Chief Clerk/Cashier, French Anthracite Co. at 18. General Manager, Swansea office, at 20. Colliery Agent, Coal Factor, Coal Exporter, Pit Wood Importer, Shipowner (18 ships). Chair: William Jenkins & Co; Gwalia Land & Property Developments Ltd. Director of several companies. Member: Council of Chamber of British Shipping, London. Vice-President: Pilots Assn. of Great Britain; British Sailors Society; Swansea YMCA. Chair/Secretary, Swansea Sailors Society. Member: Court of Referees; Court, National Museum of Wales; University of Wales, Swansea. Chair, West Glamorgan & Carmarthenshire Congregational Assn. Founder Member & thrice President, Swansea Chamber of Trade. Founder-President, Swansea Festival of Music. President: Swansea & West Wales Adult Deaf & Dumb Mission; Royal Welsh Agricultural Show; Swansea Trustee Savings Bank. MFH. Llandybie & Penllergaer Hunt. Hon. Member, Gorsedd of Bards. Swansea Vice-Consul: Denmark 1916-23, Greece 1919-53. Swansea BC 1927-54; Mayor, 1947-49. Of Swansea. Died 23 October 1968.

JENKINS William George: MA (Oxon). Plaid Cymru, Brecon & Radnor 1970. **Mr. George Jenkins:** Born Betws, Ammanford, collier's son. Married Genevieve 2c. Educated Amman Valley Grammar School; Hertford College, Oxford (Boxing Blue). With UN Refugee Service, Beirut & Damascus. Lecturer in Commerce, Coleg Hywel Dda Technical Institute, Brecon. Chair, Brecon Branch, Plaid Cymru. Member, Plaid Cymru Executive. Contested Brecon BC 1968. Languages: Welsh, English, French. Of Llanfaes, Brecon.

JENKINS William James: JP (Pembs) 1935. Labour, Pembroke, 1922, 1923, 1924, 1929, 1935, withdrew 1931 in favour of Gwilym Lloyd-George, Ind.L. **Mr. W. J. Jenkins:** Born s of Revd John Stephen Jenkins, Baptist minister. Teacher until dismissed as a conscientious objector 1915. Farmer. Pembrokeshire RDC. Member, Council for Wales. Of Hopla, Pembs.

JENNER Alison Elizabeth: BA (Open) PGCE MEd. Liberal Democrat, South/West List 1999. **Mrs. Alison Jenner:** Born Southport, Lancs. 18 July 1952, d of Alexander Edward Clark &

Clarice Elizabeth Muriel Clark, hoteliers. Church of England/Church in Wales. Married 1976, Keith Lawrence Jenner, civil engineer, 2d. Educated Southport High School for Girls; Chester FE College; Open University; University of Wales, Swansea; University of Florence (Erasmus Placement). Community Education Officer. Joined Liberal Democrats 1979. Southwell PC. Interests: Europe, Education, Community Safety. Hobbies: Singing, Literature, Sailing. Languages: English, French, Italian, some German. Of Sketty, Swansea.

JENNER Vera Maureen: Pensioners' Party, Mid & West List 2003. **Mrs. Maureen Jenner:** Born Ystrad Rhondda 1936. Married Doctor/Consultant. Widowed. Educated Tonypandy Grammar School; Furzedown College, London. Teacher. Headteacher. Post graduate Diploma & taught at English Language Centre, Hove. Retired to Cyprus, where her husband died. Returned to UK 1997. Runs ESL (English as a Second Language) tours for overseas students. Author. Chair, Carmarthenshire Ratepayers' Assn. Membership Organiser, Carmarthenshire Pensioners Forum & Wales Pensioners (Mid & West Wales Area). Of Ferryside. *Books: Maureen Jenner, The Last Princess of Wales.*

JENNINGS Derek Geoffrey: BA LlB (Cantab). Conservative, Neath 1951; Ogmore 1955. **Mr. Geoffrey Jennings:** Born Neath 1923., s of Frederick Jennings, accountant. Married 2d. Educated Alderman Davies' School, Neath, Neath Grammar School, Downing College. Cambridge. Army 1942-46, Captain, RFA. POW 1944-45. Public Prosecutor, Naples & Trieste 1945-46. Barrister, Grays Inn 1949.

JENNINGS Samuel: JP (Merthyr). Independent Labour, Merthyr 1945. Withdrew in favour of Claude Stanfield, ILP 1935. **Mr. Samuel Jennings**: Born Dowlais 1881. Baptist Deacon & Sunday School Teacher. Married. Miner, steelworker, unemployed, went to work in Southern England 1933. CWS insurance collector. Contested BC 1914; Merthyr Tydfil BC 1930-33, 1937-; Alderman, Mayor 1941-42. President, Merthyr Tydfil Trades & Labour Council 1906, 1924, 1941. A Labour Pioneer. On Labour Short-List, November 1921. Nominated by Co-operative Party for Labour candidature at Merthyr 1934, against S. O. Davies, but lost by 3 votes. Of Dowlais. Died 24 November 1961.

JEREMIAH Gwennan Bess: Labour. Euro Wales 2004. **Ms. Gwennan Jeremiah:** Educated Crickhowell, University (Politics & Economics). Teacher, Duffryn High School, Newport. Head of IT Studies, Chepstow Comprehensive School. President, Newport branch, NAS/UWT. Joined Labour Party at 16; Secretary, Crickhowell branch; Chair, Plasnewydd ward branch, Cardiff. Shortlisted at Blaenau Gwent 2003.

JEREMY Anthony William: MA (Cantab). SDP/Alliance, Cardiff North 1983, 1987; Pro-Life Party, North List 2003. **Mr. Tony Jeremy**: Born Cardiff 5 May 1936, steelworker's son. Married 1966, Sara Hazel Jeremy (qv) 3s 2d (qv. Madeleine & William). Educated Cardiff High School; Fitzwilliam College, Cambridge. Army Officer, Middle East & Northern Ireland. Lecturer, UWIST until 1964. Solicitor 1964. Research Fellow, Law & Religion, School of Law, University of Wales, Cardiff. Founder Member, Social Democratic Party & Council for Social Democracy. S. Glam CC 1985-. Of Cardiff.

JEREMY Madeleine Ellen: Pro-Life Association, Cardiff Central 2001; Cardiff Central & South/Central List 2003. **Ms. Madeleine Jeremy:** Born Cardiff, 19 January 1973, d of Anthony William Jeremy (qv) & Sara Hazel Blair (qv) & sister of William (qv). Roman Catholic. Lone parent of boy, born 1996. Educated Cheltenham Ladies College; Welsh College of Music & Drama (Diploma in Acting). Worked for various charities & part time in Marketing. Hobbies: Shakespeare, Reading, Travel. Languages: English, French. Of St. Mellons, Cardiff.

JEREMY Sara Hazel: BA (Nottingham) BSc (Wales). Pro-Life Association, Bridgend 200; North List 2003. **Mrs. Sara Jeremy:** Born South-

Left to right: Anthony William Jeremy, Sara Hazel Jeremy, Madeileine Jeremy, William Blair Richard Jeremy.

gate, London 7 October 1942, d of Hugh Vickie Blair, chartered accountant, and Joan Elsie (Haines), trained singer. Presbyterian, Anglican, Roman Catholic from 1997. Married 1966, Anthony William Jeremy (qv) 3s 2d. Educated Holy Family Convent, Enfield; Cardiff High School for Girls; Nottingham University 1960-63 (Social Administration, Diploma in Applied Social Studies 1966; University of Wales, Cardiff (Institutional Management). Medical Social Worker (Cardiff Royal Infirmary Neurology Unit. Hobbies: Church Activities, Sewing, Reading. Of Cardiff.

JEREMY William: BA (Exeter). Liberal Democrat, Carmarthen West & Pembrokeshire South 2001. **Mr. William Jeremy:** Born Cardiff, 23 January 1971, s of Anthony William Jeremy & Sara-Hazel (Sally) Blair (qv) & brother of Madeleine (qv). Church in Wales (Anglo-Catholic Universalist (brought up as Presbyterian, confirmed Anglican, *now pretty ecumenical Catholic-type*). Educated Westbourne House, Penarth; Cheltenham College; Exeter University (History/Politics); Cardiff School of Journalism. Assistant to Liz Lynne MP 1995. Legal Practice Executive. Consultant Mediator/Consultant Researcher. Contested Cardiff CC (Llanrumney 1999). Secretary, Wales Council, European Movement. Council Member, LLAMAU Housing Assn. Co-producer & presenter, local radio disability affairs. Vice-Chair: Wales Liberal Democrats Candidates Cttee. Interests: European affairs; Public sector reform; Education. Of Cardiff.

JOB Ronald: Socialist Labour, nurse. Personnel Assistant, Gorseinon College. Member: Unison, Swansea Trades Council. Contested Swansea BC 1997. Left Labour Party when it dropped the word *Socialism*. Of Swansea.

JOBBINS Siôn Tomos: BA (Wales). Plaid Cymru, Cardiff North 2001. **Mr. Siôn Jobbins:** Born Kitwe, Zambia 10 February 1968, s of Alan Stanley Jobbins, education adviser, & Catherine Lewis. Calvinistic Methodist. Married 2001, Siwan Gwyndaf. Educated Ysgol Bryntaf; Ysgol Gyfun Glantaf, Cardiff; University of Wales, Aberystwyth (2a History). Editor, *Cambria*. Contributor to *Barn*. Member, *Tu Chwith* editorial board. Head of Marketing, Education & Access, National Library of Wales. Chair: Plaid Cymru Youth Movement; Federation of Plaid Cymru Students. Aberystwyth TC 1994-2001, Mayor 1999-2000. Interests: International Politics, especially Eastern Europe, Welsh Language. Hobbies: Modern European History, Reading, Travel, The Arts, Politics, Welsh Football. Languages: Welsh, English, basic German, learning Spanish. Contested Cardiff CC B/E Feb. 2002. Of Aberystwyth.

JOHN Brynmor: PC 1979, LlB (London) 1954. Labour MP Pontypridd 1970-. **Rt. Hon. Brynmor John:** Born 18 April 1934, s of William Henry John, painter & decorator, & Sarah Jane John. Married Anne Pryce, d of David L. Hughes. Educated Wood Road Elementary School, Treforest; Pontypridd Boys' Grammar School; University College, London. Solicitor 1957. Chair, Welsh Labour Group 1983-84. Opposition Spokesman: Agriculture 1984; Social Services 1981-83; Northern Ireland 1979-80; Defence 1980-81. Minister of State, Home Office 1976-79. Under-Secretary, Defence 1974-76. Died 13 December 1988.

JOHN Caradog Steffan: BA (Wales) 2001. Liberal Democrat, Carmarthen East & Dinefwr & Mid & West List, 2003. **Mr. Steffan John:** Born St. Asaph, 28 July 1980, s of Eurion John, financial adviser, & Gwyneth Morfydd John, psychotherapist/social worker. Roman Catholic. Educated Ysgol Twm o'r Nant; Ysgol Glan Clwyd; University of Wales, Aberystwyth (International Affairs & Peace Strategic Studies). Liberal Democrat Assembly Group Researcher. Liberal Democrat Welsh Language Press & media Officer. Member: Welsh Liberal Democrat Campaigns & Election Cttee. Advisory Member, Policy Cttee. Interests: Welsh Language, Economic Globalisation, International Affairs. Hobbies: Archery, Chess, Supporter of Llanelli Scarlets XV & Liverpool FC. Languages: Welsh, English. Of Llwynhendy, Llanelli.

JOHN Edward Thomas: JP. Liberal MP East Denbighshire 1910-18; Joined Labour Party, July 1918; Labour, Denbigh 1918, Brecon & Radnor 1922, Anglesey B/E 1923; Joined Plaid Cymru. **Mr. E. T. John:** Born Pontypridd 14 March 1857, s of John Morgan John & Margaret John. Family Moved to Middlesborough 1871. Calvinistic Methodist. Married 1881 Margaret, d of William Rees, Pendoylan. Educated Pontypridd Wesleyan Day School. Office Boy at J. Wild & Co; Manager at 18. Managing Director, Linthorpe Dewsdale Smelting Co Middlesborough. Director, Cardiff Haemalite Ore Co. President; Celtic Congress 1918-26; National Union of Welsh Societies 1918-27. Chair, Peace Society 1924-27. Introduced Home Rule Bill, March 1914. Of Llanidian Hall, Llanfair PG. Estate £36,899. Died 16 February 1931. *Books etc: E. T. John, Wales: Its Notable Sons & Daughters, Wales: Its Politics and Economics, Home Rule for Wales, Cymru a'r Gymraeg.*

JOHN Glyn: BA (Nottingham). Plaid Cymru, Aberavon 1964, Neath 1970. **Mr. Glyn John:** Born Blaendulais, December 1931. Welsh Independent. Married Enfys, 3s. Educated Neath Grammar School; Nottingham University Army

1953-57, Lieutenant. Manager, Carmarthenshire battery company. Ex-Secretary: Plaid Cymru Economic & Industrial Research Group; West Glamorgan Regional Cttee. Member, Plaid Cymru Executive; Director of Organisation, Plaid Cymru. Contested Swansea BC 1968. Languages: Welsh, English. Of Killay, Swansea.

JOHN Gwyn: IMS 1989. Referendum Party, Cynon Valley 1997. **Mr. Gwyn John:** Born Llantwit Major 1946. Civil Servant 25 years. Llantwit Major TC. Vale of Glamorgan BC (Conservative) 1999-. Secretary: Llantwit Major AFC 30 years. Of Llantwit Major.

JOHN Huw: Plaid Cymru, Neath 1987. **Mr. Huw John:** Married 2d. Lecturer in Motor Vehicle Technology, Neath FE College. Broadcaster.

JOHN Steffan – see JOHN Caradog Steffan.

JOHN William: JP (Glam). Rhondda West B/E 1920-50. **Mr. Will John:** Born Cockett, Swansea 6 October 1878, s of Evan John, miner, & Rachel Rosser. Welsh Baptist Sunday School Teacher at 18; Deacon (at 25); Church Secretary 1900-20; one of the founders of Moriah Baptist Church, Tonypandy. Married 1906 Anna Jane, d of George & Catherine Brookes (died 1951). Educated Cockett National School. Worked in brick works at 12. Miner at 13. Moved to Clydach Vale at 14. Lodge Secretary, Llwynypia 1912-17. Financial Secretary, Rhondda Miners 1911. Checkweighman, Glamorgan Collieries, Pontypridd, 1909. Chair, Cambrian Combine Group. Miners' Agent 1912-20. Member, SWMF Executive 1912. Sentenced to one year's imprisonment for alleged part in Tonypandy riots 1911; sentence reduced to six months by Home Secretary, Winston Churchill. Member: Rhondda War Pensions Cttee. Secretary, Rhondda Belgian Relief Cttee. President, Baptist Union of Wales 1936-37. Hon. Member, Gorsedd of Bards. Secretary, Welsh Parliamentary Labour Party 19 years. PPS 1929-31. Welsh Labour Whip 1935-42. Deputy Chief Whip 1942-45. Comptroller of the Household 1942. Lord Commissioner of the Treasury 1942-45. Languages: Welsh; English. Estate £2324. Died 27 August 1956. Further Reading: *D. Ben Rees: Cymry Adnabyddus 1952-1972.*

JOHNS Daniel: OBE 1945 MSc (Wales). Agriculturalist Party, Carmarthen 1922; withdrew 1918. **Mr. Daniel Johns:** Born Llangunnog 1st January 1884, s of John Johns & Jane Rees. Welsh Independent. Married Florence, d of Colonel W. N. Jones (qv). Educated Old College School, Carmarthen; University of Wales, Aberystwyth. Farm worker. Miner. Chief Production Officer, Carmarthenshire 1914-18. Organising Secretary,

Carmarthenshire NFU 1918-31. Barrister, Middle Temple 1931. Clerk, Carmarthenshire CC 1931-49. The only candidate of the Agriculturalist Party, founded in 1908 by the NFU in England and Wales, ever to contest a Welsh seat. Of Carmarthen. Died 1952.

JOHNS Trefor: Referendum Party, Cardiff West 1997.

JOHNSON Alexander Boris de Pfeffel: MA (Oxon). Conservative, Clwyd South 1997; MP: Henley 2001. **Mr. Boris Johnson:** Born New York, 19 June 1964, s of Stanley Patrick Johnson MEP, writer, & Charlotte Mary Offlow Fawcett, painter (gs of last Interior Minister in the Imperial Turkish Government). Church of England. Married (1) Allegra, d of art dealer, Gala Serviado (2) 1993 Marina, d of Charles Wheeler, BBC correspondent, 2s 2d. Educated Eton (King's Scholar); Balliol College, Oxford (Classics; Brackenbury Scholar). President, Oxford Union. Journalist. Trainee. *Wolverhampton Express; Times* 1983. *Daily Telegraph* leader & feature writer 1987, EC correspondent 1989-94, Asst. Editor & Chief Political Columnist 1994. Political Correspondent, then Editor, *The Spectator* 1994-95. Hobbies: Painting, Cricket, Poetry, Cycling.

JOHNSON David Stanley: BA (Wales) SDP/Alliance, Islwyn 1983. **Mr. David Johnson:** Born 1947. Educated Lewis School, Pengam; University of Wales, Aberystwyth & Cardiff. Teacher: Head of English, Cwmcarn Comprehensive School. Labour election agent. Joined SDP 1981. Islwyn BC.

JOHNSON Richard Peter: BA (Wales). Natural Law Party, Mid & West List 1999, Cities of London & Westminster, 1997, Euro London 1999. **Mr. Richard Johnson:** Born Cambridge, 13 February 1952, s of Donald Edwin Johnson, town planner/architect, & Therese Andree Simone Johnson. Roman Catholic. Unmarried. Educated St. Albans RC Primary School; Larton Bush Comprehensive School; University of Wales, Aberystwyth (Politics/Economics). Hospital/Health Service Manager Queen Mary's Hospital, Roehampton 1973-84. Teacher of Transcendental Meditation 1984-87. President, Aberystwyth Students' Labour Club 1972-73. Joined Natural Law Party 1992, Chair NLP. Contested Westminster CC, Aylesbury DC, Buckinghamshire CC. Interests: Health, Education, Rehabilitation. Hobbies: Architecture, Swimming, Travel. Languages: English, French. Of London.

JOHNSTONE Robert Andrew: Natural Law Party, South/West List 1999; West Tyrone 1997. **Mr. Robert Johnstone:** Of Skelmersdale.

JONES Alec – see JONES Trevor Alec.

JONES Aled David: BA (London). BD (Wales). Conservative, Gower 1999. **Revd Aled Jones:** Married Pauline, 1d. Educated Amman Valley comprehensive School; University College, London; Welsh Independent College, Aberystwyth. Welsh Independent Minister. Ordained 1996. Pastorates Seilo, Llansawel, Crugybar & Rhydybont, Llanybydder, 1996-2000; St. David's Welsh United Church of Canada, Toronto, August 2000-03; St. Luke's, Etibicoke, Ontario 2003-. Hobbies: Watching rugby, Reading novels. Languages: Welsh, English.

JONES Allan – see JONES, David Allan.

JONES Alun – see JONES Ivor A. S.

JONES Alun Ffred: Plaid Cymru, Caernarfon 2003. **Mr. Alun Ffred Jones:** Born Llanelli 29 October 19491, s of Revd Gerallt Jones & Elizabeth Jane Griffiths, teacher (brother of Dafydd Iwan, qv). Welsh Independent. Educated Ysgol O. M. Edwards, Llanuwchllyn; Ysgol y Berwyn, Bala; University of Wales, Bangor. Teacher. Television Producer & Company Director, *Sain*. Chair: *Antur Nantlle*. Editor, *Y Ddraig Goch*. Arfon DC 1992-96. Gwynedd CC 1996 (Leader 1996-2003, Chairman). Shadow Minister, Finance, May-November 2003. Leader, Local Election 2004 Campaign 11.2003. Hobbies: Reading, Cycling, Theatre, Sport. Languages: Welsh, English. Of Llanllyfni.

JONES Alun Lloyd – see LLOYD JONES Alun.

JONES Alun Ogwen: BSc (Liverpool) PhD (Southampton) ARIC. Plaid Cymru, West Flint 1970; Cardiff West 1979. **Dr Alun Ogwen:** Born Pentre Broughton August 1939. Married 1968 Janey 1d. Educated Grove Park Grammar School, Wrexham; Liverpool University; Southampton University (Research Fellow). Lecturer in Chemistry, Flintshire Technical College. Head of Science, Rhydfelin Welsh School. Efenchtyd PC. Holywell UDC 1970-74. Secretary, Ruthin Branch, Plaid Cymru. Plaid Spokesman on Housing. Sentenced to one month in gaol for not having a road tax disk on his car, May 1969 in protest at the absence of bi-lingual disks; released during first day when someone paid his fine. Languages: Welsh, English.

JONES Alwyn K: Ecology Party, Pontypridd 1983. **Mr. Alwyn Jones:** Married 3c. Senior Lecturer, Polytechnic of Wales, Treforest.

JONES Ann – see JONES Margaret Ann.

JONES Arthur Lewis: Communist, Rhondda East 1970; Merthyr Tydfil B/E 1972, Feb. 1974. **Mr. Arthur Jones:** Born Ferndale 1917, s of David Jones. Married 2c. Toolmaker, Lines factory. AEF Shop Steward 1950; Branch Secretary 1955. Member, Merthyr Trades & Labour Council Industrial Section. Joined Communist Party 1940; Member, Welsh Executive 1956-. Merthyr Tydfil BC 1968-71. Of Merthyr Tydfil (1939). Died 1988.

JONES Arwel P: BSc (Wales). Plaid Cymru, Montgomery Feb. & Oct. 1974. **Mr. Arwel Jones:** Born Harlech 1936. Married. Educated Barmouth Grammar School; University of Wales, Aberystwyth. Physics Teacher, Llanidloes High School. Chair, Montgomeryshire Constituency, Plaid Cymru. Llanidloes BC. Interests: Welfare, Health, Pensions. Languages: Welsh, English. Of Llanidloes.

JONES Austin Ellis Lloyd (Mr. Justice Lloyd Jones): Kt 1945 MC LlB Hon. LLD (Liverpool) 1951. Conservative, Caernarfon Boroughs 1910, 1923; Flint, 1922. **Sir Austin Lloyd Jones:** Born 27 April 1884, s of Revd T. E. Jones, Rector of Hope, Flints. Educated Haileybury School; Liverpool University. Army 1914-18, Lieutenant RFA. Barrister, Inner Temple 1907, Bencher 1945. County Court Judge 1933-45. Chair, Tithe Arrears Investigation Cttee 1937-39; Cttee on County Court Procedure 1947-49. Chair, Flintshire QS 1948-. High Court Judge: Probate, Divorce & Admiralty Division 1945-48; Judge, Kings Bench Division 1948-. Died 31 March 1967.

JONES Barry – see JONES Stephen Barry.

JONES Benjamin George: CBE 1979 LlB Hon. LLD (Wales) 1983. Liberal, Merioneth 1959. **Mr. Ben G. Jones:** Born Llanarth 18 November 1914, s of Thomas Jones, farmer. Welsh Independent Deacon. Married Menna Wyn, d of Revd E. Wynn Jones, Holyhead 1s 1d. Educated Aberaeron Grammar School; University of Wales, Aberystwyth. London Solicitor 1948. Part-time Chair, Welsh Language Council 1973. Chair: London Welsh Assn; Cymdeithas Llyfrau Cymraeg Llundain; Liberal Party Council & Executive. Secretary, Hon. Society of Cymmrodorion 1965-83, Chair 1973-78. President, University of Wales, Aberystwyth 1986- (Vice-President 1978-86). Member, BBC General Council 1969. Hon. Member, Gorsedd of Bards. Languages: Welsh, English. Of London & Llanarth. Died May 1989.

JONES Brian Gwyther: National Liberal & Conservative, Gower, 1955. **Major Gwyther Jones:** Born Swansea, 1922. Educated Glanmor Grammar School, Swansea. Army 1940-45, Lieutenant, Welch Regt 1942; Major, Engineering Reserve.

Company Representative, food-importing manufacturers. Involved in youth work. Member, Conservative Party Welsh Executive. Of Three Crosses, Gower.

JONES Brisbane – see JONES Evan B.

JONES Caradog – see JONES David Caradog.

JONES Carwyn Howell: LlB (Wales). Labour AM. Bridgend 1999-. **Mr. Carwyn Jones:** Born Swansea, 21 March 1967, s of Caron Wyn Jones, Examinations Officer, & (Katherine) Janice Jones (headteacher, Bryncethin Primary School. Welsh Independent. Married 1994, Lisa Josephine, personal assistant, d of Edward & Stella Murray, 1d. Educated Brynteg Comprehensive School, Bridgend; University of Wales, Aberystwyth. Barrister 1991-99. Tutor, Centre for Professional Legal Studies, Cardiff 1977-99. Chair, University of Wales, Aberystwyth, Labour Club. Member: Fabian Society, Society of Labour Lawyers, Amnesty International, Unison, Bridgend Railway Co. Schools governor. Bridgend CBC. 1995-(Chair, Labour Group). Coity Higher ComC 1995-. Chair: Assembly South East Regional Cttee. Minister for Rural Affairs, also Assembly Business Manager 27.2.2002; Minister of Environment, Planning & Countryside 2003. Interests: Transport, Europe, Legal affairs. Hobbies: Sport, Reading, Travel, Bridgend RFC, Brynaman RFC. Languages: Welsh, English. Of Bridgend.

JONES Clayton F: Plaid Cymru, Cynon Valley B/E 1984. **Mr. Clayton Jones:** Born Ynysybwl 1953. Married Alison. Driving Instructor. Transport Manager. Established own bus, taxi & car hire company. Member: Institute of Transport Managers. Welsh Representative, National Assn. of Approved Driving Instructors. Taf Ely BC 1982. Mid Glam CC 1981. Contested Rhondda-Cynon-Taf BC (Tonteg) 1999. Joined Plaid Cymru 1968. Of Pontypridd.

JONES Colin Leonard: John Marek Independent, North List 2003. **Mr. Colin Jones**: Born Denbigh, 5 October 1946. Educated St. Asaph Grammar School. Author, local historian & community activist. Of Rhyl.

JONES Cyril Oswald: BA (Dublin). Labour, Anglesey 1924, Flint 1929, 1931. Joined Plaid Cymru 1969. **Mr. Cyril O. Jones:** Born Bethesda 1885, s of Humphrey Bradley Jones, schoolmaster, & Lucy Alice George, & brother of F. Llewellyn-Jones, MP (qv). whom he opposed at Flint. Educated Dublin University. Army 1914-18, Lieutenant RWF 1916, Captain. Solicitor. Legal Adviser, North Wales Miners' Assn 1920-. Member: NUT, TGWU. Wrexham BC 1920; Alder-

man, Mayor, Hon. Freeman 1951. Secretary, North Wales & Chester Poor Persons Cttee 26 years. Refused the OBE and MBE. Languages: Welsh; English. Of Wrexham. Died 1970.

JONES Dafydd Alun: BSc (Wales) 1951 MB ChB (Liverpool) 1957. Plaid Cymru Denbigh, 1959, 1964. **Dr. Dafydd Alun Jones:** Born Penmachno, July 1930. Married Megan. Educated Bethesda Grammar School; University of Wales, Bangor; University of Liverpool. Engaged in atomic research, 1951-52. Left on ground of conscience to read medicine. Psychiatrist, Denbigh Mental Hospital 1957. Senior Psychiatrist, Llangefni, Denbigh 1964-. Languages: Welsh, English. Of Denbigh.

JONES Dafydd Ieuan: BSc (Wales). Plaid Cymru, Ogmore, Oct. 1974, 1979. **Mr. D. Ieuan Jones:** Born Llannon, Cards 1943. Married Pamela, teacher, 2c. Educated Aberaeron Grammar School; University of Wales, Aberystwyth. Teacher (Chemistry): Maesteg Comprehensive School; Ysgol Gyfun Rhydfelin; Ysgol Gyfun Ystalyfera 1974. Founder, Maesteg *Aelwyd*. Led Learning Welsh classes at The Old Inn, Llangynwyd. Member: UCAC. Languages: Welsh, English. Of Maesteg.

JONES Dafydd Iwan – see IWAN, Dafydd.

JONES Dafydd Orwig – see ORWIG Dafydd.

JONES Daniel: BEM 1946. Labour, Barry 1955; MP Burnley1959-83. **Mr. Danos Jones**: Born Ystradgynlais 26 September 1908, s of Daniel Jones, miner. Married Phyllis, d of James Williams, 2c. Educated Ynyshir Elementary School; National Council of Labour Colleges. Miner 1920-32. Aircraft industry engineer 1936-4. Lecturer, NCLC 1948-59. AEU Organiser 1954-59. Member: CND. PPS 1964-67. Member, Estimates Cttee 1964- 66. Languages: Welsh, English. Died 16 February 1985.

JONES Darren: Plaid Cymru, Islwyn 1997. **Mr. Darren Jones:** Born 23 June 1973. Partner, Tracy, 1s. Educated Tonypandy Comprehensive School; Ystradmynach College. Accounts Administrator. Sales Samples Administrator, fabrics factory. Secretary, Plaid Cymru, Islwyn 1995-96. Contested local elections 1995. Caerphilly BC (Blackwood) 1999-. Chair: Blackwood Town Centre Development Group; Islwyn Borough Transport Ltd Board of Directors, South East Wales regional Waste Forum. Vice-Chair: National Housing & Town Planning Council. Member: Asylum Seekers Consortium SE Wales; Council, University of Wales, Court, University of Wales Cardiff. Of Blackwood.

Allan Jones.

JONES David Allan: BEd (Wales). Independent, Bridgend 1999. **Mr. Allan Jones:** Born Pyle, 28 June 1948, s of Mostyn Jones, coalminer & steelworks electrician's mate (Glam CC 1952-95) and Margaret Jenkins, Clerk to Community Council. Church in Wales. Unmarried. Educated Cynffig County School; Caerleon Training College; University of Wales, Swansea. Teacher 1971. Headteacher 1984. Cynffig ComC. 1974-. Vice-Chair, Bridgend & Ogmore YES Campaign. Joined Labour Party 1965. Secretary, Bridgend CLP 1983-89. Resigned 1998, over undemocratic system of selecting Labour candidates. Member: Côr Bro Ogwr, Welsh National Opera Community Choir, BBC National Chorus of Wales. Interests: Education, Pensions. Hobbies: Reading, Walking, Driving, Singing in choir. Of Kenfig Hill.

JONES David Brynmor: Kt 1906 PC 1912 QC 1892 LlB (London) 1874 Hon. LLD (Wales) 1919 FRHistS. Liberal MP Swansea District 1895-1914; Stroud 1892-95. **Rt. Hon. Sir D. Brynmor Jones:** Born Pentrepoeth, Swansea 12 May 1852, s of Revd Thomas Jones. Congregationalist. Married 1892, Florence Justina, widow of A. de M. Mocatta & d of Major Lionel Cohen. Educated University College School, London; University College, London. Barrister, Middle Temple 1876, Bencher 1899, Reader 1911. County Court Judge 1885-92, resigned to contest Stroud. Recorder: Merthyr Tydfil 1910-14, Cardiff 1914. Member: Welsh Land Commission 1907. Chair, Welsh Parliamentary Party 1910. Hon. Counsel & Junior Deputy Chancellor (1906-18) University of Wales. Vice-President & Council Chair, Hon. Society of Cymmrodorion. High Court Judge (Master of Lunacy) 1914. Died 6 August 1921. *Books: D. B. Jones, Essay on Home Rule and Imperial Sovereignty 1886, Address on Welsh history in the Light of Recent Research 1891, The Welsh People (with Sir John Rhys) 1900.*

JONES David Caradog: MA (Wales) 1937 FSS. Labour, Montgomery 1951, 1955, 1959. **Mr. Caradog Jones:** Born Llanidloes 1910. Presbyterian Church of Wales Elder. Educated Llanidloes Grammar School; University of Wales, Aberystwyth. Staff Tutor, University of Leeds. WEA Tutor, North Wales; Lecturer to the Forces. Lecturer in Philosophy & Politics, Manchester University. National Secretary, Assn of Tutors in Adult Education. Joined Labour Party 1930. Secretary, North Wales Labour Federation. Died 1973.

JONES David Erroll: BSc (Wales) MSc (Newcastle). Plaid Cymru, Pontypridd 1970. **Mr. Erroll Jones:** Born Tumble 1941, miner's son. Married Diane 1s. Educated University of Wales, Swansea (Maths); University of Newcastle upon Tyne (Computer Studies). In aircraft industry. Teacher at Carmarthen. Lecturer in Computer Studies, UWIST. Member, Llantwit Fardre RFC.

JONES David Fowden: JP (Caerns). Conservative, Caernarfonshire 1929. **Mr. Fowden Jones:** Born Criccieth, s of Revd Thomas Jones, & brother of Sir Robert Armstrong Jones. Married 2d. Farmer. Glaslyn RDC. Languages: Welsh, English. Of Criccieth. Estate £43,501. Died 5 May 1942.

JONES David Gwynfryn: JP (Flints). Labour, Flint 1922, 1924. **Revd D. Gwynfryn Jones:** Born Bryncrug, Tywyn 1 November 1867, s of John Jones; family moved to Penygraig, Rhondda 1874. Married 1888, Christina, d of John Lloyd, 2s. Educated Bryncrug Board School. Miner 1877-87. Student, Rhondda private school, Cardiff preparatory school. Started preaching at 17; candidacy for ministry twice rejected on health grounds. Methodist Minister. Ordained 1898. Probationer 1894, Ashton in Makerfield 1894-97, Ffynnongroyw 1897-98, Llangefni 1898-1901; Bangor 1901-1902, Chester 1902-04; ill-health took him to South Africa: Cape Town Welsh Nondenominational Church 1904-05; Llandudno 1905-09; Barmouth 1909. Superintendent, Welsh Wesleyan Assembly; Supernumerary 1911-12. Editor, *Y Gwyliedydd Newydd* 1912-40. President, North Wales Synod 1924. Secretary, North Wales Wesleyan Synod & Bookroom 1928-34, Chair 1934-38. Supernumerary 1938. President, North Wales Federation of Free Churches 6 years. Received Methodist Testimonial, 1938. Editor, *Y Winton; Ysbryd yr Oes.* Ex-Liberal, joined Labour Party 1914. Founder member, Flintshire Labour

Party. Flintshire CC 1908-. Alderman 1924-46. Languages: Welsh, English. Of Flint Mountain (1911). Died 14 December 1954.

JONES David Ian: LlB (London). Conservative, Conwy 1997, 1999; Chester 2001; AM North Wales 11 September 2002-03 (on resignation of Rod Richards). **Mr. David Jones:** Born London, 22 March 1952, s of Brynley Jones, pharmacist/army officer, & Elspeth Savage Williams, nurse. Anglican. Married Sara Eluned Jones, nurse, 2s. Educated Ruabon Grammar School; University College, London; Chester College of Law. Solicitor. Member, Convocation, University of London. Hon. Legal Adviser: St. Davids Hospice Foundation, Gwynedd, Hospice at Home, Llandudno Heritage Trust Foundation, Fundraisers, Llandudno, High School Hospital Coronary Care Unit Appeal. Trustee, Red Cross Society. Life Governor, Imperial Cancer Research Fund. Member, National Trust. Frequent broadcaster on BBC. Interests: Europe, Health, Crime, Anglo-American Relations. Hobbies: Walking, Reading, Watching Football (No time!) Languages: English, conversational Welsh, French, Italian. Adopted Parliamentary Candidate for Clwyd West, 1.10.03. Of Llandudno Junction.

JONES David Myrddin: Labour, Cardigan B/E 1932. **Revd D. Myrddin Jones:** Born Cynwil Caeio, 4 December 1871, s of David Jones, farmer, & Elizabeth Griffiths. Married 2s. Baptist Minister. Ordained 1900. Pastorates: Zoar, Beaufort 1900-10, Ebenezer, Senghenydd 1910-. A Liberal; Joined Labour Party 1918. Ebbw Vale UDC. Glamorgan CC 1919- (Chair, County Agriculture Cttee). Died 5 November 1939. Further Reading: *The Politics of Rural Wales; Howard C. Jones, The Labour Party in Cardiganshire, Ceredigion, No. 9. 1980-83.*

JONES David Richard: Conservative, Montgomery 2001, Clwyd South & North List 1999. **Mr. David Jones:** Born Welshpool, 19 December 1944, s of David Pryce Jones & Margaret Winifred Davies, farmers. Church in Wales. Married 1977, Susan Elizabeth Jones, teacher. Educated Guilsfield Church in Wales School; Welshpool Grammar School. Farmer. Friend, Mid Wales Opera. Director: Welshpool & Llanfair Light Railway; No. 1 Celita Cyf. Member: Country Landowners Assn. Chair, Montgomeryshire Conservative Assn. Montgomeryshire DC (Chairman 1992-94; Chair, Environmental Health Cttee 1985-90). Powys CC. Chair, Welshpool Working Party. School governor 1974-84. Governor, Montgomeryshire FE College 1975-79. Chair: Montgomeryshire Conservative Assn. Interests: Agriculture, Rural Affairs, Economy. Hobbies: Amateur dramatics. Languages: English, French. Of Guilsfield, Welshpool.

JONES David Thomas: MB ChB (Leeds) MRCGP 1966. Liberal Conway, Feb. & Oct. 1974. **Dr. David Jones:** Born Maenan, Dyffryn Conwy, June 1931. Married 3c. Educated Llanrwst Grammar School; Leeds University Medical School. Medical Practitioner. Asst. Senior Medical Research Officer, Welsh Hospital Board 1971-73, Clwyd Health Authority 1973-. Languages: Welsh, English. Of Colwyn Bay.

JONES Denise Idris: Labour, Merionydd/Nant Conwy 1999, 2001; AM Conwy 2003-. **Mrs. Denise Idris Jones:** Born Wrexham, 7 December 1950, d of James & Rhona Woodrow, shopkeepers. Welsh Independent (former Baptist). Married 1986, John Idris Jones, lecturer (retired) 2s. Educated Ruabon Girls' Grammar School; College of Education, Liverpool. Teacher of English & French, Grange Street School, Rhosllanerchrugog 1973. Ruthin ComC 1998-. Interests: Education, Unemployment. Hobbies: Golf, Tennis, Reading. Assembly Cttee Member: Education, Culture, Audit. Languages: Welsh, English, French.

JONES Dennis Terence: BA (Essex) 1972 PGCE (Huddersfield). Conservative, Caernarfon 1983; Meirionydd/Nant Conwy 1987. **Mr. Dennis Jones:** Born Corwen 16 August 1949. Married 1970, Janet, 1s 1d. Educated Bala Grammar School; Ysgol y Berwyn, Bala; Denbighshire Technical College; University of Essex (Politics); Huddersfield College of Education. Senior Lecturer, Politics & Public Administration, North East Wales Institute, Wrexham. Chair, Professional Assn of Teachers, Wales. Languages: Welsh; English.

JONES Douglas Arthur: Liberal, Cardiff North 1950, Bristol South 1945; Joined National Liberal Party, Nov. 1950. **Captain Douglas Jones:** Born Risca 1899. Married (2) Betty. Clerk. Army 1917-19, Captain RE. Accountant. Area Secretary, Wales & Mon. National Chamber of Trade 1926-40. Member: Unemployment Assistance Tribunal for Newport & Pontypool 1933; Newport Pilotage Board; Monmouthshire Territorial Army Assn. Founder Member, Industrial Development Council for Wales & Mon. Hon. Secretary, Leasehold Reform Assn 1937. Newport BC. 1936-45. Hotelier at Bournemouth 1955-65. Died February 1992.

JONES Dyfan Rhys: BA (Wales) 1998. Plaid Cymru, Gower 1999, Llanelli 2001. **Mr. Dyfan Jones:** Born Leiden, Netherlands, 11 November 1976, s of Dyfrig Jones, scientist. Welsh Independent. Educated Comberton Village College, Cambridge; Ysgol Gyfun Llanharri; University of Wales, Swansea (History & Politics). President, NUS Swansea 1998-99. Joined Plaid Cymru

1996. Chair, Federation of Plaid Cymru Students. Member, Plaid Cymru Council; Political Assistant, National Union of Teachers. Director, Wales-Lesotho Link. Interests: Education, Youth Issues. Hobbies: Gym, Reading, Watching sport. Languages: Welsh, English, Basic German. Of Grangetown, Cardiff (2002).

JONES Edgar Rees: KBE 1918 BA (Wales) MA (Wales) 1900. Liberal: Gower 1931; MP Merthyr Tydfil 1910-18, Merthyr 1918-22. **Sir Edgar Jones:** Born Cwmaman, Aberdare 27 August 1878, s of Revd Morgan H. Jones. Baptist. Married 1918 Mary Brackley (died 1970) 2c. Educated University of Wales, Cardiff. Lecturer in English Literature. Barrister, Grays Inn 1912. Controller, Priority Dept. Ministry of Munitions 1915-18. Chair: Welsh Consultative Council of Health 1920-22; National Food Canning Council. President, World Trade Alliance. Of Wattstown, then of Roundabouts, Sussex. Languages: Welsh, English. Died 16 June 1962. *Books etc: Edgar R. Jones: My Election Experiences 1910, The Meaning of Literature, The Art of the Orator: Selected Speeches, Changes in the Map of Europe.* Further Reading: *D. Ben Rees: Cymry Adnabyddus 1951-1972.*

JONES Edward: JP DL (Mon) CE. Conservative: North Mon 1886. **Mr. Edward Jones:** Born 1836, s of William Jones, Talybont-on-Usk. Married 1868 Susan Mary (died 1925) d of John Williams, Abercynic, Brecon, 5s 1d (1881). Engineer & Coalowner: Chair, Partridge, Jones & Co. Chair: South Wales & Mon Coalowners' Assn; South Wales & Mon Coal Conciliation Board. Pontypool UDC. Pontypool Board of Guardians. Monmouthshire CC Alderman. Estate £140,223. Of Pontypool. Died 4 September 1903.

JONES Edward: Conservative: Merthyr Tydfil 1970. **Mr. Edward Jones:** Born Merthyr Tydfil 1940, retailer's son. Married 2c. Educated Cyfarthfa Castle Grammar School, Merthyr Tydfil. Retailer (family business). Chair, Merthyr Tydfil Action & Study Group. Contested BC elections 1970. Of Merthyr Tydfil.

JONES Edwin: Liberal, Anglesey Feb. 1974. **Mr. Edwin Jones:** Born October 1917. Nonconformist lay preacher. Married 2c. Educated Froncysyllte Junior School; Rhodes University, South Africa. Senior Police Officer. Barrister (Inner Temple). Executive Officer, Law Society. Languages: Welsh, English. Of Connahs Quay.

JONES Edwyn Gwynne: Liberal: Anglesey 1964, Merioneth 1966. **Mr. Gwynne Jones:** Born Newtown, February 1928, s of Revd W. E. Jones, Presbyterian Minister. Presbyterian Church of Wales Elder, Lay Preacher 1952. Married Dyfnwen 2d. Educated Newtown Grammar

School; Bangor Normal College. Army 1949-51, Sergeant RAEC Teacher. Head of Religious Education & Deputy Head, Holyhead Comprehensive School. President, Anglesey Branch NUT. Chair: North Wales Liberal Federation 1963-65; Liberal Party of Wales 1965-66. Member, Schools Council Panel on Religious Education. Languages: Welsh, English.

JONES Eifion L. – see LLOYD-JONES Eifion.

JONES Elin: BSc Econ MSc (Wales). Plaid Cymru AM. Ceredigion 1999-. **Miss Elin Jones:** Born Llanwnen, 1 September 1966, d of John Jones, farmer, & Avril Jones. Educated Llanwnen Primary School; Lampeter Comprehensive School; University of Wales, Cardiff; University of Wales, Aberystwyth (Agricultural Economics). Economist, Rural Development Board for Wales 1991. Development Manager, Welsh Development Agency. Branch Chair, Unison. Aberystwyth TC. 1991- (Mayor 1997-98, Chair, Finance Cttee. 1994-96). Director: Radio Ceredigion 1995, Wes Glei Cyf (television production co). Member: Côr ABC. Chair, Ceredigion Plaid Cymru 1994-96. Vice-President, Plaid Cymru 1994-96, Chair, 2000-. Shadow Spokesperson on Rural Affairs 2000-02, Shadow Economic Development Minister, March 2002. Chair, Economic Development & Transport Cttee. Of Aberystwyth (1989).

JONES Elwyn Vernon: BA (Hull) DipEd (London). Liberal Democrat, Merthyr Tydfil & Rhymney and South/East List 1999; Swansea East 1997; Edmonton 1992. **Mr. Elwyn Jones:** Born Gwent, 25 September 1938, of mining family. Unmarried. Educated Lewis School, Pengam; Hull University; Kings College, London. Teacher. Founder/Chair, Southgate SDP. Chair, Enfield SDP 1984-87. Campaign Manager, South Wales-West Euro Election 1993. Member: Welsh Liberal Democrat Policy Cttee 1997. Secretary, Swansea & Gower Liberal Democrats 1996-97. Contested Swansea CCC (Mynyddbach) 1999. Hobbies: Painting, Drawing, Singing, Music, Sport. Of Tycoch, Swansea.

JONES Errol – see JONES David Errol.

JONES Evan Brisbane: British Party: Carmarthen Oct. 1974. **Mr. Brisbane Jones:** Born New Quay 1890. Welsh Independent deacon. Married. Widowed. Draper at Church Village until c.1955. Treasurer, Pontypridd Liberal Assn. After the 1974 election he founded the Keep Britain United Assn and advertised for and financed a candidate in 1979. Languages: Welsh, English. Retired to New Quay, Ceredigion.

JONES Evan Davies: 1st Bart 1917 JP DL (Pembs) Hon. LLD (Wales) 1917 MICE. Coalition

Liberal MP Pembroke 1918-22, PPC Llandaff & Barry 1918, withdrew October after 3rd son and son-in-law killed in France. **Major, Sir Evan D. Jones:** Born Fishguard 18 April 1853, s of Thomas Jones, Pentower & Martha Davie. Anglican. Married (1) Cecily (died 1913) d of Jacob Evans, 3c (plus 3s killed in France) (2) 1914 Lily d of James Railton. Educated Privately, University College, Bristol. Civil Engineer. Director, Topham, Jones & Railton, civil engineers. Major RE (TA). Member: War Office Cttee, Organisation of Civilian Labour for Defence of London 1914-18. Board of Trade Controller for Dyes and Petrol 1917-19. Chair, Transport Board 1918-19. Controller of Mines 1919-20. High Sheriff of Pembrokeshire 1911. Treasurer & Vice-President, National Library of Wales. Member: Council: University of Wales, Cardiff & Aberystwyth, Court of the University of Wales. President, Federation of Civil Engineering Contractors 1935-37. Lord Lieutenant of Pembrokeshire 1931-44. Pembrokeshire CC Alderman, Chair 1926-27. Languages: Welsh, English. Of Pentower, Fishguard & London. Died 20 April 1949.

JONES Evan Rowland: Liberal MP Carmarthen District 1892-95. **Major Evan R. Jones:** Born Tregaron 30 September 1840, s of William Jones, Penal, & Mary Rowland. Married 1867, Kate Alice, d of William & Jane Evans, Flanagan. Educated Tregaron & Llangeitho schools. Emigrated to USA at age of 15. Served in American Civil War 1861-65: private, Wisconsin Regt. Commissioned. *Hero of Gettysburg*. US Consul, Newcastle & Cardiff 23 years. Editor/Proprietor, *Shipping World*. President, Hon. Society of Cymmrodorion. Governor, University of Wales, Cardiff. Languages: Welsh, English. Of London. Estate £9113. Died 16 January 1920.

JONES Frederick W. F. – see FAREY-JONES F. W.

JONES Gareth: OBE 1991 BA DipEd (Wales). Plaid Cymru AM. Conwy 1999-2003. **Mr. Gareth Jones:** Born Blaenau Ffestinog, 14 May 1939, s of Thomas Jones, quarryman, & Catherine Louisa Jones. Welsh Independent. Married 1967 Jane Myra Davies, antiques dealer, 1s 3d (1d died). Educated Ysgol Sir Ffestiniog; University of Wales, Swansea (Geography). Teacher (Geography) Ysgol Sir Ffestiniog 1963, Ysgol Dyffryn Nantlle 1964-74. Deputy Principal, Snowdonia National Park Study Centre 1975. Headteacher, John Bright School, Llandudno 1976-93. Educational Consultant 1993. Conwy BC (Craigydon Ward) 1998-99. Member, Court, Coleg Harlech. School governor. Chair: Assembly Education Cttee & Standards Cttee. Interests: Gaining full national status for Wales. Languages: Welsh, English, French, Spanish. Of Llandudno.

JONES Gareth John: BA 1989 MA (Cantab). Conservative, Llanelli 2003. **Mr. Gareth J. Jones:** Born Beddau, 20 February 1964, s of Walter Clifford Jones, miner/lorry driver/fitter/Royal Mint worker, & Florence Mary Jones, teacher. Church in Wales. Educated Beddau Primary School; Bryn Celynnog Comprehensive School, Cardiff; Downing College, Cambridge. Solicitor in City of London 1989-91. Cardiff Barrister 1992. Joined Conservatives 1986. Treasurer/Chair, Kilburn Branch. Hobbies: Reading, Travel, Charitable Activities. Languages; Welsh (semi), English. Of Llantrisant.

JONES Gareth M.- see MORGAN-JONES G.

JONES Gerwyn – see JONES William Gerwyn.

JONES Gillian Marion: Plaid Cymru, South/East List 1999. **Mrs. Gillian Jones:** Born Tredegar, 4 February 1955, d of Norman Thompson, engineer, & Mary Lucy Thompson. Baptist. Married 1977, divorced 1986, 1d. Educated Higher Education. Optical Technician. Caerphilly CBC (Vice-Chair: Planning Cttee. Member: Bargoed Police Liaison Cttee. Chair: Caerphilly Constituency & local branch, Plaid Cymru. Interests: Equal Opportunities, Social Services, Housing. Hobbies: Travel, Reading. Of Bargoed.

JONES Graham P: Ecology Party: Cardiff West 1983; Green Party, South Wales Euro 1989. **Mr. Graham Jones:** Born Cardiff 1941. Married 1s. Social worker. Joined Green Party 1979. Contested local elections. Of Ely, Cardiff.

JONES Graham Selwyn: Forward Wales Party, Euro Wales 2004. **Mr. Graham Jones:** USDAW branch secretary. Community campaigner. Contested Wrexham CBC 2004. Of Coedpoeth, Wrexham.

JONES Griffith Winston Guthrie: QC 1963 LlB (Wales) 1935 MA (Cantab). Conservative & National Liberal: Wrexham B/E 1955. **Mr. Guthrie Jones:** Born 24 September 1914, s of Rowland Guthrie Jones (Liberal Agent, Merioneth 1922) & Mary Elizabeth Griffith. Married (1) 1959, Anna Maria McCarthy, County Mayo (died 1969) (2) Janet, d of Commander H. O. L'estrange. Educated Dolgellau Grammar School; Bootham School, York; University of Wales, Aberystwyth; St Johns College, Cambridge. Barrister, Grays Inn 1939. Royal Artillery 1940-46. Deputy Chair, Cumberland Quarter Sessions 1963-71. Recorder of Bolton 1968-71. Crown Court Recorder 1972-74. On Liberal short-list, Caernarfon Boroughs, May B/E 1945. Languages: Welsh, English. Of Culleenmore, Co. Sligo.

JONES Gwenan: BA 1909 MA (Wales) PhD (Minnesota). Plaid Cymru: University of Wales 1945. **Dr Gwenan Jones:** Born Cwm Tryweryn 1889. Unmarried. Presbyterian Church of Wales. Educated Bala Grammar School; University of Wales, Aberystwyth; Bryn Mawr College, Pennsylvania (Research & Study); University of Minnesota (Research Student/lecturer). Welsh Teacher: Pontypool 1910-14. Lecturer, Junior College, Missouri 1918-20. Lecturer in Education, University of Wales, Aberystwyth 1918-49. Girls' Camps Organiser, 1927-39. Editor, *Yr Efrydydd* 1935-53. President: Undeb Cymru Fydd, Chair: Churches' Joint Cttee for Welsh Girls Sent to Work in English Factories; Council, Urdd Gobaith Cymru. 1st President, UCAC. Warden, Welsh Guild of Graduates. Member: Merioneth Education Cttee, Cardiganshire Youth Cttee. Languages: Welsh, English. Of Llandre. Died 1971.

JONES Gwilym Haydn: Conservative MP Cardiff North 1983-97. **Mr. Gwilym Jones:** Born Chiswick 22 September 1947, s of Evan Haydn Jones & Mary Elizabeth Gwenhwyfar Moseley. Anglican. Married 1974, Linda Margaret John, 2c. Educated St. Clement Dane Grammar School; Whitchurch High School; Caerphilly Technical School. Insurance Broker. Director, Bowring Wales Ltd 1980-92. Liveryman, Welsh Livery Guild, 1993. Chair, Cardiff North West Conservative Assn. Founder/Chair, Friendship Force in Wales 1978-81. Vice-President, Kidney Research Unit for Wales Foundation. Chair: South Wales Passenger Transport Operators. Cardiff CC 1969-72, 1973-83. Member: Select Cttee Welsh Affairs 1983-85, Secretary: Welsh Conservative MPs 1984-92, All Party Group for Replacement of Animals in Medical Experiments 1987-92, PPS 1991-92. Under-Secretary for Wales 1992-97. Rowed for Wales in Speaker's Regatta 1986. Sub-Postmaster, Penyrheol Post Office, Caerphilly, 1997. Hobbies: Golf, Model Railways, Watching Wales Win at Rugby. Of Tongwynlais.

JONES Gwynoro Glyndwr: BScEcon. Labour MP. Carmarthen 1970-74. Joined SDP 1981. SDP: Gower B/E 1982, 1983, Carmarthen 1987. Rejoined Labour Party and sought Assembly nomination 1999 & Aberavon 2000. **Mr. Gwynoro Jones:** Born 21 November 1942, s of John G. Jones, Cefneithin. Presbyterian Church of Wales lay preacher, ex-chapel organist. Married 1967, Laura Miles (divorced 1991) 3c. Educated Gwendraeth Grammar School; University of Wales, Cardiff. Market Research Officer, Needle Bearing Co Llanelli 1966-67. Research & Publicity Officer, Wales Labour Party 1969-70. Economic Section Gas Board, 1967-69. PPS 1974. Council of Europe & Western European Union 1974. Head, Research & Intelligence Unit, West Glamorgan County Council, Oct. 1974. Asst Education Officer, Development Forward Planning 1977-88. Capital & Property 1988-93. Managing director: EPPC/Severn Crossing Ltd; West Wales Business Services Ltd; N-Media Ltd. Partner, Education Policy Publicity Consulting (education policy & marketing consultancy) 1993-. Broadcaster & S4C interviewer. Affiliate Inspector, Audit Commission. External Adviser, performance management OFSTED. Business excellence inspector. Lay inspector of schools 1993. Vice-Chair, District Council Assn 1974. 1st Chair SDP Wales 1982-85, 1987-88, Member SDP National Cttee 1981-84. Joint Chair, Alliance Cttee Wales 1983-88. Member: Council for Social Democracy 1982-88, Liberal Democrat Federal Executive 1983-90, European Movement, Charter 88. On Labour Party's List of Candidates Feb. 2000. President, National Eisteddfod 1974. Hobbies: Current affairs, Sport. Member: Glamorgan Cricket Club. Languages: Welsh, English. Of Swansea. *Books etc: G. G. Jones, The Record Put Straight 1973, SDP and the Alliance in Wales (1981-86) 1986.*

JONES Helen Ceri: Liberal Democrat, Neath 2003. **Miss Helen Ceri Jones:** Born Bromsgrove, 12 October 1974, d of William Trevor Jones, Haulage Logistics, & Glenys Wynne Jones, teacher. Educated Royal Welsh College of Music & Drama (HND Popular Music). Administrator. Traffic Warden. Member: UNISON. Secretary, Welsh Liberal Democrats Policy Cttee. Vice-Chair & Minute Secretary, Swansea & Gower Liberal Democrats. Interests: Policing, Crime, Public Services, Animal Welfare. Hobbies: Tennis, Music, Cats. Of Morriston, Swansea.

JONES Helen Mary: BA PGCE (Wales). Plaid Cymru: Islwyn, 1992; Montgomery 1997; Llanelli 2003. AM. Llanelli 1999-2003, Mid & West List 2003-. **Ms. Helen Mary Jones:** Born Cefn Coch, 29 June 1960, d of John Merfyn Jones & Daphne Jones, 1d. Educated Llanfair Caereinion High School; Colchester High School; University of Wales, Aberystwyth (History). Special Education Teacher, Gwent 1982-87. Wales Organiser, Action Aid 1987-91. Cynon Valley Crime Prevention Bureau 1991-93. Project Director: NACRO 1993-94; Dr. Barnado's Youth Justice Project 1994-96. Deputy Director, Equal Opportunities Commission for Wales 1996-99. Member, National Cttee. Welsh Women's Aid. Joined Plaid Cymru 1979. Member: Oxfam, Amnesty International, CND. Patron: Llanelli Male Voice Choir. Vice-President: Heart of Wales Travellers Assn. Member, Welsh Assembly Planning Cttee. Chair, Plaid Cymru Assembly Group 1999-2000. Shadow Minister: Social Inclusion & Equal Opportunity 1999; Environment, Transport & Equal Opportunities 2000-02; Education & Lifelong Learning, March 2002; Environment, Planning & Country-

Helen Mary Jones.

side, 5.11.2003. Group Spokesperson on Parliament for Wales Campaign 5.11.2003. Contested Plaid Cymru leadership 2000, Assembly group leadership 2003. Interests: Social policy, Equal opportunities, Economic development, Rural & international issues, Third World Development. Hobbies: Cooking, Playing with my Daughter, Sitting in the Garden. Languages: Welsh, English. Of Trimsaran.

JONES Henry: Labour: Anglesey 1935. **Mr. Henry Jones:** Born Holyhead 1878, s of Hugh & Margaret Jones, 12 Lower Park Street. Presbyterian Church of Wales Elder & lay preacher. Clerk, Marine dept Holyhead. Trade Union Official (TASS) Holyhead rail and Harbour. Holyhead UDC 1909-, Chair 1915, Father of the Council 1937. Anglesey CC 1919-, Chairman 1937, Alderman 1938. Chair: Anglesey Joint Standing Cttee; Anglesey CLP; WEA TCC Wales. Vice-Chair, Unemployment Independent Executive. Member, Council, University of Wales, Bangor Freemason Grand master. Persuaded Cledwyn Hughes (qv) to join Labour. Languages: Welsh, English. Died 6 November 1939.

JONES Henry Evans – see EVANS JONES H.

JONES Henry Haydn: Kt 1937 JP (Merioneth). Liberal MP Merioneth 1910-45. **Sir Haydn Jones:** Born Ruthin 1862, s of Joseph Haydn Jones & Catherine Daniel (brother of Revd Dr. J. D. Jones, Bournemouth). Calvinistic Methodist. Married Gwendolen, d. of Lewis D. Jones, Chicago. Edu-

cated Tywyn Board School; Tywyn Academy. Iron Merchant & Slate Quarry Owner. Merioneth CC Alderman 1903-49. Hon. Director of Education, Merioneth. Chair, Welsh Parliamentary Party 1934. Issued with Coalition Coupon in 1918 but repudiated it. Signed the nomination papers of the 1950 Merioneth Conservative Candidate. Languages: Welsh, English. Of Tywyn, Merioneth. Estate £70,800 Died 2 July 1950. *Published a collection of hymns, Cân a Moliant.*

JONES Hugh William: VRD BSc PhD CPhys FInstP ASA Peng MINCEUK. UK Independence Party, Preseli 2001. **Professor Hugh Jones:** Born Liverpool 12 March 1923, s of Joseph Redfern Jones, policeman, & Mary Jones. Married 1947 Dorothy, 1d. Agnostic. Educated St. Helens Technical College; Royal Navy Engineering College, London University. Physicist engineer. Professor/Head of Departments of Applied Physics in UK & Canada. RNVR & RNR; Lieut-Commander (E) RNR (Ret). President, national scientific assns. Member: Amnesty International. Volunteer worker in developing countries. Of Swansea.

JONES Huw M. – see MORRIS-JONES H.

JONES Hywel Glynne: BA (Wales) 1928 LlB (London). Labour: West Flint 1955. **Mr. Hywel Glynne Jones:** Born Wrexham 1906, s of Cyril O. Jones (qv). Married 4c. Educated Alun School, Mold; University of Wales, Aberystwyth; London University. Solicitor, 1929. Army 1939-45, RAC. & Judge Advocate General's Dept. Chair, Dee, Clwyd & Severn Tourist Assn. Joined Labour Party 1923. Languages: Welsh, English. Of Gresford.

JONES Hywel William Wyn: BSc MSc (Wales). Plaid Cymru, Cardiff North 2003. **Mr. Wyn Jones:** Born Cardigan, 15 March 1953, s of Benjamin Percy Jones, farmer, & Daisy Jones, housewife. Welsh Independent. Married Heulwen Jones, 1s 3d. Educated Cynwyl Elfed Primary School; Queen Elizabeth Grammar School, Carmarthen; University of Wales, Aberystwyth (Electronic Physics). Information Systems Consultant. Election Agent. Interests: Transport, Economic Development. Hobbies: Sport, Gardening, DIY, Choral Singing. Languages: Welsh, English. Some French. Of Whitchurch, Cardiff.

JONES Idwal (Labour) – see JONES James Idwal.

JONES Idwal: Pensioners' Party, Mid & West List 2003. **Mr. Idwal Jones:** Born Bangor. Army. Police at Salford. President & Chair: National Assn of Retired Police Officers. Of Lancashire. Withdrew after nominations closed.

Ieuan Wyn Jones.

JONES Ieuan Wyn: LlB. Plaid Cymru: Denbigh Oct. 1974, North Wales Euro 1995; MP Ynys Môn 1987-2001; AM. Ynys Môn 1999-. **Mr. Ieuan Wyn Jones:** Born 22 May 1949, s of Revd John Jones, Baptist Minister, & Mair Jones, nurse. Baptist. Married 1949, Eirian Llwyd, 2s 2d. Educated Pontardawe Grammar School; Ysgol y Berwyn, Bala; Liverpool Polytechnic. Solicitor 1974-87. National Chair, Plaid Cymru 1978-82, Vice-Chair 1975-79. Whip 1992-95. Plaid Cymru Assembly, resigned, May 2003. Leader, Assembly Group, September 2003. Vice-Chair, Parliamentary Friends of Croatia 1991. Member, Royal College of Nurses Panel. Member. Select Cttees on Agriculture 1992-97, Welsh Affairs 1990-92. Director, Westminster Foundation for Democracy. Hon. Member, Gorsedd 2001. Hobbies: Sport, Local history. Languages: Welsh, English. Of Llangefni. *Books: Ieuan Wyn Jones, Europe and the Challenge for Wales 1996. Thomas Gee 1998.*

JONES Iolo ab Eurfyl: BA (Wales). Liberal: Merioneth Feb. 1974. Withdrew October 1974, because of pressure of work. **Mr. Iolo ab Eurfyl Jones:** Born Rhymney, January 1937. Married 2d. Educated Dolgellau Grammar School; University of Wales, Swansea (History). Secretary & President, College Liberal Assn. Audio-Visual Aids Officer, Merioneth County Council, then Youth & Community Officer. Rugby Union Referee. Vice-Chair, Bala Urdd National Eisteddfod. Bronze Medal for Life Saving. Languages: Welsh, English. Of Llwyngwril.

JONES Ivor Alun Samuel: LlB (Wales). Conservative: Pontypridd Feb. & Oct. 1974, Cardiff

SE 1979. **Mr. Alun Jones:** Born Gorseinon 21 December 1937, s of David & Catherine Jones. Married Jeanette Ferrier, 3c. Educated Gowerton Grammar School; University of Wales, Aberystwyth. Part-time lecturer in Law 1963-65. Solicitor 1967. Chair: Bletchley Young Conservatives. Treasurer, Pontypridd Conservative Assn. Secretary: County of Glamorgan Local Medical Cttee; Welsh Assn of Medical Cttees. Chair, South Glamorgan Health Authority, 1984-. South Glamorgan CC 1966-67. Chair, Llantwit Major RFC 1968-74, President 1974-76. Of Llanblethian.

JONES Jacqueline Edwina: Conservative, North List 1999. **Mrs. Jacqui Jones:** Born Sandbach, Cheshire, 4 March 1945, d of Thomas Ernest Benson, self-employed, & Winifred Freda Taylor. Church of England (Choir member, PPC & Treasurer, Llanfwrog). Married 1970, Thomas Stuart Jones, self-employed, 2d. Educated Independent School. Self-Employed Financial Controller, design & printing co. Ruthin TC (Mayor). Contested Denbighshire CC (Ruthin) 1999. Chair: Clwyd West Conservative Assn. Deputy Area Chair. School Governor. Hobbies: Sewing, Piano, Singing, People. Languages: English, Learning Welsh. Of Ruthin.

JONES James Idwal: BSc Econ London (external). Labour: Denbigh 1951; MP Wrexham 1954-70. **Mr. Idwal Jones:** Born 30 June 1900, s of James Jones & Elizabeth Bowyer, brother of T. W. Jones (qv). Churches of Christ lay preacher (1921). Married 1931, Catherine Humphreys, 3c. Educated Ruabon Grammar School; Bangor Normal College. Teacher 1922. Headteacher, Grange Secondary Modern School, 1938-54. Joined ILP. Member, CND. Member: Commons Group Reviewing Electoral Law & Procedure 1965. Chair: Welsh Labour Group 1960-61, Welsh Parliamentary Party 1957-58. Member: Court of the University of Wales. Hon. Member, Gorsedd. Languages: Welsh, English. Died 18 October 1982. *Books: A Geography of Wales 1938, An Atlas of Denbighshire 1950, Atlas Hanesyddol Cymru 1952, A Geographical Atlas of Wales 1955, A Historical Atlas of Wales 1955, A New Geography of Wales 1960, J. R. Jones (Ramoth) a'i Amserau 1967.*

JONES John (Jack): CBE 1948. Liberal: Neath 1929. **Mr. Jack Jones:** Born Merthyr Tydfil 28 November 1884, s of David Jones, miner, & Sarah Ann Jones. Married (1) 1908, Laura Grimes Evans of Builth (Died 1948) 5c (2) 1954 Gladys Morgan of Rhiwbina (1s killed, 1s died in War). Educated St. David's Elementary School, Merthyr Tydfil. Miner 1896-1902. Soldier 1902-06, 1914-19. Miner 1906-14. Navvy. Unemployed. Miners' Agent 1923, Manager, Albert Hall Cinema, Swansea. Lecturer, Writer, Novelist from 1934. Joined ILP 1900. Founder Member, Communist Party 1920. Member: Labour Party 1924; Liberal Party 1929-31, 1932-39; New Party 1931, Supported National Government 1939-45. Spoke for every Conservative candidate in Cardiff after 1945. Refused an invitation to contest the 1942 by-election at Llandaff and Barry as a *'Win the War'* Candidate. Lectured for Moral-Re-armament. 1st President, English section, Welsh Academy. Received a £700 award from the Welsh Arts Council Feb1970 for his *distinguished contribution to the literature of Wales for many years.* Languages: Welsh, English. Of Rhiwbina, Cardiff. Died 7 May 1970. *Books: Jack Jones: Rhondda Roundabout 1934, Black Parade 1935, Bidden to the Feast, 1938, Off to Philadelphia in the Morning 1947, Some Trust in Chariots 1948, River out of Eden 1951, Lily of the Valley 1952, Lucky Lear 1952, Time and the Business 1953, The Man David 1944, Unfinished Journey 1937, Mine and Mine 1946, Give me back my heart 1950. Further Reading: Keri Edwards: Jack Jones 1974. D. Ben Rees: Cymry Adnabyddus 1952-1972.*

JONES John Edward: BA (Wales) 1927. Plaid Cymru: Caernarfon 1950. **Mr. J. E. Jones:** Born Melin-y-Wig, 10 December 1905, s of Rice Price Jones (died 1906) & Jane Jones. Presbyterian Church of Wales Sunday School teacher. Married 1940, Olwen Hefin, d of Revd W. H. Roberts, 2c. Educated Melin-y-Wig Elementary School; Bala Grammar School; University of Wales, Bangor. Secretary, Bangor SRC. Teacher in London 1928-30. 1st Secretary, Plaid Cymru college branch 1926. Secretary, London branch 1928. Secretary/Organiser, Plaid Cymru 1930-May 1962. Retired on health grounds, 1962. Conscientious Objector on Nationalist Grounds. Editor: *Welsh Nation & Y Ddraig Goch.* Author & pamphleteer. Languages: Welsh, English. Died 30 May 1970. *Books: J. E. Jones: Tro i'r Yswisdir 1964, Llyfr Garddio 1969, 1970. Tros Cymru.* Further Reading: *Kenneth O. Morgan, Peace Movements in Wales 1899-1945, The Welsh History Review, Vol. 10, June 1981, page 426.*

JONES John Griffith: JP FCA. Conservative: Pontypridd 1922. **Major J. Griffith Jones:** Son of Griffith Rhys Jones, *Caradog,* choral leader). Anglican (chorister 30 years). Educated Llandovery College. Chartered accountant. Partner, W. W. Neal Ltd Cardiff. Chair: Rhondda Valleys & Ely Breweries Co Ltd 1923; William W. Neal Breweries Ltd Cardiff 1927; Cardiff Malting Co. Director, 11 companies. Joined Welch Regt Volunteers 1898; Captain 1899, Major 1913, retired 1913. Major, 4th Batt Welch Regt 1914-18. Member: Governing Body of the Church in Wales; Llandaff Diocesan Finance Cttee. Secretary, Ystrad & Pentyrch Hunt. Freemason: Grand Master. President: Pontypridd Conservative

Assn. Chair: Pontypridd Ratepayers' Assn. Captain, Pontypridd Golf Club 1912-13, President 1914. Pontypridd UDC. Languages: Welsh, English. Of Pontypridd. Estate £49,198. Died 21 October 1928.

JONES John Griffiths: Plaid Cymru: Ogmore 1987. **Mr. John Jones:** Born 1960. Married 4c. Educated Ogmore Grammar School; Bridgend Technical College; Neath Technical College. Colliery Electrician. NUM Lodge Official. Chair, Ogwr Plaid Cymru. Ogwr BC. The only miner contesting a Welsh seat in 1987. Of Nantymoel.

JONES John Gwynedd: OBE 1977. Liberal: Anglesey 1979. **Mr. John Gwynedd Jones:** Born 1916. Anglican. Married 1974, Ann, 2s. Educated Brynrefail Grammar School; University of Wales, Bangor. Army 1939-45. Farmer. Member, Anglesey Labour Party Executive until just before the 1979 election. Anglesey CC Ynys Môn BC Chair. Policy & Resources Cttee, Mayor 2 years. Chair, Steering Cttee to set up Ynys Môn CC. Languages: Welsh, English. Of Rhosybol. Died 6 June 1984.

JONES John Lloyd: Labour: Cardigan 1931, Exeter 1929. **Mr. J. Lloyd Jones:** Born Wrexham 1884, miner's son; family moved to Monmouthshire. Educated Victoria School, Ebbw Vale; Lewis School, Pengam; Pupil Teacher; Student, York Training College 1902-5. Teacher 1905. Headteacher, Cwm Ystwyth Primary School 1906-11, Beaufort Junior School 1911-. Hon. Secretary, Federation of Welsh Class Teachers. Monmouthshire CC 1919- (Chair: Higher Education Cttee 1930). Languages: Welsh, English.

JONES John Morgan: Labour MP Caerphilly B/E 1921-. **Mr. Morgan Jones:** Born Bargoed 3 May 1885, s of Elias Jones, miner & Sarah Evans. Baptist Lay Preacher. Married 1923, Gladys Thomas. Educated Gelligaer & Bargoed Elementary Schools; Lewis School, Pengam; Pupil teacher, Gilfach School, Pengam 1903-05; University College, Reading 1905-07 (President, Student Representative Council). Teacher: Gilfach School 1907-14, Bargoed Boys School 1914-15. President, Glamorgan Federation of Teachers 1913-15. Chair, South Wales Branch, No Conscription Fellowship & Member, National Cttee. Called up 1916, among first COs: Fined £100 under DORA for a leaflet calling for the repeal of the Conscription Act 30 May 1916, fined £2 & handed over to military authorities; Underwent court martial, detention, hard labour in camp prisons, released to work of national importance and then arrested as a deserter 18 April 1919. Released 2 August 1919. Deprived of his teaching post & refused re-instatement. Colliery labourer 1918. Joined: ILP 1908. Organising Secretary, Welsh Section, ILP. Member, ILP National Council 1921-22. Gelligaer UDC 1911-22. Glamorgan CC 1919-22. Member: Court of the University of Wales. First Great War CO to become MP. Joint Secretary, Select Cttee, India Constitutional Reforms 1933-34. Labour Whip 1922-24. Parl-Secretary, Education 1924, 1929-31. Chair, Select Cttee Public Accounts 1931-36. Member: Labour Party NEC 1922. Secretary: Welsh Labour Group 1922. Chair: Labour Party Advisory Education Cttee 1938. Estate £6,518. Of London. Died 23 April 1939. Further Reading: *Kenneth O. Morgan, Peace Movements in Wales 1899-1945, Welsh History Review, Vol. 10, June 1981, page 414.*

JONES John Owen: Conservative: Anglesey 1950. **Mr. Jack Owen Jones:** Born Brymbo 1903. Married Leah. Educated elementary schools. Colliery worker 1917, steelworker, trade union official, civil servant, accountant, farmer. Member NFU. Governor, Wrexham & East Denbs. War Memorial Hospital. Wrexham RDC. Languages: Welsh, English. Of Penycae, nr Wrexham.

JONES John Roberts: CBE 1959 MC 1918 Croix de Guerre (Belgium) Hon. LLD (Wales) BA (Wales) BA MA (Cantab). Liberal: Rhondda West 1923. **Major J. R. Jones:** Born Llanuwchllyn, 6 June 1887, s of David Jones. Welsh Independent. Educated Llanuwchllyn Primary School (pupil teacher)); Bala Grammar School; University of Wales, Bangor (1st Classics); Emmanuel College, Cambridge (1st Economics). Teacher. Army 1914-18, Royal Artillery; (Wounded 4 times, Royal Flying Corps; Military Intelligence. Member, Foreign Office Missions: Ukraine, Finland, Germany & Austria 1918-21. Barrister 1921. In practice at Shanghai 1925. Secretary, International Settlement. Lived in Hong Kong in 1930s and from 1945. President, Hong Kong Welsh Society. Hon. Member, Gorsedd. Leader, Undeb y Cymry ar Wasgar 1957. Presented Bardic Crown 1937 and Bardic Chair 1959 to National Eisteddfod. Member, Hon. Society of Cymmrodorion. Languages: Welsh, English. Died Hong Kong 15 January 1976.

JONES John Rowland: BA 1952 MA (Wales) 1956. Plaid Cymru: Anglesey 1955. **Mr. Rowland Jones:** Born Tregarth, Caerns 1931. Educated Bethesda Grammar School; University of Wales, Bangor (Secretary SRC) Research Student (Welsh) at Bangor. Languages: Welsh, English.

JONES John Tudor (John Eilian): OBE 1972 MA (Oxon). Conservative: Anglesey 1964, 1966, 1970. **Mr. John Eilian:** Born Llaneilian December 1909. Anglican. Married Eluned, 3c. Educated Llangefni Grammar School; University of Wales, Aberystwyth (did not finish course); Jesus College, Oxford. Considered Anglican priesthood but turned to journalism. Journalist, *Western*

Mail, 1924-27; Editor, *Times of Mesopotamia;* with *Daily Mail* 4 years; Founder Editor *Y Cymro* 1932-34; *Times of Ceylon* 1934; BBC 9 years: Head of Programmes (Wales), Director, European Programmes; Editor, *The Border Counties Advertiser;* Managing Editor, *Caernarfon Herald* Group 1953-83. Member, Governing Body, Church in Wales. National Eisteddfod Chaired Bard 1947, Crowned Bard 1949. Member: Gorsedd of Bards. Member, Royal Commission on the Press 1974-77. Languages: Welsh, English. Died 10 March 1985.

JONES John Tudor: BA (Open). Liberal Democrat, North List 1999, Delyn 2001. **Mr. Tudor Jones:** Born Holyhead 27 December 1952, s of Richard Hughes-Jones, steelworker, & Ceinwen Hughes-Jones. Married 1976, Sally Annette Ogle Jones, child therapist, 1s 1d. Educated Ysgol Glanrafon; Ysgol Maes Garmon, Mold; Bangor Normal College, Open University. Geography Teacher & Head of Humanities, St. David's High School, Saltney. Ysceifiog ComC. School Governor. Member: *Teledu i Bawb* campaign, Deeside Athletic Club. Chair, Delyn Liberal Democrats, Agent 1997, 1999. Chair, Conference 2002. Interests: Devolved Government, Environment. Languages: Welsh, English. Of Holywell.

JONES John Walter: BA (London). Liberal: Ogmore 1929. **Mr. John Walter Jones:** Born Ystradgynlais 1871, s of Revd John Cledwyn Jones & Elizabeth Winstone Walters. Presbyterian Church of Wales Elder. Married 1902 Helen, 3c. Educated British School; Swansea Grammar School; London University. Teacher, Pentre 1889-92, Ystalyfera, 1892-1907. Headteacher, Ystradgynlais Grammar School 1907-17; Neath Grammar School 1917-1931, 1940-45. Freemason. Chair: Neath Liberal Assn; Welsh Liberal Federation 1929. Vice-President, Liberal Party of Wales. Member: Liberal Party Executive; Central Welsh Board. President: Glamorgan Headteachers' Assn; Neath Cymmrodorion. Languages: Welsh, English. Died January 1951.

JONES Jon Owen: BSc (East Anglia) PCGE (Wales). Labour: Cardigan 1987; MP Cardiff Central 1992-. **Mr. Jon Owen Jones:** Born Maerdy, Rhondda 19 April 1954, s of Gwynfor Owen Jones, optical salesman/ex-miner & Dorothy Mary Davies, teacher. Married 1989 Alison Clement, 2s 1d. Educated Ysgol Gyfun Rhydfelin; University of East Anglia (Ecology); University College, Cardiff. Biology Teacher at Caerphilly 1977-92. President, Mid-Glam NUT. Joined Labour Party 1981. Cardiff CC (Chair, Economic Development Cttee). Member, Co-operative Party. President, Campaign for a Welsh parliament. Opposition Whip 1993-97. Government Whip 1997-98. Under-Secretary,

Wales 1998-99. Chair: House of Commons Information Cttee 1997-98. President, Camp Wales Assn 1988-91. Hobbies: Watching rugby, Natural History, Cooking, Walking. Languages: Welsh, English. Of Cardiff.

JONES Joseph: JP (Brecs) BA 1901 BD 1904 (Wales) MA (Oxon) Hon. LLD (Wales) 1949. Liberal: University of Wales 1923, Withdrew as Labour candidate in favour of Mrs. H. M. Mackenzie 1918. **Revd Professor Joseph Jones:** Born Rhydlewis 7 March 1877, s of Reuben & Jane Jones. Moved to Cwmaman, Aberdare 1882. Welsh Independent. Married 1907 Gwenllian de Lloyd, 2s 1d. Educated Rhydlewis Board School; Dinmor Edwards School, Pontypridd; University of Wales, Cardiff; Congregational Memorial College, Brecon (1st Independent to gain University of Wales BD); Mansfield College, Oxford; Exhibitioner, Jesus College, Oxford; Heidelberg University 1910. Lam. Professor of New Testament Studies, Brecon 1907, Principal 1943-. Dean of Theology, University of Wales 1931-34. Chair, Union of Welsh Independents 1946-47. Moderator, Free Church Federal Council of England & Wales 1949-50. Member: Council, Congregational Union of England & Wales, Board, London Missionary Society. Freemason. Breconshire CC Alderman, Chair, Chair, Education Cttee 31 years. Chair: Central Welsh Board. 1st Chair, Welsh Joint Education Cttee 1948. Vice-President, Assn. of Education Cttees, Member, Court & Council, University of Wales, of Brecon. Vice-President, Federation of Education Authorities. Languages: Welsh, English. Died April 1950. *Books: Esboniad ar Matthew 1913-14. Further Reading:* Pennar Davies, *'Episodes in the History of Brecknockshire Dissent'*, 62-64; Ivor Thomas Rees, *'Joseph Jones, 1877-1950', Brycheiniog, Vol. XXXV, 2003, 117-130.*

JONES Josiah Towyn: JP (Carms). Liberal MP East Carmarthenshire B/E 1912-18, Llanelli 1918-22. **Revd Towyn Jones:** Born New Quay, Cards 28 December 1858, s of John & Elizabeth Jones. Welsh Independent. Married 1885, Mary Howells, 2d. Educated elementary school. Shepherd at 11. Sailor. Started preaching at 16. Student: Towyn Grammar School at 17; Carmarthen Presbyterian College. Welsh Independent Minister, Ordained 1879: Gwernllwyn, Dowlais 1879-85, Bethel, Garnant 1885-1906, Missioner & Organiser of *"Y Gronfa"* (Union's Century £20,000 Fund) 1906-12. Received presentation of £1; Court, University of Wales, Aberystwyth. Secretary, East Carmarthenshire Liberal Assn. Member, Executive, Break down in health, 1922. Languages: Welsh, English. Estate £9,174. Died Ammanford, 16 November 1925.

JONES Laura Anne: BA (Plymouth) 2000. Conservative, Caerphilly 2003; AM South/East List

Laura Anne Jones.

2003-. **Miss Laura Anne Jones:** Born Newport 21 February 1979, d of John Dilwyn Jones, farmer, & Penelope Anne Jones, college lecturer. Educated Caerleon Comprehensive School; University of Plymouth (Politics). Public Relations Officer. Worked as hotel waitress during election campaign. Joined Conservatives 1995. Chair: South East Wales Conservative Future 2000-02. Fundraiser, Red Cross, Leukemia Research, SCOPE. Youngest AM 2003. Conservative Spokesperson on Sport 2003. Interests: Health, Education, Sport, Agriculture. Hobbies: Hockey, Swimming, Netball, Skiing, Cycling. Languages: Learning Welsh, English, French, German. Of Llanbadoc, Usk.

JONES Lewis: Kt 1944 JP (Swansea) 1934 Hon. LLD (Wales) 1954. National Liberal & Conservative, Swansea West 1950; Liberal National MP 1931-45. **Sir Lewis Jones:** Born Brynaman 12 February 1884, s of Councillor Evan Jones & Margaret Jones. Congregationalist. Married 1911, Alice Maud, d of Frederick W. Willis, Bath, 2s (one killed in army, India, 1947). Educated Ammanford Grammar School; Reading University. Teacher at Reading 1906-10. Liberal Party Agent 1910-14. Secretary, Priority Department, Ministry of Munitions 1914-17. Secretary, South Wales Siemens Steel Assn 1917-61. Member, Joint Cttee National Health Insurance, 1933. Parliamentary Charity Commissioner 1937-45. Member: BBC General Advisory Council 1952-. Vice-President, University of Wales, Swansea. Member: Court, University of Wales. Chair, Swansea RFC.

Sir Lewis Jones.

Member: Glamorgan Cricket Club. President, Swansea Chamber of Trade Estate £37,864. Languages: Welsh, English. Of Sketty, Swansea. Died 10 December 1968.

JONES Malcolm Douglas: Referendum Party: Alyn & Deeside 1997. **Mr. Malcolm Jones:** Born Newbridge, Mon 1936. Married 4c. Systems Analyst. Of Holywell (1983).

JONES Marc: John Marek Independent Party, 2003. **Mr. Marc Jones:** Born Bangor 1 June 1962. Married 1990, 2s. Educated Ysgol Maes Garmon, Mold. Journalist: local newspapers, HTV, BBC TV producer 10 years. Former member, Cymru Goch. ComC. Interests: Renewable Energy. Hobbies: Music, Poetry, Sport. Languages: Welsh, English. Of Penycae, Wrexham.

JONES Margaret (Maggie): Born South Wales. Full time official, UNISON. Chosen as Labour prospective parliamentary candidate for Blaenau Gwent in the face of strong opposition from local party members together with Llew Smith retiring MP and Peter Law AM to an all-women list (only 60 out of 700 members attended the selection meeting, 11.12.2003). Labour Prospective Parliamentary Candidate, Blaenau Gwent. Of London.

JONES Margaret Ann: Labour AM Vale of Clwyd 1999. **Mrs. Ann Jones:** Born Rhyl, 4 November 1953, d of Charles Jones & Helen Sadler. Christian. Married 1973, Adrian Jones, 1s 1d. Educated Rhyl. Grammar/High School. Emergency Call Operator, Flintshire & Clwyd Fire Service 1970-76. Control Operator/Senior Control Operator/Watch Officer, Clwyd Fire Service

1976-9. Fire Control Officer, Merseyside Fire Brigade 1991-99. National Official, Fire Brigades Union 1982. Agent for Chris Ruane MP 1997. Member: Christian Socialist Movement. Denbighshire CC 1995-99. Rhyl TC 1991-99 (Mayor 1996-97). Chair: Assembly Labour Group 1999; Assembly North Wales Regional Cttee; Local Government Cttee. Interests: Education, Tourism, Community Safety, Regeneration. Of Rhyl.

JONES Martyn David: CIBiol. MIBiol. Labour MP Clwyd South West 1992-97, Clwyd South 1997- **Mr. Martyn Jones:** Born Wrexham 1 March 1947, s of Vernon Jones, engine driver & Violet Jones. Married 1974 Rhona, d of Roger Bellis, 1s 1d, divorced 1991. Educated Grove Park Grammar School, Wrexham; Liverpool Poly, Trent Poly. Microbiologist, in Wrexham Lager Beer Co 1968-87. Joined Labour Party 1977, Chair, Clwyd Area Labour Party. Clwyd CC 1981-89. Opposition spokesman on Agriculture 1994-95, Chair: Select Cttee on Agriculture 1987-94, Wales, 1997-2001. Chair: PLP Welsh Group; Parliamentary Yacht Club. Opposition Whip 1988-92. Member: SERA, TGWU: CND Council, Christian Socialist Movement. Interests: Agriculture, Environment, Science, Ecology. Hobbies: Sailing, Target Shooting, Back Packing. Of Johnstown, Wrexham.

JONES Mary A: BA (Oxon) DipEd (Wales). Conservative: Llanelli 1970. **Miss Mary Jones:** Born Cardiff December 1927, d of W. J. Jones, Professor of Chemistry. Anglican. Educated Howells School, Llandaff; Oxford University; University of Wales, Cardiff (Greek & History). Asst. Organiser, Swansea West Conservative Assn. Teacher, International School, Lausanne 1958-60. History Teacher, Cranborne Chase School, Wilts 1962-68. Part-time Teacher, Heathfield Girls School, nr Reading, 1968-. Diocesan Missioner, Swansea & Brecon. Of Llanfrynach, nr Brecon.

JONES Maurice: United Socialists, Clwyd South 1999. **Mr. Maurice Jones:** Ex-Brymbo steelworker. Sought work in England & Germany. Unemployed at time of election. Founder Member, Wrexham Miners' Support Group 1984-85. Wanted to stand as *Welsh Socialist Alliance*, but this was not allowed. Campaigner for Workers' Rights. Contested Wrexham BC 21/9/2000. Of Rhosllanerchrugog.

JONES Michael: BSc (Wales) AIB. Plaid Cymru, South East Wales Euro 1979. **Mr. Michael Jones:** Born Aberdare 1937. Church in Wales. Married 2c. Educated Aberdare Grammar School, University of Wales, Cardiff (President, Debating Society). Accountant & Chartered Company Secretary. Army, RWF. NCO. Runner Up, BBC *Brain of Britain* 1968. Ex-PPC Bedwellty. Contested local elections (Bargoed) 1973. Member,

Diocesan Board of Finance; Church Warden & Parish Treasurer. Of Bargoed.

JONES Michael: Referendum Party, Alyn & Deeside 1997.

JONES Morgan – see JONES John M.

JONES Morgan Thomas Laugharne Griffith – see GRIFFITH JONES M. T. L.

JONES Norman: Liberal: Caerphilly 1979. **Mr. Norman Jones:** Born Newport April 1944. Educated Newport High School; Exeter & Bath Universities; Glasgow Polytechnic. Lecturer in Management Studies, Polytechnic of Wales. Joined Liberal Party 1962.

JONES Owen ap Fychan: Liberal: Neath 1950. **Dr. O. Vaughan Jones:** Born 1893, s of Welsh Independent Minister. Married. Medical Practitioner 1927. Public Assistance Medical Officer, Caernarfonshire. Medical Officer, Bangor Normal College. Member, Liberal Party of Wales Executive. Aled RDC. Caernarfonshire CC. Languages: Welsh, English. Died May 1960.

JONES Patrick E. C: BSc (Wales). Plaid Cymru: Pembrokeshire: Feb. & Oct. 1974, 1987. **Mr. Patrick Jones:** Born 3 June 1939. Married 2c. Educated Narberth Grammar School; University College of Wales, Aberystwyth. Ex-cabaret artist & singer (Country & Western). Scientific Research Officer, National Health Service, Withybush Hospital. Member: NALGO. Pembrokeshire CC 1970-75. Last President, Pembroke Liberal Assn.

JONES Peter Nicholls – see NICHOLLS JONES P.

JONES Peter W. – see WARBURTON-JONES P.

JONES Philip Parkyns: BA (Wales) 1915. Conservative: Swansea East 1929. **Major Philip Jones:** Born Morriston 1893, s of P. Jones. Educated Swansea Grammar School; Mill Hill School; University of Wales, Aberystwyth. Indian Army 1914-22. Solicitor 1924. Lecturer in Commercial and Railway Law (evening classes), Swansea Technical College. Secretary, Morriston War Memorial Cttee. Languages: Welsh, English. Of Treboeth, Swansea.

JONES Rhion Herman: LlB (Wales) BA (Oxon) 1972. Labour: Merioneth 1979. **Mr. Rhion Herman Jones:** Born Porthmadog, May 1948, s of Revd Herman Jones, Welsh Independent Minister & Ffion Mai, d of David Thomas, Bangor. Welsh Independent Lay Preacher 1966. Married Pamela Lesley Trace, hospice receptionist, 1s. 1d. Edu-

cated Ysgol Dewi Sant, Llanelli; Llanelli Grammar School; University of Wales, Aberystwyth; Balliol College, Oxford. Personnel Officer, Welsh Water Authority, Gower Area. Industrial Relations Officer: Ford Motor Company 1972-75. Industrial Relations Officer, Welsh Water Authority 1975-76. Managing Director: International HELP Desk Associates Ltd. Member: NALGO; UNA; Llafur. Interests: Devolution, Public Consultation. Hobbies: Writing articles, Singing, especially opera & oratorio, Games, Travel. Languages: Welsh, English. Of Hereford.

JONES Richard Oliver: Liberal: Merioneth 1964, Oct. 1974. **Mr. Oliver Jones:** Born Trawsfynydd, October 1916. Married Yvonne Grace 2s. Educated Ffestiniog Grammar School. Legal Staff, Merioneth County Council 1933-. Barrister, Grays Inn 1954. WEA & Extra-Mural lecturer. President, Merioneth Liberal Assn. Languages: Welsh, English. Of Dolgellau. Died 5 March 1986.

JONES Robert Ellis: BA (Wales) 1929. Plaid Cymru: Caernarfon 1955, 1964; Conway, 1966. **Mr. R. E. Jones:** Born Llangernyw, February 1908. Presbyterian Church of Wales Elder & Lay preacher. Married (1) Eirian, 3c (died) (2) 1954, Beryl. Educated Llanrwst Grammar School; University of Wales, Bangor. President: Bangor SRC 1930-31; College branch, Plaid Cymru. Teacher Talybont & Dolgarrog. Headteacher, Cwm Penmachno, Llanberis 1954-. Vice-President, Plaid Cymru. Languages: Welsh, English.

JONES Robert Owen: BSc PhD Labour: Ynys Môn 1992. **Dr. Robin Jones:** Born 10 January 1936. Married Beryl, 2c. Educated University of Wales, Bangor; Edinburgh University. Lecturer: Melbourne University, University of Wales, Bangor, Medical Research Council. Languages: Welsh, English. Of Gaerwen, Anglesey.

JONES Robert Thomas: JP (Caerns). Labour: Caernarfonshire: 1918, 1923, 1924. 1929; MP 1922-23. **Mr. R. T. Jones:** Born Blaenau Ffestiniog 1874, s of David Jones & Ellen Parry. Calvinistic Methodist Elder & Sunday School Teacher. Educated Ffestiniog elementary & higher grade schools. Quarry worker at 13. General Secretary, North Wales Quarrymen's Union 1908-24. North Wales Area Secretary TGWU 1924-33. Member: Royal Commission on Metalliferous Mines & Quarries 1910-14; Welsh Consultative Council, Health 1919-; North Wales Joint Disablement Cttee; Welsh Army Corps Executive; County Military Appeal Tribunal 1916-18; Royal Commission on Licensing in England & Wales 1929-; General Council, TUC 1921-30. Blaenau Ffestiniog UDC 1906-. Schools manager. Temperance speaker. Languages: Welsh, English. Died 15 December 1940.

JONES Robert Tudur: BA 1942 BD 1945 DD 1968 Hon. DLitt (Wales) DPhil (Oxon). Plaid Cymru: Anglesey 1959, 1964. **Revd Dr. Tudur Jones:** Born Llanystymdwy 28 June 1921, s of John Thomas Jones, railway guard & Elizabeth Jane Williams, nurse. Married Gwenllian Edwards. teacher, 5c. Educated Rhyl Grammar School; University of Wales, Bangor (History); Coleg Bala-Bangor; Mansfield College, Oxford; Strasbourg University. Welsh Independent Minister, Ordained 1948. Baker Street, Aberystwyth 1948-50. Vice-Principal & Professor of Church History, Coleg Bala-Bangor 1950-65, Principal 1965-. Joined Plaid Cymru 1939. Editor, *Y Ddraig Goch & Welsh Nation* 1951-71. Vice-President, Plaid Cymru. President, Union of Welsh Independents 1986. President, Free Church Council of Wales 1986. Moderator, Free Church Federal Council of England & Wales. President, International Congregational Fellowship. Languages; Welsh, English. Died 23 July 1998. *Books: R. Tudur Jones: Congregationalism in England 1662-1962, 1962; Hanes Annibynwyr Cymru, 1966; Vavasor Powell, 1971; Yr Undeb, 1975, Ffydd ac Argyfwng Cenedl, 1981 & 1982, The Great Reformation, 1985, Grym y Gair a Fflam y Ffydd, 1998.*

JONES Robin – see JONES Robert O.

JONES Roger K: BA (Oxon). Conservative: Ogmore, Feb. & Oct. 1974; Warley East 1979. **Mr. Roger Jones:** Born Cardiff, September 1945, s of G. F. Jones, Headteacher, Maesteg Comprehensive School & ex-Baptist minister. Married 1973, Gaynor Arlett. Educated Newport High School; Bridgend Grammar School; Wadham College, Oxford. Solicitor. Member: Solicitors' European Group. Secretary, Cardiff & District Law Society. Chair: Confederation of South Wales Law Societies. Treasurer, Ogmore Conservative Assn & Chair CPC. Of Penarth.

JONES Russell Lowell: MA BPh (St. Andrews). Labour: Llandaff & Barry 1918. **Captain Russell Jones:** Born Barry, engine driver's son. Educated St Andrew's University (Fellow of St. Andrews University). WEA Lecturer. Chief Clerk, Welsh National Memorial Assn. City of Cardiff Battalion, Welch Regt 1915. Invalided home from France. Army Education. Member, Welsh National Insurance Cttee. Of Barry.

JONES Silvan J: Labour: Conway 1959. **Mr. Silvan Jones:** Born Carmarthen, April 1925, s of Revd Professor Jones. Educated Queen Elizabeth Grammar School, Carmarthen, University of Wales, Bangor. Lecturer in Economics: Bangor - 1961; New Zealand, 1961-65. Member: Fabian Society. Llanfairfechan UDC 1952-56. Languages: Welsh, English.

JONES Stephen Barry, Baron Jones 2001: PC June 1999 BA (Wales). Labour: Northwich 1966, MP East Flint 1970-83, Alyn & Deeside 1983-2001. **Rt. Hon. Barry Jones:** Born Mancot, Flintshire 1 June 1938, s of Stephen & Grace Jones. Methodist lay preacher. Married Janet Davies of Swansea, 1s. Educated Hawarden Grammar School; University of Wales, Bangor. Army, Sergeant. Teacher (English), Deeside Comprehensive School 1961-66. President, Flintshire NUT. Regional Organiser NUT 1966-70. Chair, East Flint CLP. Member: NUPRE. Hawarden UDC. Under-Secretary, Wales 1974-79. Opposition Spokesman, Employment 1980-83. Chief spokesman on Wales 1983-87, 1988-92. Member, House of Commons Chairmen's Panel, House Intelligence & Security Cttee. Delegate, Council of Europe & WEU. Chair, Welsh Grand Cttee. Deputy Speaker, 14 December 2000. Hobbies: Soccer, Gardening, Walking, Cricket. Of Oakeshott, Flint & London.

JONES Stephen Rhys: Conservative, Cardiff Central & South Central List 1999. **Mr. Stephen Jones:** Born Abertridwr, 23 December 1960, s of Idris Rhys Jones. Church of England. Married Rebecca Evans, freelance opera singer and ex-nurse, 1s (born 28/4/99). Educated Caerphilly Grammar School; London Business School (Certificate of Corporate Finance). Merchant Banker. Director, N. M. Rothschild & Sons (Wales) Ltd. Member: Industrial Council for Wales 1992-99; Investment Cttee, University of Wales College of Medicine. Hon. Treasurer/ Membership Secretary, Cardiff Business Club. Interests: Economy, Transport. Hobbies: Reading. Languages, English, French. Of Penarth.

JONES Thomas: MBE OBE 2003. Labour, Caernarfon & North List 1999. **Mr. Tom Jones:** Born 4 March 1945. TGGU Regional Industrial Organiser. Director & Chair, Agoriad Ltd. (charity status co-assisting young people with learning difficulties into employment). Wales TUC Representative on North Wales Economic Forum. Languages: Welsh, English. Of Deiniolen, Caernarfon.

JONES Thomas Artemus: Kt 1931 KC 1919 JP (Caerns) LlB (London) FIJ. Liberal: Swansea East 1923, Macclesfield 1922, Keighley B/E 1925; PPC Merthyr Tydfil until 1913. **Sir Artemus Jones:** Born Denbigh 1871, s of Thomas Jones, stonemason. Married 1927, Mildred Mary, d of T. W. David JP of Llandaff. Educated Denbigh National School; Bedford College, London. Journalist, *Daily News & Daily Telegraph.* Barrister, Middle Temple, 1901, Bencher, 1926. Junior Counsel for Defence, Sir Roger Casement Treason Trial. Freeman, City of London. Member, Gardeners'

Company. Represented Great Britain on Anglo-Mexican Claims Commission 1928-29. County Court Judge 1930-. Chair, Caernarfonshire Quarter Sessions. Vice-President, University of Wales, Bangor. Made legal history by being awarded libel damages of £1750 against the *Sunday Chronicle* 1908. As a judge he encouraged the speaking of Welsh in court and campaigned for the 1942 Act which brought in the right to speak Welsh in court Languages: Welsh, English. Died 15 October 1943. *Books: T. Artemus Jones, Without My Wig.* Further Reading: *Kenneth O. Morgan, Peace Movements in Wales 1899-1945, The Welsh History Review, Vol. 10, June 1981, page 421.*

JONES Thomas George: KBE 1921 JP (Glam). National Federation of Discharged Soldiers & Sailors Independent Coalition: Aberavon 1918 (withdrew, 3 days before poll, in favour of the Coalition Liberal candidate); Conservative: Pontypool 1922, Ogmore 1931. **Sir Thomas George Jones:** Born Pontynewydd 5 January 1881, s of George & Jane Jones. Roman Catholic. Married 1901, May d of A. Matthews, Porthcawl, 3d. Chair & Director of companies. Proprietor: *Porthcawl & District News, Aberavon & Port Talbot News.* Chair & Managing Director, *Scottish Observer & Herald* Ltd. Voluntary Director, Ships Stores & National Kitchens, Ministry of Food 1917-20. Member: National Salvage Council, Disposal Boards, etc. Divisional Food Commissioner, South Wales 1921-41. Chief Food Officer, Wales, Midlands & Western Divisions 1941-45. President, Porthcawl Chamber of Trade 1912-14. Porthcawl UDC Chairman 1912-15. Glamorgan CC. Of Porthcawl. Died 30 November 1948.

JONES Thomas Griffiths – see GRIFFITHS-JONES M. T. L.

JONES Thomas Isaac Mardy – see MARDY-JONES.

JONES Thomas William, Baron Maelor of Rhos 1966: JP (Denbs) 1937. Labour: Merioneth 1935, MP Merioneth 1951-66; PPC Anglesey 1931, withdrew in favour of Megan Lloyd-George, Ind.L. **Mr. T. W. Jones:** Born Ponciau 10 February 1898, s of James Jones & Elizabeth Bowyer (brother of J. Idwal Jones qv). Churches of Christ. Married 1928, Flossy, d of Jonathan Thomas. Educated Ponciau Boys' School. Miner at 14. Pupil Teacher, August 1914. Joined Non-Combatant Corps as CO 1917. Court-Martialled Dec. 1917, Prison 1917-May 1919. Student, Bangor Normal College 1920-22. Teacher 1922-40. Welfare Officer, Ministry of Labour 1940-46. Welfare, Education/PR Officer, North Wales Power & Electric Co. 1946-, MANWEB -1951.

Joined ILP 1919. Chair: Wrexham Trades Council; North Wales Labour Federation. Vice-Chair, Wrexham-Maelor National Eisteddfod Cttee 1961. Hon. Member, Gorsedd 1962. Languages: Welsh, English. Died 18 November 1984. *Books: T. W. Jones, Fel Hyn y Bu 1970.*

JONES Trefor: BA MEd. Plaid Cymru: Neath 1997, 1999. **Mr. Trefor Jones:** Born Scotland, 1957, s of Dr. Seth Jones, general practitioner. Moved to Brynaman. Married Margaret, physiotherapist, 2c. Educated Ysgol Gyfun, Ystalyfera; University of Wales, Cardiff & Aberystwyth (History & Geography). Teacher. Head of Geography, Bargoed Comprehensive School. Resolfen ComC 1991- (Chairman). Neath BC 1991-96 (Group Leader). Member, Côr Meibion Dyffryn Aman. Languages: Welsh, English. Of Resolfen (1986).

JONES Trevor Alec: PC. Labour MP Rhondda West B/E 1967-74, Rhondda 1974-. **Rt. Hon. Alec Jones:** Born Clydach Vale 12 August 1924, s of Alec Jones. Married 1950, Mildred Maureen, d of William R Evans, 1s. Educated Rhondda County Boys' Grammar School, Porth. Rhondda UDC clerk 1940-42. RAF 1942-45. Student, Bangor Normal College 1945-47. Teacher: Essex 1947-49; Blaenclydach Secondary School 1949-67. Joined Labour Party, 1945. Chair, Wood Green CLP. Secretary: Rhondda West CLP 1965-67; Rhondda Branch, National Assn of Labour Teachers. Agent, Iori Thomas MP 1966. Member: Welsh Council of Labour Executive; NUT; Socialist Education Assn. Secretary, Welsh PLP. Chair, PLP Education Group 1969-70. PPS 1968-70. Under-Secretary, Health & Social Security Oct. 1974-75. Under-Secretary, Wales, June 1975-79. Of Tonypandy. Died 20 March 1983.

JONES Tudor – see JONES John Tudor.

JONES Whitney Richard David: MA PhD Liberal/Alliance: Newport West 1983. **Dr Whitney Jones:** Born 1925. Lecturer in History. Director of Historical Research & Secretary, Faculty Board, Gwent College of High Education. Retired. Chair, Rhymney Valley Liberals. Hengoed ComC 1974-79.

JONES William: Liberal MP Arfon 1885-. **Mr. William Jones:** Born Llangefni 1857, s of Richard & Alice Jones. Educated British School. Pupil Teacher. Student, Bangor Normal College 1873-75. Headteacher, Goginan 1875-79. Teacher, Wallington Road School, North London 1879-88. Unofficial tutor at Oxford 1888-94. Excommunicated from Holloway Calvinistic Methodist Church for *Modernism* 1887. Junior Lord of the Treasury, 1911-. Of Bangor & London, Died 9 May 1915.

JONES William: Liberal Unionist: Cardiganshire 1892. **Mr. William Jones:** Born Upper Caron, 12 November 1842, s of lead miner. Calvinistic Methodist Elder. Married. No c. Farm servant at 12. Apprenticed to grocer/draper at 16. Worked for Thomas Hall, Birmingham, 1862-. Set up own business as a draper. Languages: Welsh, English. Of Birmingham.

JONES William Edward: Communist: Pontypool 1964, 1966. **Mr. Eddie Jones:** Born Pontnewynydd, May 1908. Married. Educated Abersychan Grammar School. Engineer: Pontnewynydd Galvinising Sheet Works 1923. RAF 1939-45. At Girling Engineering Works 1945-. Engineering inspector. Chair: Joint Shop Stewards Cttee. Member, AEU District Cttee. President, Pontypool Trades Council 4 times. Chair, Pontnewynydd Community Assn. Joined Communist Party 1927, Member, Welsh Executive, 1930-. Pontypool UDC 1967-. Member: East Monmouthshire Advisory Cttee on National Insurance & Pensions; East Monmouthshire Cttee for Employment. Of Pontnewynydd, Pontypool.

JONES William Elwyn Edwards: Kt 1978 BA (Wales) LlB (London) Hon. LLD (Wales) 1979. Labour: Caernarfonshire 1931, 1935, Caernarfon District 1945, Conway, 1951, 1955; MP Conway 1950-51. **Sir Elwyn Jones:** Born 1905, s of Revd Robert William Jones & Elizabeth Jane Jones. Methodist. Married 1935, Dydd, d of Revd Dr. E. Tegla Davies, 3c. Educated Bootle Secondary School; Ffestiniog Grammar School; University of Wales, Bangor; London University. Solicitor 1927. Clerk to Bangor Magistrates 1934-; Town Clerk, Bangor 1939-. Caernarfonshire CC 1945-69. Member, Countryside Commission for Wales 1969. Member, Council & Court, University of Wales, Bangor, 1943-, Treasurer 1970-, Vice-President 1975-86. Languages: Welsh, English. Died 4 July 1989.

JONES William Gerwyn: Labour, Ynys Môn 2003. **Mr. Gerwyn Jones:** Born Llangefni 1959, s of William & Mair Jones. Educated Llangefni Primary & Comprehensive Schools; University of Wales, Bangor; Bangor Normal College. Teacher, Sir Thomas Jones School, Amlwch. Technician & Hydrologist, Welsh Water. Caseworker, Albert Owen MP 2001. Languages: Welsh, English. Of Bodffordd, Llangefni.

JONES William Nathaniel: JP 1904 DL 1925 (Carms). Liberal MP Carmarthen B/E 1928-29, short-listed 1923. **Lieut-Colonel W. N. Jones:** Born Ammanford, 1858, s of William Jones, Dyffryn. Wesleyan Methodist. Married Margaret (died 1932) d of Thomas Francis, Llandeilo, 1s (died 1928) 1d (married Daniel Johns qv). Senior Partner: W. N. Jones FAL & Son, Company

Chair: New Rhos Anthracite Collieries Ltd. Caerbryn Anthracite Collieries Ltd. Gwendraeth Valley Anthracite Collieries Ltd. Ammanford Gas Co. Ltd, Welsh Insurance Corporation. High Sheriff of Carmarthenshire 1924. Carmarthenshire CC 1894-, Alderman 1903-, Chair. Ammanford UDC. Chair: Llandybie School Board; Llandeilo & Amman Valley Grammar Schools Governors. Member, Joint Counties Mental Hospital Cttee. Languages: Welsh, English. Estate £75,970. Collapsed and died on way to Llanwrtyd railway station 24 May 1934. Of Ammanford. Further Reading: *J. Graham Jones, Sir Alfred Mond, Carmarthenshire and the Green Book, Welsh History Review, June 1999.*

JONES William Rhys: Communist: Swansea East 1966, 1970, Feb. & Oct. 1974, 1979, 1983. **Mr. Bill Jones:** Born Port Talbot, December 1918. Moved to Swansea 1924. Married. Educated Danygraig School, Swansea. CWS Shop Assistant 1934-50. Army (South Wales Borderers, India & Burma) 1939-45. CWS Insurance Agent 1950-. Branch Secretary, USDAW. Chair: Swansea Tenants & Residents Cttee. Joined Communist Party 1954, Swansea Communist Party. Member, Swansea Trades Council. Contested Swansea BC. Of Penlan, Swansea.

JONES Wyn – see JONES Hywel William Wyn.

JONES-CREMLYN John William: MA (Cantab). Conservative: West Carmarthenshire, Jan. & Dec. 1910, Withdrew at Gower, 1922; West Toxteth B/E July 1935. **Mr. John Jones-Cremlyn:** Born Bootle, 1878, s of David Jones, Cremlyn House, Bootle & Cremlyn, Anglesey, added Cremlyn to his name 1902. Anglican. Married Miss Campbell-Davys, Neuadd Fawr, Llandovery. Educated Liverpool College, Cambridge University. Barrister, Grays Inn 1902. Army 1914-18. Member: Manchester Diocesan Cttee for the Defence of the Church; Church of England League. Languages: Welsh, English. Of Manchester.

JONES-DAVIES David: BA (Wales) MA (Cantab). Labour: Cardigan 1955. **Mr. David Jones-Davies:** Born Tregaron, 7 February 1921, s of Dan Davies, minor. Married Eirian. Educated Tregaron Grammar School; University of Wales, Aberystwyth (1st Phil); Westminster College, Cambridge (Lewis Gibson Scholarship). Minister, Presbyterian Church of Wales: Ordained, 1946 Princes Road English Presbyterian Church, Bangor 1946-49. Further Education Officer, Caernarfonshire 1949-54, Deputy Education Officer, Rhondda 1954-59, Director of Education Anglesey, 1959-. Chair, Welsh Christian Youth Council. Languages: Welsh, English. Died 4 September 1965. Further Reading: *D. Ben Rees: Cymry Adnabyddus 1952-1974.*

Sir John Jones-Jenkins.

JONES-JENKINS John, 1st & last Baron Glantawe: 1st Bart 1886 JP (Carms) 1853 JP DL (Glam) 1854 FSA. Liberal MP Carmarthen District 1880-86. Joined Loyal & Patriotic Union 1886. Liberal Unionist MP 1895-1900 & Candidate 1886, 1892, 1900. Rejoined Liberal Party, 1905. **Sir John Jones-Jenkins:** Born 10 May 1835, s of Jenkin Jenkins, Morriston, & Sarah, d of John Jones, Clydach. Congregationalist, became Anglican. Married (1) 1854, Margaret (died 1863) d of Josiah Rees, Morriston (2) 1864, Katherine (died 1900) d of Edward Daniel, 2d. Educated privately. Tinplate worker. Industrialist: Owner: Beaufort Tinplate Works, Cwmfelin Tinplate & Steel Works. Chief Proprietor, Mumbles Railway Co. Ltd. Chair: Tirdonkin Collieries Ltd; Swansea Dock & Railway Co; Rhondda & Swansea Bay Railway Co. Director: National Accident Insurance Co. Ltd, 1894, North British & Mercantile Insurance Co. Founder, Swansea Bank, then Director: Metropolitan Bank, Midland Bank, 1914-. High Sheriff of Glamorgan 1889. Swansea BC 1865-. Mayor 1869-70, 1879-80, 1880-81. Glamorgan CC 1888-. Chair: Swansea Harbour Trust 1891-98. 1st President, Swansea Metal Exchange. Hon. Lieutenant, Royal Naval Artillery Volunteers. President, Royal Institution of South Wales 1889-90. Patron, Oddfellows. Freeman of Swansea, 1895. Languages: Welsh, English. Of Swansea & London. Estate £63,366. Died 27 July 1915.

JONES-LLOYD Arthur Edward Campbell Lloyd: MA (Oxon). Conservative: Merioneth 1964, 1966. **Mr. Campbell Jones-Lloyd:** Born Bala, March 1907, s of S. Lloyd-Jones (changed name by deed-poll). Educated Malvern College, Worcester College, Oxford. Farmer. Hoole UDC 1937, Chair 1945-46. Chair, Junior Imperial league. High Sheriff of Merioneth 1939. Of Bala & Chester.

JONES-PARRY Thomas Love Dunscombe: BA (Oxon). Liberal MP Caernarfonshire 1868-74, Caernarfon District 1882-86. **Sir Thomas Jones-Parry:** Born 6 January 1832, s of Lieut-General, Sir Love Jones-Parry, MP Caernarfon District 1837. Anglican. Married 1886, Charlotte Belle, d of H. Arnott of Rushington Manor & widow of F. A. Elliott. Educated Rugby; University College, Oxford. Landowner. Patron of one living. Captain, Royal Anglesea Militia. Caernarfonshire CC Alderman 1889. Of Madryn Castle, Caerns. Estate £38,596. Died 18 December 1891.

JONES-ROBERTS John: JP (Merioneth) LlB (Wales). Labour: Merioneth 1922, 1923, 1924, 1929. **Mr. John Jones-Roberts:** Born Ffestiniog 1889, s of Evan Roberts. Married Katie Winifred OBE JP, d of Rees Roberts. Educated Ffestiniog Grammar School; University of Wales, Aberystwyth. Solicitor Barrister, Middle Temple, 1923. Merioneth CC. Languages: Welsh, English. Of Ffestiniog.

– K –

KALETA Rachel Christina: BSc 1999 PGCE 2000 (Wales). Green Party: Wales Euro 1999. **Miss Rachel Kaleta:** Born 1978. Educated: University of Wales, Aberystwyth (1st Environmental Science); MSc. Student, University of Kent 2000. Worked as teacher and in environmental research and alternative technology. Helped clean up the *Sea Empress* oil spill. Campaigner for animal rights and against inclusion of vivisection in student teaching. Of Taliesin, Machynlleth.

KEAL Brian Ernest: BSc (Wales) ARIC AMIE. Liberal: Swansea West Feb. & Oct. 1974. **Mr. Brian Keal:** Born North Devon May 1939. Married Jean Keal, 2d. Educated Barnstable Grammar School, City University, London, University of Wales, Swansea. Chemical Engineer. Process Engineer, Jefferson Chemicals UK Ltd. Llanelli. Chair: Gower Branch, Crusaders; Keep Gower Tidy Co-ordinating Cttee. Glamorgan CC 1968-74, West Glam CC 1973-. Of Kittle, Gower (1963).

KEAL Jennifer: Vote 2 Stop the War Party, South/Central List 2003. **Ms. Jennifer Keal:** Born Southampton 23 April 1951, d of Owen George Ward, steel erector, & Elizabeth Louise Ward, housewife. Church of England. Married 1997 David Arthur James Bellamy, artist/writer (qv) 2d. Educated Secretarial School. Artist/writer. Interests: A fairer deal for Third World, Trade/Justice. Hobbies: Walking, Painting, Gardening Of Erwood. *I was asked to stand for the 2003 Welsh Assembly by the Vote 2 Stop the War Party because I feel so strongly about the injustice of the war against Iraq.*

KEELAN Peter John: Plaid Cymru Cardiff West 1987, Newport West 1992, South Wales Euro 1989. **Mr. Peter Keelan:** Born Newport, 26 December 1953. Educated Newport, City of London University, University of Wales, Aberystwyth. Librarian, University of Wales, Cardiff. AUT branch secretary & member, Welsh Executive. Joined Plaid Cymru 1979. Secretary, Cardiff West Constituency & South Glamorgan Area, Plaid Cymru; Member, National Executive 1987-91. Plaid Cymru National Co-ordinator, Anti-Poll Tax Campaign 1988-91. Member: CND Cymru, Friends of the Earth, Cardiff Trades Council. Of Cardiff.

KEENS Thomas: Kt 1934 JP DL (Beds). Liberal National: Pontypool 1931, Liberal: Aylesbury 1922, 1924, 1929, MP 1923-24. **Sir Thomas Keens:** Born Luton 1870, s of Thomas & Emma Keens, Married 1896 Lee, d of Thomas Bachelor, 3c. Educated private school. Incorporated Accountant, Senior Partner: Sheers, Shay, Keens & Co. Hon. Secretary: Luton Chamber of Commerce 1895-1923. President: Assn of Secretaries of British Chambers of Commerce, 1925, Society of Incorporated Accountants & Auditors, 1926-29. Bedfordshire CC 1901-10, Alderman 1918-, Chairman 1935-36. Of Luton. Died 24 November 1953.

KELLETT Edward Orlando: DSO 1943 FRGS. FRES. Conservative: Carmarthen 1935, MP Aston B/E 1939-. **Lieut-Colonel Edward Kellett:** Born 19 May 1902, s of Major-General Richard Orlando Kellett, of Chonacody, Co. Tipperary & Eleanor, d of Colonel H. A. Mallock. Married 1926, Helen Myrtle, d of Arthur Arthurley, of Languard Manor, Isle of Wight. Educated Cheltenham College; RMC Sandhurst. Lieutenant, Irish Guards 1922; Captain, Nottinghamshire Yeomanry 1931, Major 1940, Lieut-Colonel 1940. Killed in action, March 1943.

KELLY Brian: National Federation of the Self-Employed, South East Wales Euro 1979. **Mr. Brian Kelly:** Born London. Brought up at Tredegar. Married Joan (florist) 1s. Proprietor of a printing business. Chair: South Wales Region, National Federation of the Self Employed and Small Businesses (found 1974. Hon. National Secretary NFSE 1977-.

KELLY-OWEN Maureen: JP. Conservative, North List 1999; Cardiff South & Penarth 2001. **Mrs. Maureen Kelly-Owen:** Born Manchester 24 August 1935. Married Dale Owen, Widowed 1997. 2s. Educated St. Alma's School, Penarth, Welsh School of Architecture (Diploma in Architecture). Architect: Assistant, Glamorgan CC 1959-61; with Percy Thomas Partnership 1972-86, 1987-90; own practice 1991-. President, Royal Institute of British Architects. Penarth TC 1974-79. South Glamorgan CC 1977-81. Vale of Glamorgan BC 1999 (Chairman, Economic Regeneration & Prosperity Scrutiny Cttee). Member, Civic Trust Board for Wales. Interests: Health, Education, Family Issues. Hobbies: Enjoying art & architecture. Eating with friends, Cycling. Of Penarth.

KEMP Richard Anthony: BSc CertEd (Wales). Plaid Cymru: Pontypridd Feb. & Oct. 1974. **Mr. Richard Kemp:** Born 1942. Married 2c. Educated Aberdare Grammar School, University of Wales, Aberystwyth, Research Fellow, Leicester University -1970. Lecturer in Mathematics, Glamorgan Polytechnic 1970-. BBC. Member: Glamorgan Naturalists Council, Cttee. Llantrisant Civic Society, Friends of the Earth. Active in *Call to the Valleys* campaign.

KENNEDY Nicholas: BA (Oxon). Conservative: Llanelli 1983. **Mr. Nicholas Kennedy:** Born 6 October 1964. Educated Christ Hospital, Horsham; St. John's College, Oxford. Merchant Banker, Corporation Finance Executive. Ex-Head of Investment Research. Chairman. Cobham Conservatives 1981-83. Member, Bow Group. Elmbridge BC 1980-83. Of Cobham.

KENSLER Gwyneth Mai: BA DipEd (Wales). Plaid Cymru: Vale of Clwyd 1997. **Mrs. Gwyneth Kensler:** Born Oswestry 16 May 1942 , d of Matthew Jones Roberts, teacher, & Olwen Jones Roberts. Presbyterian Church of Wales. Married Dr. Craig Bruce Kensler of California, marine biologist, 2d. Educated Holywell Grammar School, University of Wales, Bangor. (French & Spanish); UNAM, Mexico. Teacher of French & Spanish. Taught in France, Mexico. Education Officer, RNZAF; Teacher, Howells School, Denbigh 1979. Member, Amnesty International, Friends of the Earth, Greenpeace. Denbigh TC 1995-. Denbighshire CC 1995-. Schools governor. Chair: Leisure Centre & Denbigh Regeneration Cttee. Director: North Wales Tourism; Coastal Enterprise Action. Member: Greenpeace, Amnesty International, Charter 88, Theatr Twm o'r Nant, Denbigh Music Club, Denbigh Civic Society. Joined Plaid Cymru 1991. Interests: Democracy, the Deficit & its Future. Hobbies: Music, Reading, Gardening, Walking – but no time! Languages: Welsh, English, French, Spanish. Of Denbigh.

KENYON Alan Roy Thomas: MB BCh LMSSA FRGS. Conservative: Gower 1983, Kelvingrove Feb1974. **Dr. Thomas Kenyon:** Born 22 June 1937. Married Dr. Susan Kenyon, 4c. Educated Cranleigh; St. Barts Hospital Medical School. Medical Practitioner. RAMC Officer with Australian Forces in Vietnam, SAS, Argyll & Sutherland Highlanders. Medical Officer, trawler fleet.

KENYON George Thomas: JP (Flint 1886, Denbigh & Salop) DL (Flint). 1886 BA 1864 MA (Oxon). Liberal: Denbigh District 1874, 1880, Liberal Unionist MP Denbigh District 1885-95, 1900-1906; Candidate, East Denbighshire B/E 1897. **Hon. George Kenyon:** Born Harley Street, London 28 December 1840, s of 3rd Baron Kenyon & Hon. Georgiana de Grey. Married 1875, Florence Anna, d of John Hurleston Leche of Carden Park, Chester. Educated Harrow, Christ Church, Oxford. Barrister, Middle Temple 1869. Landowner. 1st Chairman, Wrexham & Ellesmere Railway Co. Ltd. Captain, Denbighshire Yeomanry. Deputy Chancellor, University of Wales 1898-1901. Of Llanerch Panna, Flints. Estate £10,266. Died 26 January 1908. *Books: G. T. Kenyon, The Life of Lord Kenyon, Lord Chief Justice of England.*

KERBY Henry Britten: FRGS Norwegian Military Medal, Danish Underground Medal, Kt 1st Class White Rose of Finland, Commander of Polonia Institute of Poland. Conservative, Swansea West 1951; MP Arundel & Shoreham B/E 1954-. Joined Conservative Party 1945. Liberal, Spelthorne 1945. **Captain Henry Kerby:** Born Russia, 11 December 1914, s of Henry Kerby. Married 1947, Enid, d of Judge Philip Herchenroder of Mauritius, 2d. Educated Highgate School & Continent. Army 1933-38. Hon. Attache, Diplomatic Service 1939. Acting Consul, Malmo 1940-41 (Organised an espionage network in occupied Norway & Denmark; Sent to a Swedish prison for spying). War Office special agent 1941-45. Russian interpreter. Press Officer, African Explosives & Chemical Industries Ltd. 1946-50. Company Director: Marine & Aviation Developments Ltd; Sapphire Press Ltd; Tileyard Press Ltd; Martell Printing Co Ltd; Chapel Property Holding Co Ltd. Consultant: Fords of Bedford Ltd; Whyte, Gasc & Co, merchant bankers; Groveswood Securities Ltd. Vice-Chair, Instant Starters Ltd. Member, Court, Southampton University (Resigned *in protest against the sinister trend in student power*). Died 4 January 1971.

KERR Albert Calvin: MA (Oxon). Labour: Monmouth 1964. **Colonel Calvin Kerr:** Born Jedburgh, August 1909, s of a Scottish landowner & kinsman of Lord Lothian. Married Betty, 2 step-d. Educated Epsom College; Universities of London & Oxford (1st). Rugby, athletics & boxing at university. Ran (unpaid) centre for the unemployed 1934. Anglican priest, Ordained, 1937. Senior Curate, Aston, Birmingham 19370-39. Resigned 1939. RAF 1939-45. Colonel TA. Barrister, Grays Inn, 1962. Resigned from Conservative Party & joined Labour 1934. Member: Society of Labour Lawyers, NFU. Of Brockweir, Chepstow.

KERR Charles Iain, 1st Baron Teviot of Burghclere 1940: DSO 1919 MC JP (Northants) 1927 DL. Liberal: Swansea West 1929, Daventry 1923, 1923 (withdrew as PPC Daventry when MP became Speaker), Hull Central B/E 1926; Liberal National MP Monitors Burghs B/E 1932-40. **Lieut-Colonel Iain Kerr:** Born 3 May 1874, s of Charles Wyndham Rudolph Kerr & Anna Maria, d of Admiral, Sir Charles Elliott. Married (1) 1911 Muriel Canning, divorced 1930 (2) 1930 Florence Angela, d of Lt-Col. C. W. Villiers, 1s. Educated Stephen Hawtrey's School, Windsor. Mining Engineer 1892-96 (Canada 1892-94). Stock Exchange 1896 (Senior Partner, Kerr, Ware & Co). Company Director: National Bank of Scotland; Lloyds Bank; General Accident & Life Insurance; Bank Line, shipping; Western Board, Salisbury 1953-56. Hon. Treasurer: Assn of British Chambers of Commerce. Chairman, National Joint Council of Scotland. Council Member, St. Dunstans. Commissioned, Royal Horse Guards 1914. Lieutenant, Royal Company of Archers 1947. Chair: Liberal Publication Department 1930-3; Liberal National Federation 1930-31; Liberal National Party 1940-56. Lord Commissioner of the Treasury 1937-39. Comptroller of the Household 1939-40. Liberal National Chief Whip 1937-40. Of Banbury. Died 7 January 1968.

KERTON Eric R: National Front: Barry 1979. **Mr. Eric Kerton:** Born Somerset 1932. Married, 2d. RAF 1953-75. Production Engineer, aircraft equipment manufacturers.

KILLOCK James Edward: BA (Wales). Green Party, North List 1999. **Mr. Jim Killock:** Born Birmingham, 2 July 1972, s of Malcolm James Killock, civil servant, & Mary Elizabeth Barker, secretary. Educated South Bromsgrove High School, University of Wales, Bangor (History). Graphic Designer. Freelance University Tutor. Secretary, Bangor Green Party. Contested Gwynedd CC (Menai/Bangor) 1999. Interests: Economics, Sustainability, Foreign affairs, Open source software. Hobbies: World music disc jockey, Reading, Welsh. Languages: Learned Welsh, English. Of Bangor.

KINLOCH-COOKE Clement Kinloch: 1st Bart 1928, KBE 1919, Kt 1905, BA LLM (Cantab) ARIBA. Conservative MP: Cardiff East 1924-29, Devonport 1910-23. **Sir Clement Kinloch-Cooke:** Born Brighton 1854, s of Robert Hall Cooke, Assumed name of Kinloch by deed poll. Anglican. Married Florence, d of Revd Lancelot Errington. Educated Brighton College, St. Johns College, Cambridge. Barrister, Treasury Prosecuting Counsel for Berkshire, Legal Adviser, House of Lords Sweating Commission. Private Secretary, Earl of Dundee. Civil Service Commissioner for Inspectors of Factories. Newspaper Columnist: *Morning Post*, Editor, *English Illustrated Magazine, The Observer, Pall Mall Gazette, New Review*. Founder & Editor: *Empire Review*. Director, London Board, Colonial Mutual Benefit Society Ltd of Australia, Associated British Picture Corporation Ltd, Associated British Cinemas.

Vice-President, Tariff Reform League. Member, Council of Royal Empire Society. London CC 1907-10. Of London. Died 4 September 1944. *Books: C. Kinloch-Cooke, Australian Defences and New Guinea, Authorised Memoir of Princess Mary Adelaide, Duchess of Teck, Life of HM Queen Mary.*

KINGSTON Philip Thomas: BSc(Soc). Vote 2 Stop the War, South/East List 2003. **Mr. Philip Kingston:** Born Penarth, 26 January 1936, son of Paul Kingston, crane repairer, & Celia Kingston, housewife. Roman Catholic. Married 1960 Catherine Rafferty, clerical worker, 2s 1d. Educated university (Sociology). Lecturer in Social Work, Bristol University, retired 1992. Full-time campaigner: International Poverty/Trade Justice/Human Rights. Interests: Green/Socialist. Hobbies: Walking, Making preserves, Clay modelling, Poetry, Song writing. Of Penarth.

KINGZETT Brian: BA (Open). Ecology Party: Pembroke 1979, Carmarthen 1983, Gower 1992. **Mr. Brian Kingzett:** Born Birmingham 1930. Humanist. Self-employed craft consultant; ex-designer. UK Fund Raiser, Ecology Party. Member: Conservation Trust, Woodland Trust, Newport & Nevern Energy Group. Of Carmarthen, then Gowerton. Died suddenly at Walsall, 30 January 1999.

KINNOCK Glenys Elizabeth: BA (Wales) Hon. LLD (Thames Valley, Brunel & Kingston) FRSA. Labour MEP South Wales 1994-99, MEP Wales 1999-. **Mrs. Glenys Kinnock:** Born Roade, Northampton, 7 July 1944. Married 1967, Neil Kinnock (qv) 1s 1d. Educated Holyhead Comprehensive School. Primary & secondary school Teacher 1966-93. President, Coleg Harlech. Co-President, African, Caribbean & Pacific/European Union Joint Parliamentary Assn. President: One World Action. Patron: Saferworld. Council Member: Voluntary Service Overseas; Britain in Europe. Patron: Drop the Debt Campaign; Saferworld; Welsh Woman of the Year; Special Needs Advisory Project (SNAP) Cymru; UK National Breast Cancer Coalition Wales; Community Enterprise Wales; Charter Housing; The Burma Campaign UK; Crusaid; Elizabeth Hardie Ferguson Trust; Medical Foundation for the Victims of Torture; National Deaf Children's Society. Chair: Forum on Early Warning & Early Response (FEWER). Board Member: International AIDS Vaccine Initiative; World Parliamentary Magazine. Vice-President: Parliamentarians for Global Action; St. David's Day Foundation, Women of the Year Lunch. Member: European Parliament's Development & Co-operation Cttee; Citizens' Freedoms & Rights, Justice & Home Affairs Cttee. Hon. Fellow, University of Wales, Newport & Bangor. Interests: Development & Co-operation, Children's Rights, Education,

Disability Rights, Co-operative & Voluntary Sector Issues, Local Government & Europe, Human Rights, Gender Issues, Steel Industry. Hobbies: Theatre, Cooking, Grandchildren, Reading. Languages: Welsh, English. *Books: Voices for One World, 1987; Eritrea-Images of Peace & War, 1989; Namibia-Birth of a Nation, 1991; Could Do Better – Where is British Education in the European League Tables? By Faith & Daring, 1993; Zimbabwe-on the Brink, 2003.*

KINNOCK Neil Gordon: PC 1983, BA (Wales) 1965. Hon. LLD (Wales) 1992, (Glamorgan) 1996 Hon. FIHT. Labour MP: Bedwellty 1970-83, Islwyn 1983-95. **Rt. Hon. Neil Kinnock:** Born Tredegar, 28 March 1942, s of Gordon Kinnock, labourer, & Mary Howells, district nurse. Married 1967 Glenys Parry (qv) 1996, 2c. Educated Lewis School, Pengam, University of Wales, Cardiff (Industrial Relations & History), President, University Socialist Society 1964-65, SRC 1965-66, Member, Welsh Council, NUS. WEA Tutor; Organiser in Economics & Trade Union Studies 1966-70. Joined Labour Party 1957, Chairman NEC 1988. Member: Anti-Apartheid Movement, Fabian Society Executive CND, TGWU. PPS. Michael Foot 1974-75. Chairman: Welsh Labour Group 1977-78, TGWU Parliamentary Group 1974-76. Director (unpaid) *Tribune* Publications. Member: Welsh Hospital Board 1969-71, BBC General Advisory Council 1975-79. Member, Shadow Cabinet 1979-95, Spokesman on Education 1979-83, Leader of the Opposition 1983-92; Resigned after election defeat. European Commissioner 1995: Transport, 1995-99; resigned with fellow commissioners after European Parliament vote; Appointed Vice-President of the Commission with special responsibility for reform, July 1999. President, University of Wales, Cardiff 1998-2003. Vice-President, Socialist International 1984-. Hon. Professor, Thames Valley University 1993-. Hon. Fellow, University of Wales, Cardiff 1982. Freeman, Borough of Islwyn 1984. Hobbies: Opera, Male choral singing, Rugby, Theatre, Being with family. *Books etc: N. G. Kinnock: Wales and the Common Market 1971, Facts to Beat Fantasies 1978, Making our Way 1986.*

KNEE Kenneth Gordon: Conservative: Caerphilly 1951, East Flint 1955. **Mr. Kenneth Knee:** Born Derby, December 1919. Married Educated Bemrose School. Derby. RAF 1939-45: Squadron Leader (Lecturer in Leadership & Social Psychology). Manager, plastics factory. Hotel Proprietor. Llanwern. President, Glamorgan Group, Young Conservatives 1950-51.

KNOWLES Michael: Conservative: Merthyr Tydfil Feb. 1974, Brent East Oct. 1974, Nottingham East 1992; MP Nottingham East 1983-92. **Mr. Michael Knowles:** Born 21 May 1942. Roman Catholic. Married 3c. Educated Clapham College, London. Export & Home Sales Manager, 1964-, Consultant, PPA International. Joined Young Conservatives 1959. Chairman, Surbiton CPC. Kingston BC 1971-83, Leader 1974-83. PPS 1985-87. Member, Select: Euro Legislation 1988-89, Defence 1991-92, Severn Bridges Bill 1991-92. Joint Secretary, Conservative MPs Home Affairs Cttee 1987-89. Secretary, all party Friends of Northern Cyprus Group. Of Surbiton.

KNOWLES Timothy: ACA. Conservative: Swansea East 1966. **Mr. Timothy Knowles:** Born Cardiff 17 May 1938, s of Cyril William Knowles & Winifred Alice Hood. Married 1967 Gaynor Hallett, 1c. Educated Bishop Gore Grammar School. Chartered Accountant. Company Secretary, Louis Marks & Co. Ltd. 1960-68. Controller, Medco Valemite Ltd 1968-69. Company Secretary, HTV Ltd. 1969-75, Financial Director 1975-81, Asst Managing Director 1981-86. Director, HTV Group 1978-86, Managing Director 1986-88. Finance Director, Exports Credits Guarantees Dept. Insurance Services Group (for privatisation) 1990-91. Financial Consultant, NCM (UK) Holdings 1991-92. Member: SWEB, 1981-82, Welsh Water Authority, 1982-89. Director Welsh Water plc. 1989-. Vice-Chairman: Swansea West Young Conservatives 1962-63; Swansea West Conservative Assn; Mumbles Cricket Club. Of St. Nicholas.

– L –

LAKIN Cyril Harry Alfred: MA (Oxon). Conservative MP Llandaff & Barry B/E 1942-45. **Mr. Cyril Lakin:** Born Barry, 29 December 1893, s of Harry Lakin, of Highlight, nr Barry. Married 1916 Vera, d. of F. B. Savill, 1d. Educated Barry County School; St. John's College, Oxford. Barrister, Inner Temple. South Wales Borderers 1914-18. Asst Divisional Commissioner of Food 1918. Literary Editor, *Sunday Times, Daily Telegraph*. Assistant Editor, *Daily Telegraph* 1929-33. Killed in car crash, 23 June 1948.

LAMBERT Alfred James: Conservative: Swansea Town 1886. **Mr. Alfred Lambert:** Born Cork 1839, s of William Lambert. Married Edith, d of James Reynolds. Company Chairman: Anglo-Argentinian Railway Co. Ltd, Swansea Improvements & Tramways Co. Ltd, Imperial Tramways Co, Director: Bordeaux Tramways & Omnibus Co, Hull Street Tramways Co. Of Paddington. Died Swansea 22 September 1891.

LAMBERT Anthony: Liberal: Newport 1979, Caerphilly 1983, Staffordshire South-West Oct. 1974, Gloucestershire South 1970. **Mr. Tony Lambert:** Born 30 September 1943. Educated Hitchin Grammar School; Oxford University. Post Office Senior Manager. Member: Post Office Management Staffs Assn, SCPS. Thornbury TC 1970-. Of Thornbury.

LANGLEY John Patrick D'Arcy: BA (Wolverhampton) MA (Leeds). Pro Life Alliance, North List 2003. **Mr. John Langley:** Born Colchester, Essex, 15 October 1970, s of Thomas D'Arcy Langley, university lecturer, & Rosemary Patricia Langley, housewife. Roman Catholic. Educated St. Joseph's College, Ipswich; Suffolk College; Wolverhampton University; Leeds University. Economist. Interests: Pro-Life, Conservative. Hobbies: Computing. Languages: English, Italian, French. Of Hampstead. London.

LANGRIDGE Richard: BA (Lancaster) 1977. SDP/Alliance: Pontypridd 1983. **Mr. Richard Langridge:** Born Barry 1955. Educated Stowmarket Grammar School; Lancaster University; Post-Graduate student, Sherman Theatre, Cardiff 1979. Taught English in Italy & Libya 1980. Unemployed. BBC Wales Programme Executive Department. Press Officer, Vale of Glamorgan SDP. Press & Publicity Officer, Wales SDP.

LANSDOWN Gwenllian: BA (Oxon). MSc Econ (Wales) 2002. Plaid Cymru, Wales Euro 2004. **Miss Gwenllian Lansdown:** Born St. Asaph 1980. Educated St. Hilda's College, Oxford (French & Spanish); University of Wales, Cardiff (Political Theory). English teaching assistant, Galicia 1 year. PhD student & Postgraduate Tutor in Political Theory, Cardiff School of European Studies 2002-. Chair: Plaid Cymru Student Federation. Candidate, Cardiff CC (Plasnewydd) 2004. Of Cardiff.

LARNEY Pamela J. S: Conservative: Abertillery Oct. 1974. **Mrs. Pamela Larney:** Born 1922. Married. Educated Felixstowe Girls' College, Central London Ophthalmic College, Wolverhampton Teacher Training College. Teacher (French) at Church Stretton. Vice-Chair, Ludlow Conservative Assn. Salop CC. (Chairman 2000-01). Of Ludlow.

LATHAM Sylvia Rosena: BA (Open) 1992. Green Party, South/Central List 2003. **Miss Sylvia Latham:** Born Isleworth, Middx. 11 September 1936, d of James Latham, printer, & Rosetta Alice Lilian Latham, housewife. Free Thinker. Married, 1s 3d. Divorced. Educated Green School for Girls, Isleworth; Open University (Diplomas in Health & Social Welfare). Interests: Environment, Animal Welfare, General Green Issues. Hobbies: Animals, Gardening, Reading, Learning Classical Latin, Study. Of Ynyswen, Treorchy (1992).

LAURIE John Wimburn: CB JP (Pembs) DCL KtCommStSava (Bulgaria). Conservative: Pembroke & Haverfordwest 1892, MP 1895-1906. **Lieut-General Wimburn Laurie:** Born London 1st October 1835, s of John Laurie MP & Elizabeth Helen, d of Henry Collett, Master in Chancery. Anglican. Married Eleanor Frances Beatrice Collins of Nova Scotia, 4c. Educated Harrow; Dresden; RMA Sandhurst. Army: Ensign 1856, Major, Canada 1861, Major General 1882, Lieut-General 1887, Served in Indian Mutiny & Crimean War. Canadian MP 1892-93, 1909-10. President of the Nova Scotia Board of Agriculture 1874-80. Freemason, Grand Master: Lodge of Nova Scotia, Lodge of England 1907, South Wales 1897. Mayor of Paddington. Estate £15,520. Of London. Died 20 May 1912.

LAW Peter John: JP MIPR. Labour AM Blaenau Gwent 1999-. Mr. Peter Law: Born Abergavenny, 1 April 1948, s of John Law & Rita Mary Law. Married 1976, Patricia, d of Ronald Bolter, 2s 3d. Educated Llanfoist Primary School; Grofield Secondary School; King Henry School, Abergavenny; Nantyglo Community College; Correspondence School; Open University. Self-employed retail grocer 1964-87. Public Relations Advisor. Nantyglo & Blaina UDC 1970-74. Blaenau Gwent BC 1974-96 (Mayor 1988-89). Blaenau Gwent CBC 1995-99. Member: Gwent Police Authority; Gwent Magistrates Courts Cttee. 1st Chair, Gwent Health Trust. Member, Institute of Public Relations. Secretary for Local Government 1999-Oct. 2000. Suspended from Labour Group for voting against the Wales Millennium Centre, 5 February 2002. Hobbies: Walking, Landrovers, Countryside. Languages: Learned Welsh at Assembly, English. Of Nantyglo.

LAWRENCE Jacqueline Rita: Labour MP Preseli 1997-. **Mrs. Jackie Lawrence:** Born Birmingham 9 August 1948, d of Sidney & Rita Beale. Married. Educated Upperthorpe School; Upperthorpe College, Darlington; Open University. With TSB Bank plc. Personal Assistant to Nick Ainger MP. Secretary/Chair: Pembroke Labour Party. Dyfed CC 1993-96. Pembrokeshire CC 1995-97 (Labour Group Leader). Member: Pembrokeshire Coast National Park Authority 1993-95; Dyfed Police Authority 1994-97. Member, Christian Socialist Movement, RSPB, West Wales Naturalist Trust, TGWU. PPS on Equality Issues at Department of Trade & Industry. Select Cttee Member: Welsh Affairs 1997-99, Trade & Industry 2001-2003. Chair: Parliamentary All-Party Group for National Parks. Secretary, Welsh Labour MPs Group until 2003, President 2003. Interests: Consumer Affairs, Environment, Small business in the economy. Hobbies: Walking. Languages: Welsh (GCSE 'O' level), English, learning German & Modern Greek.

LAWRENCE James Clark: 1st Bart 1868 JP DL (London). Liberal Unionist: West Carmarthenshire 1886, Cardiff District 1900. Liberal: Lambeth North 1885; MP Lambeth 1865-68, 1868-85. **Sir James Lawrence:** Born 1820, s of Alderman William Lawrence & Jane, d of James Clark. Builder: Partner, William Lawrence & Co. Alderman, City of London. High Sheriff of London & Middlesex 1863. Lord Mayor of London 1868-69. Of London. Estate £152,098. Died 16 August 1896.

LAWRENCE Joseph: 1st Bart 1918 Kt 1902 JP. Conservative MP Monmouth District B/E 1901-06. **Sir Joseph Lawrence:** Born Zante 23 September 1848, s of Philip M. Lawrence, Ionian Islands. Married 1873, Margaret Alice, d of Joseph Jacks of Southport. Educated Owens College, Manchester. Company Chair: Linotype & Machine Ltd, International Linotype Co. Ltd, Partner, Manchester Ship Canal. Captain, Lancashire Volunteers. Sheriff, City of London 1901. Lieutenant, City of London, Surrey CC Alderman. Of London & Kenley, Surrey. Estate £26,600. Died in train 24 October 1919.

LAYTON Geraldine: Liberal Democrat: Blaenau Gwent 1997; Green Party, South/East List 2003. **Mrs. Geraldine Layton:** Born Gosport, Hampshire 18 October 1937, d of Arthur James Jolliffe, shoe repairer, & Katie Wilhelmina Harriet Layton, teacher. Quaker. Married 1959, Ernest Layton (died 1994), partner, small electrical business, 3s. Educated Gosport Grammar School; Sparsholt Agricultural College, Winchester. Helped with husband's mail-order business. Goat farmer & smallholder 1981, Mail order clerk. Gardener, auxiliary nurse. Member, Wales & Marches Goat Society. Secretary: Torfaen Liberal Democrats. Contested local elections, Blaenavon, many times. Interests: Liberal, then Liberal Democrat, 2001 slightly disillusioned with all politics. Hobbies: Farming, Comparative Religion, Climate, Gardening, Reading (quality). Of Blaenavon.

LAYTON Walter Thomas, 1st Baron Layton: of Danehill 1947 CH 1919 Kt 1930 CBE 1917, Hon. LLD Colombia 1933 Melbourne BA (London) 1904 BA (Cantab) 1907 MA (Cantab) 1911. Liberal: Cardiff South 1923, Burnley 1922, University of London 1929. **Sir Walter Layton:** Born Chelsea, 15 March, 1884, s of Alfred John Layton (both parents, professional musicians, mother 1st woman FRCO). Married 1910, Eleanor Dorothea, d. of F. P. Ormaston of Limpfield, Surrey, 7c. Educated St. George's Chapel, Windsor, Kings College School, London, Westminster City School, University College, London, Trinity College, Cambridge, Fellow of Gonville & Caius 1909, Hon. Fellow 1931). Research Lecturer, University College, London 1909-12; Fellow of University College London, Cambridge University Lecturer in Economics 1912-15; Director, Requirements and Programmes, Ministry of Munitions 1915-19; Director, Iron and Steel Trades Federation 1919-22; Editor, *The Economist* 1922-38, Company Chair: *News Chronicle* Ltd 1930-50, *Star* Newspaper Co. Ltd 1936-50, *The Economist* Ltd, Vice-Chair, *Daily News* Ltd, Deputy Chair, National Mutual Assurance Ltd. Director Tyne Tees Television. Member, Reuters Trust, Munitions Council. Director: Economic & Financial Section, League of Nations, National Federation of Iron & Steel Manufacturers, Financial Adviser, Indian Statutory Commission 1929-30, British Delegate,

World Economic Conference 1927, British Member, Organisation Cttee, Bank of International Settlements 1929, Director-General of Programmes, Ministry of Supply 1940-42, Chair, Executive Cttee, Ministry of Supply 1941-42, Chief Adviser, Programmes & Planning, Ministry of Production 1942-43, Head of Joint War Production Staff 1942-43, Vice-President, Consultative Assembly, Council of Europe 1949-57, Member, ITA 1954-56, Deputy Leader of the Liberal Peers 1952-55. Of London. Died 14 February 1966. Further Reading: *Dictionary of Liberal Biography, pages 217-219, David Hubback: No Ordinary Press Baron.*

LEADBEATER David Thomas Vincent: BA 1929 MA (Wales). Labour: West Flint 1950, 1951. **Mr. David Leadbeater:** Born Ystalyfera 1909. Married Educated Ystalyfera Grammar School; University of Wales, Aberystwyth (1st English), President of Debates 1929. Teacher (English) Mold Grammar School. Head-teacher, Mold Grammar School. Extra-Mural Lecturer. Founder, Flintshire Drama Festival 1938. Education & Welfare Officer NFS 1939-45. President, Aberystwyth Old Students' Assn 1979-80. Hobbies: Rugby player. Languages: Welsh, English. Of Mold.

LEADBETTER Jean Bibbette: BSc (Bristol). Natural Law Party Clwyd South West 1992, North List 1999; Euro North West England 1999. **Mrs. Bibbette Leadbetter:** Born 1947. Married Pete Douglas Napier Leadbetter (candidate for Chorley 1992 & Euro North West 1999). Educated Bristol University (Psychology). Designer & retailer of jewelry. Lecturer in Transcendental Meditation. Of Skelmersdale.

LEANEY John Christopher Lawrence: Referendum Party: Ceredigion 1997. **Mr. John Leaney:** Married Sue, 3c. Of Newport, Pembs (1968).

LEAVERS Frank. Social & Liberal Democrat Candidate for Vale of Glamorgan B/E 1989. **Mr. Frank Leavers:** Born 1952. Married Ann, 2c. Merchant Navy Engineering Officer, Reardon Smith Line Office, Cardiff, 4 years. SDP Organiser for Wales 1982-86. Agent, Cynon Valley & Tynebridge by-elections & Mid & West Wales Euro Election 1985. PR & Accounts Director, Cardiff Bay Corporation. Joined Liberals and stood against a SDP candidate in the by-election. A founder, Assembly for Wales Campaign. Of Cardiff.

LEBOFF Deanna Joyce: Liberal Democrat, Assembly, Mid & West list 1999. **Mrs. Deanna Leboff:** Secretary, Brecon & Radnor Liberal Democrat Assn. Member, Jews for Palestine. Of Brecon.

LEE Godfrey: BScEcon. Plaid Cymru: Newport Oct. 1974. **Mr. Godfrey Lee:** Born Newport 1951. Educated St. Julian's High School, Newport; Portsmouth Polytechnic. Asst Development Control Officer, Islwyn Borough Council. Languages: Learned Welsh, English.

LEIGHTON Diana Jennifer: Natural Law Party, South/West List 1999, Euro Yorkshire & The Humber 1999. **Mrs. Diana Leighton:** Born Bradford, Yorks. 12 January 1965, d of Percy Walter Thorpe & Freda Heinemann. Church of England. 1s 1d. Educated comprehensive school. Teacher of Transcendental Meditation. West Lancashire DC. Interests: World Peace.

LENNOX-BOYD Alan Tindal, 1st Viscount Boyd of Merton: 1960 CH 1960 PC 1951 DL 1954 BA 1927 MA (Oxon). Conservative: Gower 1929, MP: Mid-Beds. 1931-July 1960. **Rt. Hon. Alan Lennox-Boyd:** Born Loddington, Bournemouth, 18 November, 1904, s of Alan Walter Lennox-Boyd, barrister, & Florence Anne, d of Dr James Warburton Begbie (2 brothers killed in World War II, 1 died in Secret Service in Germany 1939). Married 1938 Lady Patricia Florence Susan Guinness, d. of 3rd Earl of Iveagh, 3s. Educated Sherborne School; Christ Church, Oxford (Scholar, Peit Prizeman in Colonial history). Chair, Oxford University Conservative Assn. President, Oxford Union 1926. Barrister, Inner Temple, 1941. Executive Director, Arthur Guinness, Son & Co. Ltd, Managing Director 1960-67, Joint Chair 1967-69. Parl-Sec: Labour 1938-39, Home Security 1939, Food 1940. Lieutenant RNVR 1940-43. Parl-Sec: Aircraft Production 1943-45, Minister of State, Colonies 1951-52, Minister of Transport & Civil Aviation 1952-54, Secretary of State for Colonies 1954-59. Trustee: British Museum, National History Museum. Of Ince Castle, Cornwall. Died 8 March 1983 (killed by unaccompanied learner driver). Further Reading: *Philip Murphy, Alan Lennox-Boyd (biography); Julian Amery in Political Lives, selected by Hugo Young.*

LEWIS Alexander: Referendum Party: Clwyd South 1997. **Mr. Alexander Lewis:** Born Oxford 1955. Educated Oxford. Industrial Chemist in construction chemical industry. Of Clwyd (1987).

LEWIS Benjamin T: Freedom from World Domination: Cardiff South & Penarth 1983. **Mr. Benjamin Lewis:** Wrote hymn 'The Day has Come' (tune Jerusalem). Of Penarth. *Policy: It is my firm belief that both the Tory Party and the Labour Party inevitably lead to forms of world dictatorship – either "The World is a Business" or "The World is a Communist State . . . What we want is a world where no one dominates but everyone co-operates for a better world and a better life for all the* *nations and races of humanity, so that each and everyone of us, and, also collectively as citizens of the world – can advance proudly into the future, to whatever Destiny has in store for us.*

LEWIS David: MBE 1945 JP (Brecs). Liberal: Brecon & Radnor 1945. **Mr. David Lewis:** Born 1891. Farmer. Breconshire CC 1925-, Alderman, Chair, Education Cttee 1960-63. Chair: Brecon & Radnor Liberal Assn, Council of Agriculture for Wales. Member: Welsh Agricultural Advisory Cttee, Council for Post War Reconstruction; Hill Sheep Farming Cttee. Of Cray. Died 1968.

LEWIS David Idris C: Liberal: Pontypridd 1950. **Mr. David Lewis:** Born Newbridge, Mon 1924, s of Revd W. T. Lewis, Baptist Minister. Congregational lay preacher. Married. Educated Newbridge Grammar School; Caerleon Teacher Training College. Teacher. YMCA Worker. Member NUT. Associate Member, National Assn. of Probation Officers. Interests: Child welfare, Juvenile delinquency. Of Crumlin.

LEWIS David: BSc (Wales). Conservative, Mid & West Wales Euro 1984. **Mr. David Lewis:** Born Gwent, 1935. farmer's son. Educated Grammar School; University of Wales, Aberystwyth (Agriculture & Economics). Welsh Guards. ICI 20 years. Beef & sheep farmer on family farm on father's death. Chair: UN Food & Agriculture Organisation Working Party.

LEWIS David Richard Owen: Conservative: Gower 1966, Swansea West Feb. 1974. **Mr. Richard Lewis:** Born 18 February 1940. Married Hazel Owen. Educated Oakley House School, Swansea; Craigynos School, Swansea; Mill Hill School; Swansea College of Technology (HND Mechanical Engineering). Draughtsman. Constructional Engineer. Administrative Assistant to works manager of a South Wales construction, industrial & engineering company. Chair, Wales Area Young Conservatives 1964-66. National Vice-Chair, Young Conservatives 1967-69. Of Swansea.

LEWIS Donald Jones: Liberal: Llanelli 1970. **Mr. Donald Lewis:** Born Ammanford 1932. Married 2s. Educated Amman Valley Grammar School, Swansea Technical College, Regent Street Polytechnic. Managing Director, Leo Laboratories Ltd. London. Vice-Chair, Welsh Liberal Party 1968-70. Languages: Welsh, English.

LEWIS Elizabeth: Pro Life Alliance, North list 2003. **Mrs. Elizabeth Lewis:** Born Great Harwood, Lancs. 12 December 1948, d of James Henry Rich, caretaker, & Elizabeth Ellen Rich, school dinner lady. Roman Catholic. Married 1980, Brian Edward Lewis, civil engineer, 1s. Educated Primary school, Grammar School, Teacher Training College, University – mature student (Philosophy). Housewife & Voluntary Charity Worker. Former Caring Officer & Counsellor; Lab Technician in Hospitals & Schools. Interests: Pro Life. Hobbies: Reading, Walking with dog, Bird & Butterfly Watching, Crosswords. Languages: English, French. Of Bolton, Lancs.

LEWIS Esyr ap Gwilym: QC 1971 BA 1949 MA LlB 1950 LLM (Cantab). Liberal: Llanelli 1964. **Mr. Esyr Lewis:** Born Clydach Vale 11 January1926, s of Revd Gwilym Lewis & Mary Jane May Selway. Married 1957, Anna Vidler Hoffman, d of O. W. Hoffman Bassett, Southampton, 4d. Educated Salford Grammar School; Mill Hill School 1939-44; Trinity Hall, Cambridge (1st Law, Exhibitioner 1944, Scholar 1948). Intelligence Corps. 1944-47. Lecturer in Law, Cambridgeshire Technical College 1949-50. Law Supervisor, Trinity Hall 1950-55. Barrister, Grays Inn 1951, Bencher 1978, Treasurer 1997. Leader Wales & Chester Circuit 1978-81. Circuit & Crown Court Recorder 1972-84. Circuit Judge 1984-. Senior Officer, Referees 1994-. Member: Bar Council 1965-68, Council of Legal Education 1967-73, Criminal Injuries Compensation Board 1977-84. Senior Official Referee 1994. Retired 1998. Vice-President, The Academy of Experts. Fellow of the Chartered Institute of Arbitrators. Certified Mediator in Alternative Dispute Resolution, Notre Dame Law School London, Jan. 2000.

LEWIS Gwyn Stobart: Conservative: Meirionydd/Nant Conwy 1992. **Mr. Gwyn Lewis:** Born Cwmpenmachno 10 June 1946, farmer's son. Married (1) 1d, divorced (2) engaged Nia. Educated Llanrwst Grammar School. Agricultural Merchant (Gwyn Lewis Farm Supplies) & Catering Manager, National Eisteddfod. Chair, Llanrwst Eisteddfod Finance Cttee 1989, Member, Domestic Animals Medical Council. Vice-Chair, Welsh Conservative Candidates Assn. ComC. Gwynedd CC 9 years. Languages: Welsh, English.

LEWIS Sir Herbert – see LEWIS John H.

LEWIS Herbert Clark 2nd Baron Merthyr of Senghenydd (1911). 2nd Bart 1896 JP (Pembs). Conservative: East Glamorgan 1892, Merthyr Tydfil 1895. **Mr. Herbert Lewis:** Born Aberaman. 1866, s of Sir William Thomas Lewis, 1st Baron, coal owner, & Anne, d of William Rees, Coalowner of Aberdare (& brother in law of Archbishop Green of Wales), succeeded father 1914. Married 1899, Elizabeth Anna (died 1925) d of Major-General R. S. Couchman, 1s 1d. Coal Proprietor, Company Chair & Director. High

Sheriff of Pembrokeshire 1907, Radnorshire 1914. Of Hean Castle, Saundersfoot. Estate £527,997. Died 20 March 1932.

LEWIS Herbert Mostyn: BSc (Lond) PhD. Liberal: Conway 1955, Wrexham 1950, West Ealing 1945. **Dr. Mostyn Lewis:** Born 1902, s of Rt. Hon. Sir Herbert Lewis MP (qv) & Ruth, d of W. S. Caine MP. Presbyterian Church of Wales. Married Gwen Lewis, 1d. Educated Gresham. School, Holt; Universities of London, Edinburgh & Cambridge. Missionary in Assam. Army 1939-45, Lieutenant, RASC. Lecturer in Biology, Wrexham Technical College 1948-. WEA tutor. Freelance journalist & broadcaster. *Brain of Britain*, Finalist. Member, *Round Britain Quiz* teams. President: Cambrian Archaeological Society, Cymdeithas Cerdd Dant. Languages: Welsh, English. Of Gresford. Died 10 December 1985. *Books: H. Mostyn Lewis, Stained Glass in North Wales.*

LEWIS Huw George: BSc. (Edin). Labour AM. Merthyr Tydfil & Rhymney 1999. **Mr. Huw Lewis:** Born Merthyr Tydfil 17 January 1964. Married 1995, Lynne Neagle (qv). Educated Afon Taf High School; Edinburgh University. Teacher (Chemistry) North Berwick High School & Bathgate Academy 1987-90. Parliamentary Researcher 1990-91 Chemistry Teacher, Afan-Taf High School 1991-94. Asst-General-Secretary, Labour Party, Wales 1994-99. Interests: Education, economic development. Resigned Whip Feb. 2000. Deputy Minister, Education Oct. 2000-. Of Merthyr Tydfil.

LEWIS Ian Rowland: Liberal Democrat, Ogmore 2001. **Mr. Ian Lewis:** Born Pontypridd, 20 April 1953. Married 2c. Plumber. Ex-proprietor, taxi firm, double-glazing contractor. Contested Bridgend BC 1999. Hobbies: Fly-fishing. Of Garth, Maesteg.

LEWIS Illtyd Maurice: BA (Wales). Plaid Cymru: Aberavon 1959. **Mr. Illtyd Lewis:** Born Porth, July 1927, s of Revd L. M. Lewis. Presbyterian lay preacher. Married Marilyn, divorced. Educated Neath Grammar School; University of Wales, Cardiff. Teacher of Welsh, Kenfig Hill Comprehensive School-1964. BBC 1964-. Languages: Welsh, English.

LEWIS James: see LEWIS John James.

LEWIS John: Conservative: Aberdare 1951. **Mr. Jack Lewis:** Born 1909. Educated St. Dunstan's College, London (Diploma, London Academy of Public Speaking). Company Representative, London textile firm. National Fire Service 1939-45. Tutor-lecturer, Conservative Central Office 1945-.

LEWIS John Herbert: PC 1915 GBE 1922 JP DL (Flints) Hon. LLD (Wales) BA 1879 MA 1884 (Oxon). Liberal MP Flint District 1892-1906, Flintshire 1906-18, University of Wales 1918-22. **Rt. Hon. Sir Herbert Lewis:** Born Mostyn Quay 27 December 1858, s of Enoch Lewis & Catherine Roberts. Calvinistic Methodist. Married (1) 1886, Adelaide (died 1895) d. of Charles Hughes JP of Wrexham (2) 1897, Ruth OBE d of W. S. Caine MP. Educated Denbigh Grammar School; McGill University, Montreal; Exeter College, Oxford. Solicitor, Liverpool 1882. Shipowner. Chairman, Flintshire CC 1889-93. Chair: Joint Education Cttee Intermediate Schools 1889; Central Juvenile Organisations Cttee; Dee Conservancy Board. President: Library Assn of United Kingdom 1920-21; National Library of Wales 1926-27 (Vice-President 1909-26). Member: Court of National Museum of Wales, University Colleges of Aberystwyth, Cardiff & Bangor. Constable of Flint Castle 1910. Hon. Freeman: Flint, Aberystwyth. Medal of the Hon. Society of Cymmrodorion 1927. Liberal Whip 1905-06, Parl-Secretary, Local Government Board 1909-15, Parl-Secretary, Education 1915-22. Elected Moderator of the General Assembly of the Presbyterian Church of Wales 1925, but declined. Of Caerwys, Holywell. Estate £78,174. Died 10 November 1933 Further Reading: *K. Idwal Jones: Syr Herbert Lewis, 1958, Kenneth O. Morgan, Peace Movements in Wales 1899-1945, The Welsh History Review, Vol. 10, June 1981, page 401.*

LEWIS John James: Liberal: Clwyd North-West 1983. **Mr. James Lewis:** Born Rhyl 30 June 1932. Educated Liverpool College of Art; Bradford College of Advanced Technology. Journalist, *The Guardian*. Consultant on Newspapers & Journalism, Governments of India & Sudan. Lecturer in Journalism. Chair: *Guardian* Chapel NUJ. Ex-Labour Party. Founder/Chair: Mold Liberals 1960. Member North Wales Liberal Council.

LEWIS John Robyn Jones: LlB PhD 2000 (Wales). Labour: Denbigh 1955. Resigned as Candidate 1959. Joined Plaid Cymru 1966. Plaid Cymru: Caernarfon 1970. **Dr. Robyn Lewis:** Born Llangollen, October 1929, s of Welsh soccer player & teacher, moved to Nefyn (changed name from Robert to Robyn at school). Married Gwenan Lewis. Educated Llangollen Infants School; Nefyn Primary School; Pwllheli Grammar School; Rydal School, Colwyn Bay; Coleg Harlech; University of Wales, Aberystwyth. Army, staff interpreter at NATO HQ, Fontainebleau. Member: National Union of Students Executive, National Assn. of Labour Students Executive. Solicitor 1956. WEA lecturer. Asst Recorder, Crown Court 1976. Barrister 1997. Deputy Crown Court Judge & Asst. Recorder. Law Lecturer. Chair, Plaid Cymru 1971-72, Vice-

President, 1972-77. Dwyfor RDC 1962- (Chairman 1973-75). Dwyfor DC (Chairman 1980). Hon. Legal Adviser, Gorsedd of Bards 1974. Won National Eisteddfod Prose Medal 1980. Archdruid of Wales 2002-05. Author (18 books) & Writer. Member: Cymdeithas Cyfieithwyr Cymru, Academi Gymraeg. Languages: Welsh, English. Of Nefyn. *Books: Robyn Lewis, Geiriadur Termau Cyfreithiol.*

Dr. Saunders Lewis.

LEWIS John Saunders: MA (Liverpool) Hon. DLitt (Wales) 1983. Plaid Cymru: University of Wales 1931, B/E 1943. **Dr. Saunders Lewis:** Born Wallasey, Wirral 15 October 1893, s of Revd Lodwig Lewis, Presbyterian Minister & Margaret, d of Revd Dr. John Thomas, Congregational Minister, Converted to Roman Catholicism 1932. Married 1924, Margaret Gilcrist, 1d. Educated Privately, Liscard High School for Boys, Liverpool University 1911-14, 1918-20 (1st English, French). Army, 1915-19, Lieutenant, SWB. Glamorgan librarian 1921-22. Lecturer in Welsh, University College, Swansea 1922-37, dismissed over his involvement in the burning of a shed at Penrhos Airfield 1936, Caernarfon Jury failed to agree, sentenced to nine months imprisonment for arson at Old Bailey, Wormwood Scrubs. Journalism, teaching, school inspecting & farming 1937-52. Lecturer/Senior Lecturer, University of Wales, Cardiff 1952-57. Playwright, author, broadcaster, full-time writer 1957. Columnist, *Baner ac Amserau Cymru* 1939-51. Lecturer, University of Wales, Cardiff, 1952-57. Founder-member 1925, President, Plaid Cymru 1928-39. Delivered radio lecture, *Tynged yr Iaith* 1962, which led to founding of Welsh Language Society. Languages: Welsh, English. Died 1 September 1983. *Books: Saunders Lewis,* Further Reading: *Companion to Welsh Literature (edit. Meic Stephens), which lists all his published works & studies of Saunders Lewis.*

LEWIS Julian Murray: BA 1977 MA DPhil 1981 (Oxon). Conservative: Swansea West 1983, MP New Forest East 1997-. **Dr. Julian Lewis:** Born 26 September 1951, s of Samuel (tailor) & Hilda Lewis, Jewish (family came from eastern Poland at turn of 19th century). Educated Dynevor Grammar School, Swansea; Balliol College, Oxford (PPE); St. Antony's College, Oxford (Doctoral Research, Strategic Studies 1975-77, 1978-81). Member, Labour Party 1976, to combat *Militant Tendency.* Volunteer Seaman RNR 1979-82. Research Director & Director, Coalition for Peace through Security 1981-85. Director, Policy Research Associates 1985-, Research Deputy Director, Conservative Research Dept. 1990-96. Defence & International Affairs Consultant. Parliamentary aide to MPs & peers. Treasurer, Oxford University Conservative Assn. 1971. Secretary, Oxford Union 1972. Hon. Vice-President, Greater London & West London Young Conservatives. Joint Secretary, Conservative Defence Group 1997. Member, Select Cttee on Defence 1998. Vice-Chair: Conservative Parliamentary Foreign Affairs Cttee; European Affairs Cttee. Hobbies: History, Fiction, Films, Music, Driving. *Books: Julian Lewis, Changing Direction: British Military Planning for Post War Strategic Defence 1942-47 (1988).*

LEWIS Mostyn – see LEWIS Herbert M.

LEWIS Norman Harry Evans: MIM. Liberal: Caerphilly, Oct. 1974, Brecon & Radnor 1979. **Mr. Norman Lewis:** Born December 1926. Educated Vaynor & Penderyn Grammar School, Merthyr Tydfil Grammar School. Personnel Accountant, Wales Gas. Caerphilly UDC 1967-70. Member, Institute of Administrative Management. Of Nelson.

LEWIS Owen John: JP (Mon). Conservative: Abertillery 1950. **Mr. Owen Lewis:** Born Abergavenny 1913, farmer's son (old Liberal family). Baptist lay preacher. Educated Abergavenny Grammar School. Farmer. Chair, Abergavenny Branch NFU & Member, County Executive. MFH Talybont. Chair: Monmouthshire Point-to-Point Cttee. Secretary, Abergavenny Branch, British Field Sports Society. Abergavenny RDC, Chairman. Of Llanelen.

LEWIS Pedr Rhyswil: Independent Wales Party, South/West List 2003. **Mr. Pedr Lewis:** Born Hong Kong 26 September 1923, s of Benjamin Thomas Lewis, teacher, & Mary Elen Roberts, Christian missionary & housewife. Educated Wolverhampton Grammar School. Retired. Treasurer, Independent Wales Party. Interests: To see an Independent Republic, internationally recognised Wales. Hobbies: Reading History, Poetry, Walking, Industrial sites & buildings. Languages: Welsh, English, German. Of Bridgend.

LEWIS Richard David: Conservative, Swansea East 1987; Referendum Party, Gower 1997; Independent, Gower 1999; UK Independence Party, Gower 2001, 2003; Wales Euro 2004. **Mr. Richard Lewis:** Born 25 January 1939. Church in Wales. Married 1971, Angela, 1s 2d. Educated Queens College, Taunton. RAF two years. Joined family business, D. M. Lewis & Co. Newsagent. Proprietor, Swansea Mettoy Shop. Career Change Management. Swansea CC 1973-92 (Conservative Group Leader); lost ward nomination & resigned whip. West Glamorgan CC 1987-. Contested W. Glam CC 1981. Swansea CCC; Lord Mayor 2003-04. Member: South Wales Police Authority, Swansea Area Health Authority; Governing Body, Church in Wales. Of Horton, Gower.

LEWIS Saunders – see LEWIS John S.

LEWIS Thomas Arthur: BSc (Wales). Coalition Liberal MP Pontypridd 1918-20, defeated at 1920 by-election caused by his accepting government office. National Liberal MP University of Wales 1922-23. **Mr. Arthur Lewis:** Born Nevern, Pembs. 21 September 1881, s of Revd John Maldwyn Lewis, moved to Porth when young. Baptist. Married 1919, Marjorie, d. of William Culross, barrister of Adelaide, Australia. Educated University College of Wales, Cardiff. Teacher, Porth Higher Elementary School 1904-1910. Barrister 1911. Joined Inns of Court OTC 1915. Lieutenant 1916-18. PPS 1918-20. Junior Lord of the Treasury 1920 until by-election. Estate £1,900. Languages: Welsh, English. Died 18 July 1923.

LEWIS Thomas Palesteina: JP (Caerns). Liberal: Caernarfon District 1872, MP Anglesey 1886-95. **Mr. Thomas Palesteina Lewis:** Born Cemaes 12 November 1821, s of Thomas Lewis, tenant farmer. Calvinistic Methodist Elder & Sunday School Superintendent. Married 1846, Laura, d of Henry Hughes, Llanllyfni. Educated Llanfechell Board School. Apprenticed to John Elias, shopkeeper (s of Revd John Elias) c.1834, With sister opened own shop at Bangor 1838. Became one of the chief corn & flour merchants in North Wales & Liverpool until his retirement from business in 1866. Visited Palestine 1866, and added *Palesteina* to his name to differentiate him from Thomas Lewis, Bangor. Secretary, Arfon Presbytery 30 years. Moderator, Anglesey Presbytery 1881. Temperance Speaker. Anglesey CC Alderman 1889. Languages: Welsh, English. Of Bangor. Died 2 December 1897.

LEWIS Thomas Vivian: LlB (Liverpool). Conservative: Anglesey Feb. & Oct. 1974. **Mr. Vivian Lewis:** Born October 1930. Married Verna Lewis, 1s. Educated Friars School, Bangor; Liverpool University. Solicitor 1957. Bangor CC (Liberal) 1953-74 (Chair, Housing Cttee). Mayor of Bangor 1970-72. Caernarfonshire CC 1964-74. Languages: Welsh, English. Of Bangor.

LEWIS William Russell: MA (Cantab). Conservative: Caerphilly 1959. **Mr. Russell Lewis:** Born September 1926. Anglican. Educated Caerphilly Grammar School; St. Johns College, Cambridge (History & Economics). Army 1945-48, RA & RAIC. Economist. Deputy-Head, European Community London Press Office. Director, Conservative Political Centre 1966-. With leading trade association. Chair, Bow Group 1958 (Librarian twice). Interests: Economic Policy. Of London.

LEYSHON Peter: Conservative: Rhondda Feb. & Oct. 1974, 1979. **Mr. Peter Leyshon:** Born Trealaw, October 1933. Educated Tonypandy Grammar School; Glamorgan Art Scholarship. Teacher (Art). Ex-member, Labour Party. Founder-Member, Mid-Rhondda Conservative Assn 1972. Secretary & Chair, Rhondda Conservative Assn. Executive Member: South Wales Group, Conservative Party; Wales Area, Conservative Party. Chair: Sports Council for Wales; South Wales Mountain Rescue Assn; Outdoor Pursuits Sub-Cttee, Wales Games & Sports Council. Member, Management Cttee, South West & Southern Area & North Wales Area Cttees, British Mountaineering Council. Rhondda BC 1974-77. Of Trealaw, Rhondda.

LINDLEY Clive David: SDP/Alliance: Monmouth 1983, 1987, South East Wales Euro 1984; Labour: Leominster Feb. 1974. **Mr. Clive Lindley:** Born 22 September 1934. Married 2c. Educated King Edward VII School, Lytham; Lancaster University. Founded own multi-catering company. Chair, several companies. Director: Independent Radio News (ITN), Severn Sound Radio. Chair: Democrat Newspapers, SDP. National Finance Cttee. Alliance Spokesman on Defence. *Books: Clive Lindley (selected & edited) Partnership of Principle: writings and speeches on the making of the Alliance by Roy Jenkins 1985.*

LINDSAY Henry Edzell Morgan: CB KStJ JP (Glam & Dublin) DL (Glam). Conservative: East Glamorgan 1900. **Lieut-Colonel Morgan Lindsay:** Born Tredegar Park 13 February 1857, s of Lieut-Colonel Henry Grove Lindsay, Co Dublin (ex-Chief Constable, Glamorgan) & Hon. Ellen Sarah Morgan, d of Lord Tredegar. Anglican. Married 1898, Ellen Katherine, d of George William Griffith Thomas, of Ystradmynach 5s (3 killed in war) 2d (Mrs. Stoneham qv). Educated RMA Gosport; RMA Woolwich. Officer, Royal Engineers 1876. Served, South Africa 1890-91,

Sudan 1895, South Africa 1900-02. Landowner & Company Director. Caerphilly UDC 1892-1922, Chairman. Glamorgan CC Alderman 1892-1907. Treasurer, Priory for Wales, Order of St. John of Jerusalem & Chair, Glamorgan Centre. Member, Governing Body of the Church in Wales. Member Royal Engineers Soccer XI & South of England XI 1873. President, South Wales Amateur Football Assn. Steeplechase Rider. Of Ystradmynach. Estate £7,894. Died 1 November 1935.

LINES Christopher Peter: BA (Wales). MIPR. Liberal Democrat, Monmouth & South East List 1999. **Mr. Chris Lines:** Born Guildford, 29 June 1962, s of Peter James Lines, company director, & Jane Emerson Lines, teacher/orthoptist. Agnostic (brought up Anglican). Married 1985, Clare Peace Lines, NHS Manager, 2s 2d. Educated Oundle School; University of Wales, Swansea (Politics). Public Relations Manager. Chief Executive, Liberal Democrats Wales 1998. Founder member SDP. Member, SDP Students Executive. President, University of Wales, Swansea, Liberal Democrats. Interests: Constitutional Reform, NHS, Higher Educational Environment. Hobbies: Cricket, Hill walking. Languages: English, French (O level). Of Abergavenny.

LISBURNE The Earl of: (Ernest Edmund Henry Malet Vaughan) 7th Earl of Lisburne (1776) Viscount Vaughan, Lord Vaughan (1699) JP (Cards), Conservative: Cardigan 1923. **Rt. Hon. Earl of Lisburne:** Born 8 February 1892, s of 6th Earl & Evelyn, d of Edmund Probyn, Longhope, Gloucs. Succeeded 1899. Anglican. Married (1) Regina (died 1944) d of Don Julio de Pittencourt, Chilean Attache, London 4c (2) 1961, Audrey Maureen Lesley, DStJ, d of James Meakin & widow of Hon. Robert Devereux. Educated Eton. Landowner. Army 1914-18. Captain, Welsh Guards Reserve 1918-39. Lord Lieutenant of Cardiganshire, 1924-. President, University of Wales, Aberystwyth. Member: Council, National Library. Of Trawscoed Park & London. Died 30 June 1965.

LITCHFIELD Edward John William: Referendum Party: Cardiff North, 1997. **Mr. Ted Litchfield:** Born 1952. Married Jayne 4c. Independent Financial Adviser 1949-. Ex-Merchant Navy Officer. Of Penarth.

LITTLE Frank: Liberal Democrat, Neath, 1997, Vale of Glamorgan 1999. **Mr. Frank Little:** Born 29 July 1941. Married 2d. Educated Oldershaw Grammar School, Wallasey. Freelance Computer Consultant. Member: RSPB, Archeology Cymru, Railway Development Society, Institute of Data Programme Management. Interests Child protection, Public transport, Information technology, Living world. Hobbies: Sport, Music, Cricket.

Contested Neath/Porth Talbot BC (Rhos) 1999. Of Pontardawe.

LITTLE George Spencer Ross: MBE 1982 MRCS FCMP. Conservative: Cardigan 1950. **Dr. George Little:** Born Cardiff 3 May 1907, s of Daniel Little. Married 1933, Mary Megan, d of John Evans-George, London 2c. Educated Cardiff High School; St. Bartholomew's Hospital, London. Medical Practitioner (Worksop) 1934-47. ARP 1939-45. Acting MOH Worksop. Hon. Surgeon, Victoria Hospital, Worksop. Divisional Surgeon, St. John's Ambulance Brigade, Member, BMA Council. President, West Kent Medico-Chirugical Society. Retired from medicine 1947 to farm in Cardiganshire. High Sheriff of Cardiganshire 1962. Of Blackheath & Gwbert on Sea.

LIVSEY Richard Arthur Lloyd, Baron Livsey of Talgarth 2001: CBE 1994 MSc NDA. Liberal (Democrat): Brecon & Radnor 1983, 1992, Pembroke 1979, Perth & East Perthshire 1970; MP Brecon & Radnor B/E 1985-92, 1997-2001. **Mr. Richard Livsey:** Born 2 May 1935, s of Arthur Norman Livsey, Brecon master mariner working as a canal lock keeper & Lilian Maisie James, teacher; lived at Talgarth from age of 2. Married 1964, Irene Martin, d of Ronald Earsman of Castle Douglas, 2s 1d. Educated Talgarth Primary School; Bedales School; Seale Hayne College of Agriculture; Reading University. Farm labourer at Bwlch. Agricultural Development Officer, ICI 1961-67. Farm Manager, Blairdrummond Estate, Perthshire 1967-71. Senior Lecturer, Farm Management, Welsh College of Agriculture, Llanbadarn Fawr 1971-85. Farmer (60 acres at Llanon, Cards). Deputy Director, then Development Manager, ATB-Landbase Cymru 1992-97. Chair, Brecon Jazz Festival. Member: Talgarth Male Voice Choir. Leader, Welsh Liberal Party 1988-92, 1997-. President: Brecon & Radnorshire Liberal Democrats. Hobbies: Cricket, Fishing, Rugby, Music. Languages: Learned Welsh, English. Of Llanfihangel Talyllyn. Further Reading: *John Graham Jones in Dictionary of Liberal Biography, pages 222-223.*

LLEWELLYN Daniel James Roy: Plaid Cymru: Carmarthen West & South Pembs 1997. **Mr. Roy Llewellyn:** Born Login 28 June 1937, s of Daniel John Llewellyn & Alice Mary Williams. Baptist deacon. Married Rhoswen Mary Davies, teacher & editor *Y Cardi Bach.* Educated Whitland Grammar School. British Rail clerk 1954-56. Royal Army Pay Corps 1956-58. British Rail Relief Clerk 1958-60. Youngest ever station master 1961-65. Movements Superintendent 1965-67. Asst. County Secretary, Farmers Union of Wales. Sales Representative & Advisor, international fertiliser company 1971-89. Member: Whitland Creamery Steering Cttee; Friends of the Earth; Council for Protection of Rural Wales. Dyfed CC 1989-95. Carmarthenshire CC 1995-99. Chair: West Carmarthenshire & South Pembrokeshire constituency party. Member, Whitland, Rugby Club 18 years, Chair 4 years. Interests: Environment, Agriculture, Health. Hobbies: Watching Whitland & Wales play rugby, Variety compère for charity, Cycling, Photography. Languages: Welsh, English. Of Whitland.

LLEWELLYN David Treharne: Kt 1960 BA 1938 MA (Cantab). Conservative: Aberavon 1945, MP Cardiff North 1950-59. **Sir David Llewellyn:** Born St. Fagans 17 January 1916, s of Sir David Richard Llewellyn, 1st Bart. coalowner, & Magdalen Anne, d of Revd Dr. Harries, Baptist Minister of Treherbert), brother of Sir Harry Llewellyn, horseman). Anglican. Married 1950 Joan OBE, d of R. H. Williams, Bonvilston House. Educated Eton; Trinity Hall, Cambridge. Army: ranks 1939. Commissioned, Welsh Guards, Captain. Master Printer, Journalist & Broadcaster. Member, Institute of Journalists. Under-Secretary, Home Office 1952-53. Resigned on health grounds. Of Cardiff. Died 9 August 1992. *Books: D. T. Llewellyn, Nye, the Beloved Patrician 1961, The Adventures of Arthur Artfully 1974.*

LLEWELLYN Mavis: Communist: Ogmore 1950. **Miss Mavis Llewellyn:** Born Nantymoel 1897, d of disabled miner. Educated grammar school & teacher training college. Teacher. Joined Communist Party 1930. Trainer of Civil Defence personnel 1940-45. Chair, Local Evacuation Cttee 1939. Ogmore & Garw UDC 1937-50. Languages: Welsh, English. Of Nantymoel.

LLEWELLYN Roy – see LLEWELLYN Daniel James Roy.

LLEWELLYN Trevor Wilmot: Conservative: Cardigan Feb. 1974, Gower 1979, B/E 1982. **Mr. Trevor Llewellyn:** Born Maidenhead 2 July 1947, s of Major W. H. Rhydian Llewellyn & Lady Honor Vaughan, d of Earl of Lisburne (nephew of David Llewellyn qv). Educated Eton; University College, Cardiff. Chartered Accountant. Finance Manager, BOC Ltd. Financial Director, computer services company at Maidenhead. Of Ealing & Ystrad Meurig.

LLEWELLYN William Morgan: JP (Glam) ME. Liberal: Aberdare 1923. **Mr. William Morgan Llewellyn:** Born Aberdare 11 June, 1878, s of Alderman Rees Llewellyn JP; brother of Sir D. R. Llewellyn & uncle of David Llewellyn. Succeeded his father as General Manager of Bwllfa & Merthyr Collieries, Cwmdare 1919, then Deputy-Chairman. Director, Amalgamated Anthracite Collieries Ltd. Aberdare UDC Chair 1923. Chair, Aberdare Education Cttee 1920. Master, Bwllfa Hounds. High Constable of Miskin 1923. Languages: Welsh, English. Of Cwmdare, Aberdare. Estate £290,178. Died 19 September 1943.

LLEWELLYN-JONES Edward David Walter: Labour: Montgomery 1987. **Mr. Edward Llewellyn-Jones:** Born 9 September 1949, Married 3c. Educated Durham University; Cambridge University. Teacher. Member: NAS/UWT. Ashfield BC. Kirkby DC.

LLEWELLYN-JONES Frederick Llewellyn: BA (Wales) 1924 LlB (London) DrScPol (Pecs) FREconS AIA. Member, Royal Hungarian Order of Merit. Liberal MP Flint 1929-35 (short time as Liberal National). PPC Preston 1914-18. Joined Labour Party March 1918, Re-joined Liberal Party. **Mr. F. Llewellyn-Jones:** Born Bethesda 18 April 1866, s of Humphrey Bradley Jones & Lucy George, and brother of Cyril. O. Jones (qv) who stood against him in 1929). Married 1892, Elizabeth Roberts, 5c. Solicitor 1891. Coroner for Flintshire 1901. Member, Denbigh School Board 1892-95. Chair, Holywell School Board 1894-1904. Member: Flintshire Education Cttee, Court of University Colleges of Wales, Aberystwyth & Bangor, National Library, National Museum, Welsh Consultative Health Council, Central Council for Health Education, International Law Assn, Crotius Society, London, Royal Institute of International Affairs, American Society of International Law, Society of Comparative Legislation, Medico-Legal Society of London, Hon. Society of Cymmrodorion, Fabian Society 1910. Chair, Flintshire Insurance Cttee 1912-36, Vice-Chair, Flintshire Recruiting Cttee 1915-17. 1st President, Assn of Welsh Insurance Cttees 1912. President: English, Welsh & Scottish Insurance Cttees 1924-26, 1929-31, 1934-, Welsh League of Nations Union 1933-34. Fellow of the Royal Empire Society. Hon. Member, Gorsedd. Of Mold. Died 11 January 1941.

LLEWELYN Alun: BSc Econ (Wales). Plaid Cymru, Neath 2001, 2003. **Mr. Alun Llewelyn:** Born Swansea, 4 April 1961. Baptist. Married Rhian, 2c. Educated Ysgol Gyfun Ystalyfera; University of Wales, Aberystwyth. Assistant Director, Housing Assn. Interests: Housing, Economic Development. Chair: Ystalyfera Development Trust, Tiddleywinks Community Childcare Centre. Interests: Housing, Economic Development, Community Development. Languages: Welsh, English. Of Ystalyfera.

LLEWELYN Christopher: MA PhD. Labour, Carmarthenshire East & Dinefwr 1997. **Dr. Chris Llewelyn:** Born Amman Valley 1962. Married

Julie Llewelyn. Teacher. University Lecturer. Senior Policy & Development Officer, Welsh Consumer Council. Director HTV 2000. Member: Secretary of State for Wales Strategy Advisory Group; The Consumers in Europe Food Advisory Cttee 1998. Chair: Carmarthen East & Dinefwr CLP. Mayor of Glanamman. Interests: Jobs, Education, Health.

LLEWELYN Gareth Owain: LlB BSc. Plaid Cymru: South Wales Euro 1994, Pontypridd 1997. **Mr. Owain Llewelyn:** Born 3 October 1953. Married 2c. Educated Ysgol Dyffryn Ogwen; University of Wales, Aberystwyth; Chester College of Law; Glamorgan University. Senior Chartered Surveyor. Service Director, Chestertons plc. Joined Plaid Cymru, 1977. Taf-Ely BC 1991-94. Languages: Welsh, English. Of Pontypridd.

LLEWELYN Leonard Wilkinson: KBE 1917 JP (Mon). Officer, Legion d'Honneur (France), Officer of Leopold (Belgium), Order of St. Stanislav (Russia). Conservative: Pontypool 1918. **Sir Leonard Llewelyn:** Born Aberaman 11 June 1874, s of Llewelyn Llewelyn JP & Jane, d of Col. Wilkins of Risca. Anglican. Married 1899, Edith d of Edward Jones JP DL of Snatchwood Park (qv) 4c. Spent early years in Chile where his father was mineral adviser to the Chilean government. General Manager & Agent, Cambrian Combine. Company Director: Naval, Britannic, Glamorgan & Fernhill Collieries. High Sheriff of Monmouthshire 1920. Freemason. 1st Silver Medal of Royal Humane Society for saving life in mines. Of Malpas Court, Newport. Estate £205,187. Died 1 June 1924.

LLOYD Allan William: SDP/Alliance: Rhondda 1983. **Mr. Allan Lloyd:** Born Pontypridd 1936, s of miner/deacon. Married 5c. Senior Tutor & Head of Careers Dept. Lady Hawkins School, Kington. Principal, Kington FE College. Mayor of Kington. Leominster DC. Chair, Hereford & Worcester County Careers Advisory Cttee.

LLOYD Catherine Ann: Independent Wales Party, South/East List 2003. **Miss Catherine Lloyd:** Born Abergavenny, 9 August 1975, d of Raymond Trevor William Lloyd, miner, mining deputy & mines rescue captain & Helen Elizabeth Lloyd, housewife (gd of Clarence Lloyd, member of the International Brigade in Spanish Civil War). Partner, Steve Baker, musician & metal fabricator. Educated Abertillery Comprehensive School; Crosskeys FE College. Constituency Secretary, Independent Wales Party. Administration & Customer Care. Student at University of Wales, Newport (Caerleon) 2003-. Interests: Welsh Republic. Hobbies: Archeology, History, Folklore. Languages: Learning Welsh, English. Of Abertillery.

LLOYD Charles Ellis: Labour: Llandaff & Barry 1924, 1931, 1935, MP 1929-31. **Mr. C. Ellis Lloyd:** Born Newport, s of Charles Lloyd & Mary Ellis. Anglican. Educated St. Woolos Board School, Newport; Bridgend National School; Bridgend Grammar School. Solicitor's Clerk. Solicitor. Barrister, Grays Inn 1926. District Coroner, Ogmore. Journalist & Novelist. Founder-Member NUJ. President, South Wales Branch NUJ. Member, Authors' Society. Of Bridgend. Died 7 May 1939. *Books: C. E. Lloyd, Scarlet Nest, A Master of Dreams.*

LLOYD David Alun: MA BD (Wales). Plaid Cymru: West Flint 1966. **Mr. Alun Lloyd:** Born Foel, Mont. 1926. Welsh Independent. Married. Educated Llanfair Caereinion High School; University of Wales, Bangor, Bala-Bangor Congregational College. Trained for the Ministry but did not proceed on health grounds. Teacher (History) Ruabon Grammar School, then Beaumaris until 1968. Lecturer in Welsh & Drama, Trinity College, Carmarthen 1968-74. Publicity Officer, Gwynedd County Council, 1974. Second-Hand Book dealer, Bangor. Editor, *Y Ddraig Goch* 1970-74. Political Columnist, *Y Cymro*; Editor, *Yr Herald Gymraeg*. Smallholder. Languages: Welsh, English. Of Llanfair PG until 2000, then Brynsiencyn. Died 22 June 2002. *Books: D. Alun Lloyd, Eryr y Glyn (drama).*

LLOYD David Gareth Beechey: MA (Durham). Liberal Democrat, Preseli, 1999, Mid & West Euro 1994, Neath B/E 1991. **Mr. David Lloyd:** Born Wells, Somerset, 7 March 1945, s of Glyn Raymond Beechey Lloyd, civil engineer & farmer, & Ivy Elaine Lloyd, hotelier. Church in Wales. Married 1987, Gail Elizabeth Lambourne, publisher, 2s 1d. Educated Croesgoch Primary School; Selwyn House Prep School, Begelly; Wrekin College, Durham University (Law & Economics). Hotelier. Awarded Gold Medal of Welsh Tourist Board 1981, as pioneer of Winter Marketing of Tourism. Barrister. Member: Court of University of Wales. Lay Inspector of Schools (OHMCI). Voluntary Co-ordinator, Pembrokeshire Cancer Support Group. Director, Pembrokeshire Initiative Board, 10 years. Founder: Pembrokeshire Tourist Federation 1977, St. Davids Tourist Federation 1970. Secretary, Eisteddfod Genhedlaethol Penfro 2002. Joined Liberal Party 1974. Dyfed CC. 1981-86. Interests: Community Development. Hobbies: Current affairs, Cricket, Rugby, Reading poetry, Listening to classical & Celtic folk music. Languages: Welsh, English. Of St. Davids.

LLOYD David Glyn: MBE. Conservative: Meirionydd/Nant Conwy 1979, 1983, North Wales Euro 1979. **Mr. David Lloyd:** Born 25 September 1935. Married Joan Lloyd, 4s. Educated Llangollen Grammar School. Journalist with *Wrexham Leader, Birmingham Post, Western Mail* & Broadcaster. Public Relations Officer NFU. Shropshire CC. (Vice-Chair, Education Cttee). Oswestry BC. Selattyn & Gobowen PC. Vice-Chair: Border Counties Archeology Group. Member: North Wales Projects Cttee, Prince of Wales Cttee. Languages: Welsh, English. Of Oswestry.

LLOYD David Philip: BSc 1979 PGCE 1980 (Wales). Liberal Democrat, Delyn 1997, 2003; Vale of Clwyd 1999. **Mr. Phil Lloyd:** Born Oswestry, 25 November 1957, s of Geoffrey William Lloyd, electrician, & Glenys Evelyn Lloyd, florist. Church in Wales. Married 1979, Ceris Lloyd, teacher, 1s 1d. Educated Llandisiilo Cirw Primary School; Welshpool High School; University of Wales, Cardiff (Zoology & Environmental Studies). Teacher. Vaccine Specialist 17 years. Pharmaceutical Industry Salesman. Mold TC. 1991- (Mayor 1998-99). School governor. Chair & Secretary, Mold Liberal Assn. Chair, Liberal Democrats, Wales; contested presidency, January 2002. Freemason, Master of 2 Lodges. Interests: Rebuilding Community Trust. Hobbies: Golf, Walking. Languages: Welsh, English. Of Mold.

LLOYD David Rees: MB ChB 1980 Dip. Therapeutics 1995 MRCGP 1989. Plaid Cymru, Swansea West 1992, 1997, 1999, 2003; AM. South/West List 1999-. **Dr. Dai Lloyd:** Born, Tywyn, Merioneth, 2 December 1956, s of Aneurin Rees Lloyd & Dorothy Grace Lloyd. Married 1982, Dr. Catherine, d of David & Rachel Jones, 2s 1d. Educated Lampeter Comprehensive School; Welsh National School of Medicine. Junior Hospital Doctor 1980-84. Medical Practitioner at Fforestfach 1984-99. S4C magazine doctor. Member: BMA Welsh Council; Royal College of Medical Practitioners Welsh Council. President, Alzheimer's Disease Society. Vice-President, Plaid Cymru. Shadow Minister: Health & Social Services 1999-2003; Finance, Local Government & Public Services, 5.11.2003. Chair, Plaid Cymru Assembly Group 2000-. Swansea CCC. B/E 1998-. Interests: Health, Education. Hobbies: Walking, Watching rugby, football & cricket. Languages: Welsh, English. Of Tycoch, Swansea.

LLOYD Harold Montague: Conservative: Rhondda Jan. & Dec. 1910, PPC East Glam 1910-14. Labour: Cardiff East 1924. **Mr. Harold Lloyd:** Born Cardiff 28 April 1877, s of Thomas Symonds Lloyd & Anne Louise Morgan. Anglican. Married 1901, Rowena Ethel, d of James Moreland, of Mewham Grange, Stockton on Tees. Educated Bath. Solicitor 1900, Struck off the Roll of Solicitors for *three cases of unprofessional conduct* and sentenced to five years hard labour for embezzlement 1928. Released from Maidstone Gaol 30/1/1932. Of Lavernock. *Books: Harold M. Lloyd, Murder, Mystery and Mirth.* Further Reading: *W. H. Allen, 1952. Articles in Weekly Mail & Cardiff Times 1952; Reports of trial, Weekly News & Cardiff Times, 26/5/28, 16/6/1928, Weekly Mail & Cardiff Times, 26/5/1928.*

LLOYD Ifor Dillwyn: UK Independence Party, Caernarfon 2001. **Mr. Dilwyn Lloyd:** Born Caernarfon 1965. Married Alwena Lloyd (midwife) 2d. Nurse at Ysbyty Gwynedd 15 years. Devotes time to local charities. ComC. 1996. Chair, North Wales Branch UKIP. Of Carmel, Gwynedd.

LLOYD Jennifer: MB BS (London) 1961. Liberal: Barry 1974 Feb. & Oct. **Dr. Jennifer Lloyd:** Born April 1937. Married Dr. Lloyd. 2d. Educated Howells School, Llandaff; Benenden School; London University. Asst Psychiatrist, Addiction Unit, Whitchurch Hospital. Cttee Member, Addiction Research Foundation of Wales. Chair: Cardiff & District Branch, Migraine Trust.

LLOYD John Conway: Kt 1938 MC 1915 JP (Brecs) MA (Oxon). Conservative: Breconshire Dec. 1910. **Lieut- Colonel, Sir John Lloyd:** Born 19 April 1878, s of Colonel Thomas Conway Lloyd, Dinas Brych, & Katherine Eliza Campbell-Davys. Married 1903, Marion Clive, d of Major General William Clive Jenkins, 1s 2d (one son killed over France 1940, one drowned in *HMS Thetis* 1939). Educated Eton; Christ Church, Oxford. Landowner. High Sheriff of Breconshire 1906. Chairman, Breconshire Quarter Sessions 1934-. Joined Militia 1909. Captain SWB 1914. Deputy Provost Marshal, Rhine 1919. Colonel 1919. 1st Chairman, Powys Police Authority 1953- Director, Breconshire ARP 1939-45. Brecon BC 1909-. Breconshire CC 1913-. Founder Secretary, Brecon Museum. Of Abercynrig, nr. Brecon. Died 30 May 1954.

LLOYD Kenneth John: Conservative: Caerphilly 1950. **Mr. Kenneth Lloyd:** Born 1919. Married, 3c. Educated Rugby School. Freelance journalist & broadcaster. Partner, Midland Advertising Co. Army 1939-45 (RA, RASC & Army Bureau of Current Affairs). Member: Birmingham Publicity Assn; Birmingham Chamber of Trade. Interests: Empire & Foreign Affairs. Of Birmingham.

LLOYD Marteine Owen Mowbray: 2nd Bart (1863) JP DL (Pembs, Cards & Carms). Conservative: West Carmarthenshire 1885. **Sir Marteine Lloyd:** Born Bronwydd, 8 February 1851, s of Sir Thomas Lloyd, lineal descendant of Martin of

Tours, 18th generation direct descendant of Edward I. Succeeded father 1877. Married Katherine Helena, d of Alexander Dennistown, of Golfhill, Lanark, 3d (1 son killed on Somme). Anglican. Landowner (100,000 acres in 4 counties). 24th Lord of the Manor of Kemes, only remaining Lord Marcher. Freemason. Hon. Captain, Pembrokeshire Yeomanry 1874-77. High Sheriff of Cardiganshire, 1881. Member, National Hunt Cttee. Resigned as Liberal Association President to stand as Conservative. Of Bronwydd, Henllan, Cards & Newport Castle, Pembs. Estate £109,658. Died 4 April 1933.

LLOYD Morgan: QC 1873 JP (Merioneth) MA (Edin). Liberal: Beaumaris 1868, MP Beaumaris 1874-85, Independent Liberal: Merioneth 1885, Liberal Unionist: Anglesey 1892. **Mr. Morgan Lloyd:** Born Trawsfynydd 14 July 1820, s of Morris Lloyd, farmer. Calvinistic Methodist, became an Anglican. Married (1) 1848 Mary (died 1859) d of Admiral, Hon. Charles Elphinstone Flemming (2) Priscilla d of James Lewes, Cwmhyar, Cards. Educated Bala Theological College; Edinburgh University. Started training as a surveyor, then candidated for Calvinistic Methodist Ministry but did not seek ordination. Barrister, Middle Temple 1847, Bencher 1875. A founder, Bangor Normal College. Deputy Secretary, Movement for a Welsh University. Hon. Secretary, University of Wales, Aberystwyth. Languages: Welsh, English. Of Brook Green, Middx. Estate £921. Died 5 September 1893. Further Reading: *R. Emyr Price, Lloyd George & Merioneth Politics, Cymdeithas Hanes Sir Feirionydd, Cyfrol VII, Rhif 2, 1978.*

LLOYD Nicholas John William: Referendum Party: Cardiff Central 1997. **Mr. Nicholas Lloyd:** Born 1962. Married Deborah Lloyd. Educated Whitchurch High School; North Staffs Poly. Cardiff solicitor. Former Financial Services Adviser. Of Sully.

LLOYD Paul Lewis: BSc (Dundee). Natural Law Party, South/East List 1999. **Mr. Paul Lloyd:** Born, Maidstone, Kent, 9 July 1964, s of Leslie Brian Hunt, computer systems designer, & Patricia Mary Taylor, care assistant. Non-specific religion. Unmarried. Educated Weydon Lane Comprehensive School, Farnham; Farnham FE College; Kingston Polytechnic (SRC member); Dundee University (Biochemistry). Graphic Designer/Copywriter. Ex-member: CND, Friends of the Earth. Interests: Left of Centre, Environmental, Human Rights: against GM Food, Pro-devolution, Pro-Organic Farming, Great believer in People & People's rights, Opposes manipulation of government by large companies. Hobbies: Yoga, Sports. Of Skelmersdale.

LLOYD Philip – see LLOYD, D. P.

LLOYD Raymond Trefor William: Independent Wales Party, South/Central List 2003. Of Abertillery.

LLOYD Rhys Gerran: Baron Lloyd of Cilgerran 1973 CBE 1953 QC 1961 JP (Surrey) BA 1929 MA (Cantab) 1932 BSc (London) 1929. Liberal: Anglesey. **Mr. Gerran Lloyd:** Born Cilgerran, August 1907, s of James Griffith Lloyd. United Reformed Church. Married 1940, Phyllis Mary, d of Ronald Shepherd JP of Chickworth. Educated Sloane School, Chelsea; Selwyn College, Cambridge (Hon. Fellow 1967). Scientific Research 1939-45. Barrister, Grays Inn 1939, Middle Temple 1954. Company Director: Strayfield International Ltd, Morgan Marine Ltd, Brancondale Properties Ltd. Member, Surrey Education Cttee, Vice-President, Home Counties Liberal Federation. Hon. Treasurer, Liberal Party of Wales. Director, Welsh Liberal Election Campaign 1970. Chair, Liberal Party Panel on Law Reform 1965. President, Liberal Party 1973-74. Liberal Whip (Lords) 1973-75. Founder Vice-President 1970 Cranstown Project, Esher (Drug Rehabilitation Unit), Executive Chair 1973. President: Institute of Patentees & Inventors 1975, Mobile Radio Users' Assn 1986. Of Esher, Surrey. Died 30 January 1991.

LLOYD Taliesin John: OBE JP. Labour: Merthyr Tydfil 1970. **Mr. Tal Lloyd**: Born Rhondda, February 1917. Presbyterian Church of Wales. Married. Educated Hendrefadog School, Rhondda. Engineer. Divisional Organiser AUEW 1952-. Merthyr Tydfil BC 1945- (Chair, Education Cttee), Mayor of Merthyr Tydfil. Of Merthyr Tydfil.

LLOYD Valerie: MEd BEd (Wales) RGN RNT. Labour, AM. Swansea East B/E 2001-. **Mrs. Valerie Lloyd:** Born Swansea 1943. Church in Wales. Married Bob Lloyd (Lord Mayor of Swansea) 2d. Educated Gors Primary School, Swansea; Swansea High School for Girls; University of Wales, Swansea. Nurse in London, Swansea & Zambia, Teacher at Swansea & Bahrain. Senior Lecturer in Nursing, University of Wales, Swansea. Swansea CC 1999 (Lady Mayoress). Member: Socialist Health Assn, RSPB. Interests: Education, Health. Hobbies: Watching Cricket. Of Morriston.

LLOYD-DAVIES Henry: Conservative, Ceredigion 1999, Swansea East 1992. **Mr. Henri Lloyd Davies:** Born Cardiff, 12 December 1946, s of Henry George Lloyd Davies, medical practitioner, and Emmeline Mary Thomas, Nurse. Church in Wales (Treasurer, pcc). Married 1977, Norma Yvonne Davies, optician, 2s 2d. Educated

Rugby School; Bath University (Diploma, Industrial Admin). With TI Group 1969-71. Managing Director, Clegan Publishers 1971-87. Managing Director Bryneithen Estates Ltd. 1987-. General Commissioner of Income Tax. Life Vice-President, Royal Welsh Agricultural Show. Governor, University of Wales, Cardiff 1979-81. Life Member, Royal Yachting Assn. President, Merthyr Tydfil & Rhymney Conservative Assn; Aberaeron Young Conservatives. Chair: Carmarthen East & Dinefwr Conservative Assn; Conservative Political Centre in Wales; Conservative Party Wales 1999-. Governor, University of Wales, Cardiff. President: Llandeilo Agricultural Society. Vice-President: Welsh Agricultural Society. Founder Chair, Llandeilo Heart Foundation. Life Member, Royal Yachting Assn. Contested Cardiff CC for Plaid Cymru. Interests: Devolution. Hobbies: Sailing (member, Aberaeron Yacht Club), Country sports, Walking with family. Languages: Welsh Learner, English. Of New Inn, Llandeilo.

LLOYD-DAVIES Henry James: BSc (Liverpool). Conservative, 2003. **Mr. Harri Lloyd Davies:** Born Cardiff, 27 January 1981, s of Henri Lloyd Davies (qv) & Norma Yvonne Davies. Church in Wales. Educated Ysgol Teilo Sant, Llandeilo; Llandaff Cathedral School; Rugby School; Liverpool University (Maths). Trainee Chartered Accountant. Deputy Chair: Carmarthen East & Dinefwr Conservative Assn. Hobbies: Rugby, Football, Cricket. Languages: Welsh, English. Youngest candidate in 2003 election. Of New Inn, Llandeilo.

LLOYD-EDWARDS Norman: RD 1971 Bar 1980 DL (Glam) 1978 JP 1990 KStJ 1988 ADC LlB (Bristol). Conservative: Rhondda West 1964, Cardiff South-East 1966, 1970. **Captain Norman Lloyd-Edwards:** Born Troedyrhiw, 13 June 1933, s of Evan Stanley Edwards & Mary Leah Lloyd. Anglican. Educated Quakers Yard Grammar School; Monmouth School for Boys; Bristol University. Vice-President, Bristol University Conservative Assn. Joined RNVR 1952, Royal Navy 1958-60. Commander. Wales Division RNR 1981-84. Naval ADC to the Queen 1984. Solicitor (partner 1960-93, Consultant 1993). President: Cardiff Junior Chamber of Commerce. Member: Navy League, Royal Navy Assn. Governor: Llandaff Technical College, Welsh College of Drama & Music, Reardon Smith Nautical College, Church in Wales Schools Management Cttee. Chair: Cardiff Sail Training Assn; Wales Cttee. Duke of Edinburgh Award 1981; National Rescue Training Council 1983; Cardiff Festival, Glamorgan TAVRA 1987-90. President: South Glam Scouts 1989, Cardiff Assn. National Trust 1990, King George's Fund for Sailors 1990; Christian Aid (Cardiff & District) 1992-; South-East Wales Community Foundation 1993-; Cardiff Branch, National Trust. Founder Master, Welsh Livery Guild 1992-. Patron, British Red Cross (South Glam) 1991. Chapter Clerk, Llandaff Cathedral, Prior for Wales, Order of St. John of Jerusalem 1989. Member: Welsh Arts Council 1983-89; BBC Advisory Council, Wales 1987-90. Cardiff CC 1963-87 (Deputy Chair, Education Cttee 1968; Chair, Youth Cttee). Deputy Lord Mayor 1973-74, Lord Mayor 1985-86. Lord Lieutenant of South Glamorgan, August 1990 (Vice-Lieutenant 1986-90). Vice-President, Welsh National College of Music & Drama. Hon. Colonel, Royal Regiment of Wales. Hobbies: Table talk, Gardening. Of Llandaff.

Rt. Hon. David Lloyd George.

LLOYD-GEORGE David: 1st Earl Lloyd George of Dwyfor: Viscount Gwynedd 1945 OM 1919 PC 1905 JP (Caerns) 1910 Hon. DCL (Oxon) Hon. LLD (Wales, Sheffield, Edinburgh). Grand Cordon, Legion d'Honneur (France) 1920. Liberal MP Caernarfon District B/E 1890-1945, (Ind.L. 1931-45). **Rt. Hon. David Lloyd George:** Born Manchester 17 January 1863, s of William George, teacher (died 1865) & Elizabeth Lloyd; brought up by uncle William Lloyd at Llanystumdwy. Churches of Christ/Baptist. Married (1) 1898 Margaret GBE JP (died 1941) d of Richard Owen, farmer, of Mynydd Ednyfed, Criccieth 5c (2) 1943 Frances Louise Stevenson CBE. (His secretary, died 1972). Educated Llanystymdwy National School. Articled 1877, Solicitor 1884. Caernarfonshire CC Alderman 1889. Constable of Caernarfon Castle 1908. Chairman, Caernarfonshire Quarter Sessions 1929. Chancellor for Wales, Priory of Order of St. John of Jerusalem 1918. President, Baptist Union of Wales, 1908-09. Hon. Member, Gorsedd. President of the Board of Trade 1905-08, Chancellor of the Exchequer 1908-15, Minister of Munitions 1915-16, Secretary of State for War 1916, Prime Minister 1916-22. Leader of the Liberal Party 1923-31. Of Criccieth, Churt & London. Languages: Welsh, English. Died 26 March 1945. *Books: David Lloyd George, War Memoirs (6 vols) 1933-36, The Truth about the Peace Treaties (2 vols) 1938. Further Reading: John Hugh Edwards, From Village Green to Downing Street, 1908; Herbert du Parcq, Life of David Lloyd George (4 vols) 1912; Beriah Gwynfe Evans, The Romance of David Lloyd George 1916; Harold Spender, The Prime Minister 1920; Walter Roche, Mr. Lloyd George 1920; E. T. Raymond, Mr. Lloyd George 1922; Sir Charles Mallet: Mr. Lloyd George, a study 1930; Watkin Davies, Lloyd George 1863-1914, 1939; E. Morgan Humphreys, David Lloyd George 1943; A. J. Sylvester, The Real Lloyd George 1947; Sir Alfred T. Davies, The Lloyd George I Knew 1948; Malcolm Thompson, Lloyd George, The Official Biography 1948; Thomas Jones, Lloyd George 1951; Frank Owen, Tempestuous Journey 1954; William George, My Brother and I, 1958; Richard Lloyd George, Lloyd George 1960; Charles Mowat, Lloyd George, 1964; Martin Gilbert, ed. Lloyd George 1968; A. J. P. Taylor, Lloyd George, Rise & Fall 1961, Lloyd George: Twelve Essays 1971, (ed) Lloyd George: A Diary by Frances Stevenson 197; Lord Beaverbrook, The Decline & Fall of Lloyd George 1963; Donald McCormick, The Mask of Merlin 1963; Kenneth O. Morgan, David Lloyd George, Welsh Radical as World Statesman 1963, new edition, 1982, (ed) Lloyd George: Family Letters 1973; W. R. P. George, The Making of Lloyd George 1976; C. J. Wrigley, David Lloyd George & The British Labour Movement 1976; David Woowward, Lloyd George and the Generals 1983; Olwen Carey-Evans, Lloyd George was my Father 1985; John Grigg, The Young Lloyd George 1973, Lloyd George the People's Champion 1902-11, 1978, Lloyd George, From Peace to War, 1985; Bentley B. Gilbert, David Lloyd George, A Political Life, 1987 and 1992; Peter Rowland, Lloyd George 1975; Martin Pugh, Lloyd George 1998; Chris Wrigley, Lloyd George 1992; John Campbell, Lloyd George, the Goat in the Wilderness 1992.*

LLOYD-GEORGE Gwilym: 1st Viscount Tenby of Bulford 1957: PC 1941 TD 1952 JP (Pembs) Hon. LLD (Wales) MA (Cantab). Liberal & Conservative, Pembroke, 1950. Liberal MP Pembroke: 1922-24, 1929-50 (Ind Lib. 1931-50). Liberal & Conservative MP Newcastle upon Tyne North B/E 1950-57. **Major, Rt. Hon. Gwilym Lloyd-George:** Born Criccieth 4 December 1894, s of Rt. Hon. David Lloyd George MP & Dame Margaret (Owen). Married 1921, Edna Gwenfron, d. of David Jones, Denbigh, 2s. Educated Eastbourne College; Jesus College, Cambridge, Hon. Fellow 1955, played cricket for college & regiment. Army 1914-18, Commis-

sioned RA. Civil Engineer. Managing Director, United Newspapers (Daily Chronicle) 1923; Junior Whip 1923-24, Parl-Sec, Board of Trade 1931 (one month), 1939-41, Parl-Sec, Food 1941-42, Minister of Fuel & Power 1942-45, Minister of Food 1951-55, Home Secretary, 1955-57, Minister for Welsh Affairs 1954-57. Liberal Whip withdrawn 1946. President: University College, Swansea; London Welsh RFC; FA of Wales 1963; Fleming Fund for Medical Research 1962. Member, Board of Decca 1962. Chair, Council on Tribunals 1961. Freeman, City of London, Cardiff, Tenby. Languages: Welsh, English. Died 14 February 1967. Further Reading: *Dictionary of Liberal Biography. Pages 228-230.*

LLOYD-GEORGE Megan Arvon: CH 1966 JP (Anglesey) Hon. LLD (Wales) 1949. Liberal MP Anglesey 1929-51 (Ind. Liberal 1931-45). Joined Labour Party 1955. Labour MP Carmarthen B/E Feb. 1957-. **Lady Megan Lloyd-George:** Born Criccieth, 22 April 1902, d of Rt. Hon. David Lloyd George MP & Dame Margaret Owen. Educated Garrett's Hall, Banstead & Paris. Criccieth UDC until 1955, Chair 1954-55. President, Women's Liberal Federation 1936. Member: British Council, National Federation of Women's Institutes; Waste Food Board, Ministry of Supply 1942; General Advisory Council BBC 1952. Welsh Church Commissioner 1942. Member, Speaker's Panel of Chairmen 1964. President, Parliament for Wales Campaign 1955; Council for the Protection of Rural Wales. Deputy Leader, Parliamentary Liberal Party 1949-50, Chair, PLP Agriculture Cttee 1964. Hon. Member, Gorsedd. Languages: Welsh, English. Of Criccieth. Died 14 May 1966. Further Reading: *Emyr Price, Megan Lloyd George 1983, Mervyn Jones: A Radical Life: the biography of Lady Megan Lloyd George 1991; Dictionary of Liberal Biography, pages 230-232.*

LLOYD JONES Alun: Plaid Cymru, Bridgend 1992, Preseli 1997, Mid & West List 1999. **Mr. Alun Lloyd Jones:** Born Aberystwyth, 4 June 1946, s of David Stephen Jones, Bio-Chemist/ICI Agricultural Adviser, & Mair Lloyd Jones, teacher. Calvinistic Methodist. Married Evelyn Mary Jones, asst. trading standards officer, 2s 1d. Educated Ysgol Gymraeg Aberystwyth; Ardwyn Grammar School, Aberystwyth; FE & Technical College; distance learning. Senior Medical Representative, Pfizer Ltd, retired. Sub-postmaster, Llanfarian. Chair: Plaid Cymru Ceredigion Executive. Member, Plaid Cymru National Council. Ceredigion DC 1991-95. Ceredigion CC 1994- (Group Leader until 1999 when not re-elected). Resigned from group to sit with Independents & expelled from party 1999. (Cabinet Member, Environment Services & Housing). Interests: Health, Environment, Public Protection.

Hobbies: Game-fishing, Gardening, Photography, Rough-shooting. Languages: Welsh, English, conversational French. Of Llanfarian.

LLOYD JONES Eifion: BA (Wales). Plaid Cymru: Clwyd South West 1987, 1992. **Mr. Eifion Lloyd Jones:** Born Aberaeron 13 October 1948, s of railway signalman & a teacher. Married Leah Owen, singer, 3s 1d. Educated Ysgol Eifionydd, Porthmadog; University of Wales, Aberystwyth (Law, but gave it up); University of Wales, Bangor (Welsh Literature). Lecturer, Bangor Normal College. North West Programmes Executive HTV. Lecturer in Communications Studies, in Television, Head of Department, Bangor. Member, National Eisteddfod Council 1986-. Chair, Denbigh National Eisteddfod 2000. Member: UCAC, Cymdeithas yr Iaith, Cymuned. Hobbies: Supporting Welsh language & culture, Playing golf. Languages: Welsh, English. Of Denbigh.

LLOYD-MOSTYN Henry Richard Hywel: JP 1880 DL (Caerns). Conservative: Flintshire 1885. **Colonel, Hon. Henry Lloyd-Mostyn:** Born 1857, s of Hon. Thomas Edward Mostyn Lloyd-Mostyn & Lady Augusta Nevill, d of 4th Earl of Abergavenny. Anglican. Married 1883, Hon. Pamela Georgina Douglas-Pennant, d of Lord Penrhyn. Educated Eton, RMC Sandhurst. Landowner. Lieutenant RWF 1878, Lieut-Colonel RWF (Militia) 1903-08, Cheshire Regt 1909-12. Raised & commanded 17th RWF 1915. Trustee, Llandudno & District General Hospital. Of Llandudno. Died 3 September 1938.

LLOYD-PRICE John Lloyd: JP (Flints). Conservative: Flint District 1900. **Mr. John Lloyd-Price:** Born Flintshire, 1848, s of John Price, Holywell, added Lloyd by deed-poll 1897. Anglican. Married 1873, Elizabeth, d of Edward Hutchfield. Landowner. High Sheriff of Flintshire 1909. Of Holywell.

LLOYD-WILLIAMS Huw Ceiriog: Liberal: Cardigan 1970. **Lieut-Commander Huw Lloyd-Williams:** Born Tregaron, February 1928, farmer's son. Presbyterian Church of Wales. Married 1968, Cecilia Anne Williams, Newport, Mon. 2s 1d. Educated Tregaron Grammar School; RNC. Greenwich. Royal Navy 1944-67. Wales Regional Manager, Nationwide Building Society. Farmer. Ceredigion CC 1995-. High Sheriff of Dyfed. Languages: Welsh, English. Of Talsarn. Died 30 March 1998, after long illness.

LLWYD Elfyn: LlB (Wales). Plaid Cymru MP Meirionydd/Nant Conwy, 1992-. **Mr. Elfyn Llwyd:** Born Betws-y-Coed 26 September, 1951, s of Huw Meirion Hughes & Hefina Hughes, dropped surname Hughes by deed-poll 1970.

Elfyn Llwyd.

Presbyterian Church of Wales. Married 1974, Eleri, d of Huw Lloyd Edwards, dramatist, 1s 1d. Educated Ysgol Dyffryn Conwy, Llanrwst; University of Wales, Aberystwyth; Christleton College of Law, Chester. Solicitor. Barrister, Grays Inn 1997. President: Gwynedd Law Society 1990-91. Chair, Trustees Mawddach Hatchery. Vice-Chair: NSPCC Wales. Hon. Member, Gorsedd 1998. Member, Select Cttee on Welsh Affairs. Plaid Cymru Whip. Leader, Plaid Cymru MPs 2000. President: Dolgellau RFC, Clwb Rygbi y Bala, Llanuwchllyn FC, Betws y Coed FC. Governor, University of Wales. Hobbies: Pigeon Breeding, Rugby, Choral Singing, Fishing. Languages: Welsh, English. Of Llanuwchllyn.

LOGAN David Andrew John: JP 1992. Conservative, Conwy 2001. **Mr. David Logan:** Born Eastbourne, 2 December 1961, s of John Alistair Andrew Logan, farmer, & Joan Bibby Logan, housewife. Married 1986, Philippa Elizabeth (Philly), nurse, 3s 1d. Educated Eastbourne College; Royal Agricultural College, Cirencester (Diploma). Farmer (250 acres family farm). Set up agricultural contracting business 1987, wound up on becoming candidate 2000. Management Consultant. Wealden DC 1995-2001, 2003- (Chair, Leisure, Tourism & Arts Cttee 1997-01, Deputy Leader; Chair, Strategic Planning & Economic Development Cttee 1999-01; Portfolio Holder, Finance & Assets). Interests: Farming, Tourism, Taxation, Wales, Crime. Hobbies: Family, Cooking, Fishing. Languages: English, French. Of Sussex.

LORT-PHILLIPS John Frederick: JP DL (Pembs). Conservative: Pembroke & Haverfordwest Dec. 1910. **Lieut-Colonel John Lort-Phillips:** Born

189

Pembrokeshire 27 November 1854, s of Richard Ilbert Lort-Phillips & Frederica Maria Louisa, d of Baron de Rutzen. Anglican. Married 1898 Hon. Maud, widow of Sir Andrew Walker (Maid of Honour to Queen Victoria). Landowner, steeplechaser & owner of large stud farm (succeeded uncle, George Lort-Phillips MP 1866). Hon. Major, Pembrokeshire Yeomanry 18 years. High Sheriff of Pembrokeshire 1880. Pembrokeshire CC 1888. Master of Hounds: Croom 1882, North Warwickshire 1883, Pembrokeshire 1888-1903. Of Lawrenny Castle. Estate £190,945. Died 15 May 1926.

LORT-PHILLIPS Patrick Henry: DSO 1942 Bar 1945 DL (Pembs) 1950. Liberal: Ebbw Vale B/E 1960, Gloucester B/E 1957, 1959. Joined Labour Party 23 Nov. 1963 & sought candidature. Rejoined Liberals 1972. **Lieut-Colonel Patrick Lort-Phillips:** Born May 1922, s of Major-General Shoubridge. Changed name by deed-poll to inherit estate. Married 1936, Katherine Florita, d of Pascoe Glyn. Educated Eton; RMC Sandhurst. Lieutenant, Grenadier Guards 1939. Lieut-Colonel 1942. Farmer, journalist & author. President: Pembroke Liberal Assn. Joint Treasurer, Liberal Party. Pembroke DC 1948-55. Of Lawrenny. *Writings: The Myth of the Independent Deterrent (copy typescript) 1959.*

LORT-WILLIAMS John Rolleston: Kt 1927 KC 1922 LlB (London). Conservative: Pembrokeshire 1906, B/E 1908, Stockport Dec. 1910, MP Rotherhithe 1918-23. **Sir John Lort-Williams:** Born Walsall 1881, s of Charles William Williams, solicitor. Married 1923, Dorothy, d of Edward Russell, Hampstead. Educated Merchant Taylors School; London University. Barrister, Middle Temple 1904. President, Hardwicke Society 1911. Recorder, West Bromwich 1923-24, Walsall 1924-28. Pusine Judge, High Court of Judicature, Bengal 1927-44. Middlesex Imperial Yeomanry 6 years. London CC 1907-10. Died 6 June 1966.

LOUGHOR Lewis: Kt 1929 JP. Conservative MP Cardiff East 1922-23, Cardiff Central 1924-29. **Sir Lewis Loughor:** Born Llandaff 1 October, 1871, s of Thomas Loughor & Charlotte, d of David Lewis, Radyr Farm. Anglican. Unmarried. Educated Cardiff Secondary School; Cardiff Technical College. Started as office boy with Evan Jones & Co. (13 years there). Shipowner. Chair, Lewis Loughor & Co Ltd 1910-, Whitehouse Precast Concrete Ltd, Dan-y-Bryn Estates Ltd. Director: Ben Evans & Co Ltd Swansea. Chair: Cardiff & Bristol Channel Shipowners Assn 1919, Shipping Federation, Cardiff District 1918-19, National Trimming Board of Enquiry re Hours of Coal Trimmers & Tippers under Industrial Courts Act 1919. Freemason. Liveryman,

Worshipful Company of Wheelwrights. Governor, Cardiff Royal Infirmary, Royal Hamdryad Seamen's Hospital. High Sheriff of Glamorgan 1931. Cardiff RDC 1934-54, Chair 1942-43. Glamorgan CC 1922-48. Of Radyr, Cardiff. Died 28 August 1955. Further Reading: *John Loughor: The Loughors of Glamorgan 1952.*

LOVAT-FRASER James Alexander: MA LLM (Cantab). Labour: Llandaff & Barry 1922, Bristol Central 1924; MP Lichfield 1929-31 (National Labour 1931-). Joined Labour Party 1917. Withdrew as Conservative PPC Rhondda 1900, PPC Blackfriars 1914-17. **Mr. James Lovat-Fraser:** Born Bishopriggs, Lanarkshire 16 March 1868, s of John Fraser. Anglican. Educated Trinity College, Cambridge. Barrister, Inner Temple 1891. Barry UDC 1905-07. Cardiff CC 1907-12. Chair, South Wales Council, Wales Housing Assn. Member, National Council of Maternity & Child Welfare. Hon. Secretary, State Children's Assn. Director, South Wales Public House Trust Co. Of London. Died 1938. *Books: J. A. Lovat-Fraser. John Stuart, 3rd Earl of Bute (biography) 1912.*

LOVERDIGE Angela Wendy: BA. Green Party, North List 1999. **Miss Angela Loveridge:** Born Birmingham, 5 June 1967, d of Audrey Pamela Loveridge, bookkeeper. Educated comprehensive school & university (Humanities). Diploma in Applied Statistics & Computing. Post Graduate Diploma in & Teaching English as a Foreign Language. Volunteer at Greenhouse (information centre), Bangor. Joint Convenor, Buildings Group, Moel-y-Ci sustainable enterprise groups. Interests: Green Party. Hobbies: Camping, Walking, Swimming, Bird watching, Reading, Writing. Languages: Learning Welsh, English, Greek, Russian. Of Bethesda, Gwynedd.

LOVERIDGE John Warren: Kt 1988 JP 1973 MA (Cantab) FRSA FRAGS MRIAC. Conservative, Aberavon, 1951; MP Hornchurch 1970-74, Upminster 1974-83. Liberal PPC: 1947-49, resigned to join Conservative Party. **Sir John Loveridge:** Born Cheshire, 9 September 1925, s of C. W. Loveridge & Emily Malone. Married 1954, Marguerite JP d of E. J. Chivers 4c. Educated privately; St. John's College, Cambridge. Aircraft Research, 1946. Principal, St. Godric's Secretarial College, London 1954-. Landowner & farmer. Company Director: Crescent Properties (Hampstead) Ltd 1959. Senior partner in family business (agriculture, education & property). Hampstead BC 1953-59. Treasurer, Hampstead Conservative Assn. Vice-Chair, Conservative MPs Smaller Businesses Cttee 1974. Member: Select Cttees: Expenditure, Procedure. Of Axmouth & London.

LOVILL John Roger: Kt 1987 CBE 1983 DL (E. Sussex) 1983. Conservative: Ebbw Vale 1966. **Sir**

John Lovill: Born 26 September 1929, s of Walter Thomas Lovill & Elsie Page. Married 1958, Jacqueline Parker, 4c. Educated Brighton, Hove & Sussex Grammar School. Bank Clerk, Lloyds Bank 1945, S. G. Wartburg Ltd. 1951-55. Deputy General Manager, Securicor 1955-60. Company Director: Municipal General Insurance Co 1984-. Managing Trustee, Municipal General Insurance Co 1988- (Chair, 1993-). Chair: Nationwide Small Business Property Trust, 1988-. Vice-Chair: Prime Health Ltd. 1992-. Former Chair: Brighton Pavilion Conservative Assn, South East Area Young Conservatives. East Sussex CC 1967-89, Leader, 1973-77. Chair: Sussex Police Authority 1976-79, Local Authority Conditions of Service Advisory Board 1978-83, Assn of County Councils 1983-86. President: Sussex Assn of Local Councils 1987-. Vice-President, National Assn of Local Councils, 1991-93. Leader, Conservative Assn of County Councils, 1981-83. Of Beddingham, nr. Lewes.

LOW Nicholas: Natural Law Party: Wrexham 1997. **Mr. Nicholas Low:** Born Lancashire 1952. Educated Bolton School; University of Wales, Bangor; Lancaster University. Teacher of Transcendental Meditation 1980-. Minister of All Possibilities, Research & Development, City Parliament of Lancaster & Morecambe in Age of Enlightenment.

LOWELL William: New Party: Pontypridd 1931. **Mr. William Lowell:** A Cardiff Surveyor. Formerly Leader, Conservative Party, Cardiff Parliament. Resigned from Conservative Party to join the New Party.

LUCAS Ian Colin: BA (Oxon) 1982. Labour MP Wrexham 2001-; North Shropshire 1997. **Mr. Ian Lucas:** Born Gateshead, 18 September 1960, s of Colin Lucas, process engineer, & Alice Scott, part-time cleaner. Married 1986, Norah Anne Sudd, teacher, 1s 1d. Educated Greenwell Junior High School, Gateshead; Newcastle Royal Grammar School; New College, Oxford (Jurisprudence); Chester College of Law. Solicitor. Asst Solicitor at Putney, 1983-86, Chester 1986-87, Birkenhead 1987-89, Wrexham 1989-92, Oswestry 1992-97. Principal 1997-2000, Partner 2000-. Marford ComC 1987-91. School Governor. Chair, housing charity. Non-executive director, Robert Jones & Agnes Hunt Orthopaedic & District Hospital NHS Trust, Gobowen. Joined Labour Party 1986. Chair, Wrexham CLP 1992-93. Secretary: North Shropshire Labour Party 1993-200. Member: Fabian Society, Spinal Injuries Assn. Interests: Economic Affairs, Home Affairs, Environment, Development. Hobbies: Football (Sunderland & Wrexham supporter), Constitutional history. Languages: English, German. Of Oswestry.

LUKE Alwyn Cadwallader: Independent, Preseli 1999. **Mr. Alwyn Luke:** Born Trecwn 28 June 1930, son of James Luke, farmer, & Elizabeth Luke. Church in Wales. Married 1955, Leonora Hamilton 1s 1d. Educated Trecwn Junior School; Fishguard Grammar School. Farmer & Hotelier. Haverfordwest RDC 1951-73. Preseli DC (Chairman). Pembrokeshire CC (Chairman 1998-99). Member: South Wales Electricity Consultative Council. Governor, University of Wales, Swansea. Hobbies: Singing Baritone, Choral music, Music. Languages: Welsh, English. Of Goodwick.

LUMLEY Karen Elizabeth: Conservative, Delyn 1997, Delyn & North List 1999, Redditch 2001. **Mrs. Karen Lumley:** Born Barnsley 28 March 1964, d of John Derek Allott, headteacher, & Sylvia Speck, nurse. Church of England. Married 1984 Richard Gareth Lumley, geologist, 1s 1d. Educated Rugby High School; East Warwickshire FE College (Business Studies). Trainee Accountant, Ford Motor Co. 1982-84. Asst. Accountant, John Bull Group, Wrexham 1984-85. Office Manager, Fairhood Engineering Co 1998-2000. Company Secretary, RKI Geological Services Ltd 1987. Deputy-Chair: Wales Young Conservatives 1991-93; Conservative Party Wales 1999-2000; North Wales Euro Conservative Council 1994; Wrexham Conservative Assn. Member: Conservative Women's National Cttee. 1995-97; Welsh Conservative Policy Group 1993. Chair, Managers, Wrexham Pupil Referral Unit 1995-. Treasurer, Wrexham Branch, Save the Children Fund 1996-2000. Member: Urban Investment Grant Panel 1994-97. Wrexham/Maelor BC. 1991-96 (Conservative-Independent Group Leader). Clwyd CC 1993-96. Wrexham CBC 1994-2000. Redditch BC. Conservative Spokesperson on Welsh Local Government. Shortlisted at Shrewsbury 1997. Interests: Education, Devolution, Health Service. Hobbies: Reading, Knitting, Jet Skiing. Languages: English, French. Of Wrexham, then Redditch.

LYNAM James Francis: Conservative: Swansea East 1950, Merthyr Tydfil 1951. **Mr. Jim Lynam:** Born Swansea, November 1907. Married. Educated Oystermouth Junior School; Swansea Grammar School (Ashridge Diploma in Industrial Admin & Imperial Affairs). Buyer, non-ferrous metal refiners. South Wales & Mon representative, Midlands non-ferrous metal refiners. Member, Royal Metal Exchange, Swansea 1926-. Army, 1939-45, Queens Royal Regiment. Chair: Glamorgan Branch, Junior Imperial League, West Glamorgan Conservative Advisory Cttee on Local Government. Hon. Secretary, Swansea East Conservative Assn. Vice-Chair, Swansea West Conservative Men's Assn. Of Swansea, moved to Whitchurch 1951. Died 1984.

– M –

MacASKILL Dominic James: Communist, South Wales Central List 1999, 2003. **Mr. Dominic MacAskill:** Full-time Secretary, Unison, in Rhondda/Cynon/Taf. Leading campaigner for Social Services, NHS & Care for the Elderly. Secretary, Wales area, Communist Party of Britain 1997-March 2002; Chair party's 3-man secretariat March 2000. Secretary, Rhondda Cynon Taf Stop the War Coalition. Of Pontypridd.

Rt. Hon. Ramsay Macdonald.

MACDONALD James Ramsay: PC 1924 PC (Canada) 1929 JP FRS 1930 Hon. DCL (Oxon) Hon. LLD: Glasgow, Edinburgh. Labour MP Aberavon 1922-29, Leicester 1906-18, Seaham 1929-31. Contested Southampton 1895, Leicester 1900, West Leicester 1918. National Labour MP Seaham 1931-35, Scottish Universities 1936-. **Rt. Hon. Ramsay Macdonald:** Born Lossiemouth 12 October 1866, s of Anne Ramsay & John Macdonald, ploughman. Married Margaret Ethel (died 1910), d of Dr John Hall Gladstone FRS, 2s 3d. Educated Drainie Board School. Farm labourer for a short time. Pupil Teacher at 16. Worked at Bristol church young men & boys guild 1885. Unemployed 1886. Cyclists' Touring Club envelope addresser 1886-87. Breakdown 1887. Private Secretary to Thomas Lough 1888-91. Journalist: Editor, *Socialist Library, Socialist Review.* Joined Social Democratic Federation 1885, Fabian Society 1886. Secretary, Labour Representation Cttee 1900-12, Treasurer 1912-24. Chair, ILP 1906-09. Chair, Parliamentary Labour Party 1910-14 (Resigned on outbreak of war) 1922-. Founder member, Union of Democratic Control 1914. London CC (Finsbury) 1901-04. Member, Royal Commission on Indian Public Services, 1912-14. Leader of the Opposition 1922-23, 1924-29. Prime Minister & Foreign Secretary 1923-24. Prime Minister 1929-35 (Labour 1929-31, National Government 1931-35). Lord President of the Council 1935-. Died on sea voyage 9 November 1937. *Books etc: James Ramsay Macdonald: What I Saw in South Africa 1903; Socialism and Society 1905, Socialism 1907, The Awakening of India 1910, The Labour Party and Electoral Reform: Proportional Representation and the Alternative Vote (with G. H. Roberts & W. C. Anderson) 1913, The Social Unrest 1913, The Government of India 1919, Wanderings and Excursions 1925, At Home and Abroad 193.* Further Reading: *Lord Elton, Life of James Ramsay Macdonald 1939; David Marquand: Ramsay Macdonald, 1976; A. Morgan: James Ramsay Macdonald 1987; B. Sachs, Ramsay Macdonald in Thought and Action, 1952.*

MacDONALD Victoria: JP (Cheshire) 1983. BA CertEd (Liverpool). Liberal Democrat, Conwy 2001. **Mrs. Vicky MacDonald:** Born Thames Ditton, 13 October 1945. Church of England. Married 1s 1d, divorced 1985. Educated Deganwy Primary School; Penrhos College, Colwyn Bay; St. Winifred's School, Llanfairfechan; Calder College of Education; Liverpool University (Sociology). Curator, Royal Cambrian Academy, Conwy, 1993-99; Owner, Mercier Gallery, Llandudno, 1989-93. Aberconwy BC 1994-96. Conwy TC 1995-99 (Mayor 1997-98). Member: Electricity Consumer Cttee for Merseyside & North Wales 1990-95; Rail Users Consultative Cttee for Wales 1993-94; Llandrillo College Arts Advisory Cttee 1998-; Arts Council of Wales Visual Arts Advisory Panel 1998-; Fundraising Cttee. St. David's Hospice, Llandudno 1998-2001. Hobbies: Walking, Keeping fit, Theatre, Cinema, Music, Creative writing, Reading. Languages: English, French, some Italian. Of Deganwy.

MacKAY Gwendolyne Claire: BA. Independent Wales Party, South/West List 2003. **Miss Gwendolyne MacKay:** Born Cannes 1 October 1972, d of Iver Mackay, translator, & Carys Mackay, nurse. Religion: WICCAN. Educated University

(Environmental Conservation). Teacher. Interests: Social Reform, Ecoliteracy, Education. Hobbies: Reading, Writing, Yoga, Surfing. Of Skewen.

MacKENZIE Hettie Millicent: MA (Wales). Labour: University of Wales 1918. **Professor Millicent Mackenzie:** Born Bristol, 1863, d. of W. W. Hughes, Clifton, Bristol. Married 1898, Professor John S. MacKenzie Professor of Logic & Philosophy, University of Wales, Cardiff. Educated University of Wales, Cardiff. Teacher, Sheffield Girls' High School-1891. Lecturer in Education, University of Wales, Cardiff 1891-1904, Professor of Education 1904-14, Hon. Dean of Education, National Service Scheme 1916-22. Of London & Brockweir, Chepstow. Estate £5,572. Died 10 December 1942.

MACKENZIE-SMITH Catherine Joanna: Christian Democratic Party: Wales Euro 2004. **Mrs. Catherine Mackenzie-Smith:** Born Abergavenny, 17 July 1939, d of Denis Joseph Quinlan, physician & surgeon, and Mary Patricia Quinlan, physician. Roman Catholic. Married 1967, Christopher Anthony MacKenzie-Smith, RN officer & school proprietor, 3s 1d. Educated Convent of the Sacred Heart, Woldingham; College of Law, London; Inns of Court School of Law; University of Grenoble. Barrister 1960; specialises in International Law, member of European Circuit. Private practice from 1995. Formerly: Legal Assistant to the Treasury Solicitor; Assistant Legal Adviser, Country Landowners' Assn; Nationwide Used Car Assn. Interests: Christian Democracy, European Union. Hobbies: Riding. Languages: English, French. Of London. *Books: The Rule of Law, but whose Law; A Time for More Harmony.*

MacPHERSON Neil: United Socialist, Mid & West List. **Mr. Neil Macpherson:** Mid & West Wales Secretary, Fire Brigades Union. Of Ynystawe, Swansea.

MADDOCKS Ronald Jones: Conservative: Abertillery 1959, Caerphilly 1964, 1966. **Mr. Ronald Maddocks:** Born Bargoed 1910. Married 2s. Educated Bargoed Grammar School; Cardiff Technical College; Newport Technical College. Auctioneer & Auditor until 1939. Joined Curran group of companies. Colonial Service, Nigerian Treasury 1943-. Barrister, Grays Inn 1952. Lecturer, Monmouthshire Technical College. Interests: Education, Colonial affairs, Finance, Child delinquency. Of Cross Keys. Died 1970.

MAGGS Catherine Ellen: Referendum Party: Swansea East 1997. **Mrs. Catherine Maggs:** Born Morocco 1948, lived in UK since 1961 & Swansea since 1972. Married Neil Maggs. Joint Owners, Family Pet Food Store & Garden Centre at Port Talbot. Of Sketty, Swansea.

MAHONEY Monica Emma: MA. Plaid Cymru, Bridgend 2001. **Mrs. Monica Mahoney:** Born Yonkers NY 9 June 1963, d of William Boehringer, church decorator/artist, & Ernesta Castelli, cook. Roman Catholic. Married 1994 Christopher Mahoney 1d. Educated Tobe-Coburn College, New York; Emerson College, Boston; Mesa College, Mesa, Arizona; Bridgend FE College; University of Glamorgan 2001-05. Production Associate/Production Co-ordinator/Associate Producer, American Broadcasting Co. New York (*Good Morning America & ABC Sports* 1989-93) (Emmy Award 1993). Freelance Producer, Carlton YV GMTV 1993-94. Writer-Producer, KSAZ-TV, Phoenix, Arizona (*Arizona Morning*) 1994-95; Freelance Field Producer, Reuters International, Reuters Television/TV Tokyo, Harpo Productions, *The Oprah Winfrey Show* Jan-Aug 1995. Contributor BBC Wales & Radio Wales, March 1998-. Marketing Officer, Mid Glamorgan Careers Ltd 1998-2000. Account Manager, Multimedia PRM Nov. 2000-March 2001. Project Imitator, Rhondda-Cynon-Taf & Porthcawl, *Regeneration How,* July 2001. *Community Enterprise Wales* August 2001-Jan. 2002. Volunteer Co-ordinator, Plaid Cymru 2001; Chair, Bridgend Branch 2000-01; Regional Co-ordinator, Bridgend, Ogmore, Vale of Glamorgan 2000-01; Director of Communications. Gave up active politics. Millennium Award Support Worker, Wales Council for Voluntary Services 2003-. Interests: Community regeneration, Racial equality. Hobbies: Gardening, Walking, Cooking, Films. Languages: Learning Welsh, American. Italian, German. In UK since 1993. Of Porthcawl.

MAINWARING Charles Salusbury: JP DL (Denbs) MA (Oxon) 1870. Conservative: West Denbighshire 1885. **Colonel Charles Mainwaring:** Born 7 July 1845, s of Townsend Mainwaring (MP Denbigh District 1841-47, 1857-) Marchwiel Hall & Galltfannau, & Anna Maria, d of John Lloyd Salusbury of Galltfanau, Married 1901, Gertrude, 1s, 1d. Educated Eton; Christ Church, Oxford. Landowner. Colonel, RWF Volunteers, Royal Denbighshire Militia, Denbighshire Yeomanry. Denbighshire CC. Member, Court, University of Wales. Of Cerrig y Drudion. Died 14 June 1920.

MAINWARING Sharon: Labour: Caernarfon 1992. **Mrs. Sharon Mainwaring:** Born 31 December 1953. Married 3c. Educated Ystalyfera Grammar School. Deputy-Director, Shelter Cymru. Secretary, District Labour Party. Member TGWU/ACTTS. Lliw Valley BC 1983-. Languages: Welsh, English.

MAINWARING William Henry: Labour MP Rhondda East B/E 1933-59. **Mr. Will Mainwaring:** Born Fforestfach, Swansea, 1885, s of

William Mainwaring. Marxist. Married 1914, Jessie, d of Thomas Hazell, Oxford. Educated St. Peter's National School, Cockett. Miner 1897. Student at Central Labour College; Lecturer & Vice-Principal 1919-24. Miners Agent 1924-34. Secretary SWMF Minority Group 1909-13. Secretary, Reform Cttee & Joint-author *The Miners' Next Step* 1912. Contested MFGB General Secretaryship. Appointed Secretary, International Mineworkers' Federation but never took up the post. Great War CO. Member, Royal Commission on Rhodesia & Nyassaland. Languages: Welsh, English. Of Penygraig. Died 1971.

MAITLAND William Fuller – see FULLER-MAITLAND W.

MAJOR Mark Andrew: Conservative, Newport East 1999. **Mr. Mark Major:** Born Cardiff 1974. Lived in Northern Ireland 1975-78, Newport 1978. Engaged to Samantha (1999). Educated Caldicott Comprehensive School, Newport College. Worked with father as commercial catering equipment manufacturers. Researcher & Press Relations Officer to David Davies AM. Joined Conservatives, 1990, Deputy Chair: Newport Young Conservatives. Deputy-Chair/Organising Secretary, Newport East Conservative Assn. Contested Newport BC 1995, 1999. Hobbies: Squash, Reading, Surfing. Of Newport.

MANN Christopher John: Labour: Brecon & Radnor 1992, 1997. **Mr. Chris Mann:** Born London 1 October, 1950, s of John Peter Mann & June Elizabeth Finnie. Married 1981, Melanie Sutton, 2c. Educated Kingsbury High School, Dundee University. Probation Officer, Merthyr Tydfil. Powys CC 1985-, Group Leader 1989-; Chair, Social Services Cttee 1985-2002. Member, Brecon & Radnor Community Health Council. 1st Chair: Powys Health Authority 1 April 2003. Governor, University of Wales. Languages: Learned Welsh, English. Of Brecon (1982).

MANN Colin Peter: Plaid Cymru, Cardiff North, 1999. **Mr. Colin Mann:** Born Wrexham, 29 June 1943, s of Verdun George Mann, head gardener, & Sarah Ellen Gwendoline Mann, nurse. Church in Wales. Married Constance Diane Mann, Clerical Officer, 1s 1d. Educated primary & secondary Modern Schools; technical college. (Teaching Certificate, Financial Planning Certificate, MLIA (Dip). Financial Adviser. Joined Plaid Cymru 1968. Member, National Executive. Mid Glamorgan CC 1977-96. Llanbradach ComC. 1985-; Caerphilly CBC (Llanbradach) 1996- (Deputy Group Leader; Deputy Leader of the Council 1999. Cabinet Member for Resources 1999; Chair: Appointments Cttee. Vice-Chair: Community Council Liaison Cttee). Schools Governor. Leader, Plaid Cymru Group,

Welsh Local Government Assn. Member: Court, University of Wales, Cardiff 1999-2003, Consortium of Local Authorities Wales, National Assn of Councillors (Wales). Interests: Finance, Environment, Sustainability. Hobbies: Garden, Music, Theatre. Languages: Learning Welsh, English. Of Llanbradach.

MANNING James Lionel: OBE 1974. Conservative: Pontypridd 1951, Enfield East 1955. Joined Liberal Party. **Mr. Jim Manning:** Born Bristol, January 1914, s of L. V. Manning. Married Amy Manning, of Newport, 2d. Educated Loughborough Grammar School. Freelance Journalist & Broadcaster: Sports Editor: *South Wales Argus* 4 years, *The Sunday Chronicle*. Sports Columnist, *Evening Standard* 1969. Vice-Chair, Central London Branch, NUJ 1952. Army 1939-45, Welsh TA Field Artillery. Died 19 January 1974.

MANSEL Courtenay Cecil: 11th Bart (1661) JP (Carms). Conservative: Carmarthen B/E 1928, University of Wales 1929. Joined the Conservative Party 1926 when on Liberal short-list. Liberal: Penury & Falmouth 1922, 1924, Coventry 1918; MP Penrhyn & Falmouth 1923-24. **Captain, Sir Courtenay Mansel:** Born Maesycrugiau, 25 February 1880, s of Richard Mansel Mansel & Maud Margaretta, d. of John Jones, Maesycrugiau. Succeeded father 1892. Reverted to grandfather's original name of Phillips 1903-08. Anglican. Married 1906, Mary Philippa Agnes Germaine, d. of Frederick Littlewood, 3s. RAF 1916-18, Captain, Unemployed List. Barrister, Middle Temple 1918. Landowner. Vice-President, Carmarthen Liberal Assn.-1926. Of Maesycrugiau Manor. Estate £96,316. Died 4 January 1933.

MARDY JONES Thomas Isaac: FREconS. Labour MP Pontypridd B/E 1920-May 1931. Ind Labour. Pontypridd 1931. **Mr. Mardy Jones:** Born Brynaman 1881, s of Thomas Isaac Jones & Gwen Jones. Married 1911, Margaret d of John Mordecai, St. Hilary, 2d, (separated 1933). Educated Ferndale Board School; Ruskin College, Oxford 1902-05. Miner 1893. Checkweighman, Maerdy 1907. Miners' Agent. Parliamentary Agent SWMF 1909-20. Hon. Secretary, South Wales Labour MPs 1914. Author & Lecturer: Tours of India, Middle East & South Africa 1928-46. Staff Officer, Ministry of Supply 1942-44. Public Lecturer, World Affairs. NCB Official Lecturer, Economics of Coal Industry. Company Chair, British Lignite Mining & Briquettes Ltd. Pontypridd UDC. Resigned seat in 1931 on being found guilty of misusing MPs' travel warrants by giving them to his wife to use – he believed he was entitled to do so. Cardiff ticket collector gave him the chance to pay for his wife, The Speaker & other prominent MPs begged him to *"get off his high horse"* but he refused *"on principle"*. Languages: Welsh, English. Of Pontypridd. Died 26 August 1970. *Books etc: T. I. Mardy Jones, Character, Coal and Corn: The Roots of British Power 1949, India as a Future World Power 1952.*

MAREDUDD Siân Rosemarie (Janet Power): BSc (Bristol). Plaid Cymru, Brecon & Radnor 1983, Monmouth 1987. **Ms. Siân Maredudd:** Born Croydon, March 1933. Married Dr. Power, Llandrindod general practitioner, 6c. Educated Bristol University (Geography), Teacher (Geography & Business Studies), Retired. Joined Plaid Cymru 1972. Llandrindod TC 1974-. Mayor of Llandrindod. Member: General Cttee Welsh Assn of Community Councils; RSPB; Radnorshire Wild Life Trust; Abbey Cwmhir Heritage Trust. Contested Powys CC 1999. Conducted 1983 campaign from bed after a road accident. Of Llandrindod (1974).

Dr. John Marek.

MAREK John: BSc PhD (London). Labour MP Wrexham 1983-2001, Labour AM Wrexham, 1999-2003; Independent AM Wrexham 2003-. Labour, Ludlow Oct. 1974. **Dr. John Marek:** Born 24 December 1940, s of Czech parents: John Marek, draughtsman, & Rose Marek. Married Anne Pritchard (acts as his secretary). Educated Chatham House Grammar School, London; London University. Lecturer in Mathematics, University of Wales, Aberystwyth 1966-83. Ceredigion DC 1979-83. Opposition Spokesperson: Social Security 1985-87, Treasury, Economic Affairs & Civil Service 1985-87, Member, Select Cttee Welsh Affairs, 1983-86, Public Affairs Cttee, 1985, Catering Cttee. Treasurer, Commonwealth Parliamentary Assn. Chair, All Party Aviation Group 1989-90. Deputy Presiding Officer, Welsh National Assembly 2000. Welsh international Bridge & Chess player. Failed to secure Labour re-nomination, 21 February 2003. Founded Forward Wales/Cymru Mlaen Party, 10.11.2003. Languages: English, Czech. Of Wrexham.

MARKS Dennis Howard: BA (Oxon) 1967. Legalise Cannabis Party: Neath, Norwich North & Norwich South, 1997. **Mr. Howard Marks:** Born Kenfig Hill 1946, s of Dennis Marks, ship's captain, & Edna Marks, teacher. Married 4c. Educated Garw Grammar School; Balliol College, Oxford (Physics & Diploma in History & Philosophy of Science 1968). Married (1) 1967, Ilze 2d (divorced), (2) 1980 Judy, 1s 1d. Drugs Baron & Business Man. Recruited by MI6, 1972. Tried in Amsterdam 1964 but released. Three Years UK Prison Sentence, London (Wandsworth 1980-82), arrested in Spain & extradited to USA: two sentences of 15 years & 10 years respectively in Terre Haute Prison, Indiana, 1988, released, April 1995. Campaigning to legal cannabis so as to reduce the danger of taking 'hard' drugs. Languages: Welsh, English. *Books: Howard Marks: Mr. Nice (autobiography) 1997; Book of Dope Stories 2001.*

MARLAND Paul: BA 1963 BComm. Conservative: Bedwellty 1970, West Gloucestershire, Feb. & Oct. 1974, Forest of Dean 1997; MP West Gloucestershire 1979-97, Euro Candidate 1999. **Mr. Paul Marland:** Born 19 March 1940, s of Alexander G. Marland & Elsa May Lindsey Marland. Married (1) 1965, Penelope Anne Barlow (divorced 1982) 3c. (2) 1984, Caroline Ann Rushton. Educated Gordonstoun School; Trinity College, Dublin; Grenoble University. With Hope Metal Windows 1964-65, London Press Exchange 1965-66. Farmer, 600 acres 1967-. Unpaid Chair, Marlands English Waters Ltd. Member of Lloyds. Parliamentary Adviser to several companies. Chair, Countryside Forum's Sports Cttee. PPS 1981-86. Chair: Conservative MPs Agriculture Cttee 1989-97. North Cotswold RDC. Member: Bow Group, Monday Club. Of Temple Guiting, Gloucs.

MARQUAND David Ian: A FRHistS 1986. Labour: Barry 1964, MP Ashfield 1966-77; Joined SDP 1981, SDP/Alliance: High Peak 1983. **Professor David Marquand:** Born Cardiff, 20 September 1934, s of Professor, Rt. Hon. H. A. Marquand MP (qv) & Rachel Eluned, d of D. J. Rees. Agnostic. Married 1959, Judith, d of Dr. M. Reed, 2c. Educated Emmanuel School, Battersea, Magdalen College, Oxford, St. Antony's; College, Oxford (Research Fellow 1962-64); Berkeley University, California (teaching assistant 1958-59); St. Catherine's College, Cambridge. Lecturer in Politics, Sussex University 1964-66, Journalist,

Broadcaster & Author, Leader-Writer, *The Guardian* 1966-, Professor of Contemporary History & Politics, Salford University 1978-91, Professor of Politics 1991, & Director, Political Economy Research Centre, Sheffield University 1993-, Joint Editor, *The Political Quarterly* 1987-, Principal, Mansfield College, Oxford, 1999-2002. Member: Advisory Board, Government & Opposition; International Advisory Board, New Political Economy; Fabian Society Executive 1963-. Endorser, Action for Justice Citizens' Imitative 1994. PPS 1966-69. Member: House of Commons Estimates Cttee 1966-69. Vice-Chair, PLP Economic Affairs Group. Member, Council of Europe, SDP Steering Cttee. Re-joined Labour Party when it abolished Claude IV on Nationalisation. *Books: Rethinking Ramsay Macdonald 1977, Parliament for Europe 1979; The Unprincipled Society 1988; The Progressive Dilemma 1991; The New Reckoning; (with David Butler), European Elections and British Politics 1981; (edit. With Anthony Sheldon), The Ideas that Shaped Postwar Britain 1996; (edit with Ron Nettler), Religion and Democracy 2000; (with Colin Crouch), The Politics of 1992: Beynod the Single European Market.*

MARQUAND Hilary Adair: PC 1949 BA 1923 MA 1928 DSc 1938 (Wales). Labour MP Cardiff East 1945-50, Middlesbrough West 1950-62. **Rt. Hon. Hilary Marquand:** Born Cardiff, 24 December 1901, s of Alfred Marquand, Shipowner, & Mary Adair. Married 1929, Rachel Eluned, d of D. J. Rees, Ystalyfera, 3c. Educated Cardiff High School; University of Wales, Cardiff (double 1st), state scholarship, Gladstone & Cobden Prizeman. Laura Spelman Rockefeller Fellow in Social Sciences, USA 1925-26. Lecturer in Economics, Birmingham University 1926-30. Professor of Industrial Relations, University of Wales, Cardiff 1930-45. Director, Industrial Survey, South Wales 1930, 1936. Studied industrial relations, USA 1932-33. Visiting Professor of Economics, Wisconsin University 1938-39. Acting Principal, Board of Trade, 1940-41. Deputy Controller, Wales, Ministry of Labour 1941-42. Labour Adviser, Ministry of Production 1943-44. Joined Labour Party 1920. Secretary for Overseas Trade 1945-47. Paymaster-General 1947-48. Minister of Pensions 1948-50. Minister of Health 1950-51. Chair, Information Cttee London Conference, Inter Parliamentary Union 1957. Member, Council of Europe & WEU 1957-59. Sidney Hillman Lecturer, University of Wisconsin 1956. Director ILO Studies, Geneva 1962-65. Deputy-Chair, Prices & Incomes Board 1965-68. Died 6 November 1972, after two-year illness. *Books: H. A. Marquand: Dynamics of Industrial Combination 1931, Industrial Survey of South Wales (joint) 1932, Industrial Relations in the USA 1934, South Wales Needs a Plan 1936, Second Industrial Survey of South Wales 1937, Organised Labour in Four Continents (edit) 1939.*

MARS-JONES William Lloyd: Kt 1969 MBE 1945 QC 1957 MA (Cantab) LlB Hon. LLD 1973 (Wales). Labour: Denbigh 1945. **Sir William Mars-Jones:** Born 1915, s of Alderman Henry Mars-Jones & Jane Mars-Jones, Llansannan Post Office. Welsh Independent. Married 1947, Sheila Cobon. Educated Denbigh Grammar School; University of Wales, Aberystwyth (1st Law); St. John's College, Cambridge. President, Aberystwyth Student Representative Council 1936-37. Member, Cambridge Footlights. Royal Navy 1939-45, Lieut-Commander RNVR 1945. Barrister, Grays Inn 1941, Bencher 1964, Treasurer 1982. Recorder of Birkenhead 1959-64, Swansea 1964-67, Cardiff 1967-69. Deputy-Chair, Denbighshire Quarter Sessions 1962-69. Member, Bar Council 1962. Judge of the High Court 1969-90. President, North Wales Arts Assn. 1976-. President, University of Wales, Bangor, 1983-. President, University College of Wales, Aberystwyth, Old Students Assn. 1973. Hon. Member, Gorsedd 1971. Languages: Welsh, English. Died 10 January 1999.

MARSDEN Morfudd Rosina: Socialist Labour Party, South/Central List 2003. **Mrs. Ina Marsden:** Born Aberystwyth 25 April 1930, d of John Thomas, nurseryman & baker. Married 1953 James Peter Marsden, university lecturer, 1s 1d. Educated Llanbadarnfawr Primary School; Ardwyn Grammar School, Aberystwyth. Social Worker. Joined Labour Party 1970. Member, Communist Party 1983-84. Interests: Socialism, Racial Equality. Hobbies: International Affairs, Conspiracy Theories, Gardening, Collecting China, Grandchildren. Languages: Welsh, English. Of Roath Park, Cardiff.

MARSHALL Huw: Plaid Cymru: Cardiff Central 1992. **Mr. Huw Marshall:** Born Wrexham, 28 February 1969. Married 2c. Educated Ysgol Morgan Llwyd, Wrexham, Television Producer. Company Director, Television Production Co.

MARSHALL R. Keith: MA (St. Andrews). Liberal Democrat, North Wales Euro 1989. **Mr. Keith Marshall:** Born Perth, Scotland, 1945. Married June, 3c. Educated St. Andrews University. Lecturer in French, University of Wales, Bangor, 1970. President, Bangor branch AUT 1988-; Conwy SLD. Chair: Bangor branch UNA. Founder-Chair, Welsh Branch, Liberal International. Member: Bangor CAB Management Cttee; Women's Aid Transitional Houses Management Cttee; Welsh Centre for International Affairs Standing Cttee; Liberal Party Executive 1985-88. Bangor CC 1983-87 (Mayor 1986-87). Gwynedd CC.

MARTIN Peter: Conservative: Torfaen 1983. **Mr. Peter Martin:** Born Wales 1941. Married 1s.

Educated St. Anselm's College, Birkenhead; Sheffield University; London School of Economics. Advisor, British Institute of Management. Richmond BC 1982-. Of Richmond on Thames.

MARTIN-JONES David Henry James: MBE MA (Oxon). Conservative: Neath 1970, Coventry North 1966. **Mr. David Martin-Jones:** Born Yorkshire, December 1921. Married 3c. Educated Haileybury School; Christ Church, Oxford. Planning Engineer: Smiths Industries Ltd (Aviation Division) Cheltenham; RAF Fighter Pilot 1939-45, Squadron Leader. Air Ministry for short period. Chair, Cheltenham Conservative Assn 1964-65. Cheltenham BC 1965- (Chair, Estates, Highways & Development Cttee). Deputy Mayor 1970. Of Cheltenham.

MARTINEAU Hubert Melville: JP (Berks). Liberal: Monmouth 1918. **Mr. Hubert Martineau:** Born 1888, s of Sir Philip Martineau & Alice Margaret, d of Judge Vaughan Williams, Miskin Manor (cousin to Sir Rhys Rhys-Williams, qv). Married d of Nelson Morris, cattle breeder & farmer, USA Educated Eton. Farmer & Landowner, 300 acres. Commissioned, Royal Berkshire Regt 1914-16, Welsh Guards 1916-18. Of Hollyport, Berks.

MASTERS Alan: Liberal Democrat, Torfaen 2001. **Mr. Alan Masters:** Born London 1953. Married 1983 Michelle Reed, 1s 2d. Educated Fairfax High School, Southend; Southend College of Technology; Harrow College of Technology; University of Wales, Cardiff; Inns of Court School of Law, London. Barrister, Middle Temple, 1979, Irish Bar 1993. Human Rights & Common Law Lawyer. Chair, Cardiff Union of Liberal Students 1994-76. President, Union of Welsh Liberal Students 1975-78. Member: Cardiff North & Central Liberal Democrats; Cardiff Travellers' Rights Group. Chair, Welsh Liberal Democrats Federal Appeal Cttee. Agent, Mike German, 1979. Interests: Civil Rights, Transport. Hobbies: Watching Soccer and Rugby, Science Fiction, Orienteering, Chess, Humour. Of Ickenham.

MATHER-JACKSON Henry: 3rd Bart CBE JP MA (Cantab). Liberal, South Monmouthshire 1885; Liberal Unionist, Flint District 1886. **Sir Henry Mather-Jackson:** Born 19 October 1855, s of Sir Henry Mather Jackson, Bart, High Court Judge (Liberal MP Coventry), succeeded 1881. Anglican. Married 1886, Ada Frances, d of General E. Somerset, 4c. Educated Harrow; Trinity College, Cambridge. Barrister. Company Chair, railways, docks, coal, steel. Company Director railways, coal, steel, insurance, estates, harbours. Monmouthshire CC Alderman 1895. Chair, Monmouthshire C.O. Appeal Tribunal 1915-18. Chair,

Monmouthshire Quarter Sessions. Of Llantilio Court, Abergavenny & London. Estate £8,293. Died 23 March 1942.

MATHIAS Alun John: BA (Reading). Independent Christian, South Wales Central List 1999. **Mr. Alun Mathias:** Born Cardiff, 5 July 1960, s of Colin John Mathias, civil servant, & Joan Frances Summers, civil servant. Christian. Married 1984. Catherine Mary Thomas, teacher. Educated Caerphilly Grammar School; Reading University. Tax Consultant. Member: Movement for Christian Democracy. Hobbies: Cinema, Football. Languages: English, French. Of Thornhill, Cardiff.

MATHIAS Ernest A. Robert: Liberal: Pontypool, 1950, Feb. & Oct. 1974. **Mr. Robert Mathias:** Born Pontnewydd, April 1916. Married 4c (2 sets of twins). Educated Abersychan Grammar School; City & Guilds Engineering College, London. Member, College Rugby XV & Athletics Team. Engineer. Fleet Air Arm 1941-46, Lieut-Commander. Chief Maintenance Officer UNRRA 1945-. Consulting Engineer: Australia. Consulting Engineer, Cwmbran Development Corporation, Suspended by Development Corporation for standing for Parliament 1974 but then restored to post. Member, NALGO. Member, NAGLO branch skittles team. Of Pontypool.

MATHIAS Richard: 1st Bart 1916 Kt 1913 JP DL (Mon). Independent Anti-Socialist, Merthyr 1922 (with official Liberal & Conservative backing); Withdrew as Liberal Candidate for Merthyr, 1924. Liberal MP Cheltenham 1910-11, election declared void on appeal. **Sir Richard Mathias:** Born Aberystwyth 1 June 1863, s of John Mathias, shipowner, & Jane Davies. Married 1898, Annie, d. of Evan Hughes, Cardiff, 1s. Educated Ardwyn Grammar School, Aberystwyth. Banking 15 years. Called to the Bar, Lincolns Inn 1896. Shipowner. Company Director: J. Mathias & Co, Cambrian Steam Navigation Co, London Steamship Owners Assn. Member: Cardiff Chamber of Commerce, Gloucester Chamber of Commerce, Cardiff Shipowners Assn. Life Member: Institute of Directors, Monmouthshire Chamber of Agriulture, Hon. Society of Cymmrodorion. Governor, University College, Cardiff. High Sheriff of Monmouthshire 1923. Declared Bankrupt 1934. Languages: Welsh, English. Of St. Mellons. Died 26 October 1942.

MATTHEWS David: JP Swansea. Coalition Liberal MP Swansea East B/E 1919-22. **Mr. David Matthews:** Born Morriston 1868, s of William Matthews (died 1886) & Elizabeth Matthews. Welsh Independent. Married 1892, Lilian (died 1949) d of John & Elizabeth Morris, 2d. Founded own company 1886, David Matthews

Ltd. Iron & Steel Merchant. Company Director, Tinplate Works, Clydach. Swansea BC 1896-; Alderman (Chair, Parliamentary Cttee 1911-33, Building Sub-Cttee, which planned civic centre of 1933, Deputy Group Leader). Mayor of Swansea 1909-10-11. Languages: Welsh, English. Of Swansea. Died 26 February 1960.

MATTHEWS Edward Gwynne: BA (Wales) 1966 MEd (Liverpool). Plaid Cymru, Denbigh Feb. 7 Oct. 1974. **Mr. Gwynne Matthews:** Born Dyffryn Clwyd, 26 October 1943, s of Glyn & Blodwen Matthews. Married Mair Matthews, 2c. Educated Denbigh Grammar School; University of Wales, Bangor (1st Phil). President: Bangor SRC 1967-68, University of Wales Central SRC. Plaid Cymru Organiser, North East Wales, 1968-. Spokesman on the Common Market, Plaid Cymru Director of Policy. Teacher. Lecturer, University of Wales, Bangor. Branch Chair, Abbeyfield Society. Chair, Maestryfan Youth Club Management Cttee, Denbigh. Member, Hegel Society of America. Languages: Welsh, English. Of Denbigh. *Books: E. Gwyn Matthews, Hegel, 1984, Yr Athro Alltud – Syr Henry Jones, 1852-1922, Sir Ddinbych, 2003.*

MATTHEWS John: BSc (Soc) (Wales). Green, South Wales Central List 1999, 2003, Wales Euro 1999. **Mr. John Matthews:** Born Mountain Ash, 21 February 1949, son of Vivian Powell Matthews, shoemaker. Married 1968, Patricia June Matthews, solicitor, 1s 1d. Educated secondary school; University of Wales, Cardiff (Sociology). Support Worker (Learning Difficulties). Cynon Valley BC 1983-89. Labour Party member & Councillor. Joined Green Party 1994. General Secretary, Green Party Wales 1997. Interests: All Green Issues. Hobbies: Keeping Fit, Cycling. Of Abercynon.

MATTHEWS Terri-Anne: BSc (Wales) PGCE (Warwick). Conservative, Islwyn & South/East List 2003. **Mrs. Terri-Anne Matthews:** Born Blackwood 30 October 1962, d of Ronald Henry Morris, teacher, & Patricia June Morris, teacher. Church of England. Married 1986, Paul Matthews, 1s 1d. Educated Pontllanffraith Grammar School; Gwent College, Crosskeys; University of Wales, Cardiff (Maths); Warwick University. Teacher, Monmouth Comprehensive School. Lecturer in Mathematics, Gwent College. Agent 2001. Deputy Chair: Islwyn Conservative Assn. Secretary, 3rd Newbridge Scout Group. Member, Gwent Tennis League. Interests: Education, Environment. Of Newbridge.

MAW-CORNISH Jane: LRAM. Liberal Democrat: Cardiff South & Penarth 1999. **Mrs. Jane Maw-Cornish:** Born Torquay, 21 January 1948, d of Michael St. Leger Falconer, teacher, & Damaris Anne Falconer, teacher. Roman Catholic. Married

1996, David Charles Maw-Cornish, engineer, 3d. Training Consultant. Joined Liberal Party 1974. Contested Penarth TC 1991, Vale of Glamorgan BC 1999. Vale of Glamorgan BC By-election 11.5.2000. Interests: Equality Issues, Open Government, Housing. Hobbies: Gardening, Collecting Antiques. Languages: English, French, Spanish, Greek. Of Penarth.

MAYBURY Philip Alfred: Conservative: Llanelli 1964. **Mr. Philip Maybury:** Born Macclesfield, August 1929. Married 2s. Educated Kings School, Macclesfield. Journalist. RAF 1947-49. Chair, Swansea East Conservative Assn. Member: Swansea Spastic Assn. Management Cttee, Swansea Old Peoples Welfare Cttee, Welsh Area, Conservative Party. Associate Member, Conservative Commonwealth Council. Secretary, Welsh Area Council NUJ. Treasurer, Swansea Branch NUJ. Of Morriston, Swansea.

MAYNE Richard Charles: CB FRGS FRHS JP (Middlesex, Westminster & Haverfordwest) Legion of Honour (France) Order of Medije (Turkey). Conservative Pembroke & Haverfordwest 1885, MP 1886-92. **Rear-Admiral Richard Mayne:** Born 7 July 1835, s of Sir Richard Mayne, Commissioner, Metropolitan Police, & Georgiana, d of T. Carrick. Anglican. Married 1870, Sabine, d of Thomas Dent. Educated Eton. Royal Navy 1848-79. Served in Crimea & Maori War & in exploring & surveying in the Pacific. Retired as Rear Admiral. Estate £10,934. Died 29 May 1892, suddenly at Lord Mayor of London's Banquet.

McALLISTER Linda Jane: BScEcon (London) PhD (Wales). Plaid Cymru, Bridgend 1987, Ogmore 1992. **Dr. Linda McAllister:** Born 10 December 1964. Educated Bryntirion Comprehensive School, Bridgend; London School of Economics. Part-time Tutor & Post-Graduate Student, University of Wales, Cardiff. Lecturer, Senior Lecturer, Institute of Public Administration & Management, University of Liverpool; Director PAM. BBC Political Analyst, National Assembly & European Elections 1999, 2000. Member, Cardiff Ladies Football XI. Member, Plaid Cymru 1979-92. Chair, Plaid Cymru Youth Movement 1989. The youngest candidate in the 1987 election. Member, Richard Commission (Welsh Assembly Government Consultation on the Powers of the National Assembly). Languages: English. Of Laleston. *Books: Laura McAllister: Plaid Cymru, the Emergence of a Political Party, 2001.*

McBRIAR Wilfred: Liberal: Wrexham 1966, 1970. **Mr. Wilfred McBriar:** Born Whitefield, Manchester June 1918. Married Educated All Saints School, Whitefield. Stock Controller,

Firestone Tyre & Rubber Co. Caernarfon until 1956, British Celanese, Wrexham 1956-. Branch Chair TGWU Caernarfon & Wrexham Vice-Chair, British Celanese Works Council. Secretary, Welsh Liberal Trades Unionists, Member: Welsh Liberal Party Executive; Liberal Party Council 1983-. Spokesman on Industrial Affairs. Languages: Learned Welsh, English. Lived at Conwy and then Wrexham.

McBRIDE David Ian: BSc (Wales) ACA. Liberal Democrat: Blaenau Gwent 1987, Devon West & Torridge 1992. **Mr. David McBride:** Born 23 July 1960. Educated Stockport School; University of Wales, Swansea. Chartered Accountant. Member: Liberal Party Council 1978-82, 1983-87; Welsh Liberal Democrat Executive 1989-90; Liberal Party Council.

McBRIDE Neil: Labour MP Swansea East B/E 1963-. **Mr. Neil McBride:** Born Neilstown, Renfrewshire 13 April 1910, s of Neil McBride. Roman Catholic. Married 1937, Delia, d of James Maloney of Paisley. Educated elementary schools; National Labour College. Brass Finisher, James Brown & Co. Clydebank -1963. Joined AEU 1937, Labour Party 1940. Tutor-Lecturer, National Labour College. Member, Co-operative Party. Chair, Paisley Labour Party 1950-52. Paisley BC Secretary, PLP Trade Union Group 1964-66. Alternate Delegate, Council of Europe & WEU 1964-66. Chair, PLP Transport Cttee 1964-66. Vice-Chair, PLP Social Services Group 1964-66. Asst. Govt. Whip 1966. Lord Commissioner of the Treasury 1969-70. Of Brynhyfryd, Swansea. Died 9 September 1974.

McCARTHY Francis Joseph: Conservative: Aberavon 1979. **Mr. Frank McCarthy:** Born October 1943. Roman Catholic. Married Dorothy SRN 1d. Educated St. Illtyd's College, Cardiff. Senior Audio Supervisor, BBC Radio Outside Broadcasting. Cardiff CC 1970-74. S. Glam CC 1973- (Deputy Leader, Chair, Education Cttee). Trade Unionist since 1964. Of Cardiff.

McCONVILLE Ronald Llewellyn: Liberal: Aberavon 1997, South/West List, 1999. **Mr. Ronald McConville:** Born Croydon, 5 May 1935, s of John James McConville, trader, & Lizzie Hannah Jones, nurse. Baptist, not active. Married 1958, Joan Taylor, secretary, divorced, 2d. Educated elementary & senior schools. Newsagent-Bookseller-Stationer for 37 years, retired. Member, Friends of the Earth. Branch Secretary, Federation of Retail Newsagents, 15 years. Chair-Treasurer-Secretary, Aberavon Liberal Democrats. Election Agent 1992. Hobbies: Sailing, Gardening. Of Taibach, Port Talbot.

McEVOY Neil John: Labour, South/East List 2003. **Mr. Neil McEvoy:** Born Cardiff 4 April 1970, s of Mal McEvoy, welder. & Diane Saleh, homecare assistant. Roman Catholic. Educated Comprehensive School, College, University. Languages Teacher at Pontypool. Member: Credit Union, Race Equality First. Joined Labour Party 1987. Cardiff CC (Riverside), Vice-Chair, Cardiff Labour Group. Resigned from Labour Party & joined Plaid Cymru, November 2003. Soccer Player: Fairwater Boys XI, Hannon Wanderers XI (founder). Interests: Environment, Devolution, Community Socialism, e.g. credit unions. Hobbies: All Sports, Plays Football, Cardiff City fan. Languages: Welsh, English, French, Spanish. Of Cardiff.

McGLYNN Bernard: Conservative: Swansea West 1955, Aberdare. **Mr. Bernard McGlynn:** Born Swansea 1924. Married. Educated Dynevor Grammar School; Swansea Technical College; Cardiff Technical College. Apprentice, Stewarts & Lloyds, Landore. Merchant Navy engineer officer 1944-51. Industrial Lubricating Engineer. Oil Company Representative 1951-. Youth Leader. Chair, Swansea West Conservative Assn. Member: Conservative Commonwealth Council, British Legion, Mumbles Traders & Development Assn. Contested Swansea BC. Of Swansea.

McKAY Ronald William Gordon: LlB 1926 MA 1927 (Sydney). Independent Labour: Llandaff & Barry B/E 1942; Labour: Frome 1935; MP North West Hull 1945-50, Reading North 1950-51. **Mr. Ronald Mackay:** Born Moulton, NSW, 3 September 1902, s of Alexander William Mackay. Married 1946, Doreen Armstrong, 1s. Educated Sydney Grammar School; University of Sydney. Lecturer in Philosophy & History, St. Paul's College, Sydney University. Lecturer in Economics. Solicitor, New South Wales 1926, England 1934. Came to UK 1934. Managing Director, Tarran Industries. Left Labour Party to join Common Wealth Party (Chair-1944), Re-joined Labour Party 1944. Executive Member, Proportional Representation Society. Delegate, Council of Europe. Of London. Died 15 January 1960.

McKENNA Reginald: PC 1907 MA (Cantab). Liberal: Pontypool 1918, Clapham 1892; MP North Monmouthshire 1895-1918. **Rt. Hon. Reginald McKenna:** Born London 6 July 1863, s of William Colombian McKenna & Emma, d of Charles Hanby. Congregationalist. Married 1908, Pamela (died 1943), d. of Sir Herbert Jekyll, 2s. Educated On the Continent; King's College School, London; Trinity Hall, Cambridge (Scholar, Maths Tripos). Barrister, Inner Temple, 1887-1895. Financial Secretary, Treasury 1906-07; President of the Board of Education 1907-08; First Lord of the Admiralty 1908-11; Home Secretary 1915; Chancellor of the Exchequer

1916. A bitter opponent of Lloyd George, *he refused to join the Coalition.* Declined Bonar Law's invitation to be Chancellor of the Exchequer, 1922. Director, London & Midland Bank 1917, Chair, Midland Bank Ltd. 1919. Of Westminster. Estate £89,948. Died London, 6 September 1943. *Books: Reginald McKenna: Post-War Banking Policy (collection of speeches) 1928.* Further Reading: *Stephen McKenna, Reginald McKenna 1863-1943, A Memoir. 1948; Stephen McKenna in Dictionary of National Biography; Barry Doyle, A Dictionary of Liberal Biography, pages 237-239.*

McKINLAY Andrew: BA (Liverpool) PGDip Housing (Salford). Liberal Democrat: Bridgend 1997. **Mr. Andrew McKinlay:** Born 10 November 1962. Educated Ormonde High School, Maghul; Edge Hill College of Higher Education; Salford University. Cheltenham Housing Assn. Manager. Member, Chartered Institute of Housing. Cheltenham BC 1991- (Chair: Environment Cttee, Joint-Airport Sub-Cttee). Primary school Governor. Member: CAMRA, MSF, Gloucester County Cricket Club, Southport FC Supporters Club. Of Cheltenham.

McLEAN Alan: Kt 1933 DL (Aberdeenshire) MA (Cantab) 1905. Conservative: Caerphilly 1922; MP South West Norfolk 1923-29, 1931-35. **Major, Sir Alan McLean:** Born 5 July 1875, s of David McLean, Alford, Aberdeenshire. Married Elizabeth Blodwen, d. of Revd J. Jones. Educated Harrow; Trinity College, Cambridge. Barrister, Lincolns Inn 1902. Served, Inns Of Court OTC 1914-18. Landowner & Company Director. Chair, Lampson Paragon Supply Co, etc. Council Member, National Rifle Assn, 1912-35. Aberdeenshire CC 1938-56, Convenor 1950-55. Chair, Aberdeenshire National Service Cttee 1939-45. Of Littlewood Park, Alford, Aberdeenshire. Died 19 May 1959.

McLEAN Donald: PC 1916 KBE 1917 JP Hon. LLD (Cantab) 1920. Liberal: Cardiff East 1924, Kilmarnock 1923, Bath 1900; MP Bath 1906-Jan. 1910; Pebbles & South Midlothian 1918-22, North Cornwall 1929-. **Rt. Hon. Sir Donald MacLean:** Born Farnworth, Lancs. 9 January 1864, s of John MacLean, master cordwainer, & Agnes Macmellin (Gaelic speaker). Presbyterian Church of England. Married 1907, Gwendolen Mary, d. of Andrew Devitt JP, Oxted. (father of Donald Maclean, Soviet defector). Educated Haverfordwest Grammar School; Queen Elizabeth Grammar School, Carmarthen. Solicitor (London & Cardiff). Hon. Secretary NSPCC. Vice-President, Cardiff Free Church Council 1902-03. PPS to Master of Elibank MP, Liberal Chief Whip; Deputy Chair of Ways & Means 1911-18. Chair: Treasury Cttee on Enemy Debts

1916; London Military Tribunal 1916, Reconstruction of the Poor Law Cttee 1917; Port Labour Enquiry 1919. Chair, Liberal (Asquithian) Parliamentary Party 1918-22. President of the Board of Education 1931-. Of Westminster. Died of a heart attack, 15 June 1932. *Further Readings: Roy Douglas in Dictionary of Liberal Biography, pages 242-244.*

McLEAN James MacKenzie: Conservative MP Cardiff District 1895-1900, Oldham 1885-92; Candidate, Elgin Burghs 1880. **Mr. MacKenzie Maclean:** Born 13 August 1838, s of Alexander Maclean, Liberton, Edinburgh. Married (1) 1867, Anna Maria, d of Philip Whitehead, (2) 1900, Sara Kennedy. Editor, *Newcastle Chronicle* 1855-58. Leader Writer, *Manchester Guardian* 1858-59. Editor/Proprietor *Bombay Gazette* 1859-89. Fellow, Bombay University. Chair, Bombay TC. Part-Proprietor, *Western Mail* 1900. Chair, London & Northern Assets & Debenture Corporation, President, Institute of Journalists 1897-98. Of London. Estate £1,291. Died 22 April 1906.

McPAKE Barbara I: Green Party, Mid & West Wales 1989. **Mrs. Barbara McPake:** Born Edinburgh 1962. Married. Lecturer, University of Wales, Swansea. Member, University Labour Club. Joined Green Party 1985. Of Mount Pleasant, Swansea.

McQUEEN Mary: Liberal Democrat: Caernarfon 1997. **Mrs. Mary McQueen:** Born 6 February 1950 (cousin of Simon Hughes MP). Married, divorced. Educated St. Elphin's School, Darley Dale; St. Mary's Orthopaedic Hospital, Paddington; Oswestry Spinal Unit; London University Institute of Archeology; London University. Physiotherapist. Museum Consultant, Antiquities Conservator & studying for a Leicester University Diploma in Museum Studies. Of Talsarnau.

MEAGER David Villiers: Conservative: Swansea Town Jan. 1910. **Mr. Villiers Meager:** Born Swansea 1859, s of George Blaney Meager, Mumbles (Proprietor of Globe & Albion Dry Dock Co) & Dinah Harries. Anglican. Married 1890, Mary Edwina Milder Stuckley (died 1935) d of Charles Francis Edward Lucas, West Cross, 2s 1d. Educated Swansea Grammar School. Articled to C. H. Glascodine, solicitor (qv). Barrister, Middle Temple 1888, Clements Inn Prizeman. Deputy Clerk of Arraigns. Company Director: Cwmteg Colliery Co, Globe & Albion Dry Dock Ltd. Military Representative, Neath Town & Rural District 1915-18. Swansea BC 1885-. Of West Cross, Swansea. Estate £28,640 Died 20 November 1923.

MEGARRY Mary Kathleen: Liberal Democrat, Carmarthenshire West & Pembrokeshire South

2003. **Mrs. Mary Megarry:** Born Newport Pagnall, 13 April 1959, d of Alexander Megarry. Anglican. Married 1995, J. W. Jenkins, 1s. Fund Manager. Pembrokeshire CC. ComC. Interests: Economic Development, Tourism. Hobbies: Complementary Therapies, Reading, Travel, and Theatre. Languages: English, Basic French. Of Staylittle, Narberth.

MEGGITT James Claxton: JP (Glam) 1907. Liberal: Llandaff & Barry 1922. Backed Conservative Candidate 1935, 1945. **Mr. J. C. Meggitt:** Born Wolverhampton 1858. Congregationalist Deacon. Married 1887, Beatrice Mary, d. of J. G. Broger, Cardiff. Timber Importer. Chair, Meggitt & Jones, Cardiff. President, Bristol Channel Shipowners' Assn. Member, Barry Local Board-1894. Barry UDC 1894-1914, 1st Chairman 1894. Barry BC 1914-, Charter Mayor 1914, Deputy Mayor 1939, Freeman 1941. Glamorgan CC 1915-, Alderman. Chair, Finance Cttee, Barry National Eisteddfod. Of Barry (1892). Estate £75,996. Died 18 April c.1950.

MEIKLE Alistair H: Liberal Democrat, Cardiff North 1999. **Mr. Alistair Meikle:** Born 1942. Self-employed training consultant & driver. Qualified shipbroker & sailing instructor. Joined Young Liberals 1960s, rejoined Liberal Democrats 1997. Vice-Chair, Cardiff North Liberal Democrats. Contested Cardiff CC (Heath) 1999. Promoter/producer of major charity concerts. Hobbies: Scuba Diving, Clock & Art Collecting, Kite Flying, Car & Motorcycle Driving, Travel. Of Cardiff.

MELDING David Robert Michael: BScEcon (Wales) MA (William & Mary). Conservative: Blaenau Gwent 1992, Cardiff Central 1997, Vale of Glamorgan, 1999, 2003; AM South/Central List 1999-. **Mr. David Melding:** Born 28 August, 1962, son of Graham Melding, ex-steelworker & founder of Melding Stonecraft, & Edwina Margaret King. Roman Catholic. Educated Skewen Primary School; Dŵr-y-Felin Comprehensive School, Neath; University of Wales, Cardiff; College of William & Mary, Virginia. Member, Conservative Research Department 1986-89. Deputy Director, Welsh Centre for International Affairs. Co-ordinator, Carers National Assn in Wales 1996-99. Chair: Neath Young Conservatives 1980, University of Wales, Cardiff Conservative Assn. Vice-Chair, Neath Conservative Assn 1986. Member, Manifesto Drafting Team 1999. Chair, Governors, Cardiff special school. Conservative Spokesperson on Health & Social Services 1999-2003; Resigned to concentrate on gaining greater powers for the Assembly. Chair, Health & Social Services Cttee May 2003. Interests: Community Care, Carers, Health, Special Needs Education, Devolution & its consequences, Electoral Systems, Europe, Defence, NATO, Aid & Debt in Developing World, Street Children, Collective Security, Small Businesses, Tourism, Rural Economy. Hobbies: Swimming, Golf, Reading, Dry Sherry, Bull Fighting. Of Barry.

MENDEL Paul David: JP 1955-83. Conservative: Pontypool 1964. **Mr. Paul Mendel:** Born 14 October 1930, s of Eric Lazarus Mendel & Esther Graber. Jewish. Married (1) Marion Leigh (divorced 1967), 2c (2) 1989, Rosalind Adler. Educated Byron House School, Highgate; St. Christopher's School, Letchworth. Army 1949-51, Captain, RMP. Director, family motor business at Hampstead 1951-. Middlesex CC 1961-64. Barnet BC 1964-. Director, Defence & Group Relations, Board of Deputies of British Jews 1982-84. Director, Council of Christians & Jews 1992-98 (Asst. Director 1985-87, Deputy Director 1987-92). Member: Inter-Faith Network 1987-98, Executive, International Council of Christians & Jews. Languages: English, Hebrew. Of London.

MERCER David Jeremy: LlB (Nottingham) 1970. Conservative: Swansea East Feb. & Oct. 1974, Swansea West 1979. **Mr. David Mercer:** Born 15 April 1940. Married Julie Mercer, 1d. Educated Oakleigh House School, Swansea; Craig-y-Nos School, Swansea; Christ College, Brecon; Dynevor Grammar School, Swansea; University of Nottingham; Guildford College of Law. Solicitor. Political Secretary, Swansea West Young Conservatives. Editor, Wales & Mon Young Conservatives *Newsbeat*. Member: Society of Conservative Lawyers, Lawn Tennis Umpires Assn, Swansea Junior Chamber of Trade, Swansea Council of Social Services. Wales Junior Tennis Champion 1968. Of Swansea.

MEREDITH John Wynn: LlB (Wales) LAMPTI. Plaid Cymru: Anglesey 1966. **Mr. John Meredith:** Born October 1932. Educated Ardwyn School, Aberystwyth; University College of Wales, Aberystwyth. Solicitor, with Flintshire County Council, then in practice at Llandudno, 1960. Member: NALGO; Legal Assn of Town Planning Assn; Plaid Cymru Executive. Gwynedd CC. Languages: Welsh, English.

MEREDITH Walter Reynallt: Liberal: Abertillery 1929. **Mr. Walter Meredith:** Miner. Chair, Tirpentwyn Lodge SWMF.

MEREDYTH William Herbert: BA (London) FRGS. Conservative: Swansea Town 1885, West Monmouthshire 1892. **Mr. William Meredyth:** Born London 1863, s of William Leodore Colomiati Meredyth MD FRCS & Eliza, d of Richard Robinson, Whaley, Derbyshire. Educated London University. Foreign Office 1884. Secretary, Welsh Conservative Union c.1888. Of London & Bath. *Further Reading:* Ivor Thomas Rees, 'Whatever Happened to Young William', *Journal of Gwent History Society, 2005.*

MERRIMAN Edward John: Plaid Cymru: Abertillery B/E 1965, Ogmore 1970, Feb. & Oct. 1974, 1983. **Mr. Ted Merriman:** Born Nantymoel, May 1922. Married Ada Merriman, 2c. Miner at 14. London Milkman 1937-40. Miner 1940-69. Asst. Secretary & Vice-Chair, Western Colliery Lodge, NUM. Organising Secretary, Western Colliery Coal Hewers Assn. Vice-Chair, Ocean Checkweighers Fund. Joined Plaid Cymru 1939. Ogmore & Garw UDC 1961-64, 1966-69. Ogmore DC 1974-. Glamorgan CC 1966-70. Mid-Glam CC 1973- (Leader, Plaid Cymru Group). Sentenced to a month' imprisonment with Trefor Morgan & Hywel Lewis by Aberystwyth magistrates, 1940, for refusing to stand for *God save the King* at a cinema. Died July 1995.

MEWIES Sandra Elaine: BA (Open). Labour, Delyn 2003 & North List 2003. **Mrs. Sandy Mewies:** Born Wrexham, 16 February 1950, d of Tom Oldland, credit controller, & Margaret Mewies, nursing auxiliary. Married 1976, Paul Mewies, 1s. Educated Grove Park Girls' Grammar School, Wrexham; Open University. Journalist 20 years. Schools lay inspector. Former Director, Wales European Centre, Brussels. Member: Board, North Wales Probation Service; Council of Museums in Wales. Wrexham BC 1986-2003, Mayor 2001-02 (Chair, Social Services). Chair, European & External Affairs Cttee May 2003. Hon. Fellow, North East Wales Institute. Of Wrexham.

MEYER Anthony John Charles: 3rd Bart (1910) MA (Oxon). Officeur de Legion d'Honneur (Fr). Conservative MP West Flint 1970-83, Clwyd North West 1983-92 (failed to secure re-nomination), Eton & Slough 1964-66. **Sir Anthony Meyer:** Born 27 October 1920, s of Sir Frank Meyer Bart. & Georgina Seeley. Married 1941, Barbadee Violet, d of A. C. Knight, 3c. Educated Eton; New College, Oxford. Scots Guards, 1945-46. Foreign Office 1946-52: First Secretary, Paris 1953, Moscow 1956, London 1958. Director of Research, Common Market Campaign. Lloyds Underwriter. Trustee, Royal Shakespearian Theatre. Joint-Secretary Conservative MPs Housing & Local Govt Cttee 1965-66. PPS 1970. Stood against Margaret Thatcher for party leadership 1989. Policy Director, European Movement. Vice-Chair, British Section, Franco British Council. Joined Pro-Europe Conservative Party, then went over to Liberal Democrats with Pro-Europe Conservatives 11 December 2001. Of Llanasa. *Books etc: A. J. C. Meyer: A European Technological Community 1966, Europe: Should We Join?*

MEYER Peter Charles: Conservative, South/Central List 1999. **Mr. Peter Meyer:** Of Cardiff. Chair: South Wales Central Conservatives.

MEYER Peter John Herman: FCA. Conservative: Rhondda 1983, South/East List. **Mr. Peter Meyer:** Born Cardiff, April 1936. Married 2c. Educated Cardiff High School; University of Wales, Cardiff. Chartered Accountant. South Glam CC 1973- (Deputy Chair, Education Cttee). Member: Welsh Joint Education Cttee, Business Education Council, South Wales Area MSC (special projects). Contested Cardiff CC (Penylan) 1999. Member, University Dental Hospital NHS Trust (Chair, Audit & Charitable Fund Cttees).

MICHAEL Alun Edward: PC 1998 JP BA (Keele). Labour & Co-operative MP Cardiff South & Penarth 1987-, AM Mid & West List, 1999-2000, resigned to concentrate on Westminster. **Rt. Hon. Alun Michael:** Born Bryn Gwran, Ynys Môn, 22 August 1943, s of Leslie Michael (shopkeeper) & Elizabeth Michael. Anglican. Married 1966, Mary d of Ambrose Crawley, 2s 3d. Educated Colwyn Bay Grammar School; Keele University (English & Phil). Journalist, *South Wales Echo* 1966-71. Youth Worker, Cardiff CC 1971-74, Youth & Community Worker (Grangetown & Butetown) 1974-87. Cardiff CC 1973-89. Chair, Cardiff Junior Bench 1986-87. Chair, Welsh Labour M.Ps. 1995-, All Party Penal Affairs Group, Alcohol Misuse Group, Vice-Chair, Anglo-German Group, Chair, Somalia. Group, Political Co-ordinator, by-elections, Vale of Glamorgan, Neath & Monmouth, 1991. Hon. President, Cardiff Bay Business Forum, Wales/North America Business Forum. Vice-President, YHA. Labour Whip 1987-88, Opposition Spokesperson: Wales 1988-92, Home Affairs 1992-97, Co-operative Party NEC 1988-92, Minister of State, Home Office (responsible for criminal policy) 1997-98, Secretary of State for Wales, 27/10/1998-99, First Secretary, Assembly, 1999-2000. Lost vote of confidence, January 2000. Minister of Agriculture 2001-. Hobbies: Long-Distance Running, Mountain Walking, Opera, Listening to Classical Music, Reading. Languages: Welsh, English.

MICHOLLS Edward Emmanuel: Conservative: Monmouth District 1906. **Mr. Edward Micholls:** s of Emmanuel Montefiore Micholls, barrister (died 1926) & Ada, d of Maurice Beddington JP. Of Caerleon.

MIDDLEHURST Tom: Labour AM Alyn & Deeside 1999-2003. **Mr. Tom Middlehurst:** Born Ormskirk 25 June 1936, s of James & Agnes Middlehurst. Married (1) 2d (2) 1986 Patricia Middlehurst. Educated Ormskirk Grammar

School; Wigan Technical College; Liverpool Polytechnic. Worked for Pilkington Glass, NCB and clothing manufacturer. Local government since 1971. Flintshire CC Leader. Chair, Welsh Local Government Assn, Flintshire Skills Task Group. Founder Member, North Wales Economic Forum. Secretary for Higher Education, 1999-2000. Resigned in protest at forming coalition with Liberal Democrats. Hobbies: Crown Green Bowls, Of Ewloe.

MIERS Henry Nathaniel: JP (Glam, Brecs). Conservative: West Glam. 1885. **Mr. Henry Miers:** Born Clydach 6 September 1848, s of Richard Hill Miers, Ynispenllwch, & Elizabeth Jane, d of John Bonnor, Denbighshire, (descendent of Robert de la Mere, Lord of the Manor of Mere, 1176). Anglican. Married 1870, Lydia Kate, do of John Miles Probyn JP 3s 4d (1s killed 1915). Educated Westminster School & Abroad. Tinplate Manufacturer & Proprietor, Onllwyn Collieries. Landowner (11,292 acres, income £18000 pa). Liveryman of the Worshipful Company of Tinplate Workers, Freeman of the City of London, Inland Revenue & Land Tax Commissioner. Boy Scouts' Commissioner. Member, Governing Body of the Church in Wales. Chair: Rhwngddwyclydach School Board 1875. Gower Conservative Assn 1923. Patron, living of Cadoxton juxta Neath. Lord of the Manors of Caegurwen, Neath Ultra & Cilybebyll. Of Ynispenllwch, Clydach (1870) & London. Estate £58,189. Died 10 October 1926.

MILBANK Powlett Charles James: 2nd Bart (1882) JP DL (North Riding). Conservative MP: Radnorshire 1895-1900. **Sir Powlett Milbank:** Born Edinburgh, 1st May 1852, s of Sir Frederick A. Milbank, & Alexina, d of Sir Alexander Don, Bart. Succeeded 1888. Anglican. Married Edith Mary, d of Sir Richard Green-Price, Bart. (qv). Educated Eton. Landowner. Lord Lieutenant of Radnorshire 1895-, MFH Radnorshire & West Herefordshire 1902. Languages: English. Of Norton Manor, Herefordshire, & Barnard Castle. Estate £195,132. Died 30 June 1918.

MILLAR Darren David: Conservative, Vale of Clwyd 2003 & North List 2003. **Mr. Darren Millar:** Born Manchester July 1977; moved to Tywyn 1988. Pentecostal lay preacher. Married Rebekah Millar, 1s 1d. Educated Ysgol Emrys ap Iwan, Abergele; Llandudno Technical College. Accountant. Assistant Director, North Wales, charity for the deaf. Worked previously in construction, care home & telecommunications industries. Joined Conservative Party 1992. Chair: Clwyd North West Young Conservatives. Tywyn & Kinmel TC 1999 (youngest Mayor in Wales). Hobbies: Reading, Comedy Sketch Writing. Of Bodelwyddan.

MILLINGTON Julia Jayne: Pro-Life Party, North List 2003; North-West England Euro 2004. **Ms. Julia Millington:** Lawyer 7 years. In television until 2003. Political Director, Pro-Life Party 2003-. Chair, North West Area, Pro-Life Party 2002-03. Of Tarporley, Cheshire, until moving to London in 2003.

MILLINGTON Mary Elizabeth: Socialist Labour, Islwyn 2001; South/East List 2003. **Ms. Mary Millington:** Born Luton 12 March 1948, d of the Revd Edward Reginald Charlwood. Anglican, & Pamela Dale, teacher. Pagan. Married 1970, Peter Thomas Millington, Information Scientist, 1d. Educated School of St. Helen & St. Katherine, Abingdon; College of Sarum St. Michael, Salisbury. Primary School Teacher; studying Welsh at University. Anti Nuclear Activist: Lived at Greenham Women's Peace Camp 1982-90. Member: Women's International League for Peace & Freedom; Palestine Solidarity Campaign (Women's International Peace Service volunteer on West Bank during 2003 election). Interests: Campaign for Peace & Justice. Hobbies: Walking, Welsh literature. Languages: Learned Welsh, English. Of Newport.

MILLS David: Liberal Democrat: Bridgend 1992. **Mr. David Mills:** Born 20 July 1960. Educated Bridgend Grammar School; Seale Hayle Agricultural College. Superstore Manager, National Education Officer, RSPCA. Environmental Campaigner. Of St. Brides Major.

MILLS Robert Henry: Independent, Montgomery 2003. **Mr. Bob Mills:** Born Montgomeryshire. Educated, Kerry Primary School; Newtown High School. Welsh Guards 10 years. Businessman. Organiser, Newtown Horse Show. Newtown & Llanuwchhaearn TC 1993-. Powys CC. Interests: Health Service, Tourism. Of Newtown.

MILLWARD Edward Glyn: BA MA 1954 PhD (Wales). Plaid Cymru: Cardigan 1966, Montgomery 1970. Resigned as PPC, Montgomery, Dec. 1973, because of pressure of work. **Dr. Tedi Millward:** Born Cardiff 28 June 1930, s of David Price Millward & Margaret Evelyn Millward. Welsh Independent. Married Sylvia Theresa Humphreys, 1s 1d. Educated Cathays High School, Cardiff; University of Wales, Aberystwyth (1st Welsh). Research Assistant, University of Wales, Bangor 1954-58. Lecturer in Welsh: Barry 1958-59, Swansea 1959-61, Aberystwyth 1961-; Reader. Secretary, Law Section, Welsh Book Council. Member, Language & Literature Cttee Board of Celtic Studies. Hon. Member, Gorsedd of Bards 1978. Aberystwyth BC 1964-68. Vice-President, Plaid Cymru. Spokesman on Water. Editor, *Bro* (local newspaper). Languages: Welsh, English. Of Waunfawr, Aberystwyth.

MILN David Leslie: JP (Cheshire). Liberal National, Wrexham 1945. **Mr. David Miln:** Born 1900, s of George Peddie Miln. Presbyterian Church of Wales Elder. Educated Privately; Kings School, Chester; Edinburgh University. Chair & Managing Director, Miln & Co. (Chester) Ltd. Chair & Director, Associated Seeds Ltd (Chester). Sole Proprietor, Leslie Trading Co. Racehorse Owner. Member, UNA Executive. Hon. Secretary, Chester Society of Natural Sciences. Fellow: Linnean Society, National Institute of Agricultural Botany, Cambridge, Royal Horticultural Society. President, Chester Male Voice Choir 1946-50. Of Chester.

MINNIGIN Nina Samantha: Vote 2 Stop the War, Mid & West 2003. **Mrs. Nina Minnigin:** Born Kingston upon Hull, 3 March 1966, d of Arthur Minnigin, stage set designer, & Christine Moore, hypnotist. Married 1s 1d. Widowed. Educated Sevenoaks School for Girls; Hull College of Further Education; University of Humberside. General Assistant, outdoor education center, & part-time child-minder. Member: Mountain Rescue Team. Campaigner on Homelessness, Ireland. Prisons & Single Mothers. Interests: Ireland, Women's Rights. Hobbies: Diving, Caving, Mountaineering, Climbing. Languages: Welsh, English.

Ali Miraj.

MIRAJ Mohammed Ali: BSc 1996 MSc (London) ACA. Conservative, Aberavon 2001. **Mr. Ali Miraj:** Born London 31 October 1974, s of Adil Miraj, engineer, & Rosman Ansara, medical practitioner. Muslim. Educated Haberdashers' Aske Boys School; London School of Economics (International Relations); (Politics of the World Economy 2000); Harvard University (Political Philosophy). Chartered Accountant,

with Barings Investment Bank. Hillingdon BC 1998-. Member: Conservative Central Office Race Relations Advisory Team. Deputy Chair: Ruislip-Northwood Conservative Assn. Associate Member, Royal Institute of International Affairs. Interests: Foreign & Economic Policy, International Affairs. Hobbies: Impersonating People, Listening to House Music, Socialising. Languages: English, Urdu, Arabic, French, German. Adopted as candidate for Watford 2003. Of London.

MITCHELL Ian Randall: Independent (Rural Business Campaign), Brecon & Radnorshire 2001. **Mr. Ian Mitchell:** Born Llantwit Major. Married (2) Christina (interior designer of Llandrindod) 2s 2d. Chartered Accountant. Leader, Powys Rural Business Campaign. Founder Chair, Llandrindod Wells Town Trust. A founder, Llandrindod Wells Victorian Festival. Hobbies: Sport, Great Outdoors, Socialising, Accepting a Challenge. Of Brecon.

MOELWYN-HUGHES Huw: UK Independence Party: Islwyn B/E 1995, Newport West 1997, 2001, 2003. **Mr. Huw Moelwyn-Hughes:** Married 3c. Solicitor, 1965-2000, retired. Ex-member, Labour Party, Founder member, UK. Independence Party. Agent, Swansea East Assembly B/E September 2001. Secretary, UKIP Welsh Cttee. Chair, Dolman Theatre, Newport. Supporter of Welsh National Opera & Royal Shakespearian Theatre. Of Newport.

MOGFORD David J: BSc (Wales) DPhil (Oxon). Plaid Cymru, Bedwellty 1974, Oct. **Dr. David Mogford:** Born Newport 1948. Educated Newport High School; University College of Wales, Swansea (1st Biology); Oxford University. Biologist. Researcher-Teacher at Pisa University. Languages: English, Italian.

MOHINDRA Gotz: Conservative Prospective Parliamentary Candidate, Cardiff Central 2004. **Mr. Gotz Mohindra:** Born 1977. Director: Deal Commodity Corn Ltd until June 2002; Chromex Group (furniture company). Director/secretary, seven other companies which are dormant. Of London.

MOLSON Arthur Hugh Elsdale, Baron Molson 1961: PC 1956 MA (Oxon). Conservative: Aberdare 1929, MP Doncaster 1931-35, High Peak B/E 1939-61. **Rt. Hon. Hugh Molson:** Born 29 June 1903, s of Major J. E. Molson MP. Anglican. Married 1939, Nancy, d of W. H. Astington, Bramhall, Cheshire. Educated RN Colleges, Osborne & Dartmouth; Lancing College; New College. Oxford. President, Oxford Union 1925. Political Secretary, Associated Chambers of Trade of India 1926-29. Barrister, Inner Temple 1931.

Army 1941-42. Member, Central Housing Advisory Commission 1943-45. Parl-Secretary, Works, 1951-53. Jt Parl-Secretary, Transport 1953-57. Minister of Works 1957-59. Chair, Council for the Protection of Rural England 1968-71; President 1971-. Member, Monckton Commission on Rhodesia & Nyassaland 1960. Of Chinley via Stockport, Kelson & London.

MÔN-HUGHES Robert Glyn: BA (Wales). Conservative, North Wales Euro 1994, Birkenhead 1992. **Mr. Glyn Môn-Hughes:** Born 4 July 1956, s of Revd R. G. Môn-Hughes, Welsh Independent Minister. Educated Birkenhead School; University of Wales, Bangor; Trinity Hall, Cambridge. Public Relations Executive. Publicity Officer, BBC Philharmonic, Manchester 1989-90. Media Officer, Birkenhead Conservative Assn. Member: Gorsedd, Institute of Welsh Affairs. Of Birkenhead.

MONAGHAN Susan Marie: Referendum Party: Islwyn 1997. **Mrs. Susan Monaghan:** Born Lancashire 1943. Married 1s 1d. Housewife, ex-estate agent. Of Newport (1981).

MOND Alfred Moritz, 1st Baron Melchett 1928: 1st Bart 1910 PC 1913 FRS MA (Oxon) Hon. LLD. (St. Andrews Manchester) Hon. DCL (Durham) Hon. DSc (Oxford, Paris). Liberal MP Swansea Town 1910-18, Swansea West 1918-23, Carmarthen B/E Aug. 1924-28, Chester 1906-1910; candidate for Salford South 1900. Joined Conservative Party 1926 & crossed floor of the Commons and was adopted as Conservative ppc for Carmarthen. **Rt. Hon. Sir Alfred Mond:** Born Farnworth, Lancs 23 October 1868, s of Dr. Ludwig Mond, FRS (millionaire scientist, died 1909) & Frida Lowenthal. Jewish Agnostic (Founder, Cartesian Club). Married 1893, Violet Florence Mabel DBE, d. of Henry James Goetze, 1s. Educated Cheltenham College, St. John's College, Oxford (failed Tripos), Edinburgh University (Law). Barrister, Inner Temple 1894; Practised briefly on the North Wales & Chester circuit. Industrialist. Director of his father's nickel & chemical business 1895. Chair: Mond Nickel Co, ICI 1926-, Amalgamated Collieries Ltd. Director: South Staffs Mond Gas (Power & Heating) Co. Ltd, Westminster Bank, Industrial Financial Investment Corporation. Part-Owner, *Westminster Gazette & English Review*. Treasurer: Free Trade Union; Disestablishment Campaign Cttee. Chair, Chemical Industries Section, Franco-British Exhibition, London, 1908. Manager, British Institution 1924-25. Chair, Imperial War Museum. President, World Power Conference 1928. Vice-President, Infants Hospital, London. Founder-President, Institute of Fuel. President, Empire Economic Union. Chair, Economic Board for Palestine. First Commissioner of

Works 1916-21, Minister of Health 1921-22. Gave £5,000 pa to Zionism. Of, Melchett Court, nr. Romsey, Hants, London. Languages: English, German. Estate £1,029,673. Died 27 February 1930. *Books: Alfred Mond: Industry and Politics 1927; Imperial Economic Unity 1930, Questions of Today and Tomorrow (republished articles) 1912. Further Writings: J. Graham Jones, Sir Alfred Mond, Carmarthenshire and the Green Book, Welsh History Review, June 1999; Herbert Bolitho, Alfred Mond, first Lord Melchett, 1933; G. M. Bayliss, PhD thesis (Wales 1969, The Outsider: Aspects of the Political Career of Alfred Mond, first Lord Melchett (1868-1930; John Graham Jones in Dictionary of Liberal Biography, pages 263-266.*

MONGER Herbert: Liberal Unionist, Swansea District 1892. **Mr. Herbert Monger:** Born, Sketty Swansea 1862, s of William & Jane Monger, gs of Hafod copperworks manager. Anglican. Solicitor. Swansea BC Alderman. Member: Turnpike Abolition Trust. Of Hafod, Swansea.

MOON Madeleine: Labour Prospective Parliamentary Candidate for Bridgend, 24 January 2004. **Mrs. Madeleine Moon:** Born 1950, Social Worker. Mayor of Porthcawl. Bridgend CBC. Of Porthcawl.

MOORE Andrew: MA (Oxon). Plaid Cymru: Bedwellty Feb. 1974. **Mr. Andrew Moore:** Born Garw Valley, July 1947. Educated grammar school; Balliol College, Oxford (Bio-chemistry). Senior Biochemist, Radcliffe Hospital, Oxford.

MOORE Anthony: BCom (Cork). Natural Law Party: Pontypridd 1997. **Mr. Anthony Moore:** Born 1968. Educated Cork University. Lecturer, Aberdeen University 1990-93. Health Economist, Mid Glam Health Authority 1993-96. Administrator, Welsh National Centre for Transcendental Meditation, Cardiff. Treasurer, Natural Law Party.

MOORE William Lyndon: JP 1928 DL (Mon) 1917. Coalition Liberal: Newport B/E 1922. **Mr. Lyndon Moore:** Born Newport 1857, s of Lawrence R. Moore, Contractor. Anglican. Married Marion, 2s (1 killed in war) 1d. Educated Bedford School. Articled, Bradford & London. Solicitor 1883. Coroner for Newport 1892. Retired 1924. President: Coroners Society of England & Wales; Newport Chamber of Commerce 1901. Chair: Newport Advisory Cttee for Appointing Magistrates. Member, Newport Harbour Board. Freemason, Grand Master. Of Newport. Estate £25,650. Died 25 March 1935.

MORELAND Robert John: BA (Nottingham). Conservative: Pontypool Oct. 1974; MEP Staffordshire 1979-84. **Mr. Robert Moreland:** Born 21

August 1941, s of Samuel John Moreland & Norah Mary Haines (member of *England's Glory Matches* family). Educated Glasgow Academy; Dean Close School, Cheltenham; Nottingham University (Econ); Institute of World Affairs & Commerce; Warwick University. Civil Servant: government of Nova Scotia 1966-67; New Brunswick 1967-72. Senior Economist, West Central Scotland Planning Study 1972-74. Management Consultant, Touche, Ross & Co London 1974. Consultant: Westminster Conferences Ltd 1985-; Strategy Network International 1988-93; Prima Europe 1993-. Westminster CC 1990- (Chief Whip 1993-94; Chair, Environment Cttee 1994). Chair, Bow Group European Cttee 1977-78. Vice-Chair, Conservative Group for Europe 1985-88. Member, Economic & Social Cite. European Community 1986. Chair, Regional Policy & Town and Country Planning Section 1990. Of London.

MORGAN Adrienne: BSc (Wales) PhD (London). Vote 2 Stop the War, South/Central List 2003. **Dr. Adrienne Morgan:** Born Purley, 5 November 1955, d of David Elias Julian Morgan, chemical engineer, & Ann G. Morgan, teacher. Atheist. Educated University of Wales, Swansea; Kings College, London. Medical Research Scientist 20 years. IT consultant & Lecturer. Vice-Chair, British CND. Member, Amicus. Member, Labour Party until expelled for standing in this election. Interests: Left of Centre Politics. Hobbies: Singing, Star Trek, Art, Travel. Languages: English, French. Of London.

MORGAN Andrew Paul: Plaid Cymru, Caerphilly 1983. **Mr. Paul Morgan:** Born Tremorfa, Cardiff 1948. Married Pauline, 2c. Educated Howardian High School, Cardiff; University of Wales, Cardiff. Teacher; Deputy Head, Basseleg Comprehensive School. Secretary, Cardiff Central Plaid Cymru. Member: Rumney RFC; CND Cymru, Amnesty International.

MORGAN Arthur John: JP DL (Mon) JP (Brecs). Conservative: Breconshire 1880, 1885. **Hon. Arthur Morgan:** Born 27 August 1840, s of 1st Baron Tredegar & Rosamund Mundy. Anglican. Educated Eton. Of London. Died 9 November 1900.

MORGAN Benjamin Charles Leslie: BSc (London). Plaid Cymru, Pontypool B/E 1958, 1859. **Mr. Leslie Morgan:** Born Griffithstown, Pontypool 1922. Married June, 5c. Educated Pontypool Grammar School; Abersychan Grammar School; University of London 1945-48. Left school to be a railway worker 1938; Served RAF & Free French Air Force, 1939-45. Industrial Chemist. Of Cwmbran.

MORGAN Charles Courtenay Evan, 1st Viscount Tredegar 1926; 3rd Baron Tredegar (1859) 5th Bart 1792 OBE 1919 CBE 1925 JP DL (Mon) FSA FRCI. Conservative: South Monmouthshire 1906. **Colonel, Hon. Evan Morgan:** Born Ruperra Castle, Glam 10 April 1867, s of Hon. F. C. Morgan MP (qv); succeeded uncle to barony 1913. Anglican. Married 1890, Lady Catherine Carnegie, d of Earl of Southesk, 2c. Educated Eton. Landowner (40,000 acres). Lieut-Colonel, Royal Engineers; Hon. Colonel; Served in Boer War. Captain RNVR 1914-19, OC Bristol. ADC King George V 1925-26. Master of Foxhounds. Lord Lieutenant of Monmouthshire 1933. Of Ruperra Castle, Monmouthshire, & Dorking. Estate £389,685. Died, Ritz Hotel, London, 8 May 1934.

MORGAN Dafydd Elystan, Baron Elystan-Morgan: LlB (Wales) 1953. Plaid Cymru, Wrexham B/E March 1955; 1955, 1959; Merioneth 1964. Joined Labour Party 4 August 1965. Labour MP Cardigan 1966-74; Candidate Feb. & Oct. 1974. **Mr. Elystan Morgan:** Born Llandre 7 December 1932, s of Dewi & Olwen Morgan (nephew of Iwan Morgan qv). Presbyterian Church of Wales Elder. Married Alwen, d of William Roberts, 2c. Educated Ardwyn School, Aberystwyth; University College of Wales, Aberystwyth. Solicitor 1956 (at Wrexham). Barrister, Grays Inn 1971. Chair, Welsh Parliamentary Party 1967-69. President, Welsh Local Authorities Assn 1967-68. Under-Secretary, Home Affairs 1968-70. Circuit Judge 1987-. Languages: Welsh, English. Of Landre, Aberystwyth.

MORGAN David: Communist, North List 2003. **Mr. David Morgan:** Tutor in History, University of Wales, Bangor. Anti War Campaigner. Member, Executive, Young Communist League. Member: Communist Party Welsh Cttee. Of Bangor.

MORGAN David Eirwyn: BA BD (Wales) MA DPhil (Oxon). Plaid Cymru: Llanelli: 1950, 1951, 1955, 1959. **Revd Dr. Eirwyn Morgan:** Born Penygroes, Carms. 23 April 1918, s of David Morgan, miner, & Rachel Morgan. Married 7 April 1943, Mair Ellis Jones, d of Ellis Jones, Bancffosfelen, 1s 1d. Educated Amman Valley Grammar School; University College of Wales, Swansea; Presbyterian College, Carmarthen; Regents Park College, Oxford; Fulbright Scholar/Ecumenical Fellow, Union Seminary, New York 1961-62. Welsh Baptist Minister, Ordained 1944; Bancffosfelen 1944-56, Llandudno 1956-67, Professor of New Testament Studies, Bangor Baptist College 1967-80, Principal 1971-80. Won Chair, Urdd National Eisteddfod, Carmarthen 1935. Preached at World Young Baptist Conference, Oslo 1957. Joint-Editor *Mawl yr Ifainc*. Editor: *Seren Cymru* 1962;

Y Ddraig Goch 1954-59. Member: Plaid Cymru Executive, Federal Union of European Nationalities 1955. President: Baptist Union of Wales; Arfon Baptist Assn; North Wales Free Church Federal Council 1964. Vice-President, Llandudno Eisteddfod 1963. Secretary, Mudiad Heddwch Cymru 1950s. Member, Executive, Peace Pledge Union 1954-59. Founder Secretary, Welsh Hymn Society. Languages: Welsh, English. Died 30 August 1982.

MORGAN David Watts: CBE 1920 DSO 1918 JP ME 1900. Labour MP, Rhondda East 1918-. **Lieut-Colonel David Watts Morgan:** Born Skewen 18 December 1864; s of Thomas Morgan & Margaret Davies. Calvinistic Methodist. Married (1) Amy Blanche Morgan (2) 2s 4d. Educated Elementary Schools at Skewen, Neath & Swansea; evening classes. Lived at Wattstown from 1880. Educated National School. Miner at 11; Mining Engineer 1900-14 but never became a manager. Checkweigher at National Colliery. Rhondda Miners' Agent 1898-1918. Saved 18 lives at Senghenydd Pit Explosion 1913. Joined Welch Regiment as Private 1914; Major 1917; Lieut-Colonel 1918. Rhondda UDC. Glamorgan CC 24 years (Candidate 1899; 1900), Alderman, Chair 1926-28. Freemason. Chair, Welsh Parliamentary Party. Languages: Welsh, English. Of Porth. Estate £1313. Died 23 February 1933. *Books etc: D. W. Morgan: Compensation Act Treatise, Miners' Tables on Wages, Handbook on Safety in Mines.* Further Reading: *Chris Williams, Democratic Rhondda.*

MORGAN Donald: Plaid Cymru: Rhondda Oct. 1974. **Mr. Don Morgan:** Born 1937, miner's son. Married 1s. Educated Blaenclydach School; Queen Elizabeth Training College, Leatherhead. Freelance Quantity Surveyor. Secretary, Llwynypia & Glyncornel Hospitals League of Friends; Member; UNA; Board of Management, Rest Convalescent Home, Porthcawl; Rhondda Action Cttee; Trade Union Employment Sub-Cttee; contested local elections. Member, UNA.

MORGAN Frank John: Conservative, Mid & West List 1999. **Mr. Frank Morgan:** Of Bwlch, Brecon.

MORGAN Frank Leslie: MBE 1973 CBE 1987 BA (Wales). Conservative: Montgomery 1959 (Resigned as PPC for West Bromwich to contest Montgomery). **Mr. Leslie Morgan:** Born Llanfair Caereinion 7 November 1926, s of Edward Arthur & Beatrice Morgan. Welsh Independent. Married 1962. Victoria Stoker Jeffrey 3c. Educated Llanfair Caereinion Grammar School; University College of Wales, Aberystwyth (Economics). Army 1945-48, Captain, Army Reserve 1948-59. Graduate trainee & parts executive,

Coventry motor industry 1950-56. Chair & Managing Director, Morgan Bros. (Mid Wales) agricultural merchants 1959-. Member, Council for Wales 1970-79. Deputy Chair, Mid Wales New Town Development Corporation 1973-77. Chair: Mid Wales Development Corp/Development Board for Rural Wales 1981-89. Director: Development Corporation for Wales 1981-83; Wales Advisory Board, Abbey National 1982-90. Member: Welsh Development Agency 1981-89; Wales Tourist Board 1982-89; Infrastructure Cttee British Tourist Authority 1982-89; Design Council Welsh Cttee 1981-85. Vice-Chair, Warwick & Leamington Young Conservatives. Chair, Montgomeryshire Conservative Assn 1964-74, President 1974-80, 1989-. Chair: Policy Cttee Campaign for Montgomeryshire. Languages: Welsh, English. Of Llangyniew, Welshpool.

MORGAN Frederick Courtenay: JP (Glam) DL (Mon) VD. Conservative MP: Monmouthshire 1874-85; South Monmouthshire 1885-1906. **Colonel, Hon. Frederick Morgan:** Born Brighton 24 May 1834, s of 1st Baron Tredegar & Rosamund, d of General Godfrey Basil Mundy, 4c. Anglican. Married 1858, Charlotte Anne, d of Charles Alexander Williams of Balgray, Dumfries. Educated Winchester. Captain, Rifle Brigade (1860-70. Lieut-Colonel, Monmouthshire Volunteers 1860-70; Hon. Colonel, 1881. Monmouthshire CC 1888-. Of Ruperra Castle & London. Estate £15,801. Died 8 January 1909.

MORGAN George Hay: KC 1913 BSc (London) 1894. Coalition Liberal: Abertillery B/E Dec. 1920, Ipswich 1918, Penryn & Falmouth 1922, Salford West 1923; MP Truro 1906-18. **Mr. G. Hay Morgan:** Born Hay-on-Wye 1866, s of Walter & Ann Morgan. Baptist. Married 1911 Margaret, d of Henry Lewis, Pontynewynydd. Educated Pontypool Baptist College; University of Wales (1st student to enter Parliament), Cardiff; University College, London. Pupil Teacher - 1887; Baptist Minister, Ordained 1890. Woodberry Down Baptist Church 1890-1900. Barrister 1899. Member, Drapers Company. Director, Abbey Road Building Society; Tottenham Gas Co. Of London. Estate £11,223. Died 24 January 1931.

MORGAN George Osborne: 1st Bart 1892 PC QC 1869 JP (Denbs) BA 1848 MA Oxon) 1860. Liberal MP Denbighshire 1868-85; East Denbighshire 1885-. **Rt. Hon. Sir George Osborne Morgan:** Born Gothenburg 8 May 1826, s of Revd Morgan Morgan, Chaplain 1821-35, later Vicar of Conwy, & Fanny Nonnen of Gothenburg. Anglican. Married 1856, Emily, d of Leopold Reiss, Eccles. Educated Friars School, Bangor; Shrewsbury School; Worcester & Balliol Colleges, Oxford 1st Classics) Fellow of University College

1850-57. Barrister, Lincolns Inn 1853; Bencher 1869; Treasurer 1890; Examiner in Equity, Inns of Court 1877. Judge Advocate General 1880-85 (abolished flogging in the army). Under-Secretary, Colonies 1886. Governor, Shrewsbury School. Of London & Brymbo Hall, Wrexham. Estate £11,490. Died 25 August 1897. *Books: G. O. Morgan: A Treatise on Chancery Practice (with Lord Davey), A Treatise on Chancery Costs, Translation of Virgil's Eclogues into English Hexameters.*

MORGAN Herbert: BA (Wales) MA (Oxon). Labour: Neath 1918. **Revd Herbert Morgan:** Born Banwen 15 September 1875, s of John David Morgan (worked for Thomas & Evans) & Mary Kemyes. Educated Rhondda Grammar School, Porth; Water Board clerk; Pontypridd Academy; University of Wales, Cardiff 1898-1902; Mansfield College, Oxford; Proctor Travelling Scholarship; Marburg University. Began preaching at 20. Baptist Minister, Ordained 1906: Castle Street, London 1906-12; Tyndale, Bristol 1912-20. Director of Extra-Mural Studies, University of Wales, Aberystwyth 1920-40. President: University of Wales Labour Party 1918; Mansfield College Old Students Assn. Warden, Guild of Graduates, University of Wales 3 years. Temperance speaker. Member: Fellowship of Reconciliation; Heddychwyr Cymru. President, Baptist Union of Wales 1945-46; President, Carmarthenshire Cardiganshire Baptist Assn 1945-46. Languages: Welsh, English. Estate £22,737. Died September 1946. *Books: Herbert Morgan: The Social Task in Wales (joint author); Esboniad ar Rannau o Esaia; Diwydiant yng Nghymru.*

MORGAN Horace Alexander: MA (Cantab). Liberal: Wrexham 1923. Joined Conservative Party; Nominated for Cardiff North 1950. **Mr. Horace Morgan:** Born 1889, s of William Morgan, boot & shoe merchant of Brighton. Methodist. Married Beatrice Morgan 1s 1d. Educated Cambridge University 1910-14. Missionary in Newfoundland 1908. Army 1914-18, Captain RAOC. Joined Economic League 1918. Director, Public Economy Assn. Chair, National Union of Ratepayers Assns. Of Cardiff. Died 23 October 1951.

MORGAN Hywel Rhodri: PC 2000 BA 1961 MA (Oxon) MA (Harvard) 1963. Labour MP Cardiff West 1987-2001, AM Cardiff West, 1999-. **Rt. Hon. Rhodri Morgan:** Born 29 September 1939, s of Professor Thomas John Morgan & Huana Morgan. Married 1967, Julie (qv) d of Jack & Grace Edwards, 1s 2d. Educated Whitchurch Grammar School; St. John's College, Oxford (PPE); Harvard University. WEA Tutor-Organiser 1963-65. Research Officer: Cardiff City Council, Welsh Office & Dept. Environment 1965-71. Economic Adviser, Dept. of Trade &

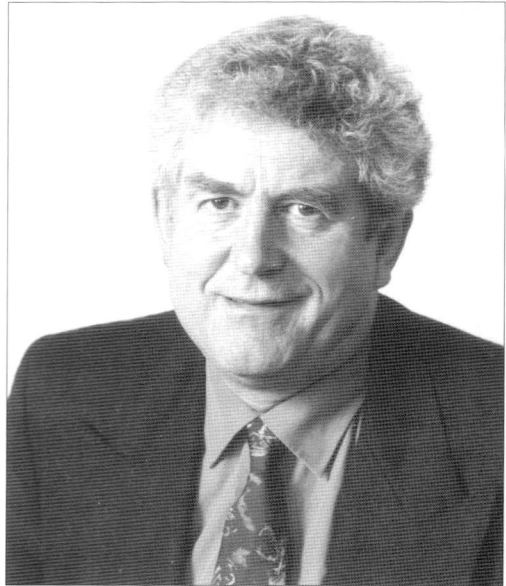

Rt. Hon. Rhodri Morgan.

Industry 1972-74. Industrial Development Officer, S. Glamorgan CC 1974-80. Industrial Analyst, Head of Press & Information Bureau, European Commission in Wales 1980-87. President: Fairwater RFC. Joined Labour Party 1960. Opposition Spokesperson: Energy 1989-92, Wales 1992-97. Select Cttee Member: Energy 1987-89, Members Interests 1987-89. Chair, Select Cttee on Public Administration. Vice-Chair, all party asthma group, Treasurer, Lords & Commons Tennis Club. The Spectator's "Inquisitor of the Year" Award 1998. Contested Labour Assembly Leadership 1998, 1999. Of Michaelston-le-Pit, Dinas Powys. Assembly Secretary for Economic Development, 1999. First Secretary Feb. 2000, First Minister Oct. 2000-. Hobbies: Sports & Athletics, Wildlife, Woodcarving. Languages: Welsh, English, French, German, some Spanish. Of Michaelston-le-Pit, Dinas Powys.

MORGAN Iwan James: BA 1926 MA 1929 (Wales). Commander, Order of Three Stars (Latvia). Labour: Cardigan 1945, 1950. **Mr. Iwan Morgan:** Born Tondu 1904, s of John James Morgan (Headteacher. Garw Grammar School). Presbyterian Church of Wales. Married Esme Lewis, Caerau. Educated Bridgend Grammar School; University of Wales, Aberystwyth (Economics). Lecturer, extra-mural & Coleg Harlech (Economics & International Affairs). Director of Extra Mural Studies, University of Wales, Cardiff 1935-. Member of Plaid Cymru in 1930s but disagreed with Saunders Lewis' view of socialism and joined Labour Party. Member, National Library Court & Council. Languages: Welsh, English. Died 1 April 1966.

MORGAN John Dilwyn: BSc (Manchester) LlB (Bristol). Conservative: Rhondda West 1970. **Mr. Dilwyn Morgan:** Born 1939, s of Breconshire farmer. Married Frances 1d. Educated Christ College, Brecon; Manchester University; Bristol University. RAFVR pilot. Worked in Ellesmere Port Oil Refinery. Solicitor. Kensington & Chelsea BC.

MORGAN John Harold: Liberal: Newport Feb. & Oct. 1974. **Mr. John Morgan:** Born Tredegar, February 1929. Married 3c, divorced. Educated Tredegar Grammar School; Pembroke College, Cambridge. Chartered Engineer & Naval Architect; One of the world's leading corrosion experts. Managing Director, three engineering companies. Member, Hon. Society of Cymmrodorion. Fellow of the Institute of Directors in Wales.

MORGAN John Lloyd: KC 1906 JP (Carms) 1885 BA (Cantab) 1884. Liberal MP West Carmarthenshire 1892-1910. **Mr. J. Lloyd Morgan:** Born Carmarthen 13 February 1861, s of Revd Professor William Morgan & Margaret, d of Thomas Rees, Llandeilo. Congregationalist. Educated Greenhill School, Tenby; Tattenhall College; Owens College, Manchester; Trinity Hall, Cambridge. Barrister, Inner Temple, 1884. Recorder of Swansea 1908-11. County Court Judge, 1911-26. Languages; Welsh, English. Of Carmarthen & London. Died 17 May 1944. *Books: John Lloyd Morgan: The Life of the Rev. William Morgan.*

MORGAN Jonathan Barrie Robert Winston: LlB (Wales) MSc Econ. Conservative: Merthyr Tydfil & Rhymney 1997, Cardiff North 1999, 2003. AM South/Central List 1999-. **Mr. Jonathan Morgan:** Born 12 July 1974. Anglican. Educated Bishop of Llandaff Church in Wales High School, Cardiff; University of Wales, Cardiff. With European Fund Secretariat with FFORWM Ltd (Welsh FE Colleges Assn) 1997-98. European & External Funding Officer, Coleg Glanhafren FE 1998-99. Chair: Cardiff North Young Conservatives 1992-95, Wales Conservative Students 1995-96, Wales Young Conservatives 1997-98. Deputy Chair, Cardiff North Conservative Assn 1998-. Member, South Wales Conservative Euro Council 1993-. Deputy Chair, Cardiff North Conservative Assn 1998-99. Contested Cardiff CC 1996. Spokesperson on Education & Culture; Health, Social Services & Assembly Business, May 2003. Conservative Prospective Parliamentary Candidate, Cardiff North, 2004. Interests Education, European Union, Regional Policy, Constitutional Affairs. Hobbies: Theatre, Eating Out, Golf, Music. Of Cardiff.

MORGAN Julie: BA (London) Dip. Social Admin (Manchester) CSQU (Wales). Labour Cardiff North 1992; MP. Cardiff North 1997-. **Mrs. Julie Morgan:** Born Cardiff 2 November 1944, d of Jack & Grace Edwards. Married 1967 Hywel Rhodri Morgan (qv) 1s 2d. Educated Dinas Powys Primary School; Howells School, Llandaff; Kings College, London, Manchester University; University of Wales, Cardiff. Asst. Director, Childcare, Dr. Barnado's, Wales. Principal Social Services Officer & Development Officer, W. Glam CC 1983-87. Senior Social Worker, Barry Social Services 1985-87. Asst. Director, Child Care, Barnados's 1987-. Cardiff CC. South Glam CC (Chair, Equal Opportunities Cttee). Member; Anti Apartheid Movement; Nicaragua Solidarity Campaign. Chair: All Parties Group on Clinical Depression. Hobbies: Swimming. Of Michaelston-le-Pit, Dinas Powys.

MORGAN Lewis: JP. Conservative, South Glamorgan, Jan. & Dec. 1910. **Mr. Lewis Morgan:** Born Llanwit Fardre 30 August 1860, s of David Morgan, hotelier & ex-collier, & Jane Williams (brother of Morgan Morgan (qv). Anglican. Married 1886, Mary, d of Peter Williams, engineer & shipowner, 1s 2d. Educated private school at Bridgend. Solicitor 1893. Registrar of County Court & Cardiff District Registry. Company Chair, Welsh National Insurance Co Ltd. Cardiff CC 1896, Alderman (Chair, Education Cttee; Leader, Conservative Group). Lord Mayor 1908-09. Member, Council of University of Wales, Cardiff; Central Welsh Board. Hon. Sec. Cardiff Conservative Assn 25 years. Freemason (Grand Master & Provincial Deacon). Hobbies: Golf (Captain & Vice-President, Porthcawl Golf Club). Languages: Welsh, English. Estate £6353. Died 19 April 1914.

MORGAN Mair Eluned: Labour MEP Mid & West Wales 1994-99, MEP Wales 1999-. **Ms. Eluned Morgan:** Born Cardiff 1972, d of Canon Bob Morgan (Leader, South Glam CC; resigned from Labour Party over Iraq, Feb. 2003). Married. Educated Atlantic College; University of Hull, University of Strasbourg. TV Researcher. Member, National Assembly Advisory Group 1998-99.

MORGAN Mark Edwin: Referendum Party, Caerphilly 1997. **Mr. Mark Morgan:** Born Mountain Ash 7 January 1959, s of Thomas James Morgan, toolmaker, & Phyllis Doreen Watts, nurse. Church of England. Married 1988 Dawn Morgan, IT analyst, 3d. Educated secondary school (BUOH PCert P405 P402). Army: Staff Sergeant RAMC 1975-94. Vehicle Assembler; Environmental Scientist (asbestos). Interests: European Issues: Environment. Hobbies: Computers, Internet, Reading; Watercolour Painting. Languages: English, little Welsh, German. No political activity after 1997. Of Caerphilly.

MORGAN Morgan: Kt 1887 JP (Cardiff). Conservative: South Glamorgan 1892. **Sir Morgan Morgan:** Born 1843, s of Morgan Morgan, farmer, of Cilposte, Carms. Anglican. Married 1874, Elizabeth Margretta, d of James Buckley of Penyfai, Llanelli (1s died in War 1915). Solicitor 1866. Educated Christ College, Brecon; Oxford University. Solicitor 1866. Company Chair: Thompson & Sheahall Ltd. Director: Cowbridge & Aberthaw Railway Co; Merchants Exchange, Cardiff. Cardiff BC 1881-; Mayor 1887-88. Languages: Welsh, English. Of Cardiff & Castell Gorfod, Glam. Estate £15,170. Died 6 December 1894.

MORGAN Morgan: JP (Cardiff) 1895 FAI. Conservative: Ebbw Vale 1922, Upton 1929; PPC Rhondda East 1920-22. **Colonel Morgan Morgan:** Born Llantwit Fardre April 1865, s of David Morgan, hotelkeeper & ex-collier, & Jane Williams (brother of Lewis Morgan qv). Anglican. Married 1889, Mdme. Hypolytte Reneaume, 1s. Educated Llantwit Fardre Elementary School. Miner 1875. Estate agent 1889. Barrister 1902. Cardiff BC 1887-; Deputy Mayor 1897. Founder, Institute of Patentees 1919, President 1923-24. Standing Counsel, Seamen's Union. Freemason. President: Rhondda Conservative Assn. Vice-President, Glamorgan Conservative Assn. Captain & Vice-President, Porthcawl Golf Club. Freemason (Grand Master & Provincial Grand Deacon, Prince of 31st Degree). Hobbies: Shooting, Golf. Languages; Welsh English. Estate £6,553. Died 1 September 1935.

MORGAN Paul – see MORGAN A. P.

MORGAN Peter Trevor Hopkin – see HOPKIN-MORGAN Peter Trevor.

MORGAN Philip Steven Eric: Referendum Party: Cardiff South & Penarth 1997. **Mr. Steven Morgan:** Anglican. Married 4c. Travel Agent. In wine trade 25 years. Of Penarth.

MORGAN Rowland G: BSc (Manchester). Liberal: Bedwellty Feb. & Oct. 1974; Weston Super Mare 1979; Woodspring 1983. **Mr. Rowland Morgan:** Born 2 December 1934. Married 3c. Educated Tredegar Grammar School; Manchester University. Chartered Civil Engineer. Lecturer in Civil Engineering, Bristol University. Member AUI.

MORGAN Sidney Royston: Plaid Cymru: South East Wales Euro 1984, Pontypridd B/E 1989. **Mr. Sid Morgan:** Born 1944. Married 2c. Educated Caerphilly Grammar School; University of Wales, Swansea. Administrator in Education & Health Service. Development Manager, Hafod Housing Assn. Senior Vice-President, Plaid Cymru 1983-;

Chair. Caerphilly DC 1973-. Mid-Glam CC. Of Ystrad Mynach.

MORGAN Stephen: Plaid Cymru, Blaenau Gwent 1983, 1987. **Mr. Stephen Morgan:** Born 1956. Married Julie Morgan. 1c. Chargehand Electrician, Pantteg Steel Works. Brynmawr TC 1982. EEPTU shop steward. Branch Secretary. Nantyglo & Blaina Plaid Cymru. Of Brynmawr.

MORGAN Talmai Philip: MA (Cantab). Conservative: Blaenau Gwent 1983. **Mr. Talmai Morgan:** Born 7 January 1953. Married. Educated Gowerton Grammar School; Emmanuel College, Cambridge (Economics & Law). Barrister 1976. Barings (Guernsey) 1988-94. Managing Director, Bermuda Trust (Guernsey) of Bank of Bermuda 1994-99. 1st Director of Fiducing Services & Enforcement, States of Guernsey 1999-. Vice-Chair: Westminster Young Conservatives; Greater London Young Conservatives. Of London.

MORGAN Trefor Richard: Plaid Cymru: Ogmore 1945, B/E 1946; Abertillery 1955; Brecon & Radnor 1964, 1966; Independent Welsh Nationalist: Merthyr Tydfil 1950. **Mr. Trefor Morgan:** Born 28 January, 1914, s of Samuel Morgan & Edith Richards, one of 7 children. Baptist. Married 1943, Gwyneth, d of Arthur & Mary Evans, Aberdare, 4c. Educated elementary school. Miner 1928. Insurance agent. Farmer. Founded Undeb Co Aberdare and set up a small industrial estate at Hirwaun. Company Director & Insurance Broker. Set up *Gronfa Glyndŵr yr Ysgolion Cymraeg* 1963, to enable children to have Welsh language education. Bought Bryntirion, Laleston, to open Ysgol Glyndŵr, a Welsh language boarding school, 1968, but the scheme ended with his death. Sentenced to a month's imprisonment by Aberystwyth magistrates 1940 with Ted Merriman & Hywel Lewis for refusing to stand in a cinema for *God save the King*. Languages: Welsh, English. Died Bridgend 3 January 1970.

MORGAN Walter Harold: Liberal: Denbigh District 1895; South Glamorgan 1900. **Mr. Walter Morgan:** Born Pontypridd 1853, s of William Morgan JP, Tynewydd, Treherbert. Married Catherine Morgan 2d. Solicitor 1876; Founded Morgan, Bruce & Nicholas, Pontypridd. Clerk: Ystradyfodwg & Pontypridd Main Sewage Board; Ystradyfodwg District Council 1877-1901. Glamorgan CC Alderman, Chair 1895. Of Trefforest. Suffered abuse for opposing 'a hero' of the Boer War in the election, which affected his health. Died 1901. Further Reading: *Chris Williams, Democratic Rhondda.*

MORGAN Wendy Ellen: Labour, South Wales Central List 1999. **Mrs. Wendy Morgan:** HND.

MBPS (CertOccTesting A & B) MIPB. Born Maidstone 9 April 1951, d of Matthew Henry Barrett, teacher, & Jean Rosemary Baldwin, social worker. Married (1) 1970 Morgan, divorced 1988 (2) 1994 Dan Leslie Buckler, duty manager, 1s 1d. Educated Maidstone Girls Grammar School; University of Glamorgan (Glam Polytechnic). Personnel Manager. Voluntary Service Co-ordinator, Mencap Cymru. Member: Labour National Policy Forum. Chair: Wales Labour Women's Cttee. Rhondda-Cynon-Taf CBC -1999 (Chair: Personnel Cttee). Interests: Equality of Opportunity, Socialism, Feminism Hobbies: Allotment Gardening, Travelling, Politics. Languages: Welsh, English, Spanish, German, Italian & British Sign Language. Of Pontypridd.

MORGAN William Geraint Oliver: QC 1971 LlB (Wales) MA (Oxon). Conservative: Merioneth 1951, Huyton 1955; MP Denbigh 1959-83. **Mr. Geraint Morgan:** Born Llanfihangel Aberlythic, Llandeilo, 2 November 1921. Married 1957 J. S. M. Maxwell, 4c. Educated Llandeilo Grammar School; University of Wales, Aberystwyth; Trinity Hall, Cambridge. Royal Suffolk Regt. 1939; Major, Royal Marines. Barrister, Grays Inn 1947. Recorder, Crown Court 1972-. Chair, Welsh Parliamentary Party 1965-66. Hon. Member, Gorsedd of Bards 1969. Supported Plaid Cymru candidate 1983. Languages: Welsh, English. Of Prescott. Died 2 July 1995. *I wasted the prime years of my life in the service of the Conservative Party (quoted in Welsh Nation, June 1984).*

MORGAN William John: MB ChB (Edin) 1970 FRCS (Edin) 1975. Conservative, Newport West 2001. **Dr. Bill Morgan:** Born India, 27 January 1946. Married, separated. 2s 1d. Educated Windsor Comprehensive School; Edinburgh University). Independent Accident & Emergency Consultant 2000-; A&E Consultant, Royal Gwent Hospital 1980-2000. Chair, Newport West Conservative Assn. Rogerstone ComC 1998-. Interests: Health Service, Education. Hobbies: Golf, Bird Watching: Running [ran Welsh Marathon 3 times]. Of Bassaleg, Newport (1980).

MORGAN William Prichard: Liberal MP Merthyr Tydfil B/E 188-1900 (defeated by Keir Hardie); Independent Liberal: Jan. 1910; Independent: East Fife 1918 (against H. H. Asquith). **Mr. W. Prichard Morgan:** Born Usk, 25 July 1844, s of William Morgan, Wesleyan lay preacher. Earned half-a-crown a week on leaving school. Ran away to sea & returned home to a Newport Solicitor's office. Solicitor 1865, at Newport. Emigrated to Queensland 1867 and broke stones at six shillings a day. Went to Gympie Goldfield 1867; set up Solicitor's Office; bought gold and mine shares. Speculated for gold in Korea. Re-

turned to Wales 1887, developed Morgan Gold Mine & formed Merioneth Gold Co Defeated the official Liberal candidate in the by-election, being backed by the local Unionists and licensed victuallers and with much working class support in Aberdare. Of Englefield Green, Surrey. Estate £1,694. Died July 1924.

MORGAN-EDWARDS Brian – see EDWARDS B. M.

MORGAN-JONES Gareth: BSc MSc (Wales) PhD (Nottingham). Plaid Cymru: Aberdare 1970. **Dr. Gareth Morgan Jones:** Born Rhostryfan 1939. Educated Caernarfon Grammar School; University College of Wales, Aberystwyth; Nottingham University. Research in Canada 1964-66. National Research Council of Canada Fellowship in Biosystematics, Havard University & Waterloo University, Ontario 1970-71. Botanist; Commonwealth Mycological Institute, Kew 1966-68. Asst General Secretary, Plaid Cymru 1968-70. Joint Founder, Plaid Cymru Research Group; Plaid Spokesman on the Arts. Member, UNA Welsh Executive. Languages: Welsh, English. Of Swansea.

MORGAN-RICHARDSON Charles Evans Davis: JP (Pembs) 1901. Liberal Unionist: Cardiganshire 1906. **Mr. Charles Morgan-Richardson:** Born St. Davids 11 September 1857, s of Canon Thomas Richardson & Jane, d of David Evans, Treffgarne Hall, Pembs. Added Morgan by deed-poll on death of Mrs. Morgan 1880 to inherit the Treforgan estate of Thomas Morgan. Married 1882, Evelyn Beatrice, d of Sir Henry More Browning, Bart. Educated Berkhampstead School. Articled in conveyancing to Thomas Morgan. Landowner & Farmer. Cardigan BC. Mayor 1897-1900. Cardiganshire CC 1888-. President, Cardiganshire Unionist Assn 1910. Treasurer, Welsh Liberal Unionist Assn. Of Rhoshill, Pembs. Interests: Shooting. Of Boncath. Estate £29,418. Died 28 September 1913.

MORLEY Charles: BA 1870 MA (Cantab) 1874. Liberal MP Breconshire 1895-1906; Candidate: East Somerset 1892. **Mr. Charles Morley:** Born 1847, s of Samuel Morley MP & Rebecca, d of Samuel Hope, Liverpool (brother of Rt. Hon. Arnold Morley MP). Educated Trinity College, Cambridge. Director, Holborn Viaduct Land Co. Hon. Secretary, Royal College of Music. Of Shockerwick Hall, Bath & London. Estate £297,158. Died 27 October 1917.

MORRIS Alan: Pro-Europe Conservative, Wales Euro 1999. **Mr. Alan Morris:** Of Hereford.

MORRIS David: Conservative prospective parliamentary candidate, Carmarthenshire West &

Pembrokeshire South, 20003. **Mr. David Morris:** Hairdresser. Conservative Prospective Candidate, Carmarthenshire East & Dinefwr 2004. Of Leigh, Lancashire.

MORRIS David Richard: Labour: Brecon & Radnor 1983; MEP South West Wales, 1984-99. **Revd David Morris:** Born Llanelli, 28 January 1930. Married 2c. Educated Stebonheath Secondary School, Llanelli. Foundry labourer 1944-51. Student at United Theological College, Aberystwyth; University of Wales, Swansea. Minister, Presbyterian Church of Wales, Ordained 1958: Rhayader & Sychnant, then Newport 1958-62. Educational Adviser, Newport BC 1962-74; Gwent Education Authority 1974-84. Newport BC. Member: European Parl Cttees: Agriculture, Fisheries & Food (Senior Vice-President, Fisheries Sub-Cttee); Environment. Vice-President, Parliament for Wales Campaign. Member: TGWU, Tribune Group, Socialist Educational Assn, Socialist Health Assn. Chair, CNDCymru. Of Swansea.

MORRIS Elfyn Lloyd: BA (Wales). Liberal: Conway 1970. **Mr. Elfyn Lloyd Morris:** Born Breconshire 1939, s of Revd Thomas Lloyd Morris, Presbyterian Minister. Married 1c. Educated University of Wales, Aberystwyth. Teacher (Geography). Co-Author, *Liberal Plan for Wales*. Secretary: Welsh Liberal Party; Policy Directorate of Welsh Liberal Party. Member, Merioneth European Conservation Year Cttee 1974. Bala UDC 1964, Chair 1970-71. Languages: Welsh, English.

MORRIS John, Baron Morris of Aberavon 2001: KG 2003 PC 1970 Kt 1999 QC 1970 Hon. LLD (Wales) 1983 LlB (Wales) MA (Cantab). Labour MP Aberavon, 1959-2001. (Short-listed at Cardigan & Carmarthen). **Rt. Hon. Sir John Morris:** Born Talybont, Cards. November 1931, s of David William Morris, farmer, & Mary Olwen Morris, Penywern. Presbyterian Church of Wales. Married Margaret, d of Edward Lewis, OBE. Llandysul publisher, 3d. Educated Ardwyn School, Aberystwyth; University of Wales, Aberystwyth; Gonville & Caius College, Cambridge; Academy of International Law, The Hague. Army 1947-49; Lieutenant, Welch Regt. Barrister Grays Inn 1954; Holker Senior Exhibitioner. Legal Adviser & Deputy General Secretary, Farmers' Union of Wales. Joined Labour Party 1951. Member, Council, British Socialist Agricultural Society. Hon. Member, Gorsedd of Bards. Vice-President, Hon. Society of Cymmrodorion. UK Delegate, Council of Europe 1963-64. Chair: National Pneumoconiosis Jt Cttee 1964-66; Joint Review of British Railways 1966 National Road Safety Advisory Council 1967. Parl-Secretary, Power 1964-66; Parl-Secretary,

Transport 1966-68; Minister of State, Defence (Equipment) 1968-70; Secretary of State for Wales 1974-79. Opposition Spokesman: Wales 1979-83; Legal Affairs 1983-97. Attorney General, 1997-99. Member, Cttee of Privileges 1984-87, 1989-97. Vice-Chair, MPs' Barristers Group. Member, Courts: University of Wales, Aberystwyth & Swansea. Chancellor of the University of Glamorgan 2001. Lord Lieutenant of Dyfed 2003. Languages: Welsh; English. Interests: Agriculture; Defence, Coal & Steel. Hobbies: Fishing, Reading, Shooting. Languages: Welsh, English.

MORRIS Lewis: Kt 1895 JP MA (Oxon) 1858. Officer of the Redeemer of Greece. Liberal: Pembroke & Haverfordwest 1886. Withdrew at Carmarthen District, 1892; made several attempts to seek parliamentary candidature. **Sir Lewis Morris:** Born Carmarthen 23 January 1833 s of Lewis Edward William Morris. Married 1868, Florence Julia Pollard, 3c. Educated Queen Elizabeth Grammar School, Carmarthen; Sherborne School; Jesus College, Oxford (1st Classics). Chancellor Professor 1858. Barrister, Lincolns Inn, 1861-80. Joint-Secretary, University of Wales, Aberystwyth 1878; Treasurer 1889-96; Vice-President 1896-1907; Deputy Vice-Chancellor, University of Wales. Jubilee and Coronation Medallist 1902. English poet. Languages: Welsh, English. Estate £13,416. Died 10 November 1907. *Books: Lewis Morris: Sons of Two Worlds 1872-74-75, The Epic of Hades 1876-77, Gwen, a drama in monologue 1879, The Ode of a Life 1880, Songs Unsung 1883, Gycia, a drama 1886, Songs of Britain 1887, A Vision of Saints 1880, Songs without Notes 1894, Idylls and Lyrics 1896, Harvest Tide 1901, The New Rambler 1906.*

MORRIS Paul Raymond: Conservative, Swansea East 2001. **Mr. Paul Morris:** Born Swansea 7 January 1959. Married 1c. Educated Penlan Comprehensive School. Group Administrator, Assembly Conservative Group. Ex-Securities Clerk, HSBC Bank. Chair, Swansea West Conservative Assn. Contested Swansea CC, West Glam CC. Interests: Law & Order, Europe, Economy. Hobbies: Reading, Cinema, Theatre. Of Swansea.

MORRIS Percy: CBE 1963 JP (Swansea) 1939. Labour: Swansea West 1935; MP 1945-64. **Mr. Percy Morris:** Born Manselton, Swansea, 6 October 1893, s of Thomas & Emma Morris. Congregationalist Lay Preacher & Deacon. Married (1) 1920 Elizabeth, d of William Davies (killed in blitz 1941) (2) 1956 Catherine Evans. Educated Dynevor Grammar School, Swansea. Railway Clerk 1908. President, Railway Clerks Assn 1943-45; Transport Salaried Staffs Assn 1953-. Deputy Regional Commissioner for Civil Defence 1941-45. Swansea BC 1927- (Leader,

Labour Group; Chair, Parliamentary Cttee 1935-). Alderman 1942. Deputy Mayor 1943-44. Mayor 1955-56. Freeman 1958. President, Swansea Labour Assn. Member, National Assistance Board 1961-66, Deputy Chair 1965-66. Member, Western Area, British Transport Commission 1960-62. Deputy Chair, Supplementary Benefits Commission 1966-67. Member: Council, University of Wales, Swansea. Chair, Swansea & West Carmarthenshire English Congregational Assn 1927-45. Of Swansea. Died 7 March 1967.

MORRIS Peter Alban: BEd MA 1998 (Wales) FETC LCGI. Referendum Party, Neath 1997; Conservative, Swansea East 2001, 2003. **Mr. Peter Morris:** Born Gorseinon, 19 April 1954, s of Leslie James Morris, civil servant, & Audrey Martha Bateman MBE. Anglican. Married 1975, Monica Stopford, probation officer, divorced, 2c. Educated Gregg High School, Swansea; Llanelli Grammar School; Swansea Institute (Business); UWIST (Leisure, Tourism, Management). Winner of Winston *Churchill Fellowship*, which enabled him to visit USA 20 times in 15 years. Police Officer, retired after injury. Photographic Technician, University of Wales, Swansea. Teacher: St. Michael's Independent School, Llanelli; ICT teacher, Bishop Gore Comprehensive School, Swansea. Leader West Glamorgan Age Concern. Vice-Chair, South Wales (Western) Branch, International Police Assn. Joined Referendum Party 1995. South Wales Hon. Organiser, Referendum Movement 1998. Joined Professional Assn of Teachers 1992; Chair: Swansea & Port Talbot Federation & Member Council. Deputy-Chair: Llanelli Conservative Assn Vice-Chair, Conservative Welsh Executive 2002-; Member, National Council. Member: User Group of the Blood Pressure Assn; Network Rail. Conservative candidate, Llanelli Rural Council (Hengoed) B/E 27 June 2002. Member: Swansea community Orchestra. Hobbies: Travelling, especially to USA, Garden Railway, Playing Violin. Languages: Welsh, English. Of Llanelli.

MORRIS Rhys Hopkin: Kt 1954 MBE 1917 KC 1932 BA (Wales) LlB (London). Independent Liberal, Cardigan 1922; Liberal MP 1923-32; MP Carmarthen 1945-. **Major, Sir Rhys Hopkin Morris:** Born Maesteg, 5 September 1888, s of Revd John Morris & Mary Hopkin. (Both parents died 1904). Welsh Independent. Married 1918, Gwladys Perris Williams OBE DLitt. d of W. H. Williams, Llanrwst, 1d. Educated Maesteg Grammar School; University of Wales, Bangor (Philosophy); University College, London (Law). President, Bangor Student Representative Council 1911. Teacher at Barged. Barrister, Middle Temple 1920. Lieutenant RWF 1914; Chief Recruiting Officer for Wales-1918. Metropolitan Magistrate 1932-36. BBC Regional Director for

Major, Sir Rhys Hopkin Morris.

Wales 1936-45 Court Member: University of Wales; National Library; National Museum. Member, Parliamentary Delegation to East Africa 1928; Palestine Commission 1929. Deputy Chair of Ways & Means, 1951-. Languages: Welsh, English. Of Sidcup. Died November 1958. *Books: R. Hopkin Morris: Dare or Despair, Welsh Politics 1927.* Further Reading: *T. J. Evans: Rhys Hopkin Morris: The Man and his Character, 1957; John Emmanuel and D. Ben Rees, Bywyd a Gwaith Syr Rhys Hopkin Morris 1980, D. Ben Rees: Cymry Adnabyddus 1952-1972. Dictionary of Liberal Biography.*

MORRIS Robert Jonathan: Socialist Labour, South/East List 1999, 2003. **Mr. Robert Morris:** Born Tredegar, 14 February 1966. Married 2c. Construction Worker 20 years. Regional Organiser, UCATT. Of Sheffield.

MORRIS Robert Jones: JP (Merioneth). 1896 Conservative: Merioneth Jan. 1910. **Mr. Robert Morris:** Born Porthmadog 19 December 1855, s of W. E. Morris & Jane Jones. Anglican. Lifelong church organist. Married 1893, Edith Isabel, d of William Ansell, Corsgydol. Educated Porthmadog Grammar School; Liverpool Institute. Farmer. Member: Merioneth County CO Appeal Cttee 1916-19; Merioneth County Agricultural Cttee; Governing Body of the Church in Wales. Merioneth CC Alderman. Of Talsarnau. Died January 1945.

MORRIS Wayne: Conservative, South Wales West List 1999. **Mr. Wayne Morris:** Contested Neath/Port Talbot BC (Baglan) 1999. Agent, Aberavon 2001. Of Port Talbot.

MORRIS-JONES Huw William: JP (Caerns) 1949 BA 1933 MA (Wales) BLitt (Oxon) 1937. Labour: Merioneth 1945; Joined SDP 1981. **Professor Huw Morris-Jones:** Born 1 May 1912, s of William Oliver & Mary Jones. Presbyterian Church of Wales. Married 1942, Gwladys Evans 2c. Educated Alun Grammar School, Mold; University of Wales (double 1st); Oriel College, Oxford. Education Officer, South Wales Council for Social Service 1937-39. Lecturer in Philosophy, Nottingham University 1939-42; University of Wales, Bangor 1942-59; Senior Lecturer 1959-66. Professor of Social Theory & Institutions 1966-77. Member, Broadcasting Council for Wales 1957-67; Chair: Welsh Advisory Cttee Independent Broadcasting Authority 1976-82; Welsh Fourth Channel Authority 1981-82. Languages: Welsh, English. Died 1989.

MORRIS-JONES John Henry: Kt 1937 MC 1918 JP 1918 DL (Denbs) LRCP LRCS (Edin) LRFPS (Glasgow). Liberal MP Denbigh 1929-31; Liberal National MP 1931-50. **Sir Henry Morris-Jones:** Born Waunfawr, Caerns. 2 November 1884, s of Captain Morris Jones & Ann Jones. Presbyterian, became an Anglican. Married 1931 Leila Augusta Paget-Marsland. Educated Caernarfon Grammar School; Menai Bridge Grammar School; St. Mungo's College, Glasgow. Medical Practitioner 1908-29. Captain, RAMC 1914-19. Denbighshire CC. Colwyn Bay UDC, Chair. Freeman. High Sheriff of Denbighshire 1938, High Sheriff Designate 1929-30. Chair: National Liberal Party Executive 1953-54; Welsh Parliamentary Party 1941-42. Asst. Whip 1932-35. Lord Commissioner 1935-37. Liberal National Whip withdrawn Feb. 1942-May 1943. Member, Governing Body, Church in Wales, 1950-62. Languages: Welsh, English. Of Royston, Herts. Died 9 July 1972. *Books: J. H. Morris-Jones: Surgical Experiences at Wimereux, France (with Hugh Lett), Doctor in the Whips' Room (autobiography) 1955.*

MORSE John Howard: British National Party: Cardiff North 1992, Bournemouth West 1983, East Midlands Euro 1999. **Mr. John Morse:** Born 1943. Bus driver. Third in command, BNP. Editor, *The British Nationalist.* Prosecuted 1986, for a series of articles saying that black people were more likely to commit crimes than white people; sentenced to 12 months at Wormwood Scrubs; reduced to four months on appeal.

MORSE Richard: BSc PGCE Dip Computing. United Socialist, South Wales East List 1999, Newport West 2003. **Mr. Richard Morse:** Born Cwmbran, 15 September 1957, son of Richard Gordon Morse, factory worker-shopkeeper-company director, & Jean Olwen Myfanwy Morse, housewife. Atheist. Married 1992 Mary Kathleen Murphy, teacher, 2s 1d. Educated Croesyceiliog

Comprehensive School, Cwmbran; University of North London (Chemistry); University of Kingston. Teacher. Secretary: Torfaen Trades Union Council, Mynwy/Casnewydd/Torfaen Branch, UCAC. Member: Executive, Gwent Autistic Society. Interests: Socialism/Trade Unionism. Languages: Welsh, English. Of Cwmbran.

MORT David Llewellyn: Labour MP Swansea East B/E 1940-, Eccles 1929-31, Candidate: Bilston 1935. **Mr. David Mort:** Born Briton Ferry 25 March 1888, s of Henry Mort. Congregationalist. Married (1) 1912, Hannah (died 1947) d of Thomas Perrett (2) Mrs. W. J. Davies. (2) Educated elementary schools. Steelworker. South Wales Secretary, Iron & Steel Trades Confederation 1915-. Briton Ferry UDC 1922-25. Neath BC 1925-29. PPS 1942-43. Of Swansea. Died 1 January 1963.

MORUS Gwilym: Green, North Wales List 1999. **Mr. Gwilym Morus:** Of Bangor.

MOSELEY Thomas Hywel: MA LLM QC. Plaid Cymru. Mid & West Wales Euro 1979. **Professor Hywel Moseley:** Born Carno 27 September 1936, s of Revd Luther Mosely & Megan Eluned Moseley. Welsh Independent. Married 1960, Monique Germaine Theresa Drifin, 3d. Educated Caterham School; University of Wales, Aberystwyth; Queens College, Cambridge (1st Law). National Service 1954-56. Barrister (Grays Inn) 1964. Practised at Cardiff 1964-89 and London 1977-89. Recorder 1981-89. Lecturer in Law 1960-65. Professor of Law, University of Wales, Aberystwyth 1970-82. Judge 1989-. Hon. Legal Adviser: National Eisteddfod, Urdd Gobaith Cymru. Member: Court of University of Wales; Insolvency Rules Cttee 1993-97. Languages: Welsh, English.

MOSS Samuel: JP BA 1878 MA BCL 1880 (Oxon). Liberal MP East Denbighshire 1897-1910. **Mr. Samuel Moss:** Born Llansannan 13 December 1858, s of Enoch Moss, Rossett. Congregationalist. Married 1895, Eleanor, d of E. B. Samuel, Wrexham 6c. Educated Worcester College, Oxford. Barrister, Lincolns Inn 1880. Denbighshire CC Alderman 1889, 1st Vice-Chair 1889-92; 2nd Chair 1892-95 Chester CC. Asst. Boundary Commissioner 1887. County Court Judge 1906. Of London & Chester. Died 14 May 1918. *Books: Samuel Moss: English Land Laws 1886.*

MOWAT James: MA (Cantab) FRGS. Liberal Unionist: South Glamorgan 1886. **Mr. James Mowat:** Born 1845, s of James Ryder Mowat, first Secretary, Great Northern Railway. Married 1874, Fanny Louise, d of William Ackroyd, Stourbridge. Educated Harrow; Gonville & Caius College, Cambridge. Barrister 1871. Member,

Central Liberal Assn. Founder Member, National Liberal Club. Of Kensington.

MULLETT Richard Clive: BSocSc (Birmingham). Conservative: Rhondda East 1970. **Mr. Richard Mullet:** Born 1942. Educated George Dixon Grammar School, Birmingham; Birmingham University. Asst Lecturer in Economics, Bristol University; Birmingham College of Commerce; WEA Lecturer. Bristol CC. Of Bristol North.

MULLINS Thomas: LlB (Ireland). Natural Law Party, North List 1999, Down North 1997, Euro Ulster 1999. **Mr. Thomas Mullins:** Born Dublin, Ireland, 13 April 1948, s of Thomas Mullins, businessman, & Eileen Kennedy. Roman Catholic. Married 1980, Sarah Mullins, 1d. Educated University College, Dublin. Chair: Northern Ireland Natural Law Party. Hobbies: Sport, Cinema. Languages: English, Irish. Of Dublin, Ireland.

MUNFORD Daniel: BA (London) 1990. Liberal Democrat: Vale of Clwyd 1997. **Mr. Daniel Munford:** Born Montgomeryshire 28 September 1968. Married 1997, Siân Jones of Oswestry. Educated Fitzalan Comprehensive School; Oswestry Grammar School; University College, London (2a. History). Political Researcher, Alex Carlile MP. Teacher of English in Tokyo & Paris. Partner, Market Research Business. Holder, Pilot's licence. Chair, Montgomeryshire Liberal Democrats. Joined Conservative Party 2001. Of Berriew, Welshpool.

MUNGHAM Geoffrey: BA (Leicester) BLitt (Oxon). Labour, Cardiff Central 2003. **Mr. Geoffrey Mungham:** Labour, Cardiff Central 2003. Born Portsmouth 18 March 1943, s of Thomas Edward Mungham, labourer, & Marie Ethel Mungham, shop assistant. Roman Catholic. Educated: secondary modern School; University of Leicester; University of Oxford. Senior Lecturer, Welsh School of Journalism, Media & Cultural Studies. Worked at various times in Brazil, Canada, China, Denmark, Kosovo, Netherlands, South Korea, and USA. Cardiff CC 1985-95 (Chair: Finance Cttee 1987-94). Hon. Consul, Brazil. Director, Cardiff Community Housing Assn. Member: Welsh Consular Assn; Institute of Welsh Affairs; Campaign for Press & Broadcasting Freedom; Society of Labour History. Interests: Education & Government Finance. Hobbies: Military History, International Travel. Died in hotel whilst on lecture visit to University of Utrecht, November 2003. *Books: Co-author: Redesigning Democracy: The Shaping of the Welsh Assembly (2001); The Fog of War, the Media and the Battlefield (1987).*

MUNRO Patrick Mackenzie: MA (Oxon). Conservative MP Llandaff & Barry 1931-. **Mr. Patrick Munro:** Born 9 October 1883, s of Patrick Munro, Bonar Bridge. Anglican. Married 1911, Jessie Margaret d of Edward F. Martin, Abergavenny. Educated Leeds Grammar School; Christ Church, Oxford (Open Scholarship; 2nd History); Oxford Rugby Blue 1903, Captain 1905. Member, Scottish Rugby XV 1905-06, 1906-07, 1911 (Captain 1907, 1911). President: Vincents Club, Oxford 1906-07; Scottish Rugby Union 1919. Sudanese Civil Service: 1907-29; Governor, Darfur Province 1923-24; Khartoum Province 1924-29. Army, 1914-18; Private, Home Guard 1940-. PPS. 1935. Asst. Whip 1937. Lord Commissioner 1937-42. Of London & Bwlch, Brecon. Estate £5,263. Died, House of Commons, 3 May 1942.

MURPHY Brendan: LlB (Manchester). Conservative: Vale of Clwyd 2001; Hazel Grove 1997; Euro NE England, 1999. **Mr. Brendan Murphy:** Born Loughton, Essex, 9 September 1941, s of Phelim Murphy (from milkman to shipping company sales manager, & Elizabeth Mary Murphy, from servant/maid to senior civil service administrator). Roman Catholic. Married 1966 Iris Roper (died 2003). Educated Salesian College, Cheshire; St. Bonaventure's, London; Faculty of Law, Manchester; Henley on Thames Management College. Ex-Journalist. Managing Director, PulseTech (behavioural research consultancy). Information Manager, NHS 1970-73. Head of Communications & Marketing, Stockport BC 1973-85. Head of Public Affairs & Corporate Communications, Dŵr Cymru 1989-. Conservative Central Office Researcher 1989-91. Macclesfield TC. Cheshire CC. 1993-97. Primary School Governor. Governor, Royal School for the Deaf. Member: RSPCA; RSPB; World Life Nature Fund. Interests: Preserving Liberty, Justice & Social Responsibility, Protecting the Individual from oppressive bureaucracy or political control, Enhancing human diversity, Conserving our heritage & environment, Maintaining public morality, Europe, Social Services, Planning Policies, Taxation. Hobbies: Music, Piano Playing, Gardening, Indoor Plants, Swimming, Walking my dogs. Languages: Welsh (but not very well), English, French, Italian, Spanish.

MURPHY Mary Gwyneth: JP (Glam) 1962. Liberal: Pontypridd 1970, Feb. & Oct. 1974. **Mrs. Mary Murphy:** Born Pontypridd 1930 d of Edwards. Welsh Independent deacon. Married Bernard Murphy, Clerk to UDC. Educated Pontypridd Grammar School; St. Mary'sTraining College, Bangor. Teacher, Maths & PE, Ysgol Gyfun Rhydfelin. Chair, Liberal Party of Wales 1966-67. 1st Secretary, Welsh Liberal Party 1967-68. Treasurer, South Wales Liberal Federation. Pontypridd UDC 1963-74; Taf-Ely BC 1973. Mid-

Glam CC 1973. Languages: Welsh, English. Of Pontypridd.

MURPHY Michael J: Conservative: Swansea East 1970. **Mr. Michael Murphy:** Born Swansea, July 1945. Married March 1970, Jane Murphy. Educated Dunbarton House School, Swansea; Swansea College of Technology. Post office Telephone Engineer. Member: Conservative Advisory Cttee for Trade Unionism in Wales; Cttee Welsh Assn of Boys Clubs. Vice-Chair, Swansea Branch, Post Office Engineering Union; Suspended for helping clean Guildhall during a cleaners' strike, Oct.-Nov. 1970. Resigned from union Nov. 1970. Hobbies: Active sportsman. Of Swansea.

MURPHY Paul Peter: PC BA MA (Oxon). Labour MP, Torfaen 1987-; Contested Wells 1979. **Rt. Hon. Paul Murphy:** Born Usk 25 November 1948, s of Ronald Murphy, miner, & Marjorie Murphy. Roman Catholic. Unmarried. Educated St. Francis School, Abersychan; West Mon. School, Pontypool; Oriel College, Oxford. Co-operative Society Trainee Manager 1970-71. Lecturer in History & Government, Ebbw Vale FE College 1971-87. Member: Co-operative Party; WEA; Socialist Education Society, TGWU. Secretary, Torfaen CLP 1974-87. Torfaen BC 1973-87 (Chair, Finance Cttee 1976-86). Treasurer, Labour Against a Welsh Assembly 1978. Opposition Spokesman: Defence 1995-97; Wales 1988-94; Northern Ireland 1994-95. Member: Select Cttee on Welsh Affairs 1988. Minister of State, Northern Ireland 1997-99. Secretary of State for Wales 1999-2002. Secretary of State for Northern Ireland, Nov. 2002. Hon. Fellow, Oriel College, Oxford. Hobbies: Listening to music, Cooking. Of Cwmbran.

MURRAY Michael: Prospective Conservative candidate for Gower, December 2003. **Mr. Mike Murray:** Married Menna (of Llangennith) 2s. Educated Wycliffe School, Gloucs. Chartered Surveyor. Of Oxfordshire.

MURRAY Peter: UK Independence Party, Clwyd West 2003. **Mr. Peter Murray:** Married 1963 June Gough-Roberts 5c. Army. Clerk of Works-Surveyor. Conway CBC (Ind. Kinmel Bay). Mayor of Kinmel Bay. Of Rhyl.

MYTTON Devereux Herbert: JP DL (Mont) 1895 Hon. LLD (Wales). Conservative: Montgomery 1886, 1892. **Captain Devereux Mytton:** Born Baraset. Bengal 9 September 1832, s of Richard Herbert Mytton & Charlotte, d of General J. A. Paul Macgregor. Anglican. Married 1873, Emma Lydia, d of Edmund Story, 5s 1d. Captain 85th Foot. Landowner. High Sheriff of Montgomeryshire 1873. Montgomeryshire CC (Chair 1906-10). Of Garth, Welshpool Estate £11,834. Died 14 February 1910.

NANNEY Hugh John Ellis – see ELLIS-NANNEY H. J.

NAISH Bronwen: ARMCM. Conservative, Caernarfon & North List 1999, Caernarfon 2001. **Ms. Bronwen Naish:** Born Burley, Hants. 19 November 1939, d of Ernest Frederick Edward Naish, naval officer, millowner & farmer. Church of England. Married 1959, Roger Best, 2s 3d. Educated Bodedern Primary School; Holyhead Grammar School; Royal Manchester College of Music. Sub-principal Double Bass, Northern Sinfonia Orchestra 1965-78. London Solo debut 1972. Specialised in performances for primary school audiences 1972-94. LEA peripatetic cell/ bass tutor, NE England and Gwynedd, 25 years. Published book 1981, two albums of solo bass music with *Sain*. Vice-Chair: Caernarfon Conservative Assn. Interests: Economy, Agriculture, And Political Definitions. Hobbies: DIY, Gardening, Beekeeping. Languages: Welsh, English. Of Cwm Pennant, Gandolbenmaen.

NATHAN Harry Louis, 1st Baron Nathan of Cheyt 1940: PC 1946 JP DL (London) FBA 1960 FREconS FRStatS FRSA1955 FRGS. Labour, Cardiff South 1935; Liberal: Whitechapel & St. Georges 1924. MP North-East Bethnal Green 1929-35, Supported National Government 1931, Crossed floor 1933, Joined Labour 1934. MP Wandsworth Central B/E 1937-40. **Colonel, Rt. Hon. Harry Nathan:** Born London, 1889, s of Michael Henry Nathan JP. Jewish. Married 1919, Eleanor Joan Clara Stettauer, 1s 1d. Solicitor. Joined Volunteers (TA) 1908. Army1914-18, 1939-43. Hon. Colonel TA 1937 & Air Commodore AAF. President: Royal Society of Arts 1961-63; Royal Geographical Society 1957-60; Geographical Assn 1958; Assn of Technical Institutes 1958; London & Middlesex Archaeological Society 1946-49; Old Pauline Club 1957-70; Anglo-Israeli Club; Hillel Foundation. Chair: Westminster Hospital 1948; Cttee on Charitable Trusts 1950; Queen Elizabeth Coronation Forest; Executive British Cancer Campaign 1954. Member: Board of Deputies of British Jews; Jewish Agency under Mandate for Palestine; Royal Institution for International Affairs. Trustee, Hillel Foundation. Master: Patten Makers Company 1951-56; Gardeners' Company 1958-60. Lieutenant, City of London. Liberal Whip, resigned Feb. 1933. Under-Secretary, War 1945-46. Minister of Civil Aviation 1946-48. Chair, Dock Labour Board. Of Churt & London. Died 1963.

NAYLOR John Murray: JP (Mont) 1913 MA (Oxon). Conservative: Montgomery 1929. **Captain John Naylor:** Born Liverpool 20 July 1888, s of John Naylor, Leighton Hall, Welshpool. Anglican. Married (1) 1912, Winifred Williamson, d of Baron Forres, 2c, divorced 1940 (2) 1941, Ruth Anita, d of Ernest Freshfield Dent, 1c. Educated Eton; Trinity Hall, Cambridge. Barrister, Inner Temple 1912. Landowner. Lieutenant, Montgomeryshire Yeomanry 1902-1912. Captain, City of London Rifle Brigade 1914-18. Montgomeryshire CC 1911-31, Chair, 1922-23. High Sheriff of Montgomeryshire 1914. Of Leighton Hall, Welshpool & Forfar.

NAYLOR Robert Anderton: Conservative: Caernarfon District 1906. **Mr. Robert Naylor:** Born Grappenhall 1847. Timber Merchant. Newspaper: *Thought to be a Liberal Unionist; No sense of politics; no oratory; no links with Wales or knowledge of the constituency.* Of Warrington.

NEAGLE Lynne: BA (Reading). AM Torfaen 1999-. **Ms. Lynne Neagle:** Born Merthyr Tydfil 18 January 1968, d of Colin Harvey Neagle, coach builder, & Frances Mary Hounihan. Christian. Married 1966, Huw George Lewis (qv). Educated Cyfarthfa High School, Merthyr Tydfil; University of Reading (French & Italian). Set up Rape & Sexual Abuse Support Service. Volunteer Housing Rights Worker, Shelter Cymru. Information Projects Officer, Mid Glamorgan Assn of Voluntary Organisations 1993-94. Research Assistant to Glenys Kinnock MEP 1994-97. Carers Development Officer, Voluntary Action Cardiff 1997-98. Chair: Assembly Labour Group; All Party Group on Cancer. Member, Health & Social Services Cttee. Interests: Health, Social Services, Housing, Regeneration of South Wales Valleys. Languages: English, French, Italian. Of Merthyr Tydfil.

NEAL David Kent: MRAC. Conservatory Party, Clwyd 1997, North List 1999. **Mr. David Neal:** Born Swanley, Kent, 23 September 1949, s of Horace Charles Frederick Neal, shopkeeper, & Diane Neal. Educated grammar school; Royal Agricultural College, Cirencester. Married 1970 Pamela Neal, training executive, 2s 1d. Antique furniture restorer. Founder & Leader, Conservatory Party, 1997 General Election. Hobbies: Cycling, Training, Gardening, Yoga. Languages: English. French. Of Peniel, Denbigh.

NEALE Gareth John Jarvis: CBE BA (Wales) LlB (London). Conservative: Rhondda West B/E 1967; Brecon & Radnor1970, Cardiff West Feb1974, Cardiff South & Penarth 1987. **Mr. Gareth Neale:** Born Bristol 12 April 1935, s of Stanley J. Neale & Gwenllian Margaret Jones. Married Anne Bryant 2c. Educated Barry High School; University of Wales, Aberystwyth (Econ); London University (Law). Barrister. Research Officer, Development Corporation of Wales. Methods Officer, Rolls Royce. Asst. Data & Processing Manager, Mettoy. Lecturer in Liberal Studies, Llandaff Technical College-1968; Brecon Technical College 1968-70. Industrial Arbiter, British Foods biscuit factory, Gwent 1970-.Management Services Manager & Industrial Relations Consultant. Head of Business Studies, Cross Keys College 1979-. Scoutmaster. Chair: Barry Young Conservatives; Business Productivity Group (British Productivity Council); Cardiff & District Productivity Assn. Major RWF (TA) until 1961, Welch Regt (TA) 1961-. South Glam CC 1973- (Group Leader 1985-91). Cardiff CC 1979-95, B/E 1998- (Deputy Lord Mayor 1991-92). Chair, Wales Conservative Local Government Cttee 1986. Of Rhiwbina, Cardiff.

NEALE Stuart Kensley: Plaid Cymru: Monmouth 1970. **Mr. Stuart Neale:** Born Cardiff 1939. Married. Educated Penarth Grammar School. Librarian 3 years. Student, Welsh College of Music & Drama 3 years. Television actor 3 years. Forestry Commission manual worker 1965-. Branch Secretary, National Union of Agricultural Workers. Member: local trades council, UNA. Secretary, Monmouth District Cttee Plaid Cymru. Contested Abergavenny BC. Chair, Craft Forum Wales. Member, Board, Arts Training Wales. Of Abergavenny.

NEATHERCOTE Ernest Tom: CBE 1923 JP DL (Sussex) FCS FZS FRGS. Conservative: Gower 1924, Cardiff South 1929. **Mr. Ernest Neathercote:** Born Ely, Cambridge 8 August 1880. Married 1904, Ada Jackson, 1s. Educated Soham School. Pharmaceutical Chemist & Manufacturer: Chair: Savory & Moore Ltd, John Kay Ltd, J. E. Hanger & Co Ltd, Artificial Limbmakers Ltd, Pharmaceutical Products Ltd, Laurence Press Ltd, Moores Stores Ltd, Metcalfs Stores Ltd, Kemp Stores Ltd, E. B. Jones & Co Ltd, Hays Grocery Stores Ltd. Governing Director: G. S. Mascall, Son & Co Ltd. Managing Director: Knoll Ltd. Chair: Prince of Wales General Hospital, North London, Pharmacy Board of Examiners 1919-24. President: Pharmaceutical Society of Great Britain 1919-24, International Pharmaceutical Conference 1923. Member: North East Metropolitan Hospital Board. Governor: St. Barts Hospital, Royal Veterinary College, Royal Agricultural Society of England. Liveryman,

Farriers Company. Weybridge UDC Chair 1914-20. West Sussex CC. Of Horsham, Sussex. Died 28 July 1950.

NEWBURY John: Liberal Democrat, Swansea West 1997, 1999. **Mr. John Newbury:** Born Swansea 3 January 1939, s of Ivor Lloyd Newbury. Copper works furnaceman, & Violet Mary Newbury, shop assistant/canteen assistant. Roman Catholic. Married 1965, Eileen Mary Newbury, 1s 1d. Educated Brynhyfryd Junior School, Swansea; Bishop Gore Grammar School; Pontardawe Technical College. Electrician 40 years. Trained in coal industry; worked in car manufacturing, copper mining, Zambia (4 years). Merchant Navy Officer (Esso deep sea oil-tankers) 2 years. Electricity generation. EPTU shop steward 1974-83. Member AEU. Founder Member SDP. Agent. Secretary/Chair, Swansea & Gower Liberal Democrats. Dunvant ComC 1983-. Swansea CC 1987-96, 1997-. Patron & Member, Management Cttee, Dunvant RFC XV. Chair & Trustee: Dunvant Unemployed & Social Centre. Member, Dunvant Working Men's Club. Hobbies: Watching Rugby & Cricket, Reading. Of Dunvant, Swansea.

NEWNES George: 1st Bart 1895 JP. Liberal MP Swansea Town 1906-1910, Newmarket 1885-95. **Sir George Newnes:** Born 13 March 1851 s of Revd T. Mold Newnes, Matlock. Congregationalist. Married 1875, Priscilla, d of Revd J. Hillyard. Educated Silcoates School; City of London School. Apprenticed to a fancy goods warehouse; manager, Manchester branch; wrote for various periodicals; Founded *Tit-Bits* 1881, *Review of Reviews* 1891, *The Strand Magazine* 1892, Westminster Gazette 1903 (connected too with *Strand Musical Magazine, World Wide Magazine, Picture Magazine, The Million & The Daily Courier*. Company Chair, George Newnes Ltd. publishers. Estate £174,153. Died 9 June 1910.

NEWTON-DUNN William Francis: BA1963 MA (Cantab) MBA (Fontainebleau) 1966. Conservative: Carmarthen Feb. 1974, Cardiff West Oct. 1974; MEP Lincolnshire 1979-94; Candidate: Lincolnshire & Humberside South 1994; MEP 1999. **Mr. William Newton-Dunn:** Born 3 October 1941, s of Lieut-Colonel Owen Frank Newton-Dunn & Barbara Brook (family originated from Kidwelly). Atheist. Married 1971, Anna Terez Arki, TV programme producer, 1s 1d. Educated Marlborough College; Gonville & Caius College, Cambridge (Natural Science), Member, College Rugby XV; Sorbonne (Language Diploma 1960); Insead Business School, Fontainebleau. Worked in Industry 1963-79. Chair, Vauxhall Conservative Political Centre. Chair: British Conservative MEPs 1993-94. Vice-Chair: EU Common Security & Defence Policy. Member: Cttee on Foreign Affairs,

Human Rights. Substitute: EU Cttee on Citizens' Freedoms. & Rights, Justice & Home Affairs, EU Delegation for Relations with Israel. Joined Liberal Democrats 21 November 2000. Interests: Europe. Hobbies: Writing. Languages: English, French, German. Of Navenby, Lincoln.

NIBLOCK Michael J: PhD (London). Conservative: Aberdare Feb. 1974. **Dr. Michael Niblock:** Born 1941. Educated Leighton Park School; London School of Economics. Worked at a Bermondsey settlement; Lecturer in Politics, Bristol University 1959-62; Head of Foreign Affairs Section, Conservative Central Office 1962-.

NICHOLAS Thomas Evan: Labour & Pacifist: Aberdare 1918. **Revd T. E. Nicholas:** Born Crymych 6 October 1879. Married Mary Alys Hopkins 2c. Educated Gwynfryn Academy, Ammanford; Work at 13: shop & "The Swan Inn", Crymych. Treherbert 1879. Welsh Independent Minister, Ordained 1901; Llandeilo 1901-03; Dodgeville USA 1903-04; Glais 1904-14; Llangybi 1914-18. Welsh Editor, *Merthyr Pioneer* 1911. Served apprenticeship and became a dentist at Aberystwyth 1918. Joined No-Conscription Fellowship 1914 and opposed the war. Summoned for sedition under DORA for his address at a Keir Hardie Memorial Service 1915 but the case was withdrawn; detained under DORA 1940. Organised Cardiganshire farm labourers in a strong union. Marxist. Joined Communist Party 1921. Winner of three bardic chairs. Languages: Welsh, English. Died 19 April 1971. *Books: T. E. Nicholas: Salmau Werin 1909, Cerddi Gwerin 1912, Cerddi Rhyddid 1914, Dros eich Gwlad 1920, Terfysgoedd Ddaear 1939, Llygad y Drws 1940, Canu'r Carchar 1942, Y Dyn a'r Gaib 1944, Dryllio'r Delwau 1941, 'Rwyn gweld o bell 1963.* Further Reading: *J. Roose Williams (edit), T. E. Nicholas, Proffwyd Sosialaeth a Bardd Gwrthryfel 1971; David Howell: Nicholas of Glais, The People's Champion; Kenneth O Morgan, Peace Movements in Wales 1899-1945; Meic Stephens (edit) Companion to Welsh Literature; Robert Pope, Building Jerusalem 1997, pages 41-48.*

NICHOLLS George: Conservative: Rhondda East 1950. **Mr. George Nicholls:** Born 1909. Methodist lay preacher. Married 2s. Educated elementary schools. Special constable 1939-45. Chair, Auxiliary Police Assn. Eastleigh BC.

NICHOLLS-JONES Paul: Liberal Democrat: South East Wales Euro 1989, Rhondda 1992; Independent: Cynon Valley B/E 1984; Independent (The Welshman): Chesterfield B/E 1984. **Mr. Paul Nicholls-Jones:** Born 8 April 1958. Unmarried. Educated Secondary Modern School; Open University. Ex-seaman, auxiliary nurse & fireman. Owner of burglar alarm company & insurance salesman. Of Gelli, Rhondda.

NICHOLSON Robert Douglas: Independent (Farmers' Support), Brecon & Radnorshire 2001. **Mr. Bob Nicholson:** Born 1937. Married. Educated Abertillery Mining & Technical Institute. Self-employed Instrument/Electrical Engineer. Worked for Rolls Royce (Aero) 1962-65. With truck design, power station, onshore gas terminal, Greater Cairo Wastewater Project & various water treatment & supply works 10 years etc. in Canada, Egypt, Europe & UK. Contact member, National Assn for Child Support Action (NCSA). Volunteer Therapist, Sarajevo. Involved with Epynt disaster protests (Foot & Mouth) 2001.

NORTHCOTT Peter James: People's Representative, South/West List 1999. **Mr. Peter Northcott:** Born Plymouth, 19 September 1950, s of Eric Janes Northcott, mason, & Peggy Anita Northcott, nurse. Atheist. Married 1975, Cecilia Margaret Northcott, 2s. Educated Grammar School, Art College. Graphic Designer. Interests: Currently disillusioned with the system. Hobbies: Running, Tai Chi, Travel. Of Swansea.

NUTT Ingrid Ann: Independent, Torfaen 1999. **Mrs. Ingrid Nutt:** Born Griffithstown, Pontypool, 30 August 1945, d of Harry Frederick Morgan, engine driver, & Bertha Morgan. Church of England. Married 1964 Carl Agar Nutt, glazier, 1s 1d (died). Shop assistant: Boots 1961. Wages Clerk, G. F. Howell 1962-66. Part times jobs from 1972. Partner with husband in glazing business & smallholder. Chair, Governors, Ysgol Onnen, Varteg, Executive Member, LATCH. Raised £25,000 for LATCH Llandough Hospital). Member: Pontypool Twinning Cttee, Gwent Construction Training Group. Vice-President, Pontypool Gleemen. President, Torfaen Amateur Athletics, Betty Eyes Singers. Owns smallholding. Of Cwmavon, Pontypool.

– O –

OAKLEY Archibald Benjamin Lloyd: Labour: Monmouth 1945, B/E 1945. **Mr. Lloyd Oakley:** Principal, Cheltenham private commercial college. Of Abergavenny.

OAKLEY Ian: BA (Durham). Conservative, South East List 1999, Newport East 2001. **Mr. Ian Oakley:** Born Solihull, 21 March 1977, son of Paul & Diane Oakley, brought up at Pontypool. Educated Rogiet Primary School, Newport, Rougemont School, Newport, Durham University, post-graduate student 2001. Financial Regulator. Chair: Monmouth Conservative Future, Durham University Conservative Assn. Contested local elections 1999. Interests: Economy, Economic Development. Hobbies: Cinema, Reading. Of Pontypool.

O'BRIEN Howard J: LlB (London) 1968. Liberal: Cardiff North 1970, Cardiff Northwest Feb. & Oct. 1974. **Mr. Howard O'Brien:** Born Cardiff, January 1947. Roman Catholic. Married Pamela O'Brien, 2s. Educated De La Salle School, Cardiff; St. Illtyd's College, Cardiff; London University (Vice-President, Student Representative Council). Solicitor 1972. Press Officer, Cardiff North Liberal Assn. Vice-Chair, Welsh Young Liberals. Member: Liberal Party National Executive, Welsh Liberal Party Executive. Of Rhiwbina, Cardiff.

O'KEEFE Barrie: Conservative, Blaenau Gwent 2003. **Mr. Barrie O'Keefe:** Born Merthyr Tydfil 28 September 1949, s of Desmond O'Keefe, building worker & Lily O'Keefe, cleaner. Roman Catholic. Married 1973, Lynda O'Keefe, 1s 1d. Fish & Chip Restaurant owner 1982- (Blaina 1980-94, Abergavenny 1995-). Chair, Gilwern Conservative Branch. Contested Llanelli PC 2002. Interests: Plight of Self-Employed, Very Small Businesses. Hobbies: Golf, Reading. Of Gilwern (1995).

OLIVER Raymond D: Liberal: Merthyr Tydfil 1979. **Mr. Ray Oliver:** Born Newport. Married.

OLIVER William Albert: Liberal Democrat: Newport East 1992. **Mr. Will Oliver:** Born 21 October, 1935. Married 1d. Educated, Sir Joseph Williamson Mathematics School, Rochester; RN Dockyards Technical College. Naval Designer at Chatham. Submarine & Warship Designer. European Community Official, Luxembourg 1970-89.

Chair: Euro Control Staff Cttee. Secretary: Euro-control Solidarity Fund. Member, Institute of Professional Civil Servants. Software Consultant. Of Pwllmeyric, Chepstow.

OGWEN Alun – see JONES: A. O.

ONIONS Alfred: JP (Mon). Labour MP: Caerphilly 1918-. **Mr. Alfred Onions:** Born St. George's, Shropshire, 30 October 1858, s of Jabez Onions, miner. Methodist. Married 1887, Sarah Ann Dix, miner's daughter, 3s 1d. Educated, St. George's National School (left at 10); evening classes at 20. Staffordshire Miner 1871; Black Vein Colliery, Risca 1883-83; Rhondda. Abercarn timberman (2 years). Checkweighman, Abercarn 1887. Secretary, Monmouthshire District 1888. Miners' Agent, Rhymney Valley 1898. Treasurer SWMF1898-. Member: MFGB Executive 1904-10; TUC Parliamentary Cttee. Mynyddislwyn School Board 1888-; Bedwellty School Board 1899-; Risca UDC, 1st Chair. Monmouthshire CC 18 years, Alderman 1919, Chair 1919-20. Of Tredegar. Estate £3267. Died 6 July 1921.

OPIK Lembit: BA (Bristol) 1987. Liberal Democrat MP: Montgomery 1997-. Candidate: Newcastle upon Tyne Central, 1992; Northumbria Euro 1994. **Mr. Lembit Opik:** Born Bangor, Co Down 2 March 1965, s of Uno Opik & Liivi Vedo, refugees from Soviet Estonia in 1950s. Educated, Royal Belfast Academical Institute; Bristol University (Philosophy); President, Student Representative Council 1985. Global Human Resources With Proctor & Gamble (Brand Assistant/Asst. Brand Manager 1988-91; Corporate Training & Organisation Development Manager 1991-96; Global human resources training manager 1996-97. Contested Newcastle upon Tyne CC 1990. Vice-Chair, Newcastle Liberal Democrats. Member: Liberal Democrat Party Federal Executive 1991. Deputy Chair: Liberal Democrats Northern Region 1993-96; English Liberal Democrats 1995-96. Member: Greenpeace; Charter 88; Amnesty International; Druridge Bay Campaign. Member: All Party Friends of the Bahai Group, Greenpeace, Charter 88. Hobbies: Astronomy, gliding, cinema, motorcycling. Of Newtown.

ORCHARD Arthur John: CBE 1922 JP (Glam) 1922. Conservative: Rhondda East 1922. **Mr. Arthur Orchard:** Born Tredegar 1874. Anglican. Married. Educated, Rhondda elementary schools.

Publican, Porth Hotel, & Farmer. Rhondda UDC 1910-. Chair: Rhondda Of Porth. Estate £30,592. Died 3 November 1924.

ORMSBY-GORE William George Arthur, 4th Baron Harlech 1876: KG 1947 PC 1927 GCMG 1938 Hon. LLD (Wales) 1947 Hon. DCL (Oxon) 1937 JP DL (Co. Leitrem) BA 1908 MA (Oxon) FRGS. Conservative MP: Denbigh District 1910-18, Stafford 1918-38. **Rt. Hon. William Ormsby-Gore:** Born 11 April 1885, s of 3rd Baron & Lady Mary Ethel Gordon, d of Marquess of Huntly. Succeeded 1938. Married 1913, Lady Beatrice Cecil, d of Marquess of Salisbury, 5c. Educated, Eton; New College, Oxford. Landowner (58,538 acres in 11 estates in 5 counties and in Ireland). Chair, Bank of West Africa; Midland Bank. Director, Union Corporation. Army 1914-18, Lieutenant 1914, Captain 1915; Intelligence Officer, Arab Bureau 1916. PPS 1917-18. Political Officer, Palestine 1918. Member, British Delegation, Peace Conference (Middle East Section) 1918. Under-Secretary, Colonies 1922-23 1924-29. Postmaster General 1931. First Commissioner of Works 1931-36. Secretary of State, Colonies 1936-38. North East Regional Commissioner, Civil Defence 1939-40. High Commissioner, South Africa, Basutoland & Swaziland 1941-44. President, National Museum of Wales 1937. Chair: Advisory Council, Victoria & Albert Museum 1933; Governors, School of Oriental & African Studies 1938-41. Trustee, British Museum 1937-; National Gallery 1927-34, 1936-41; Tate Gallery 1931-38, 1945-53. Lord Lieutenant of Merioneth 1938-57. Constable of Harlech Castle 1938-; Caernarfon Castle 1946-. Pro-Chancellor, University of Wales 1945-57. Of London & Glyn Talsarnau. Merioneth. Died 14 February 1964. *Books: W. G. A. Ormsby-Gore, Welsh Disestablishment and Disendowment 1912, Florentine Sculptors of the Fifteenth Century 1930, Guide to the Montegna Cartoons at Hampton Court 1935, Guide to the Ancient Monuments of England in 3 vols.*

O'ROURKE Hayley Emma: Socialist Labour Party, South/East List 2003. **Ms. Hayley O'Rourke:** Lives with partner, 1d. Youth Worker. Interests: Family Value, Crime, Education, Local Economies, Transport. Of Crumlin.

ORSI Giovanni Francesco: Liberal Democrat, Pontypridd 1999. **Mr. Gianni Orsi:** Born Pontypridd 6 April 1958, son of Italo Louis Orsi & Maria Orsi, restaurateurs. Roman Catholic. Married 1989, Linda Romana Margaritolli, flight attendant, 1s 1d. Educated Belmont Abbey, Hereford; Polytechnic of Wales. Caterer (run family business since 1982). Contested Mid-Glam CC 1986, Rhondda-Cynon-Taf BC 1999. Languages: English, Italian. Hobbies: Cars/Horse Racing. Of Llantwit Fardre.

ORWIG Dafydd: BA (Wales). Plaid Cymru: Caernarfon 1959. **Mr. Dafydd Orwig:** Born September 1928. Dropped *Jones* from name. Presbyterian Church of Wales. Educated Brynrefail Grammar School; University of Wales, Aberystwyth. Teacher (Geography), Blaenau Ffestiniog Grammar School, Dyffryn Ogwen Grammar School. Lecturer in Geography, Bangor Normal College. 1st President, Plaid Cymru Youth Section. Caernarfonshire CC 1973-; Gwynedd CC 1974 (Chair, Education Cttee 1985-87). 1st Chair, Reconstituted Gwynedd CC 1996. Chair: European Board of Lesser-Used Languages; Welsh Books Council (1994); WJEC Language & Culture Cttee; Teaching Welsh to Adults Cttee. Of Bethesda. Languages: Welsh, English. Died 10 November 1996. *Books: Dafydd Orwig (edit) Yr Atlas Gymraeg.* Further Reading: *Ieuan Wyn, Cofio Dafydd Orwig.*

O'SHAUGHNESSY Nicholas Jackson: MA (Oxon) MPhil (London) MBA (St. Columba NY) PhD (Cantab). Conservative: Swansea East 1983. Professor **Nicholas O'Shaughnessy:** Born Derby 26 June 1954, s of Professor John O'Shaughnessy, Columbia University NY, & Marjorie O'Shaughnessy, teacher. Anglican. Educated Bedford School; Sorbonne University, Paris; London University; Oxford University (President, Oxford Union 1978); Columbia University NY; Cambridge University. Analyst. American Economic Foundation 1980. Lecturer, UWIST. Lecturer, Cambridge & Fellow, Hughes Hall. Professor of Marketing, Keele University. Informal Adviser, Prime Minister John Major. Interests: Higher Education. *Books: Nicholas O'Shaughnessy: The Phenomenon of Political Marketing (1990), Politics & Propaganda: Weapons of Mass Destruction (Michigan); The Idea of a University Revisited (1992).*

OSMOND Osi Rhys: MEd (Wales). Plaid Cymru: Pembroke 1983, 1987. **Mr. Osi Rhys Osmond:** Born Blackwood 1943. Married Linda Osmond, 2s. Educated, Newport College of Art; Cardiff College of Art; University of Wales, Cardiff. Artist. Art Teacher at Narberth. Lecturer, Carmarthen College of Art. Carmarthenshire CC B/E 2001. Languages; Learned Welsh, English. Of Clunderwen (1983), then Llansteffan.

O'SULLIVAN Richard M. S: Conservative: Ogmore 1983. **Mr. Richard O'Sullivan:** Born 1956. Educated, Bloxham School, Banbury; Christ Church, Oxford; Inns of Temple School of Law. Barrister 1988. Investment Consultant. Lambeth BC 1982-. Of London.

O'SULLIVAN Taran Mina: Respect Unity Coalition, Wales Euro 2004. **Ms. Taran O'Sullivan:** Secretary, Cardiff Stop the War Coalition. Organiser & political activist. Of Pentrebane, Cardiff.

O'TOOLE Carole Georgina Tetley: BA (Wales) MA (Liverpool). Liberal Democrat, Wrexham 2001, North List 2003. **Mrs. Carole O'Toole:** Born Cardiff 5 December 1942, d of Landon Ronald Owens, shop proprietor, & Florence Victoria Owens, clerical worker. Church of England. Married 1975, Antony James O'Toole, barrister, 1s 1d. Educated grammar school; University of Wales, Bangor; University of Liverpool DipVG Diploma in Social Work. Adult Literacy Tutor. Social Worker. Chair: Wrexham Liberal Democrats. Acton ComC. Member: Amnesty International, WEA. Interests: Education, Social Welfare. Hobbies: Philosophy. Languages; English, some French. Of Wrexham.

OUBRIDGE Graham Edwin: Green Party: Carmarthen 1987, Swansea West 1983, South/West List 1999. **Mr. Brig Oubridge:** Born London, 20 July 1951, son of Raymond Barrington Oubridge, radiographer, & Marjorie Irene Giddins, teacher. 2s 2d. Educated Latymer Upper School, Hammersmith; Imperial College, London. Smallholder (160 acres) 1979 & founder of its Tipi village of 15 adults & 50 children (the longest established & largest eco-village in UK). Company Director (Festival Organiser). Joined Ecology Party 1979, Co-Chair: UK Green Party 1986-88. Llanfynydd ComC. 1987-91. Peace activist. Member: CND Cymru, Nuclear Free Wales, National Council for Civil Liberties. Interests: Sustainable Development, Planning, Civil Liberties. Hobbies: Watching rugby.

OWEN Albert: BA (York). Labour, Ynys Môn, 1999; MP Ynys Môn 2001-. **Mr. Albert Owen:** Born Bangor 1959, s of William Owen & Doreen Woods. Married 1983, Angela Margaret Magee, 2d. Educated Llangainoch Primary School; Holyhead Comprehensive School; Coleg Harlech; York University (Politics). Merchant Seaman 1976-92. Port worker at Holyhead 10 years. Student 1992-97. Manager, Advice & Training Centre for the Unemployed 1997-2001. Director, *Digartref Mon.* Chair: Llangain Village Hall; Holy Island Millennium Group; Ynys Môn New Deal Forum; Member: 1999 National Eisteddfod Appeal Cttee; Holyhead-Dun Laoghaire Link. Governor, Coleg Harlech. Languages: Welsh, English. Of Llaiangoch, Holyhead.

OWEN Ann: MA (Wales) 2001. Plaid Cymru, Alyn & Deeside & North List 1999. **Mrs. Ann Owen:** Born Bangor, 30 July 1959, d of William Corbett Thomas, welder, & Mary Wyn Thomas, nurse. Presbyterian Church of Wales. Married Gruffydd Siôn Owen, trust manager, 1s 2d. Nurse 1977, Midwife, health visitor. Professional Officer, MSF (Queensferry based union for community nurses and health visitors in Wales) 1997-. Chair: Dwylo Da Cyf. (community co-operative providing nursery and childcare). Director, Antur Nantlle cyf. (enterprise agency promoting economic development), Director/Chair: Dwylo Da cyf, Cymad cyf. Director, Plaid Cymru Equal Opportunities 2001-, Social Service Policy Director 2001. School governor. Trustee: Gwynedd Children & Families Forum. Member: Gwynedd Early Years Partnership. Chair: Wales Professional Nursing Forum; Welsh Nursing & Midwifery Society. Interests: Community Economic Development, Health 7 Social Services. Hobbies: walking, reading. Languages: Welsh, English. Of Pontllyfni, Caernarfon.

OWEN Arthur H. – see HUMPHREYS OWEN: A. E.

OWEN Charles Edward Jones: JP DL (Merioneth) MA (Oxon). Conservative: Merioneth 1895. **Mr. Charles Owen:** Born 1857, s of Revd Edward Owen & Catherine, d of Hugh Jones, Hengwrt Ucha. Anglican. Married Mary Maitland, d of John Vaughan, Nannau (qv). Educated, Eton; Christ Church, Oxford. Landowner. High Sheriff of Merioneth1890. Merioneth CC 1892-. Of Hengwrt Ucha, Dolgellau & Aberhiraeth Hall, Cemaes, Mont. Estate £34,887. Died Great Western Hotel, Paddington 25 February 1906.

OWEN David: MBE 1947 JP (Carms). Labour: Carmarthen 1951. **Mr. David Owen:** Born April 1895. Married. Educated, elementary schools. Started work at 14. Engine driver. Branch secretary, ASLEF 12 years. Secretary, Carmarthen CLP. Chair: South West Wales Rivers Board. Member: Council for Wales. Carmarthen BC 1931- (Leader, Labour Group), Alderman, Mayor. Languages: Welsh, English. Of Carmarthen.

OWEN David Ieuan: BSc (Essex) 1980 BSc (Wales) 1983. Plaid Cymru: Gower B/E 1982, Neath 1983. **Mr. Ieuan Owen:** Born Brynaman 1953. Married Diana (orthoptist) 3c. Educated Swansea Valley; University of Essex; University of Wales, Swansea (Economics). Shopkeeper & Owner, Coal Retail Business. Company Secretary, Llanelli family contractor company. Member, Plaid Cymru Executive. President, University of Wales, Swansea, Athletic Union. Chair: Lliw Valley Rights & Advice Training Services Group. Llangiwg ComC. 1977-. Member: Brynaman RFC. Languages: Welsh, English. Of Pontardawe.

OWEN David James: Liberal: Neath Oct. 1974. **Mr. David Owen:** Born Neath April 1930. Married 4c. Educated Neath Grammar School; Queen Elizabeth Grammar School, Carmarthen; University of Wales, Aberystwyth. Farmer 1954-. Member: NFU Cardiganshire Cttee; Welsh Council, Co-operative Movement. Chair, local farmers'

Co-operative. Languages: Welsh, English. Of Bronant, Ceredigion.

OWEN David J: BSc (Liverpool). Plaid Cymru: Delyn 1987. **Mr. David Owen:** Born Dyffryn Clwyd 5 December, 1949. Married 4c. Educated Denbigh High School; Liverpool University. Quality Assurance Engineer, Rockware plc. Languages: Welsh, English. Of, Mold.

OWEN David Philip: Conservative: Llanelli 1950; Liberal: East Surrey 1945. **Mr. Philip Owen:** Born North Wales 1920, (gs of poet, Ceiriog). Army 1939-45. Accountant. Company Director (opened silk screening factory at Llanelli). Cttee Member, Textile Institute. Of Surrey.

OWEN Edward Teilo: Labour: Carmarthen B/E August 1924, 1924. **Revd E. T. Owen:** Born Eglwysfach 14 February 1876, labourer's son. Married 1911 Sarah Ann (Sally) Tompkins, Llandeilo, 2s. Educated elementary school; Glamorgan miner for a while; Machynlleth Grammar School; Richmond Methodist College. Welsh Independent Minister, Ordained 1906: Battersea Rise 1906-10; Saron, Llangeler 1910-25; Siloh, Cwmgwrach 1925-49. Chair, South Glamorgan Welsh Independent Assn 1935. Founder-President, Carmarthen Constituency Labour Party. Fined £20 under Emergency Act, 1926 Strike. Languages: Welsh, English. Died 25 January 1956.

OWEN Eric Cyril Hammersley: LlB (Liverpool) 1968. SDP/Alliance: Alyn & Deeside 1987; Cheshire West Euro 1984. **Mr. Eric Owen:** Born Gresford 7 December 1946, miner's son. Anglican Lay Reader. Married Diana, 2c. Educated Grove Park School, Wrexham; Liverpool University. Lecturer, Southport Technical College-1969. Barrister, Lincolns Inn 1969. Author. Chair SDP Christian Forum; Vice-Chair, SDP Wales. Plaid Cymru PPC 1977. ComC 1983-86. Drafted constitution for Wales SDP. Languages: Learned Welsh, English. Of Wrexham.

OWEN Geraint Degwel: Plaid Cymru, Aberavon 2003. **Mr. Geraint Owen:** Born Morriston Hospital, 6 March 1966, son of Degwel Owen, senior lecturer, & Alma Marilyn Owen, teacher. Baptist. Married Annette Lee Owen, airworker, 1s. Educated Gowerton Comprehensive School; University of Wales, Swansea. Teacher & Professional Actor. Head of Drama Department, Neath/Port Talbot College. Interests: Health, Community, Economic Development. Blaenrhondda ComC. Chair: Neath Constituency Plaid Cymru. Hobbies: Walking Dalmatians, Reading. Languages: Welsh, English.

OWEN Glyndwr Edward: Plaid Cymru: Aberdare Feb. & Oct. 1974. **Mr. Glyn Owen:** Born Mountain Ash 1932, s of Edward Owen, miner. Married Jean George 1s. Educated, Miskin Senior School. Railway worker 1947-50. RAF 1952-54. Merchant Navy 1954-. Miner. Joint Owner with wife of a clothes shop. Plaid Cymru Regional Director, East Glamorgan. Aberdare election agent 1970. Aberdare UDC 1969-74. Aberdare DC 1974-. Glamorgan CC 1971-74. Mid-Glam CC 1973-. Retired from politics 1985 because of his wife's health. Languages: Learned Welsh, English. Of Cwmbach, Aberdare.

OWEN Gomer: Liberal: West Flint 1955. **Mr. Gomer Owen:** Born early 1880s. Retired bank clerk. Took part in every election since 1910. Secretary, West Flint Liberal Assn. Stood at the last minute when the association decided not to put up a candidate.

OWEN Goronwy: Kt 1944 DSO 1916 JP DL (Caerns) MA (Wales). Liberal MP Caernarfonshire 1923-31; Ind.L. 1931-45; National Liberal Candidate, South Derbyshire 1922. **Colonel, Sir Goronwy Owen:** Born Aberystwyth 22 June 1881, s of Abraham Owen & Margaret Sylvanus Williams. Married 1925, Mrs. Gladwyn Owen-Jones. Educated Ardwyn School, Aberystwyth; University of Wales, Aberystwyth. Teacher 1903-14. RWF 1914-18, Captain 1914, Major 1916, Colonel 1946. Barrister, Grays Inn 1919. Caernarfonshire CC Alderman 1945. High Sheriff of Caernarfonshire 1950-51. Freeman of Conway 1943. Chair: Agricultural Wages Cttee, Anglesey, Caernarfonshire, Merioneth & Montgomery; Caernarfonshire & Anglesey Territorial Army Assn. Liberal Chief Whip & Comptroller of the Household 1931. Chair, Gwynedd Police Authority 1955-56. Languages: Welsh, English. Of Llanrug. Died 26 September 1963.

OWEN Gwilym G. Vaughan: OBE FOB. Conservative: Clwyd South West 1992, Ynys Môn 1997. **Mr. Gwilym Owen:** Born 13 December 1938. Married Susan, fashion model, 2c. Educated Tywyn Grammar School. Business Consultant. Ex-Midland Bank Area Manager, Cardiff: earlier at Caernarfon, Oswestry. Financial Secretary, National Eisteddfod. President, Cardiff Council of Bankers. Member, Welsh Language Board; Secretary of State for Wales advisory group; Hon. Treasurer, Celtic Film & TV Associates. National Eisteddfod winner. Hobbies: Rugby, Cricket, Football, Gardening. Languages: Welsh, English. Of Oswestry.

OWEN Gwynfor: Plaid Cymru, North List 1999. **Mr. Gwynfor Owen:** Of Tremadog, Porthmadog.

OWEN Henry: JP (Merioneth). Liberal Unionist: Merioneth 1892. **Mr. Henry Owen:** Born 1856. Nonconformist. Tenant Farmer. Languages: Welsh,

English. Of Dolgoed, Caerns. Died, Corris, 25 February 1895 (found dead in bed at Slaters' Arms).

OWEN Lyn: United Socialists, North List 1999. **Ms. Lyn Owen:** Of Wrexham.

OWEN Peter H: BA (London) CertEd (Wales). Labour & Co-operative: Cardiff North West 1979; Weston super Mare Oct. 1974. **Mr. Peter Owen:** Born May 1927. Married 2c. Educated Penarth Grammar School; Trinity College, Carmarthen; London University. Royal Marines 1945-47. Senior Lecturer in Law & Liberal Studies, Rumney College, Cardiff. Chair, Cardiff Branch, ATTI 1969. Member: NATFHE; Cardiff Trades Council. Cardiff CC 1973-76 (Deputy Chair, Liaison & Tattoo Cttees). Rugby player: Old Penarthians XV; Trinity College, XV; Wheatsheaf XV 1949-51. Member, Whitchurch Cricket XI. Association Football Referee. Welsh Rugby Union Coach. Of Rhiwbina, Cardiff.

OWEN Philip C: Liberal/Alliance: Merthyr Tydfil & Rhymney 1983. **Mr. Philip Owen:** Born 1952. Educated Builth Wells Comprehensive School; Christ College, Brecon; Durham University; Cambridge (Cambridge Rowing Blue; Duke of Edinburgh Award). Business Manager. Joint Founder: Durham University Liberal Club, Rugby Young Liberals; Brecon Area Organiser, Liberal Party 1979-82. Of Beaufort.

OWEN Philip Loscombe Wintringham: QC 1953 TD 1950 JP (Mont) 1949 Cheshire 1961 MA (Oxon). Conservative: Montgomery 1945. **Captain Philip Owen:** Born 10 January 1920, s of Rt. Hon. Sir Wintringham Stable & Lucie Haden Freeman; changed name by deed poll 1942. Roman Catholic, converted from Anglicanism 1944. Married 1949, Elizabeth Jane, d of Lewis Trelawney Widdicombe of Effingham, 3s. Educated Winchester; Christ Church, Oxford. Army 1939-45, Captain. Barrister Middle Temple 1949. Deputy Chair, Quarter Sessions: Montgomeryshire 1959-71; Cheshire 1961-71. Recorder of Merthyr Tydfil 1971; Crown Court Recorder 1971-82; Leader, Wales & Chester Circuit 1975-77. Chair: Advisory Board, Misuse of Drugs Act 1974. Legal Assessor: General Medical Council 1970, General Dental Council 1970-; Royal Institute of Chartered Secretaries 1973-. Director, Swansea City AFC 1976-87. Vice-President, Montgomery Conservative Assn. President: Montgomeryshire Society 1974-75. Trustee & Cttee Member, Young Musicians Symphony Orchestra. Of London & Llanbrynmair.

OWEN Robert Roy: Conservative: Merioneth Feb. & Oct. 1974. **Mr. Roy Owen:** Born Tremadoc, November 1941. Educated, John Bright Grammar School, Llandudno; Open University. Clerk, Midland Bank. Accident underwriter, NFU & Avon Assurance Companies 5 years. Manager, Quinton Hazell, Colwyn Bay. Treasurer, Conway Conservative Assn. School governor. Member: Post & Telecommunications Panel CBI; British Institute of Management. Conway BC, Mayor. Aberconwy DC. Languages: Welsh, English. Of Deganwy.

OWEN William John: Liberal: Newport 1950, 1951. **Mr. John Owen:** Born Carmarthen 1922. Married. Educated Queen Elizabeth Grammar School, Carmarthen; University of Wales Law School, Swansea; Inns of Court Law School. Barrister, Lincolns Inn. Town Clerk of Carmarthen. RAF 1940-45, Flight Lieutenant. Languages; Welsh, English. Of Llanelli.

OWEN-JONES David Roderic: LlB LLM (London) FRSA. Liberal: Carmarthen Feb. & Oct. 1974, Rugby & Kenilworth 1983. **Mr. Roderic Owen-Jones:** Born Caernarfon 16 March 1949, s of John Eryl Owen-Jones OBE & Mabel Clara, d of Grant McIlvride, Aimer, Rajputana. Educated Caernarfon Grammar School; Llandovery College; University College, London. President, London University Liberal Federation. Barrister Lincolns Inn 1972. Legal Assistant, European Commission on Human Rights 1972. Acting Metropolitan Magistrate. Executive Member, London Liberal Party. Member: Howard League for Penal Reform; Assn of Liberal Lawyers; Council of the Hon. Society of Cymmrodorion. Contested Wandsworth BC 1982. Languages: Welsh, English. Of London.

OWENS Richard Manning Sims: Liberal: Swansea East B/E 1963, Gower Oct. 1974. **Mr. Richard Owens:** Born Llansamlet 1922. Married 2c. Educated, Glanmor Grammar School, Swansea; Swansea College of Art; Cardiff Technical College. RAF 1939-45. Local government planning assistant 1945-48. Building Surveyor & Estate Agent 1958. Resigned as PPC for Brecon & Radnor, August 1964, to set up a company to manufacture Canadian style houses. Hotelier, Glanafon Park Hotel, Pontardawe. Vice-President, Pontardawe RAF Assn. Secretary, Glamorgan Young Farmers Clubs. Member: Glamorgan Agricultural Executive Cttee, Executive, South Wales Tourism Cttee, Post Office Advisory Cttee. President: Swansea Junior Chamber of Commerce. Secretary, Welsh Liberal Candidates Assn Languages: Welsh, English.

– P –

PADLEY Walter Ernest: Labour MP. Ogmore 1950-79; ILP Acton B/E 1943. **Mr. Walter Padley:** Born, Chipping Norton, 24 July 1916, s of Ernest Padley, grocery clerk. Married 1942, Sylvia Elsie Wilson 2c. Educated Chipping Norton Grammar School; Ruskin College, Oxford. Clerk with CWS. Joined Distributive Workers Union 1933. President USDAW 1948-64. Joined ILP 1932, Member, ILP National Executive 1941-46. Joined Labour Party 1946; Member, Labour NEC 1956- Chair 1966-67, Chair, Overseas Sub-Cttee. Minister of State, Foreign Office 1964-67. Of London. Died 15 April 1984. *Books: W. E. Padley: The Economic Problem of the Peace 1944, Am I My Brother's Keeper 1945, Britain: Pawn or Power? 1947, USSR; Empire or Free Union 1948.*

PAGE Norah: Liberal Democrat, South/West List 1999. **Mrs. Norah Page:** Born Stroud, 21 December 1952, d of Frederick James Theyer, gardener/handyman, & Viva King Theyer. Church of England. Educated: Heolgam Secondary Modern School, Bridgend; Bridgend Girls Grammar School. Married 2s divorced. Company Secretary & Director. Secretary: Bridgend Liberal Democrats, Agent 2001. Porthcawl TC. Bridgend BC (Chair: Education & Leisure & Community Services Scrutiny Cttee). Hobbies: Life Saving, involved in many charity organizations. Of Nottage, Porthcawl.

PAGE-HARRIS Martha Jayne: Socialist Labour, Mid & West list 1999. **Mrs. Martha Page-Harris:** d of Peter & Trisha Bowen (qv) & Miriam Bowen (qv). Of Llandissilio, Clynderwen.

PAICE James Edward Thornton: Conservative: Caernarfon 1979; MP Cambridgeshire South-East 1987-. **Mr. James Paice:** Born, 24 April 1949, s of Edward & Winifred Paice. Married, 1973, Ava , d of Stuart & Sarah Paterson, 2s. Educated, Framlingham College, Suffolk; Essex College of Agriculture (National Diploma in Agriculture 1970). Farm Manager 1970-73. Stock Breeder & Branding Contractor. Training Officer, Framlingham Farmers Ltd 1979-82; Training Manager 1982-85, Non-executive director 1985, Director 1989-94. Chair, Eye Young Conservatives 1976-78. Treasurer, Eye Conservative Assn. Governor, Framlingham College. Suffolk Coastal DC 1976-87 (Chair 1982-83). Public Affairs Adviser, Dixons plc. Parliamentary Adviser, National Training Federation. PPS 1989-95. Jt Sec Conservative MPs Employment Cttee 1988-89; Member, Select Cttee Employment 1987-90. Chair, All Party Racing & Bloodstock Cttee 1992-. PPS 1989-94. Under-Secretary: Education 1994-95, Education & Employment 1995-7. Opposition Spokesman on Agriculture 1997-. Hobbies: Windsurfing, Shooting, Racing.

PAINTSELL Wendy: Forward Wales Party. Wales Euro 2004. **Ms. Wendy Paintsell:** Journalist & broadcaster. National Secretary, Forward Wales Party. Contested Wrexham CBC 2004. Of Wrexham.

PALFREY Colin F: JP 1975 BA MA MEd PhD. Plaid Cymru Cardiff Northwest Feb. & Oct. 1974, Cardiff North 1992 1997. **Dr. Colin Palfrey:** Born, Cardiff 8 July 1939. Married, 2d. Educated, Whitchurch Grammar School, University College, London, Kings College, London. Adult Education Lecturer, Open University. Tutor, Alltyrun Technical College, Newport. Education Consultant. Research Officer, Gofal Housing Trust at School of Health, University of Wales, Swansea. Co-founder, Swansea Poverty Action Network (research group to improve mental health services in the community). Poet & classical guitarist. Caerphilly UDC Dec. 1970-74. Rhymney Valley DC 1974-. Caerphilly CC. Plaid Spokesman on Home Affairs. Member: Gwent Probation Cttee, Bench Liaison Cttee.

PALMER: David L: BSc. Natural Law Party: Cardiff North 1992; Gravesham 1997. **Mr. David Palmer:** Born Southall 24 December 1961, s of Leslie Palmer, costs accountant, & Joyce Mary Bessie Sizer, nurse. Anglican. 1c. Engineer: British Aerospace, Royal Aircraft Establishment, Aberporth, Race Electrics, Llantrisant. Mahambo Foundation 1989-92. Joined Natural Law Party 1992. Hobbies: Transcendental Meditation & Yoga, Flying.

PALMER John Kelvin: Vote 2 Stop the War, South Central List 2003. **Group Captain Kel Palmer:** Born Wilmslow, Cheshire, 10 June 1930, son of John Kelvie Stoddart-Palmer, market gardener, & Ellen Stoddart-Palmer, photographer. Baptist. Married (1) 2s (2) 1997 Rosemary Yvonne Palmer, 4c. Educated Manchester Grammar School. RAF 1946-83: technical apprentice 1946; RAF College; Staff College, Flying College. Exchange Officer USAF, Texas & Vietnam War;

Group Captain Kel Palmer.

served in Ministry of Defence Directorate of Operational Requirements; Director, Department of Air Warfare; Chief of Nuclear Plans, SHAPE. On retirement joined Defence Industry to assume responsibility for major programmers. Chair: Youth Facility, Community Trust Partnership; Residents' Assn. Secretary, Welsh Tenants Assn. Hobbies: Football, Rugby, Writing Crime Fiction, Travel, Flying. Languages: English, French, German. Of Mountain Ash.

PALMER Roger Graham – see GRAHAM PALMER Roger.

PARDOE-THOMAS Bertie: JP (Mon). Independent Democrat: South Mon B/E 1917, Newport 1918. **Mr. Bertie Pardoe-Thomas:** Born, Newport 23 July 1866, s of Revd John Pardoe-Thomas & Ann French, 3c. Nonconformist. Married, 1903 Rose Ann Turner (Died 1928) 1d. Educated, Chandlers School, Newport. Shipowner: Chair, Pardoe-Thomas & Co, White Cross Line. President, Newport Chamber of Commerce 1919. Master, Worshipful Company of Glaziers. Member: Bristol Channel Shipowners' Assn. Newport BC. Chair: Newport Harbour Commissioner. Of Newport. Estate £45,436. Died 14 March 1937.

PARISH Neil Quentin Gordon: Conservative: Torfaen 1997; MEP South West England 2000. **Mr. Neil Parish:** Born, Bridgwater, 26 May 1956, farmer's son. Married, Sue (language teacher) 2c. Educated, Brynmore School; Taunton Technical College. Farmer (3000 acre family farm) 1972 & Businessman. Somerset CC 1984-93, Sedgemoor DC 1983-95, Group Deputy-Leader 1990-95. Chair, Pawlett PC. School Governor. Chair, Bridgwater Conservative Assn 1997-99 (Deputy Chair: 1995-97). Member: Bridgwater NFU. Member: Euro Parliament Agriculture Cttee. Deputy Group Whip. Hobbies: Music; Swimming. Of Pawlett, Bridgwater.

PARKER Neil Martin: BA (Durham) 1993, MscEcon (Wales). Liberal Democrat, Monmouth 2001. **Mr. Neil Parker:** Born Portsmouth, 12 January 1971. Partner Helen. Educated, Kings College, Taunton; Durham University (Spanish); University of Wales, Cardiff (European Politics). Army 1989. Languages teacher: Christ College, Brecon 1995-98, Monmouth School, 1998. Interests: Education, Health. Transport. Hobbies: Sports, Music. Of Wyesham nr Monmouth.

PARKER Stanley C: Conservative: Ebbw Vale 1945. **Mr. Stanley Parker:** Born, Cardiff. Financial Journalist 1930-39. Agent-Organiser, North Paddington Conservative Assn 1935. RAF 1939-45 (Middle East 1940-45), Flight Lieutenant RAFVR. Investment Trust Manager 1945. Member, Glamorgan Wanderers Rugby XV.

PARRI Brynach: BA DipEd (Wales). Plaid Cymru, Brecon & Radnorshire 2001, 2003. **Mr. Brynach Parri:** Born Brecon 20 August 1944, miner's son. Married. Educated, Brecon Boys Grammar School; University of Wales, Cardiff (German & Swedish) & Bangor; Hamburg University. Teacher (Jersey, Flintshire, Carmarthen, Aberaeron, Cologne, Llanharri); joint owner of Teifi passenger boat service. Runs translation service in European & Business Languages (transferred from Cardiff to Brecon 1995). Teacher of Welsh at Coleg Powys. Member: Institute of Linguists. Cttee Member: Brecon Museum; Brecon Welsh Society. Lampeter BC. Interests: Tourism; Education; Europe; Local Government. Hobbies: Reading, Philately, Local History, Poetry, Walking. Languages: Welsh, English, German, Swedish. Of Brecon.

PARRI Meurig: Plaid Cymru: Cardiff West 1983. **Mr. Meurig Parri:** Born, Caerleon 1967. Lives with partner 2c. Educated, England. Army, Commissioned in RAF Regiment. Returned to Wales 1973. Accountant, Oxfam. Administration Manager, Chapter Arts Centre, Cardiff. Clerk, St. Thomas worker's co-operative. Plaid Cymru Organiser, Pontypridd. Chair: Cardiff Voluntary Social Services 1970-74. Member: CND Cymru; TGWU; War on Want, Cymdeithas yr Iaith. Contested West Glam CC (St. Thomas) 1997.

PARRY Colin: BSc (Wales). Labour: Ynys Môn 1987. **Mr. Colin Parry:** Born, 3 October 1939, (brother of Glenys Kinnock MEP qv). Married, 3c. Educated, Holyhead Comprehensive School; University of Wales, Cardiff. Research Chemist, Canada 6 years; Production Controller, Anglesey Aluminium-1984. Owner, village supermarket 1984. Languages: Welsh, English.

PARRY Gordon Samuel David, Baron Parry of Neyland: 1975 DL (Dyfed) 1993 DipAd

(Liverpool) FRSA. Labour: Monmouth 1959, Pembroke 1970, Feb. & Oct. 1974. **Mr. Gordon Parry:** Born, Molleston, Narberth, 30 November 1925, s of Revd Thomas Lewis Parry, Baptist Minister & Anne Evans. Married, 1948, Glenys Catherine, d of Jack Leslie Incledon 1d. Educated, Pembroke Dock Grammar School; Trinity College, Carmarthen; Liverpool University. Teacher 1946-62; Student, Liverpool Institute of Education 1962-65; Warden, Pembrokeshire Teachers Centre 1965-67. Neyland UDC 1948-65, Chair 1955. Director: Milford Dock Co (Chair 1984-91; President 1991-). Chair: Marine Leisure Co 1984. Director: Seacon 1990-97; Marriott UK 1997-98. Chair: Clean World International 1991, Taylor Plan Services 1988. Director, Seacon. President: Wales Spastics Society, Pembrokeshire Spastics Society. Vice-President, Mentally Handicapped Society for Wales. Chair: Keep Wales Tidy Campaign Consultative Cttee. President: British Institute of Cleaning; Tidy Britain Group. Member: Welsh ITV Authority, Welsh Independent Broadcasting Authority, General Council, Independent Broadcasting Authority, Wales Development Agency, Welsh Arts Council, Schools Council for Wales. Chair, Wales Tourist Board. Hon. Fellow: James Cook University, Australia; Trinity College, Carmarthen. Of Llangwm, Haverfordwest. *Books: Autobiography, A Legacy for Life 1996.* Died 8 September 2004.

PARRY Ian Huw: BScEcon (Wales) FCA. Liberal Democrat, Cynon Valley 2001; Bristol North West 1997. **Mr. Ian Parry:** Born, Reading, 12 May 1962. Married, Sue, chartered accountant, 2c. Educated Meadway School, Reading; University of Wales, Cardiff. Chartered Accountant, Higher Education Funding Council. Director, Coteval Ltd. Chair: Union of Liberal Students, Cardiff 1983-85; Welsh Liberal Youth Movement 1984-85; Member: Bristol North West Liberal Democrat Executive 1990-97; Western Counties Executive 1990-97. Bristol CC 1991-95. Hobbies: Reading, Theatre, Watching rugby.

PARRY John Dafydd Hughes – see HUGHES PARRY John Dafydd.

PARRY M. Keith: Plaid Cymru, Bridgend 2003. **Mr. Keith Parry:** Born Cardiff, 3 January 1952. Married 2c. Educated Howardian High School, Cardiff; University of Wales, Swansea. Railway Worker. Contested Local Elections. Branch Secretary, Plaid Cymru. Interests: Constitutional Development of Wales, Social Policy, Communications, International Affairs. Hobbies: Walking, Swimming, Travel, Local History.

PARRY Owen: JP 1949 BA 1922 MA (Wales). Labour: Merioneth 1950. **Mr. Owen Parry:** Born,

Bethel, Caerns. s of Ellis Parry. Married. Educated Caernarfon Grammar School; University of Wales, Bangor. North Wales Regional Officer, National Council of Social Service. BBC Wales Education Officer/Programme Director. Merioneth CC. Chair, Merioneth Council of Youth & Further Education Service. Languages: Welsh, English. Of Llanegryn.

PARRY Ruth Eluned: Liberal Democrat: Meirionydd/Nant Conwy 1992; North Wales Euro 1994. **Miss Ruth Parry:** Born, Cardiff 7 April 1945. Educated Bangor Girls Grammar School; Cardiff College of Education (CertEd). Teacher Bryntaf Welsh School, Cardiff, 2 years; & Benghazi 2 years. Cardiff Supply Teacher. BBC 1973, Producer-Presenter, *Merched yn Bennaf.* Owner/director, *Si-Lwli* children's nursery. A Conciliator, South Glamorgan Family Health Service Authority. Member, Welsh consumers Council until 1991. Parliamentary Officer, Country Landowners' Assn Wales, 1999. Languages: Welsh, English.

PARRY Susan Marilyn: BA MA PGCE. Natural Law Party: Ynys Môn 1992; Assembly North List 1999. **Mrs. Susan Parry:** Born, Bangor, 23 November 1946, d of Trevor William Robert Parry, Flight Engineer RAF, & Lorna Myfanwy Parry, teacher. Church of England. Married 1969 Edwin Roberts, headteacher, divorced 1984, 2s 2d. Educated, Grammar School; Teacher Training College; University (Fine Arts; MA film & Television Production). Art Teacher. College Lecturer & Artist/film maker. Interests: Environmental/Green/Natural Law. Hobbies: Sailing, Swimming, Yoga. Of Skelmersdale.

PARRY Thomas Henry: DSO 1917 JP DL (Flint) 1922 MA (Cantab) LlB (Wales) Order of the Nile. (Coalition) Liberal MP Flint District B/E 1913-18, Flint 1918-24. **Lieut-Colonel T. H. Parry:** Born, Mold 1881 s of Thomas Parry JP & Gwenllian Parry, Llys Ifor. Educated University of Wales, Aberystwyth; Christ's College, Cambridge. Barrister, Inner Temple. Officer RWF (Suvla Bay, Egypt & Palestine) 1914-18. Trustee: Welsh Troops Children's Fund; Member, Welsh Regional Pensions Council. Of Mold & London. Died 8 October 1939.

PARSONS David Huw: LlB (York). Plaid Cymru: Montgomery 1992. **Mr. Huw Parsons:** Born, 16 January 1964. Educated York University; Chester College of Law. Solicitor 1981. Member, Plaid Cymru National Executive. Llandrindod TC 1986-, Mayor 1990.

PARSONS George William: Liberal: Cardiff South East 1966; Joined National Front 1969; National Front: Cardiff South East 1970. **Mr. George Parsons:** Born, Cardiff October 1924.

Married. Educated grammar school. Company Director: Cardiff motor trader company. Chair, City of Cardiff Liberal Party. Cardiff CC 1962-65 (Liberal Group Leader). National Front council candidate 1969. Chair, National Front South Wales Area Council.

PARSONS John Humphrey: Liberal (Democrat): Merioneth 1979, Ogmore 1983, Caernarfon 1987. **Mr. John Parsons:** Born Corris, 19 April 1930. Married Dilys, 1s. Educated Machynlleth Grammar School; Liverpool University. Solicitor. Part-time clerk, Machynlleth TC. Agent to Emlyn Hooson MP. Member: Executive, Montgomery Liberal Assn. Languages: Welsh, English.

PARTRIDGE Henry Graham: OBE JP (Pembs) MA (Oxon). Conservative: Brecon & Radnor 1955; Pembroke 1959, 1964. **Mr. Graham Partridge:** Born August 1916. Married, 5c. Educated, Sherborne School; New College, Oxford. Royal Artillery 1939-43, invalided out. Farmer & Company Director: Chair, Cardigan Mercantile Co Ltd. Member, South Wales Electricity Board 1952. Chair, Pembrokeshire Branch, National Farmers Union 1953. Vice-President, Pembrokeshire Federation of Young Farmers Clubs. Member: NFU Council, Ministry of Agriculture's Statistical Cttee, Council for Wales 1971. Cardigan BC.

PASSMORE Rhiannon: Labour, Ceredigion 2003. **Ms. Rhiannon Passmore:** Lecturer in background in Social Exclusion. Musician. Teacher. Campaigner for elderly care, Welsh Arts Development. Chair: Welsh Labour Women's Cttee; Policy Forum; Member, Labour National Policy Forum. Founded TYTRA (Tysign Tenants & Residents Assn) 1998. Nominated for *Welsh Woman of the Year 2003*. Interests: Youth participation in politics, Environment, Anti-poverty. Languages: Welsh, English.

PATERSON Owen William: MA (Oxon) 1978. Conservative: Wrexham 1992; MP Shropshire North 1997-. **Mr. Owen Paterson:** Born, Whitchurch Salop 24 June 1956, s of Alfred Dobell Paterson & Cynthia Marion Owen. Anglican. Married, 1980, Hon. Rose Emily Ridley, d of Viscount Ridley, 2s 1d. Educated, Radley College, Corpus Christi College, Oxford (History). Tanner: Managing Director, British Leather Company, Birkenhead 1993-99. UK. Representative, Euro Tanning Federation. Member, Ellesmere Hospital Action Group 1988-89. Liveryman, Leather Selling Company. General Election Aide, John Biffen MP 1987. Euro Election Aide, Sir Christopher Proud 1989, 1994. Select Cttee Member: Welsh Affairs 1997. Interests: Anti Euro, Low taxes, Free trade, Privatisation. Hobbies: Trees, Racing, Poultry. Languages: English, French, German. Of Ellesmere.

PATON Rosse Malcolm Ritson: MA (Oxon). Welsh Independent: Llandaff & Barry B/E 1942; Liberal: Brecon & Radnor 1950. **Mr. Malcolm Paton:** Born Pontypool, s of John Paton, industrialist. Married, 2c. Educated, Winchester; Trinity College, Oxford. Haulage Contractor. He announced that he would stand as an Independent Liberal after the local Liberals decide to not contest the 1950 election and then he received the backing of UK Liberal Party HQ. *In 1942 he advocated a form of Welsh nationalism.* Spoke for Gordon Parry, Labour, at Monmouth *(Western Mail 30.9.1959).* Of Crickhowell.

PATTERSON George Benjamin: MA (Cantab). Conservative: Wrexham 1970; MEP Kent West 1979-94. **Mr. Ben Patterson:** Born 21 April 1939, s of Eric James & Ethel Patterson. Married, 1970, Felicity Barbara Anne Raybould, 2c. Educated, Westminster School; Trinity College, Cambridge; London School of Economics. Tutor, Swinton Conservative College 1961-68. Editor, *CPC Monthly Report* 1965-67; Deputy-Head, London Office, European Parliament 1974-79; Principal Administrator, Internal Market Directorate General, European Parliament 1994-. Of Hawkhurst, Kent.

PATTMAN Jacqueline: Conservative: Mid & West Wales Euro 1984. **Miss Jacqueline Pattman:** Born 1951. Languages: English, French, German. Of Surrey.

PEACE David Henry: Conservative: Rhondda East 1959. **Mr. David Peace:** Born Sussex February 1928. Educated Burstow School, Surrey; Eastwood School, Scotland; Imperial College, London. Engineering Sales Executive; Research Officer, British Coal Utilisation Council. With industrial company. Joined Eastbourne Young Conservatives 1945. Asst. Secretary, Eastbourne Conservative Assn 1949-50. Chair: Cities of London & Westminster Lunch-Hour Branch 1954-57. Member: English Speaking Union.

PEARCE David Norton Idris: Kt 1990 CBE 1982 TD 1972 DL (Greater London) 1986 FRICS Hon. DSc (City 1990, Oxford Poly 1991, Salford 1991), Hon. DEng (West of Eng1994). Conservative: Neath 1959. **Sir Idris Pearce:** Born Neath 28 November 1933, s of Lemuel George, licensee, *Full Moon,* & Evelyn Mary Pierce. Married 1963, Ursula Helen Langley, 2d. Educated, Gnoll Secondary School, Neath; West Buckland School; Swansea Technical College. Lieutenant RE 1952-54, TA 1970-73, Hon. Colonel, 135 Ind Topographic Squadron RE(V)TA. 1989-94. Chartered Surveyor. Joined Richard Ellis 1959; Chair: English Estates 1989-94, Flexit Companies1993. Director: The Phoenix Initiative 1991, ITC 1992, National Mortgage Bank 1992, Higgs & Hill 1993, Dusco UK Ltd 1993, Royal Institute of

Chartered Surveyors (Member, General Council 1980-; Management Board 1984-91; Chair, Parl. & Public Affairs Cttee. 1984-89; Vice-President 1986-90; President 1990-91). Chair: International Assets Valuation Standards Cttee. 1981-86; Deputy Chair: Urban Regeneration Agency, 1993-; English Partnership. Chair: Higher Education Funding Council for Wales 1992-. Member: Universities Funding Council; Higher Education Funding Council for England; Vice-Chair: Greater London TA & VRA 1991-94; Chair: Development Board, National Art Collection Fund 1988-92. Pro-Chancellor, University of Surrey 1994-; Member: Court, City University 1987. Trustee, Rochester Bridge Trust 1991-94. Governor, Peabody Trust 1992. Centenary Fellow, Thames Poly 1991. Companion, de Montfort University 1992. Master, Worshipful Company of Tylers & Bricklayers.

PEARCE Herbert: Communist: Swansea East B/E 1963 Neath 1970, Perry Barr 1955, 1959. **Mr. Bert Pearce:** Born, Pembroke Dock January 1919, s of a Baptist lay preacher. Married (teacher of deaf children), 2c. Educated Pembroke Dock Grammar School. Lived in Birmingham 1938-58. Shop Worker. Civil Servant. Member USDAW. Member, Labour Party until 1944; Joined Communist Party 1944. Communist Party District Secretary, Birmingham & South Staffs 1945-60; Secretary, Communist Party Welsh Council 1960-. Member, Birmingham Trades Council. Contested Birmingham CC, Cardiff CC. Author of pamphlets on future of Wales & Welsh Communism. Hobbies: Classical Music, playing piano, singing baritone 'mostly in the bath'. Died 21 August 2002.

PEARSON Arthur: CBE 1959 JP (Glam) 1939. Labour MP Pontypridd B/E 1938-70. **Mr. Arthur Pearson:** Born Pontypridd 31 January 1898, s of William Pearson. Congregationalist deacon. Unmarried. Educated Elementary & central schools. Errand Boy c.1910. Chainworker 1913-38. Welsh Guards 1916-19; Pontypridd UDC 1926-38; Glamorgan CC 1928-45. Secretary: Pontypridd Trades & Labour Council. Labour Whip 1939-59; Comptroller of the Household 1945-46; Treasurer of the Household 1945-51. Of Pontypridd. Died 14 October 1980.

PEEL Jeremy Charles: MA (Oxon) 1965. Conservative: Llanelli 1966. **Mr. Jeremy Peel:** Born Farnham, Surrey, September 1934 (descendant of Prime Minister, Sir Robert Peel; gf was Civil Lord of the Admiralty). Married, 2s. Educated Eton; Christ Church, Oxford. Army, 2nd Hussars. Stockbroker. Member: Commonwealth Council; Primrose League. Of Farnham, Surrey.

PEEL Mervyn Lloyd: KBE 1922 JP (Carms) MA LlB (Cantab). Conservative: East Carmarthen-shire Jan. & Dec. 1910; B/E 1912. **Sir Mervyn Peel:** Born, Sale Old Hall, Cheshire 1856, s of John Peel of Danyrallt, Llangadog & Charlotte Louisa Frances, d of John William Lloyd JP, Danyrallt. Anglican. Married, 1886, Frances Annabella, d of Ralph Assheton, Clitheroe, 1d. Educated, Privately & Trinity College, Cambridge. Barrister, Inner Temple 1881. Staff Reporter, Law *Times* 1889-93. Landowner, succeeded to estate, 1901, on death of brother, Sir Vincent Peel. 1901. Carmarthenshire CC 1907-19. President: United Counties Agricultural Society 1908. Chair: Towy Fisheries Board; East Carmarthenshire Unionist Assn 1907-18, West Carmarthenshire Unionist Assn 1918-20, South Wales Provincial Council, National Union of Conservative & Unionist Assns. Secretary, Carmarthenshire Tariff Reform League. Hobbies: Fishing, Skating. Of Danyrallt Park, Llangadog. Estate £65,386. Died 4 January 1929.

PENNANT David Arnold Pearson: BSc (Reading). Independent, Vale of Clwyd 1999. **Mr. Arnold Pennant:** Born Chester, 12 July 1946, s of Arthur Dermot Humberston Pennant, farmer and landowner, & Ann Bankes Carver (ggs of Philip Pennant Pennant, qv). Anglican. Married 1977 Gillian Eileen Evans, 1s 1d. Educated Reading University (Agriculture). Contested Denbighshire CC (Tremeirchion) 1999. Of Tremeirchion.

PENNANT Dyfrig Huws: DSO 1916 JP (Pembs) MD (Durham) MR.CS LRCP. Liberal: Pembroke 1951. **Dr. Huws Pennant:** Born, Pontycymmer, 1 September 1890, s of William Pennant. Anglican. Married, 1917, Rachel d of Revd Thomas Davies, St. Clears, 2s (1 killed in RAF). Educated, Llandaff Cathedral School; University of Wales, Cardiff; Durham University; London Hospital. Captain RAMC 1914-19. Medical Practitioner at Solfa 25 years. Retired to farm 40 acres. Member: Welsh Regional Hospital Board 1948. Chair: West Wales Mental Health Management Cttee 1948. High Sheriff of Pembrokeshire 1948. Pembrokeshire CC Alderman, Chair, Education Cttee 3 years; Chair 1950-51. Governor: University of Wales, National Library & National Museum of Wales. Member, Council, Welsh National School of Medicine.

PENNANT Philip Pennant: JP DL (Flints) BA1857 MA (1860 (Cantab). Conservative: Flint District 1880, 1885, 1892, 1895; Flintshire B/E 1886. **Captain Philip Pennant:** Born 5 August 1834, s of Revd George Pearson, Castle Camps, Yorks & Catherine, d of Philip Humberton, Chester. Anglican. Changed his name to Pennant, 1860, in order to inherit the estate of his godfather, David Pennant. Married, 1862, Mary Frances, d of Col. Edward Banks, 1s 3d. (Aunt of

Sir Eldon Bankes (qv). Educated, Charterhouse; St. John's College, Cambridge. Landowner. Member, Denbighshire Asylum Visitors Committee 40 years. Flintshire CC, Chair, Flintshire Quarter Sessions. Constable of Flint Castle. Chair, 2nd Welsh Conference on Education, 1 June 1906. Of St. Asaph. Estate £32,760. Died 2 October 1910.

PENNAR Andreas Meirion: BA PhD (Wales). Plaid Cymru: Swansea West 1983. **Dr. Meirion Pennar:** Born Cardiff 1947, s of Revd Dr. Pennar Davies (qv) & Rosemarie Pennar Davies. Married, 1s divorced. Educated Dynevor Grammar School, Swansea; University of Wales, Swansea. Lecturer in Welsh, University of Wales, Lampeter. Editor, *Taliesin Poems*; Translator: *The Black Book of Carmarthen*. Languages: Welsh, English. Of Swansea.

PENNEFATHER John de Fontenblanque: 1st Bart 1924 JP. Conservative: North Monmouthshire 1900; MP Kirkdale 1915-29. **Sir John Pennefather:** Born 1856, s of Major Kingsmill Pennefather, Co. Tipperary. Anglican. Married, Madeleine Emily Messeline, d of Sir Robert Stewart. Educated Ireland. Landowner. Master of Hounds. Of Virginia Water, Surrey. Estate £48,164. Died 8 August 1933.

PENRI-WILLIAMS Hugh Henning: BScEcon (Wales) CIA CISA CCSA. Liberal: Pontypridd 1979. **Mr. Hugh Penri-Williams:** Born Hitchsenbach, Germany, s of Major William Penri-Williams, born Patagonia, died 1975). Married 1985, Myriam Therese Gaston Janssens, nurse, 1s. Educated St. George the Martyr Primary School, London; St. Marylebone Secondary School, London; Jung-Stilling Gymnasium, Hilchenbach; University of Wales, Aberystwyth (mature student at time of election). Vice-President, Welfare, Students Union, Aberystwyth (Hon. Life Member). Worked in world banking & insurance. Chief Security Officer, Alcatel, Paris; Security, Fraud, IS Audit. Ex-Chair, European (now Information) Security Forum. International Lecturer & Post Graduate Teacher in Belgium. Interests: Human Rights, International Conflicts & Terrorism. Hobbies: Railways, especially steam locos, Sports (spectator), British humour. Languages: English, German, French, Dutch. Of Brussels.

PENSTONE Michael John Alfred: Conservative: East Flint Feb. & Oct. 1974. **Mr. Michael Penstone:** Born, 1938. Married, 3c. Educated, Holyhead Grammar School, Law Society School of Law. Solicitor 1966 (Colwyn Bay). Chair, Holyhead Young Conservatives. Of Deganwy.

PERKINS Susanna Jennifer: BA CertEd 1998 (Wales). Plaid Cymru, Wales Euro 1999. **Miss**

Susanna Perkins: Born Birmingham 1977. Educated University of Wales, Aberystwyth. Women's Officer, University of Wales, Aberystwyth Students. Chair: Plaid Cymru Students Federation.

PERRY Roy James: BA (Exeter). Conservative: Swansea West 1992; MEP Wight & Hants South 1994-. **Mr. Roy Perry:** Born, 12 February1943, s of George & Dora Perry. Married 1966, Veronica, d of George Hammell, 2d. Educated, Tottenham Grammar School; Exeter University (Govt). Junior Executive, Marks & Spencer 1964-66. Senior Lecturer in Government & Politics, Southampton Technical College 1966-94. Director, Trident International. Test Valley BC 1979-94 (Leader 1988-94). Eastleigh BC 1970-74. Member. European Parliament Cultural Cttee. Vice-President, European Inter-Isles Group. Member, Budgetary Control Cttee 1995. Vice-President, Assn of District Councils. Of West Mellow, Romsey.

PETERSEN David Thomas: NDD ATC RCA. Plaid Cymru, Brecon & Radnor & Mid & West List 1999. **Mr. David Petersen:** Born Cardiff 25 February 1944, s of Jack Petersen, World Champion Boxer. Church in Wales. Married Bronwen Petersen, 3s 1d. Broadcaster, Artist & Blacksmith. With sons deigned images for Welsh definitive issue postage stamps 1999. Designed & made National Eisteddfod Crown 2002. Branch Chair, Plaid Cymru. Founder/Chair: Antur Cwm Taf a Thywi. Interests: Cultural and National (Wales). Hobbies: Music. Of St. Clears.

PETROU Michael Demetrios: Labour: Cardiff North 1979. **Mr. Michael Petrou:** Born 1946, s of a Cypriot father & Abertillery mother. Married, 2 c. London Solicitor. Lambeth BC 1971-74 (Deputy Leader). Joined Labour Party 1966. Of Streatham.

PHIBBS Charles: Kt 1936 JP (Merioneth) OStJ. Conservative: Merioneth 1929, 1931, 1935. **Sir Charles Phibbs:** Born, Kingstown, Ireland 27 May 1878, s of Sir Charles Phibbs, Bunaweddan Co. Sligo. Anglican. Married 1908, Beatrice Gwendoline, d. of Walter Lanyon Nicholls, Birkenhead, 2s. Educated Rossall School. Farmer & Land Agent in Ireland, 1894-1922. Landowner & Farmer. County Commissioner, Order of St. John of Jerusalem. President, Merioneth Conservative Assn. Merioneth CC 1955; Alderman, Chair 1950-51. Of Plas Gwynfryn, Llanbedr (1922). Died 2 July 1964.

PHILIPPS Charles Edward Gregg: 1st Bart 1887 JP (Carms. & Pembs). Conservative: Pembrokeshire 1885, 1886, 1892. **Lieut-Col Sir Charles Philipps:** Born Huddersfield 1840, s of Edward

Fisher, Spring Dale, Yorkshire, & Jane, d of Dominic Gregg, Coleraine. Anglican. Married, 1868, Mary Philippa, d of Revd J. H. A. Philipps, Piston Castle and assumed the name of Philipps by royal licence 1876, in compliance with his father-in-law's will. Educated, Cheltenham College. Barrister 1868. Landowner. Chair, Milford Haven Sea Fisheries Cttee. Member: House of Laymen, Province of Canterbury, then Governing Body of the Church in Wales. Lord Lieutenant of Haverfordwest 1876. Chair: Pembrokeshire Quarter Sessions & Standing Joint Cttee 1912-. High Sheriff, Pembrokeshire 1882. Lieut-Colonel (Ret) Pembrokeshire Yeomanry. Pembrokeshire CC, Chair 1898-1903. Alderman & Mayor of Haverfordwest 1897-99. President, Tenby Golf Club. Interests Shooting & Golf. Estate £92,386. Died 5 June 1928.

PHILIPPS John Wynford, 1st Viscount St. Davids 1918: 1st Baron St. Davids 1908. 13th Bart of Picton 1621 PC 1914 GBE 1922 JP (Pembs & Suffolk) MA (Oxon). Liberal MP Pembrokeshire B/E 1898-1908, Mid-Lanarkshire B/E 1888-92. **Rt. Hon. Sir Wynford Philipps:** Born 30 May 1860, s of Revd Sir John Erasmus Philipps, Bart & Hon. May, d of Hon. & Revd S. Best (sister of 5th Baron Wynford). Anglican. Married (1) 1888 Norah, d of J. Gerstenberg (died 1915) (2) 1916 Elizabeth Frances, d of Hon. Paulyn Rawdon-Hastings (Baroness Strange of Knockin & Hungerford de Moleyns). Educated, Felsted School; Keble College, Oxford. Barrister 1886. Landowner. Company Chair, Buenos Aires & Pacific Railway Co. President, Welsh National Liberal Council 1907. Chair, Unemployment Grants Cttee. Lord Lieutenant of Pembrokeshire 1911-32. Hon. Captain, Pembrokeshire Imperial Yeomanry. Of Lydstep Haven, Penally; Roch Castle; Landwade House, Exning, Newmarket, Suffolk, & London. Estate £123,736. Died 28 March 1938.

PHILIPPS Owen Cosby 1st & last Baron Kylsant: of Carmarthen 1920, GCMG 1918 DL (Pembs) JP (Carms. & Pembs) KStJ Grand Cross of Spanish Red Cross. Liberal: Montgomery District 1895, Darlington 1898; MP Pembroke & Haverfordwest 1906-Dec. 1910; Conservative MP Chester B/E 1916-18, City of Chester 1918-22. **Sir Owen Philipps:** Born 25 March 1863, s of Revd Sir John Erasmus Philipps Bart, & Hon. Mary Best, d of Lord Wynford (brother of John Wynford Philipps (qv). Anglican. Married 1902, Mai Alice Magdalene CBE. d of Thomas Morris DL. 3d. Educated, Newton College, Devon. Shipowner: Chair & Managing Director: Royal Mail Steam Packet Co. Director: Union Castle Line and associated companies (500 ships). Landowner (6000 acres in Carmarthenshire & Pembrokeshire). President: Federation of

Chambers of Commerce of the British Empire; Chamber of Shipping of the United Kingdom. Vice-President: Royal Colonial Institute; Liverpool School of Tropical Medicine. Chair, Port of London Authority 1909-13. Chair, Wales & Mon. Conservative Council. Lord Lieutenant of Haverfordwest. Sub-Prior for Wales, Knights of St. John of Jerusalem 1912-29. MFH. Carmarthenshire 1912-26; Vice-Admiral of North Wales & Carmarthenshire 1929; Hon. Captain RNR. High Sheriff of Pembrokeshire 1904. Chair, Church in Wales Finance Cttee. Short-listed at Gower 1900. Sentenced to one year's imprisonment for false communication of commercial information, July 1931. Of Coomb, Llangain, Amroth Castle & London. Estate £62,567. Died 5 June 1937.

PHILIPPS Richard Hanning: MBE 1945 JP DL (Pembs). Conservative: Brecon & Radnor B/E 1939. **Major, Hon. Hanning Philipps:** Born 17 February 1904, s of 1st Baron Milford (gs. of Sir James Erasmus Philipps 12th Bart, brother of Wogan (Communist 2nd Baron). Married, 1930, Lady Marion Violet Dalrymple, d. of 12th Earl of Starr, 2c. Educated, Eton. Lieutenant, Welsh Guards 1939, Major 1944. Hon. Colonel, Pembrokeshire Yeomanry 1959. Chair then President, Schweppes Ltd; Schweppes (Overseas) Ltd; Director: Northern Securities Trust Ltd; Duns & Bradstreet Ltd, Milford Steam Trawling Co Ltd, Picton Land & Investment Ltd. Lord Lieutenant of Pembrokeshire 1958-74; Vice-Lieutenant, 1957. Trustee, Picton Castle Trust. President, Pembrokeshire Order of St. John. Chair, Milford Haven Conservancy Board. Of Picton Castle, Haverfordwest; London, & Jean Cap Ferrat, France. Died 29 January 1998.

PHILLIPS A. Glenn: Plaid Cymru: Aberavon 1983. **Mr. Glenn Phillips:** Born 1956. Educated University of Wales, Aberystwyth. Teacher; Unemployed. Secretary: Gower Plaid Cymru 1980-82; Plaid Cymru Trade Union Organisation. Member, CND Cymru. Languages: Learned Welsh, English. Of Trebanos, Pontardawe.

PHILLIPS David Marc: Plaid Cymru: Llanelli 1992, 1997; Mid & West Wales Euro 1984; Euro Wales, 1999. **Mr. Marc Phillips:** Born Merthyr Tydfil 8 December 1953. Married, Elaine Senior, 2s. Educated Cyfarthfa High School. Community Worker, Glyncoch, Pontypridd. Development Officer, Urdd Gobaith Cymru 1977-86. Director, Dyfed Assn. of Voluntary Services 1986-95. Chief Executive, Tenovus 1995-2002. National Co-ordinator, BBC Children in Need Appeal 2002-. School Governor. National Chair, Plaid Cymru 1995-99; Vice-President 1993-95. Secretary, Cymdeithas yr Iaith Gymraeg. Ex-Chair, Wales Rural Forum. UK Representative,

Trans European Rural Network. Member, Welsh Language Board 2003-. Hobbies: Politics, Current affairs, Music, International travel. Languages: Welsh, English. Of Cardiff.

PHILLIPS Elizabeth Fletcher: Referendum Party: Brecon & Radnor 1997; UK Independence, Brecon & Radnor 2001, 2003; Wales Euro 2004. **Mrs. Liz Phillips:** Born 13 February 1948, d of James Piper, Civil Servant, & Bessie Piper, Accountants Manager. Church of England (church organist, Rhayader). Married 1989 Charles Phillips, Rhayader greengrocer. Educated Folkestone County Grammar School. Company Director, Wales Sales & Marketing. Formerly Sales Manager: Jacksons Fencing; Security, Debenhams Group. National Retail Operations Manager, Group 4 Total Security. UK Independence Party, Wales Euro 2004. Hobbies: All things political, Walking, Golf, Cooking, Gardening, Music. Languages: Some Welsh, English, French. Of Rhayader (1989).

PHILLIPS Gerald Stewart: Independent: Pembroke 1983. **Mr. Gary Phillips:** Born 1956 s of Gilroy Phillips, hotelier, Mayor of Tenby & Chair of Bring Back Pembrokeshire Campaign. Based his campaign on his 70,000 page book, "MP", written during a three month stay in hospital after a hang-gliding accident in Norfolk, August 1979, whilst an engineering student at the Polytechnic of Wales *Policies World Government which would lead to multilateral disarmament; return of capital & corporal punishment; improved transportation; road projects; energy conservation; 'Bring Back Pembrokeshire.'*

PHILLIPS Harry: Conservative: Mid Glamorgan 1900. **Mr. Harry Phillips:** Anglican lay reader. Treasurer, Dockers' Union. West Ham BC Alderman & Deputy Mayor.

PHILLIPS Ian Robert: BA (Oxon). UK Independence Party, Carmarthen West & South Pembrokeshire, 2001. **Mr. Ian Phillips:** Born London 2 August 1946, s of Harold Phillips, Banker, & Viola C. Phillips. Brought up an Anglican, now New Age. Married 1972-87, Anne Phillips. Educated Sevenoaks School; Magdalen College, Oxford (Natural Philosophy-Physics). Science teacher. Own property business. Worked for Referendum Party 1997. Organiser, Democracy Movement. Interests: Vision for a world of co-operating but fully independent nation states; Cultural Relations with USSR, Organic growing. Hobbies: Complementary Medicine; Psychology. Languages: English, Russian. Of Tenby.

PHILLIPS Marc – see PHILIPS David Marc.

PHILLIPS Michael: Liberal Democrat: Neath 1992. **Revd Michael Phillips:** Born Briton Ferry

5 July, 1958. Royal Navy until 1977 (invalided out after accident). Non-Stipendiary Minister, Free Presbyterian Church. President, Port Talbot Free Church Council. Co-ordinator, Glamorgan Christian Ecology Group. Of Cwmafan.

PHILLIPS Neil David: BSc. Natural Law Party, South/West List 1999. **Mr. Neil Phillips:** Born Cardiff, 17 September 1949, son of Lloyd George Phillips & Dorris Bessie Rossiter. Educated university. Engineer (Member of the Institute of Engineers of Australia). Marketing Consultant. South Gloucs DC. Interests: Local, National & Global Development, using the scientifically proven 'Maharishi effect'. Hobbies: Personal Development, Investment (Stock Market). Languages: Welsh (once, learned it at school), English, some French. Of Downend, Bristol.

PHILLIPS Paul Gregory: Independent, South/Central List 1999. **Mr. Paul Phillips:** Born 1956. Married 3c. Researcher/Copy Writer. Of Church Village, Pontypridd. Ruptured his Achilles tendon during the campaign. *Standing on a ticket of ensuring fair distribution of economic aid to essential services in the constituency . . . believes in free education from nursery to degree level, improved pay and conditions for all health professionals and allied staff, and more accountability, responsibility and consultation in local government. (Western Mail).*

PHILLIPS Simon Kristen: Green, North List 1999. **Mr. Simon Phillips:** Born 1974. Secretary, Llanelli Green Party. Contested Carmarthenshire CC 1999. Of Llanelli.

PHILLIPS William Francis: BA 1906 BD (Wales) 1909 BLitt (Oxon) 1911. Liberal: West Glamorgan, Dec. 1910. **Revd W. F. Phillips:** Born Dwygyfylchi 1 September 1877, s of William Phillips (died 1893) & Mary Jane Phillips. Work at 16: Clerk, Elder Dempster Line; London & Lancs Fire Insurance, Liverpool. Educated Bala Theological College; University of Wales, Cardiff; Jesus College, Oxford. Presbyterian Minister: Ordained 1891: Havelock Street, Newport; Tenby; Swallow Lane, Liverpool; retired because of ill health, March 1919. Organising Secretary, Dr. Barnado's Homes 1919. Journalist & Writer as *John Colwyn) Liverpool Daily Post, London Daily Mail, Daily Dispatch* etc. Author, Playwright & Drama Adjudicator. Editor, *The Torch* (Forward Movement) & *The Grail.* Member, South Wales Young Liberal Federation. Founder/editor, *Y Gwerin/Monthly Democrat* 1912, to oppose the socialist elements in the SWMF. Languages: Welsh, English, Died 16 August 1920.

PHILPOTT Howard L: Conservative: Caerphilly 1992. **Mr. Howard Philpott:** Born Splott, Cardiff 29 January 1966. Married, Jane. Educated Willow

High School; University of Wales, Cardiff. Owner, family furniture & printing companies. Contested Cardiff CC (Heath) 1999. Of Splott, Cardiff.

PIERCE Griffith Hughes: Conservative & National Liberal: Wrexham 1959, 1964, 1966; Widnes 1970; PPC Ardwick May 1953-April 1955. **Mr. Griffith Pierce:** Born Newton Le Willows, January 1920, Welsh parents. Anglican lay reader. Married Margaret 4c. Educated Newton Le Willows Grammar School. LMS. railway clerk c.1935; Royal Army Corps of Signals 1940-45; Student at Didsbury Teacher Training College 1946-48; Teacher 1948. RNVR officer 1946-53. Official Amateur Boxing Assn. Vice-President, Wales & Mon. Young Conservatives. Organiser of poll on Sunday opening.

PILE Aubrey Willis: JP (Swansea). Liberal: Cardiff East 1935; Declined to stand in Swansea East 1951. **Mr. Willis Pile:** Born, Swansea 1892. Methodist lay preacher. Married, Hetty, 1s. Educated Swansea Grammar School. Ship's broker & Shipowner. Fellow, Chartered Institute of Shipbrokers. Member: Swansea Pilotage Cttee; Swansea Post Office Advisory Cttee. Bristol Channel Cttee. President, Swansea Chamber of Commerce (twice). Grand Master, Penrice Lodge of Freemasons 1927. Member, Swansea Cricket & Football Club Cttee. Member: Court of University of Wales; Council of University College, Swansea. Swansea BC 1935-70, Mayor 1964-65. Elocutionist. Polio Victim. Of Swansea. Died August 1970.

PINTO Fiona Karen: Pro Life Alliance, South/East List 2003; Welwyn-Hatfield 2001; North-West England Euro 2004. **Miss Fiona Pinto:** Born 1980, member of a Goan family. Roman Catholic. Educated Magdalen College, Oxford. President: Oxford University Pro Life. UK Director, Student Life Net (national network campaigning for pregnant and parenting students) 2000-02. Political Researcher, Paul Marsden MP. Asst. General Secretary, Goan Community Assn.

PIPER Craig Stuart: Conservative, Cardiff Central 2003. **Mr. Craig Piper:** Born Plymouth 1978. Fiancée/Partner Nicola. Educated Heles School, Plymouth. Financial Underwriter, Black Horse Finance, Cardiff. Joined Conservative Party 1995. Secretary, South Devon Young Conservatives 2 years. Hobbies: Football fan, Music, Walking, Computing. Of Cardiff (2000).

PITMAN Raymond Charles: Conservative: Bedwellty 1950; Joined Liberal Party 1952, PPC Brecon & Radnor until 1964. **Mr. Raymond Pitman:** Born Risca 1914, s of T H Pitman (gs. Sir Charles Edwards, Labour MP QV). Congrega-

tionalist. Married 1940, Doris M. d of Rosser Williams, Pentwynnen, 3c. Journalist. Lay Pastor, Sardis & Siloh Churches, Garndiffaeth, Army 1939-45; Chief Education Instructor. Secretary-Treasurer, Welsh Conservative Candidates Assn 1950. Vice-Chair, Liberal Party of Wales 1965-6.

PLAISTED Norman Gordon John: Pro Life Alliance, South/East List 2003. **Mr. Norman Plaisted:** Born Newport, 13 August 1941, s of Cyril Plaisted, welder, & Amealia Plaisted, housewife. Roman Catholic. Married 1966 Angel Plaisted, 1s 1d. Educated secondary school. Security Guard. Member: Society of St. Vincent de Paul. Interests: Promoting Pro Life & Pro-Family causes. Hobbies: Keep Fit, Reading, Studying Political Parties. Of Newport.

PLANT Kevin James: Plaid Cymru: Wrexham 1997. **Mr. Kevin Plant:** Born Wrexham 28 September 1965. Married Jane, 1s. Educated St. Mary's School, Brymbo; Ysgol Bryn Alyn, Wrexham. Employee at electrical goods distributors. Member of a band. Vice-Chair, Wrexham Constituency, Plaid Cymru. Contested Wrexham BC 1999. Of Wrexham.

PLATT Henry: CB JP DL (Caerns). Conservative: Arfon 1885, 1886, Caernarfon District 1900. **Colonel Henry Platt:** Born Oldham 26 December 1842, s of John Platt MP & Alice Radcliffe. Married 1889 Eleanor d of Richard Sykes, Edgeley, Stockport, 2c. Educated, Cheltenham College; Frederich Wilhelm Schule, Berlin. Company Director, Platt & Co machine makers. Partner, Williams Bank. 1st Mayor of Bangor 1862. High Sheriff of Caernarfonshire 1877. Of Gorddinog, Aber. Estate £407,539. Died 13 October 1914.

PLOWS Alexandra Jane: BA (London) 1991 MA 1999 PhD (Wales). Green, North List 1999. **Dr. Alexandra Plows:** Educated Goldsmiths College, London University (English literature), University of Wales, Bangor (Social Research & Sociology). PhD student at Bangor. Research Assistant, University of Keele. Centre for Economic & Social Aspects of Genomics (Lancaster & Cardiff Universities) at Cardiff. Contested Gwynedd CC. (Deiniol) 1999. Interests: Environment, Feminism. Languages: Learned Welsh, English, French. *Books: Joint Author, Explaining the Fuel Protests.*

POIRRIER Joy A: Referendum Party, Carmarthen West & South Pembrokeshire 1997. **Mrs. Joy Poirrier:** Born London 1939. Married, 2c, widowed. Air Stewardess, Cabin Crew Staff Manager, Laker Airways, retired.

POLE David Graham: MA (Edin). Labour: Cardiff South 1922, Cardiff Central 1924, East

Grinstead 1918, Edinburgh South B/E 1920, Derbyshire South 1931; MP Derbyshire South 1929-31. **Major Graham Pole:** Born, Edinburgh 1 December 1877, s of Captain John Pole. Atheist. Married, Jessie Hair, d. of G. Hair Pagan, Sheriff-Clerk of Fife. Educated Edinburgh High School; Edinburgh University. Edinburgh Solicitor 1901-14; Notary Public 1903; Solicitor in House of Lords & Privy Council (Indian Appeals) 1913-26. Edinburgh University Volunteers 1899, Lieutenant 1901; Captain TA 1912; Northumberland Fusiliers 1914-18, Major 1916; temp Lieut-Colonel; Invalided out. Treasurer, National Labour Club 1928-30; MPs All-Party Commerce Cttee 1929-31. PPS 1931. Vice-Chair, Labour Party Machinery of Government Cttee, British Cttee on India & Burma Affairs. Member, Burma Round Table Conference 1931-32; Parliamentary Correspondent & Director, *New India*, Madras; London Correspondent, *Modern Review*, Calcutta. Chair, North London Rent Tribunal. Director, Ratsours Ltd, Max Arc Electricals. Of London & Farnham. Died 26 November 1952.

POLE-CAREW Reginald: KCB 1900 CB 1887 CVO 1901 JP DL (Cornwall) BA (Oxon). Conservative: Pembroke & Haverfordwest 1906, Bodmin Jan. 1910; MP Bodmin Dec. 1910-1916. **Lieut-General, Sir Reginald Pole-Carew:** Born 1 May 1849, s of W. H. Pole Carew of Antony & Frances Anne, d of John Bullet of Morval. Married, Lady Beatrice Butler, d of 3rd Marquess of Ormonde, 4c. Educated Eton; Christ Church, Oxford. Officer, Coldstream Guards 1869-99. Private Secretary to Governor of New South Wales 1876-77. ADC Viceroy of India 18781-79. ADC various generals (Afghan & South African wars) ADC Duke of Connaught 1882. Military Secretary Madras; ADC Commander in Chief, India 1888-90. Colonel, 2nd Battalion, Coldstream Guards 1895-99. Major-General 1905. Inspector General of Territorials 1914. Estate £15,444. Died 19 September 1924.

POLLITT Harry: Communist: Rhondda East 1935, 1945, 1950; Seaham 1929; Whitechapel & St. George's B/E 1930; Clay Cross B/E 1933. **Mr. Harry Pollitt:** Born Droylesden 22 November 1890, s of Samuel Pollitt & boiler shop operator & Mary Louise Pollitt (Died 1939). Educated Droylesden Elementary School; attended Moravian Sunday School. Married, Marjorie (Contested Hendon North 1950); 1s. 1d. Half-time work at 12 at Bensons Mill. Cotton worker 1902. Apprentice at Gorton Tank railway locomotive building plant 1905. Boiler Maker. shop steward at Levenshulme. Joined: Boilermakers' Society 1912 (London District Secretary, 1919). Joined ILP1909. Secretary, Openshaw Socialist Society 1911. Branch Secretary, British Socialist Party 1912. Mother gave him *Das Kapital* as 21st birth-

day present. Opposed Great War: worked in Southampton Shipyard but refused to load munitions. National Organiser, *Hands off Russia Movement* September 1919. Founder member, Communist Party 1922. Secretary, National Minority Movement 1924-29Kidnapped by a fascist gang to keep him from a Liverpool meeting March 1924. Arrested 1924, four days before his wedding. Imprisoned under Incitement to Mutiny Act 1925. Arrested 1934 for speeches against treatment of the unemployed, but released. Deported from Belfast 1933. General Secretary, Communist Party of Great Britain 1929-57 (removed from office 1939 because he opposed the party's war policy; reinstated when USSR entered the war 1941). Party Chair 1950; President 1956. Died 27 June 1960, on liner *Orion* on way home from Australia. *Books: Harry Pollitt: Serving My Time, 1940.*

PONSONBY Vere Brabazon, 9th Earl of Bessborough (1739); Baron of Bessborough; Viscount Duncannon (1723); Baron Ponsonby (1749); Baron Duncannon (1834) PC 1931 GCMG 1931 CMG 1919 JP DL (Kilkenny) KStJ Hon. LLD. (McGill, Toronto) 1921 Hon. FRIBA MA (Cantab) Grand Officer, Legion d'Honneur (France) Orders: St Anne, Russia; Leopold II, Belgium; SS Maurice & Lazarus, Italy; Redeemer, Greece. Conservative: Carmarthen District 1906; MP Cheltenham 1910, Dover B/E 1913-20. **Hon. Vere Ponsonby:** Born, 1880 s of 8th Earl & Blanche Vere, d of Sir John Guest, Bart. Succeeded father 1920. Anglican. Married 1912 Roberte de Neuiflize CStJ, d of Baron Jean de Neuiflize. Educated Cambridge. Barrister, Inner Temple 1903. Lieutenant, Bucks Yeomanry. Major TA. Governor General of Canada 1931-35. President Council, Foreign Bondholders 1936. Chair: League Loans Cttee 1937; Cheltenham Ladies College Governors; Chichester Diocesan Fund; Church of England Advisory Cttee; Council for Empire Settlement; Hotels & Restaurants Assn; Franco British Society. Company Chair: Rio Tinto Co. Of Rowlands Castle, Hants. Died 1956.

POOLEY Michelle: BSc (Wales). Plaid Cymru: Swansea East 1997. **Miss Michelle Pooley:** Born Zimbabwe 13 March 1971. Educated Convent High School, Harare; University of Wales, Swansea (Computer Studies). Manager, Playtime Ltd 1990-91; Women's Officer, University of Wales Swansea 1991-94. Women's Officer, NUS Wales 1994-96. Plaid Cymru Women's Officer. Member: Shelter Cymru Housing Group; All Wales Aids Network; West Glamorgan Mental Health Network; Management Cttee Swansea Women's resource & training centre.

POPE Ambrose T: Liberal: Ebbw Vale 1979, South East Wales Euro 1979. **Mr. Ambrose Pope:**

Born October 1923. Educated elementary school; technical college. RAF 1941-46. Mechanical engineer. AUEW shop steward, British Steel Corporation, Ebbw Vale. Member, Tredegar Orpheus Male Voice Choir. President: Hilltop Senior Citizens Assn. Chair: 1158 ATC Squadron. Ebbw Vale UDC (RA).

POPHAM Anthony Govan: Freedom Party, Gower 1997, Independent, Llanelli 1999. **Mr. Tony Popham:** Born Wales 1954. Married 3s. Businessman. Member: Amnesty International, Friends of the Earth, League Against Cruel Sports, World Vision, Samaritans. Elmbridge BC [Molesley Residents Assn] (Chair: Environmental Affairs Overview & Scrutiny Cttee). Of East Moseley, Surrey.

Mrs Annie Powell.

POWELL Annie: Hon. MA (Wales). Communist: Rhondda East 1955, 1959, 1964, 1966. **Mrs. Annie Powell:** Born Ystrad Rhondda, September 1906, d of headteacher. Brought up at Methodist Central Hall. Married, Trefor Powell, Co-operative Society employee. Educated Pentre Grammar School; Barry Training College. Teacher at Pontypridd-1971. Briefly a member of Plaid Cymru and Labour Party. Joined Communist Party 1938. Chair, Welsh Executive, Communist Party; Member, Communist Party National Executive-1965; Rhondda BC 1955-57, 1959-65, 1967-; Mayor 1979-80 (1st Communist Mayor in UK); Hon. Alderman. Languages: Welsh, English. Of Llwynypia. Died 28 August 1986.

POWELL Dapho Llewellyn: LlB (Wales). Liberal: Ogmore 1929. **Mr. Dapho Powell:** Born Bridgend 6 July 1884, s of William Powell JP. Congregationalist. Educated Ilford Modern School; private tutor; University of Wales, Aberystwyth. Married 1915, Gladys Siddle d. of George Chitham, Cardiff Shipowner. Solicitor 1907, Barrister 1923. Member, South Wales Fisheries Board. Secretary, Central Glamorgan Branch NSPCC. Vice-Chair, Governors, Bridgend County School. Liberal Agent, Ogmore 1922. Financial Secretary, North Wales YMCA. Freemason. Bridgend UDC. Glamorgan CC 1922-23. Of Bridgend.

POWELL John Francis: BA BD (Wales). Conservative: Rhondda East 1929. **Mr. J. Francis Powell:** Born 1890, s of John Powell, Dyffryn Works, Morriston, & Sarah Powell. Calvinistic Methodist. Married Winnie, 1s. Educated Swansea Grammar School; University of Wales, Aberystwyth (Latin & History), Aberystwyth Theological College. Minister, Presbyterian Church of Wales. Ordained 1922: Briton Ferry 1922-25. Field Ambulance Brigade in Serbia 1914-18. Barrister, Grays Inn 1926. Lecturer in Law, University of Wales, Cardiff & Swansea. Freemason. Member, Morriston Cricket XI. Of Treboeth, Swansea. Languages: Welsh, English. Died 27 January 1942.

POWELL John Lewis: QC 1990 MA 1972 LlB (Cantab). Labour: Cardigan 1979. **Mr. John Powell:** Born Ammanford 14 September 1950, s of Gwyn Powell & Lillian Mary Griffiths. Married, Eva Zufia Lomnicka, lecturer in Law, 3c. Educated Christ College, Brecon (Pantyfedwen Scholar); Amman Valley Grammar School; Trinity Hall, Cambridge. VSO Thailand 1968; Israeli Kibbutz 1969; Travelled widely. Lecturer in Law; Barrister, Middle Temple 1974 (Harmsworth Scholar), Bencher. Attorney of the Turks & Caicos Islands. Deputy High Court Judge. Recorder. Member: Bar Council Executive; Society of Labour Lawyers, Royal Institute for International Affairs, Welsh Centre for International Affairs, European Movement, Fabian Society International Cttee, NATFHE. President, Society of Construction Law 1991-93. Chair: Bar Law Reform Cttee 1997-98. Joined Labour Party 1973 Languages: Welsh, English. Of Rhandir Trapp, Llandeilo. *Books:John L. Powell (with Roger Stewart QC), "The Hon. Mr. Justice Jackson", 2002.*

POWELL Meirion: Plaid Cymru: Gower Oct. 1974. **Mr. Meirion Powell:** Born 1947. Educated University of Wales, Aberystwyth. With Malawi Agricultural Services. In tourist industry. Languages: Welsh, English.

POWELL Michael: Liberal Democrat, Pontypridd 2003. **Mr. Mick Powell:** Married. Educated Polytechnic of Wales. Plumber. Quantity Surveyor. Rhondda/Cynon/Taf BC. Interests: Education. Environment, Health, Safety in Work. Member: RSPB. Hobbies: Meccano. Of Pontypridd.

POWELL Michael E: Conservative: Caerphilly 1987. **Mr. Michael Powell:** Born 23 May 1948. Married, 2 stepchildren, divorced 1999. Educated Bridgend Grammar-Technical School; Exeter University. Teacher in a comprehensive school; took administrative post in education. Owner, driving school & music business. Bridgend TC 1979-; Mayor 1984-85. Ogwr BC 1979-83. Laleston ComC 1979-85. Of Sarn, Bridgend.

POWELL Percy Lunniss: BA (Wales) 1953. Conservative: Ogmore 1951. **Mr. Sandy Powell:** Born, Cardiff January 1921. Married. Educated Newport private school; Southlea Preparatory School, Malvern; Haileybury College; University of Wales, Cardiff. Army (Middle East) 1940-45. Industrial Relations Trainee 1956-58. Schoolmaster 1958-66. Branch Manager, Imperial Life Assurance Co of Canada Ltd 1966-. Vice-Chair, Glamorgan Young Conservatives. Cardiff CC 1950-56.

POWELL Raymond: Kt 1996. Labour MP: Ogmore 1979-. **Sir Ray Powell:** Born Treorchy, 19 June 1928, s of Albert Ernest (miner) & Lucy Powell. Married 1949, Marion Grace Evans, 1s 1d (Janice, AM. Ogmore qv). Educated Pentre Grammar School; National Council of Labour Colleges; London School of Economics. Fireman, British Rail 1946-50. Shop Manager 1950-56. Own butcher's shop 1956-66. Secretary/Agent to Walter Padley MP1967-79 (voluntary 1969-79). Administrative Officer, Penybanc Main Sewerage Board 1974-97. Senior Administrative Officer, Welsh Water Authority 1974-79. NCLC Lecturer. Chair: South Wales Euro CLP 1980-. Member, Executive, Labour Party in Wales 1970-80, 19883-90 (Chair 1977). Member USDAW 50 years. Ogwr BC 1973-79. Jt Chair (ex-Secretary), All Party Fairs & Showgrounds Group 1989. Vice-Chair: All Party Retail Industry Parl. Group. Member: Select Cttee. Welsh Affairs 1982-85, Commons Services Sub-Cttee 1987-89. Chair, Commons Accommodation & Works Cttee 1991-97. Secretary, Welsh Labour MPs 1984-; Anglo-Bulgarian Parl Group 1984-. Treasurer, Anglo-Romanian Parl. Group 1984-. Vice-Chair, PLP Agriculture Cttee 1986-87. Opposition Whip. Sought nomination for Rhondda, Died 7 December 2001.

POWELL Walter Rice Howell: JP DL (Pembs & Carms) MA (Oxon). Liberal: Carmarthenshire 1874; MP: Carmarthenshire 1880-85; West Carmarthenshire, 1885-92. **Mr. Walter Powell:** Born 4 April 1819, s of Walter Rice Howell Powell & Mary, d of Joshua Powell. Anglican. Married (1) 1840 Emily Anne (Died 1846), d of Henry Skrine, 2c (2) Catherine Anne Prudence, d of Grismond Phillips, Cwmgwili 1c. Educated Private Tutor; Christ Church, Oxford. Landowner. High Sheriff of Carmarthenshire 1849. Secretary, Llanboidy Agricultural Show. Originator, United Counties Benefit Society. Master of Hounds 50 years. of Maesgwynne, Whitland. Estate £6,343. Died 25 June 1889.

POWELL William Denston: Pro Europe Conservative, Wales Euro 1999. **Mr. William Powell:** Chair, Wales European Movement. Joined Liberal Democrats. Of Hereford.

POWER Janet – see MAREDUDD Siân.

POWLESLAND John James: Labour: Swansea West 1918. **Mr. John Powlesland:** Born Plymouth 1863. Married Mary, 1c. Railway worker, Great Western Railway. Branch Secretary, National Amalgamated Labourers' Union 1899, District Secretary 1900, South Wales Organiser until 1907. South Wales Secretary, National Transport Workers' Union 1907-21; Transport & General Workers Union 1921-31. Swansea BC 1912-16; Alderman 1916. President, Swansea Labour Federation 1909. Chair: Board, Swansea & South Wales Institute for the Blind; Industrial School. Vice-Chair, Swansea Labour Club & Institute. Of Swansea. Died 26 October 1936.

PREECE Aneurin Jason Marsden: Plaid Cymru, Torfaen 2003. **Mr. Aneurin Preece:** Born Caerphilly 18 November 1962. Educated Torfaen Welsh Unit; Ysgol Gyfun Rhydfelin; University of Glamorgan. Self-employed part time teacher in Higher Education. Plaid Cymru Campaign Manager, Torfaen 2003. Chair, Torfaen Plaid Cymru. Vice-Chair: Plaid Cymru National Assembly Regional Election Cttee. Interests: Education, Home Affairs. Hobbies: Horse riding, Golf, Gardening. Languages: Welsh, English. Of Cwmbran.

PREECE Gerald Lyndon: Conservative: Merthyr Tydfil 1966. **Mr. Gerald Preece:** Born Port Talbot, October 1931. Methodist. Educated, Glanafan Grammar School. Steel Scheduler, Abbey Steel Works. Church youth club leader. Chair: Aberavon Young Conservatives, Aberavon Conservative Assn 1966. Contested Port Talbot BC. Of Margam.

PRICE Adam Robert: BSc (Wales) 1991. Plaid Cymru: Gower 1992, MP Carmarthen East & Dinefwr 2001. **Mr. Adam Price:** Born, Carmarthen, 23 September 1968, s of Rufus Price, miner (brother of Adrian (qv). Educated Dyffryn Aman Comprehensive School; University of Wales, Cardiff; Saarland University, Saarbruken. Manager: Aberystwyth Business Venture Project Oct. 1983. Research Fellow, City & Regional Planning, University of Wales, Cardiff 1991-93. Project Manager 1995-96. Founder/Managing Director, Newidiem (largest indigenous economic development consultancy in Wales). Founder/Secretary, Plaid Cymru Student Federation.

Adam Price.

Director of Policy; Director of Political Education 1995-9. Member, Plaid Cymru Executive. Interests: Economic, Rural Development, Pensions, Social Policy. Hobbies: Contemporary Culture, Good Friends, Good Food, Travel. Languages: Welsh, English. Of Treganna, Cardiff.

PRICE Adrian: Plaid Cymru: Llanelli 1987. **Mr. Adrian Price:** Born Amman Valley 1965, s of Rufus Price, miner (brother of Adam Price qv). Educated Dyffryn Aman Comprehensive School; University of Wales, Aberystwyth. Teacher, Amman Valley Comprehensive School. Member, UCAC. Languages: English, Welsh.

PRICE Charles William Mackay: Kt 1931 DL (Pembs). Conservative: Pembroke 1923, 1929, 1931; MP 1924-29. **Major Sir Charles Price:** Born Haverfordwest, 22 November 1872, s of James Price & Margaret Mackay. Anglican. Married 1897 Gwyndolin, d of Major J. Figula, Hove. Educated Clifton College, Bristol. Solicitor. Queens Royal Regt 1914-19. Middlesex CC 1907-11. Pembrokeshire CC 1922-. Chair, Pembrokeshire Conservative Assn -1950; President 1950. Member, Governing Body of the Church in Wales. Forestry Commissioner 1929. Of Haverfordwest. Died 6 July 1954.

PRICE Emyr: BA MA DipEd 1967 (Wales) MScEcon (London) 1980. Plaid Cymru: Conwy 1979. **Mr. Emyr Price:** Born Bangor 7 May 1944. Married Mair. 2s 1d. Educated Pwllheli Grammar School; Ysgol Gyfun Eifionydd; University of Wales, Bangor; London School of Economics. Teacher Brynrefail Grammar School 1967. Senior Lecturer, Bangor Normal College 1967-82. Editor *Y Faner* 1982. Hobbies: Cricket. Languages: Welsh, English. Of Bethel. *Books: Emyr Price: Fy Hanner Canrif I (autobiography), Lloyd George y Cenhed-*

PRICE Gerald Alexander Lewin: QC 1992 MA (Oxon). Conservative: Newport Feb. & Oct. 1974, Gower 1987. **Mr. Lewin Price:** Born Bridgend 13 September 1948, s of Denis Lewin Price & Patricia Rosemary Metcalfe, Porthcawl. Lay preacher. Married 1974, Theresa Elizabeth (Tessa) Iremonger-Watts, 2s. Educated Haileybury; Hertford College, Oxford; London College of Law. Barrister, Middle Temple, 1969; Cardiff practice 1970-74; Bermuda 1977-84. Stipendiary Magistrate 1971-81. Chief Stipendiary Magistrate & Senior Coroner 1981-84. Private practice, Cardiff 1984-. Chair: Liquor Licence Authority, Land Valuations Appeals Tribunal, Price Controls Commission, & Jury Revising Tribunal 1981-84. Crown Court Recorder 1990. Circuit Judge May 2000. Member: Commonwealth Magistrates & Judges Assn 1984-, Royal Yachting Assn; Royal Commonwealth Society; Glamorgan Lawn Tennis Club. Hobbies: Motorboats, the Balearics, Classical Music, Country Life.

PRICE Huw: LlB (Wales). Liberal Democrat, Cynon Valley 1997, South/East List 1999, Caerphilly 2003. **Mr. Huw Price:** Born Trecynon, 13 January 1969, s of Norman Hay Price, photographer. Unmarried. Educated Aberdare Boys Comprehensive School; University of Wales, Aberystwyth; York College of Law. Solicitor. Joined Liberal Party 1984. Secretary, Cynon Valley Liberal Democrats. Vice-President: Rhondda/Cynon/Taf Liberal Democrats 1997. Vice-Chair, Caerphilly Liberal Democrats. Caerphilly CBC (St. Martins) 1999-. Interests: Transport, Social Services. Hobbies: Playing Bowls, Sport, Travel, Shortwave Radio. Of Caerphilly.

PRICE John Barry: Labour: Montgomery 1979. **Mr. John Price:** Born 1942. Post Office Engineer. Chair, Chester & North Wales Post Office Unions. Secretary, North Wales & Chester Post Office Engineering Unions Co-ordinating Cttee. Member: Chester & District Trades Council. Chester CC (Labour Chief Whip 1965, Deputy Leader, Leader). President, Walled Towns Friendship Circle. Chair, Chester Community Safety Partnership. Member, North West Regional Assembly. Cheshire CC 1974-. Vice-Chair, Chester CLP. Press Officer, Cheshire County Labour Party. Treasurer, Chester Co-operative Party. Of Chester.

PRICE Peter Nicholas: BA (Southampton) 1963. Conservative: Aberdare 1964, 1966; Caerphilly 1970; MEP West Lancashire 1979-84, London SE 1984-95. Joined Liberal Democrats 6 December 1997. Contested Euro Wales 1999. **Mr. Peter Price:** Born Aberdare 19 February 1942, s of Revd Dewi Emlyn Price & Kate Mary Price, teacher.

Humanist. Married 1988, Joy Jassodra Bhola, operating theatre nurse, 1d. Educated, Aberdare Grammar School; Southampton University; Guildford College of Law; King's College, London (DipECLaw 1999). Solicitor 1966-79. Asst. Solicitor, Glamorgan CC 1967-68. European Strategy Counsel 1994. Part-time Chair, Employment Tribunal, Sept,2000. Director, CJA Consulting Ltd 2000. Non-Executive Director: Ravensbourne NHS Trust 1998-99; Bureau Veritas Quality International Ltd (BVQI) 1991-2001. Chair, Aberdare Young Conservatives 1958-59. Wales Area Young Conservatives. Convenor, Wales Young Conservative Policy Group. Vice-Chair: National Young Conservatives 1971-72; Wales Area, Conservative Party. Secretary: South Wales Group British Humanist Assn; Cardiff 2000 Planning Cttee; Royal Institute of International Affairs 1997-. Chair: Cardiff New Theatre Society. Member: National Long Term Planning Group; Family Planning Assn; European Movement Council; board of Wales in Europe 2001-; Institute of Welsh Affairs 1996-. Vice-President, Llangollen International Eisteddfod 1981-. Chair: European Parl Budgetary Control Cttee 1989-95. Governor, Thames Valley University 1996-. Standing Orders Commissioner, Welsh Assembly 1998-99. Member: [Richards] Commission on the Powers & Electoral Arrangements of the National Assembly 2002-04; Wales Public Law & Human Rights Assn 2000-; Foreign Secretary's Advisory Cttee on People's Europe preparing for British Presidency 1997-98. Joint Leader, Conservatives say YES, 1997. Awarded Hon. Membership of European Parliament, July 1994. Trustee, Ysgol Gymraeg Llundain. Of Cardiff.

PRICE J. Ll. – see LLOYD PRICE J.

PRICE Susan: Independent Wales, South/East List 2003. **Ms. Susan Price:** Abertillery Branch Secretary, Independent Wales Party.

PRICE Thomas Phillips: JP (Mon & Essex) BA 1867 MA (Oxon) 1869. Liberal MP North Monmouthshire 1885-95. **Captain Thomas Price:** Born 14 June 1844, s of Canon William Price, Vicar of Llanarth, Mon & Mary, d of Sir Thomas Phillips. Anglican. Married, (1) 1882 Frances Ann (died 1897) d of Revd John Charles Bowlatt (2) Frances Celia (died 1926) d of Maximilian Konetam. Educated Winchester; University College, Oxford. Barrister, Inner Temple 1869. Landowner. High Sheriff of Monmouthshire 1882. Captain, Royal Mon Engineers Militia 1879-83. Of Trilley Court, Mon, Kelvedon & Chelsea. Estate £ 60,907. Died 28 June 1932.

PRICE-ROWLANDS Gwynn: LlB (Liverpool) LLM (London). Conservative: Ynys Môn 1992.

Mr. Gwynn Price-Rowlands: Born Bangor 18 January, 1951, s of Emyr Price & Aileen Mar. Married 1991 Dr. Catherine Evans. Educated Friars School, Bangor; Brynhyfryd School; Liverpool University; London University. North Wales Public Speech Champion. Solicitor 1976. Barrister 1985. Languages: Welsh, English.

PRICE-WHITE David Algernon Price: TD 1946 BA (Wales). Conservative: Conway 1950; MP Caernarfon Boroughs 1945-50. **Lieut-Colonel David Price-White:** Born Bangor 5 September 1906, s of Price FFoulkes White & Charlotte Bell. Anglican. Married, 1934, Gwyneth Harries 1s 1d. Educated Friars School, Bangor; University of Wales, Bangor. Solicitor 1932-56. Principal Assistant, General Electricity Board, Midland Regional HQ 1957. TA 1928-39, Army 1939-45. Caernarfonshire CC 1939-41. Bangor CC. Languages: Welsh, English. Of Colwyn Bay. Died 6 March 1978.

PRICHARD Wilfred Augustus: MBE MC 1918 BA 1920 MA (Cantab). Conservative: Rhondda West 1929. **Captain Wilfred Prichard:** Born Resolven, s of Dr. R. D. Prichard JP. Married 1928, Freda, d of B. Warmeford, Halsey House, London. Educated Resolven Board School; Monmouth Grammar School, Trinity College, Cambridge (Engineering). Army 1914-18 (3 years in France), Lieutenant 1915. Barrister Grays Inn 1922. Conservative Agent, Pontypridd 1924. Joined RAFVR 1939, Flight-Lieutenant 1940; Director, RAF Legal Service 1939-45. Penarth UDC 1934-; Chair 1936-37.

PRIESTLEY Christopher Fearne: JP (Anglesey). Conservative: Anglesey 1900. **Mr. Christopher Priestley:** Born 1843, s of John Priestley, Hirdrefiog, & Jane, d of Col. Richard Edwards, Nanhoron. Anglican. Married, Annabella Sarah Wynn Griffith. Landowner. President, Anglesey Constitutional Assn (Merger of Conservative & Liberal Unionist Assns) 1886. Anglesey CC. Of Hirdrefeiog, Llangefni. Estate £7,739. Died 31 October 1908.

PRIESTLEY Francis John Lloyd: JP (Merioneth) 1906 Croix de Guerre (France). Conservative: Eifion. Jan. 1910. **Lieut-Colonel Francis Priestley:** Born, s of Henry Samuel Priestley & Lucy, d of Sir Robert Cunliffe (nephew of C. F. Priestley [qv]). Anglican. Married 1902, Pearl, d of Colonel Llewelyn England Sidney Parry DSO, Pengwern, Rhuddlan, 3c. Educated Shrewsbury School. Landowner. High Sheriff of Caernarfonshire 1906, Merioneth 1910. Lieut-Colonel, Denbighshire Yeomanry 1917-18. Of Ymlwch, Criccieth, then Dolfnig, Penrhyndeudraeth. Estate £3,128 plus settled land. Died 28 January 1940.

PRIOR Michael J: Conservative: Cardiff West 1992. **Mr. Michael Prior:** Born 6 May 1955. Married 1982, Karen, 2s. Educated St. George's School, Weybridge; Durham University. Solicitor 1981 (Cardiff). South Glam CC 1989-. Wenvoe ComC 1977-91. Chair, Welsh Conservative Candidates Assn.

PRITCHARD John L: BA (Wales). Conservative: Wrexham Feb. & Oct. 1974, Norwood 1979. **Mr. John Pritchard:** Born, Lewisham July 1946. Married 1c. Educated Haberdasher Aske's School; St. David's College, Lampeter. Local Government Officer, Lewisham Borough Housing Department. Queen's Scout. Member RNAS. Vice-Chair, Lewisham West CPC. Contested GLC election 1973; Bromley BC 1974-. Member NALGO.

PRITCHARD Margaret: BA DipDrama. Labour: North List 1999. **Ms. Margaret Pritchard:** Born Bethesda, 7 April 1951, d of Samuel Pritchard & Mair Menai Hughes, shopkeepers. Welsh Independent. Married 1972 John Howard Copley, university lecturer, 2d. Educated Ysgol Dyffryn Ogwen; Welsh College of Music & Drama; Open University. Broadcaster (HTV continuity desk until 1992). Charity Chief Executive. Member, Labour Party Cttee. NHS Trust Non Executive Director 8 years. School Convenor 8 years. Interests: Health, Education. Hobbies: Gardening, Reading. Languages: Welsh, English.

PRITCHARD William Alexander: Green Party: Meirionydd/Nant Conwy 1992. **Mr. Bill Pritchard:** Born Bristol, 4 February 1943, s of Robert Edward Pritchard, shipping insurance surveyor, & Jean McBratney, physiotherapist. Church of England. 1d. Educated Truro School. Various jobs since coming to Wales. Clr. 1990-94. Supported Plaid Cymru 1997. Hobbies: Walking, cycling. Languages: English, once spoke Spanish & Hebrew. Of Barmouth.

PRITCHARD-RAYNER George: JP DL (Anglesey) JP (Warwickshire) 1874. Conservative: Anglesey 1880, 1885, 1886, Withdrew 1874. **Captain George Pritchard-Rayner:** Born, Llangwyllog 13 September 1843, s of Henry Pritchard JP DL Trescawen (of Mynydd Parys copper) & Martha, d of John Moulsdale. Anglican. Married 1871, Sarah Mary Brady-Rayner, d of John Brady MP Cambridge, 5c. (1s Died of typhoid in Boer War); Added name of Rayner by deed-poll. Educated, Eton. Landowner (spent £40,000 on new mansion & estate improvements). Captain, 5th Dragoons. High Sheriff of Anglesey 1878. Chair, Anglesey Chamber of Agriculture. President: Anglesey Agricultural Society. Noted conjurer – raised £1600 for charity in London; used conjuring skills in election meetings. Of Trescawen, Anglesey. Estate £15. Died 18 July 1893.

PROBERT Arthur Reginald: Labour MP: Aberdare B/E 1954-74. **Mr. Arthur Probert:** Born 1909, s of Albert John Probert, publican. Married 1938, Muriel, d of William Taylor, 2d. Educated Aberdare Boys' Grammar School. Local Government Officer, Aberdare UDC Housing Dept. RAFVR 1939-45. Secretary, Aberdare Trades & Labour Council 1949-54. Member TGWU. Secretary, Welsh PLP 1956-59. PPS 1965-66; Member: Public Accounts Cttee 1964-66. Opposition Whip Nov. 1959-Dec. 1960, Resigned in opposition to Labour's nuclear policy. Member, Speaker's Panel of Chairmen. Chair, Welsh Grand Cttee. 1970. Died 14 February 1975.

PROCTOR David: Socialist Labour Party: Swansea West 1997. **Mr. Dave Proctor:** Born, Castleford, W. Yorks. 1956. Partner, Lynne. Yorkshire Mineworker 22 years. Electrician, Tower Colliery 1989-92. WEA Tutor, Trade Union Studies 1992. NUM Branch Chair. Member, NUM Yorkshire Regional Executive. Officer, Swansea West Labour Party. Secretary, South Wales Area, Socialist Labour Party. Of Tycoch, Swansea (1994).

PROFUMO Joseph Alexander, 3rd Baron Profumo (Italy): Liberal: South Mon 1892. **Baron Alexander Profumo:** Born Italy, 1860, son of 2nd Baron Profumo, banker (related to Italy's first Minister of Finance). Married. Educated at a private school. Entered commercial life at 19. Founder/Managing Director, Provident Life Assn. Total Abstainer. Vice-President, Norwood Band of Hope Union. Of London. Estate £183,456. Died Grand Hotel, Paris, 11 June 1911.

PROSSER John: Conservative, Merthyr Tydfil 2003. **Mr. John Prosser:** Born married Christine. Educated Cyfarthfa Castle Grammar School, Merthyr Tydfil; Polytechnic of Wales. European Chartered Mechanical Engineer. Worked in Food, Pharmaceutical & Petrochemical Industries. Ran own consultancy. University Lecturer. General Manager, sauce manufacturing co. Chair: Penarth Male Voice Choir (compiled history). Civil Defence Adviser, Buckingham. Member: Royal British Legion, RAF Assn. Governor, Moose International Abergavenny Lodge 309. Founder Member: Abergavenny Eisteddfod, Abergavenny Petanque Society. Abergavenny TC (Chair: Events Cttee; Council Rep. On Oestringen Twining Cttee). Member: Gwent Assn of Local Councils Cttee. Of Abergavenny.

PROTHERO-BEYNON Hilda Edith: MBE 1972. Conservative: Carmarthen 1970. **Mrs. Hilda Protheroe-Beynon:** Born, Llanelli November 1909, d of Percy Rees, stockbroker (great gd of Revd David Rees, Capel Als). Anglican. Married (1) John G. Protheroe-Beynon OBE JP (2) Fenner-Clayton. Educated privately. Housewife & Farmer. Member, Carmarthenshire NFU Executive.

Founder 1st Burry Port Girl Guides. Of Laugharne. Died 4 January 2000, after very long illness.

PRYCE-JONES Pryce: Kt. 1887 JP(Mont). Conservative MP: Montgomery District 1885-86, 1892-95; retired in favour of his son Edward (qv). **Sir Pryce Pryce-Jones:** Born Newtown, 16 October1834, illegitimate s of William Jones, solicitor, & Mary Ann Goodwin, nearest living relative of Robert Owen at his funeral. Anglican. Became Pryce-Jones by deed poll 1887. Married 1859, Eleanor, d of Edward Rowley-Morris, 4s 4d. Apprenticed, Newtown draper at 12; took business over 1859. Wool entrepreneur & mail order pioneer (Royal Welsh Warehouses, Newtown); (boasted of 300,000 customers around the world, inc. Florence Nightingale & Queen Victoria). Developed own parcel post system. Business sold to Great Universal Stores 1953. Suggested parcel post to Postmaster General at a dinner 1882. Director, Welshpool & Llanfair Railway Co. High Sheriff of Montgomeryshire 1891. Of Dolerw, Newtown. Estate £7,902. Died 11 January 1920.

PRYCE-JONES Pryce Edward:1st Bart 1918 TD JP DL (Mont) BA 1889 MA 1892 (Oxon). Conservative: Montgomery District 1906, Jan. 1910, MP 1895-1906; Dec. 1910-18. **Colonel, Sir Edward Pryce-Jones:** Born, Newtown 6 February, 1861, s of Sir Pryce Pryce-Jones (qv) & Eleanor, d of Edward Rowley-Morris. Anglican. Married Beatrice, d of Herbert Hardie, Oxford House, Chester, 2c. Educated Liverpool College; Oxford University. Barrister, Inner Temple 1892. Wool Entrepreneur. Company Chair: mail order company. Landowner. Captain, Montgomeryshire Yeomanry 1883-95; Raised & Commanded 5th Vol Batt. SWB 1895-1908, Hon. Colonel SWB 1908.Junior Deputy Vice-Chancellor, University of Wales 1911-13. Joint Treasurer, Inter Parliamentary Union 1911-18. Of Milford Hall, Newtown. Estate £13,683. Died 22 May 1926.

PRYS Gwilym Roger: MA (Oxon). Conservative: Caernarfon 1966. **Mr. Roger Prys:** Born September 1912. Educated, Monmouth School; Keble College, Oxford. Solicitor at Rhyl. Founder-Secretary, Industrial Assn for Wales & Mon. Secretary, North Wales Productivity Council.

PRYS-DAVIES Gwilym, Baron Prys-Davies of Llanegryn 1982: LlB 1949 LLM (Wales) 1952 Hon. LLD (Wales) 1996 OStJ. Labour: Carmarthen: B/E March 1966. **Mr. Gwilym Prys-Davies:** Born Oswestry 8 December, 1923, s of William & Mary Matilda Davies. Presbyterian Church of Wales. Married 1951, Llinos Evans, 3d. Educated Tywyn Grammar School; University of Wales, Aberystwyth. Royal Navy 1942-46. Solicitor; Senior Partner 1957-87; Consultant.

Legal Adviser: Coal Industry Benevolent Fund; National Union of Mineworkers; lawyer involved with Aberfan disaster; Christian Education Movement in Wales. Member: Plaid Cymru 1947-50; Welsh Republican Movement 1950; Labour Party 1953; Fabian Society1953; Council for Wales1967-9; Welsh Cttee Independent Television Authority, Court of the University of Wales. Chair, Welsh Hospital Board 1968-74. Vice-President, Hon. Society of Cymmrodorion 1992-. Adviser to Secretary of State for Wales 1974-78. Opposition Spokesman in Lords on Health 1983-89; Northern Ireland 1985-997; legal affairs 1990. Member: Economic & Social Cttee EEC 1978-82. Vice-President, Coleg Harlech 1989. President, University of Wales, Swansea 1997. First peer to take oath of allegiance in Welsh. Languages: Welsh, English. Of Tonteg, Glam.

PUDNER David Huw: BEd. United Socialist, Aberavon 1999; Welsh Socialist Alliance, Neath 2001. **Mr. Huw Pudner:** Born, 28 June 1950, s of Ivor Pudner, steelworker, & Catherine Pudner, nurse. Married 1974, Heather, university administrator, 1s 1d. Educated Rhydhir Secondary Modern School, Neath Abbey. Teacher. Member, Labour Party, resigned to join Socialist Workers' Party 1992. Agent: Aberavon 2001, Swansea East Assembly B/E September 2001. Organised Skewen Park Family Day 1985-94. Founder Member, Stop the Crymlyn Burrows Incinerator Campaign. Member: Anti-Nazi League.; CND; Anti-Apartheid activist. ComC. Interests: Education, Health, Nuclear, Anti Capitalist Movement. Hobbies: Schools rugby coach. Of Skewen.

PUGH Alan: BA CertEd DipComp Studies (Wales). Labour AM Clwyd West 1999. **Mr. Alan Pugh:** Born Penygraig, 9 June 1955, son of Maurice Thomas Pugh, miner, & Violet Jane Pugh, nurse. Married 1978, Janet 1s 1d. Educated Tonypandy Grammar School; Polytechnic of Wales, University of Wales, Cardiff. Lecturer in Accounting, Bridgend College, 1983-87. Senior Lecturer/Section Head, Newcastle College 1987-92. Head of Business Studies, Llandrillo College 1992-95. Head of Academic Development 1995-96. Head of Learning Development & Asst. Principal, West Cheshire College 1996-99. Member: Snowdonia Society, Austrian Alpine Club. Qualified Mountain Leader. Labour Whip 1999. Deputy Minister, Economic Development 30.4.2001. Minister for Culture, Sport & Languages of Wales, May 2003. Interests: Post school education, Information & commercial technology. Hobbies: Opera, Mountaineering. Languages: Learning Welsh, English. Of Colwyn Bay.

PUGH David: JP (Carms) JP DL (Cards) BA (Oxon) 1828. Liberal MP: Carmarthenshire 1857-68, East Carmarthenshire 1885-. **Mr. David Pugh:**

Born March 1806, s of Lieut-Colonel David Heron Pugh MP of Greenhill and Manoravon & Elizabeth, d of William Beynon. Anglican. Unmarried. Educated Rugby School; Balliol College, Oxford. Barrister, Inner Temple 1837.

PULESTON John Henry: Kt 1887 JP DL Conservative: Caernarfon District 1892; MP: Devonport 1874-92. **Sir John Puleston:** Born Llanfair Dyffryn Clwyd 2 June, 1930, s of John Puleston & Mary, d of John Jones, Talsarn (descendant of Sir Roger de Puleston). Anglican. Married 1857, Margaret (Died 1902) d of Revd E. Lloyd. Educated Ruthin Grammar School; Kings College, London. Journalist, then banker in USA 1855-60. Colonel in American Civil War. Lord Lieutenant of London; Constable of Caernarfon Castle. Vice-President, Hon. Society of Cymmrodorion. Treasurer, National Eisteddfod Assn 1880-1907 & Chair, National Eisteddfod General Cttee. Chair, City of London Conservative Assn. Of Ffynogion, Ruthin & London. Died 19 October 1908.

PULLIN John: SDP/Alliance Candidate for Pembroke 1983. **Revd John Pullin:** Born Garw Valley 1939. Married Yvonne, 1s 2d. Educated Newport schools; University of Wales, Cardiff; Cardiff Baptist College. Baptist Minister. Ordained 1961: Cwmparc 1961, Penarth -1968, Cianorte, Brazil 1970-71, Jaguariava 1971-74, Cacares Matagrosso, Brazil (coffee growing area in Amazon Valley) 1974-78, Deer Park, Tenby 1978-89; Paranaiba 1989-92, Campogrande 1992-. President, Sul-Mato-Grossense Baptist Convention 2003. Planned to join Labour Party on returning home in 1978 but joined SDP instead. Short-listed at Bridgend when selected for Pembroke.

PULMAN Angela: MSc (Wales). Plaid Cymru, Ogmore 2001. **Ms. Angela Pulman:** Born, Merthyr Tydfil, 25 March 1951. Lives with partner 2c. Educated Cyfartha Grammar School, Merthyr Tydfil; University of Wales, Cardiff (Economics). Community Economic Development Officer. Held a number of roles related to social & economic regeneration projects; ex-economic research, PR & marketing consultant in public/local government sector. Chief Executive, Community Enterprise Wales. Director, *Glas Cymru* July 2001. Economic Adviser, Plaid Cymru. Interests: Social Exclusion, Women's Rights, Young People. Hobbies: History, Reading, Learning Danish, Walking, Food. Of Merthyr Tydfil.

PURNELL David Cuthbert: Conservative: Rhondda East 1964; Aberdare 1970. **Mr. David Purnell:** Born Cardiff, 1932, s of Alderman O C Purnell KSG CBE JP DL Lord Mayor of Cardiff. Roman Catholic. Married 1959 Helen Croke of

Neath, 3c. Educated De la Salle School, Cardiff; St. Illtyd's College, Cardiff; Oratory School, Woodcote. Estate Agent-1958. Office Manager, Funeral Directors, 1958, Director. Cardiff CC 1958-, Alderman 1970, Lord Mayor. South Glam CC, Chairman (Chair, Public Works & Planning Cttee. 1966, resigned 1969 because of his opposition to a 55 million-city re-development scheme). Vice-President: Riverside Ward Conservative Assn; Carlton Group. Governor: St. Illtyd's College, Heathfield House School, Cardiff College of Music & Drama. Sea-scoutmaster. Of Cardiff. Died 17 February 1979.

PYM Francis Leslie, Baron Pym of Sandy 1987: PC 1970 MC 1945 DL (Cambs) 1973 MA (Cantab). Conservative: Rhondda West 1959; MP Cambridgeshire B/E 1961-1983, Cambridgeshire SE 1983-87. **Rt. Hon. Francis Pym:** Born Abergavenny 13 March, 1922, s of Leslie Ruthven Pym MP (qv) & Iris Rosalind, d of Charles Orde. Anglican. Married 1949, Valerie, d of F. J. H. Dalglish, 4c; Educated Eton; Magdalene College, Cambridge (Hon. Fellow 1979). Army 1939-45, Captain, 9th Lancers. Trainee, Lewis Ltd 1947-49. General Manager, Merseyside Dairies 1949-52. Managing Director, George Holloway & Webb, agricultural stand erectors) 1953-61. Landowner in Huntingdonshire & Bedfordshire. Secretary, Cambridge University Conservative Assn 1941. Chair: Liverpool Young Conservatives 1948-49, Hereford Divisional Conservative Assn. Member, Liverpool Education Cttee. Herefordshire CC 1958-61. Member, Court of Liverpool University 1949-53. PPS 1962. Asst Whip 1962-64, Opposition Whip 1964-67. Deputy Chief Whip 1967-70. Chief Government Whip & Parliamentary Secretary to the Treasury 1970-73. Secretary of State for Northern Ireland 1973-74. Paymaster General 1981. Lord President of the Council & Leader of the Commons 1981-82. Secretary of State for Foreign & Commonwealth Affairs 1982-83. Asked to resign by Mrs. Thatcher after the 1983 election. Chair: English Cable Enterprises 1990-95; Diamond Cable Communications 1995-99; Philip N. Christie & Co 1990-93. Director: Christie Brockbank Shipton Ltd 1994-99. President, Atlantic Treaty Assn 1985-87. Chair, English Speaking Union 1987-92. Of Sandy, Beds.

PYM Leslie Ruthven: MA (Cantab) JP DL (Mon). Conservative MP Monmouth B/E 1939-. **Mr. Leslie Pym:** Born Wentworth, Lancs 1884, s of Rt. Revd Walter Ruthven Pym, Bishop of Bombay. Anglican. Married 1914, Iris Rosalind, d. of Charles Orde of Suffolk (qv Francis L. Pym). Educated, Bedford School; Magdelene College, Cambridge. Land Agent. President, Land Agents Assn 1935. PPS. Lord Commissioner of the Treasury 1942-45. Of Aberpergwm Lodge, Abergavenny & London. Died 10 July 1945.

– Q –

QUIN Jeremy Mark: BA (Oxon). Conservative: Meironydd/Nant Conwy 1997. **Mr. Jeremy Quin:** Born Buckinghamshire 24 September 1968, s of an agricultural merchant. Married Arabella, book publisher. Educated St. Albans School; Hertford College, Oxford (Modern History). President, Oxford Union. Member, Prime Minister's Euro Election Team 1974. Parliamentary assistant & election aide, Peter Lilley MP 1990-93. Joined Nat.West Securities 1990. Asst-Director, corporate stockbroking department. Deutsche Bank (Brewing, Pubs & Spirits). Joined Conservative Party 1983. Area Chair, Young Conservatives. Co-founder/Chair, Millennium Group 1993. Secretary, Coningsby Club. Master, Beagle Pack. Member: Countryside Alliance.

QUINTAVALLE Josephine Mary: Pro Life Alliance, South/Central List 2003; Kensington & Chelsea 2001; South-West Surrey 1997; South-East England Euro 2004. **Countess Josephine Quintavalle:** Born New Zealand. Married Count Qunitavelle 5s (1s, Bruno Quintavalle, Holborn & St. Pancras 2001). Worked with local charities including drug addicts & the homeless. Director: Scottish Pro-Life Alliance. Director: UK Pro-Life Alliance. Founder & Chief Counsellor, CORE (comment on Reproductive Ethics) 1994-2000. Co-ordinate campaign against cloning. Worked with homeless & drug addicts. Of Chelsea (1980).

– R –

RADCLIFFE Henry John: JP (Glam) 1906. Liberal: Merthyr Tydfil 1906. **Mr. Henry Radcliffe:** Born Merthyr Tydfil 1857, s of Rees Radcliffe & Sarah Davies. Calvinistic Methodist. Married Mary (died 1920) 1s. Educated Miss Morgan's School & Evan Williams' School, Thomastown, Merthyr Tydfil. Shipowner. Chair & Director, shipping, dry dock and estate companies. Largest landowner in Glamorgan. President: South Glamorgan Liberal Assn. Chair: Cardiff Shipowners Assn; Shipping Federation; Glamorgan Council of Agriculture. Languages: Welsh. English. Last minute nomination 1906. Estate £1,200,000. Of St. Mellons. Died 16 December 1921.

RADCLIFFE John: Conservative: Abertillery 1951. **Mr. John Radcliffe:** Born March 1900. Educated Stoneyhurst. Army. RAF 1939-45. Teacher of Public Speaking.

RADFORD Jacqueline: BA BSc (Open). Liberal Democrat, Ogmore & South/West List 2003. **Mrs. Jacqueline Radford:** Married, Stephen Radford (making & publishing video of wrecks around Welsh coast). Educated University of Wales, Swansea (American Studies). 30 years in banking; voluntary redundancy, Christmas 2001. Postgraduate MA Student. Of Maesteg.

RAFFAN Keith William Twort: BA 1971 MA (Cantab) 1977. Conservative MP Delyn 1983-87; Candidate: Feb. 1974, East Aberdeenshire Oct. 1974. Joined Liberal Democrats. Liberal Democrat: Highlands & Islands Euro B/E 1998; MSP Mid Scotland & Fife Region 1999-. **Mr. Keith Raffan:** Born Aberdeen 21 June 1947, s of Dr. Alfred William Raffan TD & Dr. Jean Crampton Twort. Educated Robert Gordon's School, Aberdeen; Trinity College, Glenalmond; Corpus Christi College, Cambridge. Parliamentary Correspondent, Daily *Express* 1981-83. Television Interviewer/Political Commentator 1997-. Member, NUJ. President: Welsh Conservative Trade Unionists 1984-87, Welsh Young Conservatives 1987-90. National Chair, PEST 1970-74. Vice-Chair, Conservative Party Organisation Cttee 1985-89. Executive, British Atlantic Group of Young Political Leaders 1970. Select Cttee Member: Wales 1983-92. Vice-President: Clwyd Pre-School Playgroups Assn 1983-; Delyn & Deeside Multiple Sclerosis Society. Hobbies: Architecture, Cinema, Travel, Hill-Walking, Eating, Working-out.

RAIKES Henry St. John Digby: CBE 1920 KC 1921 JP DL. Conservative: East Denbighshire 1895, Mid-Derbyshire 1900. **Mr. Henry Raikes:** Born 1863, s of Rt. Hon. Henry Cecil Raikes MP. Anglican. Married Annie Lucinda, d of General "Dan" MacKinnon (son MP). Educated Charterhouse School; Trinity College, Cambridge. Barrister, Inner Temple 1887. Recorder of Kings Lynn 1905-. Chair, Derbyshire Quarter Sessions 1912. Of Derby & London. Estate £8,252. Died 1 May 1943.

RAIZ Raja Gul: Welsh Socialist Alliance: Cardiff Central 2003; Respect Unity Coalition, Wales Euro 2004. **Mr. Raja Gul Raiz:** Muslim. Secretary, Dar-ul-Isra Mosque, Cardiff. Member, UK Islamic Mission. Works for Cardiff CAB.

RAJAN Kunnathur Thiruvenatachari: MB BS (Madras) 1958. UK Independent Party, Rhondda 2003. **Dr. K. T. Rajan:** Born Calcutta, India, 22 September 1932, s of Kunnathur M F Chari, civil servant, & Chem Bagammal, housewife. Hindu. Married 1987, Marca Elizabeth Rajan, occupational therapist, 1s 2d. Educated Christian Medical College, Vellore; Welsh National School of Medicine (DipChestDiseases 1961); Kings College, Cambridge. Researched pneumoconiosis at Llandough Hospital. Consultant physician & rheumatoligist, retired. Fundraiser for Athritis. Fellow, Rhondda Medical Society. Established Osteoporosis Service in Wales. Interests: Health issues affecting Rhondda, Liberal Democrats, UK Independence Party, National Health Service. Hobbies: Water Colour Painting, Travel. Languages: English, Hindi, Tamil. Of Cardiff.

RAMSAY Nicholas Harvey: MA (Durham). Conservative, Torfaen 2003. **Mr. Nicholas Harvey:** Born Newport, 10 June 1975, son of Graham George Harvey, marine electrical engineer, & Caroline Ann Davies, housewife. Church of England. Educated Croesyceiliog Comprehensive School, Cwmbran; St. John's College, Durham (English & Philosophy); University of Wales, Cardiff (Diploma in Linguistics). AM Support Staff, National Assembly. Chair: Monmouth Conservative Assn. Hobbies: Pub Quizzing, Tennis. Languages: English, some German. Of Llanfrechfa, Cwmbran.

RAMSAY-WAYE: Sheila: Liberal Democrat, Ogmore 1999, Gower 2001. **Mrs. Sheila Ramsay-**

Waye: Born 1935. 1s. Hairdresser (self-employed 20 years). Community Placement Carer & Regional Clinical Hypnotherapist. Core Trainer, West Glamorgan Social Services & Lecturer at Llanelli & Afan Colleges. Stress Management Consultant & Relaxation Therapist. Interests community voluntary services. Joined Liberal Democrats 1998. Hobbies: DIY, Car & Motorcycle Maintenance, Complimentary Therapies, Reading, Politics, Watching Ballet, Listening to all sorts of music. Of Pontardawe.

RANDELL David: Liberal MP West Glamorgan B/E 888-1900. **Mr. David Randell:** Born Llanelli 1854, s of John Randell, merchant. Calvinistic Methodist. Married 1890 Sarah Ann, d of Richard George, Llanidloes manufacturer, 1s 1d. Educated Revd Thomas James School, Llanelli; Dr. Condon's School, New Wandsworth. Solicitor 1876. Solicitor, SWMF. Carmarthenshire CC Alderman 1889; Llanelli BC. Stood in by-election as Labour and Home Rule Candidate, with support of miners & tinplate workers; active in tinplate union litigation. Languages: Welsh, English. Of Llanelli & London. Estate £2,989. Died 5 June 1912.

RANDERSON Jennifer Elizabeth: BA PGCE (London). Liberal/Liberal Democrat: Cardiff South & Penarth, 1987, Cardiff Central 1992, 1997, AM Cardiff Central 1999-. **Mrs. Jennie Randerson:** Born Paddington 26 May 1948. Married 1970 Dr. Peter Randerson, lecturer, 1s 1d. Educated Wimbledon High School; Bedford College, London University; London Institute of Education. Teacher: Sydenham High School 1970-72, Spalding High School 1972-74, Llanishen High School 1974-76. Lecturer in Business Studies & Manager, Coleg Glan Hafren 1976-2000. Company Director, L'Avenir Ltd. Chair: Octavia Trust. Cardiff CC 1983-95, Cardiff CCC 1994-99 (Leader of the Opposition). 1st Chair, Welsh Liberal Democrats 1988, President. Member: NATFHE, Charter 98, Friends of the Earth, All Mod Cons. Chair, School Governors. Minister of Culture, Sport & Welsh Language, October 2000-2003; Acting Deputy Prime Minister 2001. Spokesperson for Economic Development, May 2003. Hobbies: Travel, Gardening, Concerts. Of Cardiff.

RANELAGH John O'Beirne-: MA (Oxon) PhD (Kent). Conservative: Caerphilly 1979. **Dr. John O'Beirne-Ranelagh:** Born 3 November 1947, s of James O'Beirne Ranelagh & Elaine Lambert O'Beirne Ranelagh. Married 1974, Elizabeth Grenville, d of Sir William Hawthorne. Educated St. Christopher's School, Letchworth; Cambridge College of Arts & Technology; Christ Church, Oxford; Eliot College, Kent University. Credit Analyst, Chase Manhattan Bank 1969-70.

Campaign Director Onset Housing Assn 1971. Studentship in History, Kent University 1972-74. Research Officer, Conservative Research Department 1975-79 (Margaret Thatcher's speech writer). Assoc. Producer, Ireland, a Television History, BBC TV 1979-81. Secretary to the Board 1981-83; Commissioning Editor, Channel Four TV Co. 1981-88. Deputy Chief Exec & Director of Programmes, TV2 Denmark 1988. Exec Producer & Writer, CIA, BBC TV/NRK/Primetime 1989-92. Associate, Hydra Associates 1989-91. Director, Broadcasting Research Unit 1988-90. Consultant: TV2 Norway 1991- & TV1 Portugal 1992-94. Member: ITV Commission 1994-99; TMS Executive Cttee 1984-87; Political Cttee. UNA 1978-90. Governor, Danesford School 1977-81. Hobbies: old Bentley cars; Quarter Horses. Of Grantchester, Cambridge. *Books: John O'Beirne-Ranelagh, Science, Education & Industry 1978;* with Richard Luce, *Human Rights & Foreign Policy 1978; Ireland – an Illuminated History 1981.*

RATHBONE William VI: JP DL (Lancs) Hon. LLD (Victoria) 1895. Liberal MP Caernarfonshire 1880-85; Arfon 1885-95; Liverpool 1868-80; Contested Lancashire SW 1880. **Mr. William Rathbone:** Born Liverpool, 11 February 1819, s of William Rathbone V, & Elizabeth, d of Samuel Greg of Manchester, (of a Quaker family which later became Unitarian) Married (1) 1847, Lucretia (died 1859) d of Samuel Stillman Gaer, Liverpool (2) 1866, Emily, d of Acheson Lyle, Lord Lieutenant of Londonderry, 10c. Partner: Rathbone Bros & Co. Merchants & Shipowners, & Ross T. Smyth. Formerly with Nichol, Duckworth 7 Co. Liverpool, & Baring Brothers, London. President, University College of Liverpool 1892; University College of North Wales, Bangor 1894-1900; Vice-President 1884-92; Vice-President, Queens College, Liverpool. Freeman, City of Liverpool 1891. Of Liverpool & London. Died 1 March 1902. Further Reading: *Rathbone Papers, Special Collections and Archives, University of Liverpool. Rathbone Letters University of Wales, Bangor, Department of Manuscripts; Bishopsgate Institute, London; Liverpool Records Office & Family History Service. Eleanor Rathbone: William Rathbone, a Memoir, 1905; Sheila Marriner: The Rathbones of Liverpool, 1961.Gwen Hardy, William Rathbone and the Early History of District Nursing, Hesketh Ormskirk 1981.*

RAW-REES Dafydd Ffredric: BA (Wales). Liberal Democrat, Merionydd/Nant Conwy 2001. **Mr. Dafydd Raw-Rees:** Born 1948. Married Jane, 2d. Educated University of Wales, Aberystwyth (History). Poultry Farmer. Member: East Dyfed Health Authority; West Wales Valuation Tribunal. Interests: Care of the Elderly; Student Grants. Hobbies: Sport, Rugby, Athletics, Golf, Reading, Theatre, Film. Languages: Welsh, English. Of Llandre, Ceredigion.

RAW-REES William Thomas Kinsey: MBE Conservative: Ceredigion & North Pembs 1983. **Mr. Tom Raw-Rees:** Born 1931. Anglican church warden. Married Anne, 2s 1d. Educated Llandovery College; University of Wales, Aberystwyth (Nuffield Agricultural Scholar; Agricultural Management). Merchant Navy. Student. Farmer 1957 & leading turkey producer. Aberystwyth RDC. Ceredigion DC 1974-97 (Chairman 1976-77, Vice-Chairman 1998-99). Ceredigion CC Chairman 1999-2000). Chair: Ceredigion NFU; Dyfed Branch, Council for the Protection of Rural Wales; Mid Wales Tourism; Ceredigion Farming & Forestry Wildlife Group, Wales Farming & Forestry Wildlife Group. UK Vice-Chair, Farming & Forestry Wildlife Group. Member, Development Board for Rural Wales 1981. Associate, Council of Awards, Royal Agricultural Society. A founder, Welsh Food Centre, Horeb, Llandysul. Member Llandovery College rugby XV, Aberystwyth RFC XV. Vice-Chair, Aberystwyth RFC. Chair, Aberystwyth Round Table. Of Borth. Died suddenly 9 December 2000.

RAWLINGS Frances: Communist, South/East List 1999, 2003. **Mrs. Frances Rawlings:** Born Cardiff, 12 September 1945. Married 1981, David Rawlings. Educated grammar school. Social & Community Worker. Fundraising Officer, SNAP Cymru (Independent Parental Support Service). Unison Shop Steward. Member: Cardiff Partnership Management Board. Branch Secretary & Executive Member, Communist Party of Britain. Campaigner against poverty, low pay & racism. Interests: Women's Issues. Hobbies: Reading, Art & Design. Of Roath, Cardiff.

RAYNER Bryan J: BA (Wales). Labour: Pembroke 1987. **Mr. Bryan Rayner:** Born Eastbourne 28 July 1936. Married Nora, 1s. Educated Eastbourne Technical School; University of Wales, Swansea. Residential Supervisor. Metropolitan Police 1953-57; Military Police 1954-56; Metropolitan Police CID 1956-73. Power Worker. Grocer at Burry Port 1975; Insurance Agent. Dyfed CC 1981- (Deputy Leader, Leader, Labour Group).

RAYNER George Pritchard – see PRITCHARD-RAYNER G. P.

RECONTRE Noel: Independent Womble: Cynon Valley B/E 1984. **Mr. Noel Recontre:** Born Burma, 1918. Came to Aberdare 1954. Educated Catholic Brothers Boarding School; Treforest School of Mines. NCB Work Study Engineer for 15 collieries based at Tondu; Made redundant 1973. Of Aberdare. *Policy (Aberdare Leader) There are two Labour Parties, left and moderate; two Liberal Parties – David Steel & S.D.P. – 1st cousin to the Tory Party; There is no Tory Party, only Mrs. Thatcher & Wets and that smells of dictatorship; . . . will not bash the unions, need for consultation; need for jobs self-evident; ban coal imports; against ad-lib nationalisation; Bible says, "when the righteous are in authority, the people rejoice" and also "You cannot serve two Masters – the rich and the Kingdom of Heaven"; in the Kingdom of Heaven you will only find the meek, poor, humble and unemployed; it is no place for the arrogant. A thriving mining community will bring trade to the shops. 'Why Womble?' – The Wombles of Wimbledon are happy people. Only happy people can make other people happy. Miserable and cheerless people make other people miserable.*

REECE Francis Bertram: CBE 1958 MA (Cantab). Conservative: Aberavon 1929. **Mr. Bertram Reece:** Born Ruthin 1888, s of Canon J. F. Reece. Anglican. Married (1) Gladys Catherine (Died 1939) d of Ephraim Wood DL JP, Conway 1d; (2) 1940 Dorothy Alice Macbeth, widow of Captain W.A. Low & d of Dr. A Macbeth Elliot. Educated Rossall School; St. John's College, Cambridge (Classical Exhibitioner). Barrister, Inner Temple 1914. Recorder of Birkenhead 1935-43. Metropolitan Magistrate 1943-61. Chair: Home Office Poisons Board 1946-58; Preventative Detention Advisory Board. Of Bramley, Surrey, & London. Died 4 April 1971.

REED Edward James: KCB 1880 CB 1868 JP (Pembs & Glam) FRS MICE MIME Knight Commander, St. Joseph of Austria 1874 Knight of St. Stanislaus (Russia) Order of Medjide (Turkey) Order of Rising Sun (Japan). Liberal MP Pembroke 1874-80; Cardiff District 1880-95. Contested Hull B/E Oct. 1873; Joined Unionists in support of Tariff Reform 1904, Con/LU PPC Cardiff District 1905. **Sir Edward Reed:** Born 20 September 1830, s of John & Elizabeth Reed, Sheerness Dockyard. Anglican. Married 1851, Rosetta, d of Sir Norman Barnaby, Sheerness. Educated Harrow; School of Mathematics & Construction, Portsmouth. Chief Royal Navy Constructor 1863-70. Lord Commissioner Feb-July 1886. Chair, Cttee to Determine Load Line of Steamships 1884. Member, Council of Civil Engineers. Of Ascot & Kensington. Estate £19,611. Died 20 November 1906. *Books: E. J. Reed: Our Iron-Clad Ships 1869, Letters from Russia 1875-1876, Japan 1880, The Stability of Ships 1884, Fort Minster MP 1885, Modern Ships of War (with Admiral Simpson) 1885, Poems 1902.*

REES David: Liberal: Pontypridd 1923. **Mr. David Rees:** Born Mountain Ash 1872. Calvinistic Methodist Elder. Married 1903, Elizabeth, d of Lewis Williams, Llantwit Fardre, 3c. Solicitor's Clerk 1884; Solicitor 1894, partner in W. R. Davies & Co. Solicitor to South Glamorgan NFU. Coroner for East Glamorgan 1908.

Joined Liberal Party 1903. Chair, Pontypridd Divisional Liberal Assn. Languages: Welsh, English. Of Llantwit Fardre. Died 1959.

REES David – see REES Winstone David.

REES David Benjamin: BA BD MScEcon (Wales) MA PhD (Liverpool). Labour: Conway 1974, Feb. & Oct. **Revd Dr. D. Ben Rees:** Born Llanddewi Brefi 1 August 1937, s of John Rees, labourer/roadman & Ann Jane Benjamin. Married Meinwen Llewelyn, teacher, 2s. Educated Tregaron Grammar School; University of Wales, Aberystwyth; United Theological College, Aberystwyth. Minister, Presbyterian Church of Wales. Ordained 1962: Abercynon, Penrhiwceiber & Merthyr Tydfil 1962-68; Heathfield Road Church, Liverpool 1968-. Author & Writer. Lecturer, WEA & Liverpool University Celtic Studies. Open University Tutor. Joined Labour Party 1955. Treasurer, Cardiganshire Labour Party 1960-62. President: Liverpool Free Church Council 1971-72. Member: NATSOPA, Christian Socialist Movement, Cymdeithas y Cymod, Hon. Society of Cymmrodorion, Cymdeithas Cadw Dydd yr Arglwydd, Executive, Labour Cttee for Electoral Reform. Member, Editorial Board, Peacelinks (FoR). Founder, reformed Liverpool Fabian Society (Secretary 1974-72. Languages: Welsh, English. Of Liverpool. *Books: D. Ben Rees: Haneswyr yr Hen Gorff 1981,Chapels in The Valley, the sociology of Welsh nonconformity 1975, Pregethu a Phregethwyr 1996, The Liverpool Welsh and their Religion 1984, Samuel Roberts 1987, Life and Work of Owen Thomas 1812-91, 1996. The Rotarians of Toxteth 1998, The Welsh of Merseyside Vol. 1, 11996, The Welsh of Merseyside in the Twentieth Century Vol. 2, Cymry Lerpwl a'r Cyffiniau 1996, Cymry Lerpwl a'r Cyffiniau yn yr Ugeinfed Ganrif, Graces for all Occasions.*

REES David Felix: Labour, Brecon & Radnorshire 2003. **Mr. David Rees:** Born 1957. Married Marie (Senior Radiographer) 2d. Head of School of Computing & BSc Course, Swansea Institute of Higher Education. Member, NATFHE Welsh Regional Council. Languages: Learning Welsh, English. Of Cwmafan, Port Talbot.

REES Denis Gilbert: BScEcon. Liberal: Cardiff North 1964; Ludlow B/E 1960; Oswestry 1959. **Lieut-Colonel Dai Rees:** Born Swansea December 1908, s of Congregational Minister. Married. Educated Caterham School; University of Wales, Aberystwyth; McGill University, Montreal. Army 1939-48. Unilever Africa 1948-56. Chief Information Officer, Wales, Kompass Register. Joined Liberal Party 1930. Chair: South Wales Liberal Federation. Member: Welsh Rugby Union; National Industrial Development Council for Wales. Pembroke BC -1939, Mayor 1938-39.

REES Diane: JP 1988. Conservative, Cardiff South & Penarth 2003. **Mrs. Diane Rees:** Born, Cardiff 1950. Married John Rees QC, 4c. Educated Canton High School for Girls; Kings College, London, Cambridge College of Art & Technology. Teacher. Businesswoman & part-time legal adviser. Joined Conservatives 1991. Deputy Chair: Cardiff North Conservative Assn. Old St. Mellons ComC (Chair 1998-2000). Contested Cardiff CCC 1999, 2001. Hobbies: Gardening, Walking dog, Watching son play rugby. Of Cardiff.

REES Dorothy Mary: DBE 1975 CBE 1964 JP (Glam). Labour MP Barry 1950-51. **Dame Dorothy Rees:** Born Barry, 1898. Married David Rees (died 1938). Educated Barry Grammar School; Barry Training College. Teacher. Liaison officer, Ministry of Food 1939-45. Barry BC. Glamorgan CC 1934-; Alderman; Chair 1964-65. Freeman of Barry 1956. Chair: Morgannwg Hospital Management Cttee; Barry National Eisteddfod 1966-68. Member: Welsh Joint Education Cttee; National Advisory Cttee for National Insurance; Welsh Teaching Hospitals Board. PPS Edith Summerskill, 1950-51. Languages: Welsh, English. Died 1987.

REES Edward Christopher: BA (Wales) LesL (Toulouse). Plaid Cymru: Gower 1955; Swansea East B/E 1963, 1964, 1966; Merthyr Tydfil 1970. **Mr. Chris Rees:** Born Swansea, May 1931 (cousin of J. E. H. Rees MP qv). Married Nan, 1s 2d. Educated Taunton School; University of Wales, Swansea (Welsh 1951, French 1954); (Member, College Rugby XV) University of Toulouse. Sentenced to 18 months imprisonment as nationalist CO to national service 1954-55. Teacher, Brynmawr Comprehensive School 1960-69. Administrative Secretary, Welsh Joint Education Cttee 1969. Director, Welsh Language Teaching Centre, Cardiff 1983-96. Introduced the Israeli system for learning Hebrew to Welsh. Joined Plaid Cymru 1952, Vice-President 1964. Languages: Learned Welsh, English, and French. Died 8 December 2001, after long illness.

REES Francis John: JP (Carms). Conservative: Llanelli 1931. **Mr. Francis Rees:** Born 1879, s of William Rees; clerk, Llanelli Steel Works. Clerk, Llanelli Steelworks 1896. Company Secretary, Managing Director (1912), Chair, Llanelly Foundry Co, Kidwelly Tinplate. Director: tinplate, galvinising & colliery companies. President: Swansea Metal Exchange. Chair: South Wales Siemens Steel Assn. High Sheriff of Carmarthenshire 1927-28. Chair, Executive, Llanelli National Eisteddfod. President, Llanelli RFC; Vice-President, Federation of British Industry. Vice-President, Welsh War Prisoners' Fund. Llanelli BC 1918-. Mayor 1926-27. Of Llanelli. Estate £37,866. Died 28 August 1934.

REES Graham: Liberal Democrat, Vale of Clwyd. **Mr. Graham Rees:** Born Birmingham 26 March 1945, s of George Rees, coal miner, & May Rees, cotton worker. Church of England. Married 1968, Gillian Mary Rees, typist, 1s 1d. Educated secondary modern school. British Gas Engineer 1960-94, Retired 1994. Joined Liberal Democrats 1999, Member, Welsh Executive. Aberconwy BC 1991-. Conwy BC (Cabinet member) 1999. Soccer administrator over 30 years (Chair, Conway United Football Club; Director. League of Wales; Executive Officer, North Wales Football Assn). Interests: Crime, Environment. Executive Member, North Wales Coast FA. Interests: Crime, Environment. Hobbies: Football; Reading; Walking. Of Glanconwy.

REES Griffith Caradog: Liberal: Denbigh District Dec. 1910; MP Arfon B/E 1915-18. **Mr. Caradog Rees:** Born Birkenhead 1858, s of Griffith Rees (asst overseer). Calvinistic Methodist. Unmarried. Educated Liverpool Institute. Solicitor 1895-1903. Barrister, Middle Temple 1903. PPS 1915. Of Rhos on Sea & London. Estate £9,241. Died 20 September 1924.

REES Hefin Ednyfed: Labour: Meirionydd/ Nant Conwy 1997. **Mr. Hefin Rees:** Born Liverpool 30 June 1969, s of Revd D. Ben Rees (qv) & Meinwen Llewelyn. Presbyterian Church of Wales. Married 1995 Dr. Bethan Wyn Jones. Educated King David High School, Liverpool; Durham University. Barrister, Inner Temple 1995. Joined Labour Party 1988. Member: Fabian Society, Society of Labour Lawyers. Hammersmith & Fulham BC 1998-. Languages: Welsh, English. Of London.

REES Ioan Bowen: MA (Oxon) Hon. LLD (Wales) 1997. Plaid Cymru: Conway 1955, 1959; Merthyr Tydfil 1964. **Dr. Ioan Bowen Rees:** Born Dolgellau 3 January 1929, s of Aurfryn Maudie Rees & Kate Olwen Parry. Welsh Independent. Married Wynn Meredith, 3c. Educated Dolgellau Grammar School; Boothams School, York; Queens College, Oxford. Army 1947-50, Lieutenant. Solicitor. Asst Solicitor, Lancashire County Council 1956-58. Prosecuting Solicitor, Cardiff City Council 1958-62. Cardiff City Prosecutor 1962-68. Asst Clerk, Pembrokeshire County Council 1965-67; Deputy-Clerk 1967-73. County Clerk, Dyfed 1973-74. County Clerk, Gwynedd 1974-80. Chief Executive, Gwynedd County Council 1980-91. Secretary, North Wales Probation Cttee 1980-91. Haldane Medal 1968. Member: Council, University of Wales, Aberystwyth 1977-78. President, Bethesda RFC 1974; Gwynedd Law Society 1984-88. Hon. Member, Gorsedd 1980. Chair, Welsh Mountain Leadership Training Board 1980-90. UK Member, European Bureau for Lesser-Used Languages 1982-88. Chief Executive Advisor on National Parks, County Councils Assn 1984-90. Member: University Grants Commission Welsh Advisory Cttee on Teacher Training in Wales. Chief Executive, Exchange with Zimbabwe, Council, Institute for Welsh Affairs 1989-91; Cttee to shape Welsh Assembly Dec. 1997. Languages: Welsh, English. Of Llanllechid. Died May 1999.

REES John David: 1st Bart 1920 KCIE 1910 CIE 1890 CVO 1908 JP 1907. Liberal MP Montgomery District 1906-Dec. 1910; Joined Conservatives November 1910; Conservative: Kilmarnock B/E 1911; MP East Nottingham B/E 1912-. **Sir John D. Rees:** Born 16 December 1854, s of Lodwick William Rees, Abergavenny. Married 1891, Hon. Mary Catherine Dormer, d of General, Hon. Sir James Dormer & sister of 13th Baron Dormer. Indian Civil Service 1897-1900 (Magistrate, Judge; British Representative, Maharaja of Travancore; Member, Legislative Council). Chair, Central African Co Ltd. Director, Prisoners of War Information Bureau 1915-20. Silver Medallist, Royal Society of Arts. Member, staff of Earl Marshal at 1910 Coronation. A fanatical opponent of women's suffrage. Of London. Estate £84,637. Died 2nd June 1922, fell from London-Glasgow express at Chesterfield. *Books: J. D. Rees: Tours in India, Duke of Clarence in South India, Current Political Problems, The Mahommedans, The Real India, Modern India.*

REES John Edward Hugh: FRICS FRVA Conservative: Swansea West 1966; MP 1959-64. **Mr. Hugh Rees:** Born Swansea 8 January 1928, s of D. Emlyn Rees, coal exporter (cousin of E Chris Rees, qv). Married 1961, Gillian Milo-Jones (died 1978) 2s. Educated Parc Wen Junior School, Swansea; Glanmôr Grammar School, Swansea; Bromsgrove School. Welsh Regt 1946-49; Lieutenant RA. Chartered Surveyor, Chartered Auctioneer & Estate Agent. Chair, Glamorgan Group Young Conservatives 1954-56; Wales & Mon Young Conservatives 1956-58; Swansea East Conservative Assn 1957-58. PPS 1960-62. Asst Whip 1962-64. UK Representative, EEC Economic & Social Cttee 1972-78. Director, Abbey National plc 1976-91. Chair, Abbey Housing Assn Ltd. 1980-82. Member, Welsh Development Agency 1980-86. Trustee, Ffynnone School Trust 1973- (Chair 1977-85). Governor: National Museum of Wales. Of Newton, Swansea. Found dead in car, 2 December 2003.

REES Kenneth Denver: Liberal: Llanelli 1979, 1983, 2001, 2003. **Mr. Ken Rees:** Born Tumble May 1944. Married 1c. Educated Coleshill Secondary-Technical School, Llanelli; Llanelli Technical College. Planning Engineer & Draughtsman. Supervisor, British Steel Corporation/Corus 1995-2001. Member: TASS/AEW. Secretary, Bynea

RFC; Llanelli District League of Hospital Friends. Area Co-ordinator, Home Watch. School governor. Chair, Llanelli Liberal Democrats. Dyfed CC. Llanelli TC (Mayor 2001). Contested Carmarthenshire CC (Lliedi) 1999. Languages: Welsh, English. Of Llanelli.

REES Peter John Wynford, Baron Rees of Goytre 1987: PC 1983 QC 1969 MA (Oxon). Conservative: Abertillery1964, B/E 1965; West Derby 1966; MP Dover & Deal 1970-83, Dover 1983-87. **Rt. Hon. Peter Rees:** Born 9 December 1926, s of Major-General Wynford Dagger Rees & Rosalie Innes. Married Anthea Wendell. Educated Stowe School; Christ Church, Oxford. Scots Guards 1939-45; Staff of GOC Trieste 1944-48. Barrister, Lincolns Inn 1953. Goytre PC. Minister of State, Treasury 1979-81. Minister of State, Trade 1981-83. Chief Secretary, Treasury 1983-85. Deputy Chair, Leopold Joseph Holdings plc 1985. Chair: Economic Forestry Group 1989-93, Duty Free Confederation 1987. Company Chair: General Cable Ltd 1990-95; Westminster Industrial Brief 1990-92; Scottish Marine Oil plc (LASMO) 1988-94. Director: James Finlay Ltd 1986-92, Fleming Mercantile Investment Trust 1987, Bradford Cable Communications Ltd 1988. Of Abergavenny & London.

REES Timothy: BA (Open). Natural Law Party: Islwyn B/E 1995. **Mr. Timothy Rees:** Born Carmarthen 1951. Educated Llandeilo Grammar School; Carmarthen Technical College (OND Engineering); Open University (Maths). Worked in forestry, agriculture, local government, probation service. Studying for Master's degree.

REES William Daniel: Liberal: Swansea West 1924. **Mr. William Rees:** Born 1878, s of Morgan Rees, tinplate worker & trade unionist of Cwmbwrla, Swansea. Married Coal Factor & partner in a milk business. Swansea BC 1921- (Chair, Water Cttee); Independent Party Whip, Alderman, Mayor 1937-38. US Vice Consul 18 years. Of Swansea. Estate £755. Killed in blitz; believed to have died 19 February 1941; body found 26 February 1941.

REES Winstone David: UK Independence Party, Wales Euro 1999; Referendum Party, Hampshire North East 1997. **Mr. David Rees:** Aircraft Engineer. Of Greatham, Hants.

REES HUGHES Loti: JP (Carms). Labour: Cardigan 1959. **Mrs. Loti Rees-Hughes:** Born 1908. Sunday School Teacher. Married (1) Hopkins (died) (2) Alderman W. Douglas Hughes, Teacher, lecturer, broadcaster. Carmarthenshire CC 1946-67; Alderman -1967. Languages: Welsh, English.

REID Clive Burton: Plaid Cymru. Swansea East 1983, 1987. **Mr. Clive Reid:** Born 1941. Married, 3c. Educated Barry Grammar School; Welsh National School of Pharmacy. RAMC 1959-61. Worked in London 2 years. Representative, drug company until 1968. Own pharmacy at Morriston 1968, Chair: West Glamorgan Pharmaceutical Cttee; Swansea West branch, Plaid Cymru.

REID Sara Eirwen: Plaid Cymru, South/West List 1999. **Ms. Sara Reid:** Born 1962, d of Clive Reid (qv). Married Nick Bacon. Ex-Playgroup Leader & College Lecturer. National Co-ordinator, Wales, of a charity. College researcher. Asst. Children's Officer, Wales. Contested Swansea CCC (Sketty) 1999. Interests: Child & Family Services, Housing. Of Sketty. Swansea.

REID Stephen Henry: MA (Cantab) 1972. Conservative: Rhondda 1987, Eastleigh B/E 1994, 1997. **Mr. Stephen Reid:** Born 16 August 1951. Married Terry 2s. Educated Queen Mary School, Basingstoke; FitzWilliam College, Cambridge. Data Processing Manager: a London college of further education. Basingstoke & Deane DC 1978-95, Council Leader; Chair, Housing Cttee. Chair, Wessex Area Young Conservatives 1976-78.

RENDEL Stuart, 1st & last Baron Rendel 1894: JP BA 1857 MA 1859 (Oxon) Knight of Charles XII (Spain) Officer, Order of Charles Albert (Italy). Liberal MP Montgomeryshire 1880-94. **Mr. Stuart Rendel:** Born Plymouth 2 July 1834, s of James Meadow Rendel FRS & Catherine Rendel. High Anglican. Married Ellen, d of W. Egerton Hubbard, Horsham, 4d. Educated Eton; Oriel College, Oxford (4th class). Barrister, Lincolns Inn 1861. Company Chair: Armstrongs, armaments manufacturers. President, University of Wales, Aberystwyth 1895-1913 & a major benefactor. Purchased land as a gift for the site of the National Library of Wales. Chair, Welsh Parliamentary Party 1888. President: North Wales Liberal Federation 1886; Welsh National Liberal Council 1887; Welsh Parliamentary Liberal Assn 1888 (Unofficial leader, Welsh Liberal MPs). Close friend of Gladstone. His election gave the Wynn family its first defeat in the county since 1799. Of Plas Dinam, Mont, London & Chateau de Thorenc nr Cannes etc. Estate £652,328. Died 4 June 1913. *Books: F. E. Hamer (ed): The Personal Papers of Lord Rendel 1931.*

RENDLE John Emlyn: MA (Oxon). Conservative: Abertillery 1970. **Mr. Emlyn Rendle:** Born 1931, steelworker's son. Baptist lay preacher. Educated Newbridge Grammar School; Abertillery Technical College; Coleg Trefecca; Bognor Regis Training College; London University;

Regents Park College, Oxford. Stock & Invoice Clerk, Abertillery 3 years. Royal Artillery 1949-51. Lecturer in Religious Education, St. Osyth's College of Education, Clacton-1970, resigned, January 1970, to prepare for the election. Co-founder-secretary, Aberbeeg Boys Club. Member: ACTD; English Speaking Union.

REYNOLDS John Arthur: BScEcon (London, external) 1962. Labour: Cardiff North 1964; nominated for Caerphilly B/E 1968. **Mr. John Reynolds:** Born Roath, Cardiff, October 1925. Married 1952, Dorothy, 2c. Educated elementary schools. Railway clerk 1941-52; Fleet Air Arm 1943-46; student, Trinity College, Carmarthen 1952-54;Teacher 1954-65; Lecturer in Government, Cardiff College of Food Technology & Commerce 1965-. Joined Labour Party 1945. Chair: Cardiff North CLP. Contested city elections 1951.

REYNOLDS Neal John: BA (Open). UK Independence, Newport East 2001, 2003. **Mr. Neal Reynolds:** Born Erith, Kent 14 March 1962, s of Stanley Walter Edwin Reynold, engineer, (mother died 1964) & adoptive mother, Anne Marie Reynolds, nurse. Anglican. Educated Graham Road Comprehensive School; Mid Kent FE College 1978-82; Open University 1996-02 (Humanities). Production worker at a Chepstow quarry. Trade Union Shop Steward & Branch Secretary. Open University student. Joined UK Independence Party 1994. Treasurer & Chair: Gwent UK Independence Party. Interests: Democracy, Accountable Government, Reducing Bureaucracy. Hobbies: Social History, The Arts, Sport. Of Chepstow.

RHYS David: MA (Oxon). Conservative: East Denbighshire Jan. 1910; Denbigh 1923; Mid-Derbyshire Dec. 1910. **Mr. David Rhys:** Born Llanarth, Ceredigion. Calvinistic Methodist. Married Charlotte, d. of John Wade, Llanelli, 2s. Educated Christ College, Brecon, University of Wales, Aberystwyth, Jesus College, Oxford. Senior Master, Llanelli Grammar School. Barrister, Inner Temple. Commissioner for Civil Liberties, North Wales 1914-18. Heston & Isleworth BC 1940-, Mayor 1945. Anti-Disestablishment. Languages: Welsh, English. Of Hounslow, Middx.

RHYS Manon: BA (Wales). Plaid Cymru: Clwyd North West 1983. **Ms. Manon Rhys:** Born Trealaw 1987, d of James Kitchener Davies (qv) & Mair Rees. Married Richard Lloyd Jones (divorced) 2c; Partner T. James Jones. Educated Rhondda County Girls' Grammar School, Porth; Ysgol Glan Clwyd; University of Wales. Freelance researcher & writer; television script writer (*Y Palmant Aur etc)* author, reviewer. Co-Editor,

Taliesin. Tutor, Creative Writing & Script Modules, Dept of Welsh, University of Wales, Cardiff. Editor: *Taliesin (joint), Cyfres y Cewri, Storïau'r Troad.* Adjudicator, Denbigh National Eisteddfod. CND activist. Involved in Greenham Common demonstrations. Languages: Welsh, English. *Books: Cwtsho (short stories) 1998; Cysgodion (novel) 1993; Pobl y Cwm, Iar Fach yr Haf, Palment Aur, Cwilt Racs (tv scripts), editor: Storïau'r Troad, Ar fy myw, Detholiad o Waith Kitchener Davies (with M Wynn Thomas) Editor, Cyfres y Cewri I (Gwasg Gomer), Tridiau ac Angladd Corostshen 1996.*

RHYS-ROBERTS Thomas Ensor Rhys: QC 1972 GM. Conservative: Pontypridd 1950, Newport 1951**. Lieut-Colonel Thomas Rhys-Roberts:** Born London 22 April 1910, s of Arthur Rhys Roberts & Hannah E. Jones. Married 1939 Barbara Ruth Eccles 1s. Educated Westminster School; RMC Sandhurst. Army Officer 1925-35, 1939-45. Seconded to Foreign Office (British Embassy, Athens). Barrister 1938. Deputy Stipendiary Magistrate, Cardiff 1953-Of Llanblethian. Died 6 June 1975.

RHYS-WILLIAMS Brandon Meredith: 2nd Bart. 1918. Conservative: Pontypridd 1959; Ebbw Vale B/E 1964, MP South Kensington B/E 1968-74, Kensington 1974-. **Sir Brandon Rhys-Williams:** Born Miskin Manor 17 November 1927, s of Sir Rhys Rhys-Williams (qv) & Lady Juliet Rhys-Williams (qv). Anglican. Married 1961, Caroline, d of L. A. Foster. Educated Eton; Bolton Technical College. Lieutenant, Welsh Guards 1946-48. ICI sales staff 1948-62. Asst. Director, Spastics Society 1962-63. Consultant, Management Selection Ltd 1963. Member, Bow Group. Vice-President: British Cttee, League for European Co-operation. President: East Glamorgan Branch, Welsh Guards Old Comrades Assn 1955. Secretary: Conservative MPs Health & Social Security Cttee. 1970; Conservative MPs Finance Cttee. Member: Select Cttee on Social Services 1979-83. Member, European Parliament 1973-84. Of London. Died 18 May 1988.

RHYS-WILLIAMS Juliet Evangeline: DBE 1937 DStJ 1937. Liberal National: Pontypridd B/E 1937; Liberal: Ilford North 1945. **Lady Rhys-Williams:** Born 17 December 1898, d. of Clayton Glyn & Elinor Glyn (novelist). Married 1921, Sir Rhys Rhys-Williams. (qv), 1s, Brandon (qv) (1 son killed Tunisia 1943) 2d. Educated The Links, Eastbourne. Private Secretary to Director of Training & Staff Duties 1918. Asst. Secretary to War Cabinet Demobilisation Cttee 1919. Private Secretary to Sir Rhys Rhys-Williams MP 1918-20. Hon. Treasurer, Queen Charlotte's Hospital Anesthetic Fund 1928-39. Hon. Secretary, Joint Council of Midwifery 1934-39. Member: Inter-Departmental Cttee on Abortion 1937-38; Bishop of Llandaff's Cttee which sought ways to alleviate poverty in the Rhondda valley in the 1930s. Asst Commercial Relations Officer, Ministry of Information 1939-40. Assistant Section Officer, WAAF 1940-45. Hon. Secretary, Women's Liberal Federation 1943; Chair, Liberal Party Publications & Publicity Cttee 1940-46; Hon. Secretary, Economic Section, Congress of Europe, The Hague 1948; United Europe Movement 1947-48. Governor, BBC 1952-56. Director, *Economic Digest* 1954-58. Vice-President, Economic Research Council. Chair: Cwmbran Development Corporation 1955-60. Of Miskin Manor & London. Died 18 September 1964.

RHYS-WILLIAMS: Rhys: 1st Bart 1918 DSO 1915 KC 1913 JP (Glam) 1888 BA (Oxon) Order of St. Vladimir (Russia). National Liberal: Pontypridd 1922, Coalition Liberal MP Banbury 1918-22. **Colonel, Sir Rhys Rhys-Williams:** Born Miskin Manor 1865, s of Judge Gwilym Williams & Emma, d of William Williams, Aberpergwm (uncle of Hubert Martineau (qv). Married 1921, Juliet Evangeline (qv) d. of Clayton Glyn, 1s.(Brandon qv; 1s killed, Tunisia 1943) 2d. Barrister, Inner Temple 1890. Landowner. Welsh Guards 1914-17. Military Attaché, Teheran 1915-17. Asst. Director-General, War Office 1917-19. Parl-Secretary, Transport 1919-20. Chair, Glamorgan Quarter Sessions 1906-44. Recorder of Cardiff 1922-30. Assistant Charity Commissioner. Hon. Colonel, 53rd Welsh Division RE (TA) 1928. President, Rhondda Centre Cttee, Order of St. John. Glamorgan CC. Of Miskin Manor & London. Died 29 January 1958.

RICHARD Henry: MP Merthyr Tydfil 1868-. **Revd Henry Richard:** Born Tregaron, 3 April 1812, son of Revd Ebenezer Richard, Teacher, scholar, bard & Calvinistic Methodist minister (1811), & Mary, d of William Williams. Married 1866, Margaret Matilda Farley, d of a prosperous merchant. Educated, Llangeitho Grammar School and John Evans' Commercial and Mathematical School, Aberystwyth. Draper's assistant at 14. Trained for the Ministry at Highbury Theological College, London. Ordained 1835. Minister, Marlborough Congregational Church, Old Kent Road, London 1835-50. Secretary, the Society for the Promotion of Permanent and Universal Peace (The Peace Society) 1838-85. Attended Brussels Peace Conference 1848. Chairman, Congregational Union of England and Wales 1877-78. Appointed in 1844 to visit the Congregational Churches of Wales to bring about a union between English and Welsh Nonconformists. Declined Liberal nomination for Cardiganshire 1865. Member: The Liberation Society; National Education League; Anti-Slavery Society. A champion of Wales & of Welsh Nonconformity in particular. Opposed the Crimean War. Member, Depart-

Revd Henry Richard.

mental Cttee to Enquire into higher education in Wales & Mon., 1880; Lord Cross Commission on Education 1886-88. Known as the Apostle of Peace & the Member for Wales. Interests: Peace, Welsh Affairs. Languages: Welsh, English. Died at Treborth, Bangor, home of Richard Davies (qv) 30 August 1888. *Books: Defensive War, 1846 & 1890; Memoirs of Joseph Sturge 1864; Letters on Social and Political Conditions in Wales 1866 & 1884; The Recent Progress of International Arbitration.* Further Reading: *C. S. Miall, Henry Richard, 1899; L. Appleton, Memoirs of Henry Richard 1889; etc.*

RICHARD Ioan Merritt: People's Representative Party, South/West List 1999. **Mr. Ioan Richard:** Born Woking, Surrey 6 June 1944, s of Trevor

Ioan Richard.

250

Richard, colliery worker, & Maud Richard. Married 1969, Katherine Iris Richard, teacher, 2s 1d. Educated Pontardawe Grammar School; Trinity College, Carmarthen (mature student). Worked in coal, tinplate & steel industries. Teacher (Science). Mynydd Mawr ComC. Swansea CCC. Ex-member, Plaid Cymru. Founder Secretary, People's Representative Party 1999. Interests: Left-of-centre Welsh nationalism. Hobbies: Reading non-fiction, Hill walking. Local history. Languages: Welsh, English. Of Craigcefnparc.

RICHARDS Aneurin – see RICHARDS, W. A.

RICHARDS David Leigh: Welsh Socialist Alliance, Swansea West 2003. **Mr. Leigh Richards:** Born Swansea 1966. Secretary, YES to Assembly Campaign. Convener, Swansea Coalition Against War. Left Plaid Cymru to join the Welsh Socialist Alliance because of the WSA's 'unstinting support for Socialist policies'.

RICHARDS David Robert: Communist: Pontypridd B/E 1989. **Mr. David Richards:** Born Gloucestershire 1950, of valley parents. Educated Cheltenham College of Art. His animated film *Agoraphobia* won a 1972 award. Recruited from college as a full-time Communist Party worker. Welsh Secretary, Communist Party of Great Britain. Of Penarth.

RICHARDS David William: BA (Wales) MA 1917 PhD (London) 1943. Labour: University of Wales 1929. **Revd. Dr. David Richards:** Born Capel Isaac 1894. Married 4s. Educated Llandeilo Grammar School; University of Wales, Aberystwyth (Maths). Teacher at Pwllheli. Welsh Independent Minister. Ordained 1917: Saron, Bedwas 1917-20, & Peniel, Trethomas 1918-20; Griffithstown 1920-24; Seion, Abercanaid 1924-27; Bethel, Penclawdd 1927-31; & WEA & YMCA Lecturer. Lecturer, Birmingham University Extra-Mural Dept 1931. Won National Eisteddfod prizes on philosophical subjects, Neath, Corwen, Barry. Languages; Welsh, English. Died Leamington Spa, 24 April 1949 (Suicide).

RICHARDS Delyth: BEd. Plaid Cymru, Mid & West List 1999. **Mrs. Delyth Richards:** Born Swansea 25 March 1952, d of David Wyn Evans, coalminer, & Hilda Mary Evans, seamstress. Welsh Baptist. Married 1976, David Wynallt Richards, teacher, 3s. Educated Gwendraeth Valley Grammar School; Trinity College, Carmarthen. Teacher. Lecturer, FE College. Secretary, Dyffryn Aman Branch, Plaid Cymru, Chair: East Carmarthen & Dinefwr Forum. Betws ComC. Interests: Conservation, Welsh Culture. Hobbies: Walking. Languages: Welsh, English. Of Betws, Ammanford.

RICHARDS Dorothy L: Plaid Cymru: Cynon Valley 1987. **Mrs. Dorothy Richards:** Born 1949. Married 2d. Senior Social Worker, Mid Glam CC. NALGO Shop Steward. Member, CND Cymru. Languages: Learned Welsh, English.

RICHARDS Gwilym John David: MA (Oxon). Conservative: Llanelli Feb. & Oct. 1974. **Mr. Gwilym Richards:** Born Tenby 1930 Anglican. Married Margaret, 5c. Educated Llandysul Grammar School; St. Catherine's College, Oxford (Justinian Bracegirdle Exhibitioner). Army 1959-61. Solicitor 1961 (Newcastle Emlyn). Chair: Carmarthen Divisional Conservative Assn; West Wales Area Conservative Cttee. Languages: Welsh, English. Of Cilgwyn, Newcastle Emlyn. Died 8 March 2001.

RICHARDS Hugh Wynne: Green Party: Brecon & Radnor 1992. **Mr. Hugh Richards:** Born Cardiff 1945; Married Margaret, 2s. Independent Planning, Design & Environment Consultant. Moved to constituency 1976.

RICHARDS John Winterson: LlB (Bristol) 1985 MBA (Wales) 1987. Conservative: Rhondda 1992. **Mr. John Winterson Richards:** Born Cardiff, 19 June 1969, s of Alun Thomas Richards, solicitor, & Patricia Winterson Lloyd, antiques dealer & fair organiser. Christian. Unmarried. Educated Llanishen High School, Cardiff; Bristol University; UWIST. Managing Director: Winterson Richards, Management Consultants. Company Director: Cardiff Market, Cardiff City Bus. Trustee: local Charity for Special Relief. Member: local Police Consultative Cttee; Council, Institute of Welsh Affairs. Chair: Lisvane Branch, Conservatives 1991-95. Member: Conservative National Local Government Cttee. Cardiff CC 1986-96 (Leader of Opposition 1995-96). South Glam CC 1995-99. Member: Court, University of Bristol. Retired from active politics in 1999. Subsequently more active in charity fundraising & writing. Interests: Enterprise, Local Government, Defence. Hobbies: Hill Walking, Opera, Billiards, History. Languages: English, some Welsh, little French & German. Of Lisvane, Cardiff.

RICHARDS Leigh – see RICHARDS, David Leigh.

RICHARDS Philip Brian: LlB (Bristol). Plaid Cymru, Cardiff North Feb. 7 Oct. 1974; Aberdare 1979; Cynon Valley 1997. **Mr. Phil Richards** *(Phil Bach):* Born Nottingham, 3 August 1946, s of Glyn Bevan Richards, teacher, & Nancy Gwenhwyfar Richards, teacher. Presbyterian Church of Wales. Married 1971, Dorothy Richards, divorced 1968, 2c. (2) 1994, Julia Richards. Educated Cardiff High School; Bristol University. Barrister, Inner Temple 1969. Circuit Judge. Chair:

Plasnewydd Residents Assn; Plasnewydd Assn for the Care of the Elderly; Plaid Cymru Steel Action Group. Plaid Cymru Spokesperson on Housing. Part-time Chair SSAT 1987. Editor, *Welsh Nation* 1980-89. Chair: Governors, Ysgol Rhydfelin. Vice-President, Mountain Ash RFC. Hobbies: Politics, Literature, Music, Sport, Cinema, Opera, Theatre, Welsh History. Languages: English, some Welsh. Of Mountain Ash.

RICHARDS Robert: BA (Wales) MA (Cantab). Labour MP Wrexham 1922-24, 1929-31, 1935-. **Professor Robert Richards:** Born Llangynnog, Montgomeryshire 7 May 1884, s of John Richards slate quarryman & Ellen Richards. Methodist Sunday School Teacher. Married Mary Myfanwy (died 1950) d of Thomas Owen. Educated Llanfyllin Grammar School; University of Wales, Aberystwyth; St. John's College, Cambridge. Lecturer in Political Economy, Glasgow University 1909-11. External Lecturer in Economics, University of Wales, Bangor 1911-22. Tutor in Economics & Political Science, Bangor 1931-35. War Office 1916-. Dept of Agriculture -1919. Under Secretary of State for India 1924. Joint Regional Commissioner for Wales ARP 1939-45. Historian & Author. Chair, Welsh Antiquarian Society 1943-53, President 1953. Vice-President, Hon. Society of Cymmrodorion 1951. Declined Governorship of Malta & a peerage. Languages: Welsh, English. Died 22 December 1955.

RICHARDS Roderick: BScEcon (Wales). Conservative: Clwyd West 1997, Vale of Glamorgan B/E 1989, Carmarthen 1987; Clwyd West 1997, 1999; MP Clwyd North-West 1992-99; AM North List 1999-2003. **Mr. Rod Richards:** Born Llanelli 12 March 1947, son of Ivor George Richards & Lizzie Jane Evans. Married 1975, Elizabeth Knight, 3c. Educated Llandovery College; University of Wales, Swansea (1st Economics). Royal Marines Lieutenant 1969-71. Ministry of Defence Intelligence Staff 1977-83. BBC news & current affairs presenter 1983-89. Special Adviser to Secretary of State for Wales (David Hunt) 1990. Hotelier. Member, Development Board for Rural Wales; Welsh Consumer Council; Member, Special Forces Club; Llanelli Rugby Club. PPS 1993-94. Member, Select Cttee. Welsh Affairs 1992-93. Under-Secretary for Wales 1994-96; Resigned, 1996, because of personal matters. Elected Leader of Welsh Conservatives, 10 November 1998; Resigned July 1999. Whip withdrawn 2000. Hobbies: Keen rugby & cricket supporter. Resigned Assembly seat, 10 September 2002. Languages: Welsh, English. Of Cardiff.

RICHARDS Sioned Mair: Labour, Mid & West List 1999. **Ms. Sioned Richards:** Born 27 April 1958. Works for Jackie Lawrence MP. Carmarthenshire CC. Carmarthen TC (Mayor 1998-99).

Member, Welsh consumer Council. Languages: Welsh, English. Of Carmarthen.

RICHARDS Thomas: PC 1918 JP (Mon 1907 & Brecs) KStJ 1918. Labour MP West Mon B/E 1904-18; Ebbw Vale 1918-20. **Rt. Hon. Tom Richards:** Born Beaufort 8 June 1858, s of Thomas Richards & Mary Joseph. Welsh Independent. Married 1880, Elizabeth Eleanor, d of David Thomas. Educated Beaufort British School. Miner at 12. Founder/Secretary Ebbw Vale Miners' Assn 1884-88. Miners' Agent, Ebbw Vale, 1888-98. General Secretary, SMWF 1898-. President, Treasurer. Jt Secretary, Sliding Scale Board. Member, MFGB Executive 1903-11, 1921- (Vice-President 1924-30; President 1929-31). President: Miners' International. Member: Labour Party National Executive. Ebbw Vale UDC 1895- (Chairman 1901-02). Monmouthshire CC Alderman 1904 (Chairman 1924). Member: Llangattock School Board. School governor. Active in recruiting 1915-18. Took Liberal Whip until 1909. Chair, Welsh Parliamentary Party 1918-20. Member, Joint conference on Industrial Reorganisation & Industrial Relations 1928-29. Languages: Welsh, English. Of Cardiff. Estate £1,948. Died November 1931.

RICHARDS Timothy: LlB (Wales) GGCE. (Manchester). Plaid Cymru, Bedwellty 1979; United Socialists, Caerphilly 1999. **Mr. Tim Richards:** Born Cardiff 25 May 1950, s of Thomas Hugh Richards, journalist & Welsh dramatist, & Aelwen Eluned Richards. Agnostic. Married 1979, Judith Mary Stubbings, French teacher, 2s. Educated Rhiwbina Junior School, Cardiff; Whitchurch Grammar School, Cardiff; Dynevor Grammar School, Swansea; University of Wales, Aberystwyth; University of Manchester. Lecturer in Law, Rumney College of Technology/Coleg Glan Hafren & freelance journalist. Worked for Oxfam's Third World First. Joined Plaid Cymru 1974, Secretary, Caerphilly constituency party until 1979. Chair: Welsh Socialist Republican Movement 1979. A founder of Cymru Goch, Chair 1987. Founder/Chair: Rhymney Valley Miners' Support Group 1984-85. Founder, South Wales Anti-Nuclear Alliance against Hinckley Point PWR Proposal. National Organiser, Wales against the Poll Tax. Editor, *Y Faner Goch.* Chair/Secretary: Coleg Hafren Branch NATFHE. Aber Valley ComC (Ind. Welsh Socialist) 1986-88. Contested Caerphilly CBC (Aber Valley) 1999. Governor, Ysgol Ifor Bach, Senghenydd 1986-2000. Interests: Socialist, Green, Welsh Republican for independence and a bit of an anarchist too. Hobbies: Freelance journalist & poet (Red Poets Society), Photography, Drawing, History (written class history of Wales), Unsuccessful scriptwriter for TV.LOL. Languages: English, tried to learn Welsh. Of Abertridwr.

RICHARDS W. Aneurin: BSc (Wales) CE ME FIWSP. Plaid Cymru: Abertillery Feb. & Oct. 1974, Islwyn 1983. **Mr. Aneurin Richards:** Born miner's son. Married 2c. Educated elementary school; University of Wales, Cardiff. Crosshands Colliery at 16. Senior Mining Engineer, NCB East Wales Headquarters, Ystradmynach. Vice-President, Newbridge RFC. Plaid Cymru Housing Spokesman; Chair, Islwyn Plaid Cymru. Islwyn DC 1973-83. Languages: Welsh, English. Of Newbridge.

RICHARDSON Ernald Edward: MA Oxon). Conservative: East Carmarthenshire 1895, 1896. **Captain Ernald Richardson:** Born 31 July 1869, s of Colonel John Crow Richardson, Glanbrydan Park (family of copper magnates) & Theresa Eden d of Revd Edward Serecold. Anglican. Married 1898, Eirene Caroline, d of Colonel Ynyr Henry Burgess & Hon. Mrs. Parkhauser, Co. Tyrone, 3s 1d. Educated Eton; Christ Church, Oxford. Landowner (considerable property). Chair, Tominol Copper Co Mexico. Director, English Copper Smelters. Captain, Royal Carmarthenshire Artillery, Militia. Served South African War, Pembrokeshire Yeomanry 1899-1901. Of Glanbrydan Park, Manordeilo, Langland & Pantygwydr, Swansea. Estate £155,793. Died Mexico, of enteric fever, 7 July 1909.

RICHARDSON Josephine: Labour: Monmouth 1951, 1955; Hornchurch 1959; Harrow 1964; MP Barking Feb. 1974-. **Miss Jo Richardson:** Born Newcastle upon Tyne 28 August 1923, d of John Joseph Richardson (Liberal, Darlington 1929). Agnostic. Educated Southend High School for Girls. Private Secretary: Ian Mikardo MP & John Freeman MP 1945-. Chair: Parliamentary Staffs Group, CAWU. Secretary, Labour MPs' groups: Keep left; Only One Way; Victory for Socialism, Tribune. Catering Manager, Aldermaston March. Export Sales Manager, Ian Mikardo & Co Ltd. Member: APEX; ASTMS; Co-operative Party. Vice-Chair CND. Joined Labour Party 1945. Member, Labour NEC 1979-91. Hornsey BC 1950-62, Alderman 1955. Hammersmith BC 1962-65. Opposition Spokesperson on Women's Rights 1983-. Died 1 February 1994.

RICKETTS William Kenneth Ronald: ARICS. Conservative: Rhondda East 1966. **Mr. William Ricketts:** Born Cardiff 1940. Methodist Sunday School teacher. Married Eirian Anna Seaborn Davies MBE FSCP, Director Clinical Services, Cardiff (died 1998) of Caernarfon, 1s. Educated Dulwich College. Chartered Surveyor, Auctioneer & Estate Agent. Property Correspondent, *South Wales Echo*; Lecturer in Estate Management & Property Valuation, Glamorgan College of Technology. Member, Glamorgan Cricket Club. Resigned from list of prospective candidates

1967 because of disagreement with party policy. Died May 1999.

RILEY Jeffrey J: Conservative: Alyn & Deeside 1992. **Mr. Jeffrey Riley:** Born Cheshire, 4 February 1962. Married Jean. Educated Ewloe Green Primary School; Hawarden High School. Sales Manager, local building company. Conservative Agent, Cardiff South & Penarth, & Oxford East. Chair, CCA.

RIPPETH Thomas Peter: BSc (Reading) MSc PhD (Wales). Liberal Democrat, North list 1999, Wrexham 2003. **Dr. Thomas Rippeth:** Born Hexham, Northumberland 29 July 1966, s of Noel George Rippeth, science teacher, & Ione Hanson, college lecturer. Non-practising Methodist. Partner. Educated Rykon on Tyne Junior School; comprehensive schools; University of Reading; University of Wales, Bangor. Research Scientist, School of Oceanic Studies. Awarded 5 year Advanced Fellowship by UK Natural Environment Research Council, March 2002 'to support his research in the study of turbulent ,mixing of sea waters and its impact on physical, biological and sedimentoligical processes'. Chair: North Wales Liberal Democrats. Member: Liberal Democrat Federal Executive, Welsh Executive. Contested Gateshead MBC 1988, 1990, 1991, Ynys Môn CC (Cwm Cadnant). Interests: Environment, Social Justice. Hobbies: Playing in a Jazz Band, Hill Walking, Gardening. Of Northop.

RITCHIE Clayton Lee: Liberal Democrat, South/West List 1999. **Mr. Clayton Ritchie:** Born Bridgend, 2 May 1976, son of Philip Ritchie, college lecturer, & Kathryn Sharpe, teacher. Married 1999, Claire Ritchie, hostel worker/manager 2d. Educated university (business studies). Retail Manager, Joined Police Force, October 2000, and thus withdrew from politics. Contested Bridgend CBC (Newcastle) 1999. Hobbies: Travel. Of Bridgend.

ROBERTS Aled Owen: JP (Liverpool). Liberal MP Wrexham 1931-35; Contested East Toxteth 1929, B/E 1939. Resigned as Liberal PPC Wrexham, March 1945 & joined Conservative Party. Conservative: Kirkdale 1945. **Mr. Aled Roberts:** Born Liverpool 17 July 1889, s of Robert Roberts. Presbyterian Church of Wales Elder. Married Ione Ruth (Died). Army 1914-19; Captain RWF. Lieut-Colonel, Home Guard 1940-45. Insurance Broker & Underwriter (manages pensions, insurance etc. for Presbyterian Church of Wales). Company Director: Morris & Jones Ltd, Provincial Insurance Co. Ltd, Monument Insurance Co. Ltd, Clarence Building Society. Board Member: MANWEB. Treasurer, National Eisteddfod, Liverpool 1929. Liverpool CC 1936- (Deputy Leader, Liberal Group. Of Aigburth, Liverpool. Languages: Welsh, English. Died 1949.

ROBERTS Anne Grace: Liberal: Caerphilly 1929. Joined Labour Party; Labour short-list Cardigan 1932. **Miss Grace Roberts:** Born Ruthin, d of Robert Roberts, trader. Presbyterian Church of Wales. Married 1930, George Arthur Bowen-Jones, bank manager, St. Dogmaels. Private Secretary to Ellis Davies MP. Welsh Organiser, Independent Liberal Party (Asquith). Journalist & lecturer. Author, short stories in Welsh & English. Member, Cambrian Archaeological Assn. Languages: Welsh, English.

ROBERTS Caroline: Conservative: Cardiff South & Penarth 1997. **Miss Caroline Roberts:** Born Surrey 30 November 1953. Educated Walthamstow Hall, Sevenoaks; Manchester University. Director of Public Affairs, Brewers & Licensed Retailers Assn. Chair, Battersea Conservative Assn. Member, Conservative Greater London Executive. Member: National Trust, National Arts Collections Fund, Institute of Public Relations. School governor 1989-. Action Aid sponsor.

ROBERTS David Iorwerth: BA MEd. Independent, Assembly, Vale of Clwyd 1999. **Mr. David Roberts:** Born Bangor, 13 December 1942, s of Owen Gwilym Roberts, quarryman, & Lizzie May Roberts, nurse. Methodist. Married 1966 Patricia Lydia Roberts, 1s 1d. Educated John Bright Grammar School, Llandudno, Bangor Normal College, Liverpool University, Open University. Teacher, Ysgol Glan Clwyd 1975-96, Freelance Worker in Education 1996. St. Asaph TC 1996- (Mayor 1998-99, 2000-01). Secretary: Rhyl AFC, Golf Club Wheelchair Charity Cttee. Interests: General Interest in Politics. Hobbies: Golf, Walking. Languages: Welsh, English. Of St. Asaph.

ROBERTS David Leonard: LlB (London) 1979 AKC. SDP/Alliance: Meirionydd/Nant Conwy 1983, 1987. **Mr. David Roberts:** Born Aberdyfi 1957 farmer's son Educated Tywyn School; Kings College, London; London School of Law. Solicitor. Joined father as mixed stock farmer. Youth Leader. Chair: Meirionydd branch FUW. Member: NFU; Tourist Enterprise; Campaign for the Protection of Rural Wales; Coast Railway Action Group; CLA Parliamentary & Legal Cttee; FUW Parliamentary & Land Use Cttee. Secretary, Gwynedd SDP. Member, SDP Welsh Council. Languages: Welsh, English. Of Aberdyfi.

ROBERTS Dominica: BA (Oxon) 1960. Pro Life Party 2003; Bracknell 1997, 2001; South-East England Euro 2004. **Mrs. Dominica Roberts:** Born Liverpool 27 October 1937, d of Richard Haddow Forrest, circuit judge, & Monica Constance Neville, housewife. Roman Catholic. Mar-

ried 1960 Timothy Wace Roberts (qv) 2s 3d (son John contested Burton 2001). Educated Convent HCJ, Mayfield; St. Anne's College, Oxford (Jurisprudence). Chartered Patent Attorney. Leader, Pro Life Party & Spokeswomen on Euthanasia. Member, Bracknell LIFE. Given election deposit of £500 as Ruby Wedding present by husband 2000. Hobbies: Reading, Opera. Languages: Tiny amount of Welsh, English, French, German, Latin.

ROBERTS Edward Alun: LlB (Wales). Plaid Cymru: Pontypridd 1979. **Mr. Alun Roberts:** Born Penygraig 1947. Married 2s. Educated Rhondda Grammar School, Porth; University of Wales, Aberystwyth. Solicitor. SWEB solicitor.

ROBERTS Emrys Owen: CBE 1976 MBE 1946 LlB (Wales) 1938 BA 1933 MA (Cantab). Liberal MP Merioneth 1944-51. **Mr. Emrys Roberts:** Born Caernarfon 22 September 1910, s of Owen Owens Roberts & Mary Grace Williams. Baptist. Married 1948 Anne Elizabeth Tudor, 2c. Educated Caernarfon Grammar School; University of Wales, Aberystwyth (1st Law); Gonville & Caius College, Cambridge (1st Law); Clements Inn Prize; S. T. Evans Prize]; Geneva School of International Law. RAF 1941-45, Squadron Leader. Solicitor 1936. Barrister, Grays Inn 1944. Director: Tootall, Broadhurst, Lee & Co Ltd 1958-; English Calico Co Ltd 1970-. Secretary, English Sewing Cotton Co 1966-. President: National League of Young Liberals 1946-48; Liberal Party of Wales 1949-51. Member, Council of Europe 1950-51. Hon. Legal Adviser, National Eisteddfod of Wales. Chair, National Eisteddfod Council 1964-67. Member: Legal Council on Status of the Welsh Language in the Law Courts; Duke of Norfolk's Investiture Cttee. 1969. Chair, Mid-Wales Development Corporation 1969-77. Member: Development Board Agency 1977-81; Development Corporation of Wales 1978-81; Court, University of Wales, Aberystwyth 1972-88. Vice-President, Hon. Society of Cymmrodorion. Short-listed at Caernarfon Boroughs, May B/E 1945. Languages: Welsh, English. Of Cardiff. Died 29 October 1990. *Books: E. O. Roberts: The Law of Restrictive Trade Practices and Monopolies (joint).*

ROBERTS Emrys Puw: MA (Wales). Plaid Cymru: Newport B/E 1956; Cardiff North 1959, 1964; Ebbw Vale B/E 1960; Merthyr Tydfil B/E 1972; Feb. & Oct. 974. **Mr. Emrys Roberts:** Born Royal Leamington Spa November 1931, Welsh father & English mother; Moved to Cardiff 1942. Married Mary Gough, 4c, divorced. Educated Cathays High School, Cardiff. Inland Revenue Officer 1947-49. CO on nationalist grounds 1952, imprisoned for 3 months. University of Wales, Cardiff 1952-55. President, Student Representative

Council. Extra mural Lecturer. Youth Secretary/ Asst. Secretary, Plaid Cymru, General Secretary, resigned in disagreement over policy. Organising Secretary, CND Cymru. Organiser, Tyneside Eisteddfod 1966-68. Editor, *Caerphilly Advertiser* 1968-69. PRO Wales Hospital Board 1969-72, resigned post to contest Merthyr Tydfil by-election. Public Relations Consultant. Secretary: South Gwent Community Health Council 1974-93; Assn of Welsh Community Health Councils 1988-92. District Health Manager, Gwent Health Authority 1993-96. Welsh Representative, Council on Tribunals 1999-. 1st Chair, CND Cymru. Treasurer, Rhymney Valley MIND. Merthyr Tydfil BC B/E 1975-79, Leader of the Council 1976-79. Languages: Learned Welsh at school, English.

ROBERTS Eric Randolph: Plaid Cymru, Cardiff South-East 1979; Welsh Independent Socialist & Ecologist, Vale of Glamorgan B/E 1989. **Mr. Eric Roberts:** Born Penarth 1933. Married 4c widowed. Educated Dinas Powys Elementary School. Army 1949-66. Bus driver. Taxi driver. Welsh Rugby XV dressing room steward. Chair, Cardiff SE Plaid Cymru. Member: Plaid Cymru Executive; South Wales Leasehold Reform Group; TGWU. Contested Cardiff CC 1977. Of Dinas Powys.

ROBERTS Ernest Handforth Goodman: Kt 1936 KC 1949 MA (Oxon). Conservative: Flint 1923, 1929; MP 1924-29. **Sir Ernest Goodman Roberts:** Born Penyffordd, Flints 20 April 1890, s of Hugh Goodman Roberts. Anglican. Unmarried. Educated Malvern; Trinity College, Oxford. President, Oxford Union 1914. Army 1914-19, Captain RWF; Court Martial Officer. Barrister Inner Temple 1916. Deputy Chair, Flintshire Quarter Sessions 1949-61. Chief Justice, High Court of Judicature, Rangoon 1936-48. Judge & Commissioner of Assize 1949-55. Member, Governing Body of the Church in Wales 1920-36, 1947-59. Chancellor: Diocese of Bangor 1947-59; Chelmsford 1950-. Of Mold. Died 14 February 1969. *Books: E. H. G. Roberts, Principles of the Law of Contract 1923.*

ROBERTS Fflur Gwenllian: BSc (Wales). Plaid Cymru, North List 1999. **Ms. Fflur Roberts:** Born Bangor, 27 August 1970, d of John Roberts, headteacher, & Kathleen Mary Roberts, teacher. Presbyterian Church of Wales. Married 1999, Edward Bryn Jones, business development manager. Educated Ysgol Glan-y-Mor, Pwllheli; University of Wales, Cardiff (Chemistry). President, Cardiff SRC. Marketing & Communications Manager, National Trust, Wales. Member, Court of the University of Wales. Bethesda ComC. Interests: Environment, Education, Culture & Language. Hobbies: Walking, Welsh

Language theatre, Current Affairs. Languages: Welsh, English. Short-listed for Ynys Môn 2000. Of Bethesda.

ROBERTS Gareth Harrison: Independent Wales Party, Blaenau Gwent & South/East List 2003. **Mr. Gareth Roberts:** Born Tredegar, 9 March 1955, s of John Daniel Roberts, electrician, & Elizabeth Millicent Roberts, nurse. Christian. Educated Georgetown Junior School, Tredegar; Gaveston Hall School; Brighton Technical College. Customer Care Manager, MacDonald's, Merthyr Tydfil. Member, Plaid Cymru 1970-2000. Joined Independent Wales Party 2000. Branch Chair; Vice-Chair, Blaenau Gwent Constituency; IWP Transport Spokesman. Contested local elections. Interests: Transport, Welsh Language. Hobbies: Railways, Languages, Watching TV. Languages: Welsh, English. Of Tredegar.

ROBERTS George Fossett: Kt 1935 CB OBE TD JP DL (Cards) 1929 Hon. LLD (Wales). Conservative: Cardiganshire Jan. 1910. **Colonel, Sir George Fossett Roberts:** Born Aberystwyth 1 November 1870, s of Alderman David Roberts & Maria Roberts. Anglican. Married 1896, Mary (Died 1947) d of John Parry, Glanpaith, 2d. Educated Cheltenham private school. Managing Director, David Roberts & Son, Brewers, Aberystwyth 1890-1935. Army 1914-19; Hon. Colonel. 102 Field Brigade RA1933. Chair, Cards TA Assn. High Sheriff of Cardiganshire 1911. Aberystwyth BC 30 years; twice Mayor. Cardiganshire CC. Vice-President: University of Wales, Aberystwyth. President: National Library of Wales; Cardiganshire Conservative Assn; Aberystwyth AFC. District Commissioner, Scouts. 1st Chair, Mid Wales Hospital Management Cttee 1948-51. Member, Governing Body of the Church in Wales. Of Aberystwyth. Died 1953.

ROBERTS Goronwy Owain, Baron Goronwy-Roberts 1974: PC 1968 MA Wales) 1938 FRSA 1968. Labour MP Caernarfonshire 1945-50; Caernarfon 1950-74. **Rt. Hon. Goronwy Roberts:** Born Bethesda, 20 September 1913, s of E. E. & Amelia Roberts. Presbyterian Church of Wales elder. Married Marian Ann, d of David & Elizabeth Evans, Tresalem, Aberdare, 1d. Educated Bethesda Grammar School; University of Wales, Bangor (1st English); Fellow of the University of Wales 1938. Research at King's College, London & on the Continent 1937-39. Army 1940-41; Army Reserve 1941-44. Youth Education Officer, Caernarfonshire 1941-44. Lecturer, Youth Leadership, University of Wales, Swansea 1944-45. Chair, Hughes a'i Fab, publishers 1955-59. Member of Courts: University of Wales, Aberystwyth; National Library, National Museum. Chair: Welsh Economic Planning Council 1964-66; Technical Education Cttee of

Council for Education in the Commonwealth 1966-67. Trustee, Oppenheimer Trust for Ex-Servicemen 1952-58. Deputy Chair, House of Commons Library Cttee. Member, Speaker's Panel of Chairmen 1963-64. Member: Fabian Society. Freeman: Royal Borough of Caernarfon 1972. Company Director: Ansvar Insurance Co. Ltd 1971-74. Minister of State: Wales 1964-66; Education & Science 1966-67; Foreign Office 1967-69; Board of Trade 1969-70; Foreign Office 1974. Hobbies: Walking, Music, Collecting year books. Languages: Welsh, English. Died 23 July 1982.

ROBERTS Gwilym Effrwd: JP (Luton) BSc (Wales) PhD FIS. Labour: Conway 1964, Ormskirk 1959, South Bedfordshire 1970; Cannock & Burntwood 1987; MP South Bedfordshire 1966-70; Cannock Feb. 1974-83. **Dr. Gwilym Roberts:** Born 7 August 1928, s of William & Jane Ann Roberts. Married 1954, Mair Griffiths. Educated Brynrefail Grammar School; University of Wales, Bangor. Lecturer, Scientific Management Techniques, College of Advanced Technology –1957. Principal Lecturer, Hendon College of Technology 1957-66. Business Analyst, Economic Forecasting, Market & Operational Research 1957-. Company Director: Method Advisory Services Ltd. Polytechnic consultant. Member: Institute of Statisticians. Adviser, NATFHE. PPS 1976-79. Languages: Welsh, English. Of Luton.

ROBERTS Henry: MSc (Wales). Plaid Cymru: Llanelli 1979. **Mr. Harri Roberts:** Born Caernarfon July 1953. Educated Caernarfon Grammar School; University of Wales, Swansea. President SRC & University of Wales Central SRC. Computer Consultant. Plaid Cymru Director of Research. Languages: Welsh, English.

ROBERTS Hugh Griffith: Labour: Meirionydd/Nant Conwy 1987. **Mr. Hugh Roberts:** Born Barmouth 25 April 1948, s of owner/editor, *Barmouth Advertiser,* & a nurse. Christian. Married. Educated Ysgol Ardudwy, Harlech; Ysgol y Gader, Dolgellau; Bangor Normal College. Teacher. Head Warden, Snowdonia National Park 1972-. Youth & Schools Officer, Snowdonia Park Authority. Urdd Gobaith Cymru Instructor. Secretary, Urdd Gobaith Cymru Senate. Member: NACRO Advisory Cttee for Gwynedd, NALGO. Chair: Farming, Forestry & Wildlife Advisory Group's Education & Publicity Cttee for Gwynedd. Member, Labour Party, 1980-91. Joined Plaid Cymru, February 1991. Languages: Welsh, English.

ROBERTS Humphrey: Plaid Cymru: Caernarfon 1966. **Mr. Wmffra Roberts:** Born Talsarn, Dyffryn Nantlle 1940. Married Educated Penygroes Grammar School. Railway clerk 1955-58.

Army 1958-60. Clerk in travel agency, bought out owners when they were going to close it and set up Snowdon Travel Agency, Caernarfon 1960. Chair, Caernarfon Chamber of Commerce. Gwyrfai RDC 1961-73. Gwynedd CC 1973-. Languages: Welsh, English. Of Penygroes, Gwynedd. Died 22 January 1976.

ROBERTS Hywel Eifion Prichard: DL Clwyd 1988 1951 QC 1971 LlB (Wales) BCL (Oxon). Liberal: Denbigh 1951. **Mr. Eifion Roberts:** Born, Anglesey, 22 November 1927, s of Revd E. P Roberts & Margaret Jones (brother of Sir Wyn Roberts, qv). Married Buddug, d of G J Williams, Menai Bridge. Educated Beaumaris Grammar School; University of Wales, Aberystwyth; Exeter College, Oxford. RAF Flying Officer, Education. Barrister, Grays Inn 1952. Deputy Chair, Quarter Sessions: Anglesey 1966-71; Denbighshire 1970-71. Crown Court Recorder 1971-75. Asst Boundary Commissioner, Wales 1967-69. Vice-President & Chair of Council, University of Wales, Bangor. Member for Wales, Crawford Cttee on Broadcasting. Languages: Welsh, English. Of Llai, Wrexham.

ROBERTS Hywel Heulyn: JP (Cards) 1968. Plaid Cymru, Carmarthen 1959. **Mr. Hywel Heulyn Roberts:** Born Liverpool 16 March 1919, s of John Roberts. Welsh Independent. Married Margaret Eluned Davies 1s 3d. Educated Liverpool Institute High School. Bank clerk 1935-49. District Manager, feeding stuffs manufacturer 1949. Part-time Organiser, Plaid Cymru. Owner, shop & petrol station. Cardiganshire CC 1952, Alderman 1962, Chair 1967-68, 1971-72; Chair, Finance Cttee 1964-73. Dyfed CC 1973-89; Chair 1973-76. Chair: Cardigan Bay Resorts Assn; South West Wales Hospitals Management Board Finance Cttee; Plaid Cymru Finance Cttee 1964-71; Cardiganshire Constituency, Plaid Cymru; Welsh Folk Museum 1971-73, Dyfed-Powys Police Authority 1980-82. Member: Welsh County Councils Assn; Welsh Joint Education Cttee; Court & Council, University of Wales; Governing Body: Welsh National School of Music & Drama; Welsh College of Librarianship; Managing Cttee, Welsh Theatre Company. Chair, Cardiganshire Welsh Independent Assn. Hon. Member, Gorsedd 1976. Languages: Welsh, English. Of Synod Inn.

ROBERTS Hywel W: BSc (Wales) DipEd DipStats. Plaid Cymru: Wrexham Feb. & Oct. 1974. **Mr. Hywel Roberts:** Born Liverpool September 1938. Married Carole, lecturer in Statistics. Educated Moelwyn School, Blaenau Ffestiniog; University of Wales, Aberystwyth (Maths). Lecturer in Administration, Leeds Polytechnic 1963. Senior Lecturer, Slough College of Technology; City of London Polytechnic School of Business Studies

-1972. Head of School of Management, Business & Trade Union Studies, Flintshire College of Technology 1972-. Chair, London Branch, Plaid Cymru 1969-72. Plaid Cymru Representative; Home Office Conference on Electoral Law; Union of European Nations. Plaid Cymru Spokesman on Education. Member, ATTI. Leader, Wrexham Area Rent Campaign. Wrexham-Maelor DC. Languages: Welsh, English.

ROBERTS Ieuan Wyn Prichard, Baron Roberts of Conwy 1997: PC 1991 Kt MA (Oxon). Conservative MP Conwy 1970-97. **Rt. Hon. Sir Wyn Roberts:** Born Anglesey 10 July 1930, s of Revd E. P. Roberts, Presbyterian minister & Margaret Jones (brother of H. E. P. Roberts qv). Married 1956, Enid Grace Williams, 3s. Educated Beaumaris Grammar School; Harrow School; University College, Oxford. Sub-Editor, *Liverpool Daily Post* 1952-54; News Assistant BBC 1954-57; Welsh Controller, TWW Ltd. 1957-68; Programme Director, Harlech Television 1968-69. Resigned to contest Conwy election. Governor: National Museum; National Library; University of Wales, Aberystwyth. PPS 1970-74; Opposition Spokesman, Wales 1974-79; Under-Secretary, Wales 1979-87; Minister of State, Wales 1987-96; Vice-President, Assn of District Councils 1975-79. President, Welsh National School of Medicine. Welsh Poet. Hon. Member, Gorsedd 1966. Hon. Fellow: University of Wales, Bangor 1995, Aberystwyth 1997. Hobbies: Welsh Poetry, Gardening. Languages: Welsh, English. Of Conwy.

ROBERTS James: British National Party. Wales Euro 2004. **Mr. James Roberts:** RAF & RAAF 14 years. Worked in engineering & sales. Of Prestatyn (1990).

ROBERTS John: JP (Denbs & Liverpool) 1873. Liberal MP Flint District B/E 1874-90. Mr. John Roberts: Born Liverpool 14 July 1835, s of David Roberts, Tanyrallt, Denbs. Calvinistic Methodist Elder. Married 1861, Katherine, d of Revd John Hughes. Educated Brighton College. Timber Merchant. President, North Wales Calvinistic Methodist Synod. Languages: Welsh, English Of Abergele & Liverpool. Estate £165,562. Died 24 February 1894.

ROBERTS John Bryn: JP DL (Caerns). Liberal MP Eifion 1895-1906. **Mr. J. Bryn Roberts:** Born Bangor 8 January 1843, s of Daniel Roberts & Anne, d of Griffith Jones, Plas Gwananas. Calvinistic Methodist Elder. Educated Cheltenham College. Solicitor 1868. Barrister 1889. Deputy Chair, Caernarfonshire Quarter Sessions. Caernarfonshire CC Alderman 1889. County Court Judge 1906. Supported the establishment of the pro-Asquith Welsh Liberal Federation.

Languages: Welsh, English. Of Bangor, & London. Sent letter of support to Revd E. T. Owen, Labour candidate at Carmarthen B/E (*Carmarthen Journal* 8/8/1924). Estate £33,262. Died 14 April 1931.

ROBERTS John Hamlet Shelton: Conservative: Flint District B/E 1913. **Major Hamlet Roberts:** Born Llanllyfni 1880, s of Dr. Evan & Mary Roberts, Penygroes, Arfon. Married Mary. Solicitor at Caernarfon. Barrister 1913. Lieutenant TA 1913. Army 1914-8; Major RWF. Conservative agent, Eifion Jan. 1910. Languages: Welsh, English. Of Chelsea. Died 11 June 1945.

ROBERTS John Herbert, 1st Baron Clwyd of Abergele 1919: 1st Bart 1908 JP1885 BA (Cantab) 1884: MA 1888. Liberal MP West Denbighshire 1892-1918. **Sir Herbert Roberts:** Born Liverpool, 8 August 1863, s of John Roberts (MP Flint 1878-92) & Catherine, d of Revd John Hughes, Liverpool. Calvinistic Methodist Elder. Married 1893 Hannah, d of W. S. Caine MP 3s. Educated Privately & Trinity College, Cambridge. Timber Merchant. President, North Wales Temperance Society. Secretary, Welsh Liberal MPs 1906-12, Chair 1912-18. Welsh Church Commissioner 1914-. Chair, British Cttee Indian National Congress. Languages: Welsh, English. Of Bryngwenith, Abergele & London. Died 19 December 1955.

ROBERTS: John P. T: LlB (Liverpool). Liberal: Cardiff North-West 1979. **Mr. John Roberts:** Born Prestatyn, 1947. Educated Liverpool University. Solicitor (London). Chair, Liberal Party of Wales.

ROBERTS John Rice: JP DL (Anglesey) MA. Conservative: Anglesey 1895; PPC 1890 resigned. **Mr. John Rice Roberts:** Born Aberffraw 1837. Anglican. Married Jane Anne 1d. Solicitor. Town Clerk, Beaumaris. Clerk, Anglesey County Council. Clerk of the Peace 1902-12. Chair, Anglesey Conservative Assn. President, Anglesey Harriers. Anglesey CC 1892, Vice-Chair. Of Rhiwlas, Pentraeth. Estate £38,006. Died 19 July 1920.

ROBERTS John Roger, Baron Roberts of Llandudno 2004: BA (Wales). Liberal (Democrat): Conwy 1979, 1983, 1987, 1992, 1997; Euro Wales, 1999. **Revd Roger Roberts:** Born Llanrwst 23 October 1935, s of Thomas Charles & Alice Ellen Roberts. Married Eirlys Ann, 1s 2d. Educated John Bright Grammar School, Llandudno; University of Wales, Bangor; Handsworth Theological College, Birmingham. Superintendent Minister, Llandudno Circuit. Chair, Union of University Liberal Societies. President: Welsh Liberal Party 1981-84; Welsh Liberal Democrat Party 1990-91. Federal Vice-President, Liberal

Democrat Party. Vice-President, Welsh Liberal Democrats, January 2002. Aberconway BC 1976-87 (Chair, Environmental Health; Group Leader). Member: Fund for Human Need. Chair, Wales Water Lifeline. Regular contributor, Radio 2 *Pause for Thought*. Languages: Welsh, English. Of Llandudno.

ROBERTS Llewelyn Emyr: Liberal: West Flint 1959. **Mr. Emyr Roberts:** Born 1906. Married. Educated Mold Grammar School. Bank Clerk. Of Rhyl.

ROBERTS Michael Hilary Adair: BA Wales). Conservative: Aberdare B/E 1954; Cardiff South East 1955, 1959; MP Cardiff North 1970-74; Cardiff North West Feb. 1974. **Mr. Michael Roberts:** Born Aberystwyth May 1927, s of Revd T. A. Roberts, later Rector of Neath. Anglican. Married Mrs. Eileen Evans, d of C. H. Billing, 3c. Educated Neath Grammar School; University of Wales, Cardiff. RAF Education Officer. Teacher. 1st Headteacher, Bishop of Llandaff Secondary School, Cardiff 1963-70. Hon. Coach, Welsh Rugby Union. Member: Bow Group. President, Cardiff Branch NUT. Chair: Welsh Area CPC. Jt Vice-Chair, Conservative MPs' Education Cttee 1974. Opposition Whip 1974. Under-Secretary, Wales 1979-. Of Whitchurch, Cardiff. Died 10 February 1983.

ROBERTS Nia: BSc. CPA EPA CPhys. MInstP. Labour, North Wales List 1999. **Ms. Nia Roberts:** Born Bangor, 4 January 1963, d of John Roberts, farmer, & Marian Edwards, singer. Unitarian. Married 1992 Dr. John Nye, R & D Director, 1s 1d. Educated Ysgol Parc y Bont, Llanddaniel; Ysgol David Hughes, Menai Bridge; Victoria University of Manchester (Physics). Chartered Patent Attorney. Hobbies: Writing, Languages, Singing. Languages: Welsh, English, Dutch, French, German. Of Llandudno.

ROBERTS Owen Meurig: Conservative: Anglesey 1951, 1959; Caernarfon 1955. **Mr. Meurig Roberts:** Born Bangor March 1904. Lay preacher. Married 3c. Educated Friars School; Bangor; University of Wales, Bangor. Hospital Services Organiser, Caernarfonshire & Anglesey 1936-48. Secretary, Anglesey & Caernarfonshire General Hospital, Bangor 1948-. Associate, Institute of Hospital Administrators. Chair, local health service branch, NALGO. Caernarfonshire CC 1946-49. Bangor CC 1945-, Mayor. Languages: Welsh, English. Of Bangor.

ROBERTS Richard Cowan: OBE 1915 KStJ 1922. Conservative: Wrexham 1922. **Colonel Richard Roberts:** Born Rhosrobin 1875. Married (wife died 1967). Anglican. Solicitor 1900. (Senior Partner R. C. Roberts & Russell). Clerk: Wrexham RDC & Joint Fever Hospital 1911-22, Bromfield Magis-

trates1933-54; Denbighshire Lieutenancy 20 years. Under Sheriff of Denbighshire in 1950s. Captain, 4th Denbighshire RWF (TA) 1904-14; RWF 1914-18, Major 1918; wounded, 1915; Deputy Director General of Recruiting, Ministry of National Service 1916-18. Organised training for disabled soldiers 1919. Director of Pensions for Wales 1919-22 (resigned post to contest the election). Joint Hon. Secretary, Gresford Colliery Disaster Fund 1934. Wrexham BC 1910-19. Vice-Chair, Wrexham Conservative Assn. 1945-. President: Chester & North Wales Branch, Law Society; Chester & North Wales Branch, Justices Clerks Society. Founder-Member, Wrexham Golf Club; Captain 1926. Of Wrexham.

ROBERTS Richard Owen: LlB (London). Conservative: Anglesey, December 1910, 1923. **Mr. Richard Roberts:** Born London 3 September 1876, s of William Roberts, private hotelier, & Jane Parry. Married Gladys Hughes, 3c. Educated Kings College School; Kings College, London. Solicitor, London General Omnibus Co. Barrister, Inner Temple. County Court Judge 1924. Contested London CC 1910, 1913. Died 12 September 1929.

ROBERTS Shelagh Marjorie: DBE 1981 Peerage 1/1/1992. Conservative: Caernarfon 1964; MEP London S.W. 1979-; technical disqualification led to a by-election at which she was re-elected. **Dame Shelagh Roberts:** Born Port Talbot 13 October 1924, d of bank manager. Educated Milford Haven Grammar School; Ystalyfera Grammar School; St. Wyburn School, Birkdale. Civil Servant. Inland Revenue c.1942-. Asst. Secretary, Society of Civil Servants. Part-time industrial relations officer, Industrial Relations Consultant. Chair, Conservative Party Conference 1976; National Conservative Women's Advisory Cttee 1972-75. Greater London CC 1970-81 (Chair, Planning & Communications Cttee). Kensington & Chelsea BC 1953-71 (Chair, Housing Cttee). Member: Race Relations Board 1973-77, Panel of Industrial Tribunals 1973-79. Chair: London Tourist Board & Convention Bureau 1989-92. Died 16 January 1992.

ROBERTS Thomas W: Communist: Merthyr Tydfil Oct. 1974. **Mr. Tom Roberts:** Born 1927. Educated Twynrodyn; Queens Street School, Merthyr Tydfil; Quakers Yard Technical College. Bricklayer. Secretary, Merthyr Tenants & Residents Assn. Member: UCATT; Welsh Cttee, Communist Party; Merthyr Tydfil Trades & Labour Council. Of Twynrodyn, Merthyr Tydfil.

ROBERTS Timothy Peter: BA (Oxon). Conservative: Alyn & Deeside 1997. **Mr. Timothy Roberts:** Born Cheltenham, 18 February 1971, (gs of Aled Roberts MP qv). Educated Cleeve

School, Cheltenham; St. Hugh's College, Oxford. Research Associate, Adam Smith Institute. Head of Research, Walker, Crips, Weddle, Beck plc city stockbrokers 1991. Vice-Chair, National Association of Conservative Graduates 1995-. Treasurer, Westminster Young Conservatives.

ROBERTS Timothy Wace: MA (Oxon) CPA EPA. Pro-Life Party, Mid & West Wales List 2003. **Mr. Timothy Roberts:** Born Winchester, 29 July 1937, son of Charles Wace Roberts, Lloyds Underwriter, & Felicity Mary Roberts, housewife. Roman Catholic. Married 1961, Dominica Mary Forrest (qv), chartered patent attorney, 2s 3d (son John contested Burton 2001). Educated Mourne Grange Preparatory School, Kilkeel, Co. Down; Sedbergh School; Trinity College, Oxford (Scholar; Chemistry). Chartered Patent Attorney/ Intellectual Property Consultant. Member: European Plant Variety Rights Office Appeal Panel; UK Government Intellectual Property Advisory Cttee. Editor, *European Patents Handbook*. President, Chartered Institute of Patent Agents 20001-02. Interests: Pro-Life. Hobbies: Aspirant Polymath. Languages: English, French, German, Japanese, Latin, minimal Russian.

ROBERTSON Henry: JP (Denbs; Merioneth) DL (Merioneth) MA (Aberdeen) CE. Liberal MP Merioneth 1885-86; Shrewsbury 1862-65, 1874-85. **Mr. Henry Robertson:** Born Banff 1st January 1816, s of Duncan Robertson. Married 1846, Elizabeth, d of William Deene, Shrewsbury. Educated Aberdeen University. Came to Wales 1842. Civil Engineer, locomotive manufacturer, railway developer, colliery proprietor, ironmaster & landowner. Planned Chester-Shrewsbury & Ruabon-Dolgellau lines. Bought estates at Crogan, Corwen & Llandderfel. High Sheriff of Merioneth 1869. Disagreed with Gladstone's Home Rule Policy. Of Pale, Corwen, & London. Estate £185,528. Died 22 March 1888.

ROBINS Samuel John: Liberal: Pontypool 1923, Plymouth Drake 1922. **Major Samuel Robins:** Born Penarth 1868, s of John Robins, chief clerk, Taff Vale Railway, & Margaret Robins. Educated East London Training Institute for Home & Foreign Missions. Baptist Minister: Ordained 1893. Pastorates: Mount Pleasant, Cadoxton, Barry 1893-95; Blakeney 1895-98; Scapegoat Hill 1898-99; Beeston, Leeds 1905-07; Lancaster 1907-09. Resigned from Ministry & moved to Canada 1909. Private Secretary to Prime Minister of Canada. Received backing of Pontypool Conservative Assn.

ROBINSON Ann: MA (Oxon) MA PhD (McGill). Conservative, South East Wales Euro 1979. **Dr. Anne Robinson:** Born London 1937, d of Samuel James & Dora Thomas. Married Michael Finlay Robinson (Lecturer in music) 2s. Educated Halldon House School, Fulmer; Bishopshalt School, Hillingdon; St. Anne's College, Oxford; McGill University. Lecturer in Politics, University of Wales, Cardiff, & Vesting Fellow, Centre for Fiscal Studies, Bath. Academic Secretary, Study of Parliament Group. Financial Journalist, *Investors Guide* 1959-61; University Lecturer: Durham 1962-65, Bristol 1970-71, Bath 1972-75, University of Wales, Cardiff 1972-87. Senior Lecturer 1987-89. Head of Policy Unit, Institute of Directors 1989-95. Director: Great Western Holdings 1996-98, Almedia 2001. Visiting Professor, University of Bournemouth. Director-General, National Assn of Pension Funds Ltd 1995-2000. Member: Equal Opportunities Commission 1991-93; HFCW 1993-97; Economic & Social Cttee 1986-93; Welsh Arts Council 1991-93; Council, RIA Competition Commission 1993-99; Board of Academic Governors, Richmond College, London, 1992; Board Commonwealth Institute 1992-97; Council, Clifton College. Director, Welsh National Opera 1992-97. Of Shirenewtown.

ROBINSON David Alan: UK Independence Party, Swansea East 2003. **Mr. Alan Robinson:** Born Port Tennant, Swansea, 4 March 1946, son of Arthur Victor Robinson, tinplate mill inspector, & Mary Ann Robinson, housewife. Married 1965, Linda James, self-employed caterer, 1s 2d. Educated Danygraig Schools. Publican. Chair, Port Tennant & St. Thomas Residents' Assn. Contested Swansea CC 1999. Hobbies: Golf, Cycling, Rugby.

ROBINSON Dorienne Julia: Green Party, Mid & West list 2003; Wales Euro 2004; Truro & St. Austell 1997. **Ms. Dorienne Robinson:** Born 25 May 1954. Divorced 1 d. Builders' Labourer. Sports Physiotherapist. Cider Maker. Part-time Press Officer, Green Party Wales & part-time worker, Heart of Wales Credit Union. Green Party, Wales Euro 2004. Hobbies: Long distance running, Growing vegetables, Good wine. Languages: Welsh, English. Of Rhayader. *Books: Dorienne Robinson, The Straw House.*

ROBINSON Mark Noel Foster: MA (Oxon). Conservative MP Newport West 1983-87; Somerton & Frome 1992-97; Contested South Yorkshire Euro 1979. **Mr. Mark Robinson:** Born 26 December 1946, s of John Foster Robinson CBE & Margaret Paterson. Married Vivien Pilkington. Educated Harrow; Christ Church, Oxford. President, Oxford University Conservative Assn 1967. Barrister, Middle Temple. Special Assistant to Chief, UN Emergency Operation, Bangladesh 1972-73. Personal & Political Assistant, UN Secretary General (Kurt Waldheim) 1974-77. Asst Director Commonwealth Secretariat, Marlborough House 1977-83. Member, Select Cttee Foreign Affairs 1983-84; Hon. Secretary United Nations Parliamentary Group 1983-85; British-Canadian Group. Commonwealth Parliamentary Assn 1983-85. Treasurer, British-Caribbean Parliamentary Group 1984-85. Secretary, Welsh Conservative MPs. PPS 1984-85. Under-Secretary, Wales 1985-92. Member, Winston Churchill Memorial Trust 1993; Commonwealth Development Corporation-1992.

ROBINSON Sidney: JP (Glam; Somerset; Wiltshire). Liberal MP Breconshire 1906-18; Brecon & Radnor 1918-22. **Mr. Sidney Robinson:** Born Somerset 1863, s of John Robinson, Backwell House, Somerset. Married 1887, Catherine Grant (died 1935). Educated Mill Hill School. Lived in Cardiff from 1880. Company Director: Robinson, David & Co timber merchants. President, Bristol Channel Timber Importers Assn; Cardiff Liberal Assn. Cardiff BC 1895-1901, 1902-6 (Liberal Whip). Of Bath. Died 6 December 1956.

ROCH Walter Francis: Liberal MP Pembrokeshire B/E 1908-18. **Mr. Walter Roch:** Born 20 January 1880, s of Walter Francis Roch, Butterhill, Pembs. & Emily Catherine, d of W. R. H. Powell MP. Married 1911, Hon. Fflorens Mary Ursula Herbert, d of Baron Treowen (qv). Barrister, Inner Temple 1913. Landowner. Leading member, Men's League for Women's Suffrage; supported Asquith in 1915. Of Chelsea, Plas y Bridell, Cilgerran; Maesgwynne, Whitland, & later of Llanarth Court, Raglan. Died 3 May 1965. *Books etc: W. F. Roch, Welsh Disestablishment: The Case for It 1911, Mr. Lloyd George and the War.*

RODDICK George Winston: CB 31.12.2003 QC 1986 LlB LLM (London). Liberal: Anglesey 1970, Cardiff South & Penarth 1983, Newport West 1987. **Mr. Winston Roddick:** Born Caernarfon 2 October, 1940, s of William & Aelwen Roddick. Married Cennin Parry, 1s 1d. Educated Caernarfon Grammar School; University College, London; President, University College, London Liberal Society. Liverpool Policeman, Barrister, Grays Inn 1968. Holker Scholar. Asst Recorder; Crown Court Recorder 1987-. Chair: Welsh Liberal Party 1983-85, President 1988. President, Alliance in Wales; Alliance Spokesman on Welsh Education. Member, Welsh Language Board. Director & Trustee, Wales Diabetes Trust 1987. Counsellor, National Assembly of Wales Oct. 1998-2 Nov. 2003. Hon. Recorder of Caernarfon. Languages: Welsh, English. Of Cyncoed, Cardiff.

RODERICK Caerwyn Eifion: BSc (Wales). Labour MP Brecon & Radnor 1970-79. **Mr. Caerwyn Roderick:** Born Ystradgynlais15 July 1927. Baptist. Married Eirlys Mary Lewis, 1s 2d.

Educated Maesydderwen Grammar School, Ystradgynlais; University of Wales, Bangor (Maths). Teacher: Caterham School 1949-52; Chartesey School 1952-54; Brecon Boys Grammar 1954-57. Methods Study Officer, NCB Ystradmynach 1957-60. Teacher, Hartridge High School, Newport 1960-69. Lecturer in Mathematics, Cardiff College of Education 1969-70. Joined Labour Party 1955. Chair: Cardiff North CLP. District Officer NUT 1980-91. Member: NUT Welsh Secondary Education Cttee; NUT National Advisory Cttee for Comprehensive Schools; Co-operative Party. Vice-President, South Wales branch, National Society for Mentally Handicapped Children. South Glam CC 1980-86. Council Member: Royal College of Veterinary Surgeons; University of Wales, Cardiff. PPS to Leader of the Opposition. Of Rhiwbina, Cardiff.

RODERICK Evan Joshua: JP (Glam). Liberal: Aberdare 1929. **Mr. Evan Roderick:** Born Llanbadarnfawr 1877, s of John Roderick (mother Died 1881). Welsh Independent deacon. Leadminer 1890-92. Coalminer 1892-1930. Checkweighman 1892. Member of Labour Party until he joined the Liberals 1928. Rhondda UDC 1910-28; Chair 1919-20. Languages: Welsh, English. Of Clydach Vale (1893). Died February 1963.

ROFFE Melvyn Wesley: BA (York) 1985 PGCE (Durham) 1986. Liberal Democrat, South/East List 1999, Corby 1992. **Mr. Melvyn Roffe:** Born Derby, 15 June 1964, son of Brian Leslie Roffe, electrical power engineer, & Vera Maud Roffe, teacher. Anglican. Married 1988, Catherine Anne Stratford, 1s 1d. Educated Noel-Baker Comprehensive School, Derby; University of York, Durham. Teacher. Headteacher, East Midlands 2001. Agent, Monmouth 1997, 2001. East Northamptonshire DC (Leader, Lib Dem Group) 1991-93. Interests: Education, Constitution, Home Affairs. Hobbies: Politics. Languages: English, French. Of Newcastle, Monmouth (1993-2001).

ROFFE Robert William: BA (Teeside) PGCE (Wales). Liberal Democrat, Caerphilly 2001, 2003. **Mr. Rob Roffe:** Born Sunderland, 12 January 1977, s of John Robert Roffe, firefighter, & Pauline Roffe, receptionist. Nominally Church of England. Partner, Helen Forsey. Educated Monkswearmouth Comprehensive School, Sunderland; Monkswearmouth College; University of Teeside (History); University of Wales, Swansea). Tour Guide, Comeston Medieval Village 1999. Research Assistant, National Assembly Liberal Democrat Group 1999-2000. PhD research student/part time lecturer, University of Wales Institute, Cardiff. Tutor, University of Glamorgan. Joined Liberal Democrats 1994. Contested Sunderland MC 1998. Press Officer,

Rhondda/Cynon/Taf Liberal Democrats 1999-2000. Secretary/ Chair: Caerphilly Liberal Democrats. Policy Officer, Welsh Liberal Democrats 2002. Interests: education, constitutional reform, environment. Hobbies: Cinema, Theatre, Reading ,Classical music, Political history; Sunderland AFC. Languages: English, British Sign Language. Of Treforest.

ROGERS Allan Ralph: BSc (Wales) FGS. Labour MP Rhondda 1983-2001; MEP South East Wales 1979-84. **Mr. Allan Rogers:** Born Penybryn 4 October 1932, s of John Henry Rogers, miner, & Madeleine Smith. Married Ceridwen, d of Bryn James, Cefn Hengoed, 4c. Educated Gelligaer Primary School; Bargoed Secondary School; University of Wales, Swansea. Army 1951-53. Geologist. Worked in Canada, USA. & Australia. District Secretary WEA. NCB Geologist. Joined Labour Party 1948. Gelligaer UDC 1965-71; Mid-Glam CC 1970-79. Chair, Polytechnic of Wales. Vice-President, Wales Anti-Apartheid Movement. Member CND. Treasurer, Bargoed Boys Club. National Secretary, UK. Jazz Bands Federation. Opposition Spokesman: Defence & Arms. Control 1987. Select Cttee Member: Euro Legislation 1983-87; Channel Tunnel Bill 1986; Public Accounts 1983-88; Welsh Affairs 1983-87; Intelligence & Security 1994-. Secretary, World Government Group; Chair, Welsh Labour Group 1987-88. Campaign Officer 1989-. Of Hengoed.

ROGERS Anthony: Independent, Merthyr Tydfil & Rhymney 1999. **Mr. Tony Rogers:** Born Cefn Coed, s of Lance Rogers. Educated Vaynor & Penderyn Grammar School. Worked at Hy-Mac, Rhymney, NCB Works, Lodge Secretary NUM. AEUW Shop Steward. Merthyr Tydfil BC (Labour) 1976- (Chair: Personnel Cttee 5 years). Resigned from Labour *Party because I realised last October that I could not be part of the regime of New Labour.* Of Merthyr Tydfil.

ROGERS Charles Coltman – see COLTMAN-ROGERS Charles.

ROGERS John Dunlop: BA (Leeds). Plaid Cymru, Ebbw Vale, Oct. 1974, East Flint 1979, Alyn & Deeside 1987, 1992, Ogmore 1997 1999. **Mr. John Rogers:** Born February 1943. Married Brenda, nurse, 1s 1d. Educated Glyndwr Secondary Modern School, Rhyl; Rhyl Grammar School; St. Mary's College, Crosby; Leeds University (English & Spanish); Seville University. Merchant Navy Seaman. Teacher (English): Merioneth, St. Richard Gwyn School 1974-88; Ysgol Gyfun Rhydfelin. Founder, Cambrian Coast Line Action Cttee. Member, Nantymoel Neighbourhood Watch Cttee; Amnesty International. Secretary, West Riding Branch, Plaid Cymru; Plaid Cymru Transport Spokesman. Of Nantymoel.

ROGERS Peter Standing: Conservative: Ynys Môn, 1999, 2003; AM North Wales List 1999-2003. **Mr. Peter Rogers:** Born Wrexham, 2 January 1940. s of Harold & Jean Rogers. Married 1973, Margaret Roberts 2s. Educated Prenton Secondary School, Birkenhead; Cheshire School of Agriculture. Farm Manager 1962-65, Sales Manager, Ciba Geiky UK 1965-72, Self-Employed Farmer 1972. Vice-President, Ynys Môn Conservative Assn. Hobbies: Sports, All Rural Activities, played rugby for Bridgend & Cardiff. Of Brynsiencyn.

ROGERS Simon Keith: AMRSH AIPRWO. Liberal Democrat, South/East List 1999, Merthyr Tydfil & Rhymney 2001, Blaenau Gwent 1999, **Mr. Keith Rogers:** Born Tredegar, 16 October 1959. Married Helen 2c. Educated Nantyglo Comprehensive School; mature student at University of Wales, Newport. Collier, Abertillery New Mine; Head Countryside Ranger, Blaenau Gwent CBC. Chair, Blaenau Gwent & Torfaen Lib Dems. Regimental Medical. Sergeant, 104 Regt RA (RV); served in Gulf War. School Parent Governor. Chair: Blaenau Gwent Group, Gwent Wildlife Trust; Trustee, Gwent Wildlife Trust. Vice-Chair, Gwent Bat Group. Contested Abertillery ComC. Interests: Environment, Crime & Policing, Health, Defence. Hobbies: Mountain Walking, Bird Watching. Of Abertillery.

ROLLS John Allan, 1st & last Baron Llangattock of the Hendre: 1892: JP DL (Mon) MA (Oxon) FSA. Conservative: North Mon 1885, 1892; MP Monmouthshire 1880-85. **Colonel John Rolls:** Born The Hendre, 19 February 1837, s of Captain John Etherington Welch Rolls & Elizabeth d of Walter Long & Lady Mary, d of Earl of Northesk. Anglican. Married 1868, Georgiana Marcia, d of Sir Charles Fitzroy Maclean Bart.4c (only son killed in France 1916). Educated Eton; Christ Church, Oxford. Landowner (6100 acres in Mon & estates in Southwark, Stoke Newington, Camberwell & Bermondsey). Breeder of shorthorn cattle and shire horses. Captain, Royal Gloucestershire Hussars. Hon. Colonel, 1st Mon Artillery Volunteers. Freemason: Provincial Grand Master, Eastern Division of South Wales & Mon. High Sheriff of Monmouthshire 1875. Monmouthshire CC. Alderman 1889-95. Jubilee Mayor of Monmouth 1887-8-9. Patron of two livings. Of The Hendre, Monmouth; Llangattock Manor; Croft y Bwla, Monmouth; & London. Estate £249,776. Died 23 September 1912.

ROSS Elaine: Green, South East 1999. **Ms. Elaine Ross:** Of Quakers Yard.

ROUT Peter: Ecology Party: Bedwellty 1979. **Mr. Peter Rout:** Born 1944. Married Diana. Driver. Organiser. Welsh Ecology Party. Of Machen.

ROWBOTTON Dorian Gerald: JP BA (Open) BA (Wales). Conservative, Swansea East B/E 2001, Swansea West 2003. **Mr. Gerald Rowbottom:** Born Swansea 2 August 1962, son of Stanley Paul Rowbottom, soldier/labourer, & Mary Eileen Purcell. Roman Catholic. Unmarried. Educated Bishop Gore School, Swansea; Open University; University of Wales, Swansea. Working on MA & MSc. Army 10 years. Qualified social worker. Director, property development co. Deputy Chair: Swansea West Conservative Assn 2001-02, Treasurer. Deputy-Chair: South Wales West Regional Conservatives 2001-. Member: Luton South & Kensington & Chelsea Conservative Assns; Conservative Wales Health Policy Review Team. Wales Conservatives Campaign Co-ordinator for Social Services. Interests: Increasing Conservative interest in National Assembly. Hobbies: Childline Cymru Counsellor. Of Swansea.

ROWDEN Gerald: Communist: Aberavon 1979. **Mr. Gerald Rowden:** Born 1954. Building worker. Secretary: Porthcawl Branch UCATT; Welsh Cttee. Communist Party.

ROWLAND Robyn Patrick Jeffrey: BA (London) MSc (Wales). Liberal Democrat: Merthyr Tydfil & Rhymney 1992; Cardiff North 1997. **Mr. Robyn Rowland:** Born 28 April 1967. Educated H. H. Dow High School, Michigan; British School, Brussels; City of London Poly (Law); University of Wales, Cardiff. Post-graduate Student. South Glam CC (Deputy Group Leader).

ROWLANDS David John: UK Independence, Monmouth 2001, Torfaen 2003, Wales Euro 2004. **Mr. David John Rowlands:** Born 28 April 1948, s

David John Rowlands.

of Thomas John Rowlands, electrician, & Annie Olwen Rowlands. Baptist. Married Keryn Anne Rowlands, 2d. Educated Pontllanffraith Grammar Technical School; Gwent College of Higher Education (HND Business Studies). Petrol Station Proprietor in Cwmbran area, 1976-. Ex-member, Plaid Cymru. Chair: Gwent UKIP; Welsh Council UKIP. 'First foray into politics'. Interests: Independence, Sovereignty of UK. UK Independence Party, Wales Euro 2004. Hobbies: Reading, Writing, Gliding Instructor. Of Croesyceiliog, Cwmbran.

ROWLANDS David William Lloyd: MA Diploma in Law (Cantab) 1959 FRICS. Independent: Montgomery 1983; UK Independence Party: North Wales Euro 1994; Wales Euro 1999, Montgomery 2001, 2003. **Mr. David Rowlands:** Born Shrewsbury, 8 February 1934, s of John Mc. Rowlands, Newspaper Proprietor & Kathleen Sheppard (family in county 200 years). Anglican. Married 1963, Barbara Musgrave, divorced 1993. Educated Shrewsbury; Trinity Hall, Cambridge. Land Agent & farmer. Llanwddyn ComC 1960-79, Chair 4 years. Montgomery DC 1973-87, Chair, Finance Cttee 7 years, Chair 3 years. Powys CC 1981-91. Chair: Antur Tanat Cain 1981-; Montgomeryshire AFC League 1961-; Powysland Club; Montgomeryshire County History Society. Vice-Chair: Wildlife Trust; Mid-Wales Housing Assn. Trustee: Clwyd-Powys Archeological Trust; Llanwddyn Community Centre. Member: Broadcasting Council for Wales 1979-83; Governing Body of the Church in Wales. Chair: St. Asaph Diocesan Parsonage Board; church treasurer. Financed his own candidature in both elections; would not sit in European Parliament if elected. Minute Secretary, UK Independence Party National Executive; Member, Welsh Council; Chair: Powys Branch UKIP. Hobbies: History, Science, Walking. Of Llanerfyl.

ROWLANDS Edward, Baron Rowlands of Merthyr Tydfil and Rhymney 2004: BA (London) 1962. Labour MP Cardiff North 1966-70; Merthyr Tydfil B/E 1972-83; Merthyr Tydfil & Rhymney 1983-2001. **Mr. Ted Rowlands:** Born Porthcawl, 23 January 1940, s of William S. Rowlands, civil engineer. Church in Wales. Married 1968, Janice Williams, Kidwelly, 2s 1d. Educated Treorchy Junior School; Rhondda County Grammar School; Wirral Grammar School; King's College, London (Modern History). Research Assistant, History of Parliament Trust 1963-64. Lecturer in Modern History & Government, Welsh College of Advanced Technology 1965-66. Under-Secretary, Wales 1969-70, 1974-75. Minister of State, Foreign & Commonwealth Office 1976-79. Member, Foreign Affairs Select Cttee 1987-97. Opposition Spokesman: Energy 1980-87; Foreign Affairs 1979-80. Treasurer, All Party Kenya Group; Secretary, United Nations Group. Booker Prize Judge 1984. Chair: History of Parliament Trust. Member: Governing Body, Commonwealth Institute 1980-92; Academic Council Wilton Park 1983-92/ Chair, History of Parliament Trust 1993-. Interests: The Disabled, Education, Overseas Aid, Publishing. Hobbies: Literature, Music, Golf. Of Porthcawl.

ROWLANDS Gwilym: Kt 1945 CBE 1929 JP (Glam). Conservative: Rhondda West B/E 1920, 1922; Caerphilly 1923, 1924; Pontypool 1929. MP Flint 1935-45. **Sir Gwilym Rowlands:** Born Penygraig, Rhondda 2 December 1878, s of Rowland Rowlands, colliery manager. Married 1908, Elizabeth Ann, d of John Mason, 1s. Educated Penygraig Board School; Heath School, Pontypridd. Colliery Worker 1893. Coal Merchant. President, Rhondda East Conservative Assn. Chair, National Council of Conservative & Unionist Assns. Rhondda UDC 1913-19, 1922-29. Of Penygraig. Languages: Welsh, English. Died 16 January 1949.

ROWLANDS Gwynn Price – see PRICE ROWLANDS G.

ROWLANDS Herbert Roy: TD 1950. Conservative: Rhondda East 1955. **Major Roy Rowlands:** Born Bromsgrove 16 August 1902, s of W. H. Rowlands. Married 1936, Elizabeth, d of Frank Sellars. Educated Rossall School. Engineer. Royal Gloucs Hussars 1939-45. Farmer. Member, NFU. High Sheriff of Herefordshire 1957. Herefordshire CC. Of Malvern.

ROWLANDS John: Plaid Cymru, Cardiff South & Penarth 1999. **Mr. John Rowlands:** Married 3c. Teacher 10 years. BBC Journalist. PR Officer, Environment Agency, Wales. Contested Cardiff CCC (Whitchurch-Tongwynlais) 1999. Chair, Menter Caerdydd. Of Cardiff (1973).

ROWLANDS Roy – see ROWLANDS Herbert Roy.

ROWLANDS William Bowen: QC 1882 BA 1859 MA (Oxon) 1865. Liberal MP Cardiganshire 1886-. **Mr. W. Bowen Rowlands:** Born 1836, s of Thomas Rowlands JP, Glenover, Pembs. Anglican, converted to Roman Catholicism. Married 1864, Adeleine Wogan, d of J. D. Brown, Haverfordwest. Educated Jesus College, Oxford (2nd classics). Church of England clergyman: Ordained Deacon 1864. Curate of Narberth & Asst master, Haverfordwest Grammar School 1864. Ordained priest 1865. Resigned Orders under Clerical Disabilities Relief Act 1870. Barrister, Grays Inn 1871; Bencher 1882; Treasurer 1889. Leader, South Wales & Chester Circuit. Member: Council for Legal Education; Bar Library

Cttee. Recorder of Swansea 1893-1900. County Court Judge 1900. A teetotaler and supporter of the United Kingdom Alliance. Of Earls Court, London. Estate £4,118. Died 4 September 1906.

ROWLINSON Paul John: MA DPhil (Oxon) PGCE (Wales). Plaid Cymru, North List 1999; Delyn 2001, 2003. **Dr. Paul Rowlinson:** Born Altrincham, 25 August 1954, son of Professor, Sir John Rowlinson FRS & Nancy Gaskell. Roman Catholic. Married Ffion Pennant Rowlinson, 1s 2d. Educated Hertford College, Oxford (Chemistry); Linacre College, Oxford (History); University of Wales, Bangor. Qualified Accountant. Freelance Consultant & Translator. Ex-chemical worker, teacher (science & economics) at Essex, Llandudno & Caernarfon. Local government officer, Gwynedd CC Finance Dept. Director, credit union. Llanrug ComC 1995- (Chair 1997-2000). Interests: Community Development, Equal Opportunities (Disability), Public Finance & Economic Policy, Local Government, Education. Vice-President, Plaid Cymru 1998. Interests: Economic Policy; Local Government; Europe. Hobbies: Music, Walking, History. Languages: Learned Welsh, English, German. Of Bethesda.

RUANE Christopher Shaun: BScEcon (Wales) 1979 PCGE (Liverpool) 1980 DipMechEd. Labour: Clwyd North West 1992; MP Vale of Clwyd 1997-. **Mr. Chris Ruane:** Born 18 July 1958, s of Michael Ruane, labourer, & Esther Ruane. Roman Catholic. Married 1994, Gillian, d of Joseph & Phyllis Roberts, 1d. Educated Ysgol Mair, Rhyl; Blessed Edward Jones High School, Rhyl; University of Wales, Aberystwyth. Teacher 1982-91; Deputy Headteacher 1991-97. Chair: Rhyl Anti-Apartheid Group; Rhyl Environment Assn. President, Clwyd NUT 1990. Treasurer, All party Objective One Group. Hobbies: Reading, Cooking.

RUNCIMAN Walter, 1st Viscount Runciman of Doxford 1937: 2nd Baron Runciman of Shoreston 1933, 2nd Bart 1906 PC 1908 BA 1892 BA 1892 MA (Cantab) 1895 Hon. DCL (Oxon) Hon. LLD (Manchester, Bristol). Liberal MP Swansea West 1924-29; Oldham 1899-1900; Dewsbury 1902-18; St. Ives 1929-31; Contested Gravesend 1898, Edinburgh North 1920; Liberal National MP St. Ives 1931-37. **Rt. Hon. Walter Runciman:** Born South Shields 19 November 1870, s of 1st Baron Runciman, self-made shipping magnate, & Ann Margaret Lawson. Wesleyan Methodist. Married 1898, Hilda d. of J. C. Stevenson MP 2s 2d. Educated Trinity College, Cambridge (1st History). Shipowner: partner in father's Moor Line 1892-1905. Deputy Chair, Royal Mail Packet Co. Ltd. Chair, United Kingdom Provident Institution 1930-31. Director, National West. President, Chamber of Shipping of UK 1926-27. Parl-Secretary: Local Government Board 1905-07.

Parl-Secretary, Treasury 1908-11. President: Board of Education 1908-11; Board of Agriculture 1911-14; Board of Trade 1914-16. Went into Opposition as a bitter enemy of Lloyd George 1916-22. President, Board of Trade 1931-37. Lord President of the Council 1937-39. Chair: Liberal Council 1927 (acted as a party within a party throughout the country, anti-Lloyd George) Sent to Czechoslovakia, July 1939, to mediate between the Czech government and the Sudation Germans, an unsuccessful prelude to the Munich Pact. Of Isle of Eigg, Doxford Hall, Northumberland, & London. Died 14 November 1949.

RUSSELL Arthur Charles: Conservative: Pontypool 1950; West Gloucestershire 1951. **Mr. Arthur Russell:** Born Glasgow 1909. Married d of an Ebbw Vale minister. Educated elementary school. Works Accountant, Cwmbran. Cwmbran Agent, Red Cross & St. John's Ambulance. Treasurer, Cwmbran ATC Squadron; Branch Secretary & Treasurer, POWs Aid Assn.

RYDER Arthur John: BA (Oxon) 1934 PhD (London). Conservative: Cardigan 1964. **Dr. Arthur Ryder:** Born April 1913. Anglican. Educated Radley College; Oriel College, Oxford; London School of Economics. Teacher with British Council in Egypt, Palestine & Syria. Civilian education officer BOAR 1946-52. Lecturer in Modern History, St. David's College, Lampeter 1962.

RYDER Janet: BA PGCE. Plaid Cymru AM North List 1999. **Mrs. Janet Ryder:** Born Sunderland 21 June 1955, d of James Spooner, design technical draughtsman, & Audrey Varah Spooner, personal secretary. Religion (blank). Married 1978 Peter Ryder (qv) 2d. Educated St. Anne's Convent High School, Newcastle on Tyne, North Counties College of Education. Teacher, Little Weighton Primary School 1987-88, Coleford Primary School, Hull 1988-89. Member: North Wales Fire Authority 1995-99, Board, Denbighshire Voluntary Services 1995-99. Ruthin TC 1992-, Mayor 1998-2001. Denbighshire CC 1994-99 (Chair: Children's & Families Cttee; Early Years Working Group; Early Years Partnership). Member: Merched y Wawr; Gweini; Canolfan Awelo; North Wales Race Equality Network; Plaid Cymru Councillors Assn; Plaid Cymru Executive 1995-2000. Shadow Minister: Local Government & Housing, Communities Regeneration & Social Inclusion 2000; Local Government & Communities 2002; Education & Lifelong Learning, 5.11.2003. Interests: Housing, Local Government, Regeneration. Hobbies: Rugby League. Languages: Learned Welsh, English. Of Ruthin.

RYDER Peter: Plaid Cymru, Wrexham 2003. **Mr. Peter Ryder:** Born Middlesborough 12 July 1952. Married Janet Spooner (qv) 3c. Educated Northern Counties College of Education. Teacher. Chair/Secretary Vale of Clwyd Plaid Cymru. Regional Co-ordinator, North Clwyd, Denbighshire & Colwyn, Plaid Cymru. Interests: Europe, Education, Poverty. Languages: Learned Welsh, English. Of Ruthin.

RYKALA Adam John: Plaid Cymru, Blaenau Gwent 2001. **Mr. Adam Rykala:** Born Ebbw Vale, 29 January 1969, s of Czeslaw Rykala, coal miner, & Coral Williams. Educated Nantyglo Comprehensive School; Queen Mary & Westfield College, London University (unfinished BSc); Allt-yr-Un College, Newport (HNC Computing); The Hill College, Abergavenny (FE Training Certificate). Senior Technical Analyst, Penny & Giles Controls, Cwmfelinfach. Previously worked for Nevill Hall Hospital & Blaenau Gwent CBC. Chair, Plaid Cymru Blaenau Gwent Constituency 1999; Press Officer. Member, Phil Williams campaign team, 1999. Contested Blaenau Gwent CBC (Blaina) 1999. Resigned as prospective candidate, March 2003, when made redundant by his employer. Interests: Constitution Matters, Information Technology & its effects, particularly through internet/changing working conditions, Social exclusion, Community regeneration. Hobbies: Astronomy; Playing guitar, Walking, Squash. Languages: Welsh learner, English. Of Blaina (1973).

– S –

SACKVILLE Thomas Geoffrey: BA (Oxon). Conservative: Pontypool 1979; MP Bolton West 1983-97. **Hon. Tom Sackville:** Born 1950, younger s of 10th Earl de la Warr & Anne Rachel, d of George Devas. Married 1978, Catherine Theresa, d of Brigadier James Windsor Lewis, 2c. Educated Eton; Lincoln College, Oxford. With Deltec Banking Corporation, New York 1971-74; Grindleys Bank 1974-78; International Bullion & Metal Brokers Ltd London 1973-83. Divisional manager 1978-81; Divisional director 1981-83. Director, family owned ranching business in Rhodesia. Partner in export business. Secretary, all party British-Colombian parliamentary group. Treasurer, British-Spanish parliamentary group. Member, Select Cttees: Broadcasting 1990-91; Commons Administration 1991-92. Se. Lord Commissioner 1989-92. Under-Secretary, Health 1992-97.

SADLER Peter Gethin: BScEcon (London, external) MSc DipAdmin (London). Liberal: Caerphilly B/E 1968. **Professor Peter Sadler:** Born Penarth 1926. Married 1s. Educated Penarth Grammar School; London University. Clerical assistant, Glamorgan County Council 1942. Research Student, London University. Part-time lecturer in Local Government, Cardiff Technical College. Lecturer in Economics, University of Wales, Bangor. Professor in the Economics Section, Cardiff Business School (expertise in Agricultural & Industrial Project Appraisal in developing countries. Hon. Professor.

SAIN-LEY-BERRY Peter Godfrey: BA 1968 MA (Cantab). SDP/Alliance, Swansea West 1983, Pontypridd 1987, Pembroke 1991. **Mr. Peter Sain-Ley-Berry:** Born Edinburgh, 9 May 1946, s of Godfrey Oswald Edwin Sain Ley Berry, teacher & artist, & Margaret St. Clair Miller, writer. Educated Magdalen College School, Oxford; Peterhouse, Cambridge (History & Economics). Married 1971, Jennifer Sain Ley Berry, teacher, 2d. National Institute of Industrial Psychology 1968-72. Civil Service 1972-82 (Senior Psychologist & internal consultant, Civil Service Dept; Principal, Welsh Office 1978-80). Political & Policy work, Social Democratic Party & Lib Dems 1982-92. (Secretary SDP Council for Wales 1982). Self-employed Management Consultant 1985-2000. Associate Director, Cardiff Officer, Eurofl Ltd 1988-. Editor, *EuropaWorld* 2000-. Team leader, *Devpolawar* Project 2001-02.

Manager, *VIP labels,* UK wide-label-broking co. Chair, Lloyd George Society 1989-91. Chair, Lib Dem Candidates Cttee 1989-91. Member: Standing Conference, Welsh Centre for International Affairs 1985-; Team Europe 1993-. Representative to EU Stakeholder Forum on Sustainable Development, Brussels 2002. Chair, Wales Council, European Movement 1996-2000. Vice-Chair, Cowbridge Town Twinning Cttee. Member, Institute of Welsh Affairs. Interests: European Affairs, Sustainable Development. Hobbies: Local ancient history, Amateur dramatics. Languages: English, French, little German, Spanish & Welsh. Of Cowbridge.

ST. CLAIR Lindi (*Miss Whiplash*): Corrective Party, Vale of Glamorgan B/E 1989, Monmouth B/E 1991, Richmond B/E 1989, Mid-Staffordshire B/E March 1990, Knowsley South B/E Sept 1999, Eastbourne B/E Oct. 1990, Ribble Valley B/E March 1991, Langbaurgh B/E Nov. 1991, Newbury B/E May 1993; withdrew at Arundel & South Downs 1997. **Miss Lindi St. Clair:** Born 1954. Real name, Marion Aken. *Grew up around Monmouth (election address).* 20 years in prostitution. Leading campaigner for prostitutes' rights. Founded Corrective Party 1988. Contested Greenwich BC (Charlton). Planned to contest many seats in 1992 until she was declared bankrupt after being sued by the Inland Revenue. Bankruptcy discharged 1997. *Books: Lindi St. Clair, It's only a game (autobiography).*

SALISBURY Robert Andrew: LlB (Liverpool). Conservative, Clwyd 1999. **Mr. Robert Salisbury:** Born Holywell, 18 February 1948, son of Walter Andrew, policeman, & Ms. Roberts. Church in Wales. Married 1s 3d. Educated local primary schools; Mold Grammar School; Liverpool University. Solicitor, Senior Partner at Rhyl. Chair, North Wales CBI Cttee. President, Chester & North Wales Law Society. Interests: Seeing the Conservatives do well. Hobbies: Sport. Languages: Welsh (a bit), English, French, German. Of St. Asaph.

SALKELD Anthony: BA (Wales). Plaid Cymru, Newport West 2001. **Mr. Anthony Salkeld:** Born Caerleon, 6 December 1966, son of Michael Salkeld, furniture fitter, Roman Catholic. Partner, Kathleen Campbell. 2s 2d. Educated St. Joseph's School, Newport; University of Wales, Cardiff (Ancient & Medieval History). Constituency

Manager for Jocelyn Davies AM. Chair: Plaid Cymru Newport Branch; Newport West Constituency Party. Contested Newport CBC (Shaftesbury) 1999. Interests: Poverty & deprivation, Environment & Transport, Welsh Language & Culture. Hobbies: Philately, Collecting Roman coins & military medals. Of Newport.

SALT Geoffrey John: BSc PGCE Natural Law Party, South/Central List 1999. **Mr. Geoffrey Salt:** Born Birmingham, 18 July 1950, son of Thomas Melville Salt, ICI sales manager, & Mary Winifred Jeffries. Roman Catholic. Educated University (Logic with Physics). Systems. Programmer. Trustee, Maharishi Foundation (Wales) charitable trust. Hobbies: Guitar, Meditation. Languages: English, some French & Spanish Of Windsor.

SAMBROOK Paul: Plaid Cymru, Mid & West list 2003. **Mr. Paul Sambrook:** Archeologist. Of Eglwyswrw.

SAMSON Edward Marlay: KBE 1920 CBE 1918 KC 1919 JP DL (Pembs) JP (Glam) MA (Oxon) KStJ. Conservative: Pembrokeshire Jan. & Dec. 1910. **Sir Marlay Samson:** Born 27 March 1869, s of Louis Samson JP DL Scotchwell, Haverfordwest. Anglican. Educated Harrow; Trinity College, Oxford (History). Barrister, Inner Temple 1893. Chair, Haverfordwest Quarter Sessions 1909-; Pembrokeshire Quarter Sessions 1924-43. Recorder of Swansea 1918-23. Swansea Stipendiary Magistrate 1923-. Chancellor, Diocese of St. Davids 1909, Swansea & Brecon 1923-29. Of Swansea & Haverfordwest. Died 3 April 1949.

SAMUEL Howell Walter: KC 1931. Labour: Swansea West 1922, 1924, 1931; MP1923-24, 1929-31. **Mr. Walter Samuel:** Born Fforestfach, Swansea 1881, s of Thomas Samuel, tinplateworker. Presbyterian Church of Wales. Married (1) 1911 Harriet Sawyer Polkinghone, teacher (died 1939) (2) 1941 Annie Gwladys, widow of Sir Henry Gregg & d of David Morlais Samuel, Swansea. Educated Cockett National School. Miner & Tinplate Worker 1892-1914. Member SWMF Lodge Executive. Industrial injury led to study. Secretary, Swansea Labour Association. Barrister, Middle Temple 1915. Recorder of Merthyr Tydfil 1930-33. Chair, Radnorshire Quarter Sessions 1933-. Chair, South Wales Conscientious Objectors Appellate Tribunal 1939-45. Of Swansea. Died 5 April 1953.

SAMUEL Wynne Islwyn: LlB LLM (London). Plaid Cymru: Neath B/E 1 945, 1945; Aberdare B/E 1946, 1950, 1951; Pembroke 1970, Withdrew because of ill health at Merthyr Tydfil 1964. **Mr. Wynne Samuel:** Born Ystalyfera1912, orphaned & brought up by his maternal grandfather (Revd William Jones, Soar, Ystalyfera) and his aunt. Baptist (deacon at 22) & lay preacher. Married 1d. Educated Ystalyfera Grammar School. Offered place with Glamorgan Cricket Club staff but his aunt shattered his dreams. Audit Clerk, Swansea Town Hall c.1938, Dismissed 1940 for refusing to sign a statement declaring complete support for the war. Appeared before South Wales CO Tribunal, September 1940 & registered unconditionally as a CO. Full time Organiser, Plaid Cymru Dec. 1940-50. Editor, *Welsh Nation*. Secretary, Ystradgynlais National Eisteddfod 1952-54. Took external Diploma in Public Administration & law degrees. Barrister, Grays Inn 1956. Offered a post with UNO at Geneva. Lecturer in Law, Chester Technical College 1964. Pontardawe UDC 1947-56. Town Clerk of Tenby 1965-. President: West Glamorgan Welsh Baptist Assn 1950, Baptist Union of Wales 1960-61. Member, Council of BBC in Wales. Languages: Welsh, English. Died June 1960.

SANDERS Charles Fletcher: JP (Cardiff) Hon. LLD (Wales) 1933 FSSA FAL. (National) Liberal: Cardiff Central 1922. **Mr. Charles Sanders:** Born Cardiff 23 July 1857, s of William Sanders JP Mayor of Cardiff 1889-90. Wesleyan Methodist. Married Margaret Colerick Herne, 4s 1d. Educated private & public schools in Cardiff. Incorporated Accountant. Chair: William Sanders & Sons: Auctioneers, Estate Agents & Surveyors, & Senior Manager Secretary, Principality Building Society. President: Cardiff Free Church Council. Chair: Cardiff Temperance & Band of Hope Union 30 years; Cardiff Central Liberal Assn. Vice-President, Cardiff Liberal Assn. Executive Member, Magistrates Assn. Member: Cardiff Board of Guardians 1898, Llandaff School Board 1900. Cardiff BC 1895-, Alderman 1928, Lord Mayor 1933-34. Of Cardiff. Estate £17,233. Died 24 January 1936.

SANDFORD-HILL Brian: LHS (Dublin). Conservative Candidate for Rhondda West 1966, Nominated to stand as Independent Conservative against Nigel Fisher MP Surbiton 1970 but withdrew. **Dr. Brian Sandford-Hill:** Born Exeter 1935. Married. Educated Monkton House School, Cardiff; Christ College, Brecon; Royal College of Surgeons, Dublin. Army 1953-55, TA 1955-61. Medical Practitioner (at Rumney, Cardiff1962-). Cardiff CC 1969-72. Whip withdrawn Nov. 1969. Rejected as Conservative candidate 1972 because of far-right views. Ind-Con candidate, Cardiff CC 1973.

SANDY E. Christopher: ACA. Conservative: Neath 1979. Joined Conservatives 1975. Liberal: Dorset South Oct. 1974. **Mr. Christopher Sandy:** Born April 1949. Educated Bishop Wordsworth School, Salisbury; Crawford School, Wimborne.

Chartered Accountant. Editor, Conservative Party's *Small Business News*.

SARGEANT Carl: Labour, North List 2003; AM Alyn & Deeside 2003. **Mr. Carl Sargeant:** Born St. Asaph, 27 July 1968, son of Malcolm Sargeant, heavy goods vehicle driver, & Sylvia Sargeant. Church of England. Married 1991, Bernie Sargeant, classroom assistant, 1s 1d. Educated Connahs Quay High School. Process Operator, chemical company, quality environment auditor. Part-time Fire Fighter. Connahs Quay TC. Governor, Deeside College & schools. Interests: Sports. Hobbies: Music. Of Connahs Quay.

SAUNDERS David W. J: Plaid Cymru: Aberavon 1992. **Mr. David Saunders:** Born Pyle 2 November 1942. Married Sylvia, 3d. Educated Cirencester Grammar School; Swansea Technical College. Professional motorbike racer. London fireman. Transport manager, Remploy Ltd. Neath Abbey. Clydach ComC 1990. Member, TGWU. Replaced as Euro Candidate 1994; he and his wife resigned from Plaid Cymru and gave up their seats on the Community Council. Cost prevented his contesting the Euro seat as an Independent. Of Clydach (1973).

SAUNDERS Gwenno Margaret: Independent, Aberavon 2003. **Miss Gwenno Saunders:** Born Cardiff, 23 May 1981, d of Timothy Simon Saunders, Cornish Poet, & Lyn Mererid, translator. Educated comprehensive school. Joined Sean Eireann, Macmahon Academy of Irish Dance at 5. Singer (in Welsh & Cornish), entertainer & television artist. People's Choice award at Alternative Eurovision Song Contest, Holland. November 2003. Languages: Welsh, English, Cornish, Erse. Of Cardiff.

SAUNDERS-DAVIES Arthur Picton: JP DL (Pembs). Conservative: Pembrokeshire 1895. **Mr. Arthur Saunders-Davies:** Born 26 July 1862, s of Arthur Henry Saunders-Davies & Fanny, d of Grismond Phillips (gs of David Arthur Saunders-Davies MP Carmarthenshire 1842). Anglican. Married 1899, Mabel Daughady, d of William Harrison Woodruff, Tacoma, Washington, USA 1s 1d. Landowner. High Sheriff, Pembrokeshire 1880. Landowner. Captain, Pembrokeshire Yeomanry. Of Boncath. Estate £137,883. Died 18 November 1922.

SAVILLE Elizabeth: BA PGCE (Wales). Plaid Cymru, North list 2003. **Ms. Liz Saville:** Born Woolwich, London, 16 December 1964, d of Nicholas Saville, computer programmer, & Nancy Saville, teacher. Married 1994, Dewi Wyn Roberts, 2d. Educated Blackheath High School; Avery Hill College; University of Wales, Aberystwyth (Celtic Studies). Director, Sgiliaith Bilingualism Centre, Coleg Meirion Dwyfor. Languages: Welsh, English. Interests: Decentralisation in all its aspects. Hobbies: Horses, Reading, Walking. Languages: Welsh, English, Irish, French. Of Morfa Nefyn.

SAVOURY Anne: Pro-Life Alliance, Cardiff South & Penarth 2001, South/Central List 2003. **Miss Anne Savoury:** Roman Catholic. Nurse, with experience of caring for the terminally ill. Lives with a severe physical disability (registered 1984) – uses wheelchair. Voluntary worker with SPUC, handicap Division. RCIA Catechist at local church. Pro-Life speaker, specializing in disability since 1987. Of Splott, Cardiff.

SAYEED Reehana: Socialist Labour Party, South/East List 2003. **Ms. Reehana Sayeed:** 2d Youth Worker at Oakdale & driver, mobile information service.

SCARBOROUGH Frances Ethel: Conservative: Ebbw Vale 1935. **Miss Frances Scarborough:** Pianist, Composer, Conductress & Authoress. Of Barnet, Herts.

Arthur Scargill.

SCARGILL Arthur: Socialist Labour Party: Newport East 1997; London Euro, 1999; Hartlepool 2001, South/East List 2003. **Mr. Arthur Scargill:** Born 11 January 1938, s of Harold & Alice Scargill. Anglican. Married 1961, Anne, d of Elliott Harper, 1d. Educated Worsborough Dale School; White Cross Secondary School; Leeds University. Miner, Woolley Colliery 1953. Member, NUM branch cttee. 1960; Member, NUM Nat Executive 1972-. President, Yorkshire NUM 1973-. General Secretary NUM 1992-2002 (President 1981); Member, TUC General Council 1986-88. Member: Young Communist League 1955-62, Co-operative Party 1963, CND, Labour Party 1966-95; Labour Party NEC 1966-95. Resigned to form the Socialist Labour Party in protest at Labour's abandonment of its traditional socialism. Of Pontefract.

SCHIAVONE Anthony Owen Gruffydd: Plaid Cymru: Clwyd South-West 1983. **Mr. Toni Schiavone:** s of Vito & Eluned Schiavone. Married Dawn c. Teacher (Geography) Ysgol Dyffryn Conwy. Asst Director, Basic Skills Agency. Member: CND Cymru, Cymdeithas yr Iaith. Plaid Cymru spokesman on Welsh Language. Member, Wales World Book Day Steering Cttee 2003. Languages: Welsh, English. *Books: Toni Schiavone (with Patrick Wiegland), Atlas Gynradd 2, 1983.*

SCORGIE Mervyn Nelson: BScEcon (London). Conservative: Neath 1964. **Mr. Mervyn Scorgie:** Born London 1915. Anglican. Educated King Edward VI School, Southampton; London School of Economics 1945-. Barrister, Inner Temple 1948. Apprenticed to Boots the Chemists –1945. Joined Abbots Laboratories Ltd 1949, General Manager 1949-54, Managing Director 1954-Jan. 1964 when he resigned to fight Neath. Chair: Conservative South East Political Centre; CPC National Advisory Cttee; Greater London CC 1970-. Of London.

SCOTT Anne-Marie: Natural Law Party, Mid & West List 1999, Euro, North West England 1999. **Ms. Nanne Scott:** Born Newmarket, Canada, 31 May 1956, d of George Potter, tool designer, & Jean Potter. Married, separated, 3s 1d. Teacher. Interests: Natural Law Party Programmes (30 years). Hobbies: Arts & Crafts, Walking, Swimming, Movies. Author of *Children's Book of Natural Law.* Of Skelmersdale.

SCOTT-CATO Sarah Margaret: BA MA (Oxon) MSc (Open) PhD (Wales) 2000. Green Party: Preseli 1997, 1999; Mid & West List 2003; Wales Euro 2004. **Dr. Molly Scott-Cato:** Born Wrexham 21 May 1963, d of David Brian Curtis, management consultant, & Mary French, physics teacher. Married 1987 Raymond Scott, divorced 1994, 2s. Partner, Chris Busby (qv) 3c. Educated Bath High School; St. Hugh's College, Oxford (PPE); Open University; University of Wales, Aberystwyth. Economist at University of Wales, Aberystwyth (Study of Future of Work), writer, editor & homemaker. Joined Green Party 1988. General Secretary. Then Chair, Wales Green Party. Member: Policy Cttee, Editor Green Wales. Party Speaker on Economics. Green Party, Wales Euro 2004. Interests: Poverty, Economic Policy, Social Policy. Hobbies: Opera, Reading, Tennis, Swimming, Music. Languages: Welsh (limited), English. *Seven Myths* about Work 1997, jt. editor, *Beyond Supply and Demand to Meeting People's Needs,* 1999.

SCOTT-HOPKINS James Samuel Rawdon: Kt 1981. Conservative: Bedwellty 1955; MP North Cornwall 1959-66, West Derbyshire B/E 1967-79;

MEP Hereford & Worcester: 1979-94. **Major, Sir James Scott-Hopkins:** Born Shiplake on Thames 29 November 1921, s of Lieut-Col. Rawdon Scott-Hopkins. Married 1946, Geraldine Elizabeth Mary Hargreaves CBE 3c. Educated Eton; New College, Oxford. Army 1939-50; Commissioned 1st Gurkhas 1942-49. Farmer 1950. Chair, Outlook Ltd. 1968 (went into voluntary liquidation). Marketing Consultant. Jt-Parl-Secretary, Agriculture, Fisheries & Food 1962-64. Deputy-Leader, Conservative MEPs Group & Spokesman on Agriculture 1973-79. Vice-President 1976-79 (Chair 1979-82), European Democratic Group. Of London & English Bicknor, Gloucs.

SCREEN Cerian Rebecca: Socialist Labour, South/Central List 1999, 2003. **Ms. Cerian Screen:** Born Wrexham 14 January 1971, d of Liz Screen (qv). Agnostic. Married 1997 Andreas Gotthard, divorced 2002. Educated Cardiff comprehensive school; Welsh Agricultural College (HNC Equine Studies 1993). Science Student, University 2003-. Part-time Riding Instructor. Animal Rights Activist. Campaigner against student tuition fees. Interests: Animal Rights, Environmental Issues. Hobbies: Horses, Dogs, Walking, Travelling. Languages: Very little Welsh, English, German, some Spanish. Of Splott, Cardiff.

SCREEN Elizabeth Anne: BA PGCE (Wales). Socialist Labour, South/Central List 1999, Newport East 2001; South/West list 2003. **Ms. Liz Screen:** Born Newport 20 November 1942, d of David Phillips, machinist & ex-merchant seaman. Married 1964, Divorced 2d (qv Cerian). Educated Newport High School; University of Wales, Cardiff (Languages). Teacher (French & German). Member, Labour Party until 1996. Joined Socialist Labour Party 1996. Secretary: Welsh Region, Socialist Labour Party, National Women's Section, Member, National Executive. Contested local elections. Member: CND. Peace activist. Interests: Environment, Education, Social Justice. Hobbies: Politics, Grandson. Languages: English, French, German. Of Cardiff.

SEAGER William Henry: Kt 1918 JP (Cardiff) DL (Glam). Coalition Liberal MP: Cardiff East 1918-22. **Sir William Seager:** Born Cardiff 13 March 1862, s of William Seager & Mary Jane Berry. Methodist. Married 1890, Margaret Annie, d. of John Elliot of Cardiff, 2s. Educated Wesleyan Day School. Started work at 13. Own store 1893. Shipowner, Merchant & Company Director. Chair, Tempus Shipping Co. Ltd; Sir William Seager & Sons Ltd; Seager Shipping Supplies Ltd; Victory Shipping Co. Ltd; Ropners Shipbuilding Ltd; Southern Steamship Underwriting Assn. Chair: Cardiff & Bristol Shipowners Assn; Cardiff Pilotage Authority. Vice-Chair, Cardiff

Shop Store Merchants Assn; Cardiff Institute for the Blind. Vice-President, South Wales One-Man-Business Federation; United Kingdom Commercial Travellers Assn. President: Cardiff Shipbrokers Institute; Chamber of Shipping of the United Kingdom 1928. Council Member: Cardiff Chamber of Commerce; Council of the Shipping Federation. Governor & Trustee, King Edward VII Hospital, Cardiff; Governor, Royal Hamadryad Hospital for Seamen; Queens College, Taunton; Farrington Girls School, Chislehurst. Vice-President: Cardiff Liberal Assn. President, Cardiff Sunday School Union. High Sheriff of Monmouthshire 1932-33. Of Lisvane, Cardiff. Estate £180,418. Died 10 March 1941.

SEATON Arthur: Independent Conservative: Pontypridd, 1918, withdrew a few days before polling in favour of Coalition Liberal, T. A. Lewis. **Captain Arthur Seaton:** Born Pontypridd 1871, s of William Seaton, 1 of 4c. Contractor. Captain, RE.

SELBY David Mark: BA. Liberal Democrat, Mid & West List 1999. **Mr. David Selby:** Born Hitchin, Herts. 21 April 1953, s of John Alan Selby, engineer, & Valerie Selby, part-time shop assistant. Married 1993 Rhian Selby, 2d. Senior Manager. Chair, Newtown Liberal Democrat Assn. Newtown TC. Of Newtown.

SELIGMAN David Joseph: OBE 1.1.2001 LlB (Wales) Labour: Cardiff West 1983. **Mr. David Seligman:** Born Riverside, Cardiff 21 April, 1928. Jewish. Married Philippa, 2s. Educated Canton High School, Cardiff; University of Wales, Aberystwyth; London University; Hebrew University, Jerusalem. Royal Engineers 1946-49. Solicitor. Company Director, Cefn Estates. Cardiff CC 1973-91. Member: CAB; Cardiff Assn for Mental Health; St David's Hall & New Theatre Trusts; Council of National Museum & National Library; Race Relations Conciliation Cttee for Wales & South West England; Advisory Cttee for Race Relations; Race Equality Council. Director, Welsh National Opera. Launched Cardiff duty solicitors' scheme for police prisoners in early 1970s. Of Llandaff, Cardiff.

SENIOR David Hugh: BA (Kent). Plaid Cymru, Montgomery & Mid & West List 1999, 2003; Montgomeryshire 2001. **Mr. David Senior:** Born Newtown 2 July 1963. Educated Forden Primary School; Newtown High School; University of Kent (Biology); University of Wales, Aberystwyth. Science Teacher of Children with special needs, Cruckton Hall School, Shrewsbury, 1991. Former Self-Employed Builder 1985-91. Joined Plaid Cymru 1984. Vice President, South Clwyd Constituency, Maldwyn Constituency. Interests: Redefining of political boundaries to create real democracy and reduce conflict. Hobbies: Walking, Climbing. Of Welshpool.

SHACKLAND David Peter: MA (Edin) PhD 1993 (Cantab). Liberal Democrat: Caernarfon 1999. **Dr. Peter Shackland:** Born 1963. Married. Educated Edinburgh University 1982-86 (anthropology); Cambridge 1988-90. Social Anthropologist, specialising in modern Turkey. Assistant, then Acting Director, British Institute of Archeology, Ankara 1992-95. Hon. Research Fellow, Middle East Studies Centre, SOAS 1994. Lecturer in Social Anthropology, University of Wales, Lampeter 1994-. Recorder, Archeology & Anthropology Section (H), British Assn for the Advancement of Science 1997. ERSC grant of £42,000 in order to devote himself to full-time research 2000-01. Writer of several papers on religion in Turkey. Contested Ceredigion CC 1999. Interests: International Affairs, Islam, Turkey. Hobbies: Antiquarian Books, Walking. Languages: English, French, Turkish. Of Aberystwyth.

SHARP Michael E: Labour: Vale of Glamorgan 1983. **Mr. Michael Sharp:** Born 3 June 1939. Married Brenda, 3c. Educated Derbyshire state schools; Nottingham College of Further Education; Nottingham Technical College; Coleg Harlech; Nottingham University (Politics). Probation Officer. Labour Agent, Barry 1979. Member, TGWU; Nat Assn of Probation Officers. Director: Business Technical Centre; Cardiff Marketing Ltd; Vale Enterprises; Cardiff Bay Development Corporation, April 1999. Vale of Glamorgan BC. South Glamorgan CC (Labour Chief Whip). Of Barry.

SHAW Michael William: Independent: Brecon & Radnor 1999. **Mr. Michael Shaw:** Born Bicknall, Shropshire, 6 November 1940, son of D. H. Shaw & Sarah Ann Evans, newsagents. Church of England. Married 1961, Lisbeth Anne Shaw, school administration officer, 2s 1d. Financial Consultant. Radnor DC. Lived in Radnorshire from 1937. Of Knighton.

SHAW Timothy: BSc (Reading). Green Party, Mid & West List 1999, 2003. **Mr. Tim Shaw:** Born Horsham, Surrey, 4 January 1950, s of Nevil Shaw, artist, & Audrey Phyllis Shaw, housewife. Educated Holcombe Road & Troy Town Schools, Rochester; Chatham Technical High School for Boys; Reading University (Physics & Meteorology). Master Craftsman. Contested local election. Interests: Environment. Hobbies: Gardening, Cricket, Chickens, Music & Having Fun. Of Llanwrda.

SHELDON Iain James: UK Independence Party, Mid & West List 2003. **Mr. Iain Sheldon:** Born 1940. Married Joan. Royal Naval Fleet Air Arm.

Trained in aerospace engineering. Aerospace Experimental Work, Concorde etc. Works Manager. Farmer; semi-retired on 10-acre smallholding. Interests: Environment, Local Politics. Hobbies: Trains, shows & judges dogs. Of Cilcennin nr. Aberaeron.

SHEPHERD Michael: Socialist Party: Cardiff South & Penarth 1997. **Mr. Mike Shepherd:** Born Cardiff 1973. Married 2c. Chair: CRISIS (Cardiff Royal Infirmary-Save its Services).

SHEPPARD John: Plaid Cymru: Pembroke 1966. **Mr. Jack Sheppard:** Born London 1911. Married Educated elementary schools; Wimbledon Technical College. Post Office Engineer 1936-; at Swansea 1937-39; Haverfordwest 1939-. Member, Labour Party 1945,expelled 1962 because of CND membership. Joined Plaid Cymru 1966. Pembrokeshire County Secretary CND 1951. Haverfordwest RDC 1945-; Pembrokeshire CC.

SHERRINGTON Catherine: BSc. Labour, Conwy 1999. **Ms. Catherine Sherrington:** Born 21 December 1962. Bank Clerk. Primary School Teacher at Llandudno. Mature Student (environmental studies). Interests: Education, Economic Development, Social Exclusion. Languages: Welsh, English.

SHERRINGTON Emlyn Jones: BA (Wales). Labour: Denbigh Feb. 1974, Caernarfon Oct. 1974. **Mr. Emlyn Sherrington:** Born Llanberis 1938. Married 3c. Educated Llanberis Primary School; Brynrefail Grammar School; University of Wales, Aberystwyth. Researcher, Board of Celtic Studies. Lecturer, Modern Political History, University of Wales, Bangor. Member: ASTMS, Bangor & Beaumaris Trades Council. Chair, North Wales Disablement Incomes Group. Caernarfonshire CC. Languages: Welsh, English.

SHIPTON Martin: Wales on Sunday Objective One Funding, Ceredigion B/E 2000. **Mr. Martin Shipton:** Born 1956. Journalist. Joined *Western Mail* 1994. Chief Reporter, *Wales on Sunday*. BT Welsh Journalist of the Year 1999 and 2000. *I did not spend years attending tedious party meetings or sucking up to people I secretly despise. Instead, I got a quick call into the editor's office and an instant selection process was engineered. I've got this idea and within minutes I was a prospective parliamentary candidate. . . Our aim is simply to show the strength of feeling in Wales on the key issue of match funding.*

SHORE K. Alan: BSc PhD (Liverpool) MIEE SMIEEE MOSA FinstP. Plaid Cymru: Alyn & Deeside 1983. **Dr. Alan Shore:** Married Elizabeth, 1d. Research Fellow, Applied Physics, UWIST 1975-76. Applications Programmer, Dept Computing, UWIST 1976-79. Lecturer in Electrical Engineering & Electronics, Liverpool University 1979-83. Lecturer, Electrical Engineering, Bath University 1983-86. Senior Lecturer 1986-90, Reader 1990-95, Professor (Personal Chair) April 1995. Professor of Electronic Engineering, University of Wales, Bangor, September 1995-. Co-founder/Programmer Cttee Chair: Annual International Conference on Semiconductor & Integrated Optolelectronics, UWCC Cardiff 1987-92. Joint Guest Editor, Special Issue of the *IEEE Proceedings*. Chair: Institute of Physics (Wales) 2002-05. Visiting Professor: Dept of Physics, Macquarie University, Sydney 1998; Centre for Laser Applications, Macquarie 2000; Visiting Researcher, ATR Advanced Communications Research Laboratory, Kyoto, Japan 2001. Rhymney Valley DC.

SHORT Cherry Rose Pamela: Labour, Monmouth, 1999; Mid-West List 2003. **Mrs. Cherry Short:** Born Jamaica, 10 November 1952, lived in South Wales since 1959. Married Christopher Albert Short (qv). Probation Officer 13 years. Commissioner for Race Relations, Wales. Chair: Wales Cttee, Commission for Racial Equality. Lecturer on issues of equality. Senior Fellow Institute of Government & Public Affairs. Member: Industrial Tribunal, New Deal Task Force. Cardiff CC. (Chair: Environmental Security Cttee). Interests: Tourism, Agriculture, Economic Development of Wales. Of Barry Island.

SHORT Christopher Albert: Labour: Monmouth 1983. **Mr. Christopher Short:** Born Derby 15 April 1947, s of Albert Edgar Short & Helen Mary Jones. Came to Wales 1967. Married 1987, Cherry Rose Pamela Lewis (qv) 3c. Educated Bemrose Grammar School, Derby; University College, London; Institute of Advanced Legal Studies. Left school at 16. Cardiff Solicitor 1972-2000. Governor, South Glam Institute HE. Member: RAAF; APEX, Amnesty-International, CND. Treasurer & Vice-President, Cardiff TUC. Treasurer, South Glamorgan Miners' Support Fund 1984-85. Chair: Wales Anti-Apartheid Movement 1981-89; Friends of the Earth Cymru 1991; Conference & Elections Cttee, National Council for Civil Liberties; Trade Union Studies Unit, Llandaff. Vale of Glamorgan BC 1987 (Chair, Finance & Policy Cttee 1991). Of Barry.

SHREWSBURY Martyn John: BA (Manchester) BA (Wales) FRAI. Liberal (Democrat): Swansea East 1983, Llanelli 1987, Swansea West 1992; Green Party, Swansea West 2001; South/West List 2003; Wales Euro 2004. **Mr. Martyn Shrewsbury:** Born 7 April 1938. (Brought up an Anglican). Married Tina, 1 s. Educated Burton Grammar School; Dynevor Comprehensive School, Swansea; Manchester University; University of Wales,

Martyn Shewsbury.

Swansea. Teacher of English as a Foreign Language. Educational Consultant & Psychotherapist. Chair, Sketty Residents Assn 1991-92. Chair: West Glamorgan Liberal Assn 1985-86. Joined Green Party 1999. Green Party, Wales Euro 2004. Of Swansea.

SHREWSBURY Sandra Christina: Green Party, Gower 2001. **Mrs. Tina Shrewsbury:** Born Port Talbot. Emigrated to Australia as a teenager; traveled widely in 1980s; returned to UK 1990. Married, Martin Shrewsbury (qv). Part-time student for BA in Ceramics. HND (industrial design ceramics). Worked in marketing & as magazine editor. Green Party spokesperson on animal welfare and education. Member: RSPCA, PSPB, Soil Assn, Amnesty International. Of Swansea.

SIMNER Percy Reginald Owen Abel: KCB 1963 CB 1934 DSO 1917 & Bar TD DL (London) BA 1900 MA (Oxon). Conservative: West Glamorgan Jan. 1910. **Lieut-Colonel, Sir Percy Simner:** Born 1878, s of Abel Simner, Friog, Merioneth & Westminster. Married 1948, Irene, d of Kenhelm Preedy. Anglican. Educated Pocklington; Exeter College, Oxford. Barrister, Lincolns Inn 1903. Inns of Court OTC 1914. Lieut-Colonel 1916. Hon. Colonel, Berkshire Home Guard. Commander, City of London TA & AFA 1942-48. Commander, Army Cadet Corps 1932-46. Westminster CC 1906-22. London CC. A founder/Vice-President, Junior Imperial League. Member, Council, London Welsh Conservative & Unionist Assn. Prime Warden, Fishmongers Company. Senior Master of the Supreme Court & King's Remembrancer. Freeman, City of London. Of Kensington & Friog, Merioneth. Died 11 January 1963.

SIMMONDS David Timothy: BA (Durham). Conservative, Caerphilly 2001. **Mr. David Sim-**

monds: Born Canterbury, 22 February 1976, s of Ian Rory Simmonds, local government officer, & Veronica Joan King, local government officer. Roman Catholic. Single. Educated Cardinal Newman RC School, Pontypridd; Durham University. Manager, Cornhill Ltd. Hillingdon BC (Chair, Social Services 2000; Deputy Leader). Chair: Durham University Conservative Assn. Deputy Chair: Uxbridge Conservative Assn. Interests: Defence, Law & Order, Health, Social Services, Economy. Hobbies: Driving, Cooking for friends. Languages: English, French.

SIMONS Emrys: LlB (Wales). Conservative: Rhondda West 1951; Cardiff West 1955. **Mr. Emrys Simons:** Born Porth1911, coalminer's son. Married 1s 1d. Educated Rhondda County Grammar School, Porth; University of Wales, Aberystwyth (Law & Economics). Solicitor 1936. Private, Royal Engineers 1940. Lieutenant, Royal Artillery 1941, Captain. Chair, Pontypridd District Cttee Conservative Party.

SINCLAIR Geoffrey A: Liberal Democrat, Mid & West Wales1989. **Mr. Geoffrey Sinclair:** Born Cheshire 1943 of farming family. Married Mary. Land Use Consultant, specializing in hill farming, environment & urban renewal. Lived in Mid Wales from mid 1960s.

SINCLAIR Karen: Labour AM, Clwyd South 1999. **Mrs. Karen Sinclair:** Born Wrexham 20 November 1952. Married 1973 Mike, 1s 1d. Educated Grove Park Girls' Grammar School, Wrexham; Cartrefle College, Wrexham. CAB Adviser. Contracted Care Manager, Wrexham Social Services 1990-99. Glyndwr DC 1988-95, Denbighshire CC 1997-99. Assembly Labour Chief whip. Assembly Business Manager May 2003-. Hobbies: Family, Local Politics, Horse Riding. Of Llangollen.

SINGH Moira Anne: Labour, South/East List 2001. **Mrs. Moira Singh:** Born 7 March 1953. Married Paul Singh, psychiatric nurse, divorced, 2c. Teacher 16 years. Progress File Manager, Careers Wales West. Education Co-ordinator. Swansea CCC (Uplands) 1999-. (Deputy Cabinet Member for Finance). Chair, School Governors. Vice-Chair: Swansea West Labour Party. Of Swansea.

SINNETT Rhys: Plaid Cymru, Preseli 2001. **Mr. Rhys Sinnett:** Born Haverfordwest 27 July 1962. Married 2c. Educated Milford Haven Grammar School. Health Promotion Specialist for drug & alcohol education, Dyfed/Powys Health Authority. Worked for 12 years at Cardiff, Manchester & North Wales. Interests: Health, Social Affairs, Home Affairs, Drug & Alcohol Abuse. Hobbies: Local quiz league. Cinema, Music. Returned to

Milford Haven 1995. Milford Haven TC. Regional Vice-President, Plaid Cymru. Agent, Preseli 1999. Of Milford Haven.

SIXSMITH Charles Frederick Gilbourne: LRCP LRCS (Edin). Independent Coalition: Llandaff & Barry 1918. **Dr. Charles Sixsmith:** Born Cavan, Ireland 1861. Married 4s. Educated Edinburgh University. Medical Practitioner 1885 (at Melton, Barry from 1894). ENT specialist, Barry schools. Lecturer in Ambulance and Nursing Work, Glamorgan CC. Surgeon, Barry Hospital. Barry UDC. Cardiff Board of Guardians. One of three on Labour short list 1918. Stood as The Resident Candidate and Workmen's Friend. Withdrew a few days before poll in favour of Major William Cope, Coalition Conservative. Contested Glamorgan CC as Labour, March 1919. An authority on horses and horse breeding. Died 4 April 1936.

SKEET Trevor Herbert Harry: Kt 1986 LlB (NZ). Conservative: Llanelli 1955, Stoke Newington & Hackney North 1951, Willesden West 1964; MP Willesden West 1959-64, Bedford 1970-73, Bedfordshire North 1983-97. **Sir Trevor Skeet:** Born Auckland, New Zealand 28 January 1918, s of Harry May Skeet & Lucy Kate Sims. Married 1958, Elizabeth Mary, d of M. H. Gilling. Educated Kings College, Auckland; University of New Zealand. New Zealand Army: Sergeant, NZ Eng; Lieut. NZ Anti-Aircraft. Sub-Lieut. NZRNR 1939-45. Solicitor & Barrister, New Zealand Supreme Court. Barrister, Inner Temple 1947. Writer & Industrial Consultant. Joined Conservative Party on arriving in UK 1946. Vice-Chair, Conservative MPs Power Cttee. Chair: Conservative MPs Trade Cttee. 1971-74. Member: Council, Royal Commonwealth Society 1952; CBI Technical Legislation Cttee; Select Cttee on Wealth Tax 1974-76. Secretary, all party Airships Group 1971-78. Chair: Conservative MPs Middle East Cttee 1973-78; Steering Cttee, Parliamentary Scientific Cttee 1985-88. Co-Chair, All party Minerals Group 1971-97. Of Milton Ernest, Beds.

SKELLY Peter: Socialist Labour Party: Pontypridd 1997. **Mr. Peter Skelly:** Born Dundee 31 May 1953, s of Francis Skelly, jute spinner, & Thomasina Perkins, millworker. Roman Catholic. Married 1978 Georgina Skelly, 3s 1d. Railway track worker. Branch Secretary, RMT 1989. President, Welsh Region RMT twice & member, National Executive 1993-96. *Currently politically unattached* (October 2001). Interests: Economics. Hobbies: Social History; Biographies; Snooker; Football (watching Cardiff City FC). Of Pontyclun.

SLEEMAN Deidre: Natural Law Party, Mid & West List 1999, Woking 1997. **Ms. Deidre Sleeman:** Of Mentmore, Beds.

SMART Christopher Blake: Conservative, Assembly, Ogmore & South/West List 1999, Neath 2003. **Mr. Chris Smart:** Born 1950. Married Kay. Journalist. Started on *Glamorgan Gazette*. Worked extensively in radio. Founded own Mid Glamorgan Press Agency 1973. Joined Conservatives 1970. Media Co-ordinator to Rod Richards when Welsh Conservative Leader. Chair: Maesteg AFC. Hobbies: Soccer, Rugby. Of Nottage, Porthcawl.

SMART Marrilyn Jane: OBE. Conservative South/East List 1999. **Ms. Marrilyn Smith:** Vice-Chair, Monmouth Conservative Assn.

SMART Russell: SDP/Alliance: Bridgend 1983, 1987. **Mr. Russell Smart:** Born Rhondda, 9 August 1931, s of ex-Rhondda miner. Married. Educated Rhondda Technical School, left at 14; Coleg Harlech; University of Wales, Cardiff (graduated at 37). Toolmaker 20 years. Civil Servant. Senior Lecturer in Economics, Polytechnic of Wales. Member: SDP Welsh Council; AUEW; NATFHE. Of Bridgend (1963).

SMITH Andrew Mark: Conservative: Cynon Valley 1992, 1997. **Mr. Andrew Smith:** Born Guildford 5 July 1962, s of George Smith. Roman Catholic. Educated St. Columba's School, Bexleyheath. Civil servant, Ministry of Agriculture, Fisheries & Food 1978-82. Deputy Managing Director/Company Secretary, Ian Greer Associates. Group Managing Director, IGA Holdings 1982-. Policy Partnership, London. Member: Bow Group; Conservative Group for Europe; Royal United Service Institute for Defence Studies; Greater London Conservatives' Task Force 1990. Contested Tower Hamlets BC 1990. School governor. Vice-President, Cynon Valley Conservative Assn. Of Aberdare.

SMITH Brian Edward: Labour: South/East List 1999. **Mr. Brian Smith:** Born Cwmbran, 7 August, 1940, s of Albert Edward Smith, production worker ALCAN, & Ethel Mavis Gilmore, domestic. Church in Wales. Married 1964 Jean Margaret Davies, secretary, 2s. Educated Llantarnam Comprehensive School; Crumlin FE College; Cardiff Art College; London Polytechnic (Finals, City 7 Guilds, Industrial Photography. Industrial photographer ICI, 23 years. Personnel Services Manager, Lucas. Retired. Joined Labour Party 1964. Torfaen BC 1984- (Labour Group Leader, Leader of the Council). Spokesperson on Europe, Welsh Local Government Assn. Chair: Welsh European Programme Executive Ltd; All Wales Welsh Local Government Assn Working Party on Structural Funds. President: Cwmbran New Town Caged Bird Society. Member: Europe Cttee of the Regions; Assembly of the European Regions Executive;

Welsh Local Government Leaders Co-ordinating Cttee; National Local Government Assn Policy & Strategy Cttee; Coalfield Communities Campaign; TGWU 19 years. Interests: Europe. Hobbies: Collecting Cranberry Glass Jugs, UK Stamps & Paperweights. Of Fairwater, Cwmbran. Died 25 July 2004.

SMITH Dewi Hywel Garrow-: Liberal Democrat: Cardiff West 1999, Vale of Glamorgan 2001. **Mr. Dewi Smith:** Born Barry 8 April 1964, s of Courtenay Frederick Smith, police officer, & Williams. 1s 1d. Educated Ysgol Gyfun Rhydfelin; Ysgol Uwchradd Tregaron; Welsh College of Music and Drama (Post Graduate Stage Management, prize for best student). Theatricals. Business Manager. Part-time Lecturer, Coleg Glan Hafren. Interests: Environment, Foreign Affairs. Contested Cardiff CCC (Radyr/Morganstown) 1999. Hobbies: Fitness, Archery, Reading. Languages: Welsh, English. Of Cardiff.

SMITH John Ian: OBE 1982 ACA. Conservative: Bedwellty 1951. **Mr. John Smith:** Born East Lothian 1912. Educated Skerry's College; Heriot Watt College, Edinburgh. Economic League Lecturer for Yorkshire & Lincolnshire; Chartered Accountant. Of London.

SMITH John William Patrick: BscEcon (Wales). Labour: Vale of Glamorgan 1987, 1992; MP B/E 1989-92; 1997-. **Mr. John Smith:** Born Penarth 17 March 1951, s of John Henry Smith, window cleaner, & Margaret Mary Collins. Married 1971 Kathleen Mulvaney, 2s 1d. Educated Fairfield Primary School, Penarth; Penarth Grammar School; Gwent College of Higher Education; University of Wales, Cardiff. RAF 1968-71. Carpenter/Joiner, Vale BC 1971-76. Mature Student 1976-83. Lecturer in Business Studies, University of Wales, Cardiff 1983-85 1988-92. Chief Executive, Gwent Image Partnership 1992-97. Joined Labour Party 1972. Member: WEA, AUT, MSF. Chair: Labour Party Wales 1988-89, Wales Anti-Apartheid Movement. Vale of Glamorgan BC 1979-91 (Labour Group Leader, 1983-88). Member, Select Cttees: Broadcasting 1991-92; Wales 1990-92. Vice-Chair, Welsh Labour MPs 1991-92. PPS Deputy Leader of the Opposition 1989-92. PPS 1997-99. Hobbies: Swimming, Walking, Rugby, Boating, Camping. Of Barry.

SMITH Kathleen J: Conservative: Caernarfon 1970. **Miss Kathleen Smith:** Born Luton June 1929. Educated Luton High School. Farming 6 years. Repertory until 1956. Prison Service: Asst. Governor, Holloway Prison 1957-60. Left prison service to write, farm & press for prison reform. Author, playwright & hill farmer. Languages: Learned Welsh, English. Of Clynnog (1968).

SMITH Llewelyn Thomas: BSc MSc (Wales). Labour MP Blaenau Gwent 1992-; MEP South-East 1984-94. **Mr. Llew Smith:** Born Newbridge, 16 April 1944, s of Ernest & Cissie Smith. Married 1963, Pamela, d of Russell & Lilian Williams, 2s 1d. Educated Greenfield Secondary Modern School, Newbridge; Coleg Harlech; University College of Wales, Cardiff. Labourer: Pilkington Glass & George Wimpey. Computer Operator, British Steel. WEA Tutor/Organiser. Member: CND; Labour European Safeguards Campaign (anti Euro). Joined Labour Party 1964. Chair, Abertillery CLP; Welsh Executive, Labour Party. Announced his decision not to contest the next election 2003. Hobbies: Soccer, Cricket. Of Newbridge, Gwent.

SMITH: Marilyn Ann – see WAKEFIELD M. A.

SMITH Paul – see SMITH Stephen Paul.

SMITH Robert: BA PhD 1995 PGCE 1994 (Wales). Labour, South/ West List 1999. **Dr. Robert Smith:** Born Aberystwyth, 27 October 1968, son of J. B. Smith & Llinos O. W. Vaughan. Calvinistic Methodist elder. Married 1994 Ann Griffith, 1s. Educated Ysgol Gyfun Penweddig, Aberystwyth; University of Wales, Swansea. Head of Research & Evaluation, Wales, National Foundation for Educational Research. Lecturer, Centre for Welsh & Celtic Studies, University of Wales, Aberystwyth. Secretary: Llafur, Society for Welsh Labour History, Lliw Valley District Labour Party, Ffaldybrenin Ward Labour Party, Llwchwr Branch WEA. Llwchwr TC 1991- (Labour Whip). School Governor. Interests: Education, Local Government, Economic Development. Hobbies: Vegetable Gardening, Reading, History. Languages: Welsh, English. Of Kingsbridge, Gorseinon.

SMITH Samuel: JP (Liverpool & Kirkudbright) MA (Edin). Liberal MP Flintshire B/E March 1886-1906, Liverpool 1882-85. Contested Abercromby 1885. **Rt. Hon. Samuel Smith:** Born Kirkcudbright 1836, s of James Smith JP South Carlton, Borgue, Kirkudbright. Presbyterian. Married 1866, Melville (died 1893) d of Revd John Christianson DD, Biggar. Educated Edinburgh University. Cotton Broker 1860-84. Liverpool CC 4 years. President, Chamber of Commerce 1876. Founder, Liverpool Gordon Institute for Seamen in memory of his son. Of Liverpool & Perthshire. Estate £111,107. Died Calcutta, 26 December 1906. *Book: Samuel Smith, My Life Work.*

SMITH Stephen Paul: BScEcon (Wales) CQSW OSW. Local Socialist, Torfaen 1999; Plaid Cymru, Torfaen 2001. **Mr. Steve Smith:** Born Pontypool, 24 May 1952, s of Lewis John Smith & Ivy

Georgina Saunders, factory workers. Married 1973, Linda Walker, checkout operator, 1 s. Educated St. Albans RC Secondary School; Gwent HE College; University of Wales, Cardiff. Day Centre Operator. Chair-Secretary-Treasurer, Labour Party Branch. Chair, Torfaen CLP. Chair: North Torfaen Branch, Plaid Cymru. Pontypool ComC 1985-87. Torfaen BC & CBC 1986-99, Mayor 1996-97. Interests: Economics, Housing. Hobbies: Growing Vegetables, Angling, Reading. Of Penygarn, Pontypool.

SOSKICE Frank, Baron Stow Hill of Newport 1966: Kt 1945 PC 1947 KC 1945 MA (Oxon). Labour MP Newport B/E 1956-66, Birkenhead 1945-50; Neepsend B/E April 1950-55; Contested Bebington 1950. **Rt. Hon. Sir Frank Soskice:** Born 23 July 1902, s of David Soskice (g-gs. of painter, Ford Madox Brown). Married 1940, Susan Isabella, d of William Cloudsley Hunter, 2s. Educated St. Paul's School; Balliol College, Oxford (Classics). Barrister, Inner Temple 1926; Bencher 1945. Oxfordshire & Bucks Light Infantry 1939-45. Lord Privy Seal 1966-70. Of Hampstead. Estate £131,700. Died 1979.

SOUTTER Elizabeth: Referendum Party: Delyn 1997. **Mrs. Elizabeth Soutter:** Married David Souter (Deputy Regional Campaign Manager, Referendum Party) 2c. Owner of a property & maintenance business. Of Flint Mountain (1966).

SPANSWICK Edward H: Plaid Cymru: Monmouth Feb. 1974. **Mr. Ted Spanswick:** Married June, 2c; Engineer. AUEW shop steward. Army 1939-45. Contested Chepstow UDC Convenor, Gwent Regional Council, Plaid Cymru. Produced & distributed 18000 Anti-European Community leaflets during Pontypridd by-election 1985. Of Pontypridd. *Papers at National Library.*

SPEHT Robert: BSc (Wales) 1997 MSc (Loughborough). Liberal Democrat, Swansea East 2001. **Mr. Rob Speht:** Born Pontefract, 1972. Educated University of Wales, Swansea (Mechanical Engineering & German); Manheim Technical University; University of Loughborough (Renewable Energy Systems). Senior Project Manager, Sustainable Energy Ltd Swansea 1998. Director, EnergyTech. Ltd 2001-. PhD Student at De Montfort University, Leicester. Joined Liberal Democrats 1991. Contested Swansea CC 1995, 1999. Interests: Community Development, Environment, Sustainability, Transport; 'Digital' divide. Hobbies: Cycling, Walking. Liberal Democrat Prospective Parliamentary Candidate, Swansea East 2003. Of Brynmill, Swansea (1991).

SPENCE Thomas Heriot: MA (Edin). Independent Labour: Ogmore 1987. **Mr. Thomas Spence:** Born 1940. Married 4c. Educated George Watson College, Edinburgh; Edinburgh University. Businessman. Contested Ogwr BC.

SPENCER Richard H: Communist: Cardiff South East 1979. **Mr. Richard Spencer:** Born 1917. Senior Lecturer in French, University of Wales, Cardiff. Branch President AUT.

SPICER Albert: 1st Bart 1906 PC 1912 JP DL (Essex). Liberal: Monmouth District 1900 B/E 1901; MP 1892-1900. Central Hackney 1906-18. Contested Walthamstow 1886. **Rt. Hon. Sir Albert Spicer:** Born Woodford 6 March 1847, s of Sir James Spicer JP DL. Congregationalist. Married 1879, Jessie, d of D. Stewart Dykes, Grove Hill, Surrey. Educated Mill Hill School; London University; Heidelberg University. Paper Manufacturer & Company Director 60 years. Director, London Missionary Society 1873- (Treasurer 1885-1900). 1st lay Chairman, Congregational Union of England and Wales 1893 (1st Chair of the Council). President, Sunday School Union 1900. Of London. Estate £74,590. Died 20 December 1934.

SPINK Jonathan Howard: BSc MSc Diploma in Law PGCE (London). Green Party, Ogmore B/E 14 Feb. 2002. **Mr. Jonathan Spink:** Born 1963. Partner, Sophie, 2c Educated University College, London (Applied Physics), London School of Economics (Sea Use, Law & Policy Making); Polytechnic of Central London; London Institute of Education. Non-practising barrister. Science teacher in Tower Hamlets 1994-97. Software engineer. Worked for Sony, Bridgend, 1997-. Volunteer European Proliferation Centre (campaigning against nuclear proliferation) 1986-90. Elections Officer, Bridgend Green Party. Secretary: Bridgend Campaign for Democracy. Of Bridgend (1997).

SQUIRES Michael: AMIMechE. UK Independence Party, Carmarthen East & Dinefwr, 2001. **Mr. Mike Squires:** Born Abersychan 26 January 1946, s of George W. T. Squires, civil engineer, & Winifred Alice Squires, secretary. Married 1973, Glynis Roberts, teacher. Educated West Monmouth Grammar School, Pontypool; Newport & Mon College of Technology. Design Engineer. Deputy chief engineer, Newport Forge, Bedwas, 22 years. Own business (design & manufacture of mechanical handling equipment) 1979-2001. Organic farming (cattle suckling herd) 1979-. Royal Naval Reserve, South Wales division 7 years. Member: UKIP Welsh Cttee. Chair, UKIP Dyfed Branch. Interests: Retention of the Sovereignty of Britain, Animal Welfare, GM Crops, Globalisation is the route to world domination. Hobbies: Vintage Cars, Reading, music. Languages: English, French & German (O level). Of Llanarthne.

STANFIELD Claude: JP (Merthyr Tydfil). ILP: Merthyr 1935; Refused 1945 ILP nomination to support Samuel Jennings, Ind Lab. **Mr. Claude Stanfield:** Born Troedyrhiw. Miner. Chair, Treasurer & Arbitrator, SWMF. Checkweighman. Insurance agent; President, National Amalgamated Union of Life Assurance Workers. Merthyr Tydfil BC (Plymouth ward) 1932-35, 1947-; Alderman; Mayor. Joined ILP 1921. Joined Labour when ILP branch was wound up in 1950. Died 19 February 1948.

STANTON Charles Butt: CBE 1920 JP (Glam) 1920. Labour: East Glamorgan Dec. 1910; Independent Labour/Coalition MP Merthyr Tydfil B/E 1915-18; National Democratic & Labour Party MP: Aberdare 1918-22. National Liberal , Aberdare 1922. **Mr. Charlie Stanton:** Born Aberaman 7 April 1873, s of Thomas and Harriet Stanton. Married 1893, Alice Maud Thomas, 1s (1 killed in war). Educated Aberaman British School. Docker. Miner. Miners' Agent, Aberdare 1899-. Member, MFGB Executive 1911. Leader, Powell Dyffryn Strike 1910. 1st Secretary, Aberdare Socialist Society 1895. President, South Wales ILP & Socialist Federation. Leader (with Ben Tillett) Socialist National Defence League 1915-18. Founder, British Workers' National League 1916 (Vice-President) & National Democratic Party. Backed in 1915 by-election by the Liberals and Conservatives on the *'straight war ticket, to fight against the Huns for our Homeland'*; 1918 manifesto was *'Make Germany pay and expel all aliens'.* Polled NDP's highest vote. Joined Liberal Party 1928. Journalist & Lecturer, early 1920s. Violin playing publican in old inn at Hampstead. Later worked in Hollywood movies as Archbishop of Canterbury & often as *an English butler.* High Constable of Miskin, 1920. Governor, University College, Cardiff; University College of Wales, Aberystwyth. Glamorgan CC. Hobbies: Painting, Music (violinist) & Reading. Estate £437. Died 6 December 1946. *Books etc: C. B. Stanton, Facts for Federationalists, Maxims for Miners, Why We Should Agitate?*

STEAD Peter Price: BA (Wales). Labour: Barry 1979. **Professor Peter Stead:** Born Barry 22 August 1943, s of John Stead, Police superintendent, & Elivira Stead. Baptist. Married Elizabeth Hilton. Educated Barry Grammar School; Gowerton Grammar School; University of Wales, Swansea (1st History). Lecturer in History: University of Wales, Swansea 1966-97; Wellesley College, Visiting Professor, University of Glamorgan. Member: Swansea Health Executive 1966-68; Welsh Council Film Cttee. 1972-74; Executive Welsh Academy 1992 (Fellow), Institute of Welsh Affairs. Joined Labour Party 1964. Of Derwenfawr, Swansea. *Books: Peter Stead: Coleg Harlech 1976, Film and the Working Class 1979 and 1981, Richard Burton, So Much, So Little 1991, Dennis Potter 1994, Hymns and Arias: Great Welsh Voices 2001, Acting Wales: Stars of Stage and Screen 2002, More Heart and Soul: The Character of Welsh Rugby* (edit with Huw Richards & Gareth Williams) 1999.

STEEL Timothy Michael: Labour: Monmouth 1979. **Mr. Timothy Steel:** Born Frimley, Surrey 10 January 1944, s of W. J. F. Steel, comprehensive school head; mother a primary school head. Married Christine Thomas of Haverfordwest 1s 1d. Educated Royal Grammar School, Guildford. Marketing Manager, Leyland Cars. Managing Director of a group of companies. Chair of four companies and director of 5th. Joined Labour Party 1969. Member: TGWU: Co-operative Party.

STEPHEN Campbell: MA 1907 BD 1910 BSc 1915 (Glasgow). ILP: Merthyr B/E June 1934, Camlachie 1931; MP Camlachie, Labour 1922-31, ILP 1935-July 1947. Joined Parliamentary Labour Party 21 October 1947. Labour, Ayr Burghs 1918. **Revd Campbell Stephen:** Born Caithness 29 March 1884, s of Alexander Stephen, farmer. Married 1945, Dorothy (MP Norwich 1922-24) d of George Jewson. Educated Townhead Public School; Allan Glen's School; Glasgow University; Glasgow United Free Church Theological College. United Free Church Minister, Ordained 1911: Maxwelltown & Park, Adrosson 1911-18; Resigned charge in order to work for socialism. Teacher of Mathematics, Strathmungo Higher grade School, Glasgow 1919-22. Suspended from the Commons, 27 June 1923. Barrister 1924. Member, Governing Body, British Film Institute. Died 25 October 1947.

STEPHENS Alfred: Kt 1923 JP (Carms). Conservative: Carmarthen 1923, B/E 1924. **Sir Alfred Stephens:** Born Llanelli 7 June 1871, s of Daniel Stephens JP & Catherine Stephens, Kidwelly. Anglican. Married Emily Margaret, d. of W. R. Bryant, 5d. Educated Castle Street School, Kidwelly; Queen Elizabeth Grammar School, Carmarthen; Owens College, Manchester; University College, Cardiff; Lycee de Caen. Company Chair: Stephens Silica Brick Co. Ltd. Director: Bynea Steel Co; Gorse Galvinising Works; *Carmarthen Journal* Ltd. Chair, Towy Fishery Board; Teifi & Aeron Fishery Board. Carmarthenshire CC 1898-, Chairman. Kidwelly BC 1896-; Mayor 1902-03-04, 1926-27-28. Member, Lord Lieutenant of Carmarthenshire Advisory Cttee. Chair, Carmarthen Conservative Assn. President: Kidwelly Quins RFC; Kidwelly Cricket Club. Of Kidwelly. Estate £144,682. Died 28 November 1938.

STEPHENS Michael: BA MA DLitt 2000 (Wales). Plaid Cymru, Merthyr Tydfil 1966; South/Central

List 1999. **Professor Meic Stephens:** Born Trefforest, 23 July 1938, s of Herbert Arthur Lloyd Stephens, power station turbine driver, & Alma Symes. Nominally Calvinistic Methodist. Married 1965, Ruth Wynn Meredith, 1s 3d. Educated Pontypridd Grammar School for Boys; University of Wales, Aberystwyth (English); University of Rennes. Journalist, *Western Mail* 1966-67. Launched magazine, *Poetry Wales*. 1st Director of Literature, Welsh Arts Council 1967-90. Professor of Welsh Writing in English, University of Glamorgan. Member: Cymdeithas yr Iaith; Plaid Cymru Executive; Hon. Society of Cymmrodorion; Linguistic Minorities in Europe. Hon. Member, Gorsedd 1979. Fellow of The Welsh Academy Hon. Fellow, University of Wales, Lampeter. Poet, writer, translator. Hobbies: Minority languages, The media, Radnorshire etc. Languages: Learned Welsh, English, French. Of Whitchurch, Cardiff. *Books: Editor, New Companion to the Literature of Wales 1998, Joint-Editor, Writers of Wales Series (University of Wales Press), Editor: 2nd Edition, Oxford Guide to Great Britain and Ireland, 1992. Author: The Literary Pilgrim in Wales, 2000, etc.*

STEVENS Christopher: BA (Wales). Conservative, Islwyn & South East List 1999. **Mr. Chris Stevens:** Born 22 September 1977, s of Adrian Stevens, motor dealer, & Sonia Woods, NHS manager. Church of England. Educated Blackwood Comprehensive School; Coleg Gwent; University of Wales, Newport (History & European Studies). Insurance Adviser. Civil Servant, National Assembly. Chair: Islwyn Conservative Assn 1995-2000 (Vice-Chair 2000-; Agent 1997). Contested Caerphilly CBC B/E 1998. Hobbies: Reading, Cinema, Keep Fit, Eating Out. Of Pengam.

STEVENS Frank Thomas: MA (Cantab). Conservative: Brecon & Radnor 1964, 1966. **Mr. Frank Stevens:** Born May 1921. Anglican. Educated Felsted School; Trinity Hall, Cambridge. Royal Navy 1940-45. Lieutenant RNVR. Farmer. Of Eardisley, Herefordshire.

STEWART Robert: Communist: Caerphilly B/E 1921 (1st UK Communist Candidate); Dundee 1924, 1929. **Mr. Bob Stewart:** Born Dundee. Married. Newspaper seller. Jute worker. Ship's joiner. Leader, Dundee Socialist Prohibition Fellowship. Prison in Great War for opposing war; 77 days for sedition in 1921 *on pretty flimsy evidence.* Founder Member of the Communist Party. Member, Communist Party Central Cttee 1922. Party representative in Moscow, he smuggled back thousands of pounds to help Communist cause in UK. Dismissed 1923, by order of the Communist International. Acting Party Secretary 1925-26 (Secretary Inkpin in prison).

STOCK Peter: Conservative, Mid & West List 1999. **Mr. Peter Stock:** Born Swansea, 10 May 1936, s of David Rees Stock, wholesale fruiterer, & Florence May Bennett. Church of Wales. Married 1960, Margaret Cynthia Howells, clerk, 3d. Educated secondary schools at Haverfordwest & Milford Haven. General Manager, wholesale electrical suppliers. Preseli DC (Chairman 1994-95), Pembrokeshire CC (Chairman 1997-98). Interests: Social Services, Tourism, Economic Development. Hobbies: Gardening, Football, DIY, Dominoes. Of Haverfordwest.

STODDART Helen: BA (York) MSc (Sheffield). Conservative, Carmarthenshire East & Dinefwr 1999. **Miss Helen Stoddart:** Born 1965. Educated Milford Haven Grammar School; University of York (Economics & Statistics); University of Sheffield (Statistics); University of Wales, Cardiff (Diploma in Journalistic Studies). Trainee Investment Analyst. Research Assistant, small business centre 1987-89. Part-time Lecturer in Statistics, Sheffield & Huddersfield Polytechnics. Press Officer, Mid Wales Tourist Initiative. With family launched *West Wales Mercury* 1992 (chief sub-editor & football editor), sold interest 1999. Of Milford Haven.

STODDART Robert Michael: LlB (Wales). Anti-Federalist Party: Pembroke 1992. **Mr. Michael Stoddart:** Born Wigton, Cumbria, 1 February 1940, s of John Pattinson Stoddart, businessman, & Jean Harker. Married 1964 Vivien Mary Matthews, journalist, 1s 2d (qv. Helen). Educated Nelson Tomlinson Grammar School, Wigton; Keele University; University of Wales, Cardiff. Managing Director, R M Stoddart Construction 1966-80. Director, Parkhouse Dairies 1971-82. Property Developer & Consultant. Founded *West Wales Mercury* October 1992 (with family); sold interest, April 1999. Preseli DC. Only candidate in Wales of Alan Sked's Anti-Federalist Party. Interests: European Integration. Free Trade. Hobbies: Golf, Bridge, Rugby. Of Milford Haven.

STOLARSKA Karolina Maria: BA (Durham) 2000. Pro-Life Party South/West List 2003. **Miss Karolina Stolarska:** Roman Catholic. With Family Publications of Oxford. Secretary, Student Lifenet Cttee. Of Acton, London.

STONEHAM Nellie J: MBE 1943. Conservative: Caerphilly 1935. **Mrs. Nellie Stoneham:** Born d of Colonel Morgan Lindsay (qv). Anglican. Married Gerald T. Stoneham (Squadron Leader). Chair, Caerphilly Conservative Women's Assn 1923-. Officer Commanding, AFS London 1940-41. Superintendent, Women's Studies NFS Staff College.

STRINGFELLOW Mark: British National Party. Wales Euro 2004. **Mr. Mark Stringfellow:** East

Midlands Regional Organiser, BNP. Contested Bolsover BC 2003. Of Bolsover.

STUCHBURY Oliver Piers: MA PhD (Cantab). Conservative: Rhondda East 1951. Joined Labour Party 1960. **Dr. Oliver Stuchbury:** Born London January 1927. Educated Radley College; Kings College, Cambridge. Grenadier Guards 1946-48, Lieutenant. Solicitor. Managing Director, Save & Prosper Unit Trust 1959-67. Resigned to take up honorary post at Labour Party H.Q. as Head of Fund Raising. Launched Golden Prize Clubs 1968. Personal Assistant, Ivor Richard MP1964. Lecturer in Philosophy, Colorado University; Sussex University. GLC Alderman 1973.

SUMMERS Glyndwr John: Independent, Rhondda 1999, 2001. **Mr. Glyndwr Summers:** Born London 6 June 1946, s of Kenneth G Summers, British Rail shunter, & Currie. Roman Catholic. Married 1971, Lynwen, planning officer, 1s 1d. Educated Edgware Junior School, London; Pontyclun Junior School 1955; Pant Secondary Modern School; Bridgend & Rhondda FE Colleges. Apprentice Toolmaker & General Engineer. Mechanical Engineer. Experienced redundancy & unemployment. Technician, Physics & Astronomy Dept. University of Wales, Cardiff. Member, Ystradyfodwg Bowls Club (Captain 1999, Vice-Chair), Rhondda Bowls Management Cttee. Interests: Better future for the Rhondda, Wales & UK. Hobbies: Bowls, DIY, Swimming. Lived in Rhondda from 1971. Of Trealaw.

SUMMERS James Woolley: JP (Denbighshire, Flintshire, Lincolnshire) Liberal MP Flint District 1910-. **Mr. James Summers:** Born Dukinfield, Ashton under Lyne 24 March 1849, s of John Summers. Married 1883, Edith, d of Hugh Mason MP. Company Director. Chair, John Summers & Co. Stalybridge BC. Flintshire CC 1904-10. Of Flintshire. Estate £170,483. Died 1 January 1913.

SUTCH David Edward (Lord David Sutch): Monster Raving Loony Party: Vale of Glamorgan B/E 1989, Monmouth B/E 1991, Islwyn 1992 B/E 1995; National Teenage Party: Stratford on Avon B/E 1963. Young Ideas Party: Huyton 1966, Cities of London & Westminster 1970; Go to Blazes Party, Stafford & Stone Oct. 1974. Founded Monster Raving Loony Party 1983: Bermondsey B/E 1983, Finchley 1983, Penrith & The Border 1983, Chesterfield 1986, Fulham B/E 1986, Newcastle under Lyme 1986, Kensington B/E 1986, Govan b/E 1986, Epping forest B/E 1986, Epping Forest B/E 1988, Richmond B/E 1989, Bootle B/E 1990, Mid-Staffs B/E 1990; Knowsley South B/E 1990, Huntingdon 1992,

Yeovil 1992; Newbury B/E 1993; Christchurch B/E 1993; Rotherham B/E 1994; Bradford South B/E 1994; Eastleigh B/E 1994, Perth & Kinross B/E 1995, Littleborough & Saddleworth B/E 1995, Hemsworth B/E 1996, Staffs SE B/E 1996, Winchester B/E Nov. 1997. **Lord David Sutch (Screaming Lord Sutch):** Born Kilburn, 10 November 1940, s of Annie Sutch & a policeman killed in the Blitz; changed name to Lord David Sutch by deed-poll 1988. Partner, Yvonne Elwood. 1s. Partner, Yvonne Elwood (planned to marry at Las Vegas in October 1999). Educated Salisbury Road Secondary Modern School, Kilburn. Self-employed window cleaner 1955. Rock & Roll entertainer, pop singer & business manager. Founded Radio Sutch 1984, which became Radio City. Did not contest 1997 election because of mother's illness. Died June 1999 (found hanged 16 June 1999 (suicide). *Books: Lord David Sutch. (with Peter Chippendale) Life as Sutch: The Official Autobiography of a Monster Raving Loony 1991.*

SWAYNE Desmond Angus: Conservative: Pontypridd 1987, West Bromwich West 1992; MP New Forest West 1997-. **Mr. Desmond Swayne:** Born Abergavenny 20 August 1956. Anglican. Married August 1992. Educated Bedford School; St. Andrews University; Open University. Teacher (Economics), Wrekin College & Charterhouse. Company Director, Brick Sculptures Ltd. Computer Systems. Development Manager, Royal Bank of Scotland. TA Officer, Warwickshire & Worcestershire Yeomanry Squadron. President, St. Andrew's Conservative Assn. Member, Prayer Book Society; Bow Group. Prison Visitor.

SWEENEY Walter: BA (Hull) MPhil (Cantab) CertEd TEFL. Conservative MP Vale of Glamorgan 1992-97; Contested Stretford 1983. **Mr. Walter Sweeney:** Born Dublin, 23 April 1949, s of Patrick Anthony Sweeney, veterinary surgeon, & Jane Yerbury, headteacher. Married Nuala Maire Kennan, consultant radiologist, 2d. Educated Lawrence Sheriff School, Rugby; University of Aix-Marseille; University of Hull; Darwin College, Cambridge; Life Member, Cambridge University Conservative Assn. Solicitor 1976. Law Lecturer. Solicitor, at Barry 1989-92; Beverley 1998-. Joined Conservative Party 1964. Chair, Rugby Young Conservatives1965. Vice-Chair, Rugby Conservative Assn. Chair, Rugby CPC 1970. Rugby BC 1974-77. Bedfordshire CC 1981-89. Select Cttees Member: Wales 1990-92; Home Affairs 1992-97; Channel Tunnel Rail Link 1995-96; Secretary, Conservative MPs Home Affairs Cttee 1994-97; Jt. Vice Chair, Conservative Legal Cttee 1995-97 (Secretary 1993-97); Vice-Chair, All Party Penal Affairs Group 1993-97. Hobbies: Rugby, Flying, Theatre.

SWETENHAM Edmund: QC 1880 JP (Denbs) BA1845 MA 1848 (Oxon). Conservative: Caernarfon District 1885; MP: 1886-. **Mr. Edmund Swetenham:** Born Somerford Booths, Cheshire 15 November 1822, s of Clement Swetenham & Eleanor, d of John Buelar (gs of Roger Comerbach, who changed his name to Swetenham in order to inherit the estate of his great uncle, Edward Swetenham, Somerford Booths, Cheshire). Married (1) 1851 Elizabeth, d of Wilson Jones, Hartsheath Park, Surrey (MP Denbigh District 1835-41 (2) 1868, Gertrude (died 1876) d of Ellis Cunliffe (Gd Sir Foster Cunliffe). Educated Macclesfield Grammar School; Brasenose College, Oxford. Barrister, Lincolns Inn 1848; Bencher 1882. Of Wrexham. Estate £28,636. Died 19 March 1880.

SWIFT Mary Shackerley: Natural Law Party: Clwyd North-West 1992. **Mrs. Mary Swift:** Married 1d. Part-time teacher & writer of children's stories. Of Skelmersdale.

SYMONDS Michael Andrew: FRICS. Liberal: Islwyn 1992. **Mr. Andrew Symonds:** Born 6 January 1939. Married 5c. Chartered Surveyor. School governor.

– T –

'Kit' Mansel Talbot.

TALBOT Christopher Rice Mansel: JP (Glam) BA 1824 MA (Oxon) FRS 1831 FLS. Liberal MP Glamorgan 1830-85, Mid Glamorgan 1885-. **Mr. "Kit" Mansel Talbot:** Born Penrice Castle, Gower, 10 May 1803, s of Thomas Mansel Talbot & Lady Mary Lucy Fox-Strangways, d of 3rd Earl of Ilchester. Inherited the estate 1824. Anglican. Married 1835, Lady Charlotte Butler (died 1846) d of Earl of Glengall, 1s 3d. Educaborne 1811; Harrow 1814-17; private tutor & Oriel College, Oxford (1st Maths). Landowner, Industrialist & Company Director. Chair, South Wales Railway until it merged with Great Western Railway; Director, GWR (invested £1 million). Proprietor: Chester & Birkenhead Railway; Great Western Hotel; (invested £3m in railways by 1890). Elected to Parliament in succession to his mother's 2nd husband, Sir Christopher Cole MP 1817-30. Father of the House of Commons 1874-. Raised 1st Corps, Glamorgan Rifle Volunteers 1859, Colonel. Founder, Royal Institution of South Wales 1835; President 1856-57; Vice-President 1857-70. President: Swansea Farmers Club. Vice-Commodore, Royal Yacht Squadron 1850-61. Lord Lieutenant of Glamorgan 1848-. Gave his name to Port Talbot. Declined a peerage, Nov. 1869. Of Margam Castle (20,000 acres), Penrice Castle & Llandough (14,000 acres); Rents £44,000 pa. Estate £1,399,172. Died 17 January 1890.

TAMI Mark Richard: BA (Wales) 1985. Labour MP Alyn & Deeside 2001. **Mr. Mark Tami:** Born Enfield, 3 October 1962, s of Michael John Tami & Patricia Tami. Married 1994 Sally Ann Daniels, 2s. Educated Enfield Grammar School; University of Wales, Swansea (History). Clerical Officer, NAGO; Head of Research & Communications, AEEU 1986-99, Policy 1999-2001. Member: Labour Party national policy forum; Fabian Society; TUC General Council 1999-2000; *First Past the Post* Campaign. Hobbies: Football (Norwich City), Cricket, Fishing, Antiques.

TANNER Roger D: BSc (Southampton). Plaid Cymru, Pontypool Feb. & Oct. 1974. **Mr. Roger Tanner:** Born October 1949. Educated Cardiff High School; Southampton University; University of Wales, Bangor (research in politics). With ICI. Planning Officer, Monmouthshire County Council. Member NALGO. Book reviewer, *Times Higher Educational Supplement*. Languages: Learned Welsh; English.

TARBET Stephen H: BA (Wales). Labour: Cardiff North 1987. **Mr. Stephen Tarbet:** Born 23 October 1954. Unmarried. Educated Canton High School, Cardiff; University of Wales, Swansea; Cardiff College. Teacher (History of Economics; Business Studies) Stanwell Comprehensive School, Penarth. Secretary: Cardiff West CLP, South Glam Area Labour Party. President, South Glam NUT 1986-87. Chair, Canton Branch, GMBTU. Of Cardiff.

TAYLOR Andrew Robert: Conservative: Blaenau Gwent 1987, South Wales Euro 1989, Newport West 1992. **Mr. Andrew Taylor:** Born 14 February 1961. Educated Tredegar Comprehensive School; University College, Cardiff. Barrister, Grays Inn. Member, Council for Legal Aid, London. Chair, Abergavenny Lawn Tennis Club; Secretary, Tredegar RFC 1987-88. Member: Monmouthshire Lawn Tennis Team; Penpergwm Croquet Club 1986-89; Stow Park Lawn Tennis Club 1989. Joined Young Conservatives 1978. Secretary: Welsh Conservative Candidates Assn, Welsh Conservative Policy Group. Hobbies: Rugby, Cricket, Drama, Music. Of Basseleg, Newport.

TAYLOR John: BEd CertEd. Plaid Cymru, South/East List 1999. **Mr. John Taylor:** Born Abertridwr 24 September 1950, s of William

George Taylor, Chief Petty Officer, RN & Civil Servant, & Gertrude Evans, nurse. Baptist. Educated Caerphilly boys Grammar School; Glamorgan College of Education; Glamorgan Polytechnic. Teacher. Chair: Cwmaber Branch, Plaid Cymru. Member, Plaid Cymru National Council. Rhymney Valley DC 1983-96. Aber Valley ComC. 1985-. Caerphilly CBC 1999- (Cabinet Member for Transport & Planning, Chair: Standing Advisory Council on Religious Education). Chair: Aber Valley Area Forum, Schools Governors. Member: National Housing & Town Planning Council; Disability Wales; Public Consortium of Non Metropolitan Authorities; Road Safety Council for Wales. Hobbies: Amateur Drama. Languages: some Welsh, English, French. Of Abertridwr.

TAYLOR Mary: Conservative, South/East List 1999. **Mrs. Mary Taylor:** Born Abergavenny 29 October 1943, d of Trevor James Edwards, Royal Navy, & Gladys Mary Jones. Church in Wales. Married 1960, Michael Eric Taylor, consultant, London teaching hospital, 1d. Educated Abergavenny High School; Middlesex Hospital. Nurse: hospital, industry, nursery, nursery school. Home carer to father-in-law. Joined Young Conservatives 1950. Area Young Conservative Organiser, South Lewisham 1996, Brecon & Radnor 1993. Chair: Lewisham East Conservative Assn; Mid & West Euro Conservatives 1996. Treasurer, Brecon & Radnor Conservative Assn 1997. Powys CC 1995-99. Vale of Gwyrney ComC, Chairman 1995-96. Member: Brecon Beacons National Park Authority; Brecon & Radnor Community Health Council; Abergavenny & Crickhowell CAB; Crickhowell & District Dial a Ride; Red Cross branch; Caring in the Community, Management Cttee; Home for Unmarried Mothers. School Governor. Guider. Secretary, Llangenny PCC. Promoter of Organic & Local Food. Interests: Environmental Issues, Food Safety, Promoting Women. Hobbies: Swimming, Quilting, Cookery, Food Issues, Women's Issues. Of Crickhowell.

TAYLOR Neil Harding: Plaid Cymru: Flint East Feb. 1974, Flint West Oct. 1974, Clwyd North-West 1992. **Mr. Neil Taylor:** Born Scunthorpe, 11 March 1941. Educated John Bright Grammar School, Llandudno; Liverpool Poly; Chester College of Law. Machine Operator. Clerk in lawyer's office 1973. Legal Executive. Solicitor. Field Officer, North Wales Unemployment Resources & Advice Centre 1982-. Conservative for 30 years. Joined Plaid Cymru 1963. Rhyl TC 1974-89. Rhuddlan BC 1976-87, Mayor 1984-85. Clwyd CC 1981-84. Chair, Plaid Cymru Clwyd County Cttee. Member, Shotton Steelworks Defence Cttee. Founder-Chair, Clwb y Triban, Rhyl. Vice-Chair, Clwyd Assn. of Chambers of Trade 1976-. Backed by Geraint Morgan, ex-

Conservative MP. Plaid Cymru Spokesman on the Constitution. Of Rhyl (1973).

TAYLOR Paul: Independent, Islwyn 2001; Tinker Against the Assembly, South/East List 2003. **Mr. Paul 'Tinker' Taylor:** Born Tredegar, 18 February 1952, s of Brinley Taylor, miner, & Annie Taylor. Deist. Married (1) 1s (2) 1996 Jennifer Anne Taylor, teacher. Educated Lewis Boys' School, Pengam. Licensee & Restaurateur. Interests: Leader, Tinker against the Assembly Party, General concern about the state of the Nation. Founded Caerphilly Reality Party 2004, with slogan *Vote Reality, we're sick of politics.* Of Penmaen, Blackwood.

TAYLOR Reginald: Independent, Montgomery 2001; Green Party, Mid & West Wales List 2003. **Mr. Reg Taylor:** Born Liverpool 14 February 1935, s of Reginald Taylor, French Polisher. Married 1955 Margaret Dorren, staff nurse, 3s 1d. Educated secondary modern school. Montgomeryshire DC (Vice-Chair, Establishment Cttee). Powys CC. Member, Montgomeryshire Health Council 1991, Chair 1994-. Chair: Welsh Assn of Health Councils 1995-; Community Health Council's Health Information Advisory Group; Wales; Working Group on Employment & Resources for Welsh Community Health Councils. Hon. Member of Gorsedd 2001, *Reg o Lerpwl.* Interests: Agriculture; Devolution, with tax & law making powers; Pensions, Health, Environment, Abolish Tuition Fees; Anti European Union; Anti Fox Hunting. Hobbies: Football. Languages: some Welsh, English. Of Newtown.

TELFER Teresa: Green Party, South/East List 2003. **Mrs. Teresa Telfer:** Born Guernsey, 13 January 1950, d of Richard & Maureen Angell. Roman Catholic. Married 1996 Ian Telfer, Postman, 1s 2d. Married 3c. Educated Larkfield Grammar School, Chepstow. Postwoman. Vegan & Animal Rights Campaigner. Interests: Animal Rights, Saving Environment. Hobbies: Swimming, Walking, Reading. Languages: English, French (O Level). Of Sudbrook, near Chepstow.

TEMPLE-MORRIS Owen Temple: Kt KC 1937. Conservative: Caerphilly 1929, MP Cardiff East 1931-42. **Sir Owen Temple-Morris:** Born Cardiff 1896, s of Dr. Frederick Temple Morris & Florence, d of Colonel C. L. Owen, Portsmouth. Anglican. Married 1927, Vera, d of D. Hamilton Thompson, 1s (Peter qv). Educated privately. Solicitor 1920-25. Barrister, Grays Inn 1925. Post Office Prosecuting Counsel 1931-37. Recorder of Merthyr Tydfil 1936-42. Acting Recorder of Swansea 1940-42. Chair of Quarter Sessions: Haverfordwest 1942-48; Carmarthenshire 1942-50, Breconshire 1948-55, Monmouthshire 1950-69. Vice-President: Wales & Mon Conservative &

Unionist Assn 1931-42. Chair: Wales & Mon Conservative Education Cttee 1938-42; Wales & Mon Conservative Clubs Advisory Cttee 1929-42. Chancellor, Diocese of Llandaff 1935-79. Hon. Lay Secretary, Llandaff Diocesan Conference 1927-32. Member: Governing Body of the Church in Wales; Hon. Society of Cymmrodorion. Chief Commandant, Cardiff Volunteers, Special Constabulary 1935-45. Chair & Secretary, Commandants of Special Constabulary No. 8 Region 1942-45. Hon. Treasurer, Cardiff Centre, Order of St. John of Jerusalem. County Court Judge 1942-. Died 25 April 1985.

TEMPLE-MORRIS Peter, Baron Temple-Morris of Llandaff 2001: MA (Cantab). Chevalier du Tastevin 1991. Conservative: Newport 1964, 1966; Norwood 1970; PPC Epping until boundaries redrawn 1968). MP Leominster Feb. 1974- 2001; Resigned from the party 22 November 1997, after the Whip was withdrawn to sit as an Independent on the Labour side of the Commons; Joined Labour Party 1998. **Mr. Peter Temple-Morris:** Born Cardiff, 12 February 1938, s of Sir Owen Temple-Morris (qv) and Vera, d. of D. Hamilton Thompson. Anglican. Married Tahere, d of Senator Khozeime Alam, Teheran (Chamberlain to the Shah of Iran) 2s 2d. Educated Malvern College; St. Catherine's College, Cambridge. Worked in a solicitor's office for 2 years before university. Judge's Marshal to Mr. Justice Finnemore. Chair, Cambridge University Conservative Assn 1960-61. Member, Cambridge University Afro-Asian Expedition 1961. Member: Young Barristers' Cttee, Bar Council 1962-63. Barrister 1962. Solicitor 1989. Second Counsel, Inland Revenue, SE Circuit 1971. Member, Bow Group; Conservative Overseas Bureau's Group, Council of Europe 1963-. Chair, North Kensington Conservative Assn. Member Select Cttees: Agriculture 1982-83, Foreign Affairs 1987-90, Consolidation Bills 1991. Chair: British-Irish inter-parliamentary body 1983-, Afghanistan Support Cttee 1981-82; British-Lebanese Parliamentary Group 1992-94; British Netherlands Group 1980; British Iranian Group 1989-; British South African All Party Group 1989-. Vice-Chair, GB-Russian Centre 1993. Jt Chair, All Party Release of Hostages Parl Group 1990-. Jt Vice-Chair, Conservative MPs Foreign Affairs Cttee. 1982-90. Jt. Vice-Chair, Conservative MPs Northern Ireland Cttee. 1989. Co-founder, British-Irish Parliamentary Body. Chair, British Group IPU 1982-85. Member, Executive, Society of Conservative Lawyers 1968-71, 1990-. National Treasurer, UN Assn (UK) 1987-97. Hon. Vice-President, 1997-. Freeman, City of London. Liveryman, Basketmakers Co; Barbers Co 1993. Governor, Malvern College. Hon. Citizen: New Orleans, Havana. Nat Treasurer UNA 1987. Of Huntington, Hereford.

TERLEZSKI Stefan: CBE 1992. Conservative: Cardiff SE Feb. & Oct. 1974, South Wales Euro 1979; MP Cardiff West 1983-87. **Mr. Stefan Terlezski:** Born Antoniwka, Eastern Ukraine 27 October 1927, s of Oleska Terlezski (factory manager who spent 25 years in a Siberian labour camp) & Olena Terlezski (who took part in the Warsaw uprising, taken by Gestapo to a concentration camp & then forced labour 1941; Served in German Land Army 1944-45; Joined Russian Army 1945, Deserted 1946; Joined British Catering Corps, Vienna 1947-49). Naturalised British Subject 1965 (parents & sister banished to Siberia 1952). Roman Catholic. Married Mary, 2d. Educated Cardiff High School; Cardiff College of Food Technology & Commerce. Managing Director, The Cedars Hotel, Llanishen. Management Consultant. Chair, Cardiff City AFC 1975-77. Cardiff CC 1968-74. Cardiff DC 1973-83. South Glamorgan CC 1973-85. Deputy Chair: College of Food Technology & Commerce, Glamorgan Polytechnic. Member: South Wales Police Authority 1975-80, Welsh Joint Education Cttee 1975-85. Chair: Keep Britain in Europe Campaign 1973-75; Conservative Group for European Movement 1973-75; Foreign Affairs Forum 1974. Vice-President, Young Conservatives, Wales 1975-80. UK Representative, Convention Cttee for the Prevention of Torture and Inhuman or Degradation Treatment & Punishment 1989. Languages: English, Ukrainian, Polish, Russian & German. Of Cyncoed, Cardiff.

TERRELL Thomas: QC 1898 FCS. Liberal: Pembroke & Haverfordwest 1900. **Mr. Thomas Terrell:** Born Paris 1852, s of Judge Thomas Hall Terrell. Anglican. Married 1880, Emma, d of Edward Oke Spooner FRCS 1d. Barrister, Grays Inn 1879, Bencher 1896, Treasurer 1904. Of Muswell Hill, London. Estate £571. Died 27 April 1928.

TESTER Debra Ann: Independent Wales Party. Mid & West List 2003. **Ms. Debra Tester:** Of Abercrave.

TETT Henry Lewis: Conservative: Bedwellty 1945. **Mr. Lewis Tett:** Company Director. Lieutenant, Royal Artillery, Newport Anti-Aircraft Force. Withdrew as Independent National Unity Candidate, Newport B/E May 1945.

THEUNISSEN Evelyn Edwina: BSc. UK Independence, Clwyd South 2001, 2003. **Mrs. Edwina Theunissen:** Born Wrexham, d of Jack Davies. Married 3c. Educated (Environment Science). Runs family farm. Librarian. Involved in home education nationally. Worked in South Africa. Mayoress of Wrexham (father, Mayor) 1983-84. Joined UKIP 1996. Of Marchwiel, Wrexham.

THOMAS Abel: QC 1891 JP (Pembs) BA (London) 1870. Liberal MP East Carmarthenshire 1892-1910. **Mr. Abel Thomas:** Born 15 February 1848, s of Revd Theophilus Evan Thomas JP & Mary John, Trehale. Married 1875, Bessie (died 1890) d of Samuel Pollack, London, 1s 2d. Educated Clifton College, Bristol. Barrister, Middle Temple 1873, Bencher 1900. Chair, Pembrokeshire Quarter Sessions. Languages: Welsh, English. Of London. Estate £7,257. Died 23 July 1912.

THOMAS Abraham Garrod: Kt 1912 DL (Mon) 1897 JP (Cards Mon & Newport) MB MS 1876 MRCS (England) 1876 MD (Edin) 1878 Hon. LLD Wales) 1922. Liberal MP South Monmouthshire 1917-18. **Sir Garrod Thomas:** Aberaeron 5 October 1853, s of Lewis Thomas & brother of John Aeron Thomas MP (qv). Congregationalist. Married 1879, Eleanor, (died 1926) d of R. H. Richards, Newport. Educated Universities of Edinburgh, Berlin & Vienna. Consultant Physician, Royal Gwent Hospital, Newport 1877-1912. Chair: *South Wales Argus* Ltd. Chair: Royal Gwent Hospital Board; Newport Property Owners' Assn. Newport BC. 1889-92. Newport School Board 1889-92. High Sheriff of Cardiganshire 1900. President: Monmouthshire Congregational Assn; Free Church Council of Wales 1918; South Wales & Mon Branch BMA1900-01; Newport Liberal Assn. Co-Treasurer & Vice-President, University of Wales, Aberystwyth. Member, Court & Council, University of Wales, Cardiff. Languages: Welsh, English. Of Newport & London. Died 30 January 1931.

THOMAS Adolphus Daniel: Plaid Cymru: Wrexham 1951. **Mr. Dan Thomas:** Born Llanerchymedd 20 February 1899, s of workhouse master. Presbyterian Church of Wales elder & lay preacher (ex-Anglican). Married (1) Elizabeth Watcyn Jones, Llanuwchllyn (died 1953) 1s 2d (one daughter married Gwynfor Evans (qv) (2) Menna Williams. Educated Abergele Elementary School; Abergele Grammar School. Bank clerk, Maritime Bank, Liverpool 1905. Bank Manager retired 1947. Member, Bank Officers Guild & National Union of Bank Employees, 33 years; Acting President, 4 years. Persuaded by George M. Ll. Davies to join the Territorials 1911, whom he arrested 1917, an act he bitterly regretted for the rest of his life. Army 1914-18: Lieutenant; France, then Recruiting Officer for Recruiting. Moderator of Presbytery; North Wales Assembly, Presbyterian Church of Wales. President, North Wales Free Church Federal Council 1969-70. Joined Labour Party, then Plaid Cymru. Financial Secretary, Plaid Cymru, Treasurer 1951-56. Llangollen UDC. Pwllheli BC. Languages: Welsh, English. Died 11 June 1974.

THOMAS Alan Peter: Conservative: Swansea West Oct. 1974. **Mr. Alan Thomas:** Born Cardiff, 1936. Roman Catholic. Married Julie, 2c. Educated St. Illtyd's College, Cardiff; University of Wales, Cardiff; London School of Economics. Financial Journalist & Stockbroker. RAF 1954-56. Private pilot's licence. Richmond on Thames BC 1968-71. School governor. Member: Bow Group; Gas Consultative Council; Arts Council; London Airport Liaison Cttee.

THOMAS Alfred, 1st & last Baron Pontypridd 1912: Kt 1902 JP (Glam & Cardiff) DL (Glam). Liberal MP East Glamorgan 1885-1910. **Sir Alfred Thomas:** Born Llwyn-y-Grant Farm, Penylan, Cardiff 16 September 1840, s of Daniel Thomas, contractor. Baptist Deacon & Sunday School superintendent. Educated Weston School nr Bath. Contractor. Cardiff BC 1875-86, Alderman, Mayor 1881-82. Freeman of Cardiff 1887. President: Baptist Union of Wales 1886; University of South Wales & Mon. 1st President, National Museum of Wales. Chair, Welsh Parliamentary Party 1897-1910. Introduced the National Institutions Bill 1892, to set up an elected National Council for Wales and appoint a Secretary of State. Teetotaller. Languages: Welsh, English. Of Cardiff. Died 14 December 1927.

THOMAS Alun Clydwyn: Communist: Neath 1950. **Mr. Alun Thomas:** Born Nantymoel 1907. Went to USA 1912. Educated USA & Canada. Returned to Wales 1924 & took an engineering course at University of Wales, Swansea. Miner. Scholarship to Central Labour College but expelled for *extremist views*. Communist Party West Wales Organiser until 1951. Secretary, Communist Party Welsh Area Council 1951-53. Wholesale Egg Merchant. Glamorgan CC 1946-49. Neath RDC. Of Neath Abbey. Died 1956.

THOMAS Andrew Martin: Liberal Democrat: Wrexham 1992; 1997. **Hon. Andrew Thomas:** Born 15 October, 1965, s of Donald Martin Thomas (qv). Married Jodie. Educated Darland Comprehensive School; Yale Sixth Form College, Wrexham; Cambridge University; Inns of Court School of Law. Barrister. Member, Welsh Liberal Democrat Consumer Affairs Group.

THOMAS Ann Pamela: LlB (London). Conservative: Swansea East B/E 1963, Willesden West 1966. **Miss Pamela Thomas:** Born May 1929, d. of Revd Llewellyn Thomas, Vicar of Glasbury. Anglican. Educated Rodean School; Kings College, London. Barrister, Lincolns Inn 1955. Lecturer in Law, Holborn College of Law, Language & Commerce. Member: Bow Group; ATTI. Secretary, Inns of Court Conservative Assn 1963-. Kensington & Chelsea BC (Chair, Housing Cttee). Contested GLC 1958.

THOMAS Catherine Bailey: Labour, Llanelli 2003. **Mrs. Catherine Bailey:** Born Llanelli 1963.

Married Wayne David MP (qv) separated. Educated Dafen Primary School; Llanelli Girls Grammar School; University of Glamorgan; University of Wales, Cardiff. Environmental Co-ordinator. Political Aide to Julie Morgan MP. Ex-Aide in European Parliament. Languages: Welsh, English. Of Gwynfe.

THOMAS Dafydd Elis – see ELIS THOMAS Dafydd.

THOMAS Daniel Clive Byron: BA (Exeter) 2002. Conservative, Cynon Valley & South/Central list 2003. **Mr. Daniel Thomas:** Born Newport 30 April 1981, s of Clive Byron Thomas & Nicola Joan Thomas. Church of England. Educated Blackwood Comprehensive School; Gwent Tertiary College, Crosskeys; University of Exeter (Politics). Investment Reviewer, Private Banking. Chair: Islwyn Conservative Future 1999-2002; Exeter University Conservative Students 2000-02. Vice-Chair: Exeter Conservative Assn 2000-02. Member, Air Training Corps 9 years (Lord Lieutenant's Cadet 2000). Interests: British Constitution, Welfare, Education, Economy. Hobbies: Reading Rugby, Outdoor pursuits Shooting. Of Blackwood.

THOMAS Daniel Geraint: MA (Oxon). Plaid Cymru: Aberavon Oct. 1974, 1979. **Mr. Geraint Thomas:** Born Carmarthen, December 1949. Married. Educated Carmarthen Grammar School; Jesus College, Oxford; Hebrew University, Jerusalem. Consultant Economist. Asst Planner, Economic Development, Swansea City Council. Economist with Plastics firm. Member, Royal Economic Society. Secretary: Swansea Branch, NALGO; Welsh Branch, National Council for Civil liberties. Of Swansea.

THOMAS David Albert Terence: BA Lampeter) BA MA (Oxon) MTh PhD. Liberal: Cardiff North 1974, Feb; Withdrew as Carmarthen PPC 1979; SDP: Pontypridd B/E 1989; South Wales Euro 1989, Joined Labour 1991. Revd **Dr. Terry Thomas:** Born Drefach, Felindre, 26 May 1931, s of Albert John Thomas & Olwen Evans. Anglican. Married 1956 Rosemary Carole Davies, 3s. Educated Llandysul Grammar School; St. David's College, Lampeter; St. Catherine's College, Oxford; Serampore University, India. Ordained 1958. Diocese of St. Davids 1958-6. Church Missionary Society, India 1961-71. Sociologist; Arts Tutor, Open University 1971. Secretary, British Society of Religions 1987. Director, North American Paul Tillich Society 1988-91. Fellow, Royal Asiatic Society. Chair, local Residents Assn. Member, AUT. Hobbies: Angling, classical music, Spain. Languages: Welsh, English. Of Lakeside, Cardiff. *Publications: Terry Thomas: The British, Their Religious Beliefs and Practices 1988; The Encounter of Religions and Quasi Religions 1989.*

THOMAS David Alfred, 1st Viscount Rhondda, of Llanwern 1918: 1st Baron Rhondda 1910 PC 1916 JP 1881 DL (Glam) BA 1880 MA 1883 (Cantab). Guy Medal, Royal Statistical Society. Liberal MP Merthyr Tydfil B/E 1888 -Jan. 1910; Cardiff District Jan.-Dec. 1910. **Rt. Hon. D. A. Thomas:** Born Aberdare 26 March 1856, s of Samuel Thomas, Ysguborwen, coalowner, & Rachel, d of Morgan Joseph ME. Congregationalist-Agnostic. Married 1882, Sibyl Margaret, d of George Haig, Penaithen, Radnorshire, 1d. Educated Dr. Hudson's School, Clifton; Gonville & Caius College, Cambridge (Boxing Blue). Entered Mining Industry at Clydach Vale 1889. Coal Owner. Proprietor: Cambrian Combine (Cambrian, Albion, North's Navigation Collieries), & David Davis & Sons. Chair, Barry Dock Co. Landowner. President: South Wales Liberal Federation, 1893-97; Cardiff Chamber of Commerce 1895. Member: Ystradyfodwg Board of Health. Leading member, National Men's League for Women's Suffrage 1907. President, Board of Trade 1916-17. Board of Trade Controller for Food 1917-18. Of Llanwern, Newport & London. *The colossus of the South Wales Economy in his day.* Estate £883,645. Died 3 July 1918. *Books etc: D. A. Thomas, Some Notes on the Present State of the Coal Trade in the United Kingdom with Special Reference to that of South Wales and Monmouthshire 1896, The Growth and Direction of Our Foreign Trade in Coal During the Last Half Century 1903, The Industrial Struggle in Mid-Rhondda 1911. Further Reading: J. Vyrnwy Morgan: Life of Viscount Rhondda 1918, Viscountess Rhondda: D. A. Thomas Viscount Rhondda 1921.*

THOMAS David Emlyn: Labour MP Aberdare B/E 1946-. **Mr. Emlyn Thomas:** Born Maesteg, s of James Thomas, miner, 16 September 1892. Welsh Independent deacon. Married 1923, Bessie Thomas, teacher (died 1993) 1s 2d. Educated Maesteg Grammar School. Colliery clerk 1906-1. SWMF Official 1911-36. SWMF Aberdare District Secretary 1934-36. Miners' Agent 1936-46. Chair, Welsh Labour Group 1949-50. Member, Trecynon Choral Union. Of Trecynon, Aberdare. Languages: Welsh, English. Died 20 June 1964.

THOMAS David Eryl: MA (Oxon). SDP/Alliance: Ynys Môn 1983. **Mr. Eryl Thomas:** Born Ammanford, 27 September 1951, s of Enoch Thomas (later Head, Cardigan Grammar School). Educated Cardigan Grammar School; Amman Valley Grammar School; Jesus College, Oxford (PPE). Barrister, Grays Inn. Member, Liberal Democrat Economic Panel. Languages: English: Welsh. Of Cardigan.

THOMAS David John: Plaid Cymru: Newport East 1983. **Mr. David Thomas:** Born 1959. Tinplate Inspector, British Steel Corporation, Ebbw Vale. Chair: TGWU branch; Ebbw Vale Trades Council. Member, Labour Party; Joined Plaid Cymru.

THOMAS David Nicholas: Conservative, Blaenau Gwent & South/East List 1999; East Carmarthen & Dinefwr 2001; Carmarthenshire West & Pembrokeshire South 2003. **Mr. David Thomas:** Born Cwmgors 17 November 1941. Educated, St. Edmund's School, Canterbury; West London College of Commerce. Married Margaret Thomas, teacher, 1d. Worked for Shell Oil, Armstrong World Industries & Forbo Group. Principal, Towy Products 1989. Ex-marketing director, floor-covering companies. Former member, Plaid Cymru. Chair: Neath Conservative Assn. Deputy Chair, Gower Conservative Assn –1978; Mid & West Euro Tories 1978; South West Euro Conservatives 1998-. Chair: West Glamorgan Conservative Local Government Cttee. Contested W.Glam CC 1993. Member: Rotary; European Movement; English Speaking Union. Hobbies: Sport. Reading, Current Affairs. Languages: Welsh, English. Of Southgate, Gower.

THOMAS David Rees Dyfrig: BA (Wales). Plaid Cymru: Pembroke 1964. **Mr. Dyfrig Thomas:** Born, Cardigan, 13 July 1941, s of David John Aneurin Thomas, farmer, & Anne Jane Thomas, housewife. Welsh Independent. Married 1970, Marged Phillips, nurse. Educated Capel Iwan Primary School. Welsh book shop proprietor at Llanelli 1970- & Swansea (Ty Tawe) & teacher of Welsh in adult classes. Member, Plaid Cymru Youth Cttee; Agent for Pembroke 1966, 1970; Llanelli 1983. Llanelli TC 1999-. Contested Carmarthenshire CC (Ty Isha) 1999. Interests: Social Justice, Environment, Welsh Language. Hobbies: Reading, Internet/Computer, Chess, Walking. Languages: Welsh; English. Of Caedbach, Llanelli.

THOMAS David Rowland: KC 1931. Liberal: Merthyr 1923, Canterbury B/E 1911. **Mr. Rowland Thomas:** Born Merthyr Tydfil 1889. Presbyterian Church of Wales. Married d of William Evans, General Manager GKN steel. Educated Merthyr Tydfil elementary, higher grade & intermediate schools. Worked in Post Office, Cardiff, London, 1903. Journalist. Private Secretary (to Sir Edwin Cornwall, then Sir Albert Spicer). Barrister, Middle Temple 1909; Bencher. Recorder of Carmarthen 1935-41. Metropolitan Magistrate 1941-54. Languages: Welsh, English. Died 1955.

THOMAS David Wynford: LlB (Wales). Liberal: Pembroke 1970, Colchester Feb. 1974, Swansea

East 1983. **Revd Wynford Thomas:** Born Loughor, 19 March 1948. Unmarried. Educated Gowerton Grammar School; University of Wales, Aberystwyth (Deputy President SRC 1968-69, Student Member, University Court); Queen's College, Birmingham. Represented Wales on Duke of Edinburgh's Commonwealth Expedition to Canada 1967. Joined Liberal Party 1964. Chair, Welsh Young Liberals. Member, Executive, Liberal Party of Wales; Liberal Party Council. Lecturer in Law, Chelmsford. Ordained Church in Wales Deacon 1979; Priest 1980. Curate, St. Mary's with Holy Trinity & St. Mark's 1979-83; Priest in charge, St. Mark's, Waunwen 1973-79 Licensed to Office 1990. President, Manselton Council of Churches 1984-85. Lecturer, Swansea Technical College. National Trust Manager. Smallholder. Joined United Reformed Church. Of Swansea.

THOMAS David Wynne: Labour: Montgomery 1970. **Mr. Wynne Thomas:** Born Bethesda, 3 January 1941. Married 2c. Educated Ysgol Dyffryn Ogwen, Bethesda; Caernarfonshire & Denbighshire Technical Colleges. Apprentice Mechanical Engineer 1957. Design Draughtsman 1960-67. Student, Bolton College of Education (Technical) 1967-68. Lecturer in Mechanical Engineering, Rumney Technical College, Cardiff 1968-. Joined Labour Party 1962. Conwy Agent 1966. Bethesda UDC 1960-67. Member: AEU; ATTI; DATA; NALGO. Languages: Welsh, English. Of Cardiff.

THOMAS Dewi Wyn Hughes: Plaid Cymru: Aberdare 1964. **Mr. Dewi Thomas:** Born March 1925. Married 1d. Educated Aberdare Grammar School; Miner 1940-43; RAF 1943-45; Miner 1945-; Student, Treforest Technical College; Civil Engineer. Surveyor, Glamorgan Education Dept Hirwaun. Vaynor & Penderyn RDC 1963-64.

THOMAS Donald Martin, Baron Thomas of Gresford 1997: OBE 1982 QC 1979 MA LlB (Cantab). Liberal (Democrat): West Flint 1964. 1966, 1970; Wrexham Feb. & Oct. 1974, 1983, 1987. **Mr. Martin Thomas:** Born Meliden, Prestatyn 13 March 1967, s of Hywel Thomas, Town Inspector Superintendent & Olwen Thomas. Married 1961, Nan Kerr (died 2000) 3s (Andrew qv) 1d. Educated Grove Park School, Wrexham; Peterhouse, Cambridge. Wrexham Solicitor 1961-6. Lecturer, Flint Technical College 1966-68. Barrister, Grays Inn 1967 (defended in Brighton bomb case), Bencher 1989. Deputy Circuit Judge 1974-76. Crown Court Recorder 1976-. Deputy High Court Judge 1985-. A founder of the Welsh Liberal Party. President: Wrexham Liberal Assn. Vice-Chair: Welsh Liberal Party, 1967-74, Chair, 1969-74, 1977-80. President: Welsh Liberals 1977-79; Welsh Liberal Democrats 1993-94. Chaired session of Liberal Party Assembly, which decided to unite with SDP 1987. Vice-Chair, Marcher Sound Radio Ltd. 1991-. Member, Criminal Injuries Compensation Board; Welsh Rugby Coach & Referee. Hobbies: Rugby, Rowing, Golf, Music making, Fishing. Of Gresford, Wrexham.

THOMAS Dyfrig – see THOMAS David Rees Dyfrig.

THOMAS Eifion: BScEcon (Wales) 1977. Plaid Cymru: Gower 1979. **Mr. Eifion Thomas:** Born Llanelli, 1947. Married. Educated Ysgol Dewi Sant, Llanelli; Llandybie Grammar School; Ammanford Grammar School; Llanelli Technical College (ONC). In industry, 1963-72. Worked at Esso & Gulf oil refineries, Milford Haven; Coleg Harlech 1972-74; University of Wales, Swansea 1974-77 (Economics). Graduate Design Draughtsman. Spent time at Kibbutz Engedi. TU Official 3 years at Teddington Bellows, Pontarddulais. Joined Plaid Cymru 1964. Secretary, Gower Plaid Cymru. Contested West Glam CC 1977. Languages: Welsh, English. Of Gorseinon.

THOMAS Elwyn R: BA (Wales) DipSocSc (London). Liberal: Caernarfon 1950. **Mr. Elwyn Thomas:** Born Tywyn, Merioneth 1923, farmer's son. Educated Tywyn Grammar School; University of Wales, Aberystwyth (Economics); London School of Economics. Royal Navy 1941-45. Social Worker at Bristol & London 1949-50. Farmer. Director: Royal Welsh Agricultural Society. Member, Liberal Party Executive. Languages: Welsh, English.

THOMAS Gareth: LlB (Wales) Labour MP Clwyd West 1997-. **Mr. Gareth Thomas:** Born Bangor 25 September1954, s of William Thomas, toolmaker, & M. M. Humphreys. Presbyterian Church of Wales. Married 1987 Sioned Wyn, d of H. Jones, separated, 1s 1d. Educated Rock Ferry High School, Birkenhead; University of Wales, Aberystwyth; Council for Legal Education, London. Worked in insurance industry in UK and overseas. Loss Adjuster: Toplis & Harding; Guardian Royal Exchange. Barrister 1986. Member: MSF, Amnesty, SERA, SLL, Co-operative Party, Fabian Society. Flintshire CC 1995-97. Supports devolution & Proportional Representation. Failed to gain Assembly nomination 1999. PPS Paul Murphy, Secretary of State for Wales 2001. Interests: Wales, Agriculture, Work & Pensions, Home Affairs. Hobbies: Drama, Welsh History, Architecture, Gardening. Languages: Welsh, English, French.

THOMAS Garrod – see THOMAS Abraham G.

THOMAS Geraint – see THOMAS Daniel Geraint.

THOMAS Graham F: BA (Wales). Labour: Monmouth 1950. **Mr. Graham Thomas:** Born Cwmafan 1921. Married Ismay (Labour Party Welsh Women's Organiser) 2d. Educated elementary schools; University of Wales, Cardiff (History). Asst. Organiser, Further Education, Glamorgan -1951. WEA & YMCA Lecturer. Education Officer, Government of Sudan 1951-; Kenya. Education Officer, ICI Billingham. Lecturer, Slough College of Further Education. Warden, Buckinghamshire Adult Education College. Joined Labour Party 1937. *Books: Graham Thomas, Sudan 1950-85.*

THOMAS Griffith Bowen: Labour & Christian Socialist: Pembroke 1918. **Mr. G. B. Thomas:** Born Llanuwchchwydog 1867. Quarry Contractor. Secretary, Cilgerran District War Pensions Cttee.

THOMAS Gwenda: Labour AM Neath 1999-. **Mrs. Gwenda Thomas:** Born Cwmrhydyceirw, 22 January 1942, d of Helmas Evans, stonemason, & Menai Parry, housewife. Baptist. Married 1939 Morgan John Thomas, 1s. Educated Pontardawe Grammar School. Civil servant. Local organiser, Blood Transfusion Service. Supporter: Barnados, NSPCC, Mind. Represented Parent/Teachers Assn of Wales on Welsh Language Development Cttee. West Glamorgan CC (Chair, Social Services Cttee). Neath/Port Talbot BC (Chair: Social Services Cttee). Interests: Children's Issues, Social Services, Education. Hobbies: Reading, spending time with the family. Languages: Welsh, English. Of Gwauncaegurwen.

THOMAS Huw – see THOMAS Hywel Gruffydd.

THOMAS Huw Rhys: BA BD CertEd (Wales) 1972. Labour: Denbigh 1979. **Revd Huw Rhys Thomas:** Born Penrhos, Ystradgynlais 22 September 1949, s of W. J. Thomas & Renee Evans, shopkeepers. Married 1983, Nia (teacher) d of Revd Walford Llewelyn; 1s. Educated Maesydderwen Comprehensive School; University of Wales, Swansea (2a. Politics); Coleg Coffa, Aberystwyth 1972-73. Teacher (RE) John Bentiles School 1974-77. Church Secretary. Welsh Independent Minister, Ordained 1984. Gosen, Trebanos 1984-87; Soar, Blaendulais 1985- & Tabernacl, Skewen 1987-; Joined Labour Party 1968. On Aberavon parliamentary candidate list 2000. Languages: Welsh, English. Of Bryncoch.

THOMAS Hywel Gruffydd: LlB (Wales) MA (Cantab). Liberal: Llanelli 1950, Carmarthen 1970; Declined nomination for Rhondda West B/E 1967. **Mr. Huw Thomas:** Born Pembrey, September 1926. Married Anne (niece of Clement Davies MP) 3c. Educated Kidwelly Grammar School; University of Wales, Aberystwyth; Queens College, Cambridge. Vice-President, Cambridge

University Liberal Society. Barrister. ITA Newscaster. Television Consultant to UK & overseas companies. Liberal Agent, Carmarthen 1955. Languages: Welsh, English.

THOMAS Hywel Rhodri Glyn: BA BD MTh (Wales). Plaid Cymru: Carmarthen 1992, Carmarthenshire East & Dinefwr 1997, AM Carmarthenshire East & Dinefwr 1999-. **Revd Rhodri Glyn Thomas:** Born Wrexham 11 April 1953; s of Revd T. Glyn Thomas, Welsh Congregational Minister, & Eleanor Roberts, nurse. Married 1975, Marian Gwenifair (Welsh Adviser, Pembs CC) d of Gwilym Iorwerth Davies & Mary Sarah Green, educational adviser, 2s 1d. Educated Bodhyfryd School, Wrexham; Ysgol Morgan Llwyd, Wrexham; University of Wales, Aberystwyth (Welsh); Coleg Bala-Bangor, Lampeter (American Theology). Welsh Independent Minister, Ordained, 1978. Bethlehem, St. Clears & Elim, Llanddowror 1978-; added Capel Mair, St. Clears & Gibeon 1992. Managing Director, Cwmni Sgript Cyf (television programme production) 1989-96. Welsh Spokesman, Forum of Private Business. Director of Sgript Cyf. (Language Consultants). ComC. Chairman 1996-97. Chair: CND Cymru 1984-88; NSPCC, Mid & South West Wales Liaison Cttee (Member, British Council, NSPCC); school governors. Chair, Assembly Culture Cttee. Deputy Leader, Plaid Cymru Group. Shadow Minister: Environment, Planning & Countryside; Health 5.11.2003. Contested Assembly Group Leadership, September 2003. Interests: Culture; Sport; Rural Economy. Hobbies: Running, All Sport. Languages: Welsh; English. Of Llangynin, St. Clears.

THOMAS I. Emlyn: Liberal: Merioneth 1970. Joined Conservatives 1976. Conservative: Cardigan 1979. **Mr. Emlyn Thomas:** Born Carmarthen 1923. Married Gwenda, 2s 1d. Educated Llandovery College; Wolverhampton Technical College. Carmarthenshire County Secretary, Farmers Union of Wales 1957-66. General Secretary, Farmers Union of Wales 1966-68. General Secretary, Welsh Liberal Party Sept 1968-March 1970. Managing Director, plastics co at Llanybydder 1971. Secretary, Lampeter & District Self-Employed Action Group 1974, Chair 1975. Chair, All Wales Self Employed & Small Businesses Action Group. Member, Small Businesses Bureau. Languages: Welsh, English.

THOMAS Ian: United Socialist, South/East List 1999. **Mr. Ian Thomas:** Born Tredegar, 16 June 1965, s of Colin Arthur Thomas, miner, & Maureen Thomas, sew factory operative. Agnostic. Partner, Jill Bowen, social worker, 1d. Educated Blackwood Comprehensive School; Crosskeys College (night school). Fabricator, British Coal. Psychiatric Nurse. Joined Socialist Workers Party 1989. Joint Asst. Secretary, Cardiff & Vale Branch,

Unison. Interests: SWP, *Searchlight* (anti-Nazi magazine). Hobbies: Football, Reading, Films. Languages: Welsh (tipyn bach/ little), English. Of Pontllanffraith.

THOMAS Iorwerth Rhys: Labour MP Rhondda West 1950-. **Mr. Iori Thomas:** Born Clydach Vale, 22 January 1895, s of David William Thomas. Marxist & militant atheist. Married (1) Annie Mary d of D. J. Davies, Rhondda (died 1956) 1s 1d (2). Educated Cwmparc Elementary School. Miner 1908-14. Army 1914-18. Miner 1919-22. Checkweighman, Park & Dare Collieries 1922-50. Lodge Chair SWMF. Joined Labour Party 1918. Imprisoned for three months following disturbances at Parc & Dare collieries during General Strike 1927. Rhondda UDC 1928-51, Chairman 1938-39. Chair, Rhondda ARP Cttee 1940-45. Member, South Wales Electricity Board 1947-50. Languages: Welsh, English. Of Cwmparc. Died 3 December 1966.

THOMAS James Purdon Lewes, 1st Viscount Cilcennin of Caeglais 1955: PC 1951 MA (Oxon) KStJ. Conservative: Llanelli 1929, MP Hereford 1931-55. **Rt. Hon. J. P. L. Thomas:** Born Llandeilo 13 October, 1903, s of J. Lewes Thomas, Caeglas, & Anna Louise Purdon (Co. Clare). Unmarried. Educated Rugby School; Oriel College, Oxford. Assistant Private Secretary, Rt. Hon. Stanley Baldwin MP 1931. PPS 1932-40. Lord Commissioner 1940-43. Financial Secretary, Admiralty 1943-45. First Lord of the Admiralty 1951-56. Vice-Chair, Conservative Party 1945-51. Governor, Rugby School. Chair, Weekend Television. Lord Lieutenant, Herefordshire, 1957-. Of Colwell, Herefordshire & London. Died 13 July 1960. *Papers: Carmarthenshire Record Office (Correspondence and Papers 1936-60); Birmingham University Information Services, Special Collections, Papers pf (Robert) Anthony Eden, including correspondence with Thomas 1957-61; British Library: Correspondence with Paul Vychan Emrys-Evans MP 1937-60).*

THOMAS Jeffrey: QC 1974 LlB (London). Labour: Barry 1966; short-listed, Abertillery B/E 1965; MP Abertillery 1970-83. SDP/Alliance: Cardiff West 1983. **Mr. Jeffrey Thomas:** Born Abertillery, 12 November 1933, s of Jack Thomas, head-teacher, Married 1960, Margaret Jenkins. Educated Abertillery Grammar School; Kings College, London. President, University of London Union 1955-56. Barrister, Grays Inn 1957. Army 1959-61: Deputy Director, Army Legal Services, BAOR 1961. Crown Court Recorder 1975-. Joined Labour Party 1953, SDP 1981, Rejoined Labour Party 1988. Member: Justice, Fabian Society, CAWU, Court of National Museum, National Library & University of Wales, Aberystwyth. Vice-President: Western Valleys Sewage Board, North Monmouthshire Rugby Union. Contested Barnet UDC & Hertfordshire CC

1964-67. Member, Select Cttee on Conduct of Members 1976-77. PPS 1976-79. Chair, Welsh Labour Group 1980-81. Vice-Chair, UK Branch, Inter-Parliamentary Union 1979-82. Chair, British-Caribbean Assn. Died 1989.

THOMAS John Aeron: JP (Swansea). Liberal MP West Glamorgan 1900-06. **Mr. John Aeron Thomas:** Born Llanarth, Cards 1850, s of Lewis & Jane Thomas, Pantyrerod, & brother of Sir Abraham Garrod Thomas (qv). Congregationalist. Married 1880, Eleanor (died 1935), d of John Lewis JP. Dolgoy, Llandeilo. Educated Llwyn Rhydowen Grammar School; Milford Haven Grammar School. Solicitor 1878. Colliery Owner. Company Director: Weaver & Co (Millers); Swansea Cold Storage Co; William Edwards (Drapers); Cambrian Cold Storage Co. Chair: Bryn Tinplate Co, Berthlwyd Colliery Co, New Berthlwyd Colliery Co, Lime Firms. Ltd, Emlyn Anthracite Co, Garwen Granite Quarries, Limestone Products Ltd, Emlyn Brick Co, Ingram & Co (Coal Exporters), Aeron Thomas & Co (Timber Importers), Swansea United Breweries Ltd, Phoenix Patent Fuel Ltd. Swansea BC Mayor 1897-98, Alderman 1898. President, Swansea Cymmrodorion. Vice-President, Swansea Liberal Assn. Of Swansea & London. Languages: Welsh, English. Died three days after wife, 1 February 1935. Further Reading: *Kenneth O Morgan, The "Khaki Election" in Gower, Gower Journal, 1960.*

THOMAS John Maldwyn: Kt 1968 JP Glam FCIS. Liberal: Aberavon 1950, PPC West Flint, 1962-64. **Sir Maldwyn Thomas:** Born Taffs Well 17 June 1919, s of Daniel & Gwladys Thomas. Welsh Independent deacon. Married 1975, Maureen Elizabeth. Educated Porth Secondary School. Royal Army Service Corps 1939-45. With Lewis & Tyler Ltd. Cardiff 1940-56. Barrister, Grays Inn 1953 & 1987. Solicitor 1965. Company Secretary, Signode Ltd Swansea 1956-1959. Commercial Agreements Manager UK Atomic Energy Authority, Risley 1959-64, Rank Xerox. Secretary 1964-70, Managing Director & Chief Executive 1970-72, Chair 1972-79. Chair, European Govt Business Relations Council 1978-79. Director, Westland Helicopters Ltd 1989-94. Chair, Aberavon Divisional Liberal Assn. President, Welsh Liberal Party. Porthcawl UDC 1953-59. President, London Welsh Assn –2001. Vice-President, London Welsh RFC. Trustee, London Welsh School. Of Regents Park, London. Died August 2002.

THOMAS John Richard: BA (Wales). Plaid Cymru: Wrexham 1964, 1966, 1983. **Mr. John Thomas:** Born Llanaber, 11 February 1928, s of Richard Thomas, agricultural labourer, & Kate Roberts. Presbyterian Church of Wales elder. Married 1956, Mair, headteacher, d of E. Miles

Jones. Educated Barmouth Primary School; Barmouth Grammar School; University of Wales, Aberystwyth (Geography). Teacher (Geography), Rhosllanerchrugog Secondary School 1956-65. Deputy Head, Ysgol Morgan Llwyd, Wrexham 1966-88. Wrexham-Maelor DC 1973- (Mayor, 1981-82). Clwyd CC 1987-. President, UCAC 1976-77. Member, Executive, National Eisteddfod 1961. Chair, Executive, Wrexham National Eisteddfod 1977. Member: Court of the University of Wales, Bangor & Cardiff. Interests: Economic, social & cultural matters. Hobbies: Photography, Drama, Travel. Languages: Welsh; English. Of Rhosllanerchrugog.

THOMAS John Stradling: Kt 1985 BSc (London). Conservative: Aberavon 1964; Cardigan 1966; MP: Monmouth 1970-. **Sir John Stradling Thomas:** Born 10 June 1924, s of Roger Thomas & Catherine Delahaye. Married 1951, Freda Rhys Evans, 3c. Educated Bryntirion School, Bridgend; Rugby School; London University; Royal Veterinary College. Hon. Associate, Royal College of Veterinary Surgeons & British Veterinary Assn. Barrister, Inner Temple. Farmer & Company Director. Chair, Carmarthen Branch NFU. Member: NFU Council; NFU Welsh Council 1963-70. Carmarthen BC 1961-64. Member, Bow Group. President, Federation of Conservative Clubs 1984. Select Cttees Member: Civil List 1970-71, Trade & Industry, Commons Service Cttee 1979-83. Assistant Whip 1971-72. Lord Commissioner 1973-74. Opposition Whip 1974-79. Treasurer of the Household & Deputy Chief Whip 1979-83. Minister of State, Wales 1983-85. Associate MRCVS. Hon. Member BVA. Died 29 March 1991.

THOMAS Kathleen Patricia: Conservative, South East List 1999. **Mrs. Kay Thomas:** Born Cwmbran, 27 Feburary 1948, d of Patrick Cunningham, foundry worker, & Mary Elizabeth Meehan. Roman Catholic. Married 1979, Keith Timothy Thomas, naval officer, 3s 2d. Educated Our Lady of the Angels RC School. Product Advisor (worked mostly in customer services with local and national companies). Post Office Clerk. Practitioner of Complimentary Medicines. Adult Literacy Trainer. Sign Language Communicator. Teachers Aid Volunteer. Women's Aid Volunteer. Secretary & Deputy Chair: Torfaen Conservative Assn. Contested Torfaen BC B/E Interests: Health, Education. Hobbies: *Coronation Street,* Complimentary Medicines, Music, Theatre. Of Old Cwmbran.

THOMAS Keith L: Labour: Clwyd North West 1987. **Mr. Keith Thomas:** Born 27 August 1929. Married 2c. Educated Lincoln School; Liverpool Poly. Microbiologist. Laboratory technician at Lincoln & Ipswich then spent four years in India with World Health Organisation. Came to North

Wales 1962, and worked at Conwy, Rhyl & Ysbyty Glan Clwyd, Bodelwyddan. Retired 1984. Part-time Lecturer in Trade Union Studies. Liaison Officer, County Labour Party & Clwyd CC Labour Group. Secretary, North Wales Branch, ASTMS. .

THOMAS Kenneth Pryce: BA (Wales) 1938. Plaid Cymru: Aberdare 1959. **Mr. Ken Thomas:** Born December 1915. Welsh Independent lay preacher & deacon. Married 3d. Educated Tonypandy Grammar School; University of Wales, Cardiff; St. David's College, Lampeter. Teacher (History & RE), Pontypridd. Secretary, Treorchy branch, Plaid Cymru. Contested local elections. Of Treorchy.

THOMAS Leigh Simon: BSc (Wales). Plaid Cymru, Islwyn 2001. **Mr. Leigh Thomas:** Born Tredegar, 17 October 1970, s of Carey Gwilym Frederick James Thomas, carpenter/joiner, & Pearl Susan Thomas, publican. Married 1998, Paula Jane Davies, hairdresser/beautician. Educated Blackwood Comprehensive School; Crosskeys FE College; University of Wales, Cardiff (Geology), Equal Opportunities Sabbatical Officer 1993, Welsh Affairs Convenor & Spokesperson 1992, President SRC 1994-95. With FT, London, 1994-98. Senior Account Manager, NTL Media. Member, Labour Party 1994-98. Joined Plaid Cymru 1998; Chair, Blackwood branch 2000-01; Islwyn Constituency 2001-02; Member, National Council, 1999-2001. Founder Member, SWS society, London. Interests: Training & Youth Opportunities; Student hardship, Poverty, Environment, Constitutional affairs. Languages: English; Welsh learner; Basic French. Hobbies: Computers, Rugby, Sports, Reading, Pressurised DIY, Socialising. Of Blackwood.

THOMAS Merfyn: TD. Conservative, Assembly North List, 1999. **Major Mervyn Thomas:** Born Bangor, 15 September 1942, son of Owen Thomas, railway shunter, & Mair Ena Williams, ladies' hairdresser. Church in Wales. Married 1966 Diana Mair Thomas, 2d. Educated Friars Grammar School, Bangor; HMS. Conway. Deck Officer, Merchant Navy 1962-64. Family Business 1964-78. Partner/Director, Terry Platt Wine Merchants, Llandudno Junction 1987-92. Wine Consultant & Lecturer, Grants of St. James 1992-94. Ministry of Defence, undergraduate management training 1994. Regional Manager, East Anglia & London, NAAFI, 1994-96. Consultant, Prudential Assurance Corporation 1996-. Major, Territorial Army. Retired. Holds Private Pilots Licence. Fund Raiser: KRUFTS (Kidney Research) & Cancer Research. School Governor. Chair, PTA. Languages: Welsh, English. Of Beaumaris.

THOMAS Nigel Matthew: LlB (Wales) MA (Cantab). Conservative: Carmarthen 1979, 1983; Southport 1987. **Mr. Nigel Thomas:** Born St. Clears 18 March1952. Educated Whitland Grammar School; University of Wales, Aberystwyth; Emmanuel College, Cambridge. Chair, University of Wales, Aberystwyth, Conservative Assn; University Conservative Assn. Barrister. Asst Secretary, Society of Conservative Lawyers 1978. Editor, *The Encyclopaedia of Capital Taxation.* Tutor in Land Law, University College, London.

THOMAS Noel Bell: MB ChB (Edinburgh & Cambridge) MA (Cambridge) 1965 DObst RCOG 1970 DCH (England) 1972. Ecology Party: Ogmore 1983. **Dr. Noel Thomas:** Born Maesteg 1945. Married 2s. Educated Edinburgh University. Medical Practitioner. Member, Medical Campaign against Nuclear Weapons. Joined Ecology Party 1973. Obtained highest vote ever recorded for the Ecology Party. Of Maesteg.

THOMAS Noel Kennedy: BA (Wales) PhD (Birmingham). Liberal: Brecon & Radnor Feb. & Oct. 1974. **Dr. Noel Thomas:** Born Wrexham, December 1929. Married Jackie, 2c. Educated Grove Park Grammar School, Wrexham; University of Wales, Bangor; Birmingham University. Taught in Finland, Cyprus, Swaziland & South Africa; Principal Lecturer in English, Westhill College of Education, Birmingham. President, Selly Oak Liberal Assn.

THOMAS Owen: Kt 1917 JP1894 DL (Anglesey) 1919. Labour/Coalitionist MP Anglesey 1918-. Resigned from Labour Party Oct. 1920. Liberal: Oswestry 1895. **Brigadier, Sir Owen Thomas:** Born Llanfechell, Anglesey 18 December 1858, s of Owen Thomas, Carrog, substantial farmer & Ellen, d of William Jones-Roberts. Welsh Independent Deacon. Married 1887, Fredericka Wilhelmina Shelton Perhouse, 4s 1d (3 sons killed in Great War). Educated Llanfechell National School; Clwyd Bank Academy, Ruthin, Liverpool College (1872). Freemason. Worked on family farm 1876, Estate Steward until 1898. Chair, Anglesey Liberal Assn 1892. Founded Rifle Volunteers at Cemaes 1887. Militia Captain 1886, Manchester Regt, then RWF; Army Captain 1893; Major 1894; South African War (Colonel); Great War; Brigadier-General 1914; Raised Welsh Brigades. Farmer & Managing Director. General Manager & Director, East African Estates 1908. Secretary, Cemaes Regatta. Chief Officer, Cemaes Life Saving Apparatus Station 1876. Chair, Anglesey Welsh Independents Assn. 1894. President, Anglesey Agricultural Society 1894. Member, Royal Commission on Causes of Rural Depression 1893-97. High Sheriff of Anglesey 1893. Anglesey CC Alderman 1888-. Backed by Anglesey Conservatives in 1922. Languages: Welsh, English. Of Llanfechell (1888). Estate £15,377. DIED 6 March 1923. *Books: Owen Thomas, Agricultural Prospects of South*

Africa. Further Reading: *David A. Pretty, "Rhyfelwr Môn", Gwasg Gee, 1989.*

THOMAS Owen John: MA (Wales) 1990 CertEd 1971. Plaid Cymru: Cardiff North 1979, Cardiff Central 1999, 2003; AM South/Central List 1999-. **Mr. Owen John Thomas:** Born Cardiff, 3 October 1939, son of John Owen Thomas, pharmacist, & Evelyn Jones. Married (1) 1d (2) 1985 Siân Wyn Thomas, 3s. Educated Howardian High School, Cardiff; Glamorgan College of Education, Barry. Tax Officer, Inland Revenue 1956-61/Chemical Analyst 1961-68. Primary school teacher 1971-79. Deputy Head, Cathays Primary School 1989-99. Chair: Cardiff Region UCAC, Cardiff District Plaid Cymru, Plasnewydd Leaseholders Assn. Joined Plaid Cymru 1959. Contested Cardiff CC. Shadow Minister, Culture, Sport & Welsh language. Interests: Education, Employment. Hobbies: Walking, Listening to light music, Reading, Writing, Psephology, Study of election statistics, Local history, Rugby, Welsh baseball. Languages: Welsh, English. Of Cardiff.

THOMAS Paul Selwyn: ACA 1954. Conservative: Pontypool B/E 1958, 1959. **Mr. Paul Thomas:** Born Cornwall, August 1930. Anglican. Married Patricia SRN 2d. Educated Truro Cathedral School. Chartered Accountant. Chair, Cornwall YCs Federation. Member, Young Conservatives National Advisory Cttee. Vice-Chair, Western Area Young Conservatives; Cornwall Federation of Conservative & Unionist Assns. Truro UDC 1953-58. Of Perranporth.

THOMAS Peter John Mitchell, Baron Thomas of Gwydir 1987: PC 1964 QC 1964 MA (Oxon). Conservative MP Conway 1951-64, Hendon South 1970-87. **Rt. Hon. Peter Thomas:** Born Llanrwst 31 July 1920, s of David Thomas, solicitor, & Anne Gwendoline Mitchell. Married 1947, Frances Elizabeth Theresa (died 1985) d. of Basil Dean & Lady Mercy Greville, 4c. Educated Llanrwst Grammar School; Epworth College, Rhyl; Jesus College, Oxford. RAF 1939-45. POW 1941-45. Barrister, Middle Temple 1947, Master of the Bench 1971, Emeritus 1991. Deputy Chair of Quarter Sessions: Cheshire 1966-70; Denbighshire 1968-70. Arbiter, Court of Arbitration, International Chamber of Commerce, Paris 1974-8. Crown Court Recorder 1974-88. Company Director. Joined Conservative Party 1938. PPS 1954-59. Parl-Secretary. Labour 1959-61. Under-Secretary, Foreign Affairs 1961-63. Minister of State, Foreign Affairs 1963-64. Secretary of State for Wales 1970-74. Chief Opposition Spokesman on Wales 1974-75. Chair, Conservative Party Organisation 1970-72. President, National Union of Conservative & Unionist Assns 1974-7. Chair, Select Cttees: Members' Salaries 1981-82; Standing Orders. Member, Select Cttee on Conduct of Members 1977; Select Cttee on Procedure (Sup-

ply) 1982. Hon. Member, Gorsedd 1965. Member, Historic Buildings Council for Wales 1965-67. Vice-President, Hon. Society of Cymmrodorion. Hon. Fellow, Jesus College, Oxford 2001. Of Elstead, Surrey.

THOMAS Ralph Morton: LlB (Wales). Conservative: Ogmore 1964, 1966. **Mr. Ralph Thomas:** Born Treorchy, April 1929, s of John Thomas, Estate Agent. Married Sheila, 2s. Educated Pentre Grammar School; University of Wales, Aberystwyth. Army, 1947-40, Lieutenant RASC. Solicitor. Chair, Rhondda Young Conservatives 1951. Secretary, Glamorgan Federation of Angling Clubs. Bridgend UDC 1962- (Leader; Chair, Town Planning & Development Cttee). Chair, Bridgend Town Hall Trust. Vice-President, Pontypridd & District Law Society 1969-71.

THOMAS Rhodri – see THOMAS Hywel R. G.

THOMAS Richard Clement Charles: MA (Cantab). Liberal: Gower Feb. 1974, Carmarthen 1979; Mid-Wales Euro 1979. **Mr. Clem Thomas:** Born Brynaman 28 January 1929, s of D. J. Thomas, butcher. Married 1954, 3s 1d, divorced (2) Joyce. Educated Blundells School; St. Johns College, Cambridge. Farmer & Managing Director, Meat Company. Rugby Correspondent, *The Guardian, The Observer;* broadcaster. Captain, Welsh Secondary Schools Rugby XV, Swansea XV, Welsh XV; Cambridge Blue; Member, British Lions XV. Treasurer, Swansea Liberal Assn; Liberal Party of Wales Social Cttee. Member, Cttee of Welsh National Sports Assn for the Disabled; Cttee, Welsh National Council for the Disabled; Member: Anti-Apartheid Movement. Languages: Welsh, English. Of Southgate, Gower. Died 5 September 1996.

THOMAS Robert John: 1st Bart 1918 JP DL (Denbs). (Coalition) Liberal MP: Wrexham 1918-22; Anglesey 1923-29. **Sir Robert Thomas:** Born 23 April, 1873, s of William & Catherine Thomas. Calvinistic Methodist Elder. Married 1905, Marie Rose (died 1948) d. of Arthur Burrows, 2s 1d. Educated Bootle College; Liverpool Institute; Tettenhall College, Staffs. Ship & Insurance Broker & Underwriter. Founder & Hon. Secretary, North Wales Heroes Memorial Hospital. High Sheriff of Anglesey 1918. Anglesey CC. Member, Council, University College, Bangor. Discharged as a Bankrupt, Nov. 1935. Of Holyhead. Died 27 September 1951.

THOMAS Roger: UK Independence Party, South/East List 2003. Married 1991, 2c. Railway Electrician 1985. Of Portskewett.

THOMAS Roger Gareth: Labour MP: Carmarthen 1979-89. **Dr. Roger Thomas:** Born Garnant, 14 November 1925, s of Evan J. Thomas, miner,

& Beryl Thomas. Married Indeg, d of Revd Thomas, Welsh Independent Minister, 1s 1d. Educated Ammanford Grammar School; London Hospital Medical School. Medical Practitioner. Captain RAMC 1949-52. Joined Labour Party 1970. Member, Fabian Society. Dyfed CC 1977-79. Opposition Spokesman on Welsh Affairs. Member, Select Cttee on Welsh Affairs 1979-. Died 1 September 1994.

THOMAS Siân Elizabeth: BA MA MEd (Wales). Plaid Cymru, Mid & West list 2003. **Mrs. Siân Thomas:** Born Ystradgynlais, 14 March 1950, d of Sulwyn L. A. M. Lewis, headmaster & founder of UNESCO in Wales, & Margaret Glenys Daniel, teacher. Married 1981, David Oliver Thomas, teacher. Educated Ystalyfera Grammar School; University of Wales, Aberystwyth (Education & Philosophy), University of Wales, Swansea; Trinity College, Carmarthen. (DipRE DipVoc Counselling). Lecturer in Information Technology. Author. Examiner, OCR Examination Board. Carmarthenshire CC (Chair, Plaid Cymru Group; Chair, Gwendraeth Area Cttee; Vice-Chair, Environment Scrutiny). Joined Plaid Cymru 1966; Member, National Executive. Member: Court, University of Wales, Aberystwyth; Diabetes UK Campaigners Network. Interests: Green Issues, Women's Issues, Equality Issues. Hobbies: Swimming, Foreign Exchanges. Of Castell y Rhingyll, near Crosshands. *Books: Siân Thomas, Tri llawlfyr ar ddysgu IT: Prosesu Geiriau;Taenlen; Bas Data; Barddoniaeth, Storïau Byrion.*

THOMAS Simon: BA (Wales). Plaid Cymru, Mid & West List 1999, MP Ceredigion B/E 2000-. **Mr. Simon Thomas:** Born Aberdare, 20 December 1963 (gs of Emrys Jones, Labour UDC). Married, Gwen, d of Professor Gareth Alban Davies 1s 1d. Educated Aberdare Boys County Grammar School; University of Wales, Aberystwyth (Welsh); College of Librarianship, Aberystwyth (DipLib Wales). With Wales Council for Voluntary Action 1994-200. Policy & Research Officer, Plaid Cymru Group, Rhondda/Cynon Taf BC. Director of Policy & Research, Plaid Cymru 1995-98. Manager, Jigso, rural regeneration programme. Asst Curator, National Library. Ceredigion CC (Penparciau). Member, Plaid Cymru Policy Team. Interests: Sustainable Development, rural development culture & language. Hobbies: Walking, Cycling, Family Life. Languages: Welsh, English. Of Aberystwyth.

THOMAS Stephen Vaughan: BA (Oxon) MSc (Wales) Plaid Cymru, Monmouth 2003. **Mr. Stephen Thomas:** Born Morriston 14 February 1959, s of Kenneth Mostyn Vaughan Thomas, sub-postmaster, & Thelma Theophilus Thomas, shopkeeper. 1d. Educated Llandovery College; Jesus College, Oxford; University of Wales, Cardiff. Director, Welsh Centre for International Affairs. Chair: Plaid Cymru, Cardiff West 2001-. Interests: International Development, Foreign Policy. Hobbies: Cricket, Walking. Languages: Welsh, English, French, Portuguese. Of Pontcanna, Cardiff.

Rt. Hon. George Thomas.

THOMAS Thomas George 1st & last Viscount Tonypandy 1983: PC 1968 Hon. DCL Oxford 1983 Hon. LLD Asbury College Kentucky 1976, Southampton 1977, Wales 1977, Birmingham 1978, Oklahoma 1981, Liverpool 1982, Leeds 1983, Keele 1984, Warwick 1984, Open University 1984. Hon. DD Centenary Univ. Lousiana 1982. Data Setoa Negara, Brunei 1971. Grand Cross of the Peruvian Congress 1982. Gold Medal for Democratic Services, Carinthia 1982. Silver Medal of St. Paul & St. Barnabas, Cyprus 1989. Labour MP: Cardiff Central 1945-50; Cardiff West 1950-83. **Rt. Hon. George Thomas:** Born Port Talbot 1909, s of Zachariah Thomas, miner, & Emma Jane Tilbury (died 1972). Methodist lay preacher. Unmarried. Educated Tonypandy Grammar School; University College, Southampton. Teacher. President, Cardiff Teachers' Assn (NUT). Executive Member, NUT 1940-45; National Union of Labour Teachers. Special Policeman 1940-45, sergeant. President: British Heart Foundation; National Brotherhood Movement 1955; Luton Industrial College 1982l College of Preceptors 1984-87; National Children's Home 1990- (Chair 1983-89). Vice-President, Methodist Conference 1960-61. Joined Labour Party 1924. Chair, Welsh PLP 1950-51. 1st Chair, Welsh Grand Cttee 1951. Member, Speaker's Panel of Chairmen 1951-64. PPS 1951. Under-Secretary, Home Affairs 1964-66. Minister of State, Wales 1966-67. Minister of State, Commonwealth Office 1967-68. Secretary of State for Wales 1968-70. Chief Opposition Spokesman, Wales 1970-74. Chair of Ways & Means & Deputy Speaker 1974-76. Speaker of the House of Commons 1976-83. Governor, University of Wales. Jt Chair: Commonwealth Societies Council 1984-87. Chair, Bank of Wales 1989-91. Freeman: Rhondda 1970, Cardiff 1975, City of London 1980, Paphos 1989. Hon. Fellow: University of Wales, Cardiff 1973, College of Preceptors 1977, Polytechnic of Wales 1982, St. Hugh's College Oxford, 1983, Hertford College, Oxford 1983, Faculty of Building 1983, Westminster College, Oxford 1990, Trinity College, Carmarthen 1994. Hon. Companion, Leicester Polytechnic 1989. William Hopkins Bronze Medal, St. David's Society NY 1982. Opposed European integration. President, Campaign Against a Welsh Assembly 1997. Cancer 1988. Died 21 September 1997. *Books: T. G. Thomas, The Christian Heritage in Politics 1960, George Thomas Mr. Speaker 1965, My Wales 1986.*

THOMAS William David: Liberal: Rhondda East B/E March 1933. **Mr. W. D. Thomas:** Born Maerdy, s of miner killed underground. Porth Solicitor 1928. Rhondda UDC 1929. Died 24 December 1941.

THOMAS William Stanley Russell: MA MB BChir (Cantab) MRCS LRCP. Liberal: Brecon & Radnor 1955, Ilford 1931, Central Aberdeenshire 1935, Ross & Cromarty B/E 1936, Southampton 1945, Middlesborough East 1950, Liberal National MP: Southampton B/E 1940-45; PPC East Ham North 1931; Hillsborough 1937-40. **Dr. Russell Thomas:** Born Talgarth 5 February 1896, s of David & Mary Thomas. Married 1922, Kathleen Maud, d. of Raymond Bennett. Educated Brecon County School; Christ's College, Brecon; Queens College, Cambridge; Guy's Hospital. Medical Practitioner. Barrister, Lincolns Inn 1930. RNVR 1914-18. Member, Select Cttees: National Expenditure 1942-45; Public Petitions 1942-44. Vice-President, National Federation of Property Owners. National Chair, RSPCA 1951-52. Chair, London Area, Liberal National Party 1937-45. Caterham & Wallington UDC. Of Warlingham. Died 21 March 1957.

THOMAS Wynne – see THOMAS David Wynne.

THOMASON Kenneth Roy: LlB (London). Conservative: Newport East 1983; MP Bromsgrove 1992-97. **Mr. Roy Thomason:** Born 14 December 1944, s of Thomas Roger & Constance Dora Thomason. Married 1969, Christine Ann Parsons 4c. Educated Cheney School, Oxford; London University. Solicitor 1969. Partner 1970-91, Senior Partner 1979-91, Horden & George, Bournemouth. Companies Adviser Member, Pension Trust Panel. Chair: Bournemouth West Conservative Assn 1981-82; Wessex Advisory Cttee, Conservative Party 1983-86. Bournemouth BC 1970-92 (Leader 1974-82), Chair: Policy, Ways and Means & Finance Cttees). Member, Association of District Councils1987-91 (Council Member 1979-91, Leader 1981-87; Chair 1987-91, Chair, Housing & Environmental Health Cttee 1983-

87). Vice-Chair, National Local Government Advisory Cttee 1988-91. Member, National Union Executive Cttee 1988-91. Member: Select Cttee on Environment 1992-97; Jt Statutory Instrument Cttee 1992-97; Conservative Parl Environment Cttee 1993-97.

THOMPSETT Alan Colin: Referendum Party: Newport West 1997. **Mr. Colin Thompsett:** Born Ebbw Vale 1932. Married Annie, nurse, 3c. Educated Usk Farm Institute; Seale-Hayne Agricultural College. Worked in heating, plumbing & financial services. Of, Abergavenny.

THOMPSON Frank Robert: BA DipEd (Hull). Labour: Monmouth Feb. 1974, South Norfolk 1964; Wells 1970. **Mr. Frank Thompson:** Born Newark 1 January 1938, s of Arthur Richard Thompson. Married Deidre Skinner, teacher, 1s 1d. Educated Magnus Grammar School, Newark; Hull University (English). Teacher & Careers Counsellor at a comprehensive school. Principal, Swindon FE College. Lecturer in Liberal Studies, East Mon. FE College. Retired 1990. Member: NUT, NALGO, Co-operative Party, Fabian Society. Gloucestershire CC 1981-. Deputy Group Leader 1982-, Assn of County Councils Executive. Of Trelleck.

THOMPSON Samuel: Conservative: West Denbighshire, December 1910. **Mr. Sam Thompson:** Born New York 5 April 1878 (father died before he was born; mother returned to Bryncoch, Cardiganshire). Anglican. Cardiganshire leadminer at 12. Coalminer at Tylorstown. Joined Tylorstown Conservative Club 1897. Chair, Rhondda Conservative Assn 1902-03. Joined staff of National Union of Conservative & Unionist Assns. Languages: Welsh, English.

THOMSON Alan: BSc MSc (Wales). United Socialist, South West List 1999, Swansea East B/E 2001, 2003. **Mr. Alan Thomson:** Born London, 25 September 1969, s of John Lawrence Thomson & Bridget Thomson. Atheist. Married 2000, Michelle Thomson, 2s 1d. Educated Thomas Tallis Comprehensive School, Kidbrooke, London; University of Wales, Swansea (American Management Studies, Computer Studies). Computer Technician, Swansea College. Unison Shop Steward. Member: Socialist Workers Party. Agent, Aberavon 1999, Swansea West 2001. Interests: Revolutionary Socialist. Of Birchgrove, Swansea (1988).

THORNEYCROFT George Edward Peter, Baron Thorneycroft of Dunston 1967: PC 1951. Conservative MP: Monmouth B/E 1945-66; Stafford, B/E 1938-45. **Captain, Rt. Hon. Peter Thorneycroft:** Born Dunston, Staffs. 26 July 1909, s of Major George E. M. Thorneycroft & Dorothy, d. of Sir William Franklyn. Married (1) 1938, Sheila

Wells Paget, 1s, divorced 1949 (2) 1949, Countess Carla Roberti, 1d. Educated Eton; RMA Woolwich. Royal Artillery 1930-33, 1939-45. Barrister, Inner Temple 1934. Parl-Secretary, Transport 1945. President, Board of Trade 1951-57. Chancellor of the Exchequer 1957-58 (resigned with Enoch Powell & Nigel Birch in disagreement over policy). Minister of Aviation 1960-62. Minister of Defence 1962-64. Chair, Conservative Party 1973-81. Chair, Pirelli Ltd; A.E.G. Unit Trust (Managers) Ltd. Chair: Commonwealth Trust Fund. Died 1994. *Papers at Southampton University. Books: G. E. P. Thorneycroft, The Amateur: A Companion to Watercolour 1985.*

THRAVES Alec: BA (Wales). United Socialists, Swansea West & Mid & West List 1999, Swansea West 2001. **Mr. Alec Thraves:** Born Swansea 12 March 1950, s of Alec Thraves, factory worker, & Pearl Thraves, school cleaner. Atheist. Married divorced, 1s 2d. Educated Penlan Comprehensive School, Swansea; University of Wales, Newport (DipTUStudies); University of Wales, Swansea (Politics). Fitter & Turner/Technician. Political Organiser (Wales), Socialist Party. Member, Labour Party 1974, expelled 1994. Member, Swansea Trades Council. Interests: Overthrowing Capitalism. Hobbies: Weight Training, Walking, Travelling. Of Swansea.

TIARKS John Christopher: MB BChir 1963 MA1964 (Cantab) MRCGP (St. Thomas) 1972. Protect the Health Service Candidate, Vale of Glamorgan BE 1989. **Dr. Chris Tiarks:** Born 1948. Married. Educated Cambridge University; St. Thomas' Hospital, London. Medical Practitioner of Peterston super Ely. Resigned to contest the by-election. Founded the National Health Service Supporters Party, December 1989, with plans to fight 50 seats but the party had a disastrous result in the Mid Staffordshire B/E March 1990 and faded away. Took on a one-doctor practice on the Isle of Eigg after the by-election, then at Bourne End. Member, BMA Council. Deputy Chair: General Practitioners Cttee, Scotland. Of Bourne End, Herts.

TILBY Henry Albert: OBE JP. Conservative: Flint District Jan. 1910. **Mr. Henry Tilby:** Born Deptford 1867 (father died 1877). Anglican. Pupil teacher at 13. Worked at confectioner's at weekends. Won scholarship to a London college but did not take it up. Student at Trinity College, Carmarthen. Head-teacher, Clwyd Street National School, Rhyl 1888-1904. President: Rhyl & Holywell Teachers' Assn, North Wales Council of Organised Teachers, Member NUT Executive. Secretary/Agent, Flintshire Conservative Assn 1904-11. Clerk of the Peace & Clerk to Flintshire County Council 1911-32. Joint Secretary. Rhyl National Eisteddfod 1904. Rhyl UDC 1894- (Chair,

Finance Cttee) Chairman 1900. Established munitions factories & raised a RWF battalion in Great War. Local Organiser, Church Defence League. Member, St. Asaph Diocesan Schools Board. Of Rhyl. Retired to Thames Ditton 1932.

TILLETT Benjamin: Labour: Swansea Town Jan. 1910; Bradford West 1892, Eccles 1906; Pro-War-Ind Labour MP, Salford North B/E 1918. Labour MP Salford North 1918-24, 1929-31. **Mr. Ben Tillett:** Born Lower Easton, Bristol 1st September 1860, s of Benjamin Tillett, labourer, & Elizabeth Lane (died 1861). Brought up by series of stepmothers & other relatives; tried twice to run away before age of 6. Congregational lay preacher. Barely literate until 17; became voracious reader. Married 1882, Jane Tompkins (died 1926) 2d. Brickyard Worker at 6. Ran away at 8 & joined circus. Brought home by sister a year later & sent to National School at Stafford; expelled after a few days for 'assaulting a teacher who struck him'. Fishing boats at 12, Royal Navy at 13 (invalided out at 16). Merchant Navy, Tea Porter, London Docks. Formed Union of Tea Porters & General Dock Labourers (with 300 members. Founder/General Secretary, Dock, Riverside & General Workers' Union 1877-1922. International & Political Secretary TGWU 1922-. Instigated & Led London strikes 1889. Helped found London CC, Alderman 1892-98. Imprisoned and deported at Antwerp & Hamburg when involved in dockers' disputes. Member: War Emergency Workers' National Cttee President TUC 1929. Freemason. Joined MRA in last years; close friend of Frank Buchman. Estate £168. Died 27 January 1941. *Books: Ben Tillett: Memories and Reflections (autobiography) 1931. Further Reading: George Light: Ben Tillett, Fighter & Pioneer (pamphlet) 1941. David Cleaver, The General Election Contest in the Swansea Town constituency, January 1910 – the Socialist Challenge; Llafur 1990, Vol. 5, No. 10, page 29.*

TITHERINGTON Ian Richard: BEng (Wales). Plaid Cymru, South/West List 1999, Swansea West 2001. **Mr. Ian Titherington:** Born Swansea, 1 August 1966, son of Harrison Titherington, Accountant, & Elizabeth Iris Davies, Secretary. Church in Wales. Partner, Anna. Educated Sketty Primary School; Olchfa Comprehensive School; Polytechnic of Wales. Civil Engineer. Worked in local government. Unison Shop Steward. Secretary, Swansea West Plaid Cymru, Agent 1999. Member, Plaid Cymru National Executive, Secretary, Undeb (Plaid Trade Union Section), Press Officer, Plaid Cymru Swansea West. Contested Swansea CC (Sketty) 1999. Ex-Media Officer, Dunvant RFC XV. Interests: Transport, Environment, International development, Health. Hobbies: Weight training, Surfing, Socialising Of Sketty, Swansea.

TIVERTON Viscount (Hardinge Goulburn Giffard), 2nd Earl of Halsbury: Viscount Tiverton (1898), Baron Tiverton 1885. KC 1923 MA (Oxon). Conservative: Carmarthen District 1906. **Viscount Tiverton:** Born 1880, s of 1st Earl (Contested Cardiff District 1874) & Wilhelmina, d of Henry Woodfall. Anglican. Married 1907, Esme, d of James S. Wallace. Major RAF 1918. Barrister, Inner Temple. Recorder of Carmarthen 1923-. Died 15 September 1943.

TOFARIDES George David: Socialist Labour, Mid & West List 1999, Euro List 1999. **Mr. George Tofarides:** Of Hay on Wye.

TOUHIG James Donnelly: Labour/Co-op MP: Islwyn B/E 1995-; Richmond & Barnes 1992. **Mr. Don Touhig:** Born Abersychan 5 December 1947. Roman Catholic (Papal Knight of Order of St. Sylvester). Married 4c. Educated St. Francis RC School, Abersychan; East Mon FE College. Journalist 1968-76, General Manager/Editor in Chief, *Free Press* Group 1988-92. General Manager (business development) Bailey Group 1992-93; Bailey Print 1993-95. Gwent CC 1973-95 (Chair, Finance Cttee). Secretary, Welsh Labour MPs 1995-. Chair, All Party Alcohol Misuse Group 1996-. Parliamentary Adviser, Police Federation. Member: Co-operative Party Council; Labour Party Welsh Executive; Mencap, Mensa. Press officer, Glenys Kinnock, 1994 Euro election. Member: Welsh Affairs Select Cttee 1996-97. Secretary, Welsh Labour Group 1995-99/Vice-Chair, All Party Penal Affairs Cttee. Secretary: All Party Police Group. PPS to Chancellor of the Exchequer 1997-99, resigned 27/7/99 after document's leak & suspended from the House July 7 1999. Hobbies: Cooking for family & friends, Reading, Music, Visiting France. Of Hafod-yr-ynys.

TOWNSEND Charles Edward: BA (Leicester) MBA (Wales). Liberal Democrat, Blaenau Gwent 2001. **Mr. Ed Townsend:** Born Wallasey, 28 August 1951, s of Eric Charles Townsend, schoolmaster, & Hilda Myfanwy Townsend, road safety officer. Married 1976, Carmel Townsend 2s 4d. Educated Wallasey Grammar School; Horace Mann School, New York; University of Leicester (Politics); Cardiff Business School. Journalist, Merseyside 1973-77. Press Officer, Dunlop & National Girobank 1977-80. Journalist, *Daily Post* 1980-85. Press & PR Manager, BT 1985. PR Consultant. Chair: Birkenhead Lib Dems. Contested Wirral BC, Newport BC; Gwent CC. President: Newport Chamber of Commerce. Chair: Welsh Liberal Democrat Candidates Cttee 2001-. Secretary, Welsh Lib Dem Campaigns Cttee 2000-. Member, Welsh Liberal Democrats National Executive. Interests: Transport, Social Justice. Hobbies: Canoeing, Walking, Cooking.

Languages: Learning Welsh, English, French, German. Of Newport.

TOYE John William Andrew: MIBM. Liberal Democrat: Newport West 1992. **Mr. Andrew Toye:** Born 1961. Married 3c. Educated Gwent HE College. Army 5 years. Taught business studies. Management consultant. Owner, photographic & marketing business. South Glam CC. Of Michaelston y Fedw.

TRAHERNE Cennydd George: KG 1970 Kt 1964 JP 1946 DL (Glam) 1946 TD 1950 Hon. LLD (Wales) 1966 KStJ GCStJ 1991 MA (Oxon). Conservative: Pontypridd 1945. **Colonel, Sir Cennydd Traherne:** Born Coedarhydyglyn nr. Cardiff, 14 December 1910, s of Comdr. Llewellyn Edmund Traherne & Dorothy, d of G F S Sinclair. Anglican. Married Olivera Rowena, d. of James Binney & Lady Margaret Binney, Bampisford Hall, Cambs. Educated Wellington College; Brasenose College, Oxford. Barrister, Inner Temple 1938. TA 1934. Army 1939-45/ Major; Deputy Asst Provost Marshal, 2nd British Army 1945, 53rd Division Provost Co TMP 1947-49. Hon. Colonel TA 1953-58, 1962-67, 1971-75. Landowner, Farmer & Forester. Director: Guest, Keen & Nettlefold 1954-; Cardiff; Commercial Bank of Wales 1972-88. Chair, Wales Gas Consultative Council 1958-71. Lord Lieutenant: Glamorgan 1952-74, Mid, South & West Glamorgan 1974-85. Deputy Chair, Glamorgan Quarter Sessions 1949-52. Chancellor, Order of St. John of Jerusalem. President: British Empire Games Cardiff 1958; Welsh College of Advanced Technology 1957-65; Welsh National School of Medicine 1970-83; University of Wales College of Medicine 1983-87 (Hon. Fellow 1989). Chair, Representative Body of the Church in Wales 1965-77. Cardiff RDC, Chairman. Peterston super Ely PC., Chairman. Hon. Member, Gorsedd. Hon. Freeman: Cowbridge 1984, Cardiff 1985. Languages: Learned Welsh, English. Of Coedarhydyglyn, nr Cardiff. Died January 1995.

TREDINNICK David Arthur Stephen: BA MBA (Cape Town) MLitt (Oxon) 1980. Conservative: Cardiff South & Penarth 1983; MP Bosworth 1987-. **Mr. David Tredinnick:** Born 19 January 1950, s of Stephen Victor Treddinick & Evelyn Mabel Watts. Married 1983 Rebecca Jane, d of Roland Shott, 2c. Educated Ludgrove School, Wokingham; Eton; Mons Officer Cadet School; Graduate School of Business Studies, Capetown University; St. John's College, Oxford. 2nd Lieutenant, Grenadier Guards 1968-71. Trainee, E. B. Savoury Miln & Co Stockbrokers 1972. Account Executive, Quadrant International 1974. Salesman, Kalle Infotec UK 1976. Sales Manager, Word Processing 1977-78. Consultant, Baird Communication, NY 1978-79. Marketing Manager, Q1 Europe Ltd 1979-81. Research Assistant,

Kenneth Warren MP & Angela Rumbold MP 1981-87. Manager, family owned Malden-Mitcham Properties 1985-88, Daneswood Properties. Chair, Anglo-East European Co. Ltd 1990-; Ukraine Business Agency 1992-97. PPS 1991-97. Jt Secretary, Conservative MPs Defence Cttee, Foreign & Commonwealth Cttee 1990-91. Chair, British-Atlantic Group Young Politicians 1990-91. Co-Chair, Future of Europe Trust 1988-. Treasurer: All-party Parliamentary Group for Alternative & Complementary Medicine. Member, Standing Cttees: Housing 1997-. Chair: Select Cttee on Statutory Instruments 1997-; Select Cttee for Channel Tunnel Rail Link Act 1995-96. *Papers at Worcestershire Record Office.*

TREFOR-EDWARDS John: Liberal: Caernarfon 1979. **Mr. John Trefor-Edwards:** Born Birkenhead, 1931. Married a harpist, 1s 1d. Legal Executive, Liverpool Solicitors. 1st Secretary/President, Birkenhead United Welsh Society. Member of Gorsedd (blue order 1950). Languages: Welsh, English. Of Birkenhead.

TREGONING John Simmons: JP (Carms). Conservative: Carmarthen District 1885. **Mr. John Tregonning:** Born Launceston, Cornwall 1868, s of John Simmons Tregonning, Llanddue. Anglican. Married Sophia Morris of Liverpool. Came to Llanelli 1866. Tinplate Manufacturer. Director, John S Tregoning & Co Llanelli. Of Ferryside, then Launceston. Died 13 July 1933.

TREGONING Nicholas: BA (Manchester) Liberal Democrat, Swansea East 2003; Wales Euro 2004. **Mr. Nick Tregoning:** Born 2 February 1952, son of Major Arthur Tregoning MM, Royal Engineers, & Beatrice Tregoning, teacher. Christian. Married 1975. Educated Stoneham Grammar School; University of Manchester. Manager, Swansea University Students' Union. Regional Manager, Peter Black AM. Elections Officer, Swansea & Gower Liberal Democrats; Secretary, South Wales West Liberal Democrat Executive. Swansea CC. Liberal Democrat, Wales Euro 2004. Interests: Third World Development, Economic Development, Environment, Education, Credit Unions. Hobbies: Walking, Badminton, Theatre, Music, Reading. Languages: English, French. Of Dunvant, Swansea.

TRENBERTH Siân: Natural Law Party, South East List 1999. **Ms. Siân Trenberth:** Of Cardiff.

TRIVEDI Nimisha: United Socialists, South/Central List. **Ms. Nimi Trivedi: Born** Uganda, of Asian family. Came to Wales when expelled by General Amin. Partner Martin Chapman (qv) 1s, Social Services Worker at Pontypridd. Unison Shop Steward & branch secretary. Of Splott, Cardiff, then Brynmill, Swansea.

TROLLOPE David Norman: People's Representative, South West List 1999. **Mr. David Trollope:** Of Sketty, Swansea.

TRUE Arthur: Communist: Rhondda West 1966, B/E 1967, 1970; Rhondda Feb. & Oct. 1974, 1979, 1983, 1987. **Mr. Arthur True:** Born Treherbert December 1920. Married Gladys 1s. Educated Penyrenglyn Junior Boys School; Treherbert Senior School. Miner 1935-47. Member, Fernhill Colliery Lodge NUM. Re-habilitation course as electrician. ETU Shop steward & Convenor, Margam Steelworks, Cwm Colliery, Llanwern Sites, British Railways. Secretary, Treorchy ETU branch 6 years; Member, ETU Area Cttee 1962. Joined Communist Party 1944. Secretary, Rhondda Area Cttee. Member, Communist Party National Executive 1965-. Secretary, Local Residents Cttee opposing Rhondda Re-Development Plan. School governor. Vice-Chair, Treherbert Hospital League of Friends. Contested local elections 1959-67. Rhondda BC B/E June 1967-74. Mid-Glam CC 1973-. Of Treherbert, Rhondda.

TUCK Ralph: OBE. Conservative, Abertillery 1979, South East List 1999. **Mr. Ralph Tuck:** Born Tredegar, 4 November 1921, son of Arthur Tuck, colliery examiner, & Abigail Tuck. Church in Wales. Married 1948, Magdalene Matthews, 1s 2d. Educated Tredegar Grammar School. Security Officer. Member, TGWU Branch Executive. Chair: Wales Area Conservative Trade Union Cttee, Blaenau Gwent Conservative Assn (2001). TC 1974-79. Hobbies: Voluntary Sector.

TUCKER Janet Rosemary: BA PGCE (Wales). Green Party, South/Central List 2003. **Mrs. Jan Tucker:** Born Haverfordwest 1 January 1953, d of Oswald Perkin Jones, retailer, & Francis Mary Jones, sub postmistress. Christian. Married 1976, Charles Robert Tucker, engineer, 2s. Educated Fishguard Secondary School; University of Wales, Swansea. Director, Fair Do's/Siopa Teg (previously Canolfan Traidcraft) only Traidcraft shop in Wales. Former Traidcraft regional representative; hon. representative for Wales. Interests: Environment, Social Justice, especially for Third World. Hobbies: Reading, Walking, Music. Languages: Welsh, English, French.

TUCKER Margaret: Plaid Cymru: Ogmore 1964. **Mrs. Margaret Tucker:** Born April 1943. Married Michael Tucker (Glamorgan County Treasurer's Dept) divorced. Educated Cathays High School, Cardiff. Housewife. Secretary, Plaid Cymru Youth Section; Member, Plaid Cymru Executive.

TURNBULL Lisa: Plaid Cymru, Aberavon, 2001. **Mrs. Lisa Turnbull:** Born London, 19 September 1974. Married. Educated Stantonbury, Milton Keynes; University of Wales, Aberystwyth. Plaid

Cymru Policy Researcher, National Assembly. Interests: Health; Community Development Hobbies: Sci-Fi, Hill Walking. Of Cardiff.

TURNER Dorothy Marianne: Cert.Ed. Conservative, South/Central 1999. **Mrs. Dorothy Turner:** Born West Bromwich, 6 October 1945, d of James William Jones, surveyor, & Gladys Mary Morris, secretary. Church of England. Married 1968, Martin James Turner, company director, 1s 1d. Educated Oldbury Grammar School, Worcs; City of Birmingham College of Education. Secretary. Joined Conservative Party 1960. South Glam CC 1986-98 (Shadow Chair of Education. Hobbies: Needlework, Antiques, Reading. Of Penarth.

TURNER Kathryn: Green, North List 1999. **Ms. Kathryn Turner:** Of Talwrn, Llangefni.

TURNER Lee: Green, South West 1999. **Mr. Lee Turner:** Born Kings Lynn, Norfolk, 20 January 1969, s of Leonard Turner, driver, & Elizabeth Ann Smith. Church of England. Married 1990 Barbara Ann turner, trainee teacher, 1s 1d. Educated comprehensive school & college. (Dip. Arboriculture, Advanced Dip. Env. Management). Environmentalist. Senior Manager, Community Regeneration for Groundwork Bridgend. School governor. Hobbies: My children, Old motorbikes, Sailing, Music, Wood turning. Of Penyfai, Bridgend.

TURNER Nicholas Robin: Direct Customer Services Party, Carmarthen West & South Pembrokeshire 2001. **Mr. Nick Turner:** Born 1958. Married 4c. Worked in agriculture, building & construction and shot blasting. Of Meidrim, St. Clears.

TURNER Noel Geoffrey: Plaid Cymru, Torfaen 1999. **Mr. Noel Turner:** Born Bridgend, 6 February 1947, s of Noel David Jeffries Turner, soldier, & Doris Margaret Williams. Church in Wales. Married 1975, Pauline Jane Turner, clerk, 1s 1d. educated Army schools in UK & Europe; Pontypool FE College; Newport FE College. Payroll Clerk. Worked at Girlings, Cwmbran 24 years. Joined Plaid Cymru 1966. Blackwood TC. Caerphilly CBC (Pengam) 1999- (Chair: Environmental & Housing Scrutiny Cttee). Interests: Environment, Housing, Transport. Hobbies: Cars, Gardening, Computers, Travel. Of Fleur de Lis.

TURNER Suzanne Jayne: Independent, Mid & West List 1999. **Ms. Suzy Turner:** Born 1974. Married 2c. *I don't have a political programme but I think there should be some representatives from people like myself – a young person who is thinking of the problems of everyday life.* Of Meidrim, St. Clears.

TURNER Vivien Margaret Conor: BScEcon MA MSc RGN HV. Green Party, South/Central 1999. **Mrs. Vivien Turner:** Born Cardiff 30 January 1947, d of Arthur Connor Lysaght, surgeon, & Jacqueline Lois Douglas Heard, Conservative Party worker. Married 1974, Duncan Turner, university lecturer, 1s. Educated direct grant secondary school; University of Wales, Swansea; University of Manchester; University of Wales, Cardiff. Curriculum Manager, FE. Member: NATFHE. MSF. Hobbies: Sailing, Walking, Painting, Music. Languages: English, French, Spanish (now poor). Contested Cardiff CCC (Canton) 1999. Of Canton, Cardiff.

TUTTON Andrew James: Independent Ratepayers, Aberavon 2001. **Mr. Andrew Tutton:** Born Bedlinog, 20 August 1954, s of Leslie Malcolm Tutton, blacksmith, & Shirley Maureen Bolwell. Church in Wales. Married 1999 Tracie Keylock Tutton 2s 2d. Educated Dyffryn Comprehensive School, Port Talbot; Bridgend Tertiary College. Crane Driver at Port Talbot Steelworks. Neath/Port Talbot BC. Interests: I stood for election as a Ratepayer so that I could represent the people without party influences. Hobbies: Watching rugby. Of Port Talbot.

TWILLEY Norman J: Conservative: Wrexham 1987. **Mr. Norman Twilley:** Born 4 February 1945. Married 2c. Educated Westminster School. Management Consultant. Editor & Publisher, *Conservative Micro News*. Mid-Sussex DC 1984-.

TWITCHEN John: Conservative, Islwyn 1987. **Mr. John Twitchen:** Born 19 February 1945. Married. Educated Westcliff High School; Law Society's College of Law. Solicitor 1967.

TYLER Richard Hugh: Liberal Democrat, Mid & West List 1999. **Mr. Richard Tyler:** Born Swansea, 21 April 1946, s of Thomas Edward Tyler, headteacher, & Gladys Fay Tyler, nurse. Church in Wales. Married 1969, Gaynor Tyler, nonstipendiary priest, 2s 1d. Educated Llandrindod Wells Grammar School; University of Wales, Aberystwyth. Solicitor/Mediator. Chair: Brecon & Radnor Liberal Democrats 1999-2001; Rhayader Liberal Democrats. Powys CC 2001-. With his wife, runs a small retreat house at home. Interests: Beating the Tories. Hobbies: Farming, Walking, Reading, Poetry. Languages: English, rudimentary French. Of Llanwrthwl.

TYRRELL Thomas Robert Victor: Conservative, Pontypridd 1955. **Mr. Thomas Tyrrell:** Born Cardiff, 1921. Educated Clive Hall College, Cardiff; Canton High School, Cardiff. Office boy c. 1935. Civil Defence 1939-40. RAF 1940-45. Manufacturer's representative. Housing Society Director. Interests: Trade Unions, Industrial Relations, Social Services. Of Cardiff.

– U –

UNDERDOWN Emmanuel Maguire: QC 1886. Conservative: Monmouth District 1895. **Mr. Emmanuel Underdown:** Born 183-, s of Emmanuel Montefiore Underdown, Sidmouth & Ada, d of Maurice Beddington JP. Married (1) 187- Selina, d of Peter Pollard, 1c (2) 1876, Maria, d of Leopold Eherenfich 1s. Barrister, Inner Temple 1861, Bencher 1894. Hon. Counsel, Society of Authors. Chair of seven foreign companies, mainly in Central & South American Railways. Director, Alexandra Dock Co Newport. Almost became a professional singer. Patron of opera. Friend of artist, Whistler. High rank in Freemasonry. 'In India at the time of the Mutiny, Spain in the troubles of the 70s and Cuba at one of its most exciting periods. Of Backenham Hall, Mundford, Norfolk & London. Estate £108,556. Died at Strand Underground Station 11 April 1913.

UNGOED-THOMAS Arwyn Lynn: Kt 1951 KC 1947 MA (Oxon). Labour: Carmarthen 1950; MP Llandaff & Barry 1945-50, Leicester NW B/E 1950-62. **Sir Lynn Ungoed-Thomas:** Born Carmarthen 26 June 1904, s of Revd Evan Ungoed-Thomas, Welsh Baptist Minister, & Katherine Howells. Married 1933, Dorothy d of Jasper Travers Wolfe, Co. Cork 2s 1d; Educated Queen Elizabeth Grammar School, Carmarthen; Haileybury School; Magdalen College, Oxford. Member: Welsh Rugby XV reserve 1924 Barrister, Inner Temple 1929 (Exhibitioner); Bencher 1951. Member, General Council of the Bar 1946. Chair, Chancery Bar Assn. Army 1939-45, Major RA. & General Staff. Member: Cttee on Leasehold Reform 1948; Cttee on Naval Courts Martial 1949; Statute Law Revision Cttee. President, Hardwicke Society. UK Delegate, Council of Europe & WEU 1949. Solicitor General 1949-51. Judge of the High Court, April 1962. Of London. Died 4 December 1972.

UNWIN David Alan: Conservative, Bridgend 1987, Ogmore 1997, South/West List 1999. **Mr. David Unwin:** Born London, 21 January 1947, son of William Henry Unwin, accountant, & Doris Edna Fisk, clerk. Church of England. Unmarried. Educated Southgate Grammar School. Worked at Royal Mint, London & Llantrisant 20 years. Distribution & Shipping Agent 1970-83. Conservative Agent, Bridgend 1983-87. Manager, Brackla Nordor Sports Equipment Manufacturers & Red Dragon Sports Mail Order. Company Secretary, Parc Slip Opencast Coal Site 11 years. Joined Conservatives 1970. Vice-President, Bridgend Conservative Assn. Ogwr BC 1976-96. Mid-Glam CC 1977-85. St. Brides ComC 1979. Bridgend TC 1984- (Mayor 1990-91). Bridgend CBC 1997-99. Hon. Election Agent: South West Euro 1994, Bridgend 1997, 1999, 2001. Interests: Transport, Housing. Hobbies, Philately, Railways, Travel. Of Ogmore by Sea.

UPWARD Allen: Independent Liberal/Labour: Merthyr Tydfil 1895. **Mr. Allen Upward:** Born Worcester, banker's son. Congregationalist. Educated Trinity College, Dublin. Barrister; Columnist in a Merthyr newspaper; Novelist, author & poet. Member of Gorsedd as *Maenhir*. Withdrew candidature in 1892; described himself as 'the only Liberal (Merthyr candidate) never to be a Tory'. After his defeat at Merthyr he fought on the Greek side in the war with Turkey and then spent six years as a political officer in North West Nigeria. Announced his decision to contest Chelsea as an Anti-Coalition candidate with Labour and Liberal backing in 1918 but did not stand. Died January 1926 (shot himself in the heart at Verwood near Wimborne). Further Reading: *David A. Pretty: John Owen (ap Ffermwr) and the Labour Movement in Wales (Morgannwg XXXVIII 1996).*

– V –

Revd Valentine Lewis.

VALENTINE Lewis Edward: BA 1919 MA 1921 Hon. DD 1986 (Wales). Plaid Cymru: Caernarfonshire 1929. **Revd Lewis Valentine:** Born Llandulas, Denbighshire, 1 June 1893, s of Revd Samuel Valentine (quarryman & Baptist minister) & Mary Valentine. Married 1925, Margaret E. Jones, 1s 1d. Educated Llandulas Parish School; Colwyn Bay Grammar School; Uncertificated Teacher, 2 years; University of Wales, Bangor; Bangor Baptist College 1913-16, 1918-21; President, Student Representative Council 1919-20. RAMC 1916-18; France 1/10/16; gassed on the Somme 23/10/1917. Became a pacifist. Founder, *Cymdeithas Heddwch Cymru* (Peace Society of Wales) 1937. Welsh Baptist Minister. Ordained, 1921: Tabernacl, Llandudno 1921-47; Penuel, Rhosllanerchrugog 1947-70; retired. Failed to be appointed to Professor of Old Testament Studies at Bangor Baptist College 1943. President, Byddin Ymreolaeth Cymru 1924-25; Plaid Cymru 1925-26 (Vice-President 1935-38). Contested Llandudno UDC 1926. Imprisoned for part in *"burning of Penbryn airfield"* 1937. Editor, *Seren Cymru* 1951-74; Poet. President: Arfon Baptist Assn 1932-33; Denbigh, Flint & Merioneth Assn 1942-43; Baptist Union of Wales 1962-63. Died Rhos on Sea, 5 March 1986. *Books: Dyddiadur Milwr a Gweithiau Eraill (edit. John Emyr 1988), Dyrchafwn Gri (edit. Idwal Wyn Jones) 1994, Articles in 'Y Geiriadur Beiblaidd 1926';*

Detholiad o'r Salmau 1937. Further Reading: *Isaac Jones, Adnabod Deg (edit. Derec Llwyd), Densil Morgan, Cewri'r Canrif.*

VALERIO Paul Harold: Conservative: Neath 1966, Swansea West 1999. **Mr. Paul Valerio:** Born Swansea, 10 May 1940, son of Eric B Valerio, restaurateur/businessman, & Elfina De Marco. Roman Catholic. Married Dorothy, 2s. Educated Swansea Grammar School; Swansea Technical College. Managing Director, Valmatics, family owned automatic vending machine company. Joined Young Conservatives 1958, Chair: Wales & Mon Young Conservatives 1964. Member: Young Conservatives National Advisory Cttee; Executive, National Union of Conservative & Unionist Assns 1993-98. Chair: Swansea West Conservative Assn 1991-93 (President 1993); Wales Area Conservative Local Government Cttee 1993-95. Vice-Chair: Mid & West Wales Euro Conservatives 1992. Welsh Conservative Spokesperson on Tourism 1997. Deputy Chair: Conservative Party, Wales. Swansea BC 1968-96 (Leader, Conservative Group 1978-88), last Mayor 1981-82, 1st Lord Mayor 1982-83. West Glam CC 1972-82. President: Swansea Rotary Club; South Wales Rotary Club 1998-99. Vice-President, Swansea Branch, Royal British Legion. School governor, -2001. Member: South Wales Electricity Board 1984-87. Chair: South Wales Electricity Council 1984-87. Member: RNLI. Hobbies: Amateur Radio, Country Walking Of Reynoldston, Gower.

VARLEY Peter Ashley Clifford: MSc PhD (Wales). Green Party, South/East List 2003. **Dr. Peter Varley:** Born 13 June 1957, s of Clifford Varley & Julia Baker. Freelance Computer Programmer. Worked for Armstrong Healthcare (surgical robots); Midstep Project. Member: Newport One World Week Co-ordinating Cttee; local trade justice group; Stop the War Coalition. Hobbies: Chess (Gwent County Champion 7 times, member Wales team 2000, 2001). Contested Newport BC B/E September 2001. Hobbies: Chess. Of Newport.

VAUGHAN John: JP DL (Merioneth) MA (Oxon). Conservative: Merioneth 1886. **Mr. John Vaughan:** Born 1829, s of John Vaughan, Madras Civil Service (died 1842); Succeeded grandfather, Robert Vaughan MP. Anglican. Married 1863, Anne Elinor d of Edward Owen, Garthangharad,

2s 2d. Educated Shrewsbury School; Oxford University. Landowner. High Sheriff of Merioneth 1890. Of Nannau. Estate £63,467. Died 29 June 1900.

VAUGHAN John Edward: JP1889 DL (Glam) JP (Brecs) MA (Oxon). Conservative: Mid-Glamorgan 1885. **Lieut-Colonel John Vaughan:** Born Lanelay, Llanharan 27 September 1868, s of Vaughan Hanning Vaughan Lee MP Dillington Park, Ilminster, Somerset. Dropped name of Lee. Anglican. Married 1888, Alice Elizabeth, d of Major Waller Ashe 1s 2d. Educated Harrow; New College, Oxford. Royal Scots Fusiliers 1884: Burma, South African & Great War. Hon. Lieut-Colonel 1909. OC Swansea Garrison 1914-16. Landowner. High Sheriff, Breconshire 1901. Glamorgan CC 1888-1928. Vice-Commodore, Bristol Channel Yacht Club. Member: Rheola Cricket XI. Vice-Chair, Neath Conservative Assn. Of Rheola, Vale of Neath. Estate £18,792. Died 30 March 1929.

VAUGHAN Robert: KBE 1937 JP DL (Merioneth). Conservative: Merioneth 1924. **Sir Robert Vaughan:** Born 15 September 1866, s of John Vaughan (qv), Nannau & Anne Elinor Owen. Anglican. Married 1904, Patricia Steuart, d of Major-General, Sir Frederick Goldsmid. Educated Eton; Downton Agricultural College. Merioneth CC Alderman 1931; Chair 1935-36. Chair: Merioneth NFU. Member: Merioneth War Agricultural Executive Cttee 1919-20. Recruiting Officer, Merioneth & Montgomery 1914-19. Vice-Chair, Merioneth Quarter Sessions. Of Dolgellau. Estate £25,733. Died 16 January, 1941.

VAUGHAN-DAVIES Matthew Lewis 1st & last Baron Ystwyth of Tanybwlch 1920: JP DL (Cards). Liberal MP Cardiganshire 1895-1920; Joined Liberal Party 1892; Conservative Candidate 1885. **Mr. Matthew Vaughan-Davies:** Born 17 December 1840, s of Matthew Davies, Tanybwlch. Anglican. Married 1889, Mary [Minnie] (died 1926), of Swansea, widow of Alexander Jenkins, & d of Thomas Powell. A leading Conservative in Cards. until his marriage to this wealthy Swansea Liberal widow. Educated Harrow (one year); Landowner. Patron of Llanerchaeron living. Master of Foxhounds; Chair, Llanilar Bench. High Sheriff of Cardiganshire 1875. Chair, Welsh Parliamentary Party 1920-21 Of Tanybwlch & London. Estate £24,385. Died 21 August 1935.

VERITY Lynn Helen Stuart: LlB LLM Diploma in International Law (London). Conservative, South Wales Central Euro 1994. **Mrs. Lynn Verity:** Born Bristol. Married. Educated London University. Aviation Industry (British Caledonian & British Airways) 15 years. Solicitor. Former

JP & school governor. Hobbies: Cricket, Theatre. Of London.

VERMA Marcello Kumar: BSc MBA. Liberal Democrat: Cynon Valley 1992. **Mr. Marcello Verma:** Born Cardiff. 4 October 1968, s of Prabat Kumar Verma (qv) & Concetta Verma. Catholic/ Hindu Interfaith. Married 1996 Ashumali Verma 1s 1d. Educated Chabyan Grove School, Salisbury; Polytechnic of Wales (Estate Management). Estate Agent Management Consultant & Part-time Lecturer. Officer, Cardiff South & Penarth Liberal Democrats. Joined Labour Party 1996. Interests Housing. Hobbies: Golf. Of Cardiff.

VERMA Peter – see VERMA Prabhat K.

VERMA Prabhat K: JP BSc MBA MEd FIMinEng CCM MIMgt. Liberal Democrat: Merthyr Tydfil 1987, South Wales Euro 1989, Cardiff South & Penarth 1992. Labour, South/Central List 2003. **Mr. Peter Verma:** Born India Monghyr, Bihar, 15 November 1941, s of Nagendranath Verma, advocate, & Ramkali Devi. Hindu, married to a Catholic. Married 1972, Concetta Verma 2c. Educated India; University of Wales, Cardiff. Mining Engineer. Mining Consultant. Management Consultant & Part-time Lecturer UWIST. Member, Wales Council for Voluntary Action. Founder, Plasnewydd Ward Liberal Assn. Joined Labour Party 1996. Labour candidate, Cardiff CC (Cyncoed) 1999. Interests: Housing, Health. Hobbies: Voluntary Work. Languages: English; Hindi; Urdu. Of Cardiff.

VERNON Wayne Anthony: BEng 1990 MEng (Wales) CE. Plaid Cymru: Cardiff Central 1997 **Mr. Wayne Vernon:** Born Wrexham 17 December 1967. Married 1d. Educated Bryn Alyn School, Gwersyllt; Yale Sixth Form College, Wrexham; University of Wales, Cardiff. Engineer, British Steel Corporation, Llanwern. Chair, Cardiff District Cttee Plaid Cymru 1993-96; Blaenau Gwent PC 1998; Elections Co-ordinator, Blaenau Gwent. Member, Plaid Cymru National Council. Of Ebbw Vale.

VICKERS Simon: Referendum Party: Vale of Clwyd 1997. **Mr. Simon Vickers:** Born North West England. Educated Shrewsbury; USA. Travel Agent, *Suncare Travel Specialists* of Rhyl, Chester & Liverpool. Of Rhuddlan.

VICKERY Alfred Robert: Plaid Cymru Candidate for Newport 1970, 1979; Assembly, Newport East, 1999. **Mr. Bob Vickery:** Born Pill, Newport May 1935. Baptist deacon. Married Hazel, 1s 2d. Educated Newport High School; Newport Technical College. Royal Navy 9 years, Petty Officer. Electrician SWEB 1950- Managing

Director, IRC Components, Tredegar. Joined Plaid Cymru 1953; Chair, Plaid Cymru Monmouthshire County Cttee; Election Agent 1997. Governor, Ysgol Gynradd Casnewydd. Member: Saracens RFC Cttee. Resigned from Plaid Cymru 2000. Died 2 July 2001.

VINCENT Hugh Corbet: Kt 1924 MA (Cantab). Conservative: Caernarfon District Jan. 1910. **Sir Hugh Vincent:** Born 1863, s of Revd James Vincent, Vicar of Caernarfon. Married Bronwen Adelaide, d of Canon Thomas Warren Trevor, 5c. Educated Sherborne School; Trinity College, Cambridge. Member, Wales Rugby XV. Solicitor 1886 (Carter, Vincent & Co. Bangor & Caernarfon). Clerk to Bangor Magistrates. Company Chair: Amalgamated Slate Assn Ltd. 3 times Mayor of Bangor. Caernarfonshire CC 1909. Chair, Bangor Chamber of Trade. Member, Governing Body of the Church in Wales. Of, Bangor. Estate £41,888. Died 2 February 1931.

VINER George Scotchford: Labour: Cardiff North 1959. **Mr. George Viner:** Born May 1912. Married 1936, Nancy, d of Gwilym Gray, 1d. Educated Wallington County School. Journalist: Chief South Wales Representative, *Daily Herald* 1929-. TA (NCO). 14th Army 1939-45, Major; Secretary, NUJ Cardiff Branch & Wales District Council. Member, NUJ Appeals Cttee Chair, *Cymric Democrat* Publishing Society. Joined Labour Party 1936. Of Cardiff (1932).

VIPASS Brenda Muriel: UK Independence Party, Torfaen 2001, Caerphilly 2003. **Mrs. Brenda Vipass:** Born Sheffield 30 October1929, daughter of Percy Robinson, silversmith, & Edith Helena Robinson. *Evangelist (Was Methodist but been to many others, last was Baptist).* Married (1) 1947 Leslie Sims, miner (divorced 1950) 4s 1d (2) 1962 Janis Vipass (miner, Latvian,(died 1981) 2d. [One daughter founded a mission in Latvia in 1991 to help the many street children – Brenda visits to help]. Naaffi HQ assistant; housewife; Traffic Patrol Warden; Gallup Poll Interviewer 1971-79. Campaigned for Handicapped Children since 1953; founder 'Peterlee Friends of Handicapped Children' 1953. Campaigner for charities aiding elderly & disabled. Became disabled herself. Moved to Wales 1999. Interests: Rights of the Disabled. Hobbies: Whist, Gardening, Family. Of New Inn, Pontypool (2001).

VIVIAN Frank G: Independent Labour: Carmarthen District B/E 1912. **Mr. Frank Vivian:** Born Llanelli 1859, s of William Frank Vivian, gasworks foreman. Educated Market Street Schools & Privately. Apprenticed at gasworks. Consultant Gas Engineer. Claimed to be standing as ILP candidate but was repudiated by party HQ. Of Llanelli

VIVIAN Henry Hussey 1st Baron Swansea 1893: 1st Bart 1882 JP1859 DL (Glam) MA (Cantab) FGS. Liberal MP Glamorgan 1857-885; Swansea District 1885-93; Truro 1852-57. **Sir Hussey Vivian:** Born Marino, Singleton Park, Swansea, 6 July 1821, s of Major John Henry Vivian (MP. Swansea 1822-55) & Sarah, d of Arthur Jones, The Priory, Reigate. Anglican. Married (1) 1847, Jessie Dalrymple (died 1848) d of Ambrose Goddard MP. & gd of Duke of St. Albans; 1s (2) 1853, Caroline Elizabeth (invalid from 1854, died 1868) d of Sir Montague Cholmely, Bart. (3) 1870, Averil, d of Captain Richard Beaumont RN. & gd of Lord Macdonald. Educated Eton (unhappy at school); France & Germany 1838-40; at Le Havre lived in same house as Friedrich Engels, with whom he became friendly); Trinity College, Cambridge. Metallurgist (copper, gold, silver, nickel). Ran Liverpool Office of family firm, 1842-45; Manager, Hafod Works 1845 (introduced new type of furnace). Took out patents for non-ferrous metals other than copper: zinc 1843, Gold 1850, Nickel & Cobalt 1851. Began extracting gold and silver from copper ore 1856; opened zinc works 1868; began smelting copper 1869. Set up own company of H. H. Vivian & Co. & opened White Rock Works 1871. Industrialist & Company Director: Rhondda & Swansea Bay Railway Co. Declined Swansea Mayoralty. 1st Chair, Glamorgan County Council from 1889. Lieut-Colonel, 4th Glamorgan Rifles 11 years; President: Royal Institution of Wales (twice); Cambrian Archeological Assn 1861-62; Swansea Training College for School Mistresses; Vice-President, University College, Cardiff. Chair, Swansea Harbour Trust. Of Singleton Abbey, Swansea, & London. Estate £215,032. Died 28 November 1894.

VOISEY Matthew Colin: Conservative, South West 1999. **Mr. Matthew Voisey:** Chair Ogmore Conservative Assn 2001. Of Pencoed, Bridgend.

VON RUHLAND Christopher John: HD (Tech) BSc MIBiol MPhil. Green Party, Cardiff Central 1997, South West List 1999. **Mr. Chris Von Ruhland:** Born Ruislip, Middlesex 2 August 1962, son of Joseph Von Ruhland, civil engineer, & Anne Sever, nurse. Atheist. Married 1992, Jane Von Ruhland, accountant, 1s 1d. Educated Hayden Comprehensive School, Northwood; NE Surrey College of Technology; Portsmouth Poly; South Glamorgan Institute of Higher Education. Research Technician. Scientist. Green Party Branch Chair/Secretary, Treasurer. Contact, South Wales Green Party Vegan & Vegetarian Group. Contested Cardiff CCC (Heath) 1999. Interests: Green Politics, specifically Transport & Energy. Hobbies: DIY, Aikido, Woodturning/Carpentry. Languages: English, some German, French, Japanese. Of Cardiff.

– W –

WAINWRIGHT Owen: Independent Conservative: Conwy 1992, Conservative PPC Ynys Môn 1978. **Mr. Owen Wainwright:** Born Criccieth 1941. Educated Ruthin School. Married 1s 1d, divorced. Joined family retail furnishers, Birmingham 1958. Hotelier, with brother: bought Dinorben Arms. Hotel, Amlwch 1961, Eagles Hotel, Llanrwst 1971, Tynycoed Hotel 1978, Gwydir Hotel 1984. Anglesey CC. Gwynedd CC. Member: Army Council for Wales; International Centre for Welsh Affairs. Chair: Amlwch Chamber of Trade; Anglesey Chamber of Trade. Resigned as PPC *because of pressure of work and disagreements with constituency party officers*. Of Betws-y-Coed. Further Reading: *D. Elwyn Jones, Y Rebel Mwyaf, page 23.*

WAKEFIELD Marilyn Ann (Smith): Ecology Party/Green Party: Ceredigion 1983, Vale of Glamorgan B/E 1989, Ceredigion & Pembrokeshire North 1987. **Mrs. Marilyn Wakefield:** Born 1958, (née Smith). Married 1s. Educated Cornell University (parapsychology). Unemployed 1983. Member: Green Party Council; CND Cymru; 300 Group; Aberteifi Peace Group. Of Ferwig, Cardigan.

WAKEFIELD Simon John: BSc 1975 PhD 1981 (Leeds) FGS. Liberal Democrat: Cardiff South & Penarth 1997. **Dr. Simon Wakefield:** Born Maidstone, Kent, 10 February 1954, s of John Roger Wakefield, newsagent/confectioner, & Ruth Kathleen Willis, housewife. Church of England/ Church in Wales. Married 1985,Vivien C. M. Jones, teacher/librarian, 2s, divorced 2002. Educated Maidstone Grammar School; Leeds University (Earth Sciences). Marine Geochemist. Lecturer in Chemical Oceanography, University of Wales, Swansea 1978-79. Lecturer in Marine Geochemistry, University of Wales, Cardiff 1989-. Director of Teaching in Earth Sciences & Deputy Head of Department, University of Wales, Cardiff. Researches into deep-sea sediments. Participated on 12 deep-sea cruises on UK & Russian vessels. West Glam CC (SDP) 1985-89. Cardiff CC 1999-. Chair: Swansea West SDP, Cardiff Central Liberal Democrats 1994-. Member: UK Challenger Society Cttee & education sub-cttee; Geological Society of London Marine Studies Group Cttee. Consultant: Open University Oceanography course team, World Wildlife Trust, Greenpeace, Friends of the Earth, Charter 88, Campaign for Protection of Rural Wales,

Amnesty International, AUT. Interests: Education, Environment, Regeneration, Conservation, Electoral Reform. Hobbies, Music, Sport. Of Cyncoed, Cardiff.

WALKER Greg – see WALKER Hugh Gregory.

WALKER Helen: Socialist Labour, South/Central List 2003. **Ms. Helen Walker:** Active equal opportunities campaigner. Of Blaengarw.

WALKER Hugh Gregory: BA (Bristol). Conservative, Cardiff Central 2001. **Mr. Greg Walker:** Born Caerphilly, 10 August 1976. Anglican. Educated Llanishen High School; Bristol University. Research Assistant: Francis Maude MP. Financial Officer, Woolwich Building Society. Research Officer: Jonathan Morgan AM & David Melding AM. Chair, Bristol University Conservative Assn. Member: St. Martin's, Roath PCC, Chapter Arts Centre, Friends, Welsh National Opera. Hobbies: Tennis, Watching rugby & soccer (Cardiff City XI & Cardiff RFC). Of Cardiff.

WALKER James: JP (Lanarkshire) 1922-29. Labour MP Newport 1929-31, Motherwell 1935-. Contested: Rotherham 1918, 1922. **Mr. James Walker:** Born Glasgow 1883, s of John Walker. Married 1910, Ada, d of John Chivers. Educated Ruskin College, Oxford. Steelworker. Organiser, Iron & Steel Trades Assn 25 years. Chair, Scottish TUC. Glasgow CC 1914-31. Of Norbury, London. Died 5 January 1945.

WALKER John Andrew: British National Party, Wales Euro 2004. Married 2c. RAF (Logistics) Sealand 23 years. Civil Servant. Member TGWU. Territorial Army (Royal Welsh Fusiliers & REME). Contested Wrexham BC by-election 2003. Lived in Wales from 1981.

WALKER John Richard: UK Independence Party, North List 2003. **Mr. John Walker:** Born London 1952. Educated Bradford Grammar School; University. Teacher. Engineer. Forestry/ Farming. With Welsh Office Agriculture Dept. Self-employed computer engineer at Clwt-y-Bont, Llanberis. Ex-Conservative. UKIP North Wales PR Officer. Of Caernarfon 1985).

WALKER John Sneddon: Green Party, North list 2003. **Mr. John Walker:** Born Nottingham, 16 September 1964, s of George Sneddon Walker, bricklayer, & Rita Mary Sneddon, warehouse-worker. Member, Anthroposophy Society (Have my own spirituality). Married 1998 Michaela Ann Walker, housewife, 1s, divorcing. Mentor/Technical Assistant, IT Access & Training, Lifelong Learning Project, & Youthworker & Playworker. Interests: Monetary Reform, Free Trade, Environment, Power at Local Level. Hobbies: Music, Sport, Tennis (Rhyl Men's Team Captain), Reading, Walking, Nature, Computers. Languages: Learning Welsh, English, Learning German. Extremely active environmentalist campaigner & human & animal rights activist. Of Rhyl.

WALKER Susan: BA (Oxon) MSc (London). Green Party: Montgomery 1997, Mid & West 1999, Wales Euro 1999. **Ms. Sue Walker:** Partner, Sean Featherstonhaugh, 1s 1d. Educated Oxford University (Physics); Imperial College, London (Marketability of electric cars). Worked at Energy Technology Support Unit, Harwell, & National Radiological Protection Board. Independent Energy Consultant & Open University Staff Tutor in Environmental Management. Established energy resource center at Llanidloes. Editor, Green Party's *Green Wales*. Of Newtown.

WALLACE Wellesley Theodore Octavius: MA (Oxon). Conservative, Pontypool, Feb. 1974; Battersea South, Oct. 1974, 1979. **Mr. Theo Wallace:** Born 10 April 1938, s of Dr. Caleb Paul Wallace & Dr. Elizabeth Rainsford (née Pigott). Roman Catholic. Married 1988, Maria Amelia, d of Sir Ian Abercromby Bart. 1 s 1d. Educated, Charterhouse; Christ Church, Oxford. Barrister, Inner Temple 1963; Member, Lincolns Inn 1973. 2nd Lieutenant, Royal Artillery 1958. Lieutenant, Surrey Yeomanry TA 1959-62. Chairman, VAT & Duties Tribunal 1989-. Special Commissioner, Income Tax, 1992-. Deputy-Chair, Battersea South Conservative Assn. Vice-Chair, Greater London CPC Cttee. Hon. Secretary, Taxation Sub-Cttee, Society of Conservative Lawyers 1974-92. Trustee, Trinity Fields Trust Wandsworth. Member Royal Institute of International Affairs, Conservative Group for Europe. Hobbies: Lawn Tennis, Ski-ing, Golf. Of 46 Bellville Road, London SW11 6QZ & Whitecroft, West Clandon GU4 7DT. *Books: (with John Wakeham) The Case against Wealth Tax* 1968.

WALLER Claire Margaret: BA (Wales) 2001. Liberal Democrat, Aberavon 2003. **Miss Claire Waller:** Born Reading, 5 January 1980, d of Kenneth Charles King Waller, actuary, & Susan Mary Waller, housewife. Christian. Partner, Dr. Steven John Moss, chemical engineer. Educated, Kendrick Girls' Grammar School; University of Wales, Swansea (Classics). Asst Regional Manager, Peter Black AM. Joined Liberal Democrats 1996. Chair: University of Wales Swansea Liberal

Democrats. Treasurer: Swansea & Gower Liberal Democrat Executive. Member: Young Liberal Democrat Society Wales Executive. Interests: Education, Environment. Hobbies: Dark Age re-enactment, singing, amateur dramatics, scuba diving. Languages: Welsh, English, French, Latin. Of Swansea.

R. C. Wallhead.

WALLHEAD Richard Collingham: Labour MP Merthyr 1922- (ILP 1931-33). Contested Coventry 1918. **Mr. R. C. Wallhead:** Born Islington, 28 December 1869 s of Richard Wallhead, railway porter, & Mary Love (died 1873). Married 1892 Ellen, d of Frederick Staines, 2d (Muriel Nichol MP). Educated St. Edmund's Elementary School, Romford. Clerk, Great Eastern Railway, 1881. Decided to train as water-colourist & designer. Unemployed in early 1890s. Decorator at Wilmslow. Evening student at Manchester School of Art. Set up own decorator crafts business & acquired shop, but business failed. Journalist. Joined ILP 1894. Manager, *The Labour Leader,* Manchester 1906-21. Full-time (freelance) propagandist 1908. Sentenced to 4 months imprisonment (DORA) 1917 for making anti-war socialist speeches, after refusing to pay a fine. Member ILP National Council. Chair ILP 1920-23. Member, Executive, International Socialist Bureau (2nd International). Hon. Organiser, ILP Scouts 1910. Manchester CC 1919-21. Resigned from ILP to take Labour Whip 1933. Estate £1,064. Of London. Died 27 April 1934.

WALLIS Anthony Peter: Conservative: Abertillery 1966. **Mr. Peter Wallis:** Born May 1929. Married 1s. Educated Beverley Secondary Modern School; Wimbledon Commercial College. Insurance Broker. TA Officer. Treasurer/Vice-Chair, South Eastern Area Young Conservatives. Of Seaford, Sussex.

WALSH Arthur Henry John, 3rd Baron Ormathwaite (1868): Bart (1804) GCVO 1920 KCVO 1912, Grand Cross of the Order of Francis Joseph (Austria) Grand Cross of the Sacred Treasure (Japan) Grand Cross of the White Eagle (Serbia) Commander Legion d'Honneur (France). Conservative MP Radnorshire 1885-92. **Hon. Arthur Walsh:** Born London 1859, s of 2nd Baron & Lady Emily Somerset, d of Duke of Beaufort. Succeeded father 1920. Married 1890, Lady Clementine Frances Anne Pratt, d of Marquess Camden. Educated Eton. Lieutenant, Life Guards 1878-86. Equerry in Waiting, Duke of Clarence. HM Master of Ceremonies 1910-20. Landowner (26,300 acres in Radnorshire & Berkshire. Lord Lieutenant of Radnorshire. President, Radnorshire TA Assn. Of Penybont Hall, Radnorshire, Eywood Titley, Herefordshire & London. Died 13 March 1937.

WALTER Robert John: BSc (Aston) 1971. Conservative: Bedwellty 1979; MP Dorset North, 1997-. **Mr. Robert Walter:** Born Mumbles, Swansea, 1948. Married Sally 1970 (died 1995) 2s 1d. Educated Colstons School, Bristol; Lord Weymouth School, Warminster; Aston University. Insurance Investment Executive. Sheep Farmer, South Devon. Director & Vice-President, Aubrey G. Langston & Co 1986. Former member of Stock Exchange. Visiting Lecturer in East/West Trade, University of Westminster. Chair: Warminster Young Conservatives 1965-67, Aston University Conservative Assn 1967-69, Westbury Young Conservatives 1974-75. Vice-Chair, Westbury CPC 1974. Freeman of the City of London 1983. Liveryman, Needlemakers' Company 1983. Founder-President, Wiltshire Europe Society. Member: NFU, National Sheep Assn, Royal Agricultural Society of Wales. Junior Spokesman on Wales 1999. Member, Select Cttee: Health 1997. Treasurer, All Party Group on Charities & the Voluntary Sector. Vice-Chair, Conservative Parliamentary Agriculture Cttee 1997. Secretary: Conservative European Affairs Cttee 1997, Positive European Group 1997. Treasurer: British-Japanese Parliamentary Group 1997, All-party Group on Charities 1997. Chair: Governors, Tachbrook School.

WALTERS David Alun: Plaid Cymru, Cynon Valley 2003. **Mr. David Walters:** Born Aberdare 1970. Educated Polytechnic of Wales. Solicitor. Secretary, Cynon Valley Constituency, Plaid Cymru. Interests: Environment, Education. Of Trecyon, Aberdare.

WALTERS David Russell: BA (Kent). Conservative: Islwyn 1997. **Mr. Russell Walters:** Born London, 14 July 1961, s of Raymond Walters, teacher, & Rachel Edith Walters, teacher. Welsh Independent. Married 1997, Elizabeth Kimber, secretary, 1s. Educated Cwmdare Primary School, Aberdare; Aberdare. Boys Grammar School; Kent University (Politics & Government). Executive Director, Democracy Movement. Director, Campaign for Freedom in Europe. Conservative Chief of Staff in Scotland 1989-. Political Adviser, Seychelles Democratic Party 1992-93. Research Associate, Adam Smith Institute 1982-83-. Member, Secretary of State's Welsh Manifesto Advisory Group. Member, National Young Conservative Advisory Cttee. Treasurer, Holborn & St. Pancras Conservative Assn 1994. Interests: International Affairs, Civil Liberties, Europe. Hobbies: Reading, Walking, Chinese Cooking. Of London.

WALTERS Ira Gwilym: BScEcon (Wales). Labour: Conwy 1983. **Mr. Ira Walters:** Born Gorseinon, 16 February 1960, s of Vivian John Walters, stock controller, & Marion Evans, shop assistant. Welsh Baptist. Married 1982, Janette, nursery teacher, d of Jack Britton & Megan Shallish, Penygraig, 2s 1d. Educated Gowerton Boys' Grammar School; Penyrheol Comprehensive School; University of Wales, Aberystwyth. Research Officer EEPTU 1981=88. Personnel & management roles 1988-. General Manager, MEG (UK) 1995-. Secretary, Llwchwr Labour Party Young Socialists 1975-78; UW Aberystwyth Labour Club 1979-81. Chair, Welsh Organisation of Labour Students 1980-81. Member, EETPU Parliamentary Panel 1984-88. Secretary, St. Paul's Cray Branch Labour Party 1985-87. Chair, Chislehurst CLP 1986-87. Regional Secretary, EETPU Greater London Political Advisory Cttee 1986-88. Bromley BC 1986-88. Interests: Manufacturing industry, Industrial Relations, Welsh Affairs, Europe. Hobbies: Reading, DIY (grudgingly), Gardening, Caravanning, Outdoors, Music. Youngest candidate in 1983 election. Shortlisted, Carmarthen 1987, Barking 1987. Languages: Welsh, English.

WALTERS Leslie James: Conservative: Neath Feb. 1974, Merthyr Tydfil Oct. 1974. Joined SDP 1981. **Mr. Leslie Walter:** Born Maesteg, 1937. Married Mary, d of Arthur Phillips, Neath wholesale greengrocer, 3c. Educated Cowbridge Grammar School; Bridgend & Margam Technical College. Analytical Chemist, British Steel Corporation, Abbey Works, Port Talbot. Member BISAKTA. Merthyr Mawr ComC. Bridgend TC. Penybont RDC -1974. Ogwr BC 1974-. Chair, Penybont South Conservative branch. Of Bridgend.

WALTERS Nicholas M: Conservative, Merthyr Tydfil & Rhymney 1987. **Mr. Nicholas Walters:** Born 16 May 1957, s of Dennis Walters MP for Westbury. Roman Catholic. Educated Downside School; Exeter University. Public Relations Consultant & Director, Good Relations Group plc. Member: Executive, National Assn of Conservative Students 1984-86, Chair: Exeter University Conservative Students. Member: Institute of International Affairs.

WALTERS Russell – see WALTERS David Russell.

WANHILL Stephen Robert Charles: BA PhD (Wales) DUS (Southampton) FTS FHCIMA Liberal: Cardiff West 1970. **Professor Stephen Wanhill:** Born Portsmouth 26 January 1945, s of Robert Sidney Wanhill, police officer, & Mary Wanhill, housewife. Married 1975, Eluned Lewis. Educated Portsmouth; RMC Sandhurst; University of Wales, Bangor (1st Economics); University of Southampton. Lieutenant, RA 1964-70. Resigned commission to contest election. Professor of Tourism, University of Wales, Cardiff, Professor of Tourism Research, Bournemouth University & Head of the Unit for Tourist Research Centre of Bornholm, Denmark. Tourism Advisor to the House of Commons Select Cttee on Welsh Affairs 1985-89. Member, Wales Tourist Board 1993-95. Editor, *Journal of Tourism Economics*. Interests: Small Business Policy (Tourism). Hobbies: Military History, Opera.

Peter Warburton.

WARBURTON Peter Nigel: Natural Law Party. Mid & West List 1999, Euro South-East England 1999, Southend East 1997. **Mr. Peter Warburton:** Deputy Leader & International Affairs Spokesperson NLP. Of Mentmore.

WARBURTON-JONES Peter: MA (Cantab). Conservative: East Flint 1979. **Mr. Peter Warburton-Jones:** Born 1946. Educated Trinity College, Glenalmond; Madrid University; Corpus Christi College, Cambridge. Barrister. Part-time legal adviser, newspaper group. Executive Member, Lambeth Conservative Assn. Of London.

WARDELL Gareth Lodwig: BScEcon MSc (London) FRGS. Labour MP Gower B/E 1982-97. **Mr. Gareth Wardell:** Born Tumble 29 November 1944, s of John Thomas Wardell (barber) & Jenny Ceridwen Rees. Married Jennifer Dawn Evans (teacher) 1s. Educated Gwendraeth Grammar School; London School of Economics. Teacher (Economics), Chislehurst & Sidcup Technical High School 1967-68, St. Clement Danes Grammar School 1968-70, Haberdasher Aske's School, Elstree 1970-72. Lecturer, Bedford FE College 1972-73. Senior Lecturer in Geography, Trinity College, Carmarthen 1973-82. Tutor in Social Studies, Open University. WEA Tutor. Joined Labour Party 1974. Joint Vice-Chair, All Party British-Sri Lanka Group. Joint Secretary, British-Burmese Group. Chair, Select Cttee on Welsh Affairs 1984-97. Vice-President, National Assn for Clean Air, President, Mumbles/Kinsale Twinning Assn, Penclawdd RFC, Côr Meibion Pontarddulais. Fellow & trustee, Industry & Parliament Trust. Forestry Commissioner. Hobbies: Cycling, Cross-country running. Languages: Welsh, English. Of Carmarthen.

WARDEN Michael Ian: BA (London) CertEd (Bristol). Liberal Democrat, Preseli 2003, Northern Ireland Assembly, Belfast 1982. **Mr. Mike Warden:** Born Southgate, Middx. 28 November 1936, s of Henry Eric Warden, bank official, & Marjorie Ethel Warden, housewife. Anglican. Married 1973, Jeannetta Karolina Saunders, 3s. Educated Epsom College; University College, London; Bristol University. ComC 1988-2003 (Chair: Preseli Liberal Democrats 1996-2002. Interests: Environment, Proportional Representation, Social Justice. Hobbies: Garden, Current Affairs, Drinking with Friends. Languages: English, French. Of Puncheston, Pembs.

WARLOW Eve: Liberal Democrat: Cardiff North 1992. **Ms. Eve Warlow:** Born 15 June 1947. Married 4c. Educated Jordanhill College of Education. Teacher. Chair, Cardiff North Liberal Democrats. Trustee, Lisvane Memorial Hall. Member: MENSA, Campaign for Welsh Assembly. Of Cardiff.

WARMAN John: SDP/Alliance: Neath B/E 1991; Liberal Democrat: Ogmore 1992. **Mr. John Warman:** Born Neath, 20 January 1944, s of Leonard Thomas Warman & Doris Vera Stevens, dressmaker. Church in Wales. Married Lesley Gillian Warman, researcher, 2d. Educated Cadoxton Secondary Modern School. Boilermaker, British Steel Corporation. GBMU Shop Steward. Neath BC 1972-, Mayor, 1988-89, Neath/Port Talbot BC. Member: Neath & Port Talbot Community Health Council, Water Services Cttee for Wales, Press Council 1983-89, Independent Television Commission. School governor. Hobbies: Reading. Of Cimla, Neath.

WARMINGTON Cornelius Marshall: 1st Bart 1908 QC 1882. Liberal MP West Monmouthshire 1885-95. **Sir Cornelius Warmington:** Born 5 June 1842, s of Edward Warmington, Colchester. Married 1871, Annie, d of Edward Winch, Chatham, 2s. Educated University College School, London' University College, London. Solicitor 1864, Barrister, Middle Temple 1869, Bencher 1885. Member, London University Senate. Stood down 1892, in favour of Sir William Harcourt, defeated some days earlier at Derby. Of Bayswater, London. Estate £130,644. Died 12 December 1908.

WARRENDER John Robert, 2nd Baron Bruntisfield of Boroughmuir 1942: Bart 1915 OBE 1962 MC 1943 TD 1966 JP 1955 DL 1965 (Somerset). Conservative: Pontypridd 1964. **Colonel Hon. John Warrender:** Born 7 February 1921, s of 1st Baron Bruntsifield (MP Grantham) & Dorothy, d of Lt-Col R. H. Rawson MP. Succeeded father 1993. Married 1948, Moireen (died 1976) d of Sir Walter Fendall Campbell, 4c. (2) 1977, Mrs. Shirley Crawley (died 1981) (3) 1985, Mrs. Joanne Graham. Educated Eton; RMC Sandhurst. Commissioned, Royal Scots Grays. ADC Governor of Madras 1946-48. Colonel/Deputy Brigadier, Royal Company of Archers, Queens Bodyguard in Scotland 1973-85. OC North Somerset Yeomanry/44th Royal Tank 1962-67. Somerset CC. Farmer. Chair, Thistle Holdings Ltd 1973-. Member, Council, National Trust for Scotland 1972-.

WARRICK Paul Terence Philip: Conservative: Aberavon 1987. **Mr. Paul Warrick:** Born Slough, 2 September 1944, s of Eric William Warrick, civil servant. Church of England. Married 1973, Lorna Mary Warrick, librarian, 1s 1d. Educated Cheam School; Stowe School; Neuchatel University; South West London College; College of Law (HND Business Studies, BL). Lawyer. Kensington & Chelsea BC 1982-; Cabinet Member for Service Improvement. Member, General Council, Conservative Group for Europe. Hobbies: Shooting, Sailing, Skiing, Wine & Food. Languages: English, French, Spanish. Of London.

WARRY Susan Marilyn: UK Independence Party, Pontypridd 2001. **Mrs. Susan Warry:** Born Pontypridd, 4 June 1953, d of F. Williams, miner, & G Williams. Anglican. Married 1988 Niall Warry (qv) Educated Pontypridd Grammar School. Barmaid. Joint Owner, Old Mitre Inn, Llanfoist. Hobbies: Cooking, Keep fit. Of Church Village, Pontypridd (2001).

WARRY Timothy Niall: TD 1997 FMBCI tacsc. Referendum Party: Monmouth 1997; UK Independence Party, Wales, 1999, Vale of Glamorgan 2001. **Mr. Niall Warry:** Born Chagford, Devon 20 April 1951, s of Major N. J. Warry MC & J. R.

Warry. Married (1) 2s, (2) 1988, Susan Marilyn (qv). Educated Cheltenham College. Officer, Royal Green Jackets 1969-79 (Germany, Northern Ireland, Cyprus, Canada). Joined Bass 1979. Retail Business Manager, Bass Taverns (18 pubs in Cardiff area). Self-employed Distributor. Lived at Cardiff-1996 when he bought Old Mitre Inn, Llandeilo Pertholey, Abergavenny, run by his wife (1997). Officer, Royal Regt of Wales TA 12 years. Former member, Conservative Party. Agent for his wife 2001. Interests: Get out of Europe. Hobbies: Walking my dog. Of Church Village, Pontypridd (2001).

WATERHOUSE Ronald Gough: GBE 2001 Kt 1978 QC 1969 Hon. LLD Wales) 1986 MA LLM (Cantab). Labour: West Flint 1959. **Sir Ronald Waterhouse:** Born Holywell 8 May 1926, s of Alderman Thomas Waterhouse & Dorothy Helena Gough, brother of Stuart (qv). Married Selina, d of Captain E. A. Ingram & Diana Mary Legh-Bennett. Educated Holywell Grammar School; St. Johns College, Cambridge. President, Cambridge Union 1950. RAFVR 1944-48. Barrister, Middle Temple 1952, Bencher 1977, Treasurer 1995. Member, General Council of the Bar 1961-65. Deputy-Chair, Quarter Sessions: Cheshire 1964, Flintshire 1966-71. Chair: Court of Enquiry into all aspects of Britain's Rabies Policy 1970, Agricultural Mining Act 1971-78, Local Govt Boundary Commission for England & Wales 1974-78, North Wales Child Abuse Tribunal 1997-98. Crown Court Recorder 1972-77. Presiding Judge, Wales & Chester Circuit 1980-84. Judge, Employment Appeal Tribunal 1979-87. Judge of the High Court 1977. Presiding Judge 1980-84. Member: Panel of Administrators of Singapore International Arbitration Centre 1996-. Vice-President, Zoological Society of London. President: CAB Royal Courts of Justice 1992 (Chair 1981- 92); Llangollen International Eisteddfod 1994.

WATERHOUSE Stuart G: BCom (London). Liberal: East Flint 1950. **Lieut-Colonel Stuart Waterhouse:** Born Holywell 1918, s of Alderman Thomas Waterhouse & Dorothy Helena Gough, & brother of Ronald (qv). Married Educated Holywell Grammar School; London School of Economics. Army 1939-45. General Manager, woollen mill. Holywell UDC 1949. Flintshire CC 1951. Member, Liberal Party Executive. Of Holywell.

WATERS Julian William Penrose: BA (Cantab) 1990. Conservative, Cynon Valley 2001. **Mr. Julian Waters:** Born Beaconsfield 27 May 1963. Married Sally 1s 1d. Educated Harrow School; Cambridge University (Law). Barrister, at Common Law; Commercial Bar 1986-. Chair: South West Surrey Conservative Assn. 1997-99. Waverley DC. Interests: Law, Economy. Hobbies: Spending time with family. Of Surrey.

WATKINS Dennis Ronald: Plaid Cymru: Wrexham 1983, Newport 1987, Bridgend 1997. **Mr. Dennis Watkins:** Married 2s. Optician. Chair, Pontypridd Trades Council. Taf-Ely BC 1987- (Chair, Finance Cttee 5 years). Rhondda/Cynon/ Taf BC. (Cabinet Member, Resources & Performance, Chair: Policy Cttee). Treasurer, Plaid Cymru. Of Llantwit Fardre.

WATKINS: Mark Christopher: Conservative, Torfaen 1992. **Mr. Mark Watkins:** Born 27 July 1961. Educated West Monmouth Boys Grammar School; University of Wales, Cardiff. Management Consultant. Chair: Torfaen Young Conservatives 1979-82.

WATKINS Tudor Elwyn, Baron Watkins of Glantawe 1970: Labour MP Brecon & Radnor 1945-70. **Mr. Tudor Watkins:** Born Abercrave 9 May 1903, s of Howell Watkins JP CC. Baptist Deacon & Lay Preacher. Married 1936 Bronwen Strather, Talgarth. Educated elementary school, Coleg Harlech. Miner 1917-25. Labour Agent, Brecon & Radnor 1925-33. General Secretary, Breconshire Assn. of Friendly Societies 1937-48. Breconshire CC Alderman. Branch Secretary NUGMW. Vice-President, Rural District Councils Assn. Chair, Brecon Beacons National Park Cttee 1974-84. Member: Welsh Panel, British Council 1954, Wales Tourist Board, Brecon & Radnor Hospital Management Cttee, Civil Aviation Advisory Cttee for Wales, Mid-Wales Industrial Development Assn. Member: Parliament for Wales Campaign, CND. Languages: Welsh, English. Of Brecon. Died 1983.

WATKINS Veronica Katherine: BSc. MSc. Liberal Democrat Newport West 1999, 2001; Ogmore B/E Feb. 2002. **Mrs. Veronica Watkins:** Born Birmingham 12 February 1957, d of Peter Anthony Hopkins, financial director & Doreen Brenda White, secretary. Roman Catholic. Married 1s 2d (divorced). Educated St. Anne's School, Southampton; Aston University (Chemical Engineering); Birmingham University (Biochemical Engineering). Teacher (IT & Biology). Constituency Manager, Mike German MEP. Researcher, Kirsty Williams AM. Joined Liberal Democrats 1986. Treasurer/Chair, South East Wales Region Lib. Dems. Contested Gwent CC & Newport BC. Newport CCC (St. Julians) 2004-. Languages: English; Welsh learner. Hobbies: Playing tenor saxophone, listening to music, decorating. Of Newport.

WATKINS-EVANS Ieuan: BA (Wales) MA LlB (Cantab). Liberal: Cardiff Central 1923, Norfolk South 1929. **Mr. Ieuan Watkins-Evans:** Born s of

Theophilus Evans, headmaster, Gelligrug Schools, Abertillery. Calvinistic Methodist. Educated University of Wales, Aberystwyth; Emmanuel College, Cambridge. Barrister, Inner Temple 1918, in practice 1929-36. Ministry of Food. Solicitor 1936. Contested Cardiff CC (Cathays) 1922. Of Newport.

WATSON Alastair Peter Lindsay: BA 1978 MA 1987 (Oxon) MBA 1990. Conservative, Cardiff North 2001. **Mr. Alastair Watson:** Born St. Helens, Lancs. 17 October1955, s of James Henderson Watson, engineer, & Marjorie Pye, teacher. Church of England. Married 1978 Sarah Rosalind Watson, 2s. Educated Merchant Taylor's School, Crosby; Oxford University; Cranfield School of Management. Production Manager, Unilever plc 1978-8. Principal Consultant, PA Consulting Group 1989-93. Managing Consultant, Pera Consulting 1993-95. Company director, Tesseract Ltd. Oxford, management consultants & training company 1995. Contested 3 local elections. Chair: Bristol North West Conservative Assn. Interests: Economy, Health, Education, Environment. Hobbies: Rowing, Skiing, Hill Walking. Of Bristol.

WATTS John Henry: JP (Bucks) 1913. Liberal Unionist: Merthyr Tydfil Dec. 1910. **Mr. John Watts:** Born 1868, s of Michael Watts, Gold Hall, Chalfont St. Peter (descendant of Isaac Watts). Married Grace, d of Frederick S. Osmond. Barrister, Inner Temple 1905. Of Marlow Park, Marlow.

WAYE Sheila Ramsay – see RAMSAY WAYE.

WEBB Basil Graham Conrade: MA Oxon). Conservative: Aberdare Oct. 1974, Stoke South 1951, 1955. **Mr. Basil Webb:** Born 1922. Married. Educated Mill Hill School; Queens College, Oxford. Barrister, Middle Temple 1964. Deputy-Recorder, Brighton Crown Court. Linguist & author. Hampstead BC 4 years. Deputy-Chair, Conservative Foreign Affairs Forum.

WEBB Harri: MA (Oxon). Plaid Cymru: Pontypool 1970. **Mr. Harri Webb:** Born Tycoch, Swansea 7 September 1920, s of William J. Webb, powerhouse stoker, & Lucy Irene, d of John & Elizabeth Gibbs. Educated Oxford Street National School; Glanmôr Grammar School, Swansea; Magdalen College, Oxford (Exhibitioner; Romance Languages). Royal Navy, 1941-45, Petty Officer, Interpreter. Member, Royal Navy Mission to French Provisional Government. Worked at: Druid Press, Carmarthen 1945-49; *Principality Educational* Bookshop, Cardiff 1949-51; Shared in owning bookshop at Bargoed 1951; Worked for Fords Motor Co; Clerk, Lionite & grocers; Cinema commissionaire; trained as librarian;

Librarian: Cheltenham 1952-54, Mountain Ash 1954-64 & Dowlais; retired 1970. Branch Chair NALGO. Joined Plaid Cymru, St. George's Day 1948. Founder Member, Welsh Republican Movement 1949 & Editor, *Welsh Republican* 1949-51. Member, Labour Party 1953-58. Re-joined Plaid Cymru 1959. Editor, *Welsh Nation* 1961-64. Member, Plaid Cymru Executive & Cilmeri Group. Member: Welsh Academy, Arts Council Welsh Panel. Founder Member, Dowlais Round Table. Poet (began writing 1941-46). Television & Radio Script Writer. Languages: Learned Welsh, English. Suffered stroke 1985. Died 31 December 1994. (*Western Mail The uncrowned poet laureate of Wales*). *Books: Harri Webb: Triad (with Meic Stephens & Peter Griffith) 1963, The Green Desert 1969, A Crown for Branwen 1974, Rampage and Revel 1977, Poems and Points 1983, Tales from Wales 1984, Collected Poems. (Ed. Meic Stephens) 1995, No Half Way House & A Militant Muse (edit. Meic Stephens) 1997; autobiographical articles in 'Planet' (Jan. 1976) & Artists in Wales. In articles & television scripts.*

WEBB Henry: 1st Bart 1916 JP DL. Liberal: Cardiff East 1922; Herefordshire, Jan. & Dec. 1910; MP Cardiff East 1923-24, Forest of Dean B/E 1911-18. **Lieut-Colonel, Sir Henry Webb:** Born Kington, Herefordshire 28 July 1886, s of Henry Webb & Hannah Jones. Married (1) 1894, Ellen MBE (died 1919) d. of W. P. Williams, Cardiff (2) 1919, Helen Kate de Paula, (son killed in France, 1917). Educated privately; Lausanne; Paris. Mining Engineer. Company Secretary, Ocean Coal Co. Company Director: Ocean Coal Co Ltd, Wilsons Ltd, Deep Navigation Collieries, Taff Merthyr Colliery. Farmer. Raised and commanded 3 army battalions 1914-18. Life Member, Cardiff Cymmrodorion Society. President, Glamorgan Cricket Club. Asst. Whip (unpaid) 1912-15. Of Holme Lacy, Hereford, & London. Estate £105,193. Died 29 October 1940.

WEBSTER-GARDNER Graham R: BSc (Warwick) FBIM. Conservative: Newport East 1987; UK Independence Party, Epsom & Ewell 2001. **Mr. Graham Webster-Gardner:** Born 4 July 1947. Educated Selhurst Grammar School, Croydon; Warwick University. Married 4c. Marketing Director, 4 companies. Secretary, Marketing Society 1981. Chair, Conservative Family Campaign. Member: National Listeners & Viewers Assn. Member, UK Independence Party National Executive Cttee. Of London.

WEEPLE James Gabriel: Conservative: Pontypool 1945. **Mr. Gabriel Weeple:** Born Glasgow 1896. Married 1939, Jessamine, d of Clr. F. H. Davies, Varteg (President & Acting Chair, Pontypool Conservative Assn). Royal Artillery 1914-18. Industrial Chemist & Paint Manufacturer.

West Ham BC. Contested London CC (Limehouse) 1937. Travelled widely in Europe & South America.

WELBY Charles William Hodder: Conservative: Caerphilly 1987. **Mr. Charles Welby:** Born 6 May 1953, s of Sir Bruno Welby 7th Bart & Jane, d of Ralph Hodder-Williams. Married 1978, Suzanna, d of Major Ian Stuart-Routledge, 3d. Educated Eton; Royal Agricultural, College, Cirencester. Farmer. TA 6 years. Of Harston Hall, Grantham.

WELCH J. Peter: BA (Wales) 1945. Conservative: Pontypool B/E 1946. **Mr. Peter Welch:** Born September 1923, s of R. E. Welch, coal merchant, Canton, Cardiff. Roman Catholic. Educated St. Illtyds College, Cardiff (Captain, Rugby XV); Cardiff Technical College; University of Wales, Cardiff. President, Student Representative Council 1946-47. Secretary: CPC South Wales & Mon. Conservative Party Education Officer Wales, September 1946. Of Canton, Cardiff.

WERE Ann: Green Party, South/East List 2003. **Mrs. Ann Were:** Born Monmouth, 7 April 1959, d of Peter John Powell, postman, & Edna Alice Powell, shop assistant. Christian. Married 1987, Martin Brian Were, computer engineer, 2s 1d. Enrolled Nurse. Nursing Officer, Residential Home for Severely Disabled Adults. Open University Student (Environmental Studies). Parent Governor, comprehensive school. Interests: Environmental Issues, Social Justice. Hobbies: Needlework, Dress Making.

WEST Christina Maria: Christian Democratic Party, Wales Euro 2004. **Ms. Christina West:** Business woman. Of Moston, Manchester.

WEST Daniel Granville, Baron Granville-West of Pontypool 1984: BA (Wales). Labour MP Pontypool B/E 1946-84. **Mr. Granville West:** Born Newbridge, Gwent 17 March 1904, s of John West & Elizabeth Bridges. Married 1937, Verna, d of J. Hopkins of Pontypool, 1s 1d. Educated Newbridge Grammar School; University of Wales, Cardiff. Solicitor 1929. RAF 1939-45, Flight-Lieutenant RAFVR. Abercarn UDC 1934-38. Monmouthshire CC 1938-47. President, South Wales & Mon Branch, Probation Officers Assn. PPS 1950-51. Chair, Advisory Council on Civil Aviation in Wales. Of Abersychan. Died 23 September 1984.

WEST Harry: Conservative: Montgomery 1950, Cardiff South-East 1951; Joined Conservative Party 1931; Liberal: Forest of Dean B/E 1925. **Mr. Harry West:** Born Blaenavon 1894, Baptist minister's son. Baptist lay preacher. Married. Educated elementary schools. Miner 1907-32. Army 1914-19, POW 1916-19. Trade Union &

Labour Organiser, Wales & Mon Conservative Council 1932-51. Director for Wales, Public Economy Assn 1951-. Of Pontyclun.

WHEATLEY William Gareth: BScEcon MEd PGCE (Wales). Plaid Cymru: Wrexham 1992. **Mr. Gareth Wheatley:** Born Gower, 2 March 1949, son of William Frederick Wheatley, sailor/salesman, & Esther Mary Wheatley, deputy matron, care home. Nonconformist. 2s. Educated Bishop Gore School, Swansea; University of Wales, Aberystwyth (Economics) & Cardiff. Senior Lecturer, North-East Wales Institute, Wrexham. Head Business Development Unit. Writer. Interests: Devolution. Languages: Learning Welsh, English. Of Wrexham.

WHEELER Olive Annie: DBE 1949 MSc (Wales) DSc (London) FPsychS. Labour: University of Wales 1922. **Professor, Dame Olive Wheeler:** Born Brecon 1885, d. of H. Burford Wheeler. Educated Brecon Grammar School; University of Wales, Aberystwyth; Bedford College, London (Psychology); Paris University. Lecturer in Mental & Moral Science, Cheltenham Ladies College. Lecturer in Education & Dean of Faculty, Manchester University. Professor of Education & Dean of the Faculty, University of Wales, Cardiff 1929-51. Professor Emeritus 1951. Fellow of the University of Wales. Member: Welsh Joint Education Cttee, Court & Appointments Board, University of Wales, Council, Welsh National School of Medicine, National Employment Council. Chair: Advisory Cttee on Youth Employment (Wales), WEA South Wales Council. South Wales Regional Adviser WRVS. Vice-President, British Federation of University Women. Of Cyncoed, Cardiff. Estate £26,000. Died September 1963.

WHIPLASH Miss – see ST. CLAIR Lindi.

WHITBY Michael J: Conservative: Delyn 1992, West Midlands Euro 1989, B/E 1987, Warley East 1983. **Mr. Michael Whitby:** February 1948. Married Gaynor, teacher. Educated James Watt Technical-Grammar School; College of Michaelhoven. Company Director, clothing & textile distributors & Lecturer in Business Studies. Vice-Chair, West Midlands CPC. Secretary, West Midlands Conservative Clubs Advisory Cttee 1986. Member, National Federation of Self-Employed & Small Businesses. Sandwell BC 1984-86. Of Pentre Halkyn.

WHITE Eirene Lloyd, Baroness White of Rhymney 1970: MA (Oxon) Hon. LLD (Wales 1979, Queens University Belfast 1981, Bath 1983). Labour, Flint 1945; MP East Flint 1950-70. **Rt. Hon. Eirene White:** Born Belfast 7 November 1909, d of Dr. Thomas Jones CH, Secretary

to Great War Coalition Cabinet. Brought up at Barry. Married 1947, John Cameron White, journalist (died 1968). Educated St. Paul's Girls School; Somerville College, Oxford (Hon. Fellow 1966). Civil Servant, Ministry of Labour & Department of Education 1933-37, 1941-45. Political Correspondent, *Manchester Evening News* 1945-49. Member, Labour Party NEC 1947-53, 1958-72 (Chair 1968-69). President, National Council of Women, Wales; Council for the Protection of Rural Wales 1974-89; Nursery Schools Assn 1964-66. Vice-President, National Union of Students; Commonwealth Countries League; Town & Country Planning Assn 1983-91; Council for the National Parks 1985-. Chair: Fabian Society 1959-60; International Cttee, National Council of Social Service 1973-77; Coleg Harlech 1974-84; Advisory Commission on Oil Pollution at Sea 1974-78; Land Authority for Wales 1975-80. Deputy-Chair: Metrication Board 1972-76. Member: National Joint Cttee of Working Women's Assns 1948-52, 1958-60, 1963-68; Court of National Museum of Wales 1950-70; Council of University of Wales, Aberystwyth 1973-85; Council of University of Wales, Bangor 1977-80, Council of UWIST 1981-93 (Chair 1983-88, President 1987-88, Vice-President 1988-93); University Grants Commission 1977-80; Cinematograph Film Council; Royal Commission on Environmental Pollution 1974-84; British Waterways Board 1974-80; Governor: British Film Institute; National Film Theatre. Minister of State, Foreign Office 1966-67; Minister of State, Wales 1967-70. Deputy Speaker, House of Lords 1979-89. Principal Deputy Chairman of Cttees 1979-82. Hon. Fellow, University of Wales, Cardiff 1989. Of London & Treberfydd, Bwlch, Powys. Died January 2000. *Books: Eirene White, The Ladies of Gregynog.*

WHITEBEAM Robin Franklyn Welch: BSc (Wales). Green Party, North List 1999. **Mr. Robin Whitebeam:** Born Norton-Juxta-Kenpsey (Pershore) Worcestershire, 3 April 1969, s of Douglas Victor Welch, soldier, & Heather Gillian Davies, secretary, housing co-operative. Anglican. Married 1997, Tonya Rees, artist, 3s 1d. Educated University of Wales, Bangor (Agroforestry). Agroforester. Contested Gwynedd CC 1999. Chair, Bangor Green Party. Interests: Re-modelling of British farming & forestry, re-establishment of urban & countryside social & business links. Hobbies: Building environment – friendly houses, walking. Languages: English.

WHITING Stephen James: BA PGCE (Wales). Conservative: Rhondda 1997. **Mr. Stephen Whiting:** Born 17 March 1969. Educated Chislehurst & Sidcup Grammar School; University of Wales, Swansea; Cardiff Institute of Higher Education. Conservative Research Department,

Cardiff 1991-93. Teacher 1993-. Chair: Swansea West Central Branch. Secretary, Cardiff South & Penarth Conservative. Executive. Contested Swansea CC 1990, South Glam CC 1993, Cardiff CC 1999. Barnado's fundraiser. Languages: Learning Welsh, English. Of Grangetown, Cardiff.

WHITTLE Lindsay Geoffrey: BA (Wales). Plaid Cymru, Caerphilly 1983, 19987, 1992, 1997, 1999, 2001, 2003. **Mr. Lindsay Whittle:** Born Caerphilly, 24 March 1953, s of Thomas Ivor Whittle, welder, & Margaret May James, factory worker. 1 d. Educated Caerphilly Grammar/Technical School; university (Post Graduate Diploma in Housing). Worked 11 years in aluminium industry. Regional Housing Manager, St. Mellons. Vice-Chair: South Wales Housing Assns Board. Member: Court, University of Wales, Plaid Cymru National Council. Penyrheol ComC. Rhymney Valley DC 1976-96. Mid-Glam CC 1977-81. Caerphilly CBC 1996- (Group Leader, Leader of the Council 1999). Interests: Housing, Services for Senior Citizens. Hobbies: Antique Collecting, Gardening, Rugby. Of Abertridwr.

WHYATT Robert: Conservative, South East Wales Euro 1984. **Mr. Robert Whyatt:** Industrialist.

WIGGIN Alfred William: Kt 1993 TD 1970 MA (Oxon). Conservative: Montgomery 1964, 1966; MP Weston super Mare B/E 1969-97. **Sir Jerry Wiggin:** Born 24 February 1937, s of Colonel, Sir William Wiggin. Married (1) 1964, Rosemary Orr, 3c (s Bill, MP for Leominster 2001-, Spokesman on Wales 2003-) (2) Mrs. Morella Bulmer. Educated Eton; Trinity College, Cambridge (Cambridge shooting blue). Executive, management consultants. Sheep & corn farmer (Began farming 1958 (200 acres from mother, formed private company). Lloyds Underwriter-1992. RAF Pilot 1955-57. TA 1957-, Major, Royal Yeomanry, 1975-78, Hon. Colonel, Warwickshire & Worcestershire Yeomanry (A) Squadron, Royal Mercian & Lancastrian Yeomanry 1992. PPS 1970-74. Parl-Secretary, Agriculture, Fisheries & Food 1979-81. Under-Secretary, Armed Forces 1981-83. Chair: Select Cttee on Ag. Jt. Vice-Chair, British-Chinese Parliamentary Group. Jt Secretary: British-Turkish Parliamentary Group, Conservative MPs Defence Cttee 1974-75, Agriculture Cttee 1975-79. Chair: West Country Conservative MPs. House of Commons Conservative Spokesman on Wales 2003-. President, Wells Conservative Assn. Of Axbridge, Somerset.

WIGLEY Dafydd Wynne: PC. BSc (Manchester). Plaid Cymru: Merioneth 1970, North Wales Euro 1984; MP Caernarfon 1974- 2001; AM Caernarfon 1999-2003. **Rt. Hon. Dafydd Wigley:** Born Derby 1 April 1943, s of Elfyn Edward Wigley, County

Treasurer, & Myfanwy Batterbee, brought up at Bontnewydd. Methodist. Married Elinor Bennet, harpist, d of Edward Bennett Owen, Dolgellau, 1s 1d (2s died). Educated Caernarfon Grammar School; Rydal School, Colwyn Bay; University of Manchester. Costs Accountant. Executive, Mars Chocolate. Financial Controller, Hoover Co. Merthyr Tydfil. Senior Costs & Accountant & Industrial Economist 1971-74. President, South Caernarfonshire Creamery 1989. Director, Alpha Cyssylltiadau 1981. Joined Plaid Cymru 1962. Founder Member, Plaid Cymru Research Group 1966. Director of Research. Whip 1987-87. President 1981-84, 1991-2000 (resigned on health grounds). Merthyr Tydfil BC 1972-74. Member: Electoral Reform Society. President: Caernarfon Town AFC; Spastic Society of Wales. Vice-President: Council for the Disabled, National Federation of Industrial Development Authorities 1981. Member: Select Cttee on Welsh Affairs 1983-87, All Party Disablement Group. Sponsored Disabled Persons Act 1981. Awarded Grimshaw Memorial Award 1992 by National Federation for the blind. Co-ordinator, 2003 Election in the Valleys, March 2002. Director, S4C November 2003. Pro-Chancellor, University of Wales, 4 December 2003. Vice-President, Hon. Society of Cymmrodorion 2003. Interests: Economic Development, Disability Issues, Europe. Hobbies: Football, Rugby, Tennis, Chess, Gardening, Walking, Writing. Languages: Welsh, English, basic French. *Book: Dafydd Wigley, An Economic Plan for Wales (with Phil Williams) 1970, O Ddifri, Dal Ati, Maen I'r Wal (autobiography 3 vols), Working for Wales 2001.*

WILKINS Anna: Pro-Life Alliance, South/Central List 2003. **Ms. Anna Wilkins:** Of London.

WILKINSON Brian: Communist: Pontypool 1970. **Mr. Brian Wilkinson:** Born Northampton 1935. Married 3c. Moved from Scotland to Newport 1969. Junior railway clerk. Railway signal engineer. Asst Area Railway Manager.

WILLEY Richard Frederick: BA PhD (Cantab). Labour, Brecon & Radnor B/E 1985, 1987. **Dr. Richard Willey:** Born 27 November 1944, s of Rt. Hon. Fred Willey MP. Partner, 1s. Educated, Cambridge University. With Community Relations Council, London; Research Fellow, Australian Institute of Aboriginal Affairs; Educational Researcher & Writer. Chair, Brecon & Radnor Labour Party. Radnor DC. Died after fall, 29 August 1987.

WILLIAMS Alan John: PC 1977 BSc Econ (London) 1954 BA (Oxon). Labour MP Swansea West 1964-, Contested Poole 1959. **Rt. Hon. Alan Williams:** Born Caerphilly 14 October 1930, s of Emlyn Williams, ex-miner/local government officer, & Violet Russ. *Christian with no particular Denomination.* Married Patricia Mary Rees of Blackwood, 2s 1d. Educated Cardiff High School; Cardiff College of Technology; London University; University College, Oxford (PPE). Member, NUS Delegation to USSR 1954. RAF Education Officer 1948-50. Lecturer in Economics, Welsh College of Advanced Technology 1960-64. Broadcaster, Journalist & Company Director. Joined Labour Party 1950. Member, ATTI, Fabian Society, Co-operative Party. PPS 1966-67. Chair, Welsh PLP 1966-67. Under-Secretary: Economic Affairs 1967-69; Technology 1868-70. Opposition Spokesman, Higher Education & Science 1970-74. Minister of State: Prices 1974-76, Industry 1976-79. Opposition Spokesman: Wales 1979-80, Civil Service 1980-83, Trade & Industry 1983-84, House of Commons Affairs 1984-87, Wales 1987-88; House of Commons Affairs & Deputy Campaigns Co-ordinator 1988-89. Member: Public Accounts Cttee 1966-67, Standards & Privileges Cttee 1997-2001. Jt Chair: All Party Minerals Cttee 1979-86. Parliamentary Adviser: Institution of Plant Engineers; Assn of First Division, Civil Servants; TSSA. Chair, Public Accounts Commission. Interests: Economic Policy, Royal Family. Hobbies: Golf. Of Swansea & London.

WILLIAMS Alan Wynne: BA 1966 DPhil 1969 (Oxon). Labour MP Carmarthen 1987-97, Carmarthenshire East & Dinefwr 1997-2001. **Dr. Alan Wynne Williams:** Born Cwmffrwd, 21 December 1947, s of Tom & Mary Hannah Williams. Married 1973, Marian Williams. Educated Carmarthen Grammar School; Jesus College, Oxford (1st Chemistry). Senior Lecturer in Environmental Studies, Trinity College Carmarthen 1971-87. Joined Labour Party 1977. Secretary, Carmarthen Labour Party 1981-84. Carmarthen election agent 1983. Member, Select Cttees: Science & Technology 1992-97, Welsh Affairs 1987-92, Consolidation Bills 1987-92. Jt. Vice-Chair, PLP environment cttee. 1990-. Member, NAFTHE, SERA, Greenpeace, Friends of the Earth. Hobbies: Reading, Watching sport. Languages: Welsh, English. Of Penybanc, Ammanford.

WILLIAMS Albert Clifford: BEM 1957 JP (Mon) 1952. Labour MP Abertillery B/E 1965-70. **Mr. Cliff Williams:** Born Abertillery 28 June 1905, s of Albert Williams, miner. Married 1930, Beatrice Ann, d of Charles Garbett. Educated elementary schools. Colliery Repairer. Chair: Western Lodge, NUM 1936-46. Chair: Monmouthshire Health & Welfare Cttee, Usk River Board 1945-65. Member: North Monmouthshire Hospital Management Cttee, Monmouthshire Joint Workshops for the Blind, Welsh Water Authority. Monmouthshire CC 1946-64, Alderman 1964-65 (Vice-Chair

Centre Sub-Cttee). Vice-Chair, Sports Council for Wales. Of Blaina. Died April 1979.

WILLIAMS Arthur James: JP (Cardiff) 1932. Labour: Cardiff East 1918, 1922. **Mr. Arthur Williams:** Born nr. Pontypool 30 November 1880, s of James Edward Williams, railway signalman. Married 1914, Gladys Agnes Russell (died 1947) 1s. Educated Pantymoile National School; Ruskin College, Oxford 1907-08. Sold buns at Pontypool Station at 10. Railway Worker 1894. Railway Guard. South Wales & Mon Area Organiser, Amalgamated Society of Railway Servants 1909, then NUR. Chair: Cardiff East Labour Party, Cardiff Co-operative Party. Vice-President, National Federation of Old Age Pensioners Assns. Cardiff CC 1927-30, 1935- (Leader, Labour Group) Alderman 1959-, Lord Mayor 1958-59. Of Rhiwbina, Cardiff. Died 10 October 1962.

WILLIAMS Arthur John: JP (Glam) DL1893. Liberal MP South Glamorgan 1885-95; Contested Birkenhead 1880. **Mr. Arthur Williams:** Born 1836, s of Dr. John Morgan Williams, Bridgend & Caroline Augusta, d of T. Whitesmith of Bawtry. Married 1877 Rose Harriette Thompson, d of Robert Crawshay, Cyfarthfa. Educated Privately. Barrister, Inner Temple 1867. Member, Select Cttee on Crown Lands. Secretary, Royal Commission on Accidents in Mines 1885. Hon. Sec Legal Aid Assn & Law Amendment Society. A founder, National Liberal Club. Of Bridgend. Estate £9,290. Died 12 September 1911.

WILLIAMS Arthur Osmond: 1st Bart 1909 JP DL (Caerns). Liberal MP Merioneth 1900-1910; Contested West Manchester 1885. **Sir A. Osmond Williams:** Born Castell Deudraeth 17 March 1849, s of David Williams (MP Merioneth 1868, died 1869) & Annie Loveday Wynn-Williams. Anglican. Married 1880, Frances Evelyn, d of J. W. Greaves of Berricote, Warwickshire. Educated Eton. Landowner. Lord Lieutenant of Merioneth. Chair, Merioneth Quarter Sessions. Constable of Harlech Castle. Merioneth CC Chairman 1903-06. Died 28 January 1927.

WILLIAMS Arthur Ronald: Independent, Carmarthen West & South Pembrokeshire 2003. **Mr. Arthur Williams:** Born, Newport, Gwent. Married 2d. RAF. TA. Part-time Salvation Army envoy. Motor industry. Special Constable. Interests: Attract large companies & new jobs to the area, Increase funding for NHS, Proper hospital in Tenby, NHS dentists, Road & rail links, Remove unfair regulations & restrictions on farming industry, Free education for all. Hobbies: Most sports, Reading, Keeping fit, Church. Of Whitlow, Saundersfoot.

WILLIAMS Benjamin Francis – see FRANCIS-WILLIAMS Benjamin.

WILLIAMS Betty Helena: BA (Wales). Labour: Caernarfon 1983, Conwy 1987; MP Conwy 1997. **Mrs. Betty Williams:** Born Dyffryn Nantlle 31 July 1944. Welsh Independent Deacon. Married Evan Williams, 2s. Educated Ysgol Dyffryn Nantlle; Bangor Normal College. Secretarial Work. Freelance Journalist. Joined Labour Party 1964. ComC 1967-83. Arfon BC 1970-91, Mayor 1990-91. Gwynedd CC 1976-97 (Chair: Social Services Cttee). Member: Môn/Gwynedd Victim Support Group, Arfon Carers' Group, Electricity Users Council, Gas Consumers Council, Welsh Joint Education Cttee, Health Education Advisory Cttee for Wales, Snowdonia National Park Cttee (Northern), Court, University of Wales. Chair, National Eisteddfod local Finance Cttee. Hon. Fellow, University of Wales, Bangor. Interests: Devolution, Feminist issues. Languages: Welsh, English.

WILLIAMS Brynle: Conservative, Clwyd West 2003, AM North List 2003, **Mr. Brynle Williams:** Born Cilcain, nr. Mold, 9 January 1949, son of George Williams, farmer, & Maenwen Williams, housewife. Calvinistic Methodist. Married 1971, Frances Mary Williams, 1s 1d. Educated Ysgol Uwchradd Maes Garmon, Mold. Farmer. President: Denbighshire & Flintshire Agricultural Society. Chair: Flintshire FUW. Member: Royal Welsh Agricultural Council. Conservative spokesman on Rural Affairs. A leading figure in the protest against petrol prices 2000. Interests: The Welsh Language, rural affairs. Hobbies: Showing & judging Welsh cobs & ponies, spending time with wife & children. Languages: Welsh, English. Of Cilcain.

WILLIAMS Brynmor: BA (Lampeter) 1931 BD 1940 MTh 1941 (London). Labour: Cardigan 1951. **Revd Brynmor Williams:** Born Seven Sisters 27 August 1906. Married 1928, Annie Elizabeth Price, 1s. Educated elementary schools; St. David's College School; St. David's College, Lampeter (1st Theology), Learned German to read theology. Miner 1920-. Ordained: Priest of the Church in Wales 1933. Curate of Clydach 1933-40. Vicar of Llanganten with Llanynis 1940-48. Vicar of Llansamlet 1948-74. Chaplain to the Forces 1940-45. Extra Mural Lecturer, University of Wales, Swansea 1960-. Examining Chaplain, Bishop of Swansea & Brecon 1958-. Member, Brecon Advisory Labour Council. Made history as the first UK Anglican priest to stand for Parliament. Languages: Welsh, English. Died 10 June 1989.

WILLIAMS Catherine: Pro-Life Alliance: Caerphilly 1997. **Mrs. Catherine Williams:** Married 4c. Lives in Cardiff, children attend school in Caerphilly. Stood on an anti-abortion platform.

WILLIAMS Christmas Price: JP (Denbs) BSc (Manchester). Liberal, Wrexham 1923; MP Wrexham 1924-29. **Mr. C. P. Williams:** Born Christmas Day 1881, s of Peter Williams, Managing Director, Brymbo Steel Works & Mary Price. Welsh Independent. Married 1909, Marion, d. of Thomas Davies. Educated Wrexham & Mold; Victoria University, Manchester. Engineer. Worked at Sheffield, Warrington & Africa as fitter & draughtsman. Managing Director, Brymbo Steel Works. Languages: Welsh, English. Of Wrexham. Died 18 August 1965.

WILLIAMS Dafydd J: BSc (Exeter) MSc (London). Plaid Cymru, South Wales Euro 1979. **Mr. Dafydd Williams:** Born Rumney. Cardiff, 1933. Educated Cardiff High School; Exeter University; London School of Economics. Economist. South Wales Organiser, Plaid Cymru. General Secretary, Plaid Cymru 1971-92. Member: Cardiff Philharmonic Choir. Languages: Welsh, English, French, Spanish, Irish. Of Cardiff.

WILLIAMS Daniel Geraint: OBE 1986 BA Leeds). Liberal: Caernarfon 1955, PPC Shipley 1950. Joined Plaid Cymru April 1960. **Mr. Geraint Williams:** Born 1921, s of Revd Daniel Williams. Presbyterian lay preacher. Educated Bala Grammar School; Loughborough Training College; Leeds University. Executive Member, Leeds Liberal Club. Army 1939-45, RA & RAEC. Teacher (English & PE), Holyhead. Headteacher, Castell Alun High School, Mold. Chair: Anglesey Branch, Incorporated Assn of Assistant Masters 1952-53. Languages: Welsh, English.

WILLIAMS David: JP (Swansea). Labour: Swansea East 1918, B/E 1919, MP 1922-. **Mr. David Williams:** Born Swansea 8 September 1865, s of David Williams, copper worker. Anglican choirmaster. Married 1889, Elizabeth Colwill, 5c. Educated Kilvey Copper Works School. Page boy, Grenfell family 1877-79 (sacked for organising staff strike). Apprentice boiler maker 1879. Boiler Maker. Chair, Swansea & District Co-operative Society from its inception, President 1900-. Member, Western Sectional Cttee CWS. Swansea BC 1898- (1st Labour Clr), (Chair, Health Cttee), Alderman, Mayor 1912-13. Hon. Freeman 1924. Of St. Thomas, Swansea. Estate £911. Died 22 January 1941.

WILLIAMS David Ellis: JP (Mon). Conservative: North Monmouthshire Dec. 1910. Lieut-Colonel Ellis Williams: Born Cwmdu, Brecs. 1854, s of Jenkin Williams & Margaret Morgan. Anglican. Married 1887, Laura, d of Isaac Butler JP Pantteg, Mon. Steel Manufacturer. Director,

Baldwins Steel. Army 1914-18. TA: OC. 4th Welsh Brigade RFA. Freemason. President, North Monmouthshire Conservative Assn, Pontypool Conservative Assn. Chair, Pantteg UDC. Of Griffithstown, Pontypool.

WILLIAMS David Elwyn: Plaid Cymru: Gower 1997. **Mr. Elwyn Williams:** Born 1958. Carmarthen Insurance Broker & part-time beef farmer. Treasurer, Carmarthen Plaid Cymru. President, Carmarthen Young Farmers Club. Of Carmarthen.

WILLIAMS David Henry: Liberal: Gower 1918, B/E 1920. **Mr. David Williams:** Born Three Crosses, Gower 1873, s of John Williams, farmer. Welsh Congregationalist deacon. Married Phoebe Elizabeth Annie (Nancy), d of Revd James Thomas, Baptist Minister, Penclawdd, & sister of Mrs. Lily Folland (qv). Educated Borough Road Teacher Training College, London. Teacher. Headteacher: Three Crosses School, Herbert Road School, Neath. Secretary, Gower Liberal Assn 1900. Of Three Crosses and then Neath.

WILLIAMS David James: JP 1938-39. Labour MP Neath B/E 1946-64. **Mr. D. J. Williams:** Born Gwauncaegurwen 3 February 1897, s of Morgan Williams, miner, & Margaretta Jones. Married d of James Alexander. Educated Gwauncaegurwen elementary school; Central Labour College 1919-21. Unemployed 1921. Ruskin College, Oxford 1922-23. Miner 1911-. Lecturer, Scottish Labour College 1924-31. Miner, 1931-. Checkweighman & Lodge Secretary, Gwauncaegurwen 1931-45. Chair: Anthracite Miners' Combine Cttee. Member, SWMF Executive. Joined Socialist Labour Party 1917, ILP 1922 (Oxford branch propaganda secretary). Pontardawe RDC 1931-45, Chair 1938-39. Member: Board of Guardians. Secretary, Welsh Labour MPs. Languages: Welsh, English. Died 12 September 1982. *Books etc: D. J. Williams, Capitalist Combination in the Coal Industry 1924.*

WILLIAMS David John: Liberal Democrat, Wales Euro 2004; Ashford 1997; East Sussex & Crawley Euro 1994. **Mr. John Williams:** Born Usk, 25 June 1949. Educated King Henry VII Grammar School, Abergavenny; Hatfield Polytechnic. Medical Translator & Public Affairs Consultant. Regional Chair, German Liberal Party (Frei Demokratishe Partei) in 1980s.

WILLIAMS David John Delwyn: LIB (Wales). Conservative: Montgomery 1970, 1979, 1983, Cardigan Oct. 1974; MP Montgomery 1979-83. **Mr. Delwyn Williams:** Born 1 November 1938, s of David Lewis Williams & Irene Violet Gwendoline Williams. Married 1963, Olive Elizabeth Jerman, 2c. Educated Welshpool Grammar School; University of Wales, Aberystwyth. Solicitor &

Company Director. Secretary, Welsh Conservative MPs 1982-83. Member, Select Cttee on Wales, Statutory Instruments Cttee. Jt Sec All-Party Leisure & Recreation Industry Cttee. President, Welshpool Chamber of Trade. Rotarian. Member, British Field Sports Society. Race Horse Owner. Of Welshpool.

WILLIAMS David Leonard: MB ChB (Liverpool) 1949 MRCGP. Liberal: Denbigh Feb. & Oct. 1974. **Dr. David Williams:** Born 26 December 1926, s of Dr. John Williams, Birkenhead. Married a teacher, 4c. Educated Birkenhead School; Liverpool University. RAF. Medical Practitioner. Flintshire CC. President: North Wales Branch BMA. Member: General Medical Services Cttee 1968-. Welsh Liberal Spokesman, Health. Languages: Learned Welsh, English. Of Holywell.

WILLIAMS David Meurig: BSc MSc CEng MBCS MCIPD MIQA MISTC. Liberal Democrat, Rhondda 1999. **Mr. Meurig Williams:** Born Church Village, 11 November 1950, s of Thomas Richard Williams, headteacher, & Eunice James, teacher. Methodist. Married 1991, Margaret M. Gray, clinical psychologist. Chartered Information Systems Engineer. Human Resources Manager, Lloyds TSB. Consultant in Training & Development. Voluntary tutor at local library. Windlesham PC 1995. School governor 2001. Interests: Transport, Education & Training, Disability Issues. Hobbies: Church, Community Activities, Bee-Keeping, Voluntary Work, History. Languages: some Welsh, English. Of Bagshot, Surrey.

WILLIAMS David Rhys: BA Nottingham. Labour: Caernarfon 1987, Meirionydd/Nant Conwy 1992. **Mr. Rhys Williams:** Born Tregaron 21 January 1948. Married Margaret, 2d. Educated Pontypridd Grammar School; Exeter University; College of William & Mary, Virginia; Nottingham University. Worked in England & USA. Returned to Wales 1976. Teacher (Head of English, Lampeter Comprehensive). Regional Officer for Wales NUT. Chair, Ceredigion & North Pembs Labour Party. Tregaron ComC. President, Dyfed NUT. Poet in Welsh & English. Of Tregaron.

WILLIAMS David Rowland: JP Labour: Carmarthen 1923, West Derby 1922, Wolverhampton East 1924, 1929. **Mr. Rowland Williams:** Born Blaenau Ffestiniog 1876, s of John & Ellen William. Calvinistic Methodist. Married 1902, Katherine Maude Geldart. GWR Engine driver. Bala UDC. Brotherhood & Temperance speaker. Languages: Welsh, English.

WILLIAMS Dewi: BA (Lancaster). Liberal: Caernarfon Oct. 1974. **Mr. Dewi Williams:** Born

Dyffryn Clwyd, 1946, farmer's son. Married Rhiannon, teacher, 2c. Educated elementary school; left school at 15; Llysfai Farm Institute; Coleg Harlech; Lancaster University (History). 1st Chair, Lancaster University Welsh Society; Liverpool School of Law; Copenhagen Farm College. Solicitor at Denbigh 1974. Languages: Welsh, English. Of Rhyl.

WILLIAMS Edward John: PC 1945 KCMG 1952 JP (Glam 1937 & New South Wales). Labour MP Ogmore B/E 1930-46. **Rt. Hon. Sir Ted Williams:** Born Victoria, Ebbw Vale 1 July 1890, s of Emmanuel Williams, miner, & Ada James. Baptist. Married 1916, Evelyn, d of David James, 2d. Educated Victoria & Hopkinstown Elementary Schools. Miner, Great Western Collieries 1902-14. Secretary, Great Western Collieries 1909-13, Student, London Labour College 1913-15. Unemployed 1916. Miner 1917-18. Labour Colleges provincial lecturer 1916. Miner 1917. Checkweighman 1918. Miners' Agent, Garw Valley 1919-31. Secretary: Pontypridd ILP 1914-18, Pontypridd Branch, No Conscription Fellowship, Hands off Russia Council. Glamorgan CC 1927-31, 1937-. PPS 1940-45. Minister of Information 1945-46. High Commissioner to Australia 1946-52. Member, National Insurance Disputes Tribunal 1954-59. Estate £7406. Died 16 May 1963.

WILLIAMS Eifion Wyn: Labour, Caernarfon 1997, North List 1999. **Mr. Eifion Williams:** Born Bwlch-y-Groes, Wrexham, 14 September 1970. Educated Ysgol Morgan Llwyd, Wrexham; Plasgoch FE College; University of Wales, Aberystwyth. Parliamentary Assistant, Joe Wilson MEP; Researcher, Alan Williams MP. Director, Moonlight Theatre, Aberystwyth. Chair: University of Wales, Aberystwyth, Labour Club 1992-93; All-Wales Labour Forum. Contested Wrexham CBC (Llangollen Rural) 2004. Languages: Welsh, English, German. Hobbies: Travel, cooking. Of Bwlchgwyn.

WILLIAMS Eilian Stuart: LlB (Wales). Plaid Cymru: Clwyd West 1999, Ynys Môn 2001, North List 2003. **Mr. Eilian Williams:** Born Porth Amlwch 26 January 1950. Married 2d. Educated Ysgol Uwchradd Syr Thomas Jones; Ysgol Uwchradd Holyhead; Ysgol Uwchradd Llangefi; University of Wales, Aberystwyth. Solicitor. Holyhead 1974. Ynys Môn CC. Plaid Cymru, Wales Euro 2004. Interests: Law, Legal Justice System, Agriculture, Small Businesses, Health, Defence, Europe. Hobbies: Painting, Literature, Art. Of Holyhead.

WILLIAMS Elfed – see WILLIAMS Huw Elfed.

WILLIAMS Elwyn (Plaid Cymru) – see WILLIAMS David Elwyn.

WILLIAMS Elwyn: Conservative: Caernarfon 1997; UK Independence Party, Caernarfon & North List 2003. **Mr. Elwyn Williams:** Born Llanberis 9 March 1935. Married Naomi Williams, 2c. Educated John Bright Grammar School, Llandudno; Friars School, Bangor; Bala Grammar School. RAF 1953-56. Nigeria 1956-82: Standard Bank 1956-82, redundant. Senior Management, Balfour Williamson. Financial Controller, Ashamu Group of 10 Nigerian companies. Made a chief of the Yoruba tribe after saving the life of the King of Osogobo. Sheep Farmer at Penygroes 1985. Co-founder, Cymmrodorion Society of Nigeria. Secretary & President, Conservative 2000 Group. Joined UKIP 2002. Member: UKIP Wales Agriculture Sub-Cttee. Languages: Welsh, English. Of Penygroes, Gwynedd. *Books: Elwyn Williams, Oyinbo Banki, A White Chief's Nigerian Odyssey 1996.*

WILLIAMS Ernest Nefyl Coppack: Plaid Cymru: West Flint 1959, 1964. **Mr. Nefyl Williams:** Born Connahs Quay May 1911. Married Myfanwy, 1s. Educated Hawarden Grammar School; Cartefle Training College, Wrexham 1945-47. Worked at Shotton Steelworks c.1927-45, established a staff trade union. Teacher (Art), Mold Grammar School. Languages: Learned Welsh, English. Of Sychdyn, Mold. Died 12 February 1983.

WILLIAMS Eryl Wynn: Plaid Cymru: Clwyd West 1999, 2001. **Mr. Eryl Williams:** Born 13 November 1955. Presbyterian Church of Wales. Educated Llysfasi Agricultural College. ComC. Glyndwr DC. Clwyd CC. Denbighshire CC 1995- (Group Leader), Chairman 1997-98, Leader of the Council 2003-. Chair: Clwyd Young Farmers Organisation, Young Farmers, England & Wales 1988-89 (Vice-President 1996-97). School Governor. Member: BBC Wales Agriculture Advisory Cttee 1991-95, North Wales Economic Forum, North Wales Tourist Board, Clwydfro Enterprise Agency, Ruthin Choir. Plaid Cymru Spokesman: Agriculture. Languages, Welsh, English. Of Clawddnewydd, Ruthin.

WILLIAMS Euryn Ogwen: BA (Wales). Plaid Cymru: Barry 1970. **Mr. Euryn Ogwen Williams:** Born Penmachno 22 December 1942, s of Alun Ogwen Williams, headteacher & Lilian Evans, professional singer. Welsh Independent. Married Jenny 1s 1d. Educated Llanrwst Grammar School; Alun Grammar School, Mold; University of Wales, Bangor (Philosophy & Psychology). President: Bangor Student Representative Council; University of Wales Central SRC 1964. Founder Editor, *Y Dinesydd*. Television Producer/Director: TWW Ltd 1964-67. Head of Religion & Sport, Harlech TV Ltd. 1967-. Independent Producer (BBC HTV & various corporations). Head of Programmes S4C 1981-91. Adviser to Gaelic television in Scotland &

Ireland 1991-. Digital development adviser S4C. Founder/Director, Digital College. In co-operation with National Assembly developed community project using wireless broadband in rural communities. Plaid Cymru Spokesman on Broadcasting. National Eisteddfod Chaired Bard. Hon. Fellow, University of Wales, Lampeter 2003. Poet & writer. Interests: Television, Broadband, Religions & Religious Matters. Hobbies: Sport, Politics. Languages: Welsh, English. Of Barry.

WILLIAMS Francis John Watkin: 8th Bart. QC 1951 MA (Cantab) JP (Denbs) 1951. Conservative, Anglesey 1935. **Sir Francis Williams:** Born 24 January 1905, s of Col. Lawrence Williams. Succeed to baronetcy on death of his brother 1971. Anglican. Married 1932, Brenda Beryl, d of Sir John Jarvis, Bart., 1d. Educated Malvern College; Trinity College, Cambridge. Barrister, Middle Temple, 1928. Contested London CC (Southwark) 1928. Hon. Secretary, United Club 1935. Wing-Commander RAFVR. Deputy Chairman of Quarter Sessions: Anglesey 1949-60 (Chairman 1960-95), Cheshire 1952-95, Flintshire 1953-61 (Chairman 1961-95). High Sheriff of Denbighshire 1957, Anglesey 1963. Recorder of Birkenhead 1950-95, Chester 1958-95. Chair, North Wales Area, Medical Appeal Tribunal 1954-57. Chancellor of the Diocese of St. Asaph 1966-83. Freeman, City of Chester 1960. Of Denbigh. Died 5 January 1995.

WILLIAMS Gareth Stephen: BA (Cantab). Labour, Wales Euro 1999, 2004. **Mr. Gareth Williams:** Born Crickhowell, 28 April 1960, s of Graham Williams, headteacher, & Iris Mary Williams, teacher. Partner, Michael John Penn. Educated King Edward's School, Birmingham; Trinity Hall, Cambridge (double 1st History). Second Secretary, British Embassy, Stockholm. Desk Officer, Central Africa, Foreign & Colonial Office. Head, Welsh Development Agency & Enterprise Wales. Policy Adviser, Socialist Group in European Parliament 3 years in early 1990s. Head of European Affairs, Birmingham City Council. Director of Research, ECOTEC Research & Consulting Ltd (European regional development & environmental policy). Economic Development Consultant. Special Adviser, Alun Michael (Secretary of State for Wales & First Secretary, Assembly) 1998-2000. Director, GJW Wales. Secretary, Ludlow CLP 1983-2001. Ludlow TC 1999-. Joined Labour Party c.1980. Chair: Shropshire County Labour Party. Labour, Wales Euro 2004. Member, Samaritans. Hobbies: Walking, Cinema. Languages: picking up Welsh by osmosis, English plus five other languages. Of Ludlow.

WILLIAMS Gareth Victor: Plaid Cymru: Clwyd South 1997. **Mr. Gareth Victor Williams:** Born 13

December 1953. Married 1997. Educated Maes Garmon School, Rhyl; University of Wales Institute of Education, Cyncoed, Cardiff; North East Wales Institute (Diploma in Youth Club Work). Teacher & School Governor, Abergele Secondary School. Contested Flintshire CC 1999. Interests: Environment, Disabled Issues, Welsh Language. Languages: Welsh, English.

WILLIAMS George Clark: 1st Bart 1955 KC 1934 JP (Carms) Hon. LLD (Wales) BA (London) 1898. (National) Liberal: Llanelli 1922. **Sir George Clark Williams:** Born 2 November 1878, s of Samuel & Martha Williams, Llanelli. Congregationalist. Educated Bishops Stortford, University of Wales, Aberystwyth. Solicitor 1902-08. Barrister, Inner Temple 1909. Judge of the County Court (Glamorgan) 1939-48. Deputy Chair, Carmarthenshire Quarter Sessions. Deputy National Insurance Commissioner 1948-50. Lord Lieutenant of Carmarthenshire 1948-50. Life-Governor, University of Wales, Aberystwyth. Member, Council of University of Wales, Swansea. Languages: Welsh, English. Died 15 October 1958.

WILLIAMS Glyn: SRN SCM. Labour: Meirionydd/Nant Conwy 1983. **Mr. Glyn Williams:** Born Rhosllanerchrugog 8 April 1939. Educated Wrexham Technical College; Goldsmiths College, London University. Senior Lecturer in Industrial Relations, Woolwich FE College. Greenwich BC. Member: NTFHE, NUPE. Languages: Welsh, English. Of Greenwich.

WILLIAMS Godfrey Herbert John: JP (Glam) 1901. Conservative: Mid-Glamorgan Jan. 1910. **Mr. Godfrey Williams:** Born 6 January 1875, s of Morgan Stuart Williams JP FSA & Josephine Lucy Marie, d of William Herbert of Clytha. Anglican. Married 1901, Hon. Miriam Isabel Thellusen, d of 5th Baron Rendelsham, 4d, divorced 1923 (2) 1924 Mrs. Ethel Regina Ogilvy Spence & d of David J. Van Ham. Educated Eton. Landowner & Governing Director, Aberpergwm Colliery. Patron Aberpergwm living. Lieutenant RNVR 1914-18. Chair, Neath RFC. Languages: Welsh, English. Of Aberpergwm & St. Donats Castle. Died 7 April 1956. Further Reading: *Elizabeth F. Belcham, About Aberpergwm.*

WILLIAMS Goronwy Wyn: JP (Caerns) 1959. Conservative: Caernarfon 1950. **Mr. Goronwy Wyn Williams:** Born Porthmadog, 1913. Married. Educated Porthmadog Grammar School; Sir John Cass Technical Institute, London. Research Worker, Woolwich Arsenal 1930-34. Managing Director, Glaslyn Foundry. Porthmadog UDC Chair 1948-49. Chair, Ffestiniog Group, Wales Gas Board. Languages: Welsh, English. Of Porthmadog.

WILLIAMS Graham R: Communist: Pontypool Feb. 1974. **Mr. Graham Williams:** Born 1934. Married 2c, Fitter, British Steel Corporation, Pantteg Works, Pontypool. Convenor, Craftsmen's Cttee. Member, AUEW Blackwood District Cttee, Pontypool Trades Council. Local secretary, Campaign for Comprehensive Education. Contested local elections. Of Pontypool.

WILLIAMS Gwyn O: Plaid Cymru: Monmouth 1979, 1983. **Mr. Gwyn Williams:** Born Brynmawr 1947. Married Glenys Margaret (died 1978) 2c. Educated Brynmawr Grammar School; University of Wales, Aberystwyth & Cardiff. Teacher (Geography) Bucks & Abergavenny. With Hydrology Dept, Wye Water Authority. Deputy-Head, Ebbw Vale Senior Comprehensive School. Part time National Park warden. Member, Brynmawr & Aylesbury rugby XVs. Joined Plaid Cymru 1969. Llanfoist PC 1970-73. Of Govilon.

WILLIAMS Huw: Respect Unity Coalition. Wales Euro 2004. **Mr. Huw Williams:** Local Government Worker. Shop Steward. Organiser, Blackwood Stop the War Coalition. Of Blackwood.

WILLIAMS Huw D. Windsor – see WINDSOR-WILLIAMS H. D.

WILLIAMS Hubert Llewelyn: KC 1938 DL (Glam) 1954 JP (Swansea) 1948 MA (Oxon). Liberal: Carmarthen 1922, Liberal National PPC Gower 1939. **Mr. H. Llewelyn Williams:** Born 1890 s of Mayberry Williams (nephew of W. Llewelyn Williams MP qv). Married 1915, Hilda, d of T. Lumley-Davies & Lady (David Charles) Roberts. Educated Llandovery College; Oriel College, Oxford. Army 1914-18. Lieutenant Royal Garrison Artillery. Barrister, Middle Temple 1920, Master of the Bench 1947. Recorder of Carmarthen 1941-50. Stipendiary Magistrate, Swansea 1950-. Chair, Glamorgan Quarter Sessions 1949-61. Of Langland Bay. Died 11 May 1964.

WILLIAMS Huw: Conservative, Blaenau Gwent 2001. **Mr. Huw Williams:** Born Northampton, 5 May 1962. Married Margrit Williams (qv) 1s 1d. Educated Royal College of Mines; Imperial College, London. Investment Analyst in Oil, Chemicals, Mining & Metals at Deutsche Bank Secondary School Governor. Member, Community Health Council. Hobbies: Rugby, Golf, Family. Of Brecon.

WILLIAMS Huw Elfed: Plaid Cymru, Clwyd West 2001. **Mr. Elfed Williams:** Born Dolgellau, 15 March 1963, s of Thomas Isaac Williams, bank manager, & Doris Jones. Calvinistic Methodist.

Married 1999, Tracey Siân Alford Williams, physiotherapist, 1 d. Educated Ysgol Gyfun Dyffryn Conwy; North Wales HE Institute; Welsh Agricultural College, Aberystwyth. Wales Regional Officer (part-time), CHILD (National Infertility Support Network) 2001- & part-time Social Worker, Royal Agricultural Institute 1999-. Ex-marketing & research officer, computer company. Member: Denbighshire Children & Disabilities Group, Care Co-ordinator Cttee. Chair: Denbighshire & Conwy Plaid Cymru 1998-2001. Ruthin TC. Interests: Children's Issues, Disabilities, Charities, Agriculture. Hobbies: Climbing, Cycling, Far Eastern Cooking. Languages: Welsh, English. Of Ruthin.

WILLIAMS Hywel: BA (Wales). Plaid Cymru, Clwyd West 1999; MP Caernarfon 2001-. **Mr. Hywel Williams:** Born Pwllheli, 14 May 1953. Married (divorced) 3d. Educated Ysgol Glanymor, Pwllheli; University of Wales, Cardiff & Bangor. Freelance Lecturer, Social Policy; consultant & author on social work & social policy. Manager, *Gofal Cymru*. Founder, All-Party Parliamentary Group on Lesser Used Languages. Languages: Welsh, English. Interests: Social Policy, Culture & Language, The Arts. Hobbies: Reading, Walking.

WILLIAMS Janet: BSc. United Socialists, North List 1999; Forward Wales, Wales Euro 2004. **Miss Janet Williams:** Born Wrexham, 29 August 1965, d of Humphrey Williams, landscape gardener, & Margaret Rose Pennington. Partner, Andrew James Radford, author & organic landscape designer, 1s 1d. Educated Cefnmawr Primary School, Wrexham; Egerton Primary School, Knutsford; Knutsford County High School; University (Agriculture). Environmental campaigner/lobbyist. Contested Wrexham CBC 1999. Hobbies: Ponies, Horse Riding, Voluntary Work. Languages: English. Of Wrexham.

WILLIAMS John: JP (Glam). Labour MP Gower 1906-. **Revd John Williams:** Born Aberaman 1861, s of David Williams, collier. Ordained Baptist Minister. Married 1882, Elizabeth, d of Daniel Jones, Aberaman, 4s 5d. Educated Aberaman British School. Pupil teacher at 12. Coached by Minister & attended evening classes. Door Boy, Plough Colliery, Aberaman at 12. Miner, Grocer, Aberaman Co-op. Surface Worker, Abergwawr, Aberaman, Middle Dyffryn & Fforchaman pits. Checkweighman, Lady Windsor Colliery, Ynysybwl 1887-. Miners' Agent, General Secretary, Amalgamated Society of South Wales Colliery Workers 1890, Agent, West Ogmore & Gilfach Goch. Member, SWMF Executive 1898-. Lecturer in Economics. Mountain Ash UDC. Governor, University of Wales, Cardiff. Poet. Member of Gorsedd as *Eryl Glan Glawr*. In the 1900 General Election he supported Liberal candidate, John Aeron Thomas, against Labour's John Hodge. Languages: Welsh, English. Of Sketty, Swansea. Estate £2,460. Died Swansea, 20 June 1922. Further Reading: *Unpublished biography by his daughter at West Glamorgan Archive; Kenneth O Morgan, Wales in British Politics 1963.*

WILLIAMS John (Lib. Dem) – see WILLIAMS David John.

WILLIAMS John A: MB ChB (Liverpool). Liberal, Caernarfon 1970. **Dr. John Williams:** Born July 1926. Educated. Friars' School, Bangor; University of Liverpool School of Medicine. Medical Practitioner.

WILLIAMS John David: Liberal: Wrexham 1945; Labour: Montgomery 1950. **Mr. John Williams:** Born 1898. Educated Holywell Grammar School; Skerry's College, Liverpool. Sales executive officer. Army 1939-45. Farmer. Merioneth CC.

WILLIAMS John Eaton Wynford: ABIM RSA MIHeatB. Plaid Cymru: Aberdare 1966. **Mr. Eaton Williams:** Born Aberdare 1907, s of Samuel Williams, carpenter & builder. Welsh Independent Deacon. Married Marion Thomas, Swansea, 1s. Educated Ysgol Comin, Aberdare; Aberdare Grammar School. (Diploma in Advanced Economic Theory). London 1926-. Clerk of Works, Pontypridd & Rhondda National Health & Welfare Cttee. Builders' Agent. Army 1939-45 Captain. Aberdare UDC (Protectionist) 1957-64. Joined Plaid Cymru 1965. Languages: Welsh, English. Died August 1975.

WILLIAMS John Ellis: JP (Glam). Liberal: Pontypridd 1945. **Mr. J. Ellis Williams:** Born Ferryside 13 September 1892, s of Revd W. H. Williams, Baptist minister. Baptist deacon. Married 1923 Mabel Blizzard, 1d. Educated Kidwelly Grammar School; Teacher Training College. Teacher 1913, Headteacher, Retired 1953. President: Glamorgan Federation NUT, Pontypridd Liberal Assn. Chair, Liberal Party of Wales. Secretary: Pontypridd Cymmrodorion. Hon. Member, Gorsedd. Member, Welsh Cttee UNESCO. Langauges: Welsh, English. Died June 1965.

WILLIAMS John Henry: JP (Carms) MD (Oxon) LCA 1902. Labour: East Carmarthenshire Dec. 1910, B/E 1912, Llanelli 1918; MP Llanelli 1922-. **Dr. J. H. Williams:** Born Liverpool 1869, s of Captain Evan Williams & Jane Williams, Pwll, Llanelli. Baptist. Married Ann, d of William Thomas, Pwll. Educated Cardiff; Oxford University; London Hospital. Medical Practitioner. Carmarthenshire CC. Burry Port UDC Chair-man. Chair, Carmarthenshire Public Health Authority. Languages: Welsh, English. Of Burry Port. Estate £3,615. Died 7 February 1936.

WILLIAMS John Lasarus: MA (Wales). Plaid Cymru: Anglesey 1970, 1979. **Mr. John Lasarus Williams:** Born Llangoed 29 October 1924. Presbyterian Church of Wales Elder. Married Beti Jones, 3c. Educated Beaumaris Grammar School; University of Wales, Bangor (1st Welsh, MA Educational Psychology). Royal Navy 1943-46. Teacher, David Hughes Comprehensive School, Beaumaris, Lecturer in Welsh, Bangor Normal College. Founder, Union of Language Workers. Aethwy RDC. Gwynedd CC 1963-81 (Chair: Further Education Cttee. 1988-). Member: Court of the University of Wales. Vice-Chair, Anglesey National Eisteddfod. Languages: Welsh, English. Of Llanfairpwll. Died 13 June 2004. *Books: John Lasarus Williams: The Land of the Long Long Name, Syr John Morris Jones 1862-1929.*

WILLIAMS John Nigel: ACA. Conservative: Bedwellty 1966. **Mr. Nigel Williams:** Born June 1928. Educated St. Julian's High School, Newport. Chartered Accountant. Treasurer, Newport Conservative Assn. Contested local elections.

WILLIAMS Kevin: Green Party, South/East List 1999. **Mr. Kevin Williams:** Of Treharris.

WILLIAMS Kirsty – see WILLIAMS Victoria Kirstin.

WILLIAMS Llewelyn Griffith: MA. Liberal, Denbigh 1922. **Revd Llew G. Williams:** Born Penygroes, Dyffryn Nantlle 1883. Calvinistic Methodist. Quarry Worker on leaving school. Educated Bala & Aberystwyth Theological Colleges. Minister, Presbyterian Church of Wales. Pastorates: Ysbyty Ystwyth & Barry. Resigned 1918. Stood out against the Great War from its beginnings. Journalist 1920-. London Correspondent, *Baner ac Amserau Cymru.* Author of *Y Genedl's London Letters.* Contributor to *Welsh Outlook.* Suffered from poor health all his life. Died 5 December 1925.

WILLIAMS Llewelyn: BA (Wales). Labour MP Abertillery 1950-. **Revd Llywelyn Williams:** Born Llanelli 2 June 1910, s of William Williams, miner. Married 1938, Elsie, d of Gordon Macdonald MP (Lord Macdonald of Gwaenysgor) 1s 1d (d MEP). Educated Llanelli Grammar School; University of Wales, Swansea (1st Welsh); Presbyterian College, Carmarthen. Welsh Independent Minister. Ordained 1936: Bethesda, Bangor 1936-42, Tabernacle, Abertillery 1942-46, Tabernacl, Kings Cross, London 1946-50. WEA lecturer. Former member, Plaid Cymru. Chair: Welsh Parliamentary Party. Welsh Labour Group.

Delegate, Council of Europe `952-53. Languages: Welsh, English. Estate £5,568. Bequeathed body for medical research. Languages: Welsh, English. Collapsed in Newport street & died 5 February 1965. *Books, Llywelyn Williams, Hanes y Tabernacl, Kings Cross 1947.* Further Reading: *D. Ben Rees: Cymry Adnabyddus 1952-1972.*

WILLIAMS Louis Hedley: Liberal Democrat, Mid & West List 1999. **Mr. Louis Williams:** Powys CC (Chair: Political Structures Working Party). Hon. Secretary, Montgomeryshire Liberal Democrat Assn. Of Newtown.

WILLIAMS Mark Fraser: BA (Wales) 1987. Liberal Democrat: Monmouth 1997, Ceredigion B/E 2000. **Mr. Mark Williams:** Born Hertford, 24 March 1966. Married Helen Wyatt, 1d. Educated Richard Hale School, Hertford; University of Wales, Aberystwyth (Politics); Plymouth University. Liberal Democrat Research Assistant, House of Lords 1987-92. Constituency Assistant to Geraint Howells MP 1987-92. Teacher: Madron Daniel School 1993-96, Forches Cross School, Barnstable 1996-200, Deputy Headteacher, Llangors School 2000-. President, Ceredigion Liberal Democrats. Member: NASUWT. Liberal Democrat Prospective Parliamentary Candidate, Ceredigion 2003. Interests: Wales, Education, Environment. Hobbies: Walking, Camping, Reading biographies. Languages: Learning Welsh, English. Of Brecon.

WILLIAMS Margrit Anna: Conservative: Blaenau Gwent 1997. **Mrs. Margaret Williams:** Born 9 May 1964. Married Huw Williams (qv) 1s 1d. Educated Southend High School for Girls; Queens School, Rheindalen, Germany; London Guildhall University. Global Investment Strategist. Wandsworth BC 1990-94. Member: Society of Financial Advisers. Member, Conservative London Local Govt Advisory Cttee. Conservative, Wales Euro 2004. Of Brecon.

WILLIAMS Meurig – see WILLIAMS David Meurig.

WILLIAMS Nefyl – see WILLIAMS Ernest Nefyl Coppack.

WILLIAMS Nigel: LlB (Buckingham). Plaid Cymru: Gower 1983, Swansea West 1987. **Mr. Nigel Williams:** Born Mumbles 1955. Married Sara. Educated Harrow School; Buckingham University. Development Manager, Business Consultant. Interests: Wales in Europe. Hobbies: Supporting Swansea RFC XV. Languages: Welsh, English, French. Of Horton, Gower.

WILLIAMS Noel: Plaid Cymru: Rhondda East 1959. **Mr. Noel Williams:** Born Pwllheli, December 1927. Married. Educated Pwllheli

Grammar School; Trinity College, Carmarthen. On leaving school worked eight years as lathe operator, asphalt worker, builder's labourer, social worker, reporter, then went to college. Teacher, Cardiff school. BBC Newsreader. Executive member, Nottingham WEA. Asst. Secretary UCAC. Hobbies: Poet, amateur dramatics. Languages: Welsh, English. Of Cardiff.

WILLIAMS Owain: Independent Wales Party, North List 2003. Left Independent Wales Party after Plaid Cymru's statement that 'it believed in Independence', March 2004, to sit on Gwynedd County Council as an Independent Nationalist. **Mr. Owain Williams:** Born Bangor, 10 August 1935, s of Griffith Williams, farmer, & Jane Mary Williams, housewife. Calvinistic Methodist. Married 1988, Doran Williams, teacher, 2s 3d. Educated Pistyll & Nefyn Primary School; Pwllheli Grammar School. Farmer & Businessman. Member, Plaid Cymru. Member, Mudiad Amddiffyn Cymru (Wales Defence Force) – involved with Emyr Llewelyn Jones in causing an explosion at Tryweryn Dam site & of blowing up a pylon in protest at the sentence imposed on Emyr Llewelyn Jones 1963. Founder & Chair, Independent Wales Party. Gwynedd CC (Clynnog). Interests: To establish the IWP as a credible alternative. Hobbies: Walking, Travel. Languages: Welsh, English, German. Of Llanllyfni. *Books: Owain Williams, Cysgod Tryweryn (autobiography).*

WILLIAMS Owen Glyn: LlB (Wales). Liberal: Swansea West 1964, Pembroke 1966. **Mr. Glyn Williams:** Born February 1921. Presbyterian Church of Wales Elder. Married Gwenan, 1s 1d. Educated Ffestiniog Grammar School; University of Wales, Aberystwyth (University Boxer). Army 1940-45, Lieutenant, Royal Signals. Solicitor (Luton until 1950, Kenya 1950-52, Ammanford 1952-). Treasurer, South Wales Liberal Federation. Member: Liberal Party of Wales Executive. Languages: Welsh, English. Died 18 October 1999.

WILLIAMS Owen John: MA (Oxon). Conservative: Ceredigion & North Pembs 1987, 1992, Mid & West Wales Euro 1989, Carmarthenshire West & South Pembs 1997, Meirionydd/Nant Conwy 1999, Euro Wales 1999, Ceredigion 2003, Euro Wales 2004. **Mr. Owen J. Williams:** Born 17 May 1950. Married. Educated Ysgol Abermad; Harrow; University College, Oxford (Modern History). Barrister 1974. Company Chair: O. J. Williams Ltd (family group of companies). Member, Hon. Society of Cymmrodorion, Institute of Directors, United Counties Agricultural Society. Director, Dyfed Health Authority. President, St. Clears Senior Citizens Club. Burgess of Laugharne. Conservative, Wales Euro 2004. Interests: Small

Businesses, Agriculture, Europe. Hobbies: Racing, Rugby, Music. Languages: Welsh, English. *Books: O. J. Williams, Strengthening the Union.* Of Chelsea & St. Clears.

WILLIAMS Paul James: Conservative, Rhondda 2003. **Mr. Paul Williams:** Born Usk 1953. Roman Catholic. Married Elizabeth (nurse) 2s. Educated St. Albans Comprehensive School, Pontypool; South Gwent FE College; De La Salle College, Manchester. Lyricist, light & stage designer for rock groups *Iron Child* & *Touch*. With Dept. of Industry's Business Statistics Office; Norfolk Social Services; Burton's Biscuits. First Administrator, Maddermarket Theatre, Norwich. Political Research & Media Officer to William Graham AM. Member: St. John's Ambulance, Gwent Talking Newspaper, Hospital Radio, 'Stencil' Community Art Assn. Branch Officer: CPSA, BFAWU. Chair: Roman Catholic Parish Advisory Council, Cwmbran. Secretary, Torfaen Conservative Association. Contested Torfaen BC 1999. Interests: Education, Health, Promoting Arts, Culture, Tourism. Of Cwmbran.

WILLIAMS Penri G: Plaid Cymru: Vale of Glamorgan 1987. **Mr. Penri Williams:** Born 1951. Married 2d. Educated Cowbridge Grammar School; Polytechnic of Wales. Electrical Engineer (Aberthaw Power Station 1974). Mid-Glam CC B/E Nov. 1976- Contested Cardiff CC (Pentyrch) 1999. Pentyrch ComC (Chairman). Editor, *Tafod Elai.* Of Pentyrch.

WILLIAMS Philip James Stradling: MA PhD (Cantab). Plaid Cymru, Caerphilly 1964, B/E 1968, 1970, Feb. & Oct. 1974, 1979, Blaenau Gwent 1999; AM South/East List 1999-2003. **Dr. Phil Williams:** Born Tredegar, 11 January 1939, s of Glyndwr Williams, primary school headteacher. Married, Ann Green, 1s 1d. Educated, Lewis School, Pengam; Clare College, Cambridge (double 1st). Research Fellow in Radio Astronomy, Cavendish Laboratory 1964-67. Lecturer in Electronics, University of Wales, Aberystwyth, 1967, Senior Lecturer, Professor. Chair, Cambridge University Socialist Club 1960. Joined Plaid Cymru 1961. Director of Research, Plaid Cymru 1967-; Vice-President 1968-69,1976-78, Chair 1970-76. Member, ASTMS. Member, University of Wales Court. Shadow Secretary for Economic Development 1999, Hobbies: Jazz, playing alto saxophone, dancing, hill-walking, history, poetry. Died 10 June 2003.

WILLIAMS Rhys – see WILLIAMS David Rhys.

WILLIAMS Rhys Tudor John: Labour: Ynys Môn 1983. **Mr. Tudor Williams:** Born 1939. Presbyterian Church of Wales. Married Siân 3c. Solicitor. Member: Fabian Society, Society of Labour Lawyers, TGWU/CTSS. Joined Labour Party 1972. Languages: Welsh, English. Of Wrexham.

WILLIAMS Richard Charles: Liberal: Monmouth 1929. **Revd Richard Williams:** Born Swansea, 24 February 1881. Congregationalist. Married 1905, Gwen Morfydd Gabe (died 1919). Educated University College, Reading. Ordained Swansea, 1905. London Missionary Society Missionary: (1) Teacher at Central School, Hope Fountain, Matabeleland, & 1st trainer of African teachers in Southern Rhodesia but the scheme ended because of the lack of government support & farmed school's 2,400 acres 1905-09 (2) Port Moresby, Papua/New Guinea 1909-11, signed 1911. Primary School Teacher and Headmaster at Swansea. Chair, Swansea West Liberal Assn (1945). Chair & Vice-President, Welsh Area Young Liberals. Of Sketty, Swansea.

WILLIAMS Richard David Mansel: Plaid Cymru, South/West list 2003. **Mr. Richard Williams:** Born Gilfach Goch, 24 December 1948, s of Richard Edward Williams, music teacher, & Sylvia Lorna Williams, civil servant. Church in Wales. Married (1) 1s 1d (2) Dawn Williams, unemployed, 1 step s, 1 step d. Educated Llandrindod Wells School for the Deaf; Cardiff College of Food Technology & Commerce (City & Guilds Diploma in Confectionary & Breadmaking). UPVC Fabricator. Llantrisant ComC 1983-1987. Tonyrefail ComC 1991-95. Contested Blaenau Gwent BC 1999. Chair: Pontypridd Deaf Club 1983-87; Blackpool Deaf Club 1987-90; South Wales Area, British Deaf Assn. 1996-99. Secretary, Cardiff Deaf Sports & Social Club 1992-2003. Interests: Welsh Parliament, Disability (Civil Rights & Equal Human Rights). Hobbies: Astronomy, Nature, Documentary Political History, Space Exploration, Darts (plays in local league). Of Ebbw Vale (1996).

WILLIAMS Robert: Labour: Aberavon 1918, Coventry 1922. **Mr. Robert Williams:** Born Swansea, 1881, s of dock labourer. Married 1921, Stella Pearlman, 1d. Educated elementary school. Dock labourer. Coal trimmer. President, National Amalgamated Labourers Union. Secretary, National Transport Workers Federation 1912-25. President, International Transport Workers' Union 1920-30. Labour Propaganda Officer *Daily Herald* 1930. Labour Party NEC 1918-21, 1922-(Chair 1926). Swansea BC 1910-12. A founder member, Communist Party of Great Britain 1920, expelled 1921 for supporting the compromise over the threatened strike of rail and transport workers in support of the miners. Died (found dead in a gas filled room at Kings Road, Chelsea) 1st February 1936.

WILLIAMS Robert: BSc HND (Eng). United Socialist. South/West List 1999. Aberavon 2003. **Mr. Rob Williams:** Born Neath, 2 December 1969, s of Richard Williams, forestry foreman, & Fay Lewis, school crossing officer, & gs of Glyn Williams, President, South Wales Area NUM. Atheist. Married 1992, Linda Ann Williams, social worker, 1s 1 step-s. Divorced 1995. Educated Cymer Afan Comprehensive School; Neath FE College; Swansea Institute (part-time degree course in engineering). Car worker, Ford. Production worker, Vistew. Leader, Port Talbot Anti-Poll Tax Union. Secretary, Port Talbot branch, Socialist Party. Member, Socialist Party Wales Executive. Member: TGWU. Hobbies: Supports Liverpool FC. Languages: English. Of Glyncorrwg.

WILLIAMS Robert Arwel Wyn: Liberal Democrat: Caernarfon 1992. **Mr. Arwel Williams:** Born 28 April 1956. Presbyterian Church of Wales Elder. Educated Brynhyfryd School, Ruthin; North East Wales Institute; West Cheshire College. Local Government Legal Officer. Member, Caernarfon Male Voice Choir. Languages: Welsh, English.

WILLIAMS Robert Coleman: MA (Oxon). Conservative: Caerphilly B/E 1968, Cardiff West 1970, PPC Carmarthen 1967-68 but resigned to contest Caerphilly B/E **Mr. Robert Williams:** Born Bridgend 1940, s of railway clerk. Married Christina Hobhouse 2d. Educated Cowbridge Grammar School; Jesus College, Oxford. Member: Oxford University Air Squadron. RAFVR pilot. Commissioned in Welch Regt & Royal Monmouthshire RE. TA Officer. Lecturer, Worcester College, Mass. Business Consultant in USA. Freelance television interviewer researcher. Lecturer in English, Trinity College, Carmarthen. Managing Director, Atlantic & Western Consultants, Swansea. Governor: Royal Hospital & Home for Incurables, Putney. *Books: R. C. Williams, A Concordance of the Collected Poems of Dylan Thomas.*

WILLIAMS Roger Hugh: MA (Cantab). Liberal Democrat, Carmarthenshire West & South Pembrokeshire 1999; MP Brecon & Radnor 2001-. **Mr. Roger Williams:** Born 22 January 1948. Married 2c. Educated Christ College, Brecon; Selwyn College, Cambridge (Agriculture). Farmer. Inspector of Schools. Chair: Brecon & Radnor NFU; Mid-Wales Agri-Food Partnership; Brecon Beacons National Park. Vice-Chair: Powys TEC; Development Board for Rural Wales 9 years. Member: FUW; Brecknock Access Group (for disabled people). Powys CC (Llangors) 1981, Interests: Education, Health, Agriculture. Hobbies: Rugby, Countryside.

WILLIAMS Shane: BA. Labour, Islwyn 1999. **Mr. Shane Williams:** Born 2 January 1968. Educated City of Birmingham Polytechnic (Government). Political Assistant to Don Touhig MP. Joined Labour Party 1983, Youth Officer, then Press Officer, Islwyn Labour Party.

WILLIAMS Siân: Welsh Socialist, South East Wales Euro 1994. **Miss Siân Williams:** Born 1961. Partner, Alun, 2d. Unemployed. Nominated by *Cymru Coch (Red Wales)*, founded 1987, to fight for a free socialist Wales. Of Pontlottyn.

WILLIAMS Stanley: LlB (Liverpool). Labour: Denbigh 1959, 1954. **Mr. Stanley Williams:** Born Froncysyllte April 1911. Educated Ruabon Grammar School, Liverpool University. Solicitor, Bootle 1934-50, Ruabon 1952. Lieutenant RAMC 1939-45. Chair & Treasurer, Bootle Trades Council, Member, Advisory Cttee NOISE. Bootle BC 1934-39, 1946-50. Ruabon PC. Denbighshire CC.

WILLIAMS Thomas Alfred: Communist, North List 1999. **Mr. Tom Williams:** Of Flint. Died 2000.

WILLIAMS Thomas Howell – see IDRIS T. H. W.

WILLIAMS Thomas Jeremiah: Liberal: Gower 1906, MP Swansea District B/E 1915-18, Swansea East 1918-. **Mr. Jeremiah Williams:** Born Morriston 1872 s of William Williams MP (qv) of Maesygwernen Hall & Margaret Jeremiah. Welsh Independent Deacon. Married 1912, Laura Alica, d of Thomas Marlow, 1d. Educated Swansea Grammar School; University College School, London; Firth College, Sheffield. Barrister, Grays Inn 1902. Tinplate Manufacturer. Chair, Beaufort Works Ltd. Director: Mumbles Railway Co, Western Colliery Co, Dunvant-Penlan Collieries. Property owner: estates at Morriston, Enfield & Blackheath. Languages: Welsh, English. Estate £101,444. Of Maesygwernen Hall, Morriston. Died after a long and painful illness, 12 January 1919.

WILLIAMS Tudor – see WILLIAMS Rhys T. J.

WILLIAMS Victoria Kirsten: BA (Manchester) 1993. Liberal Democrat, Ogmore 1997; A.M. Brecon & Radnor 1999, **Ms. Kirsty Williams:** Born Taunton, Somerset, 19 March 1971, d of Edward G. Williams & Pamela M. Hall. Anglican. Married 2000, Richard Rees, farmer, 1d. Educated St. Michael's School, Llanelli; Universities of Manchester (American Studies) & Missouri. Accounts Executive, Cardiff Design Co; Marketing Executive. Deputy President, Liberal Democrats Wales 1997-99. Member, National Assembly Advisory Planning Cttee

Ms. Kirsty Williams.

1997. Chair: Assembly Health & Social Services Cttee 1999-2003; Standards Cttee 2003-. Liberal Democrat Business Manager 2000. Interests: Health, Agriculture, Young People. Hobbies: Horse riding, helping on the farm. Of Felinfäch, Powys.

WILLIAMS Waldo Goronwy: BA (Wales). Plaid Cymru: Pembroke 1959. **Mr. Waldo Williams:** Born Haverfordwest 30 September 1904, s of J. Edwal Jones, primary school headteacher & Angharad, d of John Jones (niece of Professor, Sir Henry Jones). Both parents were pacifists. Baptist, joined Society of Friends 1953. Moved to Mynachlogddu at 7 and learned Welsh. Married 1942 Linda Llewelyn (died 1943) 2c. Educated Prendergast Primary School, Haverfordwest; Narberth Grammar School; University of Wales, Aberystwyth (English). Teacher: Dinas primary school 1927-28, Solfach 1928-, Supply in 30s, Registered as CO (though too old) 1942 and made exempt but lost Pembrokeshire teaching post. Botwnog Grammar School 1942-45, Kinbolton, Hunts, Chippenham & Lyneham 1945-50. Returned to Wales 1950. Teacher: Pembroke Dock RC 1963 then Barham, Abergwaun RC & Goodwick Primary Schools. Retired Dec. 1970. WEA & Extra Mural Lecturer. Member ILP. Adjudicator for Chair, Bala Eisteddfod 1967. Developed a sense of guilt over the Korean War and withheld tax *until the last conscript is discharged.* Twice sent to prison (once for six weeks), September 1960 for refusing to pay £15/6/0 income tax. Furniture seized but bought by Quakers. Suffered a seizure January 1971. Died 20 May 1971. *Books: Waldo Williams: Dail Pren 1956, Cerddi'r Post a Beirdd Penfro 1961. Studies: Dafydd Owen, Dal Pridd y Dail Pren 1972. Further*

Reading: *James Nicholas, Waldo Williams 1975; edit. James Nicholas, Teyrnged 1977; Ned Thomas, Waldo Williams (Llais y Llenor); Robert Rhys, Waldo Williams (Cyfres y Meistri) 1987, Chwilio am Nodau'r Gân 1992; Dyfnallt Morgan, Waldo Williams, Thema yn ei Waith 1974; D. Ben Rees, Cymry Adnabyddus 195-72.*

WILLIAMS William: JP (Glam 1887 & Swansea). Liberal MP Swansea District B/E 1883-95. **Mr. William Williams:** Born Morriston 1840, s of William Williams, tinplate worker. Welsh Independent deacon. Married (1) 1860s d of Mr. Jeremiah, Cwmdu, Cwmbwrla, 3s 2d (2) 1894, widow of Revd Mr. Phillips of Morriston & d of Thomas Bowen of Morriston, 1d. One of the world's largest tinplate manufacturers. Went at 12 to work at Upper Forest Tinplate Works, leg amputed in accident, Manager, Swansea Tinplate Works. Works' Proprietor at 42. Chief Proprietor: Upper Forest Steel & Tinplate Co, Worcester & Morlais Tinplate Works, Morriston. The largest employer in the area. Chair: Glamorganshire Banking Co until amalgamation with Capital & Counties Bank of which he became a director. Board of Guardians. Swansea BC 1879-88, Mayor of Swansea. Glamorgan CC 1888. Languages: Welsh, English. Of Maesygwernen Hall, Morriston, & London. Estate £69,173. Died 21 April 1904.

WILLIAMS William Edwin: JP (Mon) FRCS. Conservative: West Monmouthshire 1886, 1895. Declined nomination 1900. **Dr. Edwin Williams:** Born 1846, s of John Jones Williams, Llanhilleth. Married 1898, Adeleine Mary, d of Frederick Walpole JP, Medical Practitioner. Chair, West Monmouthshire Conservative Assn. Of Abertillery, then Govilon.

WILLIAMS William Gwyn: BSc (Reading). Liberal Democrat: Clwyd North West 1992, Clwyd West 1997. **Mr. Gwyn Williams:** Born Ruthin 30 October 1960, s of Gwilym Clwyd Williams, Y Wern (farmer), & Olwen Jones. Anglican. Married 1995, Nia, d. of D. Cyril Jones, headteacher & college lecturer & election agent to Gwynfor Evans MP, & Anita Jones, teacher & translator, Pumsaint, 1s 1d. Educated Ruthin School; Reading University. Farmer. Company Director: NJEC plc, Cadwyn plc, Clwydero plc. Chair: Clwyd South West Liberal Democrat Executive; Welsh Liberal Democrat Executive 1990. Clwyd CC 1986-97. Denbighshire CC 1997-99 (Vice-Chair: Education Cttee, Liberal Democrat Group Leader). Vice-Chair, Governors, Llysafasi Agricultural College. Member: Clwyd Health Authority. Member: Amnesty International, NFU, FUW. Hobbies: Gardening, Music, Reading. Languages: Welsh, English. Of Llanbedr Dyffryn Clwyd.

WILLIAMS William Henry: BSc (London) FREconS FCS FRGS. Liberal: Bedwellty 1918, 1923; Aberavon 1924, 1929. **Captain Henry Williams:** Born Manchester 18 April 1876, s of William Williams, Foryd. Married 1904, Emily Watkin, Llanfair Caereinion. Educated Bangor Normal College; King's College, London; University College, London; London School of Economics. Fought in Russo-Japanese War 1905. Army 1914-18, Captain, Cheshire Regt, Military Representative, Monmouthshire 1916. Legal Adviser, Welsh Region, Ministry of National Service-1918. Lecturer in Pure Mathematics, Birmingham Municipal Technical College. Barrister, Middle Temple. Secretary, Cttee of Inquiry, Anglo-Chinese Education. Assistant to the Director of Education, Hong Kong. President, Welsh Federation of Discharged Soldiers & Sailors. Secretary, Newport Development Assn. Of Newport, Mon.

WILLIAMS William Hywel: MA (Cantab). Conservative: Aberavon 1992, Resigned from Conservative Party 1998. **Mr. Hywel Williams:** Born Bangor, 3 June 1954, s of Revd W Raymond Williams (qv). Educated Llandeilo Grammar School; Bishop Gore Grammar School, Swansea; St. Johns College, Cambridge. Teacher: sixth form master & house tutor, Rugby School. Adviser to John Redwood MP 1993-97. Resigned from Conservative Party. Journalist & broadcaster. Languages: Welsh, English. *Books: Hywel Williams, Guilty Men, Conservative Decline & Fall 1992-97 (1998).*

WILLIAMS William Lewelyn: BA 1889 MA BCL (Oxon) FRHistS KC 1912. Liberal Cardigan B/E 1921; MP Carmarthen Boroughs 1906-18. Born Llansadwrn, 10 March 1867, s of Morgan Williams, farmer, & Sarah Davies. Welsh Independent. Married 1891, Elinor Jenkins. Educated Llandovery College; Brasenose College, Oxford (2nd History). A founder, Dafydd ap Gwilym Society. Journalist, *South Wales Star* (Editor), Barry 1889, *South Wales Daily Post, South Wales Daily News, The Star* (Asst Editor) London. Historian & Author in Welsh & English. Barrister, Lincolns Inn 1897. Bencher of Lincolns Inn. Recorder of Swansea 1914-15, Cardiff 1915-22. Chair, Welsh National Eisteddfod Assn. Hon. Secretary, Farmers' Defence League. Supported the War in 1914 because of the invasion of Belgium but became disenchanted; vigorously opposed Conscription Act & Defence of the Realm Act. Became a bitter opponent of David Lloyd-George. Hobbies: Fishing, golf, Eisteddfod, archaeology. Of London. *Books: Gwilym Benni Bach, Gŵr y Dolan (novels), 'Slawer Dydd (reminiscences), Making of Modern Wales.* Died 2 November 1922.

WILLIAMS William Raymond: BA MA BD (Wales). Plaid Cymru: Llanelli: Feb. & Oct. 1974. **Revd Raymond Williams:** Born Five Roads, Llanelli, s of Labour alderman. Married 2s (qv W. Hywel Williams). Educated Llanelli Grammar School; University of Wales, Swansea (Welsh); Carmarthen Presbyterian College; Coleg Bala-Bangor; University of Wales, Bangor. Army 1945-48, Lieutenant, Registered as CO when on Reserve List, at commencement of Korean War 1950. Welsh Independent Minister, Ordained 1953: Ebeneser, Deiniolen & Maesydref 1953-56, Capel Newydd, Llandeilo 1956-69. Teacher (Biblical Studies): Glanafan Comprehensive School, Port Talbot 1969-71, Gwendraeth Grammar School 1971-. Part-time extra mural lecturer, University of Wales, Aberystwyth. Member, Bible Society's Team for translating New Testament into Modern Welsh. Languages: Welsh, English. Of Sketty, Swansea.

WILLIAMS-DRUMMOND Hugh Henry John: 1st Bart 1922 CMG 1918 JP (Devon). Conservative: West Carmarthenshire B/E 18 July 1889. **Brigadier, Sir Hugh Drummond:** Born 29 November 1859, s of Sir James Williams-Drummond, 3rd Bart. Edwinsford, Llandeilo (dropped Williams). Anglican. Married 1889, Gertrude Emily d of Hon. Mark Kerr Rolle, 1d. Landowner. Chair: Southern Railway Co. Director: National Provincial Bank, Budleigh Railway Co, London & South Western Railway Co 1910. Member of the Royal Company of Archers, Sovereign's Bodyguard in Scotland. Lieutenant, Rifle Brigade. Lieut-Colonel, North Devon Imperial Yeomanry. Of London & Midlothian. Estate £28,497. Died 1 August 1924.

WILLIAMS-WYNN Arthur Watkin: JP DL (Mont) MA (Oxon). Conservative: Montgomeryshire Jan. 1910. **Lieut-Colonel Arthur Williams-Wynn:** Born London 1856, s of Charles Watkin Williams-Wynn & Lady Annora Charlotte Pierpoint, d of Earl Manvers. Anglican. Married Alice Mary, d of Hon. George Wentworth FitzWilliam, 1s 2d. (1s killed in France). Educated Westminster School; Christ Church, Oxford. Private Secretary, Viscount Cross. Landowner. Major (Hon. Lieut-Colonel) Montgomeryshire Yeomanry. High Sheriff of Montgomeryshire 1901. Montgomeryshire CC. Of Llansantffraid, Mont. Died February 1946.

WILLIAMS-WYNN Charles Watkin: JP DL (Mont) BA 1843 MA 1845 (Oxon). Conservative: Montgomeryshire 1880, 1885, MP: 1862-80. **Lieut-Colonel Charles Williams-Wynn:** Born 4 October 1822, s of Rt. Hon. Charles Watkin Williams-Wynn (MP Montgomeryshire 1796-99, Old Sarum 1799-99) & Mary, d of Sir Foster Cunliffe, Bart. Married 1853, Lady Annora Charlotte

Pierrpont, d of 2nd Earl Manners. Educated Westminster School; Christ Church, Oxford. Barrister, Lincolns Inn 1846. Deputy Chair, Montgomeryshire Quarter Sessions. Recorder of Oswestry April 1880. Chair, Lands Improvement Co. Lieut-Colonel, Montgomeryshire Yeomanry 1877. Of Llansantffraid, Mont. & London.

WILLIAMS-WYNN Herbert Lloyd Watkin: 7th Bart (1658) CB 1902 JP (Mont, Denbs, Merioneth, Salop) DL (Denbs) MA (Oxon). Conservative: East Denbighshire 1885 1886, 1892; MP Denbighshire B/E May 1885. **Colonel, Sir Watkin Williams-Wynn:** Born Cefn. 5 June 1860, s of Colonel Herbert Watkin Williams-Wynn (MP: Montgomeryshire 1850) & Anna Lloyd. Anglican lay reader. Married 1884, Louise Alexandra, d of his uncle, Sir Watkin, 6th Bart, 1s 2d, divorced 1898. Succeeded uncle/father-in-law 1885. Educated Wellington College; Trinity College, Cambridge. Landowner (145,800 acres). Company Director: Great Western Railway, Provincial Insurance Co. High Sheriff of Denbighshire 1890. Lord Lieutenant of Montgomeryshire 1891-. Chair, Denbighshire Quarter Sessions 1905. Member, Governing Body of the Church in Wales. Captain, Montgomeryshire Yeomanry 1884, Lieut-Colonel 1889. Raised troops for the Boer War. Denbighshire CC 1888-. Patron of seven livings. The last MP in the Wynnstay tradition. Estate £363,847. Died Wynnstay, 24 May 1944.

WILLIAMS-WYNN Robert William Herbert Watkin: 9th Bart (1658) KCB 1938 CB 1922 DSO 1902 KStJ MA (Oxon). Conservative: Montgomeryshire B/E 1894, 1895, 1900. **Colonel, Sir Robert Watkin Williams-Wynn:** Born Plas-y-Cefn, St. Asaph 3 June 1862, s of Colonel Herbert Watkin Williams-Wynn MP (qv) & Anna, d of Edward Lloyd, Cefn Meriadog. Succeeded nephew 1950. Married 1904, Elizabeth Ida, d of George W. Lowther, Swillington, Yorks 4c. Educated Wellington College, Christ Church; Christ Church, Oxford. Army: Imperial Yeomanry 1882-, Boer War 1899-1901. Colonel, Montgomeryshire Yeomanry 1907-17. District Commander, Egypt 1917-19. Hon. Colonel 61st/69th Regt Medium Artillery 1923. Lord Lieutenant of Denbighshire 1928. MFH Flint & Denbigh 1888-1946. Estate £943,410. Died Plas-y-cefn, 23 November 1945.

WILLIAMS-WYNN Watkin: 6th Bart (1658) JP DL (Denbs Merioneth, Montgomeryshire, Salop) MA (Oxon). Conservative: West Denbighshire 1885, MP Denbighshire 1841-85. **Sir Watkin Williams-Wynn:** Born Chilwen Cotton, Warwickshire, 22 May 1820, s of 5th Bart. Married 1852, Marie Emily, d of his uncle, Rt. Hon. Sir Henry Watkin Williams-Wynn MP, 2d. Succeeded

father 1840. Educated Westminster School; Christ Church, Oxford. Landowner. Cornet, 1st Life Guards 1839-41. Lieut-Colonel/OC Montgomeryshire Yeomanry 1844-77. Lieut-Colonel, 1st Royal Denbighshire Rifle Volunteers 1861, (Hon. Col 1877), ADC Queen. North Wales Grand Master, Freemasons. Member, Gorsedd, *Eryr Erryrod Eryri*. Steward of Queen's lordships & manors of Bromfield & Yale 1845. President, Hon. Society of Cymmrodorion. Patron of seven livings. *No record of his having spoken in the House, popular with his tenants.* Of Wynnstay, Ruabon; Glan Llyn, Bala; Llangedwyn near Oswestry & London. The largest landowner in Wales. Estate £106,809. Died Wynnstay, 9 May 1885.

WILLIAMS-WYNNE John Francis: CBE 1972 DSO 1945 TD JP 1950 DL 1953 VL 1954 MA (Oxon) FRAgS. Conservative: Merioneth 1950. **Lieut-Colonel John Williams-Wynne:** Born London 8 June 1908, s of Major Francis R. Williams-Wynne & Beatrice Cooper. Anglican. Married 1938, Margaret Gwendolen (died 1938) d of Revd George Roper, 3c. Educated Oundle School; Magdalen College, Oxford (Mechanical Sciences). Royal Artillery, 1929-49. OC Merioneth & Montgomery LAA (TA) 1951-54. Farmer & Landowner. Lord Lieutenant: Merioneth 1957-74, Gwynedd 1974-80. Vice-Lieutenant Gwynedd 1980-85. Chair, Advisory Cttee, Ministry of Agriculture Advisory Farm, Trawscoed 1953-76. Part-time member: MANWEB 1953-6, National Parks Commission 1961-66, Forestry Commission 1963-65. Member: Regional Advisory Cttee North Wales Conservancy Forestry Commission, 1950-63, County Agric Exec Cttee. 1953-663, 1967-71, Gwynedd River Board 1957-63, Forestry Cttee of GB 1966-73, Home Grown Timber Advisory Cttee 1966-76, Prince of Wales Cttee for Wales, 1970-79. President: Timber Growers Organisation 1974-76, Merioneth Branch, County Landlords' Assn 1979, Royal Welsh Agricultural Society 1968 (Chair of Council 1971-77). Chair: BBC Wales Agricultural Advisory Cttee 1974-79. Member: Airline Users Cttee CAA 1973-79, School of Agriculture Cttee University of Wales, Bangor 1982. Of Tywyn, Merioneth.

WILLIAMS-WYNNE William Robert Charles: JP (Merioneth) FRICS. Conservative: Montgomery 1974, Feb. & Oct. **Mr. William Williams-Wynne:** Born London, 17 February 1947, s of Lt-Col. J. F. Williams-Wynne (qv) & Margaret Gwendolin, d of Revd George Roper. Anglican. Married 1975, Hon. Veronia Margaret Buxton, 3d. Educated Abermad; Packwood Haugh; Eton. Studied hill farming, two years in New Zealand. Army, ten months 1967. Chartered Surveyor at Kettering. Tenant Hill Farmer, Merioneth 1965. Chair: Williams-Wynne Farms Ltd, Mount Pleasant Bakeries, Bilston 1983-85 etc, Chair, Merioneth

Conservative Assn 1977-79. President, Wales Young Conservatives 1973. Founder, Welsh Mule Society (President 1980-86). President: Welsh Agricultural Sales & Export Council 1985-87, Europa Club, Lands Tribunal. Chair: Historic Houses Wales Assn, Welsh Agricultural Sales & Export Council. Member: National Parks Commission, Prince of Wales Cttee. Youngest JP in UK when appointed. Hobbies: Building aircraft, Flying, Modern British art. Of Tywyn, Gwynedd.

WILLIS Carole Anne: BA (Wales). Plaid Cymru, South/Central List 1999, 2003. **Mrs. Carole Willis:** Born, Matlock, 18 August 1950, d of Edward Thomas Walker, wholesale florist, & Lillian Mason. Welsh Independent. Married 1974, Eric Lawrence Willis, businessman, 1s 3d. Educated Mynyddbach Girls' Comprehensive School, Swansea; University of Wales, Aberystwyth (Welsh). Plaid Cymru Branch Chair & Agent. Pentyrch ComC. Taff-Ely DC. Interests: More of an organiser than a politician. Hobbies: Singing in Côr Godre'r Garth, Opera, Walking. Languages: Welsh, English, some French. Of Groesfaen, Pontyclun.

WILLOCK John: Socialist Labour Party, Llanelli 1997. **Mr. John Willock:** Born 1950. 3c. Worked 14 years at Troste Tinplate Works, Llanelli. Training Officer, Carmarthenshire College of Technology & Art. Chairman, Llangennech Community Council. Secretary: Llanelli Right to Work Campaign, Llanelli & District Branch CCTA, Llangennech & Bryn Forum. Chair: Llanelli CAB, Llangennech Players. Resigned from Labour Party to join Arthur Scargill's Socialist Labour Party. Member, Llanelli Forum Co-ordinating Cttee.

WILLOTT Alison Leyland: BA (Durham) CertEd (London). Liberal Democrat, Cynon Valley 1999, Monmouth 2003; Wimbledon 1992, 1997. **Mrs. Alison Willott:** Born 21 February 1946. Married Bill Willott (Chief Executive, Welsh Development Agency 1998-) 2s 2d (Jenny qv). Educated Wimbledon High School; Cheltenham Ladies College; Durham University (1st Classics); Kings College, London. Professional Messo-Soprano Soloist 1976-. Teacher (Classics & English), London Oratory School. Civil Servant 1969-74 (Board of Trade; Diplomat, Foreign & Commonwealth Office; Principal, Dept of the Environment). Member: Liberal Democrat National Executive; Federal Finance Cttee. Merton BC (Group Leader 1994-98). Contested Monmouthshire CC (Caerwent) 1999. Member, AMMA. Interests: Environment, Education, Getting women into Parliament, Electoral Reform, Equity & justice for Third World. Hobbies: Gardening (RHS Certificate in Horticulture), Homeopathy, Computing, Reading, Music, Writing, Walking. Of Monmouth.

WILLOTT Jennifer Nancy: MA (Durham) MSc (London). Liberal Democrat, Cardiff Central 2001. **Miss Jenny Willott:** Born Wimbledon, 19 May 1974, d of Brian Willott (chief executive, Welsh Development Agency) & Alison Willott (qv). Educated Wimbledon High School; Durham University (Classics); London School of Economics (3rd World Development). Project Manage, Oxfam: spent 5 months in NE India: external consultant, Aditihii NGO India, 1995. Office Manager, Lembit Opik MP 1997-2000. Researcher, Welsh Assembly Liberal Democrats 2000-01. Head of Advocacy, UNICEF UK. Merton BC 1998-2000. Interests: International Development, Education, Environment. Hobbies: Travel, Music, Reading, Acting. Re-adopted as parliamentary candidate for Cardiff Central 2003. Languages: English, basic Hindi, fluent French, Spanish. Of Cardiff.

WILSON Alistair Taylor Macintosh: MA Cantab) LMSSA. Communist: Aberdare 1950, 1966, Feb. & Oct. 1974. **Dr. Alistair Wilson:** Born Trecynon 1913. Married 3c. Educated Downing College, Cambridge; University College, Exeter; Welsh National School of Medicine. Medical Practitioner 1940, & farmer. Joined Communist Party 1932. Member: Welsh Executive 1943-45, Party Appeals Cttee. 1961-66. Secretary, South Wales Branch. Socialist Medical Assn. Editor, *Cyffro*. Chair, The Geriatrics Society. Of Llwydcoed, Aberdare.

WILSON Anthony Joseph: BEd (Wales). Labour: Montgomery 1983; MEP North Wales 1993-99, withdrew after being placed No 5 on 1999 Nominations List. **Mr. Joe Wilson:** Born Birkenhead, 6 July 1937, s of Joseph Samuel Wilson & Eleanor Annie Jones. Congregationalist. Married 1960, June Mary, d of Charles Sockett, 3c; divorced 1988 (2) 1998 Susan Kathleen Bentley. Educated Capel Mawr, Criccieth; Wood Road School, Birkenhead; Birkenhead School; Loughborough College (DLC); University of Wales, Aberystwyth. National Service, RAPC 1957-59, Teacher, Guernsey 1966-66. Manager, St. Mary's Bay School Journey Centre, Kent 1966-69. Lecturer in Physical Education, North East Wales Institute of Higher Education 1966-89. Joined Labour Party 1969; constituency secretary & chair. Played in North Wales Basketball League. Wrexham-Maelor DC 1969-72, 1979-89. Vice-Chair: Cttee of Welsh District Councils. Interests: Housing, Agriculture. Hobbies: Basketball, Tennis, Camping. Languages: English, some French. Of Wrexham.

WILSON John Richard: Communist: Caerphilly, 1929. **Mr. Jock Wilson:** Born Argyll. Member, ILP. Joined Communist Party. Communist Party Organiser, South Wales. Retired on health grounds

1927. Member, Left *Wing Group*. Contested General Secretaryship 1924.

WILSON Robert: Conservative, Carmarthen West & South Pembrokeshire, 2001, Bolton NE 1997. **Mr. Rob Wilson:** Born Oxfordshire 4 January 1965. Married 1s. Educated Wallingford School; University of Reading (President Reading NUS). Managing Director, 3hree Communication Ltd. (specialists in design & public relations for IT industry). Ex-Managing Director, market, design & PR Co. Adviser to David Davis MP. Reading BC 1992-96 (Deputy Group Leader). Interests: Inward Investment, Technology. Hobbies: Sport, Travel, Current Affairs. Prospective candidate for Reading East 2003. Of Reynoldston, Gower.

WILSON Stanley W: BA (Open). Liberal Democrat: Caerphilly 1992, Newport West 1997, Redcar 2001. **Mr. Stan Wilson:** Born 12 November 1931. Methodist steward. Married Stella, 2s. Educated King Alfred's College, Winchester. Teacher (retired). Learning Resource Centre Manager. Former youth worker & member, CYSA national executive. Redcar BC 1963-66. Langbaurgh DC 1987-. Member: Redcar Local Development Agency, Welsh Liberal Democrats Executive. Cricket league umpire. Amateur member, Darlington FC XI. Of Redcar, Cleveland.

WINDSOR-WILLIAMS Huw Dawkin: Independent, South west Wales Euro 1979. **Mr. Huw Windsor Williams:** Born Swansea. Married 2c. Educated Uppingham School. Royal Artillery (Gunner to 2nd Lieutenant). Worked in Steel Industry & Farming. Studied Law in London. Solicitor. Member, International Bar Assn. Of Neath.

WINSTONE James: JP (Mon). Labour: Monmouth District 1906, Merthyr Tydfil B/E 1915, Merthyr 1918 & PPC. Merthyr. **Mr. James Winstone:** Born Machen 9 February1863, s of William (stonemason, died young) & Hannah Winstone (father died at early age). Baptist. Teetotaller. Married 1886, Sarah Jane Iven, 7c. Educated elementary school. Worker at brickworks (aged 8) 1871. Miner at Risca United Colliery 1873 (sacked for union activities). Checkweighman at Risca. Miners Agent, Eastern Valley 1901. A founder SWMF, Vice-President 1912-; President 1920. Representative of British Trade Unions to Canada1917. President, South Wales Branch, Plebs League. Risca UDC (Chair). Abersychan UDC (Chair 1911). Pontypool Board of Guardians. Monmouthshire CC 1906, Alderman 1919, Chairman 1920 (Vice-Chair, Education Cttee). Governor, University of Wales. Taken ill (appendicitis) at strike negotiations in London and died at a nursing home. *The Times* recorded that 25,000 attended his funeral. Died London, 27 July 1921. *See Anthony Mor-O'Brien, Keir Hardie, C B Stanton and the First World War, Llafur 1985, Vol. 4, No. 5, pp. 31-42.*

WINTER Mary: MA (Reading). Communist: Aberdare 1979, Cynon Valley B/E 1984. **Mrs. Mary Winter:** Born Swansea, 1946. Married 2c. Educated Glanmôr Grammar School, Swansea; Reading University. Senior Social Service Officer, Mid-Glam. County Council. Deputy Editor *Cyffro*, Welsh Marxist magazine. NALGO shop steward, Chair: Welsh Cttee Communist Party, Aberdare Health Centre Patients Cttee, Taf-Cynon Housing Assn. Member, CND Cymru. Of, Aberdare.

WITHERDEN Melvin John: MA (Cantab). Green Party: South East Wales Euro 1984, 1989, Torfaen 1987; Green Party/Plaid Cymru: Monmouth B/E 1991, 1992. **Mr. Melvin Witherden:** Born Maidenhead, Berks, 11 January 1948, s of John Frank Gavin Witherden, engineer, & Doris Winifred Print. Partner, Susan Margaret Pickananle, charity worker, 3s. Educated Maidenhead Grammar School; Oundle School; St. Catherine's College, Cambridge (English). Community Development Worker/consultant. Pioneered development of community businesses in South Wales, for providing jobs, training places & voluntary workers with the unemployed. Ex-Journalist: *South Wales Argus, Western Mail*. Member NUJ. Secretary, Torfaen Green Party. Founder-member/General Manager, Cwmbran Community Press. Secretary: British Earth Sheltering Society. A founder, Vote 2 Stop the War Party March 2003. Founder member, Torfaen Anti-Poll Tax. Of Coed Efa, Cwmbran.

WITHERS Michael Charles: Conservative: Pontypridd 1970. **Mr. Michael Withers:** Born October 1931. Married 1d. Educated Convent School, Bath. Company Director: Withers (Bristol) Ltd pharmaceutical firm. Trustee: investment trust. Chair, Bath Young Conservatives. Bristol CC 1956-. Of Bristol.

WOOD Aaron John: Referendum Party: Pontypridd 1997. **Mr. John Wood:** Born Cefn Hengoed, 9 February 1950, s of Robert John Wood, coal miner, & Beryl Priscilla Walker. Church of England. Married 1984, Christine Jacqueline Wood, hotelier, 2s 2d. Licensed trade since 1976. Hotel Proprietor. Languages: English, Spanish. Of The Legends Hotel, Pontyclun.

WOOD Cynthia Kay: MSc (London). Conservative: Wrexham 1983, Newham NE 1979. **Mrs. Kay Wood:** Born 21 March 1943. Married 1s. Educated Queens School, Chester; Oldfrey Fleming School of Speech Therapy; Guys Hospital Medical School, London University. Speech Therapist. Ward Chair, Kensington Conservative Assn, Administrative-Secretary, Conservative Medical Society. Hon. Treasurer & Councillor, College of Speech Therapy. Member NALGO.

WOOD Leanne: BA (Wales). Plaid Cymru: Rhondda 1997, 2001; AM South/Central List 2003. **Ms. Leanne Wood:** Born Penygraig 13 December 1971. Lives with partner. Educated Tonypandy Comprehensive School; Glamorgan University (Public Admin); University of Wales, Cardiff (Post Graduate Diploma in Social Work 1997). Probation Assistant, Mid-Glam Probation Service 1994-95. Probation tutor, University of Wales, Cardiff 2000-. Rhondda-Cynon-Taf BC 1995-. School Governor. Vice-President, Rhondda-Cynon-Taf Plaid Cymru. Shadow Minister for Social Justice & Regeneration, May 2003. Interests: Crime, Criminal Justice, Europe, Trade Unions, Youth & Women's Issues, Poverty, Public Expenditure. Hobbies: Gardening, Socialising, Reading. Of Penygraig, Rhondda.

WOOD Steven John: Labour: Montgomery 1992. **Mr. Steve Wood:** Born 29 February 1952. Married Janet, 2c. Educated state schools. Police Officer 1971-76. South Shropshire Social Work Team Leader. Member NUPE.

WOOD Thomas: JP (Brecs). Conservative: Breconshire 1892, 1895. **Colonel Thomas Wood:** Born 1 June 1853, s of General Thomas Wood, Gwernyfed (MP Middlesex 1837-42). Married 1863, Hon. Rhona Cecilia Emily, Tollemache, d of 1st Baron Tollemache, 2s 2d. Educated Eton. Landowner. High Sheriff of Breconshire 1886. Lieut-Colonel SWB (TA). Captain, Grenadier Guards. Breconshire CC 1888-1904. Of Gwernyfed Park, Brecs. & later of Norwich. Died 26 September 1933.

WOODIN Pamela: Socialist Labour, Wales Euro 1999.

WOODWARD Edward Stanton: Labour, Meirionydd/Nant Conwy & Mid & West List 2003. **Mr. Eddie Woodward:** Born Wirral, 1954. Newsagent. Conwy BC (Cabinet Member, Economic Development). Llanrwst TC. Mayor. Hobbies: Keen sportsman. Of Llanrwst.

WOODWARD Georgiana R: National Front: Newport 1979. **Mrs. Georgiana Woodward:** Born Newport 1927. Married 4c. Educated Alexandra High School, Newport. Cocktail Bar Receptionist & Housewife. Of Newport.

WOOLGROVE Christopher F: Liberal Democrat, South Wales East Euro 1994. **Mr. Chris Woolgrove:** Born London 1950. Married 1d.

Educated University of Wales, Cardiff. Ex-PE Teacher. Working for Sports Manufacturer. Marketing Consultant. Secretary, Monmouth Liberal Democrats. Of Monmouth,

WOOTTON Matthew Leon James: BA. Green Party, South/East List 2003. **Mr. Matthew Wootton:** Born 10 March 1978, s of Ian Christopher Wootton, chartered chemist, & Sarah Ann Hunt, market researcher. Unmarried. Educated Dulverton Primary School, Eltham; Colle's School, London SE12; University College, Northampton; Welsh National College of Music & Drama, Cardiff. Wales Green Party Media Officer. Publications Co-ordinator, Green Party of England & Wales Executive 2003-. Interests: Globalisation/localisation, International development. Hobbies: Playing cello, Singing. Languages: Learning Welsh, English. Of Bargoed.

WORKER Christopher: BA (Wales). Liberal Democrat: Islwyn 1997. **Mr. Chris Worker:** Born Aberystwyth 26 April 1954. Married 1c. Educated Easingfold Comprehensive School, York; University of Wales, Aberystwyth. Trained as teacher. Arts Centre Manager. Previously in warehousing, security and farming. Director, Equal Support in Wales. Joined Liberal Democrats 1992. Chair, Liberal Democrat Arts Policy Cttee. Member, Railway Development Society, National Campaign of the Arts. Member: Ceredigion Objective One Forum. Of Aberystwyth.

WORLEY Graham: Liberal Democrat, Meirionydd/Nant Conwy, 1999. **Mr. Graham Worley:** Born 1973. Educated comprehensive school & university. Network Manager. IT team leader at 23. Braymer Prize twice. Joint Manager, Ocean Sciences Computer Facility, University of Wales, Bangor. Interests: Rural economy, Education. Hobbies: Technology, Cycling, Walking, Swimming, Sailing, Music. Languages: Welsh, English. Of Trawsfynydd.

WORRALL Thomas F: Labour: Llandaff & Barry 1923, shortlisted 1918. **Mr. Tom Worrall:** Born Llanwrda 1866. Educated Oxford. Teacher 1918. Of Rhoose.

WORTH Nigel: Green Party: Clwyd South West 1992. **Mr. Nigel Worth:** Born 1937. Married 3c. RAF Pilot. Local Authority Conservation Officer. Worked with Play Groups & Adventure Playground Movement. Hobbies: sings in choir, member, Nantglyn Drama Group. Languages: Learned Welsh, English. Of Nantglyn.

WORTH Stanley George: Independent Disarmament: Cardiff North 1959. **Mr. Stanley Worth:** Born London, 21 September 1912. Unmarried. Educated St. Paul's School. RE 1939-

45, Major. Surveyor. District Estates Manager, British Rail, Cardiff 1953-. Member: UNA, Cardiff Lawn Tennis Club, Penarth Badminton Club. *Policy: Half of navies of USA USSR & GB to be sunk at same time.* Of Cardiff.

WRIGHT John Roper: 1st Bart 1920 VD JP DL (Glam). Conservative: Swansea District 1895, Swansea Town Jan. & Dec. 1910. **Colonel, Sir John Wright:** Born 12 March 1843, s of William Roper Wright of Croston, Lancs. Anglican. Married (1) 1870, Jessie Eliza, d of Charles Wilson (2) 1897, Alice, d of B. W. Stephens, Edgartown, 1s 1d. Apprentice at Soho Engineering Works, Preston. Steel Engineer. Industrialist & Company Director. Came to Wales 1867. Manager, Landore Siemens Steel Co. Formed Wright, Butler & Co, Lased Elba Steel Works, Gowerton. Purchased Pantteg Steel Co, Swansea Haematite Iron Co, Primitive Iron Ore Mine, Bilbao, Cwmavon Estate, Collieries & Steelworks, Phoenix Sheet & Galvanising Works, Pontypool. Amalgamated with E. M. & W. Baldwin, Stourpourt, & Alfred Baldwin, Pantteg (with Bryn Navigation Colliery, Port Talbot & Blackwall Galvanising Co. Blackwall) to form Baldwins Ltd 1902. Vice-Chair 1902, Chair, Baldwins Steel Co 1908, Port Talbot Docks & Railway Co, Swansea Metal Exchange. Erected Crumlin Burrows Steel Works 1910. Hon. Colonel: 1st Mon. Artillery Volunteers 1890-93, Glam RGA 1894-1903, 4th Welsh Brigade RFA 1912-13. Of Hendrefoilan, Sketty, Swansea, then Widcombe Manor, Bath. Estate £137,978. Died 25 July 1926.

WRIGHT Matthew Gerald: AMCIM. Conservative, Alyn & Deeside & North Wales List 2003. **Mr. Matthew Wright:** Born Stockton on Tees 1962. Partner/Fiancée Susan. Educated Teeside Poly. Worked in manufacturing industry. Director, Business Solutions Division, Enterprise plc. Senior Consultant, Qinetiq. Member: Institute of Welsh Affairs, Institute of Small Business Affairs. Affiliate, North Wales Branch, Chartered Institute of Marketing, Tory Green Initiative. Branch Organiser, Salmon & Trout Assn. Hobbies: Fishing, Walking dog, Pub meals. Of Nannerch.

WRIGHT Oliver Cecil: Conservative: Swansea East 1964, Northampton 1966, Brentford & Chiswick 1970. **Lieut-Commander Oliver Wright:** Born May 1925. Anglican. Married Jean 2s. Educated Reading School; Thames Nautical Training College; HMS *Worcester*; RNC Greenwich. Royal Navy 1943-61, Admiralty Liaison Officer for South Wales. Retired 1961. Hon. Secretary, Cardiff Mission to Seamen. Regional Director, Wild Life Trust, 1962-64. Company Director, family motor company, Reading 1964. Member, ASSET, British Olympic Assn, Organizing Cttee

British Olympic Games 1948, Institute of Navigation, Institute of Advanced Motorists, World Wild Life Trust Executive 1961-64. Vice-President, Navy League. Chair, Reading Branch SSAFA. Of Reading.

WYKES Francis Charles: MA (Cantab). UK Independence Party, Ynys Môn, 2001, 2003. **Mr. Frank Wykes:** Born Truro, 7 April 1937, s of Charles Henry Wykes, civil servant, & Iris Hunt. Church of England. Married 1962 Pauline Phyllis Cutress, 1s 1d. Educated Tonbridge School; Cambridge University (science & engineering). RAF 1955-57. With RhoAnglo Mine Services, Zambia copper belt 2 years; then with Johson & Matthey, London metal refiners. With Motor Industry Research Assn 25 years. Dept of Transport executive agency inspector 11 years. Retired on inheriting aunt's Anglesey property. Editor of an electric vehicle magazine. Left Conservative Party & joined UK Independence Party. Secretary, North Wales Branch UKIP. Interests: Anti Euro, Anti EU, Green Issues. Hobbies: Cycling, Contract Bridge, Gardening, Foreign Travel. Languages: English, French. Of Bodorgan.

WYN Eurig: Plaid Cymru MEP Wales 1999-2004; prospective parliamentary candidate Ynys Môn 2004. **Mr. Eurig Wyn:** Born 10 October 1944, s of Albert & Alvira Davies. Married 1972 Gillian Wyn, 1s 1d. Educated University of Wales, Aberystwyth. Journalist/Press Officer, BBC Wales 1970-75. Organiser, Plaid Cymru 1975-78. Development Officer, Community Co-operative Movement 1978-82. Freelance Journalist 1982-85. Gwynedd CC (Waunfawr) 1990-99. Leader, Plaid Cymru Group, Welsh Local Authorities Assn. President & General Secretary, European Free Alliance group. Member, European Committee of the Regions. Languages: Welsh, English. Of Waunfawr.

WYN-ELLIS Nesta M: Liberal, North Wales Euro 1979, Spelthorne 1966, Brighton Pavilion B/E 1969, Chipping Barnet Feb. & Oct. 1974. **Miss Nesta Wyn Ellis:** Born November 1940. Educated Llanrwst Grammar School; Liverpool University (Botany & Zoology). Secretary, South East Young Liberal Federation. Journalist, author, novelist, poet, composer, astrologer. Singer (90 minutes show, *Saison d'amour*). Cover Girl in *Hot Gossip*. Books: Nesta Wyn-Ellis: John Major, The Baker's Daughter, Dear Elector – the Truth about MPs, Britain's Top 100 Eligible Bachelors, Love Notes (Poems). Moved to Paris 2000.

WYNDHAM-QUIN Windham Henry: 5th Earl of Dunraven & Mount Earl: Viscount Adair 1822, Viscount Mount Earl 1816, Baron Adair 1800. CB 1903 DSO 1900. JP. Conservative MP South Glamorgan 1895-1906. **Colonel Windham**

Wyndham-Quin: Born 1857, s of Captain, Hon. W. H. Wyndham-Quin & Caroline, d of Admiral Sir George Tyler, Succeeded cousin 1926. Married 1895, Lady Eva Constance Aline Bourke (died 1940) d of Earl of Mayo 3c. Educated Eton; RMC Sandhurst. Lieutenant, 16th Lancers 1878. ADC General Hon. Robert Bourke, Governor of Madras (wife's uncle) 1886-89. Adjutant, Royal Gloucester Hussars 1890-94. Major, 16th Lancers 1893. Raised & commanded (Lieut-Col) Glamorgan Imperial Yeomanry. Commandant, Lines of Communication 1915. Landowner in Glamorgan & Ireland. Director, Great Western Railway. High Sheriff of Kilkenny 1914. Governor, National Museum of Wales. President, Bridgend National Eisteddfod 1940. Of Dunraven Castle, Southern down, Glam. Co. Limerick & London. Died 23 October 1952. *Books: W. H. Wyndham-Quin, Sir Charles Tyler GCB Admiral of the White 1912, The Yeoman Cavalry of Gloucester and Monmouth 1897, The Foxhound in County Limerick.*

WYNNE Alfred William Ernest: JP (Swansea) 1922. Conservative: Swansea West 1929. **Mr. Alfred Wynne:** Born Liverpool 22 November 1876, s of Alfred George Wynne & Maria Pritchard. Anglican. Married 1904, Florence Mary Ellery 2d. Educated St. Margaret's School, Anfield; Emmanuel School, Battersea. Managing Director, Farr, Wynne & Co, coal exporters. Director: Letricheux & David Ltd, Swansea Constructional Builders Ltd. Vice-Chair, Henderson's Welsh Anthracite Collieries Ltd. President, Swansea Chamber of Commerce 1918. Chair: Institute of Shipping, Swansea Trimming Board, Coal Trade Benevolent Assn, Swansea District, National Maritime Board, Swansea West Conservative Assn 1922. Director, South Wales Coal Exporters Assn. Executive Member, Great Britain for Supply of Coal to France & Italy. Member, Court of University of Wales, Swansea. Swansea BC. Member: Clyne Golf Club, Glamorgan Cricket Club. Of West Cross. Swansea.

WYNNE William Robert Maurice: JP (Merioneth & Mont) 1862 DL Merioneth. Conservative: Merioneth 1885, MP Merioneth 1865-68. **Mr. William Wynne:** Born 15 February 1840, s of William Watkin Edward Wynne (MP Merioneth 1852- 65) & Mary, d of Robert A Slaney MP, Walford Manor, Shropshire. Anglican. Married Winifred Frances, d of W Kendall & widow of R. I. Williamson. Educated Eton. Landowner. Lieutenant, Scots Guards 1860-65. High Sheriff of Merioneth 1886. Chair, Merioneth Quarter Sessions. Lord Lieutenant of Merioneth 1891. Constable of Harlech Castle. Of Peniarth, Tywyn, & London. Estate £129,965. Died 25 February 1909.

WYNNE-EDWARDS Thomas Alured: VD 1905 JP DL (Denbs). Conservative: Denbighshire 1895. **Lieut-Colonel Thomas Wynne-Edwards:** Born Denbigh, 1855, s of John Copner Wynne-Edwards, solicitor (died 1886) & Maria, d of Wood Gibson, of Hope, Lancs. Anglican. Married 1885, Isabel Gertrude, d of J. Parry-Jones, Plas Clough. Engineer & Estate Agent. Lieutenant, Denbighshire Volunteers 1882. Lieut-Colonel & OC 1900-08, Hon. Colonel 1905. OC 4th RWF 1908-13. Member, War Office Advisory Cttee Territorial Force 1908-13. Commandant, Prisoner of War Detention Centre 1914. Raised & Commanded 16th & 21st RWF 1915-18. Denbigh BC, Mayor 1890-92. Denbighshire CC 1892-98. Member, Governing Body of the Church in Wales. Of Plas Nantglyn, Denbigh. Died 1925.

WYNNE-WILLIAMS Valerie: Plaid Cymru: Barry Feb. & Oct. 1974. **Mrs. Valerie Wynne-Williams:** Born Cwmllynfell, miner's daughter. Married Michael Wynne-Williams, slate quarry & factory owner, 3d. Educated Cwmllynfell Primary School; Pontardawe Grammar School; King's College Hospital, London. Captain, Kings College Hockey Team, Welsh AAA Hurdles Champion. Physiotherapist. Editorial Staff of Keidrych Rhys' *Wales.* Granada Television Compere. Actress, Interior Decorator. Director, Theatr Ardudwy, Harlech. Director, Oriel Cymru Gallery. Chair, Criccieth Festival. Languages: Welsh, English.

– Y –

YEO Frank Ash: JP (Glam) 1877. Liberal MP Gower 1885-. **Mr. Frank Yeo:** Born 18 August 1832, s of Thomas Yeo of Bideford. Congregationalist deacon. Married (1) 1863, his cousin, Sarah d of Richard Cory (2) 1868, Mary, d of George Daws of Northallerton. Educated Bideford. Joined commercial staff of Cory, Sons & Co. Joined commercial staff of Cory, Sons & Co. at Swansea 1854. Coal Owner & Industrialist: Partner, Cory, Yeo & Co. (Sank Penrhiwceiber Colliery, then deepest mine in Wales). Chair, Swansea Harbour Trust 1878-86. Swansea BC Alderman, Mayor 1874, 1886. Of Swansea (1854). Estate £68.965. Died 4 March 1888.

YEO Timothy Stephen Kenneth: MA (Cantab) 1971. Conservative: Feb. 1974, MP Suffolk South 1983-. **Mr. Timothy Yeo:** Born 20 March 1945, s of Dr. John Kenneth Yeo & Norah Margaret Yeo. Married 1970, Diane Helen, d of Brian Richard FRCS 1s 1d. Educated Charterhouse; Emmanuel College, Cambridge (History Exhibitioner). Asst Treasurer, Bankers Trust Co 1970-73. Director: Worcester Engineering Company Ltd 1975-80. Director, Spastics Society 1980-83 (Member, Exec Council 1984-86. Company Chair & Investment Manager, Securities Selection. Freelance Journalist. Member: Select Cttee on Social Services 1985-90. Vice-President, Tanzania Development Trust 1980. Chair, Tadworth Court Children's Hospital Trust 1984-90; Member, Independent Development Council of Mental Handicap. Chair, VAT Reform Group 1982. PPS 1989-90. Under-Secretary, Environment 1990-93, Minister of State, Environment 1993-97. Opposition Spokesman on Environment, Transport & The Regions 1997-98; Shadow Minister of Agriculture, Fisheries & Food 1998-2003; Shadow Secretary of State for Public Services, Health & Education 2003-. Captain, Parliamentary Golf Team.

YORK-WILLIAMS John: Liberal, Rhondda 1987. **Mr. John York-Williams:** Born 1942. Married. Educated Porth Grammar/Technical School; University of Wales, Cardiff. Corporate Marketing Manager.

YOUNG James Anthony: BA (Liverpool). Green Party, Swansea East 2001, South/West List 2003. **Mr. Tony Young:** Born Swansea 14 May 1943, s of Patrick Young, gardener, & Kathleen Young, housewife. Educated St. Joseph's Primary School, Swansea; Bishop Gore Grammar School; University of Liverpool (Hispanic Studies); Saltley College, Birmingham Former teacher (England, Ireland, Spain, Swansea). Distributor, Betterwear UK Ltd. Joined Green Party 2000. Agent: Swansea East B/E September 2001. Local Party Development Officer. Interests: Future of Mankind, both spiritually and materially; Peace through Global Disarmament; Restructuring of Global Governance; Human Rights; Environmental Issues. Hobbies: Irish Music, Culture & History, Indigenous Cultures. Languages: English, French, Spanish, Portuguese, Irish. Of Penlan, Swansea.

YOUNG Rochfort M: BSc Econ ACA. Conservative, South East Wales Euro 1989; Rochdale, October 1974. **Mr. Rochfort Young:** Born 1945. Educated Harrow; Trinity College, Dublin. Chartered Accountant. Former Personal Assistant, John Marshall MEP. Vice-Chair: National Assn of Conservative Graduates. Member: Royal Commonwealth Society sub-cttee on the integration of Commonwealth citizens into the community.

– Z –

ZIMMERN Alfred Eckhard: Kt 1936 MA (Oxon) Hon. LLD Aberdeen Hon. DLitt Bristol & Hartford USA Hon. LittD. Melbourne. Labour: Caernarfon Boroughs 1924. **Professor, Sir Alfred Zimmern:** Born Surbiton 1879, s of Adolph & Matilda Zimmern. Married 1921, Lucie, d. of Pastor Maurice Hirsch. Educated Winchester; New College, Oxford; Berlin University. Classicist. Lecturer in Ancient History New College 1903, Fellow & Tutor 1904-09. Under-Secretary, Joint Cttee. on Oxford & Working Class Education 1907-08. Staff Inspector. Board of Education 1912-15. Political Intelligence Dept Foreign Office 1918-19. Wilson Professor of International Politics, University College of Wales, Aberystwyth 1919-21 (resigned). Acting Professor of Political Science, Cornell University 1922-23. Deputy-Director, League of Nations Institute of Intellectual Co-operation Paris 1926-30. Montague Burton Professor of International Relations, Oxford 1930-44. Deputy-Director of Research, Foreign Office 1943-45. Adviser, Information & External Relations, Ministry of Education 1945. Executive Secretary & later Adviser UNESCO Preparatory Commission 1946. Secretary General, Constituent Conference UNESCO 1945-46. Director, Hartford, Connecticut, Center of World Affairs 1948. Visiting Professor, Trinity College, Hartford 1947-49. Died 24 November 1957. *Books: A. E. Zimmern: The Greek Commonwealth, politics & economics in fifth-century Athens, My Impressions of Wales, The Third British Empire, The League of Nations and the Rule of Law 1918-35, The economic weapon in the war against Germany, The prospects for democracy and other essays, Solon & Croesus, and other Greek essays, The Greatness and Decline of Rome, America & Europe, and other essays, The American road to world peace.*